HISTORICAL REGISTER

OF

Officers of the Continental Army

DURING

THE WAR OF THE REVOLUTION

April, 1775, to December, 1783

By FRANCIS B. HEITMAN

Reprint of the

New, Revised, and Enlarged Edition

of 1914

With Addenda

By ROBERT H. KELBY, 1932

CLEARFIELD

Reprinted for
Clearfield Company by
Genealogical Publishing Co.
Baltimore, Maryland
1997, 2000, 2003, 2005, 2006, 2008

ISBN-13: 978-0-8063-0176-1
ISBN-10: 0-8063-0176-7

Made in the United States of America

Originally published: Washington, D.C., 1914
Reprinted: Genealogical Publishing Co., Inc.
Baltimore, 1967, 1973, 1982
Library of Congress Catalogue Card Number 67-22180

TABLE OF CONTENTS

PREFACE

In preparing the first edition of the Historical Register of Officers of the Continental Army, which was published in 1893, the compiler examined all the records then available in the several executive departments in Washington and supplemented the data obtained from this source by such as could be gathered from documents published by the Government and also those printed by States and individuals.

An Act of Congress of July 27, 1892, provided for the transfer to the War Department for preservation and indexing of the revolutionary records in the Treasury and Interior Departments, and an Act of March 2, 1913, directed the Secretary of War to collect or copy "the scattered military records of the Revolutionary War," including those of State troops, etc. Under those acts many revolutionary records were transferred to the War Department. Others not in the possession of the Government were loaned to the Department to be copied and returned. As a result of this legislation, the Government has now a fair collection of the Army records of the Revolutionary War.

This collection is, however, far from complete. All official records filed in the War Department when it was burned November 8, 1800, were then destroyed. Many other records or documents have been lost or destroyed through various causes and still others have become, through lack of care, so torn and mutilated as to be of little or no value for reference. Very few rolls or other records pertaining to the troops of Georgia and the two Carolinas have been found, most of them having probably been captured or destroyed by the enemy during the almost continuous fighting in those States.

A good many records are in possession of historical or other societies, libraries, and individuals and have not been sent to the War Department to be copied. For these reasons a complete list of the names of all the participants in that glorious struggle for our independence, either of officers, or of soldiers who shouldered the musket, can never be compiled.

There are in existence many records pertaining to the Militia during the War. These are fragmentary, and an examination of such of them as could be found shows that they consist principally of pay accounts for service for short periods of from two days to three months, but unfortunately the dates, or even the years in which the service was rendered, are rarely shown.

The compiler was allowed access to all the records on file in the War Department bearing on the Revolutionary War, and this enabled him not only to correct and more fully complete the data contained in the former volume, but to add the names of several thousand officers with a more or less complete record of their services.

The records given in this volume are not strictly official, for much of the data has not been obtained from official records, but in order to complete as far as possible the service of each officer, other sources of reliable information have been consulted and the data obtained therefrom included. (Many officers of the Militia and State troops who were mentioned by name in reports of battles, campaigns, etc., or of whom a list was furnished at the time, appear in this volume. The rank such officers held at the time mentioned only is stated, as many no doubt attained subsequently a higher grade.)

(The compiler has devoted much time and labor to the preparation of this work, in the examination of records of various sorts such as returns, rolls, orderly books, pay accounts, etc., many of which are not in the possession of the Government, but have been loaned to him by societies and individuals.)

This NEW EDITION contains the records of 14,000 Officers, there being 6,000 NEW names not recorded in the former edition, and of the 8,000 Officers mentioned in the old edition, a great many records have been revised, augmented and completed.

FRANCIS B. HEITMAN.

Signers of the Declaration of Independence.

Alphabetical list of the 56 Signers of the Declaration of Independence, showing from what State, when and where born, and when died. **(Names also appear in list of Continental Officers.)**

NAMES	From State Of	Born in	Died
Adams, John	Mass.	Mass., Oct. 31, 1735	July 4, 1826
Adams, Samuel	Mass.	Mass., Sept. 22, 1727	Oct. 2, 1803
Bartlett, Josiah	N. H.	Mass., Nov. 21, 1727	May 19, 1795
Braxton, Carter	Va.	Va., Sept. 10, 1736	Oct. 10, 1797
Carroll, Charles	Md.	Md., Sept. 20, 1737	Nov. 14, 1832
Chase, Samuel	Md.	Md., April 17, 1741	June 19, 1811
Clark, Abraham	N. J.	N. J., Feb. 15, 1726	Sept. 15, 1794
Clymer, George	Pa.	Pa , 1739	Jan. 23, 1813
Ellery, William	R. I.	R. I , Dec. 22, 1727	Feb. 15, 1820
Floyd, William	N. Y.	N. Y., Dec. 17, 1734	Aug. 4, 1821
Franklin, Benjamin	Pa.	Mass., Jan. 17, 1706	April 17, 1790
Gerry, Elbridge	Mass.	Mass., Dec. 6, 1715	Nov. 23, 1814
Gwinnett, Button	Ga.	England, 1732	May 27, 1777
Hall, Lyman	Ga.	Conn., 1725	Oct. 19, 1790
Hancock, John	Mass.	Mass., Jan. 12, 1737	Oct. 8, 1793
Harrison, Benjamin	Va.	Va., April 5, 1740	April 24, 1791
Hart, John	N. J.	N. J., 1708	May 9, 1799
Hewes, Joseph	N. C.	N. J., 1730	Nov. 10, 1799
Hayward, Thomas	S. C.	S. C., 1746	March 6, 1809
Hooper, William	N. C.	Mass., June 17, 1742	Oct. 11, 1790
Hopkins, Stephen	R. I.	R. I., March 7, 1707	July 13, 1785
Hopkinson, Francis	N. J.	Pa., Sept. 21, 1737	May 9, 1791
Huntington, Samuel	Conn.	Conn., July 3, 1731	Jan. 5, 1796
Jefferson, Thomas	Va.	Va., April 2, 1743	July 4, 1826
Lee, Francis Lightfoot	Va.	Va., Oct. 14, 1734	April 3, 1797
Lee, Richard Henry	Va.	Va., Jan. 20, 1732	June 19, 1794
Lewis, Francis	N. Y.	Wales, March, 1713	Dec. 30, 1802
Livingston, Philip	N. Y.	N. Y., Jan. 15, 1716	June 12, 1778
Lynch, Thomas, Jr.	S. C.	S. C., Aug. 5, 1749	Oct., 1779
McKean, Thomas	Del.	Pa., March 19, 1734	June 24, 1817
Middleton, Arthur	S. C.	S. C., June 26, 1742	Jan. 1, 1788
Morris, Lewis	N. Y.	N. Y., 1726	Jan. 22, 1798
Morris, Robert	Pa.	Eng., Jan. 20, 1734	May 8, 1806
Morton, John	Pa.	Pa., 1724	April, 1777
Nelson, Thomas, Jr.	Va.	Va., Dec. 26, 1738	Jan. 4, 1789
Paca, William	Md.	Md., Oct. 31, 1740	1799
Paine, Robert Treat	Mass.	Mass., March 11, 1731	May 11, 1814
Penn, John	N. C.	Va., May 17, 1741	Sept. 14, 1788
Read, George	Del.	Md., Sept. 17, 1733	Sept. 21, 1798
Rodney, Caesar	Del.	Del., Oct. 7, 1728	June 29, 1784
Ross, George	Pa.	Del., 1730	July 16, 1799

Rush, Benjamin	Pa.	Pa., Dec. 24, 1745	April 19, 1813
Rutledge, Edward	S. C.	S. C., Nov. 23, 1749	Jan. 23, 1800
Sherman, Roger	R. I.	Mass., April 19, 1721	July 23, 1793
Smith, James	Pa.	Ireland, 1720	July 11, 1806
Stockton, Richard	N. J.	N. J., Oct. 1, 1730	Feb. 28, 1781
Stone, Thomas	Md.	Md., 1743	Oct. 5, 1787
Taylor, George	Pa.	Ireland, 1716	Feb. 23, 1781
Thornton, Matthew	N. H.	Ireland, 1714	June 24, 1803
Walton, George	Ga.	Va., 1740	Feb. 2, 1804
Whipple, William	N. H.	Mass., Jan 14, 1730	Nov. 28, 1785
Williams, William	Conn.	Conn., April 18, 1731	Aug. 2, 1811
Wilson, James	Pa.	Sctd., Sept. 14, 1742	Aug. 28, 1798
Witherspoon, John	N. J.	Sctd., Feb. 5, 1722	Sept. 15, 1794
Wolcott, Oliver	Conn.	Conn., Nov. 26, 1726	Dec. 1, 1797
Wythe, George	Va.	Va., 1726	June 8, 1806

GENERAL OFFICERS

OF THE

CONTINENTAL ARMY

Arranged According to Rank, with Period of Service in the Grade.

General and Commander-in-Chief.

George Washington, 15th June, 1775, to 23d December, 1783.

Major Generals.

Artemus Ward, 17th June, 1775, to 23d April, 1776.
Charles Lee, 17th June, 1775, to 10th January, 1780.
Philip Schuyler, 19th June, 1775, to 19th April, 1779.
Israel Putnam, 19th June, 1775, to 3d June, 1793.
Richard Montgomery, 9th December, 1775, to 31st December, 1775.
John Thomas, 6th March, 1776, to 2d June, 1776.
Horatio Gates, 16th May, 1776, to 3d November, 1783.
William Heath, 9th August, 1776, to 3d November, 1783.
Joseph Spencer, 9th August, 1776, to 13th January, 1778.
John Sullivan, 9th August, 1776, to 30th November, 1779.
Nathaniel Greene, 9th August, 1776, to 3d November, 1783.
Benedict Arnold, 17th February, 1777, to 25th September, 1780.
William Alexander, 19th February, 1777, to 15th January, 1783.
Thomas Mifflin, 19th February, 1777, to 25th February, 1779.
Arthur St. Clair, 19th February, 1777, to 3d November, 1783.
Adam Stephen, 19th February, 1777, to 20th November, 1777.
Benjamin Lincoln, 19th February, 1777, to 29th October, 1783.
Paul J. G. de M. Lafayette, 31st July, 1777, to 3d November, 1783.
Philip De Coudray, 11th August, 1777, to 15th September, 1777.
John De Kalb, 15th September, 1777, to 19th August, 1780.
Robert Howe, 20th October, 1777, to 3d November, 1783.
Alexander McDougall, 20th October, 1777, to 3d November, 1783.
Thomas Conway, 13th December, 1777, to 28th April, 1778.
Frederick W. A. Steuben, 5th May, 1778, to 15th April, 1784.
William Smallwood, 15th September, 1780, to 3d November, 1783.
Samuel H. Parsons, 23d October, 1780, to 22d July, 1782.
Henry Knox, 15th November, 1781, to 20th June, 1784.
Louis L. Duportail, 16th November, 1781, to 10th October, 1783.
William Moultrie, 15th October, 1782, to 3d November, 1783.

Brigadier Generals.

Horatio Gates, 17th June, 1775, to 16th May, 1776.
John Thomas, 22d June, 1775, to 6th March, 1776.
Richard Montgomery, 22d June, 1775, to 9th December, 1775.
David Wooster, 22d June, 1775, to 2d May, 1777.
William Heath, 22d June, 1775, to 9th August, 1776.
Joseph Spencer, 22d June, 1775, to 9th August, 1776.
John Sullivan, 22d June, 1775, to 9th August, 1776.
Nathaniel Greene, 22d June, 1775, to 9th August, 1776.
Joseph Frye, 10th January, 1776, to 23d April, 1776.
Benedict Arnold, 10th January, 1776, to 17th February, 1777.
John Armstrong, 1st March, 1776, to 4th April, 1777.
William Thompson, 1st March, 1776, to 3d September, 1781.

Andrew Lewis, 1st March, 1776, to 15th April, 1777.
James Moore, 1st March, 1776, to 9th April, 1777.
William Alexander, 1st March, 1776, to 19th February, 1777.
Robert Howe, 1st March, 1776, to 20th October, 1777.
Frederick W. de Woedtke, 16th March, 1776, to 28th July, 1776.
Thomas Mifflin, 16th May, 1776, to 19th February, 1777.
Hugh Mercer, 5th June, 1776, to 11th January, 1777.
James Reed, 9th August, 1776, to — September, 1776.
John Nixon, 9th August, 1776, to 12th September, 1780.
Arthur St. Clair, 9th August, 1776, to 19th February, 1777.
Alexander McDougall, 9th August, 1776, to 20th October, 1777.
Samuel H. Parsons, 9th August, 1776, to 23d October, 1780.
James Clinton, 9th August, 1776, to 3d November, 1783.
Adam Stephen, 4th September, 1776, to 19th February, 1777.
Christopher Gadsden, 16th September, 1776, to 2d October, 1777.
William Moultrie, 16th September, 1776, to 15th October, 1782.
Lachlan McIntosh, 16th September, 1776, to 3d November, 1783.
William Maxwell, 23d October, 1776, to 25th July, 1780.
William Smallwood, 23d October, 1776, to 15th September, 1780.
Matthias A. R. De Fermoy, 5th November, 1776, to 31st January, 1778.
Prud Homme De Borre, 1st December, 1776, to 14th September, 1777.
Henry Knox, 27th December, 1776, to 15th November, 1781.
Francis Nash, 5th February, 1777, to 7th October, 1777.
Enoch Poor, 21st February, 1777, to 8th September, 1780.
John Glover, 21st February, 1777, to 22d July, 1782.
John Paterson, 21st February, 1777, to 3d November, 1783.
Anthony Wayne, 21st February, 1777, to 3d November, 1783.
James M. Varnum, 21st February, 1777, to 5th March, 1779.
John P. De Haas, 21st February, 1777, to 3d November, 1783.
William Woodford, 21st February, 1777, to 13th November, 1780.
Peter Muhlenberg, 21st February, 1777, to 3d November, 1783.
George Weedon, 21st February, 1777, to 11th June, 1783.
George Clinton, 25th March, 1777, to 3d November, 1783.
Edward Hand, 1st April, 1777, to 3d November, 1783.
Charles Scott, 1st April, 1777, to 3d November, 1783.
Ebenezer Learned, 2d April, 1777, to 24th March, 1778.
Jedediah Huntington, 12th May, 1777, to 3d November, 1783.
Thomas Conway, 13th May, 1777, to 28th April, 1778.
Casimir Pulaski, 15th September, 1777, to 11th October, 1779.
John Stark, 4th October, 1777, to 3d November, 1783.
Louis L. Duportail, 17th November, 1777, to 16th November, 1781.
Jethro Sumner, 9th January, 1779, to 3d November, 1783.
James Hogun, 9th January, 1779, to 4th January, 1781.
Isaac Huger, 9th January, 1779, to 3d November, 1783.
Mordecai Gist, 9th January, 1779, to 3d November, 1783.
William Irvine, 12th May, 1779, to 3d November, 1783.
Daniel Morgan, 13th October, 1780, to 3d November, 1783.
Otho H. Williams, 9th May, 1782, to 16th January, 1783.
John Greaton, 7th January, 1783, to 3d November, 1783.
Rufus Putnam, 7th January, 1783, to 3d November, 1783.
Elias Dayton, 7th January, 1783, to 3d November, 1783.
Charles T. Armand, 26th March, 1783, to 3d November, 1783.

TROOPS AT VALLEY FORGE, PA.

1777-1778

List of General and Field Officers who belonged to Brigades and Regiments as arranged and encamped at Valley Forge, Pennsylvania, in the winter and spring of 1777 and 1778.

REGIMENT	COLONEL	LIEUT. COLONEL	MAJOR
Brig. Gen. William Woodford's Brigade.			
7th Va.........A. McClanachan		Holt Richardson	John Webb
11th Va.......Daniel Morgan		John Cropper	Thomas Snead
Brig. Gen. Charles Scott's Brigade.			
8th Va.........Abraham Bowman		John Markham	Alexander Morgan
12th Va.......James Wood		John Neville	George Slaughter
Continental ...Wm. Grayson		Levin Powell	John Thornton
Brig. Gen. Anthony Wayne's Brigade.			
1st Pa.........James Chambers		Thomas Robinson	James Moore
2d Pa..........Henry Bicker		Henry Miller	Wm. Williams
7th Pa.........Wm. Irwin		David Grier	Samuel Hay
10th Pa.......George Nagel		Adam Hubley	James Grier
Second Pennsylvania Brigade.			
4th Pa.........,Lambert Cadwalader		Wm Butler	Thomas Church
5th Pa.........Francis Johnston		Persifer Frazer	James Taylor
8th Pa.........Daniel Broadhead		Stephen Bayard	Frederick Vernon
11th Pa.......Richard Humpton		Caleb North	Francis Mentges
Brig. Gen. Enoch Poor's Brigade.			
3d N. H.......Alexander Scammell		Henry Dearborn	James Norris
1st N. H......Joseph Cilley		George Reid	Wm. Scott
2d N. H.......Nathan Hale		Jeremiah Gilman	Benjamin Titcomb
2d N. Y.......Philip Van Cortland		Fred'k. Weisenfels	Nicholas Fish
4th N. Y.......Henry B. Livingston		Pierre R. de Roussi	Benjamin Ledyard
Brig. Gen. John Glover's Brigade.			
4th Mass.......William Shepard		Ebenezer Sprout	Warham Parks
1st Mass......Joseph Vose		Elijah Vose	Thomas Cogswell
13th Mass....Edward Wigglesworth		·Dudley Coleman	John Porter
15th Mass.....Timothy Bigelow		Henry Haskell	Hugh Maxwell
Brig. Gen. Ebenezer Learned's Brigade.			
2d Mass........John Bailey		Ezra Badlam	Andrew Peters
9th Mass......James Wesson		James Mellen	....
8th Mass......Michael Jackson		John Brooks	William Hull
Brig. Gen. John Paterson's Brigade.			
10th Mass.....Thomas Marshall		Joseph Thompson	Nathaniel Winslow
14th Mass.....Gamaliel Bradford		Barakieh Bassett	Samuel Tubbs
11th Mass.....Benjamin Tupper		Noah M. Littlefield	Wm. Lithgow
12th Mass.....Samuel Brewer		Samuel Carlton	Tobias Fernald
Brig. Gen. George Weedon's Brigade.			
2d Va.........Christian Febiger		Richard Parker	Ralph Faulkner
4th Va.........Isaac Read		Thomas Gaskins	Isaac Beall
10th Va.......John Green		Lewis Willis	Samuel Hawes
3d Va.........Thomas Marshall		William Heth	John Hays
14th Va.......Charles Lewis		....	George Stubblefield and S. J. Cabell
Brig. Gen. Peter Muhlenberg's Brigade.			
1st Va.........James Hendricks		Robert Ballard	Edmund B. Dickinson
5th Va.........Josiah Parker		Abraham Buford	Thomas Gaskins

9th Va........George Matthews	Burgess Ball	John Fitzgerald
6th Va........John Gibson	Charles Simms	Samuel Hopkins
13th Va.......Wm. Russell	Richard Campbell	Richard Taylor
German Regt.....................	Ludowick Weltner	Daniel Burchardt

Brig. Gen. William Maxwell's Brigade.

1st N. J........Matthias Ogden	David Brearley	Joseph Morris
2d N. J........Israel Shreve	Wm. De Hart	Daniel Piatt and
		Richard Howell
3d N. J........Elias Dayton	Francis Barber	Joseph Bloomfield
4th N. J.......Ephraim Martin	David Rhea	John Conway

Brig. Gen. Thomas Conway's Brigade.

3d Pa..........Thomas Craig	Rudolph Bunner	John Huling
6th Pa........Robert Magaw	Josiah Harmar	Jeremiah Talbot
9th Pa........Richard Butler	Matthew Smith	Francis Nichols
12th Pa.......Wm. Cooke	Neigel Gray	....
Continental ...Wm. Malcolm	Aaron Burr	Albert Pawling
Continental ...Oliver Spencer	Ebenezer Lindsley	....

Brig. Gen. Jedediah Huntington's Brigade.

5th Conn.......Philip B. Bradley	Matthew Mead	Jonathon Johnson
2d Conn.......Charles Webb	Isaac Sherman	Hezekiah Holdridge
7th Conn.......Heman Swift	....	John Sedgwick

Brig. Gen. James M. Varnum's Brigade.

1st R. I........Christopher Greene	Adam Comstock	Samuel Ward
2d R. I........Israel Angell	Jeremiah Olney	Simeon Thayer
8th Conn.......John Chandler	Thomas Dyer	David Smith
4th Conn.......John Durkee	Giles Russell	....

Brig. Gen. Lachlan McIntosh's Brigade.

1st N. C........Thomas Clark	Wm. Davis	John Walker and
		James Emmet
2d N. C........John Patten	Selby Harney	Hardy Murfree
4th N. C.......Thomas Polk	James Thackston	John Armstrong
3d N. C.......Jethro Sumner	Caleb Brewster	Henry Dixon
5th N. C.......Edward Buncombe	Wm. L. Davidson	Thomas Hogg
6th N. C.......Gideon Lamb	Wm. Taylor	John B. Ashe
8th N. C.......James Armstrong	Levi Dawson	Pinketham Eaton
7th N. C.......James Hogun	Robert Mebane	Wm. Fenner
9th N. C.......John P. Williams	John Luttrell	Wm. Polk

Brig. Gen. Henry Knox's Artillery Brigade.*

1st Cont. Art..Charles Harrison	Edward Carrington	Christian Holmer
2d Cont. Art...John Lamb	Eleazer Oswald	Sebastian Bauman
3d Cont. Art...John Crane	John Popkin	....
4th Cont. Art..Thomas Proctor	John Strobagh	Thomas Forrest

The following two regiments appear to have not been attached to any of the Brigades.

| Continental ...David Henley | Wm. Tudor | Wm. Curtis |
| Continental ...Henry Jackson | David Cobb | John S. Tyler |

Note.—Most of the four regiments of the Continental Dragoons, parts of two regiments of Artillery Artificers, and of the Engineers and Sappers and Miners were there, but the specific data is incomplete.

---

*Only parts of the 1st and 2d Continental Artillery were at Valley Forge.

Aides-de-Camp and Military Secretaries

TO

GENERAL WASHINGTON

Baylies, Hodijah, A. D. C., 13th May, 1782, to 23d December, 1783.
Baylor, George, A. D. C., 15th August, 1775, to 9th January, 1777.
Carey, Richard, A. D. C., 21st June, 1776, to ———?
Cobb, David, A. D. C., 15th June, 1781, to 1st January, 1783.
Fitzgerald, John, A. D. C., November, 1776, to 6th July, 1778.
Fitzhugh, Peregrine, A. D. C., 2d July, 1781, to 23d December, 1783.
Grayson, William, Assistant Secretary, 21st June, 1776, A. D. C. 24th August, 1776, to 11th January, 1777.
*Hamilton, Alexander, A. D. C., 1st March, 1777, to 23d December, 1783.
Hanson, Alexander C., Assistant Secretary, 21st June, 1776, to ———?
Harrison, Robert H., A. D. C., 5th November, 1775, to 16th May, 1776, and Secretary, 16th May, 1776, to 25th March, 1781.
Humphreys, David, A. D. C., 23d June, 1780, to 1st April, 1783.
Johnson, George, A. D. C., 20th January, 1777, to 15th August, 1777.
Laurens, John, A. D. C., 6th September, 1777, to 27th August, 1782.
McHenry, James, Assistant Secretary, 15th May, 1778, to 30th October, 1780.
*Meade, Richard K., A. D. C., 12th March, 1777, to 23d December, 1783.
Mifflin, Thomas, A. D. C., 4th July, 1775, to 14th August, 1775.
Moylan, Stephen, A. D. C., 5th March, 1776, to 5th June, 1776.
Palfrey, William, A. D. C., 6th March, 1776, to 27th April, 1776.
Randolph, Edmund, A. D. C., 15th August, 1775, to 25th March, 1776.
Reed, Joseph, Secretary, 4th July, 1775, to 16th May, 1776.
Smith, William S., A. D. C., 6th July, 1781, to 23d December, 1783.
Thornton, Presley P., A. D. C., 6th September, 1777, to ———?
Tilghman, Tench, Volunteer Secretary and Acting A. D. C., 8th August, 1776, to 21st June, 1780, and A. D. C., 21st June, 1780, to 23d December, 1783.
Trumbull, Jonathan, A. D. C., 27th July, 1775, to 15th August, 1775.
Trumbull, Jonathan, Jr., Secretary, 8th June, 1781, to 23d December, 1783.
Varick, Richard, Private Secretary, 25th May, 1781, to 23d December, 1783.
*Walker, Benjamin, A. D. C., 25th January, 1782, to 23d December, 1783.
Walker, John, A. D. C., 17th February, 1777, to 22d December, 1777.
Webb, Samuel B., A. D. C., 21st June, 1776, to 1st January, 1777.

———

*These were probably relieved at an earlier date; records incomplete.

Field Officers

OF

REGIMENTS OF THE CONTINENTAL LINE

Note.—The appointment of the first and termination of service of the last field officer of each regiment or battalion, as a general rule, indicates the term of service of each organization. While many of the regiments of the Continental Line bore a numerical designation, they were, however, generally known and designated in orders and correspondence by the names of their respective colonels or commanders. The term battalion, instead of regiment, appears to have been the general designation.

The dates here given are not in all cases dates of rank, but only the periods they belonged to the battalion; for date of rank and continuity of service see alphabetical list.

It will be observed that in many cases the successive order is somewhat irregular, which is owing to many causes, viz: absence of complete records; the several rearrangements made by law: by the authority of the commanding generals of the different departments, and by the appointment or promotion in the place of those absent on detached duty, sick, prisoners of war, etc., and who on return of such absence were returned to their former, or assigned to other, regiments.

In addition to the list of regiments or battalions herewith there were others belonging to the Continental Line—the Pulaski Legion, Lee's battalion of Light Dragoons, Armand's Partisan Corps, Corps of Engineers, Sappers and Miners, and Rangers, but only few rolls or lists of these are on file, not sufficient to make an approximately correct roster of field officers, hence they are omitted; such names, however, as were found of these organizations appear in the alphabetical list.

ARTILLERY

Gridley's and Knox's Regiment of Artillery.

Colonel Richard Gridley, 19th May, 1775, to 17th November, 1775.
Colonel Henry Knox, 17th November, 1775, to 27th December, 1776.
Lieutenant-Colonel William Burbeck, 19th May, 1775, to 25th May, 1776.
Lieutenant-Colonel David Mason, 25th May, 1776, to — December, 1776.
Major David Mason, 19th May, 1775, to 25th May, 1776.
Major Scarborough Gridley, 19th May, 1775, to 24th September, 1775.
Major John Crane, 10th December, 1775, to 1st January, 1777.
Major John Lamb, 9th January, 1776, to 1st January, 1777.

First Artillery.

Colonel Charles Harrison, 30th November, 1776, to 17th June, 1783.
Lieutenant-Colonel Edward Carrington, 30th November, 1776, to 17th June, 1783.

Major Christian Holmer, 30th November, 1776, to 1st January, 1783.
Major Wm. Brown, 31st January, 1781, to 17th June, 1783.

Second Artillery.

Colonel John Lamb, 1st January, 1777, to 17th June, 1783.
Lieutenant-Colonel Eleazer Oswald, 1st January, 1777, to 28th June, 1778.
Lieutenant-Colonel Ebenezer Stevens, 30th April, 1778, to 17th June, 1783.
Major Sebastian Bauman, 12th September, 1778, to 17th June, 1783.

Third Artillery.

Colonel John Crane, 1st January, 1777, to 17th June, 1783.
Lieutenant-Colonel John Popkin, 15th July, 1777, to 17th June, 1783.
Major William Perkins, 12th September, 1778, to 1st November, 1779.

Fourth Artillery.

Colonel Thomas Proctor, 5th February, 1777, to 18th April, 1781.
Lieutenant-Colonel John Strobagh, 3d March, 1777, to 2d December, 1778.
Lieutenant-Colonel Thomas Forrest, 2d December, 1778, to 7th October, 1781.
Lieutenant-Colonel Andrew Porter, 1st January, 1782, to 17th June, 1783.
Major Thomas Forrest, 5th February, 1777, to 2d December, 1778.
Major Benjamin Eustis, 2d December, 1778, to 6th October, 1781.
Major Andrew Porter, 19th April, 1781, to 1st January, 1782.
Major Isaac Craig, 7th October, 1781, to 17th June, 1783.
Major Francis Proctor, Jr., 1st January, 1782, to 1st January, 1783.

Corps of Artillery.

Colonel John Crane, 17th June, 1783, to 3d November, 1783.
Major Sebastian Bauman, 17th June, 1783, to 20th June, 1784.

ARTILLERY ARTIFICER REGIMENTS.
Baldwin's.

Colonel Jeduthan Baldwin, 3d September, 1776, to 29th March, 1781.
Major Jeremiah Bruen, 12th November, 1779, to 29th March, 1781.

Flower's.

Colonel Benjamin Flower, 16th July, 1776, to 28th April, 1781.
Major Joseph Seayres, 16th July, 1776, to 30th August, 1780.
Major Charles Lukens, 8th March, 1777, to 30th August, 1780.

CANADIAN REGIMENTS.

First Canadian.

Colonel James Livingston, 20th November, 1775, to 1st January, 1781.
Lieutenant-Colonel Richard Livingston, 18th December, 1776, to 2d November, 1779.
Major George C. Nicholson, 1st April, 1777, to 1st January, 1781.

Second Canadian.

(*Also called "Congress' Own."*)

Colonel Moses Hazen, 22d January, 1776, to 1st June, 1783.
Lieutenant-Colonel Edward Antil, 22d January, 1776, to 1st May, 1782.
Lieutenant-Colonel Joseph Torrey, 1st May, 1782, to 1st June, 1783.
Major John Taylor, 13th November, 1776, to 10th February, 1779.
Major Joseph Torrey, 9th January, 1777, to 1st May, 1782.
Major Tarlton Woodson, 1st May, 1777, to 1st March, 1782.
Major James R. Reid, 1st September, 1777, to 1st June, 1783.
Major Lawrence Olivia, 1st May, 1782, to 1st June, 1783.
Major Anthony Selin, ————, to 1st January, 1783.

CONNECTICUT LINE.

First Connecticut.

Colonel David Wooster, 1st May, 1775, to 25th June, 1775.
Lieutenant-Colonel Andrew Ward, 1st May, 1775, to 20th December, 1775.
Major Jabez Thompson, 1st May, 1775, to 20th December, 1775.

(*Not in service in* 1776.)

Colonel Jedediah Huntington, 1st January, 1777, to 12th May, 1777.
Colonel Josiah Starr, 27th May, 1777, to 1st January, 1781.
Colonel John Durkee, 1st January, 1781, to 29th May, 1782.
Colonel Zebulon Butler, 1st January, 1783, to — June, 1783.
Lieutenant-Colonel Samuel Prentiss, 1st January, 1777, to 27th May, 1778.
Lieutenant-Colonel David F. Sill, 13th March, 1778, to 1st January, 1781.
Lieutenant-Colonel Thomas Grosvenor, 1st January, 1781, to 1st January, 1783.
Lieutenant-Colonel Ebenezer Huntington, 1st January, 1783, to — June, 1783.
Major David F. Sill, 1st January, 1777, to 5th March, 1778.
Major Christopher Darrow, 15th April, 1778, to 27th August, 1780.
Major Abner Prior, 7th August, 1780, to 1st January, 1781.
Major Joseph A. Wright, 1st January, 1781, to June, 1783.
Major Wills Clift, 1st January, 1781, to 1st January, 1783.
Major Robert Warner, 29th May, 1782, to 1st January, 1783.
Major John P. Wyllys, 1st January, 1783, to — June, 1783.

Second Connecticut.

Colonel Joseph Spencer, 1st May, 1775, to 25th June, 1775.
Colonel Samuel Wyllys, 1st July, 1775, to 10th December, 1775.

Lieutenant-Colonel Samuel Wyllys, 1st May, 1775, to 1st July, 1775.
Lieutenant-Colonel Roger Enos, 1st July, 1775, to 10th December, 1775.
Major Roger Enos, 1st May, 1775, to 1st July, 1775.
Major Return J. Meigs, 1st July, 1775, to 10th December, 1775.

(Not in service in 1776.)

Colonel Charles Webb, 1st January, 1777, to 13th March, 1778.
Colonel Zebulon Butler, 13th March, 1778, to 1st January, 1781.
Colonel Heman Swift, 1st January, 1781, to — June, 1783.
Lieutenant Colonel Isaac Sherman, 1st January, 1777, to 28th October, 1779.
Lieutenant-Colonel Joseph Hait, 28th October, 1779, to 1st January, 1781.
Lieutenant-Colonel Jonathan Johnson, 1st January, 1781, to — June, 1783.
Major Hezekiah Holdridge, 1st January, 1777, to 25th May, 1778.
Major Amos Walbridge, 28th April, 1777, to 1st January, 1781.
Major Theodore Woodbridge, 1st January, 1781, to 1st January, 1783.
Major David Smith, 1st January, 1783, to — June, 1783.

Third Connecticut.

Colonel Israel Putnam, 1st May, 1775, to 19th June, 1775.
Colonel Experience Storrs, 1st July, 1775, to 10th December, 1775.
Lieutenant-Colonel Experience Storrs, 1st May, 1775, to 1st July, 1775.
Lieutenant-Colonel John Durkee, 1st July, 1775, to 10th December, 1775.
Major John Durkee, 1st May, 1775, to 1st July, 1775.
Major Obadiah Johnson, 1st July, 1775, to 16th December, 1775.

(Not in service in 1776.)

Colonel Samuel Wyllys, 1st January, 1777, to 1st January, 1781.
Colonel Samuel B. Webb, 1st January, 1781, to — June, 1783.
Lieutenant-Colonel Zebulon Butler, 1st January, 1777, to 13th March, 1778.
Lieutenant-Colonel Thomas Grosvenor, 13th March, 1778, to 1st January, 1781.
Lieutenant-Colonel Ebenezer Huntington, 1st January, 1781, to 1st January, 1783.
Lieutenant-Colonel Ebenezer Gray, 1st January, 1783, to — June, 1783.
Major Thomas Grosvenor, 1st January, 1777, to 13th March, 1778.
Major Wills Clift, 25th May, 1778, to 1st January, 1781.
Major John P. Wyllys, 1st January, 1781, to 1st January, 1783.
Major Joseph A. Wright, 1st January, 1783, to — June, 1783.

Fourth Connecticut.

Colonel Benjamin Hinman, 1st May, 1775, to 20th December, 1775.
Lieutenant-Colonel George Pitkin, 1st May, 1775, to 20th December, 1775.
Major Samuel Elmore, 1st May, 1775, to 20th December, 1775.

(Not in service in 1776.)

Colonel John Durkee, 1st January, 1777, to 1st January, 1781.
Colonel Zebulon Butler, 1st January, 1781, to 1st January, 1783.
Lieutenant-Colonel Giles Russell, 1st January, 1777, to 5th March, 1778.
Lieutenant-Colonel John Sumner, 28th April, 1777, to 1st January, 1781.

Lieutenant-Colonel Ebenezer Gray, 1st January, 1781, to 1st January, 1783.
Major John Sumner, 1st January, 1777, to 28th April, 1777.
Major Benjamin Throop, 1st May, 1778, to 1st January, 1781.
Major Abner Prior, 1st January, 1781, to 28th December, 1781.
Major Joseph A. Wright, 28th December, 1781, to 1st January, 1781.

Fifth Connecticut.

Colonel David Waterbury, 1st May, 1775, to 13th December, 1775.
Lieutenant-Colonel Samuel Whiting, 1st May, 1775, to 18th November, 1775.
Major Thomas Hobby, 1st May, 1775, to 13th December, 1775.

(*Not in service in* 1776.)

Colonel Philip B. Bradley, 1st January, 1777, to 1st January, 1781.
Lieutenant-Colonel Matthew Mead, 1st January, 1777, to 25th May, 1778.
Lieutenant-Colonel Jonathan Johnson, 25th May, 1778, to 1st January, 1781.
Lieutenant-Colonel Isaac Sherman, 1st January, 1781, to 1st January, 1783.
Major Jonathan Johnson, 1st January, 1777, to 25th May, 1778.
Major Albert Chapman, 5th March, 1778, to 1st January, 1781.
Major David Smith, 1st January, 1781, to 1st January, 1783.
Major Benjamin Throop, 1st January, 1781, to 1st January, 1783.

Sixth Connecticut.

Colonel Samuel H. Parsons, 1st May, 1775, to 10th December, 1775.
Lieutenant-Colonel John Tyler, 1st May, 1775, to 10th December, 1775.
Major Samuel Prentiss, 1st May, 1775, to 10th December, 1775.

(*Not in service in* 1776.)

Colonel William Douglas, 1st January, 1777, to 28th May, 1777.
Colonel Return J. Meigs, 12th May, 1777, to 1st January, 1781.
Lieutenant-Colonel David Dimon, 1st January, 1777, to 18th September, 1777.
Lieutenant-Colonel Ebenezer Gray, 15th October, 1778, to 1st January, 1781.
Major Ebenezer Gray, 1st January, 1777, to 15th October, 1778.
Major Eli Leavenworth, 27th May, 1777, to 1st January, 1781.

Seventh Connecticut.

Colonel Charles Webb, 6th July, 1775, to 10th December, 1775.
Lieutenant-Colonel Street Hall, 6th July, 1775, to 19th December, 1775.
Major Jonathan Lattimer, 6th July, 1775, to 19th December, 1775.

(*Not in service in* 1776.)

Colonel Heman Swift, 1st January, 1777, to 1st January, 1781.
Lieutenant-Colonel Josiah Starr, 1st January, 1777, to 27th May, 1777.
Lieutenant-Colonel Hezekiah Holdridge, 25th May, 1778, to 1st January, 1781.

Major John Sedgwick, 1st January, 1777, to 10th February, 1778.
Major Theodore Woodbridge, 10th February, 1778, to 1st January, 1781.

Eighth Connecticut.

Colonel Jedediah Huntington, 6th July, 1775, to 10th December, 1775.
Lieutenant-Colonel John Douglas, 6th July, 1775, to 19th December, 1775.
Major Joel Clark, 6th July, 1775, to 18th December, 1775.

(*Not in service in* 1776.)

Colonel John Chandler, 1st January, 1777, to 5th March, 1778.
Colonel Giles Russell, 5th March, 1778, to 28th October, 1779.
Lieutenant-Colonel Thomas Dyer, 1st January, 1777, to 11th April, 1778.
Lieutenant-Colonel Joseph Hait, 15th September, 1777, to 28th October, 1779.
Lieutenant-Colonel Isaac Sherman, 28th October, 1779, to 1st January, 1781.
Major Joseph Hait, 1st January, 1777, to 15th September, 1777.
Major David Smith, 13th March, 1778, to 1st January, 1781.

Swift's Connecticut Battalion.

Colonel Heman Swift, 3d June, 1783, to 25th December, 1783.
Lieutenant-Colonel Ebenezer Huntington, 3d June, 1783, to 25th December, 1783.
Major John P. Wyllys, 3d June, 1783, to 25th December, 1783.

CONTINENTAL REGIMENTS OF INFANTRY, OR "FOOT"

The following twenty-seven regiments were organized for one year from January 1, 1776. The States opposite each in parentheses ( ) show where they were raised.

First Continental Infantry. (Pennsylvania.)

Colonel William Thompson, 1st January, 1776, to 1st March, 1776.
Colonel Edward Hand, 7th March, 1776, to 31st December, 1776.
Lieutenant-Colonel James Chambers, 7th March, 1776, to 31st December, 1776.
Major Anthony J. Morris, 1st January, 1776, to 25th October, 1776.
Major James Ross, 25th October, 1776, to 31st December, 1776.

Second Continental Infantry. (New Hampshire.)

Colonel James Reed, 1st January, 1776, to 9th August, 1776.
Lieutenant-Colonel Israel Gilman, 1st January, 1776, to 31st December, 1776.
Major Nathan Hale, 1st January, 1776, to 31st December, 1776

Third Continental Infantry. (Massachusetts.)

Colonel Ebenezer Learned, 1st January, 1776, to 31st December, 1776.
Lieutenant-Colonel William Shepard, 1st January, 1776, to 31st December, 1776.
Major Ebenezer Sprout, 1st January, 1776, to 31st December, 1776.

Fourth Continental Infantry. (Massachusetts.)

Colonel John Nixon, 1st January, 1776, to 9th August, 1776.
Colonel Thomas Nixon, 9th August, 1776, to 31st December, 1776.
Lieutenant-Colonel Thomas Nixon, 1st January, 1776, to 9th August, 1776.
Major Andrew Colburn, 1st January, 1776, to 31st December, 1776.

Fifth Continental Infantry. (New Hampshire.)

Colonel John Stark, 1st January, 1776, to 31st December, 1776.
Lieutenant-Colonel Thomas Poor, 1st January, 1776, to 31st December, 1776.
Major John Moor, 1st January, 1776, to 31st December, 1776.

Sixth Continental Infantry. (Massachusetts.)

Colonel Asa Whitcomb, 1st January, 1776, to 31st December, 1776.
Lieutenant-Colonel William Buckminster, 1st January, 1776, to 22d June, 1776.
Major John G. Frazer, 1st January, 1776, to 31st December, 1776.

Seventh Continental Infantry. (Massachusetts.)

Colonel William Prescott, 1st January, 1776, to 31st December, 1776.
Lieutenant-Colonel Johnson Moulton, 1st January, 1776, to 31st December, 1776.
Major Henry Woods, 1st January, 1776, to 31st December, 1776.

Eighth Continental Infantry. (New Hampshire.)

Colonel Enoch Poor, 1st January, 1776, to 31st December, 1776.
Lieutenant-Colonel John McDuffee, 1st January, 1776, to 31st December, 1776.
Major Joseph Cilley, 1st January, 1776, to 31st December, 1776.

Ninth Continental Infantry. (Rhode Island.)

Colonel James M. Varnum, 1st January, 1776, to 31st December, 1776.
Lieutenant-Colonel Archibald Crary, 1st January, 1776, to 31st December, 1776.
Major Christopher Smith, 1st January, 1776, to 31st December, 1776.

Tenth Continental Infantry. (Connecticut.)

Colonel Samuel H. Parsons, 1st January, 1776, to 9th August, 1776.
Colonel John Tyler, 10th August, 1776, to 31st December, 1776.
Lieutenant-Colonel John Tyler, 1st January, 1776, to 10th August, 1776.
Lieutenant-Colonel Samuel Prentiss, 12th August, 1776, to 31st December, 1776.
Major Samuel Prentiss, 1st January, 1776, to 12th August, 1776.
Major James Chapman, 15th August, 1776, to 15th September, 1776.

Eleventh Continental Infantry. (Rhode Island.)

Colonel Daniel Hitchcock, 1st January, 1776, to 31st December, 1776.
Lieutenant-Colonel Ezekiel Cornell, 1st January, 1776, to 31st December, 1776.
Major Israel Angell, 1st January, 1776, to 31st December, 1776.

Twelfth Continental Infantry. (Massachusetts.)

Colonel Moses Little, 1st January, 1776, to 31st December, 1776.
Lieutenant-Colonel William Henshaw, 1st January, 1776, to 31st December, 1776.
Major James Collins, 1st January, 1776, to 31st December, 1776.

Thirteenth Continental Infantry. (Massachusetts.)

Colonel Joseph Read, 1st January, 1776, to 31st December, 1776.
Lieutenant-Colonel Ebenezer Clap, 1st January, 1776, to 31st December, 1776.
Major Calvin Smith, 1st January, 1776, to 31st December, 1776.

Fourteenth Continental Infantry. (Massachusetts.)

Colonel John Glover, 1st January, 1776, to 31st December, 1776.
Lieutenant-Colonel Gabriel Johannet, 1st January, 1776, to 31st December, 1776.
Major William R. Lee, 1st January, 1776, to 31st December, 1776.

Fifteenth Continental Infantry. (Massachusetts.)

Colonel John Paterson, 1st January, 1776, to 31st December, 1776.
Lieutenant-Colonel Seth Read, 1st January, 1776, to — August, 1776.
Major Henry Sherburne, 1st January, 1776, to 31st December, 1776.

Sixteenth Continental Infantry. (Massachusetts.)

Colonel Paul D. Sargent, 1st January, 1776, to 31st December, 1776.
Lieutenant-Colonel Michael Jackson, 1st January, 1776, to 31st December, 1776.
Major Jonathan W. Austin, 1st January, 1776, to 13th November, 1776.

Seventeenth Continental Infantry. (Connecticut.)

Colonel Jedediah Huntington, 1st January, 1776, to 31st December, 1776.
Lieutenant-Colonel Joel Clark, 1st January, 1776, to 19th December, 1776.
Major Elihu Humphreys, 1st January, 1776, to 31st December, 1776.

Eighteenth Continental Infantry. (Massachusetts.)

Colonel Edmund Phinney, 1st January, 1776, to 31st December, 1776.
Lieutenant-Colonel Samuel March, 1st January, 1776, to 31st December, 1776.
Major Jacob Brown, 1st January, 1776, to 31st December, 1776.

Nineteenth Continental Infantry. (Connecticut.)

Colonel Charles Webb, 1st January, 1776, to 31st December, 1776.
Lieutenant-Colonel Street Hall, 1st January, 1776, to 31st December, 1776.
Major John Brooks, 1st January, 1776, to 31st December, 1776.

Twentieth Continental Infantry. (Connecticut.)

Colonel Benedict Arnold, 1st January, 1776, to 10th January, 1776.
Colonel John Durkee, 12th August, 1776, to 31st December, 1776.
Lieutenant-Colonel John Durkee, 1st January, 1776, to 12th August, 1776.
Lieutenant-Colonel Thomas Knowlton, 12th August, 1776, to 16th September, 1776
Major Thomas Knowlton, 1st January, 1776, to 12th August, 1776.
Major Thomas Dyer, 19th August, 1776, to 31st December, 1776.

Twenty-First Continental Infantry. (Massachusetts.)

Colonel Jonathan Ward, 1st January, 1776, to 31st December, 1776.
Lieutenant-Colonel Benjamin Tupper, 1st January, 1776, to 31st December, 1776.
Major Timothy Bigelow, 1st January, 1776, to ——?
Major James Mellin, 15th August, 1776, to 31st December, 1776.

Twenty-Second Continental Infantry. (Connecticut.)

Colonel Samuel Wyllys, 1st January, 1776, to 31st December, 1776.
Lieutenant-Colonel Rufus Putnam, 1st January, 1776, to 31st December, 1776.
Major Levi Wells, 1st January, 1776, to 31st December, 1776.
Major Hezekiah Holdridge, 3d September, 1776, to 31st December, 1776.

Twenty-Third Continental Infantry. (Massachusetts.)

Colonel John Bailey, 1st January, 1776, to 31st December, 1776.
Lieutenant-Colonel John Jacobs, 1st January, 1776, to 31-st December, 1776.
Major Josiah Haden, 1st January, 1776, to 31st December, 1776.

Twenty-Fourth Continental Infantry. (Massachusetts.)

Colonel John Greaton, 1st January, 1776, to 31st December, 1776.
Lieutenant-Colonel Joseph Vose, 1st January, 1776, to 31st December, 1776.
Major Jotham Loring, 1st January, 1776, to 31st December, 1776.

Twenty-Fifth Continental Infantry. (Massachusetts.)

Colonel William Bond, 1st January, 1776, to 31st August, 1776.
Lieutenant-Colonel Ichabod Alden, 1st January, 1776, to 31st December, 1776.
Major Nathaniel Cudworth, 1st January, 1776, to 31st December, 1776.

Twenty-Sixth Continental Infantry. (Massachusetts.)

Colonel Loammi Baldwin, 1st January, 1776, to 31st December, 1776.
Lieutenant-Colonel James Wesson, 1st January, 1776, to 31st December, 1776.
Major Daniel Wood, 1st January, 1776, to 10th August, 1776.
Major Isaac Sherman, 10th August, 1776, to 31st December, 1776.

Twenty-Seventh Continental Infantry. (Massachusetts.)

Colonel Israel Hutchinson, 1st January, 1776, to 31st December, 1776.
Lieutenant-Colonel Benjamin Holden, 1st January, 1776, to 31st December, 1776.
Major Ezra Putnam, 1st January, 1776, to 31st December, 1776.

THE SIXTEEN ADDITIONAL CONTINENTAL REGIMENTS.

These regiments or battalions were authorized by the Resolve of Congress, 27th December, 1776; they were not numbered, but were known by the names of their respective colonels, were raised at large, and are here arranged in the alphabetical order of the names of their commanders.

Forman's.

Colonel David Forman, 12th January, 1777, to 1st July, 1778.
Lieutenant-Colonel Thomas Henderson, 12th January, 1777, to — October, 1777.
Major William Harrison, 1st May, 1777, to 1st July, 1778.
(*This regiment never was fully completed, and on July 1, 1778, was disbanded and officers and men transferred mainly to the New Jersey Line.*)

Gist's.

Colonel Nathaniel Gist, 11th January, 1777, to 1st January, 1781.
Lieutenant-Colonel ———?
Major ———?
Major Nathaniel Mitchell, 22d April, 1779, to 1st January, 1781.

Grayson's.

Colonel William Grayson, 11th January, 1777, to 22d April, 1779.
Lieutenant-Colonel Levin Powell, 11th January, 1777, to 15th November, 1778.
Lieutenant-Colonel John Thornton, 15th November, 1778, to 22d April, 1779.

Major David Ross, 11th January, 1777, to 20th December, 1777.
Major John Thornton, 20th March, 1777, to 15th November, 1778.
Major Nathaniel Mitchell, 23d December, 1777, to 22d April, 1779.
 (*Regiment was consolidated with Gist's Regiment, 22d April, 1779.*)

Hartley's.

Colonel Thomas Hartley, 1st January, 1777, to 16th December, 1778.
Lieutenant-Colonel Morgan Connor, 9th April, 1777, to 16th December, 1778.
Major Adam Hubley, 12th January, 1777, to 12th March, 1777.
Major Lewis Bush, 12th March, 1777, to 15th September, 1777.
 (*Regiment transferred to the Pennsylvania Line, 16th December, 1778, and designated the Eleventh Pennsylvania.*)

Henley's.

Colonel David Henley, 1st January, 1777, to 22d April, 1779.
Lieutenant-Colonel William Tudor, 1st January, 1777, to 9th April, 1778.
Major William Curtis, 1st January, 1777, to 20th May, 1778.
Major Lemuel Trescott, 20th May, 1778, to 22d April, 1779.
 (*Regiment was consolidated with Jackson's Regiment, 22d April, 1779.*)

Jackson's.

Colonel Henry Jackson, 12th January, 1777, to 23d July, 1780.
Lieutenant-Colonel David Cobb, 12th January, 1777, to 23d July, 1780.
Major John S. Tyler, 1st February, 1777, to — March, 1779.
Major Lemuel Trescott, 22d April, 1779, to 23d July, 1780.
 (*Regiment was transferred to the Massachusetts Line, 23d July, 1780, and designated the Sixteenth Massachusetts.*)

Lee's.

Colonel William R. Lee, 1st January, 1777, to 24th January, 1778.
Lieutenant-Colonel William S. Smith, 1st January, 1777, to 22d April, 1779
Major Joseph Swasey, 1st January, 1777, to 9th July, 1778.
 (*Regiment was consolidated with Jackson's Regiment, 22d April, 1779.*)

Malcolm's.

Colonel William Malcolm, 30th April, 1777, to 22d April, 1779.
Lieutenant-Colonel Aaron Burr, 4th January, 1777, to 31st March, 1779.
Major Albert Pawling, 27th January, 1777, to 22d April, 1779.
 (*Regiment was consolidated with Spencer's Regiment, 22d April, 1779.*)

Patton's.

Colonel John Patton, 11th January, 1777, to 3d February, 1778.
Lieutenant-Colonel John Park, 11th January, 1777, to 29th October, 1778.
Major Peter Scull, 11th January, 1777, to 1st January, 1778.
Major Joseph Prowell, 1st January, 1778, to 13th January, 1779.

    (Regiment broken up in January, 1779; part of it was transferred to the 11th Pennsylvania and the remainder to the Delaware Regiment.)

Rawlings'.

Colonel Moses Rawlings, 12th January, 1777, to 2d June, 1779.
Lieutenant-Colonel ———?
Major Alexander Smith, 11th September, 1777, to 6th September, 1780.

    (No rolls, returns, or lists of this regiment were found, but from correspondence, orders, &c., it would appear that it never was fully organized. It was originally raised in 1776 in Maryland and Virginia as Stephenson's Maryland and Virginia Rifle Regiment, and reorganized in 1777 as one of the sixteen additional Continental Regiments.)

Sherburne's.

Colonel Henry Sherburne, 12th January, 1777, to 1st January, 1781.
Lieutenant-Colonel Return J. Meigs, 22d February, 1777, to 12th May, 1777.
Major William Bradford, 12th January, 1777, to 1st January, 1781.

Spencer's.

Colonel Oliver Spencer, 15th January, 1777, to 1st January, 1781.
Lieutenant-Colonel Eleazer Lindsley, 15th January, 1777, to 27th May, 1779.
Lieutenant-Colonel William S. Smith, 22d April, 1779, to 1st January, 1781.
Major John Burrowes, 22d July, 1779, to 1st January, 1781.

Thruston's.

Colonel Charles M. Thruston, 15th January, 1777, to 1st January, 1779.
Lieutenant-Colonel ———?
Major ———?

    (No rolls, returns, or lists of this regiment were found; it would appear, however, that the regiment never was fully organized, and that it was merged into Gist's Regiment, 22d April, 1779.)

Warner's.

Colonel Seth Warner, 5th July, 1776, to 1st January, 1781.
Lieutenant-Colonel Samuel Safford, 5th July, 1776, to 1st January, 1781.
Major Elisha Painter, 5th July, 1776, to 11th October, 1778.
Major Gideon Brownson, 16th July, 1779, to 1st January, 1781.

(*This regiment was organized under the Resolve of Congress of July 5, 1776; not being attached to any of the States, it was regarded in 1777 as one of the sixteen additional Continental Regiments.*)

Webb's.

Colonel Samuel B. Webb, 1st January, 1777, to 1st January, 1781.
Lieutenant-Colonel William S. Livingston, 1st January, 1777, to 10th October, 1778.
Lieutenant-Colonel Ebenezer Huntington, 10th October, 1778, to 1st January, 1781.
Major Ebenezer Huntington, 1st January, 1777, to 10th October, 1778.
Major John P. Wyllys, 10th October, 1778, to 1st January, 1781.

(*Regiment was transferred to the Connecticut Line January 1st, 1781, and designated the Third Connecticut.*)

German Battalion.

Colonel Nicholas Haussegger, 17th July, 1776, to 19th March, 1777.
Colonel DeArendt (Baron), 19th March, 1777, to 1st January, 1781.
Lieutenant-Colonel George Stricker, 17th July, 1776, to 29th April, 1777.
Lieutenant-Colonel Ludowick Weltner, 29th April, 1777, to 1st January, 1781.
Lieutenant-Colonel William Klein, 3d September, 1778, to 21st June, 1779.
Major Ludowick Weltner, 17th July, 1776, to 29th April, 1777.
Major William Klein, 17th July, 1776, to 3d September, 1778.
Major Daniel Burchardt, 9th April, 1777, to 2d July, 1779.
Major George Hubley, 9th April, 1777, to 7th February, 1779.

(*This battalion or regiment was organized under the Resolve of Congress of May 25, 1776. It was raised in Pennsylvania and Maryland, but, not belonging to any State, it was regarded in 1777 as one of the sixteen additional regiments.*)

CORPS OF INVALIDS.

Also Called Invalid Regiment or Battalion.

(*Organized under the Resolve of Congress, June 18, 1777.*)

Colonel Lewis Nicola, 20th June, 1777, to — June, 1783.

DELAWARE LINE.

Delaware Regiment.

Colonel John Haslet, 19th January, 1776, to 3d January, 1777.
Colonel David Hall, 5th April, 1777, to 17th May, 1782.

Lieutenant-Colonel Gunning Bedford, 19th January, 1776, to 1st January, 1777.
Lieutenant-Colonel Charles Pope, 5th April, 1777, to 13th December, 1779.
Lieutenant-Colonel Joseph Vaughan, 14th December, 1779, to close of war.
Major Thomas McDonough, 22d March, 1776, to 1st January, 1777.
Major Joseph Vaughan, 5th April, 1777, to 14th December, 1779.
Major John Patten, 14th December, 1779, to close of war.

LIGHT DRAGOONS.

First Dragoons.

Colonel Theodoric Bland, 31st March, 1777, to 10th December, 1779.
Colonel Anthony W. White, 16th February, 1780, to 9th November, 1782.
Lieutenant-Colonel Benjamin Temple, 31st March, 1777, to 10th December, 1779.
Lieutenant-Colonel Anthony W. White, 10th December, 1779, to 16th February, 1780.
Major John Jameson, 31st March, 1777, to 1st August, 1779.
Major Epaphras Bull, 1st August, 1779, to — September, 1781.
Major John Swan, 21st October, 1780, to 9th November, 1782.
        (*Consolidated with Third Regiment 9th November, 1782.*)

Second Dragoons.

Colonel Elisha Sheldon, 12th December, 1776, to close of war.
Lieutenant-Colonel Samuel Blagden, 7th April, 1777, to 1st August, 1779.
Lieutenant-Colonel John Jameson, 1st August, 1779, to close of war.
Major Samuel Blagden, 24th December, 1776, to 7th April, 1777.
Major Benjamin Talmadge, 7th April, 1777, to close of war.

Third Dragoons.

Colonel George Baylor, 9th January, 1777, to close of war.
Lieutenant-Colonel Benjamin Bird, 14th March, 1777, to 20th November, 1778.
Lieutenant-Colonel William A. Washington, 20th November, 1778, to 9th November, 1782.
Major Alexander Clough, 8th January, 1777, to 28th September, 1778.
Major Richard Call, 2d October, 1778, to 9th November, 1782.
Major John Belfield, — ——, 1780, to 9th November, 1782.
Major John Swan, 9th November, 1782, to close of war.
        (*The First and Third Regiments were consolidated 9th November, 1782, and thereafter the consolidated regiment was known as Baylor's Dragoons.*)

Fourth Dragoons.

Colonel Stephen Moylan, 5th January, 1777, to close of war.
Lieutenant-Colonel Anthony W. White, 15th February, 1777, to 10th December, 1779.

Lieutenant-Colonel Benjamin Temple, 10th December, 1779, to close of war.
Major William A. Washington, 27th January, 1777, to 20th November, 1778.
Major Moore Fauntleroy, 1st August, 1779, to ——?
Major David Hopkins, ——, 1780, to ——?

GEORGIA LINE.

First Georgia.

Colonel Lachlan McIntosh, 7th January, 1776, to 16th September, 1776.
Colonel Joseph Habersham, 16th September, 1776, to 21st March, 1778.
Colonel Robert Rae, 21st March, 1778, to close of war.
Lieutenant-Colonel Samuel Elbert, 7th January, 1776, to 5th July, 1776.
Lieutenant-Colonel Francis H. Harris, 5th July, 1776, to 17th September, 1776.
Lieutenant-Colonel Thomas Chisholm, 21st March, 1778, to ——?
Major Joseph Habersham, 7th January, 1776, to 5th July, 1776.
Major Francis H. Harris, 5th July, 1776, to 17th September, 1776.
Major John McIntosh, 14th September, 1776, to 1st April, 1778.
Major John Habersham, 1st April, 1778, to close of war.

Second Georgia.

Colonel Samuel Elbert, 5th July, 1776, to close of war.
Lieutenant-Colonel Stephen Drayton, 7th January, 1776, to 5th July, 1776.
Lieutenant-Colonel John Stirk, 5th July, 1776, to 20th March, 1778.
Lieutenant-Colonel Daniel Roberts, 21st March, 1778, to 18th November, 1779.
Lieutenant-Colonel Benjamin Porter, 18th November, 1779, to ——?
Major Joseph Pannill, 5th July, 1776, to 16th April, 1778.
Major Benjamin Porter, 16th April, 1778, to 18th November, 1779.
Major Francis Moore, 18th November, 1779, to ——, 1782.

Third Georgia.

Colonel James Screven, 5th July, 1776, to 20th March, 1778.
Colonel John Stirk, 20th March, 1778, to close of war.
Lieutenant-Colonel Robert Rae, 5th July, 1776, to 21st March, 1778.
Lieutenant-Colonel John McIntosh, 1st April, 1778, to close of war.
Major Daniel Roberts, 5th July, 1776, to 21st March, 1778.
Major Joseph Lane, 2d April, 1778, to — October, 1780.

Fourth Georgia.

Colonel John White, 1st February, 1777, to — October, 1781.
Lieutenant-Colonel Thomas Hovenden, 1st February, 1777, to 16th April, 1778.

Lieutenant-Colonel Joseph Pannill, 16th April, 1778, to 22d October, 1782.
Major Thomas Chisholm, 1st February, 1777, to 21st March, 1778.
Major Philip Lowe, 18th June, 1778, to 1st October, 1780.

MARYLAND LINE.

Smallwood's Maryland Regiment.

Colonel William Smallwood, 14th January, 1776, to — December, 1776.
Lieutenant-Colonel Francis Ware, 14th January, 1776, to — December, 1776.
Major Thomas Price, 14th January, 1776, to — December, 1776.
Major Mordecai Gist, 14th January, 1776, to — December, 1776.

First Maryland.

Colonel Francis Ware, 10th December, 1776, to 18th February, 1777.
Colonel John H. Stone, 18th February, 1777, to 1st August, 1779.
Colonel Otho H. Williams, 1st January, 1781, to 9th May, 1782.
Lieutenant-Colonel John H. Stone, 10th December, 1776, to 18th February, 1777.
Lieutenant-Colonel Patrick Sim, 18th February, 1777, to 10th June, 1777.
Lieutenant-Colonel Uriah Forrest, 10th April, 1777, to 1st August, 1779.
Lieutenant-Colonel Peter Adams, 1st August, 1779, to 1st January, 1781.
Lieutenant-Colonel John Stewart, 10th February, 1781, to — December, 1782.
Lieutenant-Colonel Levin Winder, 1st January, 1783, to 12th April, 1783.
Major Patrick Sim, 10th December, 1776, to 18th February, 1777.
Major Thomas Woolford, 20th February, 1777, to 17th April, 1777.
Major Levin Winder, 17th April, 1777, to 1st January, 1781.
Major William Sterrett, 10th April, 1777, to 15th December, 1777.
Major Alexander Roxburg, 7th April, 1780, to 1st January, 1781.
Major John Eccleston, 1st January, 1781, to 12th April, 1783.
Major Jonathan Sellman, 9th May, 1782, to 12th April, 1783.

Second Maryland.

Colonel Thomas Price, 10th December, 1776, to 21st April, 1780.
Colonel John Gunbey, 1st January, 1781, to 12th April, 1783.
Lieutenant-Colonel Thomas Woolford, 17th April, 1777, to 22d October, 1779.
Lieutenant-Colonel John E. Howard, 22d October, 1779, to 12th April, 1783.
Major Benjamin Ford, 10th December, 1776, to 17th April, 1777.
Major John Stewart, 17th April, 1777, to 10th February, 1781.
Major John Dean, 1st January, 1781, to 6th November, 1781.
Major Wm. D. Beall, 6th November, 1781, to 1st January, 1783.

Third Maryland.

Colonel Mordecai Gist, 10th December, 1776, to 9th January, 1779.
Lieutenant-Colonel Nathaniel Ramsay, 10th December, 1776, to 1st January, 1781

Lieutenant-Colonel Peter Adams, 1st January, 1781, to 12th April, 1783.
Major Uriah Forrest, 10th December, 1776, to 10th April, 1777.
Major Archibald Anderson, 10th June, 1777, to 15th March, 1781.
Major Henry Hardman, 1st January, 1781, to 1st January, 1783.
Major Thomas Lansdale, 19th February, 1781, to 12th April, 1783.

Fourth Maryland.

Colonel Josias C. Hall, 10th December, 1776, to 1st January, 1781.
Lieutenant-Colonel Samuel Smith, 22d February, 1777, to 22d May, 1779.
Lieutenant-Colonel Edward Tillard, 22d May, 1779, to 1st January, 1781.
Lieutenant-Colonel Thomas Woolford, 1st January, 1781, to 1st January, 1783.
Major Samuel Smith, 10th December, 1776, to 22d February, 1777.
Major John E. Howard, 22d February, 1777, to 11th March, 1778.
Major John Dean, 11th March, 1778, to 1st January, 1781.
Major Levin Winder, 1st January, 1781, to 27th April, 1781.
Major Alexander Roxburg, 1st January, 1781, to 1st January, 1783.
Major John Lynch, 8th September, 1781, to 1st January, 1783.

Fifth Maryland.

Colonel William Richardson, 10th December, 1776, to 22d October, 1779.
Lieutenant-Colonel James Hindman, 10th December, 1776, to 4th April, 1777.
Lieutenant-Colonel John E. Howard, 11th March, 1778, to 22d October, 1779.
Lieutenant-Colonel Thomas Woolford, 22d October, 1779, to 1st January, 1781.
Lieutenant-Colonel Benjamin Ford, 1st January, 1781, to 27th April, 1781.
Lieutenant-Colonel Levin Winder, 27th April, 1781, to 1st January, 1783.
Major Thomas Smith, 10th December, 1776, to 12th March, 1778.
Major John Eccleston, 10th December, 1777, to 1st January, 1781.
Major John Davidson, 12th January, 1781, to 1st January, 1783.
Major Benjamin Brookes, 16th March, 1781, to 1st January, 1783.

Sixth Maryland.

Colonel Otho H. Williams, 10th December, 1776, to 1st January, 1781.
Lieutenant-Colonel Henry Shyrock, 10th December, 1776, to 17th April, 1777.
Lieutenant-Colonel Benjamin Ford, 17th April, 1777, to 1st January, 1781.
Major Edward Tillard, 10th December, 1776, to 22d May, 1779.
Major Henry Hardman, 22d May, 1779, to 1st January, 1781.

Seventh Maryland.

Colonel John Gunby, 17th April, 1777, to 1st January, 1781.
Lieutenant-Colonel John Gunby, 10th December, 1776, to 17th April, 1777.

Lieutenant-Colonel Peter Adams, 20th February, 1777, to 1st August, 1779.
Lieutenant-Colonel Uriah Forrest, 1st August, 1779, to 23d February, 1781.
Major Peter Adams, 10th December, 1776, to 20th February, 1777.
Major Daniel J. Adams, 1st April, 1777, to 8th June, 1779.
Major Adam Grosh, 8th June, 1779, to 7th April, 1780.
Major Alexander Roxburg, 7th April, 1780, to 1st January, 1781.

Maryland Battalion.

Colonel John Gunby, 12th April, 1783, to 15th November, 1783.
Lieutenant-Colonel John Eccleston, 12th April, 1783, to 15th November, 1783.
Major Alexander Roxburg, 12th April, 1783, to 15th November, 1783.

MASSACHUSETTS LINE.

NOTE.—*The following twenty-seven battalions were organized immediately after the Lexington Alarm; they appear not to have been numbered, but were known by the names of their respective commanders.*

D. Brewer's.

Colonel David Brewer, 17th June, 1775, to 24th October, 1775.
Lieutenant-Colonel Rufus Putnam, 17th June, 1775, to — December, 1775.
Major Nathaniel Danielson, 17th June, 1775, to — December, 1775.

J. Brewer's.

Colonel Jonathan Brewer, 19th May, 1775, to — December, 1775.
Lieutenant-Colonel William Buckminster, 19th May, 1775, to — December, 1775.
Major Nathaniel Cudworth, 19th May, 1775, to — December, 1775.

Bridge's.

Colonel Ebenezer Bridge, 27th May, 1775, to — December, 1775.
Lieutenant-Colonel Moses Parker, 27th May, 1775, to 4th July, 1775.
Major John Brooks, 27th May, 1775, to — December, 1775.

Cotton's.

Colonel Theophilus Cotton, 27th May, 1775, to — December, 1775.
Lieutenant-Colonel Ichabod Alden, 27th May, 1775, to — December, 1775.
Major Ebenezer Sprout, 27th May, 1775, to — December, 1775.

Danielson's.

Colonel Timothy Danielson, 27th May, 1775, to — December, 1775.
Lieutenant-Colonel William Shepard, 27th May, 1775, to — December, 1775.
Major David Leonard, 27th May, 1775, to — December, 1775.

Doolittle's.

Colonel Ephraim Doolittle, 27th May, 1775, to — October, 1775.
Lieutenant-Colonel Benjamin Holden, 27th May, 1775, to — December, 1775.
Major William Moore, 27th May, 1775, to 17th June, 1775.

Fellows'.

Colonel John Fellows, 31st May, 1775, to — December, 1775.
Lieutenant-Colonel Nahum Eager, 31st May, 1775, to — December, 1775.
Major Benjamin Tupper, 31st May, 1775, to 4th November, 1775.

Frye's.

Colonel James Frye, 19th May, 1775, to — December, 1775.
Lieutenant-Colonel James Brickett, 20th May, 1775, to — December, 1775.
Major Thomas Poor, 20th May, 1775, to — December, 1775.

Gardner's.

Colonel Thomas Gardner, 2d June, 1775, to 3d July, 1775.
Colonel William Bond, 3d July, 1775, to — December, 1775.
Lieutenant-Colonel William Bond, 2d June, 1775, to 3d July, 1775.
Major Michael Jackson, 2d June, 1775, to — December, 1775.

Gerrish's.

Colonel Samuel Gerrish, 19th May, 1775, to 19th August, 1775.
Lieutenant-Colonel Loammi Baldwin, 19th May, 1775, to — December, 1775.
Major James Wesson, 19th May, 1775, to — December, 1775.

Glover's.

Colonel John Glover, 19th May, 1775, to — December, 1775.
Lieutenant-Colonel Gabriel Johannet, 19th May, 1775, to — December, 1775.
Major William L. Lee, 19th May, 1775, to — December, 1775.

Heath's.

Colonel William Heath, 19th May, 1775, to 22d June, 1775.
Colonel John Greaton, 1st July, 1775, to — December, 1775.
Lieutenant-Colonel John Greaton, 19th May, 1775, to 1st July, 1775.
Major Jotham Loring, 19th May, 1775, to — December, 1775.

Learned's.

Colonel Ebenezer Learned, 19th May, 1775, to — December, 1775.
Lieutenant-Colonel Danforth Keyes, 19th May, 1775, to — December, 1775.
Major Joseph Vose, 19th May, 1775, to 1st July, 1775.
Major Jonathan Holman, 1st July, 1775, to —— December, 1775.

Little's.

Colonel Moses Little, 19th May, 1775, to — December, 1775.
Lieutenant-Colonel Isaac Smith, 19th May, 1775, to — December, 1775.
Major James Collins, 19th May, 1775, to — December, 1775.

Mansfield's.

Colonel John Mansfield, 27th May, 1775, to 15th September, 1775.
Lieutenant-Colonel Israel Hutchinson, 27th May, 1775, to — December, 1775.
Major Ezra Putnam, 27th May, 1775, to — December, 1775.

Nixon's.

Colonel John Nixon, 19th May, 1775, to — December, 1775.
Lieutenant-Colonel Thomas Nixon, 19th May, 1775, to — December, 1775.
Major John Butterick, 19th May, 1775, to — December, 1775.

Paterson's.

Colonel John Paterson, 27th May, 1775, to — December, 1775.
Lieutenant-Colonel Seth Read, 27th May, 1775, to — December, 1775.
Major Jeremiah Cady, 27th May, 1775, to ——, 1775.

Phinney's.

Colonel Edmund Phinney, 19th May, 1775, to — December, 1775.
Lieutenant-Colonel Samuel March, 19th May, 1775, to 1st August, 1775.
Major Jacob Brown, 19th May, 1775, to — December, 1775.

Prescott's.

Colonel William Prescott, 19th May, 1775, to — December, 1775.
Lieutenant-Colonel John Robinson, 19th May, 1775, to — December, 1775.
Major Henry Woods, 19th May, 1775, to — December, 1775.

Read's.

Colonel Joseph Read, 18th May, 1775, to — December, 1775.
Lieutenant-Colonel Ebenezer Clap, 18th May, 1775, to — December, 1775.
Major Calvin Smith, 18th May, 1775, to — December, 1775.

Sargent's.

Colonel Paul D. Sargent, 19th May, 1775, to — December, 1775.
Lieutenant-Colonel Aaron Cleveland, 19th May, 1775, to — December, 1775
Major John A. Austin, 19th May, 1775, to — December, 1775.

Scammon's.

Colonel James Scammon, — May, 1775, to — December, 1775.
Lieutenant-Colonel Johnson Moulton, — May, 1775, to — December, 1775.
Major Daniel Wood, — May, 1775, to — December, 1775.

Thomas'.

Colonel John Thomas, 19th May, 1775, to 30th June, 1775.
Colonel John Bailey, 1st July, 1775, to — December, 1775.
Lieutenant-Colonel John Bailey, 19th May, 1775, to 1st July, 1775.
Lieutenant-Colonel Thomas Mitchell, 1st July, 1775, to — December, 1775.
Major Thomas Mitchell, 19th May, 1775, to 1st July, 1775.
Major John Jacobs, 1st July, 1775, to — December, 1775.

Walker's.

Colonel Timothy Walker, 23d May, 1775, to — December, 1775.
Lieutenant-Colonel Nathaniel Leonard, 23d May, 1775, to — December, 1775.
Major Abiel Mitchell, 23d May, 1775, to — December, 1775.

Ward's.

Colonel Artemus Ward, 23d May, 1775, to 17th June, 1775.
Colonel Jonathan Ward, 17th June, 1775, to — December, 1775.
Lieutenant-Colonel Jonathan Ward, 23d May, 1775, to 17th June, 1775.
Lieutenant-Colonel Edward Barnes, 17th June, 1775, to — December, 1775.
Major Edward Barnes, 23d May, 1775, to 17th June, 1775.
Major Timothy Bigelow, 15th June, 1775, to — December, 1775.

Whitcomb's.

Colonel Asa Whitcomb, 3d June, 1775, to — December, 1775.
Lieutenant-Colonel Josiah Whitney, 3d June, 1775, to ——?, 1775.
Major Ephraim Sawyer, 3d June, 1775, to — December, 1775.

Woodbridge's.

Colonel Benjamin R. Woodbridge, 16th June, 1775, to — December, 1775.
Lieutenant-Colonel Abijah Brown, 16th June, 1775, to — December, 1775.
Major William Stacey, 16th June, 1775, to — December, 1775.

First Massachusetts.

Colonel Joseph Vose, 1st January, 1777, to 3d November, 1783.
Lieutenant-Colonel Elijah Vose, 21st January, 1777, to 3d November, 1783.

Major Elijah Vose, 1st January, 1777, to 21st January, 1777.
Major Thomas Cogswell, 1st January, 1777, to 26th November, 1779.
Major Joseph Pettingill, 1st January, 1781, to 3d November, 1783.

Second Massachusetts.

Colonel John Bailey, 1st November, 1776, to 21st October, 1780.
Lieutenant-Colonel Benjamin Tupper, 1st November, 1776, to 7th July, 1777.
Lieutenant-Colonel Ezra Badlam, 7th July, 1777, to 1st January, 1781.
Lieutenant-Colonel Ebenezer Sprout, 1st January, 1781, to 3d November, 1783.
Major Andrew Peters, 1st January, 1777, to 1st July, 1779.
Major Hugh Maxwell, 1st July, 1779, to 1st August, 1782.
Major Caleb Gibbs, 1st January, 1781, to 3d November, 1783.
Major Robert Oliver, 1st January, 1783, to 3d November, 1783.

Third Massachusetts.

Colonel John Greaton, 1st November, 1776, to 7th January, 1783.
Colonel Michael Jackson, 12th June, 1783, to 3d November, 1783.
Lieutenant-Colonel Jotham Loring, 1st January, 1777, to 12th August, 1779.
Lieutenant-Colonel William Hull, 12th August, 1779, to 3d November, 1783.
Lieutenant-Colonel James Mellen, 7th January, 1783, to 12th June, 1783.
Major Edward Williams, 1st January, 1777, to 25th May, 1777.
Major John Popkin, 1st January, 1777, to 15th July, 1777.
Major Robert Oliver, 1st November, 1777, to 1st January, 1783.
Major Seth Drew, 1st January, 1783, to 12th June, 1783.
Major Billy Porter, 12th June, 1783, to 3d November, 1783.

Fourth Massachusetts.

Colonel William Shepard, 1st January, 1777, to 1st January, 1783.
Colonel Henry Jackson, 1st January, 1783, to 3d November, 1783.
Lieutenant-Colonel Ebenezer Sprout, 1st January, 1777, to 29th September, 1778.
Lieutenant-Colonel William Stacey, 29th September, 1778, to 1st January, 1781.
Lieutenant-Colonel James Mellen, 1st January, 1781, to 7th January, 1783.
Lieutenant-Colonel Ezra Newhall, 7th January, 1783, to 3d November, 1783.
Major Warham Parks, 1st January, 1777, to — July, 1778.
Major Libbeus Ball, 1st November, 1777, to 27th October, 1780.
Major Nathan Rice, 1st January, 1781, to 12th June, 1783.
Major Lemuel Trescott, 12th June, 1783, to 3d November, 1783.

Fifth Massachusetts.

Colonel Rufus Putnam, 1st November, 1776, to 7th January, 1783.
Lieutenant-Colonel David Henley, 1st November, 1776, to 1st January, 1777.

Lieutenant-Colonel Thomas Farrington, 1st January, 1777, to 26th May, 1777.
Lieutenant-Colonel Ezra Newhall, 17th May, 1777, to 7th January, 1783.
Lieutenant-Colonel David Cobb, 7th January, 1783, to 12th June, 1783.
Major Ezra Newhall, 1st November, 1776, to 17th May, 1777.
Major Jonathan Allen, 17th May, 1777, to 6th January, 1780.
Major Moses Ashley, 6th January, 1780, to 1st January, 1783.
Major Moses Knap, 1st January, 1783, to 12th June, 1783.
Major John Burnham, 9th January, 1783, to 12th June, 1783.

Sixth Massachusetts.

Colonel Thomas Nixon, 1st January, 1777, to 1st January, 1781.
Colonel Benjamin Tupper, 1st January, 1783, to 12th June, 1783.
Lieutenant-Colonel Calvin Smith, 1st November, 1776, to 10th March, 1779.
Lieutenant-Colonel Daniel Whiting, 29th September, 1778, to 1st January, 1781.
Lieutenant-Colonel Calvin Smith, 1st January, 1781, to 12th June, 1783.
Major Joseph Thompson, 1st November, 1776, to 19th December, 1777.
Major Peter Harwood, 19th December, 1777, to 16th October, 1780.
Major John Spurr, 16th October, 1780, to 1st January, 1781.
Major John Porter, 1st January, 1781, to 12th October, 1782.
Major Moses Ashby, 1st January, 1783, to 12th June, 1783.

Seventh Massachusetts.

Colonel Ichabod Alden, 1st November, 1776, to 10th November, 1778.
Lieutenant-Colonel William Stacey, 1st November, 1776, to 29th September, 1778.
Lieutenant-Colonel John Brooks, 11th November, 1778, to 12th June, 1783.
Major Daniel Whiting, 1st January, 1777, to 29th September, 1778.
Major Samuel Darby, 29th September, 1778, to 1st January, 1783.
Major Billy Porter, 1st January, 1781, to 12th June, 1783.
Major Lemuel Trescott, 1st January, 1783, to 12th June, 1783.

Eighth Massachusetts.

Colonel Michael Jackson, 1st January, 1777, to 12th June, 1783.
Lieutenant-Colonel John Brooks, 1st November, 1776, to 11th November, 1778.
Lieutenant-Colonel Tobias Fernald, 6th March, 1779, to 1st January, 1781.
Lieutenant-Colonel Ezra Badlam, 1st January, 1781, to 1st August, 1782.
Lieutenant-Colonel Hugh Maxwell, 1st August, 1782, to 12th June, 1783.
Major William Hull, 1st January, 1777, to 12th August, 1779.
Major James Keith, 12th August, 1779, to 1st January, 1783.
Major Samuel Darby, 1st January, 1783, to 12th June, 1783.

Ninth Massachusetts.

Colonel James Wesson, 1st November, 1776, to 1st January, 1781.
Colonel Henry Jackson, 1st January, 1781, to 1st January, 1783.
Lieutenant-Colonel James Mellen, 1st November, 1776, to 1st January, 1781.
Lieutenant-Colonel David Cobb, 1st January, 1781, to 1st January, 1783.
Major Ezra Badlam, 1st November, 1776, to 7th July, 1777.
Major Joseph Pettengill, 26th July, 1779, to 1st January, 1783.
Major Lemuel Trescott, ·1st January, 1781, to 1st January, 1783.

Tenth Massachusetts.

Colonel Thomas Marshall, 6th November, 1776, to 1st January, 1781.
Colonel Benjamin Tupper, 1st January, 1781, to 1st January, 1783.
Lieutenant-Colonel Ephraim Jackson, 6th November, 1776, to 19th December, 1777.
Lieutenant-Colonel Joseph Thompson, 19th December, 1777, to 1st January, 1781.
Lieutenant-Colonel Tobias Fernald, 1st January, 1781, to 1st January, 1783.
Major John Woodbridge, 6th November, 1776, to 31st October, 1777.
Major Nathaniel Winslow, 1st November, 1777, to 26th October, 1780.
Major Billy Porter, 26th October, 1780, to 1st January, 1781.
Major Moses Knap, 1st January, 1781, to 1st January, 1783.

Eleventh Massachusetts.

Colonel Ebenezer Francis, 6th November, 1776, to 7th July, 1777.
Colonel Benjamin Tupper, 7th July, 1777, to 1st January, 1781.
Lieutenant-Colonel Noah M. Littlefield, 6th November, 1776, to 1st January, 1781.
Major William Lithgow, 1st January, 1777, to 29th July, 1779.
Major Moses Knap, 5th November, 1778, to 1st January, 1781.

Twelfth Massachusetts.

Colonel Samuel Brewer, 6th November, 1776, to 29th September, 1778.
Lieutenant-Colonel Samuel Carlton, 6th November, 1776, to 28th September, 1778.
Lieutenant-Colonel Ebenezer Sprout, 29th September, 1778, to 1st January, 1781.
Major Tobias Fernald, 6th November, 1776, to 6th March, 1779.
Major Thomas Barnes, 6th March, 1779, to 7th November, 1780.

Thirteenth Massachusetts.

Colonel Edward Wigglesworth, 1st January, 1777, to 10th March, 1779.
Lieutenant-Colonel Nathan Fuller, 1st January, 1777, to 28th June, 1777.
Lieutenant-Colonel Dudley Coleman, 3d July, 1777, to 10th March, 1779.

Lieutenant-Colonel Calvin Smith, 10th March, 1779, to 1st January, 1781.
Major Dudley Coleman, 1st January, 1777, to 3d July, 1777.
Major John Porter, 30th May, 1777, to 1st January, 1781.

Fourteenth Massachusetts.

Colonel Gamaliel Bradford, 1st January, 1777, to 1st January, 1781.
Lieutenant-Colonel Barakiah Bassett, 19th November, 1776, to 1st January, 1781.
Major Samuel Tubbs, 1st January, 1777, to 11th November, 1778.
Major Joseph Morse, 11th November, 1778, to 15th December, 1779.
Major John Wiley, 15th December, 1779, to 1st January, 1781.

Fifteenth Massachusetts.

Colonel Timothy Bigelow, 1st January, 1777, to 1st January, 1781.
Lieutenant-Colonel Henry Haskell, 1st January, 1777, to 1st July, 1779.
Lieutenant-Colonel Andrew Peters, 1st July, 1779, to 26th November, 1779.
Lieutenant-Colonel Thomas Cogswell, 26th November, 1779, to 1st January, 1781.
Major David Bradish, 1st January, 1777, to 21st July, 1777.
Major Hugh Maxwell, 7th July, 1777, to 1st July, 1779.
Major William H. Ballard, 1st July, 1779, to 1st January, 1781.

Sixteenth Massachusetts.

(See Jackson's Additional Continental Regiment prior to 23d July, 1780.)

Colonel Henry Jackson, 23d July, 1780, to 1st January, 1781.
Lieutenant-Colonel David Cobb, 23d July, 1780, to 1st January, 1781.
Major Lemuel Trescott, 23d July, 1780, to 1st January, 1781.

NEW HAMPSHIRE LINE.

First New Hampshire.

Colonel John Stark, 23d April, 1775, to — December, 1775.
Lieutenant-Colonel Isaac Wyman, 23d April, 1775, to — December, 1775.
Major Andrew McClarey, 23d April, 1775, to 17th June, 1775.
Major John Moore, 18th June, 1775, to — December, 1775.

(See Fifth Continental Infantry for 1776.)

Colonel John Stark, 8th November, 1776, to 23d March, 1777.
Colonel Joseph Cilley, 2d April, 1777, to 1st January, 1781.

Colonel Alexander Scammell, 1st January, 1781, to 6th October, 1781.
Lieutenant-Colonel Joseph Cilley, 8th November, 1776, to 22d February, 1777.
Lieutenant-Colonel George Reid, 2d April, 1777, to 5th March, 1778.
Lieutenant-Colonel Jeremiah Gilman, 5th March, 1778, to 24th March, 1780.
Lieutenant-Colonel Benjamin Titcomb, 24th March, 1780, to 1st January, 1781.
Lieutenant-Colonel Henry Dearborn, 1st January, 1781, to 1st March, 1782.
Major George Reid, 8th November, 1776, to 2d April, 1777.
Major Jeremiah Gilman, 2d April, 1777, to 20th September, 1777.
Major William Scott, 20th September, 1777, to 1st January, 1781.
Major Jason Wait, 1st January, 1781, to 1st March, 1782.

Second New Hampshire.

(Also called Third New Hampshire in 1775.)

Colonel Enoch Poor, 20th May, 1775, to — December, 1775.
Lieutenant-Colonel John McDuffee, 20th May, 1775, to — December, 1775.
Major Joseph Cilley, 20th May, 1775, to — December, 1775.

(See Eighth Continental Infantry for 1776.)

Colonel Enoch Poor, 8th November, 1776, to 21st February, 1777.
Colonel Nathan Hale, 2d April, 1777, to 23d September, 1780.
Lieutenant-Colonel Nathan Hale, 8th November, 1776, to 2d April, 1777.
Lieutenant-Colonel Winborn Adams, 2d April, 1777, to 19th September, 1777.
Lieutenant-Colonel Jeremiah Gilman, 20th September, 1777, to 5th March, 1778
Lieutenant-Colonel George Reid, 5th March, 1778, to 1st March, 1782.
Major Winborn Adams, 8th November, 1776, to 2d April, 1777.
Major Benjamin Titcomb, 2d April, 1777, to 24th March, 1780.
Major Amos Morrill, 24th March, 1780, to 1st March, 1782.
Major Caleb Robinson, 6th October, 1781, to 1st March, 1782.

Third New Hampshire.

(Also called Second New Hampshire in 1775.)

Colonel James Reed, 28th April, 1775, to — December, 1775.
Lieutenant-Colonel Israel Gilman, 1st June, 1775, to — December, 1775.
Major Nathan Hale, 23d April, 1775, to — December, 1775.

(See Second Continental Infantry for 1776.)

Colonel Alexander Scammell, 8th November, 1776, to 1st January, 1781.
Lieutenant-Colonel Andrew Colburn, 8th November, 1776, to 20th September, 1777.
Lieutenant-Colonel Henry Dearborn, 19th September, 1777, to 1st January, 1781.
Major Henry Dearborn, 8th November, 1776, to 19th September, 1777.
Major James Norris, 20th September, 1777, to 5th July, 1780.
Major Jason Wait, 5th July, 1780, to 1st January, 1781.

New Hampshire Battalion.

Lieutenant-Colonel George Reid, 1st March, 1782, to 3d November, 1783
Major Amos Morrill, 1st March, 1782, to 3d November, 1783.
Major Jason Wait, 1st March, 1782, to 8th December, 1782.
Major James Carr, 8th December, 1782, to 3d November, 1783.

NEW JERSEY LINE.

First New Jersey.

Colonel William Alexander, 7th November, 1775, to 1st March, 1776.
Colonel William Winds, 7th March, 1776, to 20th November, 1776.
Colonel Silas Newcomb, 28th November, 1776, to 1st January, 1777.
Colonel Matthias Ogden, 1st January, 1777, to 21st April, 1783.
Lieutenant-Colonel William Winds, 7th November, 1775, to 7th March, 1776.
Lieutenant-Colonel Matthias Ogden, 7th March, 1776, to 1st January, 1777.
Lieutenant-Colonel David Brearley, 1st January, 1777, to 4th August, 1779.
Lieutenant-Colonel John Conway, 5th July, 1779, to 1st January, 1781.
Lieutenant-Colonel Francis Barber, 1st January, 1781, to 7th January, 1783.
Major William DeHart, 7th November, 1775, to 1st January, 1777.
Major Joseph Morris, 1st January, 1777, to 7th January, 1778.
Major Daniel Piatt, 4th January, 1778, to 16th April, 1780.
Major John N. Cumming, 16th April, 1780, to 29th December, 1781.
Major Jonathan Forman, 20th November, 1781, to 11th February, 1783.
Major Nathaniel Bowman, 11th February, 1783, to — April, 1783.

Second New Jersey.

Colonel Wiliam Maxwell, 8th November, 1775, to 23d October, 1776.
Colonel Israel Shreve, 28th November, 1776, to 1st January, 1781.
Colonel Elias Dayton, 1st January, 1781, to 7th January, 1783.
Colonel Francis Barber, 7th January, 1783, to 11th February, 1783.
Lieutenant-Colonel Israel Shreve, 31st October, 1775, to 20th November, 1776.
Lieutenant-Colonel David Rhea, 28th November, 1776, to 1st January, 1777.
Lieutenant-Colonel William DeHart, 1st January, 1777, to 20th November, 1781
Lieutenant-Colonel John N. Cumming, 20th November, 1781, to — April, 1783.
Lieutenant-Colonel Jonathan Forman, 11th February, 1783, to — April, 1783.
Major David Rhea, 8th November, 1775, to 20th November, 1776.
Major Richard Howell, 28th November, 1776, to 7th April, 1779.
Major John Ross, 7th April, 1779, to 1st January, 1781.
Major John Hollingshead, 1st January, 1781, to 27th November, 1781.
Major Samuel Reading, 27th December, 1781, to — April, 1783.
Major Richard Cox, 6th January, 1783, to — April, 1783.

Third New Jersey.

Colonel Elias Dayton, 18th January, 1776, to 1st January, 1781.
Lieutenant-Colonel Anthony W. White, 18th January, 1776, to 20th November, 1776.
Lieutenant-Colonel Francis Barber, 28th November, 1776, to 1st January, 1781.
Major Francis Barber, 18th January, 1776, to 20th November, 1776.
Major Joseph Bloomfield, 28th November, 1776, to 29th October, 1778.
Major John Conway, 29th October, 1778, to 5th July, 1779.
Major John Hollingshead, 4th August, 1779, to 1st January, 1781.

Fourth New Jersey.

Colonel Ephraim Martin, 28th November, 1776, never joined.
Lieutenant-Colonel David Brearley, 28th November, 1776, to 1st January, 1777.
Lieutenant-Colonel David Rhea, 1st January, 1777, to 1st July, 1778.
Major Ebenezer Howell, 28th November, 1776, to 17th February, 1777.
Major Thomas Morrell, 17th February, 1777, to 29th October, 1777.
Major John Conway, 29th October, 1777, to 29th October, 1778.

(Rolls, returns, and lists of this regiment are very incomplete; the regiment was broken up about July, 1778.)

---o---

NEW YORK LINE.

First New York.

Colonel Alexander McDougall, 30th June, 1775, to 3d November, 1775.
Colonel Rudolphus Ritzema, 28th November, 1775, to 28th March, 1776.
Colonel Goose Van Shaick, 8th March, 1776, to 3d November, 1783.
Lieutenant-Colonel Rudolphus Ritzema, 30th June, 1775, to 28th November, 1775.
Lieutenant-Colonel Herman Zedwitz, 8th March, 1776, to — November, 1776.
Lieutenant-Colonel Cornelius Van Dyke, 21st November, 1776, to 3d November, 1783.
Major Herman Zedwitz, 15th July, 1775, to — March, 1776.
Major Joseph Benedict, 8th March, 1776, to 27th April, 1776.
Major Barnabas Tuthill, 27th April, 1776, to 4th September, 1776.
Major Christopher Yates, 21st November, 1776, to 1st January, 1778.
Major Benjamin Ledyard, 29th April, 1778, to 26th March, 1779.
Major John Graham, 26th March, 1779, to 3d November, 1783.

Second New York.

Colonel Goose Van Shaick, 28th June, 1775, to 8th March, 1776.
Colonel James Clinton, 8th March, 1776, to 29th August, 1776.

Colonel Philip Van Cortland, 21st November, 1776, to 3d November, 1783.
Lieutenant-Colonel Peter Yates, 30th June, 1775, to 8th March, 1776.
Lieutenant-Colonel Peter Gansevoort, 19th March, 1776, to 3d November, 1776.
Lieutenant-Colonel Frederick Weisenfels, 21st November, 1776, to 13th January, 1779.
Lieutenant-Colonel Pierre R. de Roussi, 28th June, 1779, to 29th March, 1780.
Lieutenant-Colonel Robert Cochrane, 30th March, 1780, to 3d November, 1783.
Major Peter Gansevoort, 30th June, 1775, to 19th March, 1776.
Major John Visscher, — October, 1775, to 26th June, 1776.
Major Nicholas Fish, 21st November, 1776, to 3d November, 1783.

Third New York.

Colonel James Clinton, 30th June, 1775, to — March, 1776.
Colonel Rudolphus Ritzema, 28th March, 1776, to 21st November, 1776.
Colonel Peter Gansevoort, 21st November, 1776, to 1st January, 1781.
Lieutenant-Colonel Edward Fleming, 30th June, 1775, to 2d August, 1775.
Lieutenant-Colonel Cornelius D. Wynkoop, 2d August, 1775, to — March, 1776.
Lieutenant-Colonel Frederick Weisenfels, 8th March, 1776, to 21st November, 1776.
Lieutenant-Colonel Marinus Willet, 21st November, 1776, to 1st July, 1780.
Lieutenant-Colonel Jacobus S. Bruyn, 1st July, 1780, to 1st January, 1781.
Major Cornelius D. Wynkoop, 30th June, 1775, to 2d August, 1775.
Major Henry Brockholst Livingston, 2d August, 1775, to 8th March, 1776.
Major Lewis DuBois, 25th November, 1775, to 8th March, 1776.
Major John Fisher, 8th March, 1776, to 21st June, 1776.
Major Robert Cochrane, 21st November, 1776, to 30th March, 1780.
Major James Rosekrans, 1st March, 1780, to 1st January, 1781.

Fourth New York.

Colonel James Holmes, 30th June, 1775, to — December, 1775.
Colonel Cornelius D. Wynkoop, 8th March, 1776, to — November, 1776.
Colonel Henry Beekman Livingston, 21st November, 1776, to 13th January, 1779.
Lieutenant-Colonel Philip Van Cortland, 30th June, 1775, to 21st November, 1776.
Lieutenant-Colonel Pierre R. de Roussi, 21st November, 1776, to 28th June, 1779.
Lieutenant-Colonel Frederick Weisenfels, 13th January, 1779, to 1st January, 1781.
Major Barnabas Tuthill, 30th June, 1775, to — March, 1776.
Major John Visscher, 8th March, 1776, to 26th June, 1776.
Major Benjamin Ledyard, 21st November, 1776, to 29th April, 1778.
Major Joseph McCracken, 29th May, 1778, to 11th April, 1780.
Major John Davis, 11th April, 1780, to 1st January, 1781.

Fifth New York.

Colonel Lewis DuBois, 21st November, 1776, to 22d December, 1779.
Colonel Marinus Willett, 22d December, 1779, to 1st January, 1781.

Lieutenant-Colonel Jacobus S. Bruyn, 21st November, 1776, to 1st July, 1780.
Major Samuel Logan, 21st November, 1776, to 1st January, 1781.

NORTH CAROLINA LINE.

Note.—*The records of the North Carolina regiments are very meager, owing no doubt to the constant and arduous campaigns in the Carolinas, Georgia, and Virginia, in which the regiments participated, with frequent loss of all their baggage and records. Hence the following list is incomplete, and arrangement defective.*

First North Carolina.

Colonel James Moore, 1st September, 1775, to 1st March, 1776.
Colonel Francis Nash, 10th April, 1776, to 5th February, 1777.
Colonel Thomas Clark, 5th February, 1777, to close of war.
Lieutenant-Colonel Francis Nash, 1st September, 1775, to 10th April, 1776.
Lieutenant-Colonel Thomas Clark, 10th April, 1776, to 5th February, 1777.
Lieutenant-Colonel Wm. Davis, 5th February, 1777, to 1st June, 1778.
Lieutenant-Colonel Robert Mebane, 1st June, 1778, to 8th June, 1779.
Lieutenant-Colonel Hardy Murfree, 1st April, 1778, to July, 1782.
Lieutenant-Colonel John B. Ashe, 2d November, 1778, to ———.
Lieutenant-Colonel Wm. L. Davidson, 9th June, 1779, to 1st February, 1781.
Major Wm. Davis, 10th April, 1776, to 5th February, 1777.
Major Caleb Granger, 5th February, 1777, to 26th April, 1777.
Major John Walker, 26th April, 1777, to 22d December, 1777.
Major James Emmet, 22d December, 1777, to 1st June, 1778.
Major John B. Ashe, 1st June, 1778, to 2d November, 1778.
Major John Nelson, 6th February, 1782, to close of war.

Second North Carolina.

Colonel Robert Howe, 1st September, 1775, to 1st March, 1776.
Colonel Alexander Martin, 10th April, 1776, to 22d November, 1777
Colonel John Patten, 22d November, 1777, to 1st January, 1783.
Lieutenant-Colonel Alexander Martin, 1st September, 1775, to 10th April, 1776.
Lieutenant-Colonel John Patten, 10th April, 1776, to 22d November, 1777.
Lieutenant-Colonel Selby Harney, 22d November, 1777, to 6th February, 1782.
Major John Patten, 1st September, 1775, to 10th April, 1776.
Major John White, 20th April, 1776, to 1st February, 1777.
Major Hardy Murfree, 1st February, 1777, to 1st April, 1778.
Major Reading Blount, 6th February, 1782, to close of war.

Third North Carolina.

Colonel Jethro Sumner, 15th April, 1776, to 9th January, 1779.
Lieutenant-Colonel Wm. Ashton, 15th April, 1776, to 4th October, 1777.

Lieutenant-Colonel Lott Brewster, 25th October, 1777, to 15th March, 1778.
Lieutenant-Colonel Henry Dixon, 12th May, 1778, to 20th June, 1779.
Lieutenant-Colonel Robert Mebane, 7th June, 1779, to close of war.
Major Samuel Lockhart, 15th April, 1776, to 12th October, 1777.
Major Henry Dixon, 8th July, 1777, to 12th May, 1778.
Major Pinketham Eaton, 22d November, 1777, to 24th May, 1781.
Major James Emmet, 15th February, 1778, to 1st June, 1778.
Major Thomas Hogg, 1st June, 1778, to ———.
Major Griffith J. McRae, 11th September, 1781, to close of war.

Fourth North Carolina.

Colonel Thomas Polk, 16th April, 1776, to 28th June, 1778.
Lieutenant-Colonel James Thackston, 15th April, 1776, to 1st Janurary, 1781.
Major Wm. L. Davidson, 15th April, 1776, to 4th October, 1777.
Major John Armstrong, 6th October, 1777, to 17th July, 1782.
Major John Nelson, 3d February, 1778, to 6th February, 1782.
Major George Doherty, 13th October, 1781, to — February, 1782.
Major Thomas Donahoe, 6th February, 1782, to close of war.

Fifth North Carolina.

Colonel Edward Buncombe, 15th April, 1776, to 19th October, 1777.
Lieutenant-Colonel Henry Irwin, 15th April, 1776, to 4th October, 1777.
Lieutenant-Colonel Wm. L. Davidson, 4th October, 1777, to 9th June, 1779.
Major Levi Dawson, 15th April, 1776, to 19th October, 1777.
Major Thomas Hogg, 12th October, 1777, to 1st June, 1778.
Major Reading Blount, 12th May, 1778, to 6th February, 1782.

Sixth North Carolina.

Colonel John A. Lillington, 15th April, 1776, to 6th May, 1776.
Colonel Gideon Lamb, 26th January, 1777, to 1st June, 1778.
Lieutenant-Colonel Wm. Taylor, 15th April, 1776, to 1st January, 1781.
Lieutenant-Colonel Archibald Lytle, 1st February, 1781, to close of war.
Major Gideon Lamb, 15th April, 1776, to 26th January, 1777.
Major John B. Ashe, 26th January, 1777, to 1st June, 1778.
Major Thomas Donahue, 13th October, 1781, to 6th February, 1782.
Major George Doherty, 17th July, 1782, to close of war.

Seventh North Carolina.

Colonel James Hogun, 26th November, 1776, to 9th January, 1779.
Lieutenant-Colonel Robert Mebane, 26th November, 1776, to 1st June, 1778.

Major Lott Brewster, 26th November, 1776, to 25th October, 1777.
Major Wm. Fenner, 24th October, 1777, to 1st June, 1778.

Eighth North Carolina.

Colonel James Armstrong, 26th November, 1776, to 1st June, 1778.
Lieutenant-Colonel James Ingram, 26th November, 1776, to 8th July, 1777.
Lieutenant-Colonel Samuel Lockhart, 12th October, 1777, to 19th October, 1777
Lieutenant-Colonel Levi Dawson, 19th October, 1777, to 1st June, 1778.
Major Selby Harney, 26th November, 1776, to 22d November, 1777.

Ninth North Carolina.

Colonel John P. Williams, 7th April, 1777, to 1st June, 1778.
Lieutenant-Colonel John Luttrell, 27th November, 1776, to 1st June, 1778.
Major Wm. Polk, 27th November, 1776, to ———.

Tenth North Carolina.

Colonel Abraham Shepard, 17th April, 1777, to 1st June, 1778.
Lieutenant-Colonel Adam Perkins, 17th April, 1777, to 1st June, 1778.
Major ——— ———, — — ———, ———, — — ———, ———.

(It appears that a new Tenth North Carolina was organized in 1779 as a State regiment.)

PENNSYLVANIA LINE.

Thompson's Pennsylvania Rifle Battalion.

Colonel William Thompson, 25th June, 1775, to 1st January, 1776.
Lieutenant-Colonel Edward Hand, 25th June, 1775, to 1st January, 1776.
Major Robert Magaw, 25th June, 1775, to 1st January, 1776.

(Reorganized and designated First Continental Infantry, 1st January, 1776, and again reorganized as the First Pennsylvania, 1st January, 1777.)

Miles' Pennsylvania Rifle Regiment.

Colonel Samuel Miles, 13th March, 1776, to 27th August, 1776.
Lieutenant-Colonel James Piper (1st battalion), 13th March, 1776, to 27th August, 1776.

Lieutenant-Colonel Daniel Brodhead (2d battalion), 13th March, 1776, to 25th October, 1776.

Major Ennion Williams (1st battalion), 13th March, 1776, to 4th February, 1777.

Major John Patton (2d battalion), 13th March, 1776, to 11th January, 1777.

(Note.—*Between October, 1775, and January, 1776, six battalions were organized in Pennsylvania, and numbered from 1 to 6, inclusive; in the autumn of 1776, these battalions were reorganized and five additional regiments were raised, when the First Pennsylvania battalion was designated the Second Pennsylvania; the Second the Third; the Third the Fourth; Fourth the Fifth; Fifth the Sixth, and Sixth the Seventh. In January, 1777, the First Continental Infantry was reorganized as the First Pennsylvania. In the following list they are given as designated after the reorganization, although in the Alphabetical List they are shown as they were at the time.*)

First Pennsylvania.

(*See Thompson's Pennsylvania Rifle Battalion for* 1775, *and First Continental Infantry for* 1776.)

Colonel Edward Hand, 1st January, 1777, to 1st April, 1777.
Colonel James Chambers, 12th April, 1777, to 17th January, 1781.
Colonel Daniel Brodhead, 17th January, 1781, to 3d November, 1783.
Lieutenant-Colonel James Ross, 1st January, 1777, to 11th June, 1777.
Lieutenant-Colonel Thomas Robinson, 11th June, 1777, to 1st January, 1783.
Lieutenant-Colonel Josiah Harmar, 1st January, 1783, to 3d November, 1783.
Major Henry Miller (See Alphabetical List).
Major James Moore, 20th September, 1777, to 1st January, 1783.
Major Frederick Vernon, 1st January, 1783, to 3d November, 1783.

Second Pennsylvania.

(*First Pennsylvania Battalion, November,* 1775, *to October,* 1776.)

Colonel John Bull, 25th November, 1775, to 22d January, 1776.
Colonel John P. De Haas, 22d January, 1776, to 21st February, 1777.
Colonel James Irvine, 12th March, 1777, to 1st June, 1777.
Colonel Henry Bicker, 6th June, 1777, to 1st July, 1778.
Colonel Walter Stewart, 1st July, 1778, to 1st January, 1783.
Colonel Richard Humpton, 1st January, 1783, to 3d November, 1783.
Lieutenant-Colonel James Irvine, 25th November, 1775, to 25th October, 1776.
Lieutenant-Colonel Anthony J. Morris, 25th October, 1776, to 12th March, 1777.
Lieutenant-Colonel Jonathan Jones, 12th March, 1777, to 5th April, 1777.
Lieutenant-Colonel Henry Miller, 1st March, 1777, to 8th December, 1778.
Lieutenant-Colonel John Murray, 10th December, 1778, to 17th January, 1781.
Lieutenant-Colonel Caleb North, 17th January, 1781, to 1st January, 1783.
Lieutenant-Colonel Thomas Robinson, 1st January, 1783, to 3d November, 1783.
Major David Grier, 1st June, 1776, to 2d October, 1776.
Major Jonathan Jones, 25th October, 1776, to 12th March, 1777.
Major William Williams, 12th March, 1777, to 28th June, 1778.

Major John Murray, 1st July, 1778, to 10th December, 1778.
Major James Hamilton, 10th December, 1778, to 1st January, 1783.
Major James Moore, 1st January, 1783, to 3d November, 1783.

Third Pennsylvania.

(Second Pennsylvania Battalion, January to October, 1776.)

Colonel Arthur St. Clair, 3d January, 1776, to 9th August, 1776.
Colonel Joseph Wood, 7th September, 1776, to 31st July, 1777.
Colonel Thomas Craig, 1st August, 1777, to 1st January, 1783.
Colonel Richard Butler, 1st January, 1783, to 3d November, 1783.
Lieutenant-Colonel William Allen, 4th January, 1776, to 24th July, 1776.
Lieutenant-Colonel Joseph Wood, 29th July, 1776, to 7th September, 1776.
Lieutenant-Colonel Thomas Craig, 29th September, 1776, to 1st August, 1777.
Lieutenant-Colonel Rudolph Bunner, 1st August, 1777, to 28th June, 1778.
Lieutenant-Colonel William Williams, 28th June, 1778, to 17th April, 1780.
Lieutenant-Colonel Christopher Stuart, 17th April, 1780, to 17th January, 1781.
Lieutenant-Colonel Josiah Harmar, 17th January, 1781, to 1st January, 1783,
Lieutenant-Colonel Stephen Bayard, 1st January, 1783, to 3d November, 1783.
Major Joseph Wood, 4th January, 1776, to 29th July, 1776.
Major William Butler, 7th September, 1776, to 30th September, 1776.
Major Josiah Harmar, 1st October, 1776, to 6th June, 1777.
Major William West, 25th October, 1776, to 16th November, 1776.
Major Rudolph Bunner, 6th June, 1777, to 1st August, 1777.
Major John Huling, 1st August, 1777, to 1st July, 1778.
Major Thomas L. Byles, 1st July, 1778, to 16th April, 1780.
Major William Alexander, 16th April, 1780, to 1st January, 1783.
Major James Grier, 1st January, 1783, to 3d November, 1783.

Fourth Pennsylvania.

(Third Pennsylvania Battalion, January to October, 1776.)

Colonel John Shee, 3d January, 1776, to 27th September, 1776.
Colonel Lambert Cadwalader, 25th October, 1776, to 22d January, 1779.
Lieutenant-Colonel Lambert Cadwalader, 4th January, 1776, to 25th October, 1776.
Lieutenant-Colonel William Butler, 30th September, 1776, to 1st January, 1783.
Major Henry Bicker, 4th January, 1776, to 25th October, 1776.
Major Marion Lamar, 30th September, 1776, to 20th September, 1777.
Major Thomas Church, 4th September, 1777, to 17th January, 1781.
Major Frederick Vernon, 17th January, 1781, to 1st January, 1783.
Major Evan Edwards, 17th January, 1781, to 1st January, 1783.

Fifth Pennsylvania.

(Fourth Pennsylvania Battalion, January to October, 1776.)

Colonel Anthony Wayne, 3d January, 1776, to — January, 1777.
Colonel Francis Johnston, 27th September, 1776, to 17th January, 1781.
Colonel Richard Butler, 17th January, 1781, to 1st January, 1783.
Lieutenant-Colonel Francis Johnston, 4th January, 1776, to 27th September, 1776.
Lieutenant-Colonel Persifor Frazer, 4th October, 1776, to 9th October, 1778.
Lieutenant-Colonel Francis Mentges, 9th October, 1778, to 1st January, 1783.
Major Nicholas Haussegger, 4th January, 1776, to 17th July, 1776.
Major Thomas Robinson, 2d October, 1776, to 7th June, 1777.
Major Christopher Stuart, 7th June, 1777, to 17th April, 1780.
Major James Taylor, 23d September, 1777, to 3d April, 1778.
Major George Tudor, 17th April, 1780, to 17th January, 1781.
Major Thomas L. Moore, 17th January, 1781, to 1st January, 1783.

Sixth Pennsylvania.

(Fifth Pennsylvania Battalion, January to October, 1776.)

Colonel Robert Magaw, 3d January, 1776, to 17th January, 1781.
Colonel Richard Humpton, 17th January, 1781, to 1st January, 1783.
Lieutenant-Colonel Joseph Penrose, 3d January, 1776, to 25th October, 1776.
Lieutenant-Colonel Henry Bicker, 5th December, 1776, to 6th June, 1777.
Lieutenant-Colonel Josiah Harmar, 6th June, 1777, to 9th August, 1780.
Lieutenant-Colonel Stephen Bayard, 17th January, 1781, to 1st January, 1783.
Major George Nagel, 5th January, 1776, to 25th October, 1776.
Major Samel Benezet, 3d October, 1776—never joined.
Major John Beatty, 12th October, 1776, to 28th May, 1778.
Major Jeremiah Talbot, 25th September, 1777, to 17th January, 1781.
Major James Grier, 17th January, 1781, to 1st January, 1783.

Seventh Pennsylvania.

(Sixth Pennsylvania Battalion, January to October, 1776.)

Colonel William Irvine, 9th January, 1776, to 12th May, 1779.
Lieutenant-Colonel Thomas Hartley, 10th January, 1776, to — November, 1776.
Lieutenant-Colonel David Grier, 2d October, 1776, to 12th May, 1779.
Lieutenant-Colonel Morgan Connor, 12th May, 1779, to — January, 1780.
Lieutenant-Colonel Josiah Harmar, 9th August, 1780, to 17th January, 1781.
Major James Dunlop, 10th January, 1776, to 25th October, 1776.
Major Samuel Hay, 5th October, 1776, to 21st February, 1778.
Major Francis Mentges, 1st July, 1778, to 9th October, 1778.
Major James Parr, 9th October, 1778, to 17th January, 1781.

Eighth Pennsylvania.

Colonel Aenas Mackey, 20th July, 1776, to 14th February, 1777.
Colonel Daniel Brodhead, 12th March, 1777, to 17th January, 1781.
Lieutenant-Colonel George Wilson, 20th July, 1776, to — February, 1777.
Lieutenant-Colonel Richard Butler, 12th March, 1777, to 7th June, 1777.
Lieutenant-Colonel James Ross, 11th June, 1777, to 22d September, 1777.
Lieutenant-Colonel Stephen Bayard, 23d September, 1777, to 17th January, 1781.
Major Richard Butler, 20th July, 1776, to 12th March, 1777.
Major Stephen Bayard, 12th March, 1777, to 23d September, 1777.
Major Frederick Vernon, 7th June, 1777, to 17th January, 1781.

Ninth Pennsylvania.

Colonel James Irvine, 25th October, 1776, to 12th March, 1777.
Colonel Anthony J. Morris, 12th March, 1777, to 7th June, 1777.
Colonel Richard Butler, 7th June, 1777, to 17th January, 1781.
Lieutenant-Colonel George Nagel, 25th October, 1776, to 7th February, 1777.
Lieutenant-Colonel Matthew Smith, 7th February, 1777, to 23d February, 1778.
Lieutenant-Colonel Caleb North, 1st July, 1778, to 17th January, 1781.
Major John Patton, 25th October, 1776, to 11th January, 1777.
Major Matthew Smith, 11th January, 1777, to (See Alphabetical List).
Major Francis Nichols, 7th February, 1777, to 12th May, 1779.
Major Thomas L. Moore, 12th May, 1779, to 17th January, 1781.

Tenth Pennsylvania.

Colonel Joseph Penrose, 25th October, 1776, to 7th February, 1777.
Colonel James Chambers, 12th March, 1777, to 12th April, 1777.
Colonel George Nagel, 7th February, 1777, to 1st July, 1778.
Colonel Richard Humpton, 1st July, 1778, to 17th January, 1781.
Lieutenant-Colonel James Dunlop, 25th October, 1776, to 23d January, 1777.
Lieutenant-Colonel Adam Hubley, 12th March, 1777, to 13th February, 1779.
Lieutenant-Colonel Samuel Hay, 21st February, 1778, to 17th January, 1781.
Major Henry Bicker, 25th October, 1776, to 5th December, 1776.
Major Adam Hubley, 6th December, 1776, to 12th January, 1777.
Major Caleb North, 12th March, 1777, to 22d October, 1777.
Major James Grier, 23d October, 1777, to 17th January, 1781.

Eleventh Pennsylvania.

Colonel Richard Humpton, 25th October, 1776, to 1st July, 1778.
Lieutenant-Colonel Francis Gurney, 21st August, 1776, to 22d October, 1777.

Lieutenant-Colonel Caleb North, 22d October, 1777, to 1st July, 1778.
Major Francis Mentges, 25th September, 1776, to 1st July, 1778.

*(This regiment was incorporated with the Tenth Pennsylvania 1st July, 1778.
and on 16th December, 1778, Hartley's Additional Continental Regiment was designated as the Eleventh Pennsylvania.)*

Colonel Thomas Hartley, 16th December, 1778, to 13th February, 1779.
Lieutenant-Colonel Morgan Connor, 16th December, 1778, to 12th May, 1779.
Lieutenant-Colonel Adam Hubley, 13th May, 1779, to 17th January, 1781.
Major Evan Edwards, 10th December, 1778, to 17th January, 1781.
Major Joseph Prowell, 13th January, 1779, to 5th June, 1779.

Twelfth Pennsylvania.

Colonel William Cooke, 28th September, 1776, to 7th March, 1778.
Lieutenant-Colonel Neigel Gray, 27th September, 1776, to 2d June, 1778.
Major James Crawford, 28th September, 1776, to 10th November, 1777.

(Regiment was incorporated with Sixth Pennsylvania July 1, 1778.)

Thirteenth Pennsylvania.

*(Organized as the Pennsylvania State Regiment, and by Resolve of Congress
of 12th November, 1777, it was designated as the Thirteenth Pennsylvania, and was
incorporated with the Second Pennsylvania July 1, 1878.)*

Colonel John Bull, 2d May, 1777, to 17th June, 1777.
Colonel Walter Stewart, 17th June, 1777, to 1st July, 1778.
Lieutenant-Colonel Lewis Farmer, 2d May, 1777, to 1st July, 1778.
Major Lewis Farmer, 14th March, 1777, to 2d May, 1777.
Major John Murray, 14th March, 1777, to 1st July, 1778.
Major Francis Murray, 2d May, 1777, to 1st July, 1778.

RHODE ISLAND LINE.

First Rhode Island.

Colonel James M. Varnum, 3d May, 1775, to — December, 1775.
Lieutenant-Colonel James Babcock, 3d May, 1775, to — December, 1775.
Major Christopher Greene, 3d May, 1775, to — December, 1775.

(See Ninth Continental Infantry for 1776.)

Colonel James M. Varnum, 1st January, 1777, to 27th February, 1777.
Colonel Christopher Greene, 27th February, 1777, to 14th May, 1781.
Lieutenant-Colonel Adam Comstock, 1st January, 1777, to — April, 1778.
Lieutenant-Colonel Samuel Ward, 26th May, 1778, to 1st January, 1781.
Lieutenant-Colonel Jeremiah Olney, 1st January, 1781, to 14th May, 1781.
Major Henry Sherburne, 1st January, 1777, to 12th January, 1777.
Major Samuel Ward, 12th January, 1777, to 26th May, 1778.
Major Silas Talbot, 1st September, 1777, to 14th November, 1778.
Major Ebenezer Flagg, 26th May, 1778, to 14th May, 1781.
Major Coggeshall Olney, 25th August, 1781, to 14th May, 1781.
Major John S. Dexter, 25th August, 1781, to 14th May, 1781.

Second Rhode Island.

Colonel Daniel Hitchcock, 3d May, 1775, to — December, 1775.
Lieutenant-Colonel Ezekiel Cornell, 3d May, 1775, to — December, 1775.
Major Israel Angell, 3d May, 1775, to 31st December, 1775.

(See Eleventh Continental Infantry for 1776.)

Colonel Daniel Hitchcock, 1st January, 1777, to 13th January, 1777.
Colonel Israel Angell, 13th January, 1777, to 1st January, 1781.
Lieutenant-Colonel Israel Angell, 1st January, 1777, to 13th January, 1777.
Lieutenant-Colonel Jeremiah Olney, 13th January, 1777, to 1st January, 1781.
Major Simeon Thayer, 1st January, 1777, to 1st January, 1781.

Third Rhode Island.

Colonel Thomas Church, 3d May, 1775, to — December, 1775.
Lieutenant-Colonel William T. Miller, 3d May, 1775, to — December, 1775.
Major John Forrester, 3d May, 1775, to — December, 1775.

Olney's R. I. Battalion.

Lieutenant-Colonel Commandant Jeremiah Olney, 14th May, 1781, to 3d November, 1783.
Major Coggeshall Olney, 14th May, 1781, to 17th March, 1783.
Major John S. Dexter, 14th May, 1781, to 3d November, 1783.

SOUTH CAROLINA LINE.

Records are very meager of the South Carolina Line and arrangement is imperfect.

First South Carolina.

Colonel Christopher Gadsden, 17th June, 1775, to 16th September, 1776.
Colonel Charles Pinckney, 16th September, 1776, to close of war.
Lieutenant-Colonel Isaac Huger, 17th June, 1775, to 16th September, 1776.
Lieutenant-Colonel ——, from ——, to ——?
Lieutenant-Colonel William Henderson, 1st January, 1781, to close of war.
Major Owen Roberts, 17th June, 1775, to 14th November, 1775.
Major Francis Marion, 14th November, 1775, to 16th September, 1776.
Major Adam McDonald, 16th September, 1776, to ——, 1777.
Major William Cottrell, 16th September, 1776, to ——.
Major Thomas Pinckney, 1st May, 1778, to close of war.

Second South Carolina.

Colonel William Moultrie, 17th June, 1775, to 16th September, 1776.
Colonel Isaac Motte, 16th September, 1776, to close of war.
Lieutenant-Colonel Isaac Motte, 17th June, 1775, to 16th September, 1776.
Lieutenant-Colonel Francis Marion, 16th September, 1776, to close of war.
Major Alexander McIntosh, 17th June, 1775, to 14th September, 1776.
Major Peter Horry, 16th September, 1776, to 30th November, 1778.
Major William Scott, 1st May, 1777, to close of war.
Major Charles Motte, 2d April, 1779, to 9th October, 1779.

Third South Carolina (Rangers).

Colonel William Thompson, 17th June, 1775, to close of war.
Lieutenant Colonel William Henderson, 16th May, 1776, to 11th February, 1780.
Lieutenant-Colonel Alexander McIntosh, —— in 1780.
Major James Mayson, 17th June, 1775, to 16th May, 1776.
Major Samuel Wise, 18th May, 1776, to 9th October, 1779.

Fourth South Carolina (Artillery).

Colonel Owen Roberts, 16th September, 1776, to 20th June, 1779.
Colonel Barnard Beekman, 20th June, 1779, to close of war.
Lieutenant-Colonel Owen Roberts, 17th June, 1775, to 16th September, 1776.

Lieutenant-Colonel Barnard Elliott, 16th September, 1776, to 25th October, 1778
Major William Cottrell, — May, 1776, to 16th September, 1776.
Major Barnard Beekman, 16th September, 1776, to 20th June, 1779.
Major Ephraim Mitchell, 20th June, 1779, to ——.
Major Thomas Grimball, 12th May, 1780, to close of war.

Fifth South Carolina (Rifles).

Colonel Isaac Huger, 16th September, 1776, to 9th June, 1779.
Lieutenant-Colonel Alexander McIntosh, 16th September, 1776, to ——, 1780.
Major Benjamin Huger, 16th September, 1776, to 11th May, 1779.
Major Edmund Hyrne, 12th May, 1779, to 1st January, 1781.

Sixth South Carolina.

No rolls or returns of this regiment were found.

VIRGINIA LINE.

First Virginia.

Colonel James Read, 13th February, 1776, to 29th September, 1777.
Colonel James Hendricks, 29th September, 1777, to 10th February, 1778.
Colonel Richard Parker, 10th February, 1778, to 8th May, 1780.
Colonel William Davis, 12th February, 1781, to close of war.
Lieutenant-Colonel William Christian, 13th February, 1776, to 18th March, 1776.
Lieutenant-Colonel Francis Eppes, 18th March, 1776, to 27th August, 1776.
Lieutenant-Colonel John Green, 22d March, 1777, to 26th January, 1778.
Lieutenant-Colonel Robert Ballard, 4th October, 1777, to 14th September, 1778
Lieutenant-Colonel Burgess Ball, 14th September, 1778, to 12th February, 1781.
Lieutenant-Colonel Samuel Hopkins, 12th February, 1781, to close of war.
Major Frances Eppes, 13th February, 1776, to 18th March, 1776.
Major Andrew Leitch, 18th March, 1776, to 1st October, 1776.
Major John Green, 13th August, 1776, to 22d March, 1777.
Major Robert Ballard, 22d March, 1777, to 4th October, 1777.
Major Edmund B. Dickinson, 26th October, 1777, to 28th June, 1778.
Major James Lucas, 23d April, 1778, to 14th September, 1778.
Major Richard C. Anderson, 14th September, 1778, to ——?

Second Virginia.

Colonel William Woolford, 13th February, 1776, to 21st February, 1777.
Colonel Alexander Spotswood, 21st February, 1777, to 9th October, 1777.
Colonel Christian Febiger, 9th October, 1777, to 1st January, 1783.
Lieutenant-Colonel Charles Scott, 13th February, 1776, to 7th May, 1776.
Lieutenant-Colonel Alexander Spottswood, 7th May, 1776, to 21st February, 1777.
Lieutenant-Colonel Richard Parker, 10th February, 1777, to 10th February, 1778.
Lieutenant-Colonel Charles Dabney, from 16th February, 1778, to 14th September, 1778.
Liuetenant-Colonel Charles Simms, 14th September, 1778, to 7th December, 1779
Lieutenant-Colonel Richard Taylor, 7th December, 1779, to 12th February, 1781.
Liutenant-Colonel Gustavus B. Wallace, 12th February, 1781, to close of war.
Major Alexander Spotswood, 13th February, 1776, to 7th May, 1776.
Major John Markham, 7th May, 1776, to 23d December, 1776.
Major Morgan Alexander, 23d December, 1776, to 22d March, 1777.
Major Ralph Faulkner, 22d March, 1777, to 30th April, 1778.
Major Thomas Posey, 30th April, 1778, to 14th September, 1778.
Major Thomas Massie, 14th September, 1778, to 25th June, 1779.
Major Charles Pelham, 25th June, 1779, to 12th February, 1781.
Major Smith Snead, 12th February, 1781, to close of war.

Third Virginia.

Colonel Hugh Mercer, 13th February, 1776, to 5th June, 1776.
Colonel George Weedon, 13th August, 1776, to 27th February, 1777.
Colonel Thomas Marshall, 21st February, 1777, to 4th December, 1777.
Colonel William Heth, 30th April, 1778, to 12th February, 1781.
Colonel Abraham Buford, 12th February, 1781, to close of war.
Lieutenant-Colonel George Weedon, 13th February, 1776, to 13th August, 1776.
Lieutenant-Colonel Thomas Marshall, 13th August, 1776, to 21st February, 1777.
Lieutenant-Colonel William Heth, 1st April, 1777, to 30th April, 1778.
Lieutenant-Colonel Charles Fleming, 28th June, 1778, to 14th September, 1778.
Lieutenant-Colonel Thomas Gaskins, 14th September, 1778, to ——?
Lieutenant-Colonel Richard C. Anderson, from ——, to ——?
Major Thomas Marshall, 13th February, 1776, to 13th August, 1776.
Major Charles West, 1st February, 1777, to 6th July, 1778.
Major James Lucas, 14th September, 1778, to ——?
Major John Hays, 23d April, 1778, to 12th February, 1781.
Major William Lewis, 12th February, 1781, to close of war.

Fourth Virginia.

Colonel Adam Stephen, 13th February, 1776, to 4th September, 1776.
Colonel Thomas Elliott, 3d September, 1776, to 19th August, 1777.
Colonel Robert Lawson, 19th August, 1777, to 17th December, 1777.

Colonel Isaac Read, 17th December, 1777, to 4th September, 1778.
Colonel John Neville, 14th September, 1778, to close of war.
Lieutenant-Colonel Isaac Read, 13th February, 1776, to 13th August, 1776.
Lieutenant-Colonel Robert Lawson, 13th August, 1776, to 19th August, 1777.
Lieutenant-Colonel William Taliaferro, 1st February, 1777, to 1st February, 1778.
Lieutenant-Colonel Thomas Gaskins, 16th May, 1778, to 14th September, 1778.
Lieutenant-Colonel Robert Ballard, 14th September, 1778, to 4th July, 1779.
Lieutenant-Colonel Samuel J. Cabell, 4th July, 1779, to 12th February, 1781.
Lieutenant-Colonel Richard Campbell, 12th February, 1781, to 8th September, 1781.
Lieutenant-Colonel William Darke, 12th February, 1781, to 1st January, 1783.
Major Robert Lawson, 13th February, 1776, to 13th August, 1776.
Major John Sayers, 13th August, 1776, to 22d March, 1777.
Major Isaac Beall, 21st February, 1777, to 19th June, 1778.
Major George Gibson, 4th January, 1777, to 5th June, 1777.
Major Charles Fleming, 5th June, 1777, to 28th June, 1778.
Major Andrew Russell, 19th June, 1777, to 14th September, 1778.
Major John Brent, 4th October, 1777, to 4th May, 1778.
Major William Croghan, 14th September, 1778, to close of war.

Fifth Virginia.

Colonel William Peachy, 13th February, 1776, to 7th May, 1776.
Colonel Charles Scott, 7th May, 1776, to 1st April, 1777.
Colonel Josiah Parker, 1st April, 1777, to 12th July, 1778.
Colonel William Russell, 14th September, 1778, to close of war.
Lieutenant-Colonel William Crawford, 13th February, 1776, to 14th August, 1776
Lieutenant-Colonel Josiah Parker, 13th August, 1776, to 1st April, 1777.
Lieutenant-Colonel William Davies, 21st February, 1777, to 5th April, 1778.
Lieutenant-Colonel Abraham Buford, 1st April, 1777, to 14th September, 1778.
Lieutenant-Colonel Holt Richeson, 14th September, 1778, to 10th May, 1779
Lieutenant-Colonel John Webb, 4th July, 1779, to 12th February, 1781.
Lieutenant-Colonel Oliver Towles, 12th February, 1781, to 1st January, 1783
Lieutenant-Colonel Samuel Hawes, 1st January, 1783, to close of war.
Major Josiah Parker, 13th February, 1776, to 13th August, 1776.
Major George Johnson, 13th August, 1776, to 15th August, 1777.
Major Burgess Ball, 10th February, 1777, to 17th December, 1777.
Major Thomas Gaskins, 5th November, 1777, to 16th May, 1778.
Major David Stephenson, 4th May, 1778, to 14th September, 1778.
Major John Webb, 14th September, 1778, to 4th July, 1779.
Major Thomas Hill, 4th July, 1779, to 12th February, 1781.
Major William Moseley, ——, to 12th February, 1781.
Major Joseph Crockett, 12th February, 1781, to close of war.

Sixth Virginia.

Colonel Mordecai Buckner, 13th February, 1776, to 9th February, 1777.
Colonel John Gibson, 25th October, 1777, to 14th September, 1778.

Colonel John Green, 14th September, 1778, to 1st January, 1783.
Lieutenant-Colonel Thomas Elliott, 13th February, 1776, to 3d September, 1776, and 19th August, 1777, to 22d September, 1777.
Lieutenant-Colonel James Hendricks, 13th August, 1776, to 29th September, 1777.
Lieutenant-Colonel Charles Simms, 29th September, 1777, to 14th September, 1778.
Lieutenant-Colonel Samuel Hawes, 14th September, 1778, to 1st January, 1783.
Major James Hendricks, 13th February, 1776, to 13th August, 1776.
Major Richard Parker, 13th August, 1776, to 10th February, 1777.
Major James Johnson, 1st April, 1777, to 15th August, 1777.
Major Oliver Towles, 15th August, 1777, to 29th November, 1777.
Major Samuel Hopkins, 29th November, 1777, to 19th June, 1778.
Major Richard C. Anderson, 10th February, 1778, to 14th September, 1778.
Major Thomas Ridley, 14th September, 1778, to 12th February, 1781.
Major David Stephenson, 12th February, 1781, to 1st January, 1783.

Seventh Virginia.

Colonel William Dangerfield, 29th February, 1776, to 13th August, 1776.
Colonel William Crawford, 14th August, 1776, to 4th March, 1777.
Colonel Alexander McClanachan, 22d March, 1777, to 13th May, 1778.
Colonel Daniel Morgan, 14th September, 1778, to 13th October, 1780.
Colonel John Gibson, 12th February, 1781, to 1st January, 1783.
Lieutenant-Colonel Alexander McClanachan, 29th February, 1776, to 22d March, 1777.
Lieutenant-Colonel William Nelson, 7th October, 1776, to 25th October, 1777.
Lieutenant-Colonel Holt Richardson, 18th October, 1777, to 14th September, 1778.
Lieutenant-Colonel John Cropper, 14th September, 1778, to 16th August, 1779.
Lieutenant-Colonel Samuel J. Cabell, 12th February, 1781, to 1st January, 1783.
Lieutenant-Colonel Thomas Posey, 11th September, 1782, to 1st January, 1783.
Major William Nelson, 29th February, 1776, to 7th October, 1776.
Major John Cropper, 7th October, 1776, to 26th October, 1777.
Major William Davies, 22d March, 1777, to 20th March, 1778.
Major John Webb, 26th January, 1778, to 14th September, 1778.
Major Thomas Posey, 14th September, 1778, to 11th September, 1782.
Major Charles Pelham, 12th February, 1781, to 1st January, 1783.
Major Samuel Finley, 11th September, 1782, to 1st January, 1783.

Eighth Virginia.

Colonel Peter Muhlenberg, 1st March, 1776, to 21st February, 1777.
Colonel Abraham Bowman, 22d March, 1777, to — December, 1777.
Colonel John Neville, 11th December, 1777, to 14th September, 1778.
Colonel James Wood, 14th September, 1778, to 1st January, 1783.
Lieutenant-Colonel Abraham Bowman, 1st March, 1776, to 22d March, 1777.
Lieutenant-Colonel John Markham, 22d March, 1777, to 26th October, 1777.
Lieutenant-Colonel Charles Fleming, 14th September, 1778, to 15th December, 1778.
Lieutenant-Colonel Samuel J. Cabell, 15th December, 1778, to 4th July, 1779.

Lieutenant-Colonel Jonathan Clark, 10th May, 1779, to 1st January, 1783.
Major Peter Helphenstone, 1st March, 1776, to 7th August, 1776.
Major William Taliaferro, 7th August, 1776, to 21st February, 1777.
Major William Darke, 4th January, 1777, to 12th February, 1781.
Major Morgan Alexander, 22d March, 1777, to 16th May, 1778.
Major William Croghan, 16th May, 1778, to 14th September, 1778.
Major Jonathan Clark, 14th September, 1778, to 10th May, 1779.
Major Andrew Waggoner, 15th December, 1778, to 12th February, 1781.
Major John Poulson, 12th February, 1781, to 1st January, 1783.

Ninth Virginia.

Colonel Charles Fleming, 2d March, 1776, to — August, 1776.
Colonel Isaac Read, 13th August, 1776, to 10th February, 1777.
Colonel George Matthews, 10th February, 1777, to 14th September, 1778.
Colonel John Gibson, 14th September, 1778, to 12th February, 1781.
Lieutenant-Colonel George Matthews, 4th March, 1776, to 10th February, 1777.
Lieutenant-Colonel John Sayres, 30th January, 1777, to 4th October, 1777.
Lieutenant-Colonel George Lyne, 4th October, 1777, to 14th November, 1777.
Lieutenant-Colonel Burgess Ball, 17th December, 1777, to 14th September, 1778.
Lieutenant-Colonel Richard Campbell, 14th September, 1778, to 12th February, 1781.
Major Matthew Donovan, 4th March, 1776, to 27th January, 1777.
Major John Fitzgerald, 28th January, 1777, to 6th July, 1778.
Major James Knox, 6th July, 1778, to 30th September, 1778.
Major Richard Taylor, 14th September, 1778, to 7th December, 1779.
Major John Poulson, 12th May, 1779, to 12th February, 1781.
Major William Taylor, 7th December, 1779, to 12th February, 1781.

Tenth Virginia.

Colonel Edward Stevens, 12th November, 1776, to 31st January, 1778.
Colonel John Green, 26th January, 1778, to 14th September, 1778.
Colonel William Davies, 14th September, 1778, to 12th February, 1781.
Lieutenant-Colonel Lewis Willis, 13th November, 1776, to 1st March, 1778.
Lieutenant-Colonel Samuel Hawes, 1st March, 1778, to 14th September, 1778.
Lieutenant-Colonel Samuel Hopkins, 14th September, 1778, to 12th February, 1781
Major George Nicholas, 13th November, 1776, to 26th September, 1777.
Major Samuel Hawes, 4th October, 1777, to 1st March, 1778.
Major Thomas Ridley, 1st March, 1778, to 14th September, 1778.
Major Samuel J. Cabell, 14th September, 1778, to 15th December, 1778.
Major William Lewis, 12th May, 1779, to 12th February, 1781.

Eleventh Virginia.

Colonel Daniel Morgan, 12th November, 1776, to 14th September, 1778.
Colonel Abraham Buford, 14th September, 1778, to 12th February, 1781.

Lieutenant-Colonel Christian Febiger, 13th November, 1776, to 26th September, 1777.
Lieutenant-Colonel George Nicholas, 26th September, 1777, to 27th November, 1777.
Lieutenant-Colonel John Cropper, 26th October, 1777, to 14th September, 1778.
Lieutenant-Colonel Gustavus B. Wallace, 14th September, 1778, to 12th February, 1781.
Major William Heth, 13th November, 1776, to 1st April, 1777.
Major Levin Joynes, 10th February, 1777, to 11th December, 1777.
Major Thomas Snead, 1st April, 1777, to 8th March, 1778.
Major Thomas Massie, 20th February, 1778, to 14th September, 1778.
Major David Stephenson, 14th September, 1778, to 12th February, 1781.
Major Joseph Crockett, 20th May, 1779, to 12th February, 1781.

Twelfth Virginia.

Colonel James Wood, 12th November, 1776, to 14th September, 1778.
Lieutenant-Colonel John Neville, 12th November, 1776, to 11th December, 1777.
Lieutenant-Colonel Levin Joynes, 11th December, 1777, to 14th September, 1778.
Major Charles Simms, 12th November, 1776, to 29th September, 1777.
Major George Slaughter, 4th October, 1777, to 23d December, 1777.
Major Jonathan Clark, 10th January, 1778, to 14th September, 1778.

Thirteenth Virginia.

Colonel William Russell, 19th December, 1776, to 14th September, 1778.
Lieutenant-Colonel John Gibson, 12th November, 1776, to 25th October, 1777.
Lieutenant-Colonel Richard Campbell, 20th February, 1778, to 14th September, 1778.
Major George Lyne, 12th November, 1776, to 4th October, 1777.
Major Richard Campbell, 10th August, 1777, to 20th February, 1778.
Major Richard Taylor, 4th February, 1778, to 14th September, 1778.

Fourteenth Virginia.

Colonel Charles Lewis, 12th November, 1776, to 28th March, 1778.
Colonel William Davies, 20th March, 1778, to 14th September, 1778.
Lieutenant-Colonel Samuel Hopkins, 19th June, 1778, to 14th September, 1778.
Major Abraham Buford, 13th November, 1776, to 1st April, 1777.
Major George Stubblefield, 1st April, 1777, to 22d February, 1778.
Major Samuel J. Cabell, 20th December, 1777, to 14th Septetmber, 1778.

Fifteenth Virginia.

Colonel David Mason, 12th November, 1776, to 31st July, 1778.
Colonel Abraham Buford, 15th May, 1778, to 14th September, 1778.
Lieutenant-Colonel James Innis, 13th November, 1776, to ——?
Lieutenant-Colonel Gustavus B. Wallace, 20th March, 1778, to 14th September 1778.
Major Holt Richardson, 13th November, 1776, to 18th October, 1777.
Major Gustavus B. Wallace, 4th October, 1777, to 20th March, 1778.
Major Francis Taylor, 20th March, 1778, to 14th September, 1778.

(NOTE.—*There are but few rolls, returns, and lists of Virginia troops and not of uniform dates, hence the above list appears somewhat irregular as to consecutive order, which is in a measure due to the absence of orders directing transfers, &c.*)

In September, 1778, the number of Virginia regiments were reduced from fifteen to eleven and designated as follows: The Ninth was incorporated with the First; the Sixth with the Second; the Fifth with the Third, and the Eighth with the Fourth; the Seventh was designated the Fifth; Tenth the Sixth; Eleventh the Seventh; Twelfth the Eighth; Thirteenth the Ninth; Fourteenth the Tenth, and Fifteenth the Eleventh.

JACKSON'S CONTINENTAL
or
FIRST AMERICAN REGIMENT.

Colonel Henry Jackson, 3d November, 1783, to 20th June, 1784.
Lieutenant-Colonel William Hull, 3d November, 1783, to 20th June, 1784.
Major Caleb Gibbs, 3d November, 1783, to 20th June, 1784.

THE LAST SOLDIER OF THE REVOLUTION.

In the Annual Report of the Commissioner of Pensions for the year 1874 appears the following paragraph: "With the death of Daniel T. Bakeman, of Freedom, Cattaraugus County, N. Y., April 5, 1869, the last of the pensioned soldiers of the Revolution passed away."

ALPHABETICAL LIST OF OFFICERS

OF THE

CONTINENTAL ARMY

Including many officers of the Militia, during the war of the Revolution, 1775 to 1783, showing the various ranks they held, from when and how long they served, when and where wounded, taken prisoner, exchanged, died, &c., and all cases in which thanks, swords, or medals were awarded by Congress.

Following the name of each officer will be found the State or country in parentheses ( ) from which appointed, or State in which the organization was raised, in which service was rendered.

A

Aaron, William (Ga). Captain of a Georgia regiment in 1776-77.

Abbe, Richard (Conn). Ensign 7th Connecticut, 1st January, 1777; resigned 6th February, 1778. (Died 1807.)

Abbe, Thomas (Conn). 1st Lieutenant of Mott's Connecticut State Regiment, June to December, 1776; Captain 3d Connecticut, January, 1777; retired 15th November, 1778. (Died 1811.)

Abbey, Aaron (Mass). 2d Lieutenant of Ward's Massachusetts Regiment, 23d May to December, 1775.

Abbot, Abiel (N. H.). Paymaster of Baldwin's Regiment, New Hampshire Militia, September, 1776, to March, 1777; served subsequently as Major New Hampshire Militia. (Died 1809.)

Abbot, George (Mass). Regimental Quartermaster of Gardner's Massachusetts Regiment, June to December, 1775.

Abbot, Isaac (Mass). 2d Lieutenant of Frye's Massachusetts Regiment, April to December, 1775; wounded at Bunker Hill, 17th June, 1775. (Died August, 1836.)

Abbot, John (Conn). Ensign 4th Connecticut, 1st January, 1777; resigned 27th December, 1777.

Abbot, Joseph (Mass). Ensign Sargent's Massachusetts Regiment, May to December, 1775; Captain, Major and Lieutenant-Colonel Massachusetts Militia, March, 1776 to 1782. (Died 1814.)

Abbot, Josiah (Mass). Ensign 10th Massachusetts, 19th October, 1781; transferred to 2d Massachusetts, 1st January, 1783, and served to 3d November, 1783. (Died February, 1837.)

Abbot, Stephen (Mass). Ensign 8th Continental Infantry, 1st January, 1776; 1st Lieutenant 11th Massachusetts, 6th November, 1776; Captain, 28th May, 1778; transferred to 8th Massachusetts, 1st January, 1783, and served to June, 1783. (Died 1813.)

Abbott, James (Conn). Ensign of Ely's Regiment, Connecticut Militia, June, 1777; taken prisoner on the Long Island Expedition, 10th December, 1777; exchanged 17th December, 1781. (Died 1799.)

Abbott, John (Vt). Colonel Vermont Militia in 1781.

Abbott, Joshua (N. H.). Captain 1st New Hampshire, 24th April to December, 1775; Captain 5th Continental Infantry, 1st January to 31st December, 1776; Captain New Hampshire Militia, 1777-1778. (Died March, 1815.)

Abbott, Nathaniel (Mass). 1st Lieutenant 11th Massachusetts, 1st January, 1777; Captain, September, 1777; no record of service after September, 1778.

Abbott, Samuel (Conn). Colonel Connecticut Militia in 1779.

Abbott, Seth (Conn). 2d Lieutenant Sullivan's Connecticut State Regiment, July to December, 1776.

Abbott, Thomas (N. Y.). Lieutenant 2d Canadian (Hazen's) Regiment, 3d November, 1776; omitted — May, 1777.

Abeel, James (N. Y.). Captain of Lasher's Regiment, New York Militia, June to December, 1776. (Died 1825.)

Abel, Elijah (Conn). Captain of Bradley's Connecticut State Regiment, June to December, 1776.

Abel, Rufus B. (Conn). Ensign 1st Connecticut, 1st January, 1777; Regimental Paymaster, 1st June, 1777; 2d Lieutenant, 1st June, 1778; resigned 15th April, 1779.

Abney, Nathaniel (S. C.). Captain 3d South Carolina (Rangers), June, 1775 to —.

Abney, William (S. C.). Lieutenant 3d South Carolina (Rangers) in 1777.

Acker, Seybert (N. Y.). Captain New York Militia, 1778-1779.

Ackley, Bezaleel (Conn). 2d Lieutenant 22d Continental Infantry, 1st January to 31st December, 1776.

Adair, John (S. C.). Major South Carolina Militia; Aide-de-Camp to General Sumter, 17th May, 1779-1781. (Died 19th May, 1840.)

Adams, Aaron (N. H.). Captain in Stickney's New Hampshire Regiment in 1777. (Died 1819.)

Adams, Amos (Mass). Chaplain of David Brewer's Massachusetts Regiment, — May, 1775. Died 5th October, 1775.

Adams, Benjamin (Conn). Ensign 22d Continental Infantry, 1st January, 1776; 2d Lieutenant, 10th August to 31st December, 1776. (Died 1816.)

Adams Benjamin (N. H.). Surgeon's Mate New Hampshire Militia in 1780.

Adams, Caleb Greenleaf (N. H.). Surgeon 2d New Hampshire, 20th May to — December, 1775; Surgeon 8th Continental Infantry, 1st January to 31st December, 1776.

Adams, Daniel Jenifer (Md). 1st Lieutenant of Captain Beall's Independent Maryland Company, 14th January, 1776; Brigade Major to General Beall of the Maryland Flying Camp, 27th August to 1st December, 1776; Major 7th Maryland, 10th December, 1776; resigned 8th June, 1779. (Died November, 1796.)

Adams, David (Conn). Surgeon 4th Connecticut, 25th March, 1778; retired 1st January, 1781.

Adams, Ebenezer (R. I.). Served as a volunteer in the expedition to Quebec in December, 1775; Captain of Elliott's Regiment, Rhode Island State Artillery, 12th December, 1776, to June, 1777. (Died 1799.)

Adams, Edward (Ga). Lieutenant Georgia Militia, 24th August, 1776, to —, 1777.

Adams, Elijah (Conn). Surgeon's Mate 3d Connecticut, May to December, 1775.

Adams, Francis (Pa). 2d Lieutenant 10th Pennsylvania, 4th December, 1776; 1st Lieutenant, 18th April, 1777; cashiered 25th May, 1778.

Adams, Henry (Mass). Surgeon's Mate 9th Massachusetts, 1st January, 1777; transferred to 3d Massachusetts 1st January, 1781; Surgeon 6th Massachusetts, 14th May, 1781; resigned 17th August, 1782. (Died June, 1793.)

Adams, Jervis (Md). Lieutenant and Regimental Quartermaster 1st Continental Artillery, 22d November, 1777; resigned 9th February, 1779.

Adams, John (Mass). A signer of the Declaration of Independence. First Vice-President of the United States, 30th April, 1789, to 4th March, 1797, and Second President of the United States, 4th March, 1797, to 4th March, 1801. (Died 4th July, 1826.)

Adams, John (Mass). Lieutenant and Captain of Johnson's Regiment Massachusetts Militia, 1776 and 1777. (Died 1813.)

Adams, John (N. H.). Ensign 2d New Hampshire, 8th March, 1781; 2d Lieutenant 1st New Hampshire, 6th October, 1781; retained in Jackson's Continental Regiment 3d November, 1783, and served to 20h June, 1784; (Died 1847.)

Adams, Joel (Conn.). Ensign of Mott's Connecticut State Regiment June to December, 1776. Lieutenant in 1778. Wounded at Lake George 18th September, 1777. (Died 1820.)

Adams, Joseph (Mass). Surgeon's mate of Read's Massachusetts Regiment, 24th April, to December, 1775; Surgeon's mate 13th Continental Infantry, 1st January to 31st December, 1776

Adams, Joshua (Conn.). Ensign of Silliman's Connecticut State Regiment, July to December, 1776.

Adams, Josiah (Mass). Paymaster 12th Continental Infantry, 22d September to 31st December, 1776.

Adams, Nathan (Del). Captain Delaware Regiment, 19th January, 1776. (Died 27th March, 1776.)

Adams, Nathan (Mass). Lieutenant 7th Massachusetts, 1st January, 1777; deserted 1st October, 1777.

Adams, Oliver (Conn). Ensign 3d Connecticut, 1st January, 1777; resigned 12th December, 1777.

Adams, Peter (Md). Captain of Smallwood's Maryland Regiment, 14th January, 1776; Major 7th Maryland, 10th December, 1776; Lieutenant-Colonel 20th February, 1777; Lieutenant-Colonel commandant, 1st Maryland, 1st August, 1779; transferred to 3d Maryland, 1st January, 1781, and served to April, 1783.

Adams, Robert (Pa). Captain 6th Pennsylvania Battalion, 9th January, 1776; killed in the action at Isle aux Noix, Canada, 24th June, 1776.

Adams, Samuel (Mass). A signer of the Declaration of Independence. (Died 3d October, 1803.)

Adams, Samuel (Mass). Surgeon of Fellow's Massachusetts Regiment, May to December, 1775; Surgeon 18th Continental Infantry, 1st January to 31st December, 1776; Surgeon 3d Continental Artillery, 14th May, 1778; Hospital Physician and Surgeon, 6th October, 1780, and served to close of war. (Died 6th March, 1819.)

Adams, Samuel (N. H.). Ensign 2d New Hampshire, 8th November, 1776; Lieutenant 9th October, 1777; transferred to 1st New Hampshire, 1st January, 1783, and served to close of war. Brevet Captain 30th September, 1783. (Died 1813.)

Adams, Silas (Mass). 1st Lieutenant of Little's Massachusetts Regiment, 19th May to December, 1775; Captain Massachusetts Militia in 1777. (Died 1800.)

Adams, William (Conn). Ensign 6th Connecticut, May to December, 1775; 1st Lieutenant 20th Continental Infantry, 1st January, 1776; Regimental Paymaster 7th September to 31st December, 1776; Paymaster 4th Connecticut, 1st January, 1777; 2d Lieutenant 24th July, 1777; 1st Lieutenant 1st May, 1779; transferred to 1st Connecticut 1st January, 1781; cashiered 19th June, 1781.

Adams, Wm. (Md). Ensign Maryland battalion of the Flying Camp, July to December, 1776; 1st Lieutenant 4th Maryland, 10th December, 1776; transferred to 1st Maryland 1st January, 1783; retained in Maryland battalion April, 1783, and served to 15th November, 1783; Brevet Captain 30th September, 1783.

Adams, William (Md). Had been an officer in the Navy prior to 1778; 2d Lieutenant 7th Maryland, 14th April, 1778; 1st Lieutenant, 8th June, 1779; transferred to 2d Maryland, 1st January, 1781, and served to April, 1783.

Adams, Winborn (N. H.). Captain 2d New Hampshire, 23d May to — December, 1775; Captain 8th Continental Infantry, 1st January, 1776; Major 2d New Hampshire, 8th November, 1776; Lieutenant-Colonel, 2d April, 1777. Killed at Bemus' Heights 19th September, 1777.

Adams, William (N. Y.). Surgeon of Malcolm's New York State Regiment, 23d July to — December, 1776; Surgeon Hospital Department, 1777-1780.

Adams, William (Pa). Surgeon 4th Continental Artillery 1st April, 1777; resigned 7th May, 1779; reappointed 1st October, 1779; resigned 31st July, 1780.

Addison, John (Md). Lieutenant-Colonel 3d Maryland Battalion of the Flying Camp, 27th June to 1st December, 1776.

Addoms, Jonas (N. Y.). Second Lieutenant 2d Continental Artillery, 20th August, 1781; transferred to corps of artillery 17th June, 1783, and served to 3d November, 1783. (Died 1837.)

Aden, Ebenezer (Va). Captain and Major Virginia Militia, 1777-1778. (Died 26th March, 1806.)

Ahl, John Peter (Pa). Surgeon's Mate of Armand's Partisan Corps, 1777 to 1781. (Died 13th July, 1827.)

Aiken, James (N. H.). Captain New Hampshire Militia in 1780.

Ainsworth, Jedediah (Conn). Surgeon's Mate 8th Connecticut, 10th June, 1778; transferred to 5th Connecticut, 1st January, 1781, and served to — June, 1782.

Aitkin, James (N. C.). Chaplain 4th North Carolina; 5th April, 1777; in service in July, 1777. Name also spelled Atkin.

Albarty, Frederick (N. C.). Ensign North Carolina Regiment in 1781. (Died 29th August,, 1831.)

Albright, Philip (Pa). Captain of Miles' Regiment, Pennsylvania Riflemen, 19th March, 1776; resigned 23d January, 1777.

Albro, James (R. I.). Ensign Rhode Island Militia in 1775; Captain of Stanton's Rhode Island State Regiment, 12th December, 1776, to March, ₁777.

Alden, Austin (Mass). Private in Phinney's Massachusetts Regiment May to December, 1775; Ensign 18th Continental Infantry, 1st January, 1776; Lieutenant 12th Massachusetts, 6th November, 1776; cashiered 17th February, 1778. (Died 23d March, 1804.)

Alden, Ichabod (Mass). Lieutenant-Colonel of Cotton's Massachusetts Regiment, 23d April to December, 1775; Lieutenant-Colonel 25th Continental Infantry, 1st January, 1776; Colonel 7th Massachusetts, 1st November, 1776. Killed at Cherry Valley 10th November, 1778.

Alden, John (Conn). Ensign 20th Continental Infantry, 1st January to 31st December, 1776.

Alden, Judah (Conn). Captain of Webb's Additional Continental Regiment, 1st January, 1777. Killed on Staten Island, 22d August, 1777.

Alden, Judah (Mass). 2d Lieutenant of Cotton's Massachusetts Regiment, May to December, 1775; 1st Lieutenant 23d Continental Infantry, 1st January to 31st December, 1776; Captain 2d Massachusetts, 1st January, 1777; Brevet Major, 30th September, 1783; served to 3d November, 1783. (Died 2d March, 1845.)

Alden, Roger (Conn). Adjutant 5th Connecticut, 1st January, 1777; Brigade Major to General Huntington, 13th July, 1777, to 1st April, 1780; Captain Lieutenant 2d Connecticut, 15th June, 1778; Captain, 1st September, 1779; Major and Aides-de-camp to General Huntington, 1st April, 1780; resigned 8th February, 1781; Military Storekeeper United States Army, 20th January, 1825. Died 5th November, 1836.

Alderson, Simeon (N. C.). Captain 5th North Carolina, 17th April, 1776; retired 1st June, 1778.

Alderson, Thomas (N. C.). Ensign 5th North Carolina, 3d May, 1776, to ——.

Aldrich, George (N. H.). 2d Lieutenant 3d New Hampshire, 23d May to — December, 1775; 1st Lieutenant 2d Continental Infantry, 1st January, 1776; Captain of Whitcomb's New Hampshire

Rangers, 4th November, 1776; retired 1st January, 1781.

Aldrich, Levi (Mass). Ensign in Lexington Alarm, April, 1775; 1st Lieutenant of Read's Massachusetts Regiment, May to December, 1775.

Aldrich, William (R. I.). Lieutenant of Hitchcock's Rhode Island Regiment, 3d May to December, 1775.

Alexander, Abram (S. C.). 1st Lieutenant South Carolina Militia under General Sumter, 1780-81. (Died 1816.)

Alexander, Andrew (Del). Lieutenant of the Delaware battalion of the Flying Camp, July to December, 1776.

Alexander, Archibald (Va). Surgeon's Mate 10th Va, May, 1776; Surgeon, 24th August, 1777; taken prisoner at Brandywine, 11th September, 1777; retired 14th September, 1778. (Died 1822.)

Alexander, Charles (N. C.). 2d Lieutenant 4th North Carolina, November, 1776; 1st Lieutenant, 20th January, 1777, to ——.

Alexander, George (Va). 2d Lieutenant 1st Virginia State Regiment, May, 1778; 1st Lieutenant, 1st November, 1779, and served to January, 1780.

Alexander, George D. (Va). Surgeon of Grayson's Continental Regiment, 14th March, 1777; retired 22d April, 1779.

Alexander, Henry (R. I.). Ensign and Lieutenant of Richmond's and Tallman's Rhode Island State Regiments in 1776 and 1777.

Alexander, Hezekiah (N. C.). Paymaster 4th North Carolina, 16th April, 1776; 1st Lieutenant, 20th January, 1777; retired 1st June, 1778.

Alexander, James (Ga). 1st Lieutenant of Captain Phoenix's Company Georgia Artillery, 6th November, 1776; Captain Georgia Militia in 1780.

Alexander, James (S. C.). Captain South Carolina Militia, 1780-81.

Alexander, John (N. H.). Lieutenant of Bedel's New Hampshire State Regiment, 15th December, 1777, to 1st April, 1778.

·**Alexander, John** (Pa). 2d Lieutenant 6th Pennsylvania Battalion, 9th January, 1776; 1st Lieutenant, 10th February, 1776; Captain, 7th Pennsylvania, 20th March, 1777; transferred to 4th Pennsylvania, 17th January, 1781; resigned 11th July, 1781. (Died 4th August, 1804.)

Alexander, Morgan (Va). Captain 2d Virginia, 27th November, 1775; Major, 23d December, 1776; transferred to 8th Virginia, 22d March, 1777; resigned 16th May, 1778; Colonel Virginia Militia, 1781-1782. (Died 1783.)

Alexander, Nathaniel (Mass). 2d Lieutenant of Brewer's Massachusetts Regiment, May to December, 1775; 1st Lieutenant 6th Continental Infantry, 1st January, 1776; Captain 13th Massachusetts, 13th November, 1776; retired 11th April, 1779. (Died 16th February, 1829.)

Alexander, Nathaniel (S. C.). Surgeon — South Carolina Regiment, 1778-1782. (Died 8th March, 1808.)

Alexander, Philip (Va). Captain Virginia Militia in 1781.

Alexander Reuben (N. H.). Captain New Hampshire Militia in 1777.

Alexander Robert (N. C.). Captain North Carolina Militia, 1776.

Alexander, Samuel (Ga). Captain of a Georgia Regiment in 1777.

Alexander, Samuel (N. Y.). 1st Lieutenant and Regimental Quartermaster, 2d Canadian (Hazen's) Regiment, 3d November, 1776; omitted June, 1777.

Alexander, Thomas (Mass). Captain Massachusetts Militia in the Canadian Campaign, 1775 and 1776. (Died 23d March, 1801.)

Alexander, Thomas (Pa). 2d Lieutenant 7th Pennsylvania, 2d June, 1778; dropped as having been appointed Brigade Quartermaster.

Alexander, Walter (Md.) Captain, 4th Maryland Battalion of the Flying Camp, July to December, 1776.

Alexander, William (Md). 1st Lieutenant 5th Maryland, 10th December, 1776. Died 27th August, 1777.

Alexander, William (Earl of Stirling), (N. J.). Colonel 1st New Jersey, 7th November, 1775; Brigadier-General Continental Army, 1st March, 1776; taken prisoner at Long Island, 27th August, 1776; exchanged — September, 1776; Major-General Continental Army, •19th February, 1777.

By the Act of Congress of 24th September, 1779, it was "Resolved, that the thanks of Congress be given to Major-General Lord Stirling, for the judicious measures taken by him to forward the enterprise (attack of work on Paulus Hook), and to secure the retreat of the party."

By the Act of 28th January, 1783, it was "Resolved, that the President signify to the commander-in-chief, in a manner the most respectful to the memory of the late Major-General, the Earl of Stirling, the sense Congress entertain of the early and meritorious exertions of that General in the common cause, and of the bravery, perseverence and military talents he possessed; which, having fixed their esteem for his character, while living, induce a proportionate regret for the loss of an officer who has rendered such constant and important services to his country." (Died 15th January, 1783.)

Alexander, William (N. C.). Ensign 10th North Carolina, 10th May, 1781; Lieutenant, 8th September, 1781; transferred to 4th North Carolina, 6th February, 1782, and served to close of war.

Alexander, William (Pa). 1st Lieutenant 6th Pennsylvania Battalion, 9th January, 1776; Captain, 1st June, 1776; Captain 7th Pennsylvania, 1st January, 1777, to rank from 1st June, 1776; Major 3d Pennsylvania, 16th April, 1780; retired 1st January, 1783.

Alexander, William (Va). Captain Virginia Militia in 1781.

Allexander, William Lee (N. C.). Captain of a North Carolina Regiment in 1779 and 1780.

Alger, William B. (N. Y.). 2d Lieutenant 4th New York, 21st August, 1775, to — January, 1776; served subsequently as an officer New York Militia.

Alger, John (Vt). Captain Vermont Militia in 1777.

Allain, —— Mons. (France). Served as a volunteer in Armand's Partisan Corps; Brevet Lieutenant Continental Army 13th January, 1779, and retired from the service.

Allard, Shadrach (N. H.). 1st Lieutenant New Hampshire Militia in 1776

Allen, Abraham (N. J.). Ensign of Dye's Regiment New Jersey Militia; taken prisoner at Bargin Point, 16th January, 1779.

Allen, Adoniram (S. C.). Captain South Carolina Partisan Rangers, 1780 to 1782.

Allen, Archer (Va). Captain Virginia Militia, 1779-1781.

Allen, Benjamin (Mass). Sergeant of Gridley's Regiment Massachusetts Artillery, June to December, 1775; 1st Lieutenant 3d Continental Artillery, 1st February, 1777; resigned 13th March, 1778.

Allen, Charles (N. C.). Ensign 2d North Carolina, 20th October, 1775; Lieutenant, 8th June, 1776; Captain, —, 1777; transferred to 5th North Carolina, 1st June, 1778, and served to ——.

Allen, Daniel (Conn). 2d Lieutenant 3d Connecticut, 1st May to 18th December, 1775; Captain of Ward's Connecticut State Regiment, 14th May, 1776; Captain 3d Connecticut, 1st January, 1777; resigned 1st June, 1779.

Allen, David (Mass). 1st Leutenant of Gridley's Regiment Massachusetts Artillery, June to December, 1775; Captain-Lieutenant of Knox's Regiment Continental Artillery, 1st January, 1776; Captain 3d Continental Artillery, 1st January, 1777; resigned 13th September, 1778.

Allen, David (N. H.). Surgeon's Mate 1st New Hampshire, 1st May, 1782, to April, 1783.

Allen, David (Va). Ensign 5th Virginia, 26th March, 1777; 2d Lieutenant, 10th December, 1777; transferred to 3d Virginia, 14th September, 1778; 1st Lieutenant, 19th June, 1779; taken prisoner at Charleston, 12th May, 1780; exchanged July, 1781; served to close of the war.

Allen, Ebenezer (N. H.). 1st Lieutenant Green Mountain Boys, 27th July, 1775, to — January, 1776; served subsequently as Captain and Colonel of a battalion New Hampshire Rangers and Militia. (Died 26th March, 1806.)

Allen, Ebenezer (N. Y.). Major New York Militia, 1776-1779; dismissed 3d May, 1779.

Allen, Ebenezer (Vt). Captain Vermont Militia in 1776 and 1777.

Allen, Edward (Va). Ensign 4th Virginia, September, 1776; 2d Lieutenant, 12th January, 1777; 1st Lieutenant, 4th October, 1777; retired 30th September, 1778.

Allen, Ethan (N. H.). Lieutenant-Colonel and commander of the Green Mountain Boys; captured Fort Ticonderoga 10th May, 1775, "by the authority of the Great Jehovah and the Continental Congress"; taken prisoner at Montreal, 25th September, 1775; exchanged 6th May, 1778. He received the brevet rank of Colonel, Continental Army, 14th May, 1778, "in reward of his fortitude, firmness and zeal in the cause of his country, manifested during his long and cruel captivity, as well as on former occasions." Major-General Vermont Militia in 1779. (Died 13th February, 1789.)

Allen, Gabriel (R. I.). Lieutenant of Stanton's Rhode Island, State Regiment, 12th December, 1776, to March, 1777.

Allen, Heber (N. H.). Captain Green Mountain Boys, 27th July to — December, 1775. (Died 1782.)

Allen, Heman (N. H.). Captain Green Mountain Boys, July to December, 1775. (Died — May, 1778.)

Allice, Henry (Pa). Captain 3d Pennsylvania Battalion, 5th January, 1776; resigned 27th February, 1776.

Allen, Hudson (Va). Captain Virginia Militia in 1781.

Allen, Ira (N. H.). 1st Lieutenant Green Mountain Boys, 27th July, 1775, to — January, 1776; Colonel Vermont Militia in 1780. (Died 7th January, 1814.)

Allen, Jacob (Mass). Sergeant in Lexington Alarm, April, 1775; 1st Lieutenant of Thomas' Massachusetts Regiment, May to December, 1775; Captain 23d Continental Infantry, 1st January to 31st December, 1776; Captain 2d Massachusetts, 1st January, 1777. Killed at Bemus' Heights, 19th September, 1777.

Allen, James (Mass). 1st Lieutenant in Lexington Alarm, April, 1775; Captain of Thomas' Massachusetts Regiment, May to December, 1775; Captain Massachusetts Militia, 1776-1780.

Allen, James (Mass). Lieutenant of Malcolm's Continental Regiment, 22d January, 1777; Brigade Quartermaster, 1st January, 1778, to April, 1779.

Allen, James (Pa). Ensign 6th Pennsylvania, 2d June, 1778; retired 1st January, 1780 (name also spelled McAllen).

Allen, Jeremiah (S. C.). Captain South Carolina Militia in Marion's Brigade, 1780-1781.

Allen, John (Mass). 2d Lieutenant of Brewer's Massachusetts Regiment, May to December, 1775; Ensign 14th Continental Infantry, 1st January, 1776, to December, 1776; Colonel Massachusetts Militia, 1777-1781.

Allen, John (N. H.). Captain New Hampshire Militia, 1776.

Allen, John (N. J.). 2d Lieutenant of Spencer's Continental Regiment,

24th May, 1777; Regimental Adjutant, 30th May, 1777; dismissed 9th June, 1778.

Allen, John (N. C.). Lieutenant 5th North Carolina, 1st October, 1776, to ——.

Allen, John (Va). Captain of Taylor's Regiment Virginia Convention Guards and Issuing Commissary at Albemarle, Va., January, 1779, to November, 1782. (Died 1838.)

Allen, John Baptist (N. Y.) Captain 1st Canadian (Livingston's) Regiment, 20th November, 1775; cashiered 16th September, 1778.

Allen, Jonas (Mass). 1st Lieutenant of Doolittle's Massachusetts Regiment, May to December, 1775.

Allen, Jonathan (Mass). Captain of Fellows' Massachusetts Regiment, 19th May to December, 1775; Captain 21st Continental Infantry, 1st January to 31st December, 1776; Captain 5th Massachusetts, 1st January, 1777; Major, 17th May, 1777. Killed 6th January, 1780, while hunting.

Allen, Jonathan (Mass). Ensign of Brewer's Massachusetts Regiment, May to December, 1775; 1st Lieutenant 2d Massachusetts, 1st January, 1777; resigned 7th June, 1778.

Allen, Jonathan (Mass). Adjutant 8th Massachusetts, 1st January, 1777; discharged by sentence of court-martial 9th June, 1778.

Allen, Joseph (Mass). 2d Lieutenant of Walker's Massachusetts Regiment, May to December, 1775. (Died 1814.)

Allen, Lathrop (N. Y.). Private and Sergeant in 2d New York, May to December, 1775; Lieutenant in 2d New York, December, 1775, to March, 1776; Captain in Elmore's Regiment Connecticut Militia, 15th April, 1776, to — April, 1777. (Died 12th August, 1826.)

Allen, Matthew (R. I.). Captain Lieutenant in Church's Rhode Island Regiment, 3d May to — December, 1775.

Allen, Moses (Ga). Chaplain Georgia Brigade in 1776; taken prisoner at Sunbury, 9th January, 1779, and while trying to escape, shortly after he was drowned.

Allen, Moses (S. C.). Deputy Judge Advocate General Southern Departments, 29th May, 1778, to ——.

Allen, Nathaniel Coit (Mass). Paymaster 10th Massachusetts, 6th November, 1776, to 12th October, 1782; Ensign, 10th August, 1778; Lieutenant,

10th October, 1778; Captain, 12th October, 1782; transferred to 7th Massachusetts, 1st January, 1783; transferred to 4th Massachusetts, 12th June, 1783, and served to 3d November, 1783.

Allen, Noah (Mass). Lieutenant in Lexington Alarm, April, 1775; 1st Lieutenant of Fellows' Massachusetts Regiment, May to December, 1775; 1st Lieutenant 6th Continental Infantry, 1st January, 1776; Captain, 2d October, 1776; Captain 13th Massachusetts, 1st January, 1777, to rank from 2d October, 1776; transferred to 1st Massachusetts, 1st January, 1781; retired 1st August, 1782, with rank of Major.

Allen, Noel (R. I.). Ensign 1st Rhode Island Regiment, 28th June to — December, 1775; 1st Lieutenant 9th Continental Infantry, 1st January, 1776. Killed at Harlem Plains, 16th September, 1776.

Allen, Parmalee (Mass). 1st Lieutenant 3d Massachusetts, 1st January, 1777; omitted in September, 1777, with remark 'never joined regiment.' He was Captain Vermont Rangers in 1777. (Died 1806.)

Allen, Richard (N. C.). Captain North Carolina Militia at King's Mountain, October, 1780. (Died 10th October, 1832.)

Allen, Richmond (Va). Lieutenant-Colonel Virginia Militia, 1781-1782.

Allen, Robert (Mass). Captain 7th Massachusetts, 1st January, 1777; resigned 3d September, 1778. (Name also spelled Allin.)

Allen, Samuel (Mass). Ensign in Lexington Alarm, April, 1775; 2d Lieutenant of Fellow's Massachusetts Regiment, April to December, 1775; 1st Lieutenant 21st Continental Infantry, 1st January to 31st December, 1776; 1st Lieutenant 9th Massachusetts, 1st January, 1777; resigned 18th April, 1778. (Died 1801.)

Allen, Simeon (Conn). 1st Lieutenant of Mott's Connecticut State Regiment, June to December, 1776.

Allen, Stephen (N. Y.). Lieutenant 2d Continental Artillery, 1st January, 1777, and served to June, 1783.

Allen, Thomas (N. H.). Chaplain of Warner's Continental Regiment, 16th February, 1777; resigned 16th July, 1777.

Allen, Thomas (N. C.). Captain 1st North Carolina, 1st September, 1775; resigned 15th August, 1776.

Allen, Thomas (N. C.). 1st Lieutenant 3d North Carolina, 17th March, 1778; taken prisoner at Charleston 12th May, 1780, and died in prison 26th August, 1780.

Allen, Vial. (R. I.). Lieutenant Rhode Island Militia, August, 1775, to March, 1776.

Allen, Walter (N. C.). Ensign 5th North Carolina, 28th March, 1777; Lieutenant, 4th October, 1777, to ——.

Allen, William (Pa). Captain 1st Pennsylvania Battalion, 27th October, 1775; Lieutenant-Colonel 2d Pennsylvania, 4th January, 1776; resigned 24th July, 1776, and joined the enemy.

Allen, William Jr. (Pa). 1st Lieutenant 1st Pennsylvania Battalion of the Flying Camp, July to December, 1776. Wounded at Long Island 27th August, 1776. (Died 1794.)

Allen, William (R. I.). Ensign 2d Rhode Island, June to December, 1775; 1st Lieutenant 11th Continental Infantry, 1st January to 31st December, 1776; 1st Lieutenant 2d Rhode Island, 1st January, 1777; Captain, 13th January, 1777; transferred to 1st Rhode Island, 1st January, 1781; retained in Olney's Rhode Island Battalion, 14th April, 1781; Brevet Major, 30th September, 1783; served to 3d November, 1783.

Allen, William (R. I.). Lieutenant Rhode Island Militia, 3d August, 1775; 2d Lieutenant of Tallman's Regiment Rhode Island Militia, 12th December, 1776, to —— March, 1777.

Allin, Thomas (R. I.). Captain of Tallman's Rhode Island State Regiment, 12th December, 1776, and served as Deputy Quartermaster General on General Greene's staff to close of war. (Died 1800.)

Alling,' John (Pa). Lieutenant of Baldwin's Artillery Artificer Regiment, 10th June, 1777; discharged 20th August, 1778.

Alling, Joseph (N. J.). Captain New Jersey Militia in 1776.

Alling, Stephen (N. Y.). 2d Lieutenant 2d Continental Artillery, 5th February, 1777; 1st Lieutenant, 20th September, 1779; resigned 19th December, 1782. (Died 30th April, 1828.)

Allison, Benjamin (Pa). Surgeon 1st Pennsylvania Battalion, 13th June, 1776; resigned 1st January, 1777.

Allison, Francis (Pa). Surgeon 12th Pennsylvania, 14th October, 1776; Hospital Surgeon and Physician, December, 1776, to July, 1781. (Died 1813.)

Allison, Henry (Ga). 1st Lieutenant 2d Georgia, 27th April, 1778; retired 22d October, 1782.

Allison, James (Md). 2d Lieutenant 3d Maryland, 20th February, 1777, to ——. Was in service in October, 1778.

Allison, John (Va). Major 1st Virginia State Regiment, 3d March, 1777; Lieutenant-Colonel, 1st February, 1778; served to February, 1781.

Allison, Richard (Pa). Surgeon's Mate 5th Pennsylvania, 15th March, 1778; transferred to 1st Pennsylvania, 1st January, 1783, and served to close of the war; Surgeon's Mate United States Infantry, 12th August, 1784; Surgeon, 24th July, 1788; Surgeon 1st Infantry United States Army, 29th September, 1789; Surgeon of the Legion, 7th April, 1792. Honorably discharged 1st November, 1796.

Allison, Robert (Pa). Private 7th Pennsylvania, 1776; Sergeant, 15th February, 1777; Ensign of Hartley's Continental Regiment, 1st February, 1778; 2d Lieutenant, 1st October, 1778; regiment designated 11th Pennsylvania, 16th December, 1778; 1st Lieutenant, 16th March, 1780; transferred to 3d Pennsylvania 17th January, 1781; served to close of war. (Died 24th April, 1836.)

Allison, Robert (Pa). Ensign 1st Pennsylvania Battalion, 19th January, 1776; 2d Lieutenant, 4th May, 1776; resigned 1st January, 1777.

Allison, Robert (S. C.). Captain South Carolina Militia in 1781.

Allison, William (N. Y.). Colonel New York Militia; taken prisoner at Ft. Montgomery 6th October, 1777.

Allison, William (Pa). Ensign 12th Pennsylvania, 20th May, 1777; resigned 31st October, 1777.

Allison, William (Va). Lieutenant-Colonel 1st Virginia State Regiment, May, 1779, to January, 1780.

Allman, Lawrence (Pa). 1st Lieutenant 4th Continental Artillery, 1st April, 1777; Captain Lieutenant, —— December, 1777; resigned 14th February, 1780.

Allyn, John (Conn). Ensign of Wolcott's Connecticut State Regiment, December, 1775, to February, 1776; Adjutant of Gay's Connecticut Regiment, 20th June to 25th December, 1776; Captain Connecticut Militia in 1777. (Died 1829.)

Allyn, Robert (Conn). Sergeant 1st Connecticut, 10th February, 1777; Ensign, 1st November, 1777; 2d Lieutenant, 1st July, 1780; transferred to 5th Connecticut, 1st January, 1781; retired 1st January, 1783. (Died 1811.)

Allyn, Simeon (Conn). 1st Lieutenant of Mott's Connecticut State Regiment, June to December, 1776; Captain Connecticut Militia. Killed at Groton Heights, 6th September, 1781.

Allyn, Timothy (Conn). 1st Lieutenant of Webb's Continental Regiment, 1st January, 1777; Captain Lieutenant, 8th April, 1780; transferred to 3d Connecticut, 1st January, 1781; Captain, 8th February, 1781; retired 1st January, 1783.

Alner, James (N. Y.). 1st Lieutenant 1st New York, 28th June, 1775; Captain, 31st December, 1775, to — January, 1776; Major of Malcolm's Regiment New York Militia, June to December, 1776.

Alston, John (S. C.). Captain South Carolina Militia in 1775.

Allston, William (S. C.). Captain 2d South Carolina, 1779 to 1781. (Died 26th June, 1839.)

Alon, William (Pa). 1st Lieutenant 1st Pennsylvania Battalion of the Flying Camp, July to December, 1776.

Alvord, Job (Mass). 1st Lieutenant 21st Continental Infantry, 1st January to 31st December, 1776; Captain 4th Massachusetts, 1st January, 1777; retired 1st April, 1779; Captain Massachusetts Militia in 1780.

Amberson, William (Pa). 2d Lieutenant 8th Pennsylvania, 1st January, 1777; 1st Lieutenant, 2d October, 1777; wounded at Brandywine, 11th September, 1777; Aide-de-camp to General Lafayette in 1778 and 1779. (Died 13th December, 1829.)

Ambrose, Nathaniel (N. H.). Captain New Hampshire Militia, 1777-1778.

Ament, Eldred (N. Y.). Ensign 3d New York, 21st November, 1776; resigned 23d December, 1778.

Ames, Benjamin (Mass). Captain of Frye's Massachusetts Regiment, 19th April to December, 1775. (Died 1809.)

Ames, Jotham (Mass). Sergeant of Bailey's Massachusetts Regiment, May to December, 1775, and in the 23d Continental Infantry in 1776; 1st Lieutenant 2d Massachusetts, 1st January, 1777; Brevet Captain, 30th September, 1783, and served to close of war.

Ames, Seth (Mass)'. Surgeon's Mate of Thomas' Massachusetts Regiment, 1st September to December, 1775; Surgeon 13th Continental Infantry, 1st January to 31st December, 1776. (Died 1809.)

Amis, Thomas (N. C.). Commissary 3d North Carolina, 22d December, 1776, to —.

Amis, William (N. C.). Commissary 3d North Carolina, 6th May, 1776. Retired 1st December, 1776.

Amos, Aquilla (Md). Ensign 2d Maryland Battalion of the Flying Camp, July to December, 1776.

Ancrum, —— (S. C.). Major South Carolina Militia; wounded at Stono Ferry, 20th June, 1779. (See Aneram—believed to be same.

Anderson, Archibald (Md). 2d Lieutenant of Hindman's Independent Maryland Company, 14th January, 1776; 1st Lieutenant, September, 1776; Captain of 2d Maryland, 10th December, 1776; Major 3d Maryland, 10th June, 1777; Brigade Major Maryland Brigade, 16th June, 1778; killed at Guilford, 15th March, 1781.

Anderson, Augustine (N. J.). Ensign of Spencer's Continental Regiment, 17th February, 1777; omitted November, 1777. (Died 1834.)

Anderson, Daniel (Pa). Lieutenant 11th Pennsylvania. Dismissed 3d April, 1778. (Died 16th August, 1822)

Anderson, Daniel (S. C.). Captain South Carolina Militia, 1779 to 1782.

Anderson, David (Va). Ensign 1st Virginia, 2d October, 1775, to —.

Anderson, Enoch (Del). 2d Lieutenant Delaware Regiment, 13th January, 1776; wounded at Long Island, 27th August, 1776; Captain, 3d December, 1776; resigned 1st March, 1779. (Died 4th March, 1820.)

Anderson, Enoch (Pa). 1st Lieutenant 11th Pennsylvania, 30th September, 1776; Captain, 7th October, 1777; cashiered, 3d April, 1778.

Anderson, Ephraim (N. J.). Major New Jersey Militia in 1775; Adjutant 2d New Jersey, 28th October, 1775, to 10th November, 1776; Captain 2d New Jersey, 29th November, 1776; killed at Short Hills, 26th June, 1777.

Anderson, Evan, (Pa). Captain Pennsylvania Militia, 1780-1781.

Anderson, Isaac (Pa). Lieutenant Pennsylvania Militia, 1777-1780. (Died 1838.)

Anderson, James (Pa). Lieutenant of 4th Continental Dragoons; was a prisoner; exchanged December 22, 1780; when and where taken prisoner not stated.

Anderson, James (Del). Ensign Delaware Battalion of the Flying Camp, July to December, 1776.

Anderson, James (N. H.). 2d Lieutenant 1st New Hampshire, 23d April, 1775; 1st Lieutenant, 29th July to — December, 1775.

Anderson, James (N. J.). Captain New Jersey Militia in 1777.

Anderson, James (N. J.). 2d Lieutenant 2d New Jersey, 28th October, 1775, to 20th November, 1776; 2d Lieutenant 2d Canadian (Hazen's) Regiment, 8th April, 1777; taken prisoner at Staten Island, 22d August, 1777; rejoined regiment in August, 1780; served to June, 1783; 1st Lieutenant to rank from 1st February, 1778.

Anderson, James (Vt). Captain Vermont Militia, 1778 to 1780.

Anderson, James (Va). Captain and Major Virginia Militia in 1777 and 1778.

Anderson, John (N. J.). Captain of Phillips' Regiment, New Jersey Levies, in 1776.

Anderson, John (N. J.). 1st Lieutenant 3d New Jersey, 7th February, 1776; Captain 4th New Jersey, 28th November, 1776; resigned 5th June, 1778.

Anderson, John (Pa). Colonel Pennsylvania Militia in 1778.

Anderson, John (S. C.). Captain South Carolina Militia, 1775-1776.

Anderson, John (Va). 1st Lieutenant 5th Virginia, 7th March, 1776; Captain, 12th August, 1777; transferred to 3d Virginia, 14th September, 1778; transferred to 5th Virginia ,1st January, 1781; retired, 1st January, 1783.

Anderson, Joseph Inslee (N. J.). Ensign 3d New Jersey, — May, 1776; 2d Lieutenant, 19th July, 1776; 1st Lieutenant, 29th November, 1776; Captain, 26th October, 1777; transferred to 1st New Jersey, 1st January, 1781; retained in New Jersey Battalion, — April, 1783; was Regimental Paymaster, 26th October, 1777, to close of the war; Brevet Major, 30th September, 1783. (Died 17th April, 1837.)

Anderson, Nathaniel (Va). Sergeant 5th Virginia, 28th January, 1776; Ensign, 1st May, 1776; 2d Lieutenant, 11th

December, 1776; 1st Lieutenant, 21st December, 1777; transferred to 3d Virginia, 14th September, 1778; Captain-Lieutenant, — —, 1780; retired 12th February, 1781.

Anderson, Patrick (Pa). Captain Pennsylvania Musket Battalion, 15th March, 1776; regiment designated Pennsylvania State Regiment, 1st October, 1776, and 13th Pennsylvania, 12th November, 1777; superceded, 20th October, 1777.

Anderson, Richard (Md). 1st Lieutenant 1st Maryland Battalion of the Flying Camp, August, 1776; 1st Lieutenant 7th Maryland, 10th December, 1776; Captain, 15th November, 1777; transferred to 4th Maryland, 1st January, 1781; wounded at Cowpens 17th January, 1781; retired 1st January, 1782. (Died 29th June, 1835.)

Anderson, Richard Clough (Va). Captain 5th Virginia, 7th March, 1776; wounded at Trenton, 2 January, 1777; Major 6th Virginia, 10th February, 1778; transferred to 1st Virginia, 14th September, 1778; wounded at Savannah, 9th October, 1779; taken prisoner at Charleston, 12th May, 1780; was on parole until retired, 12th February, 1781, with rank of Lieutenant-Colonel 3d Virginia. (Died 16th October, 1826.)

Anderson, Robert (S. C.). Captain 3d South Carolina (Rangers), November, 1775, to May, 1779; Major and Lieutenant-Colonel in 1781. (Died 1813.)

Anderson, Simon (N. C.). Captain 5th North Carolina, 16th April, 1776, to ——.

Anderson, Thomas (Conn). Sergeant 1st Connecticut, 1st January, 1777; Regimental Quartermaster, 1st January, 1778; 2d Lieutenant, 1 June, 1778; 1st Lieutenant, 20th June, 1779; transferred to 5th Connecticut, 1st January, 1781; resigned 5th December, 1782. (Died 15th December, 1822.)

Anderson, Thomas (Del). Sergeant Delaware Regiment, 1st January, 1777; Ensign, 1st September, 1778; Regimental Quartermaster, 10th September, 1778; 2d Lieutenant, 11 September, 1779; 1st Lieutenant, 1st January, 1781; retired 1st June, 1782.

Anderson, Walker (Va). 2d Lieutenant 1st Continental Artillery, 12th Arpil, 1778, to ——.

Anderson, William (N. J.). Ensign 4th New Jersey, 17th February, 1777, to 1st July, 1778; Ensign 1st New Jersey, 21st June, 1781, and served to — April, 1783.

Anderson, William (Pa). 2d Lieutenant of Montgomery's Pennsylvania Battalion of the Flying Camp; taken prisoner at Fort Washington, 16th November, 1776.

Anderson, John (S. C.). 1st Lieutenant South Carolina Dragoons, 5th April, 1781; retired July, 1781.

Andrews, Abraham (R. I.). Ensign of Tallman's Rhode Island Regiment of Militia, 12th December, 1776, to — March, 1777.

Andrews, Ammi (N. H.). Sergeant 1st New Hampshire, 23d April, 1775; 2d Lieutenant, 18th June, 1775; taken prisoner at Quebec, 31st December, 1775.

Andrews, Hezekiah (Conn). 2d Lieutenant of Gay's Connecticut State Regiment, June to December, 1776.

Andrews, James (Conn). Ensign 2d Connecticut, 1st January, 1777; 2d Lieutenant, 1st October, 1777; 1st Lieutenant, 1st May, 1778; resigned 1st August. 1779.

Andrews, Joseph (Mass). Sergeant of Knox's Regiment Continental Artillery, 1st January, 1776; 1st Lieutenant 3d Continental Artillery, 1st February, 1777. Died 22d November, 1777, of wounds received at Brandywine, 11th September, 1777.

Andrews, Richard (N. C.). Ensign 2d North Carolina, 1st November, 1777; 2d Lieutenant, — March, 1778; taken prisoner at Fort Fayette, 1st June, 1779; exchanged 26th March, 1781; 1st Lieutenant, 10th May, 1780; wounded at Eutaw Springs, 8th September, 1781, and rendered no subsequent service.

Andrews, Robert (Va). Chaplain 2d Virginia, — March, 1777, to ——.

Andrews, William (Conn). Ensign of Elmore's Connecticut State Regiment, 15th April, 1776; 2d Lieutenant 3d Continental Artillery, 1st January, 1777; taken prisoner at Fort Fayette, 1st June, 1779; exchanged 19th March, 1781; 1st Lieutenant, 13th September, 1780, and served to — June, 1783. (Died 14th March, 1816.)

Andrews, William (Conn). 2d Lieutenant 8th Connecticut, 28th April, 1777; resigned 21st March, 1778. (Died 19th July, 1824.)

Andrus, Epaphras (Conn). 2d Lieutenant 8th Connecticut, 6th July to 18th December, 1775.

Aneram, George (Va). Lieutenant 1st Continental Artillery, 1st January, 1777; retired — —, 1778. (See Ancrum.)

Angell, Abiather (Mass). Captain of Brewer's Massachusetts Regiment, May to December, 1775; Captain of Warner's Continental Regiment, 5th July, 1776; resigned 1st August, 1777. (Died, 1830.)

Angell, Israel (R. I.). Major of Hitchcock's Rhode Island Regiment, 3d May to — December, 1775; Major 11th Continental Infantry, 1st January to 31st December, 1776; Lieutenant-Colonel 2d Rhode Island, 1st January, 1777; Colonel 13th January, 1777; retired 14th May, 1781. (Died — May, 1832.)

Angell, James (R. I.). Colonel Rhode Island Militia, 1775.

Angell, John (N. J.). 1st Lieutenant 1st New Jersey, 1st January, 1777; Captain, 4th October, 1777; retired March, 1779.

Angell, John (R. I.). Captain of Hitchcock's Rhode Island Regiment, 3d May to — December, 1775.

Angell, Nehemiah (R. I.). Ensign 2d Rhode Island, June to December, 1775.

Angell, Samuel (R. I.). Captain Lieutenant of Elliott's Regiment, Rhode Island State Artillery, 12th December, 1776, to — March, 1777.

Annable, Edward (Mass). Sergeant 13th Massachusetts, 1st January, 1777; Ensign, 30th March, 1779; 2d Lieutenant, 1st October, 1780; transferred to 3d Massachusetts, 1 January, 1781; resigned 7th June, 1781. (Died 1836.)

Annin, Wm. (Mass). Surgeon 6th Massachusetts, 1st January, 1777; transferred to 5th Massachusetts, April, 1779; resigned 1st February, 1780.

Annis, John William (Pa). Lieutenant of Artillery Pennsylvania Militia; wounded and taken prisoner at Bristol, 17th April, 1778.

Anspach, Peter (N. Y.). Lieutenant 2d Continental Artillery, 30th August, 1781; retired June, 1783.

Antes, Philip Frederick (Pa). Colonel Pennsylvania Militia in 1777. (Died 1801.)

Anthony, Burrington (R. I.). Captain Rhode Island Militia, 1775-1777.

Antignac—See d'Antignac.

Antil, Edward (N. Y.). Lieutenant-Colonel 2d Canadian (Hazen's) Regiment, 22d January, 1776; taken prisoner at Staten Island, 22d August, 1777; exchanged 2d November, 1780; resigned 1st May, 1782. (Died 1789.)

Aorson, Aaron (N. Y.). 1st Lieutenant 2d New York, 21st June, 1775;

resigned — July, 1776; Captain 3d New York, 21st November, 1776; transferred to 1st New York, 1st January, 1783; Brevet Major, 30th September, 1783; served to close of war.

App, Michael (Pa). Ensign Pennsylvania Musket Battalion, 20th March, 1776; wounded and taken prisoner at Long Island, 27th August, 1776; exchanged 9th December, 1776; no subsequent service.

Apperson, Richard (Va). 2d Lieutenant 6th Virginia, 11th March, 1776; 1st Lieutenant, 7th August, 1776; Captain, 26th September, 1777; retired as Major 14th September, 1778.

Applethwaite, John (Va). Surgeon's Mate 9th Virginia, — December, 1776; resigned 18th July, 1777.

Appleton, Abraham (N. J.). Surgeon's Mate 2d New Jersey, 21st December, 1775, to — November, 1776; 2d Lieutenant 2d New Jersey, 5th February, 1777; 1st Lieutenant, 1st December, 1777; retained in New Jersey Battalion, — April, 1783; Brevet Captain, 30th September, 1783, and served to 3d November, 1783.

Archbald, Edward (N. Y.). 1st Lieutenant 14th Continental Infantry, 1st January to 31st December, 1776; Captain Lieutenant 2d Continental Artillery, 1st January, 1777; resigned 25th June, 1781.

Archer, George (Pa). 3d Lieutenant 1st Pennsylvania, 6th August, 1776, to — .

Archer, Henry (Md). Cornet of Lee's Battalion of Light Dragoons, 1st January, 1779; Captain, 1781, and served to close of war.

Archer, John (Md). Volunteer Aide-de-Camp to General Wayne at Stony Point, 1st June, 1779, and was brevetted Captain Continental Army, 26th June, 1779, for being the bearer of General Wayne's letter announcing the victory at Stony Point. (Died 28th September, 1810.)

Archer, John (Va). Captain and Major Virginia Militia, 1777 and 1778.

Archer, Joseph (Pa). 2d Lieutenant of Captain Nelson's company of the 1st Pennsylvania Battalion, 12th July, 1776, to — January, 1777.

Archer, Joseph (Va). 2d Lieutenant 2d Virginia, 25th December, 1776; wounded at Brandywine, 11th September, 1777, and died 11th October, 1777.

Archer, Joshua (Pa). 2d Lieutenant 11th Pennsylvania, 21st April, 1777; superceded 1st January, 1778.

Archer, Peter Field (Va). Ensign 2d Virginia, — May, 1778; 2d Lieutenant, 29th May, 1780; 1st Lieutenant, 18th February, 1781; retired 1st January, 1783.

Archer, Richard (Va). Ensign 3d Virginia, 28th November, 1780, and served to close of war.

Archer, Thomas (Va). 2d Lieutenant 1st Virginia, 22d February, 1776; 1st Lieutenant, 25th February, 1776, to — .

Archibald, Alexander (Va). Surgeon's Mate, 10th Virginia, November, 1776; Surgeon, 24th August, 1777; taken prisoner at Brandywine, 11th September, 1777; retired 14th September, 1778. (Died 1822.)

Archibald, Edward (Mass). Lieutenant of Glover's Massachusetts Regiment, May to December, 1775.

Arell, David (Va). 1st Lieutenant 3d Virginia, 8th February, 1776; Captain, 28th September, 1776; resigned 14th February, 1778.

Arendt, Henry Leonard Philip Baron de (—). Colonel German Regiment, 19th March, 1777; granted leave 18th August, 1778, for 12 months for the benefit of his health, and did not rejoin regiment.

Armand, Tuffin Charles (Marquis de la Roueire), (France). Colonel 3d Cavalry, Pulaski Legion, 10th May, 1777; succeeded Count Pulaski in command of the Legion, 11th October, 1779, and on 21st October, 1780, the designation of the command was changed to "Armand's Partisan Corps," which he commanded to the close of the war. Appointed Brigadier-General Continental Army, 26th March, 1783. By the act of 27th February, 1784, it was "Resolved, whereas, the United States in Congress assembled are well informed, and entertain a just sense of the great bravery, intelligence, zeal and activity manifested during the couse of the late war with Great Britain, by Brigadier-General Armand, Marquis de Roueire, in the service of the United States, and, whereas, it also apears by a letter from the late commander-in-chief, dated at Philadelphia, 15th December, 1783, addressed to the said General Armand, that, superadded to general merit for good conduct, vigilance, and bravery, General Armand has, in a variety of instances, particularly signalized himself as an excellent officer and great partisan, and frequently rendered the United States very valuable services. Resolved, that the President write a letter to General Armand, Marquis de la Roueire, expressive of the high sense Congress are impressed with, of the services he has rendered the United States in the course of the late war with Great Britain, and of the entire approbation the United States in Congress assembled entertain of his bravery, activity, and zeal so often evidenced in the cause of America." (Died 30th January, 1793.)

Armistead, Thomas (Va). 1st Lieutenant 1st Virginia State Regiment, 15th September, 1777; Captain, 6th April, 1778, and served to — January, 1780.

Armistead, William (Va). Ensign 11th Virginia, 11th March, 1776; Cornet 1st Continental Dragoons in 1777; 1st Lieutenant, ——; Captain, 1782; retired 9th November, 1782.

Armitage, Benjamin (Pa). 2d Lieutenant 3d Pennsylvania Battalion, 8th January, 1776; taken prisoner at Fort Washington, 16th November, 1776.

Armitage, George (N. Y.). Lieutenant 2d Canadian (Hazen's) Regiment, 3d November, 1776; omitted 1st March, 1777.

Armitage, Shubert (Pa). 3d Lieutenant 4th Continental Artillery, 12th May, 1779; 2d Lieutenant, 16th October, 1779; resigned — March, 1780. (Died 27th December, 1823.)

Armor, James (Va). 2d Lieutenant 4th Virginia, 3d January, 1777; omitted August, 1777.

Armor, Thomas (Pa). 2d Lieutenant 1st Continental Infantry, March to December, 1776; 2d Lieutenant 1st Pennsylvania, 1st January, 1777, to 4th June, 1778.

Armstrong, Alexander (N. Y.). 1st Lieutenant of Hoisington's Battalion of Rangers, from —— to ——.

Armstrong, Andrew (N. C.) Lieutenant 6th North Carolina, 16th April, 1776; Captain, 12th October, 1777; served to ——.

Armstrong, Archibald (Va). Ensign 9th Virginia, 31st August, 1776; 2d Lieutenant, 10th May, 1777; superceded 1st August, 1777.

Armstrong, Edward (N. Y.). 1st Lieutenant of Malcolm's Continental Regiment, 5th April, 1777; wounded at Monmouth, 28th June, 1778; retired 23d April, 1779. (Died 14th May, 1824.)

Armstrong, Elijah ·(R. I.). Ensign Rhode Island Militia in 1776.

Armstrong, George (Md). 1st Lieutenant 3d Maryland, 10th December, 1776; Captain Lieutenant, 12th August, 1778; Captain, 11 February, 1780; transferred to 1st Maryland, 1st January, 1781; killed at Ninety-Six, 18th June, 1781.

Armstrong, Henry (Pa). 2d Lieutenant of Hoisington's Battalion of Rangers, 14th August, 1779, to 1st January, 1781.

Armstrong, James (N. C.). Captain 2d North Carolina, 1st September, 1775; Colonel 8th North Carolina, 26th November, 1776; retired 1st June, 1778; Colonel of a North Carolina State Regiment; wounded at Stono Ferry, 20th June, 1779.

Armstrong, James (N. C.). Lieutenant and North Carolina Dragoons, October, 1777, to January, 1781.

Armstrong, James (Pa). Regimental Quartermaster 2d Pennsylvania Battalion, 20th February, 1776; 2d Lieutenant, 21st May, 1776; 1st Lieutenant 2d Cavalry, Pulaski Legion, 1st April, 1777; Captain, 1st January, 1779; taken prisoner at Dorchester, S. C., 13th December, 1781, and was a prisoner to close of war.

Armstrong, James Francis (N. J.). Private New Jersey Militia in 1776; Chaplain 2d Canadian (Hazen's) Regiment, 3d November, 1776; Brigade Chaplain, 1 May, 1777; resigned 12th February, 1778. (Died 1801.)

Armstrong, John (N. C.). Colonel North Carolina Militia; wounded at Stono Ferry, 20th June, 1779.

Armstrong, John (Pa). Served as a volunteer in the Canada Expedition and at Quebec in 1775; Major and Aide-de-Camp to General Mercer to 3d January, 1777; served subsequently as a volunteer in various capacities to the close of the war; Brigadier-General, United States Army, 6th July, 1812; resigned 13th January, 1813; Secretary of War, 13th January, 1813, to 27th September, 1814. (Died 1st April, 1843.)

Armstrong, John (Pa). Brigadier-General Continental Army, 1st March, 1776; resigned 4th April, 1777; Brigadier-General Pennsylvania Militia, 5th April, 1777; Major-General Pennsylvania Militia, 9th January, 1778, to close of war. (Died 6th March, 1795.)

Armstrong, John (Pa). Sergeant in the Pennsylvania Line in 1776; Sergeant 12th Pennsylvania, 1st January, 1777; Ensign, 13th March, 1777; 2d Lieutenant, 11th September, 1777; transferred to 3d Pennsylvania, 1st July, 1778; 1st Lieutenant, 12th May, 1779; served to close of the war; Ensign United States Infantry Regiment, 12th August, 1784; Lieutenant 1st United States Infantry, 29th September, 1789, Captain, 26th September, 1790, in 1st Sub Legion, 4th September, 1792; Major, 27th September, 1792; resigned 3d March, 1793. (Died 1816.)

Armstrong, John (N. C.). Captain 2d North Carolina, 1st September, 1775; Major 4th North Carolina, 6th October, 1777; Deputy Adjutant General to General Gates, 3d August, 1780; wounded at Stono Ferry, 20th June, 1779; Lieutenant-Colonel 1st North Carolina, 17th July, 1782; retired 1st January, 1783.

Armstrong, John (R. I.). Ensign 11th Continental Infantry, 1st January, 1776; 2d Lieutenant, 10th August to 31st December, 1776.

Armstrong, Joseph (Pa). Colonel Pennsylvania Militia; killed at Harlem, 16th November, 1776.

Armstrong, Richard (Va). Ensign 9th Virginia, 10th May, 1777; superseded 11th August, 1777.

Armstrong, Robert (S. C.). 1st Lieutenant 1st South Carolina, 17th June, 1775, to ——.

Armstrong, Samuel (Mass). Ensign 8th Massachusetts, 1st January, 1777; 2d Lieutenant, 7th October, 1777; Regimental Adjutant, 1st June, 1778, to 26th April, 1780; Regimental Paymaster, 27th April, 1780, to 12th June, 1783; transferred to 3d Massachusetts, 12th June, 1783, and served to 3d Novhmber, 1783. (Died 10th December, 1810.)

Armstrong, Thomas (N. C.). 1st Lieutenant 5th North Carolina, 16th April, 1776; Captain, 25th October, 1777; wounded and taken prisoner at Fort Fayette, 1st June, 1779; exchanged — December, 1779; taken prisoner at Charleston, 12th May, 1780; exchanged — July, 1781; Aide-de-Camp to General Sumner, 11th February, 1782, to close of War; Brevet Major, 30th September, 1783.

Armstrong, Thomas (Pa). Lieutenant of Erwin's Battalion Pennsylvania Flying Camp, July to December, 1776; taken prisoner at Fort Washington, 16th November, 1776.

Armstrong, William (N. C.). Ensign 1st North Carolina, 4th January, 1776;

2d Lieutenant, 10th April, 1776; 1st Lieutenant, 1st January, 1777; Captain, 20th August, 1777; wounded at Ramsour's Mill, 20th June, 1780; transferred to 3d North Carolina, 6th February, 1782; retired 1st January, 1783.

Armstrong, William (Pa). 2d Lieutenant of Lewis' Pennsylvania Battalion of the Flying Camp, July to December, 1776; Ensign 7th Pennsylvania, 9th March, 1777; resigned 25th November, 1777.

Arndt, John (Pa). Captain of Baxter's Battalion Pennsylvania Flying Camp, July to December, 1776; wounded and taken prisoner at Long Island, 27th August, 1776. (Died 1814.)

Arnett, William (Md). Lieutenant 5th Maryland, 6th June, 1778. Died February, 1779.

Arnold, Benedict (Conn). Captain in the Lexington Alarm, April, 1775; at Ticonderoga and at Crown Point, 10th May, 1775; appointed by General Washington Colonel of the Continental Army, 1st September, 1775; wounded at Quebec, 31 December, 1775; Colonel 20th Continental Infantry, 1st January, 1776, to rank from 1st September, 1775; Brigadier-General Continental Army, 10th January, 1776, and Major-General 17th February, 1777. By the resolve of Congress of 20th May, 1777, it was "Resolved, that the Quartermaster-General be directed to procure a horse and present the same, properly caparisoned, to Major-General Arnold, in the name of this Congress, as a token of their approbation of his gallant conduct in the action against the enemy in their late enterprise to Danbury, in which General Arnold had one horse killed under him and another wounded."

By resolution of Congress of 4th November, 1777, it was "Resolved, that the thanks of Congress, in their own name, and in behalf of the inhabitants of the thirteen United States, be presented to Major-General Gates, commander-in-chief of the Northern Department, and to Major Generals Lincoln and Arnold, and the rest of the officers and troops under his command, for their brave and successful efforts in support of the independence of their country, whereby an army of the enemy of 10,000 men has been totally defeated, one large detachment of it, strongly posted and entrenched, having been conquered at Bennington; another repulsed with loss and disgrace from Fort Schuyler, and the main army of 6,000 men, under Lieutenant-general Burgonye, after being beaten in different actions and driven from a formidable post and strong entrenchments, reduced to the necessity of surrendering themselves upon terms, honorable and advantageous to these States, on the 17th of October last, to Major-General Gates." Deserted to the enemy 25th September, 1780, and his name dropped from the rolls of the army, by Order of Congress, 4th October, 1780. (Died 14th June, 1801.)

Arnold, Benjamin (R. I.). Ensign 2d Rhode Island, 17th February, 1777; dismissed 6th February, 1778.

Arnold, David (R. I.). Captain Rhode Island Militia, August, 1778. Died in September, 1778.

Arnold, Houlman (Pa). Lieutenant of Ottendorff's Battalion, 9th December, 1776, to ——. (Was in service July, 1780.)

Arnold, James (Conn). Captain 1st Connecticut, 1st May to 7th December, 1775; Lieutenant-Colonel of Douglas' Connecticut State Regiment, 20th June to 29th December, 1776; served subsequently as Major Connecticut Militia.

Arnold, James (Conn). 1st Lieutenant of Daulas' Connecticut State Regiment, June to December, 1776.

Arnold, James (N. H.). Captain New Hampshire Militia in 1776.

Arnold, John . (Mass). Sergeant of Peterson's Massachusetts Regiment May to December, 1775; Ensign 15th Continental Infantry, 1st January, 1776; deserted — August, 1776.

Arnold, Jonathan (R. I.). Surgeon Hospital Department, 1776 to 1781 (Died 1793.)

Arnold, Joseph (R. I.). Ensign of Varnum's Rhode Island Regiment, 3d May to — December, 1775; 1st Lieutenant 1st Rhode Island, 1st January, 1777; Captain Lieutenant, 1st June, 1778; Captain, — 1780; resigned 9th November, 1779. (Died 1840.)

Arnold, Noyes (Mass). Sergeant in Crane's Regiment Massachusetts Artillery, 15th May, 1776; 2d Lieutenant, 1st December, 1776; 1st Lieutenant 3d Continental Artillery, 1st February, 1777; killed at Quaker Hill, 23d August 1778.

Arnold, Philip (R. I.). Ensign of Richmond's Rhode Island State Regiment, 15th January, 1776; Lieutenant, 19th August, 1776; resigned 30th September, 1778.

Arnold, Samuel (R. I.). 2d Lieutenant 1st Rhode Island, 11th February, 1777; resigned 30th September, 1778.

Arnold, Thomas (R. I.). Lieutenant of Babcock's Rhode Island State Regiment, 15th January, 1776; Captain 1st Rhode Island, 21st March, 1777; wounded at Monmouth, 28th June, 1778; transferred to Invalid Regiment, 1st November, 1779, and served to 23d April, 1783. (Died 8th May, 1821.)

Arnold, William (R. I.). Major Rhode Island Militia in 1775 and 1776.

Arrants, Harman (Md). 2d Lieutenant 4th Maryland Battalion of the Flying Camp, July to December, 1776.

Arthur, Barnabas (Va). Ensign 5th Virginia, 26th February, 1776, to ——.

Arthur, Francis (Ga). 2d Lieutenant 1st Georgia, 7th January, 1776, to ——.

Arthur, James (Md). Lieutenant 2d Maryland, 17th June, 1781; resigned April, 1782.

Arundell, Dohickey (Va). Captain of a Company of Virginia Artillery, 5th February, 1776; killed in the action at Gwyn's Island, Chesapeake Bay, 8th July, 1776, by the bursting of a mortar.

Ashby, Anthony (S. C.). 1st Lieutenant 2d South Carolina, 17th June, 1775; 1st Lieutenant, 10th February, 1776; Captain, 28th November, 1776; resigned 16th February, 1778; Captain South Carolina Militia, wounded and taken prisoner at Augusta, Ga., 18th September, 1780; he and 12 others were hanged by the British.

Ashby, Benjamin (Va). Ensign 11th Virginia, 30th November, 1776; Regimental Quartermaster, 1st January, 1777; 2d Lieutenant, 1st June, 1777; regiment designated 7th Virginia, 14th September, 1778; 1st Lieutenant, 13th March, 1779; transferred to 3d Virginia, 1st January, 1781; retired 1st January, 1783.

Ashby, John (Va). Captain 3d Virginia, 18th March, 1776; wounded at Germantown, 4th October, 1777; resigned 30th October, 1777; Major Virginia Militia, 1780-1781.

Ashby, Nathaniel (Va). Ensign 3d Virginia, 18th March, 1776; 2d Lieutenant, 8th October, 1776; resigned 14th November, 1777.

Ashby, Stephen (Va). Captain 12th Virginia, 9th September, 1776, regiment designated 8th Virginia, 14th September, 1778; retired 1st January, 1781.

Ashe, John (N. C.). Brigadier-General North Carolina State Troops. His command was defeated at Briar Creek 3d March, 1779; was betrayed into the hands of the enemy at Wilmington, North Carolina, 1st February, 1781; suffered severe confinement until he died 24th October, 1781.

Ashe, John, Jr. (N. C.). Captain 4th North Carolina, 16th April, 1776 to ———.

Ashe, John Baptista (N. C.). Captain 6th North Carolina, 16th April, 1776; Major 6th North Carolina, 26th January, 1777; transferred to 1st North Carolina, 1st June, 1778; Lieutenant-Colonel, 2d November, 1778; served to ———. (Died 27th November, 1802.)

Ashe, Samuel (N. C.). Lieutenant and Paymaster 1st North Carolina, 1st September, 1775; resigned 16th April, 1776; Captain 1st Troop North Carolina Dragoons State Troops, 7th March, 1777, to 1st January, 1781. (Died 1814.)

Ashe, Samuel, Jr. (N. C.). Ensign 1st North Carolina, ———, 1779; taken prisoner at Charleston, 12th May, 1780; exchanged 14th June, 1781; Lieutenant, 23d January, 1781; ——— in 3d North Carolina in February, 1782; served to close of war. (Died 3d November, 1835.)

Asher, William (Va.). Ensign of Clark's Illinois Regiment in 1781.

Ashley, Barnabas (Mass). Ensign 10th Massachusetts, 6th November, 1776; 2d Lieutenant, 1st November, 1777; discharged 24th March, 1778. (Died 8th May, 1833.)

Ashley, Daniel (N. H.). 1st Lieutenant Baldwin's Regiment, New Hampshire Militia, September to December, 1776.

Ashley, Israel (Mass). Surgeon Massachusetts Militia in 1777. (Died 1814.)

Ashley, Martin (N. H.). Surgeon New Hampshire Militia, 1777-1778.

Ashley, Moses (Mass). Lieutenant in Lexington Alarm, April 1775; 1st Lieutenant of Fellowes' Massachusetts Regiment, 23d May, 1775; Captain, 5th November, 1775; Captain 15th Continental Infantry, 1st January to 31st December, 1776; Captain 1st Massachusetts, 1st January, 1777, to rank from 5th November, 1775; Major 5th Massachusetts, 6th January, 1780; transferred to 6th Massachusetts, 1st January, 1783, and served to 12th June, 1783. (Died 25th August, 1791.)

Ashley, Oliver (N. H.). Captain New Hampshire Militia, 1777-1778.

Ashley, Samuel (N. H.). Colonel New Hampshire Militia, 1779-1780.

Ashley, William (Mass). Sergeant of Fellow's Massachusetts Regiment, April to December, 1775; 2d Lieutenant 21st Continental Infantry, 1st January to 31st December, 1776.

Ashman, James (N. J.). 2d Lieutenant 2d New Jersey, 27th November, 1775. (Died 11th September, 1776.) Name also spelled Ashmore.

Ashmead, Jacob (Pa.). 1st Lieutenant 1st Pennsylvania Battalion, 27th October, 1775; Captain 2d Pennsylvania, 6th September, 1776; resigned 16th May, 1780. (Died 1814.)

Ashmead, John (Md.). Captain Maryland Militia in 1777.

Ashmore, James—see Ashman.

Ashton, Charles Jr. (Va.). Ensign 5th Virginia, 9th March, 1776, to ———.

Ashton, James (N. Y.). Major New York Militia, 1777-1778.

Ashton, John (Pa.). Sergeant of Miles' Pennsylvania Rifle Regiment, 21st March, 1776; Ensign 9th Pennsylvania, 4th December, 1776; 2d Lieutenant, 3d March, 1777; retired 1st July, 1778.

Ashton, John (Va.). Ensign 5th Virginia, 9th March, 1776, to ———. (Died 26th August, 1831.)

Ashton, Joseph (N. Y.). 1st Sergeant of Lamb's Company New York Artillery, 16th July, 1775; taken prisoner at Quebec 31st December, 1775; exchanged in August, 1776; 2d Lieutenant 2d Continental Artillery, 1st January, 1777; Regimental Adjutant, 1st June, 1777, to 16th January, 1781; 1st Lieutenant, 12th September, 1778; Captain Lieutenant, 19th April, 1781; transferred to Corps of Artillery, 12th June, 1783, and served to 20th June, 1784; Captain United States Infantry, 12th August, 1784; Captain 1st Infantry, United States Army, 29th September, 1789; Major 2d Infantry, 29th December, 1791; in 2d Sub-Legion, 4th September, 1792; resigned 27th November, 1792.

Ashton, William (N. C.). Lieutenant-Colonel 3d North Carolina, 15th April, 1776; resigned 25th October, 1777.

Aspinwall, William (Mass). Hospital Surgeon, 1775 to 1778.

Atkin, James (N. C.). See **Aitkin.**

Atkinson, Amos (Mass). Private in Lexington Alarm, April, 1775; 2d Lieutenant of Little's Massachusetts Regiment, 19th May to December, 1775; 1st Lieutenant 12th Continental Infantry, 1st January to 31st December, 1776.

Atkinson, Cornelius (N. Y.). Lieutenant New York Militia; reported as being a prisoner in 1779; when and where taken not stated.

Atkinson, Moses (R. I.). Ensign 9th Continental Infantry, 1st January, 1776; 2d Lieutenant, 10th August to 31st December, 1776. (Died 1813.)

Atkinson, Samuel (N. H.). 1st Lieutenant 1st New Hampshire, 3d May to December, 1775.

Atkinson, Wilton (Pa). Regimental Quartermaster 12th Pennsylvania, 11th January, 1777, to ——.

Atlee, Samuel John (Pa). Colonel of the Pennsylvania Musket Battalion, Militia, 21st March, 1776; wounded and taken prisoner at Long Island, 27th August, 1776, exchanged 6th August, 1778; did not re-enter the service (Died 7th November, 1786.)

Atwater, Reuben (Conn). Major Connecticut Militia, 1776 and 1777.

Atwell, Thomas (Va). Lieutenant-Colonel Virginia Militia, 1777-1778.

Augustus, Lewis (S. C.). Captain Lieutenant South Carolina Regiment; taken prisoner at Iron Hill 1st September, 1777.

Austin, Aaron, Jr. (Conn). 2d Lieutenant 4th Connecticut, 1st May to December, 1775; 1st Lieutenant of Burrall's Connecticut State Regiment, 19th January, 1776; Captain, 17th September, 1776; and served to January, 1777. (Died 15th July, 1829.)

Austin, Aaron (N. Y.). 1st Lieutenant 1st New York, 28th June, 1775, to — January, 1776; 1st Lieutenant of DuBois' New York Regiment, 26th June, 1776; Captain 3d New York, 21st November, 1776, to ——.

Austin, Caleb (N. Y.). Surgeon's Mate 2d Continental Artillery, 1st January, 1777; resigned 22d November, 1778. (Died 4th October, 1822.)

Austin, John (Mass). Sergeant in Gridley's Regiment Massachusetts Artillery, June to December, 1775, and in Knox's Regiment Continental Artillery in 1776. Sergeant 3d Continental Artillery, 1st January, 1777; 2d Lieutenant, 17th May, 1782, and served to June, 1783.

Austin, Jonathan Williams (Mass). Major of Sargent's Massachusetts Regiment, 20th April to December, 1775; Major 16th Continental Infantry, 1st January, 1776; dishonorably discharged 13th November, 1776. (Died ——, 1778.)

Austin, Joseph (Conn). Ensign 2d Connecticut, 1st January, 1777; 2d Lieutenant, 8th December, 1777; 1st Lieutenant, 1st June, 1778; resigned 1st August, 1779.

Avery, Amos (Conn). 2d Lieutenant 3d Connecticut, 1st May to 15th December, 1775.

Avery, Daniel (Conn). Ensign Connecticut Militia, ——; killed at Groton Heights, 6th September, 1781.

Avery, David (Mass). Chaplain of Paterson's Massachusetts Regiment, April to December, 1775; Chaplain 15th Continental Infantry, 1st January to 31st December, 1776; Chaplain of Sherburne's Continental Regiment, 15th February, 1777; Brigade Chaplain 15th August, 1778; resigned 4th March, 1780. (Died 1817.)

Avery, Ebenezer (Conn). Lieutenant Connecticut Militia, ——; killed at Groton Heights, 6th September, 1781.

Avery, Elijah (Conn). Captain Connecticut Militia, ——; killed at Groton Heights, 6th September, 1781.

Avery, Elisha (Conn). Deputy Commissary-General of Issues, 18th June, 1777; resigned 6th August, 1777.

Avery, Park, Jr. (Conn). Lieutenant Connecticut Militia, ——; wounded at Groton Heights, 6th September, 1781.

Avery, Simeon (Conn). Ensign 1st Connecticut, 1st January, 1777; 2d Lieutenant, 1st January, 1778; Regimental Adjutant, 15th November, 1778, to 1st January, 1781; 1st Lieutenant, 1st June, 1779; transferred to 5th Connecticut, 1st January, 1781; retired 1st January, 1783. (Died 1796.)

Avery, Thomas (Conn). 2d Lieutenant 10th Continental Infantry, 1st January to 31st December, 1776; 1st Lieutenant 1st Connecticut, 1st January, 1777; wounded at Germantown 4th October, 1777; retired 15th November, 1778. (Died 4th May, 1825.)

Avery, Waitstill (N. C.). Colonel North Carolina Militia, 1778 to close of war. (Died 1821.)

Avery, William Halley (Va). 1st Lieutenant 6th Virginia, 1st March, 1776; Captain, 4th January, 1777; resigned 28th June, 1778.

Awtry, Alexander (Ga). Captain Georgia Militia, 1778-1780.

Awtry, John (Ga). Captain Georgia Militia, 1778-1780.

Axon, Samuel Jacob (S. C.) Hospital Surgeon's Mate, May, 1776; Surgeon 1st South Carolina, 4th January, 1777, and served to close of war. Taken prisoner at Charleston, 12th May, 1780. (Died 1827.)

Axon, Richard F. (S. C.). 1st Lieutenant 4th South Carolina, mentioned in 1779-1780.

Axtell, Ebenezer (N. J.). Ensign 1st New Jersey, 29th November, 1776; omitted — May, 1777.

Axtell, Henry (N. J.). Major New Jersey Militia, 1776-1777. (Died 1818.)

Ayer, Thomas (S. C.). Captain South Carolina Militia, 1777-1781. Died 1781.

Ayers, Jonathan (Mass). 2d Lieutenant 9th Massachusetts, 1st January, 1777; deranged, 26th September, 1778.

Aylett, William (Va). Deputy Commissary-General of Stores, 27th April, 1776; Deputy Commissary-General of Purchases, 18th June, 1777, and served to 24th July, 1782.

B.

Babbitt, Elijah (R. I.). 2d Lieutenant of Elliott's Regiment, Rhode Island State Artillery, 12th December, 1776, to — March, 1777.

Babbitt, Nathan (—). Surgeon's Mate Hospital Department in 1779-1780. (Died 1826.)

Babcock, Christopher A. (R. I.). Hospital Surgeon's Mate, 11th October, 1777. Died 2d November, 1780.

Babcock, Henry (R. I.). Colonel Rhode Island State Regiment, 15th January, 1776; dismissed — May, 1776. (Died 7th October, 1800.)

Babcock, James (R. I.). Lieutenant-Colonel of Varnum's Rhode Island Regiment, 3d May to — December, 1775. (Died 1781.)

Babcock, Joshua (R. I.). Ensign 1st Rhode Island, June to December, 1775; Ensign of Tallman's Rhode Island State Regiment, 12th December, 1776, to — March, 1777.

Babcock, Joshua (R. I.). Major-General Rhode Island Militia. (Died 1st April, 1803.)

Babcock, Oliver (Conn). Ensign 6th Connecticut, 1st May, 1775; 2d Lieutenant, 1st July to 10th December, 1775; 1st Lieutenant 10th Continental Infantry, 1st January, 1776; wounded and taken prisoner at Fort Washington, 16th November, 1776; exchanged 10th January, 1777. Died 25th January, 1777.

Bachelder, Archelaus (N. H.). 1st Lieutenant 27th Continental Infantry, 1st January to 31st December, 1776. (Name also spelled Bachelor.)

Bachelder, Benjamin (N. H.). Ensign of Long's Regiment New Hampshire Militia, July to December, 1776.

Bachelder, James (Mass). Surgeon's Mate 6th Continental Infantry, 1st January, 1776, to ——.

Bachenstone, Andrew (Pa). Ensign of Captain Weaver's Company, guarding prisoners at Lancaster, 13th January, 1777; 2d Lieutenant, 30th October, 1777; retired — November, 1777.

Backus, Ebenezer (Conn). Major Commanding Battalion Connecticut Light Horse, — August to — November, 1776.

Bacon, Abner (Conn). 1st Lieutenant of Chester's Connecticut State Regiment, June to December, 1776; Captain 4th Connecticut, 1st January, 1777; retired 15th November, 1778. (Died 10th September, 1822.)

Bacon, Asa (Conn). Captain of Chester's Connecticut State Regiment, June to December, 1776.

Bacon, Charles (Mass). Ensign of Read's Massachusetts Regiment, May to December, 1775.

Bacon, David (R. I.). 1st Lieutenant of Tallman's Regiment Rhode Island Militia, 12th December, 1776. (Died 13th January, 1777.)

Bacon, Elias (Mass). Sergeant in Lexington Alarm, April, 1775; 2d Lieutenant of Read's Massachusetts Regiment, May to December, 1775; 1st Lieutenant 13th Continental Infantry, 1st January to 31st December, 1776. (Died 20th July, 1828.)

Bacon, Jacob (Mass). Surgeon's Mate of Scammon's Massachusetts Regiment, May to December, 1775; Surgeon's Mate 7th Continental Infantry, 1st January to 31st December, 1776. Was a prisoner, where and when taken not stated; exchanged October, 1778.

Bacon, John (Mass). Lieutenant of a company of Minute Men; killed at Concord 19th April, 1775.

Bacon, John (Mass). 1st Lieutenant of Paterson's Massachusetts Regiment, May to December, 1775; 1st Lieutenant 15th Continental Infantry, 1st January to 31st December, 1776; 1st Lieutenant of Baldwin's Artillery, Artificer Regiment, 9th November, 1778, to ——.

Bacon, John, Sr. (Ga). Captain Georgia Company of Riflemen, 8th January to August, 1776.

Bacon, John, Jr. (Ga). 1st Lieutenant Georgia Company of Riflemen, 8th January to August, 1776.

Bacon, Oliver (N. H.). Sergeant 2d New Hampshire, — March, 1777; taken prisoner at Skenesborough 7th July, 1777, rejoined regiment 1st August, 1779; Ensign ——, 1781; Lieutenant, 13th April, 1782, and served to close of war. (Died 25th March, 1835.)

Bacon, Thomas (Ga). 3d Lieutenant of Georgia Company of Riflemen, 8th January to August, 1776.

Bacon, William (Mass). Captain of Glover's Massachusetts Regiment, 19th May to — December, 1775; Major Artificer Regiment in 1776; Colonel Massachusetts Militia in 1779.

Bacot, Peter (N. C.). Ensign 1st North Carolina, 19th September, 1776; 2d Lieutenant, 8th February, 1777; 1st Lieutenant, 4th October, 1777; taken prisoner at Charleston, 12th May, 1780, exchanged 14th June, 1781; Captain, 8th September, 1781; served to close of war. (Died 13th August, 1821.)

Bacot, Samuel (S. C.). Lieutenant of Marion's South Carolina Rangers; taken prisoner at Charleston, S. C., 12th May, 1780, but shortly after escaped.

Bacques, James (Md). 1st Lieutenant of Dorsey's Company, 1st Continental Artillery, 3d September, 1779, and served to June —, 1783.

Badger, Joseph, (N. H.). Colonel New Hampshire Militia, 1776-1778; Brigadier General New Hampshire Militia, 1780 to 1783. (Died 4th April, 1803.)

Badlam, Ezra (Mass). Lieutenant in Lexington Alarm, April, 1775; Captain of Gridley's Regiment Massachusetts Artillery, 25th June to — December, 1775; Captain 26th Continental Infantry, 1st January, 1776; Major 9th Massachusetts, 1st November, 1776; Lieutenant-Colonel 2d Massachusetts,

7th July, 1777; transferred to 8th Massachusetts, 1st January, 1781; retired 1st August, 1782. (Died 5th April, 1788.)

Badlam, Stephen (Mass). Captain Lieutenant of Gridley's Regiment Massachusetts Artillery, May to December, 1775; Captain of Knox's Regiment Continental Artillery, 10th December, 1775, to — December, 1776. (Died 25th August, 1815.)

Badlam, William (Mass). Private in Gridley's Regiment Massachusetts Artillery, May to December, 1775; private in Knox's Regiment Continental Artillery, 21st September, 1776, to February, 1777; Quartermaster of the Artillery under General Knox, 21st September, 1776, to 1st February, 1777.

Bagby, James (N. C.). Lieutenant North Carolina Militia, 1780-1781.

Bagley, Josiah (N. Y.). Ensign 3d New York, 21st November, 1776; Lieutenant, 1st March, 1780; transferred to 1st New York, 1st January, 1783, and served to close of war.

Bagnell, Richard (Mass). Corporal in Lexington Alarm, April 1775; Sergeant in Cotton's Massachusetts Regiment, April to December, 1775; Sergeant 25th Continental Infantry; 1st January to 31st December, 1776; Ensign 7th Massachusetts, 1st January, 1777; Lieutenant, 1st July, 1779; resigned 25th July, 1782.

Bailey, Adams (Mass). Sergeant in Lexington Alarm, April, 1775; Quartermaster of Thomas' Massachusetts Regiment, May to December, 1775; 2d Lieutenant 23d Continental Infantry, 1st January to 31st December, 1776; 1st Lieutenant and Paymaster 2d Massachusetts, 1st January, 1777; Captain, 1st November, 1778, and served to 3d November, 1783. (Died 26th July, 1824.)

Bailey, Amos (Mass). Sergeant in Lexington Alarm, April, 1775; Sergeant Major of Garrish's Massachusetts Regiment, April to December, 1775; 2d Lieutenant 26th Continental Infantry, 1st January to 31st December, 1776.

Bailey, Benjamin (N. C.). Ensign 7th North Carolina, 28th November 1776; Lieutenant, 22d December, 1776; transferred to 1st North Carolina, 1st June, 1778; Captain, 8th September, 1781; transferred to 3d North Carolina, 1st January, 1782; retired 1st January, 1783.

Bailey, Fry (N. H.). Ensign of Bedel's New Hampshire regiment, January to September, 1776.

Bailey, Gídeon (Conn). 2d Lieutenant 6th Connecticut, 1st January, 1777; resigned 1st July, 1779.

Bailey, Hezekiah (Conn). Ensign 3d Connecticut, 1st January, 1777; 2d Lieutenant, 14th April, 1778; resigned 29th June, 1779.

Bailey, Hudson (Mass). Sergeant 10th Massachusetts, 12th December, 1776; Ensign 14th Massachusetts, 8th October, 1779, and resigned 26th September, 1780.

Bailey, Jacob (Vt). Brigadier General Vermont Militia in 1776. (Died 1816.)

Bailey, John (Md). 1st Lieutenant 3d Maryland, 20 February, 1777; wounded at Savannah, 9th October, 1779; resigned 11th February, 1780.

Bailey, John (Mass). Lieutenant-Colonel of Thomas' Massachusetts Regiment — May, 1775; Colonel, 1st July, 1775; Colonel 23d Continental Infantry, 1st January, 1776; Colonel 2d Massachusetts, 1st November, 1776; resigned 21st October, 1780. (Died 27th October, 1810.)

Bailey, John (Va). Captain of Clark's Illinois Regiment, 1779-1782.

Bailey, Lemuel (R. I.). 1st Lieutenant 3d Rhode Island, 28th June, 1775; 1st Lieutenant and Captain of Richmond's Regiment Rhode Island Militia in 1776.

Bailey, Luther (Mass). Corporal in Lexington Alarm, April, 1775; Adjutant of Thomas' Massachusetts Regiment, May to December, 1775; 2d Lieutenant and Quartermaster 23d Continental Infantry, 1st January to 31st December, 1776; 1st Lieutenant and Adjutant 2d Massachusetts, 1st January, 1777; Captain, 7th July, 1777, and served to close of war; Brevet Major, 30th September, 1783. (Died 12th May, 1820.)

Bailey, Montjoy (Md). Captain 7th Maryland, 10th December, 1776; resigned 14th September, 1778. (Died 22d March, 1836.) (Name also spelled Bayley.)

Bailey, Robert (S. C.). Captain 3d South Carolina, March, 1778; killed at Savannah 9th October, 1779.

Bailey, Robert C.—See Baillir.

Bailey, Samuel (Va). Paymaster 11th Virginia, 15th February, 1777, to ——; resigned 12th August, 1777.

Bailey, Thomas (Mass). 2d Lieutenant 3d Continental Artillery, 1st January, 1777; 1st Lieutenant, 12th April, 1780; retired 1st January, 1781.

Baillie, Robert C. (S. C.). 2d Lieutenant 3d South Carolina, March, 1778. Killed at Savannah 9th October, 1779.

Baillivey, Christian Francis Alexander, Jr. (Mass). Ensign 15th Massachusetts, 1st January, 1777; resigned 9th January, 1778.

Baird, Absalom (Pa). Surgeon of Baldwin's Artillery Artificer Regiment, 20th' March, 1780; retired 29th March, 1781. (Died 27th October, 1805.)

Baird, Benjamin (N. J.). Major and Lieutenant-Colonel New Jersey Militia in 1777. (Died 1778).

Baird, James (N. C.). Captain North Carolina Militia in 1776.

Baird, Samuel (Pa). 2d Lieutenant 1st Pennsylvania, 2d June, 1778. Died February, 1780.

Baird, William (N. J.). Captain and Major New Jersey Militia, 1777-1779. (Died 1794.)

Bakeman, John (N. Y.). Adjutant 1st Canadian (Livingston's) Regiment, 18th December, 1776; retired — August, 1779.

Baker, Amos (Conn). Surgeon's Mate of Bradley's Connecticut State Regiment, May to December, 1776.

Baker, David (N. J.). 1st Lieutenant of Spencer's Continental Regiment, 1st May, 1777; resigned 6th April, 1778.

Baker, David (Massachusetts). Private in Lexington Alarm, April, 1775; Sergeant of Heath's Massachusetts Regiment, May to December, 1775; Sergeant 24th Continental Infantry, 1st January, 1776; 2d Lieutenant, 8th October, 1776; 1st Lieutenant 9th Massachusetts, 1st January, 1777; resigned 28th December, 1777.

Baker, Henry (Md). 2d Lieutenant 5th Maryland, 1st August, 1781; transferred to 2d Maryland, 1st January, 1783; retained in Maryland Battalion, April, 1783, and served to 15th November, 1783.

Baker, Hugh (Pa). Lieutenant Pennsylvania Militia, ——; was a prisoner in 1780.

Baker, James (Pa). 3d Lieutenant 1st Pennsylvania Battalion of the Flying Camp, July to December, 1776. (Name also spelled Barker.)

Baker, James (Va). Ensign; killed at Stony Point 1st June, 1779.

Baker, Jesse (S. C.). 1st Lieutenant 2d South Carolina, — January, 1777; Captain, 2d October, 1778; was in 3d South Carolina in May, 1780; taken prisoner at Charleston 12th May, 1780.

Baker, John (Ga). Captain Georgia Riflemen, 8th January, 1776; Colonel Georgia Militia; wounded at Bull Swamp 8th November, 1778, and was in service to January, 1783.

Baker, John (Mass). Captain of Little's Massachusetts Regiment, May to December, 1775; Captain 12th Continental Infantry, 1st January to 31st December, 1776.

Baker, John (Mass). 1st Lieutenant of Baldwin's Artillery Artificer Regiment, 18th February, 1778, to ——.

Baker, John (Mass). Lieutenant of Colonel W. R. Lee's Continental Regiment 1st July, 1777; resigned 1st March, 1779.

Baker, John, Jr. (Mass). Sergeant in Lexington Alarm, April, 1775; Captain in Gerrish's Massachusetts Regiment, April to December, 1775.

Baker, John, Jr. (Mass). Captain 27th Continental Infantry, 1st January to 31st December, 1776.

Baker, John (N. C.). Was Surgeon's Mate in 3d North Carolina in 1777 and 1778.

Baker, John (N. C.). 1st Lieutenant 7th North Carolina, 28th November, 1776; Captain, 6th July, 1777; retired 1st June, 1778; Colonel North Carolina Militia; wounded at Bulltown Swamp, 19th November, 1778.

Baker, Joseph (Mass). 2d Lieutenant of Prescott's Massachusetts Regiment, May to December, 1775; 2d Lieutenant 7th Continental Infantry, 1st January to 31st December, 1776; 1st Lieutenant 2d Massachusetts, 1st January, 1777; retired 1st April, 1779.

Baker, Josiah (Mass). Lieutenant of Phinney's Massachusetts Regiment, May to December, 1775.

Baker, Moses (N. H.). Major of Wingate's Regiment New Hampshire Militia in 1776.

Baker, Peter (N. C.). Lieutenant 1st North Carolina, 8th February, 1777, to ——.

Baker, Peter (Va). Sergeant of Grayson's Continental Regiment, 4th February, 1777; Lieutenant and Regimental Quartermaster, December, 1777. Died 18th June, 1778.

Baker, Remember (Conn). Captain Connecticut Militia at Ticonderoga in May, 1775; killed by Indians near St. Johns, Canada, in September, 1775.

Baker, Richard Bahon (S. C.). 1st Lieutenant 2d South Carolina, — January, 1777; Captain, 25th April, 1778; taken prisoner at Charleston 12th May, 1780; exchanged — July, 1781, and served to close of war.

Baker, Thomas (Mass). Captain Lieutenant 3d Continental Artillery, 9th November, 1776; Regimental Quartermaster, 12th April, 1777; omitted November, 1779. (Died 14th November, 1809.)

Baker, Wm. (Ga). 2d Lieutenant Georgia Rifle Company, January to August, 1776.

Baker, William (Mass). Sergeant 13th Massachusetts, 5th March, 1777; Ensign, 7th March, 1779; resigned 4th May, 1780.

Baker, William (Va). 1st Lieutenant of Grayson's Continental Regiment, 23d January, 1777; resigned 8th June, 1777.

Balch, Benjamin (Mass). Chaplain of Doolittle's Massachusetts Regiment, May to December, 1775; served subsequently as Chaplain in Navy. (Died 4th May, 1815.)

Balcolm, Joseph (Mass). Sergeant Company of Minute Men at Lexington and Concord, 19th April, 1775; Sergeant in Nixon's Massachusetts Regiment, May to December, 1775, and in Marshall's Regiment in 1776; Sergeant 6th Massachusetts, 1st March, 1777; Ensign ,12th November, 1777; Lieutenant, 20th April, 1781, and resigned 13th November, 1782. (Died 11th November, 1827.)

Baldesque, Joseph (—). Captain and Paymaster 1st Cavalry Pulaski Legion, 10th May, 1778; resigned 29th December, 1779.

Baldwin, Abraham (Conn). Chaplain 2d Connecticut, 1st February, 1777; Brigade Chaplain 1st February, 1779, to 3d June, 1783. (Died 4th March, 1807.)

Baldwin, Alexander (N. Y.). Captain New York Militia in 1775.

Baldwin, Ambrose (Conn). Ensign of Swift's Connecticut State Regiment, July to November, 1776.

Baldwin, Caleb (Conn). 2d Lieutenant 10th Continental Infantry, 1st January to 31st December, 1776; 1st Lieutenant 7th Connecticut, 1st January, 1777; Captain Lieutenant, 1st June, 1778; Captain, 1st January, 1780; transferred to 2d Connecticut, 1st January, 1781; retired 1st January, 1783. (Died 5th September, 1823.)

Baldwin, Cornelius (Va). Surgeon 8th Virginia, 20th May, 1777; taken prisoner at Charleston 12th May, 1780; exchanged — November, 1780; transferred to 1st Virginia, 1st January, 1781, and served to close of war. (Died 1827.)

Baldwin, Daniel (N. J.). 1st Lieutenant 1st New Jersey, 8th November, 1775; Captain, 29th November, 1776; severely wounded and lost a leg at Germantown 4th October, 1777; honorably discharged 1st March, 1779.

Baldwin, Elias (N. J.) 2d Lieutenant of Spencer's Continental Regiment, 19th February, 1777; omitted — July, 1777.

Baldwin, Francis (Va). Ensign 8th Virginia, 1st February, 1777; 2d Lieutenant, 10th May, 1777; resigned 8th May, 1778.

Baldwin, Henry (Md). Sergeant 3d Maryland, 26th February, 1777; Ensign and Quartermaster 3d Maryland, 27th May, 1778; Lieutenant, 11th February, 1780; transferred to 2d Maryland, 1st January, 1783; retained in Maryland Battalion, April, 1783, and served to 15th November, 1783.

Baldwin, Hezekiah (N. Y.). Captain 2d New York, 28th June, 1775, to — January, 1776.

Baldwin, Isaac (N. H.). Captain 1st New Hampshire, 23d April, 1775; killed at Bunker Hill 17th June, 1775.

Baldwin, Israel (Conn). 2d Lieutenant of Silliman's Connecticut State Regiment, June to December, 1776. (Died 1778.)

Baldwin, Jedutham (Mass). Captain Assistant Engineer Continental Army, 16th March, 1776; Colonel Engineers, 3d September, 1776; retired 20th April, 1782; was also Colonel Artillery Artificer Regiment, 3d September, 1776, to 29th March, 1781. (Died 4th June, 1788.)

Baldwin, Jesse (N. J.). Ensign 1st New Jersey, 28th October, 1776; 2d Lieutenant, 4th October, 1777; resigned 1st April, 1779.

Baldwin, Jonathan (Conn). Lieutenant-Colonel Connecticut Militia, 1777-1779.

Baldwin, Josiah (Conn). 1st Lieutenant 6th Connecticut, May to November, 1775; Captain of Mott's Connecticut State Regiment, June to December, 1776.

Baldwin, Loammi (Mass). Major of Militia at Concord, 19th April, 1775; Lieutenant-Colonel of Gerrish's Massachusetts Regiment, 19th May to December, 1775; Colonel 26th Continental Infantry, 1st January to 31st December, 1776. (Died 20th October, 1807.)

Baldwin, Nahum (N. H.). Colonel New Hampshire Militia 1776 to 1778. (Died 1788.)

Baldwin, Samuel (Conn). 1st Lieutenant of Douglas' Connecticut State Regiment, June to December, 1776. (Died 1828.)

Baldy, Stephen (Pa). Lieutenant of Klotz's Battalion Pennsylvania Militia, ——; taken prisoner at Long Island 27th August, 1776.

Balkley, John (Conn). Ensign 10th Continental Infantry, 1st January to 31st December, 1776.

Ball, Benjamin (Mass). Sergeant in Lexington Alarm, April, 1775; 2d Lieutenant of Prescott's Massachusetts Regiment, — May to — December, 1775; 2d Lieutenant 7th Continental Infantry, 1st January to 31st December, 1776; 1st Lieutenant 2d Massachusetts, 1st January, 1777; resigned 23d February, 1778.

Ball, Blackall William (Pa). Ensign 12th Pennsylvania, 16th October, 1776; 2d Lieutenant 20th May, 1777; transferred to 3d Pennsylvania, 1st July, 1778; 1st Lieutenant, 11th September, 1778; transferred to 1st Pennsylvania, 1st January, 1783, and served to close of war. (Name also spelled William B. Blackall.)

Ball, Burgess (Va). Sergeant in 5th Virginia, —, 1775, to —, 1778; Cornet of Ashe's Company North Carolina Dragoons, —, 1778, to — November, 1781; wounded at Hobkirk's Hill 25th April, 1781. (Died 1800.)

Ball, Burgess (Va). Captain 5th Virginia, 10th February, 1776; Major 5th Virginia, 10th February, 1777; Lieutenant-Colonel 9th Virginia, 17th December, 1777; transferred to 1st Virginia 14th September, 1778; taken prisoner at

Charlestown 12th May, 1780, and was on parole until retired 12th February, 1781.

Ball, Daniel (Va). Ensign 8th Virginia, 18th December, 1780; 2d Lieutenant, —, 1882; retired 1st January, 1883.

Ball, Hosea (N. C.). Ensign North Carolina Militia in 1779.

Ball, James (Va). Captain Virginia Militia, 1778-1779.

Ball, John (Conn). Ensign 19th Continental Infantry, 1st January to 31st December, 1776; 2d Lieutenant 6th Connecticut, 1st January, 1777; 1st Lieutenant, 15th November, 1778; transferred to 4th Connecticut, 1st January, 1881; retired 1st January, 1783.

Ball, John (N. Y.). 1st Lieutenant 3d New York, 21st November, 1776; resigned 30th April, 1778. (Died 1842.)

Ball, John (Va). Ensign 6th Virginia, 26th February, 1776, to ——.

Ball, Lebbeus (Mass). Captain of Danielson's Massachusetts Regiment, 27th May to — December, 1775; Captain 3d Continental Infantry, 1st January to 31st December, 1776; Captain 4th Massachusetts, 1st January, 1777; Major, 1st November, 1777; resigned 27th October, 1780. (Died 1806.)

Ball, Robert (Del). Regimental Quartermaster Delaware Regiment, 19th January to December, 1776.

Ball, Stephen (N. J.). Surgeon's Mate Hospital Department, — March, 1779, to close of war. (Died 1793.)

Ball, Thomond (Pa). Paymaster of Hartley's Continental Regiment, 15th January, 1777; resigned 16th December, 1778.

Ball, William (Va). Ensign 8th Virginia, 17th December, 1780, and retired 1st January, 1783.

Ballantine, Ebenezer (Mass). Surgeon's Mate 6th Massachusetts, 20th May, 1780, to 12th June, 1783. (Died 1823.)

Ballard, Benjamin (Mass). Assistant Commissary of Issues; dismissed 1st October, 1779.

Ballard, Jeremiah (N. J.). 2d Lieutenant 3d New Jersey, 2d April, 1776; 1st Lieutenant, 29th November, 1776; Captain, 26th October, 1777; transferred to 2d New Jersey, 1st January, 1781, and served to — April, 1783.

Ballard, John (Va). Captain Virginia Militia, 1775-1778.

Ballard, Kedar (N. C.). 1st Lieutenant 3d North Carolina, 16th April, 1776; Captain, 4th October, 1777; Regimental Paymaster, 10th October, 1779; taken prisoner at Charleston 12th May, 1780; prisoner on parole to August, 1781; retired 1st January, 1783. (Died 15th January, 1834.)

Ballard, Robert (Va). Captain 1st Virginia 7th October, 1775; Major, — May to 22d March, 1777; Lieutenant-Colonel, 4th October, 1777; transferred to 4th Virginia 14th September, 1778; resigned 4th July, 1779.

Ballard, William (Va). Lieutenant of Virginia Regiment in 1780-1781.

Ballard, William Hudson (Mass). Captain of Frye's Massachusetts Regiment, 19th May to December, 1775; Captain 6th Continental Infantry, 1st January to 31st December, 1776; Captain 7th Massachusetts, 1st January, 1777; Major 15th Massachusetts, 1st July, 1779; retired 1st January, 1781. (Died — December, 1814.)

Ballaseure, James (R. I.). Surgeon's Mate, 26th May, 1777; resigned 1st February, 1778.

Ballew, David (Va). Ensign 2d Virginia, 3d March, 1776; Lieutenant, April, 1777. Died 13th May, 1778.

Balliet, Stephen (Pa). Colonel Pennsylvania Militia, 1777. (Died 1821.)

Ballou, Reuben (R. I.). Captain in Tallman's Regiment, Rhode Island Militia, 12th December, 1776, to March, 1777; Major Rhode Island Militia, 1779-1781. (Died 1803.)

Balmain, Alexander (Va). Chaplain 13th Virginia, 20th February, 1777; Brigade Chaplain, 22d May, 1778, and served to June, 1780.

Balme, Mottin de la (France). Lieutenant-Colonel of Horse Continental Army, 26th May, 1777; Colonel and Inspector-General of Cavalry, 8th July, 1777; resigned 11th October, 1777.

Baltzel, Charles (Md). 1st Lieutenant German Battalion, 12th July, 1776; Captain, 10th May, 1777; wounded at Germantown, 4th October, 1777; retired 1st January, 1781.

Baltzel, John (Md). Sergeant German Regiment, 1st December, 1776; Ensign, 10th August, 1777, to ——.

Bamper, Abraham. See Bemper.

Bamper, Jacob (N. Y.). 2d Lieutenant 2d New York, 21st November, 1776; resigned 21st July, 1777; Cornet 4th Continental Dragoons, 12th August, 1778; Regimental Quartermaster, — September, 1778; omitted May, 1779.

Bancker, Abraham (N. Y.). 1st Lieutenant 4th New York, 24th February to — November, 1776.

Bancker, Thomas B. (N. Y.). Captain New York Militia, 1776-1777. (Died 1807.)

Bancroft, Ebenezer (Mass). Captain in the Lexington Alarm, April, 1775; Captain of Bridge's Massachusetts Regiment, 27th May, 1775; wounded at Bunker Hill, 17 June, 1775; Major and Lieutenant-Colonel Massachusetts Militia, 1779-1781. (Died 22d September. 1787.)

Bancroft, Edmund (Mass). Sergeant of Prescott's Massachusetts Regiment, May to December, 1775; Ensign 7th Continental Infantry, 1st January, 1776; 2d Lieutenant, 27th August, 1776; 1st Lieutenant, 15th Massachusetts, 1st January, 1777. Died 25th June, 1777.

Bancroft, James (Mass). 1st Lieutenant of Mansfield's Massachusetts Regiment, May to December, 1775; 1st Lieutenant 23d Continental Infantry, 1st January, 1776; Captain, 16th July, 1770, Captain 8th Massachusetts, 1st January, 1777, to rank from 16th July, 1776; resigned 12th May, 1780. (Died 17th March, 1831.)

Bancroft, James (Mass). Ensign of Bridge's Massachusetts Regiment. — May to — December, 1775; Sergeant 8th Massachusetts, 21st March, 1777; Lieutenant, 12th May, 1780, and served to June, 1783. (Died 2d April, 1803.)

Bancroft, Lemuel (Mass). Lieutenant in Lexington Alarm, April, 1775; 2d Lieutenant of Danielson's Massachusetts Regiment, May to December, 1775.

Bancroft, Samuel (Conn). 2d Lieutenant 8th Connecticut, 6th July to 18th December, 1775; 2d Lieutenant of Wolcott's Connecticut Regiment in 1776.

Bancroft, William (Mass). Private 15th Massachusetts, 11th March, 1777; Sergeant, 1st June, 1778; Ensign, 31st March, 1779; transferred to 5th Massachusetts, 1st January, 1781; 2d Lieutenant, 9th April, 1782, resigned 25th May, 1782. (Died 17th December, 1827.)

Bangs, Isaac (Mass). Lieutenant 23d Continental Infantry, 1st January to 31st December, 1776.

Banister, Christian (Mass). 1st Lieutenant of Fellows' Massachusetts Regiment, May to December, 1775.

Banister, John (Va). Lieutenant-Colonel Virginia Militia, 1778-1781. (Died 1787.)

Banister, Seth (Mass). Adjutant of Learned's Massachusetts Regiment, May to December, 1775; Adjutant 3d Continental Infantry, 1st January to 31st December, 1776; 1st Lieutenant 4th Massachusetts, 1st January, 1777; Captain, 1st April, 1778; retired 1st January, 1883.

Bank, Joseph (Pa). Ensign of Captain Weaver's Company, guarding prisoners at Lancaster, 30th October, 1777, and served to ——.

Banks, Ebenezer (Conn). Ensign 5th Connecticut, 1st May to 11th December, 1775; 2d Lieutenant of Silliman's Connecticut State Regiment, June to December, 1776. (Died, 1777.)

Banks, John (N. Y.). Commissary of Military Stores, 1779, to — July, 1782. (Died 18th July, 1818.)

Banks, Joseph (Pa). Ensign 10th Pennsylvania, 24th February, 1777; Regimental Quartermaster, 4th December, 1777, to 1st January, 1781; Lieutenant, 3d June, 1778; retired 1st January, 1781.

Banks, Moses (Mass). Regimental Quartermaster of Phinney's Massachusetts Regiment, May to December, 1775; Quartermaster 18th Continental Infantry, 1st January, 1776; cashiered 24th July, 1776. (Died 10th October, 1823.)

Banks, Samuel (N. Y.). Ensign New York Militia ——; was a prisoner of war 2d December, 1781, to 15th February, 1782.

Bankson, Andrew (N. J.). Ensign 2d New Jersey, 5th September, 1776; 2d Lieutenant, 15th December, 1776; resigned 5th February, 1777.

Bankson, John (Pa). 1st Lieutenant 1st Pennsylvania Battalion, 5th January, 1776; Captain 2d Pennsylvania, 25th September, 1776; Regimental Paymaster, 14th October, 1778, to — January, 1881; transferred to 1st Pennsylvania, 1st January, 1883; Brevet Major, 30th September, 1783; served to 3d November, 1783.

Banning, John (Va). Captain Virginia Militia, 1779-1781.

Baraud, Matthew (Ga). Captain Georgia Militia, 1775.

Barbee, Thomas (Va). 2d Lieutenant 10th Virginia, 20th January, 1777; 1st Lieutenant, 22d March, 1777; regiment designated 6th Virginia, 14th September, 1778; taken prisoner at Charleston, 12th May, 1780; exchanged 14th June, 1781; Captain, 26th May, 1781, and served to close of war.

Barber, Caleb L. (Mass). 2d Lieutenant of Henley's Continental Regiment, 1st January, 1777; retired 23d April, 1779.

Barber, David (Conn). 2d Lieutenant 6th Connecticut, 1st January, 1777; killed in a skirmish on Long Island, 25th December, 1777.

Barber, Ephraim (Mass). Ensign 21st Continental Infantry, 1st January to 31st December, 1776.

Barber, Francis (N. J.). Major 3d New Jersey, 18th January, 1776; Lieutenant-Colonel, 28th November, 1776; wounded at Monmouth, 28th June, 1778; wounded at Newtown, 29th August, 1779; wounded at Yorktown, 14th October, 1781; transferred to 1st New Jersey, 1st January, 1781; Colonel 2d New Jersey, 7th January, 1783; accidently killed by the falling of a tree, 11th February, 1783.

Barber, George (Ga). Captain Georgia Militia in 1781.

Barber, Isaac R. (Mass). Ensign 6th Continental Infantry, 1st January, 1776; cashiered — September, 1776; 2d Lieutenant of Stevens' Battalion of Artillery, 9th November, 1776; Battalion formed part of 3d Continental Artillery in 1778; 1st Lieutenant 6th March, 1780; resigned 23d October, 1782.

Barber, John (N. C.). Captain North Carolina Militia in 1776.

Barber, Nathaniel (Mass). Commissary of Military Stores, 1st January, 1777; resigned 5th March, 1781.

Barber, Samuel (Conn). 1st Lieutenant 1st Connecticut, 1st May to December, 1775.

Barber, Samuel (Md). Regimental Adjutant 1st Maryland, 3d February, 1776; resigned 6th July, 1778.

Barber, William (Mass). Ensign of Jackson's Continental Regiment, 14th May, 1777; resigned 17 October, 1778.

Barber, William (N. J.). Ensign 3d New Jersey, 29th October, 1776; Aide-de-Camp to General Maxwell, 1st January, 1777, with rank of Captain from 14th April, 1777; Major and Aide-de-Camp to General Alexander, 7th May, 1778, to 15th January, 1783; wounded at Yorktown, 14th October, 1781. (Died 1799.)

Barber, William (N. J.). Adjutant of Jackson's Continental Regiment, 1st April, 1777; Ensign 14th May, 1777; resigned 17th October, 1778.

Barber, William (N. C.). Lieutenant 1st North Carolina, 19th April, 1776, to ——.

Barbour, James (Va). Ensign 6th Virginia, 14th October, 1780, to ——; (was in service May, 1781.)

Barbour, Thomas (Va). Major and Lieutenant-Colonel Virginia Militia, 1779-1781.

Barclay, Hugh (—). Colonel Assistant Deputy Quartermaster General, 16th January, 1777 to 1781. (Died 1807.)

Barclay, John (N. Y.). Captain New York Militia, 20th October ,1775 to ——.

Bard, Andrew (Pa). Ensign of Lewis' Pennsylvania Battalion of the Flying Camp, July to December, 1776.

Bard, John (Ga). Captain 2d Georgia, 29th November, 1776; taken prisoner at Savannah 29th December, 1778; prisoner on parole in 1779 and 1780; did not rejoin the army; removed to New York in 1779.

Bard, Thomas (Pa). 2d Lieutenant of Calderwood's Independent Pennsylvania Company, 23d January, 1777; company attached to 11th Pennsylvania, and retired 1st January, 1781.

Bard, William (Pa). 2d Lieutenant 12th Pennsylvania, 16th October, 1776, and served to ——.

Bardt, Nicholas (N. Y.). Lieutenant New York Militia; wounded at Johnstown, 25th October, 1781.

Bardwell, Jonathan (Mass). Captain of Brewer's Massachusetts Regiment, May to December, 1775; served subsequently as Captain Massachusetts Militia.

Bardwell, Perez (Mass). Lieutenant in Lexington Alarm, April, 1775; 1st Lieutenant of Fellows' Massachusetts Regiment, May to December, 1775.

Barker, Abner (N. H.). Surgeon of Bedel's Regiment New Hampshire Rangers, 29th August, 1775, to July, 1776.

Barker, James. (See Baker.)

Barker, John (Mass). 2d Lieutenant of Jackson's Continental Regiment, 1st

January, 1777; resigned 1st March, 1779. (Died 24th February, 1813.)

Barker, Joseph (Pa). 2d Lieutenant 4th Continental Artillery, 14th March, 1777; resigned 14th March, 1778.

Barker, Peter (Md). Quartermaster of Grayson's Continental Regiment, — March, 1777. Died 18th June, 1778.

Barker, Samuel (Conn). 1st Lieutenant of Ward's Connecticut State Regiment, 14th May, 1776, to — May, 1777.

Barker, Samuel (Conn). Captain 6th Connecticut ,1st January, 1777; retired 15th November, 1778. (Died 1807.)

Barker, Samuel Augustus Still (Conn). Adjutant of Douglas' Connecticut State Regiment, 20th June to 29th December, 1776; 1st Lieutenant and Adjutant 6th Connecticut, 26th December, 1776; Captain, 10th May, 1780; transferred to 4th Connecticut, 1st January, 1781; Brigade Major in 1781; transferred to 2d Connecticut, 1st January, 1782; resigned 13th April, 1782. (Died 19th November, 1819.)

Barker, Thomas. (See Baker.)

Barker, William (N. Y.). Major and Lieutenant-Colonel New York Militia, 1775-1779. (Died 1820.)

Barkley, John (Pa). Ensign 4th Pennsylvania Battalion, 8th January, 1776; 2d Lieutenant, 12th October, 1776; 1st Lieutenant 5th Pennsylvania, 1st January, 1777; Captain Lieutenant, 13th June, 1779; retired 1st January, 1781. (Name also spelled Barclay and Barckley.)

Barksdale, John (Va). Ensign 6th Virginia, 24th February, 1776; Lieutenant, January, 1778; retired 14th September, 1778; Colonel Virginia Militia, 1779-1780.

Barlow, Joel (Mass). Brigade Chaplain, 20th June, 1780, to 3d June, 1783. (Died 22d December, 1812.)

Barnam, Barnabas (N. H.). 1st Lieutenant Green Mountain Boys, 27th July to — December, 1775.

Barnard, John (Conn). Lieutenant of Wolcott's Connecticut Regiment, December, 1775 to March, 1776; 1st Lieutenant of Chester's Connecticut State Regiment, 20th June to 25th December, 1776; Captain 3d Connecticut, 1st January, 1777; retired 1st January, 1781. (Died 1813.)

Barnard, Moses (Mass). Surgeon's Mate of Whitcomb's Massachusetts Regiment, May to December, 1775.

Barnard, Timothy (Mass). Captain in Lexington Alarm, April, 1775; Captain of Little's Massachusetts Regiment — May to — December, 1775.

Barnard, William. (See Bernard.)

Barnes, Amos (Conn). 1st Lieutenant of Mott's Connecticut State Regiment, June to December, 1776.

Barnes, Asa (Mass). Captain in Woodbridge's Massachusetts Regiment, May to December, 1775; Captain 16th Continental Infantry, 1st January to 31st December, 1776; Captain Colonel Massachusetts Militia, 1779-1781.

Barnes, Daniel (Conn). 2d Lieutenant of Wooster's Connecticut Regiment, November 1775, to March, 1776; 1st Lieutenant 8th Connecticut, 1st January, 1777; Captain Lieutenant, 1st June, 1778; Captain, 20th April, 1779; resigned 21st August, 1780.

Barnes, Daniel (Mass). Captain of Ward's Massachusetts Regiment, 23d May to — December, 1775; Captain 21st Continental Infantry, 1st January to 31st December, 1776; Captain 15th Massachusetts, 1st January, 1777; retired 1st August, 1779.

Barnes, Edward (Mass). Major of Ward's Massachusetts Regiment, 23d May, 1775; Lieutenant-Colonel, 17th June to December, 1775.

Barnes, Henry (Md). Captain 6th Maryland, 1st January, 1777, to ——.

Barnes, James (Conn). 2d Lieutenant 7th Connecticut, 1st January, 1777; 1st Lieutenant, 15th November, 1778; resigned 20th June, 1779.

Barnes, John (N. Y.). 2d Lieutenant 2d New York, 28th June, 1775, to — January, 1776; served subsequently as Captain New York Rangers.

Barnes, John (Va). Private 11th Virginia, 12th February, 1776; Ensign 11th Virginia, 13th December, 1776; Regimental Quartermaster, ——, 1777, to ——, 1779; 2d Lieutenant, 7th March, 1777; transferred to 7th Virginia; 14th September, 1778; 1st Lieutenant, 13th May, 1779; retired 1st January, 1780.

Barnes, John H. (Md). Captain 1st Maryland, 10th December, 1776; resigned 20th December, 1777.

Barnes, Joseph (N. H.). Surgeon of Gilman's Regiment, New Hampshire Militia, ——, 1776, to ——, 1777.

Barnes, Joseph (N. Y.). 1st Lieutenant 1st New York, — March to — November, 1776.

Barnes, Nathaniel (Conn). Captain Connecticut Militia, 1776-1777.

Barnes, Parker (Va). Ensign 8th Virginia. Appears as in service November and December, 1776.

Barnes, Thomas (Mass). Captain of Mansfield's Massachusetts Regiment, 19th May to — December, 1775; Captain 14th Continental Infantry, 1st January to 31st December, 1776; Captain 6th Massachusetts, 1st January, 1777; Major 12th Massachusetts, 6th March, 1779; cashiered 7th November, 1780.

Barnes, Thomas (N. C.). Ensign North Carolina Militia in 1780.

Barnes, Thomas (Vt). Ensign Vermont Militia in 1777.

Barnet, James (N. H.). 2d Lieutenant 1st New Hampshire, 29th July to — December, 1775.

Barnet, James (Pa). 2d Lieutenant of Miles' Pennsylvania Rifle Regiment, 19th March, 1776; resigned 23d July, 1776.

Barnet, John (Pa). 3d Lieutenant 1st Pennsylvania Battalion of the Flying Camp, — June to — December, 1776.

Barnett, Churchill. Lieutenant 3d Continental Dragoons, 2d January, 1779, to ——.

Barnett, Jacob (S. C.). Captain South Carolina Dragoons, 5th April, 1781, to ——.

Barnett, James (Va). 2d Lieutenant 6th Virginia, 24th February, 1776; 1st Lieutenant, June, 1777; retired 30th September, 1778. (Died 1835.) (Name also spelled Burnett.)

Barnett, John (Mass). Brigade Chaplain — June, 1780, to — June, 1783. (Died 5th December, 1837.)

Barnett, Moses (N. H.). Captain New Hampshire Militia, 1776-1777.

Barnett, Robert (N. H.). Sergeant 2d New Hampshire, 23d April, 1775; Ensign, July to December, 1775; 2d Lieutenant 5th Continental Infantry, 1st January to 31st December, 1776; 2d Lieutenant Invalid Regiment, 1st June, 1779; retired 23d April, 1783.

Barnett, William (Conn). Captain 2d Continental Dragoons, 15th January, 1777; resigned 11th October, 1777.

Barnett, William (N. J.) Major New Jersey Militia in 1776; Captain 2d Continental Dragoons, 15th January, 1777; resigned 11th October, 1777.

Barnett, William (S. C.). Lieutenant 3d Continental Dragoons, 10th April, 1778, to — September, 1781.

Barnett, William M. (N. J.). Surgeon 1st New Jersey, 8th December, 1775; Hospital Surgeon, — May, 1778, and served to — June, 1782.

Barney, David (Mass). Lieutenant of Doolittle's Massachusetts Regiment, May to December, 1775.

Barney, Jabez (Mass). Ensign of Lee's Continental Regiment, 1st March, 1777; retired 22d April, 1779; subsequently served in Massachusetts Militia.

Barney, Rufus (Mass). Corporal in Walker's Massachusetts Regiment, April to November, 1775; Ensign 13th Continental Infantry, 1st January to 31st December, 1776.

Barnham, John (Mass). 1st Lieutenant of Little's Massachusetts Regiment, 19th May to December, 1775.

Barnham, Joshua (N. J.). Major New Jersey Militia; taken prisoner at West Chester, 16th March, 1777.

Barnham, Thomas (Mass). 2d Lieutenant of Brewer's Massachusetts Regiment, — May to December, 1775.

Barnitz, Jacob (Pa). Ensign of Swope's Pennsylvania Battalion of the Flying Camp, — June, 1776; wounded and taken prisoner at Fort Washington, 16th November, 1776; exchanged 16th February, 1778, and did not return to the army. (Died 1826.)

Barnum, Ellis (Conn). Sergeant of Bradley's Connecticut State Regiment, 20th June, 1776; Ensign 21st September, 1776; taken prisoner at Fort Washington 16th November, 1776; exchanged — May, 1777; 2d Lieutenant 2d Connecticut, 7th December, 1777; 1st Lieutenant, 2d September, 1779; resigned 18th March, 1780.

Barnum, Joshua, Jr. (N. Y.). Captain New York Militia, 1775; wounded and taken prisoner, when and where not stated.

Barnum, Samuel (Conn). 1st Lieutenant 7th Connecticut, 1st January, 1777; resigned 18th March, 1780.

Barnwell, John (S. C.). Captain 1st South Carolina, 17th June, 1775; was a Major in 1780; taken prisoner at Charleston, 12th May, 1780; Brigadier-General South Carolina Militia in 1781 and 1782.

Barnwell, Robert (S. C.). Captain South Carolina Militia in 1779.

Barr, John (N. Y.). Sergeant 4th New York, 1st January, 1777; Ensign, 1st June, 1778; retired 1st January, 1781; served subsequently as Lieutenant New York Levies.

Barr, Thomas (Pa). 3d Lieutenant of Captain Roman's Company Pennsylvania Artillery, 28th March, 1776; 2d Lieutenant, 15th May, 1776; Captain Lieutenant of Stevens' Battalion of Artillery, 9th November, 1776; company formed part of 3d Continental Artillery in 1778; Captain, 5th November, 1778, and served to October, 1779.

Barret, Criswell (Md). Cornet 3d Continental Dragoons, 6th February, 1777; taken prisoner at Tappan, 27th September, 1778; Lieutenant and Regimental Quartermaster, 2d· January, 1779; resigned 1st November, 1779.

Barret, Lemuel (Md). Captain of a Maryland Independent Company, 14th January, 1776, to — January, 1777.

Barret, William (N. C.). Captain 3d North Carolina, 16th April, 1776, to ——; 1st Lieutenant 3d Continental Dragoons, 10th April, 1778; Captain, — May, 1779; retained in Baylor's Consolidated Regiment of Dragoons, 9th November, 1782, and served to close of war. (Died 1815.)

Barrett, James (Mass). Captain Massachusetts Militia at Concord, 9th April, 1775. (Died 11 April, 1779.)

Barrett, James (N. Y.). Ensign 4th New York, 21st November, 1776; 2d Lieutenant, 8th November, 1777; retired 1st January, 1781.

Barrett, John, (Mass). Lieutenant Colonel Massachusetts Militia in 1775. (Died 1806.)

Barrett, Nathan (Mass). Captain Company of Minute Men, ——; wounded at Concord, 19th April, 1775; served as Major and Lieutenant-Colonel Massachusetts Militia, 1776-1779. (Died 1791.)

Barrett, Oliver (N. H.). Sergeant 4th New Hampshire, 4th December, 1776; Quartermaster Sergeant, 1st July, 1777; Ensign of Warner's Continental Regiment, 14th August, 1778; retired 1st January, 1781. (Died 1832.)

Barrett, Robert (Va). Captain Virginia Convention Guards, 13th January to 10th September, 1779.

Barrett, Thomas (N. Y.). Captain New York Militia, 1775-1776.

Barron, Isaac (Mass). Lieutenant 13th Massachusetts, 13th November, 1776; cashiered 11th May, 1778.

Barron, Jacob (Mass). Surgeon's Mate of Scammons Massachusetts Regiment, May to December, 1775; Surgeon's Mate on the Brig Freeman, 4th September, 1777; was captured and exchanged in 1778.

Baron, James (Va). Brigadier-General Virginia State Troops, 25th December, 1775, to 7th April, 1783.

Barron, John (Mass). Lieutenant Massachusetts Militia ——; killed at Concord, 19th April, 1775.

Barron, John (Vt). Lieutenant Vermont Militia in 1777.

Barron, Oliver (Mass). Captain Massachusetts Militia; wounded at Concord, 19th April, 1775.

Barron, Timothy (Vt). Captain of Bedel's Regiment Vermont Militia, 1st April, 1778, to 1st April, 1779.

Barrow, Jacob (N. C.). Lieutenant 7th North Carolina, 22d December, 1776, to ——.

Barrow, Samuel (N. C.). Lieutenant 7th North Carolina, 28th November, 1776, to ——.

Barry, Andrew (S. C.). Captain South Carolina Partisan Rangers, ——; wounded at Musgrove's Mills, 18th August, 1780. (Died 1811.)

Barry, John (S. C.). Captain South Carolina Militia in 1780.

Barry, Michael (Va). Surgeon 3d Continental Dragoons, 1st November, 1779, to ——.

Barstow, Joshua (Mass). Sergeant in Lexington Alarm, April, 1775; 2d Lieutenant of Thomas' Massachusetts Regiment, May to December, 1775.

Bartel, Peter (N. Y.). Captain New York Militia, 1775-1776.

Bartel, Philip (N. Y.). Captain New York Militia, 1775-1776.

Bartholomew, Benjamin (Md). Lieutenant and Adjutant 4th Maryland Infantry, — January, 1776; cashiered — March, 1778.

Bartholomew, Benjamin (Pa). 1st Lieutenant 4th Pennsylvania Battalion, 5th January, 1776; Captain 5th Pennsylvania, 2d October, 1776; wounded at Brandywine, 11th September, 1777; retired 1st January, 1783. (Died 31st March, 1812.)

Bartholomew, Joseph (Pa). 1st Lieutenant of Montgomery's Pennsylvania Battalion of the Flying Camp; taken prisoner at Fort Washington, 16th November, 1776.

Bartholomew, Joshua (Pa). 2d Lieutenant 9th Pennsylvania, 15th November, 1776; 1st Lieutenant, 30th November, 1777. (Died 16th March, 1778.)

Bartholomew, Moses (Pa). 2d Lieutenant 9th Pennsylvania, 15th November, 1776; 1st Lieutenant, 30th November, 1777. Died 16th March, 1778.

Bartleson, Ezra (Pa). 2d Lieutenant 2d Pennsylvania Battalion, 5th January, 1776; discharged 19th June, 1776.

Bartlett, Benjamin (N. Y.). Conductor of Stevens' Battalion of Artillery, 9th January to — August, 1777.

Bartlett, Daniel (Mass). Surgeon's Mate 4th Massachusetts, 1st January, 1777; transferred to 11th Massachusetts, 1st June, 1778; Surgeon, 12th September, 1780; retired 1st January, 1781. (Died 25th December, 1819.)

Bartlett, Daniel (Mass). Ensign 10th Massachusetts, 1st June, 1777, to ——.

Bartlett, Gershom (Vt). Lieutenant Vermont Militia in 1777.

Bartlett, John (R. I.). Surgeon Rhode Island State Troops, 15th January, 1776; Surgeon of Richmond's Regiment, Rhode Island Militia, 19th August, 1776; Physician and Surgeon-General Northern Department, 11th April, 1777; retired 1st January, 1781. (Died 3d March, 1820.)

Bartlett, Josiah (—). Surgeon's Mate Hospital Department in 1776 and 1777.

Bartlett, Josiah (N. H.). A signer of the Declaration of Independence; Colonel New Hampshire Militia, 1777-1779; subsequently Governor of New Hampshirt. (Died 19th May, 1795.)

Bartlett, Samuel (Mass). Lieutenant in Fellows' Massachusetts Regiment, April to December, 1775; Captain 21st Continental Infantry, 1st January to 31st December, 1776; Captain 9th Massachusetts, 1st January, 1777; resigned 6th March, 1778.

Bartlett, Thomas (N. H.). Captain Company of Minute Men in 1775; Lieutenant-Colonel and Colonel New Hampshire Militia, 1776 to 1782. (Died 1805.)

Bartley, John (Pa). Ensign 3d Pennsylvania, 5th January, 1776; 2d Lieutenant, 12th October, 1776; 1st Lieutenant 5th Pennsylvania, 1st January,

1777; Adjutant, 1st September, 1778; Captain Lieutenant, 13th June, 1779; retired 1st January, 1781.

Barton, John (N. C.). Captain North Carolina Militia at King's Mountain in October, 1780. (Died 1827.)

Barton, Joseph (R. I.). Lieutenant 1st Rhode Island Regiment, May to December, 1775.

Barton, Rufus (R. I.). 1st Lieutenant of Tallman's Regiment, Rhode Island Militia, 12th December, 1776, to — May, 1777.

Barton, William (Conn). Chaplain of Flower's Artillery Artificer Regiment, 1st May, 1777; retired 1st January, 1783.

Barton, William (N. J.). Ensign 4th New Jersey, 23d November, 1776; 2d Lieutenant, 17th February, 1777; 1st Lieutenant, 1st November, 1777; transferred to 1st New Jersey, 1st June, 1778; transferred to 2d New Jersey, 1st January, 1781; Captain, 28th December, 1781, and served to April, 1783.

Barton, William (Pa). Captain Lieutenant of Newman's Company, Pennsylvania Artillery, 2d December, 1776; Captain of Baldwin's Artillery Artificer Regiment, 1st May, 1777, to — March, 1783.

Barton, William (R. I.). Adjutant of Richmond's Rhode Island Regiment, 3d August, 1775; Captain, 1st November, 1775; Brigade-Major Rhode Island Troops, 19th August, 1776; Major of Stanton's Regiment Rhode Island State Troops, 12th December, 1776; Lieutenant-Colonel, 10th November, 1777. By the act of 25th July, 1777, it was "Resolved, that Congress have a just sense of the gallant behavior of Lieutenant-Colonel Barton, of a Militia Regiment of the State of Rhode Island and Providence Plantations, and the brave officers and men of his party, who distinguished their valor and address in making prisoners of Major-General Prescott, of the British army, and Major William Barrington, his Aide-de-Camp; and that an elegant sword be provided by the Commissary-General of Military Stores and presented to Liteutenant-Colonel Barton." Colonel of Stanton's Regiment, Rhode Island Militia, with rank and pay of Colonel Continental Army, 24th December, 1777, and served to close of war. (Died 22d October, 1831.)

Bartram, Job (Conn). Captain Connecticut Militia; wounded at Fairfield 7th July, 1779. (Died 19th July, 1813.)

Baskerville, Samuel (Va). Ensign 10th Virginia, 3d December, 1776; 2d Lieutenant, 2d January, 1777; 1st Lieutenant, 5th April, 1778; regiment designated, 6th Virginia; 14th September, 1778; taken prisoner at Charleston, 12th May, 1780; exchanged July, 1781; transferred to 1st Virginia, 1st January, 1781, and served to 15th November, 1783. (Died 29th August, 1830.)

Baskin, James (S. C.). Captain South Carolina Militia; wounded at Cherokutown, South Carolina, 26th June, 1776.

Baskin, William (S. C.). Captain South Carolina Militia; taken prisoner at Car's Fort, 10th February, 1779.

Bass, Joseph (Va). Lieutenant-Colonel Virginia Militia in 1777.

Bass, Samuel (Mass). Sergeant in Lexington Alarm, April, 1775; Sergeant of Marshall's Massachusetts Regiment, May to November, 1775; 1st Lieutenant 10th Massachusetts, 6th November, 1776; retired 9th April, 1779.

Bass, Samuel N., Jr. (Mass). Sergeant Lexington Alarm, April, 1775; Lieutenant Massachusetts Militia in 1776; 2d Lieutenant 3d Continental Artillery, 1st February, 1777; retired 1st January, 1781.

Bassett, Daniel (Mass). 2d Lieutenant 25th Continental Infantry, 1st January, 1776; 1st Lieutenant 14th Massachusetts, 6th November, 1776; resigned 26th November, 1777; served subsequently in Massachusetts Militia.

Bassett, Barachiah (Mass). Major Massachusetts Militia in 1776; Lieutenant-Colonel 14th Massachusetts, 19th November, 1776; retired 1st January, 1781. (Died 13th June, 1813.)

Bassett, Fortunatus (Mass). Sergeant in Gardner's Massachusetts Regiment, May to December, 1775; Sergeant 25th Continental Infantry, 1st January, 1776; 1st Lieutenant 14th Massachusetts, 6th November, 1776; omitted — June, 1778.

Bassett, Richard (Del). Captain Delaware Militia, 1779-1781; subsequently Governor of Delaware. (Died 18th September, 1815.)

Baston, William (Mass). 1st Lieutenant 18th Continental Infantry, 1st January to 31st December, 1776.

Batchelder, Archelaus (N. H.). 1st Lieutenant 27th Continental Infantry, 1st January to 31st December, 1776. (Died 18th December, 1828.)

Batchelder, Nathan (N. H.). Captain New Hampshire Militia, 1777-1778.

Batchelor, Archibald (Mass). 2d Lieutenant of Mansfield's Massachusetts Regiment, — May to — December, 1775; 2d Lieutenant 19th Continental Infantry, 1st January, 1776, to ——.

Batchelor, David (Mass). Lieutenant in Lexington Alarm, April, 1775; Captain of Read's Massachusetts Regiment, May, 1775, to December, 1775; Captain Massachusetts Militia, 1776-1779.

Batchelor, John (Mass). Lieutenant Lexington Alarm, April, 1775; Captain of Bridge's Massachusetts Regiment, — May, 1775, to December, 1775; Captain and Major Massachusetts Militia, 1776-1781.

Bateman, John (N. Y.). Adjutant 1st Canadian (Livingston's) Regiment, 18th December, 1776; left regiment 23d June, 1779, on leave for 12 months, and did not rejoin.

Bateman, William (Mass). Lieutenant and Adjutant 12th Massachusetts, 1st January, 1777; retired 1st April, 1779.

Bates, David (Conn). Captain Lieutenant of Warner's Continental Regiment, 13th February, 1777; Regimental Quartermaster, 14th November, 1778; cashiered 16th June, 1779.

Bates, David (N. Y.). 2d Lieutenant 4th New York, 21st March to — November, 1776.

Bates, Jacob (Mass). Ensign 3d Continental Infantry, 1st January, 1776, to ——.

Bates, James (R. I.). Ensign Rhode Island Militia in 1780.

Bates, Jonathan (R. I.). Lieutenant of Varnum's Rhode Island Regiment, 3d May, 1775, to December, 1775; Major Rhode Island Militia, 1779-1780.

Bates, Joseph (Mass). 1st Lieutenant 14th Massachusetts, 1st January, 1777; Captain, 8th October, 1779; transferred to 7th Massachusetts, 1st January, 1781; retired 1st January, 1783.

Bates, William (Va). Ensign 3d Virginia, 15th August, 1777; retired 14th September, 1778.

Battell, French (Del). Major Delaware Militia, 1775.

Battle, Ebenezer (Mass). Lieutenant of Gardner's Massachusetts Regiment, May to December, 1775.

Bauer, Jacob (Pa). 1st Lieutenant German Regiment, 8th July, 1776; Captain of Ottendorff's Battalion, 9th April, 1777; resigned 22d September, 1777. (Name also spelled Bower.)

Baugh, Robert (Va). Ensign and Regimental Quartermaster 15th Virginia, 28th November, 1776; resigned 11th October, 1777.

Bauman, Sebastian (N. Y.). Captain of a Company New York Artillery, 30th March, 1776; Captain 2d Continental Artillery, 1st January, 1777; Major, 12th September, 1778; transferred to Corps of Artillery, 17th June, 1783, and served to 20th June, 1784. (Died 19th October, 1803.)

Baury, Louis (De Ballerine) (France). Captain at the siege of Savannah in 1779. (Died 20th September, 1807.)

Baxter, —— (Pa). Colonel Pennsylvania Battalion of the Flying Camp. Killed at Fort Washington, 16th November, 1776.

Baxter, Andrew, Jr. (N. C.). Lieutenant North Carolina Militia; wounded at Camden 10th May, 1781. (Died 1814.)

Baxter, John (S. C.). Captain in Marion's Brigade; wounded at Quinby's Bridge 17th July, 1781.

Baxter, Joseph (Md). 2d Lieutenant of Smallwood's Maryland Regiment, 14th January, 1776; resigned May, 1776.

Baxter, William (Pa). Ensign 6th Pennsylvania, 15th February, 1777; retired 21st June, 1778.

Bayard, John (Pa). Major Pennsylvania Militia, 1775; Colonel of same, 1777-1779. (Died 7th January, 1807.)

Bayard, Stephen (Pa). Captain 2d Pennsylvania Battalion, 5th January, 1776; Major 8th Pennsylvania, 12th March, 1777, to rank from 4th October, 1776; wounded at Brandywine, 11th September, 1777; Lieutenant-Colonel, 23d September, 1777; transferred to 6th Pennsylvania, 17th January, 1781; transferred to 3d Pennsylvania, 1st January, 1783, and served to 3d November, 1783; Brevet Colonel, 30th September, 1783. (Died 13th September, 1815.)

Bayard, William (Pa). Ensign 1st Pennsylvania, 27th August, 1777. Died May, 1778.

Bayer, Michael—See Bowyer.

Bayles, Platt (N. J.). Captain and Major New Jersey Militia in 1776.

Bayley, Frye (Vt). Captain Vermont Militia in 1777; was a prisoner; when and where taken not stated.

Bayley, Jacob (Vt). Quartermaster of Bedell's Vermont Regiment, 1st April, 1778, to 1st April, 1779.

Bayley, Jacob (N. Y.). Brigadier General New York Militia. (Died 1815.)

Bayley, John (Va). Captain of Clark's Illinois Regiment, 29th March, 1780, to 1782.

Bayley, John Gideon (Vt). Captain Vermont Militia, 1777-1779.

Bayley, Joshua (N. H.). Captain New Hampshire Militia, 1777-1778.

Bayley Mountjoy—See Bailey.

Baylies, Ephraim (N. Y.). Captain New York Militia, 1776.

Baylies, Hodijah (Mass). 1st Lieutenant of Jackson's Continental Regiment, 1st March, 1777; Major and Aide-de-camp to General Lincoln, November, 1777; was taken prisoner at Charleston 12th May, 1780; Aide-de-camp to General Washington, 13th May, 1782, to 23d December, 1783. (Died 26th April, 1813.)

Baylis, Henry (Va). Ensign 6th Virginia, 15th August, 1777; Lieutenant, ——; retired 1st January, 1783.

Baylis, William (Va). Private 12th Virginia, 9th January, 1777; Regimental Paymaster, 27th August, 1777, and served as such to 15th December, 1779; Ensign 9th September, 1778; regiment designated 8th Virginia, 14th September, 1778; 1st Lieutenant, 18th February, 1781; retired 1st January, 1783. (Died 1843.)

Baylor, George (Va). Lieutenant-Colonel and Aide-de-camp to General Washington, 15th August, 1775, to 9th January, 1777; Colonel 3d Continental Dragoons, 9th January, 1777. By the act of 1st January, 1777, it was "Resolved, that a horse, properly caparisoned for service, be presented to Lieutenant-Colonel Baylor." Surprised, wounded and taken prisoner at Tappan, 28th September, 1778; exchanged ——. His regiment consolidated with the 1st Continental Dragoons, 9th November, 1782; retained in command of same and served to close of the war. Brevet Brigadier-General, 30th September, 1783. (Died — March, 1784.)

Baylor, John (Va). Lieutenant Third Continental Dragoons, 15th February, 1777; Captain, 1780, and served to close of the war. (Died 1788.)

Baylor, Walker (Va). Lieutenant Third Continental Dragoons, 28th June, 1777; Captain, — February, 1780; resigned 10th July, 1780. (Died 1823.)

Bayly, James (Ga). Lieutenant 2d Georgia, ——; on roll for August, 1778.

Baynham, John (Va). Cadet 6th Virginia, 28th February, 1776; 2d Lieutenant, 6th January, 1777. Died 21st August, 1777.

Baynham, Joseph (Va). 2d Lieutenant 3d Virginia, 18th October, 1776; resigned 31st December, 1777.

Baynton, John (Pa). Deputy Paymaster-General, 11th July, 1777; resigned 16th September, 1779.

Baytop, James (Va). 1st Lieutenant 7th Virginia, 7th March, 1776; Captain, 11th December, 1777; transferred to 5th Virginia, 14th September, 1778; resigned 12th May, 1779; Lieutenant-Colonel Virginia Militia in 1781.

Baytop, John (Va). Cadet 2d Virginia State Regiment, 12th August, 1777; Ensign, 1st June, 1778; 2d Lieutenant, 9th August, 1778; 1st Lieutenant, 1st May, 1779, and served to — January, 1782.

Baytop, Thomas (Va). Captain Lieutenant 1st Continental Artillery, 13th January, 1777; Captain, 5th February, 1778; resigned 11th December, 1779.

Beach, David (Conn). Sergeant 5th Connecticut, 1st January, 1777; Ensign, 15th December, 1777; transferred to 2d Connecticut, 1st January, 1781; Lieutenant, 15th November, 1781; retired 1st January, 1783. (Died 2d December, 1828.)

Beach, Elijah (Conn). 1st Lieutenant 5th Connecticut, 1st May to 5th December, 1775; Captain of Swift's Connecticut State Regiment, June to November, 1776.

Beach, Joseph, Jr. (Conn). Ensign of Douglas' Connecticut State Regiment, June to December, 1776. (Died 1802.)

Beach, Samuel (N. H.). Ensign of Warner's Continental Regiment, 14th April, 1777; Lieutenant, 14th September, 1778; retired 1st January, 1781. (Died 10th April, 1829.)

Beach, Wait (Conn). Ensign of Bradley's Connecticut State Regiment, June to December, 1776. (Died 1810.)

Beach, William (N. J.). 2d Lieutenant of Spencer's Continental Regiment, 18th February, 1777; 1st Lieutenant, 6th September, 1777; Captain Lieutenant, 12th April, 1779; resigned 8th July, 1779. (Name also spelled Beech.)

Beach, Zerah (Conn). Quartermaster of Burrall's Connecticut State Regiment, 30th August, 1776, to — January, 1777.

Beakley, Christian (Pa). 1st Lieutenant of Flower's Artillery Artificer Regiment, 3d February, 1777, to ——.

Beal, Benjamin (Mass). Private in Lexington Alarm, April, 1775; Sergeant in Greaton's Massachusetts Regiment, 27th April, 1775; Ensign, 22d June, 1775; 2d Lieutenant, 24th Continental Infantry, 1st January to 31st December, 1776; Captain Massachusetts Militia, 1777-1779.

Beal, John (Md). Captain of a Maryland Independent Company; dismissed 23d October, 1780.

Beale, Jeremiah (Ga). 1st Lieutenant 1st Georgia, 12th December, 1775, to ——.

Beale, Tavener (Va). 1st Lieutenant 8th Virginia, — May, 1776; resigned 1st March, 1777. (Died 1810.)

Beale, Zachariah (N. H.). 1st Lieutenant 2d New Hampshire, 18th June to — December, 1775; 1st Lieutenant 8th Continental Infantry, 1st January, 1776; Captain 3d New Hampshire, 8th November, 1776. Died 27th October, 1777, of wounds received at Fort Mercer 22d October, 1777.

Beale, Zaphaniah (Ga). 2d Lieutenant 1st Georgia, 12th December, 1775, to ——.

Beall, Elisha (Md). 2d Lieutenant of Reazin Beall's Maryland Independent Company, 14th January to December, 1776. (Died 1837.)

Beall, Isaac (Va). Captain 4th Virginia, 10th February, 1776; Major, 21st February, 1777; resigned 19th June, 1778. (Died 1797.)

Beall, Lloyd (Md). 2d Lieutenant 7th Maryland, 1st April, 1777; taken prisoner at Germantown, 4th October, 1777; 1st Lieutenant, 8th June, 1779; transferred to 1st Maryland, 1st January, 1781; Captain, 10th February, 1781; transferred to 2d Maryland, 1st January, 1783; retained in Maryland Battalion, 12th April, 1783, and served to 15th November, 1783.

Beall, Reazin (Md). Captain of an Independent Maryland Company, 14th January, 1776; Brigadier-General of the Maryland part of the Flying Camp, 16th August to 1st December, 1776.

Beall, Robert (Va). Captain 13th Virginia, 16th December, 1776; Regiment designated 9th Virginia, 14th September, 1778; transferred to 7th Virginia, 12th February, 1781; retired 1st January, 1783.

Beall, Robert (Va). Ensign 5th Virginia, 10th February, 1776; 2d Lieutenant, 16th September, 1776; 1st Lieutenant, 11th February, 1777; transferred to 3d Virginia, 14th September, 1778; Captain, 19th June, 1779; taken prisoner at Charleston, 12th May, 1780; retired 12th February, 1781. (Died 1789)

Beall, Robert (Va). 1st Lieutenant 8th Virginia, 10th December, 1775; transferred to 4th Virginia, 14th September, 1778; resigned 31st December, 1780. (Died 1788.)

Beall, Samuel (Md). 2d Lieutenant 4th Maryland, 1st August, 1781; retired 1st January, 1783.

Beall, Thaddeus (Md). 2d Lieutenant 1st Maryland Battalion of the Flying Camp, July to December, 1776; Brigade-Major to General Beall in September, 1776.

Beall, Thomas (Md). 2d Lieutenant of Bracco's Independent Maryland Company, 27th August, 1776; 1st Lieutenant 2d Maryland, 10th December, 1776; resigned 17th April, 1777. (Died 1823.

Beall, William (Pa). 1st Lieutenant of Clotz Battalion Pennsylvania Flying Camp, 6th September, 1776; taken prisoner at Fort Washington, 16th November, 1776.

Beall, William Dent (Md). 2d Lieutenant 3d Maryland Battalion of the Flying Camp, — July to 1st December, 1776; Captain 6th Maryland, 10th December, 1776; transferred to 5th Maryland, 1st January, 1781; Major 2d Maryland, 6th November, 1781; retired 1st April, 1783; Major 9th United States Infantry, 8th January, 1799; honorably discharged 15th June, 1800; Lieutenant-Colonel 5th United States Infantry, 24th April, 1812; resigned 15th August, 1812. (Died 24th September, 1829.)

Beames, John H. (Md). 2d Lieutenant of Smallwood's Maryland Regiment, 14th January, 1776; Captain 1st Maryland, 1st January, 1777; resigned 20th December, 1777.

Beamis, Eleazer (Mass). Ensign 4th Massachusetts, 1st January, 1777; Lieutenant, 5th November, 1778; resigned 18th August, 1779. (Name also spelled Bemus.)

Beanes, Colmore (Md). Surgeon's Mate 2d Maryland, 25th June, 1777; resigned 12th October, 1777.

Beanham, Joseph (Va). 2d Lieutenant 3d Virginia, 18th October, 1776; resigned 31st December, 1777.

Beard, Jonas (S. C.). Colonel South Carolina Militia, 1778.

Beard, Samuel (Pa). 2d Lieutenant 1st Pennsylvania, 2d June, 1778; omitted February, 1780.

Beardsley, Ebenezer (Conn). Surgeon's Mate 7th Connecticut, 7th July to 10th December, 1775; Surgeon 22d Continental Infantry, 1st January to 31st December, 1776; Surgeon 6th Connecticut, 1st January, 1777; resigned 1st June, 1778.

Beardsley, Gershom (N. Y.). Hospital Surgeon's Mate, 1776 to 1779. (Died 13th November, 1826.)

Beardsley, Nehemiah (Conn). Captain 5th Connecticut, 1st May to 11th December, 1775.

Beardsley, Phineas (Conn). Captain 7th Connecticut, 1st January, 1777; resigned 15th November, 1778.

Beaton, John (Pa). Captain Montgomery's Pennsylvania Battalion of the Flying Camp; taken prisoner at Fort Washington 16th November, 1776.

Beattie, David (Va). Captain Virginia Militia at Kings Mountain in October, 1780.

Beattie, Thomas (N. C.). Major North Carolina Militia, 1776.

Beattie, John (Va). Ensign Virginia Militia Regiment; wounded at King's Mountain 7th October, 1780. (Died 1814.)

Beatty, Charles Clinton (Pa). 2d Lieutenant 4th Pennsylvania Battalion, 5th January, 1776; accidentally killed 16th February, 1777.

Beatty, Erskurius (Pa). 2d Lieutenant 4th Pennsylvania, 2d May, 1777; wounded at Germantown, 4th October, 1777; 1st Lieutenant, 2d June, 1778; Regimental Paymaster, 1st June, 1779, to 17th May, 1780; Regimental Adjutant, 17th May, 1780; transferred to 3d Pennsylvania, 1st January, 1783; Regimental Paymaster, 22d May, 1783, and served to 3d November, 1783; Lieutenant United States Infantry, 12th August, 1784; Captain 1st Infantry United States Army, 29th September, 1789; Major, 5th March, 1792; in 1st Sub-Legion, 4th September, 1792; resigned 27th November, 1792. (Died 3d February, 1823.)

Beatty, John (Pa). Captain 5th Pennsylvania Battalion, 5th January, 1776; Major 6th Pennsylvania, 12th October, 1776; taken prisoner at Fort Washington 16th November, 1776; exchanged 8th May, 1778; Major 6th Pennsylvania, 1st January, 1777, to rank from 12th October, 1776; Colonel Commissary-General of Prisoners, 28th May, 1778; resigned 31st March, 1780. (Died 30th May, 1826.)

Beatty, Reading (Pa). Ensign 5th Pennsylvania Battalion, 5th January, 1776; 2d Lieutenant, 10th August, 1776; taken prisoner at Fort Washington, 16th November, 1776; exchanged 8th May, 1778, and joined the 6th Pennsylvania as Surgeon's Mate; Surgeon 11th Pennsylvania, 1st May, 1780; transferred to 4th Continental Artillery, 10th February, 1781, and served to — June, 1783. (Died 29th October, 1831.)

Beatty, Thomas (Md). 2d Lieutenant 5th Maryland, 8th September, 1781; transferred to 2d Maryland, 1st January, 1783; retained in Maryland Battalion April, 1783, and served to 15th November, 1783.

Beatty, William (Md). Colonel Maryland Battalion of the Flying Camp, July to December, 1776. (Died 1801.)

Beatty, William, Jr. (Md). Ensign 1st Maryland Battalion of the Flying Camp, July to December, 1776; 1st Lieutenant 7th Maryland, 10th December, 1776; Captain, 14th September, 1778; transferred to 1st Maryland, 1st January, 1781; killed at Hobkirk's Hill 25th April, 1781.

Beaulieu, Louis I de (France). Lieutenant 1st Cavalry Pulaski Legion, 1st March, 1779; taken prisoner at Savannah, 9th October, 1779; exchanged ——; severely wounded at Charleston, 12th May, 1780; on leave to close of war.

Beaumont, Ebenezer (Mass). Adjutant of Fellow's Massachusetts Regiment in Lexington Alarm, April, 1775; Adjutant of Warner's Continental Regiment, 5th July, 1776; Brigade-Major to General Paterson, — September, 1776; severely wounded at Ticonderoga, 6th July, 1777, and retired 12th August, 1779. (Name also spelled Bement.)

Beaumont, William (Conn). Sergeant 8th Connecticut, 20th March, 1777; Ensign, 15th December, 1777; Regimental Quartermaster, 24th May, 1778; Lieutenant, 28th October, 1779; transferred to 5th Connecticut, 1st January, 1781; retired 1st January, 1783. (Died 1807.)

Beavans, Robert (N. C.). 1st Lieutenant 2d North Carolina, May, 1776; on roll for August, 1776.

Beavers, Joseph (N. J.). Colonel New Jersey Militia, 1776-1777.

Beck, John (Va). Sergeant 13th Virginia, 8th February, 1777; Regiment designated 9th Virginia, 14th September, 1778; Ensign, 31st October, 1778; 1st Lieutenant, 15th December, 1779; transferred to 7th Virginia, 12th February, 1781; retired 1st January, 1783.

Becker, Abraham (N. Y.). 1st Lieutenant 4th New York, 21st March to — November, 1776.

Becker, David (N. Y.). Ensign 4th New York, — March to — November, 1776.

Beckham, ——. See also **Bickham**.

Beekham, Abner (Ga). Captain Georgia Artillery Company, 15th August, 1781, to 15th February, 1782. (Name also spelled Bickham.)

Beckley, John (Conn). 1st Lieutenant of Wolcott's Connecticut State Regiment, 1775-1776.

Beckwith, Ansolm (—). 1st Lieutenant; taken prisoner at Fort Washington 16th November, 1776.

Beckwith, Phineas (Conn). Quartermaster-Sergeant 4th Connecticut, 15th January, 1777; Ensign, 25th October, 1780; transferred to 1st Connecticut, 1st January, 1781; cashiered 24th October, 1782. (Died 24th July, 1822.)

Bedaulx, Charles Frederick de (France). Brevet Captain Continental Army, 10th May, 1777; Lieutenant-Colonel 1st Cavalry Pulaski Legion, 10th December, 1778, and served to ——.

Bedel, Timothy (N. H.). Captain New Hampshire Rangers, — June, 1775; Colonel New Hampshire Rangers, 23d June to — December, 1775; Colonel New Hampshire Rangers, 22d January, 1776; cashiered 1st August, 1776; Colonel and Brigadier-General Vermont Militia, —— 1777, to ——, 1781. (Died — February, 1787.)

Bedford, Gunning (Del). Major Deputy Quartermaster-General, New

York Department, 17th July, 1775; Lieutenant-Colonel Delaware Regiment, 19th January, 1776, to — January, 1777; wounded at White Plains, 28th October, 1776; was also Muster-Master-General, 18th June, 1776, to 12th April, 1777. (Died 30th September, 1797.)

Bedfield, John (Va). See **Belfield.**

Bedinger, Daniel (Va). 1st Lieutenant 11th Virginia, 14th November, 1776; taken prisoner at Brandywine 11th September, 1777; Regiment designated 7th Virginia, 14th September, 1778, but does not appear to have rejoined the Regiment. (Died 1818.)

Bedinger, Daniel (Va). Ensign 4th Virginia, 7th May, 1782, to close of war.

Bedinger, George Michael (Va). Served as a Captain of a Virginia Rifle Company, July, 1775, to ——, 1781; Major of a Militia Regiment at the battle of Blue Licks, 19th August, 1782; Major of the Levies in 1791; Major of Infantry United States Army, 11th March, 1792; assigned to 3d Sub-Legion 4th September, 1792; resigned 28th February, 1793. (Died 7th December, 1843.)

Bedinger, Henry (Va). Served as a Private and Sergeant in Hugh Stephenson's Company of Virginia Riflemen, July to October, 1775; 2d Lieutenant of Shepherd's Virginia Rifle Company, 25th July, 1776; 2d Lieutenant, 11th Virginia, 13th November, 1776; taken prisoner at Fort Washington, 16th November, 1776; was not exchanged until 25th October, 1780; promoted 1st Lieutenant, 23d September, 1777; transferred to 7th Virginia, 14th September, 1778; transferred to 3d Virginia, 12th February, 1781; Captain, 21st May, 1781, and served to close of war.

Bedkin, Henry (Pa). 1st Lieutenant in Ottendorff's Battalion, 5th December, 1776; Adjutant 4th Continental Dragoons, 24th January, 1777; Captain Pulaski Legion, 5th April, 1778; served to close of war.

Beebe, Asa (Conn). 2d Lieutenant of Wadsworth's Connecticut State Regiment, June to December, 1776.

Beebe, Bezaleel (Conn). 1st Lieutenant 1st Connecticut, 1st May to 1st December, 1775; Captain of Bradley's Connecticut State Regiment, —June, 1776; taken prisoner at Fort Washington, 16th November, 1776; exchanged — July, 1777; served subsequently as Major, Lieutenant-Colonel and Colonel Connecticut Militia, ——. (Died 29th May, 1824.)

Beebe, James (Conn). Ensign of Swift's Connecticut State Regiment, July to November, 1776; 1st Lieutenant 2d Connecticut, 1st January, 1777; Captain, 25th December, 1777; transferred to Sappers-Miners, 1st September, 1779; resigned 8th June, 1781.

Beebe, Martin (N. Y.). Major New York Militia in 1778.

Beebe, Roswell (N. Y.). 2d Lieutenant 2d New York, 28th June, 1775, to — January, 1776.

Beecher, Amos (Conn). 2d Lieutenant of Douglas' Connecticut State Regiment, June to December, 1776.

Beede, Daniel, Jr. (N. H.). Captain New Hampshire Militia, 1776.

Beeker, Cornelius (N. Y.). 2d Lieutenant 1st New York, 24th February, 1776, to ——.

Beekman, Barnard (S. C.). Captain 4th South Carolina (Artillery), 14th November, 1775; Major, 18th November, 1776; Lieutenant-Colonel, 25th October, 1778; Colonel, 20th June, 1779; taken prisoner at Charleston, 12th May, 1780; prisoner on parole to close of war.

Beekman, James (N. Y.). Captain New York Militia, 1776.

Beekman, John H. (N. Y.). 2d Lieutenant 1st New York, 28th June, 1775, to — January, 1776; served subsequently as Captain and Lieutenant-Colonel New York Militia.

Beekman, John J. (N. Y.). 1st Lieutenant and Captain New York Militia, 1775-1776.

Beekman, John M. (N. Y.). Captain New York Militia, 1775-1776.

Beekman, Samuel (S. C.). Lieutenant 2d South Carolina, March, 1780, and served to close of war.

Beekman, Theophilus (N. Y.). Captain of Lasher's Regiment New York Militia, June to December, 1776.

Beekman, Thomas (N. Y.). 2d Lieutenant of Lasher's Regiment New York Militia, June to December, 1776; Cornet 2d Continental Dragoons, 26th January, 1777; Lieutenant, 20th October, 1777; resigned in 1778.

Beekman, Tjerck—also spelled Tierick and Jerrick—(N. Y.). Ensign 2d New York, 21st November, 1776; 2d Lieutenant, 1st September, 1778; retired 1st January, 1781. (Died — December, 1791.)

Beeks, John (Va). Ensign 9th Virginia, 1st November, 1778, to ——; in service January, 1780.

Beeks, William (N. C.) Lieutenant and Adjutant 7th North Carolina, 22d November, 1777; retired 1st June, 1778.

Beeler, James (Pa). 2d Lieutenant 8th Pennsylvania, 9th August, 1776, to ——.

Beene, Jesse (N. C.). Captain North Carolina Militia at King's Mountain, October, 1780. (Name also spelled Bean.)

Beers, Nathan (Conn). Paymaster of Webb's Continental Regiment, 1st May, 1778; Regiment became 3d Connecticut, 1st January, 1783; retained in Swift's Connecticut Regiment in June, 1783, and served to 3d November, 1783. (Died 10th February, 1849.)

Beesley, Jonathan (N. J.). Captain New Jersey Militia; wounded and taken prisoner, near Bordentown, 8th May, 1778, and died in hands of the enemy in June, 1778.

Beeson, Edward (N. C.). Captain North Carolina Militia, ——, 1779.

Belcher, John (Conn). 2d Lieutenant 7th Connecticut, 6th July, 1775; 1st Lieutenant, 1st September to 12th December, 1775.

Belcher, Joseph (R. I.). Colonel Rhode Island Militia Regiment in 1775 and 1776.

Belcher, Joseph, Jr. (R. I.). Lieutenant of Babcock's Rhode Island State Regiment, 15th January, 1776, to ——.

Belcher, William (Conn). Captain Selden's Connecticut State Regiment, 20th June to 25th December, 1776; Captain 1st Connecticut, 1st January, 1777; resigned 3d January, 1778. (Died 1801.)

Belcher, William (R. I.). Ensign in Babcock's Rhode Island State Regiment, 15th January, 1776; Lieutenant, 19th August, 1776; 1st Lieutenant 1st Rhode Island, 1st January, 1777, to ——.

Belden, Ezekiel Porter (Conn). 2d Lieutenant of Bradley's Connecticut State Regiment, 20th June to 26th December, 1776; Lieutenant 2d Continental Dragoons, 20th December, 1776; Captain, 2d April, 1777; resigned 11th June, 1780. (Died 9th October, 1824.)

Belden, Thomas (Conn). Colonel Connecticut Militia, 1776-1777. (Died 1834.)

Belding, Moses (N. H.). Ensign of Wingate's Regiment New Hampshire Militia in 1776; 1st Lieutenant 3d New Hampshire, 8th November, 1776; retired 1st September, 1778.

Belding, Simeon (Conn). Quartermaster 22d Continental Infantry, 1st January to 31st December, 1776; Quartermaster 3d Connecticut, 1st January, 1777; Brigade Quartermaster, 1st July, 1777; Deputy Quartermaster-General, 25th May, 1778, to 15th November, 1781; retained his rank in the line, and was transferred to 1st Connecticut, 1st January, 1781, and resigned 15th November, 1781.

Belfield, John (Va). Lieutenant Company of Virginia Dragoons, 18th June, 1776; Captain 1st Continental Dragoons, 15th March, 1777; Major 3d Dragoons, ——, 1781; retired 9th November, 1782. (Name also spelled Bedfield.)

Belin, Allard (S. C.). Lieutenant 1st South Carolina, 1776; resigned 31st May, 1777.

Belknap, Ezekiel (N. H.). Lieutenant New Hampshire Militia, 1777.

Belknap, Jacob (R. I.). 1st Lieutenant of Tallman's Regiment Rhode Island Militia, 12th December, 1776, to — March, 1777.

Belknap, John (N. Y.). Captain 3d New York, 28th June, 1775. (Died 26th October, 1775.)

Belknap, William (N. Y.). Ensign 1st Canadian (Livingston's) Regiment, 15th April, 1776; 2d Lieutenant, 18th December, 1776; retired 1st January, 1781. (Died 18th July, 1831.)

Belknap, William (N. Y.). 2d Lieutenant of Nicholson's New York Regiment, March to November, 1776.

Bell, Beriah (Conn). 1st Lieutenant 19th Continental Infantry, 1st January to 31st December, 1776.

Bell, Frederick Mordaunt (N. H.). 1st Lieutenant 2d New Hampshire, 23d May to — December, 1775; Captain 8th Continental Infantry, 1st January, 1776; Captain 2d New Hampshire, 8th November, 1776; wounded at Stillwater, 19th September, 1776, and died from his wound 9th October, 1777.

Bell, Green (N. C.). Captain 7th North Carolina, 28th November, 1776, to ——.

Bell, Henry (Pa). 1st Lieutenant Pennsylvania Battalion of the Flying

Camp; taken prisoner at Fort Washington, 16th November, 1776.

Bell, Henry (Va). Lieutenant 3d Continental Dragoons, ——, 1780, to 9th November, 1782.

Bell, Jesse (Conn). Captain Connecticut Militia, 1776.

Bell, John (N. H.). Colonel New Hampshire Militia, 1777.

Bell, John (Va). Ensign 6th Virginia, 26th February, 1776; 2d Lieutenant, 28th December, 1776; severely wounded at Brandywine, 11th September, 1777, and did not rejoin the army. (Died 9th November, 1840.)

Bell, Jonathan (Conn). Captain Connecticut Militia, 1776.

Bell, Patterson (Pa). Colonel Pennsylvania Militia, 1777-1778.

Bell, Robert (N. C.). Ensign 10th North Carolina, 18th May, 1781; Lieutenant 8th September, 1781; transferred to 2d North Carolina, 6th February, 1782; served to close of war.

Bell, Robert (N. C.). Lieutenant 1st North Carolina; on roll for — November, 1777.

Bell, Robert (Va). Quartermaster 2d Virginia, ——; on roll for June, 1777.

Bell, Samuel (Md). Ensign of Grayson's Continental Regiment, 8th March, 1777; 2d Lieutenant, 8th June, 1777; 1st Lieutenant, 3d February, 1778; transferred to Gist's Regiment, 22d April, 1779; retired 1st January, 1781. (Died 28th March, 1828.)

Bell, Thomas (N. Y.). Ensign 2d Canadian (Hazen's) Regiment, 9th January, 1777; 2d Lieutenant, 1st September, 1777; 1st Lieutenant, — February, 1779; omitted June, 1779.

Bell, Thomas (Va). 2d Lieutenant of Grayson's Continental Regiment, 8th March, 1777; 1st Lieutenant, 8th June, 1777; Captain, 19th April, 1778; transferred to Gist's Regiment, 22d April, 1779; resigned 7th May, 1779. (Died 1791.)

Bell, William.—See Beall.

Bell, William Mordaunt (N. H.). Ensign 8th Continental Infantry, 6th September, 1776; Ensign, 2d New Hampshire, 8th November, 1776; 2d Lieutenant, 6th May, 1777; Regimental Adjutant, 18th August, 1777; 1st Lieutenant, 22d December, 1777; Captain, 21st November, 1782, and served to close of war.

Bellecour, Le Brun.—See Le Brun.

Bellew, David.—See Ballew.

Ballinger, Fred (N. Y.). Lieutenant-Colonel New York Militia; taken prisoner at Oriskany, 6th August, 1777.

Bellinger, George (Va). Served as a Volunteer Lieutenant, and was taken prisoner at the Siege of Charleston, 14th April, 1780.

Bellinger, John (N. Y.). Lieutenant New York Militia; killed at Oriskany, 6th August, 1777.

Bellinger, Peter (N. Y.). Colonel New York Militia, 1776-1783. (Died 1823.)

Bellows, Benjamin (N. H.). Colonel New Hampshire Militia in 1777 and 1778, and Brigadier General of same, 1781-1782. (Died June, 1802.)

Bellows, John (N. H.). Major New Hampshire Militia, 1777-1778. (Died 1812.)

Belt, John Sprigg (Md). 1st Lieutenant 3d Maryland Battalion of the Flying Camp, July, 1776; taken prisoner at Fort Washington, 16th November, 1776; 1st Lieutenant 4th Maryland, 10th December, 1776; Captain, 15th December, 1777; transferred to 1st Maryland 1st January, 1781; retained in Maryland Battalion, April, 1783, and served to 15th November, 1783; Brevet Major 30th September, 1783.

Beman, Ezra (Mass). 1st Lieutenant of Ward's Massachusetts Regiment, 23d May, 1775, to — December, 1775; Major Massachusetts Militia in 1777.

Bement, Ebenezer.—See Beaumont.

Bemis, Edmund (Mass). Lieutenant in Lexington Alarm, April, 1775; Captain of Whitcomb's Massachusetts Regiment, — May, 1775, to — December, 1775. (Died 1810.)

Bemper, Abraham (Pa). Ensign Pennsylvania State Regiment, 18th April, 1777; Regiment designated 13th Pennsylvania, 12th November, 1777; resigned 1st April, 1778.

Benedict, Amos (Conn). Adjutant 5th Connecticut, 1st January, 1777. Died 7th February, 1777.

Benedict, Caleb (N. Y.). Ensign New York Militia, ——; taken prisoner at Schoharie 17th October, 1780, and was a prisoner to 21st May, 1783.

Benedict, Elisha (N. Y.). Captain 2d New York, 28th June, 1775, to — January, 1776; served subsequently as Captain of Nicholson's Regiment New York Militia. (Died 1798.)

Benedict, Daniel (Conn). Captain Connecticut Militia; taken prisoner on the retreat from New York in November, 1776.

Benedict, Joseph (N. Y.). Captain 4th New York, 28th June, 1775; Major 1st New York, 8th March, 1776; resigned 27th April, 1776; served subsequently as Lieutenant-Colonel New York Militia.

Benedict, Noble (Conn). Captain 5th Connecticut, 1st May to 13th December, 1775; Captain of Bradley's Connecticut State Regiment, 30th June, 1776; taken prisoner at Fort Washington, 16th November, 1776.

Benedict, Peter (N. Y.). 1st Lieutenant 2d New York, 21st November, 1776; resigned — March, 1777.

Benedict, Samuel (Conn). 1st Lieutenant of Bradley's Connecticut State Regiment, June to December, 1776.

Beneker, John G. (Pa). 2d Lieutenant 5th Pennsylvania, 7th June, 1777; cashiered 15th November, 1777.

Benezet, Samuel (Pa). Captain 5th Pennsylvania Battalion, 5th January, 1776; Major 6th Pennsylvania, 14th February, 1777, to rank from 3d October, 1776, but does not appear to have ever joined the latter regiment; also reported as resigned.

Benham, Isaac (Conn.) Captain Connecticut Militia, 1776-1777.

Benham, Silas (Conn). 2d Lieutenant 2d Connecticut, 1st January, 1777; killed at White Marsh, 7th December, 1777.

Benison, William (S. C.). Major of Marion's Brigade; killed at Wambaw Creek 14th February, 1782.

Benjamin, Aaron (Conn). Ensign 8th Connecticut, 1st January, 1777; 2d Lieutenant, 14th February, 1778; 1st Lieutenant, 7th May, 1778; Regimental Adjutant, 1st April, 1780, to January, 1783; transferred to 5th Connecticut, 1st January, 1781; transferred to 3d Connecticut, 1st January, 1783; retained in Swift's Connecticut Regiment, 3d June, 1783, and served to 3d November, 1783; Lieutenant-Colonel 37th United States Infantry, 11th March, 1813; honorably discharged 15th June, 1815. (Died 11th January, 1829.)

Benjamin, James (Conn). Sergeant 1st Connecticut, 10th February, 1777;

Ensign, 20th June, 1779; transferred to 5th Connecticut, 1st January, 1781; retired 31st March, 1782.

Benjamin, John (Conn). Sergeant 2d Continental Artillery, 5th January, 1777; wounded at Ridgefield 27th April, 1777; 2d Lieutenant, 12th September, 1778; resigned 14th November, 1780; served subsequently as Major Connecticut Militia. (Died 1796.)

Benjamin, Peter (Va). Captain 11th Virginia, 13th December, 1776; retired 14th September, 1778.

Benjamin, Samuel (Mass). Sergeant 6th Continental Infantry, 13th January, 1776; Ensign 8th Massachusetts, 1st January, 1777; 2d Lieutenant, 3d October, 1777; 1st Lieutenant, 28th March, 1779, and served to June, 1783. (Died 14th April, 1814.)

Bennett, Caleb Prew. (Del). Private and Sergeant Delaware Regiment in 1776; Ensign Delaware Regiment, 5th April, 1777; wounded at Germantown 4th October, 1777; 2d Lieutenant, 16th August, 1778; 1st Lieutenant, 1st March, 1779, and served to close of war. (Died 9th May, 1836.)

Bennett, Christopher (R. I.). Ensign 3d Rhode Island, 3d May to December, 1775.

Bennett, Ebenezer (Mass). Adjutant of Fellow's Massachusetts Regiment, May to December, 1775; served subsequently as an officer Massachusetts Militia.

Bennett, Ignace (Pa). Lieutenant in Armand's Partisan Corps, 1780 and 1781.

Bennett, James (Conn). Sergeant-Major of 7th Connecticut, 25th January, 1777; Ensign, 1st September, 1777; 2d Lieutenant, 8th September, 1780; transferred to 2d Connecticut, 1st January, 1781; retained in Swift's Connecticut Regiment, June, 1783; and served to 3d November, 1783. (Died 14th November, 1819.)

Bennett, Matthew (Pa). Lieutenant of Baxter's Pennsylvania Battalion of the Flying Camp, 19th September, 1776; taken prisoner at Fort Washington, 16th November, 1776; exchanged 8th December, 1780, and did not return to the army.

Bennett, Patrick (Pa). Quartermaster 4th Continental Dragoons in 1777.

Bennett, Thomas (S. C.). Captain in Marion's Brigade in 1781.

Bennett, William (Va). Ensign of Grayson's Continental Regiment, 23d July, 1777; 2d Lieutenant, 1st December, 1777; resigned 13th April, 1778.

Benneville, Daniel.—See **De Benneville.**

Benny, Thomas (Mass). Surgeon's Mate 12th Massachusetts, 1st January, 1777; resigned 28th August, 1777.

Benson, Joshua (Mass). Lieutenant in Lexington Alarm, April, 1775; 1st Lieutenant of Cotton's Massachusetts Regiment, May to December, 1775; 1st Lieutenant 21st Continental Infantry, 1st January to 31st December; 1776; Captain 5th Massachusetts, 1st January, 1777; Brevet-Major, 30th September, 1783; served to close of war.

Benson Mark. (See Bentley.)

Benson, Perry (Md). 1st Lieutenant Maryland Battalion of the Flying Camp, July, 1776; 1st Lieutenant 5th Maryland, 10th December, 1776; Captain, 11th March, 1776; wounded at Nelson's Ferry, 20th August, 1780; wounded at Ninety-Six, 18th June, 1781; retained in Maryland Battalion, April, 1783, and served to 15th November, 1783; Brevet Major, 30th September, 1783. (Died 2d October, 1827.)

Benson, Robert (N. Y.). Lieutenant-Colonel and Aide-de-Camp to Governor Clinton of New York, 1777 to 1783.

Benstead, Alexander (Pa). Quartermaster of Hart's Battalion Pennsylvania Flying Camp, July, 1776; Paymaster 10th Pennsylvania, 1st December, 1776; Lieutenant, 1st March, 1780; retired 1st January, 1781.

Bent, Silas (Mass). Private in Lexington Alarm, April, 1775; 1st Lieutenant of Nixon's Massachusetts Regiment, 1st May to — December, 1775; 1st Lieutenant 4th Continental Infantry, 1st January to 31st December, 1776.

Bent, William (Mass). Captain of Heath's Massachusetts Regiment, May to December, 1775; Captain 24th Continental Infantry, 1st January to 31st December, 1776; Captain Massachusetts Militia in 1778.

Bentalou, Paul (Md). 2d Lieutenant German Regiment, 25th September, 1776; 1st Lieutenant, 21st June, 1777; resigned 10th December, 1777; Captain 1st Cavalry Pulaski Legion, 12th April, 1778; wounded at Savannah, 9th October, 1779; retired 1st January, 1781.

Bentham, James (S. C.). Lieutenant South Carolina Militia in 1775.

Bentley, David (R. I.). 2d Lieutenant of Stanton's Regiment Rhode Island Militia, 12th December, 1776, to — May, 1777.

Bentley, John (Ga). Lieutenant Georgia Militia; killed in action with Indians in Georgia in March, 1779.

Bentley, Joseph (Conn). Quartermaster Sergeant of 9th Connecticut Regiment, 19th November, 1777; Ensign, 17th March, 1778; resigned 9th April, 1780.

Bentley, Mark (Md). 1st Lieutenant 5th Maryland, 10th December, 1776; Captain Lieutenant, 21st May, 1779; resigned 1st June, 1779. (Name appears also as Benson and Benton.)

Bentley, William (Ga). Captain Georgia Militia in 1779.

Bentley, William (Va). 2d Lieutenant 5th Virginia, 7th March, 1776; 1st Lieutenant, 18th December, 1776; Captain Lieutenant, 26th December, 1776; transferred to 3d Virginia, 14th September, 1778; Captain, 1st May, 1779; taken prisoner at Charleston, 12th May, 1780, and was on parole to close of war.

Benton, Joseph (Pa). Surgeon of Hart's Battalion of the Pennsylvania Flying Camp, July to December, 1776.

Benton, Lemuel (S. C.). Lieutenant-Colonel South Carolina Militia, 1781-1783.

Benton, Selah (Conn). Ensign 19th Continental Infantry, 1st January, 1776; 2d Lieutenant, 10th August, 1776; 1st Lieutenant 8th Connecticut, 1st January, 1777; Captain, 21st August, 1780; transferred to 5th Connecticut, 1st January, 1781; transferred to 1st Connecticut, 1st January, 1783, and served to 3d June, 1783. (Died 12th May, 1812.)

Beraud, Matthew (S. C.). Major South Carolina Militia; killed at Savannah, 9th October, 1779.

Bernard, Peter (Va). Captain 2d Virginia State Regiment, 10th April, 1777; resigned 24th August, 1779.

Bernard, Richard (Va). Captain 5th Virginia, 9th March, 1776, to — May, 1777. (Died 23d January, 1785.)

Bernard, William (Va). 2d Lieutenant 7th Virginia, 29th February, 1776. Died 27th April, 1776.

Bernie, ——, Major Pulaski Legion, ——; killed at Monk's Corner, 14th May, 1780.

Berrien, John (Ga). 2d Lieutenant 1st Georgia, 7th January, 1776; 1st Lieutenant, 18th November, 1776; Captain, 27th May, 1777; Brigade Major North Carolina Brigade, 8th January, 1778; wounded at Monmouth, 28th June, 1778; Aide-de-Camp to General McIntosh, 1776 to 1778; Brevet Captain, 30th September, 1783; served to close of war. (Died 1815.)

Berry, Asahel (N. Y.). Ensign 5th New York, 21st November, 1776; resigned — July, 1777.

Berry, Ebenezer (N. J.). Captain and Major New Jersey Militia, 1177-1779.

Berry, Divan (Conn). Ensign in the Lexington Alarm, April, 1775; 2d Lieutenant of Swift's Connecticut State Regiment, July to November, 1776. (Died 1783.)

Berry, Enoch (Va). Ensign of a Virginia Regiment in 1781.

Berry, George (Va). 1st Lieutenant 13th Virginia, 16th December, 1776; regiment designated 9th Virginia, 14th September, 1778; Captain Lieutenant, November, 1778; Captain, 3d January, 1779; transferred to 7th Virginia, 12th February, 1781, and served to June, 1783. (Died 29th October, 1823.)

Berry, James (Mass). Sergeant of Gardner's Massachusetts Regiment, May to December, 1775; Ensign 25th Continental Infantry, 1st January, 1776; Ensign 10th Massachusetts, 6th November, 1776; furloughed 6th November, 1777, and did not rejoin. (Died 3d November, 1823.)

Berry, John (Mass). Ensign 11th Massachusetts, 6th November, 1776; omitted March, 1778.

Berry, Nathaniel (Va). Surgeon 1st Virginia State Regiment, 1st July, 1779; resigned 26th October, 1779.

Berry, Nicholas (Va). Surgeon Virginia State Regiment, 1st July, 1779; resigned 26th October, 1779.

Berry, Peleg (R. I.). Ensign and Lieutenant Rhode Island Militia, — November, 1775, to March, 1777.

Berry, Thomas (Del). Sergeant Delaware Regiment, 15th May, 1777; Ensign, 5th April, 1777; 2d Lieutenant, 28th January, 1778; resigned 7th September, 1778. (Died 1818.)

Berry, Thomas (Va). Captain 8th Virginia, 27th March, 1776; retired 30th September, 1778.

Berry, William (Va). Ensign 12th Virginia, 8th January, 1777; resigned 9th December, 1777.

Berryhill, William (N. C.). Lieutenant 1st North Carolina, 1st September, 1776, to ——.

Berthaud, Adam (Md). Lieutenant Maryland Militia, 1776.

Bertie, Thomas (N. C.). Ensign 8th North Carolina, 28th November, 1776, to —— —.

Berwick, Everton (Mass). 2d Lieutenant of Fellows' Massachusetts Regiment, — May to December, 1775.

Berwick, James (Va). Ensign 8th Virginia, 17th February, 1776; 2d Lieutenant, 1st October, 1776; 1st Lieutenant, 5th April, 1777; resigned 20th May, 1778

Best, John (Va). Ensign 1st Virginia State Regiment, 14th September, 1777; Lieutenant, 1st October, 1778, and served to 1st June, 1779.

Bethel, William (N. C.). Captain North Carolina Militia at Guilford, 15th March, 1781.

Betkin, Henry (Pa). Adjutant Pennsylvania Battalion of the Flying Camp, July to December, 1776; Adjutant 4th Continental Dragoons, 24th January, 1777; Lieutenant, 19th November, 1777; Captain, 5th April, 1778, and served to close of war. (Name also spelled Bedkin.)

Betson, John (Del). Ensign Delaware Regiment, 5th April, 1777; 2d Lieutenant, 14th October, 1777; resigned 2d September, 1778.

Bettin, Adam (Pa). 1st Lieutenant 3d Pennsylvania Battalion, 6th January, 1776; taken prisoner at Fort Washington, 16th November, 1776; exchanged 8th May, 1778; transferred to 10th Pennsylvania, 1st July, 1778; Captain 4th Pennsylvania, to rank from 4th October, 1776; killed 1st January, 1781, at the revolt of the Pennsylvania Line.

Betts, Isaiah (Conn). Private 2d Connecticut, 2d January, 1777; Corporal, 1st May, 1778; Sergeant, 1st February, 1780; Ensign, 3d April, 1780; transferred to 3d Connecticut, 1st January, 1781; retired 17th July, 1781.

Betts, James (Conn). 1st Lieutenant of Silliman's Connecticut State Regiment, June to December, 1776.

Betts, James (N. Y.). 1st Lieutenant 5th New York, 21st November, 1776; resigned 1st March, 1780.

Betts, Nathaniel (Mass). Sergeant 13th Massachusetts, 10th April, 1777; Sergeant-Major, 1st April, 1779; Ensign,

10th April, 1779; discharged 1st May, 1780.

Betts, Stephen (Conn.). 1st Lieutenant 7th Connecticut, 6th July to 23d December, 1775; 1st Lieutenant 19th Continental Infantry, 1st January to 31st December, 1776; Captain 2d Connecticut, 1st January, 1777; transferred to 3d Connecticut, 1st January, 1781; wounded at Yorktown, 14th October, 1781; served to close of war; Brevet Major, 30th September, 1783. (Died 23d November, 1832.)

Bevans, Giles (Pa). Ensign 4th Pennsylvania, 2d June, 1778, to ——.

Bevier, Philip DuBois (N. Y.). 1st Lieutenant 3d New York, 28th June, 1775, to — January, 1776; Captain of DuBois' New York Regiment, 26th June, 1776; Captain 5th New York, 21st November, 1776, to rank from 26th June, 1776; retired 1st January, 1781.

Beviere, de fuzon Francis (Mass). Surgeon's Mate 7th Massachusetts, 26th August, 1778; taken prisoner at Cherry Valley, 10th November, 1778; prisoner to close of war.

Bevin, .Charles (Md). Ensign 6th Maryland, 25th February, 1777; 2d Lieutenant, 7th October, 1777; 1st Lieutenant, 18th May, 1779; resigned 1st July, 1780.

Bevins, Wilder (Pa). 2d Lieutenant 4th Pennsylvania, 2d June, 1778; 1st Lieutenant, 11th May, 1779; transferred to 1st Pennsylvania, 1st January, 1783, and served to close of war. (Died 3d August, 1809.)

Bibb, Richard (Va). Captain Virginia Militia, 1776-1778.

Bibbs, —— (Ga): Lieutenant of Marbury's Regiment Georgia Militia; dismissed 12th March, 1778.

Bicker, Henry (Pa). Major 3d Pennsylvania Battalion, 4th January, 1776; transferred to 10th Pennsylvania, 25th October, 1776; Lieutenant-Colonel 6th Pennsylvania, 5th December, 1776; Colonel 2d Pennsylvania, 6th ᵀune, 1777; retired 1st July, 1778.

Bicker, Henry, Jr. (Pa). Ensign 3d Pennsylvania Battalion, 8th January, 1776; 2d Lieutenant, 1st September, 1776; taken prisoner at Fort Washington, 16th November, 1776; exchanged 8th May, 1778; Captain 4th Pennsylvania, 15th May, 1778; retired 1st January, 1783.

Bicker, Victor (N. Y.). 2d Lieutenant 1st New York, 28th June, 1775 to 31st March, 1776.

Bicker, Walter (Pa). 2d Lieutenant 3d Pennsylvania Battalion, 8th January, 1776; taken prisoner at Fort Washington, 16th November, 1776; exchanged 8th May, 1778; Captain 4th Pennsylvania, 15th May, 1778; retired 17th January, 1781. (Died 6th April, 1821.)

Bickerstaff, John (N. C.). Ensign 2d North Carolina, 8th June, 1776, to ——.

Bickford, Benjamin (R. I.). Lieutenant of Elliott's Regiment Rhode Island State Artillery, 12th December, 1776, to 1777.

Bickham, Abner (Ga). Captain Georgia Militia, 15th August, 1781, to 15th February, 1782. (Died 29th January. 1834.)

Bickham, James (Pa). Ensign Penn-State Regiment, 18th April, 1777; 2d Lieutenant, 1st August, 1777; regiment designated 13th Pennsylvania, 12th November, 1777; transferred to 2d Pennsylvania, 1st July, 1778; was in service February, 1779.

Bickham, John (Pa). 2d Lieutenant 9th Pennsylvania, 15th November, 1776; 1st Lieutenant, 3d March, 1777; retired 1st July, 1778.

Biddle, Clement (Pa). Lieutenant-Colonel Deputy Quartermaster General of the Flying Camp, 8th July to 1st December, 1776; ·Commissary-General of Forage, 1st July, 1777, to — June, 1780; Colonel Quartermaster-General of Pennsylvania, 11th September, 1781, to close of war. (Died 14th July, 1814.)

Bigelow, John (Conn). Served as a volunteer under Arnold at Ticonderoga in — May, 1775; Captain Independent Company Connecticut Artillery, 19th January to — December, 1776; served subsequently as Major Connecticut Artillery Militia. (Died 1780.)

Bigelow, Timothy (Mass). Captain in Lexington Alarm, April, 1775; Captain of Ward's Massachusetts Regiment, 23d May, 1775; Major, 17th June, 1775; taken prisoner at Quebec, 31st December, 1775; was appointed Major 21st Continental Infantry, 1st January, 1776, but did not join the regiment, as he was not exchanged until May, 1776; Colonel 15th Massachusetts, 1st January, 1777; retired 1st January, 1781. (Died 31st March, 1790.)

Biggs, Benjamin (Va). 1st Lieutenant 13th Virginia, 28th December, 1776; regiment designated 9th Virginia, 14th September, 1778; Captain Lieutenant, 7th November, 1778; Captain, 1st December, 1778; transferred to 7th Virginia, 12th February, 1781, and served to close of war.

Biggs, John (Del). Captain Deleware Militia, 1780-1781.

Bigham, John. (See Bingham.

Bilbo, John (Ga). Lieutenant of Marbury's Regiment Georgia Militia; dismissed 12th March, 1778; Captain Georgia Militia; died of wounds at Cherokee Hill, 8th May, 1780, received a few days previously.

Bill, Beriah (Conn). Ensign 3d Connecticut, 1st May to 10th December, 1775; 2d Lieutenant 20th Continental Infantry, 1st January, 1776; 1st Lieutenant, 20th June, 1776; 1st Lieutenant 4th Connecticut, 1st January, 1777; Captain, 24th November, 1777; retired 15th November, 1778.

Bill, David (Conn). Ensign of Selden's Connecticut State Regiment, June to December, 1776.

Bill, Jabez (Mass). Sergeant of Danielson's Massachusetts Regiment, May to December, 1775; Sergeant 4th Continental Infanty, 1st January to 31st December, 1776; Sergeant 4th Massachusetts, 1st January, 1777; Ensign, 1st November, 1777; Lieutenant and Regimental Quartermaster, 14th April, 1780; transferred to 4th Massachusetts, 1st January, 1781; retired 1st January, 1783.

Bill, Thomas (Conn). Ensign Lexington Alarm, April, 1775; Ensign 3d Connecticut, 1st May to 18th December, 1775; 1st Lieutenant of Burrall's Connecticut State Regiment, 19th January to — May, 1776. ·

Billings, Andrew (N. Y.). Captain 3d New York, 28th June, 1775, to — January, 1776.

Billings, Benjamin (Mass). Lieutenant 7th Massachusetts, 1st January, 1777; discharged 30th September, 1778.

Billings, Daniel (Conn). Sergeant 6th Connecticut, 5th May to 10th December, 1775; Ensign 10th Continental Infantry, 1st January to 31st December, 1776.

Billings, Samuel (Mass). Captain of Learned's Massachusetts Regiment, May 1775, to December, 1775. (Died 1789.)

Billings, Stephen (Conn). Sergeant 6th Connecticut, 8th May to 18th December, 1775; Ensign of Mott's Connecticut State Regiment, June to December, 1776; 2d Lieutenant 7th Connecticut, 1st January, 1777; 1st Lieutenand, 3d November, 1777; Captain Lieu-

tenant, 19th September, 1780; Captain, 5th October, 1780; transferred to 2d Connecticut, 1st January, 1781; retired 1st January, 1783. (Died 1814.)

Billups, Richard (Va). Captain Virginia Militia, 1776-1777.

Bingham, Elijah (Conn). Captain of Selden's Connecticut State Regiment, June to December, 1776.

Bingham, John (Pa). Private 4th Pennsylvania, 20th March, 1776; Corporal, 20th May, 1776; Sergeant 5th Pennsylvania, 1st January, 1777; Ensign, 1st June, 1778; Lieutenant, 1st February, 1779; cashiered 29th May, 1781.

Bingham, Lemuel (Conn). 2d Lieutenant 3d Connecticut, 1st May to 10th December, 1775.

Bingham, Melatiah (Conn). 2d Lieutenant 3d Connecticut, 1st May to 7th December, 1775.

Bingham, Nathaniel (Conn). Ensign 8th Connecticut, 6th July to 16th December, 1775; served as Commissary in 1777.

Bingham, Thomas (Conn). 1st Lieutenant 8th Connecticut, 1st January, 1777; resigned 15th March, 1778.

Binney, Barnabas (Mass). Surgeon Hospital Department, May, 1776; Hospital Physician and Surgeon, 6th October, 1780, to close of war. (Died 21st June, 1787.)

Bird, Benjamin. (See Burd.)

Bird, James (Pa). 2d Lieutenant 3d Pennsylvania, 1st April, 1777; resigned 3d November, 1777.

Bird, John (Ga). Lieutenant of a Georgia Regiment in service, May, 1778.

Bird, Jonathan (Conn). Surgeon Connecticut Militia in 1776 and 1777.

Bird, Mark (Pa). Colonel Pennsylvania Militia, 1776.

Bird, Richard (Md). Ensign 4th Maryland Battalion of the Flying Camp, — July to — December, 1776; 2d Lieutenant 5th Maryland, 10th December, 1776; 1st Lieutenant, 10th May, 1777; Captain Lieutenant, 1st June, 1779; Captain, 12th June, 1780; transferred to 1st Maryland, 1st January, 1781. (Died 30th September, 1782.)

Bird, William (Pa). 1st Lieutenant 2d Pennsylvania Battalion, 5th January, 1776; taken prisoner at Three Rivers, 8th June, 1776; exchanged ——; Captain 4th Continental Dragoons, 10th January, 1777; resigned 8th July, 1778.

Birdsall, Benjamin (N. Y.). Captain, Major and Lieutenant-Colonel New York Militia, 1775-1781. (Died 1828.)

Birdsall, Daniel (N. Y.). 2d Lieutenant 5th New York, 21st November, 1776; resigned 26th December, 1779.

Birge, Jonathan (Conn). Captain of Sage's Connecticut State Regiment, 20th June, 1776; wounded at White Plains, 28th October, 1776, and died of wounds, 8th November, 1776.

Bishop, John (N. J.). Sergeant 1st New Jersey, 1st March, 1777; Sergeant-Major, 1st January, 1778; Ensign, 1st February, 1779, and served to April, 1783.

Bishop, John (Pa). 1st Lieutenant of Cunningham's Pennsylvania Battalion of the Flying Camp, July to December, 1776.

Bishop, Nathaniel (Conn). 2d Lieutenant 20th Continental Infantry, 1st January to 31st December, 1776; 1st Lieutenant 4th Connecticut, 1st January, 1777; retired 15th November, 1778.

Bishop, Stephen (Conn). Ensign 8th Connecticut, 1st January, 1777; 2d Lieutenant, 16th January, 1778; resigned 9th March, 1778.

Bissell, Ebenezer Fitch (Conn). Private in Lexington Alarm, April, 1775; Lieutenant 8th Connecticut, 16th July, 1775; Captain 17th Continental Infantry, 1st January, 1776; taken prisoner at Long Island, 27th August, 1776. (Died 1814.)

Bissell, Elihu (Conn). Surgeon's Mate of Sherburne's Continental Regiment, 10th September, 1777; resigned 24th April, 1780.

Bissell, Ozias (Conn). Lieutenant in Lexington Alarm, April, 1775; 1st Lieutenant 8th Connecticut, 1st May 1775; Captain, 1st September, 1775; Captain 17th Continental Infantry, 1st January, 1776; wounded and taken prisoner at Long Island, 27th August, 1776; Captain of Moseley's Connecticut Militia Regiment, 1778; taken prisoner at Horse Neck, 26th February, 1779. (Died 1822.)

Bissell, Russell (Conn). Private in Lexington Alarm, April, 1775; Private 4th Connecticut, 23d May to 10th December, 1775; Ensign of Wells' Connecticut State Regiment; taken prisoner at Horse Neck, 15th December, 1780.

Bissell, Samuel (Mass). Ensign of Little's Massachusetts Regiment, May to December, 1775.

Bissell Samuel (R. I.). Ensign 1st Rhode Island, 3d May, 1775; 2d Lieutenant 9th Continental Infantry, 1st January, 1776; 1st Lieutenant, 13th March to 31st December, 1776. (Died 28th February, 1825.)

Bissell, Thomas (Mass). Lieutenant of Little's Massa Regiment, May to December, 1775.

Bitner, Henry (Pa). Lieutenant Pennsylvania Battalion Flying Camp, July, 1776, wounded and taken prisoner at Fort Washington, 16th November, 1776.

Bittinger, Nicholas (Pa). Captain 2d Battalion Pennsylvania Flying Camp, July, 1776; taken prisoner at Fort Washington, 16th November, 1776. (Died 1804.)

Black, James (Del). Major Delaware Militia, 1779-1781.

Black, James (N. Y.). 1st Lieutenant of Malcolm's New York Regiment, 4th July to December, 1776; Captain of Malcolm's Continental Regiment, 11th March, 1777; transferred to Spencer's Continental Regiment, 22d April, 1779, and resigned 23d April, 1779.

Black, James (Pa). Ensign 2d Pennsylvania Battalion, 5th January, 1776; 2d Lieutenant 3d Pennsylvania, 1st January, 1777; resigned 14th September, 1778.

Black, .John (Mass). Captain of Brewer's Massachusetts Regiment, — May, 1775, to ——.

Black, Samuel (R. I.). Ensign 2d Rhode Island Regiment, 3d May, 1775, to ——.

Blackall, William Ball (—). See **Ball**.

Blackburn, William (Va). Lieutenant of Campbell's Virginia Riflemen —; killed at King's Mountain, 7th October, 1780.

Blackden, Samuel (—). See **Blagden**.

Blackiston, Ebenezer (Md). 2d Lieutenant 4th Continental Artillery, 17th March, 1777; resigned 16th June, 1778. (Name also spelled Blackson.)

Blackiston, John (Md). 2d Lieutenant 2d Maryland, 17th April, 1777; resigned 30th April, 1777.

Blackleach, John (Conn). 1st Lieutenant of Bradley's Connecticut State Regiment, 20th June, 1776; taken prisoner at Fort Washington, 16th November, 1776.

Blackler, William (Mass). Captain of Glover's Massachusetts Regiment, 19th May to December, 1775; Captain Massachusetts Militia, 1776-1777. (Died 1818.)

Blackley, Ebenezer (N. C.). Surgeon's Mate 10th North Carolina; on roll for July, 1778.

Blackley, John (N. Y.). Ensign of Nicholson's New York Regiment, 21st April, 1776; 2d Lieutenant, June, 1776; 2d Lieutenant 1st Canadian (Livingston's) Regiment, 18th December, 1776; resigned 10th July, 1779. (Name also spelled Blakeley and Blackney.)

Blacklock, John (Va). Captain Virginia Militia, 1776-1777.

Blackman, Elijah (Conn). Captain of Sherburne's Continental Regiment, 1st January, 1777; resigned 1st March, 1779. (Died 15th May, 1822.)

Blackman, Nathaniel (Conn). 2d Lieutenant 5th Connecticut, 1st May to 29th October, 1775.

Blackman, Samuel, Jr. (Conn). 1st Lieutenant 1st Connecticut, 1st May to 29th October, 1775.

Blackmar, Nathaniel (R. I.). Captain 2d Rhode Island, 3d May to — December, 1775; Captain Rhode Island Militia, 1776-1777.

Blackmore, George (Va). Corporal and Sergeant 2d Virginia, May, 1776, until appointed Ensign 2d Virginia, 4th July, 1779; taken prisoner at Charleston, 12th May, 1780; Lieutenant, 18th February, 1781; exchanged — July, 1781; resigned, 1st April, 1782.

Blackney, William (N. Y.). Ensign of Nicholson's New York Regiment, March to November, 1776.

Blackson, Ebenezer.—See **Blackiston.**

Blackwell, Jacob (N. Y.). Colonel New York Militia in 1776.

Blackwell, John E. (Va). 1st Lieutenant 3d Virginia, 29th April, 1776; wounded at Brandywine, 11th September, 1777; Captain, 15th September, 1777; taken prisoner at Charleston, 12th May, 1780; prisoner on parole to close of war; Brevet Major, 30th September, 1783. (Died 1808.)

Blackwell, Joseph (Va). 2d Lieutenant 10th Virginia, 7th February, 1777; 1st Lieutenant, 30th November, 1777; regiment designated 6th Virginia, 14th September, 1788; taken prisoner at Charleston, 12th May, 1780; exchanged — June, 1781; Captain, 22d March, 1779; retired 1st January, 1783. (Died 8th September, 1823.)

Blackwell, Joseph (Va). 2d Lieutenant 3d Virginia, 29th April, 1776; resigned 14th April, 1778.

Blackwell, Robert (Pa). Chaplain Wayne's Pennsylvania Brigade 20th May, 1778; served to — January, 1781. (Died 1831.)

Blackwell, Samuel (Va). Captain Virginia Artillery in 1780.

Blackwell, Samuel (Va). Captain Virginia State Regiment, 1778 to 1781.

Blackwell, Thomas (Va). Captain 10th Virginia, 19th November, 1776; retired 14th September, 1778. (Died 28th April, 1831.)

Blackwell ,William (Va). Captain 11th Virginia, 31st July, 1776; resigned 10th January, 1778.

Blagden, Samuel (Conn). Major Aide-de-Camp to General Wooster, 17th September, 1775, to — December, 1776; Major 2d Continental Dragoons, 24th December, 1776; Lieutenant-Colonel, 7th April, 1777; resigned 1st August, 1779. (Name also spelled Blackden.)

Blague, Joseph (Conn). Captain of Wadsworth's Connecticut State Regiment, June to December, 1776.

Blaine, Ephraim (Pa). Commissary 8th Pennsylvania, 17th October, 1776; Commissary of Supplies Continental Army, 1st April, 1777; Deputy Commissary-General of Purchases, 6th August, 1777; Commissary-General of Purchases, 1st January, 1780, to 24th July, 1782. (Died 1804.)

Blair, John (N. J.). Ensign 4th New Jersey, 23d November, 1776; 2d Lieutenant 3d New Jersey, 1st May, 1777; 1st Lieutenant, 1st November, 1779; Regimental Adjutant, 1st November, 1780; transferred to 1st New Jersey, 1st January, 1781, and served to — April, 1783.

Blair, John (N. Y.). Lieutenant-Colonel New York Militia, 1778-1780.

Blair, John (Pa). 2d Lieutenant 7th Pennsylvania, 15th November, 1776; resigned — 29th April, 1779. (Also called William Blair.)

Blair, John (Va). 1st Lieutenant 1st Continental Artillery, 13th January, 1777; Captain Lieutenant, 30th November, 1777; died 18th August, 1780, of wounds received at Camden, 16th August, 1780.

Blair, John (Va). Captain 9th Virginia, 17th December, 1776. (Died 25th March, 1777.)

Blair, Samuel (Pa). Chaplain of Thompson's Pennsylvania Rifle Regiment, 9th November, 1775; Chaplain 1st Continental Infantry, 1st January to 31st December, 1776; Chaplain, 1st Pennsylvania, 1st March, 1777; resigned 11th August, 1777; Chaplain Artillery Brigade, 1st March, 1779, to 20th June, 1780. (Died 23d September, 1818.)

Blair, Thomas (Pa). 2d Lieutenant Pennsylvania Militia; wounded at Guelph's Mills, 11th December, 1777.

Blaisdell, Nicholas (Mass). Lieutenant 13th Massachusetts, 13th November, 1776; discharged 13th July, 1779.

Blaisdell, Samuel (Mass). Private in Lexington Alarm, April, 1775; Corporal and Sergeant 16th Continental Infantry, 1st January to 31st December, 1776; Sergeant, 8th Massachusetts, 1st January, 1777; Sergeant-Major, 9th October, 1777; Ensign, 26th November, 1779; retired 1st January, 1781.

Blake, Edward, Jr. (Mass). Private in Lexington Alarm, April, 1775; 2d Lieutenant of Knox's Regiment Continental Artillery, August to December, 1776; Sergeant 3d Continental Artillery, 14th February, 1777; 2d Lieutenant 3d Continental Artillery, 10th September, 1778; transferred to Corps of Artillery, 17th June, 1783, and served to 3d November, 1783. (Died 1792.)

Blake, Edward (Mass). Captain of Brewer's Massachusetts Regiment, May to December, 1775; served subsequently in Massachusetts Militia.

Blake, George (Mass). 1st Lieutenant of Fellows' Massachusetts Regiment, May to December, 1775.

Blake, James (N. Y.). 2d Lieutenant 3d New York, 21st November, 1776; omitted April, 1777.

Blake, John (Mass). Private in Lexington Alarm, April, 1775; Ensign 5th Massachusetts, 1st January, 1777; 2d Lieutenant, 1st November, 1777; resigned 14th October, 1780.

Blake, John (Pa). 1st Lieutenant of McVaugh's Regiment Pennsylvania Militia; taken prisoner at his home ,14th February, 1778.

Blake, John (S. C.). 1st Lieutenant 1st South Carolina, 17th June, 1775, to ——.

Blake, Jonathan (N. Y.). Captain of Malcolm's New York Regiment, June

to November, 1776; Captain of Baldwin's Artillery Artificer Regiment, 1777; cashiered, 25th August, 1779.

Blake, Joseph (Mass). 2d Lieutenant Knox's Regiment Continental Artillery, 20th December, 1775; taken prisoner at Fort Washington, 16th November, 1776; exchanged ——; Captain Lieutenant 3d Continental Artillery, 1st January, 1777. Died 28th October, 1778.

Blake, Nathan (Mass). Ensign 13th Continental Infantry, 1st January to 31st December, 1776.

Blake, Steward (Mass). Private in Lexington Alarm, April, 1775; 2d Lieutenant of Fellows' Massachusetts Regiment, — May to December, 1775.

Blake, Thomas (N. H.). Ensign 1st New Hampshire, 8th November, 1776; 2d Lieutenant, 12th May, 1778; 1st Lieutenant, 24th March, 1780, and served to close of war.

Blake, Timothy (N. H.). Sergeant 1st New Hampshire, 23d April, 1775; Ensign 5th Continental Infantry, 1st January, 1776; 2d Lieutenant, 14th August to 31st December, 1776.

Blakeley, Christopher (Pa). 1st Lieutenant of Baldwin's Artillery Artificer Regiment, 3d February, 1777; Captain Lieutenant, 3d December, 1777; omitted — May, 1778.

Blakeley, Gabriel (Pa). 1st Lieutenant of Watt's Pennsylvania Battalion of the Flying Camp, — July, 1776; taken prisoner at Long Island, 27th August, 1776; exchanged 22d November, 1780.

Blakeley, John. (See Blackley.)

Blakeley, Tilley (Conn). 1st Lieutenant of Gay's Connecticut State Regiment, June to December, 1776.

Blakeney, John. (See Blackley.)

Blakeney, William (Va). Captain Virginia Militia, 1779-1781. (Died 14th July, 1821.)

Blakesley, James (Conn). 1st Lieutenant 1st Connecticut, 1st May to 1st December, 1775; Captain New York Militia in 1780. (Died 1782.)

Blakesley, Josiah (Conn). Ensign of Sage's Connecticut State Regiment, June to December, 1776.

Blakesley, Tilley (N. H.). 1st Lieutenant Green Mountain Boys, 27th July to December, 1775; 1st Lieutenant of Warren's Continental Regiment, 16th April, 1776; deserted 18th July, 1777.

Blanchard, Andrew (Mass). Quartermaster of Baldwin's Artillery Artificer Regiment, 7th December, 1777, to 1st July, 1780.

Blanchard, Elias (R. I.). Ensign 1st Rhode Island, 10th February, 1777; resigned 30th September, 1778. (Died 8th November, 1822.)

Blanchard, James (N. H.). Quartermaster 3d New Hampshire, 8th November, 1776, to 1st June, 1778; Regimental Paymaster, 1st June, 1778, to 1st January, 1781; rank of 2d Lieutenant from 22d May, 1779; retired 1st January, 1781.

Blanchard, Jeremiah (Mass). 1st Lieutenant of Bridge's Massachusetts Regiment, 29th April to November, 1775; served subsequently in Massachusetts Militia. (Died 1824.)

Blanchard, John (Mass). 1st Lieutenant 9th Massachusetts, 1st January, 1777; Captain, 1st March, 1777; transferred to 4th Massachusetts, 12th June, 1783; Brevet Major, 30th September, 1783; served to 3d November, 1783. (Died 9th August, 1821.)

Blanchard, John (Mass). Surgeon's Mate Hospital Department in 1776.

Blanchard, Rynear (N. J.). 1st Lieutenant 3d New Jersey, 8th March, 1776; resigned 13th September, 1776.

Blanchard, Samuel (Mass). Surgeon's Mate of Gerrish's Massachusetts Regiment, 8th June to — December, 1775.

Blanchard, William (Mass). 1st Lieutenant of Bridge's Massachusetts Regiment, May to December, 1775; 1st Lieutenant 11th Continental Infantry, 1st January to 31st December, 1776.

Blanchard, William (Vt). 1st Lieutenant Vermont Militia; taken prisoner 3d May, 1782; where, not stated.

Bland, Theodorick (Va). Captain of a Company Virginia Light Dragoons, 14th June, 1776; Major Light Dragoons, 4th December, 1776; Colonel 1st Continental Dragoons, 25th November, 1776; resigned 10th December, 1776. (Died 1st June, 1790.)

Blankenburg, Frederick (Pa). 1st Lieutenant 1st Pennsylvania Battalion, 27th October, 1775, to ——.

Blanton, Rowland (N. C.). Ensign 7th North Carolina, 28th November, 1776, to ——.

Blauvelt, Abraham J. (N. J.). Captain New Jersey Militia in 1776.

Bledsoe, Anthony (Va). Major and Colonel Virginia Militia, 1776-1779.

Bleeker, John J. (N. Y.). Captain New York Militia, 1775-1776.

Bleeker, John N. (N. Y.). Assistant Deputy Commissary-General Northern Department, 3d August, 1775, to ——; was also Captain New York Militia in 1775. (Died 1825.)

Bleeker, Leonard (N. Y.). 2d Lieutenant 1st New York, 28th June, 1775; 1st Lieutenant, 14th May, 1776; Captain 3d New York, 21st November, 1776; Brigade Major to General Clinton, 19th June to 22d August, 1779; Brigade Major under Lafayette, May to October, 1781; transferred to 1st New York, 1st January, 1783; Brevet Major, 30th September, 1783; served to 3d November, 1783. (Died 9th March, 1844.)

Blewer, George (Pa). 2d Lieutenant 4th Pennsylvania, December, 1776; taken prisoner at Germantown, 4th October, 1777; exchanged 29th January, 1781; 1st Lieutenant, 16th May, 1778; transferred to 1st Pennsylvania, 1st January, 1783, and served to close of war.

Bliss, Brenton (R. I.). Ensign of Lippitt's Rhode Island Regiment of Militia, 19th August, 1776, to January, 1777.

Bliss, Elias (Conn). Ensign of Wadsworth's Connecticut State Regiment, June to December, 1776.

Bliss, John (Conn). 2d Lieutenant of Swift's Connecticut State Regiment, July to November, 1776.

Bliss, Joseph (Mass). 2d Lieutenant 3d Continental Artillery, 1st February, 1777; transferred to Corps of Artillery, 17th June, 1783; Paymaster of the Corps of Artillery, 29th January, 1784, and served to 20th June, 1784. (Died 1819.)

Bliss, Samuel (Mass). Captain of Walker's Massachusetts Regiment, — May, 1775, to December, 1775.

Bliss, Thomas Theodore (Mass). Captain of Patersen's Massachusetts Regiment, May to December, 1775; Captain 15th Continental Infantry, 1st January, 1776; taken prisoner at the Cedars, 18th May, 1776; Captain 2d Continental Artillery, 1st January, 1777; taken prisoner at Monmouth, 28th June, 1778; exchanged 9th January, 1781, and did not rejoin regiment.

Bliss, William (R. I.). Ensign Rhode Island Militia in 1781.

Bliven, Isaac Ross (R. I.). Surgeon of Lippitt's Rhode Island Regiment, 19th August, 1776, to January, 1777.

Bliven, John (N. Y.). Major New York Militia ——; wounded and taken prisoner at Oriskany, 6th August, 1777, and died in captivity.

Blodget, Caleb (N. H.). Private 2d New Hampshire, 1st April, 1777; Sergeant, 20th July, 1777; Ensign, 16th September, 1777; Regimental Quartermaster, 1st January, 1781; transferred to 1st New Hampshire, 1st June, 1782, and served to close of war. (Drowned 12th August, 1789.)

Blodget, James (Mass). 2d Lieutenant of Brewer's Massachusetts Regiment, — May, 1775, to December, 1775.

Blodget, Samuel (N. H.). 2d Lieutenant 6th Continental Infantry, 1st January, 1776; 1st Lieutenant, 18th June, 1776; Captain 2d New Hampshire, 8th November, 1776; wounded at Skenesborough, 7th July, 1777; resigned 22d December, 1777. (Died 1st September, 1807.)

Blodget, Silas (Conn.). Sergeant in the Lexington Alarm, — April, 1775; 2d Lieutenant 2d Connecticut, 1st May to 18th December, 1775; 1st Lieutenant 2d Connecticut, 1st January, 1777; resigned 17th June, 1778. (Died 27th August, 1824.)

Blodget, William (R. I.). Secretary to Rhode Island Troops in 1775; 2d Lieutenant 11th Continental Infantry, 1st January, 1776; Aide-de-Camp to General Greene, 29th June, 1776, to — January, 1777.

Bloodgood, William (N. Y.). Ensign 1st New York, 19th June, 1781; resigned 3d December, 1782. (Died 1810.)

Bloom, Daniel (Pa). Sergeant 2d Pennsylvania Battalion, 5th January to — December, 1776; served subsequently as Lieutenant Pennsylvania Militia.

Bloom, Jacob (N. Y.). Captain New York Militia; taken prisoner at Long Island 27th August, 1776.

Bloomfield, Jarvis (N. J.). Private 3d New Jersey, 14th March, 1777; wounded at Germantown, 4th October, 1777; Ensign, 1st May, 1777; 2d Lieutenant, 1st November, 1777; Regimental Adjutant, 7th July, 1780; resigned 31st October, 1780.

Bloomfield, Joseph (N. J.). 1st Lieutenant New Jersey Light Infantry, May, 1775; Captain 3d New Jersey, 9th February, 1776; Deputy-Judge-Advocate-General, 17th November, 1776, to 29th October, 1778; Major 3d New Jersey, 28th November, 1776; resigned

29th October, 1778; Brigadier General, United States Army, 27th March, 1812; honorably discharged 15th June, 1815. (Died 3d October, 1823.)

Bloomfield, Moses (N. J.). Hospital Surgeon, 14th May, 1777; Hospital Physician and Surgeon, 6th October, 1780; resigned 13th December, 1780. (Died 14th August, 1791.)

Bloomfield, Samuel (N. J.). Surgeon's Mate 3d New Jersey in 1777.

Blount, Jacob (N. C.). Paymaster North Carolina Militia in 1777.

Blount, James (N. C.). Captain 2d North Carolina, 1st September, 1775, to ——.

Blount, Jesse (N. C.). Commissary 8th North Carolina, 11th December, 1776, to ——.

Blount, Reading (N. C.). Captain 3d North Carolina, 16th April, 1776; Major 5th North Carolina, 12th May, 1778; transferred to 2d North Carolina 1st June, 1778; transferred to 1st North Carolina, 1st January, 1781; served to close of war. (Died 12th October, 1807.)

Blount, Thomas (N. C.). Lieutenant 5th North Carolina, 28th April, 1777, to ——.

Blount, William (N. C.). Paymaster 3d North Carolina, 11th December, 1778, to ——. (Died 21st March, 1800.)

Blow, Michael (Va). Colonel Virginia Militia, 1777-1781.

Blow, Richard (Va). 1st Lieutenant 4th Virginia, 11th March, 1776, to ——. (Died 3d February, 1833.)

Bluen, John (N. Y.). Major New York Militia, —— ;taken prisoner at Moses Kill 2d August, 1777; released 1st December, 1777.

Blunt, Jacob (Ga). 2d Lieutenant 1st Georgia, 12th December, 1775, to ——.

Blunt, John (R. I.). 1st Lieutenant 11th Continental Infantry, 1st January, 1776; wounded and taken prisoner at Long Island 27th August, 1776; exchanged ——. (Died 18th May, 1804.)

Blunt, Whitmal (N. C.). Lieutenant 4th North Carolina, 20th November, 1776, to ——.

Blunt, William (Va). Colonel Virginia Militia, 1779-1781.

Blyth, Joseph (N. C.). Surgeon 1st North Carolina, 12th July, 1776; taken prisoner at Charleston 12th May, 1780;

exchanged 14th June, 1781; in 4th North Carolina in February, 1782, and served to close of war.

Blyth, Samuel (N. C.). Ensign 1st North Carolina, 28th March, 1776; 2d Lieutenant, 7th July, 1776; resigned 16th May, 1778.

Boadley, George (N. C.). Captain 3d North Carolina, 19th September, 1778, to —— ; in service January, 1780.

Boardman, Benjamin (Conn). Chaplain 2d Connecticut, 1st May to 10th December, 1775; Chaplain 20th Continental Infantry, 1st January to 31st December, 1776.

Boardman, Joseph (Conn). Captain Connecticut Militia in 1777.

Boarman, Henry (Md). 1st Lieutenant 3d Maryland Battalion of the Flying Camp, — July to December, 1776.

Boden, William (Mass). Lieutenant of Bullard's Massachusetts Regiment, June to November, 1775; 1st Lieutenant 18th Continental Infantry, 1st January, 1776, to 31st December, 1776.

Bodie, Lodowick (Va). Surgeon's Mate 2d Virginia State Regiment, — September, 1777, to January, 1781.

Bodwell, Eliphalet (Mass). 2d Lieutenant of Frye's Massachusetts Regiment, — May, 1775, to ——.

Boemper, Abraham (Pa). Ensign Pennsylvania State Regiment, 28th April, 1777, to ——.

Boffee, Thomas (N. H.). 2d Lieutenant 2d Continental Infantry, 1st January to 31st December, 1776. (Died 10th January, 1820.)

Bogardus, Benjamin (N. Y.). 2d Lieutenant of Graham's Regiment, New York Militia, July to November, 1776; 2d Lieutenant 3d New York, 21st November, 1776; resigned 26th May, 1782. (Died 1812.)

Bogart, Henry (N. Y.). 2d Lieutenant 2d Continental Artillery, 1st February, 1777; resigned 24th February, 1778.

Bogart, Isaac (N. Y.). 2d Lieutenant 4th New York, May to November, 1776; 1st Lieutenant 3d New York, 21st November, 1776; resigned 10th February, 1778; served subsequently as Captain New York Militia. (Died 1818.)

Bogart, Nicholas N. (R. I.). Surgeon's Mate Olney's Rhode Island Battalion, 1st May, 1781, and served to close of war.

Boggs, Andrew (Pa). 2d Lieutenant 1st Battalion Pennsylvania Flying Camp; wounded at Long Island 27th August, 1776.

Bohan, Joseph (Ga). Captain Pulaski Legion, 1779-1780.

Bohannon, Ambrose (Va). Captain Lieutenant 1st Continental Artillery, 13th January, 1777; Regimental Paymaster, 1st June, 1778; served to — June, 1783.

Boileau, Pierre Anable (Canada). Ensign 2d Canadian (Hazen's) Regiment, April, 1778; Lieutenant, September, 1778; retired 1st January, 1782.

Bois, Pierre Francois de (France). Brevet Major Continental Army, 7th October, 1776; resigned 9th April, 1779, and granted leave to return to France.

Bolling, Wood.—See **Bouldin.**

Bolster, Isaac (Mass). Captain of Learned's Massachusetts Regiment, May to December, 1775; Captain Continental Infantry, 1st January to December, 1776.

Bolton, John (Mass). Lieutenant Artillery Artificer Regiment, 6th September, 1777; discharged 1st July, 1779.

Bolton, Robert (Md). 2d Lieutenant of Forman's·Continental Regiment, 5th March, 1777; resigned 7th January, 1778.

Bond, George P. (S. C.). Lieutenant-Colonel South Carolina Militia, 1775.

Bond, Hance (Va). Captain Virginia Militia, 1780-1781.

Bond, James (Md). 1st Lieutenant 3d Maryland Battalion of the Flying Camp, July to December, 1776.

Bond, Nathaniel (Mass). Surgeon of Glover's Massachusetts Regiment, 21st April to December, 1775; Captain 14th Continental Infantry, 1st January to 31st December, 1776; Surgeon Hospital Department, 1777, to ——.

Bond, Thomas (Mass). 1st Lieutenant of Ward's Massachusetts Regiment, April to December, 1775; served subsequently in Militia.

Bond, Thomas, Jr. (Pa). Purveyor Hospital Department, 6th October, 1780, to close of war. (Died 3d April, 1784.)

Bond, William (Md). 1st Lieutenant 3d Maryland Battalion of the Flying Camp, July 26 to December, 1776; was subsequently killed by Indians.

Bond, William (Mass). Lieutenant-Colonel in Lexington Alarm, April, 1775; Lieutenant-Colonel Gardner's Massachusetts Regiment, 2d June, 1775; Colonel, 3d July to — December, 1775; Colonel 25th Continental Infantry, 1st January, 1776. Died 31st August, 1776.

Bond, William (N. J.). Captain in Martin's Regiment New Jersey Militia, July to November, 1776; Captain 4th New Jersey, 28th November, 1776; resigned 2d December, 1777; served subsequently as Lieutenant-Colonel New Jersey Militia.

Bonham, Absalom (N. J.). Ensign 4th New Jersey, 1st May, 1777; 2d Lieutenant, 1st November, 1777; transferred to 2d New Jersey, 1st July, 1778; 1st Lieutenant, 27th March, 1780, and served to April, 1783.

Bonham, Malachi (Md). 2d Lieutenant 2d Maryland, 12th September, 1781; retained in Maryland Battalion April, 1783, and served to 15th November, 1783.

Bonneau, —— (—). Lieutenant South Carolina Militia; wounded at Savannah 9th October, 1779. (See Boroneau.)

Bonnell, Abraham (N. J.). Lieutenant-Colonel New Jersey Militia in 1776.

Bonnell, James (N. Y.). Ensign 1st New York, 26th February to — December, 1776; 2d Lieutenant of Spencer's Continental Regiment, — February, 1777; 1st Lieutenant, 1st January, 1778; Regimental Adjutant, 1st September, 1778; Captain, 24th April, 1779; retired 1st January, 1781. (Died 1808.)

Bonnetheau, Peter (S. C.). Lieutenant Charleston Artillery in 1780.

Bonneville,' ——, Chevalier (France). Ensign Continental Army, 4th March, 1780, to ——.

Bonter, Christopher (N. Y.). Ensign New York Militia, ——; prisoner 11th June, 1781, to 18th November, 1782; where taken not stated.

Bonter, Henderson (N. Y.). Lieutenant New York Militia, ——; prisoner 11th June, 1781, to 18th November, 1782; where taken not stated.

Boody, Robert (N. H.). Captain New Hampshire Militia, 1776.

Boogh, Henry (Pa). 2d Lieutenant 11th Pennsylvania, 30th September, 1776; 1st Lieutenant, 7th September, 1777; superceded 1st February, 1778.

Booker, Gideon (Ga). 1st Lieutenant 5th Georgia, — December, 1776; Captain, 28th January, 1778; transferred to 3d Georgia, 1st June, 1778; retired 22d October, 1782.

Booker, Lewis (Va). Captain Lieutenant 1st Continental Artillery, 13th January, 1777; retired 1st January, 1783. (Died 23d December, 1814.)

Booker, Ralph (Va). 2d Lieutenant 10th Virginia, 3d December, 1776; resigned 11th July, 1777.

Booker, Richard (Va). Captain Virginia Artillery in 1781.

Booker, Samuel (Va). 2d Lieutenant 5th Virginia, 28th November, 1776; 1st Lieutenant, 15th Virginia, 14th January, 1777; Captain, 1st August, 1777; regiment designated 11th Virginia, 14th September, 1778; taken prisoner at Charleston 12th May, 1780; transferred to 4th Virginia, 12th February, 1781, and served to close of war; Brevet Major, 30th September, 1783.

Boone, Hawkins (Pa). Captain 12th Pennsylvania, 4th October, 1776; transferred to 6th Pennsylvania, 5th July, 1778; killed in action with Indians near Fort Freeland, Pennsylvania, 29th July, 1779.

Boone, John (Md). Corporal 1st Maryland, 26th May, 1777; Sergeant, 1st July, 1779; Ensign, 14th March, 1780; transferred to 3d Maryland 1st January, 1781; wounded at Eutaw Springs, 8th September, 1781; resigned 25th October, 1781.

Booth, Joseph (Conn). Ensign of Wolcott's Connecticut State Regiment, December, 1775, to February, 1776; 2d Lieutenant of Sage's Connecticut State Regiment, June to December, 1776. (Died 1810.)

Booth, Nathaniel (Conn). Sergeant 3d Connecticut, 5th February, 1777; Sergeant-Major, 25th November, 1778; Ensign, 1st August, 1780; resigned 1st July, 1781.

Borden, Joseph (N. J.). Colonel New Jersey Militia, 1776.

Borden Joseph, Jr. (N. J.). Captain New Jersey Light Horse in 1777.

Borden, Stephen (R. I.). Ensign of Babcock's Rhode Island State Regiment, 15th January, 1776, to — June, 1777.

Boreman, John (Pa). Deputy Paymaster-General Western District, 16th September, 1779, to ——.

Boroneau, —— (S. C.). Lieutenant South Carolina Militia; wounded at Savannah, 9th October, 1779. (See Bonneau.)

Boss, George.—See **Bush.**

Boss, George (Pa). Ensign 2d Pennsylvania Battalion, 4th July, 1776; Ensign and Adjutant, 4th Pennsylvania, 3d January to 30th June, 1777, and from 17th December, 1777, to 17th May, 1780; Lieutenant, 4th June, 1778; transferred to Invalid Regiment 29th January, 1781; sentenced to be discharged 13th September, 1782.

Boss, Samuel (Va). Lieutenant 3d Continental Artillery, ——; dismissed 10th December, 1781.

Bostick, John (—). Captain North Carolina Regiment in 1783.

Bostwick, Amos (Conn). Ensign 19th Continental Infantry, 1st January to 31st December, 1776. (Died 19th November, 1829.)

Bostwick, Chesley (Ga). Captain 1st Georgia, 7th January, 1776; taken prisoner at Savannah 18th October, 1779. (Name also spelled Bostick.)

Bostwick, Elijah (N. Y.). Captain New York in Militia, 1780.

Bostwick, Elisha (Conn). Sergeant 7th Connecticut, 12th July to 21st December, 1775; 2d Lieutenant, 19th Continental Infantry, 1st January to 31st December, 1776.

Bostwick, Isaac (Conn). Captain 7th Connecticut, 6th July to 6th December, 1775; Captain 19th Continental Infantry, 1st January to 31st December, 1776.

Bostwick, Nathan (Conn). Ensign 7th Connecticut, 1st January, 1777; resigned 12th November, 1777. (Died 10th August, 1829.)

Bostwick, Oliver (N. Y.). Lieutenant New York Militia; wounded 2d July, 1780; where not stated. (Died 30th July, 1815.)

Bostwick, Reuben (Conn). Captain of Silliman's Connecticut State Regiment, June to December, 1776.

Bostwick, William (N. J.). 1st Lieutenant 3d New Jersey, 29th November, 1776; resigned 26th September, 1780.

Boswell, Machen (Va). 2d Lieutenant 1st Virginia State Regiment, —— March, 1777; 1st Lieutenant 6th October, 1777; Captain, 15th September, 1778, and served to February, 1781.

Boswell, Thomas (Va). Major Virginia Militia, 1775-1779.

Bosworth, Ichabod (Conn). Ensign of Sage's Connecticut State Regiment, June to December, 1776.

Botsford, Clemens (Conn). Ensign of Swift's Connecticut State Regiment, July to November, 1776.

Botsford, Jabez (Conn). 1st Lieutenant 5th Connecticut, 1st May to 9th December, 1775; Captain of Swift's Connecticut State Regiment, July to November, 1776.

Bott, William (N. J.). Colonel New Jersey Militia in 1776.

Bottom, Joshua (Conn). 2d Lieutenant of Ward's Connecticut State Regiment, May, 1776, to May, 1777.

Boucans, Jacobus (N. Y.). Captain, 4th New York, 21st November, 1776; omitted — March, 1777.

Boucher, John C.—See **Bucher.**

Bouchet, Dennis John du (France). Served as a Major on Staff of General Gates, July, 1777. resigned 29th December, 1777, and permitted to return to France.

Boude, Samuel (Pa). Ensign 10th Pennsylvania, 4th December, 1776; 2d Lieutenant 4th Continental Artillery, 1st February, 1777; killed at Brandywine, 11th September, 1777.

Boude, Thomas (Pa). 2d Lieutenant 4th Pennsylvania Battalion, 5th January, 1776; 1st Lieutenant 5th Pennsylvania, 1st January, 1777; Captain, 23d September, 1777; transferred to 2d Pennsylvania, 1st January, 1783; Brevet Major, 30th September, 1783; served to 3d November, 1783. (Died 24th October, 1822.)

Boudinot, Elias (N. J.). Colonel Commissary-General of Prisoners, 15th May, 1777; resigned 11th May, 1778. (Died 24th October, 1821.)

Boughton, Gould (N. Y.). Lieutenant 4th New York, 3d August, 1775, to January, 1776.

Bouldin, Wood (Va). 2d Lieutenant 14th Virginia, 20th November, 1776; 1st Lieutenant, 14th November, 1777; resigned 30th November, 1778. (Name also spelled Bolling.)

Bourguin, John Lewis (S. C.). Major South Carolina Militia, 1776. (Name also spelled Burgwin.)

Bourke, Thomas (Md). Captain 4th Maryland Battalion of the Flying Camp, July to December, 1776.

Bourne, Benjamin (R. I.). Ensign and Quartermaster of Babcock's and Lippitt's Regiments, Rhode Island Militia, in 1776 and 1777. (Died 17th September, 1808.)

Boush, —— (—). Ensign South Carolina or Virginia Rangers; killed at Savannah 9th October, 1779.

Boush, Robert (Va). Captain Virginia Militia, 1777-1778.

Boutelle, Timothy (Mass). Ensign of Whitcomb's Massachusetts Regiment, May to December, 1775.

Bowdoin, William (Mass). 1st Lieutenant of Paterson's Massachusetts Regiment, May to December, 1775; 1st Lieutenant 18th Continental Infantry, 1st January to 31st December, 1776.

Bowen, Daniel (Pa). Lieutenant Pennsylvania Militia, 1780-1781.

Bowen, Ephraim (R. I.). 1st Lieutenant 2d Rhode Island Regiment, 3d May to December, 1775; Captain 11th Continental Infantry, 1st January, 1776; Assistant Quartermaster-General, 14th September, 1776, to 1st January, 1777; served subsequently as Deputy Quartermaster-General and as Quartermaster-General Rhode Island Militia to close of war.

Bowen, John (Md). Ensign 4th Maryland, 10th December, 1776; 2d Lieutenant, 1st October, 1777; wounded at Germantown, 4th October, 1777; resigned 16th October, 1778.

Bowen, John (Pa). Cornet 4th Continental Dragoons, 12th October, 1778, to ——.

Bowen, John (Va). 2d Lieutenant 12th Virginia, 10th September, 1777; Regiment designated 8th Virginia, 14th September, 1778; Regimental Quartermaster, 1st December, 1778, to 1st May, 1779; taken prisoner at Charleston 12th May, 1780; Lieutenant, 8th February, 1781; retired 1st January, 1783.

Bowen, Joseph (R. I.). Ensign of Lippitt's Regiment Rhode Island Militia, 19th August, 1776, to March, 1777.

Bowen, Levi (Mass). Ensign of Brewer's Massachusetts Regiment, May, 1775; cashiered 11th September, 1775.

Bowen, Oliver (Ga). Captain 1st Georgia, 7th January, 1776, to ——.

Bowen, Prentice (N .Y.). 2d Lieutenant 3d New York, 21st November, 1776; Regimental Quartermaster, 28th May, 1778, to 14th July, 1780; retired 1st January, 1781; served subsequently as Captain New York Levies.

Bowen, Reece (Va). Lieutenant of Campbell's Regiment of Riflemen, Virginia Militia; killed at King's Mountain, 7th October, 1780.

Bowen, Reuben (Va). Cornet of a Company Virginia Dragoons in 1780.

Bowen, Seth (N. J.). 2d Lieutenant 2d New Jersey, 29th November, 1775; 1st Lieutenant, 29th November, 1776; 2d Lieutenant, 3d Continental Artillery, 1st March, 1777; Captain Lieutenant, 7th October, 1777; wounded at Monmouth, 28th June, 1778; resigned 26th October, 1778. (Died 1815.)

Bowen, Thomas Bartholomew (Pa). 1st Lieutenant of Miles' Pennsylvania Regiment, 6th April, 1776; Captain, 2d September, 1776; Captain, 9th Pennsylvania, 28th November, 1776; to rank from 2d September, 1776; Regimental Paymaster, 15th October, 1778; transferred to 5th Pennsylvania 17th January, 1781; retired 1st January, 1783.

Bowen, William (Va). Captain Virginia Militia, 1777-1781. (Died 1804.)

Bower, Jacob (Pa). Quartermaster of Thompson's Pennsylvania Rifle Regiment in 1775; Captain Pennsylvania Battalion of the Flying Camp, 29th July to 1st December, 1776; Captain, 6th Pennsylvania, 15th February, 1777; transferred to 2d Pennsylvania, 1st January, 1783, and served to 3d June, 1783. (Died ——, 1822.) (Name also spelled Bauer.)

Bower, John (Va). 2d Lieutenant 12th Virginia, January, 1777; retired 14th September, 1778.

Bower, William (N. Y.). Captain New York Militia; was a prisoner; when and where taken not stated.

Bowers, Jonathan (Conn). Captain Connecticut Militia; wounded at Stillwater 19th September, 1777.

Bowes, John (Va). 2d Lieutenant 4th Virginia, May, 1776, to ——.

Bowie, Daniel (Md). 1st Lieutenant of Smallwood's Maryland Regiment, 14th January, 1776; Captain, February, 1776; wounded and taken prisoner at Long Island 27th August, 1776, and died in captivity shortly afterwards.

Bowie, Fielder (Md). Captain Maryland Militia, 1775. (Died 1794.)

Bowie, John (S. C.). Captain 5th South Carolina, 1st March, 1777; wounded at Savannah, 9th October, 1779; was a Major in 1781, and served to close of war.

Bowie, Robert (Md). Captain 3d Maryland Battalion of the Flying Camp, July to December, 1776.

Bowie, William Sprigg (Md). 2d Lieutenant of Gunby's Independent Maryland Company, 14th January, 1776; 1st Lieutenant 3d Maryland Battalion of the Flying Camp, July to 1st December, 1776; Captain 4th Maryland, 10th December, 1776; wounded at Germantown 4th October, 1777; resigned 15th December, 1777.

Bowker, John (Mass). Ensign Lexington Alarm, April, 1775; 2d Lieutenant of Doolittle's Massachusetts Regiment, May to December, 1775.

Bowles, John (R. I.). Sergeant 1st Rhode Island, 29th April, 1777; Ensign, 24th June, 1777; discharged 27th December, 1777.

Bowles, Ralph Hart (Mass). Private and Corporal in Brewer's Massachusetts Regiment, July to December, 1775; Ensign 1st Massachusetts, 1st January, 1777; 2d Lieutenant, 28th March, 1777; Adjutant, 4th July, 1777, to 1st July, 1779; 1st Lieutenant, 28th February, 1779; retained in Jackson's Continental Regiment, 3d November, 1783, and served to June 20th, 1784. (Died September, 1813.)

Bowman, Abraham (N. J.). Lieutenant 2d New Jersey, 27th March, 1780; retired 1st January, 1783.

Bowman, Abraham (Va). Lieutenant-Colonel 8th Virginia, 1st March, 1776; Colonel, 22d March, 1777; resigned — December, 1777. (Died 1837.)

Bowman, Isaac (Va). "Major of Colonel Clark's Illinois Regiment; killed by Indians at Fort Patrick Henry, 14th August, 1779."

Bowman, Isaac Jr. (Va). "Lieutenant and Quartermaster of Colonel Clark's Illinois Regiment, May, 1779; taken prisoner by Indians 17th November, 1779; sold by them to a trader, carried to New Orleans and Cuba, escaped and returned to Virginia." (Died 9th September, 1826.)

Bowman, Joseph (Mass). Ensign in Lexington Alarm, April, 1775; Ensign of Ward's Massachusetts Regiment, 23d May to December, 1775; Major Massachusetts Militia, 1776-1780. (Died 1818.)

Bowman, Joseph (Va). Major of a Virginia State Regiment, 1778 to 1781.

Bowman, Joshua (N. C.). 2d Lieutenant 1st North Carolina, 1st September, 1775; 1st Lieutenant, 15th November, 1775; Captain, 18th September, 1776; wounded at Charleston, 12th May, 1780; killed at Ramsour's Mill 20th June, 1780.

Bowman, Nathaniel (N. J.). 2d Lieutenant 2d New Jersey, 11th November, 1775; 1st Lieutenant, 10th May, 1776; Captain, 11th April, 1777; Major 1st New Jersey, 11th February, 1783, and served to April, 1783.

Bowman, Samuel (Mass). Sergeant 3d Massachusetts, 7th January, 1777; Sergeant Major, 20th May, 1779; Ensign, 26th November, 1779; Lieutenant, 22d April, 1782; transferred to 1st Massachusetts 1st July, 1782, and served to 3d November, 1783.

Bowman, Phineas (Mass). 1st Lieutenant and Paymaster 15th Massachusetts, 1st January, 1777; Captain, 19th April, 1779; transferred to 5th Massachusetts 1st January, 1781, and served to close of war.

Bowman ,Solomon (Mass). 1st Lieutenant of Gardner's Massachusetts Regiment, May to December, 1775; 1st Lieutenant 25th Continental Infantry, 1st January to 31st December, 1776. (Died 1st July, 1823.)

Bowne, Benjamin (N. Y.). Major New York Militia; taken prisoner; when and where not stated.

Bowne, Peter (N. J.). Sergeant 4th New Jersey, 28th January, 1777; Ensign, 17th February, 1777, to ——.

Bowne, Thomas (Va). 2d Lieutenant 10th Virginia, 28th April, 1777; 1st Lieutenant and Regimental Adjutant, 10th October, 1777; transferred to 1st Virginia, 14th September, 1778; Captain, ——, 1780; taken prisoner at Charleston, 12th May, 1780; transferred to 6th Virginia, 12th February, 1781, and served to close of the war.

Bowyer, Henry (Va). 2d Lieutenant 12th Virginia, 10th September, 1777; Regimental Adjutant, 1st January, 1778; Regiment designated 8th Virginia 14th September, 1778; Lieutenant 1st Continental Dragoons, 18th February, 1781; retained in Baylor's Consolidated Regiment of Dragoons 9th November, 1782, and served to close of war. (Died 13th June, 1832.)

Bowyer, John (Va). Colonel Virginia Regiment of Riflemen, Militia; wounded and taken prisoner at Jamestown Ford 6th July, 1781.

Bowyer, John August Baptist (Va). Surgeon of Armand's Corps, 25th August, 1777; resigned 5th January, 1778.

Bowyer, Lambert (Md). 2d Lieutenant 6th Maryland, 1st April, 1777; resigned 8th October, 1777.

Bowyer, Michael (Md). 2d Lieutenant German Regiment, 12th July, 1776; 1st Lieutenant, — November, 1777; Captain, 25th May, 1778; retired 1st January, 1781.

Bowyer, Michael (Va). Captain 12th Virginia, 30th September, 1776; retired 14th September, 1778.

Bowyer, Peter (Pa). 1st Lieutenant German · Regiment, 12th July, 1776; Captain, 9th May, 1777; retired 1st January, 1781.

Bowyer, Thomas (Va). Captain 12th Virginia, 16th December, 1776; regiment designated 8th Virginia, 14th September, 1778; retired 1st January, 1783.

Box, Daniel (R. I.). Brigade Major Rhode Island Militia; severely injured by fall from horse in December, 1776.

Box, Philip (Ga). Appointed Commissary of Hospitals in State of Georgia 12th February, 1778, and served to ——.

Boyakin, Francis (Va). 2d Lieutenant 1st Virginia, 30th September, 1775; 1st Lieutenant, 30th August, 1776; was Captain in 1777; was in service in November, 1781.

Boyakin, Francis (S. C.).—See **Boykin.**

Boyce, Alexander (S. C.). Lieutenant 6th South Carolina, 1776; Captain, 27th June, 1778; died November, 1779, of wounds received at the siege of Savannah, 9th October, 1779.

Boyce, Thomas (N. Y.). Ensign New York Militia, ——; taken prisoner at Morisiana 4th March, 1782, and released 6th June, 1782.

Boyce, William (Va). Ensign 4th Virginia, 21st March, 1776; 2d Lieutenant, 28th September, 1776; 1st Lieutenant, 14th March, 1777; retired 30th September, 1778.

Boyd, Abraham (Md). Lieutenant-Colonel Recruiting Officer for Maryland troops, 1780-1781. (Died, 1799.)

Boyd, Adam (N. C.). Ensign 1st North Carolina, 4th January, 1776; 2d Lieutenant, 3d March, 1776; Chaplain 2d North Carolina, 1st October, 1777; Brigade Chaplain, 18th August, 1778, to June, 1780. (Died 1800.)

Boyd, Hugh (N. C.). Surgeon 4th North Carolina, 17th April, 1776, to ——.

Boyd, John (Mass). Captain of Company Minute Men in Lexington Alarm, April, 1775; Captain of Heath's Massachusetts Regiment, May to December, 1775.

Boyd, John (Pa). Volunteer in the Quebec Expedition; taken prisoner at Quebec 31st December, 1775; exchanged 1st November, 1779.

Boyd, John (Pa). 2d Lieutenant 12th Pennsylvania, 16th October, 1776; 1st Lieutenant, 20th May, 1777; transferred to 3d Pennsylvania, 1st July, 1778; Captain Lieutenant, 18th June, 1779; retired 17th January, 1781. (Died 13th February, 1832.)

Boyd, Matthew (Pa). Captain Montgomery's Pennsylvania Battalion of the Flying Camp; taken prisoner at Fort Washington 16th November 1776.

Boyd, Matthew (Pa). Lieutenant-Colonel Pennsylvania Militia, 1777-1778.

Boyd, Nathaniel (N. H.). Sergeant 1st New Hampshire, 24th April, 1775; 2d Lieutenant, 18th June to — December, 1775.

Boyd, Robert (Pa). Surgeon 1st Pennsylvania Battalion, 19th April, 1776; resigned 13th June, 1776.

Boyd, Thomas (Md). Ensign 2d Maryland, 27th October, 1779; transferred to 5th Maryland, 1st January, 1781, with rank of 2d Lieutenant; retained in Maryland Battalion April, 1783, and served to 15th November, 1783. (Died 1797.)

Boyd, Thomas (Pa). 1st Sergeant of Thompson's Pennsylvania Rifle Regiment, 25th June, 1775; taken prisoner at Quebec 31st December, 1775; exchanged — November, 1777; 1st Lieutenant 1st Pennsylvania, 14th January, 1778; killed in action with Indians near Geneseo, N. Y., 13th September, 1779.

Boyd, Thomas (Pa). 3d Lieutenant of Miles' Pennsylvania Rifle Regiment, 19th March, 1776; 2d Lieutenant, 9th August, 1776; taken prisoner at Fort Washington 16th November, 1776; resigned 22d June, 1777. (Died 1814.)

Boyd, William (Mass). Quartermaster of Ward's Massachusetts Regiment, — May to — December, 1775; Lieutenant and Quartermaster 21st Continental Infantry, 1st January to 31st December, 1776.

Boyd, William (Pa). Ensign 12th Pennsylvania, 16th October, 1776; 2d Lieutenant, 20th May, 1777; killed at Brandywine, 11th September, 1777.

Boyden, Josiah (Vt). Captain Vermont Militia in 1777.

Boyden, Thomas (S. C.). Captain 1st South Carolina, ——; resigned 21st January, 1778.

Boyer, ——. See **Bowyer.**

Boyer, Benjamin (Pa). 2d Lieutenant 2d Pennsylvania, 12th March, 1777; transferred to 8th Pennsylvania, 1st July, 1778; Adjutant, 10th April, 1779; Captain of Marines in July, 1779.

Boykin, Francis (S. C.). 1st Lieutenant 1st South Carolina, 17th June, 1775; Captain, ——, 1776, and served to close of war. Is mentioned as Major in 1781. (Died 1821.)

Boykin, Samuel (S. C.). Captain of a Company of South Carolina Indians in 1776.

Boylan, James (Pa). Captain Pennsylvania Battalion of the Flying Camp; taken prisoner at Fort Washington 16th November, 1776.

Boyle, Peter (Pa). Ensign Pennsylvania State Regiment, 18th April, 1777; 2d Lieutenant, 1st August, 1777; Regiment designated 13th Pennsylvania, 12th November, 1777; resigned 18th April, 1778.

Boynton, Ephraim (Mass). 2d Lieutenant of Whitcomb's Massachusetts Regiment, — May, 1775, to ——.

Boynton, Joseph (N. H.). Ensign 3d New Hampshire, 8th November, 1776; 2d Lieutenant, 7th October, 1777; Regimental Adjutant, 15th January, 1778; 1st Lieutenant, 1st May, 1778; transferred to 2d New Hampshire 1st January, 1781, and served to close of war. (Died 24th June, 1830.)

Boze, (—) Baron de.—See **De Boze.**

Braca, Elisha (Conn). 1st Lieutenant of Silliman's Connecticut State Regiment, June to December, 1776.

Bracco, Bennett (Md). 1st Lieutenant of Captain Beall's Independent Maryland Company, 14th January, 1776; Captain, 16th August, 1776; killed at White Plains, 28th October, 1776.

Bracco, James (Md). Ensign 7th Maryland, 17th April, 1777; Lieutenant, 14th September, 1778; resigned 3d January, 1780.

Brackenridge, Alexander (Va). 1st Lieutenant Gist's Additional Continental Regiment, 14th March, 1777; Captain Lieutenant, ——, 1778; Captain, 23d April, 1779; taken prisoner at Charleston, 12th May, 1780; prisoner un-

til June, 1781; retired 1st January, 1783.

Brackenridge, Robert (Va). 2d Lieutenant 8th Virginia, 10th August, 1777; 1st Lieutenant, 4th April, 1778; transferred to 4th Virginia, 14th September, 1778; taken prisoner at Charleston, 12th May, 1780; exchanged — July, 1781; served to close of war. (Died 11th September, 1833.)

Brackenridge, Samuel (N. J.). 2d Lieutenant 4th New Jersey, 10th December, 1776; resigned 1st November, 1777.

Brackett, Jacob (Conn). Captain of Douglas' Connecticut State Regiment, June to December, 1776.

Brackett, John (Mass). Captain of Phinney's Massachusetts Regiment, May to December, 1775.

Bradford, Andrew (Mass). Ensign and Paymaster 14th Massachusetts, 1st January, 1777, to 1st January, 1781; Lieutenant, 8th October, 1779; transferred to 7th Massachusetts 1st January, 1781; resigned 22d April, 1782. (Died 1st January, 1837.)

Bradford, Anthony (Conn). Sergeant 8th Connecticut, 9th July to 18th December, 1775; Ensign, 17th Connecticut Infantry, 1st January, 1776; taken prisoner at Long Island 27th August, 1776.

Bradford, Charles (Va). Sergeant 13th Virginia, 20th December, 1776; Quartermaster Sergeant, 1st June, 1777; Regimental Quartermaster, 12th August, 1777; retired 14th September, 1778.

Bradford, Gamaliel (Mass). Lieutenant-Colonel of Marshall's Massachusetts Regiment, 8th May to 1st December, 1776; Colonel, 14th Massachusetts, 1st January, 1777; retired 1st January, 1781. (Died 9th January, 1807.)

Bradford, Gamaliel, Jr. (Mass). Private in Marshall's Massachusetts Regiment, 28th May to 1st December, 1776; Private 14th Massachusetts, 1st January, 1777; Corporal, ——; Sergeant in 1778; Ensign, 8th October, 1779; Lieutenant, 3d September, 1780; transferred to 7th Massachusetts, 1st January, 1781; transferred to 4th Massachusetts, 12th June, 1783; retained in Jackson's Continental Regiment, 3d November, 1783, and served to June 20, 1784. (Died 7th March, 1824.)

Bradford, James (Pa). 2d Lieutenant 9th Pennsylvania, 15th January, 1777; 1st Lieutenant of Patton's Continental Regiment, — March, 1777, to rank from 14th January, 1777; Regimental Quartermaster in 1778; taken prisoner at Monmouth 28th June, 1778; transferred to 2d Continental Artillery, 21st July, 1779; Aide-de-Camp to General Alexander, 24th June to —— November, 1781; 1st Lieutenant, 25th June, 1781; Regimental Adjutant, 22d August, 1782, to — June, 1783; transferred to Corps of Artillery, 17th June, 1783, and served to 20th June, 1784; Captain United States Artillery Company, 20th October, 1786; Captain Artillery United States Army, 29th September, 1789; killed 4th November, 1791, in action with Miami Indians on the Maumee, Ohio.

Bradford, John (Mass). Captain in Lexington Alarm, April, 1775; Captain of Cotton's Massachusetts Regiment, 26th May to December, 1775; Captain Massachusetts Militia, 1777-1779. (Died 1836.)

Bradford, Joseph (N. H.) 1st Lieutenant 3 New Hampshire, 23d April, 1775. (Died July, 1775.)

Bradford, Robert (Conn). Ensign of Cook's Connecticut State Regiment; taken prisoner at Norwalk, 15th March, 1777.

Bradford, Robert (Mass). Ensign 23d Continental Infantry, 1st January to 31st December, 1776; 1st Lieutenant and Regimental Quartermaster, 2d Massachusetts, 1st January, 1777; Brigadier Quartermaster, 1st January, 1778; Captain 2d Massachusetts, 21st June, 1779, and served to 3d November, 1783. (Died ——, 1823.)

Bradford, Samuel (Mass). Captain in Lexington Alarm, April, 1775; Captain of Cotton's Massachusetts Regiment, April to December, 1775; Captain 23d Continental Infantry, 1st January to December, 1776. (Died 1777.)

Bradford, Samuel (N. H.). Sergeant-Major 1st New Hampshire, 23d April to December, 1775; 2d Lieutenant 5th Continental Infantry, 1st January, 1776; 1st Lieutenant 2d New Hampshire, 8th November, 1776; retired 1st September, 1778. (Died 23d July, 1833.)

Bradford, Samuel Killett (Va). 1st Lieutenant 1st Continental Artillery, 13th January, 1777; Captain Lieutenant, 1780, and served to ——; Aide-de-Camp to General Weedon, 1781; retired 1st January, 1783.

Bradford, Thomas (Pa). Captain Pennsylvania Militia in 1777; Deputy Commissary-General of Prisoners, 24th January, 1778, to 1780. (Died 1838.)

Bradford, William (Md). 2d Lieutenant of Stephenson's Rifle Battalion, April, 1776; 1st Lieutenant of Rawling's Regiment, 1st July, 1776; taken prisoner at Fort Washington, 16th November, 1776.

Bradford, William (N. H.). Ensign of Bedel's Regiment New Hampshire Rangers, 22d January, 1776; taken prisoner at the Cedars 19th May, 1776; 2d Lieutenant 1st New Hampshire, 8th April, 1776; resigned 24th August, 1778.

Bradford, William, Jr. (N. C.). Lieutenant-Colonel Deputy Quartermaster-General in 1778.

Bradford, William (Pa). Colonel Philadelphia Associators, wounded at Princeton, 3d January, 1777. (Died 1791.)

Bradford, William, Jr. (Pa). Captain of a Pennsylvania Battalion of the Flying Camp, July, 1776; Captain 11th Pennsylvania, 30th September, 1776; Lieutenant-Colonel Deputy Commissary-General of Musters, 10th April, 1777; resigned 1st April, 1779. (Died 23d August, 1795.)

Bradford, William (R. I.). Adjutant of Chester's Rhode Island Regiment in 1775; 2d Lieutenant and Adjutant 11th Continental Infantry, 1st January, 1776; Major and Aide-de-Camp to General Lee, 29th October, 1776; Major of Tallman's Rhode Island Militia Regiment, 12th December, 1776; Major of Sherburne's Continental Regiment, 12th January, 1777; retired 1st January, 1781. (Died 1811.)

Bradfute, John (Va). Chaplain 2d Virginia State Regiment, 1778 to 1781.

Bradfute, Wm. (Va). Lieutenant of Rawling's Continental Regiment, — July, 1776; was a prisoner in 1780; when and where taken not stated.

Bradish, David (Mass). Captain of Phinney's Massachusetts Regiment, 19th May to December, 1775; Major 15th Massachusetts, 1st January, 1777; resigned 21st July, 1779. (Died 1818.)

Bradish, James (Mass). Surgeon's Mate 9th Continental Infantry, 1st January to 31st December, 1776. (Died 18th September, 1818.)

Bradley, Abraham (Conn). Captain of Gay's Connecticut State Regiment, June to December, 1776.

Bradley, Daniel (Conn). Ensign 5th Connecticut, 2d January, 1777; 2d Lieutenant, 13th January, 1778; 1st Lieutenant, 20th July, 1780; transferred to

3d Connecticut, 1st January, 1781; retained in Swift's Connecticut Regiment, 3d June, 1783, and served to 3d November, 1783; 1st Lieutenant 2d United States Infantry, 4th March, 1791; Captain 4th November, 1791; 2d Sub Legion, 4th September, 1792; Major 4th Infantry, 19th January, 1797; honorably discharged 1st June, 1802. (Died 12th April, 1825.)

Bradley, David (Mass). 1st Lieutenant of Nixon's Massachusetts Regiment, 23d May to 16th September, 1775; Regimental Quartermaster of Knox's Regiment Continental Artillery, October, 1775; 2d Lieutenant 11th Massachusetts, 6th November, 1776; discharged 7th November, 1778.

Bradley, Gee (N. C.). 1st Lieutenant 3d North Carolina, 12th May, 1776; Captain, 19th September, 1778; taken prisoner at Charleston, 12th May, 1780; exchanged June, 1781; retired 1st January, 1783.

Bradley, James (Va). Captain 2d Virginia State Regiment, 1778 to 1781.

Bradley, Levi (Mass). Sergeant 4th Massachusetts, 30th January, 1777; Ensign. 30th March, 1779; taken prisoner at White House, 15th September, 1780; exchanged 22d December, 1780; Lieutenant, —— 1782; retired 1st January, 1783.

Bradley, Philip Burr (Conn). Colonel Connecticut State Regiment, May to December, 1776; Colonel 5th Connecticut, 1st January, 1777; retired 1st January, 1781. (Died 4th January, 1821.)

Bradley, Richard (N. C.). Paymaster 3d North Carolina, 5th March, 1777; retired 1st June, 1778.

Bradley, Stephen Row (Conn). Captain and Major Connecticut Militia, 1776-1779. (Died 9th December, 1830.)

Bradt, Henry (N. Y.). Lieutenant of Cox's Regiment New York Militia; wounded 7th August, 1777, at Herkimer, New York, on the retreat from Oriskany.

Bradwell, Nathaniel (S. C.). 2d Lieutenant 1st South Carolina, 16 March, 1778; 1st Lieutenant, 12th May, 1779, and served to close of war.

Brady, Christie (Va). 2d Lieutenant of Stephenson's Rifle Regiment, 23d July, 1776. Died 14th November, 1776.

Brady, David (Ga). Hospital Chaplain, 1779 to 1781.

Brady, John (Pa). Captain 12th Pennsylvania, 1st October, 1776; wounded at Brandywine, 11th September, 1777; resigned 9th March, 1778; assasinated by Indians at Muncy, 11th April, 1779, while recruiting for Hartley's Regiment.

Brady, Samuel (Pa). 1st Lieutenant of Captain Doyle's Independent Pennsylvania Rifle Company, 17th July, 1776; company attached to 8th Pennsylvania, — November, 1776, when appointed Captain Lieutenant to rank from 17th July, 1776; Captain, 2d August, 1779; transferred to 3d Pennsylvania, 17th January, 1781, and served to close of war. (Died 25th December, 1795.)

Brady, William (Va). Captain of Stephenson's Maryland and Virginia Rifle Regiment, 23d July, 1776, to ——; Captain 11th Virginia, 1st January, 1777, to rank from 23d July, 1776; resigned 11th March, 1778.

Bragg, Thomas (Va). Lieutenant Virginia Militia, 1780-1781. (Died 1819.)

Bragden, Josiah (Mass). Captain of Scammon's Massachusetts Regiment, May, 1775; resigned 19th August, 1775; 1st Lieutenant 11th Massachusetts, 6th November, 1776. Died 27th April, 1778.

Brahm, Ferdinand de (France). Major Engineer, 11th February, 1778; taken prisoner at Charleston, 12th May, 1780; exchanged 22d April, 1781; Brevet Lieutenant-Colonel, 6th February, 1784, and retired from the service.

Brainard, Jeremiah Gates (Conn). Ensign 7th Connecticut, 26th July, 1780; taken prisoner — July, 1780; released 22d December, 1780; transferred to 4th Connecticut, 1st January, 1781; resigned 28th April, 1781. (Died 7th January, 1830.)

Brainard, Josiah (Conn). Ensign of Selden's Connecticut State Regiment, June to December, 1776; 2d Lieutenant Connecticut Militia; taken prisoner at Norwalk, 15th March, 1777.

Bramble, William (Vt). Lieutenant Vermont Militia in 1777.

Bramhall, Joshua (Mass). Ensign 14th Massachusetts, 1st January, 1777; 2d Lieutenant, 2d October, 1777; 1st Lieutenant, 1st February, 1779; transferred to 7th Massachusetts, 1st January, 1781; transferred to 3d Massachusetts, 12th June, 1782, and served to close of war.

Brandon, John (N. C.). Captain North Carolina Militia at King's Mountain in October, 1780.

Brandon, Thomas (Pa). 1st Lieutenant 12th Pennsylvania, 4th October, 1776. Died 4th April, 1777.

Brandon, Thomas (S. C.). Captain South Carolina Militia at Kings Mountain, October, 1780, and in the South Carolina Campaign in 1781. (Died 5th February, 1802.)

Brandon, William (N. C.). Lieutenant 1st North Carolina, 1st September, 1775; resigned 8th March, 1776.

Branham, Samuel (Ga). Colonel Georgia Militia, 1779-1781.

Branton, Nicholas (Mass). Captain of Glover's Massachusetts Regiment, May to December, 1775.

Brashear, Richard (Va). Captain of Clark's Illinois Regiment, 1778 to 1781.

Brasher, Abraham E. (N. Y.). 2d Lieutenant 1st New York, 28th June, 1775, to — November, 1776. (Died —, 1782.)

Brasher, Ephraim (N. Y.). Lieutenant New York Militia, 1776.

Brasher, Henry (N. Y.). Captain of Malcolm's New York Regiment in 1776.

Brass, Lucas (N. J.). Captain New Jersey Militia, 1777-1778.

Bratt, Daniel (N. Y.). Lieutenant-Colonel New York Militia in 1775.

Brattle, Ebenezer (Mass). 1st Lieutenant of Gardner's Massachusetts Regiment, — May, 1775, to ——.

Bratton, James (Del). Ensign Delaware Regiment, 28th November, 1776; 2d Lieutenant, 5th April, 1777; 1st Lieutenant, 16th August, 1778; resigned 1st March, 1779.

Bratton, William (Pa). 1st Lieutenant 6th Pennsylvania Battalion, 9th January, 1776; Captain 7th Pennsylvania, 12th January, 1777; resigned 17th April, 1779.

Bratton, William (S. C.). Colonel South Carolina Militia, ——; Commander of the forces at the action at Williamson's Plantation, where he was severely wounded, 12th July, 1780. (Died 1815.)

Braxton, Carter (Va). A signer of the Declaration of Independence. (Died 10th October, 1797.)

Bray, Daniel (N. J.). Captain New Jersey Militia in 1777.

Bray, John (Mass). Captain of Glover's Massachusetts Regiment, May to December, 1775; Commissary in Hospital Department, 1776 to 1780.

Brayman, Christian (Va). Paymaster 1st Continental Dragoons, 27th December, 1777; Cornet in Armand's Partisan Corps, 15th January, 1780; resigned 4th January, 1781.

Brearley, David (N. J.). Captain 2d New Jersey, 28th October, 1775, to Noverber, 1776; Lieutenant-Colonel 4th New Jersey, 28th November, 1776; Lieutenant-Colonel 1st New Jersey, 1st January, 1777; resigned 4th August, 1779; served also as Colonel New Jersey Militia. (Died 16th August, 1790.)

Brearley, Joseph (N. J.). Captain 2d New Jersey, 20th November, 1775; resigned 5th February, 1777; served subsequently as Major New Jersey Militia. (Died 1805.)

Breed, Frederick (Mass). Private in Lexington Alarm, April, 1775; Ensign of Mansfield's Massachusetts Regiment, 9th May to 1st December, 1775; 2d Lieutenant 27th Continental Infantry, 1st January to 31st December, 1776.

Breckenridge. — See **Brackenridge.** Name spelled both ways.

Breed, Nathaniel (N. H.). Surgeon's Mate 3d New Hampshire, 23d May to — December, 1775; Surgeon's Mate 2d Continental Infantry, 1st January to 31st December, 1776; served subsequently as Surgeon of New Hampshire State Troops and Militia. (Died 1810.)

Breese, Samuel (N. J.). Colonel New Jersey Militia, 1776. (Died 1800.)

Brent, George P. (Va). Lieutenant of a Virginia State Regiment, 1779 to 1780.

Brent, Hugh (Va). Captain Virginia Militia, 1776-1777. (Died 1813.)

Brent, John (Va). Captain 4th Virginia, 23d February, 1776; Major, 4th October, 1777; resigned 4th May, 1778.

Brent, William (Va). Aide-de-Camp to General Alexander in 1777; Lieutenant-Colonel 1st Virginia State Regiment, 14th June, 1777; Colonel 2d Virginia State Regiment, May, 1778, to February, 1781.

Bresco, ——. Lieutenant of Horse; taken prisoner at Spencer's Tavern, 26th June, 1781.

Bressic, Thomas (Va). Captain of a Virginia State Regiment, 1777 to 1782.

Bressic, William (Va). Captain of a Virginia Regiment, 1778, to July, 1779.

Brett, John (Va). Captain Virginia Militia, 1777-1778.

Bretz, Michael (Pa). Captain Pennsylvania Militia, 1777-1778.

Brevard, Alexander (N. C.). Ensign 4th North Carolina, 27th November, 1776; 1st Lieutenant, 9th December, 1776; transferred to 1st North Carolina, 1st June, 1778; Captain, 20th October, 1780; transferred to 4th North Carolina, 6th February, 1782; retired 1st January, 1783; served as Colonel North Carolina Militia in 1779. (Died 1829.)

Brevard, Ephraim (N. C.). Surgeon 1st North Carolina, ——; taken prisoner at Charleston, 12th May, 1780. (Died 1783.)

Brevard, Joel (N. C.). Captain 9th North Carolina, 28th November, 1776; resigned 1st June, 1778.

Brevard, John (N. C.). 1st Lieutenant 9th North Carolina, 28th November, 1776, to ——.

Brevard, Joseph (N. C.). Ensign 10th North Carolina, 9th May, 1781; Lieutenant, 1st August, 1781; transferred to 2d North Carolina, 12th February, 1782; Regimental Quartermaster, 13th March, 1782; served to close of war.

Brevitt, John (Md). Lieutenant 4th Maryland, 20th September, 1780; retained in Maryland Battalion, April, 1783, and served to 15th November, 1783.

Brewer, Benjamin (N. H.). 1st Lieutenant 3d New Hampshire, 23d May to — December, 1775.

Brewer, David (Mass). Colonel Massachusetts Regiment, 17th June, 1775; cashiered 24th October, 1775.

Brewer, David, Jr. (Mass). Lieutenant of Brewer's Massachusetts Regiment, — May to December, 1775.

Brewer, Elisha (Mass). 1st Lieutenant 7th Massachusetts, May to December, 1775; Brigade-Major, 21st September to 1st December, 1775; 1st Lieutenant 6th Continental Infantry, 1st January, 1776; Captain, 27th August, 1776; Captain 9th Massachusetts, 1st January, 1777; resigned 5th July, 1779. (Died 23d July, 1827.)

Brewer, James (N. H.). 1st Lieutenant 3d New Hampshire, 23d April to — December, 1775. (Died 1832.)

Brewer, Jonathan (Mass). Colonel Massachusets Regiment, 19th May, 1775; wounded at Bunker Hill, 17th June, 1775; Colonel Massachusetts State Regiment of Artificers in 1776. (Died 1784.)

Brewer, Jonathan (N. J.). 2d Lieutenant 3d New Jersey, 29th November, 1776; Captain Lieutenant 4th Continental Artillery, 14th March, 1777; taken prisoner at Germantown, 4th October, 1777; exchanged in August, 1778; resigned 10th February, 1779.

Brewer, Moses (Mass). Ensign 12th Massachusetts, 13th November, 1776; resigned 6th October, 1777.

Brewer, Samuel (Mass). Colonel 12th Massachusetts, 6th November, 1776; cashiered 17th September, 1778. (Died 1781.)

Brewer, Samuel (Mass). 1st Lieutenant of Fellows' Massachusetts Regiment, May to December, 1775.

Brewster, Benjamin (Conn). 1st Lieutenant of Selden's Connecticut State Regiment, 20th June, 1776; wounded and taken prisoner on the retreat from New York, 15th September, 1776.

Brewster, Caleb (N. Y.). Ensign 4th New York, 21st November, 1776; 1st Lieutenant, 2d Continental Artillery, 1st January, 1777; Captain Lieutenant, 23d June, 1780; wounded on Long Island Bay, — December, 1782; served to 16th June, 1783. (Died 13th February, 1827.)

Brewster, Ebenezer (Conn). Ensign in the Lexington Alarm in April, 1775; 2d Lieutenant 6th Connecticut, 1st May, 1775; 1st Lieutenant, 1st July to 10th December, 1775; Captain 10th Continental Infantry, 1st January to 31st December, 1776.

Brewster, Ebenezer (Mass). 1st Lieutenant 4th Massachusetts, 1st January, 1777; resigned 12th April, 1778.

Brewster, Elisha (Conn). Private in the Lexington Alarm, April, 1775; Private 8th Connecticut, 11th July to 10th December, 1775; Ensign 17th Continental Infantry, 1st January to 31st December, 1776; 2d Lieutenant 1st Connecticut, 1st January, 1777; resigned 1st August, 1777; served subsequently as Captain in the Quartermaster's Department.

Brewster, Harvey, Jr. (N. Y.). Lieutenant New York Militia; wounded, taken prisoner at Fort Montgomery, 6th October, 1777; exchanged 17th December, 1780. (Died 15th March, 1830.)

Brewster, James (N. Y.). 2d Lieutenant 2d Continental Artillery, 1st January, 1777; 1st Lieutenant, 4th February, 1777; Captain Lieutenant, 8th April, 1782, and served to 16th June, 1783.

Brewster, John (N. H.). Captain New Hampshire Militia, 1776-1777.

Brewster, Jonathan (Conn). 1st Lieutenant 8th Connecticut, 6th July, 1775; Captain, 5th September to 10th December, 1775; Captain 17th Continental Infantry, 1st January, 1776; wounded and taken prisoner at Long Island, 27th August, 1776.

Brewster, Lott (N. C.). Major 2d North Carolina, 27th November, 1776; Lieutenant-Colonel 3d North Carolina, 25th October, 1777; resigned 15th March, 1778.

Brian, Andrew (Md). 1st Lieutenant of Grayson's Continental Regiment, 23d January, 1777, to ——.

Briant, David.—See **Bryant.**

Brice, Jacob (Md). Adjutant of Smallwood's Maryland Regiment, March, 1776; Captain 3d Maryland, 10th December, 1776; wounded and taken prisoner at Camden, 16th August, 1780; exchanged ——; transferred to 4th Maryland, 1st January, 1781; transferred to 1st Maryland, 1st January, 1783, and served to April, 1783.

Brice, John (Pa). Ensign 1st Pennsylvania Battalion, 20th January, 1776; Captain Lieutenant 4th Continental Artillery, 14th March, 1777; Captain, 1st June, 1778; Major and Aide-de-Camp to General Lafayette in 1778; Brevet Lieutenant-Colonel, 27th October, 1778; served to —— June, 1783. (Name also spelled Bryce.)

Brice, Peter (N. C.). Ensign 9th North Carolina, 28th November, 1776, to ——.

Brickell, Thomas (N. C.). Captain 7th North Carolina, 28th November, 1776, to ——; appears to have been taken a prisoner, but when and where taken not stated.

Brickett, James (Mass). Lieutenant-Colonel of Frye's Massachusetts Regiment, 20th April, 1775; wounded at Bunker Hill, 17th June, 1775; served subsequently as Brigadier- General Massachusetts Militia. (Died 10th December, 1818.)

Bridge, Ebenezer (Mass). Colonel Masachusetts Regiment, 19th April, 1775; wounded at Bunker Hill, 17th June, 1775; was tried for misbehavior at Bunker Hill.

Bridge, Ebenezer (Mass). 1st Lieutenant of Whitcomb's Massachusetts Regiment, —— May, 1775, to December, 1775; served subsequently as Major and Lieutenant-Colonel Massachusetts Militia. (Died 1823.)

Bridge, John (Mass). Quartermaster of Bridge's Massachusetts Regiment, May, 1775, to 1st August, 1775.

Bridges, James (R. I.). 2d Lieutenant 11th Continental Infantry, 1st January to 31st December, 1776.

Bridgham, John (Mass). Captain of Cotton's Massachusetts Regiment, April to December, 1775; Captain 23d Continental Infantry, 1st January to 31st December, 1776; served subsequently as Captain Massachusetts Militia.

Bridgham, John, Jr. (Mass). Ensign 23d Continental Infantry, 1st January to 31st December, 1776.

Bridgham, Paul (Mass). Ensign of Ward's Massachusetts Regiment, May to December, 1775.

Briffault, Augustin (France). Served as a volunteer in Armand's Partisan Corps; Brevet Lieutenant Continental Army, 13th January, 1779, and permitted to retire from the army.

Briggs, Cornelius (R. I.). Ensign of Church's Rhode Island Regiment, 3d May to —— December, 1775; served subsequently as Captain Rhode Island Militia.

Briggs, George (R. I.). Ensign of Stanton's Rhode Island State Regiment, 12th December, 1776, to —— May. 1777.

Briggs, Henry (Mass). 2d Lieutenant of Walker's Massachusetts Regiment, May to December, 1775; served subsequently as Captain Massachusetts Militia.

Briggs, John (Mass). 2d Lieutenant 4th Continental Infantry, 1st January to 31st December, 1776.

Briggs, Joseph (Va). Ensign Virginia Rangers in 1779.

Briggs, Stephen (R. I.). Ensign 1st Rhode Island, 20th February. 1777; resigned 7th January, 1778.

Briggs, William (Mass). Captain in Lexington Alarm, April, 1775; Captain of Reade's Massachusetts Regiment, April to December, 1775. (Died 11th August, 1819.)

Briggs, Zephaniah (Conn). 2d Lieutenant 5th Connecticut, 1st May to 4th December, 1775.

Brigham, Henry (Mass). Ensign 21st Continental Infantry, 1st January to 31st December, 1776.

Brigham, John (Mass). Captain of Cotton's Massachusetts Regiment, May, 1775, to ——.

Brigham, Origin (Mass). Surgeon's Mate of Warner's Additional Continental Regiment, 1st August, 1777; retired 1st January, 1781; Surgeon's Mate 2d Massachusetts, 25th April, 1781, and served to June, 1783. (Died 1815.)

Brigham, Paul (Conn). Captain 8th Connecticut, 1st January, 1777; transferred to 5th Connecticut, 1st January, 1781; resigned 22d April, 1781.

Brigham, Timothy (Mass). Lieutenant in Lexington Alarm, April, 1775; 1st Lieutenant of Ward's Massachusetts Regiment, May to December, 1775; Captain Massachusetts Militia, 1776-1777.

Bright, Robert (Va). Captain Virginia Militia in 1781.

Bright, Simon (N. C.). Captain 2d North Carolina, 1st September, 1775; resigned, 3d May, 1776.

Brindley, Francis (N. Y.). 2d Lieutenant of Nicholson's New York Regiment, 15th April, 1776; 2d Lieutenant 1st Canadian (Livingston's) Regiment, November, 1776, to rank from 15th April, 1776; 1st Lieutenant, 18th December, 1776; retired, 1st January, 1781.

Bringhurst, George (Pa). 2d Lieutenant of Lewis' Pennsylvania Battalion of the Flying Camp, July to December, 1776.

Brink, Alexander (N. Y.). 2d Lieutenant 2d New York, 29th June, 1775, to — January, 1776.

Brinkerhoff, Abraham (N. Y.). Colonel New York Militia in 1775.

Brinkerhoff, Dirck (N. Y.). Colonel New York Militia, 1775-1780.

Brinkerhoff, George (N. Y.). Captain New York Militia, 1777-1780.

Brinkerhoff, Stephen (N. Y.). Captain New York Militia in 1775.

Brinkley, John. Captain North Carolina Militia, 1780-1781.

Brinkley, Thomas (N. Y.). 1st Lieutenant 5th New York, 21st November, 1776; omitted — May, 1777.

Brinkley, William (N. C.). Captain 3d North Carolina, 16th April, 1776; retired 1st June, 1778.

Brinsmade, Daniel (Conn). Ensign 7th Connecticut, 6th July to 29th November, 1775; 1st Lieutenant of Bradley's Connecticut State Regiment, May, 1776. Died — September, 1776.

Brisban, John (Pa). Captain 2d Pennsylvania Battalion, 5th January, 1776; wounded at Three Rivers, 8th June, 1776; Captain 3d Pennsylvania, November, 1776; resigned 2d September, 1777. (Died 13th March, 1822.)

Briscoe, John Hanson (Md). Surgeon Hospital Department, 27th August, 1776; Surgeon 2d Maryland, 1st January, 1777; resigned 9th January, 1778.

Briscoe, Rueben (Va). 1st Lieutenant 3d Virginia, 23d February, 1776; Captain, 27th January, 1777; retired 30th September, 1778.

Brison.—See Bryson.

Britigney, —— Marquis de (France). Lieutenant Continental Army, 27th January, 1779, and by the act of 13th April, 1779, was recommended to the Governor of South Carolina to command a volunteer corps composed of Frenchmen residing in South Carolina, and was colonel of the same to close of the war.

Britton, Daniel (S. C.). Lieutenant South Carolina Militia in 1775.

Britton Henry (S. C.). Lieutenant South Carolina Militia in 1776.

Britton, Joseph (Md). Ensign 4th Maryland, 1st January, 1777; taken prisoner at Phillip's Heights, 6th September, 1778; 2d Lieutenant of Gist's Continental Regiment, 27th April, 1779; retired 1st January, 1781.

Britton, William (Mass). Captain of Spencer's Continental Regiment, 1st February, 1777; resigned 10th April, 1778.

Broadnax, Edward (Va). Captain Virginia Militia, 1776-1777.

Broadus, James (Va). Private and Sergeant 2d Virginia, March, 1776, to September, 1779; Ensign 2d Virginia, 25th September, 1779; retired 2d December, 1780.

Broadus, William (Va). 2d Lieutenant 1st Virginia State Regiment, 7th December, 1778, to February, 1781. (Died 1830.)

Broadwater, Charles Lewis (Va). Midshipman in United States Navy, October, 1775, to November, 1776; 1st Lieutenant 10th Virginia, 18th November, 1776; dismissed 21st April, 1778.

Brocaw, John (N. J.). Lieutenant New Jersey Militia; killed at Germantown, 4th October, 1777.

Brock, John (Va). 1st Lieutenant 10th Virginia, 2d December, 1776; retired 30th September, 1778.

Brock, Thomas (Va). Captain Virginia Militia, 1779-1781.

Brockway, Thomas (Conn). Chaplain of Selden's Regiment Connecticut Militia, 15th July to December, 1776. (Died 1807.)

Brodhead, Charles (N. Y.). Captain of Cantine's Regiment, New York Militia, 1778-1781.

Brodhead, Daniel (Pa). Lieutenant-Colonel Commandant 2d Battalion of Miles' Pennsylvania Rifle Regiment, 13th March, 1776; transferred to 4th Pennsylvania, 25th October, 1776; Colonel, 8th Pennsylvania, 12th March, 1777, to rank from 29th September, 1776. By the act of 27th October, 1779, it was "Resolved, that the thanks of Congress be given to Colonel Brodhead and the brave officers and soldiers under his command for executing (under direction of General Washington) the important expedition against the Mingo and Munsey Indians, and the part of the Senecas on the Allegheny River, by which depredations of those savages, assisted by their merciless instigators, subjects of Great Britain, upon the defenceless inhabitants of the Western frontiers, have been restrained and prevented." Transferred to 1st Pennsylvania, 17th January, 1781, and served to close of war; Brevet Brigadier-General, 30th September, 1783. (Died 15th November, 1809.)

Brodhead, Luke (Pa). 3d Lieutenant of Miles' Pennsylvania Rifle Regiment, 28th May, 1776; 2d Lieutenant, 24th October, 1776; wounded and taken prisoner at Long Island, 27th August, 1776; exchanged 8th December, 1776; Captain 6th Pennsylvania, 15th February, 1777; retired 21st June, 1778. (Died — May, 1806.)

Brodhead, Daniel, Jr. (Pa). 1st Lieutenant 3d Pennsylvania Battalion, 6th January, 1776; taken prisoner at Fort Washington, 16th November, 1776; exchanged 26th August, 1778, and died shortly afterwards.

Brodie, Lodowick (Va). Surgeon's Mate 2d Virginia State Regiment, 14th March, 1778; Surgeon, 15th August, 1778, to 2d August 1782. '

Brodrick, James (N. J.). Captain of Spencer's Continental Regiment, 3d February, 1777; wounded at Germantown, 4th October, 1777; resigned 15th April, 1780; served subsequently as Major New Jersey Militia.

Brogdan, John (N. Y.). Adjutant 1st New York, 30th June, 1775, to March, 1776; Lieutenant and Adjutant of Nicholson's New York Regiment, April to November, 1776.

Bronck, John L. (N. Y.). Major New York Militia, 1775-1779.

Bronck, Philip (N. Y.). Captain New York Militia, 1775-1776.

Bronson, Isaac (Conn). Surgeon's Mate 2d Continental Dragoons, 14th November, 1779, and served to close of war. (Died 1799.)

Bronson, Michael (Conn). 2d Lieutenant of Douglas's Connecticut State Regiment, June to December, 1776.

Brooke, Edmund (Va). 2d Lieutenant 1st Continental Artillery, February, 1781; resigned 3d October, 1781. (Died 2d June, 1835.)

Brooke, Edward (Mass). Sergeant of Baldwin's Artillery Artificer Regiment, 11th April, 1777; 2d Lieutenant, 20th May, 1779; retired 1st January, 1781.

Brooke, Eleazer (Mass). Colonel Massachusetts Militia, 1776.

Brooke, Francis John (Va). 2d Lieutenant, Lieutenant and Quartermaster 1st Continental Artillery, 1st February, 1781; retired 1st January, 1783. (Died 3d March, 1851.)

Brooke, Francis T. (Va). Major Virginia Militia, 1780-1781.

Brooke, George (Va). Colonel Virginia Militia, 1775-1780.

Brooke, Humphrey (Va). Colonel Virginia Militia, 1779-1780.

Brooke, James (Pa). Ensign 10th Pennsylvania, 15th September, 1780; transferred to 1st Pennsylvania, 17th January, 1781, and served to close of war.

Brooke, John (Pa). Major Pennsylvania Militia, 1776-1777.

Brooke, John T. (Va). Lieutenant 1st Continental Artillery, 1st February, 1781; retired 1st January, 1783.

Brookes, Benjamin (Md). Lieutenant of Gunby's Independent Maryland Company, 14th January, 1776; 1st Lieutenant 3d Battalion of the Maryland Flying Camp, July, 1776; Captain, 27th

August, 1776; Captain 3d Maryland, 10th December, 1776; wounded at Germantown, 4th October, 1777; wounded at Monmouth, 28th June, 1778; retired 1st January, 1783; Major 2d Artillerists and Engineers Regiment, 1st June, 1798. Died 9th January, 1800.

Brookes, David (Pa). Lieutenant Pennsylvania Battalion of the Flying Camp, July, 1776 ; taken prisoner at Fort Washington, 16th November, 1776; exchanged — January, 1780; Assistant Clothier-General for New York Troops, 1780 to 1782. (Died 30th August, 1838.)

Brooks, Almarin (N. J.). Sergeant 2d New Jersey, 9th February, 1777; Ensign, 17th May, 1780; retained in New Jersey Battalion, April, 1783, and served to 3d November, · 1783. (Died 25th January, 1824.)

Brooks, Caleb (Mass). 1st Lieutenant of Woodbridge's Massachusetts Regiment, May to December, 1775; served subsequently as Major Massachusetts Militia.

Brooks, Jabez (Conn). 2d Lieutenant of Mott's Connecticut State Regiment, June to December, 1776

Brooks, John (Mass). Captain of a Company of Massachusetts Minute Men at Lexington and Concord, 19th April, 1775; Major of Bridge's Massachusetts Regiment, May to December, 1775; Major 19th Continental Infantry, 1st January, 1776; Lieutenant-Colonel 8th Massachusetts, 1st November, 1776; Lieutenant-Colonel Commandant 7th Massachusetts, 11th November, 1778, and served to 12th June, 1783; Brigadier-General United States Army, 11th April, 1792; honorably discharged 1st November, 1796 (Died 2d March, 1825.)

Brooks, John (Pa). 2d Lieutenant and Adjutant 6th Pennsylvania Battalion, 9th January to December, 1776; served as Assistant Commissary of Issues, 1777 to 1780. (Died 1803.)

Brooks, Joseph Rider (Conn) Ensign of Sage's Connecticut State Regiment, June to December, 1776.

Brooks, Zachariah (Mass). Private in Lexington Alarm, April, 1775; Sergeant in Colonel Fry's Massachusetts Regiment, May to December, 1775; 1st Lieutenant 6th Massachusetts, 1st January, 1777; cashiered 27th April, 1778.

Broome, John (N. Y.). Lieutenant-Colonel of Jay's New York Regiment in 1775.

Broomfield, William (Md). 1st Lieutenant 2d Maryland, 1st January, 1777; resigned — June, 1777.

Bronson, Isaac (Conn). Surgeon's Mate 2d Continental Dragoons, 14th November, 1779, and served to close of war.

Bronson, Samuel (Conn). Captain Connecticut Militia, 1776-1777.

Brosius, Nicholas (Pa). Ensign of Keller's Battalion Pennsylvania Flying Camp, July to December, 1776.

Brossard, Celeron (Ga). Captain 2d Georgia, 26th June, 1777; granted 9 months' leave and permitted to return to France, 1st July, 1782.

Broughton, Alexander (S. C.). Captain South Carolina Militia, 1779-1782.

Broughton, Nicholas (Mass). Captain of Glover's Massachusetts Regiment, 19th May to November, 1775.

Brower, Andrew (Mass). Ensign 7th Continental Infantry, 1st January, 1776, to ——.

Brower, Garret (N. Y.). Lieutenant 2d Continental Artillery, 1st January, 1777, to ——,

Brower, Henry (Pa). Ensign 3d Pennsylvania, 25th August, 1779; retired 17th January, 1781.

Brown.—See also **Browne.**

Brown, Abijah (Mass). Major of Gardner's Massachusetts Regiment, April and May. 1775; Lieutenant-Colonel of Woodbridge's Massachusetts Regiment, 16th June to December, 1775; Lieutenant-Colonel and Colonel Massachusetts Militia, 1776-1778. (Died 1818.)

Brown, Abisha (Mass). Captain of Nixon's Massachusetts Regiment, May to December, 1775; Capt Massachusetts Militia in 1777.

Brown, Alexander (Pa). 2d Lieutenant 6th Pennsylvania Battalion, 9th January, 1776, to ——.

Brown, Andrew (Mass). Served as a Volunteer at Bunker Hill; Major Deputy Muster-Master-General Eastern Department, 23d May, 1777, to close of war. (Died 4th February, 1797.)

Brown, Andrew (Mass). Ensign 7th Continental Infantry, 1st January to 31st December, 1776.

Brown, Archibald (S. C.). Captain South Carolina Militia, 1776.

Brown, Benjamin (Mass). Captain of Gardner's Massachusetts Regiment, June to December, 1775.

Brown, Benjamin (Mass). 1st Lieutenant 7th Continental Infantry, 1st January to 31st December, 1776; Captain 8th Massachusetts, 1st January, 1777; resigned 26th July, 1779. (Died 1st October, 1821.)

Brown, Benjamin (Mass). Ensign and Quartermaster of Jackson's Continental Regiment, 12th May, 1778; resigned 22d December, 1779. (Died 5th March, 1833.)

Brown, Benjamin (S. C.). Captain 6th South Carolina in 1778 and 1779.

Brown, Bezaleel (Conn). Lieutenant in the Lexington Alarm, April, 1775; 1st Lieutenant, 5th Connecticut, 1st May to 1st December, 1775.

Brown, Bryant (Conn). Sergeant in the Lexington Alarm, April, 1775; Sergeant 3d Connecticut, 10th May to 16th December, 1775; Ensign 20th Continental Infantry, 1st January to 31st December, 1776; 2d Lieutenant 8th Connecticut, 1st January, 1777; resigned 11th April, 1778.

Brown, Caleb (Del). Ensign Delaware Regiment, 30th November, 1776; 2d Lieutenant, 5th April, 1777; 1st Lieutenant, 10th September, 1778. Died 29th January, 1780.

Brown Chad (R. I.). Colonel Rhode Island Militia, 1779-1780.

Brown, Charles (S. C.). Lieutenant 1st South Carolina, 8th December, 1778; taken prisoner at Charleston, 12th May, 1780; exchanged July, 1781, and served to close of war.

Brown, Clark (R. I.). Quartermaster 9th Continental Infantry, 1st January to 31st December, 1776; Quartermaster 1st Rhode Island, 1st January, 1777, to ——. (Died 31st January, 1819.)

Brown, Daniel (Mass). Sergeant 10th Massachusetts, 9th December, 1776; Ensign, 1st November, 1777; resigned 18th March, 1780. (Died 1840.)

Brown, Daniel (N. J.). 2d Lieutenant 1st New Jersey, 8th November, 1775. Died 8th November, 1776.

Brown, Daniel (R. I.). Surgeon's Mate 9th Continental Infantry, 1st January to 31st December, 1776.

Brown, Daniel (Va). Surgeon 14th Virginia, 8th June, 1778; resigned 26th September, 1778.

Brown, David (Mass). Captain of a Company of Minute Men at Concord, 19th April, 1775.

Brown David (Pa). 1st Lieutenant 4th Pennsylvania, 18th February, 1777; Captain Lieutenant, 16th May, 1778; Captain, 27th May, 1779; resigned 17th April, 1780.

Brown, David (N. J.). 1st Lieutenant of Spencer's Continental Regiment, 7th March, 1777; resigned 5th November, 1777.

Brown, David (N. Y.). Lieutenant New York State Troops; wounded at Horse Neck, 26th February, 1779.

Brown, Daivd (R. I.). Lieutenant Rhode Island Artillery, 1777-1778.

Brown, Ebenezer (Mass). Corporal in Greaton's Massachusetts Regiment, April to December, 1775; Sergeant in Whitney's Regiment, Massachusetts Militia, in 1776; Sergeant 2d Massachusetts, 23d December, 1776; Ensign, 28th September, 1777; wounded at Saratoga 8th October, 1777; transferred to 1st Massachusetts, 1st January, 1781; Lieutenant, 21st March, 1782, and served to 3d November, 1783. (Died 1st September, 1844.)

Brown, Eli (Conn). 2d Lieutenant of Elmore's Connecticut State Regiment, 15th April, 1776, to April, 1777.

Brown, Ezekiel (Mass). Surgeon Massachusetts Militia Regiment in 1776; Surgeon 7th Massachusetts, 1st January, 1777; retired 1st January, 1781.

Brown, Gabriel (S. C.). Captain South Carolina Militia; at King's Mountain in October, 1780.

Brown, Godfrey (R. I.). Ensign of Church's Rhode Island Regiment, 3d May to November, 1775.

Brown, Gowen (Mass). Captain of Jackson's Continental Regiment, 1st April, 1777; resigned 22d September, 1778.

Brown, Isaac (Conn). Private in the Lexington Alarm in April, 1775; Corporal 15th Connecticut, 11th May to 15th December, 1775; Sergeant of Webb's Continental Regiment, 25th February, 1777; Ensign, 16th May, 1778; resigned 10th March, 1779.

Brown, Isaac (Mass). Lieutenant of Prescott's Massachusetts Regiment, May to December, 1775.

Brown, Jabez (R. I.). Colonel Rhode Island Militia in 1778.

Brown, Jacob (Mass). Sergeant 13th Massachusetts, 1st March, 1777; Ensign, 1st January, 1778; resigned 13th April, 1780. (Died 19th January, 1834.)

Brown, Jacob (Mass). Major of Phinney's Massachusetts Regiment, May to December, 1775; Major 18th Continental Infantry, 1st January to 31st December, 1776.

Brown, Jacob (Mass). Major of Mitchell's Regiment Massachusetts Militia in the Bagaduce Expedition, July to September, 1779.

Brown, Jacob (Mass). Surgeon's Mate of Scammon's Massachusetts Regiment, May to December, 1775.

Brown, Jacob R. (Va). Ensign 1st Virginia, 15th September, 1778; taken prisoner at Charleston, 12th May, 1780; exchanged June, 1781; transferred to 5th Virginia, 12th February, 1781; Lieutenant, — June, 1781, and served to close of war.

Brown, James (N. H.). 1st Lieutenant 3d New Hampshire, 23d May to December, 1775.

Brown, —— (N. H.). Ensign 2d New Hampshire, ——; discharged 20th September, 1775.

Brown, James (S. C.). Chief Physician and Surgeon Southern Department, 22d March, 1780, to June, 1782.

Brown, James, Jr. (R. I.). Ensign of Church's Rhode Island Regiment, 3d May to December, 1775.

Brown, James S. (N. C.). Lieutenant-Colonel North Carolina Militia; was a prisoner in 1778; where and when taken not stated.

Brown, John (Conn). Lieutenant-Colonel Continental Army, 20th November, 1775; served during the campaign against Quebec in 1775 and 1776; Lieutenant-Colonel of Elmore's Connecticut State Regiment, 29th July, 1776; resigned 15th March, 1777; Colonel Regiment of New York Levies in 1780, and was killed at Fort Keyser 19th October, 1780.

Brown, John (Conn). Cornet 2d Continental Dragoons, 15th January, 1777; Lieutenant, 11th October, 1777; resigned 22d June, 1779.

Brown, John (Conn). Captain of Pettibone's Regiment Connecticut Militia, August, 1776; resigned 2d September, 1776.

Brown, John (Mass). 2d Lieutenant of Lee's Continental Regiment, 21st January, 1777; resigned 14th January, 1778.

Brown, John (Mass). Sergeant 3d Massachusetts, 1st January, 1777; Ensign, 1st July, 1777; on a list for August, 1778, he is reported as "under sentence of death for desertion"; was pardoned by a resolve of Congress 9th March, 1779.

Brown, John (N. J.). Private and Sergeant in Forman's Regiment, New Jersey Militia, 1775 and 1776; Cornet 2d Continental Dragoons, 15th January, 1777; Lieutenant, 11th October, 1777; resigned 22d June, 1779. (Died 27th August, 1828.)

Brown, John (N. Y.). Sergeant Major 2d New York, 1st January, 1777; Ensign, 1st June, 1778; resigned 27th March, 1781; served subsequently as Lieutenant New York Levies. (Died 1802.)

Brown, John (N. Y.). Lieutenant-Colonel New York State Regiment in 1775.

Brown, John (N. C.). Ensign, 1st North Carolina, 15th November, 1775; 2d Lieutenant, 4th January, 1776; Captain, 26th April, 1777; was at King's Mountain in October, 1780; on list for June, 1788, he is dropped, with remark transferred to one of the Dragoon Regiments in North Carolina.

Brown, John (S. C.). Lieutenant 3d South Carolina, ——; wounded at Beaufort, 9th February, 1779, and killed at Stono Ferry, 20th June, 1779.

Brown, John Alexander (Pa). Surgeon 9th Pennsylvania, December, 1776, to January, 1777.

Brown, John J. (Va). Surgeon's Mate 3d Virginia, 17th October, 1781, to 1st January, 1782.

Brown, Jonas (Mass). 2d Lieutenant of Ward's Massachusetts Regiment, 23d May to December, 1775.

Brown, Jonathan (Conn). Captain 2d Continental Artillery, 1st January, 1777 ;resigned 20th September, 1779.

Brown, Jonathan (N. Y.). Ensign 1st New York, 21st November, 1776; resigned 29th April, 1778. (Died 1836.)

Brown, Joseph (Conn). Ensign 5th Connecticut, 1st January, 1777; resigned 11th January, 1778. (Died 1812.)

Brown, Joseph (Mass). 2d Lieutenant 15th Massachusetts, 1st January, 1777; 1st Lieutenant, 2d April, 1779; Captain Lieutenant, 28th June, 1779; Captain, 3d February, 1780; resigned 15th November, 1780.

Brown, Joseph (Pa). Surgeon's Mate 7th Pennsylvania, January, 1777; Surgeon, July, 1777; retired 1st July, 1778. (Died 1835.)

Brown, Joseph (S. C.). Lieutenant-Colonel South Carolina Militia, 1779-1781.

Brown, Joshua (Mass). 1st Lieutenant of Prescott's Massachusetts Regiment, May to December, 1775; was wounded at Bunker Hill, 17th June, 1775; 1st Lieutenant 7th Continental Infantry, 1st January to 31st December, 1776; Captain 15th Massachusetts, 1st January, 1777; supernumerary, 1st August, 1779.

Brown, Josiah (Conn). 2d Lieutenant of Sherburne's Continental Regiment, 28th February 1777; resigned 17th April, 1780. (Died 12th August, 1826.)

Brown, Josiah (N. H.). 1st Lieutenant 3d New Hampshire, 23d May to December, 1775.

Brown, Josiah (Vt). Lieutenant Vermont Militia in 1777.

Brown, Malcolm (Ga). Captain and Aide-de-Camp to General Andrew Williamson, and deserted to the enemy with the General in July, 1780.

Brown, Morgan W. (N. C.). 1st Lieutenant 9th North Carolina, 28th November, 1776; resigned 12th October, 1777; served as a Volunteer, and was taken prisoner at Charleston 12th May, 1780. (Died 1840.)

Brown, Moses (Mass). Sergeant in Lexington Alarm, April, 1775; Captain 14th Continental Infantry, 1st January to 31st December, 1776. (Died 1820.)

Brown, Nathan (Mass). Captain of Mansfield's Massachusetts Regiment, May to December, 1775; Captain, 27th Continental Infantry, 1st January to 31st December, 1776; served subsequently as Major Massachusetts Militia. (Died 29th May, 1825.)

Brown, Nathan (N. H.). Captain New Hampshire Militia, 1776-1780.

Brown, Nathaniel (R. I.). Lieutenant-Colonel Rhode Island Militia in 1775.

Brown, Nicholas (Pa). Ensign Pennsylvania Battalion of the Flying Camp, July to December, 1776.

Brown, Oliver (Mass). Private in Lexington Alarm, April, 1775; Lieutenant of Gridley's Regiment Massachusetts Artillery, June to December, 1775; Lieutenant of Knox's Regiment Continental Artillery, 13th December, 1775; Captain Lieutenant 3d Continental Artillery, 1st January, 1777; resigned 30th April, 1779. (Died 17th February, 1846.)

Brown, Peter (Md). 2d Lieutenant 1st Maryland, 10th December, 1776; resigned 10th July, 1777.

Brown, Peter W. (Mass). Ensign 18th Continental Infantry, 1st January, 1776; 2d Lieutenant, 15th April to 31st December, 1776. (Died 23d February, 1830.)

Brown, Richard (N. H.). 2d Lieutenant 2d New Hampshire, 23d May to December, 1775; Quartermaster 2d New Hampshire, 8th November, 1776; resigned 22d August, 1778.

Brown, Richard (Pa). 3d Lieutenant of Thompson's Pennsylvania Rifle Regiment, June to 26th October, 1775; Captain 1st Battalion of Miles' Pennsylvania Rifle Regiment, 19th March, 1776; taken prisoner at Long Island, 27th August, 1776. (Died 1811.)

Brown, Richard (S. C.). Lieutenant 3d South Carolina, 17th June, 1775; 1st Lieutenant, 12th September, 1775; wounded at Beaufort 9th February, 1779.

Brown, Robert (N. J.). Captain and Lieutenant-Colonel New Jersey Militia, 1779-1781.

Brown, Robert (Pa). Lieutenant of Baxter's Pennsylvania Battalion of the Flying Camp, July, 1776; taken prisoner at Fort Washington, 16th November, 1776; exchanged 25th January, 1781. (Died 26th February, 1823.)

Brown, Robert (R. I.). Colonel Rhode Island Militia in 1775.

Brown, Robert (Va). Lieutenant of a Virginia State Regiment, 1778 to 1781.

Brown, Samuel (Conn). 1st Lieutenant 20th Continental Infantry, 1st January to 31st December, 1776.

Brown, Samuel (Conn). Surgeon's Mate, 1st Connecticut, 1st August, 1777; resigned 1st May, 1779.

Brown, Samuel (Mass). 1st Lieutenant of Thomas' Massachusetts Regiment, May, 1775; taken prisoner at Quebec, 31st December, 1775. (Died 1828.)

Brown, Samuel (Mass). 2d Lieutenant of Bridges' Massachusetts Regiment, May, 1775; wounded at Bunker Hill, 17th June, 1775.

Brown, Stephen (Conn). 1st Lieutenant 3d Connecticut, 1st May to 7th

December, 1775; Captain 20th Continental Infantry, 1st January to 31st December, 1776; Captain 4th Connecticut, 1st January, 1777; killed 15th November, 1777, in the defence of Fort Mifflin, Pa.

Brown, Sylvanus (Conn). Captain Lieutenant 5th Connecticut, 1st May to 13th December, 1775; Captain of Silliman's Connecticut State Regiment, 20th June to 25th December, 1776; Captain 8th Connecticut, 1st January, 1777; retired 15th November, 1778.

Brown, Tarlton (S. C.). Lieutenant South Carolina, ——, 1776; Captain, ——, 1777; served to ——.

Brown, Thomas (Conn). Major of Douglas' Connecticut State Regiment in 1776, and Lieutenant-Colonel Connecticut Militia in 1777.

Brown, Thomas (Ga). 1st Lieutenant 2d Georgia, ——; killed at Stono Ferry, 20th June, 1779.

Brown, Thomas (Mass). 2d Lieutenant of Little's Massachusetts Regiment, 19th May to December, 1775.

Brown, Thomas (Va). Ensign 1st Virginia, 8th February, 1776; 2d Lieutenant, — May, 1776; 1st Lieutenant, 4th October, 1776; Captain Lieutenant, 18th October, 1777, and served to ——.

Brown, Timothy (R. I.). Lieutenant of Captain Spalding's Company Rhode Island Artillery, 15th January, 1776, to May, 1777.

Brown, William (Md). Lieutenant Maryland Militia in 1776; Captain Independent Company Maryland Artillery, 20th November, 1777; Company transferred to 1st Continental Artillery, 30th May, 1778; Major 1st Continental Artillery, 31st January, 1781, and served to June, 1783.

Brown, William (N. Y.). 1st Lieutenant 1st New York, 28th June, 1775, to January, 1776, and Captain, July to November, 1776.

Brown, William (Va). Assistant Surgeon of the Flying Camp, 19th September to 1st December, 1776; Surgeon-General of the Hospital, Middle Department, 13th May, 1777; Physician and Director-General of Hospital, 6th February, 1778; resigned 21st July, 1780.

Brown, Windsor (Va). Captain 1st Virginia State Regiment, 28th February, 1777, to January, 1781.

Brown, Zephaniah (R. I.). Ensign of Richmond's Rhode Island State Regiment, 19th August, 1776; 1st Lieutenant 1st Rhode Island, 11th February, 1777; Captain, 11th November, 1779; retained in Olney's Rhode Island Battalion May, 1781, and served to 3d November, 1783.

Browne, William (Pa). Lieutenant of Miles' Pennsylvania Rifle Regiment, 8th January, 1776; 1st Lieutenant 9th Pennsylvania, 2d December, 1776; wounded at Brandywine 11th September, 1777; retired 30th September, 1778. (Died 1825.)

Brownell, Jonathan (R. I.). Captain of Church's Rhode Island Regiment, 3d May to December, 1775; wounded at Bunker Hill 17th June, 1775; Captain in Babcock's and Lippitt's Rhode Island State Regiments in 1776 and 1777. (Died 1796.)

Brownfield, Robert (S. C.). Surgeon's Mate 2d South Carolina in 1778, and served to close of war.

Browning, Isaac (Va). Captain Virginia Militia, 1780-1781.

Browning, Jacob (N. J.). Captain New Jersey Militia in 1777.

Brownlee, Alexander (Va). Ensign of Grayson's Continental Regiment, 1st November, 1777; resigned 27th January, 1778.

Brownlee, Alexander (—). Ensign, ——; killed at Guilford, 15th March, 1781.

Brownlee, John (Va). Surgeon's Mate Virginia Regiment, ——; taken prisoner at Charleston, 12th May, 1780.

Brownlee, Joseph (Pa). 3d Lieutenant 2d Battalion of Miles' Pennsylvania Rifle Regiment, 15th August, 1776; taken prisoner at Long Island 27th August, 1776; exchanged 9th December, 1776; 1st Lieutenant Pennsylvania State Regiment, 18th April, 1777; resigned 22d June, 1777. Also reported (unofficially) as having been killed by the Indians at the burning of Hannastown in 1782.

Brownlee, Wm. (Va). Sergeant of Grayson's Additional Regiment, —— March, 1777; Ensign, 8th June, 1777; 2d Lieutenant, 1st February, 1778; Regimental Quartermaster, 15th September, 1778; transferred to Gist's Regiment, 22d April, 1779; retired 1st January, 1781.

Brownson, Eli (Conn). 1st Lieutenant Connecticut Militia at the battle of Bennington, August, 1777. (Died 1830.)

Brownson, Eli (Vt). Lieutenant Vermont Militia in 1777.

Brownson, Gideon (N. H.). Captain Green Mountain Boys, 27th July to December, 1775; taken prisoner at Montreal, 25th September, 1775; Captain of Warner's Continental Regiment, 5th July, 1776; wounded at Bennington 16th August, 1777; Major, 16th July, 1779; wounded and taken prisoner at Lake George 15th July, 1779; retired 1st January, 1781. (Died 1796.)

Brownson, Nathan (Ga). Deputy Purveyor of Hospital for Southern Army, 27th March, 1781, to close of war. (Died 6th November, 1796.)

Brown, Atheniel (Vt). Ensign Vermont Militia in 1777.

Bruce, William (Md). 2d Lieutenant 1st Maryland, 10th December, 1776; 1st Lieutenant, 10th June, 1777; Regimental Adjutant, 6th June, 1778; Captain, 1st August, 1779; transferred to 5th Maryland, 1st January, 1781; retained in Maryland Battalion, April, 1783, and served to 15th November, 1783.

Bruen, Jeremiah (N. J.). Captain of Baldwin's Artillery Artificer Regiment, 2d March, 1777; Major, 12th November, 1779; retired 1st July, 1781.

Bruff, James (Md). 2d Lieutenant 6th Maryland, 10th December, 1776; 1st Lieutenant, 7th October, 1777; transferred to 5th Maryland, 1st January, 1781; Captain Lieutenant, — February, 1781; Captain, 8th September, 1781; wounded and taken prisoner at Camden 25th April, 1781; exchanged ——; served to April, 1783; Captain Artillerists and Engineers, United States Army, 2d June, 1794; Major 1st Artillerists and Engineers, 15th November, 1803; resigned 30th June, 1807.

Bruin, Peter Bryant (Va). Lieutenant of Morgan's Virginia Rifle Company, July, 1775; wounded and taken prisoner at Quebec, 31st December, 1775; exchanged — July, 1776; Captain 11th Virginia, 19th December, 1776; Major and Aide-de-Camp to General Sullivan, 9th November, 1777; regiment designated 7th Virginia, 14th September, 1778; Major, ——; served to close of war. (Died 27th January, 1827.)

Brun, Bellacour (—).—See **La Brun.**

Brunson, Isaac (Conn). Captain Connecticut Militia, 1778.

Brunson, Michael (Conn). Ensign of Wadsworth's Connecticut State Regiment, June to December, 1776.

Brusard, Celerine (Ga). Captain 4th Georgia in 1778; resigned 15th June, 1779, and returned to France.

Brush, Alexander (N. H.). Sergeant of Warner's Continental Regiment, 6th December, 1776; Ensign, 18th August, 1778; resigned 15th September, 1779.

Brussell, Philip (Pa). Major of Slough's Battalion Pennsylvania Associaters Militia, June, 1776; discharged 8th October, 1776.

Bruyn, Jacobus S. (N. Y.). Captain 3d New York, 28th June, 1775; Lieutenant-Colonel of Du Bois New York Regiment, 26th June, 1776; Lieutenant-Colonel 5th New York, 21st November, 1776, to rank from 26th June, 1776; taken prisoner at Fort Montgomery, 6th October, 1777; exchanged ——; transferred to 3d New York, 1st July, 1780; retired 1st January, 1781. (Died 12th July, 1825.)

Bryan, Benjamin (N. C.). Ensign 2d North Carolina, 27th April, 1777; 2d Lieutenant 7th North Carolina, 15th July, 1777; retired 1st June, 1778.

Bryan, Hardy (N. C.). Commissary 7th North Carolina, 11th December, 1776, to ——.

Bryan, James (Ga). Lieutenant 4th Georgia in 1777; taken prisoner at Savannah 19th October, 1779. (Died 1832.)

Bryan, Jehiel (Conn). 1st Lieutenant of Douglas' Connecticut State Regiment, June to December, 1776.

Bryan, John (N. C.). Captain North Carolina Militia; killed at his home by Tories 12th March, 1782.

Bryant, David (Mass). 1st Lieutenant of Knox's Regiment Continental Artillery, 13th December, 1775; Captain Lieutenant, — August, 1776; Captain Lieutenant 3d Continental Artillery, 1st January, 1777; Captain, 10th May, 1777. Died 12th September, 1777, of wounds received at Brandywine, 11th September, 1777.

Bryant, Job. (Mass). Private in Lexington Alarm, April, 1775; Corporal in Thomas' Massachusetts Regiment, May to December, 1775; Ensign 23d Continental Infantry, 1st January to 31st December, 1776.

Bryant, John (Mass). 1st Lieutenant in Knox's Regiment Continental Artillery, 1st January, 1776; had his arm accidentally shot off 12th July, 1776, but remained in service as Commissary of Issues to January, 1781.

Bryant, John, Jr. (N. C.). Lieutenant 7th North Carolina, 28th November, 1776, to ——.

Bryant, John (S. C.). Brigadier- General South Carolina Militia at Briar Creek, Georgia, in March, 1779.

Bryant, Matthew (N. H.). Lieutenant New Hampshire Militia, 1776-1777.

Bryce, John.—See **Brice.**

Bryer, Benjamin (N. C.). Ensign 7th North Carolina, 27th April, 1777; 2d Lieutenant, 15th July, 1777; retired 1st June, 1778.

Bryman, Christian (—).—See **Brayman.**

Bryson, John (Pa). 1st Lieutenant 7th Pennsylvania, 10th April, 1777; wounded and taken prisoner at Paramus, 16th April, 1780, and did not rejoin regiment.

Bryson, Samuel (Pa). 1st Lieutenant 7th Pennsylvania, 20th March, 1777; wounded at Germantown, 4th October, 1777; wounded and taken prisoner at New Bridge, New Jersey, 15th April, 1780; transferred to 4th Pennsylvania, 17th January, 1781; transferred to 2d Pennsylvania, 1st January, 1783, and served to close of war. (Died 19th December, 1799.)

Bubier, William (Mass). 1st Lieutenant of Glover's Massachusetts Regiment, 19th May to December, 1775; 1st Lieutenant 14th Continental Infantry, 1st January to December, 1776.

Buchanan, Andrew (Md). Brigadier-General Maryland Militia, 6th January, 1776, to ——.

Buchanan, Andrew (Va). Major Virginia Militia, 1776-1778.

Buchanan, John (S. C.). Captain 2d South Carolina, 28th September, 1777; taken prisoner at Charleston, 12th May, 1780; exchanged June, 1781, and served to close of war; Brevet Major, 30th September, 1783.

Buchanan, John (Va). 2d Lieutenant 7th Virginia, 4th April, 1776; 1st Lieutenant, 13th December, 1776; died 11th October, 1777, of wounds received at Germantown, 4th October, 1777.

Buchanan, Patrick (Va). Captain Virginia Militia, 1776-1777.

Buchanan, Robert (N. Y.). Captain Lieutenant 2d Canadian (Hazen's) Regiment, 18th November, 1776; omitted May, 1777.

Buchanan, Robert (S. C.). 2d Lieutenant 5th South Carolina, 18th April,

1776; 1st Lieutenant, 23d January, 1778; taken prisoner at Charleston, 12th May, 1780, and died a prisoner.

Buchanan, Thomas (Pa). 3d Lieutenant of Thompson's Pennsylvania Rifle Regiment, 25th June, 1775; 2d Lieutenant 1st Continental Infantry, 1st January, 1776; 1st Lieutenant 1st Pennsylvania, 1st January, 1777; Captain Lieutenant, 1st October, 1777; Captain, 23d October, 1777; resigned 15th October, 1779. (Died 13th October, 1823.)

Buchanan, William (Md). Captain and Lieutenant-Colonel Maryland Militia in 1776; Deputy Commissary-General of Purchases, 18th June, 1777; Commissary-General of Purchases, 5th August, 1777; resigned 23d March, 1778. (Died 1827.)

Buchanan, William (Va). Captain Virginia Militia, 1777-1783.

Bucher, John Conrad (Pa). Chaplain German Regiment, 8th July, 1776; resigned 1st August, 1777. (Died 1780.)

Buck, Asahel (Pa). 2d Lieutenant of Durkee's Wyoming Valley Independent Pennsylvania Company, 26th August, 1776; killed by Indians, 10th February, 1779.

Buck, Henry (Pa). Surgeon's Mate 2d Battalion of Miles' Pennsylvania Rifle Regiment, 22d March to November, 1776.

Buck, James (Pa). Surgeon's Mate of Miles' Pennsylvania Rifle Regiment, 25th October to December, 1776.

Buck, John (Mass). Ensign 12th Massachusetts, 13th November, 1776; resigned 1st July, 1779.

Buck, Jonathan (Conn). 2d Lieutenant of Sage's Connecticut State Regiment, 20th June, 1776; killed on the retreat from New York, 15th September, 1776.

Buck, Jonathan (Mass). Colonel Massachusetts Militia, 1776-1780. (Died 1795.)

Buck, Joseph (N. J.). Sergeant 2d New Jersey, February, 1777, to February, 1779; 2d Lieutenant, 1st February, 1779; 1st Lieutenant, 6th March, 1781; retained in New Jersey Battalion, April, 1783, and served to close of war. (Died 1803.)

Buck, Josiah (Conn). Quartermaster's-Sergeant 7th Connecticut, 1st March, 1777; 2d Lieutenant, 25th December, 1777; resigned 9th April, 1780.

Buck, Stephen (N. C.) Ensign North Carolina Militia, 1780-1781.

Buckholdt, Abraham (S. C.). Major South Carolina Militia in 1775.

Buckholdt, Peter (S. C.). Captain South Carolina Militia in 1776.

Buckland, Stephen (Conn). Captain Lieutenant of Bigelow's Independent Company Connecticut Artillery, 23d January, 1776; Captain of Stevens' Battalion Continental Artillery, 9th November, 1776; battalion became part of 3d Continental Artillery in 1778; resigned 10th April, 1780.

Buckley, Edward (—).—See **Bulkley.**

Bucklin, James (Mass). Ensign in Lexington Alarm, April, 1775; 2d Lieutenant of Walker's Massachusetts Regiment, May to December, 1775.

Buckman, Tjerch (—).—See **Beekman.**

Buckmaster, Joseph (Conn). Chaplain of Webb's Continental Regiment, 1st January, 1776, to ——.

Buckmaster, Richard (Mass). 2d Lieutenant of Nixon's Massachusetts Regiment, May to December, 1775; 2d Lieutenant 4th Continental Infantry, 1st January to 31st December, 1776; Lieutenant and Adjutant 6th Massachusetts, 1st January, 1777; Captain, 10th June, 1779. Died 11th November, 1779.

Buckmaster, William (Mass). Lieutenant-Colonel of Brewer's Massachusetts Regiment, May, 1775; severely wounded at Bunker Hill, 17th June, 1775; Lieutenant-Colonel 6th Continental Infantry 1st January, 1776. Died 22d June, 1776.

Buckner, Mordecai (Va). Colonel 6th Virginia, 13th February, 1776; cashiered 9th February, 1777. (Died 1800.)

Buckner, Samuel (Va). Cadet 6th Virginia, 25th August, 1776, to ——.

Buckner, Thomas (Va). Captain 7th Virginia, 28th October, 1776; retired 14th September, 1778.

Buckner, Thomas (Va). 2d Lieutenant 7th Virginia, 7th March, 1776; 1st Lieutenant, 13th November, 1776; Captain Lieutenant, — July, 1777; transferred to 5th Virginia, 14th September, 1778; Captain, 3d October, 1778; taken prisoner at Charleston, 12th May, 1780; prisoner on parole to close of war.

Buckner, William (Va). Captain Virginia Militia in 1779.

Budd, Charles (Ga). Captain of a Georgia Continental Regiment; mentioned in 1779.

Budd, Danied (N. Y.). Surgeon New York Militia; taken prisoner 20th April, 1779, at Onondegas.

Budd, Gilbert, Jr. (N. Y.). Lieutenant-Colonel, New York Militia, 1776.

Budd, John S. (S. C.). Captain Lieutenant 4th South Carolina (Artillery), 18th July, 1778; taken prisoner at Charleston, 12th May, 1780.

Budd, Joseph (N. J.). Major New Jersey Militia, 1777-1781.

Budd, Samuel (N. C.). 1st Lieutenant 2d North Carolina, 11th November, 1777; Captain, — 1779; taken prisoner at Charleston, 12th May, 1780; exchanged 14th June, 1781; retired 1st January, 1783.

Budd, Thomas (Ga). Captain 4th Georgia, November, 1776; resigned 9th January, 1778.

Buehler, Henry (Pa). 3d Lieutenant of Cunningham's Pennsylvania Battalion of the Flying Camp, 13th August to 1st December, 1776. (Died 1801.)

Buell, Ellis (Conn). Major of Sage's Connecticut State Regiment, 20th June to 25th December, 1776; served subsequently in Connecticut Militia.

Buell, Ephraim (Vt). Captain Vermont Militia, 1779.

Buell, John Hutchinson (Conn). Sergeant in the Lexington Alarm in April, 1775; Ensign 20th Continental Infantry, 1st January to 31st December, 1776; 2d Lieutenant 4th Connecticut, 1st January, 1777; 1st Lieutenant, 25th November, 1777; Captain Lieutenant, 20th May, 1779; Captain, 4th January, 1780; transferred to 1st Connecticut, 1st January, 1783, and served to June, 1783. (Died 1813.)

Buell, Matthew (Conn). Corporal 2d Connecticut, 6th May to 17th December, 1775; 2d Lieutenant of Gay's Connecticut State Regiment, 20th June to 25th December, 1776; 2d Lieutenant 2d Connecticut, 1st January, 1777; resigned 17th June, 1778.

Buell, Nathaniel (Conn.) Captain 4th Connecticut, 1st May to December. 1775; Lieutenant-Colonel of Burrall's Connecticut State Regiment, January, 1776, to January, 1777. (Died 1808.)

Buell, Solomon (Conn). Lieutenant Connecticut Militia; wounded in the

Danbury Raid, 27th April, 1777. (Died 1793.)

Buffe, David (N. J.). Lieutenant New Jersey Militia, ——; taken prisoner at Piscataway, 8th May, 1777.

Buffe, Thomas (N. H.). 2d Lieutenant 3d New Hampshire, 23d April to December, 1775.

Buffington, Samuel (Mass). 2d Lieutenant 7th Massachusetts, 1st January, 1777; 1st Lieutenant, — March, 1779; transferred to 4th Massachusetts, 1st January, 1781; retired 1st January, 1783. (Died 2d March, 1830.)

Buffington, Zadock (Mass). 1st Lieutenant of Mansfield's Massachusetts Regiment, May to December, 1775; 1st Lieutenant 27th Continental Infantry, 1st January to 31st December, 1776; served subsequently as Captain Massachusetts Militia.

Buford, Abraham (Va). Major 14th Virginia, 13th November, 1776; Lieutenant-Colonel 5th Virginia, 1st April, 1777; Colonel 15th May, 1778; transferred to 11th Virginia, 14th September, 1778; transferred to 3d Virginia, 12th February, 1781, and served to close of war. (Died 30th June, 1833.)

Buford, Henry (Va). Captain Virginia Militia in 1777.

Buford, William (N. C.). 2d Lieutenant 2d North Carolina, 15th May, 1777; 1st Lieutenant North Carolina Dragoons, 16th July, 1777; was a Captain in 1781; was wounded at Stono Ferry, 8th September, 1781, and served to close of war. (Died 1810.)

Bugg, William (Ga). 2d Lieutenant 1st Georgia, 12th December, 1775; 1st Lieutenant, May, 1776; was a Captain in 1779; was taken prisoner at White House, 15th September, 1780, and was wounded near Ogeechee Ferry, November 5th, 1781; served to close of war.

Bugg, Sherwood (Ga). Captain Georgia Militia, 1779-1782.

Bugbee, Edward (R. I.). Sergeant of Baldwin's Artillery Artificer Regiment, 12th January, 1776; 2d Lieutenant, 1st July, 1779; 1st Lieutenant, 12th November, 1779; Regimental Quartermaster, 1st July, 1780; retained in 2d Canadian (Hazen's) Regiment, 1st January, 1781; retired, 1st January, 1783. (Died 31st October, 1804.)

Buisson, —— (—).—See **Du Buyson.**

Bulkley, Edward (Conn). Ensign 10th Continental Infantry, 1st January,

1776; taken prisoner at Long Island, 27th August, 1776; exchanged 17th December, 1780; Captain of Webb's Continental Regiment, to rank from 1st January, 1777; transferred to 3d Connecticut, 1st January, 1781; Brigade-Major, February to August, 1782, and served to 3d June, 1783. (Died 1787.)

Bulkley, Elippalet (Conn). Captain of Wadsworth's Connecticut State Regiment, June to December, 1776; Lieutenant-Colonel Connecticut Militia, 1781-1782.

Bulkley, John (Conn). Ensign 10th Continental Infantry, 1st January, 1776, to ——.

Bull, Aaron (Conn). Fifer 2d Connecticut, 11th May to 1st September, 1775; Sergeant 2d Continental Dragoons, 8th March, 1777; Lieutenant, 5th November, 1778; Regimental Quartermaster, 1st December, 1778, and served to close of war.

Bull, Caleb (Conn). Captain of Webb's Continental Regiment, 1st January, 1777; resigned 23d March, 1778. (Died 1797.)

Bull, Epaphras (Conn).. Was one of the party under Arnold that captured Fort Ticonderoga, 10th May, 1775; Captain Connecticut Light Horse Militia in 1776; Captain 2d Continental Dragoons, 10th January, 1777; Major 1st Continental Dragoons, 1st August, 1779. Died October, 1781, of wounds received at Siege of Yorktown in October, 1781.

Bull Ezakiel (Pa). Surgeon's Mate of Hartley's Continental Regiment, ——, 1777; resigned 13th February, 1778; served subsequently as Surgeon's Mate and Surgeon Hospital Department.

Bull, John (Mass). 2d Lieutenant of Knox's Regiment Continental Artillery, 10th December, 1775, to January, 1777; Director of Laboratory of Stevens' Battalion Continental Artillery, 15th June, 1777, to May, 1778.

Bull, John (Pa). Colonel 1st Pennsylvania Battalion, 25th November, 1775; resigned 22d January, 1776; Colonel Pennsylvania State Regiment, 2d May, 1777; resigned 17th June, 1777; Adjutant-General of Pennsylvania, 17th June, 1777, to close of war (Died 9th August, 1824.)

Bull, Manning (N. Y.). 2d Lieutenant 4th New York, 28th June, 1775, to January, 1776.

Bull, Stephen (S. C.). Colonel and Brigadier-General South Carolina Militia, 1775, to 1782.

Bull, Thomas (Conn). Captain Connecticut Light Horse in 1776.

Bull, Thomas (N. C.). Surgeon's Mate 10th North Carolina, December, 1780 to 1783.

Bull, Thomas (Pa). Lieutenant-Colonel Pennsylvania Battalion of the Flying Camp; taken prisoner at Fort Washington, 16th November, 1776; was a prisoner 2 years.

Bull, Thomas (Pa). 1st Lieutenant 6th Pennsylvania, 15th February, 1777; Captain, 1st November, 1778; taken prisoner at Monmouth, 28th June, 1778; released February, 1780, and did not return to the army. (Died 1837.)

Bull, William (N. Y.). 2d Lieutenant of Spencer's Continental Regiment, 22d February, 1777; 1st Lieutenant, 6th April, 1777; Captain Lieutenant, 16th July, 1779; Captain, ——, 1780; retired 1st January, 1781. (Died 1817.)

Bullard, Asa (Mass). Private in Lexington Alarm, April, 1775; Private and Sergeant in Brewer's Massachusetts Regiment, May to December, 1775; Sergeant 12th Massachusetts, 14th November, 1776; Ensign, 7th October, 1777; Lieutenant, 5th July, 1779; transferred to 2d Massachusetts, 1st January, 1781, and served to 3d November, 1783. (Died 23d December, 1804.)

Bullard, Benjamin (Mass). Captain in Lexington Alarm, April, 1775; Captain in J. Brewer's Massachusetts Regiment, 19th May to December, 1775; Captain 6th Continental Infantry, 1st January, 1776; resigned 30th September, 1776.

Bullard, Isaac (Mass). 2d Lieutenant of Heath's Massachusetts Regiment, May, 1775, to ——.

Bullard, Seth (Mass). Captain in Lexington Alarm, April, 1775; Captain of Read's Massachusetts Regiment, May to December, 1775; served subsequently as Major Massachusetts Militia. (Died 1811.)

Bullard, Samuel (Mass). Colonel Massachusetts Militia, 1776-1778.

Bullen, John (Del). Commissary of Purchases and Issues, 1779-1781.

Bullit, Thomas (Va). Lieutenant-Colonel Deputy Adjutant-General Southern Department, 6th March, 1776, and with rank of Colonel from 18th May, 1776, to — September, 1778.

Bullock, Daniel (N. C). Lieutenant 9th North Carolina, 28th November, 1776, to ——.

Bullock, Rice (Va). Quartermaster 15th Virginia, 16th July, 1777; superseded, 6th May, 1778.

Bullock, Stephen (R. I.). Captain Rhode Island Militia, 1778-1779.

Bunbury, William (Va). Sergeant 3d Virginia, December, 1776; Ensign 15th August, 1777; resigned 26th November, 1777.

Bunce, Joseph (Conn). Ensign of Chester's Connecticut State Regiment, June to December, 1776.

Bunchoten, Elias van, Jr. (N. Y.). 1st Lieutenant, 3d New York, 28th June, 1775; Captain, 25th November, 1775, to January, 1776; Captain 3d New York, 21st November, 1776, to rank from 25th November, 1775; resigned 15th December, 1777; served subsequently as Major New York Levies.

Bunchoten, John Van (N. Y.). Captain New York Militia, 1777. (Died 1817.)

Bunchoten, Mathew (N. Y.). Captain New York Militia, 1777.

Bunchoten, Peter van (N. Y.). 2d Lieutenant 4th New York, 21st November, 1776; 1st Lieutenant, 9th November, 1777; retired 1st January, 1781

Buncombe, Edward (N. C.). Colonel 5th North Carolina, 15th April, 1776; died November, 1777, while a prisoner, of wounds received at Germantown 4th October, 1777.

Bunnell, Nathaniel (Conn.) 2d Lieutenant 1st Connecticut, 1st May to 1st December, 1775; Captain of Douglas' Connecticut State Regiment, 20th June to 29th December, 1776.

Bunnell, Titus (Conn). Ensign of Gay's Connecticut State Regiment, June to December, 1776.

Bunner, Jacob (Pa). Captain German Regiment, 8th July, 1776; retired 1st January, 1781.

Bunner, Rudolph (Pa). Captain 2d Pennsylvania Battalion, 5th January, 1776; Captain 3d Pennsylvania, 3d March, 1777, to rank from 5th January, 1776; Major 3d Pennsylvania, 6th June, 1777; Lieutenant-Colonel, 1st August, 1777; killed at Monmouth, 28th June, 1778.

Buntin, Andrew (N. H.). Captain New Hampshire Militia. Killed at White Plains, 28th October, 1776.

Bunting, William Black (Va). Ensign 9th Virginia, 14th February, 1776;

2d Lieutenant, 31st August, 1776. Died 1st April, 1777.

Burbank, Samuel (Mass). Private in Lexington Alarm, April, 1775; Lieutenant in Doolittle's Massachusetts Regiment, May to December, 1775; 1st Lieutenant 24th Continental Infantry, 1st January to 31st December, 1776; Captain Massachusetts Militia, 1778-1779. (Died 1808.)

Burbank, Silas (Mass). Lieutenant of Phinney's Massachusetts Regiment, May to December, 1775; 1st Lieutenant 18th Continental Infantry, 1st January to 31st December, 1776; 1st Lieutenant 12th Massachusetts, 1st January, 1777; Captain, 1st July, 1777; resigned 14th October, 1780. (Died 1814.)

Burbeck, Edward (Mass). Captain of Gridley's Regiment Massachusetts Artillery, June, 1775; Captain of Knox's Regiment Continental Artillery, 10th December, 1775, to December, 1776. (Died 1782.)

Burbeck, Henry (Mass). 1st Lieutenant of Gridley's Regiment Massachusetts Artillery, 19th May, 1775; 1st Lieutenant of Knox's Regiment Continental Artillery, 10th December, 1775; Captain Lieutenant 3d Continental Artillery, 1st January, 1777; Captain, 3d September, 1777; transferred to Corps of Artillery, 17th June, 1783; Brevet Major, 30th September, 1783, and served to 3d November, 1783; Captain 3d Company United States Artillery Battalion, 20th October, 1786; Captain Artillery United States Army, 29th September, 1789; Major, 4th November, 1791, of the Artillerists and Engineers, 9th May, 1794; Lieutenant-Colonel 1st Artillerists and Engineers, 7th May, 1798; Colonel Artillerists, 1st April, 1802 to 12th May, 1814, when retained as Brevet Brigadier-General in command; Brevet Brigadier- General, 10th July, 1812; honorably discharged, 15th June, 1815. (Died 2d October, 1848.)

Burbeck, William (Mass). Lieutenant-Colonel of Gridley's Regiment Massachusetts Artillery, 19th May, 1775; Lieutenant-Colonel of Knox's Regiment Continental Artillery, 10th December, 1775; dismissed 25th May, 1776; served subsequently as Superintendent and Comptroller of Laboratory, 1777-1783. (Died 22d July, 1785.)

Burch, Ezra (Conn). Ensign of Colonel Beebe's Regiment Connecticut Militia in 1775.

Burcham, Richard (N. J.). Ensign 4th New Jersey, 1st June, 1777; omitted March, 1778.

Burchardt, Daniel (Pa). Captain German Regiment, 8th July, 1776; Major, 7th April, 1777; resigned 2d July, 1779. (Name also spelled Burkhard.)

Burd, Benjamin (——).—See **Bird.**

Burd, Benjamin (Pa). 3d Lieutenant of Thompson's Pennsylvania Rifle Regiment, 25th June, 1775; 2d Lieutenant 1st Continental Infantry, 1st January, 1776; 1st Lieutenant, 25th September, 1776; Captain 4th Pennsylvania, 3d January, 1777; Lieutenant-Colonel 3d Continental Dragoons, 14th March, 1777; resigned 20th November, 1778. (Name also spelled Burd and Byrd.) (Died 5th October, 1823.)

Burd, Edward (Pa). Major of Haller's Pennsylvania Battalion of the Flying Camp, June, 1776; taken prisoner at Long Island, 27th August, 1776.

Burd, James (Pa). Colonel Pennsylvania Militia, 1775-1776. (Died 1793.)

Burd, Thomas (Va). 2d Lieutenant 11th Virginia, 23d January, 1777, to ——.

Burd, William (——).—See **Bird.**

Burdett, Samuel (Mass). 1st Lieutenant 8th Massachusetts, 1st January, 1777; resigned 3d October, 1777.

Burdett, William (Pa). Ensign of Baldwin's Artillery Artificer Regiment, 1st January, 1777; discharged 1st April, 1778.

Burfoot, Thomas (Va). Adjutant 14th Virginia, 12th January, 1778; 2d Lieutenant, 9th September, 1778; regiment designated 10th Virginia, 14th September, 1778; 1st Lieutenant, 16th July, 1780; Captain Lieutenant, 18th July, 1781; transferred to 1st Virginia, 12th February, 1781, and served to close of war. (Died 1820.)

Burgess, Basil (Md). Ensign 3d Maryland, 1st August, 1780; 2d Lieutenant, 18th June, 1781; transferred to 1st Maryland, 1st January, 1783; retained in Maryland Battalion, April, 1783, and served to 15th November, 1783.

Burgess, Edward (Md). Captain 1st Maryland Battalion of the Flying Camp, July to December, 1776. (Died 1809.)

Burgess, John Magruder (Md). 1st Lieutenant 3d Maryland Battalion of the Flying Camp, July to December, 1776.

Burgess, Joseph (Conn). 2d Lieutenant 8th Connecticut, 6th July to 15th December, 1775; 1st Lieutenant of Douglas' Connecticut State Regiment, June to November, 1776; served subsequently as Lieutenant and Captain Connecticut Militia. (Died 1806.)

Burgess, Joseph (Md). Ensign of Smallwood's Maryland Regiment, 14th January, 1776; 2d Lieutenant 3d Maryland Battalion of the Flying Camp, July to December, 1776; Captain 4th Maryland, 10th December, 1776. Died 17th November, 1778.

Burgess, Joshua (Md). Lieutenant 1st Maryland, 11th March, 1780; taken prisoner at Camden, 16th August, 1780; exchanged December, 1780, and served to April, 1783.

Burgess, Michael (Md). Corporal of Smallwood's Maryland Regiment, 3d February, 1776; Ensign 3d Maryland Battalion of the Flying Camp, July to December, 1776.

Burgess, Vachel (Md). Ensign 1st Maryland, 17th April, 1777; 2d Lieutenant, 20th February, 1778; resigned 22d August, 1779. (Died 30th March, 1824.) (Name also spelled Basil Burgess.)

Burgess, William (Va). Ensign 4th Virginia, 10th May, 1776; 2d Lieutenant, December, 1776. Died 18th January, 1777.

Burgwin, John Lewis.—See **Bourgwin.**

Burhaus, John (N. Y.). Sergeant 3d New York, 13th May, 1777; Ensign, 6th February, 1779; resigned 8th December, 1779.

Burke, Adam (S. C.). 2d Lieutenant of a South Carolina Regiment, —, 1776; 1st Lieutenant, ——, 1777; resigned 23d February, 1778.

Burke, Edward (Pa). 2d Lieutenant of Patton's Continental Regiment, 15th January, 1777; 1st Lieutenant, 4th October, 1777; regiment designated 11th Pennsylvania, 13th January, 1779; Captain Lieutenant, 16th March, 1780; transferred to 1st Pennsylvania, 17th January, 1781; retired 1st January, 1783.

Burke, Henry (Va). Captain Virginia Militia, 1780-1781.

Burke, Thomas (—).—See **Bourke.**

Burkhard, Daniel (—).—See **Burchardt.**

Burket, Ezekiel (R. I.). 2d Lieutenant of Elliott's Rhode Island State Regiment, 12th December, 1776, to ——.

Burkman, Thomas (Mass). Cornet 2d Continental Dragoons, 26th January, 1777; Lieutenant, 20th October, 1777; resigned 24th August, 1779. (Died — May, 1826.)

Burley, Henry (Pa). Ensign 11th Pennsylvania, 19th July, 1779; resigned 10th March, 1780.

Burley, William (Mass). Sergeant of Mansfield's Massachusetts Regiment, May to Deiember, 1775; 2d Lieutenant 11th Massachusetts, 6th November, 1776; 1st Lieutenant, 1st January, 1777; Captain Lieutenant, 25th June, 1779; taken prisoner at Young's House, 3d February, 1780; Captain, 16th October, 1780; retired 1st January, 1781.

Burlingame, Benjamin (R. I.). Ensign of Richmond's Rhode Island State Regiment, 1st November, 1775, to June, 1776.

Burlingame, Chandler (R. I.). Ensign 9th Continental Infantry, 1st January to 31st December, 1776; Lieutenant 1st Rhode Island, 9th June, 1779; Regimental Paymaster in 1780; retained in Olney's Rhode Island Battalion, 14th May, 1781, and served to close of war.

Burlington, Pardon (N. Y.). Captain New York Militia; was a prisoner, when and where taken not stated.

Burnam, Thomas (Mass). Corporal 8th Massachusetts, 24th March, 1777; Sergeant, 5th July, 1780; Ensign, October, 1780. Died 18th December, 1780.

Burnap, Nathan (Mass). Surgeon's Mate of Doolittle's Massachusetts Regiment, May to December, 1775; Surgeon's Mate 4th Continental Infantry, 1st January, 1776, to 7th March, 1776.

Burnett, James (Va).—See **Barnett.**

Burnett, John (N. J.). Lieutenant New Jersey Militia; cashiered 14th December, 1781.

Burnett, John (N. Y.). 1st Lieutenant 5th New York, 21st November, 1776; resigned 9th May, 1778; served subsequently as Captain New York Levies. (Died 1824.)

Burnett, Robert (—). Major and Aide-de-Camp to General Greene, 23d March, 1778, to close of war. (Died 1st December, 1854.)

Burnett, Robert (N. Y.). 2d Lieutenant 2d Continental Artillery, 29th June, 1781; transferred to Corps of Artillery, 17th June, 1783, and served to 3d November, 1783.

Burnham, George (N. H.). Sergeant, 2d New Hampshire, 18th March, 1777; Ensign, 20th September, 1777; resigned 8th July, 1780.

Burnham, John (Mass). Lieutenant of Little's Massachusetts Regiment, May to December, 1775; 1st Lieutenant 12th Continental Infantry, 1st January to 31st December, 1776; Captain 8th Massachusetts, 1st January, 1777; Major 5th Massachusetts, 9th January, 1783, and served to 12th June, 1783; Major 2d United States Infantry, 4th March, 1791; resigned 29th December, 1791. (Name also spelled Burnam.) (Died 8th June, 1843.)

Burnham, Joseph (Conn). Brigade Commissary, 1st January, 1781, to 1st January, 1783.

Burnham, Samuel (Mass). Private in Lexington Alarm, April, 1775; Ensign Massachusetts Militia in 1776; 2d Lieutenant 3d Massachusetts, 1st January, 1777. Died 15th March, 1782.

Burnley, Garland (Va). 1st Lieutenant 7th Virginia, 7th May, 1776; cashiered 18th July, 1778; Captain Virginia Convention Guards ,July, 1779, to June, 1781.

Burnley, Henry. Lieutenant Virginia Militia, 1780-1781.

Burnet, William (N. J.) Surgeon New Jersey Militia, 17th February, 1776; Physician and Surgeon-General Eastern Department, 11th April, 1777; Hospital Physician and Surgeon, 6th October, 1780; Chief Physicial and Hospital Surgeon, 5th March ,1781, and served to close of war. (Died 7th October, 1791.)

Burns, John (Va). 1st Lieutenant 11th Virginia, — January, 1777; resigned 1st July, 1777; Quartermaster 11th Virginia, 7th April, 1778; retired 14th September, 1778.

Burns, Robert (Pa). 2d Lieutenant 2d Battalion of Miles' Pennsylvania Rifle Regiment, 16th March, 1776; transferred to 2d Canadian (Hazen's) Regiment, 21st December, 1776; Captain, 8th April, 1777; retired 1st January, 1782.

Burnside, John (N. Y.). Sergeant 2d Continental Artillery, 3d January, 1777; 2d Lieutenant, 13th September, 1778. Died January, 1781.

Burr, Aaron (N. J.). Served as a volunteer in the Canadian campaign and at Quebec in 1775; Aide-de-Camp to General Putnam, 22d June, 1776, to January, 1777; Lieutenant-Colonel of Malcolm's Continental Regiment, 4th January, 1777; resigned 3d March, 1779; Third Vice President of the United States, 4th March, 1801, to 4th March, 1805. (Died 14th September, 1836.)

Burr, Ephraim (Mass). Captain 21st Continental Infantry, 1st April to 31st December, 1776; Captain 2d Massachusetts, 1st January, 1777; retired 1st April, 1779.

Burr, Wakeman (Conn). Ensign in the Lexington Alarm in April, 1775; 2d Lieutenant 5th Connecticut, 1st May to 12th December, 1775. (Died 1799.)

Burrall, Charles (Conn). Colonel Connecticut Militia Regiment in 1775; Colonel Connecticut State Regiment, 19th January, 1776, to January, 1777; served subsequently as Colonel Connecticut Militia. (Died 1803.)

Burrall Jonathan (Conn). Assistant to Paymaster-General Continental Army, October, 1776; Assistant Paymaster-General, June, 1779; Deputy Paymaster-General, January, 1781, to close of war. (Died 18th November, 1834.)

Burritt, Charles (Conn). 2d Lieutenant 6th Connecticut, 1st January, 1777; resigned 29th April, 1779.

Burritt, Israel (Conn). 2d Lieutenant 7th Connecticut, 1st January, 1777; dropped 24th April, 1778.

Burroughs, Benjamin (R. I.). Ensign of Richmond's Rhode Island State Regiment, 19th August, 1776, to March, 1777.

Burroughs, George (Va). Sergeant 2d Virginia, May, 1776; Regimental Quartermaster, February, 1777; retired 1 September, 1778.

Burroughs, Jeremiah (N. H.). Captain of Warner's Continental Regiment, 23d October, 1776; retired 1st January, 1781.

Burrowes, Eden (N. J.). Sergeant 1st New Jersey, December, 1776; 2d Lieutenant, 20th April, 1777; 1st Lieutenant, 4th January, 1778; retained in New Jersey Battalion April, 1783, and served to November, 1783. (Died 26th February, 1825.)

Burrowes, John (N. J.). Captain of Forman's New Jersey Regiment in 1776; Captain of Forman's Continental Regiment, 1st January, 1777; transferred to Spencer's Regiment, 22d April, 1779; Major, 22d July, 1779; retired 1st January, 1781. (Died 1810.)

Burrows, Hubbard D. (Conn). Captain Connecticut Militia; killed at Groton Heights, 6th September, 1781.

Burt, Gideon (Mass). Captain of Danielson's Massachusetts Regiment, May, 1775, to ——.

Burt, James (Mass). Captain of Whitcomb's Massachusetts Regiment, May to December, 1775; Colonel Massachusetts Militia, 1781-1782.

Burt, John (Vt). Lieutenant Vermont Militia in 1777.

Burt, Joseph (N. H.) Captain New Hampshire Militia, 1777.

Burton, Benjamin (N. H.). Ensign of Reed's New Hampshire Regiment, June to December, 1775; Ensign 2d Continental Infantry, 1st January, 1776; 2d Lieutenant, 28th September to 31st December, 1776; Captain of Sherburne's Continental Regiment, 15th March, 1777; discharged 1st June, 1779.

Burton, Hutchins (Va). 2d Lieutenant, 6th Virginia, 26th February, 1776. Died 17th January, 1777.

Burton, Isaac (Mass). Lieutenant 13th Massachusetts, 1st January, 1777; resigned 9th September, 1777.

Burton, James (Va). Ensign 2d Virginia, 6th November, 1776; 2d Lieutenant, 11th March, 1777; 1st Lieutenant, 4th May, 1778; resigned 22d December, 1778; Captain Virginia Convention Guards, 1779-1780. (Died 21st August, 1829.)

Burton, John (Pa). Ensign 2d Pennsylvania, 5th February, 1777; deserted 27th February, 1778.

Burton, John (Va). Served as Captain, Major, Lieutenant-Colonel and Colonel Virginia Militia, 1776-1782.

Burton, Robert (Va). 2d Lieutenant 1st Continental Artillery, 18th October, 1778, to ——. (Died ——, 1825.)

Burton, Said (Va). Was an Ensign 2d Virginia, 28th March, 1777, to ——.

Burton, Samuel (S. C.) Lieutenant South Carolina Militia, 1775.

Burwell, Lewis (Va). Colonel Virginia Militia, 1777-1781. (Died 1800.)

Burwell, Nathaniel (Va). Ensign 1st Virginia, 18th September, 1775; Captain 1st Continental Artillery, 30th November, 1776; Major and Aide-de-Camp to General Howe, 19th May, 1779; retired 1st January, 1783. (Died 1801.)

Burwell, Thacker (Va). Lieutenant-Colonel Virginia Militia, 1777-1778.

Bush, Alexander (N. H.). Ensign of Warner's Continental Regiment, 18th August, 1778; resigned 12th May, 1779.

Bush, George (Del). Lieutenant Delaware Battalion of the Flying Camp, July to December, 1776; Captain of Hartley's Continental Regiment, 13th January, 1777; regiment designated 11th

Pennsylvania, 16th December, 1778; transferred to 6th Pennsylvania, 17th January, 1781; transferred to 3d Pennsylvcania, 1st January, 1783, and served to close of war; Brevet Major, 30th September, 1783. (Also called Boss.)

Bush, Goodrich (Va). Captain Virginia Militia, 1779-1780.

Bush, John (N. C.). Ensign 8th North Carolina, 28th November, 1776; 1st Lieutenant, 5th August, 1777; transferred to 5th North Carolina, 1st June, 1778; Adjutant, 7th August, 1781; served to ——.

Bush, John (Pa). Ensign 6th Pennsylvania Battalion, 24th June, 1776; 1st Lieutenant 7th Pennsylvania, 20th March, 1777; Captain Lieutenant, 11th April, 1780; transferred to 3d Pennsylvania, 17th January, 1781; Captain, 11th December, 1781; retired 1st January, 1783. (Died 1806.)

Bush, John (S. C.). Lieutenant 2d South Carolina, 18th May, 1776; killed at Savannah, 9th October, 1779.

Bush, Lewis (Pa). 1st Lieutenant 6th Pennsylvania Battalion, 9th January, 1776; Captain, 24th June, 1776; transferred to Hartley's Continental Regiment, 13th January, 1777; Major, 12th March, 1777; died 15th September, 1777, of wounds received at Brandywine, 11th September, 1777.

Bush, Solomon (Pa). Captain Pennsylvania Battalion of the Flying Camp; taken prisoner at Long Island, 27th August, 1776.

Bush, Timothy (Vt). Captain Vermont Militia in 1777.

Bush, William (N. C.). Ensign 8th North Carolina, 10th April, 1777; 2d Lieutenant, 15th August, 1777; transferred to 1st North Carolina, 1st June, 1778; 1st Lieutenant, 1st February, 1779; Captain, 1781, and served to close of war. (Died 1821.)

Bushfield, Thomas (N. Y.). Ensign 2d New York, 21st November, 1776; omitted February, 1777.

Bushnell, David (Conn). Captain Lieutenant Sappers and Miners, 2d August, 1779; Captain, 8th June, 1781, and served to 3d June, 1783. (Died ——. 1824.)

Buss, Samuel (Mass). Corporal in Whitcomb's Massachusetts Regiment, April to December, 1775; Sergeant 18th Continental Infantry, 1st January, 1776; Lieutenant 10th Massachusetts, 6th November, 1776; resigned 1st April, 1779.

Bussey, Bennett (Md). Captain 2d Maryland Battalion of the Flying Camp, July to December, 1776.

Bussey, Edward (Md). Lieutenant Maryland Militia, 1777-1778. (Died 1782.)

Bussey, Isaiah (Mass). Private in Lexington Alarm, April, 1775; Ensign of Heath's Massachusetts Regiment, May to December, 1775; 2d Lieutenant 24th Continental Infantry, 1st January, 1776; 1st Lieutenant, 3d August, 1776; Captain Lieutenant 3d Continental Artillery, 1st January, 1777, and served to June, 1783. (Died — January, 1785.)

Butler, Aaron (Conn). Ensign 3d Connecticut, 1st January, 1777. Died 12th November, 1777.)

Butler, Charles (Conn). Sergeant in the Lexington Alarm, April, 1775; Ensign 2d Connecticut, 1st May to 10th December, 1775; 2d Lieutenant 22d Continental Infantry, 1st January to 31st December, 1776.

Butler, Edward (Pa). Ensign 9th Pennsylvania, 2d June ,1778; Lieutenant, 28th January, 1779; transferred to 5th Pennsylvania, 17th January, 1781, transferred to 3d Pennsylvania, 1st January, 1783, and served to 3d November, 1783; Captain of the Levies under General St. Clair in 1791; Captain United States Infantry, 5th March, 1792; assigned to 4th Sub Legion, 4th September, 1792; Adjutant and Inspector United States Army, 18th July, 1793, to 13th May, 1794; retained as Captain 4th United States Infantry, 1st November, 1796; transferred to 2d United States Infantry, 1st April, 1802. Died 6th May, 1803.

Butler, Eli (Conn). Captain Connecticut Light Horse, 1776-1777. (Died 1802.)

Butler, Henry (N. H.). Captain New Hampshire Militia in 1780.

Butler, James (S. C.). Captain South Carolina Militia; killed at Cloud's Creek, S. C., 7th November, 1781.

Butler, John (Mass). Adjutant of Brewer's Massachusetts Regiment; wounded at Bunker Hill 17th June, 1775.

Butler, John (N. C.). Brigadier General North Carolina Militia, 1780-1781.

Butler, John (S. C.). Captain of Marion's Brigade South Carolina Militia. 1779-1781.

Butler, Joseph (Md). 1st Lieutenant of Smallwood's Maryland Regiment, 14th January, 1776; wounded and taken prisoner at Long Island, 27th August, 1776, and died in captivity shortly afterwards.

Butler, Joseph (Mass). Lieutenant of a Company of Minute Men at Concord, 19th April, 1775; Captain of Nixon's Massachusetts Regiment, May to December, 1775; Captain 4th Continental Infantry, 1st January to 31st December, 1776.

Butler, Lawrence (Va). 1st Lieutenant 15th Virginia, 2d December, 1776; Captain Lieutenant, 18th March, 1777; Regiment designated 11th Virginia, 14th September, 1778; Captain, 14th May, 1779; taken prisoner at Charleston 12th May, 1780; Prisoner on parole to close of war; Major 8th United States Infantry, 24th April, 1799; honorably discharged 15th June, 1800.

Butler, Percival (Pa). 2d Lieutenant 3d Pennsylvania, 1st September, 1777; 1st Lieutenant, 23d November, 1777; transferred to 2d Pennsylvania, 1st January, 1783, and srved to close of war.

Butler, Pierce (S. C.). Major South Carolina Militia, 1777-1781. (Died 15th February, 1822.)

Butler, Reuben (Va). 1st Lieutenant of Grayson's Continental Regiment, 26th January, 1777; resigned 1st October, 1778.

Butler, Richard (Pa). Captain 2d Pennsylvania Battalion, 5th January, 1776; appointed Indian agent 17th May, 1778, and lost rank in the army; Major 8th Pennsylvania, 20th July, 1776; Lieutenant-Colonel, 12th March, 1777, to rank from 28th September, 1776; Colonel 9th Pennsylvania, 7th June, 1777; transferred to 5th Pennsylvania 17th January, 1781; transferred ,to 3d Pennsylvania 1st January, 1783, and served to 3d November, 1783; Brevet Brigadier General, 30th September, 1783; Major-General United States Levies in 1791; killed 4th November, 1791, in action with Indians near Fort Recovery, Ohio.

Butler, Samuel (Va). 1st Lieutenant 15th Virginia, 21st March, 1777; retired 14th September, 1777; served subsequently as Lieutenant of a Virginia State Regiment.

Butler, Thomas (Mass). 1st Lieutenant of Scammon's Massachusetts Regiment, May to December, 1775.

Butler, Thomas (Pa). 1st Lieutenant 2d Pennsylvania Battalion, 5th January, 1776; Captain 3d Pennsylvania, 4th October, 1776; retired 17th January, 1781; Major of the Levies under General St. Clair in 1791; wounded 4th November, 1791, near Fort Recovery, Ohio, St. Clair's defeat; Major of Infantry United States Army, 11th April, 1792; assigned to 4th Sub Legion 4th September, 1792; Lieutenant-Colonel, 1st July, 1794; assigned to 4th United States Infantry, 1st November, 1796; Colonel 2d United States Infantry, 1st April, 1802; died 7th September, 1805.

Butler, William (Pa). Captain 2d Pennsylvania Battalion, 5th January, 1776; Major, 7th September, 1776; Lieutenant-Colonel 4th Pennsylvania, 30th September, 1776; Aide-de-Camp to General Alexander, 7th May, 1778; Lieutenant-Colonel Commandant 4th Pennsylvania, 22d January, 1779; retired 1st January, 1783. (Died — 1789.)

Butler, William (S. C.). Colonel South Carolina Militia, 1780-1781. (Died 15th November, 1821.)

Butler, William (S. C.). Captain South Carolina Rangers in 1781; was the son of Captain James Butler, and avenged the killing of his father.

Butler, Zebulon (Conn). Lieutenant-Colonel 3d Connecticut, 1st January, 1777; Colonel 2d Connecticut, 13th March, 1778; transferred to 4th Connecticut, 1st January, 1781; transferred to 1st Connecticut, 1st January, 1783, and served to 3d June, 1783. (Died 28th July, 1795.)

Butterfield, Benjamin (N. H.). Ensign of Warner's Continental Regiment, 1st January, 1777; taken prisoner 7th July, 1777, where not stated, and did not rejoin regiment. (Died 1804.)

Butterfield, Isaac (N. H.). Major of Bedel's Regiment New Hampshire Rangers, 22d January, 1776;. taken prisoner at the Cedars, 19th May, 1776; cashiered 1st August, 1776.

Butterfield, James (Vt). Lieutenant of Bedell's Regiment Vermont Militia, 15th December, 1777, to 1st April, 1778.

Butterfield, Jonas (N. H.). Lieutenant of Whitcomb's Battalion New Hampshire Rangers, 14th December, 1776; discharged 17th February, 1780.

Butterfield, Thomas (N. H.). 1st Lieutenant of Whitcomb's Battalion New Hampshire Rangers, 14th December. 1776, and served to February, 1780.

Butterick, John (Mass). Major Massachusetts Militia at Concord, 19th April, 1775; Major of Nixon's Massachusetts Regiment, 19th May to December, 1775; served subsequently as Lieutenant-Colonel Massachusetts Militia. (Died 16th May, 1791.)

Buxton, James (Mass). Ensign 11th Massachusetts, 1st January, 1777; Lieutenant, 7th November, 1777; Regimental-Adjutant, 18th March, 1780; Captain Lieutenant, 26th October, 1780; transferred to 10th Massachusetts, 1st January, 1781; Captain, 1st January, 1781; retired 1st January, 1783.

Buxton, James (Va). Ensign 4th Virginia, 28th September, 1776; 2d Lieutenant, February, 1777; resigned 1st December, 1777.

Buysson, —— (—). See Du Buyson.

Byington, Daniel (Conn). 2d Lieutenant 7th Connecticut, 6th July to 18th December, 1775.

Byington, Joseph (Conn). Lieutenant Connecticut Militia in 1776; 2d Lieutenant 2d Connecticut, 1st May to 7th November, 1777. (Died 1778.)

Byles, Thomas Langhorne (Pa). Captain 3d Pennsylvania Battalion, 5th January, 1776; taken prisoner at Fort Washington 16th November, 1776; Brevet Major, 9th June, 1777; exchanged 1st March, 1778; Major 3d Pennsylvania, 1st July, 1778, to rank from 8th June, 1777; wounded at Paramus 16th April, 1780, and died 17th April, 1780.

Bynum, Turner (N. C.). Captain North Carolina Militia, 1781.

Byrd, Benjamin.—See Burd.

Byrd, Francis Otway (Va). Cadet, 17th July, 1775; Aide-de-Camp to General Lee in September, 1775; Lieutenant-Colonel 3d Continental Dragoons, 1st January, 1777; resigned 15th July, 1778. (Died September, 1800.)

Byrn, John (Va). Captain of Thruston's Continental Regiment, 4th June, 1777; resigned 1st August, 1778.

C.

Cabell, Joseph (Va). Colonel Virginia Militia, 1775-1781. (Died 1798.)

Cabell, Samuel Jordan (Va). Captain 6th Virginia, 4th March, 1776; Major 14th Virginia, 20th December, 1777; Regiment designated 10th Virginia 14th September, 1778; Lieutenant-Colonel 8th Virginia, 15th December,

1778; transferred to 4th Virginia, 4th July, 1779; transferred to 7th Virginia, 12th February, 1781; taken prisoner at Charleston 12th May, 1780; prisoner of war on parole to close of war. Brevet Colonel, 30th September, 1783. (Died 4th September, 1818.)

Cabell, William, Jr. (Va). Major Virginia Militia at Yorktown in 1881. (Died 1822.)

Cabot, Francis (Mass). 2d Lieutenant of Paterson's Massachusetts Regiment, May, 1775, to ——.

Cadwalader, John (Pa). Colonel of a Regiment Pennsylvania Militia in 1776; Brigadier-General Continental Army, 21st February, 1777, which he declined; Brigadier-General Pennsylvania Militia, 5th April, 1777, to close of war; was again appointed Brigadier-General Continental Army and Commander of the Cavalry in the service of the United States, 10th September, 1778, which he also declined. (Died 11th February, 1786.)

Cadwalader, Lambert (Pa). Lieutenant-Colonel 3d Pennsylvania Battalion, 4th January, 1776; taken prisoner at Fort Washington, 16th November, 1776; Colonel 4th Pennsylvania, December, 1776, to rank from 25th October, 1776, but was a prisoner of war on parole until he resigned, 22d January, 1779. (Died 12th September, 1823.)

Cady, Jeremiah (Mass). Major of Paterson's Massachusetts Regiment, April to December, 1775; in command of a battalion in the campaign in Canada, January to June, 1776.

Cady, Palmer (Conn). Sergeant-Major of Elmore's Connecticut State Regiment, 16th April, 1776; Ensign, October, 1776; Ensign 2d Canadian (Hazen's) Regiment, 1st February, 1777; Lieutenant, 24th March, 1778; resigned — June, 1780.

Cairy, Obediah (Va). Sergeant 9th Virginia, 20th November, 1776; Regimental Quartermaster, 15th July, 1777; retired 14th September, 1778.

Calderwood, James (Pa). Quartermaster 6th Pennsylvania Battalion, 9th January, 1776; Lieutenant in the Navy, 1st August, 1776; Captain of an Independent Pennsylvania Company, 19th January, 1777; died 13th September, 1777, of wounds received at Brandywine, 11th September, 1777.

Caldwell, Andrew (Pa). Sergeant in Captain Roman's Company Pennsyl-

vania Artillery, 20th February, 1776; 2d Lieutenant of Captain Coran's Company Pennsylvania Artillery, 1st April, 1777; resigned 22d July, 1779; Surgeon's Mate Hospital Department, June, 1780, to close of war. (Died 1797.)

Caldwell, Daniel (Mass). 2d Lieutenant of Danielson's Massachusetts Regiment, May to December, 1775; Captain Massachusetts Militia in 1776. (Died 27th March, 1777.)

Caldwell, James (N. J.). Chaplain 3d New Jersey, 9th February to November, 1776; served subsequently as an assistant to Deputy Quartermaster-General; was shot by a sentinel at Elizabethport, New Jersey, 24th November, 1781.

Caldwell, James (S. C.). Lieutenant South Carolina Militia; wounded at Cowpens, 17th January, 1781. (Died 1813.)

Caldwell, John (S. C.). Captain 3d South Carolina, 17th June, 1775; resigned 19th March, 1778.)

Caldwell, John (N. H.). Quartermaster 1st New Hampshire, 23d April to December, 1775.

Caldwell, Jonathan (Del). Captain Delaware Regiment, 15th January, 1776, to January, 1777.

Caldwell, Joseph (Del). Captain of Paterson's Delaware Battalion of the Flying Camp, July to December, 1776.

Caldwell, Robert (Pa). 1st Lieutenant of Atlee's Battalion Pennsylvania Militia, 28th March, 1776; 1st Lieutenant German Regiment, 15th July, 1776; wounded and taken prisoner at Fort Washington, 16th November, 1776; Captain, 29th November, 1776; exchanged 20th January, 1779; Captain of Marines, 20th March, 1779, to close of war. (Name also spelled Colwell.)

Caldwell, Samuel (Pa). Paymaster Philadelphia Light Horse, 1776-1777. (Died 1798.)

Caldwell, William (Mass). Paymaster 26th Continental Infantry, 13th August to 31st December, 1776.

Caldwell, William (S. C.). Captain 3d South Carolina; taken prisoner at Fort Howe, Ga., 18th February, 1777.

Calfe, John (N. H.). Captain New Hampshire Militia, 1776-1777.

Calhoun, George (Pa). Captain 10th Pennsylvania, 13th November, 1776. Died 21st March, 1779.

Calhoun, George (Va). 1st Lieutenant Company of Virginia Rangers, 8th June, 1779, to 1st January, 1781.

Calhoun, Mark (Del). Ensign Delaware Battalion of the Flying Camp, July to December, 1776.

Calhoun, Patrick (S. C.). Ensign South Carolina Militia; killed at Cherokeetown, S. C., 26th June, 1776.

Calhoun, William (Pa). 3d Lieutenant 1st Pennsylvania Battalion of the Flying Camp, July to December, 1776; 1st Lieutenant, 4th Pennsylvania, 3d January, 1777; taken prisoner at Germantown, 4th October, 1777.

Calkins, Reuben (Conn). Ensign of Burrall's Connecticut State Regiment, 23d January, 1776, to January, 1777; 1st Lieutenant 7th Connecticut, 1st January, 1777. Died 12th December, 1777.

Calkins, Stephen (Vt). Captain Vermont Militia, 1780-1781.

Calkins, William (Conn). Lieutenant of Mott's Connecticut State Regiment, June to December, 1776.

Call, Daniel (Conn). Sergeant 4th Connecticut, 23d May, 1775; Ensign, 1st September, 1775; discharged 20th December, 1775.

Call, Nathaniel (N. Y.). Lieutenant of Stevens' Battalion Continental Artillery, 1st February, 1777; battalion formed subsequently part of the 3d Continental Artillery; Captain, 19th December, 1777; resigned 10th September, 1778.

Call, Richard (Va). 1st Lieutenant 1st Continental Dragoons, 4th June, 1776; Captain, 4th December, 1776; retained in Baylor's Regiment Continental Dragoons, 9th November, 1782; Major in 1782, and served to November, 1783.

Callahan, John (N. C.). Lieutenant North Carolina Militia at King's Mountain, October, 1780.

Callender, John (Mass). Captain of Gridley's Regiment Massachusetts Artillery, May, 1775; cashiered 7th July, 1775, for misconduct at Bunker Hill; re-entered the service in Captain Peirce's Company New York Artillery in March, 1776, as a volunteer cadet; was wounded and taken prisoner at Long Island, 27th August, 1776; after his exchange the order dismissing from the service was revoked by General Washington for his brave and heroic conduct at Long Island and appointed

Captain Lieutenant 3d Continental Artillery, to rank from 1st January, 1777; transferred to Corps of Artillery, 17th June, 1783; Brevet Captain 30th September, 1783, and served to 20th June, 1784. (Died 12th October, 1797.)

Callender, Thomas (N. C.). Ensign 1st North Carolina, 6th June, 1776; 2d Lieutenant, 1st January, 1777; 1st Lieutenant, 8th July, 1777; Captain Lieutenant, 30th March, 1780; taken prisoner at Charleston, 12th May, 1780; exchanged 14th June, 1781; Captain, 12th May, 1780; retired 1st January, 1783. (Died 20th August, 1828.)

Callis, William Overton (Va). Ensign 4th Virginia, 27th September, 1776; 2d Lieutenant, 12th January, 1777; retired 30th September, 1778; Captain Virginia Militia, 1779-1780. (Died 14th March, 1814.)

Calloway, James (Va). Colonel Virginia Militia, 1780-1781.

Calmes, George (Va). 1st Lieutenant 11th Virginia, 2d March, 1777; resigned 8th November, 1777. (Died 20th November, 1834.)

Calmes, Marquis (Va). 2d Lieutenant 2d Virginia, 27th November, 1775; 1st Lieutenant, 1st February, 1776; Captain, 13th January, 1777; was a prisoner on parole in February, 1779, when and where taken not stated; resigned 8th March, 1779; Lieutenant-Colonel Virginia Militia, 1779-1781. (Died 27th February, 1834.)

Calmes, William (Va). Lieutenant Virginia Militia in 1781. (Died 1836.)

Calvert, John (S. C.). Lieutenant South Carolina Militia; wounded at Beaufort, 9th February, 1779.

Calvert, Jonathan (Md). Surgeon's Mate Hospital Department, 1776; Surgeon's Mate, 1st Continental Artillery, 30th November, 1777; resigned 8th October, 1778; served subsequently as Surgeon's Mate of 1st Virginia State Regiment, 1778-1781.

Calvert, Pierre du (Canada). The act of 10th August, 1776, provided that he be paid as an Ensign for 8 months and have the brevet rank of a Lieutenant; appointed 2d Lieutenant 2d Canadian (Hazen's) Regiment, 10th December, 1776; taken prisoner at Staten Island 22d August, 1777, and did not rejoin regiment.

Cambray, —— du Monsieur (France). Lieutenant-Colonel Corps of Engineers, 13th June, 1778; taken prisoner at Charleston, 12th May, 1780; exchanged

1781; Brevet Colonel, 2d May, 1783; permitted to return to France 30th October, 1782, on leave for 12 months.

Came, John.—See **Carne.**

Cameron, Allen (S. C.). 1st Lieutenant South Carolina Rangers, 17th June, 1775, to ——. ,

Cameron, Charles (Va). 1st Lieutenant 10th Virginia, 3d December, 1776; resigned 3d January, 1778.

Camp, Abner (Va). Captain 1st Virginia State Regiment, 10th May, 1777, to August, 1780.

Camp, John (Va). 2d Lieutenant 3d Virginia, 12th February, 1776, to ——; Captain 1st Virginia State Regiment, January, 1777, to June, 1778.

Camp, Samuel (Conn). 1st Lieutenant of Swift's Connecticut State Regiment, June to November, 1776. (Died 1810.)

Camp, Samuel (Conn). Ensign of Wadsworth's Connecticut State Regiment, June to December, 1776.

Camp, William (Va). Sergeant 1st Continental Artillery, 20th December, 1776; 2d Lieutenant, 30th November, 1777; Regimental Adjutant, 16th March, 1778; resigned 3d September, 1778.

Campbell, Archibald (Pa). 1st Lieutenant 6th Pennsylvania, 15th February, 1777; retired 1st September, 1779. (Died, 1788.)

Campbell, Archibald (Va). Ensign 4th Virginia, 17th October, 1780; Lieutenant, 15th June, 1781; transferred to 2d Virginia 1st January, 1783, and served to close of war.

Campbell, Arthur (N. C.). Colonel North Carolina Militia in 1780.

Campbell, Daniel (Pa). Ensign 3d Pa., 29th April, 1777; killed 26th June, 1777, at Short Hills.

Campbell, David (Va). Captain Virginia Militia at King's Mountain, October, 1780.

Campbell, Donald (N. Y.). Colonel Deputy Quartermaster-General New York Department, 17th July, 1775, and served to 2d June, 1784.

Campbell, Duncan (N. Y.) 2d Lieutenant 1st Canadian (Livingston's) Regiment, 18th October, 1776; wounded at Bemus Heights 19th September, 1777; left Regiment 18th June, 1779, on leave for 12 months, and did not rejoin; served subsequently as Captain New York Militia. (Died 4th January, 1807.)

Campbell, Eneas (Md). Captain 1st Maryland Battalion of the Flying Camp, July, 1776, to ——.

Campbell, George W. (N. Y.). Hospital Surgeon's Mate, 11th April, 1777, to 20th June, 1780; Hospital Physician and Surgeon, 20th September, 1781, and served to close of war. (Died 1818.)

Campbell, Jabez (N. Y.). Surgeon of Spencer's Continental Regiment, 1st January, 1777; retired 1st January, 1781.

Campbell, James (Del). Ensign Delaware Regiment, 5th April, 1777; 2d Lieutenant, 21st May, 1778; 1st Lieutenant, 1st March, 1779; taken prisoner at Camden 16th August, 1780.

Campbell, James (Md). 1st Lieutenant of Smallwood's Maryland Regiment, 14th January, 1776, to ——.

Campbell, James (N. Y.). Ensign 4th New York, 21st November, 1776; omitted May, 1777.

Campbell, James (N. C.). Ensign 4th North Carolina, 11th December, 1776; Lieutenant 10th North Carolina, 19th April, 1777; 1st Lieutenant, 21st December, 1777; Quartermaster, 10th September, 1778; transferred to 2d North Carolina, 1st June, 1778; Captain, 14th December, 1778; wounded and taken prisoner at Stono Ferry 20th June, 1779; exchanged 14th June, 1781,and served to close of war. (Name also spelled Campen.)

Campbell, James (Pa). 2d Lieutenant 1st Pennsylvania, 28th May, 1779; 1st Lieutenant, 18th July, 1780, and served to 3d June, 1783.

Campbell, John (N. J.). Assistant Commissary in Hospital Department. 18th October, 1777, to 1st December, 1780, when discharged.

Campbell, John (N. C.). 1st Lieutenant 10th North Carolina, 20th April, 1777; transferred to 4th North Carolina 1st June, 1778; Captain, 5th April, 1779; retired 1st January, 1783.

Campbell, John (N. C.). 2d Lieutenant 2d Continental Artillery, 29th June, 1781, and served to June, 1783.

Campbell, John (Pa). 2d Lieutenant 1st Battalion Pennsylvania Flying Camp, July to December, 1776.

Campbell, John (Pa). 2d Lieutenant Pennsylvania Militia; killed in action with Indians in Ohio 4th June, 1782.

Campbell, John (Va). Captain Virginia Militia at King's Mountain, October, 1780. (Died 1808.)

Campbell, John (Va). Captain Virginia Militia; killed at Moore's Creek, 27th February, 1776.

Campbell, Moses (Conn). Lieutenant in the Lexington Alarm in April, 1775; 2d Lieutenant 8th Connecticut, 6th July to 16th December, 1775.

Campbell, Peter (N. J.). Captain and Aide-de-Camp to General Dickinson, New Jersey Militia, in 1775.

Campbell, Richard (Va). Captain 8th Virginia, 19th February, 1776; Major 13th Virginia, 10th August, 1777; Lieutenant-Colonel, 20th February, 1778; regiment designated 9th Virginia 14th September, 1778; transferred to 4th Virginia 12th February, 1781; wounded at Camden 25th April, 1781; killed at Eutaw Springs, 8th September, 1781

Campbell, Robert (Md). Adjutant of the 4th Maryland Battalion of the Flying Camp, 17th August to 1st December, 1776.

Campbell, Robert (N. H.). Lieutenant of Bedel's Regiment New Hampshire Rangers; taken prisoner at the Cedars 19th May, 1776.

Campbell, Robert (N. Y.). Lieutenant New York Militia; killed at Oriskany, 6th August, 1777.

Campbell, Robert (Pa). 2d Lieutenant 2d Battalion of Miles' Pennsylvania Rifle Regiment, 19th March, 1776; 1st Lieutenant 2d Canadian (Hazen's) Regiment, 8th April, 1777; wounded and taken prisoner on Staten Island 22d August, 1777 (lost an arm); rejoined regiment 5th August, 1778, and was promoted to Captain, to rank from 3d February, 1778; transferred to Invalid Regiment 1st September, 1778; killed 4th October, 1779, where not stated.

Campbell, Robert (S. C.). Lieutenant South Carolina Dragoons, 1776-1777.

Campbell, Robert (Va). Ensign Virginia Militia at King's Mountain, October, 1780. (Died 27th December, 1781.)

Campbell, Samuel (N. Y.). Colonel New York Militia at Oriskany, August, 1777. (Died 1824.)

Campbell, Samuel (Va). 2d Lieutenant 14th Virginia, 20th November, 1776; 1st Lieutenant, 3d September, 1777. Died 27th August, 1778.

Campbell, Thomas (Pa). Captain of Swope's Pennsylvania Battalion of the Flying Camp; taken prisoner at Fort Washington, 16th November, 1776; released 9th November, 1778; Captain of Pennsylvania Rangers, 1779-1780.

Campbell, Thomas (Pa). 1st Lieutenant 4th Pennsylvania, 3d January, 1777; wounded at Germantown, 4th October, 1777; Captain Lieutenant, 11th 1779; Captain, 1st January, 1781; retired 1st January, 1783. (Died 19th January, 1815.)

Campbell, William (Md). Lieutenant Maryland Militia, 1776.

Campbell, William (Mass). Captain of Learned's Massachusetts Regiment, May to December, 1775.

Campbell, William (Pa). 2d Lieutenant 6th Pennsylvania, 1st January, 1777; wounded and taken prisoner at Germantown, 4th October, 1777; exchanged 25th October, 1780; Captain from 1st January, 1778; retired 17th January, 1781.

Campbell, William (Va). 1st Lieutenant 1st Virginia State Regiment, 21st June, 1778; Captain, 16th January, 1779, and served to January, 1781; Major and Lieutenant Colonel Virginia Militia in 1781; Captain 10th United States Infantry, 10th January, 1799; honorably discharged 15th June, 1800. (Died 25th January, 1845.)

Campbell, William (Va). Captain 1st Virginia, 15th December, 1775; resigned 9th October, 1776; Colonel Virginia Militia, 1777-1780. By the act of 13th November, 1780, it was "Resolved, That Congress entertain a high sense of the spirited and military ability of Colonel Campbell, and the officers and privates of the militia under his command, displayed in the action of October 7th, in which a complete victory was obtained over superior numbers of the enemy advantageously posted on King's Mountain, in the State of North Carolina, and that this resolution be published by the commanding officer of the Southern Army in General Order."

Brigadier General Virginia Militia, December, 1780; also commanded Shelby's Virginia Militia Regiment during the Siege of Yorktown until he died, 22d August, 1781.

Campen, James.—See Campbell.

Campfield, Jabez (N. J.). Surgeon of Spencer's Continental Regiment, 1st January, 1777; retired 1st January, 1781; Surgeon 2d Continental Dragoons, 17th August, 1781, and served to close of war.

Campfield, William (N. J.). Captain New Jersey Militia, 1776-1777.

Candler, William (Ga). Major Georgia Militia at King's Mountain, October, 1780, and in the South Carolina campaign of 1781. (Died September, 1789.)

Canfield, John (Conn). Adjutant Connecticut Light Horse, 1776-1777. (Died 1786.)

Canfield, Samuel (Conn). Lieutenant-Colonel Connecticut Militia, 1781. (Died 1799.)

Canfield, Samuel (N. H.). Captain New Hampshire Militia, 1776-1779. (Died 1789.)

Cannon, Daniel (S. C.). Captain South Carolina Militia in 1775.

Cannon, John (Pa). 2d Lieutenant 2d Pennsylvania, 1st January, 1777; resigned September, 1777.

Cannon, John (Va). Paymaster 6th Virginia, 1777; 2d Lieutenant 2d Virginia, 9th September, 1778; 1st Lieutenant, 20th October, 1779, and served to ——.

Cannon, Lewis (N. C.). Lieutenant 10th North Carolina, 19th April, 1777, to ——.

Cannon, Luke (Va). Ensign 15th Virginia, 21st July, 1777; 2d Lieutenant and Regimental Quartermaster, 1st April, 1778; Regiment designated 11th Virginia 14th September, 1778; 1st Lieutenant, 15th August, 1779; taken prisoner at Charleston, 12th May, 1780; transferred to 4th Virginia, 12th February, 1781; retired 1st January, 1783. (Died 7th February, 1829.)

Cannon, William (Mass). Captain Massachusetts Militia, 1777.

Cappelle, William (S. C.). Surgeon on Staff of General Lafayette, 1781-1782.

Canternier, John (S. C.). Captain South Carolina Dragoons, ——, 1779.

Cantine, John (N. Y.). Colonel New York Militia, 1778-1781.

Cantine, Moses (N. Y.). Captain New York Militia, 1780.

Cape, John (N. J.). 2d Lieutenant 1st New Jersey, 10th April, 1777; resigned 12th September, 1778.

Capers, William (S. C.). 2d Lieutenant 2d South Carolina, — March, 1777; 1st Lieutenant, 13th March, 1778; Captain, 1781, and served to close of war. (Died 1812.)

Capitaine, —— Monsier (France). Captain Corps of Engineers, 16th April, 1778, to rank from 1st December, 1776;

Brevet Major Continental Army, 5th November, 1778; served on Staff of General Lafayette in 1871; served to close of war.

Capron, Benjamin (Mass). 2d Lieutenant of Read's Massachusetts Regiment, May to December, 1775.

Capron, Oliver (Mass). Captain of Doolittle's Massachusetts Regiment, May to December, 1775.

Capron, Oliver (N. H.). Captain New Hampshire Militia, 1777-1778.

Carberry, Henry (Md). 2d Lieutenant of Hartley's Continental Regiment, 13th January 1777; 1st Lieutenant, 11th September, 1777; Captain, 30th November, 1778; regiment designated 11th Pennsylvania, 13th January, 1779; wounded 13th August, 1779, where not stated; retired 17th January, 1781; Captain in the Levies under General St. Clair in 1791; Captain of Infantry United States Army, 16th March, 1792; assigned to 4th Sub Legion, 4th September, 1792; resigned 10th February, 1794; Colonel 36th United States Infantry, 22d March, 1813; resigned 4th March, 1815. (Died 26th May, 1822.)

Carew, James (Mass). Adjutant of Jackson's Continental Regiment, 1st February, 1777; resigned 27th October, 1778; served subsequently in Massachusetts Militia.

Carey, Ephraim (R. I.). Ensign of Sherburne's Continental Regiment, 14th January, 1777; 2d Lieutenant, 1st October, 1777; resigned 8th April, 1780.

Carey, John D. (Md). Sergeant Maryland Militia in 1777; Ensign 2d Maryland, 4th September, 1781; 2d Lieutenant, 16th October, 1781; retired — April, 1783.

Carey, Jonathan (Mass). Sergeant 10th Massachusetts, 27th February, 1777; Ensign, 10th August, 1777; Lieutenant, 10th August, 1778; Captain Lieutenant, 30th October, 1780; transferred to 8th Massachusetts 1st January, 1781; retired 1st January, 1783.

Carey, Richard (Va). Brigade Major, 15th August, 1775; Lieutenant-Colonel Aide-de-Camp to General Washington, 21st June, 1776, to ——.

Carey, Samuel (Va). Adjutant 2d Virginia State Regiment, — June, 1778; 2d Lieutenant, 1st October, 1778, to January, 1781.

Carey, Simeon (Mass). Colonel Massachusetts Militia, 1776-1780. (Died 1802.)

Carey, William (N. H.). Captain New Hampshire Militia in 1777.

Carhart, Samuel (N. J.) Captain New Jersey Militia; was a prisoner, when and where taken not stated.

Carithers, John (Pa).—See **Carothers.**

Carle, Israel (N. J.). Captain New Jersey Light Horse in 1777.

Carleton, Joseph (—). Paymaster Pulaski Legion in 1779.

Carlevan, Andrew (—). 2d Lieutenant Pulaski Legion, 3d March, 1779, to ——; was in service in 1781. (Also called John Carlevan.)

Carlisle, Daniel (N. H.). Captain of Bedel's Regiment New Hampshire Rangers, 22d January, 1776; cashiered 9th August, 1776.

Carlisle, John (Md.) Captain 2d Canadian (Hazen's) Regiment, 3d November, 1776; taken prisoner at Staten Island, 22d August, 1777; retired 1st July, 1783.

Carlisle, Thomas (R. I.). Captain of Elliott's Regiment Rhode Island State Artillery, 12th December, 1776, to 1779.

Carlton, Moses (Mass). Prviate in Lexington Alarm, April, 1775; Sergeant 5th Massachusetts, 1st January, 1777; Ensign, 10th July, 1779; Regimental Quartermaster, 26th November, 1779; Lieutenant, 7th May, 1782; retired 1st January, 1783.

Carlton, Osgood (Mass). Regimental Quartermaster of Sargent's Massachusetts Regiment, May to December, 1775; Quartermaster 16th Continental Infantry, 1st January to 31st December, 1776; 1st Lieutenant 15th Massachusetts, 1st January, 1777; transferred to Invalid Regiment, 1st December, 1778; Regimental Quartermaster, 7th September, 1782, and served to 23d April 1783. (Died June, 1816.)

Carlton, Samuel (Mass). Lieutenant-Colonel, 12th Massachusetts, 6th November, 1776; retired 12th September, 1778. (Died March, 1804.)

Carmichael, Alexander (Pa). Ensign 11th Pennsylvania, 30th September, 1776; 2d Lieutenant, 9th April, 1777; killed at Brandywine, 11th September, 1777.

Carnaghan, James (Pa). 2d Lieutenant 2d Battalion of Miles' Pennsylvania Rifle Regiment, 16th March, 1776; taken prisoner at Long Island, 27th August, 1776; exchanged 10th December, 1776; 1st Lieutenant, 24th October,

1776; Captain Pennsylvania State Regiment, 15th January, 1777; Regiment designated 13th Pennsylvania, 12th November, 1777; transferred to 8th Pennsylvania, 1st July, 1778; transferred to 4th Pennsylvania, 17th January, 1781; transferred to 2d Pennsylvania, 1st January, 1783, and served to close of war; Brevet Major, 30th September, 1783.

Carnaghan, John (Pa). Ensign of Captain Moorehead's Company, guarding stores at Kittanning, Pennsylvania, 22d January, 1777; resigned 13th May, 1779.

Carnahan, William (Mass). Captain Massachusetts Militia, 1777.

Carne, John (S. C.). Surgeon's Mate 1st Continental Dragoons, August, 1777; Assistant Deputy Apothecary, Southern Department, 20th September, 1781, to close of war. (Name also spelled Came.)

Carnes, John (Mass). Chaplain 18th Continental Infantry, 1st January to 31st December, 1776.

Carnes, Patrick (Va). Surgeon's Mate, 1st Continental Surgeons, 31st March, 1777; Lieutenant of Lee's Battalion of Light Dragoons, 22d April, 1778; Captain, ——, 1780; served to close of war.

Carnes, Thomas Jenner (Mass). Cadet in Gridley's Regiment Massachusetts Artillery, May to December, 1775; 2d Lieutenant of Knox's Regiment Continental Artillery, December, 1775, to December, 1776; taken prisoner at Fort Washington, 16th November, 1776; Captain Lieutenant of Clark's Company North Carolina Artillery, 1st January, 1777; resigned 8th March, 1779; Captain of Marines, 9th July, 1779, to 1781.

Carnes, Zophar (N. J.). Captain New Jersey Militia, June, 1776; 1st Lieutenant 4th New Jersey, 22d December, 1776; cashiered 16th April, 1777.

Carney, Arthur (Ga). Captain 1st Georgia, 7th January, 1776; taken prisoner at St. Simon's Island, Ga., 10th August, 1777, and subsequently joined the enemy.

Carney, Martin (Va). Quartermaster 8th Virginia, 3d June, 1777; Ensign, 9th September, 1778; 2d Lieutenant 4th Virginia, 14th September, 1778; retired 1st January, 1780.

Carney, Richard (Va). Lieutenant of a Virginia State Regiment, 1778 to 1781.

Carothers, John (Pa). 2d Lieutenant 12th Pennsylvania, 1st October, 1776; killed at Germantown, 4th October, 1777. (Name also spelled Carithers.)

Carpenter, Abel (R. I.). 2d Lieutenant 2d Rhode Island, 17th February, 1777; resigned 14th April, 1779.

Carpenter, Benajah (R. I.). Captain Lieutenant of Knox's Regiment Continental Artillery, 10th December, 1775; killed at Long Island, 27th August, 1776.

Carpenter, Benjamin (N. Y.). Captain New York Militia in 1776.

Carpenter, Benjamin (Pa). Ensign 10th Pennsylvania, 4th December, 1776; 2d Lieutenant, 18th April, 1777; 1st Lieutenant, 1st November, 1777; resigned 3d June, 1778.

Carpenter, Gardner (Conn). Paymaster 17th Continental Infantry, 9th September to 31st December, 1776.

Carpenter, Increase (N. Y.). 1st Lieutenant New York Militia, 1776.

Carpenter, John (Mass). Lieutenant of Danielson's Massachusetts Regiment, May to December, 1775; 1st Lieutenant 3d Continental Infantry, 1st January to 31st December, 1776; Captain Massachusetts Militia, 1777-1779.

Carpenter, John (Pa). 2d Lieutenant 2d Battalion of Miles' Pennsylvania Rifle Regiment, 16th April, 1776; 1st Lieutenant, 9th August to November, 1776; wounded at Long Island 27th August, 1776. (Died 1798.)

Carpenter, Nehemiah (N. Y.). Quartermaster 5th New York, 21st November, 1776; taken prisoner at Fort Montgomery, 6th October, 1777; exchanged, 1779; Ensign, 5th June, 1779; transferred to 2d New York, 1st January, 1781; Lieutenant, 1782, and served to June, 1783.

Carpenter, Peter (N. C.). Ensign 8th North Carolina, 28th November, 1776, to ——.

Carpenter, Richard (Mass). 2d Lieutenant 15th Massachusetts, 1st January, 1777; resigned 26th October, 1777.

Carpenter, Samuel (Pa). Ensign 4th Pennsylvania, 3d January, 1777; cashiered 3d March, 1778.

Carpenter, Thomas (Mass). Colonel Massachusetts Militia, 1776.

Carpenter, Thomas (N. J.). Quartermaster and Paymaster New Jersey Militia, 1776 to 1780. (Died 1847.)

Carpenter, Thomas (N. Y.). Lieutenant New York Militia; wounded 8th November, 1778; place not stated.

Carpenter, Thomas (Pa). Captain Pennsylvania Militia; wounded at Brandywine, 11th September, 1777; (Died 1815.)

Carpenter, Thomas (R. I.). Colonel Rhode Island Militia 1778.

Carpenter, Wright (N. Y.). Lieutenant New York Militia; was a prisoner of war, 16th February, to 4th July, 1781.

Carr, Caleb (R. I.). Lieutenant in Richmond's Regiment Rhode Island Militia, 1st November, 1775; Captain, 19th August, 1776; also Captain of Tallman's Regiment Rhode Island Militia, 1st December, 1776, to May, 1777. (Died 3d April, 1829.)

Carr, James (N. H.). 1st Lieutenant 2d New Hampshire, 23d May to December, 1775; 1st Lieutenant 8th Continental Infantry, 1st January, 1776; Captain 2d New Hampshire, 8th November, 1776; taken prisoner at Hubbardton, 7th July, 1777; exchanged ——; transferred to New Hampshire Battalion, 1st March, 1782; Major, 8th December, 1782, and served to November, 1783. (Died 11th March, 1829.)

Carr, Jesse (N. H.). 2d Lieutenant 1st New Hampshire, 23d May to December, 1775; 2d Lieutenant 5th Continental Infantry, 1st January, 1776; marked "dead" on roll for August, 1776.

Carr, John (Md). Ensign 3d Maryland, 10th December, 1776; 2d Lieutenant, 17th April, 1777; 1st Lieutenant, ——, 1781; resigned 17th June, 1781.

Carr, John (Mass). Quartermaster 12th Continental Infantry, 1st January to 31st December, 1776.

Carr, John (Pa). Ensign 5th Pennsylvania, 1st January, 1777; resigned 4th July, 1777.

Carr, John (R. I.). Lieutenant Rhode Island Militia in 1775; Captain of Babcock's and Lippitt's Rhode Island State Regiments, 1776 to 1779.

Carr, John (Va). Ensign 1st Virginia, February, 1781, and served to close of war.

Carr, Joseph (N. Y.). Quartermaster 1st New York, 1st May to November, 1776.

Carr, Patrick (Ga). Captain and Major Georgia Militia, 1780-1783.

Carr, Samuel (Mass). Lieutenant in Lexington Alarm, April, 1775; 1st Lieutenant of Gerrish's Massachusetts Regiment, April to December, 1775; 1st Lieutenant 26th Continental Infantry, 1st January to 31st December, 1776; Captain 9th Massachusetts, 1st January, 1777; transferred to 8th Massachusetts, 3d May, 1782; retired 1st January, 1783.

Carr, Samuel (Va). 2d Lieutenant 9th Virginia, 11th March, 1776; appointed Captain of Marines, — September, 1777.

Carr, Samuel (S. C.). Captain South Carolina Rangers; mortally wounded at Long Cane, 4th December, 1780.

Carr, Thomas (Va). Colonel Virginia Militia under General Marion, 1780-1781. (Died 1820.)

Carraway, Gideon (N. C.). Lieutenant 8th North Carolina, 28th November, 1776, to ——.

Carrier, Titus (Conn). Ensign of Sage's Connecticut State Regiment, June to December, 1776.

Carrington, Clement (Va). Cornet of Lee's Battalion of Light Dragoons, ——, 1780; wounded at Eutaw Springs, 8th September, 1781; served to close of war.

Carrington, Edward (Va). Lieutenant-Colonel 1st Continental Artillery, 30th November, 1776; retired 1st January, 1783, and served as Deputy Quartermaster General, Southern Department, to close of war. (Died 28th October, 1810.)

Carrington, George (Va). Colonel Virginia Militia, 1778-1781.

Carrington, George, Jr. (Va). Lieutenant of Lee's Battalion of Light Dragoons, 1779 to June, 1783.

Carrington, Mayo (Va). Ensign 7th Virginia, 29th February, 1776; 2d Lieutenant, 2d May, 1776; 1st Lieutenant, 1st February, 1777; transferred to 5th Virginia, 14th September, 1778; Captain Lieutenant, 3d October, 1778; Captain, 12th May, 1779; taken prisoner at Charleston, 12th May, 1780, and was a prisoner on parole to close of war; was Quartermaster of General Woodford's Brigade, 16th July to 10th December, 1779, and Deputy Quartermaster-General of the Southern Army, 10th December, 1779, to 12th May, 1780.

Carroll, Butler (N. C.). Ensign 10th North Carolina, mentioned in 1777.

Carroll, Charles (Md). A signer of the Declaration of Independence. (Died 4th July, 1828, and was the last survivor of the signers.)

Carroll, Jonathan (Mass). 1st Lieutenant of Learned's Massachusetts Regiment, May, 1775, to ——.

Carsdorff, Jacob (—). Lieutenant ——; was a prisoner in 1780; when and where taken, not stated.

Carson, Andrew (N. C.). Private and Captain North Carolina Partisan Rangers under General Davidson, 1776 to 1782. (Died 29th January, 1841.)

Carson, Ebenezer (Pa). 2d Lieutenant 10th Pennsylvania, 4th December, 1776; 1st Lieutenant, 18th April, 1777; taken prisoner near Iron Hill, 4th September, 1777; released 22d December, 1780; Captain, 1st April, 1779; transferred to 1st Pennsylvania, 17th January, 1781; resigned 18th May, 1781.

Carson, John (Md). 2d Lieutenant 1st Continental Artillery, 2d May, 1779; died, 12th September, 1781, of wounds received at Eutaw Springs, 8th September, 1781.

Carson, Moses (Pa). Captain 8th Pennsylvania, August, 1776; deserted 21st April, 1777, and joined the enemy.

Carson, Richard (Pa). 1st Lieutenant 8th Pennsylvania, — August, 1776; deserted 23d February, 1777.

Carson, Samuel (Pa). Captain Lieutenant of Captain Montgomery's Independent Pennsylvania Artillery Company, 2d December, 1776, to October, 1777

Carson, William (Va). Paymaster 11th Virginia, June, 1777; retired, 14th September, 1778.

Carswell, John (Ga). 1st Lieutenant 4th Georgia ——; taken prisoner at Hickory Hill, 28th June, 1779.

Cartel, Simon (N. H.). 1st Lieutenant 1st New Hampshire, 8th November, 1776; omitted March, 1777.

Carter, Asper (Pa). Lieutenant Pennsylvania Militia; taken prisoner at Bristol, Pa., 17th April, 1778.

Carter, Benjamin (N. C.). 1st Lieutenant 4th North Carolina, 22d December, 1776; Captain, 1st January, 1779; transferred to 2d North Carolina, 6th February, 1782, and served to close of war. (Died 20th January, 1830.)

Carter, Caleb (Mass). Lieutenant of Baldwin's Artillery Artificer Regiment in 1777.

Carter, Hubbard (N. H.). Ensign 1st New Hampshire, 28th September, 1777;

Lieutenant, 5th July, 1780; resigned 30th August, 1782.

Carter, John (Conn). 2d Lieutenant of Swift's Connecticut State Regiment, July to December, 1775; Captain Connecticut Militia in 1778 and 1780. (Died 1819.)

Carter, John (Ga). Major Georgia Militia; mortally wounded at White House, Georgia, 15th September, 1780.

Carter, John (Pa). Ensign of Baxter's Pennsylvania Battalion of the Flying Camp; taken prisoner at Fort Washington, 16th November, 1776.

Carter, John Champe (Va). Ensign 7th Virginia, 18th March, 1776; resigned 13th January, 1777; Captain 1st Continental Artillery, 30th October, 1777, to ——; was in service November, 1778; taken prisoner at Charleston 12th May, 1780; prisoner to close of war; Brevet Major, 30th September, 1783.

Carter, John Hill (Va). Lieutenant 3d Continental Dragoons, 12th October, 1777; resigned 5th December, 1778.

Carter, Josiah (Mass). Major in Lexington Alarm, April, 1775, and served subsequently as Lieutenant-Colonel Massachusetts Militia. (Died 1812.)

Carter, Samuel (Va). Was a Private and Sergeant in 1st Virginia in March, 1776; Ensign in July, 1777, and served to ——.

Carter, Stephen (Mass). Ensign 2d Continental Infantry, 1st January to 31st December, 1776; 2d Lieutenant 7th Massachusetts, 1st January, 1777; resigned 11th April, 1780.

Carter, Stephen (N. H.). 2d Lieutenant 3d New Hampshire, 23d May to December, 1775.

Carter, Thomas (S. C.). 1st Lieutenant South Carolina Militia, 1775-1776.

Carter, Thomas Neale (Va). Surgeon Hospital Department in Virginia, 6th July, 1776, to 31st May, 1777; Surgeon of a Virginia State Regiment, 1779 to 1782.

Carter, William (N. J.). Ensign 2d New Jersey, 29th November, 1776; resigned 5th February, 1777.

Carter, William (Va). Surgeon in Hospital Southern Department, July, 1776, to close of war. (Died 1798.)

Cartwright, Thomas (Mass). Captain of Jackson's Continental Regiment, 1st February, 1777; Aide-de-Camp to General Heath, October, 1778, to March, 1779; died 21st August, 1783.

Carty, Abraham (Del). Ensign Delaware Regiment, 20th January to December, 1776.

Caruthers, Andrew (N. C.). Lieutenant North Carolina Militia at King's Mountain, October, 1780. (Died 1818.)

Carver, Joseph (Conn). Ensign 8th Connecticut, 6th July to 17th December, 1775

Carver, Robert (N. Y.). Quartermaster of Steven's Battalion Continental Artillery, 8th November, 1776; resigned January, 1777.

Carver, Samuel (Conn). 2d Lieutenant of Ward's Connecticut State Regiment, May, 1776, to May, 1777.

Cary, Archibald (Va). Lieutenant-Colonel and Colonel Virginia Militia, 1775-1776. (Died 1786.)

Case, William (N. H.). Ensign of Warner's Continental Regiment, 1st October, 1776; 2d Lieutenant, 1st October, 1777; resigned 1st October, 1778.

Casey, Benjamin (Va). 1st Lieutenant 12th Virginia, 9th September, 1776; Captain, 1st September, 1777; regiment designated 8th Virginia, 14th September, 1778. Died 14th April, 1779.

Casey, Gideon (R. I.). 2d Lieutenant 1st Rhode Island, 20th February, 1777, to ——; no record of service after March, 1778.

Cass, Jonathan (N. H.). Served as a private at Bunker Hill, June, 1775; Ensign 3d New Hampshire, 8th November, 1776; 2d Lieutenant, 4th August, 1777; 1st Lieutenant, 1st May, 1778; transferred to 2d New Hampshire, 1st January, 1781; Captain, 8th December, 1782, and served to close of war; Captain 2d United States Infantry, 4th March, 1791; in 2d Sub Legion, 4th September, 1792; Major, 3d Sub Legion, 21st February, 1793, which became 3d United States Infantry, 1st November, 1796; resigned 15th February, 1801. (Died 14th August, 1830.)

Casson, Charles (Va). Ensign 4th Virginia, —— February, 1777; cashiered, 3d October, 1777.

Casson, Philip (Md). Ensign 4th Maryland Battalion of the Flying Camp, July to December, 1776.

Castaing, Peter (France). 2d Lieutenant of Jackson's Continental Regiment, March, 1777; 1st Lieutenant, 24th April, 1779; regiment designated 16th Massachusetts, 23d July, 1780; transferred to 9th Massachusetts, 1st January, 1781; transferred to 3d Massachusetts, 1st January, 1783; served as Aide-de-Camp to General Duportail from October, 1779, to close of war; was taken prisoner at Charleston, 12th May, 1780.

Castle, Phinehas (Conn). Captain Connecticut Militia, 1776-1777.

Caswell, Richard (N. C.). Colonel North Carolina Partisan Rangers, 1776 and 1777; Major-General North Carolina Militia, 1780 to close of war; was also Governor of North Carolina same time. (Died 20th November, 1789.)

Caswell, William (N. C.). Ensign 2d North Carolina, 1st September, 1775; Captain 5th North Carolina, 16th April, 1776, to ——.

Cathcart, William (Pa). Surgeon 4th Continental Dragoons, 1st April, 1777; resigned 1st May, 1778.

Catlett, George (Va). Lieutenant Virginia Militia, 1779-1780.

Catlett, Thomas (Va). Ensign 2d Virginia, 19th February, 1776; 2d Lieutenant, 26th November, 1776; Captain Lieutenant, 11th March, 1777; Captain, 8th March, 1779; killed at Waxhaws, 29th May, 1780.

Catlin, Abel (Conn). Surgeon 4th Connecticut, June, 1775, to December, 1775; Surgeon Connecticut Militia in 1777.

Catlin, Benjamin (Conn). Corporal in the Lexington Alarm, April, 1775; Sergeant in Captain Chester's Company in 1775; Quartermaster of Arnold's Expedition to Canada, and was taken prisoner at Quebec, 31st December, 1775; exchanged 10th January, 1777.

Catlin, Eli (Conn). 1st Lieutenant 7th Connecticut, 6th July to 6th December, 1775; 1st Lieutenant, 19th Continental Infantry, 1st January to 31st December, 1776; Captain 5th Connecticut, 1st January, 1777; resigned 25th May, 1778.

Catlin, Thomas (Conn). Ensign 1st Connecticut, 1st May to 1st December, 1775; 2d Lieutenant of Gay's Connecticut State Regiment, 20th June, 1776; taken prisoner on the retreat from New York, 15th September, 1776. (Died 1829.)

Catouch, William (N. J.). Ensign 3d New Jersey, 29th November, 1776; 2d Lieutenant, 1st January, 1777; resigned 28th April, 1778.

Cattell, Benjamin (S. C.). Captain 1st South Carolina, 17th June, 1775, to ——; was in service in 1778.

Cattell, William (S. C.). Captain 1st South Carolina, 17 June, 1775; Major 3d South Carolina, — May, 1776; Lieutenant-Colonel 1st South Carolina, 16th September, 1776; taken prisoner at Charleston, 12th May, 1780.

Caulkins, Jonathan (Conn). Captain of Company in Lexington Alarm, April, 1775; Captain of Ely's Connecticut State Regiment, November, 1776, to March, 1777; Captain of Latimer's Regiment Connecticut Militia; wounded at Ticonderoga, 6th July, 1777. (Died 1787.)

Caustaphan, James (N. C.). Ensign 7th North Carolina, 28th November, 1776, to ——.

Cebra, William (N. Y.). 2d Lieutenant 2d Continental Artillery, 1st February, 1777; resigned 15th April, 1780.

Celeron, Lewis (——). Captain Pulaski Legion, 1st April, 1779; taken prisoner at Charleston, 12th May, 1780; resigned 1st July, 1782.

Cessna, Charles (Pa). Lieutenant-Colonel Pennsylvania Militia, 1777-1778.

Chadbourne, Silas (Mass). 2d Lieutenant 11th Hassachusetts, 6th November, 1776; 1st Lieutenant, 1st January, 1777; resigned 18th March, 1780. (Died 15th June, 1823.)

Chadwick, Edmund (N. H.). Surgeon's Mate 3d New Hampshire, 8th November, 1776; Surgeon, 1st April, 1778; resigned 19th September, 1778. (Died 1826.)

Chadwick, John (Mass). 1st Lieutenant of Danielson's Massachusetts Regiment, 28th April, to December, 1775; 1st Lieutenant 3d Continental Infantry, 1st January, 1776; wounded at White Plains, 28th October, 1776; Captain 12th Massachusetts, 6th November, 1776; retired 1st April, 1779. (Died 8th May, 1821.)

Chadwick, Joseph (Mass). Captain of Gridley's Regiment Massachusetts Artillery, May, 1775 ,to ——.

Chaillè, Moses (Md). 1st Lieutenant of Captain Watkin's Independent Maryland Company, 14th January, 1776, to ——.

Chaillè, Peter (Md). Colonel Maryland Militia in 1776.

Chalenor, Edward (Mass). Corporal of Gridley's Regiment Massachusetts Artillery, 1st May to 8th August. 1776; Ensign 5th Massachusetts, 21st November, 1776; 2d Lieutenant, 7th November, 1777; retired 1st April, 1779.

Chalker, Isaac (Conn). Surgeon's Mate 1st Connecticut, August to December, 1775.

Challis, Thomas (N. H.). Sergeant 2d New Hampshire, January, 1777; Ensign, 22d December, 1777; resigned 20th May, 1780.

Chamberlain, Benjamin (N. H.). Ensign of Bedel's Regiment New Hampshire Rangers, 22d January, 1776; taken prisoner at the Cedars, 19th May, 1776; dishonorably discharged 13th October, 1776.

Chamberlain, Ebenezer (N. H.). 1st Lieutenant of Bedel's Regiment New Hampshire Rangers, 22d January, to September, 1776.

Chamberlain, Ephraim (Conn). 1st Lieutenant 7th Connecticut, 1st January, 1777; Captain, 15th November, 1778; transferred to 2d Connecticut, 1st January, 1781; retired 1st January, 1783.

Chamberlain, Freedom (Mass). Captain of Thomas' Massachusetts Regiment, 19th May to December, 1775. (Died 1821.)

Chamberlain, James (Md). Brigadier-General Maryland Militia, 6th January, 1776, to ——.

Chamberlain, Moses (Vt). Lieutenant of Bedel's Regiment Vermont Militia, 1st April, 1777, to 1st April, 1779.

Chamberlain, William (N. J.). Colonel New Jersey Militia, 1777-1781. (Died 1817.)

Chamberlin, Abial (Vt). 1st Lieutenant Vermont Militia in 1777.

Chamberlin, Abner (Vt). Lieutenant Vermont Militia in 1777.

Chamberlin, Elias (Vt). Lieutenant Vermont Militia in 1777.

Chamberlin, Eliphalet (Conn). Ensign of Wadsworth's Connecticut State Regiment, June to December, 1776; 1st Lieutenant Connecticut Militia, 1777.

Chamberlin, Joel (Conn). Ensign in Lexington Alarm, April, 1775; 2d Lieutenant 8th Connecticut, 6th July to 18th December, 1775; 1st Lieutenant of Wadsworth's Connecticut State Regiment, June to December, 1776.

Chamberlin, John (Conn). Ensign of Sage's Connecticut State Regiment, June to December, 1776.

Chamberlin, Joseph (N. H.). 2d Lieutenant New Hampshire Minute Men, April and May, 1775.

Chamberlin, Joseph (Vt). 1st Lieutenant Vermont Militia in 1777.

Chambers, Benjamin (Md). Ensign of Smallwood's Maryland Regiment, 14th January, 1776; resigned 3d July, 1776.

Chambers, Benjamin (Pa). 1st Lieutenant 1st Continental Infantry, 1st January, 1776; Captain 2d Canadian (Hazen's) Regiment, 3d November, 1776; resigned 1st February, 1778.

Chambers, Benjamin (Pa). Private in Thompson's Pennsylvania Rifle Regiment, 27th June, 1775; 2d Lieutenant 1st Continental Infantry, 5th January, 1776; discharged — August, 1776; Ensign 1st Pennsylvania, 2d June, 1778; Lieutenant, 13th September, 1779; resigned 26th November, 1780. (Died 29th December, 1813.)

Chambers, David (N. J.). Colonel New Jersey Militia, 1776-1779.

Chambers, James (Pa). Captain of Thompson's Pennsylvania Rifle Regiment, 25th June, 1775; Lieutenant-Colonel 1st Continental Infantry, 7th March, 1776; Colonel 10th Pennsylvania, 12th March, 1777, to rank from 28th September, 1776; transferred to 1st Pennsylvania, 12th April, 1777; wounded at Brandywine, 11th September, 1777; retired 17th January, 1781. (Died 25th April, 1805.)

Chambers, Matthew (Mass). Sergeant of Glover's Massachusetts Regiment, 16th May to December, 1775; 2d Lieutenant 9th Continental Infantry, 1st January to 31st December, 1776; 1st Lieutenant 6th Massachusetts, 1st January, 1777; Captain Lieutenant, 10th June, 1779; Captain, 11th November, 1779, and served to June, 1783. (Died 30th January, 1809.)

Chambers, Stephen (Pa). 1st Lieutenant 12th Pennsylvania, 1st October, 1776; Captain, 1st March, 1777; retired 1st July, 1778. Wounded in a duel with Dr. Jacob Rieges, 11th May, and died 16th May, 1789.

Chambers, William (N. J.). 2d Lieutenant of Spencer's Additional Continental Regiment, 1st August, 1777; resigned 10th October, 1777.

Chambers, William (Pa). 2d Lieutenant 2d Pennsylvania Battalion, 5th January, 1776; resigned 5th July, 1776; Captain 2d Canadian (Hazen's) Regiment, 9th December, 1776; resigned 31st January, 1778.

Champe, William. Colonel Virginia Militia, 1777-1778.

Champion, Henry (Conn). 2d Lieutenant 2d Connecticut, 1st May to 10th December, 1775; Adjutant 22d Continental Infantry, 1st January to 31st December, 1776; Captain 3d Connecticut, 1st January, 1777; resigned 1st May, 1780, when appointed Commissary General Eastern Department and served to 1781. (Died, 1797.)

Champion, Reuben (Mass). Surgeon Massachusetts Militia. Died at Fort Ticonderoga, 27th March, 1777.

Champlin, George (R. I.). Lieutenant-Colonel Rhode Island Militia, 1775-1776.

Champlin, Samuel (R. I.). Lieutenant Rhode Island Militia in 1776.

Champney, John (Mass). Deputy Quartermaster-General, 1st April, 1778, to 23d September, 1780.

Champney, Jonathan (Mass). Sergeant in Lexington Alarm, April, 1775; Sergeant in Ward's Massachusetts Regiment, May to December, 1775; Ensign 21st Continental Infantry, 1st January, 1776; 2d Lieutenant, 12th July to 31st December, 1776; served subsequently as Major Massachusetts Militia.

Chandler, Abiel (N. H.). Adjutant 1st New Hampshire, 23d April to December, 1775; Adjutant 5th Continental Infantry, 1st January, 1776; killed at Long Island, 27th August, 1776.

Chandler, David (Mass). Lieutenant in Lexington Alarm, April, 1775; 1st Lieutenant of Frye's Massachusetts Regiment, May to December, 1775; 1st Lieutenant 16th Continental Infantry, 1st January, 1776. Died July, 1776.

Chandler, John (Conn). Lieutenant-Colonel of Silliman's Regiment Connecticut Militia, June to December, 1776; Colonel 8th Connecticut, 1st January, 1777; resigned 5th March, 1778. (Died 15th March, 1796.)

Chandler, John (Mass). 2d Lieutenant of Knox's Regiment Continental Artillery, 10th December, 1775, to December, 1776.

Chandler, John (N. H.). Captain New Hampshire Militia, 1777.

Chandler, Jonathan (N. H.). Captain New Hampshire Militia, 1775.

Chandler, Jonathan (Vt). Captain Vermont Militia in 1777.

Chandler, Joseph (N. H.). 1st Lieutenant 2d Continental Infantry, 1st January, 1776. Died 17th September, 1776.

Chandler, Thomas (Va). Captain of a Virginia State Regiment, 1777 to 1780.

Chandonnet, Francis (N. H.). Ensign 1st New Hampshire, 7th November, 1776; retired 1st September, 1778; Assistant Deputy Quartermaster-General, — October, 1778, to ——.

Chaney, Thomas (Mass). Ensign 24th Continental Infantry, 1st January to 31st December, 1776; Lieutenant 13th Massachusetts, 13th November, 1776; resigned 13th February, 1778.

Chaney, William (Mass). Sergeant-Major 15th Continental Infantry, 1st January, 1776; Ensign, 7th October, 1776; 2d Lieutenant 3d Massachusetts, 1st January, 1777; Regimental Adjutant, 11th November, 1777; resigned 28th August, 1780.

Channing, Walter (R. I.). 2d Lieutenant of Tallman's Regiment Rhode Island Militia, 12th December, 1776, to May, 1777.

Chapin, Adams (Mass). Ensign and Quartermaster 13th Continental Infantry, 1st January to 31st December, 1776. (Died 23d October, 1832.)

Chapin, Enoch (Mass). Captain of Danielson's Regiment Massachusetts Militia, May to December, 1775; Captain Massachusetts Militia, 1776.

Chapin, Israel (Mass). Captain of Fellows' Massachusetts Regiment, May to December, 1775; Colonel Massachusetts Militia, 1777-1778. (Died 7th March, 1795.)

Chapin, Leonard (Mass). 1st Lieutenant 3d Massachusetts, 1st January, 1777; retired 16th September, 1778.

Chapin, Leonidas (N. J.). Quartermaster 2d New Jersey, 18th September, 1776; resigned March, 1777.

Chapin, Noah (Conn). Ensign 2d Connecticut, 1st May to 17th December, 1775.

Chapin, Samuel (Mass). Ensign 4th Massachusetts, 1st January, 1777; 2d Lieutenant, 1st November, 1777; 1st Lieutenant, 20th March, 1779; resigned 30th May, 1781.

Chapin, Samuel (Mass). 1st Lieutenant of Paterson's Massachusetts Regiment, May to December, 1775; 1st Lieutenant 15th Continental Infantry, 1st January to 31st December, 1776.

Chapin, Seth (Mass). 1st Lieutenant of Wood's Regiment Massachusetts Militia in 1776.

Chapin, Seth (Mass). 1st Lieutenant of Sherburne's Continental Regiment, 19th July, 1777; resigned 19th April, 1780.

Chaplin, Abraham (Va). Lieutenant and Captain of Clark's Illinois Regiment, 1777 to 1781.

Chapline, Moses (Md). 1st Lieutenant 1st Maryland Battalion of the Flying Camp, July to December, 1776; 1st Lieutenant 6th Maryland, 10th December, 1776; Captain 20th February, 1777; resigned 12th October, 1777. (Died 1812.)

Chapman, Albert (Conn). Sergeant in the Lexington Alarm, April, 1775; 1st Lieutenant 5th Connecticut, 1st May, 1775, to March, 1776; Captain of Elmore's Connecticut State Regiment, 15th April, 1776; Captain 7th Connecticut, 1st January, 1777; Major 5th Connecticut, 5th March, 1778; retired 1st January, 1781. (Died 26th December, 1819.)

Chapman, Alpheus (Conn). Sergeant 7th Connecticut, 6th July, 1775; Ensign, 1st September to 10th December, 1775; 1st Lieutenant 19th Continental Infantry, 1st January, 1776; dismissed 10th June, 1776.

Chapman, Benjamin (N. Y.). Quartermaster 4th New York, 30th June, 1775, to January, 1776; served subsequently as Captain New York Militia.

Chapman, Elijah (Conn). Private in the Lexington Alarm, April, 1775; 2d Lieutenant of Ward's Connecticut State Regiment, 14th May, 1776; 1st Lieutenant 5th Connecticut, 1st January, 1777; Captain Lieutenant, 1st April, 1779; Captain, 20th July, 1780; transferred to 2d Connecticut, 1st January, 1781, and served to June, 1783. (Died 17th December, 1825.)

Chapman, Elisha (Conn). Captain of Selden's Connecticut State Regiment, 1776-1779. (Died 1825.)

Chapman, Ezra (Conn). Ensign of Baldwin's Artillery Artificer Regiment, 6th August, 1777. Died 31st August, 1778.

Chapman, Henry H. (Md). Ensign 2d Maryland, 4th September, 1781; Lieutenant, ———, 1782; retained in Maryland Battalion, April, 1783, and served to 15th November, 1783.

Chapman, Hezekiah (Mass). Chaplain of Read's Massachusetts Regiment, 18th May to December, 1775.

Chapman, James (Conn). Captain 6th Connecticut, 1st May to 10th December, 1775; Captain 10th Continental

Infantry, 1st January, 1776; Major, 15th August, 1776; killed 15th September, 1776, on the retreat from New York.

Chapman, James (Conn). Ensign of Elmore's Connecticut State Regiment, 15th April, 1776; 2d Lieutenant, 25th July, 1776; 2d Lieutenant 7th Connecticut, 1st January, 1777; 1st Lieutenant, 25th October, 1778; Captain Lieutenant, — March, 1780; resigned 8th September, 1780.

Chapman, John (R. I.). Lieutenant of Warner's Continental Regiment, 16th September, 1776; retired 1st January, 1781.

Chapman, John (Va). Captain of a Virginia State Regiment, 1778 to 1781.

Chapman, Joseph (Conn). Ensign 17th Continental Infantry, 1st January, 1776; taken prisoner at Long Island, 27th August, 1776; exchanged 10th December, 1776; 2d Lieutenant 4th Connecticut, 12th May, 1777; 1st Lieutenant, 20th January, 1778; Regimental Quartermaster, 13th September, 1778; Captain Lieutenant, 26th October, 1780; retired 1st January, 1781. (Died 9th August, 1822.)

Chapman, Nathan (Conn). Captain Connecticut Militia, 1776 .

Chapman, Nathaniel (Mass). Captain of Flower's Artillery Artificer Regiment, 7th May, 1778; retired 30th September, 1780.

Chapman, Richard (Conn). Lieutenant Connecticut Militia; killed at Groton Heights, 6th September, 1781.

Chapman, Samuel (Conn). Colonel Connecticut Militia, 1778-1779.

Chapman, Samuel (N. C.). 2d Lieutenant 8th North Carolina, 28th November, 1776; 1st Lieutenant, 1st August, 1777; transferred to 4th North Carolina, 1st June, 1778; Captain, 5th April, 1779, and served to close of war.

Chappel, Amos (Conn). 1st Lieutenant 4th Connecticut, 1st May to December, 1775.

Charles, Joseph (Mass). Sergeant 7th Massachusetts, 1st January, 1777; Ensign, 19th November, 1777; resigned 30th September, 1778.

Charlton, John W. (Md). Paymaster 6th Maryland, 22d April, 1777; resigned 1st October, 1778.

Charlton, Thomas (S. C.). 2d Lieutenant 3d South Carolina, 17th June, 1775, to ——.

Charlton, William (N. C.). Ensign 10th North Carolina, 14th March,

1779; 2d Lieutenant, September, 1779; wounded at Stono Ferry, 20th June, and died 21st June, 1779.

Charnock, William (S. C.). 1st Lieutenant 2d South Carolina, 17th June, 1775; Captain, May, 1776, to ——.

Charter, John (Conn). 1st Lieutenant of Gay's Connecticut State Regiment, June to December, 1776.

Charwick, William (S. C.). 1st Lieutenant 2d South Carolina, 17th June, 1775; Captain, 18th May, 1776, and served to ——.

Chase, Dudley Leavit (N. H.). Ensign 3d New Hampshire, 8th November, 1776; 2d Lieutenant, 7th October, 1777; 1st Lieutenant, 1st May, 1778; resigned 30th June, 1780. (Died 1814.)

Chase, Enoch (N. H.). Ensign 8th Continental Infantry, 1st January, 1776; 2d Lieutenant, 6th September, 1776; 1st Lieutenant, 2d New Hampshire, 8th November, 1776; Captain, 22d December, 1777; resigned 21st November, 1782.

Chase, John (R. I.). Surgeon's Mate 9th Continental Infantry, 1st January to 31st December, 1776.

Chase, Jonathan (N. H.). Colonel New Hampshire Militia, 1776-1778. (Died 1800.)

Chase, Joshua (Mass). Surgeon's Mate 13th Massachusetts, 1st January, 1777; resigned 23d June, 1777; Surgeon in Navy, 1778-1781.

Chase, Joshua (Mass). Private in Lexington Alarm, April, 1775; Private and Corporal in Gerrish's Massachusetts Regiment, 27th April to December, 1775; Sergeant 26th Continental Infantry, 1st January to 31st December, 1776; Ensign 9th Massachusetts, 1st January, 1777; resigned 12th April, 1778.

Chase, Josiah (N. H.). Surgeon's Mate 1st New Hampshire, 23d April to December, 1775; Surgeon's Mate 5th Continental Infantry, 1st January to 31st December, 1776; served subsequently as Surgeon New Hampshire Militia (Died September, 1823.)

Chase, Moses (N. H.). Captain New Hampshire Militia, 1777. (Died 1793.)

Chase, Samuel (Md). A signer of the Declaration of Independence. (Died 19th June, 1811.)

Chase, Samuel (Mass). Ensign of Jackson's Additional Continental Regiment, 10th May, 1777; resigned 1st February, 1778.

Chase, Solomon (N. H.). Surgeon New Hampshire Militia, 1777.

Chase, Wells (Mass). Lieutenant in Lexington Alarm, April, 1775; 1st Lieutenant of Frye's Massachusetts Regiment, May to December, 1775.

Chatham, John (—). Lieutenant, ——; was a prisoner in 1780; when and where taken, not stated.

Cheapin, Enoch (Mass). Captain of Danielson's Massachusetts Regiment, May to December, 1775.

Check or **Chick, Frederick** (Ga). Lieutenant in 2d Georgia in 1779.

Cheeney, James (Mass). Lieutenant 3d Massachusetts, 1st January, 1777; resigned 28th August, 1780.

Cheeney, Penuel (Conn). Surgeon's Mate 3d Connecticut, 1st May, 1775; Surgeon, 4th October, 1775; cashiered, 21st November, 1775.

Cheeney, Thomas (Mass). Ensign 24th Continental Infantry, 1st January to 31st December, 1776; 1st Lieutenant 13th Massachusetts, 1st January, 1777. Died 13th February, 1778.

Cheese, John (N. C.). Ensign 1st North Carolina, 12th June, 1776; 2d Lieutenant, 20th January, 1777; resigned 1st April, 1777.

Cheesboro, John (N. C.). Paymaster 6th North Carolina, 3d July, 1777; Ensign, 25th April, 1778; retired 1st June, 1778.

Cheesman, Jacob (N. Y.). Captain 1st New York, 1st July, 1775; Aide-de-Camp to General Montgomery, — August, 1775; killed at Quebec, 31st December, 1775.

Cheever, Ezekiel (Mass). Commissary of Military Stores, 17th August, 1775, to 1st January, 1781.

Cheever, John (Md). 2d Lieutenant 1st Continental Artillery, 8th September, 1779; retired, — October, 1782.

Cheever, Joseph (Mass). Sergeant in Lexington Alarm, April, 1775; 1st Lieutenant of Gerrish's Massachusetts Regiment, 19th May to December, 1775; 1st Lieutenant 26th Continental Infantry, 1st January to 31st December, 1776. (Died 23d October, 1830.)

Cherry, Samuel (N. H.). Sergeant 1st New Hampshire, 23d April to December, 1775; Ensign of Wingate's Regiment New Hampshire Militia in 1776; 1st Lieutenant 2d New Hampshire, 8th November, 1776; Captain Lieutenant, 22d December, 1777; Captain, 30th November, 1779; retired 1st January, 1783. (Died 21st October, 1825.)

Cherry, William (Va). 2d Lieutenant 4th Virginia, 10th February, 1776; 1st Lieutenant, 17th August, 1776; Captain, 29th November, 1777; retired 14th September, 1778.

Chesley, Alpheus (N. H.). Lieutenant-Colonel New Hampshire Militia, 1775-1776.

Chesley, Robert (Md). 1st Lieutenant 2d Maryland, 10th December, 1776; Captain, 10th June, 1777; taken prisoner at Fort Schuyler, 22d August, 1777; exchanged ——; transferred to 3d Maryland, 1st January, 1781, and served to April, 1783.

Chester, John (Conn). Captain in the Lexington Alarm, April, 1775; Captain 2d Connecticut, 1st May to 17th December, 1775; Major of Wolcott's Connecticut State Regiment, December, 1775, to February, 1776; Colonel Connecticut State Regiment, 20th June to December, 1776. (Died 4th November, 1809.)

Chevalier, John (Pa). Colonel Pennsylvania Militia, 1776.

Chew, Aaron (N. J.). Lieutenant New Jersey Militia; taken prisoner at his home 19th June, 1778.

Chew, John (Va). Cadet Sixth Virginia, 14th February, 1776; 2d Lieutenant, — November, 1776; 1st Lieutenant, ——, 1779; wounded at Camden 16th August, 1780, and did not rejoin regiment.

Chew, Robert B. (Va). 1st Lieutenant Virginia State Regiment, February, 1777, to January, 1780.

Chew, Samuel Lloyd (Md). 1st Lieutenant 3d Maryland Battalion of the Flying Camp, July to December, 1776; Captain 3d Maryland, 10th December, 1776, but did not accept.

Chew, William (Va). Lieutenant Virginia Militia; wounded at King's Mountain, 7th October, 1780.

Chewning, John (Va). Captain of Virginia State Dragoons, 1779-1781. (Died 1798.)

Chick or **Cheek, Frederick** (Ga). Lieutenant in 2d Georgia in 1779.

Chickley, Samuel (Pa). Ensign 3d Pennsylvania Battalion, 8th April, 1776; taken prisoner at Fort Washington 16th November, 1776; exchanged 20th April, 1778.

Child, ——. See also **Childs.**

Child, Francis (N. C.). 1st Lieutenant 6th North Carolina, 16th April, 1776; Captain, 26th January, 1777; transferred to 3d North Carolina 1st June, 1778; taken prisoner at Charleston 12th May, 1780.

Child, James (N. C.). Ensign 1st North Carolina, 1st September, 1775, to ——.

Child, James (R. I.). Ensign of Church's Rhode Island Regiment, 3d May to December, 1775; 2d Lieutenant 11th Continental Infantry, 1st January to 31st December, 1776.

Child, Jonathan (N. H.). Major New Hampshire Militia, 1775-1777.

Childs, Abijah (Mass). Private in Lexington Alarm, April, 1775; Captain of Gardner's Massachusetts Regiment, May to December, 1775; Captain 25th Continental Infantry, 1st January to 31st December, 1776; Captain 3d Massachusetts, 1st January, 1777; resigned 10th March, 1778. (Died 1823.)

Childs, Abraham (Mass). 2d Lieutenant of Gardner's Massachusetts Regiment, May to December, 1775; 1st Lieutenant 26th Continental Infantry, 1st January to 31st December, 1776; Captain 9th Massachusetts, 1st January, 1777; resigned 6th September, 1779. (Died 3d January, 1834.)

Childs, Isaac (Mass). 2d Lieutenant 11th Massachusetts, 6th November, 1776; resigned 28th March, 1779.

Childs, James (N. C.). Ensign 1st North Carolina, 1st September, 1775, to ——.

Childs, Jeremiah (R. I.). Quartermaster of Church's Rhode Island Regiment, 1775-1776.

Childs, John (Mass). 2d Lieutenant of Gardner's Massachusetts Regiment, May to December, 1775; 1st Lieutenant of Jackson's Continental Regiment, 12th May, 1777; resigned 17th October, 1778. (Died 3d September, 1825.)

Childs, Josiah (Conn). 1st Lieutenant of Chester's Connecticut State Regiment, June to December, 1776; Captain 5th Connecticut, 1st January, 1777; retired 15th November, 1778.

Childs, Nathaniel (Pa). Ensign of Lewis' Pennsylvania Battalion of the Flying Camp, July to December, 1776.

Childs, Obadiah (Conn). Corporal in the Lexington Alarm, April, 1775; Sergeant 3d Connecticut, 10th May to 16th December, 1775; Ensign of Ward's Connecticut State Regiment, May, 1776, to May, 1777.

Childs, Thomas (N. C.). Captain North Carolina Militia in 1780. (Died 15th September, 1820.)

Childs, Timothy (Mass). Surgeon of Paterson's Massachusetts Regiment, 28th June to December, 1775; Surgeon 15th Continental Infantry, 1st January to 31st December, 1776. (Died 25th February, 1821.)

Chilton, John (Pa). 1st Lieutenant 2d Pennsylvania Battalion, 5th January, 1776; resigned 11th November, 1776.

Chilton, John (Va). Captain 3d Virginia, 29th April, 1776; killed at Brandywine 11th September, 1777.

Chilton, Thomas (Va). Colonel Virginia Militia, 1779-1781.

Chimburg, Philip.—See **Clumburg.**

Chiny, ——. See **Cheeney.**

Chinn, Edward (Pa). Paymaster 2d Canadian (Hazen's) Regiment, 1st June, 1777; taken prisoner at Short Hills, 27th June, 1777; Lieutenant, 1st May, 1782, and served to June, 1783.

Chipman, John (N. H.). 2d Lieutenant Green Mountain Boys, 27th July, 1775; 1st Lieutenant of Warner's Continental Regiment, 16th September, 1776; taken prisoner at Fort George 16th November, 1776; Captain, 1st August, 1777; retired 1st January, 1781; served subsequently as Major New York Levies. (Died 28th August, 1829.)

Chipman, Nathaniel (Conn). 2d Lieutenant 2d Connecticut, 1st January, 1777; 1st Lieutenant, 29th December, 1777; retired 13th October, 1778. (Died 15th February, 1843.)

Chisholm, Thomas (Ga). Captain 1st Georgia, 7th January, 1776; Major 4th Georgia, 1st February, 1777; Lieutenant-Colonel — Regiment, 21st March, 1778, to ——.

Chisman, George (Va). Captain Virginia Militia, 1776-1777.

Chittenden, Benjamin (Conn). Ensign 6th Connecticut, 1st January, 1777; resigned 1st February, 1778.

Chittenden, Benjamin (N. Y.). 1st Lieutenant 2d New York, 28th June, 1775, to January, 1776.

Chittenden, Nathaniel (Mass). 2d Lieutenant of Thomas' Massachusetts Regiment, May, 1775, to ——.

Christ, Henry (Pa). Captain 2d Battalion of Miles' Pennsylvania Rifle Regiment, 9th March, 1776; resigned 19th March, 1777. (Died 1789.)

Christian, John (Va). Captain Virginia Militia, 1779-1781.

Christian, Henry (Va). Captain of Gaines' Regiment, Virginia Militia, in 1781. (Died 1805.)

Christian, Gilbert (Va). Captain Virginia Militia at King's Mountain, October, 1780. (Died 1793.)

Christian, William (Va). Lieutenant-Colonel 1st Virginia, 13th February, 1776; Colonel, 18th March, 1776, which he declined and retired from the service. (Died 1786.)

Christian, William (Va). 2d Lieutenant 10th Virginia, 3d December, 1776; resigned 13th January, 1778.

Christie, James (Pa). 1st Lieutenant 2d Pennsylvania Battalion ,5th January, 1776; Captain 3d Pennsylvania, 11th November, 1776, to rank from 9th August, 1776; transferred to 2d Pennsylvania, 1st January, 1783, and served to 3d June, 1783. (Name also spelled Chrystie.) (Died — June, 1807.)

Christie, John (Md). 2d Lieutenant 2d Maryland Battalion of the Flying Camp, July, 1776 to ——.

Christie, John (Pa). 1st Lieutenant 4th Pennsylvania Battalion, 5th January, 1776; Captain 5th Pennsylvania, 1st January, 1777; transferred to 3d Pennsylvania, 1st January, 1783, and served to 3d June, 1783.

Christie, Thomas (Va). Surgeon 1st Continental Artillery, 1st April, 1778, and served to June, 1783.

Christman, George (Va). Captain Virginia Militia, 1776-1777.

Christman, Nathaniel (N. C.). Captain North Carolina Militia; was a prisoner; exchanged 7th June, 1782; when and where taken not stated.

Christman, Paul (Md). Ensign German Regiment, 12th July, 1776; resigned 8th November, 1776.

Christman, Richard (N. C.). Captain North Carolina Militia in 1780.

Chronicle, William (N. C.). Major North Carolina Partisan Rangers; killed at King's Mountain, 7th October, 1780.

Chrystie, ——. See **Christie,** as name is spelled both ways.

Church, Benjamin (Mass). Director and Chief Physician of Hospital, 27th

July, 1775; dismissed 7th November, 1775. (Lost at sea 1st May, 1776.)

Church, Benjamin (R. I.). Ensign Rhode Island Militia, 15th January, 1776; Lieutenant of Richmond's Regiment Rhode Island Militia, 19th August, 1776; Captain of Tallman's Regiment Rhode Island Militia, 12th December, 1776, to May, 1777. (Died 11th September, 1798.)

Church, Charles (Mass). 2d Lieutenant of Cotton's Massachusetts Regiment, May to December, 1775; 2d Lieutenant, 23d Continental Infantry, 1st January to December, 1776; served subsequently as Lieutenant Massachusetts Militia.

Church, Isaac (Mass). Sergeant in Woodbridge's Massachusetts Militia Regiment, August, 1776; Ensign, 4th October, 1776; 1st Lieutenant 5th Massachusetts, 1st January, 1777; cashiered 20th January, 1778.

Church, Israel (R. I.). Ensign of Church's Rhode Island Regiment, 3d May to December, 1775.

Church, James Miller (N. Y.). Surgeon's Mate Hospital Department, 1776.

Church, Nathaniel (R. I.). 1st Lieutenant of Church's Rhode Island Regiment, 3d May to December, 1775.

Church, Reuben (Conn). Sergeant of Warner's Continental Regiment, 4th January, 1777; Ensign, 7th August. 1777; resigned 30th September, 1780. (Died 1834.)

Church, Samuel (N. Y.). Surgeon 2d Canadian (Hazen's) Regiment, 10th April, 1777; resigned 1st November, 1777.

Church, Thomas (Pa). Captain 5th Pennsylvania Battalion, 5th January, 1776; Major, 4th September, 1777, to rank from 1st March, 1777; retired 17th January, 1781.

Church, Thomas (R. I.). Colonel 3d Rhode Island Regiment, 3d May to December, 1775.

Church, Timothy (N. Y.). Lieutenant-Colonel and Colonel New York Militia, 1777-1780.

Church, Uriah (Conn). 1st Lieutenant of Wooster's Connecticut State Regiment, November, 1775, and of Ellmore's Connecticut State Regiment, 15th April, 1776, to April, 1777.

Churchill, Charles (Conn). 2d Lieutenant of Wolcott's Connecticut State Regiment, December, 1775, to February, 1776.

Churchill, Joseph (Conn). Captain of Sage's Connecticut State Regiment, June to December, 1776.

Churchill, Joseph (Mass). Lieutenant of Doolittle's Massachusetts Regiment, May to December, 1775; 1st Lieutenant 2d Continental Infantry, 1st January to 31st December, 1776. (Died 1797.)

Cicaty, Beraud de (Pa). Ensign 2d Pennsylvania, 5th February. 1777; resigned 13th October, 1777; Lieutenant of Cavalry, Pulaski Legion, 6th January, 1779, to ——.

Cilley, Jonathan (N. H.). Ensign 3d New Hampshire, 4th August, 1777; Lieutenant, 5th July, 1780; transferred to 1st New Hampshire 1st January, 1781, and served to close of war.

Cilley, Joseph (N. H.). Major 2d New Hampshire, 20th May to December, 1775; Major 8th Continental Infantry, 1st January, 1776; Lieutenant-Colonel 1st New Hampshire, 8th November, 1776; Colonel, 2d April, 1777; retired 1st January, 1781. (Died 25th August, 1799.)

Claflin, Samuel (Mass). Ensign 21st Continental Infantry, 1st January, 1776; 2d Lieutenant, 11th September, 1776; 2d Lieutenant 9th Massachusetts, 1st January, 1777; resigned 15th July, 1779.

Clagett, Horatio (Md). Ensign 3d Battalion Maryland Flying Camp, July to December, 1776; 1st Lieutenant 3d Maryland, 10th December, 1776; Captain, 10th October, 1777; transferred to 5th Maryland, 1st January, 1781; transferred to 1st Maryland, 2d January, 1783; retained in Maryland Battalion, April, 1783; Brevet Major, 30th September, 1783; served to 15th November, 1783.

Clagett, Samuel (Md). Hospital Surgeon's Mate in 1780.

Claghorn, George (Mass). Major Massachusetts Militia in 1781.

Claiborne, Buller (Va). 1st Lieutenant 2d Virginia, 24th October, 1775; Captain, 31st January, 1776, to 27th July, 1777; served subsequently as Brigade Major and Aide-de-Camp to General Lincoln in 1779 and 1780.

Claiborne, Dandridge (Va). Major Virginia Militia, 1777-1779.

Claiborne, Richard (Va). 1st Lieutenant 1st Continental Artillery, 13th January, 1777; Brigade Major of

Weedon's Brigade, 18th November, 1777, to ——; Deputy Quartermaster General, 1780 to 1782.

Clandenin, John.—See **Clendenin.**

Clanghorn, Eleazer (Conn). 1st Lieutenant of Burrall's Continental Regiment, 23d January, 1776; Captain Lieutenant, 6th Connecticut, 1st January, 1777; Captain, 19th April, 1779; resigned 10th May, 1780.

Clap, Daniel (N. H.). Lieutenant of Bedel's New Hampshire Regiment, July, 1776; 2d Lieutenant 1st New Hampshire, 8th November, 1776; 1st Lieutenant, 5th March, 1778; Captain Lieutenant, 5th July, 1780; retired 1st January, 1781.

Clapham, Josias (Va). Colonel Virginia Militia, 1777-1781.

Clapp, Caleb (Mass). Private of a Company of Minute Men at Lexington, 19th April, 1775; Sergeant and Sergeant-Major of Doolittle's Massachusetts Regiment, June to December, 1775; 2d Lieutenant 26th Continental Infantry, 1st January to 31st December, 1776; Lieutenant and Adjutant 9th Massachusetts, 1st January, 1777; transferred to 4th Massachusetts, 1st January, 1781; Captain, 9th April, 1782, and served to June, 1783. (Died 5th June, 1812.)

Clapp, Earl (Mass). Captain in Lexington Alarm, April, 1775; Captain of Cotton's Massachusetts Regiment, May to December, 1775; Captain 21st Continental Infantry, 1st January to 31st December, 1776. (Died 1836.)

Clapp, Ebenezer (Mass). Lieutenant-Colonel of Read's Massachusetts Regiment, 18th May to December, 1775; Lieutenant-Colonel 13th Continental Infantry, 1st January to 31st December, 1776. (Died 29th January, 1802.)

Clapp, Jonathan (Mass). Major of Pomeroy's Regiment Massachusetts Militia, 1776-1778. (Died 1782.)

Clapp, Joseph (Mass). Captain Massachusetts Militia, 1778-1780.

Clapp, Joshua (Mass). 1st Lieutenant 9th Massachusetts, 1st January, 1777; wounded at Stillwater, 19th September, 1777; Regimental Quartermaster, 18th October, 1778; transferred to 8th Massachusetts, 1st January, 1781; transferred to 3d Massauhusetts, 12th June, 1783, Brevet Captain, 30th September, 1783, and served to 3d November, 1783. (Died 5th November, 1810.)

Clapp, Stephen (Mass). Catain of Baldwin's Artillery Artificer Regiment, 6th November, 1778, to March, 1781. (Died 3d May, 1829.)

Clapsaddle, Daniel (Md). Major Maryland Militia, 1776.

Clapsaddle, August (N. Y.). Major New York Militia; killed at Oriskany 6th August, 1777.

Clark.—See **Clarke**, as these names are spelled both ways.

Clark, Abraham (N. J.). A signer of the Declaration of Independence; died 15th September, 1794.

Clark, Asahel (Conn). Ensign 5th Connecticut, 1st January, 1777; resigned 20th April, 1778.

Clark, Charles (Pa). Lieutenant Pennsylvania Militia; wounded at Guelph's Mills 11th December, 1777.

Clark, Charles (Pa). Lieutenant of Watts' Pennsylvania Battalion of the Flying Camp, July, 1776; taken prisoner at Long Island, 27th August, 1776; exchanged 29th January, 1781. (Died — March, 1813.)

Clark, Daniel (Conn). 1st Lieutenant of Sage's Connecticut State Regiment, June to December, 1776; 1st Lieutenant of Latimer's Regiment Connecticut Militia, 24th August, 1777; died 21st September, 1777, of wounds received at Stillwater, 19th September, 1777.

Clark, Edmund (Va). Ensign 6th Virginia, 21st March, 1780; taken prisoner at Charleston, 12th May, 1780; transferred to 1st Virginia, 12th February, 1781; Lieutenant, 10th June, 1781, and served to close of war.

Clark, Elijah (N. J.). Lieutenant-Colonel New Jersey Militia, 1776-1777.

Clark, Elisha (Conn). Ensign of Silliman's Connecticut State Regiment, June to December, 1776.

Clark, George Rogers (Va). Colonel Illinois Regiment Virginia Militia, 1777-1780, and Brigadier-General Virginia Militia, 1780-1783. (Died 13th February, 1818.)

Clark, Hezekiah (Conn). Surgeon's Mate 3d Connecticut, 22d June, 1778; retired 1st January, 1781.

Clark, Isaac (Vt). 1st Lieutenant Vermont Rangers in 1777.

Clark, J. C. (Ga). Lieutenant 3d Georgia, ——; on roll for August, 1778.

Clark, James (Conn). Captain in Lexington Alarm, 1775; Captain 3d

Connecticut, 1st May to 18th December, 1775. (Died 29th December, 1826.)

Clark, James (Conn). 1st Lieutenant 5th Connecticut, 1st May to 11th November, 1775; Captain of Sage's Connecticut State Regiment, June to December, 1776.

Clark, James (N. Y.). 2d Lieutenant 1st New York, March to November, 1776.

Clark, Joel (Conn). Major 8th Connecticut, 6th July to 18th December, 1775; Lieutenant-Colonel 17th Continental Infantry, 1st January, 1776; wounded and taken prisoner at Long Island 27th August, 1776, and died in captivity 19th December, 1776.

Clark, John (Mass). 2d Lieutenant of Glover's Massachusetts Regiment, 19th May, 1775; taken prisoner at Quebec 31st December, 1775; 1st Lieutenant of Lee's Continental Regiment, 10th February, 1777; resigned October, 1777. (Died 29th January, 1829.)

Clark, John (Pa). 1st Lieutenant 2d Battalion of Miles' Pennsylvania Rifle Regiment, 15th March, 1776; appointed Aide-de-Camp to General Greene, 14th January, 1777; Captain Pennsylvania State Regiment, 20th February, 1777; Regiment designated 13th Pennsylvania 12th November, 1777; transferred to 8th Pennsylvania, 1st July, 1778; transferred to 1st Pennsylvania, 17th January, 1781; transferred to 3d Pennsylvania 1st January, 1783, and served to 3d June, 1783. (Died 27th December, 1819.)

Clark, John (Pa). 1st Lieutenant 1st Continental Infantry, 1st January, 1776; Major 2d Battalion of the Pennsylvania Flying Camp, 14th September to December, 1776. (Died 27th April, 1819.)

Clark, John (Va). 1st Lieutenant 8th Virginia, 9th March, 1777; taken prisoner at Germantown, 4th October, 1777; exchanged October, 1780; retained as Captain 4th Virginia, 14th February, 1781, and served to close of war.

Clark, Jonah (Conn). Quartermaster of Douglas' Connecticut State Regiment, 22d June to 29th December, 1776.

Clark, Jonathan (Mass). Surgeon's Mate 14th Massachusetts, ——, 1777; died 8th April, 1778.

Clark, Jonathan (Mass). 2d Lieutenant 25th Continental Infantry, 1st January to 31st December, 1776; 2d Lieutenant 3d Continental Artillery, 18th January, 1777; resigned 4th November, 1777.

Clark, Jonathan (N. C.). Lieutenant North Carolina Militia, 1779-1780.

Clark, Jonathan (Va). Captain 8th Virginia, 23d January, 1776; Major 12th Virginia, 10th January, 1778; Regiment designated 8th Virginia, 14th September, 1778; Lieutenant-Colonel, 10th May, 1779; taken prisoner at Charleston 12th May, 1780, and was a prisoner on parole to close of war. (Name also spelled Clarke.)

Clark, Joseph (Conn). Corporal 1st Connecticut, 20th January, 1777; Ensign, 1st June, 1779; transferred to 5th Connecticut, 1st January, 1781; transferred to 2d Connecticut, 1st January, 1783; retained in Swift's Connecticut Regiment in June, 1783, and served to 3d November, 1783.

Clark, Matthias (N. Y.). 1st Lieutenant 1st New York, 28th June, 1775, to January, 1776; 1st Lieutenant 2d New York, 21st November, 1776; never joined the latter regiment and was dropped.

Clark, Nathaniel (Mass). 1st Lieutenant of Glover's Massachusetts Regiment, 19th May to December, 1775; 1st Lieutenant 4th Continental Infantry, 1st January to 31st December, 1776; 1st Lieutenant of Baldwin's Artillery Artificer Regiment, 1st January, 1777; Captain, 12th November, 1777, and served to ——.

Clark, Norman (Mass). Private of a Company of Minute Men at Lexington, 19th April, 1775, and in Whitney's Massachusetts Regiment, June to December, 1775; Lieutenant Massachusetts Militia in 1776; wounded at Harlem Plains 16th September, 1776; Captain Massachusetts Militia in 1777 and 1778.

Clark, Oliver (R. I.). 1st Lieutenant of 1st Rhode Island, 3d May to December, 1775; Captain 9th Continental Infantry, 1st January to 31st December, 1776; Captain 1st Rhode Island, 11th February, 1777; taken prisoner at Fort Mercer, 22d October, 1777.

Clark, Othneil (Conn). Private 2d Connecticut, 5th May to 18th December, 1775; Ensign 5th Connecticut, 1st January, 1777; 2d Lieutenant, 1st January, 1778; 1st Lieutenant, 16th August, 1779; transferred to 2d Connecticut, 1st January, 1781; died 26th June, 1782.

Clark, Peter (Md). 2d Lieutenant 3d Maryland, 20th February, 1777; resigned 13th July, 1779.

Clark, Peter (N. H.). Captain New Hampshire Militia, 1777-1778.

Clark, Reuben (Conn). Ensign of Mott's Connecticut State Regiment, June to December, 1776. (Died 1812.)

Clark, Richard (Va). 1st Lieutenant of Clark's Illinois Regiment, 4th June, 1780, to 1782.

Clark, Robert (Pa). Captain of Cunningham's Pennsylvania Battalion of the Flying Camp, June to December, 1776; Lieutenant-Colonel Pennsylvania Militia, 1777-1781. (Died 1821.)

Clark, Samuel (Vt). Captain Vermont Militia; wounded at Johnstown 24th October, 1781. (Died 26th November, 1801.)

Clark, Silas (Mass). Ensign 6th Continental Infantry, 1st January, 1776; 1st Lieutenant 11th Massachusetts, 6th November, 1776; Captain Lieutenant,. 28th May, 1778; wounded at Monmouth 28th June, 1778; Captain, 28th March, 1779; retired 1st January, 1781. (Died 13th August, 1800.)

Clark, Theophilus (Mass). Sergeant 5th Massachusetts, 10th August, 1777; Ensign, 7th November, 1777; 2d Lieutenant, 10th July, 1779; resigned 1st November, 1780.

Clark, Thomas (N. J.). 1st Lieutenant Eastern Company New Jersey Artillery, Militia, 1st March, 1776; Captain, 8th January, 1778, to ——.

Clark, Thomas (N. C.). Major 1st North Carolina, 1st September, 1775; Lieutenant-Colonel, 10th April, 1776; Colonel, 5th February, 1777; wounded at Stono Ferry 20th June, 1779; taken prisoner at Charleston, 12th May, 1780; retired 1st January, 1783. (Died 25th December, 1792.)

Clark, Thomas (N. C.). Ensign 9th North Carolina, 28th November, 1776; Lieutenant, 1st February, 1777; transferred to 4th North Carolina, 1st July, 1778; Captain, 10th February ,1779; served to ——.

Clark, Thomas (N. C.). Captain North Carolina Artillery Company, 1st January, 1777; last record of him is June, 1779.

Clark, Thomas (Va). Ensign 13th Virginia, 28th December, 1776; Lieutenant, 15th April, 1777; retired 14th September, 1778. (Died 22d February, 1822.)

Clark, Timothy (Conn). 2d Lieutenant in Sage's Connecticut State Regiment, June to December, 1776; served subsequently as Captain Connecticut Militia.

Clark, Watrous (Conn). Corporal in the Lexington Alarm, April, 1775; Sergeant-Major 3d Connecticut, 3d May to 10th December, 1775; Ensign 20th Continental Infantry, 1st January to 31st December, 1776. (Died 23d February, 1819.)

Clark, William (Conn). 2d Lieutenant 10th Continental Infantry, 1st January to 31st December, 1776.

Clark, William (Del). Captain of an independent Delaware company in 1778.

Clark, William (Md). 2d Lieutenant 7th Maryland, 1st April, 1777. "Went off without leave, 15th June, 1777."

Clark, William (Mass). 1st Lieutenant of Paterson's Massachusetts Regiment, May to December, 1775.

Clark, William (N. J.). Ensign 3d New Jersey, 30th March, 1776; 2d Lieutenant, 29th November, 1776; 1st Lieutenant, 1st May, 1777; severely wounded at Germantown 4th October, 1777, and did not rejoin the army.

Clark, William (N. Y.). Major New York Militia, 1776-1779.

Clark, William (Pa). Lieutenant-Colonel Pennsylvania Militia, 1777-1778.

Clark, William (Va). Lieutenant of Clark's Illinois Regiment, 6th June, 1780, to 1782.

Clarke.—See **Clark**, as these names are spelled both ways.

Clarke, Elijah (Ga). Colonel Georgia Militia; wounded at Aligator Creek in July, 1778, again at Wofford's Iron Works 8th August, 1780, and at Musgrove's Mill 18th August, 1780: Brigadier-General Georgia Militia, 1781-1783. (Died 1805.)

Clarke, Ethan (R. I.). Captain Rhode Island Regiment, 28th June to December, 1775.

Clarke, Jeremiah (N. Y.). 2d Lieutenant 2d New York, 21st November, 1776; resigned 17th December, 1777.

Clarke, John (Vt). Lieutenant of Bedel's Regiment Vermont Militia, 1st April, 1778, to 1st April, 1779.

Clarke, John C. (Ga). 1st Lieutenant 3d Georgia in 1777; Captain in 1779: wounded at Wofford's Iron Works 8th August, 1780, at Musgrove's Mills 18th August, 1780. and at Long Cane 11th December, 1780. He was also Colonel Georgia Militia in 1780.

Clarke, John J. (Ga). Captain 2d Georgia, ——; on roll for August, 1778 .

Clarke, Richard (Va). Lieutenant of a Virginia State Regiment, 1778 to ——.

Clarke, Thomas (R. I.). Major Rhode Island Militia, 1777-1778.

Clarke, William (Va). Lieutenant of Clark's Illinois Regiment, 1778 to 1782.

Clarkson, Matthew (Mass). Major and Aide-de-Camp to General Arnold, August, 1778, to March, 1779, and Aide-de-Camp to General Lincoln, March, 1779, to 2d July, 1782, when he was granted leave until recalled to go to the West Indies; was taken prisoner at Charleston, 12th May, 1780; Brevet Lieutenant-Colonel, 30th September, 1783. (Died 25th April, 1825.)

Claughry, John (N. Y.). Ensign New York Militia; was a prisoner, when and where taken not stated.

Clause, La —— (—). Lieutenant Pulaski Legion, ——; Brevet Captain, 19th July, 1780, and permitted to return to Europe.

Clay, Abijah (Va). 1st Lieutenant 6th Virginia, 26th February, 1776 to ——.

Clay, John (Va). Cadet 6th Virginia, 30th March, 1777, to ——.

Clay, Joseph (Ga). Lieutenant-Colonel Deputy Paymaster-General Southern Department, 6th August, 1777; elected to Congress, 26th February, 1778, and retired from the Army. (Died 16th January, 1805.)

Clay, Matthew (Va). Ensign 9th Virginia, 1st October, 1776; 2d Lieutenant 16th March, 1777; 1st Lieutenant, 23d April, 1778; transferred to 1st Virginia, 14th September, 1778; Regimental Quartermaster, 1st December, 1778; transferred to 5th Virginia, 12th February, 1781; retired 1st January, 1783. (Died 1815.)

Clay, Thomas (Va). Captain of a Virginia State Regiment, 1778 to 1781.

Clayes, Elijah (N. H.). 1st Lieutenant 3d New Hampshire, 23d April to December, 1775; 1st Lieutenant 2d Continental Infantry, 1st January, 1776; Captain 2d New Hampshire, 8th November, 1776; died 30th November, 1779, of wounds received at Chamung, 29th August, 1779.

Clayes, Peter (Mass). Sergeant of Nixon's Massachusetts Regiment, May to December, 1775; Ensign 4th Continental Infantry, 1st January to 31st December, 1776; 2d Lieutenant 6th Massachusetts, 1st January, 1777; Captain Lieutenant, 11th November, 1779; Captain, 11th April, 1780, and served to June, 1783. (Died 8th September, 1834.)

Clayland, James (N. J.). 1st Lieutenant of Forman's Continental Regiment, 9th May, 1777, to 1st July, 1778.

Claypoole, Abraham George (Pa). Ensign Pennsylvania Militia in 1776; Captain Lieutenant of Patton's Continental Regiment, 1st February, 1777; Captain, 10th June, 1778; Regiment incorporated into 11th Pennsylvania 16th December, 1778; transferred to 3d Pennsylvania 17th January, 1781; retired 1st January, 1783. (Died 1827.)

Claypoole, Samuel (Pa). 2d Lieutenant 1st Pennsylvania, 2d March, 1779; resigned 14th June, 1780.

Clayton, Edward (Md). 2d Lieutenant 7th Maryland, 20th February, 1777; dropped in June, 1777, as having been promoted to one of the Additional Continental Regiments, but did not join.

Clayton, Henry (Pa). Lieutenant of Swope's Pennsylvania Battalion of the Flying Camp, July, 1776; taken prisoner at Long Island, 27th August, 1776; released 8th December, 1780.

Clayton, Henry (Va). Adjutant 9th Virginia, — March, 1778; retired 30th September, 1778.

Clayton, John (Va). 2d Lieutenant 1st Virginia, 7th October, 1775; 1st Lieutenant, February, 1776, to ——. (Died 1826.)

Clayton, Joshua (Md) Major Maryland Militia in 1777; subsequently Governor of Delaware. (Died 11th August, 1798.)

Clayton, Philip (Va). Ensign 3d Virginia, 4th July, 1779; Lieutenant, 10th May, 1780; transferred to 7th Virginia, 12th February, 1781; retired 1st January, 1783. (Died 1807.)

Cleaveland.—See **Cleveland**, as these names are spelled both ways.

Cleaveland, Aaron (Conn). Ensign of Chester's Regiment Connecticut Militia, June to December, 1776.

Cleaveland, Ebenezer (Mass). 2d Lieutenant of Bridges' Massachusetts Regiment, 19th May to December, 1775; 1st Lieutenant 21st Continental Infantry, 1st January, 1776; Captain, 12th July, 1776; Captain 8th Massachusetts, 1st January, 1777; resigned 3d October, 1778. (Died 26th November, 1822.)

Cleaveland, Ebenezer (Mass). Chaplain of Ward's Massachusetts Regiment, 19th May to December, 1775; Chaplain 21st Continental Infantry, 1st January to 31st December, 1776. (Died 4th July, 1805.)

Cleaveland, Ephraim (Mass). 1st Lieutenant 16th Continental Infantry, 1st January to 31st December; 1776; Captain, 8th Massachusetts, 1st January, 1777; retired 30th October, 1778.

Cleaveland, John (Conn). Private 8th Connecticut, 11th July to 26th December, 1775; Private, 1st January, 1777, and Sergeant 4th Connecticut, 28th April, 1777; Ensign, 4th January, 1780; transferred to 2d Connecticut, 1st January, 1783, and served to 3d June, 1783.

Cleaveland, John (Mass). Chaplain of Little's Massachusetts Regiment, May to December, 1775.

Cleaveland, Moses (Conn). Lieutenant in the Lexington Alarm in April, 1775; Ensign 2d Connecticut, 1st January, 1777; 2d Lieutenant, 25th December, 1777; Captain Lieutenant Sappers and Miners, 2d August, 1779; resigned 7th June, 1781. (Died 16th November, 1806.)

Cleaveland, Parker (Mass). Surgeon of Sargent's Massachusetts Regiment, May to December, 1775.

Cleaveland, Timothy (Conn). Ensign 20th Continental Infantry, 1st January to 31st December, 1776; 2d Lieutenant, 4th Conñecticut, 1st January, 1777; 1st Lieutenant, 25th November, 1777; retired 15th November, 1778. (Died 1803.)

Cleaveland, William (Conn). Sergeant 6th Connecticut, 8th May to 10th December, 1775; 2d Lieutenant 10th Continental Infantry, 1st January, 1776; taken prisoner on the retreat from New York, 15th September, 1776.

Cleaves, Nathaniel (Mass). Lieutenant in Lexington Alarm, when he was wounded 19th April, 1775; 1st Lieutenant of Mansfield's Massachusetts Regiment, May to December, 1775; 1st Lieutenant 27th Continental Infantry, 1st January, 1776; taken prisoner at Fort Washington 16th November, 1776; exchanged in March, 1780.

Cleaves, Putnam (—). Captain, was a prisoner in 1782, when and where taken not stated.

Clement, Timothy (N. H.). Captain New Hampshire Militia, 1776-1777.

Clements, Henry (Va). Cornet of Virginia Dragoons, 19th June, 1776; Lieutenant 1st Continental Dragoons, 20th February, 1777; resigned 15th November, 1777; Lieutenant 1st Maryland, 25th April, 1781; transferred to 5th Maryland, 1st January, 1783; retained in Maryland Battalion April, 1783, and served to 15th November, 1783.

Clements, Mace (Va). Surgeon's Mate 7th Virginia, — February, 1777; Surgeon, 15th Virginia, 3d August, 1777; Regiment designated 11th Virginia 14th September, 1778; retired 12th February, 1781.

Clemm, William (Pa). 2d Lieutenant of Hartley's Continental Regiment, 26th May, 1777; 1st Lieutenant, 19th November, 1777, to ——; was present in January, 1778.

Clendenin, John (N. C.). Ensign 3d North Carolina, 15th April, 1776; 2d Lieutenant, 29th October, 1777; 1st Lieutenant, 23d December, 1777; Regimental Quartermaster, 14th December, 1779; taken prisoner at Charleston 12th May, 1780; exchanged 14th June, 1781; served to close of war. Brevet Captain, 30th September, 1783. (Name also spelled Clandinin and Clending.)

Cleveland, Aaron (Mass). Lieutenant-Colonel of Sargent's Massachusetts Regiment, May to December, 1773.

Cleveland, Benjamin (N. C.). Ensign 2d North Carolina, 1st September, 1775; Lieutenant, January, 1776; Captain, 23d November, 1776; retired 1st June, 1778; Colonel North Carolina Militia, August, 1778, to close of war; died — October, 1806.

Cleveland, Larkin (N. C.). Lieutenant North Carolina Militia; wounded at Lovelady Ford, N. C., 30th September, 1780.

Cleveland, Robert (N. C.). Captain North Carolina Militia at King's Mountain, October, 1780. (Died 1812.)

Clifford, —— (S. C.). Lieutenant 1st South Carolina in 1777.

Clift, Lemuel (Conn). Private in the Lexington Alarm, April, 1775; Sergeant 6th Connecticut, 6th May to 15th December, 1775; Ensign 10th Continental Infantry, 1st January, 1776; 1st Lieutenant 4th Connecticut, 1st January, 1777; Captain Lieutenant, 1st June, 1778; Captain, 20th May, 1779; transferred to 1st Connecticut, 1st January, 1781; retained in Swift's Connecticut Regiment, June, 1783, and served to 3d November, 1783. (Died 1821.)

Clift, Waterman (Conn). Captain 6th Connecticut, 1st May to 18th December, 1775; Major of Selden's Connecticut State Regiment, 20th June to 25th December, 1776.

Clift, Wills (Conn). 2d Lieutenant 3d Connecticut, 1st May to 16th December, 1775; Captain 20th Continental Infantry, 1st January to 31st December, 1776; Captain 3d Connecticut, 1st January, 1777; Major, 25th May, 1778; transferred to 1st Connecticut, 1st January, 1781; retired 1st January, 1783.

Clifton, Thomas (Virginia). Adjutant 15th Virginia, 14th April, 1777; resigned 14th October, 1777.

Clinch, James (N. C.). Ensign 2d North Carolina, 1st September, 1775, to ——.

Clinton, Alexander (N. Y.). Ensign 1st New York, 29th September, 1780; 2d Lieutenant 2d Continental Artillery, 29th June, 1781, and served to June, 1783.

Clinton, George (N. Y.). Brigadier-General Continental Army, 25th March, 1777, to 3d November, 1783; elected Governor of New York, 20th April, 1777; commanded the forces in the actions at Forts Clinton and Montgomery, 6th October, 1777; Brevet Major-General, 30th September, 1783. (Died 20th April, 1812.)

Clinton, James (N. Y.). Colonel 3d New York, 30th June, 1775, to January, 1776; Colonel 2d New York, 8th March, 1776; Brigadier-General Continental Army, 9th August, 1776; wounded at Fort Montgomery, 6th October, 1777; Brevet Major-General, 30th September, 1783; served to close of war. (Died 22d December, 1812.)

Clock, Jacob I.—See **Klock**.

Clotz, Jacob.—See **Klotz**.

Cloud, Jeremiah (Pa). 2d Lieutenant of Montgomery's Pennsylvania Battalion of the Flying Camp; taken prisoner at Fort Washington, 16th November, 1776.

Cloud, William (Va). Private and a Lieutenant Virginia Militia in 1777.

Clough, Alexander (N. J.). Adjutant 1st New Jersey, 20th November, 1775; Major 3d Continental Dragoons, 8th January, 1777; killed at Tappan, 28th September, 1778.

Clough, Gibson (Mass). Ensign 27th Continental Infantry, 1st January, 1776; taken prisoner at Fort Washing-

ton 16th November, 1776; exchanged — March, 1778.

Clough, Jeremiah (N. H.). Captain 2d New Hampshire, 24th May to December, 1775; Captain 8th Continental Infantry, 1st January to 31st December, 1776. (Died 1810.)

Cloyd, James (Pa). Ensign 5th Pennsylvania Battalion, 8th January, 1776, to ——.

Cloyd, Joseph (Va). Major of Preston's Regiment Virginia Militia in South Carolina in 1781.

Cluet Gerardus (N. Y.). Major New York Militia, 1775-1778.

Cluggage, Robert (Pa). Captain of Thompson's Pennsylvania Rifle Regiment, 25th June, 1775; Captain 1st Continental Infantry, 1st January, 1776; resigned 6th October, 1776.

Clum, Matthew (N. J.). Ensign of Phillips' Regiment New Jersey Levies in 1776; Ensign 2d New Jeresy, 5th February, 1777; resigned 15th November, 1777.

Clumberg, Philip, Jr. (Pa). Ensign 1st Pennsylvania Battalion, 27th October, 1775; 2d Lieutenant 2d Pennsylvania Battalion, 15th January, 1776; 1st Lieutenant 1st Pennsylvania, 1st January, 1777; resigned — April, 1778.

Cluverius, Gibson (Va). Captain Virginia Militia, 1775-1776.

Cluverius, James (Va). Lieutenant Virginia Militia, 1775-1776.

Clyde, Samuel (N. Y.). Lieutenant-Colonel New York Militia, 1779-1783.

Clymer, Daniel (Pa). Lieutenant-Colonel Pennsylvania Militia in 1776; Deputy Commissary-General of Prisoners, 12th December, 1777, to 1781. (Died 1810.)

Clymer, George (Pa). A signer of the Declaration of Independence; died 23d January, 1813.

Clymer, Thomas (Md). Ensign Maryland Militia in 1777.

Coachman, James (S. C.). Captain South Carolina Militia, 1775-1776.

Coates, Doctor John (Pa). Captain 11th Pennsylvania, 30th September, 1776; wounded at Piscataway, 8th May, 1777; resigned 7th September, 1777.

Coates, Isaac (Pa). 2d Lieutenant 4th Pennsylvania, 3d January, 1777; omitted August, 1777.

Coates, John (N. Y.). Surgeon of DuBois' New York Regiment, 26th

June, 1776; Surgeon 5th New York, 13th January, 1777; resigned — March, 1777. (Died 1810.)

Coates, William (Pa). Colonel Pennsylvania Militia; was a prisoner; when and where taken, not stated.

Cobb, David (Mass). Surgeon of Marshall's Massachusetts Regiment, May to December, 1775; Lieutenant-Colonel of Jackson's Continental Regiment, 12th January, 1777; regiment designated 16th Massachusetts, 23d July, 1780; transferred to 9th Massachusetts, 1st January, 1781; Aide-de-Camp to General Washington, 15th June, 1781, to 7th January, 1783; Lieutenant-Colonel Commandant 5th Massachusetts, 7th January, 1783; Brevet Brigadier-General, 30th September, 1783, and served to November, 1783. (Died 17th April, 1830.)

Cobb, Nehemiah (Mass). 2d Lieutenant of Cotton's Massachusetts Regiment, May to December, 1775; served subsequently in Massachusetts Militia.

Cobb, Samuel (Mass). Lieutenant in Lexington Alarm, April, 1775; Captain of Read's Massachusetts Regiment, May to December, 1775. (Died 1820.)

Cobb, Silas (Mass). Captain in Lexington Alarm ,April, 1775; Captain of Walker's Massachusetts Regiment, May to December, 1775.

Cobb, Simeon (Mass). 1st Lieutenant of Walker's Massachusetts Regiment, May to December, 1775.

Cobb, William (Mass). Captain of Mitchell's Regiment Massachusetts Militia in the Bagaduce Expedition, July to September, 1779.

Cobbs, Samuel (Va). 2d Lieutenant 2d Virginia, 25th September, 1776; 1st Lieutenant, January, 1777; retired 14th September, 1778.

Cobea, John (Pa). 2d Lieutenant 1st Pennsylvania Battalion, 15th January, 1776; 1st Lieutenant 2d Pennsylvania, 1st January, 1777; Captain, 11th March, 1779; retired 1st January, 1781.

Coburn, Asa (Mass). 1st Lieutenant of Danielson's Massachusetts Regiment, May to December, 1775; 1st Lieutenant 5th Continental Infantry, 1st January to 31st December, 1776; Captain 7th Massachusetts, 1st January, 1777, and served to June, 1783.

Coburn, John (Pa). Cornet 4th Continental Dragoons, 10th January, 1777, to ——.

Coburn, Peter (Mass). Captain in Lexington Alarm, April, 1775; Captain of Bridge's Massachusetts Regiment, May to December, 1775.

Cochran, David (Pa). Ensign 10th Pennsylvania, 23d April, 1777; resigned 1st September, 1777.

Cochran, James (Ga). 1st Lieutenant 1st Georgia, 12th December, 1775, to ——.

Cochran, John (Pa). Lieutenant Pennsylvania Battalion of the Flying Camp, July to December, 1776.

Cochran, John (Pa). Physician and Surgeon-General Middle Department, 11th April, 1777; Chief Physician and Surgeon of the Army, 6th October, 1780; Director-General of Military Hospitals, 17th January, 1781, and served to close of war. (Died 6th April, 1807.)

Cochran, Robert (Conn). Captain of a Connecticut Company under General Arnold at Crown Point in May, 1775; Captain of Elmore's Continental Regiment, 15th April, 1776; Major, 25th July, 1776; Major 3d New York, 21st November, 1776; Lieutenant-Colonel 2d New York, 30th March, 1780, and served to close of war. (Died 23d February, 1812.)

Cochran, William (Mass). Ensign and Lieutenant in Danielson's Massachusetts Regiment, May to December, 1775. (Drowned in 1779.)

Cocke, Collin (Va). Ensign 6th Virginia, 1st March, 1776; 2d Lieutenant, 7th August, 1776; 1st Lieutenant 2d February, 1777; transferred to 2d Virginia, 14th September, 1778; Regimental Paymaster, 16th February, 1779; Captain, 9th December, 1779, taken prisoner at Charleston, 12th May, 1780, and was a prisoner to close of war.

Cocke, John (Va). Colonel Virginia Militia, 1779-1781.

Cocke, Nathaniel (Va). Captain 7th Virginia, 7th March, 1776; resigned 13th December, 1776; served subsequently as Lieutenant-Colonel of Virginia Militia.

Cocke, Pleasant F. (Va). 2d Lieutenant 5th Virginia, 10th December, 1776; 1st Lieutenant, 12th August, 1777; transferred to 3d Virginia, 14th September, 1778; died 15th November, 1778

Cocke, William (Va). Ensign 1st Virginia, April, 1777; cashiered January, 1778.

Cockey, Edward (Md). Colonel Maryland Militia, 1776.

Cockey, Peter (Md). Ensign 3d Maryland, 1st April, 1777; died — February, 1779.

Codner, Isaac (N. Y.). 2d Lieutenant New York Militia; taken prisoner 24th June, 1779, at Crombond.

Codrick, John (Del). Ensign Delaware Battalion of the Flying Camp, July to December, 1776.

Codwise, Christopher (N. Y.). 2d Lieutenant of Lasher's Regiment New York Militia, May, 1776; 1st Lieutenant 2d New York, 21st November, 1776; retired 1st January, 1781.

Cody, Joseph (Mass). Sergeant Lexington Alarm, April, 1775; 1st Lieutenant of Read's Massachusetts Regiment, May to December, 1775.

Coe, Benjamin (N. Y.). Lieutenant Long Island Militia; taken prisoner at Long Island 27th August, 1776; exchanged December, 1776; served subsequently as Captain New York Militia (Died 1818.)

Coe, Ebenezer (Conn). Captain Connecticut Militia; wounded in the Danbury Raid, 25th April, 1777.

Coffer, John (Va). 2d Lieutenant 10th Virginia, 18th November, 1776; dismissed 21st April, 1778.

Coffield, Benjamin (N. C.). Adjutant 6th North Carolina, 17th May, 1777, to 1st July, 1778.

Coffin, Peter (N. H.). Major of Gilman's Regiment New Hampshire Militia, 5th December, 1776, to 12th March, 1777.

Cogan, Patrick (N. H.). 2d Lieutenant 5th Continental Infantry, 14th August, 1776; Quartermaster 1st New Hampshire, 8th November, 1776; died 21st August, 1778.

Cogswell, Amos (Mass). 2d Lieutenant of Gerrish's Massachusetts Regiment, May to December, 1775; 1st Lieutenant 26th Continental Infantry, 1st January to 31st December, 1776; Captain 9th Massachusetts, 1st January, 1777; transferred to 8th Massachusetts, 1st January, 1781; transferred to 3d Massachusetts, 12th June, 1783; Brevet Major, 30th September, 1783, and served to 3d November, 1783. (Died 28th January, 1826.)

Cogswell, James (Conn). Surgeon of Silliman's Connecticut State Regiment, June to December, 1776; served subsequently as Surgeon Connecticut Militia. (Died 1792.)

Cogswell, Jonathan (Mass). Colonel Massachusetts Militia, 1776-1778.

Cogswell, Samuel (Conn). 1st Lieutenant of Lee's Continental Regiment, 1st July, 1777; transferred to Jackson's Regiment, 22d April, 1779; regiment designated 16th Massachusetts, 23d July, 1780; transferred to 9th Massachusetts, 1st January, 1781; transferred to 7th Massachusetts, 1st January, 1783; transferred to 4th Massachusetts, 12th June, 1783; Brevet Captain, 30th September, 1783, and served to 3d November, 1783; (accidentally killed 20th August, 1790.)

Cogswell, Thomas (Mass). Lieutenant in Lexington Alarm, April, 1775; Captain of Gerrish's Massachusetts Regiment, 19th May to December, 1775; Captain 26th Continental Infantry, 1st January to 31st December, 1776; Major 1st Massachusetts, 21st January, 1777; Lieutenant-Colonel 15th Massachusetts, 26th November, 1779; retired 1st January, 1781. (Died 3d September, 1810.)

Cogswell, William (Mass). Private in Captain Cogswell's Company 26th Continental Infantry, January to December, 1776; Hospital Surgeon's Mate, 19th January, 1781; Chief Medical Officer of the Army. 20th June, 1784, to 12th August, 1785. (Died 1st January, 1831.)

Cohoon, William (—). Lieutenant; was a prisoner in 1780; when and where taken, not stated.

Coiler, James (Pa). 1st Lieutenant of Cunningham's Pennsylvania Battalion of the Flying Camp, July to December, 1776.

Coit, Samuel (Conn). Colonel Connecticut Militia Regiment in 1775 and 1776. (Died 4th October, 1792.)

Coit, William (Conn). Captain in the Lexington Alarm, April, 1775; Captain of the "Oliver Cromwell" in the Navy, 11th July, 1776; dismissed 14th April, 1777. (Died 16th November, 1821.)

Coit, William (Conn). Captain Connecticut Militia, —; wounded and taken prisoner at Groton Heights, 6th September, 1781. (Died 16th February, 1802.)

Colbreath, William (N. Y.). 2d Lieutenant of Nicholson's New York Regiment, March to November, 1776; Ensign 3d New York, 21st November, 1776; Lieutenant, 20th November, 1777; Regimental Quartermaster, 15th July, 1780; transferred to 2d New York, 1st January, 1781, and served to June, 1783.

Colburn, Amos (N. H.). 2d Lieutenant 3d New Hampshire, 8th November, 1776; discharged 10th August, 1778.

Colburn, Andrew (N. H.) Major 4th Continental Infantry, 1st January, 1776; wounded at Harlem Heights, 12th October, 1776; Lieutenant-Colonel 3d New Hampshire, 8th November, 1776; died 20th September, 1777, of wounds received at Stillwater, 19th September, 1777.

Colby, Ephraim (N. H.). Ensign 5th Continental Infantry, 1st January to 31st December, 1776.

Colcord, John (N. H.). Ensign 8th Continental Infantry, 1st January, 1776; 2d Lieutenant 2d New Hampshire, 8th November, 1776; 1st Lieutenant, 2d April, 1777; resigned, 14th May, 1777.

Cole, Abner (Conn). Sergeant 1st Connecticut, 20th January, 1777; Sergeant-Major, 1st March, 1779; Ensign, 20th June, 1779; transferred to 3d Connecticut, 1st January, 1781, and served to June, 1783.

Cole, Abraham (Md). 2d Lieutenant 1st Continental Artillery, 20th November, 1777; died 20th July, 1778.

Cole Archippus (Mass). Lieutenant in Lexington Alarm, April, 1775; 1st Lieutenant of Cotton's Massachusetts Regiment, May to December, 1775.

Cole, George (Md). Ensign German Regiment, 17th August, 1777; resigned 2d June, 1778. (Died 21st August, 1828.)

Cole, Ichabod. Ensign Rhode Island Militia in 1778; Lieutenant in 1781.

Cole, John (Conn). 2d Lieutenant of Wolcott's Connecticut State Regiment, December, 1775, to March, 1776; 2d Lieutenant 5th Connecticut, 1st January, 1777; resigned 9th May, 1778; Aide-de-Camp to General Paterson, 30th May, 1781, to close of war.

Cole, John (Conn). Lieutenant of Wolcott's Connecticut State Regiment, December, 1775, to February, 1776.

Cole, John (N. H.). Captain New Hampshire Militia, 1777.

Cole, John (Pa). Ensign 10th Pennsylvania, 4th December, 1776; 2d Lieutenant, 30th April, 1777; retired 1st July, 1778.

Cole, John (R. I.). Lieutenant Rhode Island Militia, August to December, 1775; 1st Lieutenant of Stanton's Regiment Rhode Island Militia, 12th December, 1776, to May, 1777.

Cole, John (Va). Ensign 2d Virginia, 4th May, 1777; 2d Lieutenant, 18th May, 1777; Captain, ———, and served to ———.

Cole, Joseph, Jr. (Mass). 2d Lieutenant of Thomas' Massachusetts Regiment, May, 1775, to ———.

Cole, Marcus (Conn). Ensign 2d Connecticut, 1st May to 10th December, 1775; 1st Lieutenant 22d Continental Infantry, 1st January to 31st December, 1776; 1st Lieutenant 1st Connecticut, 1st January, 1777; resigned 6th February, 1778.

Cole, Simeon (Mass). Captain Massachusetts Militia, 1776.

Cole, Thomas (Mass). Ensign 4th Massachusetts, 5th November, 1778; Lieutenant, 1st January, 1781; Aide-de-Camp to General Paterson, October, 1780, to June, 1783.

Cole, Thomas (R. I.). 1st Lieutenant 1st Rhode Island, 28th June, 1775; Captain 9th Continental Infantry, 1st January, 1776; Captain 1st Rhode Island, 1st January, 1777; retained in Olney's Rhode Island Battalion, 14th May, 1781; resigned 1st May, 1782.

Cole, Thomas (R. I.). Major Rhode Island Militia in 1775-1776.

Cole, Walter King (Va). Surgeon 1st Virginia State Regiment, 6th July, 1777; resigned 9th October, 1777.

Coleburn, Asa (Mass). Lieutenant of Danielson's Massachusetts Regiment in 1775; Captain Massachusetts Militia, 1776.

Coleman, Benjamin (N. C.). Captain 5th North Carolina, 30th April, 1777; transferred to 2d North Carolina, 1st June, 1778; taken prisoner at Charleston, 12th May, 1780.

Coleman, Charles (N. C.). Regimental Quartermaster, 4th North Carolina, 14th October, 1777, to ———.

Coleman, Dudley (Mass). 2d Lieutenant and Adjutant 12th Continental Infantry, 1st January to 31st December, 1776; Major 13th Massachusetts, 1st January, 1777; Lieutenant-Colonel, 3d July, 1777; resigned 10th March, 1779. (Died 16th November, 1797.)

Coleman, Edward (R. I.). 2d Lieutenant of Stanton's Regiment Rhode Island Militia, 12th December, 1776, to May, 1777.

Coleman, Edward S. (Conn). 2d Lieutenant 4th Connecticut, 1st January,

1777; 1st Lieutenant, 15th November, 1778; resigned 4th April, 1780.

Coleman, Jacob (Va). Ensign and Adjutant 9th Virginia, 5th April, 1779; Lieutenant, 20th December, 1779; transferred to 7th Virginia, 12th February, 1781; retired 2d April, 1782.

Coleman, John (N. C.). Ensign 9th North Carolina, 28th November ,1776, to ——.

Coleman, John (Va). Ensign 2d Virginia, 4th July to December, 1779.

Coleman, Nicholas (Pa). 1st Lieutenant 9th Pennsylvania, 15th November, 1776; retired 1st July, 1778.

Coleman, Noah (Conn). Surgeon 2d Connecticut, 1st May, 1777; retired 1st January, 1781.

Coleman, Richard (Va). Ensign 7th Virginia, 29th April, 1776; 2d Lieutenant, 28th December, 1776; transferred to 5th Virginia, 14th September, 1778; 1st Lieutenant, 20th May, 1778; retired 12th February, 1781.

Coleman, Robert (Pa). 2d Lieutenant of Cunningham's Battalion of the Flying Camp, July to December, 1776. (Died 1825.)

Coleman, Samuel (Va). Ensign 8th Virginia, 25th March, 1776; 2d Lieutenant, — February, 1777; 1st Lieutenant 1st Continental Artillery, 5th February, 1778; killed at Camden, 16th August, 1780

Coleman, Theophebus (N. C.). Lieutenant 7th North Carolina, 28th November, 1776, to ——.

Coles, Thomas (Mass). Ensign 4th Massachusetts, 29th September, 1779; Lieutenant, 5th November, 1782; served to June, 1783. (Died 13th October, 1844.)

Coleman, Whitehead (Va). Ensign 7th Virginia, 6th April, 1776; resigned 13th January, 1777; Captain Lieutenant 1st Continental Artillery, 13th January, 1777; Captain, 15th August, 1778, and served to June, 1783.

Coleman, Wyatt (Va). Ensign 1st Virginia State Regiment, — March, 1777; 2d Lieutenant, 6th April, 1778; 1st Lieutenant, 1st April, 1779, to January, 1781.

Colerus, Christian lebrun (France). Appointed Brevet Major Continental Army, 19th September, 1776; Aide-de-Camp to General Pulaski to 9th October, 1779.

Coles, William T. (N. C.). Captain 4th North Carolina, 16th April, 1776, to ——; was in service in July, 1776.

Colfax, William (Conn). Ensign 1st Connecticut, 1st January, 1777; 2d Lieutenant, 1st January, 1778; 1st Lieutenant, 18th March, 1778; transferred to 5th Connecticut, 1st January, 1781; transferred to 2d Connecticut, 1st January, 1783; Captain 1st April, 1783; retained in Swift's Connecticut Regiment, June, 1783, and served to 3d November, 1783. (Died 7th September, 1838.)

Colgate, John (Md). Ensign 4th Maryland, 1st June, 1777; 2d Lieutenant, 6th November, 1777; 1st Lieutenant, 4th August, 1778; resigned 1st May, 1780.

Colhoun, Andrew (Pa). 2d Lieutenant of Wilson's Battalion, guarding stores at Carlisle, 20th October, 1777, to 2d June, 1778.

Collier, Charles Miles (Va). Lieutenant and Captain of a Virginia State Regiment, 1777 to 1781. (Died 1825.)

Collier, James (Pa). 1st Lieutenant 1st Pennsylvania Battalion of the Flying Camp, July to December, 1776.

Collier, John (N. C.). Colonel North Carolina Militia, 1780-1781.

Collier, Joseph (Pa). Ensign Pennsylvania State Regiment, March, 1777; 2d Lieutenant, 18th April, 1777; regiment designated 13th Pennsylvania, 12th November, 1777; transferred to 1st Pennsylvania, 1st July, 1778; 1st Lieutenant, 17th May, 1779, and served to June, 1783. (Died 28th September, 1790.)

Collier, Richard (Pa). 2d Lieutenant 5th Pennsylvania Battalion, 8th January, 1776; Regimental Quartermaster, 9th February, 1776; 1st Lieutenant, 21st March, 1776; taken prisoner at Fort Washington, 16th November, 1776; exchanged 26th August, 1778, and did not re-enter the service.

Collier, Thomas (Va). Sergeant and Quartermaster Sergeant 2d Virginia State Regiment, 3d March, 1777, until appointed Regimental Quartermaster, 5th May, 1778; 2d Lieutenant, 22d October, 1778, and served to January, 1781.

Collins, Bartlett (Va). Ensign 2d Virginia State Regiment, ——, 1777; resigned 1st April, 1779.

Collins, Cornelius (Ga). 1st Lieutenant 2d Georgia, 15th March, 1777, and served to 22d October, 1782.

Collins, Daniel (Conn). 2d Lieutenant 12th Continental Infantry, 1st January to 31st December, 1776; 1st Lieutenant 1st Connecticut, 1st January, 1777; resigned 18th March, 1778; served subsequently as Captain Connecticut Militia. (Died 15th November, 1819.)

Collins, Daniel (Mass). 2d Lieutenant of Little's Massachusetts Regiment, 19th May to December, 1775; served subsequently as Captain Massachusetts Militia.

Collins, Francis (N. Y.). Captain New York Militia; taken prisoner at Fort Keyser, 19th October, 1780; released 21st May, 1783.

Collins, James (Mass). Major of Little's Massachusetts Regiment, 19th May to December, 1775; Major 12th Continental Infantry, 1st January to 31st December, 1776; served subsequently as Colonel Massachusetts Militia.

Collins, John (—). Deputy Commissary of Military Stores, ——; cashiered 23d March, 1778.

Collins, Jonathan (N. H.). 2d Lieutenant 2d Continental Infantry, 1st January, 1776, to ——.

Collins, Joseph (Pa). 2d Lieutenant 1st Pennsylvania, 18th April, 1779, to ——. (Died 1825.)

Collins, Joshua (R. I.). Ensign of Varnum's Rhode Island Regiment, 3d May, 1775, to ——.

Collins, Thomas (Del). Lieutenant-Colonel Delaware Militia, 1775.

Collins, Tyranis (N. Y.). Captain New York Levies; taken prisoner at Schohaire, 17th October, 1780; released 21st May, 1783

Colombe, P. de la (France). Allowed pay as Lieutenant Continental Army from 1st December, 1776; Captain, 15th November, 1777, and served as Aide-de-Camp to Generals Lafayette and De-Kalb to October, 1779; taken prisoner at Savannah, 29th December, 1778.

Colson, Jacob (Ga). Captain Georgia Militia in 1775; Captain 1st Georgia, 7th January, 1776, to ——.

Colson, Jacob (S. C.). Captain South Carolina Militia, 1775-1776.

Colston, Samuel (Va). 1st Lieutenant 5th Virginia, 26th February, 1776; Captain, 21st February, 1777; retired 14th September, 1778.

Colt, Peter (Conn). Deputy Commissary-General of Purchases, 9th August, 1777, and served to 4th July, 1782. (Died 16th March, 1824.)

Colt, William (Conn).—See **Coit.**

Colton, Charles (Mass). Captain 3d Massachusetts, 1st January, 1777; retired 16th September, 1778.

Colwell, Robert (Pa).—See **Caldwell.**

Colville, Andrew (Va). Captain Virginia Militia at King's Mountain, October, 1780. (Died 1797.)

Colyer, Israel (Mass). 1st Lieutenant of Glover's Massachusetts Regiment, 19th May, 1775, to ——.

Combs, George (N. Y.). Captain of Drake's New York Regiment of Militia in 1778; taken prisoner, ——; when and where, not stated.

Combs, John (N. J.). Captain of Forman's Additional Continental Regiment, 20th March, 1777, to ——; was in service May, 1779.

Combs, Thomas (N. J.). Captain New Jersey Militia; wounded at Bonhamton, 4th April, 1777.

Compton, Edmund (Md). Ensign 1st Maryland, 12th April, 1779; Lieutenant, 18th February, 1780; transferred to 4th Maryland, 1st January, 1781; retained in Maryland Battalion, April, 1783, and served to 15th November, 1783. (Died 28th March, 1838.)

Comstock, Aaron (Conn). Adjutant of Silliman's Connecticut State Regiment, June to December, 1776; Regimental Quartermaster 8th Connecticut, 1st January, 1777; resigned 5th March. 1778.

Comstock, Adam (R. I.). Major of Babcock's Rhode Island State Regiment, 15th January, 1776; Lieutenant-Colonel, 19th August, 1776; Lieutenant-Colonel, 1st Rhode Island, 1st January, 1777, to — April, 1778.

Comstock, James (Conn). Lieutenant Connecticut Militia; killed at Groton Heights, 6th September, 1781.

Comstock, John (Conn). 1st Lieutenant of Selden's Connecticut State Regiment, June, 1776; wounded and taken prisoner on the retreat from New York, 15th September, 1776; some records say he was killed there.

Comstock, Samuel (Conn). Captain of Silliman's Regiment Connecticut Militia, August to December, 1776; Captain 8th Connecticut, 1st January, 1777; transferred to 5th Connecticut, 1st January, 1781, and served to June, 1783.

Comstock, William (R. I.). 1st Lieutenant of Elliott's Regiment Rhode Island State Artillery, 12th December, 1776, to ——.

Conant, Ebenezer (Mass). Lieutenant of Whitcomb's Massachusetts Regiment, 3d June to December, 1775; Adjutant of Stearn's Massachusetts Militia Regiment in 1777. (Died 1783.)

Conant, Jonathan (Mass). Paymaster 10th Massachusetts, 6th November, 1776; resigned 31st December, 1779.

Concklin, Edward (N. Y.). 1st Lieutenant 4th New York, 21st November, 1776; resigned 7th November, 1777.

Concklin, Lemuel (N. Y.). 1st Lieutenant of DuBois' New York Regiment, 1st July to 20th November, 1776; served subsequently as Captain New York Militia.

Concklin, Nathaniel (N. Y.). Was a Sergeant 3d New York in 1775 and 1776; 1st Lieutenant of Dubois' New York Regiment, 26th June to November, 1776.

Concklin, Silvanus (N. Y.). 2d Lieutenant 4th New York, 21st November, 1776; 1st Lieutenant, 8th November, 1777; died 7th October, 1778.

Conder, David (Mass). Captain of Woodbridge's Massachusetts Regiment, May to November, 1775.

Condit, David (N. J.). Major and Lieutenant-Colonel New Jersey Militia, 1776; died 1777.

Condy, Jacob (Pa). Corporal 2d Pennsylvania, — January, 1777; Ensign, — February, 1777, to ——.

Condy, Thomas Hollis (Mass). 2d Lieutenant and Regimental Quartermaster of Jackson's Continental Regiment, 1st February, 1777; Regimental Adjutant, 27th October, 1778, to 9th April, 1779; 1st Lieutenant, 1st March, 1779; Regimental Quartermaster, 22d December, 1779; regiment designated 16th Massachusetts, 23d July, 1780; transferred to 9th Massachusetts, 1st January, 1781; transferred to 4th Massachusetts, 1st January, 1783; Brevet Captain, 30th September, 1783; retained in Jackson's Continental Regiment, November, 1783, and served to 20th June, 1784. (Died 29th August, 1833.)

Cone, Daniel (Conn). 2d Lieutenant 2d Connecticut, 1st May to 17th December, 1775.

Cone, Joseph (N. Y.). 1st Lieutenant 1st Canadian (Livingston's) Regiment, 18th December, 1776; cashiered 16th September, 1778.

Conger, Stephen (N. C.). Adjutant 1st North Carolina, 29th January, 1778; retired 1st June, 1778.

Conine, Philip (N. Y.). 1st Lieutenant 3d New York, 21st November, 1776; Captain Lieutenant, 7th January, 1780; retired 1st January, 1781. (Died 14th April, 1831.)

Conn, Joseph (Pa). Quartermaster 1st Pennsylvania, March, 1777; dismissed 18th December, 1777.

Conn, Samuel (N. J.). 2d Lieutenant 4th New Jersey, 1st January, 1777; 1st Lieutenant, 12th November, 1777; transferred to 2d New Jersey, 1st July, 1778; retained in New Jersey Battalion, April, 1783; Brevet Captain, 30th September, 1783; served to 3d November, 1783.

Conn, Thomas (S. C.). Lieutenant and Adjutant in Marion's Brigade in 1781.

Connell, Daniel (Del). Lieutenant Delaware Battalion of the Flying Camp, July to December, 1776.

Connell, Samuel (Del). 1st Lieutenant Delaware Battalion of the Flying Camp, July to December, 1776.

Connelly, John. (Pa). Lieutenant Pennsylvania Militia; taken prisoner at Germantown, 4th October, 1777. (Died 1827.)

Connelly, Robert (Pa). 2d Lieutenant 3d Pennsylvania, 8th January to December, 1776; Captain 4th Pennsylvania, 3d January, 1777; retired 31st August, 1778.

Conner, Daniel (Ga). Was a Lieutenant of a Georgia Regiment in 1778.

Connolly, Michael (N. Y.). 1st Lieutenant 5th New York, 21st November, 1776; Regimental Paymaster, 1777 to 1781; transferred to 1st New York, 1st January, 1781, and served to close of war.

Connor, Conrad (Pa). 1st Lieutenant of Cunningham's Pennsylvania Battalion of the Flying Camp, July to December, 1776.

Connor, Edward (S. C.). Paymaster 3d Continental Dragoons, 1st October, 1777; Cornet, 27th July, 1778; Lieutenant — December, 1779, to ——. (Died December, 1836.)

Connor, Morgan (Pa). 1st Lieutenant of Thompson's Pennsylvania Rifle Regiment, 17th July, 1775; Captain 1st Continental Infantry, 5th January, 1776; Major, 7th March, 1776; Lieutenant-Colonel of Hartley's Continental

Regiment, 9th April, 1777; Colonel Adjutant-General to General Washington, 19th April to June, 1777; regiment designated 11th Pennsylvania, 16th December, 1778; Lieutenant-Colonel Commandant 7th Pennsylvania, 12th May, 1779; granted six month's leave, 2d December, 1779, and was lost at sea in January, 1780.

Connor, Samuel (N. H.). Lieutenant-Colonel of Wingate's Regiment New Hampshire Militia in 1776 and 1777.

Connor, William (Va). Sergeant 13th Virginia, January, 1777; transferred to 9th Virginia, 14th September, 1778; Ensign, 6th April, 1779; transferred to 7th Virginia, 12th February, 1781; resigned 4th January, 1782.

Conover, Jacob (N J.). Captain New Jersey Militia; taken prisoner at Monmouth, 27th May, 1778.

Conrad, Peter (Pa). 1st Lieutenant of Stroud's Regiment Pennsylvania Militia; taken prisoner at Frankford, Pennsylvania, 10th January, 1778.

Contee, Benjamin (Md). 2d Lieutenant 3d Maryland Battalion of the Flying Camp, July to December, 1776. (Died 3d November, 1815.)

Converse, James (Mass). Colonel Massachusetts Militia, 1776-1779. (Died 1811.)

Converse, Josiah (Conn). Sergeant in the Lexington Alarm in April, 1775; Ensign 2d Connecticut, 26th June to 18th December, 1775; 1st Lieutenant in Sage's Connecticut Regiment, 20th June to 25th December, 1776; Captain Massachusetts Militia in 1777. (Died 1814.)

Converse, Josiah (Mass). Sergeant of Gardner's Massachusetts Regiment, April to December, 1775; Sergeant 24th Continental Infantry, 1st January to 31st December, 1776; Sergeant 3d Massachusetts, 1st January, 1777; Ensign, 25th November, 1779; Lieutenant, ——, 1781; resigned 21st November, 1782.

Converse, Thomas (Conn) Ensign of Burrall's Continental Regiment, 23d January, 1776; left behind, sick, on the retreat from Quebec in April, 1776; 1st Lieutenant and Adjutant 7th Connecticut, 1st January, 1777; Captain ,3d November, 1777; transferred to 2d Connecticut, 1st January, 1781; Brigade-Inspector, 14th July, 1781; retired 1st January, 1783.

Conway, Henry (Va). Captain 14th Virginia, 28th November, 1776; resigned 12th March, 1778.

Conway, James (Va). 2d Lieutenant 6th Virginia, 21st March, 1776; killed near Trenton, 28th December, 1776.

Conway, John (N. J.). Captain 1st New Jersey, 21st November, 1775; wounded at Germantown, 4th October, 1777; Major 4th New Jersey, 29th October, 1777; transferred to 3d New Jersey, 29th October, 1778; Lieutenant-Colonel 1st New Jersey, 5th July, 1779; retired 1st January, 1781.

Conway, Joseph (Va). Ensign 14th Virginia, 24th July, 1777; 2d Lieutenant, 22d December, 1777; regiment designated 10th Virginia, 14th September, 1778; taken prisoner at Charleston, 12th May, 1780; Captain Lieutenant, 15th July, 1780; transferred to 1st Virginia, 12th February, 1781, and served to close of war.

Conway, Thomas (France). (Born in Ireland). Brigadier-General Continental Army, 13th May, 1777; Inspector-General, with rank of Major-General, 13th December, 1777; resigned 28th April, 1778. (Died 1800.)

Conwell, Daniel (Del). 1st Lieutenant Delaware Battalion of the Flying Camp, July to December, 1776.

Conyers, Daniel (S. C.). Captain in Marion's Brigade in 1781-1782.

Conyers, James (S. C.). Captain South Carolina Militia, 1780-1781.

Conyngham, Cornelius (N. Y.). 2d Lieutenant 2d Continental Artillery, 1st January, 1777; resigned — October, 1777; Surgeon's Mate Hospital Department, 1778-1783; Surgeon's Mate United States Army, 15th October, 1810; resigned 31st March, 1820.

Cook, Daniel (N. J.). Captain and Major New Jersey Militia, 1778-1781.

Cook, David (Mass). 1st Lieutenant of Knox's Regiment Continental Artillery, 10th December, 1775; Captain Lieutenant 3d Continental Artillery, 1st January, 1777; Captain, 14th May, 1778, and served to June, 1783. (Died 27th October, 1823.)

Cook, Ebenezer (Mass). 2d Lieutenant of Cady's Battalion in the expedition to Canada, January to June, 1776.

Cook, Ellis (N. J.). Lieutenant-Colonel and Colonel New Jersey Militia ,1776 1780. (Died 1797.)

Cook, Ephraim (Conn). Captain Connecticut Militia, 1776-1777.

Cook, Ezekiel (N. Y.). Ensign 1st Canadian (Hazen's) Regiment, 18th December, 1776; resigned 6th April, 1780

Cook, George (N. J.). 2d Lieutenant 4th New Jersey, 28th November, 1776; omitted March, 1777.

Cook, George (N. C.). 2d Lieutenant 10th North Carolina, 19th April, 1777; 1st Lieutenant, 10th July, 1777; transferred to 1st North Carolina 1st June, 1778; taken prisoner at Charleston 12th May, 1780.

Cook, Giles (Va). Cadet 2d Virginia State Regiment in 1778.

Cook, Isaac (Conn). Captain Connecticut Militia in 1775. (Died 1790.)

Cook, Isham (Ga). Captain 2d Georgia, ——; appears in orders of 1778.

Cook, Isaac, Jr. (Conn). Captain 1st Connecticut, 1st May to 1st December, 1775; Major and Lieutenant-Colonel Connecticut Militia, 1780-1783. (Died 1810.)

Cook, James (N. C.). Ensign 2d North Carolina, 1st September, 1775; Captain 3d North Carolina, 16th April, 1776; retired 1st June, 1778.

Cook, Jesse (Conn). 2d Lieutenant 7th Connecticut, 6th July to 19th December, 1775; 1st Lieutenant and Captain of Bradley's Connecticut Regiment from 20th June, 1776; taken prisoner at Fort Washington 16th November, 1776; exchanged 25th October, 1780.

Cook, Job (N. Y.). 2d Lieutenant 1st New York, March to November, 1776.

Cook, John (Mass). 2d Lieutenant of Walker's Massachusetts Regiment, May to December, 1775.

Cook, John (N. J.). Major New Jersey Militia, ——; killed at Block House 19th July, 1780.

Cook, John (N. H.). Surgeon of Nash's Regiment New Hampshire Militia in 1776.

Cook, John (Pa). Private 12th Pennsylvania, October, 1776; Ensign 22d May, 1777; cashiered 30th January, 1778. (Died 21st February, 1823.)

Cook, John (R. I.). Ensign and Regimental Quartermaster 1st Rhode Island, 15th March, 1777; Lieutenant, 1st June, 1778; discharged 20th December, 1780.

Cook, John (Va). Captain 4th Continental Dragoons, 1780 to 1783.

Cook, Louis (N. H.). Captain of Bedel's New Hampshire Regiment 20th April to 10th June, 1776.

Cook, Moses (Pa). Lieutenant of Baldwin's Artillery Artificer Regiment, 12th May, 1777; Captain, 31st August, 1778; retired 1st May, 1779.

Cook, Oliver (Vt). Lieutenant of Bedel's Regiment Vermont Militia, 15th December, 1777, to 1st April, 1778.

Cook, Paris (Ga). Captain 3d Georgia in 1777.

Cook, Phineas (Mass). Captain in Lexington Alarm, April, 1775; Captain of Gardner's Massachusetts Regiment, May to December, 1775; Captain 25th Continental Infantry, 1st January to 31st December, 1776. (Died 1784.)

Cook, Rains (Ga). Captain 3d Georgia in 1777, and served to ——.

Cook, Richard D. (N. C.). Captain 9th North Carolina, 28th November, 1776; retired 1st June, 1778.

Cook, Samuel (Mass). Lieutenant in Lexington Alarm, April, 1775; Lieutenant in Woodbridge's Massachusetts Regiment, May to December, 1775.

Cook Simeon (N. Y.). Major New York Militia, 1775-1776.

Cook, Thaddeus (Conn). Major of Ward's Connecticut State Regiment, 14th May, 1776, to May, 1777; served subsequently as Colonel Connecticut Militia.

Cook, Thomas (N. J.). Lieutenant New Jersey Militia; taken prisoner at Light House, N. J., 13th February, 1777.

Cook, Thomas T. (Pa). 1st Lieutenant 8th Pennsylvania, 9th August, 1776; Captain, 26th July, 1777; retired 31st January, 1779. ('Died 5th November, 1831.)

Cook, .William (R. I.). Captain Rhode Island Regiment, May to December, 1775.

Cooke, John (R. I.). Lieutenant-Colonel Rhode Island Militia, 3d August, 1775; Colonel 2d Rhode Island State Troops, 12th December, 1776; resigned 16th June, 1777.

Cooke, John (R. I.). Ensign 1st Rhode Island, 1st January, 1777; 2d Lieutenant, 1st June, 1778; Regimental Quartermaster, ——, 1778; discharged — September, 1780.

Cooke, Joseph Platte (Conn). Colonel Connecticut Militia, 1776-1778.

Cooke, Nicholas (R. I.). Ensign Rhode Island Militia in 1777.

Cooke, Noah, Jr. (N. H.). Chaplain 8th Continental Infantry, 1st January to 31st December, 1776; Hospital Chaplain, 18th September, 1777, to 6th October, 1780.

Cooke, Oliver (Vt). Lieutenant Vermont Militia, 5th December, 1777, to April, 1778.

Cooke, Samuel (N. Y.). Surgeon 3d New York, 25th August, 1775, to January, 1776; Surgeon of Elmore's Continental Regiment, 15th April, 1776; Surgeon 5th New York, 15th April, 1777; retired 1st January, 1781.

Cooke, William (Pa). Colonel 12th Pennsylvania, 2d October, 1776; cashiered 4th March, 1778. (Died 22d April, 1804.)

Cooke, —— (Va). Ensign 1st Virginia, ——; dismissed 8th January, 1778.

Cooley, Abel (Mass). Private in Lexington Alarm, April, 1775; Sergeant in Danielson's Massachusetts Regiment, May to December, 1775; Lieutenant 4th Massachusetts, 1st January, 1777; died 13th June, 1778.

Cooley, Samuel (N. C.). Surgeon 5th North Carolina, 17th April, 1776; retired 1st June, 1778; Surgeon Virginia Militia in 1780.

Cooley, William (Mass). Captain Massachusetts Militia; wounded at White Plains 28th October, 1776 (Died 1825.)

Coombs, John (N. J.). Captain of Forman's Continental Regiment, 20th March, 1777; transferred to Spencer's Continental Regiment, 1st July, 1778; died 2d September, 1779.

Coombs, Thomas (N. J.). Captain New Jersey Militia, ——; taken prisoner at Bonhamton, 4th April, 1777; exchanged ——. (Died 10th March, 1798.)

Coon, James (Conn). 2d Lieutenant of Warner's Additional Continental Regiment, 1st October, 1776; 1st Lieutenant, 1st January, 1777; Regimental Quartermaster, 1st December, 1779; killed near Fort George 6th September, 1780.

Cooper, Apollos (Va). 2d Lieutenant 3d Virginia, 9th February, 1776; 1st Lieutenant, 7th August, 1776; killed at Brandywine 11th September, 1777.

Cooper, Benjamin A. (Va). Lieutenant of a Virginia State Regiment, 1779-1781.

Cooper, Ezekiel (Mass). Ensign of Hutchinson's Massachusetts Regiment, May to December, 1775; Ensign 27th Continental Infantry, 1st January to 31st December, 1776; 1st Lieutenant 5th Massachusetts, 1st January, 1777; transferred to 2d Massachusetts, 1st January, 1783; Captain, 7th January, 1783, and served to June, 1783.

Cooper, Ezekiel (N. Y.). 1st Lieutenant 3d New York, 28th June, 1775; Captain of Nicholson's Continental Regiment, 8th March, 1776, to April, 1777; served subsequently in New York Militia.

Cooper, George (S. C.). Captain in Marion's Brigade, 1781-1782.

Cooper, Gilbert (N. Y.). Colonel New York Militia, 1777-1779.

Cooper, James (Mass). 1st Lieutenant 13th Continental Infantry, 1st January to 31st December, 1776; Captain 14th Massachusetts, 1st January, 1777; retired 1st January, 1781. (Died 20th October, 1819.)

Cooper, John (Ga). Captain Georgia Militia; wounded at Bulltown Swamp 19th November, 1778; Major Georgia Militia; wounded at Four Holes, S. C., 15th April, 1781.

Cooper, John (Mass). 2d Lieutenant 3d Continental Artillery, 1st January, 1777; 1st Lieutenant, 1st May, 1777; resigned 11th February, 1779.

Cooper, John (Va). 2d Lieutenant 10th Virginia, 6th February, 1777; killed at Brandywine 11th September, 1777.

Cooper, Leonard.—See **Cowper.**

Cooper, Samuel (Conn). 1st Lieutenant 2d Connecticut, 1st May, 1775; killed at Quebec 31st December, 1775.

Cooper, Samuel (Mass). 2d Lieutenant 3d Continental Artillery, 1st February, 1777; Regimental Quartermaster, 14th May, 1778, to June, 1783; transferred to Corps of Artillery, 17th June, 1783, and was Adjutant of the same to 20th June, 1784. (Died 19th August, 1840.)

Cooper, Samuel (S. C.). Captain South Carolina Militia in Marion's Brigade, 1781-1782.

Cooper, Samuel (S. C.). Major South Carolina Militia, 1779-1781.

Cooper, Samuel (Va). Sergeant-Major 15th Virginia, 26th November, 1776; Ensign, 20th June, 1777; cashiered 21st July, 1778.

Cooper, Soloman (N. C.). Lieutenant 10th North Carolina, 20th January, 1778, to ——.

Cooper, William (N. C.). Lieutenant 5th North Carolina, 16th April, 1776, to ——.

Cooper, William (Pa). Ensign 8th Pennsylvania, 21st December, 1778; retired 1st January, 1781.

Cooper, Zibeon (Mass). Ensign 5th Massachusetts, 7th November, 1777, to ——.

Coots, James (N. C.). Lieutenant 4th North Carolina, 20th November, 1776, to ——.

Copeman, Abraham (N. Y.). Major New York Militia, 1779-1783.

Copp, John (N. Y.). 1st Lieutenant 1st New York, 28th June, 1775, to January, 1776; Captain of Nicholson's Continental Regiment, 15th April, 1776; Captain 1st New York, 21st November, 1776; resigned 14th July, 1779.

Copperthwait, Joseph (Pa). Captain Pennsylvania Militia, 1776.

Corbet, Thomas (Ga). Captain Georgia Militia; taken prisoner at Briar Creek, 3d March, 1779.

Corby, John (S. C.). Lieutenant South Carolina Militia, 1779-1780.

Cordell, John (Va). Chaplain 11th Virginia, 15th February, 1777; taken prisoner at Fort Mercer 22d October, 1777; served subsequently as Chaplain in a Virginia State Regiment, May, 1779, to 10th February, 1781.

Corden, Jesse (Md). 2d Lieutenant Maryland Battalion of the Flying Camp, July to December, 1776; Captain 5th Maryland, 10th December, 1776; resigned 7th December, 1777. (Name also spelled Cozden and Cosden.)

Coren, Isaac (Pa). 1st Lieutenant of Knox's Regiment Continental Artillery, 10th December, 1775, to December, 1776; Captain of an Independent Company Pennsylvania Artillery, 1st February, 1777; Company attached to Flower's Regiment of Artillery Artificers; cashiered 30th June, 1780.

Corey, Ephraim (Mass). 1st Lieutenant of Prescott's Massachusetts Regiment, May, 1775; cashiered 17th November, 1775; 1st Lieutenant 5th Massachusetts, 1st January, 1777; cashiered 29th October, 1777.

Corey, Hezekiah (N. H.). Ensign in Lexington Alarm, April, 1775.

Corey, James (Va). Ensign of Virginia State Troops; killed at King's Mountain 7th October, 1780.

Corey, Philip (Mass). Sergeant and Sergeant-Major 10th Massachusetts, 9th December, 1776; Ensign, 12th December, 1780; resigned 7th May, 1782. (Died 9th December, 1833.)

Corey, Timothy (Mass). Captain of Gerrish's Massachusetts Regiment, May to December, 1775. (Died 1811.)

Corliss, Jonathan (N. H.). Ensign 1st New Hampshire, 23d April, 1775; 2d Lieutenant, 23d May to December, 1775; volunteer Aide-de-Camp to General Varnum in 1778. (Died 1814.)

Cornelius, Elias (R. I.). Surgeon's Mate 2d Rhode Island, 1st January, 1777; taken prisoner at Staten Island 22d August, 1777; escaped from prison ship 16th January, 1778; rejoined his regiment and served to 14th May, 1781. (Died 13th June, 1823.)

Cornell, Ezekiel (R. I.). Lieutenant-Colonel of Hitchcock's Rhode Island Regiment, 3d May to December, 1775; Lieutenant-Colonel 11th Continental Infantry, 1st January, 1776; Deputy Adjutant-General, 1st October to 31st December, 1776; Brigadier-General Rhode Island Militia, 1777; appointed Inspector of the main army under General Washington 19th September, 1782, and served to close of war.

Cornell, Joseph (R. I.). Ensign 1st Rhode Island, 20th June, 1777; resigned 20th May, 1779. (Died 8th April, 1825.)

Corney, Louis Ethis de (—). See **De Corney.**

Cornick, Henry (Va). Captain Virginia Militia, 1778-1781.

Cornish, Joseph (Conn). 2d Lieutenant of Sage's Connecticut State Regiment, June to December, 1776.

Corse, John (Del). Sergeant Delaware Regiment; Ensign Delaware Regiment, 14th January, 1776; wounded at Long Island, 27th August, 1776; 1st Lieutenant, 3d December, 1776; Captain, 26th January, 1779; resigned 26th April, 1780.

Cortland, Philip (—). See **Van Cortland.**

Coryell, John (Pa). Major Pennsylvania Militia, 1777. (Died 1799.)

Cosden, Jesse.—See **Corden.**

Coskey, Peter (Md). Ensign 3d Maryland, 1st April, 1777; 2d Lieutenant, — September, 1777; deserted 19th May, 1778.

Costigin, Francis (N. J.). Ensign 1st New Jersey, 21st November, 1775; 2d Lieutenant, 29th November, 1776; discharged 17th April, 1777. (Died 27th July, 1821.)

Costigin, Lewis Johnston (N. J.). 1st Lieutenant 1st New Jersey, 21st November, 1775; wounded and taken prisoner in a skirmish near Fort Washington 13th November, 1776; exchanged 18th December, 1778, and did not return to the army, but served as a spy in New York City, 1779 to close of war. (Died 9th March, 1822.)

Costradum, Thomas (N. Y.). 2d Lieutenant 3d New York, 21st November, 1776; omitted February, 1777.

Cotgrave, Arthur (N. C.). 1st Lieutenant 2d North Carolina, 26th March, 1778; taken prisoner at Charleston 12th May, 1780; exchanged 14th June, 1781, and served to close of war.

Cotter, John (Va). Lieutenant 10th Virginia, ——; dismissed 21st April, 1778.

Cotton, George (Conn). Sergeant 3d Connecticut, 1st January, 1777; Sergeant-Major, 1st September, 1779; Ensign, 25th October, 1780, to rank from 25th June, 1779; transferred to 1st Connecticut, 1st January, 1781, and served to June, 1783.

Cotton, Isaac (Mass). Captain of Brewer's Massachusetts Regiment, May, 1775, to ——.

Cotton, John (Mass). Quartermaster of Cotton's Massachusetts Regiment, May to December, 1775; Ensign 23d Continental Infantry, 1st January to 31st December, 1776; 2d Lieutenant, 10th August, 1776; 1st Lieutenant 5th Massachusetts, 1st January, 1777; resigned 3d October, 1780. (Died 1st February, 1831.)

Cotton, Josiah (Mass). Ensign 25th Continental Infantry, 1st January to 31st December, 1776; (also called Joseph Cotton). (Died 7th March, 1829.)

Cotton, Josiah (N. C.). Captain 7th North Carolina, 28th November, 1776; retired 1st June, 1778.

Cotton, Moses (Mass). Private 10th Massachusetts, 7th August, 1779; Ensign 6th Massachusetts, 3d December, 1780; served to ——.

Cotton, Samuel (N. H.). Chaplain 1st New Hampshire, 9th April, 1777; resigned 7th August, 1777.

Cotton, Theophilus (Mass). Colonel Massachusetts Regiment, 27th May to December, 1775; Colonel Massachusetts Militia, 1776-1781.

Cotton, Thomas (N. C.). Captain North Carolina Militia in 1780.

Cottram, George (N. J.). Ensign 3d New Jersey, 29th February to December, 1776; Captain Lieutenant 4th Continental Artillery, 14th March, 1777; resigned 10th September, 1778. (Name also spelled Cottman.)

Couch, Alexander (N. J.). 2d Lieutenant, 1st New Jersey, 15th December, 1775; Regimental Adjutant, 28th November, 1776; died 11th December, 1778.

Couch, Ebenezer (Conn). Captain of Swift's Connecticut State Regiment, July to December, 1776.

Couch, John (Conn). Captain of Bradley's Connecticut State Regiment, 20th June, 1776; taken prisoner at Fort Washington, 16th November, 1776. (Died 1806.)

Couch, Thomas (Del). Colonel Delaware Militia, 1780-1781.

Couch, Thomas (Conn). Private in the Lexington Alarm, April, 1775; Sergeant 5th Connecticut, 8th May, 1775; Regimental Quartermaster, 11th July to 11th December, 1775.

Coudray, Philip Charles Jean Baptiste Trouson du (France). Major-General and Inspector-General of Ordnance and Military Manufactories Continental Army, 11th August, 1777; drowned 15th September, 1777.

Coughlan, Richard (N. H.). 2d Lieutenant 2d Continental Artillery, 1st January, 1777, to ——.

Coughran, John (Pa). 3d Lieutenant of Cunningham's Pennsylvania Battalion of the Flying Camp, June to December, 1776.

Coulter, John (Pa). Hospital Physician and Surgeon, 1776-1780. (Died 1823.)

Coulter, Samuel (Pa). Ensign 3d Pennsylvania, 1st April, 1777; resigned 31st October, 1777.

Coultman, Robert (Pa). Captain Lieutenant, 4th Continental Artillery, 14th March, 1777; Captain 3d March, 1779; retired June, 1783.

Council, Arthur (N. C.). Captain 6th North Carolina, 16th April, 1776; died — April, 1777.

Council, Robert (N. C.). Ensign 1st North Carolina, 4th January, 1776; 2d Lieutenant, 7th July, 1776; resigned 10th September, 1776; Ensign 1st North Carolina, 28th March, 1777; 2d Lieutenant, 8th July, 1777; Captain Company of North Carolina Dragoons, 1st July, 1778, and served to close of war.

Courtenay, Herculas (Pa). Captain Lieutenant of Proctor's Battalion Pennsylvania Artillery, 5th October, 1776; Captain Lieutenant 4th Continental Artillery, 1st January, 1777; Captain, 3d March, 1777; dismissed 3d March, 1778.

Couterier, John (S. C.). Captain South Carolina Militia, 1775.

Courtney, Philip (Va). Ensign 1st Virginia, 4th July, 1779; resigned 11th February, 1781.

Courts, John (Va). Surgeon 2d Virginia in 1780.

Courts, William (Md). Ensign of Smallwood's Maryland Regiment, 14th January, 1776; taken prisoner at Long Island 27th August, 1776; exchanged 9th December, 1776; 2d Lieutenant 1st Maryland, 10th December, 1776; 1st Lieutenant 2d Maryland, 17th April, 1777; resigned 25th April, 1777.

Covenhoven, Edward (N. J.). 2d Lieutenant 1st New Jersey in 1777.

Covenhoven, Jacob (N. J.). Captain New Jersey Light Horse; taken prisoner at Springfield 23d June, 1780.

Covenhoven, John (N. J.). Colonel New Jersey Militia, 1778.

Covenhoven, Joseph (N. J.). Captain New Jersey Militia, 1777.

Covenhoven, William (N. J.). 2d Lieutenant 1st New Jersey, 1st March, 1777; died 15th June, 1778.

Coventry, Alexander (S. C.). Regimental Quartermaster 3d South Carolina, 20th September, 1776, to ——.

Cover, Jacob (Pa). Ensign 9th Pennsylvania, 15th November, 1776; was paid to July 1, 1777.

Coverly, Thomas (Va). Sergeant 9th Virginia, 15th March, 1776; Ensign 7th November, 1776; 2d Lieutenant, 26th December, 1777; taken prisoner at Germantown 4th October, 1777; did not rejoin regiment. (Died 22d September, 1827.)

Covill, Ephraim (Mass). Sergeant 4th Massachusetts, 11th March, 1777; Ensign, 1st August, 1781; retired 1st January, 1783.

Covill, John (Mass). Surgeon's Mate Hospital Department, 1779-1783.

Covill, Samuel (Mass). Captain Massachusetts Militia, 1776.

Covill, Thomas (Mass). Sergeant 4th Massachusetts, 7th January, 1777; Ensign, 30th March, 1779; resigned 18th August, 1779; Ensign 4th Massachusetts, ——, 1781; cashiered 14th October, 1782. (Name also spelled Covel.)

Covington, James (N. C.). Lieutenant 9th North Carolina, 28th November, 1776, to ——.

Covington, William (N. C.). Adjutant 4th North Carolina, 28th March, 1777, to ——.

Cowan, David (N. C.). Lieutenant 10th North Carolina, 20th March, 1779; Captain in 1781, and served to ——.

Cowan, Edward (Ga). 1st Lieutenant 1st Georgia, 1st September, 1777; Captain, 1779, and served to close of war.

Cowan, Edward (Pa). 1st Lieutenant of Captain Weaver's Company, guarding prisoners at Lancaster, 13th January, 1777; resigned 23d August, 1777.

Cowan, Thomas (N. C.). Captain North Carolina State Troops; wounded at Eutaw Springs, 8th September, 1781. (Died 1817.)

Cowden, David.—See **Conder.**

Cowen, John (R. I.). Ensign of Lippitt's Regiment Rhode Island Militia, 12th August, 1776, to March, 1777.

Cowan, Thomas (N. C.). Captain North Carolina Militia, 1780-1781. (Died 1817.)

Cowherd, Francis (Va). Ensign 2d Virginia, 8th May, 1776; 2d Lieutenant, 1st September, 1776; 1st Lieutenant, 15th June, 1777; taken prisoner at Charleston 12th May, 1780; exchanged June, 1781; Captain, 29th May, 1780, and served to close of war. (Died 25th March, 1833.)

Cowles, Gideon (N. Y.). Lieutenant New York Militia; wounded and taken prisoner at Westchester 16th March, 1777.

Cowles, John (Mass). Captain of Woodbridge's Massachusetts Regiment, May to December, 1775; Captain Massachusetts Militia, 1776-1777. (Died 1802.)

Cowles, Solomon (Conn). 1st Lieutenant of Webb's Continental Regiment, 1st January, 1777; resigned 21st March, 1778.

Cowles, Thomas (Conn). Ensign 8th Connecticut, 1st January, 1777; resigned 15th December, 1777.

Cowne, Robert (Va). Captain Lieutenant of a Virginia State Regiment, 1778 to 1781. (Died 1829.)

Cowper, Leonard (Va). Ensign 8th Virginia, 19th February, 1776; Lieutenant, — June, 1776; Captain Lieutenant, 10th May, 1777; transferred to 4th Virginia, 14th September, 1778; Captain Invalid Regiment, 7th October, 1778, and served to 23d April, 1783.

Cox, Daniel Powell (Del). Lieutenant Delaware Battalion of the Flying Camp, July, 1776; 2d Lieutenant Delaware Regiment, 30th November, 1776; 1st Lieutenant, 5th April, 1777, and served to close of war; Brevet Captain, 30th September, 1783.

Cox, Ebenezer (N. Y.). Lieutenant-Colonel New York Militia, ——; killed at Oriskany 6th August, 1777.

Cox, Edmond (Maryland). Private of Smallwood's Maryland Regiment, 24th January, 1776; Sergeant 1st Maryland, 10th December, 1776; Regimental Quartermaster, 19th July, 1777; dismissed 3d October, 1778.

Cox, Elisha (Mass). Ensign 25th Continental Infantry, 1st January, 1776; died 25th June, 1776.

Cox, Francis (Mass). 1st Lieutenant of Mansfield's Massachusetts Regiment, May to December, 1775; 1st Lieutenant 27th Continental Infantry, 1st January to 31st December, 1776. (Died 1782.)

Cox, Isaac (Pa). Paymaster of Miles' Pennsylvania Rifle Regiment, 18th September, 1776; resigned 16th October, 1776.

Cox, James (Md). Major Maryland Militia; killed at Germantown, 4th October, 1777.

Cox, John (Pa). Assistant Quartermaster-General, 2d March, 1778; joined the Navy latter part of 1778. (Died 15th December, 1837.)

Cox, Joseph (Pa). Ensign 6th Pennsylvania, 15th February, 1777; taken prisoner at Newtown, 19th February, 1778; exchanged 29th January, 1781; was promoted 2d Lieutenant in 1778,

while prisoner of war, but never rejoined his regiment.

Cox, Richard (N. J.). 2d Lieutenant 27th Continental Infantry, 30th March, 1776; 1st Lieutenant, 29th October, 1776; Captain 3d New Jersey, 1st January, 1777; transferred to 2d New Jersey 1st January, 1781; Major 6th January, 1783; retained in New Jersey Battalion April, 1783, and served to close of war. (Died 29th October, 1841.)

Cox, Walter (Maryland). Ensign of Smallwood's Maryland Regiment, 14th January to May, 1776; Captain of Hartley's Continental Regiment, 5th February, 1777; retired — December, 1778.

Cox, William (Pa). Captain 10th Pennsylvania, 4th December, 1776; retired 1st July, 1778.

Coyl, Thomas (S. C.). Private, Corporal, and Sergeant 5th South Carolina, 11th June, 1776, until appointed 2d Lieutenant in 1777; 1st Lieutenant, 22d January, 1778, and served to ——.

Cozden, Jesse (—). See **Cosden.**

Cozens, John (N. J.). Captain New Jersey Militia; taken prisoner at his home, when not stated; exchanged 8th December, 1780.

Cozins, William (Mass). 1st Lieutenant of Scammon's Massachusetts Regiment, May, 1775, to ——.

Crabb, Jeremiah (Md). 2d Lieutenant 4th Maryland, 10th December, 1776; 1st Lieutenant, 15th December, 1777; resigned 1st July, 1778.

Craddock, John (Md). Major 2d Maryland Battalion of the Flying Camp, July to December, 1776.

Craddock, John (N. C.). Ensign 2d North Carolina, 3d May, 1776; 2d Lieutenant, 16th May, 1776; 1st Lieutenant, — January, 1777; Captain Lieutenant, 21st December, 1777; wounded and taken prisoner at Charleston 12th May, 1780; Captain, 1780; prisoner on parole until retired 1st January, 1783.

Craddock, Robert (Va). Sergeant 15th Virginia, 1st January, 1777; Regiment designated 11th Virginia, 14th September, 1778; 2d Lieutenant, 10th August, 1777; 1st Lieutenant, 4th July, 1779; taken prisoner at Charleston 12th May, 1780, and was a prisoner on parole to 1st May, 1783. He was transferred to the 4th Virginia 12th February, 1781.

Crafton, Bennett (N. C.). Adjutant 6th North Carolina, 15th April, 1776, to ——.

Crafts, Abner (Mass). Captain of Gardner's Massachusetts Regiment, May to December, 1775; Captain 24th Continental Infantry, 1st January to 31st December, 1776. (Died 1810.)

Crafts, Benjamin (Mass). 2d Lieutenant of Mansfield's Massachusetts Regiment, May to December, 1775; 2d Lieutenant 27th Continental Infantry, 1st January to 31st December, 1776.

Crafts, Edward (Mass). Captain of Gridley's Regiment Massachusetts Artillery, June to December, 1775; Captain of Knox's Regiment Continental Artillery, 10th December, 1775, to December, 1776; Colonel Artillery, Massachusetts Militia, 1777. (Died 11th December, 1806.)

Crafts, Nathaniel (Mass). Captain 2d Continental Dragoons, 20th January, 1777; resigned 1st January, 1778.

Craghead, Patrick (Mass). 2d Lieutenant of Baldwin's Artillery Artificer Regiment, 1st April, 1778, to ——.

Craig, Charles (Pa).· 1st Lieutenant of Thompson's Pennsylvania Rifle Regiment, 25th June, 1775; Captain, 9th November, 1775, Captain 1st Continental Infantry, 1st January to 31st December, 1776; Captain 4th Continental Dragoons, 10th July, 1777; wounded at Brandywine 11th September, 1777, and did not rejoin the army. (Died 1782.)

Craig, Hugh (Pa). Paymaster 11th Pennsylvania, 4th December, 1776; resigned 31st January, 1777.

Craig, Isaac (Pa). Served as Captain of Marines in 1776; Captain 4th Continental Artillery, 3d March, 1777; Major, 7th October, 1781, and served to 17th June, 1783. (Died 14th June, 1826.)

Craig, James (Va). 2d Lieutenant 8th Virginia, 3d September, 1776; 1st Lieutenant, 5th August, 1777; Captain, — July, 1778; retired 14th September, 1778.

Craig, James (Va). Ensign of Clark's Illinois Regiment in 1782.

Craig, John (Pa). 2d Lieutenant 2d Pennsylvania Battalion, 5th January, 1776; 1st Lieutenant 3d Pennsylvania, 11th November, 1776; 1st Lieutenant 4th Continental Dragoons, 22d March, 1777; Captain, 22d December, 1778, and served to close of war. (Died 29th November, 1829.)

Craig, John (Pa). 3d Lieutenant 4th Continental Artillery, 1st April, 1777; resigned 29th January, 1778.

Craig, John (Pa). Lieutenant of Baxter's Pennsylvania Battalion of the Flying Camp, July, 1776; taken prisoner at Fort Washington 16th November, 1776; exchanged 19th March, 1781.

Craig, Obadiah (Va). Sergeant 9th Virginia, 3d March, 1776; Regimental Quartermaster, 15th July, 1777; retired 30th September, 1778.

Craig, Robert (Pa). 2d Lieutenant 2d Canadian (Hazen's) Regiment, 3d November, 1776; resigned 1st February, 1778. (Died 1834.)

Craig, Robert (Va). Captain Virginia Militia at King's Mountain, October, 1780.

Craig, Samuel (Pa). 3d Lieutenant of Thompson's Pennsylvania Rifle Regiment, 25th June, 1775; 2d Lieutenant, 8th November, 1775; 1st Lieutenant 1st Continental Infantry, 1st January, 1776; Captain, 1st October, 1776; Captain 1st Pennsylvania, 1st January, 1777, to rank from 1st October, 1776; wounded at Paoli 19th September, 1777; retired 17th January, 1781.

Craig, Thomas (Pa). 2d Lieutenant of Thompson's Pennsylvania Rifle Regiment, 25th June, 1775; Regimental Quartermaster, July to December, 1775; Captain 2d Pennsylvania Battalion, 5th January, 1776; Lieutenant-Colonel, 29th September, 1776; Lieutenant-Colonel 3d Pennsylvania, January, 1777, to rank from 29th September, 1776; Colonel, 1st August, 1777; retired 1st January, 1783 (Died 14th January, 1832.)

Craig, Thomas (Pa). Regimental Quartermaster 9th Pennsylvania, 1st January, 1777; resigned — September, 1777.

Craig, William (Pa). Ensign 2d Pennsylvania Battalion, 5th January, 1776; 2d Lieutenant 3d Pennsylvania, 11th November, 1776; 1st Lieutenant, 1st January, 1777; Captain, 4th July, 1777; resigned 1st June, 1779.

Craigie, Andrew (Mass). Apothecary-General, 1st January, 1777; Apothecary Hospital Department, 6th October, 1780, to November, 1783. (Died 19th September, 1819.)

Craigie, Peter Markoe (Mass). 1st Lieutenant of Henley's Continental Regiment, 12th March, 1777; resigned 15th March, 1778.

Craighead, Patrick.—See Craghead.

· **Craighead, ——** (N. C.). Captain North Carolina Militia; wounded at Hanging Rock 6th August, 1780.

Craik, Thomas (N. C.). Deputy Commissary General, 23d November, 1776, to ——.

Craik, James (Va). Chief Hospital Physician, 6th October, 1780; Chief Physician and Surgeon of the Army, 3d March, 1781, and served to 23d December, 1783; Physician-General United States Army, 19th July, 1789; honorably discharged 15th June, 1800. (Died 6th February, 1814.)

Crain, Ambrose (Pa). 2d Lieutenant Pennsylvania State Regiment, 17th April, 1777; cashiered 20th August, 1777. (Name also spelled Crane.)

Crain, James (Va). Private and Sergeant 15th Virginia in 1776; 2d Lieutenant, 25th November, 1776; 1st Lieutenant, 1st April, 1778; Regiment designated 11th Virginia, 14th September, 1778; Captain, 5th October, 1780; transferred to 4th Virginia 12th February, 1781, and served to close of war. (Name also spelled Crane.)

Cramer, Jacob (Pa). Ensign German Regiment, 8th July, 1776; 2d Lieutenant, 15th May, 1777; 1st Lieutenant, 8th February, 1778; retired 1st January, 1781; served subsequently as Lieutenant Pennsylvania Rangers.

Crampton, Basil (Va). Surgeon's Mate of Grayson's Continental Regiment, 27th May, 1777; Surgeon 11th Virginia, 1st December, 1777; died 10th January, 1778.

Crandall, Amos (R. I.). 2d Lieutenant 9th Continental Infantry, 1st January to 31st December, 1776; 1st Lieutenant 2d Rhode Island, 1st January, 1777, to ——.

Crandall, Edward (R. I.). 2d Lieutenant of Stanton's Regiment Rhode Island Militia, 12th December, 1776, to ——.

Crandall, Joseph (R. I.). 1st Lieutenant of Elliott's Regiment Rhode Island State Artillery, 12th December, 1776, to May, 1777. (Died 2d July, 1799.)

Crane, Abner (Mass). Captain Massachusetts Militia, 1777.

Crane, Isaac (N. Y.). Lieutenant New York State Troops, ——; taken prisoner in West Chester County, New York, 16th March, 1777, and released in 1781. (Died 1810.)

Crane, Jacob (N. J.). Major and Lieutenant-Colonel New Jersey Militia, · 1777-1780.

Crane, James.—See **Crain.**

Crane, John (Mass). Captain of Gridley's Regiment Massachusetts Artillery, 3d May, 1775; Major of Knox's Regiment Continental Artillery, 10th December, 1775; wounded at Corlaers Hook 14th September, 1776; Colonel 3d Continental Artillery, 1st January, 1777; transferred to Corps of Artillery, 17th June, 1783; Brevet Brigadier-General, 30th September, 1783; served to 3d November, 1783: (Died 21st August, 1805.)

Crane, John (Mass). Surgeon 1st Massachusetts, 1st January, 1777; transferred to 6th Massachusetts, 1st January, 1781, and served to 1st January, 1783, when retired. (Died ——, 1805.)

Crane, John (Mass). 2d Lieutenant 6th Massachusetts, 1st January, 1777; 1st Lieutenant, 10th June, 1779; retired 1st January, 1783.

Crane, Joseph (N. Y.). 1st Lieutenant of Lamb's Company New York Artillery, 30th June, 1775; Captain Lieutenant of Knox's Regiment Continental Artillery, 16th March, 1776; taken prisoner at Fort Washington, 16th November, 1776.

Crane, Joseph, Jr. (N. Y.). Surgeon New York Militia, 1779-1780 (Died 1800.)

Crane, Peter (Mass). Ensign and Adjutant 24th Continental Infantry, 31st August to 31st December, 1776.

Crane, Thaddeus (N. Y.). Major New York Militia, ——; wounded at Danbury, 27th April, 1777; served subsequently as Colonel New York Militia.

Crane, William (N. Y.). 1st Lieutenant 4th New York, 3d July, 1775; wounded 2d November, 1775, by the explosion of a shell at St. Johns, Canada; was appointed Captain of Spencer's Additional Continental Regiment 12th February, 1777, but appears to have declined, and entered Navy. (Died — March, 1814.)

Cranston, Abner (Mass). Captain of Whitcomb's Massachusetts Regiment, May to December, 1775; Captain 6th Continental Infantry, 1st January to 31st December, 1776; Major 13th Massachusetts, 1st January, 1777. Died 29th May, 1777.

Crary, Archibald (R. I.). Captain Lieutenant 1st Rhode Island, 3d May to December, 1775; Lieutenant-Colonel 9th Continental Infantry, 1st January, to 31st December, 1776; Lieutenant-Colonel of Stanton's Regiment Rhode Island Militia, 12th December, 1776; Colonel 2d Rhode Island State Regiment, 16th June, 1777; resigned 7th May, 1779; Adjutant-General Rhode Island Militia, 1780 to close of war.

Craven, James (N. C.). Ensign 1st North Carolina, 12th June, 1776; 2d Lieutenant, 1st January, 1777; 1st Lieutenant, 28th July, 1777; dishonorably discharged 20th November, 1779.

Crawford, Charles (N. C.). Captain 2d North Carolina, 1st September, 1775; retired 1st June, 1778.

Crawford David (N. C.). Ensign 1st North Carolina, 10th June, 1777; Lieutenant, ——; wounded at Hanging Rock, 6th August, 1780.

Crawford, Edward (Pa). 2d Lieutenant 1st Pennsylvania, February, 1777; 1st Lieutenant, 23d March, 1778; wounded at Bull's Ferrey, 21st July, 1780; transferred to 3d Pennsylvania, 1st January, 1781, and served to June, 1783. (Died 6th March, 1833.)

Crawford, Jacob (Md). Ensign 2d Maryland, 26th January, 1780; Lieutenant, 20th February, 1781; retired 1st January, 1783.

Crawford, James (Md) Quartermaster Sergeant 5th Maryland, 20th July, 1777; Regimental Quartermaster, 14th October, 1777; resigned 20th September, 1779.

Crawford, James (Pa). Major 12th Pennsylvania, 28th September, 1776; wounded at Brandywine, 11th September, 1777; resigned 10th November, 1777. (Died 1817.)

Crawford, John (Pa). 2d Lieutenant 8th Pennsylvania, 9th August, 1776; 1st Lieutenant, 16th April, 1777; Captain, 10th August, 1779; transferred to 6th Pennsylvania, 17th January, 1781; retired 1st January, 1783.

Crawford, John (Pa). Lieutenant of Watt's Pennsylvania Battalion of the Flying Camp, July, 1776; taken prisoner at Fort Washington, 16th December, 1776; exchanged 8th December, 1780, and did not re-enter service.

Crawford, John (Va). Ensign 2d Virginia, 1st January, 1777; 2d Lieutenant, 4th May, 1777; 1st Lieutenant, 20th October, 1779; taken prisoner at Charleston, 12th May, 1780; exchanged July, 1781, and served to June, 1783. (Died 3d March, 1833.)

Crawford, Michael (Pa). 2d Lieutenant 5th Pennsylvania, 1st January, 1777; resigned 28th November, 1777.

Crawford, Robert (S. C.). Major South Carolina Militia, 1779-1781.

Crawford, Samuel (N. Y.). Lieutenant New York Militia; killed at Ward's House 16th March, 1777.

Crawford, William (N. C.). Ensign 1st North Carolina, 4th January, 1776; 2d Lieutenant, 28th March, 1776; resigned 5th August, 1776.

Crawford, William (Pa). 2d Lieutenant 5th Pennsylvania Battalion, 8th January, 1776; 1st Lieutenant 12th October, 1776; taken prisoner at Fort Washington, 16th November, 1776; Captain, 1st May, 1777; exchanged 18th December, 1780, and did not re-enter the service. (Died 1828.)

Crawford, William (Va). Lieutenant-Colonel 5th Virginia, 13th February, 1776; Colonel 7th Virginia, 14th August, 1776; resigned 22d March, 1777; served subsequently on the Western frontier in Virginia; commanded an expedition against Indians, was captured, tortured, and burned at the stake in Wyandotte County, Ohio, 11th June, 1782.

Crawford, —— (—). 1st Lieutenant, ——; killed at Fort Motte 12th May, 1781.

Crawley, Samuel (Va). Lieutenant and Captain of a Virginia State Regiment, 1778 to 1781.

Craycroft, Charles (Va). Major Virginia Militia; was a prisoner in 1782, when and where taken not stated.

Creecy, John (N. C.) Lieutenant North Carolina Militia, 1780-1781.

Creger, Valentine (Md). Captain Maryland Militia, 1776.

Cremer, Jacob.—See **Cramer.**

Crenshaw, Arthur (N. C.). Ensign 2d North Carolina, ——; taken prisoner at Charleston, 12th May, 1780; exchanged 14th June, 1781; served to ——.

Cresap, Daniel (Md). 1st Lieutenant of Stephenson's Maryland and Virginia Rifle Regiment, 11th July, 1776; taken prisoner at Long Island 27th August, 1776; was a prisoner two years, when he escaped; did not rejoin the Army. (Died 1794.)

Cresap, Joseph (Md). 2d Lieutenant 1st Company Maryland Rifles, 21st June, 1775, to 1776. (Died 1827.)

Cresap, Michael (Md). Captain 1st Company Maryland Rifles, 21st June, 1775; died 18th October, 1775.

Cressey, Mark (Mass). 2d Lieutenant of Gerrish's Massachusetts Regiment, 19th May to December, 1775; 1st Lieutenant 26th Continental Infantry, 1st January to December, 1776. (Died 4th May, 1816.)

Cresley, James.—See **Crosley.**

Creswell, Samuel (Ga). Surgeon of a Georgia Regiment in 1780.

Crimshire, John Dutton (N. Y.). Paymaster 2d Continental Artillery, 30th April, 1777; resigned 1st August, 1779.

Cripps, Whitton (N. J.). Lieutenant-Colonel and Colonel New Jersey Militia, 1776-1779.

Crittenden, John (Va). 2d Lieutenant 15th Virginia, 5th June, 1777; Regiment designated 11th Virginia 14th September, 1778; transferred to 5th Virginia — May, 1779; 1st Lieutenant, 14th May, 1779; Captain Lieutenant, —, 1780; retired 12th February, 1781. (Died 1795.)

Crittenden, Nathaniel (Mass). Sergeant in Wigglesworth's Massachusetts Regiment, May to December, 1775; 2d Lieutenant 4th Continental Infantry, 1st January to 31st December, 1776. (Died 22d May, 1828.)

Croat, Lewis (N. Y.). Captain New York Militia, 1775.

Crocker, Elijah (Mass). Lieutenant 14th Massachusetts, 6th November, 1776; resigned 16th May, 1778.

Crocker, John (Conn). Surgeon of Wolcott's Connecticut State Regiment, December, 1775, to February, 1776; — of Chester's Connecticut State Regiment, 20th June to 25th December, 1776.

Crocker, John (Mass). Surgeon of Scammon's Massachusetts Regiment, May to December, 1775.

Crocker ,Joseph (Mass). Paymaster 3d Massachusetts, 1st January, 1777; Lieutenant, 16th September, 1778; Captain, 31st March, 1780; resigned 24th July, 1781. (Died 13th November, 1797.)

Crocker, Sampson (Mass). — See **Sampson.**

Crocker, Zacheus (Mass). Lieutenant in Lexington Alarm, April, 1775; 1st Lieutenant of Woodbridge's Massachusetts Regiment, May to December, 1775; served subsequently as Captain Massachusetts Militia.

Crockett, Anthony (Va). Lieutenant Virginia Militia, 1779-1783.

Crockett, Henry (Va). Lieutenant Virginia Militia in 1778.

Crockett, Joseph (Va). Captain 7th Virginia, 4th April, 1776; Regiment designated 5th Virginia, 14th September, 1778; Major 11th Virginia, 20th May, 1779; transferred to 5th Virginia 12th February, 1781; Lieutenant-Colonel, —, 1782, and served to close of war. (Died 7th November, 1829.)

Crockett, Joshua (N. H.). Captain New Hampshire Militia, 1776.

Croghan, William (Va). Captain 8th Virginia, 9th April, 1776; Brigade Inspector of Scott's Brigade, 7th April, 1778; Major 8th Virginia 16th May, 1778; transferred to 4th Virginia 14th September, 1778; taken prisoner at Charleston 12th May, 1780; on parole to close of war.

Crombie, James (N. H.). Private Company of Minute Men in April, 1775; 1st Lieutenant of Baldwin's Regiment New Hampshire Militia, 20th September to November, 1776; 1st Lieutenant 2d New Hampshire, 8th November, 1776; retired 1st September, 1778. ,

Cromwell, Richard (Md). Lieutenant and Captain Maryland Militia, 1776-1781. (Died 1802.)

Cromwell, Thomas (Md). 2d Lieutenant 4th Maryland, 15th January, 1777; 1st Lieutenant, 20th May, 1777; Captain, 20th July, 1779; resigned 30th October, 1779.

Cronin, Patrick (N. Y.). Sergeant in the New York Line in 1775-1776; Sergeant of Malcolm's Continental Regiment, 9th July, 1777; Ensign, 15th September, 1777; Regimental Quartermaster, 20th December, 1777; retired 23d April, 1779; served subsequently as Lieutenant and Captain New York Militia. ,

Cronkhite, James (N. Y.). Captain New York Militia; taken prisoner at West Chester, 24th December, 1779.

Crook, Joseph (Mass). Lieutenant 10th Massachusetts, 26th September, 1780; transferred to 6th Massachusetts, 1st January, 1783; transferred to 2d Massachusetts, 12th June, 1783, and served to 3d November, 1783.

Crooker, Elijah (Mass). Captain of Thomas' Massachusetts Regiment, May to December, 1775; Captain 23d Continental Infantry, 1st January to 31st December, 1776.

Crooker, John (Mass). Surgeon of Scammon's Massachusetts Regiment, 28th June to December, 1775.

Cropper, Charles (Va). Ensign 9th Virginia, 5th February, 1776, to ——.

Cropper, John (Va). Captain 9th Virginia, 5th February, 1776; Major 7th Virginia, 7th October, 1776; wounded at Brandywine, 11th September, 1777; Lieutenant-Colonel 11th Virginia, 26th October, 1777; transferred to 7th Virginia, 14th September, 1778; resigned 16th August, 1779; served subsequently as Colonel Virginia Militia, 1781, to close of war. (Died 15th January, 1821.)

Crosby, Ebenezer (Conn). Surgeon at General Washington's Headquarters, October, 1776; resigned 1st January, 1781. (Died 19th February, 1789.)

Crosby, Jesse (Pa). Sergeant in Proctor's Battalion Pennsylvania Artillery in 1776; 2d Lieutenant 4th Continental Artillery, 1st April, 1777; 1st Lieutenant, 11th March, 1779; Captain Lieutenant, 11th February, 1780; wounded at Green Springs, 6th July, 1781, and rendered no subsequent service. (Died — October, 1791.)

Crosby, John (Pa). Captain Pennsylvania Militia; taken prisoner at Brandywine, 11th September, 1777. (Died 1822.)

Crosby, Josiah (N. H.). Captain 3d New Hampshire, 23d April to December, 1775. (Died 1793.)

Crosby, Samuel (Mass). Surgeon 21st Continental Infantry, 1st January to 31st December, 1776; Surgeon Massachusetts Militia, 1777-1779.

Crosby, Stephen (Conn). Captain of Sage's Regiment Connecticut Militia, 20th June, 1776; killed 15th September, 1776, on the retreat from New York.

Crosher, John (Mass). 2d Lieutenant 3d Continental Artillery, 1st January, 1777; resigned 19th May, 1779.

Crosley, Jesse (Pa). —See **Crosby**.

Cross, Joseph (Md). Sergeant 2d Maryland, 11th February, 1777; 2d Lieutenant, 6th November, 1781; retained in Maryland Battalion, April, 1783, and served to 15th November, 1783.

Cross, William (N. Y.). Captain New York Militia, 1778.

Cross, William (Pa). 3d Lieutenant of Thompson's Pennsylvania Rifle Regiment, 25th June, 1775; 2d Lieutenant 1st Continental Infantry, 1st January, 1776; 1st Lieutenant, 10th August, 1776; 1st Lieutenant 4th Continental Dragoons, 1st January, 1777; Captain 4th Pennsylvania, 3d June, 1777; resigned 14th May, 1779.

Crossman, Robert (Mass). Captain Massachusetts Militia, 1776.

Crossman, William (Mass). 1st Lieutenant 15th Massachusetts, 1st January, 1777; Captain, 20th June, 1779; cashiered 7th November, 1779.

Crothers, Anthony (Pa). Regimental Quartermaster of Patten's Continental Regiment, 16th February, 1777, to ——.

Crow, George (Pa). Ensign 5th Pennsylvania, 1st January, 1777; resigned 24th December, 1777.

Crow, Samuel (N. J.). Captain, Major and Lieutenant-Colonel New Jersey Militia, 1777-1780. (Died 1801.)

Crowle, Jacob (Pa). Captain of Hallet's Battalion Pennsylvania Militia, ——; taken prisoner at Long Island, 27th August, 1776.

Crowley, Florence (Mass). Sergeant in Knox's Regiment Continental Artillery, 27th September, 1775; 2d Lieutenant 3d Continental Artillery, 1st January, 1777; wounded at Brandywine, 11th September, 1777; 1st Lieutenant, 1st October, 1778, and served to June, 1783. (Died 1798.)

Croxall, Charles (Pa). 1st Lieutenant of Hartley's Continental Regiment, 25th May, 1777; taken prisoner at Brandywine, 11th September, 1777; exchanged 23d November, 1780, and did not re-enter service.

Crozier, John (Pa). 2d Lieutenant 3d Continental Artillery, 1st January, 1777; resigned 19th May, 1779. (Died 26th April, 1823.)

Cruise, Walter (Pa). Corporal of Thompson's Pennsylvania Rifle Regiment, 1775, and in 1st Continental Infantry in 1776; 2d Lieutenant 1st Continental Infantry, July, 1776; taken prisoner near Boston, 29th July, 1775; was a prisoner 17 months; Captain 6th Pennsylvania, 15th February, 1777; retired 21st June, 1778.

Cruit, —— (——). Lieutenant ——; killed at Waxhaw, 29th May, 1780.

Crump, Abner (Va).) Captain 1st Virginia State Regiment, 10th May, 1777; dismissed 19th October, 1777.

Crump, Goodrich (Va). 1st Lieutenant 1st Virginia, 18th September, 1775; Captain, 5th June, 1776; cashiered 19th October, 1777.

Crump, Richard (Va). Captain Virginia Artillery, 1780 and 1781.

Crutcher, Anthony (N. C.). Ensign 5th North Carolina, 27th February,

1780; Lieutenant, 18th May, 1781; transferred to 2d North Carolina, 6th February, 1782; served to close of war.

Crutchers, Henry (N. C.). Ensign 5th North Carolina, 20th August, 1777, to ——.

Crute, John (Va). 1st Lieutenant 4th Virginia, 30th November, 1779; Captain Lieutenant, ——, 1780; taken prisoner at Charleston, 12th May, 1780, and was a prisoner on parole to 1st May, 1783.

Crygier, Simon (N. Y.). Ensign 4th New York, 21st November, 1776; cashiered 6th August, 1777.

Cudney, John (N. Y.). Lieutenant of Drake's Regiment New York Militia; taken prisoner; when and where, not stated.

Cudworth, Nathaniel (Mass). Captain of a company of Minute Men at Concord, 19th April, 1775; Major of Brewer's Massachusetts Regiment, 19th May to December, 1775; Major 25th Continental Infantry, 1st January to 31st December, 1776. (Died 21st January, 1826.)

Culbertson, James (Va). 2d Lieutenant 9th Virginia, 16th March, 1776; Captain Lieutenant, 7th November, 1776; transferred to 1st Virginia, 14th September, 1778; Captain, 12th May, 1779; transferred to 5th Virginia, 12th February, 1781, and served to close of war.

Culbertson, John (Pa). Major Pennsylvania Militia, 1776-1780. (Died 1794)

Culbertson, Joseph (Pa). Ensign 6th Pennsylvania Battalion, 9th January, 1776; killed and scalped at Isle aux Noix, 24th June, 1776.

Culbertson, Robert (Pa). Lieutenant-Colonel Pennsylvania Militia, 1777. (Died 1801.)

Culbertson, Samuel (Md). Captain of Montgomery's Pennsylvania Battalion of the Flying Camp, July, 1776; taken prisoner at Fort Washington, 16th November, 1776; exchanged 2d November, 1780, and did not re-enter service.

Culbertson, Samuel (Pa). Colonel Pennsylvania Militia, 1777-1782. (Died 1817.)

Culbertson, Samuel (Va). Surgeon 12th Virginia, — March, 1777; superseded 21st April, 1778.

Culp, Daniel (Va). 1st Lieutenant 8th Virginia, 9th February, 1776; resigned 20th May, 1777.

Culpeper, —— (S. C.). Lieutenant South Carolina State Troops; wounded at Eutaw Springs, 8th September, 1781.

Culver, Daniel (Vt). Captain Vermont Militia, 1777.

Culver, Samuel (Conn). Ensign of Hooker's Regiment Connecticut Militia; taken prisoner, when and where not stated. A soldier of that name from Connecticut was taken prisoner at Fort Washington, 16th November, 1776.

Cumming, John Noble (N. J). 1st Lieutenant 2d New Jersey, 29th November, 1775; Captain, 30th November, 1776; Major 1st New Jersey, 16th April, 1780; Lieutenant-Colonel 2d New Jersey, 29th December, 1781; Lieutenant-Colonel Commandant, 11th February, 1783; retained in New Jersey Battalion, April, 1783, and served to 13th November, 1783.

Cummings, John (Mass). Ensign of Prescott's Massachusetts Regiment, May to December, 1775. (Died 1808)

Cummings, John (N. H.). 2d Lieutenant in Lexington Alarm, April, 1775.

Cummings, Jotham (N. H.). 2d Lieutenant of Bedel's Regiment New Hampshire Rangers, 6th July to December, 1775.

Cummings, Thomas (Mass). 2d Lieutenant of Prescott's Massachusetts Regiment, May to December, 1775; 1st Lieutenant 7th Contineneтal Infantry, 1st January, 1776; cashiered 23d February, 1776.

Cummings, Thomas (Mass). 2d Lieutenant 10th Massachusetts, 6th November, 1776; 1st Lieutenant, 1st November, 1777; resigned 13th October, 1778. (Died 24th October, 1825.)

Cummins, Alexander (Va). 2d Lieutenant 1st Virginia, 15th December, 1775; 1st Lieutenant, 11th November, 1776; resigned 13th June, 1778.

Cumpston, Edward (Mass). 2d Lieutenant of Paterson's Massachusetts Regiment, 3d May to December, 1775; 1st Lieutenant 15th Continental Infantry, 1st January, 1776; Adjutant 3d Massachusetts, 1st January, 1777; Captain, 11th November, 1777; resigned 24th March, 1780.

Cumpston, John (Mass). Served as a volunteer, and was taken prisoner at Quebec, 31st December, 1775; 1st Lieutenant 3d Continental Artillery, 1st January, 1777; Captain Lieutenant, 12th September, 1777; resigned 4th March, 1779. (Name also spelled Compston and Crumpton.)

Cuningham, Allen (Pa). 1st Lieutenant Montgomery's Pennsylvania Battalion of the Flying Camp, June to December, 1776; Captain Pennsylvania Militia, 1777-1778. (Died 15th May, 1801.)

Cunningham, Arthur (S. C.) Lieutenant South Carolina Militia, 1776

Cunningham, Cornelius.—See **Conyngham.**

Cunningham, Henry (N. Y.). Sergeant of Lamb's Company New York Artillery, 1775 and 1776; Sergeant 2d Continental Artillery, 3d January, 1777; Sergeant-Major, 1st May, 1778; 2d Lieutenant, 20th May, 1779; 1st Lieutenant, 8th April, 1782; Regimental Quartermaster, —December, 1782; transferred to Corps of Artillery, 17th June, 1783, and served to 20th June, 1784.

Cunningham, James (Pa). Colonel 1st Pennsylvania Battalion of the Flying Camp, July to December, 1776.

Cunningham, John (Ga). Was a Captain in 2d Georgia in 1777, and in 1782 was called Major.

Cunningham, John (Pa). 1st Lieutenant 11th Pennsylvania, 30th September, 1776; taken prisoner at Fort Washington, 16th November, 1776; resigned 21st April, 1777.

Cunningham, John (Va). Ensign 7th Virginia, 8th May, 1776, to ——.

Cunningham, Peter (Pa). Ensign 3d Pennsylvania, 17th June, 1779; retired 1st January, 1783.

Cunningham, Robert (Va). 3d Lieutenant 1st Continental Artillery, 25th September, 1777, to ——.

Cunningham, Samuel (Pa). 1st Lieutenant 11th Pennsylvania, 13th November, 1776; resigned 10th July, 1777.

Cunningham, William (Pa). Ensign of Montgomery's Pennsylvania Battalion of the Flying Camp, July to December, 1776.

Cunningham, William (Va), 1st Lieutenant 1st Virginia, 16th September, 1775; Captain, 22d April, 1776; retired 14th September, 1778.

Cunningham, William (Va). Ensign 7th Virginia, 8th May, 1776; resigned — September, 1776.

Curd, John (Va). Captain Virginia Militia, 1778-1781.

Curd, Joseph (Va). 1st Lieutenant 6th Virginia, 24th February, 1776, to ——.

Currell, Nicholas (Va). Sergeant 5th Virginia, 5th February, 1776; Ensign, 10th December, 1776; 2d Lieutenant, 12th August, 1776; resigned 15th September, 1778.

Currie, Andrew (Pa). Ensign of Montgomery's Pennsylvania Battalion of the Flying Camp; taken prisoner at Fort Washington, 16th November, 1776.

Currie, David (Pa). Ensign of Montgomery's Penneylvania Battalion of the Flying Camp; taken prisoner at Fort Washington, 16th November, 1776.

Currie, Ross (Pa). 2d Lieutenant 2d Pennsylvania Battalion, 5th January, 1776; taken prisoner at Three Rivers, 8th June, 1776; never rejoined regiment.

Currie, William (Pa). Surgeon's Mate Pennsylvania Musket Battalion Militia, 6th April, 1776; resigned 27th September, 1776. (Died ——, 1829.)

Currier, Ezra (N. H.). Captain New Hampshire Militia, 1777-1778.

Currier, John (Mass). Captain in Lexington Alarm, April, 1775; Captain of Frye's Massachusetts Regiment, April to December, 1775. (Died 1806.)

Curry.—See also **Currie,** as name is spelled both ways.

Curry, James (Va). 2d Lieutenant 8th Virginia, December, 1776; 1st Lieutenant, 24th June, 1777; transferred to 4th Virginia, 14th September, 1778; Captain, 23d September, 1779; taken prisoner at Charleston, 12th May, 1780; prisoner on parole to close of war. (Died 5th July, 1834.)

Curry, John (Mass). Ensign 10th Massachusetts, 10th August, 1777; Lieutenant, — March, 1779, and served to ——.

Curry, Joseph (N. J.). Hospital Steward in Hospital Department, 25th August, 1777; Assistant Commissary in Hospital Department, 31st December, 1778, to 23d July, 1780.

Curtis.—See also **Curtiss.**

Curtis, Benjamin (N. Y.). Surgeon 1st New York, 1st March, 1776; resigned 3d November, 1776; (Died 1784.)

Curtis, Bethuel (R. I.). 2d Lieutenant 2d Rhode Island, 11th February, 1777; resigned 3d May, 1778.

Curtis, Eleazer (Conn). Captain 4th Connecticut, 1st May to December, 1775; Major of Enos' Regiment Connecticut Militia in 1778.

Curtis, Eliphalet (Conn). 2d Lieutenant of Mott's Connecticut State Regiment, June to December, 1776.

Curtis, Giles (Conn). Ensign 6th Connecticut, 1st January, 1777; 2d Lieutenant, 17th October, 1777; 1st Lieutenant, 10th May, 1780; transferred to 4th Connecticut, 1st January, 1781; transferred to 2d Connecticut, 1st January, 1783, and served to 3d June, 1783.

Curtis, Israel (Conn). Captain of Bedel's New Hampshire Regiment, June to December, 1775; Major of Elmore's Continental Regiment, April, 1776; died 25th July, 1776.

Curtis, Jacob (Mass). Ensign of Scammon's Massachusetts Regiment, May to December, 1775.

Curtis, Jesse (Conn). Corporal in the Lexington Alarm, April, 1775; 1st Lieutenant 1st Connecticut, 1st May to 20th December, 1775; Captain Connecticut Militia, 1776-1777.

Curtis, John (Conn). Lieutenant Connecticut Light Horse, 1779-1780. (Died 1825.)

Curtis, John (N. C.). Lieutenant 5th North Carolina, 1st October, 1776, to ——.

Curtis, Joshua (N. C.). Ensign 4th North Carolina, 1st July, 1777; resigned 21st February, 1778.

Curtis, Marmaduke (N. J.). 1st Lieutenant 3d New Jersey, 29th November, 1776; resigned 28th April, 1778.

Curtis, Nathan (Conn). Captain Connecticut Militia, 1776-1777.

Curtis, Nehemiah (Mass). Captain of Mitchell's Regiment, Massachusetts Militia on the Magaduce Expedition, July to September, 1779. (Died 26th September, 1816.)

Curtis, Peter (Conn). 1st Lieutenant 2d Connecticut, 1st May to 18th December, 1775.

Curtis, Reuben (N. C.). Ensign 2d North Carolina in 1777.

Curtis, Thomas (Mass). 2d Lieutenant of Glover's Massachusetts Regiment, May to December, 1775; 2d Lieutenant 14th Continental Infantry, 1st January, 1776, to ——.

Curtis, Thomas (N. C.). Ensign 8th North Carolina, 28th November, 1776, to ——.

Curtis, William (Mass). 2d Lieutenant 25th Continental Infantry, 1st January to 31st December, 1776; 1st Lieu-

tenant 7th Massachusetts, 1st January, 1777; Captain, — April, 1780; resigned 2d September, 1780. (Died 11th October, 1821.)

Curtis, William (Mass). Captain of Glover's Regiment, May to December, 1775; Captain 14th Continental Infantry, 1st January to 31st December, 1776; Major of Henley's Continental Regiment, 1st January, 1777; resigned 20th May, 1778. (Name also spelled Courtis.)

Curtiss.—(See **Curtis**, as name is spelled both ways.)

Curtiss, Eli (Conn). Sergeant-Major 8th Connecticut, 10th April, 1777; Ensign, 17th November, 1777; 2d Lieutenand, 11th April, 1778; resigned 4th December, 1779. (Died 13th December, 1821.)

Curtiss, Samuel (Mass). Captain in Lexington Alarm, April, 1775; Captain of Learned's Massachusetts Regiment, May to December, 1775; Captain 3d Continental Infantry, 1st January to 31st December, 1776. (Died 31st March, 1822.)

Cushing, Charles (Mass.) Captain of Heath's Massachusetts Regiment, May to December, 1775; Captain 24th Continental Infantry, 1st January to 31st December, 1776. (Died 25th November, 1809.)

Cushing, David (Mass). Lieutenant-Colonel and Colonel Massachusetts Militia, 1776-1781. (Died 1800.)

Cushing, Job (Mass). Captain in Lexington Alarm, April, 1775; Captain of Heath's Massachusetts Regiment, May to December, 1775; Captain 24th Continental Infantry, 1st January to 31st December, 1776; Colonel Massachusetts Militia in 1777. (Died 1808.)

Cushing, Joseph (Mass). Brigadier-General Massachusetts Militia in 1777.

Cushing, Lemuel (Mass). Surgeon of Thomas' Massachusetts Regiment, May to December, 1775; Surgeon 23d Continental Infantry, 1st January to 31st December, 1776.

Cushing, Nathaniel (Mass). 1st Lieutenant of Brewer's Massachusetts Regiment, 10th May to December, 1775; 1st Lieutenant 6th Continental Infantry, 1st January to 31st December, 1776; Captain 1st Massachusetts, 1st January, 1777; Brigade-Major, 1st December, 1781, to April, 1782; Brevet Major, 30th September, 1783; served to close of war. (Died — August, 1814.)

Cushing, Pyam (Mass). Sergeant-Major 10th Massachusetts, 24th February, 1777; Ensign, 1st November, 1777; died 5th January, 1778.

Cushing, Seth (Mass). Major Massachusetts Militia, 1778-1780.

Cushing, Thomas Humphrey (Mass). Sergeant 6th Continental Infantry, January to December, 1776; 2d Lieutenant 1st Massachusetts, 1st January, 1777; 1st Lieutenant, 12th January, 1778; taken prisoner at ——, 14th May, 1781; exchanged ——; Brevet Captain, 30th September, 1783; retained in Jackson's Continental Regiment, November, 1783, and served to 20th June, 1784; Captain 2d Infantry United States Army, 4th March, 1791; assigned to 2d Sub Legion, 4th September, 1792; Major 1st Sub Legion, 3d March, 1793; Inspector of the Army, 27th February, 1797, to 22d May, 1798; Lieutenant-Colonel 2d United States Infantry, 1st April, 1802; Adjutant and Inspector-General, 26th March, 1802, to 9th May, 1807; Colonel 2d United States Infantry, 7th September, 1805; Brigadier-General United States Army, 2d July, 1812; honorably discharged, 15th June, 1815. (Died 19th October, 1822.)

Cushing, William (Mass). Private in Lexington Alarm, April, 1775; Sergeant in Thomas' Massachusetts Regiment, May to December, 1775; Lieutenant 14th Massachusetts, 6th November, 1776; wounded at Saratoga, 7th October, 1777; resigned 5th February, 1779.

Cushman, Solomon (Vt). Captain of Bedel's Regiment Vermont Militia, 15th December, 1777, to 1st April, 1779.

Custis, John Parke (Va). Captain Virginia Militia Volunteers; Aide-de-Camp to General Washington at Yorktown, October, 1781.

Custis, Thomas (Va). 2d Lieutenant 9th Virginia, 4th July, 1776; 1st Lieutenant, 22d July, 1776; retired 14th September, 1778.

Cuthbert, Alexander D. (Ga). Captain 3d Georgia, 2d June, 1777; taken prisoner at Briar Creek, 3d March, 1779, and served to ——

Cuthbert, Daniel (Ga).. 2d Lieutenant 1st Georgia, 7th January, 1776; 1st Lieutenant ——; Captain, ——; taken prisoner at Charleston, 12th May, 1780.

Cutler, Joseph (N. Y.). Ensign New York Militia; wounded near White Plains, 17th May, 1782.

Cutler, Manasah (Mass). Chaplain of Fransis' Massachusetts Regiment of Militia, 2d September, 1776; Chaplain 11th Massachusetts, 1st January, 1777; resigned 30th June, 1779. (Died 28th July, 1823.)

Cutter, Ammi Ruhameh (N. H.). Physician General of Hospital Eastern Department, 11th April, 1777; resigned 9th March, 1778. (Died 8th December, 1819.)

Cutter, Benoni (Conn). Private in the Lexington Alarm in April, 1775; 1st Lieutenant 3d Connecticut, 1st May to 14th December, 1775; Captain of Ward's Connecticut State Regiment, ment, 14th May, 1776, to 10th May, 1777.

Cutter, Samuel (Mass). 2d Lieutenant of Gardner's Massachusetts Regiment, May to December, 1775; 2d Lieutenant 27th Continental Infantry, 1st January to 31st December, 1776.

Cutting, John Brown (N. Y.). Surgeon's Mate Hospital Department in 1776; Apothecary of Hospital Eastern Department, 10th July, 1777, to 1779, and of the Middle Department, to 10th June, 1780. (Died 3d February, 1831.)

Cutting, Thomas (Conn). Lieutenant of Gay's Connecticut State Regiment, 20th June, 1776; killed on the retreat from New York, 15th September, 1776.

Cutts, Thomas (Mass). 1st Lieutenant of Scammon's Massachusetts Regiment, May to December, 1775; Captain Massachusetts Militia, 1776-1779.

Cuyler, Abraham (N. Y.). Major, Lieutenant-Colonel and Colonel New York Militia, 1775-1781.

Cuyler, Henry (Ga). Captain Georgia Militia, 1778-1780.

Cuyler, Jacob (N. Y.). Deputy Commissary-General of Purchases, 18th June, 1777, and served to July, 1782.

D.

Dabney, Charles (Va). Major 3d Virginia, 13th February, 1776; Lieutenant-Colonel 2d Virginia, 16th February, 1778; retired 30th September, 1778; Colonel Virginia State Regiment, 1778 to 1781.

Dade, Baldwin (Va). Cadet 3d Continental Dragoons' 10th May, 1778, to ——.

Dade, Francis (Va). Cornet 3d Continental Dragoons, 1st May, 1778; taken prisoner at Tappan, 28th September, 1778; Lieutenant, ——, 1779; Captain, ——, 1781; retired 9th November, 1782. (Died 1791.)

Dade, Robert (Va). 2d Lieutenant 3d Virginia, 6th February, 1776; died — August, 1776.

Daggett, ——. —See also **Dogett**; name is spelled both ways. ·

Daggett, Ebenezer (Conn). Ensign 7th Connecticut, 20th June, 1779; transferred to 1st Connecticut, 1st January, 1781; died 20th November, 1781.

Daggett, Henry (Conn). Private 7th Connecticut, 1st May, 1777; Regimental Quartermaster 13th October, 1777; 2d Lieutenant, 24th April, 1778; 1st Lieutenant, 15th November, 1778; transferred to 2d Connecticut, 1st January, 1783, and served to 3d June, 1783.

Daley, Daniel (S. C.) Lieutenant 1st South Carolina; taken prisoner at Briar Creek, 3d March, 1779.

Daley, Joshua (N. C.). 1st Lieutenant 7th North Carolina, 19th December, 1776; Captain, 12th October, 1777; retired 1st June, 1778.

Dallam, Richard (Pa). Deputy Paymaster-General of the Flying Camp, 17th July to December, 1776.

Dallas, Archibald (N. J.). 2d Lieutenant 1st New Jersey, 9th December, 1775; Captain of Spencer's Continental Regiment, 12th February, 1777; wounded and taken prisoner, 5th September, 1777, in Delaware, and died 6th September, 1777.

Dallas, John (Ga). Lieutenant of a Georgia Regiment in 1779.

Dalling, William (Mass). 2d Lieutenant of Read's Massachusetts Regiment, May to December, 1775.

Dalton, Joseph (N. J.). Captain Lieutenant 3d Continental Artillery, 1st January, 1777; resigned 1st July, 1777.

Dalton, Thomas Valentine (Va). Lieutenant Virginia Militia, 1780-1781.

Dames, John (Md). Captain 4th Battalion Maryland Flying Camp, July to December, 1776.

Dammon, Ebenezer (Mass). 1st Lieutenant of Bridge's Massachusetts Regiment, May to December, 1775.

Dan, David (N. Y.). 1st Lieutenant 4th New York, 28th June, 1775, to March, 1776; served subsequently as Captain of Thomas' New York Militia Regiment. (Name aslo spelled Don.)

Dana, Anderson (Conn). Lieutenant Connecticut Militia; killed at Wyoming, 3d July, 1778.

Dana, Benjamin (Mass). Sergeant 6th Continental Infantry, 11th April to 31st December, 1776; Ensign 13th Massachusetts, 13th November, 1776; 2d Lieutenant, 1st January, 1777; 1st Lieutenant, 1st February, 1778; retired 1st January, 1781. (Died 3d April, 1836.)

Dana, James (Conn). 1st Lieutenant 3d Connecticut, 1st May to 16th December, 1775; Captain of Ward's Connecticut State Regiment, 14th May, 1776, to May, 1777. (Died 1817.)

Dana, William (Mass). Sergeant in Lexington Alarm, April, 1775; Lieutenant of Gridley's Regiment Massachusetts Artillery, 25th April, 1775; Captain of Knox's Regiment Continental Artillery, 16th December, 1775, to December, 1776. (Died 1809.)

Dance, Etheldred (N. C.). Ensign — North Carolina Regiment in 1781. (Died 4th February, 1828.)

Dandridge, Alexander (Va). Lieutenant Virginia Company of Dragoons, 17th June, 1776; Captain 1st Continental Dragoons, 15th March, 1777; resigned 14th April, 1780.

Dandridge, John (Va). Captain 1st Continental Artillery, 7th February, 1777; taken prisoner at Charleston, 12th May, 1780; exchanged July, 1781; served to June, 1783.

Dandridge, Robert A. (Va). 2d Lieutenant 1st Continental Artillery, 30th October, 1777; 1st Lieutenant, 24th May, 1779, and served to June, 1783. (Died 1799.)

Dandridge, William (Va). Major Virginia Militia, 1777-1778.

Dane, Throphilus (N. H.) Colonel New Hampshire Militia, 1779.

Danforth, Asa (Mass). Sergeant in Lexington Alarm ,April, 1775; 1st Lieutenant of Learned's Massachusetts Regiment, May to December ,1775; Captain 3d Continental Infantry, 1st January to 31st December, 1776; served subsequently as Captain Massachusetts Militia.

Danforth, Eliakim (Mass). Captain 6th Massachusetts, 1st January, 1777; resigned 1st March, 1779.

Danforth, Elijah (Mass). 1st Lieutenant of Bridge's Massachusetts Regiment, May to December, 1775; Captain 6th Massachusetts, 1st January, 1777; retired 1st March, 1779.

Danforth, Jonathan (Mass). Captain of Brewer's Massachusetts Regiment, May to December, 1775; Captain 6th Continental Infantry, 1st January to December, 1776.

Danforth, Joshua (Mass). Corporal 12th Massachusetts, 15th May, 1777; Sergeant, 1st January, 1778; Ensign, 26th November, 1779; Lieutenant, 28th July, 1780; transferred to 2d Massachusetts, 1st January, 1781, and served to 3d June, 1783. (Died 3d January, 1837.)

Danforth, Samuel (Mass). Lieutenant 4th Massachusets, 1st January, 1777; resigned 20th April, 1779.

Dangerfield, William (Va). Colonel 7th Virginia, 29th February, 1776; resigned 13th August, 1776.

Daniel, Aaron (S. C.). Ensign South Carolina Militia in 1776.

Daniel, James (N. C.). Lieutenant 9th North Carolina, 28th November, 1776, to ——.

Daniel, John (Va). Ensign 8th Virginia, 9th February, 1776; resigned 5th August, 1777.

Daniel, Joseph (S. C.). Captain South Carolina Militia, 1776-1777.

Daniel, Stephen (N. C.). Ensign 1st North Carolina, 4th January, 1776, resigned 3d June, 1776.

Daniels, Japhet (Mass). 1st Lieutenant of Read's Massachusetts Regiment, May to December, 1775; 1st Lieutenant 13th Continental Infantry, 1st January to 31st December, 1776; Captain 6th Massachusetts, 1st January, 1777, and served to 3d June, 1783. (Died ——, 1806.)

Danielson, Nathaniel (Mass). Major of Brewer's Massachusetts Regiment, May to December, 1775.

Danielson, Timothy (Mass). Colonel Massachusets Regiment, 19th May to December, 1775; Brigadier-General and Major-General Massachusetts Militia, 1776 to 1782. (Died 19th September, 1791.)

Danielson, William (Conn). Colonel Connecticut Militia, 1776-1779.

Dannell, Joseph (S. C.). Captain South Carolina Militia, 1776-1778.

d'Antignac, Louis Jean Baptist, Baron (——). Captain Continental Artillery, 1st May, 1777, and served to — September, 1777.

Darby, Ephraim (N. J.). Private 4th New Jersey, 1st December, 1776; Regimental Quartermaster, 17th February, 1777; Lieutenant Regimental Quartermaster 3d New Jersey, 12th November, 1777; transferred to 1st New Jersey, 1st January, 1781; retired 1st September, 1782.

Darby, Henry (Del). Captain Delaware Regiment, 17th January to December, 1776.

Darby, Nathaniel (Va). Ensign 9th Virginia, 14th August, 1776; 2d Lieutenant, 7th March, 1777; taken prisoner at Germantown, 4th October, 1777; after exchange he joined the 5th Virginia; served to close of war.

Darby, Samuel (Mass). Captain of Scammon's Massachusetts Regiment, April to December, 1775; Captain 7th Continental Infantry, 1st January to 31st December, 1776; Captain 2d Massachusetts, 1st January, 1777; Major 7th Massachusetts, 29th September, 1778; transferred to 8th Massachusetts, 1st January, 1783, and served to 3d June, 1783. (Died 9th February, 1807.)

Darcy.—See also **Dorsey**, as name is spelled both ways.

Darcy, George (Mass). Lieutenant of Cady's Massachusetts Battalion on the Expedition to Canada, January to June, 1776.

Darcy, William (Ga). 2d Lieutenant of Captain Bickham's Company Georgia Militia, 15th August, 1781, to 15th February, 1782; Major Georgia Militia, 1782 and 1783.

Darcy, William (Ga). Major Georgia Militia, 1782.

Dare, David (N. J.). Sergeant 3d New Jersey, 7th February, 1776; Ensign, 29th November, 1776; omitted October, 1777.

Daring, Henry (Va). Ensign of a Virginia State Regiment for the war.

Darke, William (Va) Captain, 8th Virginia, 9th February, 1776; Major, 4th January, 1777; wounded and taken prisoner at Germantown, 4th October, 1777; exchanged 1st November, 1780; Lieutenant-Colonel 4th Virginia, 12th February, 1781, to rank from 29th November, 1777; retired 1st January, 1783; Lieutenant-Colonel Kentucky Militia, 1791, at St. Clair's defeat. (Died 20th November, 1801.)

Darling, Andrew (Va). 2d Lieutenant 8th Virginia, 4th March, 1776, to ——.

Darlington, Robert (Pa). Lieutenant of Watt's Pennsylvania Battalion of the Flying Camp, July, 1776; wounded and taken prisoner at Fort Washington, 16th November, 1776; exchanged 14th May, 1781, and did not return to army.

Darnall, Henry (N. C.). Lieutenant and Adjutant 5th North Carolina, 15th April, 1776; Captain, 1st October, 1776; retired 1st June, 1778.

Darragh, Charles (Pa). Ensign 2d Pennsylvania, 1st January, 1777; 2d Lieutenant, April, 1777; retired 1st July, 1778.

Darragh, Daniel (Pa). Sergeant Pennsylvania Battalion of the Flying Camp, July to December, 1776; Ensign 9th Pennsylvania, 7th December, 1776; 2d Lieutenant, 5th August, 1777; retired 1st July, 1778.

Darragh, Henry (Pa). Lieutenant Pennsylvania Battalion of the Flying Camp, July to December, 1776.

Darrow, Christopher (Conn). 1st Lieutenant 6th Connecticut, 1st May to 10th December, 1775; Captain 10th Continental Infantry, 1st January to 31st December, 1776; Captain 1st Connecticut, 1st January, 1777; Major, 15th April, 1778; resigned 27th August, 1780. (Died 1814.)

Dart, Joseph Sanford (S. C.). Deputy Clothier-General, 12th December, 1777, to ——; was Paymaster 1st South Carolina in 1780.

Darville, William (Va). Sergeant 2d Continental Artillery, 20th December, 1776; 2d Lieutenant, 30th November, 1777; resigned 10th November, 1778.

Dashiel, William Augustus (Md). Surgeon's Mate of Smallwood's Maryland Regiment, March to December, 1776; Surgeon Hospital Department, 1st June, 1778. Died 5th December, 1780.

Daugherty, Michael (Md). 2d Lieutenant 6th Maryland, 10th December, 1776; 1st Lieutenant, 12th November, 1777; cashiered 14th April, 1779; name also spelled Dougherty.

Davenport, Hezekiah (Conn). Lieutenant Connecticut Militia, ——; killed at Ridgefield, 27th April, 1777.

Davenport, Joseph (Pa). 1st Lieutenant 3d Pennsylvania Battalion, 6th January, 1776; Captain 23d March, 1776; wounded and taken prisoner at Fort Washington, 16th November, 1776.

Davenport, Opie (Va). Lieutenant of a Virginia State Regiment, 1779 to 1782.

Davenport, Thomas (Ga). Lieutenant 2d Georgia, ——, appears on roll for August, 1778.

Davenport, William (Va). Ensign 4th Virginia, 1st April, 1776, 2d Lieutenant, 28th September, 1776; retired 30th September, 1778. (Died 1832.)

Daves, John (N. C.). Quartermaster 2d North Carolina, 7th June, 1776; Ensign, 30th September, 1776; 1st Lieutenant, 4th October, 1777; wounded at Stony Point, 16th July, 1779; taken prisoner at Charleston, 12th May, 1780; exchanged June, 1781; transferred to 3d North Carolina, 1st January, 1781; Captain, 8th September, 1781; retired 1st January, 1783. (Died 12th October, 1804.)

Daves, John (N. C.). Ensign 10th North Carolina, 6th May, 1781, to ——.

David, Ebenezer (R. I.). Chaplain 9th Continental Infantry, 1st January to 31st December, 1776; Chaplain 2d Rhode Island, 10th March, 1777; omitted February, 1778. Name also spelled Davis.

Davidson, George (N. C.). Captain 1st North Carolina, 1st September, 1775; resigned 5th February, 1777.

Davidson, James (N. Y.). Regimental Quartermaster, 1st Canadian (Livingston's) Regiment, 18th March, 1777; cashiered 27th July, 1778.

Davidson, James (Pa). Surgeon 5th Pennsylvania, 5th April, 1777; retired 1st January, 1783. (Died 26th June, 1825.)

Davidson, John (Md). 2d Lieutenant of Allen's Independent Maryland Company, 14th January, 1776; Captain 2d Maryland, 10th December, 1776; Major 5th Maryland, 12th January, 1781; retired 1st January, 1783.

Davidson, Joshua (Pa). Ensign 8th Pennsylvania, 19th April, 1779, and served to ——.

Davidson, Thomas (Mass). Lieutenant 15th Massachusetts, 1st January, 1777; retired 23d April, 1779.

Davidson, Thomas (N. C.). Lieutenant North Carolina Militia, 1780-1781.

Davidson, William (Pa). 1st Lieutenant 3d Pennsylvania Battalion, 6th January, 1776; taken prisoner at Fort Washington, 16th November, 1776; exchanged 26th August, 1778.

Davidson, William Lee (N. C.). Major 4th North Carolina, 15th April, 1776; Lieutenant- Colonel 5th North Carolina, 4th October, 1777; transferred to

3d North Carolina, 1st June, 1778; transferred to 1st North Carolina, 9th June, 1779; served also as Brigadier-General North Carolina Militia, ——; killed at Cowan's Ford, 1st February, 1781.

Davie, Peter (Va). Quartermaster, 14th Virginia, 22d May, 1777; resigned 31st October, 1778.

Davie, William Richardson (N. C.). Entered the army in 1776 as a volunteer; Lieutenant of Dragoons Pulaski Legion, 5th April, 1779; Captain, — May, 1779; wounded at Stono Ferry, 20th June, 1779; Colonel of North Carolina Cavalry State Troops, 5th September, 1780, and served to close of war; Brigadier-General United States Army, 19th July, 1798; honorably discharged 15th June, 1800. (Died 18th November, 1820.)

Davies, William (Va). Captain 1st Virginia, 30th September, 1775; Deputy Muster-Master-General of the Flying Camp, 7th to 15th October, 1776; taken prisoner at Fort Washington 16th November, 1776; Major 7th Virginia, 22d March, 1777; Lieutenant-Colonel 5th Virginia, 21st February, 1777; Lieutenant-Colonel Commandant 14th Virginia, 6th April, 1778; Colonel, 20th March, 1778; Regiment designated 10th Virginia, 14th September, 1778; transferred to 1st Virginia, 12th February, 1781, and served to close of war.

Davis, Aaron (Mass). Captain Massachusetts Militia, 1775; Colonel of same in 1776. (Died 1777.)

Davis, Abner (Pa). 3d Lieutenant 2d Battalion of Miles' Pennsylvania Rifle Regiment, 28th March, 1776; resigned 19th October, 1776.

Davis, Abraham (N. C.). Adjutant 7th North Carolina, 22d December, 1776; resigned 21st November, 1777. (Name also spelled Dawes.)

Davis, Benjamin (N. H.). Ensign 2d Continental Infantry, 1st January to 31st December, 1776.

Davis, Benjamin (Pa). 1st Lieutenant of Montgomery's Pennsylvania Battalion of the Flying Camp, July, 1776; taken prisoner at Fort Washington, 16th November, 1776; released 8th December, 1780.

Davis, Benjamin (Pa). 1st Lieutenant 1st Pennsylvania Battalion, 27th October, 1775; Captain, 5th January, 1776; resigned 1st January, 1777.

Davis, David (S. C.). Lieutenant South Carolina Militia in 1776.

Davis, Ebenezer (Mass). Private in Company of Minute Men at Lexington and Concord, 19th April, 1775; Sergeant in Frye's Massachusetts Regiment, May to December, 1775; Sergeant in 9th Continental Infantry, January to December, 1776; Sergeant 9th Massachusetts, 25th March, 1777; Ensign, 2d March, 1779; Brigade Quartermaster, 15th March, 1782, to January, 1783; transferred to 8th Massachusetts, 15th February, 1781; transferred to 3d Massachusetts, 7th July, 1782; Lieutenant, 15th March, 1783, and served to 3d June, 1783. (Died 14th November, 1799.)

Davis, Harman (S. C.). 1st Lieutenant 4th South Carolina (Artillery), — May, 1776; Captain, 29th May, 1777; wounded at Savannah 9th October, 1779; taken prisoner at Charleston 12th May, 1780; prisoner on parole to close of war; Brevet Major, 30th September, 1783.

Davis, Hezekiah (Pa). Lieutenant of Montgomery's Pennsylvania Battalion of the Flying Camp, July, 1776; taken prisoner at Fort Washington, 16th November, 1776; exchanged 8th December, 1780.

Davis, Isaac (Mass). Captain Company of Minute Men; killed at Concord 19th April, 1775; first officer killed during the Revolutionary War.

Davis, Isaac (N. H.). Captain New Hampshire Militia, 1777.

Davis, Isaac (Pa). 2d Lieutenant 1st Pennsylvania, 28th May, 1779; retired 17th January, 1781.

Davis, Israel (Mass). Captain 13th Massachusetts, 1st January, 1777; cashiered 11th February, 1778.

Davis, James (Mass). Sergeant of Doolittle's Massachusetts Regiment, May to December, 1775; 2d Lieutenant 3d Massachusetts, 1st January, 1777, and served to 3d June, 1783. (Died 1817.)

Davis, James (Va). Ensign 3d Virginia, 23d February, 1776; 2d Lieutenant, 25th June, 1776; 1st Lieutenant, July, 1776; Captain, 7th August, 1776; retired 30th September, 1778.

Davis, Jesse (Va). 1st Lieutenant 11th Virginia, 17th November, 1776; Captain, 11th September, 1777; Regiment designated 7th Virginia, 14th September, 1778; retired — May, 1779.

Davis, John (Mass). Private, Corporal and Sergeant of Cotton's Massachusetts Regiment, 6th May to December, 1775; Sergeant 3d Continental Infantry, January to December, 1776; Sergeant 4th Massachusetts, 22d January, 1777; Sergeant-Major, 9th February, 1777; Ensign, 3d January, 1778; Lieutenant and Regimental Adjutant, 14th April, 1780, and served to 3d June, 1783. (Died 1816.)

Davis, John (Mass). Captain of Frye's Massachusetts Regiment, May to December, 1775; Captain Massachusetts Militia, 1778-1779.

Davis, John (N. C.).—See **Daves.**

Davis, John (N. Y.). 1st Lieutenant 3d New York, 28th June, 1775; Captain 4th New York, 21st November, 1776; wounded at Stillwater, 19th September, 1777; Major, 11th April, 1780; retired 1st January, 1781.

Davis, John (N. Y.). Captain New York Militia, ——; killed at Oriskany, 6th August, 1777.

Davis, John (Pa). 1st Lieutenant 1st Battalion of Miles' Pennsylvania Rifle Regiment, 6th April, 1776; Captain 9th Pennsylvania, 15th November, 1776; transferred to 1st Pennsylvania 17th January, 1781; retired 1st January, 1783. (Died 10th July, 1827.)

Davis, John (Pa). 1st Lieutenant 1st Battalion of Miles' Pennsylvania Rifle Regiment, 19th March, 1776; taken prisoner at Long Island, 27th August, 1776; Captain of Patton's Additional Continental Regiment, February, 1777; Regiment merged into 11th Pennsylvania, 16th December, 1778; resigned April, 1779. (Died 3d February, 1816.)

Davis, John (Pa). Surgeon 1st Battalion of Miles' Pennsylvania Rifle Regiment, 22d March, 1776; taken prisoner at Long Island, 27th August, 1776; exchanged 8th December, 1776; Surgeon of Patton's Continental Regiment, 1st March, 1777, to 16th December, 1778, and of the 11th Pennsylvania to April, 1779. (Died 13th February 1816.)

Davis, John (Pa). Colonel Pennsylvania Militia, 1778.

Davis, Jonathan (Mass). Captain in the Lexington Alarm, April, 1775; Captain of Whitcomb's Massachusetts Regiment, May to December, 1775.

Davis, Joseph (Pa). Ensign Pennsylvania Musket Battalion, 27th March, 1776; 1st Lieutenant 9th Pennsylvania, August, 1776; transferred to Hartley's Continental Regiment, 15th January,

1777; Captain, 3d June, 1778; Regiment designated 11th Pennsylvania, 16th December, 1778; killed by Indians near Wyoming, 23d April, 1779.

Davis, Joseph (Pa). Surgeon's Mate 1st Battalion of Miles' Pennsylvania Rifle Regiment, 22d March, 1776; taken prisoner at Long Island, 27th August, 1776; exchanged 8th December, 1776.

Davis, Joseph (Va). Surgeon 15th Virginia, 4th March, 1778; Regiment designated 11th Virginia, 14th September, 1778; was taken prisoner at Charleston, 12th May, 1780; transferred to 3d Virginia 12th February, 1781; retired 1st January, 1783.

Davis, Joshua (R. I.). Major Rhode Island Militia, 1775-1776.

Davis, Josiah (Mass). Lieutenant Massachusetts Militia, 1775-1776; 1st Lieutenant 11th Massachusetts, 6th November, 1776; resigned 8th November, 1777.

Davis, Llewellyn (Pa). Ensign 9th Pennsylvania, 2d February, 1779; Lieutenant, 10th August, 1779; transferred to 5th Pennsylvania, 1st January, 1781; transferred to 1st Pennsylvania 1st January, 1783, and served to 3d June, 1783.

Davis, Mordecai (Pa). Ensign 2d Pennsylvania Battalion, 5th January, 1776; died 12th August, 1776.

Davis, Ransom (S. C.). Captain South Carolina Militia in Marion's Brigade, 1780-1781.

Davis, Reuben (Mass). Corporal in Lexington Alarm, April, 1775; 1st Lieutenant of Learned's Massachusetts Regiment, May to December, 1775; served subsequently as Captain Massachusetts Militia until he died, 9th October, 1781.

Davis, Rezin (Md). Ensign Maryland Rifle Company, 21st June, 1775; Captain of Stephenson's Rifle Regiment, 11th July, 1776; taken prisoner at Fort Washington, 16th November, 1776; escaped 7th July, 1777; retained in Rawling's Continental Regiment after his escape; retired 1st January, 1781. (Name also spelled Davies.)

Davis, Robert (Mass). 2d Lieutenant 15th Continental Infantry, 1st January, 1776; 1st Lieutenant 1st Massachusetts, 1st January 1777; Captain, 4th November, 1777; resigned 1st April, 1779.

Davis, Samuel, Jr. (Pa). 1st Lieutenant 9th Pennsylvania, 15th Novem-

Davis 189 Day

ber, 1776; retired 1st July, 1778. (Died 6th April, 1824.)

Davis, Septimus (Pa). Ensign Pennsylvania Musket Battalion, 9th August, 1776; taken prisoner at Long Island, 27th August, 1776; exchanged 9th December, 1776; 1st Lieutenant of Patton's Continental Regiment, 17th January, 1777; Regiment merged into 11th Pennsylvania, 16th December, 1778; Captain Lieutenant, 13th April, 1779; resigned 24th February, 1780.

Davis, Thomas (Pa). 2d Lieutenant of Montgomery's Pennsylvania Battalion of the Flying Camp; wounded and taken prisoner at Fort Washington 16th November, 1776.

Davis, Thomas (Va). Captain 9th Virginia, 12th February, 1776; cashiered ——, 1776.

Davis, Thomas (Va). Chaplain 1st Continental Dragoons, 10th December, 1776, to .

Davis, Thomas (Va). Ensign 15th Virginia, 25th November, 1776; 2d Lieutenant, 1st August, 1777; Regiment designated 11th Virginia, 14th September, 1778; retired 30th September, 1778.

Davis, William (Mass). Lieutenant of Jackson's Additional Continental Regiment, 1st February, 1777; resigned 14th September, 1778.

Davis, William (N. C.). Captain 1st North Carolina, 1st September, 1775; Major, 10th April, 1776; Lieutenant-Colonel 1st North Carolina, 5th February, 1777; retired 1st June, 1778.

Davis, William (R. I.). 2d Lieutenant 1st Rhode Island, 11th February, 1777; dismissed 20th March, 1778.

Davis, William (S. C.). Captain South Carolina Militia in 1776.

Davis, William (Va). Colonel Virginia Militia, 1779-1781.

Dawes, Abraham (N. C.).—See **Davis**.

Dawes, Josiah (N. C.). Regimental Quartermaster 7th North Carolina, 10th July, 1777, to ——.

Dawes, William (Mass). 2d Lieutenant 10th Massachusetts, 6th November, 1776; discharged 25th May, 1778.

Dawsey, Nathan (Conn). Ensign 4th Connecticut, 1st May to — September, 1775.

Dawson, Henry (N. C.). Captain 2d North Carolina, 29th November, 1776; resigned 11th October, 1777.

Dawson, Henry (Va). Ensign and Regimental Quartermaster 7th Virginia, 31st October, 1778; Lieutenant, 22d February, 1780, and served to close of war. (Died 1815.)

Dawson, Levi (N. C.). Major 5th North Carolina, 15th April, 1776; Lieutenant-Colonel 8th North Carolina, 19th October, 1777; retired 1st June, 1778.

Dawson, Samuel (Pa). Captain 11th Pennsylvania, 30th September, 1776; transferred to 8th Pennsylvania, 1st July, 1778; died 3d September, 1779.

Dawson, William (Va). Ensign 6th Virginia, 26th February, 1776; 2d Lieutenant, — November, 1776; died — May, 1777.

Day, Aaron (N .J.). Ensign 3d New Jersey, 29th November, 1776; 2d Lieutenant, 1st January, 1777; Regimental Quartermaster, March, 1778; omitted July, 1779.

Day, Elijah (Mass). Sergeant 6th Continental Infantry, 1st January, 1776; Ensign 7th Massachusetts, 13th November, 1776; 2d Lieutenant, 19th November, 1777; transferred to 4th Massachusetts, 1st January, 1781; retired 1st January, 1783.

Day, Isaac (Conn). Surgeon's Mate 2d Connecticut, 1st June, 1777; resigned 6th October, 1778.

Day, James (Conn). Adjutant Battalion in the Lexington Alarm, April, 1775; Adjutant 6th Connecticut, 20th May to 10th December, 1775; 2d Lieutenant and Adjutant 10th Continental Infantry, 1st January to 31st December, 1776; served subsequently as Captain of Marines.

Day, John (Va). Captain Virginia Militia, 1775.

Day, Joseph (Ga). Captain 2d Georgia, 20th September, 1777, and served to close of war; Brevet Major, 30th September, 1783.

Day, Luke (Mass). 2d Lieutenant in Lexington Alarm, April, 1775; 1st Lieutenant of Danielson's Massachusetts Regiment, May to December, 1775; Captain 7th Massachusetts, 1st January, 1777, and served to 3d June, 1783.

Day, Luke (——). Captain of Company Delaware Indians, 1780-1781.

Day, Samuel (Mass). 1st Lieutenant 3d Massachusetts, 1st January, 1777; retired 27th September, 1778.

Day, Samuel (Mass). Private in Lexington Alarm, April, 1775; Private in

Read's Massachusetts Regiment, April to December, 1775; Corporal 4th Massachusetts, 1st April, 1777; Sergeant, 1st June, 1778; Ensign, 18th August, 1779; resigned 18th April, 1782.

Dayton, Elias (N. J.). Colonel 3d New Jersey, 18th January, 1776; transferred to 2d New Jersey, 1st January, 1781; Brigadier-General Continental Army, 7th January, 1783, and served to close of war. (Died 17th July, 1807.)

Dayton, Henry (R. I.). Captain Rhode Island Militia, 1779.

Dayton, Jonathan (N. J.). Ensign 3d New Jersey, 7th February, 1776; Regimental Paymaster, 26th August, 1776; 1st Lieutenant, 1st January, 1777; Captain Lieutenant, 7th April, 1779; Aide-de-Camp to General Sullivan, 1st May, 1779; Captain 3d New Jersey, 30th March, 1780; taken prisoner at Elizabethtown 5th October, 1780; exchanged ———; transferred to 2d New Jersey, 1st January, 1781; retained in Consolidated New Jersey Regiment in April, 1783, and served to 3d November, 1783. (Died 9th October, 1824.)

Dayton, Joseph (N. J.). 2d Lieutenant Western Company, New Jersey Artillery, 1st March, 1776, to ———.

Deal, ——— (S. C.). Lieutenant South Carolina Rangers, ———; wounded at Stono Ferry, 20th June, 1779.

Deams, Frederick (Md.). 1st Lieutenant 7th Maryland, 10th December, 1776; Captain, 7th February, 1777; left regiment 20th April, 1777, and resigned soon afterwards.

Deakins, Leonard (Md.). Captain 1st Maryland Battalion of the Flying Camp, July to December, 1776. (Died 1824.)

Dean, Ebenezer (Mass). 1st Lieutenant of Heath's Massachusetts Regiment, May to December, 1775.

Dean, Isaac (Mass). Colonel Massachusetts Militia, 1778-1780.

Dean, Isaac (Va). 1st Lieutenant 1st Continental Artillery, 13th January, 1777, to ———.

Dean, John (Md). Captain 4th Maryland Battalion of the Flying Camp, July to December, 1776; taken prisoner at Fort Washington, 16th November, 1776; exchanged 26th August, 1778; Captain 5th Maryland, 10th December, 1776; Major 4th Maryland, 11th March, 1778; transferred to 2d

Maryland, 1st January, 1781; died 6th November, 1781.

Dean, John (Mass). 1st Lieutenant of Cady's Battalion on the expedition to Canada, January to June, 1776.

Dean, Jonathan (Conn). Ensign of Elmore's Continental Regiment, 15th April, 1776, to April, 1777.

Dean, Samuel (Pa). 2d Lieutenant of Hart's Pennsylvania Battalion of the Flying Camp, July, 1776; 1st Lieutenant 11th Pennsylvania, 30th September, 1776; Captain, 9th April, 1777; retired 1st July, 1778.

Dean, Thomas (Mass). Corporal and Sergeant in Gridley's Regiment of Artillery, May to December, 1775; 2d Lieutenant of Knox's Regiment Continental Artillery, 10th December, 1775; 1st Lieutenant, 10th August, 1776; Captain Lieutenant 3d Continental Artillery, 1st January, 1777; retired 12th September, 1778.

Dean, William (Pa). Captain Pennsylvania Militia; killed at Crooked Billet, 1st May, 1778.

Deane, Walter (Mass). Sergeant 6th Continental Infantry, 1st January, 1776; Ensign ·13th Massachusetts, 6th November, 1776; 2d Lieutenant, 26th December, 1777; Captain Lieutenant, 4th July, 1780; transferred to 3d Massachusetts, 1st January, 1781; Captain, 1st January, 1781; transferred to 10th Massachusetts, 1st January, 1782; retired 1st January, 1783. (Died 1814.)

Deane, ——— (—). Lieutenant of Warner's Continental Regiment, 5th July, 1776; marked "dead" in September, 1776.

Dearborn, Henry (N. H.). Captain Company of Minute Men, April, 1775; Captain 1st New Hampshire, 23d April, 1775; taken prisoner at Quebec, 31st December, 1775; exchanged 10th March, 1777; Major 3d New Hampshire, 19th March, 1777, to rank from 8th November, 1776; Lieutenant-Colonel, 19th September, 1777; transferred to 1st New Hampshire, 1st April, 1781, and served to 21st March, 1783; Secretary of War, 5th March, 1801, to 7th March, 1809; Major-General United States Army, 27th January, 1812; honorably discharged 15th June, 1815. (Died 6th June, 1829.)

Dearborn, John (N. H). Captain New Hampshire Militia, 1777-1778.

Dearborn, Levi (N. H.). Surgeon New Hampshire Militia, 1777-1778.

Dearborn, Samuel (N. H.). 2d Lieutenant 1st New Hampshire, 23d May to December, 1775.

Dearborn, Simeon (N. H.). 1st Lieutenant 2d New Hampshire, 23d May to 20th July, 1775.

de Arendt, —— Baron.—See **Arendt.**

Dearborn, Stephen (N. H.). Captain New Hampshire Militia, 1777-1778.

Dearborn, Thomas (N. H.). Lieutenant New Hampshire Militia; Killed 29th August, 1778, at Quaker Hill.

Deane, Jonathan (N. J.). Major and Lieutenant-Colonel New Jersey Militia, 1776-1778.

Dearing, Ebenezer (N. H.). Captain New Hampshire Militia, 1776-1777.

Dearing, Francis (S. C.). Lieutenant South Carolina Militia; wounded at Beaufort, 9th February, 1779.

Deaver, John (Md). Lieutenant 3d Maryland, 10th December, 1776; resigned 8th April, 1779; Captain Maryland Militia, 1780-1782. (Died 1812.)

De Bedeaux, Frederick (France).— See **Bedaux.**

de Belleville, Nicholas Jacques Emanuel (France). Surgeon Pulaski Legion, 1777-1780. (Died 1831.)

De Benneville, Daniel (Va). Surgeon 13th Virginia, 25th April, 1778; retired 30th September, 1778; Surgeon Virginia State Regiment, 1778 to 1781.

De Bert, Claudius (France). Captain 3d Cavalry Pulaski Legion, 7th June, 1778, and Paymaster of Armand's Corps; Brevet Major, 6th February, 1784; served to close of war.

De Beviere, Francis.—See **Beviere.**

De Borre, Prud'Homme (France). Brigadier-General Continental Army, 1st December, 1776; resigned 14th September, 1777.

De Boze, —— Baron (—). Lieutenant-Colonel Pulaski Legion; killed at Egg Harbor, 15th October, 1778.

De Brahm, Ferdinand (France).—See **Brahm.**

De Camp, James (N. J.). Private, Corporal and Sergeant 2d New Jersey, December, 1776, to February, 1779; Ensign 2d New Jersey, 1st February, 1779; resigned 1st June, 1782.

Dechert, Peter (Pa). Captain 5th Pennsylvania Battalion, 5th January, 1776; taken prisoner at Fort Washing-

ton 16th November, 1776; resigned 1st February, 1777; served subsequently as Major Pennsylvania Militia. (Died 1784.)

De Cicati.—See **Cicati.**

De Colerus, Christian (France).—See **Colerus.**

De Corney, Louis Ethis (France). Brevet Lieutenant-Colonel of Cavalry, Continental Army, 5th June, 1780; served as Commissary-General to the French troops.

De Courcy, Edward (Md). 3d Lieutenant of Veazey's Independent Maryland Company, 14th January, 1776; wounded and taken prisoner at Long Island, 27th August, 1776; exchanged 27th September, 1777.

De Crenis, —— Chevalier (France). Lieutenant Cavalry Pulaski Legion, 1778; Brevet Lieutenant-Colonel Continental Army, 7th November, 1778; served to ——.

De Delafauché (France) Major of Engineers in 1780.

de Failly, —— Chevalier de.—See **Failly.**

de Fayals, —— (France). Lieutenant-Colonel Continental Army, 20th November, 1776.

De Fermoy, Matthias Alexis Roche (France). Brigadier-General Continental Army, 5th November, 1776; resigned 31st January, 1778.

De Fontevieux, —— Chevalier (France). Served as a volunteer in Armand's Corps in 1778; Brevet Lieutenant Continental Army, 13th January, 1779; Lieutenant Dragoons Armand's Corps, 9th March, 1780; Brevet Captain, 6th February, 1784; served to ——.

De Forrest, Isaac (Conn). Lieutenant of Silliman's Connecticut State Regiment, June to December, 1776.

Deforest, Samuel (Conn). Private 5th Connecticut, 8th May to 17th September, 1775; Sergeant 5th Connecticut, 1st January, 1777; Ensign, 15th December, 1777; Lieutenant, 27th August, 1780; transferred to 2d Connecticut, 1st January, 1783, and served to 3d June, 1783.

de Franchessin, Jacques Antoine (France). Brevet Lieutenant-Colonel Continental Army, 20th July, 1776, and directed to join the Flying Camp.

de Frauval, —— (France). Lieutenant-Colonel Continental Army, 1st December, 1776, and served to October, 1777.

De Freest, Isaac (N. Y.). 1st Lieutenant and Captain New York Militia, 1775-1776.

De Frey, Charles Baron (France). Captain 1st Cavalry Pulaski Legion, ——; taken prisoner 1st February, 1778, where not sated; released 1st July, 1778; resigned 28th November, 1781.

Degges.—See **Diggs**, as name is spelled both ways.

De Gimat.—See **Gimat.**

De Gouvion.—See **Guvion.**

De Groot, Joseph (N. Y.). 2d Lieutenant 1st New York, 25th April to November, 1776.

Deguillett, John (Canada). 2d Lieutenant 1st Canadian Regiment, 20th October, 1775; 1st Lieutenant, 18th December, 1776; dishonorably discharged 31st October, 1777.

De Haas, John Philip (Pa). Major of Pennsylvania Provincials in 1775; Colonel 1st Pennsylvania Battalion, 22d January, 1776; Colonel 2d Pennsylvania, 25th October, 1776, to rank from 22d January, 1776; Brigadier-General Continental Army, 21st February, 1777; to 3d November, 1783; Brevet Major-General, 30th September, 1780; went to Philadelphia in 1779, and rendered no subsequent service. (Died June, 1786.)

De Haas, John Philip, Jr. (Pa). Ensign 1st Pennsylvania, 6th August, 1776, to January, 1777. (Died August, 1826.)

De Hart, Balthazer (N. Y.). 1st Lieutenant 3d New York, 28th June, 1775, to January, 1776.

De Hart, Cyrus (N. J.). Ensign 4th New Jersey, 4th December, 1775, to March, 1776; Ensign 1st New Jersey, 18th September, 1776; 2d Lieutenant, 26th April, 1777; 1st Lieutenant, 4th October, 1777; Regimental Paymaster, 22d April, 1778, to January, 1781; Captain Lieutenant, 11th March, 1780; Captain, 20th December, 1780; transferred to 2d New Jersey, 1st January, 1781; retained in Consolidated New Jersey Battalion, April, 1783, and served to 3d November, 1783. (Died 7th September, 1831.)

De Hart, Jacob (Pa). Ensign 2d Pennsylvania, 2d June, 1778; 2d Lieutenant, 16th May, 1779; Aide-de-Camp ·to General De Kalb; died 25th July,

1780, of wounds received at Bulls Ferry, 21st July, 1780.

De Hart ,Maurice (N. J.). Major Aide-de-Camp to General Wayne; killed at Fort Lee 18th November, 1776.

De Hart, William (N. J.). Major 1st New Jersey, 7th November, 1775; Lieutenant-Colonel 2d New Jersey, 1st January, 1777; resigned 20th November, 1781. (Died 16th June, 1801.)

De Holtzendorf, Louis C. (—). See **Holtzendorf.**

Dehorety, Charles (Mass). See **Dougherty.**

De Huff, Abraham (Pa). Captain Pennsylvania Musket Battalion, 15th March, 1776; taken prisoner at Fort Washington, 16th November, 1776; exchanged 20th April, 1778. (Died 1821.)

Dike, Nicholas (Mass). Colonel Massachusetts Militia, 1776.

De Kalb, John Baron (Bavaria). Major-General Continental Army, 15th September, 1777; died 19th August, 1780, of eight wounds received at Camden, South Carolina, 16th August, 1780.

De Kermovan, —— ** (—). See **Kermovan.

De Keyser, Lehancius (N. C.). Adjutant 1st North Carolina, 16th September, 1775; 2d Lieutenant, 4th January, 1776; 1st Lieutenant, 3d February, 1776; resigned 10th December, 1776.

Deklawan, Charles (Va). Major of a Virginia State Regiment, 1778 to 1781.

de Kowatz, Michael (—). See **Kowatz.**

Delagard, C. H. (—). Adjutant 2d Canadian (Hazen's) Regiment, 3d November, 1776; resigned 3d October, 1777.

Delaplaine, James (Va). Cadet 3d Virginia, 1st June 1779; Eisign, 4th July, 1779; Lieutenant, 1st August, 1780; taken prisoner at Charleston 12th May, 1780; exchanged ——; transferred· to 2d Virginia 12th February, 1781, and served to close of war.

Delaplaine, Joseph (Ga). Surgeon 4th Georgia, ——; resigned 30th June, 1779. (Name also spelled Delaplaign.)

Delaplaine, Peter Emanuel (Ga). Ensign 1st Georgia, 7th January, 1776; Lieutenant, — November, 1776; Captain, 26th May, 1777; was also Major Georgia Militia in 1777; returned to France in 1778.

Delaporte, Deorame (Va). Captain Virginia Militia, 1780-1781.

de Laumoy.—See **Laumoy.**

Delavan, Daniel (N. Y.). Captain and Major New York Militia, 1775-1780.

Delavan, Nathaniel (N. Y.). Major New York Militia, 1779.

Delezeume, Joseph de (France). Assistant Engineer, 28th September, 1776, and served to 1783.

Dellient, —— (S. C.). Adjutant 2d South Carolina in 1776; Brigade Major to General Moultrie, 28th August, 1777, to ——.

De Linkensdorf, Louis (Pa). Adjutant of the German Regiment, 9th August, 1776; retired June, 1779.

Dellinger, John (N. C.). Captain North Carolina Militia, 1776.

De Mafastram, —— (France). Brevet Lieutenant Continental Army, 13th January, 1779, and permitted to return to France.

De Malmady, Francis (—). See **Malmady.**

De Marcellin, Antoine Claude (Pa). Ensign 2d Pennsylvania, 28th July, 1779; Lieutenant, 1st January, 1781; transferred to 3d Pennsylvania, 1st January, 1783; retained in Pennsylvania Battalion, June, 1783; Brevet Captain, 6th February, 1784, and served to 20th June, 1784.

de Medici, Cosmo (N. C.). See **Medici.**

Dement, William (Pa). Ensign 5th Pennsylvania Battalion, 6th January, 1776; Regimental Adjutant, 29th September, 1776; deserted 2d November, 1776. (Name also spelled Demont.)

Demerit, John (N. H.). Major New Hampshire Militia, 1777-1778.

Deming, David (Mass). 2d Lieutenant of Steven's Battalion of Artillery, 1st July, 1777; in 3d Continental Artillery, Fall of 1778; resigned 6th March, 1779.

Deming, Elijah (Mass). Captain Massachusetts Militia; wounded at Bennington 16th August, 1777.

Deming, Pownal (Conn). Sergeant Lexington Alarm, April, 1775; Sergeant 2d Connecticut, 12th May to 10th December, 1775; Sergeant 22d Continental Infantry, 1st January, 1776; Ensign, 10th August to 31st December, 1776; 2d Lieutenant 4th Connecticut, 1st January, 1777; 1st Lieutenant, 15th November, 1778; transferred to 1st Connecticut 1st January, 1781, and served to 3d June, 1783.

Deming, Seth (Conn). Lieutenant Connecticut Light Horse, 1776-1777.

Demler, Henry (N. Y.). 2d Lieutenant 2d Continental Artillery, 20th August, 1781, and served to June, 1783.

Demeré, Raymond (Ga). Lieutenant Georgia Militia; taken prisoner at Savannah, 4th March, 1776.

Dempsey, William (Pa). Lieutenant Pennsylvania Militia; taken prisoner at Guelphs Mills 11th December, 1777.

de Montfort, Julius, Count (France). 1st Lieutenant of Hartley's Continental Regiment, 23d March, 1777; Brevet Lieutenant-Colonel, 21st March, 1777; Major 1st Cavalry Pulaski Legion, 18th April, 1778; resigned 23d January, 1779. (Name also spelled de Mountfort.)

Demouth, Marcus (N .Y.). Captain New York Militia, ——; wounded and taken prisoner at German Flats, 29th October, 1780.

Denholm, Archibald (Va). 2d Lieutenant 1st Virginia, January, 1777; 1st Lieutenant, 9th August, 1777; Captain, 25th June, 1779; wounded at Hobkirk's Hill 25th April, 1781, and did not return to service.

Dening, Solomon (Mass). 2d Lieutenant of Fellow's Massachusetts Regiment, May, 1775, to ——.

Denison, Nathan (Conn). Lieutenant-Colonel Connecticut Militia, 1777; Colonel of same, 1777-1780. (Died 1809.)

Dennett, John (N. H.). 2d Lieutenant 3d New Hampshire, 8th November, 1776; 1st Lieutenant, 1st May, 1778; Captain Lieutenant, 19th July, 1779; Captain, 1st July, 1780; transferred to 2d New Hampshire, 1st January, 1781, and served to March, 1783.

Dennis, Daniel (Pa). 2d Lieutenant 10th Pennsylvania, 5th November, 1777; retired 1st July, 1778.

Dennis, Ezekiel (N. J.). Ensign 3d New Jersey, 29th November, 1776; omitted after July, 1778.

Dennis, John (N. J.). Captain of Patton's Additional Continental Regiment, January, 1777; taken prisoner at Red Bank, 22d October, 1777, and died while a prisoner 15th January, 1778.

Dennis, William (N. C.). 1st Lieutenant 8th North Carolina, 28th November, 1776; Captain, 30th September, 1777; retired 1st June, 1778.

Dennis, William (Va). Cadet 4th Virginia, 4th February, 1777; retired 1st July, 1778.

Dennison, William (R. I.). Adjutant of Elliott's Rhode Island State Regiment of Artillery, 12th December, 1776, to October, 1777. (Died 24th January, 1834.)

Denniston, Daniel D. (N. Y.). Ensign 4th New York, 9th November, 1777; Lieutenant, 11th April, 1780; transferred to 2d New York, 1st January, 1781, and served to 3d June, 1783. (Died 3d February, 1824.)

Denniston, George J. (N. Y.).. Adjutant 3d New York, 28th June to November, 1775; Ensign 3d New York, 21st November, 1776; 2d Lieutenant, 20th May, 1780; retired 1st January, 1781.

Denny, Ebenezer (Pa). Ensign 7th Pennsylvania, 4th August, 1780; transferred to 4th Pennsylvania, 17th January, 1781; Lieutenant, 23d May, 1781; transferred to 3d Pennsylvania, 1st January, 1783, and served to 3d November, 1783; Ensign United States Infantry, Harmar's Regiment, 12th August, 1784; Regimental Adjutant, 8th September, 1785; Lieutenant, 10th November, 1787; Lieutenant 1st Infantry, United States Army, 29th September, 1789; Captain, 29th December, 1791; resigned 15th May, 1792. (Died 22d July, 1822.)

Denny, John (N. Y.). Ensign 1st New York, July, 1776; 2d Lieutenant, 21st November, 1776; resigned 7th October, 1778.

Denny, Robert (Md). Private and Sergeant 7th Maryland, 10th December, 1776; Regimental Quartermaster, 30th April, 1777; Paymaster, 27th May, 1778; Lieutenant, 3d January, 1780; transferred to 5th Maryland, 1st January, 1781; retired 1st January, 1783.

Denny, Samuel (Va). Captain 1st Continental Artillery, 30th November, 1776, to ——.

Denny, Walter (Pa). Captain Pennsylvania Militia; killed at Crooked Billet, Pa., 1st May, 1778.

Denslow, Martin (Conn). Private in the Lexington Alarm, April, 1775; Corporal 8th Connecticut, 7th July to 18th December, 1775; Sergeant 5th Connecticut, 1st April, 1777; Sergeant-Major, 15th May, 1779; Ensign, 16th August, 1779; transferred to 2d Connecticut 1st January, 1781; retired 31st March, 1782. (Died 1817.)

Densmore, Eliphalet (Mass). Captain of Prescott's Massachusetts Regiment, May, 1775, to ——.

Dent, George (Md). 1st Lieutenant 3d Maryland Battalion of the Flying Camp, July to December, 1776. (Died 1812.)

Dent, Hatch (Md). Ensign of Smallwood's Maryland Regiment, 14th January, 1776; Lieutenant, March, 1776; taken prisoner at Long Island 27th August, 1776; exchanged 20th April, 1778; 1st Lieutenant 1st Maryland, 10th December, 1776; Captain 2d Maryland, 17th April, 1777; resigned 13th November, 1778.

Dent, John (Md). Brigadier-General Maryland Militia, 6th January, 1776; resigned July, 1776.

Dent, John (Va). Ensign 9th Virginia, 31st October, 1778; 2d Lieutenant, 6th April, 1779; resigned 20th November, 1880.

Dent, William (N. C.). Commissary 9th North Carolina, 11th December, 1776, to ——.

Denton, Daniel (N. Y.). Captain 3d New York, 28th June, 1775, to January, 1776; Captain 3d New York, 28th March to November, 1776.

Denton, Thomas (Va). Ensign 12th Virginia, January, 1777; dismissed — April, 1777.

Denwood, Levin (Md). Surgeon 7th Maryland, 3d October, 1779; transferred to 3d Maryland, 1st January, 1781; retained in Maryland Battalion, April, 1783, and served to 15th November, 1783.

De Peyster, William (N. Y.). Captain New York Militia, 1775. (Died 1803.)

De Peyster, W. W. (N. Y.). Ensign 1st New York, 24th February, 1776; killed by lightning 21st August, 1776.

De Pontiere, Louis (—). See **Pontiere.**

De Purcell, Henry (—). See **Purcell.**

Derby, Samuel (Mass). Captain of Scammon's Massachusetts Regiment, May to December, 1775.

Derick, Jacob Gerhard (Netherland). Captain 9th Pennsylvania, 15th November, 1776; Captain 4th Continental Artillery, 3d March, 1777; resigned 6th July, 1777; breveted Lieutenant-Colonel 5th November, 1778, "as a testimony of his merit and services in the army," granted leave until further orders 12th

July, 1780, and was honorably discharged 17th May, 1781. (Name also spelled Dirks.)

Derickson, Samuel (Del). Lieutenant Delaware Militia, 1780-1781.

De Roland, Sebastian (Pa). 2d Lieutenant of Patton's Continental Regiment, 15th January, 1777; dropped from rolls after September, 1777.

de Rouerie, Armand T. (France). See **Armand.**

de Roussi, Pierre Regnier (Canada). Lieutenant-Colonel 1st Canadian Regiment, 11th November, 1775; Lieutenant-Colonel 4th New York, 26th March, 1777, to rank from 21st November, 1776; transferred to 2d New York, 28th June, 1779; resigned 29th March, 1780. (Died 1810.)

Derringer, Henry (Pa). Captain of Lewis' Pennsylvania Battalion of the Flying Camp, July to December, 1776.

De Saussure, Henry W. (S. C.). Lieutenant 3d South Carolina, ——, 1777; wounded at Savannah, 9th October, 1779; taken prisoner at Charleston, 12th May, 1780; prisoner on parole to close of war. (Died 29th March, 1839.)

De Saussure, Lewis (S. C.). 1st Lieutenant 3d South Carolina; mortally wounded at Savannah, 9th October, 1779.

De Saussure, Victor Daniel (S. C.). Captain South Carolina Militia; taken prisoner at Charleston 12th May, 1780. (Died 1798.)

Des Espiniers, Augustus F.—See **Espiniers.**

Deshon, Richard (Conn). Captain of Selden's Connecticut State Regiment, June to December, 1776.

Detard, John Peter.—See **Tetard.**

De Treuson, —— (France). Brevet Captain Continental Army, 13th January, 1779.

De Treville, John Francis (S. C.). Was a Captain in 4th South Carolina (Artillery) in June, 1777; wounded at Savannah 9th October, 1779; taken prisoner at Charleston 12th May, 1780; exchanged 15th June, 1781, and served to close of war; Brevet Major, 30th September, 1783. (Died 1790.)

Detrich, Jacob (Pa). Ensign 2d Pennsylvania, 1st January, 1777; killed in a skirmish near Amboy, N. J., 1st April, 1777.

De Troy, Francis (——). Lieutenant Pulaski Legion, 1st June, 1778, to ——, 1780.

De Valcour, John S.—See **Valcour.**

De Van Brunne.—See **Van Brunne.**

De Veaux, Peter (Ga). Major and Aide-de-Camp to General Gates 3d August, 1780 to 1781. (Died 6th October, 1826.)

Devereaux, John (Mass). 2d Lieutenant of Glover's Massachusetts Regiment, May to December, 1775; Captain Massachusetts Militia, 1777-1778. (Died 1788.)

Devereaux, Peter (Ga). Major Georgia Militia, 1778-1780.

De Vernejoux, —— (——). See Vernejoux.

de Vienna, —— Marquis (France). Volunteer, ——; served without pay or expense to the United States during the campaign of 1778 as Aide-de-Camp to General Lafayette; Brevet Lieutenant-Colonel Continental Army, 15th July, 1778.

Devoe, Jeremiah (——). Lieutenant of Lee's Battalion of Light Dragoons, 1778-1779.

De Vrecourt, —— (—). See Vrecourt.

de Vrigney, —— (France). Captain Continental Army, 1st December, 1776; resigned 21st October, 1778.

Dewey, Daniel (Conn). Captain in Lexington Alarm, April, 1775; Captain Connecticut Militia in 1776.

Dewey, Elijah (Vt). Captain Vermont Militia in 1776 and 1777.

Dewey, Oliver (Mass). Sergeant-Major 7th Massachusetts, 8th March, 1777; Ensign, 19th November, 1777. Died 6th December, 1777.

Dewey, Samuel (Conn). Captain Connecticut Militia, 1776.

Dewey, Zebadiah (Mass). 1st Lieutenant of Brewer's Massachusetts Regiment, May to December, 1775.

De Witt, Charles (N. Y.). Colonel New York Militia, 1775. (Died 1787.)

De Witt, Charles (S. C.). Lieutenant South Carolina Militia, 1780-1781.

De Witt, Jacob (Conn). 1st Lieutenant of Selden's Connecticut State Regiment, June to December, 1776.

De Witt, John L. (N. Y.). Captain of Snyder's Regiment New York Militia, 1779-1783.

De Witt, Levi (N. Y.). Regimental Quartermaster 2d New York, 21st November, 1776; resigned 15th April, 1778.

De Witt, Simeon (N. Y.). Geographer and Surveyor, United States Army, 4th December, 1780, to close of war. (Died 3d December, 1834.)

De Witt, Thomas (N. Y.). 1st Lieutenant 3d New York, 28th June, 1775; Captain, 25th November, 1775, to January, 1776; Captain 3d New York, 26th June, 1776; Captain 3d New York, 21st November, 1776, to rank from 26th June, 1776; resigned 7th January, 1780; served subsequently as Major New York Levies. (Died 7th September, 1809.)

De Woedtke, Frederick William (Prussia). Brigadier-General Continental Army, 16th March, 1776; died 28th July, 1776.

Dexter, Daniel (R. I.). Lieutenant 1st Rhode Island, 1st June, 1778; Adjutant, 1st May, 1779; retained in Olney's Rhode Island Battalion with rank of Captain from 14th May, 1781, and served to November, 1783.

Dexter, David (R. I.). Ensign of 2d Rhode Island, 3d May to December, 1775; Captain of Babcock's Rhode Island Militia Regiment, 15th January, 1776; appointed Brigade-Major, 9th October, 1776; Captain 2d Rhode Island, 11th February, 1777; dismissed 7th January, 1779.

Dexter, Ichabod (Mass). Captain in Lexington Alarm, April, 1775; Captain in Woodbridge's Massachusetts Regiment, May to December, 1775; served subsequently in Massachusetts Militia.

Dexter, John Singer (R. I.). Lieutenant 1st Rhode Island, 3d May to December, 1775; 1st Lieutenant and Adjutant 9th Continental Infantry, 1st January to 31st December, 1776; Captain 1st Rhode Island, 1st January, 1777; Assistant to the Adjutant-General, 1st May, 1779; retained in Olney's Rhode Island Battalion, 14th May, 1781; Major, 25th August, 1781, and served to November, 1783.

Dexter, Oliver (R. I.). Ensign 2d Rhode Island, 1st February, 1777; 2d Lieutenant, 3d June, 1777; dismissed 11th September, 1778.

Dexter, Samuel (R. I.). Ensign of Lippitt's Rhode Island State Regiment, 19th August, 1776, to March, 1777.

Dexter, Thomas (Mass). Ensign 2d Massachusetts, 1st January, 1777; resigned 27th January, 1778.

Dexter, William (Mass). Served in Company of Minute Men at Lexington and Concord, 19th April, 1775; Surgeon's Mate of Ward's Massachusetts Regiment, May to December, 1775. (Died 4th December, 1785.)

Dey, Richard (N. J.). Major New Jersey Militia, 1776.

Dey, Theunis (N. J.). Colonel New Jersey Militia, 1776-1777.

Deygart, John (N. Y.). Captain New York Militia, ——; killed at Oriskany, 6th August, 1777.

Deygart, Jost (N. Y.). Captain New York Militia, 1779-1783.

Deygart, Peter (N. Y.). Major New York Militia, 1779-1783.

Diamond, Benjamin (R. I.). 1st Lieutenant of Church's Rhode Island Regiment, 3d May to December, 1775; Captain Rhode Island State Regiment, 15th January, 1776; Captain of Richmond's Rhode Island State Regiment, 19th August, 1776, to March, 1777.

Dibbell, Charles (Mass). Captain in Lexington Alarm, April, 1775; Captain of Paterson's Massachusetts Regiment, May to December, 1775.

Dick, Alexander (Va). Major 1st Virginia State Regiment, 1777 to 1781.

Dick, Jacob (Pa). Ensign Pennsylvania Battalion of the Flying Camp, July to December, 1776.

Dick, John (Pa). Sergeant of Thompson's Pennsylvania Rifle Battalion, 25th June, 1775; 3d Lieutenant 1st Continental Infantry, 1st January, 1776; 2d Lieutenant, 25th September, 1776; wounded at Fort Washington, 16th November, 1776.

Dick, Samuel (N. J.). Colonel New Jersey Militia, 1776.

Dickdom, Joseph (Va). 1st Lieutenant 8th Virginia, 25th March, 1776, to ——.

Dickenson, Benjamin (S. C.). 1st Lieutenant 2d South Carolina, 17th June, 1775, to ——.

Dickenson, Richard (N. C.). Ensign 6th North Carolina, 12th April, 1777; Lieutenant, 12th October, 1777; transferred to 1st North Carolina, 1st June, 1778; cashiered 20th November, 1779.

Dickerman, Isaac (Conn). 2d Lieutenant of Douglas' Connecticut State Regiment, June to December, 1776.

Dickerson, Nathaniel (N. C.). Lieutenant 9th North Carolina, 28th November, 1776, to ——.

Dickerson, Peter (N. J.). Captain 3d New Jersey, 5th March, 1776, to 10th November, 1776; Captain 3d New Jersey, 29th November, 1776; resigned 26th October, 1777.

Dickey, John (N. C.). Captain North Carolina Militia, 1779-1781. (Died 1808.)

Dickey, William (Pa). 2d Lieutenant 9th Pennsylvania, 15th November, 1776; resigned 31st October, 1777.

Dickinson, Daniel (N. Y.). Major and Lieutenant-Colonel New York Militia, 1775-1779.

Dickinson, Edmund B. (Va). Captain 1st Virginia, 25th February, 1776; Major, 26th October, 1777; killed at Monmouth, 28th June, 1778.

Dickinson, Joel (Conn). 1st Lieutenant of Elmore's Connecticut State Regiment, 15th April, 1776; Captain, 25th July, 1776, and served to April, 1777.

Dickinson, John (Pa). Brigadier-General Pennsylvania Militia, ——. (Died 14th February, 1808.)

Dickinson, Joseph (Conn). Sergeant in the Lexington Alarm, April, 1775; Ensign 2d Connecticut, 1st May to 6th October, 1775.

Dickinson, Philemon (N. J.). Brigadier-General New Jersey Militia, 19th October, 1775; resigned 15th February, 1777; Major-General, New Jersey Militia, 6th June, 1777, to close of war. (Died 4th February, 1809.)

Dickinson, Reuben (Mass). Captain of Woodbridge's Massachusetts Regiment, May to December, 1775.

Dickinson, Silvanus (N. Y.). Cornet 2d Continental Dragoons, 1st December, 1778; Lieutenant, — September, 1779; resigned 5th April, 1780. (Died 23d July, 1832.)

Dicks, Alexander (Va). Major Virginia Militia, 1780-1781.

Dickson, Beverly (Va). 1st Lieutenant 2d Virginia, 13th October, 1775; 1st Lieutenant, 28th January, 1776, and served to ——.

Dickson, James (Pa). Sergeant of 2d Canadian (Hazen's) Regiment, 4th March, 1776; Ensign, ——, 1781; 3d Lieutenant, 1st May, 1782, and served to June, 1783. (Name also spelled Dixon.)

Dickson, John (Del). 1st Lieutenant Delaware Regiment, 20th January to December, 1776.

Dietrich, Peter (Pa.). Ensign 2d Pennsylvania, 5th February, 1777; Lieu-

tenant, 1780; killed at Paramus, 16th April, 1780.

Dietz, Peter (N. Y.). Captain New York Militia; accidentally wounded, 9th September, 1777, and died next day.

Diffenderfer, David (Pa). Private German Regiment, 25th August, 1776; Corporal, 1st December, 1776; taken prisoner, 10th May, 1777, near Monmouth; rejoined regiment, 24th April, 1778; Ensign, 23d July, 1778; resigned 23d June, 1780.

Diffendorf, Henry (N. Y.). 2d Lieutenant 2d New York, November, 1775; 1st Lieutenant, July, 1776; 1st Lieutenant 3d New York, 21st November, 1776; killed at Oriskany, 6th August, 1777, while serving as Captain New York Militia. (Name also spelled Diefendorf.)

Digges, Cole (Va). Cornet 1st Continental Dragoons, 31st March, 1777; resigned 4th May, 1778. (Died 1817.)

Digges, Edward (Va). Captain Virginia Militia, 1778-1780.

Diggs, Anthony (N. C.). Lieutenant 5th North Carolina, 20th August, 1777; retired 1st June, 1778.

Diggs, Dudley (Va). Lieutenant of a Virginia State Regiment, June, 1779, to February, 1782.

Dill, James (Pa). 2d Lieutenant of Hartley's Continental Regiment, 13th January, 1777; killed at Brandywine, 11th September, 1777.

Dill, John (Pa). 2d Lieutenant of Thompson's Pennsylvania Rifle Battalion, 25th June, 1775; 1st Lieutenant, 15th October, 1775; served to December, 1775; 1st Lieutenant 1st Continental Infantry, 1st January 1776; resigned 1st February, 1776.

Dill, Matthew (Pa). Colonel Pennsylvania Militia, 1776.

Dill, William (Del). Ensign Delaware Battalion of the Flying Camp, July to December, 1776.

Dill, Robert (N. Y.). Paymaster of 2d Canadian (Hazen's) Regiment, 2d January, 1777; resigned 29th July, 1777.

Dillard, James (Va). 2d Lieutenant 10th Virginia, 3d February, 1777; 1st Lieutenant, 2d January, 1778; resigned 30th May, 1778; Captain Virginia Militia at King's Mountain, October, 1780, and in South Carolina in 1781. (Died 4th December, 1836.)

Dillenback, Andrew (N. Y.). Captain New York Militia, ——; killed at Oriskany, 6th August, 1777.

Dillon, James (N. J.). 1st Lieutenant 2d New Jersey, 11th November, 1775; Captain 2d New Jersey, 10th May to 10th November, 1776; Captain 2d New Jersey, 29th November, 1776; resigned 1st December, 1777.

Dillon, James (N. C.). 2d Lieutenant 7th North Carolina, 1st January, 1777; 1st Lieutenant, 12th October, 1777; transferred to 2d North Carolina, 1st June, 1778; killed at Eutaw Springs, 8th September, 1781.

Dillon, John (N. C.). Lieutenant 10th North Carolina, — February, 1779,- to —.

Dimick, Abel (Vt). Lieutenant Vermont Militia in 1777.

Dimmick, Benjamin (Conn). Corporal 10th Continental Infantry, January to December, 1776; Sergeant 2d Connecticut, 21st April, 1777; Ensign, 9th April, 1780; transferred to 3d Connecticut, 1st January, 1781; Lieutenant, 4th May, 1781; retired 1st January, 1783.

Dimon, Benjamin (R. I.). Lieutenant Rhode Island Regiment, May to December, 1775.

Dimon, David (Conn). Captain in the Lexington Alarm, April, 1775; Captain 5th Connecticut, 1st May to December, 1775; Brigade-Major to General Wooster, 13th June to 18th September, 1775, and to General Schuyler, 18th September, 1775, to December, 1776; Lieutenant-Colonel 6th Connecticut, 1st January, 1777; died 18th September, 1777, of wounds received at Brandywine, 11th September, 1777.

Dimon, Jonathan (Conn). Lieutenant-Colonel Connecticut Militia, 1777-1782.

Dinsmore, Eliphalet (Mass). Captain of Prescott's Massachusetts Regiment, May to December, 1775.

Dinwiddie, Hugh (Pa). Lieutenant-Colonel Pennsylvania Militia, 1776-1777. (Died 1777.)

Dionne, Germaine (Pa). 1st Lieutenant 2d Canadian (Hazen's) Regiment, 4th March, 1776, to June, 1783.

Dircks, Gerard Jacob (Pa).—See **Derick.**

Disney, James (Md). Captain 3d Maryland Battalion of the Flying Camp, July, 1776, to —.

Disting, Adam (Va). 1st Lieutenant 8th Virginia, ——; resigned — May, 1776.

Dix, Nathan (Mass). Private in Lexington Alarm, April, 1775; 2d Lieutenant of Baldwin's Massachusetts Regiment, May to December, 1775; 2d Lieutenant 26th Continental Infantry, 1st January, 1776; 1st Lieutenant, August, 1776; Captain 9th Massachusetts, 1st January, 1777; transferred to 8th Massachusetts, 1st January, 1781; transferred to 3d Massachusetts, 12th June, 1783; Brevet Major, 30th September, 1783, and served to 3d November, 1783.

Dix, Thomas (Va). 1st Lieutenant 1st Continental Artillery, 13th ᵀanuary, 1777; Captain Lieutenant, 15th January, 1778; retired 1st January, 1783.

Dix, Timothy (N. H.). 1st Lieutenant of Stickney's Regiment New Hampshire Militia, 5th March to 1st December, 1776; Major 14th United States Infantry, 12th March, 1812; Lieutenant-Colonel 14th Infantry, 20th June, 1813; died 4th November, 1813.

Dixon, Anthony F. (Va). Surgeon Hospital Department, 1776 to 1782.

Dixon, Charles (N. C.). Ensign 6th North Carolina, 2d April, 1777; Paymaster, 19th January, 1778; transferred to 3d North Carolina, 1st July, 1778; Lieutenant, 8th February, 1779; wounded at Eutaw Springs, 8th September, 1781; transferred to 4th North Carolina, 6th February, 1782; retired 1st January, 1783.

Dixon, Henry (N. C.). Captain 1st North Carolina, 1st September, 1775; arranged to 8th North Carolina, January, 1777; Major 3d North Carolina, 4th October, 1777; Lieutenant-Colonel, 12th May, 1778; wounded at Stono Ferry, 20th June, 1779; transferred to 2d North Carolina, 6th February, 1782; died 17th July, 1782.

Dixon, John (Conn). Captain in Sage's Connecticut State Regiment, 20th June to 25th December, 1776.

Dixon, Joseph (N. C.). Major North Carolina Militia at Kings Mountain, October, 1780. (Died 14th April, 1825.)

Dixon, Sankey (Pa). Sergeant-Major 6th Pennsylvania, March, 1777; Ensign, 2d August, 1779; Lieutenant, 12th May, 1781; transferred to 2d Pennsylvania, 1st January, 1783, and served to 3d June, 1783. (Died 1814.)

Dixon, Tilghman (N. C.). 1st Lieutenant 1st North Carolina, 20th October, 1775; Captain, 5th February, 1777; taken prisoner at Charleston, 12th May, 1780; exchanged 14th June, 1781; retired 1st January, 1783.

Dixon, Wynne (N. C.). Ensign 10th North Carolina, 1st March, 1781; 2d Lieutenant, 5th July, 1781; transferred to 1st North Carolina, February, 1782; served to close of war. (Died 24th November, 1829.)

Doan, Samuel (Pa). 1st Lieutenant 11th Pennsylvania, 13th November, 1776; Captain, 9th April, 1777; retired 1st July, 1778.

Dobbins, Hugh (N. C.). Lieutenant 9th North Carolina, ——, 1777, to 1st June, 1778.

Dobson, Henry (Md). 1st Lieutenant Maryland Battalion of the Flying Camp, September to December, 1776; Captain 6th Maryland, 10th December, 1776; transferred to 3d Maryland, 1st January, 1781; Major — Maryland, 3d June, 1781; killed 8th September, 1781, at Eutaw Springs.

Dobson, —— (N. C.). Captain North Carolina Militia; killed at Ramsour's Mill, 20th June, 1780.

Dodge, Abraham (Mass). Lieutenant Lexington Alarm, April, 1775; Captain of Little's Massachusetts Regiment, 19th May to December, 1775; Captain 12th Continental Infantry, 1st January to 31st December, 1776. (Died 17th June, 1786.)

Dodge, Barnabas (Mass). Captain of Gerrish's Massachusetts Regiment, May to December, 1775; Captain 26th Continental Infantry, 1st January to December, 1776.

Dodge, Henry (N. Y.). Sergeant in 3d New York in 1775 and 1776; 1st Lieutenant of DuBois' New York Regiment, 26th June, 1776; 1st Lieutenant 5th New York, 21st November, 1776; Captain Lieutenant, 30th March, 1780; retired 1st January, 1781. (Died 1820.)

Dodge, Isaac (Mass). 2d Lieutenant of Prescott's Massachusetts Regiment, 18th May to December, 1775; 2d Lieutenant 7th Continental Infantry, 1st January to 31st December, 1776.

Dodge, John (Mass). Ensign in Lexington Alarm, April, 1775; 1st Lieutenant of Mansfield's Massachusetts Regiment, May to December, 1775; 1st Lieutenant 27th Continental Infantry, 1st January to 31st December, 1776; served subsequently as Captain Massachusetts Militia.

Dodge, Levi (Mass). Sergeant 10th Massachusetts, 10th December, 1776; Ensign, 1st November, 1777; 2d Lieutenant, 15th December, 1778; transfer-

red to 1st Massachusetts, 1st January, 1783, and served to 3d November, 1783.

Dodge, Paul (Mass). Lieutenant in Lexington Alarm, April, 1775; 2d Lieutenant of Gerrish's Massachusetts Regiment, 19th May to December, 1775; 1st Lieutenant 26th Continental Infantry, 1st January to December, 1776.

Dodge, Reuben (Mass). Sergeant 10th Massachusetts, 10th December, 1776; Ensign, 1st November, 1777; omitted June, 1779.

Dodge, Richard (Mass). Lieutenant in Lexington Alarm, April, 1775; Captain of Gerrish's Massachusetts Regiment, 19th May to December, 1775; Captain 26th Continental Infantry, 1st January to December, 1776.

Dodge, Robert (Mass). 1st Lieutenant of Gerrish's Massachusetts Regiment, 19th May to December, 1775; Captain Massachusets Militia in 1776, and Colonel of same in 1782. (Died 15th June, 1823.)

Dodge, Samuel (N. Y.). 2d Lieutenant 5th New York, 21st November, 1776; taken prisoner at Fort Montgomery, 6th October, 1777; exchanged, ——; 1st Lieutenant, 1st October, 1777; transferred to 2d New York, 1st January, 1781; Brevet Captain, 30th September, 1783, and served to close of war. (Died 1807.)

Dodge, Samuel, Jr. (N. Y.). Sergeant 4th New York, 2d May, 1777; Ensign, 1st June, 1779; transferred to 2d New York, 1st January, 1781, and served to 3d June, 1783. (Died 27th October, 1835.)

Doggett, —— (S. C.). Captain South Carolina Militia; wounded at Stono Ferry, 20th June, 1779, and died next day.

Doggett, Arthur (Mass). Captain of Learned's Massachusetts Regiment, May to December, 1775.

Doggett, John (Mass). Colonel Massachusetts Militia, 1776-1777.

Doggett, Samuel (Mass). 2d Lieutenant of Gridley's Regiment Massachusetts Artillery, May to December, 1775; 2d Lieutenant of Knox's Regiment Continental Artillery, 1st January to 31st December, 1776. (Died 19th November, 1831.)

Doherty, George (N. C.). 1st Lieutenant 6th North Carolina, 16th April, 1776; Captain, 28th October, 1776; transferred to 4th North Carolina, 1st

June, 1778; Major, 13th October, 1781, and served to June, 1783.

Doherty, James (S. C.). Captain South Carolina Militia; killed near Beaufort, in August, 1776.

Dole, James (Conn). Private 2d Continental Dragoons, 7th May, 1777; Sergeant, 1st February, 1778; Sergeant-Major, 12th May, 1779; taken prisoner at Camden, 16th August, 1780; Cornet 2d Continental Dragoons, 14th January, 1781; 2d Lieutenant, 10th June, 1782, and served to close of war.

Dolliver, Peter (Mass). Adjutant of Sargent's Massachusets Regiment, June to November, 1775; Adjutant 16th Continental Infantry, 1st January to 31st December, 1776; Captain of Jackson's Additional Continental Regiment, 1st February, 1777; resigned 1st March, 1779. (Died 23d June, 1816.)

Dolson, Peter (N. Y.). Ensign 2d New York, 21st November, 1776; resigned 19th January, 1778.

Don, David (N. Y.).—See **Dan.**

Donaldson, John (S. C.). 1st Lieutenant 3d South Carolina, 17th June, 1775; Captain, 16th May, 1776, and served to ——.

Dondel, Michael (Pa). Captain in Thompson's Pennsylvania Rifle Battalion, 25th June, 1775; resigned 13th August, 1775.

Donlevy, John (Va). Ensign 1st Virginia State Regiment, April, 1777, to April, 1778.

Donnell, James (Mass). 1st Lieutenant of Scammon's Massachusetts Regiment, May to December, 1775; 1st Lieutenant 18th Continental Infantry, 1st January to 31st December, 1776; Captain 12th Massachusetts, 1st January, 1777; resigned 5th July, 1779.

Donnell, Nathaniel (Pa). 2d Lieutenant of Roman's Independent Company Pennsylvania Artillery, 25th March, 1776; 1st Lieutenant, 15th May, 1776; Captain of Steven's Battalion of Artillery, 9th November, 1776; company subsequently attached and formed part of the 3d Continental Artillery, and served to June, 1783. (Died 29th May, 1821.)

Donnell, Timothy (Mass). Private 1st Massachusetts, 1st January, 1777; Corporal, 31st March, 1778; Sergeant, — June, 1778; Ensign, 23d October, 1781, served to June, 1783.

Donnelly, Patrick (Md). Ensign 7th Maryland, 27th May, 1778; Lieutenant,

7th October, 1779; retired 1st January, 1781.

Donneson, William (R .I.). Adjutant of Elliott's Rhode Island Artillery Regiment, 1777-1778.

Donnom, William (S. C.). 1st Lieutenant 4th South Carolina, 16th April, 1776; Captain, ——, 1778; killed at Savannah, 9th October, 1779.

Donoho, Thomas · (N. C.). 1st Lieutenant 6th North Carolina, 16th April, 1776; Captain, 10th September, 1776; Major, 13th October, 1781, in 4th North Carolina, 6th February, 1782; served to close of war. (Died 1825.)

Donovan, Matthew (Va). Major 9th Virginia, 4th March, 1776; died 27th January, 1777.

Donovan, Richard (Md). Ensign 6th Maryland, 15th March, 1777; Regimental Adjutant, 17th April, 1777, to 16th August, 1780; Lieutenant, 1st April, 1778; killed 16th August, 1780, at Camden.

Donworth, Peter (R. I.). 2d Lieutenant 11th Continental Infantry, 1st January, 1776, to ——.

Dooley, George (Ga). Lieutenant 3d Georgia, —, 1778.

Dooley, John (Ga). Captain 1st Georgia, 12th December, 1775; resigned ——, 1776; Colonel Georgia Militia. He and his family murdered by Tories in August, 1780.

Dooley, Thomas (Ga). 1st Lieutenant 1st Georgia, 12th December, 1775; Captain, ——, 1776; killed by Indians near Oconee River, Georgia, 22d July, 1776.

Doolittle, Daniel (Conn). Ensign 1st Connecticut, 1st May to 1st December, 1775.

Doolittle, Ephraim (Mass). Colonel Massachusetts Regiment, May to October, 1775.

Doolittle, Ichabod (Conn). Captain 5th Connecticut, 1st May to 4th November, 1775.

Dormon, Jesse (Mass). Captain of Scammon's Massachusetts Regiment, May to December, 1775.

Dorothy, Charles (Mass). Lieutenant 12th Massachusetts, 10th August, 1777; resigned 9th January, 1778.

Dorr, Jonathan (Mass). Private in Lexington Alarm, April, 1775; 2d Lieutenant of Heath's Massachusetts Regiment, May to December, 1775.

Dorrance, David (Conn). Private in the Lexington Alarm, April, 1775; Sergeant 6th Connecticut, 8th May to 15th December, 1775; Ensign 10th Continental Infantry, 1st January to 31st December, 1776; 2d Lieutenant 1st Connecticut, 1st January, 1777; 1st Lieutenant, 1st January, 1778; Captain Lieutenant, 20th June, 1779; Captain, 1st July, 1780; transferred to 5th Connecticut, 1st January, 1781; transferred to 3d Connecticut, 1st January, 1783, and served to 3d June, 1783.

Dorrance, George (Conn). Lieutenant-Colonel Connecticut Militia; taken prisoner and murdered by Indians at Wyoming, 3d July, 1778.

Dorrance, George, Jr. (R. I.). Ensign of Hitchcock's Rhode Island Regiment, 3d May to December, 1775

Dorser, David (Mass). 2d Lieutenant of Little's Massachusetts Regiment, 19th May, 1775, to ——.

Dorsey, Daniel (Md). Captain 3d Maryland Battalion of the Flying Camp, July to December, 1776; Captain 4th Maryland, 10th December, 1776; resigned 5th August, 1777. (Died 1823.)

Dorsey, Ely (Md). Lieutenant of Watkins' Independent Maryland Company, 14th January, 1776; 1st Lieutenant, 3d October, 1776; Captain 2d Maryland, 10th December, 1776; taken prisoner at Staten Island, 22d August, 1777; was a prisoner on parole but never rejoined regiment.

Dorsey, John (Md). Surgeon's Mate Maryland Battalion of the Flying Camp, 20th August to December, 1776; Surgeon's Mate of Spencer's Continental Regiment, 11th January, 1777; retired 1st January, 1781.

Dorsey, John W. (Md). 2d Lieutenant 3d Maryland Battalion of the Flying Camp, July, 1776, to ——.

Dorsey, Larkin (Md). 2d Lieutenant Baltimore Artillery Company, 5th November, 1776; Cornet 4th Continental Dragoons, 25th January, 1777; resigned 4th September, 1778.

· **Dorsey, Nicholas** (Md). Ensign 4th Maryland, 10th December, 1776; 2d Lieutenant, 15th April, 1777; 1st Lieutenant, 1st April, 1778; resigned 10th November, 1778.

Dorsey, Richard (Md). 3d Lieutenant of Richardson's Maryland Battalion of the Flying Camp, 17th September to 1st December, 1776; Lieutenant 4th Continental Dragoons, 24th January,

1777; resigned 15th April, 1777; Captain Independent Company Maryland Artillery, 4th May, 1777; company attached to and formed part of the 1st Continental Artillery, 30th May, 1778; wounded and taken prisoner at Camden, 16th August, 1780; prisoner on parole to close of war; Brevet Major, 30th September, 1783. (Died 1826.)

Dorsey, Thomas (Pa). Captain 1st Pennsylvania Battalion, 27th October, 1775; 2d Pennsylvania, 25th October, 1776; resigned 1st January, 1777; Captain 4th Continental Dragoons, 10th January, 1777; omitted August, 1777.

Dorsey, Vachel (Md). Private Maryland Battalion of the Flying Camp, 20th July to December, 1776; Ensign of Hartley's Continental Regiment, 1st May, 1777; 2d Lieutenant, 17th November, 1777, and served to ——.

Doty, David (Conn). 1st Lieutenant of Burrall's Connecticut State Regiment, 19th January, 1776; appointed Wagonmaster-General of General Gates' Army, 3d August, 1776. (Died 1817.)

Doty, Samuel (Pa). 2d Lieutenant 2d Continental Artillery, 1st January, 1777; 1st Lieutenant, 9th November, 1778; transferred to 4th Continental Artillery, June, 1779; Captain Lieutenant, 7th October, 1781, and served to June, 1783.

Doubleday, Nathaniel (Mass). Lieutenant of Danielson's Massachusetts Regiment, April to December, 1775; 1st Lieutenant 16th Continental Infantry, 1st January to 31st December, 1776.

Doudel, Michael (Pa). Captain of Thompson's Pennsylvania Rifle Regiment, 24th June, 1775; resigned 15th October, 1775.

Dougherty, Charles (Mass). Ensign of Brewer's Massachusetts Regiment, 23d April, 1775; 2d Lieutenant, October, 1775; Ensign and Quartermaster 6th Continental Infantry, 1st January, 1776; 2d Lieutenant, 1st October, 1776; 1st Lieutenant 12th Massachusetts, 1st January, 1777; resigned 28th June, 1778. (name also spelled Dohauty and Doherty.)

Dougherty, John (Pa). Sergeant of Thompson's Pennsylvania Rifle Battalion, 25th June, 1775; 3d Lieutenant 1st Continental Infantry, 1st January, 1776; 2d Lieutenant, 25th September, 1776; discharged 31st December, 1776.

Dougherty, Michael (Mass). Private in Brewer's Massachusetts Regiment, May to December, 1775; Sergeant 6th

Continental Infantry, 1st January, 1776; Ensign, 5th October, 1776; 2d Lieutenant 13th Massachusetts, 1st January, 1777; resigned 26th December, 1777.

Doughty, John (N. J.). Captain Lieutenant of New Jersey Artillery Company, 1st March, 1776; Captain 2d Continental Artillery, 1st January, 1777; Aide-de-Camp to General Schuyler in 1777; transferred to Corps of Artillery, 17th June, 1783; Brevet Major, 30th September, 1783; Major of the Artillery Battalion, 7th August, 1784; Major Artillery Battalion United States Army, 20th September, 1789; Lieutenant-Colonel 2d United States Infantry, 4th March, 1791, which he declined, and retired from the service; Lieutenant-Colonel 2d Artillerists and Engineers, 1st June, 1798; resigned 26th May, 1800. (Died 16th September, 1826.)

Douglas, —— (——). Major, ——; taken prisoner at Briar Creek, 3d March, 1779.

Douglas, Ephraim (Pa). Regimental Quartermaster 8th Pennsylvania, 9th August, 1776; Aide-de-Camp to General Lincoln in March, 1777; taken prisoner at Bound Brook, 13th April, 1777; exchanged 27th November, 1780; appointed Ensign 9th Pennsylvania, 2d June, 1778; Lieutenant, 27th January, 1779; transferred to 5th Pennsylvania, 17th January, 1781; transferred to 2d Pennsylvania, 1st January, 1783, and served to June, 1783. (Died 1833.)

Douglas, John (Pa). Captain Pennsylvania Battalion of the Flying Camp, July to December, 1776; Captain 11th Pennsylvania, 13th November, 1776; resigned 7th December, 1777. (Died 1840.)

Douglas, John (Conn). Lieutenant-Colonel 8th Connecticut, 6th July to 19th December, 1775; Colonel Connecticut State Regiment and Militia, 1776-1777; Brigadier-General Connecticut Militia, June, 1777, to close of war.

Douglas, Richard (Conn). Private in the Lexington Alarm, April, 1775; Ensign and Regimental Quartermaster in Selden's Connecticut State Regiment, 20th June to 25th December, 1776; 2d Lieutenant 1st Connecticut, 1st January, 1777; 1st Lieutenant, 1st January, 1778; Captain Lieutenant, 11th August, 1780; Captain, 22d August, 1780; transferred to 5th Connecticut, 1st January, 1781; transferred to 3d Connecticut, 1st January, 1783; transferred to Swift's Consolidated Connecticut Regiment, June, 1783, and served to 3d November, 1783. (Died 1828.)

Douglas, Robert (N. C.). Lieutenant of Kingsbury's Company North Carolina Artillery, 19th July, 1777; omitted July, 1778.

Douglas, William (Conn). Captain 1st Connecticut, 1st May to 1st December, 1775; was Aide-de-Camp to General Wooster, 13th June to December, 1775; Colonel Connecticut State Regiment, 20th June to 25th December, 1776; wounded at Harlem Plains, 16th September, 1776; Colonel 6th Connecticut, 1st January, 1777; died 28th May, 1777.

Douglas, William (N. C.). Regimental Quartermaster 4th North Carolina, 10th February, 1777, to ——.

Douglass.—See **Douglas** as name is spelled both ways.

Douglass, Thomas (Pa). 1st Lieutenant 4th Continental Artillery, 1st April, 1777; Captain Lieutenant, 14th April, 1778; Captain, 12th October, 1781; retired 1st January, 1783; Captain of a Company United States Artillery, 12th August, 1784, and served to October, 1785.

Dove, William (Md). Ensign 1st Maryland, 17th April, 1777; resigned 1st December, 1777.

Dover, Andrew (Pa). 2d Lieutenant 5th Pennsylvania Battalion, 8th January, 1776; 1st Lieutenant, 4th March, 1776; taken prisoner at Fort Washington, 16th November, 1776; exchanged, 25th October, 1780, and did not re-enter service. (Died 12th December, 1831.)

Dover, John (Pa). Ensign 3d Pennsylvania Battalion, 8th January, 1776; 2d Lieutenant, March, 1776; 1st Lieutenant 4th Pennsylvania, 3d January, 1777; resigned 2d November, 1778.

Dow, Abner (Mass). 1st Lieutenant 15th Massachusetts, 1st January, 1777; Captain, 9th November, 1779; transferred to 9th Massachusetts, 1st January, 1781; cashiered 9th August, 1781.

Dow, Alexander (Pa). 1st Lieutenant of Malcolm's Additional Continental Regiment, 12th April, 1777; transferred to Flower's Regiment of Artillery Artificers, June, 1777; Captain Lieutenant, 4th April, 1780; retired 1st May, 1781.

Dow, James (Pa). 2d Lieutenant 3d Pennsylvania, 25th September, 1775, to October, 1776.

Dow, Jeremiah (N. H.). Captain New Hampshire Militia, 1777.

Dow, Reuben (Mass). Captain Company New Hampshire Minute Men, 19th April, 1775; Captain of Prescott's Massachusetts Regiment, 19th May to December, 1775; wounded at Bunker Hill, 17th June, 1775. (Died 1811.)

Dow, William (Md). Ensign 1st Maryland, 17th April, 1777; resigned 1st December, 1777.

Dowal, David (N. C.). Captain North Carolina Militia, 1776.

Downe, William (Pa). 2d Lieutenant 3d Continental Artillery, May, 1778; resigned March, 1779.

Downer, Eliphalet (Mass). Volunteer Surgeon at Lexington and Concord, 19th April, 1775; Surgeon of Heath's Massachusetts Regiment, May to December, 1775; Surgeon 24th Continental Infantry, 1st January to 31st December, 1776; served subsequently in United States Navy.

Downey, Ezekiel (Pa). Surgeon 6th Pennsylvania, 11th September, 1780; drowned 1st July, 1781.

Downey, John (Pa). Captain Pennsylvania Militia, ——; killed at Crooked Billet, 1st May, 1778.

Downes, Edward (Md). 2d Lieutenant 7th Maryland, 1st April, 1777; resigned 7th January, 1778.

Downes, Henry, Jr. (Md). 1st Lieutenant 4th Maryland Battalion of the Flying Camp, July to December, 1776.

Downes, William (Mass). 2d Lieutenant 3d Continental Artillery, 1st January, 1777; resigned 9th February, 1779, and entered the Navy as an officer of Marines.

Downing, Henry (Va). Ensign of a Virginia Regiment in 1781 and 1782.

Downing, Thomas (Mass). 2d Lieutenant of Mansfield's Massachusetts Regiment, May to December, 1775; 1st Lieutenant 27th Continental Infantry, 1st January to 31st December, 1776.

Downing, William (Pa). 2d Lieutenant 10th Pennsylvania, 4th December, 1776, to ——.

Downman, Raleigh (Ga). Captain 3d Georgia, ——; on roll for August, 1778.

Downs, David (Conn). Captain of Burrall's Connecticut State Regiment, 19th January, 1776; taken prisoner at the Cedars, 19th May, 1776. (Died 1813.)

Downs, John (S. C.). Adjutant 2d South Carolina, 12th March, 1778, to ——

Doyle, Daniel (S. C.). Lieutenant in a South Carolina Regiment in 1780.

Doyle, John (Pa). Captain of an Independent Pennsylvania Company, 6th July, 1776; company attached to and became part of the 11th Pennsylvania, 16th December, 1777; transferred to 6th Pennsylvania, 1st July, 1778; transferred to 1st Pennsylvania, 1st January, 1783, and served to 3d June, 1783.

Doyle, Sylvester (Pa). Private 9th Pennsylvania, 16th November, 1776; Surgeon's Mate, ——, 1777; discharged 25th January, 1778.

Doyle, Thomas (Pa). Regimental Quartermaster 6th Pennsylvania, 13th July, 1778; 2d Lieutenant, 1st January, 1779; wounded at Green Springs, 6th July, 1781; transferred to 1st Pennsylvania, 1st January, 1783, and served to November, 1783; Lieutenant United States Infantry, 12th August, 1784; Lieutenant 1st United States Infantry, 29th September, 1798; Captain 22d October, 1790, which became 1st Sub Legion, 4th September, 1792; Major, 29th September, 1792; honorably discharged 1st November, 1796. (Died 15th February, 1805.)

Dozier, John (S. C.). Captain South Carolina Militia in 1776.

Drake, Abraham (N. H.). Lieutenant-Colonel of Volunteers 6 weeks; mentioned as at Winter Hill in 1775; Colonel New Hampshire Militia in 1776-1777. (Died 1st August, 1781.)

Drake, Jacob (N. J.). Colonel New Jersey Militia, 1776-1777.

Drake, Jacob (Pa). 2d Lieutenant of Hart's Pennsylvania Battalion of the Flying Camp, July to December, 1776; 2d Lieutenant 3d Pennsylvania, 1st January, 1777; resigned 23d November, 1777.

Drake, John (R. I.). Lieutenant Rhode Island Militia in 1776.

Drake, Joseph (N. Y.). Colonel New York Militia, 1777-1781.

Drake, Joshua (N. Y.). 2d Lieutenant of Malcolm's Additional Continental Regiment, 25th March, 1777; 1st Lieutenant, 24th December, 1777; retired 23d April, 1779; Captain New York Militia, ——; taken prisoner at Kanassoraga, 23d October, 1780, and remained a prisoner to 21st May, 1783.

Drake, Phineas (Conn). 2d Lieutenant of Gay's Connecticut State Regiment, June to December, 1776.

Drake, Samuel (N. Y.). Colonel New York Militia, 1775-1776.

Drake, Thomas (Va). 2d Lieutenant 3d Virginia, 22d February, 1776; 1st Lieutenant, — January, 1777; killed 21st January, 1777, at Millstone, New Jersey.

Draper, George (Va). Hospital Surgeon and Physician, 6th October, 1780, to close of war.

Draper, Moses (Mass). Lieutenant in Lexington Alarm, April, 1775; Captain of Gardner's Massachusetts Regiment, May to December, 1775; Captain 25th Continental Infantry, 1st January to 31st December, 1776.

Drayton, Charles (S. C.). Captain South Carolina Artillery, 14th November, 1775, to ——.

Drayton, Glen (S. C.). Lieutenant 1st South Carolina, 17th June, 1775, to ——.

Drayton, Stephen (Ga). Lieutenant-Colonel 2d Georgia, 7th January, 1776, to 5th July, 1776.

Drayton, Stephen (S. C.). Major and Aide-de-Camp to General Howe, 29th November, 1777; Colonel Deputy Quartermaster-General Southern Department, 12th November, 1778, to ——.

Dresser, John (Mass). 2d Lieutenant of Little's Massachusetts Regiment, May to December, 1775.

Drew, John (N. H.). Captain of Wyman's Regiment New Hampshire Militia, June, 1776; Captain 2d New Hampshire, 8th November, 1776; resigned 31st August, 1778.

Drew, John (Va). Was an Ensign and 2d Lieutenant 1st Virginia in 1777; Lieutenant 1st Continental Artillery, — February, 1781; wounded at Eutaw Springs, 8th September, 1781, and served to ——.

Drew, Lebbeus (Mass). Private in Lexington Alarm, April, 1778; Sergeant of Cotton's Massachusetts Regiment, May to December, 1775; 1st Lieutenant 4th Massachusets, 1st January, 1777; taken prisoner near Schuylkill, 28th December, 1777; Captain, 14th April, 1780; resigned 10th April, 1782.

Drew, Seth (Mass). Lieutenant in Lexington Alarm, April, 1775; 1st Lieutenant of Cotton's Massachusetts Regiment, May to December, 1775; 1st Lieutenant 23d Continental Infantry, 1st January to 31st December, 1776; Captain 2d Massachusetts, 1st January, 1777; Brigade-Inspector, 13th July, 1781;

Major 3d Massachusetts, 7th January, 1783, and served to 12th June, 1783. (Died 18th May, 1824.)

Drew, Thomas Haynes (Va). 2d Lieutenant of Grayson's Additional Continental Regiment, 6th February, 1777; 1st Lieutenant, 1st February, 1778; Regimental Paymaster, 31st August, 1778, transferred to Gist's Regiment, 22d April, 1779; resigned 2d July, 1779.

Drew, Zebulon (N. H.). 2d Lieutenant 2d New Hampshire, 20th May to December, 1775.

Drewry, John (Va). Captain Virginia Militia, 1776-1777.

Driesbach, Yost (Pa). 2d Lieutenant 1st Battalion of Miles' Pennsylvania Rifle Regiment, 10th March, 1776; taken prisoner at Long Island, 27th August, 1776; exchanged 10th December, 1776; Captain of Ottendorf's Battalion Pulaski Legion, 22d February, 1777, and served to ——.

Driskill, Joseph (N. Y.). 2d Lieutenant of Steven's Battalion New York Artillery, 9th November, 1776, which became part of the 3d Continental Artillery; 1st Lieutenant, 7th May, 1779; retired 1st January, 1780.

Dritt, Jacob (Pa). Lieutenant of Swope's Pennsylvania Battalion of the Flying Camp, 23d August, 1776; taken prisoner at Fort Washington, 16th November, 1776.

Drown, Jonathan (Mass.). Lieutenant in Danielson's Massachusetts Regiment, May to December, 1775; 1st Lieutenant 16th Continental Infantry, 1st January to 31st December, 1776; Captain of Lee's Continental Regiment, February, 1777; resigned — November, 1778.

Drowne, Solomon (R. I.). Surgeon Rhode Island State Regiment, 1776-1778, to close of war. (Died 5th February, 1834.)

Drowne, William (R. I.). Lieutenant of Babcock's Rhode Island State Regiment, 15th January to November, 1776.

Druitt, John (Pa). Conductor of Artillery of Captain Roman's Company Pennsylvania Artillery, 25th March, 1776; 3d Lieutenant, 15th May, 1776; dismissed 30th July, 1776.

Drummond, James (Va.). 2d Lieutenant 9th Virginia, 5th February, 1776, to —.

Drummond, Peter (Pa.). 2d Lieutenant 10th Pennsylvania, 18th April, 1777; 1st Lieutenant, 22d November, 1777; retired 17th January, 1781.

Drury, Asa (Mass.). Captain Massachusetts Militia, 1781.

Drury, John (Va). Sergeant and Sergeant-Major 1st Virginia, November, 1776, until appointed 2d Lieutenant, 9th August 1777; 1st Lieutenant, 16th November, 1777; retired 14th September, 1778.

Drury, John (Mass). Captain Massachusetts Militia, 1778.

Drury, Jotham (Mass). Captain of Knox's Regiment Continental Artillery, 1st January to 31st December, 1776; Captain 3d Continental Artillery, 1st January, 1777; cashiered 12th March, 1778.

Drury, Luke (Mass). Captain of Ward's Massachusetts Regiment, 22d May to December, 1775.

Drury, Thomas (Mass). Captain of Nixon's Massachusetts Regiment, May to December, 1775.

Dryden, Nathaniel (Va). Ensign Virginia Riflemen, ——; killed at King's Mountain, 7th October, 1880.

Du Bois, Abraham (Pa.). 2d Lieutenant of Hart's Pennsylvania Battalion of the Flying Camp, July to December, 1776.

Du Bois, Christian (N. Y.). Lieutenant New York Militia, 1775. (Died 1807.)

Du Bois, Cornelius (N. Y.). Lieutenant-Colonel New York Militia, 1775-1779.

Du Bois, David (N. Y.). 1st Lieutenant 3d New York, 28th June, 1775; Captain, 25th November, 1775; Captain of DuBois' New York Regiment, 26th June to November, 1776.

Du Bois, Henry (N. Y.). Adjutant of DuBois' New York Regiment, 26th June, 1776; Adjutant 5th New York, 21st November, 1776; Captain Lieutenant, 1st September, 1778; Captain, 22d December, 1779; transferred to 2d New York, 1st January, 1781; resigned 4th November, 1782. (Died — January, 1804.)

Du Bois, James (N. Y.). 2d Lieutenant 3d New York, 21st November, 1776; omitted February, 1777.

Du Bois, Lewis (N. Y.). Captain 3d New York, 28th June, 1775; Major, 25th November, 1775; Major of Nicholson's New York Regiment, 8th March, 1776; Colonel, 21st June, 1776; Colonel 5th New York, 21st November, 1776, to rank from 25th June, 1776; taken prisoner at Fort Montgomery, 6th October,

1777; resigned 22d December, 1779; subsequently served as Colonel New York Levies. (Died 29th November, 1802.)

Du Bois, Zachariah (N. Y.). Major New York Militia; taken prisoner; when and where, not stated.

Du Bose, Abraham (S. C.). Captain in Marion's Brigade, 1780-1781.

Du Bose, Elias (S. C.). Lieutenant in Marion's Brigade in 1781.

Du Bose, Isaac (S. C.). 2d Lieutenant 2d South Carolina, 17th June, 1775; 1st Lieutenant, May, 1776; Captain South Carolina Dragoons, ——, 1779, to ——.

Du Bose, Samuel (S. C.). Lieutenant South Carolina Militia, 1781-1782. (Died 1811.)

Du Bouchet.—See Bouchet.

Du Buysson, —— Chevalier (France). Major Continental Army, 4th October, 1777; served as Aide-de-Camp to General De Kalb, 4th October, 1777, to 19th August, 1780; Lieutenant-Colonel Continental Army, 11th February, 1778; wounded and taken prisoner at Camden 16th August, 1780, and was prisoner on parole to close of war.

du Calvert.—See Calvert.

Du Cambray.—See Cambray.

Duclos, Francis (N. J.). Ensign 2d New Jersey, 9th December, 1775; taken prisoner at Three Rivers, 8th June, 1776; 1st Lieutenant, 2d New Jersey, 29th November, 1776; cashiered 27th October, 1778.

Ducoines, John (Ga). 1st Lieutenant 2d Georgia, 22d July, 1777; taken prisoner at Charleston 12th May, 1780; exchanged April, 1781; Captain, ——; served to close of war.

du Coudray.—See Coudray.

Duda, Lemuel (N. H.). Ensign 2d New Hampshire, ——, 1781; transferred to 1st New Hampshire, March, 1782; discharged 20th November, 1782.

Dudley, Ambrose (Va). Captain Virginia Militia, 1780-1781.

Dudley, Daniel (Conn). 2d Lieutenant of Swift's Connecticut State Regiment, June to December, 1776.

Dudley, Guilford (N. C.). Lieutenant-Colonel North Carolina Militia, 1780-1781.

Dudley, Henry (Va). Captain Virginia State Regiment, 15th October, 1777, to 1st January, 1780.

Dudley, John (Va). 1st Lieutenant and Captain 2d Virginia State Regiment, March to November, 1777.

Dudley, Moses (Conn). 2d Lieutenant of Mott's Connecticut State Regiment, June to December, 1776.

Dudley, Robert (Va). 1st Lieutenant 5th Virginia, 12th February, 1776, to ——; was in service in December, 1776.

Dudley, Thomas (N. C.). Musician 6th North Carolina in 1776; Ensign, May, 1778; transferred to 3d North Carolina, 1st June, 1778; 2d Lieutenant, 20th June, 1779; 1st Lieutenant, 1st March, 1781; wounded at Eutaw Springs 8th September, 1781; served to close of war.

Duey, Oliver (Mass). Sergeant-Major 7th Massachusetts, 8th March, 1777; Ensign, 19th November, 1777; died 6th December, 1777.

Duff, Daniel (S. C.). Lieutenant 3d South Carolina, 30th September, 1776, to ——.

Duff, Edward (Va). Surgeon 5th Virginia, 23d January, 1777; transferred to 6th Virginia, 14th September, 1778; last record of him is for November, 1779.

Duff, Henry (Del). Ensign Delaware Regiment, 29th November, 1776; 2d Lieutenant, 5th April, 1777; 1st Lieutenant, 16th August, 1778; taken prisoner at Camden 16th August, 1780; retired 17th May, 1782. (Died — May, 1789.)

Duff, Richard (Conn). Ensign 22d Continental Infantry, 1st January, 1776; wounded and taken prisoner at Fort Washington 16th November, 1776.

Duff, Thomas (Del). Major Delaware Militia, 1775.

Duffield, Andrew (Pa). Ensign of Lewis' Pennsylvania Battalion of the Flying Camp, July to December, 1776.

Duffield, John (Pa). Surgeon 3d Continental Artillery, 30th September, 1782, and served to June, 1783.

Duffield, Samuel (Pa). Surgeon Hospital Department in 1779.

Duffy, Patrick (Pa). 3d Lieutenant of Proctor's Battalion Pennsylvania Artillery, 5th October, 1776; 1st Lieutenant 4th Continental Artillery, 1st January, 1777; Captain, 29th February, 1778; dismissed 11th October, 1781.

Duffy, Timothy (N. Y.). Surgeon's Mate 2d Canadian (Hazen's) Regiment,

10th December, 1776; taken prisoner at Long Island, 22d August, 1777, and did not rejoin regiment.

Dugan, James (Pa). Ensign Pennsylvania State Regiment, 18th April, 1777; regiment designated 13th Pennsylvania 12th November, 1777; resigned 9th February, 1778.

Dugan, Jeremiah (—). Major Battalion Rangers, 28th March, 1776, to ——.

Duguid, John (Pa). 2d Lieutenant 3d Pennsylvania Battalion, 8th January, 1776; 1st Lieutenant, 13th June, 1776; taken prisoner at Fort Washington 16th November, 1776; exchanged 25th October, 1780, and did not re-enter the service. (Died — August, 1787.)

Dull, Abraham (Pa). Sergeant 2d Pennsylvania Battalion, 19th January, 1776; Ensign, 25th October, 1776, and served to January, 1777.

Dull, Casper (Pa). 1st Lieutenant of Lewis' Pennsylvania Battalion of the Flying Camp, July to December, 1776; Captain Pennsylvania Militia, 1779.

Dull, Leonard (Pa). 2d Lieutenant of Lewis' Pennsylvania Battalion of the Flying Camp, July to December, 1776.

Dumouchett, John (Ga). Lieutenant 3d Georgia in 1778.

Dunbar, Thomas (S. C.). Lieutenant 2d South Carolina, 24th February, 1777; Captain, 9th November, 1777; taken prisoner at Charleston 12th May, 1780; exchanged June, 1781; served to close of war. Brevet Major, 30th September, 1783.

Duncan, Daniel (Conn). Ensign of Silliman's Connecticut State Regiment, July to December, 1776.

Duncan, David (Va). Lieutenant of a Virginia Regiment; taken prisoner at Long Island 27th August, 1776.

Duncan, James (Pa). 2d Lieutenant 2d Canadian (Hazen's) Regiment, 3d November, 1776; 1st Lieutenant, 8th April, 1777; Captain, 25th March, 1778; retired June, 1783. (Died 24th June, 1844.)

Duncan, John (N. Y.). Captain New York Militia, ——; killed at Minnisink, 22d July, 1779.

Duncan, Matthew (Pa). Volunteer in the expedition to Canada, 25th September, 1775; taken prisoner at Quebec, 31st December, 1775; Captain 5th Pennsylvania Battalion, 5th January,

1776; taken prisoner at Fort Washington, 16th November, 1776.

Duncan, Robert (N. C.). Regimental Paymaster 4th North Carolina, 1st December, 1777; retired 1st June, 1778.

Dunckerly, Joseph (—). Deserted from the British Army; Adjutant of Henley's Continental Regiment, March, 1777; resigned 20th May, 1778.

Dungan, Thomas (Pa). Paymaster 12th Pennsylvania, 29th April, 1777; Ensign, 2d June, 1778; transferred to 6th Pennsylvania, 1st July, 1778; 2d Lieutenant, 1st January, 1781; transferred to 2d Pennsylvania 1st January, 1783, and served to 3d June, 1783.

Dunham, Azariah (N. J.). Lieutenant-Colonel New Jersey Militia in 1776.

Dunham, George (Mass). Sergeant in Lexington Alarm, April, 1775; Sergeant in Cotton's Massachusetts Regiment, May to December, 1775; 2d Lieutenant 21st Continental Infantry, 1st January to 31st December, 1776; Captain 2d Massachusetts, 1st January, 1777; resigned 21st June, 1779. (Died 19th December, 1819.)

Dunham, Levi (Mass). Sergeant in Lexington Alarm, April, 1775; 1st Lieutenant of Danielson's Massachusetts Regiment, May to December, 1775.

Dunham, Lewis Ford (N. J.). Surgeon 3d New Jersey, 8th February to October, 1776; Surgeon 3d New Jersey, 28th November, 1776; resigned January, 1780. (Died 1821.)

Dunham, Silas (Mass). Lieutenant Massachusetts Militia; killed at Whitemarsh 7th December, 1777.

Dunham, Stephen (N. J.). 1st Lieutenant 3d New Jersey, 7th February, 1776; resigned July, 1776.

Dunholm, Archibald (Va). (See **Denholm**—name spelled on rolls both ways.

Duning, Michael (N. H.). 1st Lieutenant of Warner's Continental Regiment, 1st October, 1776; taken prisoner at Stony Point, 15th July, 1779; Captain, 16th July, 1779; retired 1st January, 1781.

Dunlap, James (Pa). Captain Philadelphia Light Horse, 1776-1777. (Died 27th November, 1812.)

Dunlop, Francis (N. J.). 2d Lieutenant 2d New Jersey, 1st January, 1778; cashiered 27th October, 1778.

Dunlop, James (Pa). Major 6th Pennsylvania Battalion, 10th January,

1776; Lieutenant-Colonel, 10th Pennsylvania, 25th October, 1776; resigned 23d January, 1777; Colonel Pennsylvania Militia in 1780. (Died 15th December, 1821.)

Dunlop, William (Virginia). Chaplain 6th Virginia, 9th April, 1776, to ——.

Dunn, Abner (Pa). 2d Lieutenant of Patton's Continental Regiment, 15th January, 1777; Lieutenant, 4th October, 1777; last record of him is February, 1779.

Dunn, Abner Martin (Pa). Ensign 2d Pennsylvania Battalion, 11th November, 1776; 1st Lieutenant of McLane's Delaware Partisan Company, 13th January, 1777; Lieutenant 9th Pennsylvania, 31st May, 1779; transferred to 5th Pennsylvania 17th January, 1781; transferred to 2d Pennsylvania 1st January, 1783; transferred to 1st Pennsylvania June, 1783, and served to 3d November, 1783. (Died 1795.)

Dunn, Isaac Budd (Pa). 2d Lieutenant 2d Pennsylvania Battalion, 5th January, 1776; 1st Lieutenant, 4th July, 1776, Captain 3d Pennsylvania, 1st January, 1777; Major Aide-de-Camp to General St. Clair, May, 1781, to close of war; Brevet Major, 30th September, 1783.)

Dunn, John (N. J.). Major New Jersey Militia, 1776-1778.

Dunn, Micajah (N. J.). Lieutenant-Colonel New Jersey Militia in 1776.

Dunn, Peter (Va). 1st Lieutenant 6th Virginia, 26th February, 1776; Captain, 22d June, 1776. Died 26th December, 1777.

Dunn, Samuel (Mass). Captain of Phinney's Massachusetts Regiment, May to December, 1775. (Died 1784.)

Dunn, William (N. Y.). 2d Lieutenant 1st New York, 30th March to November, 1776.

Dunnell, Zacheus (Mass). Sergeant of Gridley's Regiment Massachusetts Artillery, June to December, 1775; 2d Lieutenant 3d Continental Artillery, 1st January, 1777; resigned 3d November, 1778.

Dunscomb, Edward (N. Y.). 2d Lieutenant of Lasher's New York Militia Regiment, January, 1776; 1st Lieutenant, May, 1776; taken prisoner at Long Island 27th August, 1776; 1st Lieutenant 4th New York, 21st November, 1776; Captain Lieutenant, 23d April, 1778; Captain, 11th April, 1780;

retired 1st January, 1781. (Died 12th November, 1814.)

Dunsmore, William (Mass). Surgeon of Whitcomb's Massachusetts Regiment, May to November, 1775.

Dunton, Moses (Mass). 1st Lieutenant of Gerrish's Massachusetts Regiment, 19th May to December, 1775.

Dunwoody, Andrew (Pa). 1st Lieutenant Montgomery's Pennsylvania Battalion of the Flying Camp; taken prisoner at Fort Washington, 16th November, 1776.

Du Plessis, de Maduit (—). See **Plessis.**

Duportail, Louis Lebique (France). Colonel Engineers, 8th July, 1777; Chief of Engineers, 22d July, 1777; Brigadier-General Engineers, 17th November, 1777; appointed Commandant of Corps of Engineers and Sappers and Miners, 11th May, 1779; taken prisoner at Charleston 12th May, 1780, and on parole to November, 1780; Major-General Chief Engineer, 16th November, 1781; retired 10th October, 1783. (Died ——, 1802.)

Duprie, Antoine (Canada). Lieutenant 2d Canadian (Hazen's) Regiment, 1st November, 1776; resigned 3d April, 1778.

Dupuy, James (S. C.). Captain South Carolina Militia at the battle of Guilford, 15th March, 1781.

Dupuy, Peter (S. C.). Lieutenant South Carolina Militia in 1780.

Durant, Edward (Mass). Surgeon of Mansfield's Massachusetts Regiment, 28th June to October, 1775; Surgeon in Hospital Department, 1776-1778.

Durfee, Benjamin (R. I.). Captain Rhode Island Militia in 1775.

Durfee, Joseph (Mass). Captain Massachusetts Militia, 1776; Lieutenant-Colonel of same, 1780-1781.

Durfee, Richard (R. I.). Captain Rhode Island Militia, 1776-1779.

Durfee, Thomas (R. I.). Ensign Rhode Island Militia, 1776-1777.

Durkee, Benjamin (Conn). Sergeant in the Lexington Alarm, April, 1775; Ensign, 20th Continental Infantry, 1st January, 1776; 2d Lieutenant, September, 1776; 2d Lieutenant 3d Connecticut, 1st January, 1777; retired 15th November, 1778; Captain Connecticut Militia, 1781-1783. (Died 1827.)

Durkee, Jedediah (Conn). Ensign of Swift's Connecticut State Regiment, July to November, 1776.

Durkee, John (Conn). Major 3d Connecticut, 1st May, 1775; Lieutenant-Colonel, 1st July to 10th December, 1775; Lieutenant-Colonel 20th Continental Infantry, 1st January, 1776; Colonel, 12th August, 1776; Colonel 4th Connecticut, 1st January, 1777; wounded at Monmouth, 28th June, 1778; transferred to 1st Connecticut 1st January, 1781; died 29th May, 1782.

Durkee, John Jr. (Conn). Ensign 20th Continental Infantry, 1st January to 31st December, 1776; 2d Lieutenant 4th Connecticut, 1st January, 1777; 1st Lieutenant, 31st July, 1777; Captain Lieutenant, 4th January, 1780; Captain, 26th October, 1780; transferred to 1st Connecticut, 1st January, 1781; retired June, 1783.

Durkee, Joseph (Conn). 2d Lieutenant of Ward's Connecticut State Regiment, 14th May, 1776, to May, 1777.

Durkee, Nathaniel (Conn). Regimental Quartermaster 7th Connecticut, 1st January, 1777; Deputy Commissary General of Purchases, 1st October, 1777, to 1781.

Durkee, Robert (Conn). Captain of an Independent Company, known as Wyoming Valley Company, 26th August, 1776; he retired from the service 23d June, 1778, his company being consolidated with Ransom's; served as a volunteer and was killed in the Wyoming Massacre, 3d July, 1778.

Dusenbury, John (N. Y.). 1st Lieutenant 3d New York, 10th January, 1776; wounded at White Plains, 28th October, 1776; Brigade Major to General J. M. Scott, April, 1777, to March, 1778, and of Parson's Brigade to February, 1782.

Dustin, Woody (N. H.). Lieutenant of Danielson's Massachusetts Regiment, May to December, 1775; 2d Lieutenant 16th Continental Infantry, 1st January, 1776; 1st Lieutenant 1st New Hampshire, 8th November, 1776; Captain, 5th March, 1778; retired 1st January, 1781. (Died 1810.)

Dustin, Moses (N. H.). 1st Lieutenant 26th Continental Infantry, 1st January, 1776; 1st Lieutenant 2d New Hampshire, 8th November, 1776; taken prisoner at Hubbardton 7th July, 1777; Captain, 20th September, 1777; retired 1st January, 1781.

Dutarque, Lewis (S. C.). 1st Lieutenant 3d South Carolina, 17th June, 1775, to ——.

Dutee, Gerauld (R. I.). Captain — Rhode Island Regiment; resigned 21st June, 1782.

Dutton, Titus (Conn). Lieutenant of Baldwin's Artillery Artificer Regiment, 23d February, 1779; omitted March, 1780.

Duval, Daniel (Va). Ensign 5th Virginia, 24th February, 1776, to ——.

Duval, Edward (Md). 2d Lieutenant 2d Maryland, 14th January, 1777; 1st Lieutenant, 17th April, 1777; taken prisoner at Germantown 4th October, 1777; killed at Camden 16th August, 1780.

Duval, Isaac Ensign 3d Maryland, 22d March, 1777; Lieutenant, 12th April, 1779; wounded at Camden, 16th August, 1780; transferred to 1st Maryland 1st January, 1781; wounded at Ninety-six 19th June, 1781; killed at Eutaw Springs, 8th September, 1781.

Duval, Jonathan Jr. (R. I.). Ensign of Richmond's Rhode Island Regiment, 1st November, 1775, and Lieutenant and Captain in Stanton's Rhode Island State Regiment, 1776 and 1777. (Died 19th August, 1824.) (Name also spelled Devol.)

Duval, William (Md). 2d Lieutenant 3d Maryland Battalion of the Flying Camp, July to December, 1776; 1st Lieutenant 4th Maryland, 10th December, 1776; died 15th April, 1777.

Du Veil, —— (—). Captain Sappers and Miners, 2d August, 1779, to ——.

Duychinck, John (N. J.). Lieutenant-Colonel and Colonel New Jersey Militia, 1776; "deserted to the enemy."

Dwight, Timothy (Conn). Brigade Chaplain, 6th October, 1777; resigned 28th January, 1779. (Died 11th January, 1817.)

Dye, Jonathan (Va). Ensign 2d Virginia, 1st January, 1777; 2d Lieutenant, 17th June, 1777; killed at Germantown 4th October, 1777.

Dyer, Asa (Mass). 1st Lieutenant of Heath's Massachusetts Regiment, May to December, 1775. (Died 1831.)

Dyer, Charles (R. I.). 2d Lieutenant of Stanton's Rhode Island State Regiment, 12th December, 1776, to —, 1777. (Died 1845.)

Dyer, Charles (R. I.). Captain of Richmond's Rhode Island State Regiment, 1st November, 1775, to ——.

Dyer, Charles (R.I.). Major and Lieutenant-Colonel Rhode Island Militia, 1775-1781.

Dyer, Christopher (R. I.). 1st Lieutenant of Babcock's Rhode Island State Regiment, 15th January, 1776; Captain of Lippitt's Rhode Island State Regiment, 19th August, 1776, to 1777.

Dyer, Edward (Md). 2d Lieutenant 2d Maryland, 14th January, 1777; 1st Lieutenant, 27th May, 1778; Captain Lieutenant, 10th September, 1780; Captain, 3d June, 1781; retired 1st January, 1783.

Dyer, Eliphalet (Conn). Colonel Connecticut Militia, 1775 and 1776, and Brigadier-General Connecticut Militia, December, 1776, to May, 1777. (Died 13th May, 1807.)

Dyer, Thomas (Conn). Captain 3d Connecticut, September to December, 1775; Captain 20th Continental Infantry, 1st January, 1776; Brigade-Major to General Parsons, 15th to 31st August, 1776; Major 20th Continental Infantry, 19th August to 31st December, 1776; Lieutenant-Colonel 8th Connecticut, 1st January, 1777; resigned 11th April, 1778.

Dyer, Walter (Md). Private 3d Maryland, 9th January, 1777; Sergeant, 26th June, 1777; Ensign 26th January, 1780; 2d Lieutenant, 1st August, 1781; retained in Maryland Battalion, April, 1783, and served to 15th November, 1783. (Died 2d April, 1819.)

Dysart, James (Pa). Ensign of Montgomery's Battalion Pennsylvania Flying Camp, July to December, 1776.

Dysart, James (Va). Captain Virginia Riflemen, ——; wounded at King's Mountain 7th October, 1780; subsequently served as Major and as Colonel Virginia Militia to close of war.

Dyson, Thomas A. (Md). Ensign 3d Maryland, 1st August, 1781; transferred to 2d Maryland, 1st January, 1783; retained in Maryland Battalion, April, 1783, and served to 15th November, 1783.

E.

Eager, George (N. H.). Surgeon's Mate of Bedel's New Hampshire Regiment, 22d January to 1st July, 1776; Surgeon of Bedel's Vermont Regiment, 15th December, 1777, to 1st April, 1779.

Eager, Nahum (Mass). Lieutenant-Colonel of Fellow's Massachusetts Regiment, May to December, 1775. (Died 1805.)

Eagery, Daniel (Mass). Captain of Danielson's Massachusetts Regiment, May to December, 1775.

Eagle, Joseph (N. C.). Ensign 4th North Carolina, 1st January, 1776; resigned 20th March, 1776.

Eakin, Samuel (Del). Chaplain Delaware Battalion of the Flying Camp, July to December, 1776.

Eames, John (Mass). Sergeant in Lexington Alarm, April, 1775; 2d Lieutenant of Nixon's Massachusetts Regiment, May to December, 1775.

Earle, John (S. C.). Captain 3d South Carolina (Rangers), 1776, and served to close of war. (Died 1815.)

Earle, Joseph (Md). Lieutenant-Colonel 4th Maryland Battalion of the Flying Camp, July, 1776, to ——.

Earle, Richard Tilghman (Md). Colonel Maryland Militia, 1776.

Earle, Samuel (Md). Ensign 4th Maryland Battalion of the Flying Camp, July to December, 1776.

Earle, Samuel (S. C.). Ensign 5th South Carolina, 11th June, 1777; 2d Lieutenant, 20th June, 1779; 1st Lieutenant, October, 1779, to January, 1781; Captain South Carolina Rangers, 1781 and 1782. (Died 24th November, 1833.)

Earl, William (N. C.). Captain North Carolina Militia, 1780-1781.

Early, Joseph (Va). 2d Lieutenant 5th Virginia, 26th February, 1776; 1st Lieutenant, —— September, 1776, and served to ——.

Eastebrooks, Joseph (N. H.). Captain of Bedel's New Hampshire Rangers, 22d January, 1776; taken prisoner at the Cedars, 19th May, 1776; died 15th June, 1776, of smallpox.

Eastman, Ebenezer (N. H.). 1st Lieutenant 1st New Hampshire, 8th May to December, 1775. (Died 27th October, 1794.)

Eastman, John (N. H.). Captain New Hampshire Militia, 1780.

Eastman, Nehemiah (Mass). Ensign 3d Massachusetts, 1st January, 1777; deserted 1st April, 1777.

Eastin, Philip.—See **Easton.**

Easton, James (Conn). Captain of Ethan Allen's forces at Ticonderoga in May, 1775; by the act of 1st August, 1776, he was promoted to Colonel of the Continental Army, to rank from 1st July, 1775; dismissed 16th July, 1779.

Easton, Philip (Va). Private 8th Virginia, 27th February, 1777; Ensign, 20th May, 1777; 2d Lieutenant, 1st October, 1777; 1st Lieutenant, 10th August, 1778; transferred to 4th Virginia, 14th September, 1778; retired 1st January, 1783. (Died 1817.) (Name also spelled Eastin.)

Easton, Richard (Va). 2d Lieutenant 8th Virginia, 27th March, 1776; 1st Lieutenant, 6th April, 1777; resigned 7th June, 1778.

Easton, Seth (N. C.). Lieutenant 7th North Carolina, 28th November, 1776, to ——.

Eaton, Aaron (Conn). Ensign of Gay's Connecticut State Regiment, June to December, 1776.

Eaton, Benjamin (Mass). 2d Lieutenant 3d Continental Artillery, 1st February, 1777, and served to June, 1783. (Died 20th August, 1819.)

Eaton, Ezra (Conn). Captain of Baldwin's Artillery Artificer Regiment, 1st January, 1777, to ——.

Eaton, John (N. H.). Ensign 3d New Hampshire, 8th November, 1776; discharged 20th August, 1778.

Eaton, John Elliot (Mass). Surgeon's Mate 5th Massachusetts, 1st June, 1777; resigned 28th November, 1777. (Died 1812.)

Eaton, Nathaniel (Mass). 2d Lieutenant of Frye's Massachusetts Regiment, May to December, 1775; 1st Lieutenant 25th Continental Infantry, 1st January to 31st December, 1776. (Died 1796.)

Eaton, Pinketham (N. C.). Captain 3d North Carolina, 16th April, 1776; Major 8th North Carolina, 22d November, 1777; retired 1st June, 1778; Colonel North Carolina Militia; wounded at Briar Creek, 3d March, 1779, and was killed at Fort Grierson 24th May, 1781.

Eaton, Thomas (S. C.). Major South Carolina Militia, 1781.

Eayres, Joseph (Pa). Major of Flower's Artillery Artificer Regiment, 16th July, 1776; retired 30th August, 1780.

Eberhard, Michael (Pa). Paymaster German Battalion, 12th July, 1776. Died 16th July, 1778.

Eborne, John (N. C.). Lieutenant 5th North Carolina, 1st October, 1776, to ——.

Eborne, Thomas (N. C.). Lieutenant 5th North Carolina, 16th April, 1776, to ——.

Eccleston, John (Md). 2d Lieutenant of Barrett's Independent Maryland Company, 14th January, 1776; 1st Lieutenant, July, 1776; Captain 2d Maryland, 10th December, 1776; Major 5th Maryland, 10th December, 1777; taken prisoner at Charleston 12th May, 1780; released 30th December, 1780; transferred to 1st Maryland 1st January, 1781; Lieutenant-Colonel, — December, 1782; retained in Maryland Battalion 12th April, 1783, and served to 3d November, 1783.

Eckerson, Cornelius (N. Y.). Lieutenant New York Militia; taken prisoner, when and where not stated.

Eckert, Valentine (Pa). Captain of a Pennsylvania Company of Dragoons; wounded at Germantown 4th October, 1777.

Eddins, Samuel (Va). Ensign 7th Virginia, 1st March, 1776; Captain Lieutenant, 1st Continental Artillery, 12th January, 1777; Captain, 1st January, 1778; retired 1st January, 1783.

Eddy, John (Pa). Ensign 6th Pennsylvania Battalion, 9th January, 1776; taken prisoner on Sorrel River, Canada, 24th July, 1776; exchanged July, 1777, and did not re-enter service.

Eddy, Joshua (Mass). Private in Cotton's Massachusetts Regiment, May to December, 1775; Ensign, 16th Continental Infantry, 1st January, 1776; Captain 14th Massachusetts, 1st January, 1777; resigned 15th October, 1778. (Died 1st May, 1833.)

Eddy, Samuel (Mass). Corporal in Lexington Alarm, April, 1775; Private 12th Massachusetts, 14th February, 1777; Sergeant-Major, 15th August, 1778; Ensign, 1st January, 1780; retired 1st January, 1781.

Eden, James (Md). Major 3d Maryland Battalion of the Flying Camp, July to December, 1776.

Edes, John Welsh (Mass). 2d Lieutenant of Gridley's Regiment Massachusetts Artillery, 13th May, 1775; 1st Lieutenant of Knox's Regiment Continental Artillery, 10th December, 1775, to 31st December, 1776.

Edes, Joseph (Mass). Sergeant of Gerrish's Massachusetts Regiment, May to December, 1775; Ensign 26th Continental Infantry, 1st January, 1776; 2d Lieutenant, 10th August, 1776; 1st Lieutenant 9th Massachusetts, 1st January, 1777; Captain, 15th September, 1780; resigned 21st June, 1781.

Edes, Thomas (Mass). Regimental Quartermaster of Gridley's Regiment Massachusetts Artillery, June to December, 1775.

Edgar, Clarkson (N. Y.). 1st Lieutenant 2d Continental Artillery, 1st February, 1777; resigned 15th December, 1777; Captain and Major New Jersey Militia, 1778-1780.

Edgar, David (N. J.). 2d Lieutenant of Forman's Regiment New Jersey Militia, July, 1776; 1st Lieutenant 4th New Jersey, 23d November, 1776; resigned 14th January, 1777; Lieutenant 2d Continental Dragoons, 25th January, 1777; Captain, 23d November, 1778, and served to close of war.

Edgar, George (N. H.). Surgeon's Mate of Bedel's Regiment, New Hampshire Rangers, January to November, 1776.

Edgerley, Edward (Md). 2d Lieutenant 2d Maryland, 14th January, 1777; Regimental Adjutant, 3d April, 1778; 1st Lieutenant, 27th May, 1778; Captain, 10th September, 1779; transferred to 5th Maryland, 1st January, 1781; killed at Eutaw Springs, 8th September,, 1781.

Edie, John (Pa). 2d Lieutenant 6th Pennsylvania Battalion, 9th January, 1776; 1st Lieutenant, 5th February, 1776; wounded and taken prisoner at Three Rivers, 8th June, 1776; exchanged 10th April, 1778, and did not re-enter service.

Edison, Thomas (Pa). 2d Lieutenant German Battalion, 7th June, 1777; dishonorably discharged, 22d May, 1778.

Edmiston, Samuel (Md). Quartermaster of the Maryland Battalion of the Flying Camp, July to December, 1776; Lieutenant and Regimental Quartermaster 5th Maryland, 10th December, 1776; resigned 14th October, 1777; Lieutenant 1st Maryland, 14th March, 1781; retained in Maryland Battalion April, 1783, and served to 15th November, 1783.

Edmond, William (Conn). 1st Lieutenant 6th Connecticut, 1st May to 15th December, 1775; Lieutenant of Sage's Connecticut State Regiment, June to December, 1776; Captain Connecticut Militia; wounded at Danbury, 25th April, 1777. (Died 1st August, 1838.)

Edmonds, William (S. C.). Lieutenant 3d South Carolina in 1777; served to ——.

Edmondson, Benjamin (Va). 2d Lieutenant 2d Virginia State Regiment, 22d September, 1777; 2d Lieutenant, 24th April, 1778; 1st Lieutenant, 1st January, 1779; served to January, 1781.

Edmondson, Robert Sr. (Va). Lieutenant Virginia Rangers, ——; killed at King's Mountain, 7th October, 1780.

Edmondson, Robert Jr. (Va). Lieutenant Virginia Rangers, ——; wounded at King's Mountain 7th October, 1780.

Edmondson, William (Va). Major Virginia Rangers, ——; wounded at King's Mountain, 7th October, 1780. (Died 30th July, 1822.)

Edmonson, Andrew (Va). Ensign Virginia Rangers, ——; killed at King's Mountain 7th October, 1780.

Edmonson, Samuel (Va). Hospital Surgeon's Mate, June, 1777, to 20th June, 1780; Hospital Physician and Surgeon, 20th September, 1781, and served to close of war. (Name also appears as Edmiston, Edmondston and as Edmunson.)

Edmonston, Thomas (Md). Ensign 1st Maryland Battalion of the Flying Camp, July to December, 1776; Lieutenant Maryland Militia in 1777.

Edmunds, Elias (Va). Major and Lieutenant-Colonel of a Virginia State Regiment, 1777, to February, 1781.

Edmunds, Nicholas (N. C.). Captain 3d North Carolina in 1777; served to ——.

Edmunds, Thomas (Va). Lieutenant and Captain of a Virginia State Regiment, 1777, to February, 1781.

Edmunds, Thomas (Va). Captain 15th Virginia, 25th November, 1776; wounded at Brandywine, 11th September, 1777; regiment designated 11th Virginia, 14th September, 1778; transferred to 3d Virginia 12th February, 1781; wounded at Eutaw Springs, 8th September, 1781; transferred to 1st Virginia, 1st January, 1783; Brevet Major, 30th September 1783; served to close of war. (Died 1791.)

Edwards, David (N. J.). Captain New Jersey Militia in 1777.

Edwards, Edward (Md). Ensign 4th Maryland, 10th December, 1776; resigned 1st November, 1777.

Edwards' Enoch (Pa). Surgeon of Lewis' Pennsylvania Battalion of the Flying Camp; taken prisoner at Fort Washington 16th November, 1776.

Edwards, Evan (Pa). 1st Lieutenant 3d Pennsylvania Battalion, 6th January, 1776; Captain, 23d March, 1776; Captain in Hartley's Additional Continental Regiment, 1st January, 1777, which was called 11th Pennsylvania, 16th December, 1778; Aide-de-Camp to General Lee in 1777; Major 11th Pennsylvania, 13th January, 1779, to rank from 10th December, 1778; transferred to 4th Pennsylvania 17th January, 1781; retired 1st January, 1783.

Edwards, John (S. C.) Captain and Aide-de-Camp to General Marion in 1781 and 1782.

Edwards, LeRoy (Va). Ensign 5th Virginia, 26th February, 1776; 1st Lieutenant, 21st February, 1777; transferred to 3d Virginia, 14th September, 1778; Captain, 19th June, 1779; taken prisoner at Charleston 12th May, 1780; prisoner to close of war.

Edwards, Marshall (Pa). Major of Lewis' Pennsylvania Battalion of the Flying Camp, July to December, 1776.

Edwards, Nathaniel (Conn). 2d Lieutenant 1st Connecticut, 1st May to 20th December, 1775; 1st Lieutenant of Bradley's Connecticut State Regiment, 20th June, 1776; taken prisoner at Fort Washington, 16th November, 1776.

Edsall, Richard (N. J.). 2d Lieutenant of Spencer's Additional Continental Regiment, 2d February, 1777; 1st Lieutenant, 27th February, 1777; Captain, 6th September, 1777; resigned 20th April, 1779. (Died 1823.)

Edwards, Richard (N. J.). Ensign of Spencer's Continental Regiment, 10th February, 1777; resigned 20th November, 1777.

Edwards, Simeon (Vt). Lieutenant Vermont Militia in 1777.

Edwards, Thomas (Mass). Private in Lexington Alarm, April, 1775; 1st Lieutenant of Jackson's Continental Regiment, 31st May, 1777; regiment designated 16th Massachusetts, 23d July, 1780; appointed Deputy Judge-Advocate of the army 9th April, 1780; Judge-Advocate of the army 2d October, 1782, and served to 3d November, 1783; he retained his rank also in the line, being transferred to the 9th Massachusetts 1st January, 1781, and to the 2d Massachusetts 1st January, 1783. (Died 4th August, 1806.)

Edwards, Thomas (Pa). Major 1st Battalion Pennsylvania Flying Camp, July to December, 1776.

Eells, Edward (Conn). Captain of Sage's Connecticut State Regiment, 20th June to 25th December, 1776; Captain 3d Connecticut, 1st January, 1777; transferred to 1st Connecticut 1st January, 1781, and served to 3d June, 1783. (Died 1787.)

Egbert, Jacob (Va). Surgeon's Mate Hospital Department, 1780-1783.

Egbert, Thomas (N. J.). Major New Jersey Militia in 1777.

Egery, Daniel (Mass). Captain of Danielson's Massachusetts Regiment, May to December, 1775; Captain 25th Continental Infantry, 1st January to December, 1776.

Egleston, Azariah (Mass). Sergeant 1st Massachusetts, 1st January, 1777; Ensign, 1st May, 1777, to rank from 1st January, 1777; Regimental Quartermaster, March, 1778; Regimental Paymaster, 4th May, 1780; Lieutenant, 30th August, 1780, and served to close of war. (Died 12th January, 1822.)

Egleston, Joseph (Va). Paymaster 1st Continental Dragoons, — March, 1777; resigned 18th November, 1777; Lieutenant and Paymaster of Lee's Battalion of Light Dragoons, 21st April, 1778; Captain, 5th September, 1779; taken prisoner at Elizabethtown, 25th January, 1780; reported as a Major in 1781; served to close of war. (Died 1811.)

Egleston, William (Va). 2d Lieutenant 5th Virginia, 20th February, 1776; 1st Lieutenant, 7th September, 1776; died 4th February, 1777.

Ehrenzeller, Jacob (Mass). Surgeon of Jackson's Continental Regiment in 1778; resigned 1st June, 1779; Surgeon of Lee's Battalion of Light Dragoons, 1st January, 1779; omitted — August, 1779.

Eichelberger, Barnet (Pa). 1st Lieutenant 6th Pennsylvania Battalion, 9th January, 1776; resigned 5th February, 1776; Captain of Hartley's Continental Regiment, 12th January, 1777, which appointment it would appear he did not accept.

Eichelberger, George (Pa). Deputy Quartermaster-General in 1777 and 1778.

Eichelberger, Martin (Pa). 2d Lieutenant of Hartley's Continental Regiment, 25th January, 1777; 1st Lieutenant, 11th September, 1777; regiment became 11th Pennsylvania, 16th December, 1778; resigned 29th March, 1779. (Died 2d October, 1840.)

Eicholtz, Jacob (Pa). Sergeant Pennsylvania Musket Battalion, 21st March, 1776; Regimental Quartermaster, August to December, 1776.

Eisenlord, John (N. Y.). Major New York Militia,——; killed at Oriskany, 6th August, 1777.

Elbert, John L. (Md). Surgeon's Mate 5th Maryland, 1st January, 1782; retired April, 1783.

Elbert, Samuel (Ga). Lieutenant-Colonel 1st Georgia, 7th January, 1776; Colonel 2d Georgia, 5th July, 1776; wounded and taken prisoner at Briar Creek, 3d March, 1779, and at Charleston 12th May, 1780; commanded a Brigade at Yorktown, June to November, 1781; Brevet Brigadier-General, 3d November, 1783; was also Brigadier-General Georgia Militia, and served to close of war. (Died 2d November, 1788.)

Elder, Robert (Pa). Colonel Pennsylvania Militia, 1777-1781.

Elderkin, Jedediah (Conn). Colonel and Brigadier-General Connecticut Militia, 1775-1779. (Died 1793.)

Elderkin, John (Conn). Regimental Quartermaster 6th Connecticut, 6th July to 10th December, 1775; 2d Lieutenant and Regimental Quartermaster 19th Continental Infantry, 1st January to 31st December, 1776; Lieutenant and Regimental Quartermaster 2d Connecticut, 1st January, 1777; resigned 29th August, 1777.

Elderkin, Vine (Conn). Captain of Mott's Connecticut State Regiment, June to December, 1776; Captain 7th Connecticut, 1st January, 1777; resigned 3d November, 1777 (Died 15th August, 1810.)

Eldred, Samuel (Mass). Sergeant in Lexington Alarm, April, 1775; Sergeant of Cotton's Massachusetts Regiment, May to December, 1775; Ensign 21st Continental Infantry, 1st January to 31st December, 1776; 2d Lieutenant 1st Massachusetts, 1st January, 1777; taken prisoner 28th December, 1777, near Schuylkill; 1st Lieutenant, 1st November, 1778; transferred to 2d Massachusetts, 1st January, 1781, and served to 3d June, 1783. (Died 18th

December, 1825.) (Also called El-dridge.)

Eldridge, Charles (Conn). Lieuten-ant Connecticut Militia, ——; wounded at Groton Heights, 6th September, 1781. (Died 1789.)

Eldridge, Daniel (Conn). Private in the Lexington Alarm, April, 1775; Ser-geant 3d Connecticut, 1st May to 18th December, 1775; 2d Lieutenant 2d Con-necticut, 1st January, 1777; resigned 4th February, 1778.

Eldridge, Eli (N. J.). Lieutenant New Jersey Militia in 1776.

Eldridge, James (Conn). 1st Lieuten-ant 6th Connecticut, 1st May, 1775; Captain, 1st July to 10th December, 1775; Captain 10th Continental Infan-try, 1st January to 31st December, 1776; Captain 1st Connecticut, 1st Jan-uary, 1777; resigned 2d January, 1778.

Elholm, Augustus Christian George (Germany). Lieutenant of Cavalry Pu-laski Legion, April, 1778, to 18th May, 1780; Captain of South Carolina Troops, February, 1781, to June, 1783.

Elkins, Henry (N. H.). Captain 2d New Hampshire, 23d May, 1775; re-signed 20th August, 1775.

Ellerbee, Thomas (S. C.). Captain in Marion's Brigade, 1780-1781.

Ellery, William (R. I.). A signer of the Declaration of Independence; died 15th February, 1820.

Ellicott, Andrew (Md). Major Mary-land Militia, 1776-1778. (Died 1820.)

Elliot, John (N. Y.). Surgeon's Mate 3d New York, 21st November, 1776; transferred to 1st New York, 1st Jan-uary, 1781, and served to 3d Novem-ber, 1783; Surgeon's Mate United States Infantry, 12th April, 1785; Surgeon's Mate 1st United States Infantry, 29th September, 1789; Surgeon 2d United States Infantry, 3d March, 1791; as-signed to 4th Sub Legion, 4th Septem-ber, 1792; assigned to 1st United States Infantry, 1st November, 1796; honor-ably discharged 1st June, 1802.

Eliot, John (Pa). 2d Lieutenant 4th Pennsylvania, 3d January, 1777; re-tired 1st January, 1778.

Elliot, Robert (R. I.). Captain Rhode Island State Artillery, 19th August, 1776; Colonel Rhode Island State Ar-tillery, 12th December, 1776, to 1st June, 1780, and subsequently served as Brigadier-General Rhode Island Militia.

Elliot, Robert (Va). 2d Lieutenant 12th Virginia, 20th March, 1777; re-tired 14th September, 1778; served sub-sequently as Captain Virginia Militia. (Died 4th January, 1838.)

Elliot, William (Del). Ensign Dela-ware Battalion of the Flying Camp, July to December, 1776.

Elliot, William (N. H.). Adjutant 2d New Hampshire, 7th November, 1776; taken prisoner at Hubbardton, 7th July, 1777, and did not return to regi-ment.

Elliott, —— (—). Lieutenant Pu-laski Legion; killed at Flat Rock, 17th July, 1780.

Elliott, Barnard (S. C.). Captain 4th South Carolina Artillery, 17th June, 1775; Major, 14th November, 1775; Lieutenant-Colonel, 16th September, 1776; died 25th October, 1778.

Elliott, Barnard (S. C.). Captain-Lieutenant 4th South Carolina (Artil-lery), 29th May, 1778; Captain, 1780; taken prisoner at Charleston, 12th May, 1780.

Elliott, Benjamin (S. C.). Captain South Carolina Militia in 1775.

Elliott, James (Pa). 1st Lieutenant of an Independent Pennsylvania Com-pany Continental Army, 27th February, 1778; Captain, 8th March, 1779; re-tired 1st January, 1781.

Elliott, James (Va). Captain Vir-ginia Militia at King's Mountain, Oc-tober, 1780; killed by an Indian, 28th December, 1780.

Elliott, John (Conn). Chaplain 2d Connecticut, 1st May, 1777; resigned 20th February, 1778.

Elliott, John (Pa). 2d Lieutenant 4th Pennsylvania, 3d January, 1777; re-signed 15th January, 1778. (Died 29th August, 1826.)

Elliott, Joseph (Conn). Captain in the Lexington Alarm, April, 1775; Cap-tain 3d Connecticut, 1st May to 11th August, 1775. (Died 9th October, 1785.)

Elliott, Joseph (Mass.). Captain Massachusetts Militia, 1781.

Elliott, Joseph (N. Y.). Captain New York Militia in 1775.

Elliott, Joseph (S. C.). 2d Lieuten-ant 1st South Carolina, 17th June, 1775; 1st Lieutenant, November, 1776; Cap-tain, 8th March, 1778; wounded and taken prisoner at Charleston, 12th May, 1780.

Elliott, Robert (Pa). Adjutant 7th Pennsylvania, 20th March, 1777; retired 1st July, 1778.

Elliott, Samuel (S. C.). Lieutenant-Colonel South Carolina Militia in 1775 and 1776.

Elliott, Thomas (S. C.). Lieutenant 1st South Carolina, 17th June ,1775; Captain in 1777; was in service April, 1782; served to ——.

Elliott, Thomas (S. C.). Lieutenant South Carolina Militia; Aide-de-Camp to General Marion in 1781.

Elliott, Thomas (Va). Lieutenant-Colonel 6th Virginia, 13th February, 1776; Colonel 4th Virginia, 3d September, 1776; transferred to 6th Virginia, 19th August, 1777; resigned 22d September, 1777.

Ellis, Amos (Mass). 2d Lieutenant of Read's Massachusetts Regiment, — to December, 1775; Captain Massachusetts Militia, 1777-1781.

Ellis, Benjamin (Conn). Surgeon's Mate 6th Connecticut, July to October, 1775.

Ellis, Benjamin (N. H.). 2d Lieutenant 3d New Hampshire, 8th November, 1776; 1st Lieutenant, 1st May, 1778; Captain, 5th July, 1780; transferred to 1st New Hampshire, 1st January, 1781, and served to 3d June, 1783. (Died 29th November, 1831.)

Ellis, Jeremiah B. (Conn). Ensign of a Connecticut Regiment; taken prisoner at Norwalk, 15th March, 1777.

Ellis, John (Conn). Chaplain 8th Connecticut, 6th July to 10th December, 1775; Chaplain 17th Continental Infantry, 1st January to 31st December, 1776; Chaplain 1st Connecticut, 1st January, 1777; Brigade Chaplain, 27th May, 1777, and served to 3d June, 1783.

Ellis, John (Mass). Ensign 24th Continental Infantry, 1st January to 31st December, 1776; Captain Massachusetts Militia, 1778.

Ellis, John (Pa). 2d Lieutenant 1st Pennsylvania Battalion, 27th October, 1775; 1st Lieutenant, 5th September, 1776; Captain of Sherburne's Continental Regiment, 1st January, 1777; dishonorably discharged 9th November, 1777.

Ellis, John (R. I.). Captain 1st Rhode Island, 1st January, 1777; dismissed 10th November, 1777.

Ellis, Joseph (N. J.). Colonel New Jersey Militia in 1776; Brigadier-General New Jersey Militia, February, 1777, which he declined; Brigadier-General New York Militia, 1777-1778.

Ellis, Paul (Mass). Ensign of Phinney's Massachusetts Regiment, 24th April to 8th July, 1775; Captain 15th Massachusetts, 1st January, 1777; killed at Monmouth, 28th June, 1778.

Ellis, Timothy (N. H.). Captain New Hampshire Militia, 1776-1780.

Ellis, William (N. J.). Captain of Newcomb's Battalion New Jersey Militia, 14th June, 1776; Major of Read's Battalion New Jersey Militia, 18th July, 1776; taken prisoner 5th April, 1778, at Cooper's Ferry; exchanged 26th December, 1780.

Ellis, William (N. H.). 1st Lieutenant 3d New Hampshire, 8th November, 1776; Captain, 4th May, 1777; resigned 30th June, 1780.

Ellison, John (S. C.). Lieutenant 3d South Carolina (Ranger's), November, 1775, to ——.

Ellison, Robert (S. C.). Captain 3d South Carolina (Ranger's), November, 1775; taken prisoner at Augusta in September, 1780, and was a prisoner to close of war.

Elmendorf, Peter, Jr. (N. Y.). Ensign of Malcolm's Additional Continental Regiment, 8th April, 1777; resigned 1st January, 1778.

Elmer, Ebenezer (N. J.). Ensign 3d New Jersey, 9th February, 1776; 2d Lieutenant 9th April, 1776; Surgeon's Mate, 28th November, 1776; Surgeon, 5th June, 1778; transferred to 2d New Jersey, 1st January, 1781; retained in New Jersey Battalion, April, 1783, and served to 3d November, 1783. (Died 18th October, 1843.)

Elmer, Eli (N. C.). 1st Lieutenant Clark's Company North Carolina Artillery, 1st January, 1777; resigned 13th February, 1780.

Elmer, Moses G. (N. J.). Surgeon's Mate 3d New Jersey, 21st August, 1778; transferred to 2d New Jersey, 1st January, 1781; retained in New Jersey Battalion, April, 1783, and served to 3d November, 1783.

Elmer, Timothy (N. J.). Captain and Major New Jersey Militia, 1776-1778.

Elmore, Samuel (Conn). Major 4th Connecticut, 1st May to 20th December, 1775; Colonel Connecticut State Regiment, 15th April, 1776, to April, 1777. (Died 1805.)

Elmore, Samuel, Jr. (Conn). 2d Lieutenant of Elmore's Connecticut State Regiment, 15th April, 1776; 1st Lieutenant, 25th July, 1776; killed 26th April, 1777, in the Danbury Raid.

Elsworth, Charles (Conn). Captain in the Lexington Alarm, April, 1775; Captain 8th Connecticut, 6th July to 18th December, 1775.

Elsworth, Peter (N. Y.). 2d Lieutenant 4th New York, 21st November, 1776; 1st Lieutenant, 2d September, 1777; Captain Lieutenant, 11th April, 1780; retired 1st January, 1781; served subsequently as Captain New York Levies.

Elsworth, Reuben (Conn). Lieutenant Connecticut Light Horse, 1776-1777.

Elton, John (—). 1st Lieutenant of Baldwin's Artillery Artificer Regiment, 11th April, 1778, to ——.

Elwell, Sawtelle (N. J.). Captain New Jersey Militia in 1776.

Ely, Abner (Conn). Sergeant 6th Connecticut, 8th May to 19th December, 1775; Ensign 6th Connecticut, 1st January, 1777; resigned 4th May, 1778; also reported as transferred to Artillery.

Ely, Christopher (Conn). 1st Lieutenant 6th Connecticut, 1st May to 10th December, 1775; Captain 10th Continental Infantry, 1st January to 31st December, 1776; Captain 1st Connecticut, 1st January, 1777; resigned 2d January, 1778.

Ely, Eli (N. C.). 1st Lieutenant 7th North Carolina, 11th December, 1776; Captain, 12th October, 1777; retired 1st June, 1778.

Ely, Elisha (Conn). Surgeon's Mate 10th Continental Infantry, 1st January, 1776; Surgeon 19th Continental Infantry, 19th July to 31st December, 1776; Captain 6th Connecticut, 1st January, 1777; resigned 28th August, 1780.

Ely, George (N. J.). Captain, Lieutenant-Colonel and Colonel New Jersey Militia, 1776 to 1783.

Ely, John (Conn). Captain 6th Connecticut, 1st May to 18th December, 1775; Colonel Connecticut Militia Regiment in 1777; taken prisoner on the Long Island Expedition, 10th December, 1777; exchanged 5th December, 1780. (Died 1800.)

Ely, Samuel (N. C.). Captain 7th North Carolina, 17th December, 1776; resigned 17th February, 1778.

Eman, John (Ga). 2d Lieutenant 1st Georgia, 7th January, 1776, to ——.

Emerson, Amos (N. H.). 1st Lieutenant 3d New Hampshire, 23d April to December, 1775; 1st Lieutenant 2d Continental Infantry, 1st January, 1776; Captain 1st New Hampshire, 8th November, 1776; resigned 24th March, 1780.

Emerson, Daniel (N. H.). Captain New Hampshire Militia, 1776.

Emerson, John (Va). Lieutenant 13th Virginia, 1st January, 1777; retired 14th September, 1778.

Emerson, Jonathan (N. H.). Ensign 2d Continental Infantry, 1st January, 1776; 1st Lieutenant 1st New Hampshire, 8th November, 1776; wounded at Stillwater, 19th September, 1777, and did not rejoin his regiment.

Emerson, Nathaniel (—). 1st Lieutenant of Baldwin's Artillery Artificer Regiment, 1st January, 1777; resigned 6th June, 1777.

Emerson, Nehemiah (Mass). Private Company of Minute Men at Lexington, 19th April, 1775; Ensign 11th Massachusetts, 6th November, 1776; 2d Lieutenant, 7th November, 1777; 1st Lieutenant, 28th March, 1779; Captain, 27th October, 1780; transferred to 10th Massachusetts, 1st January, 1781; retired 1st January, 1783. (Died 11th December, 1832.)

Emerson, Peter (N. H.). Surgeon New Hampshire Militia, 1778-1780.

Emerton, Ephraim (Mass). 1st Lieutenant of Mansfield's Massachusetts Regiment, May to December, 1775; 1st Lieutenant 27th Continental Infantry, 1st January to 31st December, 1776; served subsequently as Captain in Navy.

Emery, Benjamin (N. H.). Captain New Hampshire Militia in 1776.

Emery, Ephraim (Mass). Ensign 13th Massachusetts, 1st March, 1777; Lieutenant Regimental Paymaster, 10th April, 1779; transferred to 6th Massachusetts, 1st January, 1781, and served to 3d June, 1783. (Died 27th September, 1827.)

Emes, Worsley (Pa). 1st Lieutenant of Proctor's Battalion Pennsylvania Artillery, 5th October, 1776; 1st Lieutenant 4th Continental Artillery, March, 1777, to rank from 5th October, 1776; Captain Lieutenant, 16th July, 1777; Captain, 26th September, 1780; retired 1st January, 1783. (Died 9th July, 1802.)

Emmerson, John (Va). 2d Lieutenant 13th Virginia, 16th December, 1776; resigned — April, 1778.

Emmet, James (N. C.). Captain 3d North Carolina, 16th April, 1776; Major 1st North Carolina, 22d December, 1777; retired 1st June, 1778.

Emory, Gideon (Md). 2d Lieutenant 5th Maryland, 10th December, 1776; 1st Lieutenant, 14th February, 1777, and served to ——.

Emory, Richard (Md). Captain 5th Maryland, 10th December, 1776; Brigade-Major 1st Maryland Brigade, 14th October, 1777; resigned 27th December, 1777.

Emory, Thomas Lane (Md). 1st Lieutenant 4th Maryland Battalion of the Flying Camp, July, 1776, to ——.

Engle, Andrew (Pa). Ensign 12th Pennsylvania, 10th October, 1776; 2d Lieutenant, 11th May, 1777; wounded at Monmouth 28th June, 1778; transferred to 3d Pennsylvania, 1st July, 1778; 1st Lieutenant, 20th December, 1778; retired 1st January, 1781.

Engle, James (Pa). Sergeant 2d Pennsylvania Battalion, 19th January, 1776; Ensign, 20th September, 1776; 2d Lieutenant 3d Pennsylvania, January, 1777, and served to ——. (Was in service in August, 1777.) (Died 1821.)

English, Andrew (Mass). 1st Lieutenant 12th Massachusetts, 1st January, 1777; Adjutant, 1st April, 1779; resigned 1st August, 1780. (Died 26th May, 1832.)

English, James (Pa). Private 2d Pennsylvania Battalion, 26th February, 1776; Sergeant, 1st March, 1776; Ensign 3d Pennsylvania, 1st January, 1777, and served to ——.

English, Samuel (N. Y.). 2d Lieutenant 5th New York, 21st November, 1776; 1st Lieutenant, 1st September, 1778; retired 1st January, 1781.

Enloe, John (N. C.). Captain 5th North Carolina, 16th April, 1776; resigned 25th October, 1777.

Ennis, James (Pa).—See **Innes.**

Ennis, William (R. I.). Ensign Olney's Rhode Island Battalion, 1st April, 1781; 2d Lieutenant, 1st March, 1782; 1st Lieutenant, 1st January, 1783, and served to November, 1783.

Eno, Martin (Conn). Sergeant of Warner's Additional Continental Regiment, 16th February, 1777; Ensign, 7th

August, 1779; killed at Fort George, 11th October, 1780.

Enoch, David (Va). Captain Virginia Militia, 1779-1781.

Enos, Roger (Conn). Major 2d Connecticut, 1st May, 1775; Lieutenant-Colonel, 1st July to 10th December, 1775; Brigadier-General Vermont Militia in 1781. (Died 6th October, 1808.)

Enslin, Frederick Gotthold (Pa). 1st Lieutenant of Malcolm's Continental Regiment, 4th March, 1777; cashiered 14th March, 1778, and drummed out of service.

Ensworth, Jedediah (Conn). Surgeon's Mate 8th Connecticut, 10th June, 1778; transferred to 5th Connecticut, 1st January, 1781; resigned 15th January, 1783.

Eppes, Francis (Va). Major 1st Virginia, 13th February, 1776; Lieutenant-Colonel, 18th March, 1776; killed at Long Island, 27th August, 1776.

Eppes, William (Va). 2d Lieutenant 14th Virginia, 20th November, 1776; 1st Lieutenant, 30th August, 1777; transferred to 10th Virginia, 14th September, 1778; Captain Lieutenant, ——, 1780; retired 12th February, 1781. •

Epple, Andrew (Pa). Paymaster 11th Pennsylvania, 14th April, 1777; resigned 1st March, 1778. ,

Epple, Henry (Pa). Ensign 2d Pennsylvania Battalion, 5th January, 1776; 2d Lieutenant, 21st May, 1776; 1st Lieutenant 11th November, 1776; Captain, 4th July, 1777; resigned 9th April, 1778.

Ernest, Matthew (N. Y.). Private in 5th New York, ——, 1779, to January, 1781; Lieutenant United States Artillery, 21st October, 1786; Lieutenant Artillery Battalion United States Army, 29th September, 1789; Battalion Paymaster, 5th June to 5th November, 1790; resigned 26th July, 1791. (Died ——, 1805.)   ,

Erskine, Charles (Va). Lieutenant 4th Virginia, 5th April, 1780; wounded at Eutaw Springs, 8th September, 1781; appears as Lieutenant in Lee's Battalion of Light Dragoon's, 1781 to close of war.   ,

Erskine, John (N. Y.). 2d Lieutenant 2d Canadian (Hazen's) Regiment, 3d November, 1776; resigned 10th March, 1778.

Erskine, Robert (N. J.). Geographer and Surveyor to the Army of the

United States, 27th July, 1777; died 2d October, 1780.

Erskine, William (N. Y.). Brigadier-General New York Militia, 1776.

Erskine, William (N. Y.). 1st Lieutenant 2d Canadian (Hazen's) Regiment, 8th April, 1777; omitted November, 1777.

Erving, Henry (Mass.). Ensign 5th Massachusetts, 1st January, 1777; resigned 17th April, 1778.

Erwin, Arthur (Pa.). Colonel Pennsylvania Militia, 1776.

Erwin, David (N. J.). Surgeon's Mate New Jersey Militia, 1776-1777; Surgeon 1st New Jersey, 26th September, 1780, to ——.

Erwin, James (Pa.). Ensign 9th Pennsylvania, 20th July, 1780; transferred to 5th Pennsylvania, 17th January, 1781; transferred to 3d Pennsylvania, 1st January, 1783, and served to 3d June, 1783.

Erwin, James (S. C.). Lieutenant South Carolina Militia in 1776.

Erwin, John (Pa.). Lieutenant of Baxter's Pennsylvania Battalion of the Flying Camp, June, 1776; taken prisoner at Fort Washington, 16th November, 1776; exchanged 18th February, 1781.

Erwin, John (S. C.). Colonel South Carolina Militia in 1775.

Erwin, Joseph (Pa.). Captain 2d Battalion of Miles' Pennsylvania Rifle Regiment, 9th March to December, 1776; appointed Captain 9th Pennsylvania, 15th November, 1776, to rank from 6th April, 1776; retired 1st July, 1778.

Esdel, Benjamin (N. J.). Ensign of Spencer's Additional Continental Regiment, 12th May, 1779; retired 1st January, 1781.

Esdel, Richard (N. J.). 1st Lieutenant of Spencer's Additional Continental Regiment, 17th February, 1777; Captain Lieutenant, 6th September, 1777; Captain, ——, 1780; retired 1st January, 1781.

Eskridge, George (Va.). Ensign 15th Virginia, 25th November, 1776; resigned 14th August, 1778.

Eskridge, William (Va.). Ensign 4th Virginia, 4th May, 1777; 2d Lieutenant, 15th June, 1777; transferred to 2d Virginia, 14th September, 1778; 1st Lieutenant, 1st November, 1779; taken prisoner at Charleston, 12th May, 1780;

transferred to 1st Virginia, 12th February, 1781, and served to close of war.

Espiniers, Augustin Francois des (France). Captain Continental Army and Aide-de-Camp to Baron Steuben, 21st August, 1777; Major, 2d February, 1778; "in consideration of the services rendered by his uncle, Mons. de Beaumarchais, and of his having served with reputation in the American Army," granted six months' leave and returned to France in October, 1779.

Espy, Samuel (N. C.). Captain North Carolina Militia; wounded at King's Mountain, 7th October, 1780. (Died 29th December, 1838.)

Essaslstyne, Richard (N. Y.). Major New York Militia in 1775.

Este, Moses (N. J.). Captain New Jersey Militia; wounded at Monmouth, 28th June, 1778. (Died 1836.)

Estop, Alexander (Md.). 1st Lieutenant 6th Maryland, 10th December, 1776; resigned 10th October, 1777.

Eubank, John (S. C.). Ensign South Carolina Militia in 1775 and 1776.

Eustace, John (Va.). 2d Lieutenant 1st Virginia, 6th September, 1775; 1st Lieutenant, August, 1776; Captain, May, 1777; killed at Germantown, 4th October, 1777.

Eustace, John (Va.). Ensign 3d Virginia, 7th October, 1780, and served to close of war.

Eustace, John Skey (Ga.). Major Aide-de-Camp to General Lee, 29th October, 1776; Aide-de-Camp to General Sullivan, 7th November, 1777; Aide-de-Camp to General Greene in 1779; resigned 27th January, 1780. (Died 25th August, 1805.)

Eustis, Abraham (Mass.). 2d Lieutenant 3d Continental Artillery, 1st January, 1777; resigned 26th April, 1778.

Eustis, Benjamin (Mass.). Captain of Gridley's Regiment Massachusetts Artillery, 10th May, 1775; Captain of Knox's Regiment Continental Artillery, 10th August, 1776; Captain 3d Continental Artillery, 1st January, 1777; Major 4th Continental Artillery, 2d December, 1778; died 6th October, 1781.

Eustis, William (Mass.). Surgeon of Gridley's Regiment Massachusetts Artillery, 10th May to December, 1775; Surgeon of Knox's Regiment Continental Artillery, 10th December, 1775, to December, 1776; Hospital Physician and Surgeon, 6th October, 1780, to close of war; Secretary of War, 7th March, 1809, to 13th January, 1813. (Died 6th February, 1825.)

Evans, Andrew (Mass). Lieutenant of Brook's Massachusetts Regiment; taken prisoner at Croton River, 17th October, 1781; exchanged 20th June, 1782.

Evans, Benjamin (N. Y.). 1st Lieutenant 2d New York, 28th June, 1775; Captain of Nicholson's New York Regiment, 8th March, 1776, to April, 1777.

Evans, Charles (S. C.). Captain South Carolina Militia, 1775-1776.

Evans, Daniel (Pa). Lieutenant of Baldwin's Artillery Artificer Regiment, 3d December, 1777; Captain Lieutenant, April, 1778; omitted — March, 1779. (Died 1820.)

Evans, Edward (N. H.). Ensign 5th Continental Infantry, 1st January to 31st December, 1776.

Evans, Elijah (Md). Ensign of Stephenson's Maryland and Virginia Rifle Regiment, May, 1776; Lieutenant, 10th August, 1776; taken prisoner at Fort Washington, 16th November, 1776; Captain of Rawlin's Continental Regiment, 10th April, 1778; retired 1st January, 1781. (Died 1801.)

Evans, Ephraim (N. H.). 2d Lieutenant 2d New Hampshire, 23d May to December, 1775.

Evans, Enoch (S. C.). Lieutenant South Carolina Militia, 1780-1781.

Evans, Evan (Pa). Colonel Pennsylvania Militia, 1776.

Evans, George (Del). Major Delaware Battalion of the Flying Camp, July to December, 1776.

Evans, George (S. C.). Lieutenant 2d South Carolina, 18th August, 1779; taken prisoner at Charleston, 12th —, 1780; exchanged June, 1781, and served to close of war.

Evans, George (Va). Surgeon 3d Continental Dragoons, 20th May, 1777; taken prisoner at Tappan, 28th September, 1778; exchanged, ——; resigned 1st August, 1779.

Evans, Israel (N. Y.). Chaplain 1st New York, 3d August, 1775; Chaplain of Nicholson's New York Regiment, 8th March, 1776; Brigade Chaplain, 5th January, 1778; retired — June, 1783. (Died 9th March, 1807.)

Evans, Jean Francis (S. C.). Lieutenant 1st South Carolina, ——; resigned 12th January, 1778.

Evans, Jesse (Va). Captain Virginia Militia, 1780-1781.

Evans, John (Pa). Ensign 2d Pennsylvania Battalion, 5th January, 1776; died 29th June, 1776.

Evans, John (Va). Colonel Virginia Militia, 1777-1779.

Evans, Jonathan (Mass). Captain in Lexington Alarm, April, 1775; Captain of Frye's Massachusetts Regiment, May to December, 1775; Captain Massachusetts Militia, 1776-1779.

Evans, Moses (Vt). Lieutenant Vermont Militia; taken prisoner at Diamond Island, 5th October, 1777, and made his escape 13th May, 1778.

Evans, Peter (Va). 1st Lieutenant Virginia Militia in 1779.

Evans, Reese (Pa). Ensign 5th Pennsylvania, 1st January, 1777; resigned 6th July, 1777.

Evans, Reuben (Mass). Ensign in Lexington Alarm, April, 1775; 2d Lieutenant of Fry's Massachusetts Regiment, May to December, 1775.

Evans, Samuel (Pa). Ensign Pennsylvania State Regiment, 8th April, 1777; regiment designated 13th Pennsylvania, 12th November, 1777; served to ——.

Evans, Samuel (Pa). Captain Pennsylvania Militia in 1775.

Evans, Stephen (N. H.). Colonel New Hampshire Militia, 1776-1778.

Evans, Thomas (N. C.). Ensign 2d North Carolina, 6th June, 1776; 2d Lieutenant, 19th July, 1776; 1st Lieutenant, 15th May, 1777; Adjutant, 22d November, 1778; taken prisoner at Tappan, 28th September, 1778; exchanged 4th November, 1780; retained in 1st North Carolina, 1st January, 1781; Captain, 1st June, 1781; transferred to 4th North Carolina, 6th February, 1782, and served to close of war.

Evans, Thomas (S. C.). Paymaster 2d South Carolina in 1777; served to ——.

Evans, .Thomas .(Va).. .Surgeon's Mate, 3d Continental Dragoons, 7th June, 1777; wounded and taken prisoner at Tappan, 28th September, 1778; resigned 1st June, 1779.

Evans, William (Ga). Lieutenant Georgia Militia, 1776-1777.

Evans, William (Va). Ensign 10th Virginia, 10th December, 1776; 2d Lieutenant, 23d March, 1777; wounded at Brandywine, 11th September, 1777; 1st

Lieutenant, 13th January, 1778; regiment designated 6th Virginia, 14th September, 1778; retired 1st January, 1783.

Eveleigh, George (S. C.). 2d Lieutenant 2d South Carolina, 17th June, 1775, to ——.

Eveleigh, Nicholas (S. C.). Captain 2d South Carolina, 17th June, 1775; Colonel Deputy Adjutant-General for South Carolina and Georgia, 24th May, 1777, to ——.

Evely, Joseph(Mass). 1st Lieutenant of Little's Massachusetts Regiment, 19th May to December, 1775.

Everett, Abner (Pa). 2d Lieutenant of Baxter's Pennsylvania Battalion of the Flying Camp; taken prisoner at Fort Washington, 16th November, 1776.

Everett, Edward (N. H.). Captain of Bedel's Regiment New Hampshire Rangers, 22d January, 1776; taken prisoner at the Cedars, 19th May, 1776; Captain New Hampshire Militia in 1777.

Everett, Pelathiah (Mass). Private in Lexington Alarm, April, 1775; Sergeant 6th Continental Infantry, 1st January to 31st December, 1776; Sergeant 5th Massachusetts, 1st April, 1777; Ensign ,7th November, 1777; 2d Lieutenant, 10th August, 1778; 1st Lieutenant, 25th April, 1781; transferred to 1st Massachusetts, 12th June, 1783, and served to 3d November, 1783. (Died — October, 1821.)

Everetts, Solomon (Conn). Surgeon's Mate 6th Connecticut, 24th September, 1780; retired 1st January, 1781.

Everidge, William (Va). Ensign 2d Virginia, 4th May, 1777, to ——.

Everly, Michael (Pa). Sergeant 10th Pennsylvania, April, 1777; Ensign, 1st October, 1779; Lieutenant, 1st April, 1780; transferred to 1st Pennsylvania, 17th January, 1781; retired 1st January, 1783.

Everson, George R. (Pa). Captain Deputy Commissary of Military Stores, 18th January, 1777, to 1781. (Died 1820.)

Ewell, Charles (Va). 1st Lieutenant 1st Virginia State Regiment, 11th March, 1777; Captain, 1st June, 1778, to 1st January, 1781. (Died 1st April, 1830.)

Ewell, James (Va). Major Virginia Militia, 1776-1778.

Ewell, Thomas W. (Va). Captain 1st Virginia State Regiment, 31st January, 1777, to 1st January, 1781.

Ewell, William (N. C.). Lieutenant 5th North Carolina, 20th April, 1777, to ——. Name also spelled Hewell.

Ewing, Alexander (Va). 2d Lieutenant 14th Virginia, 3d September, 1777; regiment designated 10th Virginia, 14th September, 1778; 1st Lieutenant, 14th February, 1779; Captain, ——, 1781; Aide-de-Camp to General Greene, 1781 to close of war; wounded at Guilford, 15th March, 1781. (Died 1822.)

Ewing, George (N. J.). Ensign 3d New Jersey, 1st January, 1777; resigned 29th April, 1778; served subsequently as Lieutenant New Jersey Militia. (Died 1824.)

Ewing, George (Pa). Major Pennsylvania Militia, 1776-1777.

Ewing, Henry (Mass). Ensign 5th Massachusetts, 1st January, 1777; resigned 19th April, 1778.

Ewing, James (Md). Ensign 2d Maryland, 11th April, 1777; 2d Lieutenant, 17th April, 1777; 1st Lieutenant, 29th May, 1778; transferred to 1st Maryland, 1st January, 1781; wounded at Eutaw Springs, 8th September, 1781; Captain, 6th November, 1781; retired 1st January, 1783.

Ewing, James (Pa). Brigadier-General Pennsylvania Militia, 4th July, 1776, to ——. (Died 9th March, 1806.)

Ewing, Jasper (Pa). 2d Lieutenant and Adjutant 1st Continental Infantry, 1st January to 31st December, 1776; Brigade Major to General Hand in 1777 and 1778. (Died 1800.)

Ewing, Nathaniel (Md). 1st Lieutenant of Smallwood's Maryland Regiment, 14th January, 1776; Captain 1st Maryland, 10th December, 1776; resigned 9th February, 1779.

Ewing, Samuel (Md). Paymaster 1st Maryland, 17th April, 1777; deserted 1st July, 1780.

Ewing, Thomas (Md). Captain of Smallwood's Maryland Regiment, 14th January, 1776; Colonel 3d Maryland Battalion of the Flying Camp, July to December, 1776.

Ewing, Thomas (N. J.). Major New Jersey Militia, 1777-1778.

Eyre, Benjamin (Pa). Lieutenant-Colonel Philadelphia Artillery Regiment Militia, 1779. (Died 1781.)

Eyre, John (Pa). Colonel Philadelphia Artillery Militia Regiment, 1779.

Eysandeau, William (Mass). Ensign 15th Massachusetts, 1st January, 1777;

Lieutenant, 2d April, 1779; transferred to 5th Massachusetts, 1st January, 1781; transferred to 3d Massachusetts, 12th June, 1783, and served to 3d November, 1783.

F.

Facey, Joseph (N. H.). Ensign 3d New Hampshire, 8th November, 1776; died 2d November, 1777, of wounds received 19th September, 1777, at Bemus' Heights.

Faggot, Arthur (Mass). Captain of Learned's Massachusetts Regiment, May, 1775.

Failly, —— Chevalier de (France). Major Continental Army, 5th August, 1777; Lieutenant-Colonel, 21st August, 1777; with pay from 1st December, 1776, and served to ——.

Fairbanks, Amos (Mass). Captain of Company Minute Men in Lexington Alarm, April, 1775; Captain Massachusetts Militia, 1775-1781. (Died 1809.)

Fairbanks, George (Mass). Surgeon's Mate 14th Massachusetts, 6th November, 1776; Surgeon, 5th September, 1777; resigned 9th April, 1778.

Fairbanks, Samuel (Mass). Quartermaster-Sergeant 6th Massachusetts, 9th November, 1776; Ensign, 1st January, 1777; 2d Lieutenant, 12th November, 1777; 1st Lieutenant, 10th June, 1779; resigned 20th April, 1781.

Faircloth, William (N. C.). Lieutenant 10th North Carolina, 20th January, 1778; retired 1st June, 1778.

Fairfield, Matthew (Mass). Private in Lexington Alarm, April, 1775; 1st Lieutenant of Gerrish's Massachusetts Regiment, 19th May to December, 1775; 1st Lieutenant 24th Continental Infantry, 1st January to 31st December, 1776; Captain 13th Massachusetts, 1st January, 1777; resigned 22d November, 1777.

Fairfield, Samuel (Mass). Private in Lexington Alarm, April, 1775; Lieutenant 13th Massachusets, 1st January, 1777; resigned 13th February, 1778.

Fairlanb, Nicholas (Pa). Colonel Pensylvania Militia, 1776-1777.

Fairlie, James (N. Y.). Ensign 1st New York, 24th February, 1776; 2d Lieutenant 2d New York, 21st November, 1776; Major and Aide-de-Camp to General Steuben, July, 1778, to close of war. (Died 10th October, 1830.)

Falcon, Birkit (Md). 1st Lieutenant 4th Maryland Battalion of the Flying Camp, July, 1776, to ——.

Falconer, Andrew (Md). 1st Lieutenant 4th Maryland Battalion of the Flying Camp, July to December, 1776.

Falconer, John (N. Y.). Ensign New York Militia; taken prisoner at Monmouth, 21st October, 1776.

Falls, Edward (N. Y.). 2d Lieutenant 2d New York, 28th June to November, 1775.

Falls, —— (N. C.). Captain North Carolina Partisan Rangers, ——; killed at Ramsour's Mill, 20th June, 1780.

Fally, Richard (Mass). Lieutenant of Danielson's Massachusetts Regiment, May to December, 1775; Lieutenant Massachusetts Militia in 1776.

NFaneuil, —— Monsieur (France). Brevet Lieutenant-Colonel Continental Army, 24th March, 1777, and served to ——.

Fanning, Charles (Conn). Ensign of Selden's Connecticut State Regiment, 20th June to 25th December, 1776; 2d Lieutenant 4th Connecticut, 1st January, 1777; 1st Lieutenant, 15th November, 1778; Regimental Paymaster, 1st May, 1779, to June, 1783; retained in Swift's Connecticut Regiment, June, 1783, and served to 3d November, 1783. (Died 1837.)

Fanning, John (Conn). Surgeon's Mate Hospital Department, 11th April, 1777, to June, 1780.

Fanning, Thomas (Conn). Regimental Quartermaster 8th Connecticut, 6th July to 10th December, 1775; 2d Lieutenant and Regimental Quartermaster 17th Continental Infantry, 1st January, 1776; wounded and taken prisoner at Long Island, 27th August, 1776.

Farewell, Isaac (Conn). Ensign 3d Conecticut, 1st May to 6th November, 1775.

Farish, Robert (Va). Surgeon's Mate 1st Continental Artillery, —, 1777; Hospital Surgeon's Mate, 13th May, 1780, to 1st January, 1781.

Farley, Michael (Mass). Sergeant in Lexington Alarm, April, 1775; Regimental Quartermaster of Gerrish's Massachusetts Regiment, 19th May to December, 1775; 2d Lieutenant and Regimental Quartermaster 26th Continental Infantry, 1st January to 31st December, 1776; 1st Lieutenant and Regimental Quartermaster 9th Massachusetts, 1st January, 1777; Captain Lieutenant, 26th July, 1779; Captain, 1st January, 1780; taken prisoner at Young's House, 3d February, 1780. (Died 20th June, 1789.)

Farmer, Benjamin (Mass). 1st Lieutenant of Read's Massachusetts Regiment, May, 1775, to ——.

Farmer, Henry (Conn). 2d Lieutenant 7th Connecticut, 6th July to 21st December, 1775.

Farmer, Lewis (Pa). Captain 1st Battalion of Miles' Pennsylvania Rifle Regiment, 6th April, 1776; wounded at Long Island, 27th August, 1776; Major Pennsylvania State Regiment, 14th March, 1777; Lieutenant-Colonel, 2d May, 1777; regiment designated 13th Pennsylvania, 12th November, 1777; retired 1st July, 1778.

Farmer, Samuel (Md). Ensign 3d Maryland, 20th February, 1777; Lieutenant, 12th April, 1779; wounded and taken prisoner at Camden, 16th August, 1780.

..**Farmer, Thomas** (Conn). Ensign 6th Connecticut, 16th February, 1779; 2d Lieutenant, 28th August ,1780; transferred to 4th Connecticut, 1st January, 1781; resigned 15th November, 1781.

Farnall, William (Mass). 1st Lieutenant of Scammon's Massachusets Regiment, May, 1775, to ——.

Farnham, Zebediah (Conn). 1st Lieutenant 8th Connecticut, 6th July to 10th December, 1775; 1st Lieutenant 17th Continental Infantry, 1st January to 31st December, 1776; served subsequently in the Navy. (Died 1814.)

Farnsworth, Amos (Mass). Corporal of Prescott's Massachusetts Regiment, May to December, 1775; wounded at Bunker Hill, 17th June, 1775; Ensign of a Massachusetts Militia Regiment in 1776, and 1st Lieutenant of a company of Matrosses Massachusetts Militia, 1778, to close of war. (Died 29th October, 1847.)

Farnum, Benjamin (Mass). Captain of Frye's Massachusetts Regiment, May, 1775; wounded at Bunker Hill, 17th June, 1775; Captain 11th Massachusetts, 6th November, 1776; resigned 28th March, 1779. (Died 4th December, 1833.)

Farnum, David (Mass). Sergeant 11th Massachusetts, 24th February, 1777; 2d Lieutenant, 16th January, 1778; resigned 12th August, 1778.

Farnum, Zebediah (Conn). 1st Lieutenant 17th Continental Infantry,

1st January to 31st December, 1776; served subsequently in Navy.

Farr, John (S. C.). 2d Lieutenant 2d South Carolina, 17th June, 1775, to ——.

Farrar, Field (S. C.). 1st Lieutenant 3d South Carolina, ——, 1777; Captain, 18th December, 1778; wounded at Savannah, 9th October, 1779; taken prisoner at Charleston, 12th May, 1780; retired 1st January, 1781.

Farrar, Thomas (S. C.). 1st Lieutenant 5th South Carolina, March, 1777, to ——.

Farrer, Benjamin (Mass). Lieutenant of Read's Massachusetts Regiment, May to December, 1775.

Farrer, Jonathan (Mass). Lieutenant Company of Minute Men in the Lexington Alarm, April, 1775; Lieutenant of Nixon's Massachusetts Regiment, May to November, 1775.

Farrington, Thomas (Mass). Volunteer in the expedition against Quebec, October, 1775, to January, 1776; Captain 16th Continental Infantry, 1st January to 31st December, 1776; Lieutenant-Colonel 5th Massachusetts, 1st January, 1777; cashiered 26th May, 1777.

Farrow, Ezekiel (Mass). Ensign 3d Massachusetts, 1st January, 1777; resigned 31st March, 1777.

Farrow, Field (S. C.). Captain in a South Carolina Regiment in 1778.

Farrow, Thomas (S. C.). Captain 3d South Carolina, ——; taken prisoner at Charleston 12th May, 1780; wounded at Ninety Six 22d May, 1781; served to ——. (Died 1843.)

Farwell, Francis (N. H.). Captain New Hampshire Militia, 1777.

Farwell, Henry (Mass). Captain in the Lexington Alarm, April, 1775; Captain of Prescott's Massachusetts Regiment, April, 1775; wounded at Bunker Hill 17th June, 1775.

Farwell, Isaac (N .H.). 1st Lieutenant 3d New Hampshire, 23d May to December, 1775; 1st Lieutenant 2d Continental Infantry, 1st January, 1776; Captain 1st New Hampshire, 8th November, 1776, and served to close of war. (Died 1791.)

Fassett, Amaziah (Mass). 1st Lieutenant of Prescott's Massachusetts Regiment, May, 1775; mortally wounded and taken prisoner at Bunker Hill, 17th June, 1775.

Fassett, John (N. H.). 1st Lieutenant Green Mountain Boys, 27th July, 1775; 1st Lieutenant of Warner's Additional Continental Regiment, 5th July, 1776; Captain, 16th September, 1776; cashiered 16th October, 1776. (Died 1803.)

Fathern, Benjamin (S. C.). Lieutenant South Carolina Dragoons, 5th April to September, 1781.

Faucheraud, John (S. C.). Major and Aide-de-Camp to General Howe, 29th November, 1777 ,to ——.

Faulkner, Peter (N. J.). Private and Sergeant in Lee's Battalion of Light Dragoons, Pulaski Legion, 1778 and 1779; Ensign 2d New Jersey, 17th May, 1780; retained in New Jersey Battalion April, 1783, and served to 3d November, 1783; Captain 11th United States Infantry, 8th January, 1799; honorably discharged 15th June, 1800; Military Storekeeper, United States Army, 19th August, 1818; dismissed 20th June, 1820. (Died 20th September, 1823.)

Faulkner, Ralph (Va). Captain 5th Virginia, 1st March, 1776; Major 2d Virginia, 22d March, 1777; resigned 30th April, 1778; also shown as retired 14th September, 1778, with rank of Lieutenant-Colonel.

Faulkner, Robert (Pa). Ensign 12th Pennsylvania, 8th January, 1777; resigned 11th October, 1777.

Faulkner, William (N. J.). Captain 2d New Jersey, 11th November, 1775; died 25th April, 1776.

Faulkner, William (N. Y.). Captain New York Militia; wounded at Fort Montgomery 6th October, 1777; served subsequently as Colonel New York Militia.

Fauntleroy, Griffin (Va). 2d Lieutenant 7th Virginia, 5th March, 1776; 1st Lieutenant, 28th October, 1776; resigned 16th November, 1777; Cornet 1st Continental Dragoons, 11th November, 1777; — Lieutenant, ——; killed at Guilford 15th March, 1781.

Fauntleroy, Henry (Va). 1st Lieutenant 5th Virginia, 10th February, 1776; Captain, 15th September, 1776; killed at Monmouth 28th June, 1778.

Fauntleroy, Moore (Va). Ensign 5th Virginia, 13th February, 1776; 2d Lieutenant, 10th September, 1776; Captain 4th Continental Dragoons, 21st January, 1777; taken prisoner at Germantown 4th Ocober, 1777; Major, 1st August, 1779, and served to ——; was in service March, 1780.

Fauntleroy, Robert (Va). Ensign 5th Virginia, 10th May, 1777; resigned 30th May, 1778.

Fawn, William (N. C.). 2d Lieutenant 3d North Carolina, 15th April, 1777; 1st Lieutenant, 4th October, 1777; Captain Lieutenant, 30th March, 1780; wounded and taken prisoner at Charleston 12th May, 1780; Captain ——; retired 1st January, 1783.

Faxon, Elisha (Mass). Sergeant 14th Massachusetts 2d March, 1777; Ensign, 18th October, 1779; retired 1st January, 1781.

Fay, Jonas (N. H.). Surgeon New Hampshire Militia, 1775-1776. (Died 6th March, 1818.)

Fay, Joseph (N. H.). Ensign 3d New Hampshire, 8th November, 1776; died 2d November, 1777, of wounds received at Stillwater, 19th September, 1777.

Fay, Josiah (Mass). Captain in Lexington Alarm, April 1775; Captain of Ward's Massachusetts Regiment, 23d May to December, 1775; Captain 21st Continental Infantry, 1st January, 1776; died 8th August, 1776.

Fay, Josiah (Mass). Captain and Aide-deCamp to General Poor, 2d July, 1779, to 8th September, 1780.

Fayssoux, Peter (S. C.). Chief Physician and Surgeon of Hospital Southern Department, 15th May, 1781, to close of war.

Fayssoux, Peter (S. C.). 1st Lieutenant South Carolina Regiment, 13th July, 1778; taken prisoner at Charleston 12th May, 1780. (Died 1795.)

Fear, Edmund (N. C.). Captain North Carolina Militia at King's Mountain, October, 1780.

Fearson, John (——). Lieutenant, ——; was a prisoner in 1782; when and where taken not stated.

Fehiger, Christian (Virginia). Adjutant of Gerrish's Massachusetts Regiment, 19th May, 1775; Brigade-Major to General Arnold in the campaign against Canada, and was taken prisoner at Quebec 31st December, 1775; exchanged November, 1776; Lieutenant-Colonel 11th Virginia, 13th November, 1776; Colonel, 26th September, 1777; assigned to 3d Virginia, 9th October, 1777; served to close of war; Brevet Brigadier-General, 30th September, 1783. (Died 20th September, 1796.)

Feck, David (Pa). Private in Proctor's Battalion Pennsylvania Artillery in 1776; Ensign 9th Pennsylvania, 7th

December, 1776; Captain Lieutenant of Gibbs Jones' Company Pennsylvania Artillery, 1st June, 1778; omitted December, 1778.

Feely, Timothy (Va). Ensign 11th Virginia, 10th December, 1776; 2d Lieutenant, 1st June, 1777; 1st Lieutenant, 6th November, 1777; regiment designated 7th Virginia, 14th September, 1778; taken prisoner at Charleston 12th May, 1780; transferred to 3d Virginia 12th February, 1781; retired 1st January, 1783.

Fegan, Lawrence (Pa). Regimental Quartermaster 9th Pennsylvania, —— to 24th September, 1777.

Fell, Peter (N. J.). Lieutenant-Colonel New Jersey Militia, 1778-1779.

Fell, William E. (Pa). Cornet 4th Continental Dragoons, 10th February, 1777; omitted March, 1778.

Fellows, David (Conn). Ensign of Burrall's Connecticut State Regiment, January, 1776; Ensign 2d Canadian (Hazen's) Regiment, 6th November, 1776; died 10th December, 1779.

Fellows, John (Mass). Colonel Massachusetts Regiment, May to December, 1775; Brigadier-General of Massachusetts Militia, 1776 to 1780. (Died 1st August, 1808.)

Fellows, Joseph (Conn). Private 6th Connecticut, 12th May to 10th December, 1775; Sergeant 1st Connecticut, 1st January, 1777; Sergeant-Major, 15th November, 1778; Ensign, 1st March, 1779; resigned 29th May, 1780.

Felt, Jonathan (Mass). Private Company of Minute Men at Lexington, 19th April, 1775; Corporal in Read's Massachusetts Regiment, May to November, 1775; 1st Lieutenant 4th Massachusetts, 1st January, 1777; Captain Lieutenant, ——, 1780; Captain, 14th October, 1781; transferred to 7th Massachusetts, 3d May, 1782, and served to 3d June, 1783. (Died 5th November, 1800.)

Felt, Samuel (Conn). 2d Lieutenant 2d Connecticut, 1st May to 17th December, 1775.

Feltman, William (Pa). Ensign 10th Pennsylvania, 4th December, 1776; 2d Lieutenant of Captain Weaver's Company, guarding prisoners at Lancaster, 13th January, 1777; 1st Lieutenant, 30th October, 1777; company transferred to 10th Pennsylvania, 7th November, 1777; transferred to 1st Pennsylvania, 17th January, 1781; taken prisoner at Green Springs, 6th July, 1781; resigned 21st April, 1782.

Felton, Benjamin (Mass). Sergeant in Lexington Alarm, April, 1775; 2d Lieutenant of Learned's Massachusetts Regiment, May to December, 1775; 2d Lieutenant 3d Continental Infantry, 1st January to 31st December, 1776; served subsequently as Captain Massachusetts Militia. (Died 26th January 1820.)

Fenn, Benjamin (Conn). Lieutenant-Colonel Connecticut Militia, 1776-1777.

Fenn, Theophilus (Conn). Captain Connecticut Militia; wounded at Bunker Hill, 17th June, 1775.

Fenn, Thomas (Va). 1st Lieutenant 1st Continental Artillery, 13th January, 1777; Captain Lieutenant, 24th May, 1779; retired 1st January, 1783.

Fenner, Arthur (R. I.). Lieutenant 2d Rhode Island, June to December, 1775; Lieutenant in Babcock's Rhode Island State Regiment, 15th January, 1776; Captain in Lippitt's Rhode Island State Regiment, 19th August, 1776, to 1777; Lieutenant Rhode Island Militia in 1778. (Died 15th October, 1805.)

Fenner, Richard (N. C.). Ensign 2d North Carolina, 10th January, 1779; taken prisoner at Charleston 12th May, 1780; exchanged 14th June, 1781; Lieutenant, 12th May, 1781, and served to close of war.

Fenner, Robert (N. C.). Lieutenant 2d North Carolina 1st January, 1776; Captain, 20th May, 1777; taken prisoner at Charleston 12th May, 1780; served to close of war; Brevet Major, 30th September, 1783.

Fenner, William (N. C.). 1st Lieutenant 2d North Carolina, 1st September, 1775; Captain, 1st May. 1776; Major 7th North Carolina, 24th October, 1777; retired 1st June, 1778.

Fennimore, Thos. (N. J.). Major New Jersey Militia, 1777-1779.

Fenno, Ephraim (N. Y.). 2d Lieutenant of Knox's Regiment Continental Artillery, July to December, 1776; Captain Lieutenant 2d Continental Artillery, 1st January, 1777; taken prisoner at Fort Clinton, 6th October, 1777; transferred to Corps of Artillery, 17th June, 1783, and served to 20th June, 1784.

Fenno, John (N. Y.). Captain New York Militia, ——; taken prisoner at Fort Clinton 6th October, 1777.

Fenno, William (N. Y.). Quartermaster 2d Continental Artillery, 5th March, 1778; superseded 27th October, 1778.

Fenton, Joseph (Mass). Private 6th Continental Infantry, 9th April, 1776; Sergeant 13th Massachusetts, 14th November, 1776; Ensign 1st January, 1777; Lieutenant 15th June, 1779; died of wounds 29th March, 1780; when and where wounded not stated.

Fenton, Solomon (Conn). Ensign 2d Connecticut, 1st January, 1777; 2d Lieutenant, 24th December, 1777; 1st Lieutenant 15th May, 1778; resigned 4th April, 1780.

Fenwick, Thomas (S. C.). Lieutenant South Carolina Militia in 1775 and 1776.

Fergus, Janus (N. C.). Surgeon 1st North Carolina, 24th May, 1776; resigned — April, 1777; Surgeon's Mate 1st North Carolina, 21st February, 1782; Surgeon, 20th August, 1782, and served to close of war.

Ferguson, John (Mass). Captain of Danielson's Massachusetts Regiment, May to December, 1775. (Died 1792.)

Ferguson, William (Pa). Captain Lieutenant 4th Continental Artillery, 14th March, 1777; taken prisoner at Bound Brook 13th April, 1777; exchanged 1st December, 1780, Captain, 14th April, 1778; retired 1st January, 1783; Captain United States Artillery, 20th October, 1785; Captain Artillery Battalion United States Army, 29th September, 1789; Major Commandant Artillery Battalion United States Army, 4th March, 1791; killed 4th November, 1791, near Fort Recovery, Ohio, in action with Indians at St. Clair's defeat.

Feriole, Alexander (Conn). Ensign 2d Canadian (Hazen's) Regiment in 1777; Lieutenant, — August, 1780; retired 1st January, 1782.

Fermoy, Matthias Alexis Roche de (France). See **De Fermoy**.

Fernald, Joshua (Mass). Corporal in Scammon's Massachusetts Regiment, May to December, 1775; Sergeant 2d Massachusetts, 1st January, 1777; Sergeant-Major, 15th April, 1777; Ensign, 1st June, 1777; resigned 25th April, 1780. (Died 11th January, 1830.)

Fernald, Tobias (Mass). Captain of Scammon's Massachusetts Regiment, 19th May to December, 1775; Captain 18th Continental Infantry, 1st January, 1776; Major 12th Massachusetts, 6th November, 1776; Lieutenant-Colonel 8th Massachusetts, 6th March, 1779; transferred to 10th Massachusetts 1st January, 1781; retired 1st January, 1783. (Died 15th August, 1784.)

Fernald, William (Mass). Lieutenant of Scammon's Massachusetts Regiment, May to December, 1775.

Fernandis, James (Md). Ensign of Smallwood's Maryland Regiment, May, 1776; taken prisoner at Long Island 27th August, 1776; exchanged 24th March, 1777; 2d Lieutenant 1st Maryland, 10th December, 1776; 1st Lieutenant, 17th April, 1777; Captain Lieutenant, 1st March, 1778; resigned 15th July, 1779.

Ferrall, Micajah (N. C.). Ensign 9th North Carolina, 28th November, 1776, to ——.

Ferrebee, Joseph (N. C.). Lieutenant 10th North Carolina, 5th May, 1777, to ——.

Ferrebee, William (N. C.). Lieutenant 7th North Carolina, 28th November, 1776; transferred to 4th North Carolina, 1st June, 1778; Captain, 1st July, 1781; retired 1st January, 1783.

Ferrell, Luke L. (N. C.). Lieutenant 10th North Carolina, ——, 1778, to ——.

Ferrell, William (N. C.). Ensign 8th North Carolina, 8th September, 1777; 2d Lieutenant, 10th October, 1777; transferred to 2d North Carolina, 1st June, 1778, and served to ——.

Ferris, Nathan (Conn). 1st Lieutenant 7th Connecticut, 1st January, 1777; cashiered 25th October, 1777.

Fessenden, Haskell (—). Lieutenant and Aide-de-Camp, ——; resigned 15th August, 1780.

Few, Benjamin (Ga). Colonel Georgia Militia, 1776-1781.

Few, Ignatius (Ga). 1st Lieutenant 1st Georgia, 2d January, 1776; Captain, 21st July, 1777; taken prisoner at Amelia Island, Fla., 18th May, 1777; served to close of war; Brevet Major, 30th September, 1783. (Died 1810.)

Few, Joseph (Pa). Regimental Quartermaster 4th Continental Artillery, 1st April, 1777; resigned 31st October, 1777.

Few, William (Ga). Colonel Georgia Militia, 1778 to 1782. (Died 16th July, 1828)

Fick, David (Pa). 1st Lieutenant of Captain Jones' Company Pennsylvnia Artillery, 1st January, 1777; Captain Lieutenant, 1st June, 1778; Captain, 14th April, 1780; retired 1st January, 1781.

Fickle, Benjamin (Md). Sergeant Maryland Battalion of the Flying

Camp, July to December, 1776; wounded at Long Island 27th August, 1776; Sergeant 7th Maryland, 6th April, 1778; Ensign, 26th January, 1780; 2d Lieutenant, 19th February, 1780; wounded at Camden, 16th August, 1780; transferred to 5th Maryland, 1st January, 1781; retained in Maryland Battalion, April, 1783, and served to 15th November, 1783.

Fiddeman, Philip (Md). Captain 4th Maryland Battalion of the Flying Camp, June, 1776, to ——.

Field, Benjamin (Va). Captain of Clark's Illinois Regiment, 1778-1782; name also spelled Fields.

Field, Ebenezer (Mass). Corporal and Sergeant in Learned's Massachusetts Regiment, May to December, 1775; Ensign 3d Continental Infantry, 1st January to 31st December, 1776; 1st Lieutenant 4th Massachusetts, 1st January, 1777; Captain Lieutenant, 15th June, 1779; resigned 14th April, 1780.

Field, Henry (Va). 1st Lieutenant 8th Virginia, 26th January, 1776; resigned 3d August, 1776. (Died ——, 1777.)

Field, James (S. C.). Captain Lieutenant 4th South Carolina (Artillery), in 1779-1780; taken prisoner at Charleston 12th May, 1780.

Field, John (N. Y.). Colonel New York Militia, 1776-1780.

Field, John (R. I.). Captain Lieutenant 2d Rhode Island, 3d May to December, 1775.

Field, Nathaniel (R. I.). Ensign of Hitchcock's Rhode Island Regiment, 3d May to December, 1775.

Field, Nehemiah (R. I.). Ensign 11th Continental Infantry, 1st January, 1776, to ——.

Field, Reuben (Va). Ensign 8th Virginia, 13th February, 1776; 2d Lieutenant, — September, 1776; taken prisoner at Germantown 4th October, 1777; 1st Lieutenant, 10th January, 1778; Captain 4th Virginia, 25th May, 1781; retired 1st January, 1783.

Field, Stephen (Va). Lieutenant Virginia Militia, 1778-1780.

Filer, Abraham (Conn). Captain 8th Connecticut, 6th July to 10th December, 1775.

Filson, John (Pa). Ensign of Montgomery's Pennsylvania Battalion of the Flying Camp; taken prisoner at Fort Washington, 16th November, 1776.

Filson, Robert (Pa). 1st Lieutenant of Montgomery's Pennsylvania Battalion of the Flying Camp; taken prisoner at Fort Washington, 16th November, 1776.

Finch, Nathaniel (N. Y.). Lieutenant and Adjutant of Hathorne's New York Militia Regiment, ——; killed at Minnisink, 22d July, 1779.

Finck, Andrew (N. Y.). 1st Lieutenant 2d New York, 15th July, 1775; Captain, 16th February, 1776; Captain 1st New York, 21st November, 1776, to rank from 16th February, 1776; retired 1st January, 1781; served subsequently as Major New York Levies. (Died 3d February, 1820.)

Findale, James (Mass). 2d Lieutenant of Heath's Massachusetts Regiment, May to December, 1775.

Finley, Andrew (Pa). Ensign 8th Pennsylvania, 9th August, 1776; 2d Lieutenant 13th July 1777; 1st Lieutenant 4th October, 1777; retired 10th September, 1778.

Finley, Ebenezer (Md). Captain Lieutenant of Dorsey's Company Maryland Artillery, 4th July, 1777; company formed part of 1st Continental Artillery, 30th May, 1778; Deputy Judge Advocate Southern Department, July, 1780; retired 1st January, 1781.

Finley, James Edwards Burr (Mass). Surgeon 15th Massachusetts, 25th February, 1778; transferred to 5th Massachusetts, 1st January, 1781; transferred to 4th Massachusetts, 12th June, 1783, and served to 3d November, 1783. (Died 13th June, 1819.)

Finley, John (Pa). 1st Lieutenant 8th Pennsylvania, July, 1776; Captain, 22d October, 1777; transferred to 5th Pennsylvania, 17th January, 1781; transferred to 2d Pennsylvania, 1st January, 1783, and served to 3d June, 1783.

Finley, John H. (Pa). 2d Lieutenant 5th Pennsylvania Battalion, 8th January, 1776; 1st Lieutenant, 1st November, 1776; taken prisoner at Fort Washington, 16th November, 1776; exchanged 25th October, 1780, and did not re-enter service.

Finley, Joseph Lewis (Pa). 2d Lieutenant 1st Battalion of Miles' Pennsylvania Rifle Regiment, 6th April, 1776; Lieutenant Pennsylvania State Regiment, 24th October, 1776; Captain, 20th October, 1777; regiment designated

13th Pennsylvania 12th November, 1777; transferred to 8th Pennsylvania 1st July, 1778; Brigade-Major, 20th July, 1780; transferred to 2d Pennsylvania 17th January, 1781; transferred to 1st Pennsylvania 1st January, 1783, and served to 3d June, 1783. (Died 1839.)

Finley, Samuel (Mass). Surgeon 14th Massachusetts, 10th April, 1778; transferred to 7th Massachusetts 1st January, 1781, and served to 3d June, 1783; Surgeon 12th United States Infantry, 4th September, 1799; resigned 1st April, 1800.

Finley, Samuel (Pa). 1st Lieutenant of Proctor's Pennsylvania Artillery, 28th June, 1776; taken prisoner at Fort Washington 16th November, 1776; exchanged 2d November, 1780, and did not re-enter service.

Finley, Samuel (Va). 1st Lieutenant of Stephenson's Maryland and Virginia Rifle Regiment, 9th July, 1776; taken prisoner at Fort Washington, 16th November, 1776; Captain 11th Virginia, 20th December, 1776; transferred to 4th Virginia, 12th February, 1781; Major 7th Virginia, 11th September, 1782; transferred to 1st Virginia 1st January, 1783, and served to close of war. (Died 2d April, 1829.)

Finn, John (S. C.). Captain Lieutenant of Artillery; killed at Eutaw Springs 8th September, 1781.

Finn, Thomas (Va). 1st Lieutenant 1st Continental Artillery, 13th January, 1777; Captain Lieutenant, ——, 1780; served to close of war.

Finney, Lazarus (Pa). Ensign of Montgomery's Battalion Pennsylvania Flying Camp, July to December, 1776; Lieutenant and Captain Pennsylvania Militia, 1777-1778.

Finney, Thomas (N. C.). Ensign 2d North Carolina, 12th November, 1777; Lieutenant, 23d January, 1781; taken prisoner at Charleston 12th May, 1780; exchanged 14th June, 1781; served to close of war.

Finney, Walter (Pa). 1st Lieutenant Pennsylvania Musket Battalion, 20th March, 1776; Captain 13th July, 1776; taken prisoner at Long Island 27th August, 1776; Captain 10th Pennsylvania, to rank from 10th August, 1776; wounded at Green Springs 6th July, 1781; transferred to 3d Pennsylvania 1st January, 1783; transferred to 1st Pennsylvania June, 1783; Brevet Major, 30th September, 1783; served to 3d November, 1783; Captain United States Infantry, 12th August, 1784; resigned 1st September, 1787. (Died 17th September, 1820.)

Finnie, William (Va). Colonel and Deputy Quartermaster-General Southern Department, 28th March, 1776, and served to close of war.

Fish, Adam (Mass). Ensign Lexington Alarm, April, 1775; Lieutenant of Massachusetts Militia in 1776; 1st Lieutenant 14th Massachusetts, 1st January, 1777; Captain Lieutenant, 1st April, 1778; Captain, 8th October, 1779; resigned 14th April, 1780.

Fish, Ebenezer (Mass). Sergeant 16th Continental Infantry, 1st January to 31st December, 1776; 1st Lieutenant 8th Massachusetts, 1st January, 1777; Regimental Quartermaster, 28th September, 1778; Captain Lieutenant, 1st January, 1779; died 4th April, 1779.

Fish, Joseph (Conn). 2d Lieutenant 4th Connecticut, 1st January, 1777; dismissed 13th January, 1778.

Fish, Nicholas (N. Y.). Lieutenant and Captain in Malcolm's New York Regiment in 1775 and 1776; Brigade-Major to General Scott, 9th August, 1776; Major 2d New York, 21st November, 1776, and served to 3d June, 1783. (Died 30th June, 1833.)

Fish, Thomas (Mass). 2d Lieutenant of Learned's Massachusetts Regiment, April to November, 1775; 1st Lieutenant 3d Continental Infantry, 1st January to 31st December, 1776; Captain 4th Massachusetts, 1st January, 1777; resigned 1st July, 1779.

Fishbourne, Benjamin (Pa). Paymaster 2d Pennsylvania Battalion, 2d October, 1776; Captain 4th Pennsylvania, 3d January, 1777; transferred to 1st Pennsylvania 1st January, 1783; Aide-de-Camp to General Wayne, 1779 to 1783; served to 3d June, 1783. (Died 3d November, 1819.)

Fishburne, William (S. C.). Lieutenant in 1st South Carolina in 1778; wounded at Stono Ferry, 20th June, 1779; Captain under General Marion in 1780 and 1781.

Fisher, Frederick (N. Y.). Colonel New York Militia, ——; wounded and scalped at Johnstown, N. Y., 22d May, 1780. (Died 9th June, 1809.)

Fisher, Hendrick (N. J.). 1st Lieutenant 1st New Jersey, 16th December, 1775; Paymaster 7th Continental Infantry, 13th September to 31st December, 1776.

Fisher, Henry (Pa). Captain German Regiment, 8th November, 1776; cashiered 7th April, 1777.

Fisher, Isaac (Mass). Sergeant in Lexington Alarm, April, 1775; 2d Lieutenant of Walker's Massachusetts Regiment, May to December, 1775, and Lieutenant of Massachusetts Militia in 1776.

Fisher, John (N. Y.) Captain 2d New York, 28th June, 1775; Major 3d New York, 8th March, 1776; Lieutenant-Colonel of Nicholson's New York Regiment, 21st June to November, 1776.

Fisher, Jonathan (Mass). Lieutenant Massachusetts Militia, 1776 and 1777; died in service, 10th March, 1777.

Fisher, Joshua (Mass). Captain Massachusetts Militia, 1776.

Fisher, Samuel (Pa). Captain Pennsylvania Militia; taken prisoner at Guelphs Mills 11th December, 1777; released 8th December, 1780.

Fisk, Isaac (N. Y.). Sergeant 2d Continental Artillery, 26th April, 1777; Sergeant-Major, 19th October, 1779; 2d Lieutenant, 29th June, 1781; resigned 14th July, 1782.

Fisk, John (Conn). Ensign of Elmore's Connecticut Regiment, 15th April, 1776; resigned 2d October, 1776.

Fisk, Joseph (Mass). Private in Lexington Alarm, April, 1775; 2d Lieutenant 12th Continental Infantry, 1st January to 31st December, 1776; Surgeon's Mate 1st Massachusetts, 1st January, 1777; Surgeon, 18th March, 1779, and served to close of war. (Died 25th September, 1837.)

Fisk, Squire (R. I.). Ensign of Richmond's Rhode Island State Regiment, 1st November, 1775, to April, 1776; served subsequently as Lieutenant Rhode Island Militia. (Died 1805.)

Fisk, Thomas (Mass). 2d Lieutenant of Learned's Massachusetts Regiment, May to December, 1775.

Fisk, William (R. I.). Lieutenant of Elliott's Regiment Rhode Island State Artillery, 12th December, 1776, to June, 1777.

Fiske, Daniel (R. I.). Ensign of Tallman's Rhode Island State Regiment, 12th December, 1776, to June, 1777..

Fisley, —— (—). Lieutenant 2d Battalion, ——; killed at Stono Ferry, 20th June, 1779.

Fiss, Jacob (Pa). Ensign 11th Pennsylvania, 30th September, 1776; 2d Lieutenant, 7th September, 1777; 1st Lieutenant, 1st February, 1778; retired 1st July, 1778. (Name also spelled John Fiss.)

Fister, Henry (Md). Captain German Battalion, 12th July, 1776; dismissed 7th April, 1777.

Fitch, Andrew (Conn). Private Company of Minute Men at Lexington and Concord, 19th April, 1775; Lieutenant 3d Connecticut, 1st May to 19th December, 1775; 1st Lieutenant of Ward's Connecticut State Regiment, 14th May, 1776; Captain 4th Connecticut, 1st January, 1777; retired 1st January, 1781. (Died 28th August, 1811.)

Fitch, Asel (Conn). Surgeon's Mate 5th Connecticut, May to December, 1775.

Fitch, Ebenezer (Mass). Sergeant in Lexington Alarm, April, 1775; 2d Lieutenant of Bridge's Massachusetts Regiment, May to December, 1775; 1st Lieutenant 11th Continental Infantry, 1st January to 31st December, 1776. (Died 21st March, 1833.)

Fitch, Gerard (Mass). Ensign Quartermaster 15th Continental Infantry, 1st January to 31st December, 1776

Fitch, Jabez (Conn). Private in Lexington Alarm, April, 1775; 1st Lieutenant 8th Connecticut, 6th July to 17th December, 1775; 1st Lieutenant, 17th Continental Infantry, 1st January, 1776; taken prisoner at Long Island 27th August, 1776; was a prisoner 18 months. (Died 1812.)

Fitch, Joseph (N. Y.). 2d Lieutenant 2d New York, 28th June, 1775, to January, 1776; served subsequently as Lieutenant New York Militia.

Fitch, Stephen (Mass). 1st Lieutenant of Cady's Battalion on the expedition to Canada, January to June, 1776.

Fitch, William (N. H.). Captain Green Mountain Boys, 27th July, 1775, to ——.

Fithian, Glover (N. J.). Ensign 1st New Jersey, 29th November, 1776, to March, 1777; Captain New Jersey Militia, ——; killed 8th October, 1777 (Where not stated).

Fithian, Philip Vickers (N. J.). Chaplain New Jersey Militia, ——; killed on the retreat from New York, 15th September, 1776.

Fitzgerald, Benjamin (Pa). 2d Lieutenant 9th Pennsylvania, 15th January, 1777, to ——.

Fitzgerald, John (S. C.). Captain South Carolina Militia in 1776.

Fitzgerald, John (Va). Captain 3d Virginia, 8th February, 1776; Lieutenant-Colonel and Aide-de-Camp to General Washington, — November, 1776, to 6th July, 1778; wounded at Monmouth, 28th June, 1778; was also Major 9th Virginia, 28th January, 1777, until he resigned, 6th July, 1778.

Fitzgerald, John Henry (Va). Ensign 5th Virginia, 1st March, 1776; 2d Lieutenant, 17th September, 1776; 1st Lieutenant, 1st April, 1777; transferred to 3d Virginia, 14th September, 1778; Captain Lieutenant, 19th June, 1779; Captain, 10th May, 1780; taken prisoner at Charleston 12th May, 1780; transferred to 6th Virginia 12th February, 1781; retired 1st January, 1783.

Fitzgerald, William (Va). Captain Virginia Militia; wounded at Guilford 15th March, 1781. (Died 1818.)

Fitzhugh, Perigrine (Va). Cornet 3d Continental Dragoons, 16th June, 1778; Lieutenant, ——, 1778; taken prisoner at Tappan 28th September, 1778; exchanged 25th October, 1780; Lieutenant-Colonel and Aide-de-Camp to General Washington, 2d July, 1781, to close of war; was also Captain 3d Continental Dragoons in 1781.

Fitzhugh, William Frisby (Va). Cornet 3d Continental Dragoons, ——, 1779; Lieutenant, 2d March, 1781; transferred to Baylor's Regiment of Consolidated Dragoons, 9th November, 1782, and served to close of war. (Died 1839.)

Fitzpatrick, Patrick (Ga). 1st Lieutenant 4th Georgia in 1779 and 1780, and is mentioned as Captain in 1782.

Fitzpatrick, William (S. C.). Lieutenant 3d South Carolina in 1778; wounded at siege of Savannah in September, 1779.

Fitz-Randolph, Edward. — See **Randolph.**

Flagg, Ebenezer (R. I.). Captain 2d Rhode Island Regiment, 28th June to December, 1775; Captain 9th Continental Infantry, 1st January to 31st December, 1776; Captain 1st Rhode Island, 1st January, 1777; Major, 26th May, 1778; killed, 14th May, 1781, by Delancey's Tories in Westchester County, New York.

Flagg, Henry Collins (S. C.). Surgeon South Carolina Troops in 1775; Apothecary General Southern Department, 1779 to close of war; was taken prisoner at Charleston 12th May, 1780.

Flagg, Josiah (R. I.). Lieutenant-Colonel of Elliott's Rhode Island Artillery Regiment, 1777-1778.

Flahavan, John (N. J.). 2d Lieutenant 1st New Jersey, 16th December, 1775, to 10th November, 1776; 1st Lieutenant 1st New Jersey, 29th November, 1776; Captain, 15th December, 1776; taken prisoner 22d April, 1777, where not stated; resigned 22d January, 1779.

Flanningham, Samuel (N. J.). 1st Lieutenant 3d New Jersey, 9th February to 10th November, 1776; Captain 3d New Jersey, 30th November, 1776; resigned 26th October, 1777; served subsequently as Major New Jersey Militia.

Flaving, John (N. J.). Major New Jersey Militia; taken prisoner near Amboy, 20th April, 1777.

Fleet, John (Va). Ensign 2d Virginia State Regiment, 3d September, 1777; 2d Lieutenant, 23d April, 1778; 1st Lieutenant, 10th September, 1778, to January, 1781.

Fleming, Charles (Va). Captain 7th Virginia, 29th February, 1776; Major 4th Virginia, 5th June, 1777; Lieutenant-Colonel 3d Virginia, 28th June, 1778; transferred to 8th Virginia, 14th September, 1778; resigned 15th December, 1778.

Fleming, Frederick (Va). Surgeon's Mate 8th Virginia, 19th April, 1777, to ——.

Fleming, Edward (N. Y.). Lieutenant-Colonel 3d New York, 30th June, 1775; Colonel Deputy Adjutant General New York Department, 28th August, 1775; resigned 15th June, 1776.

Fleming, George (N. Y.). 1st Lieutenant of Knox's Regiment Continental Artillery, 16th March, 1776; Captain Lieutenant 2d Continental Artillery, 1st January, 1777; Captain, 9th November, 1778, and served to November, 1783; Brevet Major, 30th September, 1783; Military Storekeeper, U. S. A., at West Point, N. Y., 1st October, 1800; resigned 12th July, 1806. (Died 2d October, 1822.)

Fleming, James (Va). Lieutenant Virginia Militia, 1779-1780. (Died 14th May, 1833.)

Fleming, John (Va). Captain 1st Virginia, 2d October, 1775; killed at Princeton, 3d January, 1777.

Fleming, Stephen (N. J.). Lieutenant-Colonel New Jersey Militia; taken prisoner at Monmouth 27th February, 1777.

Fleming, Thomas (Va). Colonel 9th Virginia, 2d March, 1776; died 30th January, 1777.

Fletcher, —— (—). Lieutenant, ——; wounded at Hanging Rock, 6th August, 1780.

Fletcher, Joel (Mass). Captain in Lexington Alarm, April, 1775; Captain of Doolittle's Massachusetts Regiment, May to December, 1775.

Fletcher, Samuel (N. Y.). 1st Lieutenant 2d New York, 8th June, 1775, to January, 1776; served subsequently as Regimental Quartermaster New York Militia Regiment.

Fletcher, Samuel (Vt). Colonel and Brigadier-General Vermont Militia, 1779-1782. (Died 1814.)

Fleury, Francois Louis de (France). Captain Engineer 22d May, 1777. By the resolve of Congress of 13th September, 1777, it was "Resolved, whereas Congress has received information that Monsieur Lewis de Fleury, during very gallant exertions in the late battle of Brandywine, near Birmingham Meeting-House, had his horse shot under him, resolved that the Quartermaster-General present him with a horse, as a testimonial of the sense Congress have of Monsieur de Fleury's merit." Appointed Brigade-Major to Pulaski, 3d October, 1777; wounded at Fort Mifflin, 15th November, 1777; Lieutenant-Colonel Engineer, 26th November, 1777. By the resolve of Congress of 26th July, 1779, it was "Resolved unanimously, that Lieutenant-Colonel Fleury and Major Stewart, who by their situation in leading two attacks (on Stony Point), had a more immediate opportunity of distinguishing themselves, have, by their personal achievements, exhibited a bright example to their brother soldiers, and merit in a particular manner the approbation and acknowledgment of the United States; that a silver medal, emblematical of this action be struck and presented to Lieutenant-Colonel Fleury." By the acts of 1st October, 1779, it aws "Resolved, that Congress entertain a high sense of the zeal, activity, military genius and gallantry of Lieutenant-Colonel Fleury, which he has exhibited on a variety of occasions during his service in the armies of these States; wherein, while he has rendered essential benefit to the American cause, he has deservedly acquired the esteem of the army and gained unfading reputation for himself." Granted leave, 27th September, 1779, and returned to France ——.

Fling, Lemuel (Conn). Sergeant 4th Connecticut, 1st January, 1777; Sergeant-Major, 15th April, 1780; Ensign, 1st October, 1780; transferred to 1st Connecticut, 1st January, 1781; 2d Lieutenant, 13th November, 1781; resigned — September, 1782. (Died 22d October, 1824.)

Flinn, John (N. Y.). Ensign of Malcolm's Additional Continental Regiment, 29th April, 1777; resigned 9th April, 1778.

Flint, John (Mass). Lieutenant in Lexington Alarm, April, 1775; 1st Lieutenant of Bridge's Massachusetts Regiment, May to December, 1775; Lieutenant in Massachusetts Militia, 1776-1779.

Flint, Joseph (Mass). Captain Massachusetts Militia, 1776.

Flint, Royal (Conn). Paymaster of Ward's Connecticut State Regiment, 10th June, 1776, to May, 1777; Assistant Commissary of Purchases, 27th May, 1778; resigned — February, 1780. (Died 17th October, 1797.)

Flint, Samuel (Mass). Captain Massachusetts Militia; killed at Stillwater 7th October, 1777.

Flood, Benjamin ,N. H.). Captain New Hampshire Militia, 1777-1778.

Flournoy, Thomas (Va). Captain Virginia Militia, 1776-1777.

Flower, Benjamin (Pa). Commissary of Military Stores of the Flying Camp, 16th July to December, 1776; Colonel Artillery Artificer Regiment, 16th January, 1777; died 28th April, 1781.

Flower, Samuel (Mass). 2d Lieutenant of Danielson's Massachusetts Regiment, May to December, 1775; Captain 3d Massachusetts, 1st January, 1777; resigned 9th February, 1780; Major Massachusetts Militia in 1782.

Floyd, Charles (S. C.). Captain South Carolina Militia, 1775-1777. (Died 1820.)

Floyd, Ebenezer (Mass). Sergeant 1st Massachusetts, 1st January, 1777; Ensign, 23d October, 1781, and served to November, 1783.

Floyd, William (N. Y.). A signer of the Declaration of Independence; was Colonel and Major General New York Militia: died 4th August, 1821.

Foakes, Yelverton (N. C.). Lieutenant and Regimental Quartermaster 1st North Carolina, 3d February, 1776; resigned 1st August, 1776.

Foard, Hezekiah (N. C.). Chaplain 5th North Carolina, 20th April, 1777; retired 1st June, 1778.

Fogarty, Joseph (S. C.). Lieutenant South Carolina Militia in 1776.

Fogg, Jeremiah (N. H.). Regimental Adjutant 2d New Hampshire, 23d May to December, 1775; 2d Lieutenant Regimental Quartermaster 8th Continental Infantry, 1st January, 1776; Paymaster 2d New Hampshire Infantry, 8th November, 1776, to 17th October, 1779; Captain 2d New Hampshire, 9th October, 1777; transferred to 1st New Hampshire, 1st March, 1782, and served to June, 1783.

Fogg, Joseph (N. H.). Regimental Quartermaster 2d New Hampshire, 23d May to December, 1775; served subsequently in New Hampshire Militia. (Died 1822.)

Foissin, Peter (S. C.). 2d Lieutenant 2d South Carolina, 6th December, 1777; 1st Lieutenant, 13th July, 1778; taken prisoner at Charleston 12th May, 1780; served to close of war.

Foley, Mason (S. C.). Captain South Carolina Militia in 1780.

Folsom, Benjamin (N. H.). Captain New Hampshire Militia, 1775-1776.

Folsom, Nathaniel (N. H.). Major-General New Hampshire Militia, May to August, 1775. (Died 26th May, 1790.)

Folwell, John (Pa). Captain of Hart's Pennsylvania Battalion of the Flying Camp, July to December, 1776.

Fonda, Jelles A. (N. Y.). Captain New York Militia, 1777-1780.

Fonda, John L. (N. Y.). Lieutenant New York Militia in 1781.

Fondey, Douw J. (N. Y.). Ensign 3d New York, 29th May, 1779; transferred to 1st New York, 1st January, 1781, and served to 3d June, 1783; Captain, 12th United States Infantry, 8th January, 1799; Major, 15th October, 1799; honorably discharged 15th June, 1800. (Name also spelled Fonda.)

Fondey, John (N. Y.). Ensign 2d New York, 29th June, 1781; transferred

to 1st New York, 1st January, 1783, and served to 3d June, 1783. (Name also spelled Fonda.)

Fontaine, Bechet de Roche (France). Captain Engineers, 15th May, 1778, and served to ——.

Fontaine, William (Va). Captain 2d Virginia, 21st October, 1775, to March, 1776; Lieutenant-Colonel Convention Guards, June, 1779, to June, 1781.

Foot, —— (—). Lieutenant Pulaski Legion, ——; taken prisoner at Camden 16th August, 1780.

Foot, Aaron (Conn). 2d Lieutenant, 1st Connecticut, 1st May to 1st December, 1775.

Foot, Joseph (Mass). Ensign 12th Massachusetts, 1st January, 1777; Lieutenant, 6th March, 1779; transferred to 1st Massachusetts 1st January, 1781; resigned 7th July, 1782.

Foote, Moses (Conn). Lieutenant of Wadsworth's Connecticut State Regiment, June to December, 1776. (Died 1819.)

Forbes, Arthur (N. C.). Colonel North Carolina Militia; wounded at Guilford 15th March, 1781, and died in April, 1781.

Forbes, James (Pa). Sergeant 4th Pennsylvania Battalion, 18th June, 1776; Ensign 12th October to 26th November, 1776; 2d Lieutenant 5th Pennsylvania, 1st January, 1777; 1st Lieutenant, 20th September, 1777; resigned 5th November, 1778.

Forbes, John (Md). 2d Lieutenant 3d Maryland Battalion of the Flying Camp, July to December, 1776.

Forbes, John (N. C.). Captain North Carolina Militia in 1781; killed at Guilford 15th March, 1781.

Forbes, Jonathan (Mass). Ensign 4th Massachusetts, 1st January, 1777; cashiered 8th March, 1778.

Forbes, William A. (N. Y.). 1st Lieutenant 1st New York, 28th June, 1775; Captain, 16th August to November, 1776.

Forbush, Charles (Mass). Captain of Bridge's Massachusetts Regiment, May to December, 1775.

Force, Ebenezer (Conn). Private in the Lexington Alarm, April, 1775; Ensign 3d Connecticut, 1st January, 1777; resigned 28th March, 1778.

Ford, Benjamin (Md). 1st Lieutenant of Smallwood's Maryland Regiment, 14th January, 1776; Captain, May, 1776; Major 2d Maryland, 10th December, 1776; Lieutenant-Colonel 6th Maryland, 17th April, 1777; transferred to 5th Maryland, 1st January, 1781; died 27th April, 1781, of wounds received at Hobkirk's Hill, 25th April, 1781.

Ford, Chilion (N. J.). 2d Lieutenant 2d Continental Artillery, 1st February. 1777; Regimental Adjutant, 25th May, 1778; Regimental Quartermaster, 1st August, 1779; 1st Lieutenant, 1st October, 1780, and served to June, 1783. (Died 1800.)

Ford, Denham (Va). Ensign 4th Virginia, 28th September, 1776; 2d Lieutenant, 22d March, 1777; Commissary of Military Stores, 19th October, 1777; cashiered 3d January, 1778. (Name also spelled Dennis Foard.)

Ford, George (S. C.). Major South Carolina, 1775-1776.

Ford, Hezekiah (Md). Sergeant 2d Maryland, 10th April, 1777; 2d Lieutenant, 1st September, 1777; 1st Lieutenant, 16th August, 1780; transferred to 1st Maryland, 1st January, 1781, and served to April, 1783. (Died 16th February, 1833.) Name also spelled Foard.

Ford, Jacob, Jr. (N. J.). Colonel New Jersey Militia, 1776-1777; died 10th January, 1777.

Ford, Jacob (N. Y.). Captain, Major and Lieutenant-Colonel New York Militia, 1775 to 1780. (Died 1809.)

Ford, James (Mass). 1st Lieutenant of Bridge's Massachusetts Regiment, May to December, 1775.

Ford, James (N. H.). Lieutenant of Nichols' New Hampshire Militia Regiment; wounded at Bennington, 16th August, 1777.

Ford, James (S. C.). Captain South Carolina Militia in 1776.

Ford, John (Mass). Captain of Bridge's Massachusetts Regiment, May to December, 1775; Captain Massachusetts Militia, 1776-1777. (Died 1822.)

Ford, John (N. C.). Ensign 3d North Carolina, 30th November, 1778; taken prisoner at Charleston, 12th May, 1780; Lieutenant, 23d January, 1781, and served to close of war.

Ford, Joseph (Md). 2d Lieutenant of Smallwood's Maryland Regiment, 14th January, 1776; 1st Lieutenant, 16th August, 1776; Captain 1st Maryland, 10th December, 1776; resigned 6th March, 1778. (Died — December, 1812.)

Ford, Mahlon (N. J.). Ensign 3d New Jersey, 1st May, 1777; 2d Lieutenant, 26th October, 1777; 1st Lieutenant, 30th March, 1780; transferred to 1st New Jersey, 1st January, 1781; retained in New Jersey Battalion, April, 1783; Brevet Captain, 30th September, 1783, and served to November, 1783; Ensign United States Infantry Regiment, 12th August, 1784; Lieutenant United States Artillery Battalion, 17th March, 1786; Lieutenant Artillery Battalion United States Army, 29th September, 1789; Captain, 4th March, 1791; Artillerists and Engineers, 9th May, 1794, Major 1st Artillerists and Engineers, 7th May, 1798; honorably discharged 1st June, 1802. (Died 12th June, 1820)

Ford, Tobias (S. C.). Ensign 1st South Carolina in 1781; served to close of war.

Ford, William (Conn). Ensign of Wolcott's Connecticut State Regiment, December, 1775, to February, 1776.

Foreman, Alexander (N. Y.). Ensign New York Militia, ——; prisoner of war, 8th January to 11th October, 1777; where taken not stated; served subsequently as Captain New York Militia. (Died 25th December, 1831.)

Foreman, Caleb (N. C.). Lieutenant 8th North Carolina, 28th November, 1776, to ——.

Foreman, Charles (Pa). 1st Lieutenant 4th Pennsylvania, 4th December, 1776; resigned 30th April, 1777.

Foreman, Robert (Va). Paymaster 9th Virginia, — April, 1777; resigned 16th June, 1778

Forgue, Francis (Conn). Surgeon 7th Connecticut, 6th July to 10th December, 1775;. Surgeon 19th Continental Infantry, 1st January, 1776; resigned 3d July, 1776; Surgeon-General of Hospital Northern Department, 11th April, 1777; resigned 31st July, 1777.

Forman, David (N. J.). Colonel New Jersey State Regiment, 25th June, 1776; Colonel of one of the sixteen Additional Continental Regiments, 12th January, 1777, to 1st July, 1778, and Brigadier-General New Jersey Militia, ——. (Died 1812.)

Forman, Jonathan (N. J.). 1st Lieutenant of Forman's New Jersey Militia Regiment, May to November, 1776; Captain 1st New Jersey, 23d November, 1776; Major, 20th November, 1781; Lieutenant-Colonel 2d New Jersey, 11th February, 1783; retained in Consolidated

New Jersey Regiment, April, 1783, and served to 13th November, 1783.

Forman, Samuel (N. J.). Captain and Colonel New Jersey Militia, 1775-1777.

Forman, Thomas Marsh (Pa). 1st Lieutenant 10th Pennsylvania, 4th December, 1776; Captain of Forman's Continental Regiment, 1st April, 1777; Major and Aide-de-Camp to General Alexander, 12th January, 1779, to 15th January, 1783.

Forney, Peter (N. C.). Captain North Carolina Rangers, serving in South Carolina, 1780-1781. (Died 1834.)

Forrest, Andrew (Pa). 2d Lieutenant 3d Pennsylvania Battalion, 8th January, 1776; taken prisoner at Fort Washington, 16th November, 1776; exchanged 25th October, 1780, and did not re-enter service.

Forrest, Thomas (Pa). Captain of Proctor's Battalion Pennsylvania Artillery, 5th October, 1776; Major 4th Continental Artillery, 5th February, 1777; Lieutenant-Colonel, 2d December, 1778; resigned 7th October, 1781. (Died 20th March, 1825.)

Forrest, Uriah (Md). 1st Lieutenant of Gunby's Independent Maryland Company, 14th January, 1776; Captain 3d Maryland Battalion of the Flying Camp, July, 1776; Major 3d Maryland, 10th December, 1776; wounded and lost a leg at Germantown, 4th October, 1777; Lieutenant-Colonel 1st Maryland, 10th April, 1777; transferred to 7th Maryland 1st August, 1779; resigned 23d February, 1781. (Died April, 1805.)

Forrester, James (Pa). 1st Lieutenant of Hartley's Additional Continental Regiment, 13th January, 1777; Captain, 19th November, 1777; regiment designated 11th Pennsylvania, 16th December, 1778; died 16th March, 1780.

Forrester, John (R. I.). Major of Church's Rhode Island Regiment, 3d May to December, 1775.

Forshay, Thomas (Pa). Ensign 8th Pennsylvania, 1st January, 1777; omitted October, 1777.

Forster, Jacob (Mass). Chaplain of Scammon's Massachusetts Regiment, May to December, 1775; Chaplain 18th Continental Infantry, 1st January, 1776; resigned 28th February, 1776.

Forsyth, David (N. H.). Ensign 2d New Hampshire, 8th November, 1776; died 10th May, 1778.

Forsyth, James (N. J.). Ensign of Spencer's Additional Continental Regiment, 4th June, 1777; resigned 14th March, 1778.

Forsyth, Robert (Va). Adjutant 4th Virginia in 1776; Captain of Lee's Battalion of Light Dragoons Pulaski Legion, 1st July, 1778; resigned 5th September ,1779; served subsequently as Major of a Virginia Militia Regiment to close of war.

Fortney, Henry (Pa). 2d Lieutenant of Doyle's Independent Pennsylvania Rifle Company, 17th July, 1776, and served to ——.

Forthay, Thomas (Pa). Ensign 8th Pennsylvania, 1st January, 1777; deserted — February, 1777.

Fosdick, Thomas (Conn). Surgeon's Mate in Lexington Alarm in April, 1775; Surgeon's Mate 6th Connecticut, 20th May, to December, 1775. (Died 1776.)

Fosdick, Thomas (Mass). Ensign of Glover's Massachusetts Regiment, May to December, 1775; 2d Lieutenant and Adjutant 14th Continental Infantry, 1st January to 31st December, 1776. (Died 1801.)

Fosdick, Thomas Updike (Conn). Sergeant 19th Continental Infantry, 1st January, 1776; Ensign, 11th July, 1776; taken prisoner at Fort Washington, 16th November, 1776.

Foster, Achilles (Va). Regimental Quartermaster, 12th Virginia, 7th October, 1777; died 26th August, 1778.

Foster, Benjamin (Mass). Surgeon of Frye's Massachusetts Regiment, May to December, 1775; Colonel Massachusetts Militia, 1776-1781.

Foster, Daniel (—). Surgeon's Mate Hospital Department; was a prisoner in 1782; when and where taken not stated.

Foster, David (Mass). Corporal in Lexington Alarm, April, 1775; 2d Lieutenant of Whitcomb's Massachusetts Regiment, May to December, 1775; Lieutenant Massachusetts Militia, 1776 (Died 1825.)

Foster, Ebenezer (Mass). Private in Cotton's Massachusetts Regiment, May to December, 1775; Ensign 14th Massachusetts, 1st January, 1777 ;killed 19th September, 1777, at Bemus' Heights.

Foster, Elijah (Conn). 2d Lieutenant of Bradley's Connecticut State Regiment, June to December, 1776.

Foster, Eliphalet (R .I.). Ensign 11th Continental Infantry, 1st January to 31st December, 1776.

Foster, Elisha (Mass). Private, corporal and Sergeant 6th Massachusetts, 25th February, 1777, until appointed Ensign, 15th June, 1781; transferred to 2d Massachusetts, 12th June, 1783, and served to November, 1783.

Foster, Ezekiel (Mass). 2d Lieutenant of Whitcomb's Massachusetts Regiment, May, 1775, to ——.

Foster, Ezekiel (N. J.). Captain and Major New Jersey Militia, 1777-1779.

Foster, Gideon (Mass). 2d Lieutenant in Lexington Alarm, April, 1775; Captain in Mansfield's Massachusetts Regiment, May to December, 1775; Captain Massachusetts Militia in 1778. (Died 1845.)

Foster, Henry (Del). Lieutenant-Colonel Delaware Battalion of the Flying Camp, July to December, 1776; Lieutenant-Colonel Delaware Militia, 1781-1782.

Foster, Isaac (Mass). Volunteer Surgeon at Bunker Hill, June, 1775; Hospital Surgeon in 1776; Deputy Director-General of Hospital Eastern Department, 11th April, 1777; retired 6th October, 1780. (Died 27th February, 1782.)

Foster, James (Mass). Ensign 14th Continental Infantry, 1st January, 1776, to ——.

Foster, James (Va). Captain 15th Virginia, 28th November, 1776; died 15th November, 1777.

Foster, John (Mass). Sergeant and Ensign Massachusetts Militia in 1776; 2d Lieutenant 11th Massachusetts, 6th November, 1776; resigned 14th July, 1779.

Foster, John (N. Y.). Lieutenant Ulster County, New York, Militia in 1775.

Foster, John (Pa). Sergeant 5th Pennsylvania Battalion, 22d February, 1776; Ensign 6th Pennsylvania, 22d August, 1777; dismissed 18th January, 1778

Foster, John (S. C). Captain South Carolina Dragoons, 5th April to September, 1781.

Foster, John H. (Va). Ensign 2d Virginia, 18th February, 1781, and served to close of war.

Foster, Josiah (Mass). 1st Lieutenant of Bridge's Massachusetts Regiment. May, 1775, to December, 1775.

Foster, Josiah (Va). Captain Virginia Militia, 1775-1776.

Foster, Parker (Mass). 2d Lieutenant of Scammon's Massachusetts Regiment, May to December, 1775; Captain Massachusetts Militia, 1776-1777.

Foster, Richard (Va). Ensign and Adjutant 7th Virginia, January, 1777; resigned 10th ·May, 1777.

Foster, Robert (Va). Ensign 15th Virginia, 16th April, 1777; Lieutenant, 20th April, 1778; taken prisoner at Barn Hill Church, 24th April, 1778; Lieutenant, 20th April, 1778; regiment designated 11th Virginia, 14th September, 1778; transferred to 4th Virginia, 12th February, 1781; served to close of war.

Foster, Samuel (Mass). Sergeant in Lexington Alarm, April, 1775; 1st Lieutenant of Heath's Massachusetts Regiment, May to December, 1775; 1st Lieutenant 24th Continental Infantry, 1st January to 31st December, 1776; Captain 3d Massachusetts, 1st January, 1777; died 6th May, 1778.

Foster, Simpson (Va). Sergeant and Sergeant-Major 14th Virginia, 6th January, 1776; regiment designated 10th Virginia, 14th September, 1778; Ensign, 4th July, 1779; 2d Lieutenant, — November, 1779; taken prisoner at Charleston, 12th May, 1780, and died in captivity.

Foster, Thomas (Mass). Private in Lexington Alarm, April, 1775; Sergeant 8th Massachusetts, 18th March, 1777; Ensign, 26th November, 1779; Lieutenant, 6th October, 1780, and served to 3d June, 1783. (Died 16th December, 1793)

Foster, Thomas Waite (Mass). Captain of Gridley's Regiment Massachusetts Artillery, April to December, 1775, and Captain in Knox's Regiment Continental Artillery, December, 1775, to December, 1776.

Foster, Timothy (Mass). Ensign of Learned's Massachusetts Regiment, May to December, 1775.

Foster, William (Va). 2d Lieutenant 8th Virginia, 20th May, 1777; 1st Lieutenant, 14th April, 1779; transferred to 3d Virginia, 12th May, 1779; resigned 2d July, 1779.

Fouges, Francis (Conn). Surgeon 19th Continental Infantry, 1st January, 1776, to ——.

Fouke, Gerard (Md). Ensign , 3d Maryland Battalion of the Flying Camp, July to December, 1776.

Fountain, William (Va).—See **Fontaine.**

Fouquet Mark Sr. (France). Brevet Captain Continental Army, 17th November, 1777, and served to ——.

Fouquet, Mark Jr. (France). Brevet Lieutenant of Artillery, 17th November, 1777, and served to ——.

Fowkes, Yelverton (N. C.). Quartermaster 1st North Carolina, 3d February, 1776; resigned 1st August, 1776.

Fowle, Ebenezer Smith (Mass). 2d Lieutenant of Jackson's Additional Continental Regiment, 12th May, 1777; resigned 14th January, 1778; Lieutenant United States Artillery Battalion, 20th October, 1786; Lieutenant Artillery Battalion United States Army, 29th September, 1789; died 13th February, 1791.

Fowler, Ebenezer, Jr. (Conn). Ensign 1st Connecticut, 1st May to 20th December, 1775, 2d Lieutenant of Swift's Connecticut State Regiment, June to November, 1776.

Fowle, John (Mass). Ensign 13th Massachusetts, 1st January, 1777; Lieutenant, 11th April, 1779; Captain, 20th May, 1780; retired 1st January, 1781. (Died 1823.)

Fowler, John, Jr. (Conn). 1st Lieutenant 1st Connecticut, 1st May to 1st December, 1775.

Fowler, Samuel (N. H.). 1st Lieutenant of Bedel's Regiment New Hampshire Rangers, 22d January, 1776; taken prisoner at the Cedars, 19th May, 1776.

Fowler, Stephen (Mass). Sergeant Massachusetts Militia, 1776; Ensign 6th Massachusetts, 1st January, 1777; taken prisoner at Young's House, 3d February, 1780; rejoined regiment 3d November, 1780; resigned 4th April, 1782.

Fowler, Theodosius (N. Y.). Ensign 1st New York, 24th February, 1776; 2d Lieutenant, 10th August, 1776; 1st Lieutenant 4th New York, 21st November, 1776; Captain, 23d April, 1778; transferred to 2d New York, 1st January, 1781, and served to 3d June, 1783. (Died 16th October, 1841.)

Fowler, William (Conn). Ensign 5th Connecticut, 27th February, 1781; died 27th February, 1782.

Fowler, William (Va). 1st Lieutenant 5th Virginia, 1st March, 1776; Captain, 1st April, 1777; transferred to 3d Virginia, 14th September, 1778; resigned ——. 1779.

Fowles, John (Mass). Sergeant 6th Continental Infantry, 12th February, 1776; 2d Lieutenant, 14th November, 1776; 1st Lieutenant and Adjutant 13th Massachusetts, 1st January, 1777; Captain, 20th June, 1779; transferred to 3d Massachusetts, 1st January, 1781, and served to 3d June, 1783. (Died 31st December, 1823.)

Fox, Jacob (Conn). Sergeant 6th Connecticut, 5th May to 21st September, 1776; 2d Lieutenant 1st Connecticut, 1st January, 1777; retired 15th November, 1778. (Died 27th November, 1824.)

Fox, Jeremiah (Pa). 2d Lieutenant 4th Continental Artillery, 1st April, 1777; resigned 31st July, 1778.

Fox, Joseph (Mass). Adjutant of Bridge's Massachusetts Regiment, April to December, 1775; Ensign of Burrall's Connecticut State Regiment, 23d January, 1776; 2d Lieutenant, 19th September, 1776; 1st Lieutenant of Lee's Continental Regiment, 11th January, 1777; Captain, 23d June, 1777; Regimental Paymaster, 13th October, 1778; transferred to Jackson's Continental Regiment, 22d April, 1779; regiment designated 16th Massachusetts, 23d July, 1780; transferred to 9th Massachusetts, 1st January, 1782; retired 1st January, 1783. (Died 24th March, 1820.)

Fox, Nathaniel (Va). 1st Lieutenant 6th Virginia, 16th February, 1776; Captain, 19th June, 1776; retired with rank of Major, 30th September, 1778. (Died 1825.)

Fox, Nathaniel (Va). Ensign 7th Virginia, 26th February, 1776; 2d Lieutenant, 27th April, 1776; resigned 28th September, 1777.

Fox, Thomas .(Va). 2d Lieutenant 10th Virginia, 2d December, 1776; 1st Lieutenant, 30th October, 1777; regiment designated 6th Virginia, 14th September, 1778; taken prisoner at Charleston, 12th May, 1780; wounded at Quinby's Bridge, 17th July, 1781; served to close of war.

Foxwell, Charles (N. H.). 2d Lieutenant 3d Continental Infantry, 1st January to 31st December, 1776.

Foxwell, Thomas (N. H.). 2d Lieutenant 3d Continental Infantry, 1st January, 1776, to ——.

Frailey, Jacob (Pa). Surgeon's Mate Hospital Department, 1777-1778.

Franchesin, Jacque Antoine de.—See **de Franchesin.**

Francis, —— (N. C.). Captain North Carolina Partisan Rangers, ——; killed at Shallow Ford, 6th February, 1781.

Francis, Aaron (Mass). Corporal in Mansfield's Massachusetts Regiment, May to December, 1775; Regimental Quartermaster 11th Massachusetts, 6th November, 1776; Ensign, 1st March, 1778; transferred to 10th Massachusetts, 1st January, 1781; resigned 16th April, 1782. (Died 17th October, 1825.)

Francis, Ebenezer (Mass). Lieutenant in Lexington Alarm, April, 1775; Captain of Mansfield's Massachusetts Regiment, May to December, 1775; Colonel 11th Massachusetts, 6th November, 1776; killed at Hubbardton, 7th July, 1777.

Francis, George (Pa). 3d Lieutenant of Thompson's Pennsylvania Rifle Battalion, 25th June, 1775; 3d Lieutenant 1st Continental Infantry, 13th March, 1776; resigned 29th September, 1776.

Francis, John (Mass). Adjutant 11th Massachusetts, 6th November, 1776; 1st Lieutenant, ——, 1778; Captain Lieutenant, 25th June, 1779; resigned 18th March, 1780. (Died 30th July, 1822.)

Francis, Thomas (Mass). Sergeant in Lexington Alarm, April, 1775; 1st Lieutenant 11th Massachusetts, 6th November, 1776; Captain, 18th March, 1780; transferred to 10th Massachusetts, 1st January, 1781; transferred to 6th Massachusetts, 3d May, 1782; retired 1st January, 1783. (Died 9th November, 1833.)

Frank, David S. (Pa). Aide-de-Camp to General Arnold, — July, 1778, to 25th September, 1780.

Frank, Lawrence (Pa). 1st Lieutenant 4th Continental Dragoons, 1st October, 1779; Captain, ——, 1782, and served to close of war.

Franklin, Benjamin (Pa). A signer of the Declaration of Independence; died 17th April, 1790.

Franklin, James (Va). Captain 10th Virginia, 19th November, 1776; resigned 19th September, 1778.

Franklin, Jesse (N. C.). 1st Lieutenant, Captain and Major North Carolina Militia, 1776-1782. (Died — September, 1823.)

Franklin, John (N. C.). Captain North Carolina Militia at King's Mountain, October, 1780. (Died 29th September, 1823.)

Franks, David Solebury (Pa). Major Aide-de-Camp to General Arnold, May, 1778, to 25th September, 1780, and was continued as Major and Aide-de-Camp Continental Army until retired, 1st January, 1783.

Franks, Isaac (Mass). Ensign 7th Massachusetts, 22d February, 1781; resigned 22d March, 1782.

Franks, John (N. Y.). Paymaster 4th New York, 10th April, 1777; resigned 1st March, 1779; served subsequently as Commissary to New York State Troops and Militia.

Fraser, Alexander (S. C.). 2d Lieutenant 1st South Carolina, 31st January, 1778; 1st Lieutenant, 6th October, 1778; taken prisoner at Charleston, 12th May, 1780.

Frazer, Anthony (Va). Ensign 1st Virginia State Regiment, 1st March, 1777; 2d Lieutenant, 29th May, 1777; resigned 12th February, 1778.

Frazer, Falvey (Va). 1st Lieutenant 14th Virginia, 14th November, 1776. He is dropped from the records of the Regiment with the remark "supposed to have been killed at Germantown, 4th October, 1777." In an old letter published some years ago, written by a tent-mate of Lieutenant Frazer, it is stated that he was wounded at Germantown, 4th October, 1777, and that he was mortally wounded by his own brother, an officer of the British Army, at Yorktown, 14th October, 1781. (Name also spelled Fraser.)

Frazer, John (S. C.). Lieutenant 4th South Carolina (Artillery), ——, 1777; killed at Beaufort, 9th February, 1779.

Frazer, John Gizzard (Mass). Served as Assistant to Quartermaster-General, 22d September to December, 1775; Major 6th Continental Infantry, 1st January to 31st December, 1776.

Frazer, Persifor (Pa). Captain 4th Pennsylvania Battalion, 5th January, 1776; Major, 3d October, 1776, to rank from 24th September, 1776; Lieutenant-Colonel 5th Pennsylvania, 12th March, 1777, to rank from 4th October, 1776; taken prisoner at Brandywine, 11th September, 1777; escaped 17th March, 1778; resigned 9th October, 1778; appointed Clothier-General Continental Army, 15th July, 1779, which he declined; Brigadier General Pennsylvania Militia, 25th May, 1782, to close of war. (Died 24th April, 1792.)

Frazier, John (Ga). 2d Lieutenant 3d Georgia, ——, 1777; 1st Lieutenant, 4th April, 1778; wounded in action with Indians, 4th May, 1777; was a Captain in 1780, and served to ——.

Frazier, William (Md). Ensign of Hindman's Independent Maryland Company, January, 1776; 1st Lieutenant 5th Maryland, 10th December, 1776; Captain Lieutenant 1st Continental Artillery, 13th January, 1777; resigned 24th May, 1779.

Freeland, Joseph (Mass). 1st Sergeant 21st Continental Infantry, January, 1776; Ensign, 11th September, 1776, and served to ——.

Freeman, Constant (Mass). 1st Lieutenant Stevens' Battalion Continental Artillery, 9th November, 1776; battalion attached to 3d Continental Artillery in 1778; Captain Lieutenant, 1st October, 1778, and served to June, 1783; Major 1st Artillerists and Engineers, 28th February, 1795; Lieutenant-Colonel Artillerists, 1st April, 1802; transferred to Corps of Artillery, 12th May, 1814; Brevet Colonel, 10th July, 1812; honorably discharged 15th June, 1815. (Died 27th February, 1824.)

Freeman, Elijah (N. J.). 2d Lieutenant of Spencer's Additional Continental Regiment, 5th February, 1777; omitted — June, 1777.

Freeman, Edmund (N. H.). Captain New Hampshire Militia, 1777.

Freeman, Haskell (Mass). Ensign 4th Massachusetts, 1st November, 1777; wounded in Rhode Island, 29th August, 1778; Adjutant, — March, 1779; Lieutenant, 18th August, 1779; resigned 24th August, 1780.

Freeman, Jeremiah (Pa). 2d Lieutenant of Captain Roman's Independent Company Pennsylvania Artillery, 10th December, 1775; 1st Lieutenant, 10th August, 1776; Captain Lieutenant, 1st January, 1777; Retired 1st January, 1781.

Freeman, John (Ga). Lieutenant Georgia Militia, 1780. (Died 1825.)

Freeman, John (N. Y.). 2d Lieutenant 5th New York, 21st November, 1776; taken prisoner at Fort Clinton, 6th October, 1777.

Freeman, Nathaniel (Mass). Brigadier-General Massachusetts Militia, 1778, to close of war. (Died 20th September, 1827.)

Freeman, Robert (N. Y.). Major New York Militia, 1775-1777.

Freeman, Robert (Va). Paymaster 9th Virginia, 15th February, 1777, to ——.

Freeman, Thomas Davis (Mass). Corporal Massachusetts Militia, July

to December, 1775; Ensign 14th Massachusetts, 31st January, 1777; Lieutenant, 1st April, 1778; transferred to 7th Massachusetts, 1st January, 1781, and served to June, 1783.

Freer, Charles (S. C.). Captain South Carolina Militia in 1775 and 1776.

Freer, John (N. Y.). Colonel New York Militia, 1775-1777.

Frelinghuysen, Frederick (N. J.). Captain, Major and Colonel New Jersey Militia, 1775-1777. (Died 13th April, 1804.)

French, Abner (N. Y.). Lieutenant in Wynkoop's Regiment New York Militia, June to November, 1776; 1st Lieutenant 2d New York, 21st November, 1776; Captain, 1st June, 1778; retired 1st January, 1781; served subsequently as Captain New York Levies.

French, Elijah (Mass). Corporal 10th Massachusetts, 20th February, 1777; Sergeant, 1st November, 1777; Quartermaster-Sergeant, 1st January, 1780; Ensign, 20th December, 1780; transferred to 7th Massachusetts, 1st January, 1781; transferred to 4th Massachusetts, 12th June, 1783, and served to 3d November, 1783.

French, Jacob (Mass). Colonel Massachusetts Militia, 1776-1777.

French, Joseph (Mass). Ensign 10th Massachusetts, 27th March, 1781; resigned 28th July, 1781.

French, Mason (Md). Ensign of Grayson's Additional Continental Regiment, 15th February, 1777; 2d Lieutenant, 1st December, 1777; resigned 12th May, 1778.

French, Samuel (Mass). Major and Commissary Military Stores, 18th January, 1777, and served to 17th December, 1779.

French, Samuel (Va). Ensign 1st Virginia State Regiment, 20th June. 1777; resigned 30th April, 1778.

Frey, John (N. Y.). Captain 2d New York, 28th June, 1775; Brigade-Major, 15th July, 1775, to January, 1776; served subsequently as Brigade-Major to General Herkimer's New York Militia and was taken prisoner at Oriskany, 6th August, 1777, and exchanged 28th October, 1778. (Died 19th April, 1833.)

Fricker, Anthony Ernest (Pa). Ensign 11th Pennsylvania, 14th June, 1777; resigned 29th September, 1777.

Frierson, John (S. C.). Lieutenant 2d South Carolina, 9th March, 1778; taken prisoner at Charleston, 12th May, 1780; exchanged June, 1781, and served to close of war.

Fries, Henry (N. J.). 1st Lieutenant 2d New Jersey, 28th November, 1775; missing at Three Rivers, 8th June, 1776.

Frink, Calvin (N. H.). Surgeon's Mate 1st New Hampshire, 23d April to December, 1775; Surgeon of Wyman's Regiment New Hampshire Militia, 1777-1778.

Frink, Samuel (Mass). Ensign 8th Massachusetts, 5th July, 1782; transferred to 4th Massachusetts, 12th June, 1783, and served to 3d November, 1783. (Died ——, 1846.)

Frink, Thomas (N. H.). Surgeon New Hampshire Militia, 1777.

Frisbie, Elisha (Conn). Regimental Quartermaster Connecticut Light Horse, 1776-1777.

Frisbie, Philip (N. Y.). Captain and Major New York Militia, 1775-1779. (Died 1813.)

Frisby, Jonah (Mass). Lieutenant 1st Massachusetts, 1st January, 1777; resigned 16th April, 1779.

Frissell, William (Conn). Sergeant in the Lexington Alarm, April, 1775; Ensign 3d Connecticut, 1st May to 10th December, 1775; Lieutenant of Mott's Connecticut State Regiment, June to December, 1776.

Froelich, Christian (Pa). 2d Lieutenant of Ottendorff's Battalion Armand's Corps, 3d May, 1777, and served to ——

Froelich, Joseph (N. Y.). Ensign 4th New York, 21st November, 1776; 2d Lieutenant, 3d September, 1777; 1st Lieutenant ,9th November, 1777; transferred to 2d New York, 1st January, 1781, and served to November, 1783; Brevet Captain, 30th September, 1783.

Frost, Ichabod (Mass). Sergeant 13th Massachusetts, 2d March, 1777; Ensign, 1st October, 1778; discharged 9th March, 1779.

Frost, George Pepperell (N. H.). Ensign 2d New Hampshire, 8th November, 1776; 2d Lieutenant, 20th September, 1777; 1st Lieutenant, 22d December, 1777; transferred to 1st New Hampshire, 1st January, 1781; Captain, 6th December, 1782, and served to June, 1783.

Frost, John (Mass). Colonel Massachusetts Militia, 1776-1778. (Died — July, 1810.)

Frost, Samuel (Mass). Sergeant- Major 4th Continental Infantry, January, 1776; Ensign, 10th August, 1776; 1st Lieutenant 6th Massachusetts, 1st January, 1777; Regimental Adjutant, March, 1779; Captain Lieutenant, 16th October, 1780; · Captain, 12th October, 1782, and served to June, 1783. (Died 1st November, 1817.)

Frost, Stephen (Mass). 2d Lieutenant of Gardner's Massachusetts Regiment, May, 1775, to ——.

Frost, William (Mass). 2d Lieutenant of Scammon's Massachusets Regiment, May to December, 1775; 2d Lieutenant 18th Continental Infantry, 1st January to 31st December, 1776; 1st Lieutenant 12th Massachusetts, 6th November, 1776; omitted December, 1778. (Died 2d June, 1827.)

Frothingham, Benjamin (Mass). Captain Lieutenant of Gridley's Regiment Massachusetts Artillery, June to December, 1775, and of Knox's Regiment Continental Artillery, to 31st December, 1776; Captain 3d Continental Artillery, 1st January, 1777; wounded at Germantown, 4th October, 1777, and served to June, 1783. (Died 19th August, 1809.)

Frothingham, Ebenezer (Conn). Sergeant of Webb's Continental Regiment, 25th May, 1777; Ensign 16th May, 1778; Lieutenant, 26th May, 1779; Regimental Quartermaster, 27th May, 1779, to June, 1783; transferred to 3d Connecticut, 1st January, 1781, and served to June, 1783; Lieutenant United States Infantry Regiment, 15th July, 1785; Lieutenant 1st Infantry United States Army, 29th September, 1789; killed 22d October, 1790, in action with Indians at the Miami Towns near Old Chillicothe, Ohio.

Fry, Benjamin (R. I.). 1st Lieutenant of Richmond's Rhode Island State Regiment, 1st November, 1775, to May, 1776; Captain Rhode Island Militia in 1776 and 1777. (Died 1799.)

Fry, Joseph (R. I.). Major Rhode Island Militia in 1775-1776.

Fry, Richard (R. I.). Colonel Rhode Island Militia, 1776-1779.

Frye, Ebenezer (N. H.). 1st Lieutenant 1st New Hampshire, 23d April to December, 1775; 1st Lieutenant 5th Continental Infantry, 1st January, 1776; Captain 1st New Hampshire, 8th November, 1776; cashiered 6th December, 1782. (Died 1784.)

Frye, Daniel (Mass). Sergeant of Baldwin's Artillery Artificer Regiment,

4th March, 1777; 2d Lieutenant, 13th November, 1779; resigned — March, 1781.

Frye, Frederick (Mass). Ensign 1st Massachusetts, 1st February, 1781, and served to 3d November, 1783. (Died 30th January, 1828.)

Frye, Isaac (N. H.). Regimental Quartermaster 3d New Hampshire, 23d April to December, 1775; Regimental Quartermaster 2d Continental Infantry, 1st January, 1776; Captain 3d New Hampshire, 8th November, 1776; transferred to 1st New Hampshire, 1st January, 1781; retained in Jackson's Continental Regiment, November, 1783; Brevet Major, 30th September, 1783, and served to 20th June, 1784.

Frye, James (Mass). Colonel of a Massachusetts Regiment, 19th May to December, 1775; wounded at Bunker Hill, 17th June, 1775. (Died 8th January, 1776.)

Frye, Jonatham (Mass). 1st Lieutenant 8th Continental Infantry, 1st January to 31st December, 1776; 1st Lieutenant 8th Massachusetts, 1st January, 1777; resigned 17th December, 1777. 2d Lieutenant of Baldwin's Artillery Artificer Regiment, 22d March, 1780; Adjutant, 1st April, 1780; resigned 25th March, 1781.

Frye, Joseph (Mass). Major-General Massachusetts Militia, 21st June, 1775; Brigadier-General Continental Army, 10th January, 1776; resigned 23d April, 1776. (Died 1794.)

Frye, Nathaniel (Mass). Ensign 9th Massachusetts, 1st January, 1777; Regimental Quartermaster, 22d September, 1777; Regimental Paymaster, 18th October, 1778; Lieutenant, 28th August, 1780; transferred to 8th Massachusetts, 1st January, 1781; retired 1st January, 1783. (Died 17th April, 1833.)

Fulford, John (Md). Captain Maryland Militia, 1777-1778.

Fuller, Ballard (Mass). 1st Lieutenant of Frye's Massachusetts Regiment, May, 1775, to ——.

Fuller, Elisha (Mass). Ensign of Whitcomb's Massachusetts Regiment, May to December, 1775.

Fuller, Isaac (Mass). Lieutenant of Danielson's Massachusetts Regiment, May to November, 1775; 1st Lieutenant 16th Continental Infantry, 1st January to 31st December, 1776. (Died 1804.)

Fuller, Isaiah (Mass). Ensign 16th Continental Infantry, 1st January to 31st December. 1776.

Fuller, Jacob (Mass). Regimental Quartermaster of Walker's Massachusetts Regiment, May to December, 1775; Lieutenant Massachusetts Militia, 1776-1779.

Fuller, John (Conn). Chaplain of Douglas' Connecticut State Regiment, January to March, 1776.

Fuller, John (Mass). Captain of Whitcomb's Massachusetts Regiment, May to December, 1775.

Fuller, John (Mass). 1st Lieutenant 14th Massachusetts, 1st January, 1777; Captain, 16th April, 1780; transferred to 4th Massachusetts, 1st January, 1781, and served to 3d June, 1783.

Fuller, John (S. C.). Captain South Carolina Militia in 1775.

Fuller, Jonathan (Mass). Surgeon 14th Massachusetts, 1st January, 1777; deserted 16th August, 1777, and joined the enemy.

Fuller, Josiah (Conn). Sergeant in the Lexington Alarm, April, 1775; Sergeant 3d Connecticut, 12th May to 10th December, 1775; 2d Lieutenant 20th Continental Infantry, 1st January to 31st December, 1776.

Fuller, Nathan (Mass). Captain of Gardner's Massachusetts Regiment, May to December, 1775; Captain 25th Continental Infantry, 1st January, 1776; Major, 13th February, 1776; Lieutenant-Colonel 13th Massachusetts, 1st January, 1777; resigned 28th June, 1777.

Fuller, Nathaniel (S. C.). Lieutenant South Carolina Militia, in 1775.

Fuller, Richard (S. C.). 1st Lieutenant 1st South Carolina, 17th June, 1775, to ——.

Fuller, Simeon (Conn). 2d Lieutenant of Douglas' Connecticut State Regiment, June to December, 1776.

Fullerton, Edward (Pa). Surgeon Hospital Department in 1775; Surgeon Pennsylvania Battalion of the Flying Camp; taken prisoner at Fort Washington, 16th November, 1776; was a prisoner to 14th April, 1778, and on parole until he died, 5th May, 1781.

Fullerton, Humphrey (Va). Surgeon of Hospital Department in Virginia, 1776 to 1781.

Fullerton, Patrick (Pa). Ensign Pennsylvania State Regiment, 18th April,

1777; regiment designated 13th Pennsylvania, 12th November, 1777; transferred to 2d Pennsylvania, 1st July, 1778, and served to ——.

Fullerton, Richard (Pa). Regimental Adjutant 3d Pennsylvania, 1st June, 1778, to August, 1780; Ensign 3d Pennsylvania, 19th June, 1778; Lieutenant, 12th May, 1779; transferred to 1st Pennsylvania, 1st January, 1783, and served to 3d November, 1783; Brevet Captain, 1st November, 1783, "for having acted as a volunteer at an early period of the war, particularly in the action on Long Island, and at the battles of Trenton and Princeton, and having discharged the several extra appointments of Adjutant, Major of Brigade, and the important one of Assistant Adjutant General to the Southern Army, highly to the satisfaction of his General officers." (Died 16th June, 1792.)

Fullsome, Elisha (Mass) 1st Lieutenant of Whitcomb's Massachusetts Regiment, April to June, 1775.

Funk, Jacob (Pa). Ensign 4th Pennsylvania Battalion, 5th January to 26th November, 1776; Cornet 4th Continental Dragoons, 10th January, 1777, and served to ——.

Fuqua, Joseph (Va). Captain Virginia Militia in 1780. (Died 1812.)

Furman, Alexander (N. Y.). Lieutenant New York State troops; taken prisoner near King's Bridge, 8th January, 1777; exchanged 11th October, 1777, and died shortly afterwards.

Furman, John (N. Y.). 2d Lieutenant 5th New York, 21st November, 1776; taken prisoner at Fort Montgomery, 6th October, 1777; exchanged 9th November, 1780; 1st Lieutenant, 1st September, 1778; transferred to 1st New York, 1st January, 1781, and served to 3d June, 1783. (Name also spelled Foreman.)

Furnival, Alexander (Md). 2d Lieutenant of Smith's Independent Company Maryland Artillery, 14th January, 1776; 1st Lieutenant. ——; Captain, ——; retired July, 1779

Furnival, James (Mass). 2d Lieutenant of Knox's Regiment Continental Artillery, 10th December, 1775; Captain Lieutenant 3d Continental Artillery, April, 1777. when sent in arrest to General Schuyler for misconduct.

G.

Gadsden, Christopher (S. C.). Colonel 1st South Carolina, 17th June. 1775;

Brigadier-General Continental Army, 16th September, 1776; resigned 2d October, 1777; taken prisoner at Charleston, 12th May, 1780. (Died 28th August, 1805.)

Gadsden, Thomas (S. C.). 1st Lieutenant 1st South Carolina, 12th May, 1776; Captain, 6th October, 1778; killed at the Siege of Charleston, 24th April, 1780.

Gage, Isaac (Mass). Ensign 25th Continental Infantry, 1st January to 31st December, 1776; 1st Lieutenant 3d Massachusetts, 1st January, 1777; retired 16th September, 1778; Captain Massachusetts Militia in 1781.

Gage, Nathaniel (Mass). Captain of Frye's Massachusetts Regiment, April to December, 1775; Captain Massachusetts Militia in 1777.

Gaillard, Tacitus (S. C.). Colonel and Quartermaster General Southern Department, 14th June, 1776, to ——.

Gaines, James (Va). Captain Virginia Militia; wounded at Guilford, 15th March, 1781. (Died 1810.)

Gaines, Thomas (Va). Ensign 1st Virginia State Regiment, 1777-1778.

Gaines, William Fleming (Va). 1st Lieutenant 1st Continental Artillery, 13th January, 1777; Captain Lieutenant, 20th October, 1777; Adjutant, 25th August, 1778, and served to 1st January, 1783.

Gaither, Greenberry (Md). 1st Lieutenant 1st Maryland Battalion of the Flying Camp, July, 1776; 1st Lieutenant 7th Maryland, 10th December, 1776, but never joined the latter regiment.

Gaither, Henry (Md). Ensign of Smallwood's Maryland Regiment, 14th January, 1776; 1st Lieutenant 1st Maryland Batalion of the Flying Camp, 8th June, 1776; 1st Lieutenant 3d Maryland, 10th December, 1776; Captain, 17th April, 1777; Brevet Major, 5th November, 1777; transfered to 4th Maryland, 1st January, 1781; transferred to 1st Maryland, 1st January 1783, and served to April, 1783; Major in the Levies, 1791; Major United States Infantry, 11th April, 1792, assigned to 3d Sub Legion, 4th September, 1792; Lieutenant-Colonel, 1st October, 1793; assigned to 3d Infantry, 1st November, 1796; honorably discharged 15th June, 1802. (Died 23d June, 1811.)

Gaither, John (Md). 1st Lieutenant 1st Maryland Battalion of the Flying Camp, July, 1776, to ——.

Gakee, James (N. C.). Surgeon 1st North Carolina, — December, 1775; resigned — May, 1776.

Galbreath, Andrew (Pa). Major of Watts' Pennsylvania Battalion of the Flying Camp; taken prisoner at Fort Washington, 16th November, 1776. (Died 1806.)

Gale, Edward (Md). Captain Independent Company Maryland Artillery, 3d September, 1779; died 31st October, 1779.

Gale, Eli (Mass). Lieutenant of Frye's Massachusetts Regiment, May to December, 1775; Lieutenant 8th Massachusetts, 22d July, 1779, to 22d April, 1780.

Gale, Eli (Mass). 1st Lieutenant of Baldwin's Artillery Artificer Regiment, 12th November, 1779; dropped as without leave since 1st June, 1780.

Gale, Jacob (N. H.). Colonel New Hampshire Militia Regiment in 1778 and 1779.

Gale, John (Md). 2d Lieutenant 2d Maryland, 10th December, 1776; 1st Lieutenant, 15th January, 1777; taken prisoner at Staten Island, 22d August, 1777; exchanged 12th October, 1778; Captain, 10th December; 1777; transfered to 5th Maryland, 1st January, 1781; Aide-de-Camp to General Gist, 22d December, 1782, to close of war; Brevet Major, 30th September, 1783.

Gale, Samuel (Conn). Captain in the Lexington Alarm, April, 1775; Captain 6th Connecticut, 1st May to 19th December, 1775. (Died 1799.)

Gallahue, Charles (Va). Captain 11th Virginia, — January, 1777; killed at Sag Harbor, 23d May, 1777.

Gallaudet, Edgar (N. J.). 2d Lieutenant 3d New Jersey, 30th November, 1776; 1st Lieutenant, 26th October, 1777; resigned 9th December, 1778.

Galloway, James (S. C.). Lieutenant South Carolina Militia in 1776.

Galloway, John (Va). Lieutenant of a Virginia Regiment in 1780.

Gallup, Isaac (Conn). 1st Lieutenant 6th Conecticut, 1st May to 18th December, 1775; Captain 10th Continental Infantry, 1st January to 31st December, 1776. (Died 1799.)

Gallup, Joseph (Conn). Captain Connecticut Militia, 1776.

Gallup, Nathan (Conn). Major and Colonel Connecticut Militia, 1776-1782. (Died 1799.)

Goloche, James (Ga). 2d Lieutenant 1st Georgia, 12th December, 1775, to ——.

Galpin, Amos (Conn). Ensign of Sherburne's Continental Regiment, 1st January, 1777; resigned 30th April, 1780.

Galpin, Jehiel (Conn). Private 7th Connecticut, 10th July to 10th December, 1775; Sergeant-Major 6th Connecticut, 24th November, 1776; Ensign, 26th July, 1780; transferred to 4th Connecticut, 1st January, 1781; resigned 13th April, 1782.

Galpin, Seth (Conn). 2d Lieutenant of Webb's Additional Continental Regiment, January, 1777; 1st Lieutenant 9th July, 1777; retired 1st January, 1781.

Galt, John Minson (Va). Surgeon 15th Virginia, in 1777; taken prisoner at Germantown 4th October, 1777.

Galt, Patrick (Va). Surgeon of a Virginia Regiment, 1775 to 1778.

Galusha, David (N. H). 1st Lieutenant Green Mountain Boys, 27th July to December, 1775.

Galvan, William (S. C). 2d Lieutenant 1st South Carolina, May, 1776; 1st Lieutenant, 5th October, 1777; Captain, ——, 1779; Major and Inspector Continental Army 12th January, 1780, to March 26th, 1782; was also Acting aide-de-Camp to General Washington to November, 1783.

Gamble, Edmund (N. C.). Ensign 1st North Carolina, 28th March, 1776; 2d Lieutenant, 7th July, 1776; 1st Lieutenant, 20th January, 1777; transferred to North Carolina Dragoons State Regiment, 1st June, 1778, and served to close of war.

Gamble, James (Pa.) Regimental Quartermaster 7th Pennsylvania, 20th March, 1777; Ensign in 1778; Lieutenant, 1st January, 1781; transferred to 4th Pennsylvania, 1st January, 1781; transferred to 4th Continental Artillery, 1st January, 1783, and served to June, 1783; Captain Artillerist and Engineers, 2d June, 1794. Died 20th August, 1795.

Gamble, John (S. C). Major in Marion's Brigade, 1780-1781.

Gamble, Robert (Va). 1st Lieutenant 12th Virginia, 14th September, 1776. Captain 7th March, 1778; regiment designated 8th Virginia, 14th September, 1778; taken prisoner at

Camden, 16th August, 1780. Retired, 1st January, 1783.

Gamble, Thomas (Va). Captain Virginia Rangers, 7th April, 1779, to —

Gammage, William (—). Surgeons Mate Hospital Department, 1776-1777.

Gano, Daniel (N. Y.). 2d Lieutenant 1st New York, 28th June, 1775; resigned 13th July, 1776; 2d Lieutenant of Knox's Regiment Continental Artillery, August, 1776; Captain-Lieutenant 2d Continental Artillery, 1st January, 1777; resigned 12th October, 1778; served subsequently as Captain New York Levies.

Gano, John (N. Y.). Chaplain 19th Continental Infantry, 1st January, 1776; Chaplain 5th New York, 21st November, 1776, to 27th May, 1777; Brigade Chaplain, 18th August, 1778, to May, 1780. (Died 10th January, 1804.)

Gano, Stephen (N. Y.). Surgeon's-Mate 2d Continental Artillery, 15th June, 1779, to May, 1781. (Died 18th August, 1828.)

Gansel, John (Pa). Ensign 5th Pennsylvania Battalion, 8th January, to December, 1776.

Gansevoort, Leonard (N. Y.). Paymaster 2d New York, 25th September to November, 1776. (Died, 1810.)

Gansevoort, Peter (N. Y.). Major 2d New York, 30th June, 1775; Lieutenant-Colonel, 19th March, 1776; Colonel 3d New York, 21st November, 1776; by the act of 4th October, 1777, it was "Resolved, that the thanks of Congress be given to Colonel Gansevoort and the officers and troops under his command for the bravery and perseverance which they have so conspicuously manifested in the defence of Fort Schuyler, and that he be appointed Colonel-Commandant of the Fort so gallantly defended." Retired 1st January, 1781; Brigadier-General New York Militia, 26th March, 1781, to close of war; Military Agent Northern Department, 29th April, 1802; Brigadier-General United States Army, 15th February, 1809; died 2d July, 1812.

Garardeau, John Bohun (—). Deputy Commissary-General of Issues, 6th August, 1777; resigned 28th October, 1778.

Garden, Alexander (S. C.). Ensign of Lee's Battalion of Light Dragoons; Aide-de-Camp to General Greene, March, 1781, to close of war. (Died 24th February, 1829.)

Garden, Benjamin (S. C.). Lieutenant-Colonel South Carolina Militia 1775-1780.

Garden, John (S. C). Lieutenant South Carolina Militia in 1775.

Gardenier, Hermanus (N. Y). Lieutenant New York Militia; taken prisoner at Oriskany, 6th August, 1777.

Gardenier, Jacob (N. Y.). Captain New York Militia, ——; wounded at Oriskany, 6th August, 1777. (Died 9th May, 1808.)

Gardiner, Caleb (R. I.). Captain of Richmond's Rhode Island State Regiment, 1st November, 1775; Lieutenant-Colonel, 19th August, 1776, to ——.

Gardiner, Christopher (R. I.). Captain of Varnum's Rhode Island Regiment, 3d May, 1775; cashiered, 2d August, 1775.

Gardiner, Francis (R. I.). 2d Lieutenant of Stanton's Rhode Island State Regiment, 12th December, 1776, to June, 1777; served also as Captain Rhode Island Militia.

Gardiner, James (R. I.). Captain 1st Rhode Island, 3d May to December, 1775.

Gardiner, Nathaniel (N. H.). Surgeon 1st New Hampshire, 28th June, 1780. Resigned 4th July 1782.

Gardner, Aaron (Mass). Lieutenant in Lexington Alarm, April, 1775; 1st Lieutenant of Brewer's Massachusetts Regiment, April, 1775, to December, 1775; Captain and Major Massachusetts Militia, 1776-1781.

Gardner, Benjamin (Mass). Sergeant in Lexington Alarm, April, 1775; 2d Lieutenant of Mansfield's Massachusetts Regiment, May to December, 1775; 2d Lieutenant 27th Continental Infantry, 1st January, 1776; Captain-Lieutenant 5th Massachusetts, 1st January, 1777; Captain, 1st November, 1778; resigned 18th October, 1780; Captain Assistant Deputy Quartermaster-General, 19th May, 1813; honorably discharged 15th June, 1815; reinstated 3d May, 1816; resigned 19th October, 1816.

Gardner, Caleb (R. I). Captain Major and Lieutenant Colonel Rhode Island Militia, 1775-1781. (Died 1806.)

Gardner, Isaac (Mass). Captain of the Brookline Company Massachusetts Militia, ——; killed at Lexington, 19th April, 1775.

Gardner, James (Mass). Deputy Commissary of Knox's Regiment Continental Artillery, 18th September, 1776; Regimental Adjutant 3d Continntal Artillery, 1st January, 1777; Captain Lieutenant, 22d February, 1780, and served to June, 1783.

Gardner, James (N. C.). Captain 2d North Carolina, May, 1776; resigned 15th May, 1777.

Gardner, John (N. H.). Adjutant of Bartlett's New Hampshire Militia Regiment in 1780.

Gardner, Joseph (Mass). Surgeon's Mate 12th Massachusetts, 1st March, 1777; retired 1st January, 1781. (Died 1788.)

Gardner, Joseph (Pa). Captain of Montgomery's Pennsylvania Battalion of the Flying Camp; taken prisoner at Fort Washington, 16th November, 1776; Captain Pennsylvania Militia, 1777-1778. (Died 1794.)

Gardner, Matthew .(Md). Sergeant 1st Maryland, 10th December, 1776; Ensign, 17th April, 1777; resigned 4th March, 1778.

Gardner, Thomas (Mass). Colonel in Lexington Alarm, April, 1775; Colonel of a Massachusetts Regiment, May, 1775; mortally wounded at Bunker Hill, 17th June, 1775, and died 3d July, 1775.

Gardner, William (N. C.). Ensign 2d North Carolina, 1st September, 1775, to ——; 2d Lieutenant, 20th October, 1775, and served to ——.

Garland, Edward (Va). 1st Lieutenant 1st Virginia, 7th October, 1775; Captain 14th Virginia, 20th November, 1776; resigned 2d December, 1777.

Garland, Kellis (Va). 2d Lieutenant of Grayson's Continental Regiment, 23d January, 1777; 1st Lieutenant, 8th June, 1777; resigned — May, 1778.

Garland, Peter (Va). 2d Lieutenant 6th Virginia, 16th February, 1776; 1st Lieutenant, 19th June, 1776; Captain, 17th August, 1777; retired 14th September, 1778 .

Garlie, John (S. C.). Lieutenant 3d South Carolina, ——; resigned 7th October, 1777.

Garnett, Benjamin (Md). Ensign 5th Maryland, October, 1777; Lieutenant, 13th October, 1778; Regimental Adjutant, 23d September, 1779; transferred to 3d Continental Dragoons, — September, 1779, and served to 10th November, 1782.

Garnett, Henry (Va). Captain of a Virginia State Regiment, 1778 to 1781.

Garnett, Thomas (Md). 2d Lieutenant 5th Maryland, 10th December, 1776; resigned 10th December. 1777.

Garnett, William (N. Y.). Surgeon's Mate 2d Canadian (Hazen's) Regiment, ——, 1777; died 1st February, 1778.

Garrard, Charles.—See **Gerrard.**

Garrard, James (Va). Captain Virginia Militia, 1776-1777. (Died 9th January, 1822.)

Garrett, Andrew (Mass). Sergeant 7th Massachusetts, 1st March, 1777; Ensign, 1st October, 1778; taken prisoner at Cherry Valley, 10th November, 1778; was a prisoner to March, 1783; Lieutenant, 25th October, 1781; transferred to 6th Massachusetts, 1st January, 1783, and was retired 3d June, 1783.

Garrett, Morton (Pa). 1st Lieutenant Pennsylvania Musket Battalion, 20th March, 1776; Captain, 25th October, 1776; resigned 12th February, 1777.

Garrett, Nicholas (Pa). 2d Lieutenant 6th Pennsylvania, 15th February, 1777; resigned 12th September, 1777.

Garrison, Abraham (N. Y.). Lieutenant of Wempell's New York Militia Regiment, 1779-1781.

Garrison, Isaac (N. Y.). 2d Lieutenant New York Militia; taken prisoner at Fort Montgomery, 6th October, 1777. (Died 1816.)

Garrison, Joseph (N. Y.). Lieutenant of Swartwout's Regiment New York Militia in 1776.

Garrison, Richard (N. Y.). Lieutenant and Quartermaster of Hamman's Regiment New York Militia; wounded at Pine's Bridge, 7th July, 1777.

Garzia, John (R. I.). Captain Lieutenant of Elliott's Regiment Rhode Island Artillery, 12th December, 1776, to May, 1777.

Gaskins, Thomas (Va). Captain 5th Virginia, 26th February, 1776; Major, 5th November, 1777; Lieutenant-Colonel 4th Virginia, 16th May. 1778; transferred to 3d Virginia, 14th September, 1778, and served to close of war.

Gassaway, Henry (Md). Sergeant 4th Maryland, 6th December, 1779; Ensign, 26th January, 1780; transferred to 4th Maryland, 1st January, 1781; 2d Lieutenant, 25th April, 1781; transferred to 1st Maryland, 1st January, 1783; retained in Maryland Battalion, April, 1783, and served to 15th November, 1783.

Gassaway, John (Md). 2d Lieutenant 1st Maryland, 10th December,

1776; 1st Lieutenant, 17th April, 1777; Captain Lieutenant, 1st July, 1779; Captain, 2d April, 1780; taken prisoner at Camden, 16th August, 1780; prisoner on parole to close of war. (Died March, 1819.)

Gassaway, Nicholas (Md). Ensign 3d Maryland, 26th February, 1777; 2d Lieutenant, 17th April, 1777; transferred to 2d Maryland, 1st January, 1781; 1st Lieutenant, 26th December, 1782; retained in Maryland Battalion, April, 1783, and served to 15th November, 1783.

Gaston, Alexander (N. C.). Captain North Carolina Militia; murdered by Tories, 20th August, 1781; where not stated.

Gaston, Robert (N. C.). Captain 2d North Carolina, February, 1776, to ——.

Gaston, Robert (S C). Lieutenant 3d South Carolina, ——; wounded at Savannah, 9th October, 1779.

Gatchell, Samuel H. (Mass). Sergeant in Gridley's Regiment Massachusetts Artillery, 1st May, 1775; Sergeant in Glover's Massachusetts Regiment, 1st July to 31st December, 1775; Ensign 14th Continental Infantry, 1st January to 31st December, 1776; Lieutenant of Lee's Continental Regiment, 1st January, 1777; resigned 25th March, 1779.

Gates, Benjamin (Mass). 1st Lieutenant of Brewer's Massachusetts Regiment, April to December, 1775; Captain Massachusetts Militia in 1776; Captain 5th Massachusetts, 1st January, 1777; resigned 13th January, 1778.

Gates, Horatio (Va). Had been Major in British Army. Brigadier-General and Adjutant-General Continental Army, 17th June, 1775; Major-General Continental Army, 16th May, 1776. By the act of 4th November, 1777, it was "Resolved, that the thanks of Congress, in their own name, and in behalf of the thirteen Unitd States, be presented to Major-General Gates, Commander-in-Chief of the Northern Department, and to Major-Generals Lincoln and Arnold, and the rest of the officers and troops under his command, for their brave and successful efforts in support of the independence of their country, whereby an army of the enemy of 10,000 men has been totally defeated, one large detachment of it, strongly posted and entrenched, having been conquered at Bennington, another repulsed with loss and disgrace from Fort Schuyler, and the main army under General Burgoyne, after being beaten in different actions and driven from a formidable post and strong entrenchments, reduced to the necessity of surrendering themselves, upon terms honorable and advantageous to these States on the 17th Day of October last to Major-General Gates; and that a medal of gold be struck under the direction of the Board of War, in commemoration of this great event, and in the name of these United States, presented by the President to Major-General Gates." Served to close of war (Died 10th April, 1806.)

Gates, John (Md). 1st Lieutenant 2d Maryland, — December, 1776; taken prisoner on Staten Island, 22d August, 1777.

Gates, John (N. Y.). Served as Private, Corporal and Sergeant in New York Regiment, 28th July, 1775, to December, 1776; Ensign 1st Canadian (Livingston's) Regiment, 18th December, 1776; retired 20th May, 1780

Gates, Jonathan (Mass). Lieutenant of Whitcomb's Massachusetts Regiment, May to December, 1775.

Gates, J. Shepherd (Vt). Lieutenant Vermont Militia in 1777.

Gates, William (Mass). Sergeant in the Lexington Alarm, April, 1775; 2d Lieutenant of Ward's Massachusetts Regiment, 23d May to December, 1775; Captain Massachusetts Militia in 1776; Captain 15th Massachusetts, 1st January, 1777; omitted in July, 1778 (Died 7th July, 1811.)

Gatling, Levi (N. C.). Ensign 10th North Carolina, ——, 1777; Lieutenant, 12th February, 1778; cashiered 25th August, 1778.

Gaudilet, Edgar (N. J.). Ensign 3d New Jersey, 7th February, 1776; 2d Lieutenant, 29th November, 1776; resigned 25th November, 1778.

Gavet, John (R. I.). Captain Rhode Island Militia in 1775.

Gay, Fisher (Conn). Lieutenant-Colonel of Wolcott's Connecticut Regiment, December, 1775, to February, 1776; Colonel Connecticut State Regiment, 20th June, 1776; died 27th September, 1776.

Gay, John (Mass). 1st Lieutenant of Heath's Massachusetts Regiment, May to December, 1775; 1st Lieutenant 24th Continental Infantry, 1st January, 1776, to December, 1776.

Gay, Samuel (Va). Surgeon's Mate 12th Virginia, — February, 1777; resigned 20th October, 1777; Hospital Surgeon in Virginia, 1778-1781.

Gaylord, Levi (Conn). Sergeant 1st Connecticut, May to November, 1775; Sergeant of Elmore's Continental Regiment, 8th April, 1776; Ensign of Ward's Connecticut State Regiment, 17th June, 1776, to May, 1777.

Gaylord, Timothy (Conn). Sergeant in the Lexington Alarm, April, 1775; Lieutenant of Gay's Connecticut State Regiment, 20th June, 1776; killed 15th September, 1776, on the retreat from New York.

Gaynes, Simeon (Conn). Ensign of Ward's Connecticut State Regiment, 14th May, 1776, to May, 1777.

Geary, John (N. J.). Private 1st New Jersey, 1st September, 1777; Ensign, 1st February, 1779; resigned 28th March, 1783.

Geary, William (Pa). 1st Lieutenant 8th Pennsylvania, 9th August, 1776; resigned 17th April, 1777; name also spelled McGeary.

Geddes, David (Va). Paymaster of the Convention Guards in 1780.

Geddes, Henry (Del). Captain Delaware Militia, 1776-1777; served subsequently in Navy.

Gee, Charles (S. C.). Captain South Carolina Militia; wounded at Eutaw Springs, 8th September, 1781.

Gee, Howell (N. C.). Ensign 7th North Carolina, 15th April, 1777; Lieutenant, November, 1777; Captain, ——, and served to ——.

Gee, James (N. C.). 1st Lieutenant 2d North Carolina, 1st September, 1775; Captain, 3d May, 1776; died 12th November, 1777.

Geiger, George (Pa). Sergeant of Miles' Pennsylvania Rifle Regiment, 1st April, 1776; 3d Lieutenant, 24th October, 1776; 1st Lieutenant Pennsylvania State Regiment, 18th April, 1777; regiment designated 13th Pennsylvania, 12th November, 1777; retired 1st July, 1778; Colonel Pennsylvania Militia; was a prisoner in 1780; when and where taken not stated.

Geikee, James (N. C.). Surgeon 1st North Carolina, — December, 1775; resigned — May, 1776.

Geiser, Frederick (Pa). 2d Lieutenant German Battalion, 12th July, 1776; resigned — May, 1777.

Gentzler, Conrad (Pa). Ensign Pennsylvania Associaters; killed near Perth Amboy in 1776.

Geoghegan, John (Md). Ensign 6th Maryland, 20th February, 1777; resigned 20th January, 1778. (Died 20th February, 1826.)

George, George (Va). 1st Lieutenant 11th Virginia, 23d July, 1776; taken prisoner at Fort Washington, 16th November, 1776; broke his parole and did not return to the Army.

George, John (Mass). 2d Lieutenant in Lexington Alarm, April, 1775; 2d Lieutenant of Gardner's Massachusetts Regiment, May to December, 1775; 2d Lieutenant 25th Continental Infantry, 1st January, 1776; 1st Lieutenant, 9th April, 1776; 1st Lieutenant 3d Continental Artillery, 1st January, 1777; wounded at Fort Mifflin, 15th November, 1777; Captain Lieutenant, 1st October, 1778, and served to June, 1783. (Died 22d January, 1820.)

George, Joshua (Md). Captain 4th Maryland Battalion of the Flying Camp, July to December, 1776.

George, Robert (Va). Captain of Clark's Illinois Regiment, 1779 to 1782.

George, William (Va). 1st Lieutenant of Stephenson's Maryland and Virginia Rifle Regiment, 9th July, 1776; taken prisoner at Fort Washington, 16th November, 1776; appointed Captain 11th Virginia, 11th March, 1777; retired 14th September, 1778, on account of being a prisoner; exchanged 2d November, 1780.

Georges, John (Mass). Surgeon's Mate of Heath's Massachusetts Regiment, 28th June to December, 1775.

Gerard, —— (——). Brevet Lieutenant of Dragoons, Pulaski Legion, 3d September, 1778, and served with the Dragoons to 1782 at his own expense; Brevet Lieutenant-Colonel, 13th February, 1779. (Also spelled Girard.)

Gerault, John (Va). Captain of Clark's Illinois Regiment, 1779-1782.

Gerock, Samuel L. (Md). 1st Lieutenant German Battalion, 12th July, 1776; Captain, 1st July, 1777, to ——. (Is also referred to as Captain of Artillery.)

Gerrard, Charles (N. C.). Ensign 5th North Carolina, 30th April, 1777; 2d Lieutenant, 19th December, 1777; 1st Lieutenant 2d North Carolina, 1st June, 1778; taken prisoner at Charleston, 12th May, 1780; exchanged 14th June, 1781; transferred to 1st North Carolina, 1st January, 1781; served to close of war.

Gerrish, Jacob (Mass). Captain Company of Minute Men in the Lexington Alarm, April, 1775; Captain of Little's Massachusetts Regiment, May to December, 1775; Captain 1st Continental Infantry, 1st January to 31st December, 1776; Colonel Massachusetts Militia, 1777-1779.

Gerrish, Samuel (Mass). Colonel of a Massachusetts Regiment, 19th May, 1775; cashiered 19th August, 1775.

Gerry, Elbridge (Mass). A signer of the Declaration of Independence; subsequently Governor of Massachusetts, and fifth Vice President of the United States, 4th March, 1813, until his death, 23d November, 1814.

Gervas, Thomas (S. C.). Captain 2d South Carolina, ——, 1777; resigned 15th March, 1778.

Geter, —— (Ga). Lieutenant in 3d Georgia; mentioned in General Howe's order of February, 1777-1778.

Gettig, Christopher (Pa). 1st Lieutenant 12th Pennsylvania, 14th October, 1776; wounded and taken prisoner at Piscataway, 11th May, 1777; leg amputated. (Died 12th July, 1790.) Name also speller Getty.

Gettman, Frederick (N. Y.). Captain New York Militia, 1780; was a prisoner; when and where taken not stated.

Ghiselin, John (Md). 1st Lieutenant 1st Maryland Battalion of the Flying Camp, July to December, 1776; Captain 6th Maryland, 16th December, 1776; resigned March, 1777; Captain 6th Maryland, 4th July, 1777; resigned 1st June, 1779.

Gibbes, William Hasell (S. C.). Captain South Carolina Artillery; taken prisoner at Charleston, 12th May, 1780. (Died 13th February, 1834.)

Gibbons, James (Pa). Ensign 5th Pennsylvania Battalion, 8th January, 1776; taken prisoner at Fort Washington, 16th November, 1776; 1st Lieutenant 6th Pennsylvania, 15th February, 1777; Aide-de-Camp to General Irvine in 1779. By the Act of 26th July, 1779, it was "Resolved unanimously, that Congress warmly approve and applaud the cool, determined spirit with which Lieutenant Gibbons and Lieutenant Knox led on the forlorn hope (Stony Point), braving danger and death in the cause of their country, and that a brevet of Captain be given Lieutenant Gibbons." Resigned 16th May, 1781. (Died 1st July, 1835.)

Gibbons, Philip (Pa). Sergeant 1st Pennsylvania, 1st January, 1777; Ensign, 15th February, 1777; 2d Lieutenant 6th Pennsylvania, 17th October, 1777; cashiered, 10th October, 1779.)

Gibbons, William (Pa). Colonel Pennsylvania Militia, 1776-1777. (Died 1803.)

Gibbs, Benjamin (Del). 1st Lieutenant Delaware Battalion of the Flying Camp, July to December, 1776.

Gibbs, Caleb (Mass). Adjutant 14th Continental Infantry, 1st January, 1776; Captain and Commander of a Company of Washington's Guards, 12th March, 1776; Major, 29th July, 1778; transferred to 2d Massachusetts, 1st January, 1781; wounded at Yorktown, 14th October, 1781; retained in H. Jackson's Continental Regiment in November, 1783, and served to 20th June, 1784; Brevet Lieutenant-Colonel, 30th September, 1783. (Died 6th November, 1818.)

Gibbs, Churchill (Va). Sergeant 1st Virginia State Regiment, January, 1777; 2d Lieutenant, 7th December, 1778, to January, 1781.

Gibbs, Herod (Va). 2d Lieutenant 15th Virginia, 10th March, 1777; resigned 30th May, 1778.

Gibbs, John (Mass). Captain Massachusetts Militia, 1778-1779.

Gibbs, Josiah (R. I.). Lieutenant 1st Rhode Island, June to December, 1775; Captain in Richmond's and Stanton's Rhode Island State Regiments, 1776 to 1779.

Gibbs, Lemuel (Conn). 2d Lieutenant 7th Connecticut, 6th July to 19th December, 1775. (Died 1827.)

Gibbs, Samuel (Conn). 2d Lieutenant 3d Connecticut, 1st January, 1777; transferred to Invalid Regiment, 1st November, 1780; discharged 23d April, 1783. (Died 27th October, 1829.)

Gibbs, Thomas (Va). 1st Lieutenant 2d Virginia, 21st September, 1775, to ——.

Gibbs, Warham (Conn). 1st Lieutenant 4th Connecticut, 1st May to December, 1775.

Gibson, George (Va). Captain 1st Virginia, 2d February, 1776; Major, 4th Virginia, 4th January, 1777; Colonel 1st Virginia State Regiment, 5th June, 1777, to January, 1782; Colonel of the Pennsylvania and New Jersey Levies in 1791; mortally wounded 4th November, 1791, in action with Indians near Fort Recovery, Ohio (St. Clair's defeat), and died 11th December, 1791.

Gibson, James (Pa). 1st Lieutenant of Baldwin's Artillery Artificer Regiment, 17th February, 1777; Captain, ——, 1779; retired 1st May, 1781.

Gibson, John (N. Y.). 2d Lieutenant 2d Canadian (Hazen's) Regiment, 15th March, 1777; resigned 20th June, 1777.

Gibson, John (Va). Lieutenant-Colonel 13th Virginia, 12th November, 1776; Colonel 6th Virginia, 25th October, 1777; transferred to 9th Virginia, 14th September, 1778; transferred to 7th Virginia, 12th February, 1781; retired 1st January, 1783. (Died 10th April, 1822.)

Gibson, John, Jr. (Va). Ensign 9th Virginia, 11th October, 1780; transferred to 7th Virginia, 12th February, 1781; retired 1st January, 1783.

Gibson, Jonathan (Md). Ensign 5th Maryland, 10th December, 1776; 2d Lieutenant, 20th February, 1777; 1st Lieutenant, 26th January, 1778; Regimental Paymaster, 25th February, 1779; Captain, 1st May, 1780; wounded at Camden, 16th August, 1780; transferred to 4th Maryland, 1st January, 1781; wounded at Eutaw Springs, 8th September, 1781, and died of his wounds in 1782.

Gibson, Thomas (N. C.). Ensign of a North Carolina Regiment, 20th February, 1780; taken prisoner at Charleston, 12th May, 1780; exchanged 14th June, 1781.

Gibson, Woolman (Md). 1st Lieutenant 4th Maryland Battalion of the Flying Camp, July, 1776 to ——.

Giddings, Eliphalet (N. H.). Captain New Hampshire Militia, 1777-1778.

Gidley, Jasper Manduit (N. Y.). Conductor of Artillery, Steven's Battalion, 1st June, 1777, to ——.

Gifford, David (R. I.). Captain Rhode Island Militia in 1775.

Gifford, Elihu (Mass). Captain Massachusetts Militia, 1781.

Gifford, William Bernard (N. J.). 2d Lieutenant 3d New Jersey, 7th February, 1776; 1st Lieutenant, 10th August, 1776; Captain, 20th November, 1776; wounded at Monmouth, 28th June, 1778; taken prisoner at Elizabethtown, 25th January, 1780; released 22d November, 1780, and did not return to service.

Gilbank, John (S. C.). 1st Lieutenant 4th South Carolina (Artillery), July, 1777, to ——; Major South Carolina Militia; killed in the siege of Charleston in May, 1780.

Gilbert, Aaron (N. Y.). Regimental Quartermaster of Malcolm's New York Regiment in 1776. ..

Gilbert, Benjamin (Mass). Quartermaster-Sergeant 5th Massachusetts, 17th January, 1777; Ensign, 11th November, 1778; Lieutenant, 17th April, 1782; transferred to 3d Massachusetts, 12th June, 1783, and served to 3d November, 1783.

Gilbert, Benjamin (N. Y.). Ensign 1st New York, 21st November, 1776; Lieutenant, 5th April, 1781, and served to 3d June, 1783.

Gilbert, Elisha (Mass). Sergeant 15th Continental Infantry, 1st January to 31st December, 1776; Sergeant-Major 1st Massachusetts, 1st January, 1777; Ensign, 1st September, 1778; resigned 1st January, 1780.

Gilbert, Gershom (Conn). Corporal 8th Connecticut, 8th May to 13th December, 1775; Sergeant of Elmore's Continental Regiment, 15th May, 1776; Quartermaster-Sergeant 8th Connecticut, 1st January, 1777; Regimental Quartermaster, 16th January, 1778, resigned 11th March, 1778.

Gilbert, John (Conn). 2d Lieutenant of Douglas' Connecticut State Regiment, June to December, 1776; Captain Connecticut Militia; killed at New Haven, 5th July, 1779.

Gilbert, John (Conn). Captain Connecticut Light Horse, 1778-1779. (Died 1795.)

Gilbert, John (Pa). Surgeon's Mate 4th Continental Artillery ,— May, 1777; resigned October, 1777.

Gilbert, Joseph (Mass) . Sergeant in the Lexington Alarm, April, 1775; 1st Lieutenant of Prescott's Massachusetts Regiment, May to December, 1775; 1st Lieutenant 7th Continental Infantry, 1st January, 1776; Captain, 10th August, 1776; taken prisoner at Springfield, 17th December, 1776.

Gilbert, Michael (Md). 2d Lieutenant 2d Maryland Battalion of the Flying Camp, June to December, 1776; 1st Lieutenant 2d Canadian (Hazen's) Regiment, 3d November, 1776; Captain, 1st April, 1777; resigned 20th April, 1781.

Gilbert, Nathan (Conn). Captain Connecticut Militia, 1776.

Gilbert, Richard (—). 1st Lieutenant 2d Canadian (Hazen's) Regiment, 3d November, 1776; Captain in 1777, and served to ——.

Gilbert, Samuel (Mass). Sergeant in the Lexington Alarm, April, 1775; Captain of Prescott's Massachusetts Regiment, May to December, 1775; Captain 7th Continental Infantry, 1st January, 1776; taken prisoner at Fort Washington, 16th November, 1776.

Gilbert, Samuel (Mass). Surgeon's Mate 7th Massachusetts, 1st January, 1777; resigned 11th October, 1777.

Gilbert, William W. (N. Y.). Captain New York Militia, 1776.

Gilchrist, Adam (Pa). Ensign 5th Pennsylvania, 1st September, 1777; resigned 24th December, 1777.

Gilchrist, George (Va). Captain 9th Virginia, 4th July, 1776; taken prisoner at Germantown, 4th October, 1777; exchanged 2d November, 1780, and was retired 12th February, 1781, with the rank of Major.

Gilchrist, James (Pa). Ensign 5th Pennsylvania, 23d June, 1779; Lieutenant, 23d May, 1781; retired 1st January, 1783. (Died 9th March, 1791.)

Gilchrist, John (Pa). 2d Lieutenant 1st Pennsylvania Battalion of the Flying Camp; wounded at Fort Washington, 16th November, 1776.

Gilder, Reuben (Del). Surgeon's Mate Delaware Regiment, 13th January, 1776; Surgeon, 5th April, 1777, and served to close of war.

Gildersleeve, Finch (N. Y.). Ensign of Spencer's Additional Continental Regiment, 17th March, 1777; 2d Lieutenant, 16th October, 1777; 1st Lieutenant, 12th April, 1779; retired 1st January, 1781. (Died 1812.)

Giles, Aquila (Md). Major and Aide-de-Camp to General St. Clair, ——; taken prisoner at Brandywine, 11th September, 1777; released 10th November, 1780; served to close of war; Military Storekeeper United States Army, 1st November, 1817; died 8th April, 1822.

Giles, Edward (Md). Reported as a Captain in 2d Canadian (Hazen's) Regiment in 1778 and 1779; Major and Aide-de-Camp to General Morgan, 1779 to 1781; "Brevet Major Continental Army, 9th March, 1781, in consideration of his merit and services at the battle of Cowpens;" subsequently served as Aide-de-Camp to General Smallwood to close of war.

Giles, James (N. Y.). 2d Lieutenant 2d Continental Artillery, 13th January, 1777; Regimental Adjutant, 1st January, 1781; resigned 21st August, 1782. (Died August, 1825.)

Giles, John (Va). Ensign 3d Virginia, 24th October, 1780, and served to close of war.

Giles, Thomas (S. C.). Captain South Carolina Dragoons, ——; wounded at Savannah, 9th October, 1779, and at Eutaw Springs, 8th September, 1781.

Gill, Archibald (S. C.). Lieutenant South Carolina Dragoons, 5th April to September, 1781.

Gill, Erasmus (Va). Sergeant 2d Virginia, 28th August, 1776; Ensign, 28th November, 1776; 2d Lieutenant, 15th June, 1777; Captain 4th Continental Dragoons, February, 1779, to rank from 25th December, 1778; taken prisoner at the Siege of Savannah, 3d October, 1779; exchanged 22d October, 1780, and served to close of war.

Gill, Samuel (Va). Ensign 4th Virginia, 10th February, 1776; 2d Lieutenant, 28th September, 1776; 1st Lieutenant, 12th January, 1777; retired with rank of Captain, 14th September, 1778.

Gill, Thomas (S. C.). Captain South Carolina Militia, 1781.

Gillam, Robert (S. C.). Major South Carolina Militia in 1776 and 1777 in the operations against the British and Cherokee Indians, and at the Siege of Charleston in May, 1780. (Died 1795.)

Gillespie, Robert (N. C.). Ensign 4th North Carolina, ——, 1777; Lieutenant, — August, 1777; served to ——.

Gillett, Joel (Conn). Sergeant 8th Connecticut, 8th July to 18th December, 1775; Ensign 17th Continental Infantry, 1st January, 1776; taken prisoner at Long Island, 27th August, 1776.

Gillett, Jonathan (Conn). 2d Lieutenant 8th Connecticut, 6th July to 10th December, 1775; 2d Lieutenant 17th Continental Infantry, 1st January, 1776; 1st Lieutenant, 1st August, 1776; taken prisoner at Long Island, 27th August, 1776; exchanged in 1779, and died shortly after.

Gilliam, John (Va). 2d Lieutenant 4th Virginia, 14th March, 1776, to — December, 1776. ·

Gilliland, James (N. Y.). 2d Lieutenant Hamilton's Company New York Artillery, 14th March, 1776; 1st Lieutenant, 15th August, 1776; resigned — December, 1776; Captain Lieutenant Sappers and Miners, 2d August, 1779; Captain,

1st June, 1781; resigned 9th October, 1782.

Gilliland, William (N. Y.). 1st Lieutenant 1st New York, 28th June, 1775, to April, 1776; 1st Lieutenant of Lasher's Regiment New York Militia, June, 1776; taken prisoner at Long Island, 27th August, 1776. (Died 1796.)

Gillison, John (Va). Captain 10th Virginia, 18th November, 1776; wounded at Brandywine, 11th September, 1777; transferred to 6th Virginia, 14th September, 1778; taken prisoner at Charleston, 12th May, 1780; retired 1st January, 1783.

Gillon, Alexander (S. C.). Captain South Carolina Militia in 1776.

Gilman, David (N. H.). Colonel New Hampshire Militia Regiment, 1776 and 1777.

Gilman, David (N H.). 2d Lieutenant 2d New Hampshire, 8th November, 1776; cashiered 7th November, 1778.

Gilman, Francis (—). Ensign 2d Canadian (Hazen's) Regiment, 5th February, 1776; Lieutenant, 5th August, 1780; omitted — May, 1782; name also spelled Gilmand.

Gilman, Israel (N. H.). Lieutenant-Colonel 3d New Hampshire, 1st June to December, 1775; Lieutenant-Colonel 2d Continental Infantry, 1st January to 31st December, 1776.

Gilman, James (Va). Captain Virginia Militia at Cowpens in 1781.

Gilman, Jeremiah (N. H.). Captain 5th Continental Infantry, 1st January, 1776; Captain 1st New Hampshire, 8th November, 1776; Major, 2d April, 1777; Lieutenant-Colonel 2d New Hampshire, 20th September, 1777; transferred to 1st New Hampshire, 5th March, 1778; resigned 24th March, 1780. (Died 24th March, 1823.)

Gilman, John (N. H.). 2d Lieutenant 2d New Hampshire, 23d May, 1775; 1st Lieutenant, 20th July to December, 1775. (Died 25th June, 1821.)

Gilman, Nathaniel (N. H.). 1st Lieutenant 3d New Hampshire, 8th November, 1776; sick with the smallpox, and resigned 1st May, 1778. (Died 1803)

Gilman, Nicholas (N. H.). Colonel New Hampshire Militia, 1776 to 1780.

Gilman, Nicholas (N. H.). Regimental Adjutant 3d New Hampshire, 8th November, 1776; Captain 1st June, 1778; appointed Assistant Adjutant-General, 15th January, 1778; transferred to 1st New Hampshire, 1st January, 1781, and served to close of war. (Died 3d May, 1814.)

Gilman, Samuel (N. H.). Captain 2d New Hampshire, 25th May to December, 1775. (Died 1778.)

Gilman, Zebulon (N. H.). Captain New Hampshire Militia, 1776-1778. (Died 1809.)

Gilmore, James (N. H.). Captain New Hampshire Militia, 1778. (Died 1809.)

Gilmore, James (Va).—See **Gilman**; name spelled both ways.

Gilmore, William (Mass). 1st Lieutenant of Brewer's Massachusetts Regiment, May to December, 1775.

Gimat, —— de (France). Major Continental Army, 1st December, 1776; Lieutenant Colonel Aide-de-Camp to General Lafayette, August, 1777; wouned at Yorktown, 14th October, 1781; returned to France, January, 1782.

Girard.—See Gerard.

Gist, John (Md). Captain of Gist's Continental Regiment, 9th March, 1777; retired 1st January, 1781.

Gist, Mordecai (Md). Captain Baltimore Independent Company, July, 1775; Major of Smallwood's Maryland Regiment, 14th January, 1776; Colonel 3d Maryland, 10th December, 1776; Brigadier-General Continental Army, 9th January, 1779. By the act of 14th October, 1780, it was "Resolved, that the thanks of Congress be given to Brigadier Generals Smallwood and Gist and to the officers and soldiers in the Maryland and Delaware lines, the different corps of Artillery, Colonel Porterfield's and Major Armstrong's corps of Light Infantry and Colonel Armand's Cavalry, for their bravery and good conduct displayed in the action of the 16th of August last, near Camden, in the State of South Carolina." Served to close of war. (Died 9th July, 1792.)

Gist, Nathaniel (Va). Colonel Additional Continental Regiment, 11th January, 1777; taken prisoner at Charleston, 12th May, 1780; retired 1st January, 1783. (Died 1796.)

Gist Nathaniel, Jr., (Va). Ensign of Gist's Continental Regiment ——, 1779. Killed at King's Mountain, 7th October, 1780.

Gitman, Frederick (N. Y.). Captain New York Militia ——; taken prisoner at Kanassoraga, 23d October, 1780, and released 14th November, 1782.

Gitting, William (Pa). Ensign of Armand's Corps in 1779 and 1780.

Givens, Robert (Mass). 2d Lieutenant 7th Massachusetts, 1st January, 1777; 1st Lieutenant, ——, 1779, and served to June, 1783.

Gladding, Nathaniel (R. I.). Lieutenant of Elliott's Regiment Rhode Island State Artillery, 19th August, 1776; Captain Lieutenant, 12th December, 1776, to May, 1777.

Glaeton, Jacob (Pa). 2d Lieutenant of Ottendorff's Battalion Armand's Corps, 3d March, 1777, and served to ——.

Glaharí, John (N. C.). Captain 7th North Carolina, 28th November, 1776; resigned 11th October, 1777.

Glasbeech, —— Baron (——,. Volunteer Aide-de-Camp to General Morgan; brevet Captain Continental Army, 9th March, 1781, "in consideration of his merit and services at the battle of Cowpens."

Glascock, Thomas (Ga). 1st Lieutenant Georgia Regiment, 1st July, 1777; Lieutenant 1st Continental Dragoons, ——, 1779, to 10th November, 1782. (Died 9th May, 1841.)

Glass, Thomas (S. C.). 2d Lieutenant South Carolina Rangers, ——; in service 1779 and 1780.

Glatz, ——. See Klatz.

Gleason, Micajah (Mass). Captain in the Lexington Alarm, April, 1775; Captain of Nixon's Massachusetts regiment, April to December, 1775; Captain 4th Continental Infantry, 1st January, 1776. Killed at Harlem Plains, 16th September, 1776.

Gleckner, Christian (Pa). Sergeant German Regiment, 10th July, 1776; Ensign, 23d July, 1778; retired 1st January, 1781.

Glenn, Bernard (Va). Lieutenant Virginia Militia, 1780.

Glenn, John (Va). Captain-Major and Lieutenant Colonel Virginia Militia, 1776-1781.

Glenny, William (Conn). Private 10th Continental Infantry, 16th January, 1776; Sergeant 4th Connecticut, 1st January, 1777; Ensign 20th May, 1779; transferred to 1st Connecticut, 1st January, 1781; 2d Lieutenant, 1st April, 1783; retained in Swift's Connecticut Regiment, June, 1783, and served to November, 1783. (Died 1800.)

Glenny, William (N. Y.). Served as a Sergeant in 3d New York, June, 1775, to January, 1776; Ensign 2d New York, 21st November, 1776; 2d Lieutenant, 21st June, 1777; 1st Lieutenant, 5th April, 1780; killed at West Canada Creek, 30th October, 1781.

Glentworth, George (Pa). Senior Surgeon and Physician of the Middle Department, 1st November, 1777, to 11th September, 1780.

Glentworth, James (Pa). 2d Lieutenant 6th Pennsylvania 15th February, 1777; 1st Lieutenant 22d March, 1777; wounded and taken prisoner at Paramus, 16th April, 1780; transferred to 2d Pennsylvania, 1st January, 1783, served to June, 1783.

Glidden, Charles (N. H.). Ensign of Poor's New Hampshire Regiment, 23d May to December, 1775; Ensign 8th Continental Infantry, 1st January, 1776; 2d Lieutenant, 6th September to 31st December, 1776.

Glover, John (Mass). Colonel of a Massachusetts Regiment, 19th May to December, 1775; Colonel 14th Continental Infantry, 1st January, 1776; Brigadier-General Continental Army, 21st February, 1777; resigned 22d July, 1782. (Died 30th January, 1797.)

Glover, John (S. C.) Ensign 1st South Carolina ——, 1775; Lieutenant, ——, 1776; served to ..... (Died 27th March, 1821.)

Glover, Joseph (S. C.). Colonel South Carolina Militia in 1775 and 1776.

Glover, Samuel Kinsley (Va). Surgeon's Mate Hospital Department in 1775 and 1776.

Glover, Thomas (Mass). 1st Lieutenant of Doolittle's Massachusetts Regiment, May, 1775 to ——.

Glover, William (N. C.). 1st Lieutenant 6th North Carolina, 16th April, 1776; Captain, 7th May, 1776. Retired 1st June, 1778.

Godboldt, James (S. C.). Lieutenant South Carolina Militia in 1776.

Godfrey, George (Mass). Brigadier-General Massachusetts Militia in 1776 to 1781. (Died 1793.)

Godfrey, Richard (S. C.). Captain South Carolina Militia in 1781. (Died 1817.)

Godfrey, William (N. C.). Lieutenant 8th North Carolina, 28th November, 1776; resigned 15th August, 1777.

Godfrey, William Egerton (Pa). Captain-Lieutenant of Flower's Artillery Artificer Regiment, 1st July, 1777; taken prisoner; when and where not stated; retired 30th August, 1780.

Godman, Samuel (Md). 1st Lieutenant 3d Maryland Battalion of the Flying Camp, July to December, 1776; Captain 4th Maryland, 10th December, 1776. Resigned 21st May 1779. (Died 1st October, 1781.)

Godman, William (Va). 1st Lieutenand 1st Continental Artillery, 13th January, 1777; Captain-Lieutenant, 1st January, 1778; cashiered, 18th August, 1779. (Died 11th June, 1825.)

Godwin, Dinwiddie (Va). Ensign 6th Virginia, 9th April, 1776. Died 17th February, 1777.

Godwin, Henry (N. Y.). Captain 5th New York 21st November, 1776; taken prisoner at Fort Montgomery 6th October, 1777; transferred to 4th New York 20th July, 1780; retired 1st January, 1781; served subsequently as Captain New York Levies. (Name also spelled Goodwin.)

Godwin, Jonathan (Va). Ensign 1st Virginia, 30th September, 1775; 2d Lieutenant 26th January, 1776; served to ——.

Goforth, William (N. Y.). Captain 1st New York, 28th June, 1775; Major of DuBois' New York Regiment, 26th June, 1776; resigned 6th July, 1776. (Died 1807.)

Goggins, John (Va). 1st Lieutenant 5th Virginia, 12th March, 1776, to ——.

Gokins, Samuel (Va). Ensign 7th Virginia, 7th March, 1776; resigned 13th January, 1777.

Goldsborough, Greenburry (Md). Captain 4th Maryland Battalion of the Flying Camp, July, 1776, to ——.

Goldsborough, William (Md). Ensign 1st Maryland, 16th October, 1781; transferred to 2d Maryland 1st January, 1782; 2d Lieutenant, — April, 1782; transferred to 1st Maryland, 1st January, 1783; retained in Maryland Battalion, April, 1783, and served to 15th November, 1783.

Goldsmith, John (Pa). Ensign 3d Pennsylvania 21st April, 1777; deserted 31st October, 1777.

Goldsmith, Peter (Ga). Captain Georgia Militia, 1780-1781.

Goldsmith, Thomas (Md). 2d Lieutenant of Smallwood's Maryland Regi-

ment, 14th January, 1776; 1st Lieutenant in June, 1776; wounded at White Plains, 28th October, 1776.

Goldthwaite, Jacob (Mass). Ensign 13th Continental Infantry, 1st January, 1776; Lieutenant, August, 1776; 1st Lieutenant 3d Continental Artillery, 1st January, 1777; Captain-Lieutenant, 6th March, 1780; resigned 13th September, 1780.

Golson, Lewis (S. C.). Major South Carolina Militia in 1775.

Gomath, Jacob.—See Grometh.

Gooch, John (R. I.). Captain 9th Continental Infantry, 1st January to 31st December, 1776; Assistant Deputy Quartermaster-General, 14th July, 1777, and served to ——.

Gooch, Thomas (Del). Colonel Delaware Militia, 1775.

Good, Jacob (Md). Captain 1st Maryland Battalion of the Flying Camp, June, 1776, to ——.

Goodale, Ezekiel (N. H.). 2d Lieutenant 3d New Hampshire, 8th November, 1776; resigned 30th April, 1778. (Died 10th July, 1827.)

Goodale, Nathan (Mass). Lieutenant of Brewer's Massachusetts Regiment, May to December, 1775; 1st Lieutenant 13th Continental Infantry, 1st January to 31st December, 1776; Captain 5th Massachusetts, 1st January, 1777; wounded and taken prisoner at King's Bridge, 30th August, 1778; exchanged, 9th October, 1780; transferred to 1st Massachusetts, 12th June, 1783; brevet Major, 30th September, 1783; served to 3d November, 1783. (Died 1793.)

Goode, Samuel (Va). Lieutenant Virginia Dragoons, 1776-1779. (Died 14th November, 1822.)

Goodell, Silas (Conn). Sergeant 3d Connecticut, 5th May to 10th December, 1775; Ensign 20th Continental Infantry, 1st January to 31st December, 1776; 2d Lieutenant 3d Connecticut, 1st January, 1777; 1st Lieutenant, 24th April, 1778; transferred to 1st Connecticut, 1st January, 1783, and served to 3d June, 1783.

Goodenow, David (N. H.). 2d Lieutenant of Whitcomb's New Hampshire Rangers, 17th February to 28th July, 1777.

Goodenow, Ithamar (Mass). 1st Lieutenant of Woodbridge's Massachusetts Regiment, May, 1775, to ——.

Goodenow, Levi, (Vt). Captain Vermont Rangers, 1777.

Goodenow, Micah (Mass). 1st Lieutenant of Nixon's Massachusetts Regiment, May to December, 1775; 1st Lieutenant 5th Continental Infantry, 1st January to 31st December, 1776.

Goodin, Christopher (N. C.). Lieutenant 6th North Carolina, 16th April, 1776; transferred to 3d North Carolina 1st June, 1778; Captain — January, 1779. Killed at Eutaw Springs, 8th September, 1781.

Goodloe, Robert (N. C.). Captain North Carolina Militia, 1779-1780. (Died 1797.)

Goodman, Moses (Conn). Private in the Lexington Alarm, April, 1775; Sergeant 8th Connecticut, 8th July to 10th December, 1775; Ensign 17th Continental Infantry, 1st January to 31st December, 1776. (Died 1831.)

Goodman, Simeon (Mass). Ensign 18th Continental Infantry, 1st August to 31st December, 1776.

Goodman, William (N. C.). Captain 4th North Carolina 1st October, 1776. Killed at Eutaw Springs, 8th September, 1781.

Goodman, William (Va). Ensign Virginia Militia, 1780-1781.

Goodrich, Benjamin (Mass). 2d Lieutenant of Cady's Battalion on the expedition to Canada January to June, 1776.

Goodrich, Daniel (Mass). Captain of Cady's Battalion on the expedition to Canada, January to June, 1776.

Goodrich, Ezekiel (Mass). 2d Lieutenant 8th Massachusetts, 1st January, 1777; killed at Saratoga, 7th October, 1777.

Goodrich, John (Va). 1st Lieutenant 4th Virginia, 1st April, 1776; resigned 6th January, 1777; Captain Virginia Militia, 1779-1780.

Goodrich, Levi (Conn). Sergeant 3d Connecticut 23d January, 1777; Quartermaster Sergeant 1st April, 1780; Ensign 29th June, 1780; transferred to 4th Connecticut 1st January, 1781; resigned 24th October, 1781.

Goodrich, Ozias (Conn). Private in the Lexington Alarm, April, 1775; Private 2d Connecticut, 12th May to 17th December, 1775; Corporal 3d Connecticut, 1st January, 1777; Sergeant, 1st August, 1778; Ensign, 1st July, 1779; transferred to 1st Connecticut, 1st January, 1781; retained in Swift's Connecticut Battalion, June, 1783, and served to 3d November, 1783.

Goodrich, Samuel (Mass). Regimental Quartermaster, 27th Continental Infantry, 1st January, 1776; 1st Lieutenant 11th Massachusetts, 6th November, 1776; Captain-Lieutenant 25th June, 1779; resigned 14th July, 1779. (Died 27th March 1820.)

Goodrich, Silas (Mass). 1st Lieutenant of Brewer's Massachusetts Regiment, May, 1775, to ——.

Goodrich, Stephen (Conn). Lieutenant in the Lexington Alarm, April, 1775; 1st Lieutenant 2d Connecticut, 1st May to 10th December, 1775; 1st Lieutenant 22d Continental Infantry, 1st January to 31st December, 1776. (Died 23d September 1823.)

Goodrich, William (Mass). Captain in the Lexington Alarm April, 1775; Captain of Glover's Massachusetts Regiment, May to December, 1775; taken prisoner at Quebec, 31st December, 1775; Brigade Major of Putnam's Brigade, 1st March to July, 1777; served subsequently in Massachusetts Militia.

Goodrich, William (Mass). 1st Lieutenant 10th Massachusetts, 1st January, 1777; resigned 14th July, 1779. Major Massachusetts Militia in 1780.

Goodridge, Samuel (Conn). Regimental Quartermaster 19th Continental Infantry, 1st January, 1776 to ——.

Goodwin, Charles (Conn). Ensign of Gay's Connecticut State Regiment, June to December, 1776.

Goodwin, Dinwiddie.—See Godwin.

Goodwin, Francis Le Baron (Mass). Surgeon's-Mate 14th Massachusetts, 1st January, 1777; transferred to 9th Massachusetts, 1st January, 1781; transferred to 3d Massachusetts, 1st January, 1783, and served to 3d June, 1783. (Died 19th February, 1816.)

Goodwin, .Jedediah (Mass). 1st Lieutenant of Scammon's Massachusetts Regiment, May, 1775, to December, 1775. Captain Massachusetts Militia, 1776-1781.

Goodwin, John (N. C.). Lieutenant North Carolina Militia, 1781.

Goodwin, John (S. C.). 1st Lieutenant 1st South Carolina, 12th July, 1778; taken prisoner at Charleston, 12th May, 1780.

Goodwin, Joseph (Va). Lieutenant 1st Virginia, — May, 1776. Died 30th January, 1777.

Goodwin, Nathaniel (Conn). Captain 2d Connecticut, 1st January, 1777; died

1st May, 1777, of wounds received at Crompo Hill, 28th April, 1777.

Goodwin, Robert (S. C.). Captain 2d South Carolina (Rangers), 17th June, 1775 to——; Colonel South Carolina Militia in 1778; wounded at Charleston, 12th May, 1780.

Goodwin, Simeon (Mass). Sergeant in Scammons' Massachusetts Regiment, May to December, 1775; Sergeant, 18th Continental Infantry, 1st January, 1776; Ensign 1st August to 31st December, 1776.

Goodwin, Stephen (Conn). Captain of Gay's Connecticut State Regiment, 20th June to 25th December, 1776. (Died 1788)

Goodwin, Uriah (S. C.). Lieutenant 3d South Carolina — May, 1776; Captain 1st September, 1777; wounded at Stono Ferry, 20th June, 1779; taken prisoner at Charleston, 12th May, 1780; exchanged — November, 1780. Killed at Eutaw Springs, 8th September, 1781.

Gookin, Daniel (N. H.). Sergeant-Major 2d New Hampshire, 15th November, 1776; Ensign, 6th May, 1777; Lieutenant, 12th July, 1780; retired 12th March, 1782 (Died 24th September, 1831.)

Goosley, Willaim (Va). Captain Virginia Militia, 1775-1777.

Gordon, Ambrose (Va). Paymaster 3d Continental Dragoons, 1st November, 1779; wounded at Eutaw Springs, 8th September, 1781; retained in Baylor's Consolidated Regiment of Dragoons, 9th November, 1782, and served to close of war.

Gordon, Arthur (Va). 1st Lieutenant 13th Virginia, 19th December, 1776; regiment designated 9th Virginia, 14th September, 1778, and served to —— (Was in service in January, 1780)

Gordon, Charles (N. C.). Major North Carolina Partisan Rangers, ——; wounded at King's Mountain, 7th October, 1780. (Died 24th March, 1799.)

Gordon, Coe (Del). 2d Lieutenant of the Delaware Battalion of the Flying Camp, July to December, 1776; 2d Lieutenant Delaware Regiment, 2d December, 1776. Resigned 4th April, 1777. (Died 1792.)

Gordon, Daniel (N. H.). Captain New Hampshire Militia, 1776-1780

Gordon, James (Conn). Captain of Douglas' Connecticut State Regiment, January to March, 1776.

Gordon, James (Del). 2d Lieutenant Delaware Regiment, 19th January to December, 1776. (Died 1792.)

Gordon, James (N Y.). Lieutenant-Colonel New York Militia; taken prisoner at Schoharie, 17th October, 1780; released 19th November, 1782. (Died 17th January, 1810.)

Gordon, James (Pa). Ensign 10th Pennsylvania, 4th December, 1776; 2d Lieutenant, 18th April, 1777; resigned — December, 1777.

Gordon, John (S. C.). 2d Lieutenant 5th South Carolina ——, 1777; 1st Lieutenant 21st January, 1778; Adjutant of Lee's Battalion of Light Dragoons in 1780; killed at Eutaw Springs, 8th September, 1781.

Gordon, Joshua (Mass). Captain of Mitchell's Regiment, Massachusetts Militia on the Bagaduce expedition, July to September, 1779.

Gordon, Peter (N. J.). Captain New Jersey Militia in 1777; served subsequently as Major in Quartermaster's Department.

Gordon, Roger (S. C.). Lieutenant South Carolina Militia in Marion's Brigade in 1781.

Gordon, Thomas (Md). Ensign 3d Maryland, 20th February, 1777; resigned 1st July, 1778.

Gordon, William (N. J.). 2d Lieutenant 3d New Jersey, 5th March, 1776; 1st Lieutenant, 19th July, 1776; Captain, 29th November, 1776. Died 15th April, 1777.

Gore, Daniel (Pa). Lieutenant Pennsylvania Militia; wounded (lost an arm) at Wyoming, 3d July 1778. (Died 1806)

Gore, Obadiah (Conn). 1st Lieutenant 3d Connecticut, 1st January, 1777; retired 1st January, 1781. (Died 22d March, 1821.)

Gore, Silas (Pa). Ensign Pennsylvania Militia. Killed at the Wyoming massacre, 3d July, 1778.

Gorget, John F. (S. C.). Captain-Lieutenant 4th South Carolina (Artillery), 30th May, 1778; taken prisoner at Charleston, 12th May, 1780.

Gorham, Nehemiah (Conn). Private 5th Connecticut, 19th May to 12th December, 1775; Ensign 5th Connecticut, 1st January, 1777; 2d Lieutenant, 15th December, 1777; 1st Lieutenant, 7th April, 1780; transferred to 2d Connecticut, 1st January, 1781, and served to 3d June, 1783.

Gorham, Shubael (Mass). 1st Lieutenant of Little's Massachusetts Regiment, 19th May to December, 1775; 2d Lieutenant of Elmore's Connecticut State Regiment, 15th April, 1776; 1st Lieutenant, 25th July, 1776, and served to April, 1777.

Gorham, Stephen (Mass). Sergeant in Lexington Alarm, April, 1775; 2d Lieutenant of Learned's Massachusetts Regiment, May to December, 1775; 1st Lieutenant 7th Massachusetts, 1st January, 1777; resigned 5th December, 1777; Lieutenant Massachusetts Militia, 1778-1779.

Gorman, Joseph (Pa). Sergeant of Miles' Pennsylvania Rifle Regiment, 29th March, 1776; Ensign Pennsylvania State Regiment, 18th April, 1777; regiment designated 13th Pennsylvania, 12th November, 1777; retired 1st July, 1778.

Gorton, Israel (R. I.). Captain 2d Rhode Island Regiment, 28th June to December, 1775.

Gorton, Thomas (R. I.). Captain of Babcock's Rhode Island State Regiment, 19th August, 1776, to May 1777; Lieutenant-Colonel Rhode Island Militia, 1777-1780.

Gosner, Peter (Pa). 2d Lieutenant 1st Pennsylvania Battalion, 15th January, 1776; 1st Lieutenant 2d Pennsylvania, 1st January, 1777; Captain, 26th September, 1777; retired 1st January, 1781.

Goss, John (Mass). Lieutenant New Hampshire Minute Men in the Lexington Alarm, April, 1775; 1st Lieutenant of Prescott's Massachusetts Regiment, May, 1775; Surgeon 5th Continental Infantry, 1st January to 31st December, 1776.

Gosselin, Clement (Canada). Captain 2d Canadian (Hazen's) Regiment, 4th March, 1776; wounded at Yorktown 4th October, 1781; retired June, 1783. (Died 7th August, 1823.)

Gosselin, Louis (Canada). Ensign 2d Canadian (Hazen's) Regiment, ——, 1779; served to June, 1783.

Gostelow, Jonathan (——). Major Commissary of Military Stores, 1st February, 1777, to ——.

Gough, John (S. C.). Lieutenant South Carolina Militia in 1776.

Gough, Richard (S. C.). Captain South Carolina Dragoons in 1779 to 1782.

Gould, Abraham (Conn). Captain and Lieutenant-Colonel Connecticut Militia, 1775-1777; killed at the Danbury Raid, 26th April, 1777.

Gould, Benjamin (Mass). Corporal; wounded at Lexington, 19th April, 1775; Sergeant in Little's Massachusetts Regiment, May to December, 1775; Ensign 12th Continental Infantry, 1st January to 31st December, 1776; Captain Massachusetts Militia, 1777-1780. (Died 30th May, 1841.)

Gould, David (Va). Hospital Surgeon, 8th September, 1777; Senior Hospital Surgeon in Virginia, 11th October, 1779; died 12th July, 1781.

Gould, Ebenezer Brewster (Mass). Private in Lexington Alarm April, 1775; Corporal in Danielsen's Massachusetts Regiment, April to December, 1775; Sergeant 3d Continental Infantry, 5th January, 1776; Ensign 10th August, 1776; 1st Lieutenant 4th Massachusetts, 1st January, 1777. Resigned 12th April 1778.

Gould, George (Mass). Captain of Danielson's Massachusetts Regiment, May to December, 1775.

Gould, Jacob (Mass). Captain in Lexington Alarm, April, 1775; Captain of Heath's Massachusetts Regiment, May to December, 1775; Captain 24th Continental Infantry, 1st January, 1776 to December, 1776. (Died 1809.)

Gould, James (Md). Ensign 5th Maryland, 20th February, 1777; Lieutenant, 11th March, 1778; Regimental Quartermaster, 20th September, 1779; transferred to 3d Maryland, 1st January, 1781; killed at Eutaw Springs, 8th September, 1781.

Gould, James (Mass). Lieutenant of Woodbridge's Massachusetts Regiment, May to December, 1775.

Gould, James (N. H.). Sergeant and Sergeant-Major and 2d Lieutenant of Bedel's New Hampshire Regiment, 15th June, 1775, to April, 1776; 1st Lieutenant of Baldwin's New Hampshire Regiment, May to November, 1776; 1st Lieutenant 1st New Hampshire, 8th November, 1776; severely wounded at Bemus Heights, 19th September, 1777, and never rejoined regiment.

Gould, John (Mass). Ensign 12th Continental Infantry, 1st January to 31st December, 1776.

Gould, Joshua (Mass). Ensign in Lexington Alarm, April, 1775; 2d Lieutenant of Heath's Massachusetts Regiment, April to December, 1775; 2d

Lieutenant 24th Continental Infantry, 1st January to 31st December, 1776.

Gould, Nathan .(Conn). Surgeon's-Mate of Douglas' Connecticut State Regiment, 3d July to 29th December, 1776.

Gould, Samuel (Mass). 2d Lieutenant of Woodbridge's Massachusetts Regiment, May, 1775, to ——.

Gould, Theophilus (Mass). Private in Lexington Alarm, April, 1775; Lieutenant of Frye's Massachusetts Regiment, May to December, 1775.

Gourley, Thomas (Pa). 2d Lieutenant of Miles' Pennsylvania Rifle Regiment, 16th March, 1776; 1st Lieutenant 9th Pennsylvania, 15th November, 1776; Captain 3d March, 1777; resigned 23d May, 1778.

Gouvion, Jean Baptiste Obrey de (France). Major Engineer on staff of General Lafayette, 8th July, 1777; Lieutenant-Colonel, 17th November, 1777; brevet Colonel, 16th November, 1781; retired 10th October, 1783. (Died 11th June, 1792.)

Gove, Nathaniel (Conn). Sergeant in the Lexington Alarm, April, 1775; 2d Lieutenant 8th Connecticut, 6th July to 17th December, 1775; 1st Lieutenant 17th Continental Infantry, 1st January, 1776; taken prisoner at Long Island, 27th August, 1776.

Govert, Jacque Paul (France). Captain-Lieutenant Continental Artillery, 18th September, 1776, and served to ——.

Grace, Arnold (Pa). Lieutenant Pennsylvania Militia, was a prisoner in 1780; when and where taken not stated.

Grace, Ernest.—See Greece.

Grace, John (Mass). Ensign 1st Massachusetts, 13th November, 1776; 2d Lieutenant, 14th June, 1777; 1st Lieutenant, 4th November, 1777; retired 1st January, 1783.

Grace, Richard, (Md). Sergeant of Watkin's Maryland Company, 25th January, 1776; 1st Lieutenant 2d Maryland, 10th December, 1776; Captain 17th April, 1777; taken prisoner at Staten Island, 22d August, 1777, and did not rejoin regiment.

Graff.—See Graeff. (Name spelled both ways.)

Graeff, George (Pa). Captain of Kachleine's Battalion Pennsylvania Militia; wounded and taken prisoner at Fort Washington, 16th November, 1776, and died in captivity.

Grafton, John (Va). Lieutenant of a Virginia Regiment; wounded at Savannah, 9th October, 1779.

Graham, Alexander (Pa). Ensign 5th Pennsylvania Battalion, 9th August, 1776; 2d Lieutenant 8th Pennsylvania, 13th July, 1777; 1st Lieutenant, 1st April, 1779. Resigned 1st March, 1779.

Graham, Andrew (N. Y.). Surgeon New York Militia, ——; taken prisoner at White Plains, 28th October, 1776;, and was a prisoner to November, 1781. (Died, 1785.)

Graham, Archibald (Va). Ensign 13th Virginia, 1st February, 1777; resigned 19th November, 1777.

Graham, Charles (N. Y.). 1st Lieutenant 4th New York, 28th June, 1775, to January, 1776; Captain 2d New York, 21st November, 1776; retired 1st January, 1781. (Died 12th February 1838.)

Graham, George (N. Y.). Suregon's Mate 4th New York, 2d May to November, 1776.

Graham, George (N. C.). Ensign 1st North Carolina, 1st September, 1775; 2d Lieutenant, 4th January, 1776; resigned 15th April, 1776; served subsequently as Captain North Carolina Rangers.

Graham, Isaac Gilbert (Mass). Surgeon's-Mate 7th Massachusetts, 18th July, 1781; transferred to 2d Massachusetts, 12th June, 1783, and served to 3d November, 1783. (Died 1st September 1848.)

Graham, John (N. Y.). Lieutenant-Colonel New York Militia; killed at Westchester, 16th September, 1778.

Graham, John (N. Y.). Captain 2d New York, 30th June, 1775; Captain of Nicholson's Continental Regiment, 16th February, 1776; Captain 1st New York, 21st November, 1776, to rank from 16th February, 1776; Major, 26th March, 1779 and served to close of war. (Died 7th May, 1832.)

Graham, Jonathan G. (Conn). Surgeon's-Mate 2d Connecticut, 6th October, 1778; Surgeon 7th Connecticut, 23d March, 1779; resigned 1st January, 1780.

Graham, Joseph (N. C.). Served as Lieutenant and Captain North Carolina Rangers from September, 1778; Major North Carolina Partisan Rangers, 1780; wounded at Charlotte, 26th September, 1780. (Died 12th November, 1836.)

Graham, Morris (N. Y.). Colonel New York Militia, 1776-1780.

Graham, Richard (N. C.). Lieutenant 2d North Carolina, 8th June, 1776; Captain January, 1778; retired 1st June, 1778.

Graham, Sheldon (Conn). Regimental Quartermaster of Wolcott's Connecticut State Regiment, December, 1775, to February, 1776.

Graham, Stephen (Va). Hospital Surgeon's Mate, 1780 to 1782.

Graham, Walton (Va). 2d Lieutenant 13th Virginia, 12th February, 1777; retired 14th September, 1778; served subsequently as Captain Lieutenant of a Virginia State Regiment. (Died 1829.)

Graham, William (Pa). Ensign 6th Pennsylvania Battalion, 9th January to December, 1776.

Graham, William (N. C.). Colonel North Carolina Militia, 1776 to 1781. (Died 3d May, 1835.)

Graham, William (Va). Surgeon's Mate 2d Virginia, 3d March, 1777; retired 14th September, 1778.

Grameth, Jacob (Md)—See Grometh.

Grainger, Caleb (N. C.). Captain 1st North Carolina, 1st September, 1775; Major, 5th February. 1777; resigned 26th April, 1777.

Grainger, John (N. C.). 1st Lieutenant 2d North Carolina, 1st September, 1775, to ——.

Granberry, George (N C). Captain 3d North Carolina, 16th April, 1776, to ——.

Granberry, John (N. C.) Lieutenant 3d North Carolina, ——, 1777, to ——.

Granberry, Thomas (N C.). Captain 3d North Carolina, 16th April, 1776; was taken prisoner; when and where not stated. (Died 20th May, 1830.)

Granger, Asher (Mass). Private in Lexington Alarm, April, 1775; Regimental Quartermaster of Danielson's Massachusetts Regiment, May to December, 1775; 2d Lieutenant 3d Continental Infantry, 1st January to 31st December, 1776.

Granger, Bildad (Conn). Private in the Lexington Alarm, April, 1775; 1st Lieutenant 8th Connecticut, 1st January, 1777; retired 15th November, 1778. (Died 1820.)

Granger, John (Mass). Captain of Learned's Massachusetts Regiment. May, 1775, to December, 1775. (Died 1783.)

Granger, Samuel (Conn). 1st Lieutenant of Wolcott's Connecticut State Regiment, December 1775, to February, 1775; 1st Lieutenant of Ward's Connecticut State Regiment, 14th May, 1776; Captain 2d Connecticut, 1st January, .1777; resigned 24th December, 1777.

Grannis, Enos (Conn). Private of Elmore's Connecticut State Regiment, May, 1776, to May, 1777; Sergeant of Baldwin's Artillery Artificer Regiment, 13th September, 1777; Lieutenant, 12th November, 1779; retired 1st January, 1781.

**Grant, —— ** (Ga). Captain Georgia Militia; killed in action near Ogechee Road, 21st May, 1782.

Grant, Benjamin (N. H.). Lieutenant New Hampshire Militia, September, 1775; 2d Lieutenant of Bedel's Regiment New Hampshire Rangers, 22d January, 1776. Died 20th May, 1776, of smallpox.

Grant, Benoni (Conn). Sergeant of Warner's Additional Continental Regiment, 27th February, 1777; Ensign, 14th August, 1778; retired 1st January, 1781.

Grant, Christopher (Mass). Lieutenant of Gardner's Massachusetts Regiment, May to December, 1775.

Grant, Daniel (Conn). Ensign 4th Connecticut, 1st May to 10th December, 1775

Grant, Eleazer (N. Y.). 2d Lieutenant 2d New York, 28th June, 1775, to January, 1776; served subsequently as Regimental Quartermaster, New York Militia Regiment.

Grant, George (Pa). 3d Lieutenant 1st Battalion of Miles' Pennsylvania Rifle Regiment, 19th March, 1776; 1st Lieutenant 9th Pennsylvania, 15th November, 1776; Captain, 3d March, 1777; died 10th October, 1779.

Grant, Gilbert (R. I.) Lieutenant of Lippitt's Rhode Island Militia Regiment, 19th August, 1776; 1st Lieutenant 2d Rhode Island, 1st January, 1777, to ——.

Grant, Jesse (Conn). Sergeant 7th Connecticut, 8th July to 19th December, 1775; 2d Lieutenant 19th Continental Infantry, 1st January, 1776; wounded and taken prisoner at Fort Washington, 16th November, 1776; exchanged 25th October, 1780, and did not re-enter service.

Grant, John (N. H.). Captain Green Mountain Boys, 27th July to November, 1775; Regimental Quartermaster of Jackson's Continental Regiment, 1st

June, 1777, to 23d April, 1779; subsequently served as Quartermaster of New Hampshire State and Militia forces. (Died November, 1825.)

Grant, Peter (Va). 1st Lieutenant of Grayson's Additional Continental Regiment, 11th February, 1777; Captain, 20th August, 1777; resigned 19th April, 1778.

Grant, Reuben (N. C.). Ensign 6th North Carolina, 16th April, 1776; Lieutenant, 6th June, 1776; served to ——.

Grant, Thomas (Mass). Captain of Glover's Massachusetts Regiment, 19th May to December, 1775; Captain 14th Continental Infantry, 1st January, 1776; taken prisoner at Fort Washington, 16th November, 1776.

Grant, Thomas (N. C.). Ensign 6th North Carolina, 16th April, 1776, to ——. (Died 1828.)

Gratten, John (Va). 2d Lieutenant 8th Virginia, 25th March, 1776, to ——.

Graule, Jacob (Pa). Captain Pennsylvania Battalion of the Flying Camp, July, 1776, to ——.

Graves, Aaron (Mass). Captain Massachusetts Militia, 1777.

Graves, Abner (Mass). Lieutenant in Lexington Alarm, April, 1775; 1st Lieutenant 9th Massachusetts, 1st January, 1777; resigned 17th June, 1778.

Graves, Asa (Mass). Private 6th Continental Infantry, 1st January to 31st December, 1776; Sergeant 6th Massachusetts, 1st January, 1777; Ensign, 15th June, 1780; transferred to 1st Massachusetts, 12th June, 1783, and served to November, 1783. (Died 6th October, 1823.)

Graves, Crispus (Mass). Ensign of Phinney's Massachusetts Regiment, April 24 to December, 1775; 2d Lieutenant 18th Continental Infantry, 1st January, 1776; 1st Lieutenant, 18th May to 31st December, 1776; 1st Lieutenant Massachusetts Militia in 1778.

Graves, Ebenezer (Mass). 2d Lieutenant of Glover's Massachusetts Regiment, 19th May to December, 1775; 2d Lieutenant 14th Continental Infantry, 1st January to 31st December, 1776.

Graves, Francis (N. C.). Regimental Quartermaster 8th North Carolina, 1st September, 1777; Lieutenant 10th North Carolina, 26th October, 1777; transferred to 3d North Carolina, 1st June, 1778; 1st Lieutenant, 14th July, 1779; transferred to 1st North Carolina, — July, 1780; taken prisoner at Charleston, 12th

May, 1780; exchanged 14th June, 1781, and served to close of war.

Graves, John (Va). Ensign 8th Virginia, 19th February, 1776; 2d Lieutenant, 25th March, 1776; resigned 21st April, 1778; served subsequently as Major Virginia Militia.

Graves, Jonathan (N. Y.). Captain New York Militia, 1775-1776.

Graves, Joseph (S. C.). Lieutenant South Carolina Militia in 1776.

Graves, Ralph (Va). Lieutenant of a Virginia State Regiment, 1779 to 1781.

Graves, Silvanus (Conn). Major Connecticut Militia, 1776.

Graves, William (Mass). 1st Lieutenant 14th Continental Infantry, 1st January, 1776, to ——.

Gray, —— (——). Lieutenant 2d Continental Artillery; dismissed 8th February, 1778; name also spelled Grey.

Gray, Ebenezer (Conn). 2d Lieutenant 3d Connecticut, 1st May to 10th December, 1775; 1st Lieutenant and Regimental Quartermaster 20th Continental Infantry, 1st January, 1776; Brigade Major to General Parson's Brigade, 31st August to December, 1776; Major 6th Connecticut, 1st January, 1777; Lieutenant-Colonel, 15th October, 1778; transferred to 4th Connecticut, 1st January, 1781; transferred to 3d Connecticut, 1st January, 1783, and served to 3d June, 1783. (Died 18th June, 1795.)

Gray, Ebenezer (Mass). 2d Lieutenant 1st Massachusetts, 1st January, 1777; died 19th June, 1777.

Gray, Francis (Va). Ensign 6th Virginia, 15th October, 1780; 2d Lieutenant, 15th October, 1781; retired 1st January, 1783. (Died 24th April, 1827.)

Gray, Frederick (S. C.). Was a Lieutenant and Captain in a South Carolina Regiment in 1777 and 1778.

Gray, George (Va). Ensign 3d Virginia, 9th May, 1776; Lieutenant 4th Continental Dragoons, 10th January, 1777; Captain 7th December, 1777; resigned 12th May, 1779. (Died 1823.)

Gray, Henry (S. C.). 2d Lieutenant 2d South Carolina, 15th June, 1776; wounded at Sullivan's Island, 28th June, 1776; Paymaster 2d South Carolina, 14th December, 1777; Captain, — 1778; wounded at Savannah, 9th October, 1779; taken prisoner at Charleston, 12th May, 1780. (Died 20th July, 1824.)

Gray, Hugh (Mass). Private in Sargeant's Massachusetts Regiment, 24th April to December, 1775; 1st Lieutenant 10th Massachusetts, 6th November, 1776; killed at Saratoga, 3d August, 1777.

Gray, Isaac (Mass). Lieutenant in Lexington Alarm, April, 1775; Captain of Brewer's Massachusetts Regiment, May to December, 1775; Captain Massachusetts Militia in 1777. (Died 1787.)

Gray, James (N. H.). Sergeant-Major 1st New Hampshire, 23d April to December, 1775; Captain 3d New Hampshire, 8th November, 1776; retired 1st June, 1778; Major and Deputy Commissary-General of Issues, 19th October, 1778; resigned 16th November, 1780.

Gray, James (S. C.). 1st Lieutenant 2d South Carolina, ——; died 22d October, 1779, of wounds received at Savannah, 9th October, 1779.

Gray, James (Va). Captain 15th Virginia, 22d November, 1776; regiment designated 11th Virginia, 14th September, 1778, and served to ——. (Was in service in 1780.)

Gray, James Woolford (Md). Ensign 3d Maryland Battalion of the Flying Camp, 8th August, 1776; 3d Lieutenant, August, 1776; 1st Lieutenant 5th Maryland, 10th December, 1776; Captain, 25th December, 1777; taken prisoner at Savannah, 9th October, 1779; exchanged 10th February, 1781; transferred to 3d Maryland, 1st January, 1781; retained in Maryland Battalion, April, 1783, and served to 15th November, 1783; Brevet Major, 30th September, 1783.

Gray, John (Md). 2d Lieutenant 2d Maryland, 20th February, 1777; resigned 20th March, 1777.

Gray, John (Mass). 1st Lieutenant of Brewer's Massachusetts Regiment, May to December, 1775; Captain of Mitchell's Massachusetts Regiment in the Bagaduce Expedition, July to September, 1779. (Died 27th May, 1796.)

Gray, John (N. C.). Captain 3d North Carolina, 16th April, 1776; retired 1st June, 1778.

Gray, Matthew (Mass). 1st Lieutenant of Learned's Massachusetts Regiment, May, 1775, to ——.

Gray, Neigal (Pa). Lieutenant-Colonel 12th Pennsylvania, 5th October, 1776; cashiered, 2d June, 1778. (Died ——, 1786.)

Gray, Pardon (R. I.). Lieutenant-Colonel Rhode Island Militia in 1775.

Gray, Peter (S. C.). 1st Lieutenant 2d South Carolina, March, 1777; Captain, 30th December, 1778; taken prisoner at Charleston, 12th May, 1780; exchanged June, 1781, and served to close of war.

Gray, Richard (N. Y.). Captain New York Militia; was a prisoner; when and where taken not stated.

Gray, Robert (N. Y.). Ensign 1st Canadian (Livingston's) Regiment, 2d February, 1777; deserted 15th August, 1777, and joined the enemy.

Gray, Robert (Pa). Regimental Quartermaster Pennsylvania Musket Battalion, 22d March, 1776; Captain Pennsylvania State Regiment, 28th February, 1777; regiment designated 13th Pennsylvania, 12th November, 1777; retired 1st July, 1778.

Gray, Samuel (Pa). 2d Lieutenant 4th Pennsylvania, 3d January, 1777; retired 1st July, 1778.

Gray, Silas (N. Y.). 2d Lieutenant 4th New York, 21st November, 1776; 1st Lieutenant, 13th March, 1777; Captain, 11th April, 1780; retired 1st January, 1781; served subsequently as Captain New York Levies. (Died 19th January, 1820.)

Gray, Thomas (Conn). Surgeon's Mate of Douglas' Connecticut State Regiment, December, 1775, to March, 1776; Surgeon 4th Connecticut, 1st January, 1777; resigned 31st October, 1777.

Gray, Thomas (R. I.). Captain 3d Rhode Island, 28th June to December, 1775; served subsequently as Lieutenant-Colonel Rhode Island Militia. (Died ——, 1803.)

Gray, William (Pa). 1st Lieutenant 1st Battalion of Miles' Pennsylvania Rifle Regiment, 15th March, 1776; taken prisoner at Long Island, 27th August, 1776; exchanged 8th December, 1776; Captain 4th Pennsylvania, 3d January, 1777; retired 17th January, 1781. (Died 18th July, 1804.)

Gray, William (Va). Lieutenant 1st Continental Dragoons' ——; was a Captain in 1781, and served to ——.

Graybell, Philip (Md). Captain German Battalion, 8th July, 1776; resigned 12th March, 1778.

Graydon, Alexander (Pa). Captain 3d Pennsylvania Battalion, 5th January, 1776; taken prisoner at Fort

Washington, 16th November, 1776; paroled 7th July, 1777; exchanged 15th April, 1778, and rendered no further service. (Died 2d May, 1818.)

Graydon, Andrew (Pa). Ensign 3d Pennsylvania Battalion, 13th June, 1776; supposed to have been killed at Fort Washington, 16th November, 1776.

Grayson, John (S. C.). 1st Lieutenant 4th South Carolina (Artillery), 30th November, 1779; taken prisoner at Charleston, 12th May, 1780.

Grayson, Spence (Va). Chaplain of Grayson's Additional Continental Regiment, May, 1777; retired 22d April, 1779. (Died 1798.)

Grayson, William (Va). Assistant Secretary to General Washington, 21st June, 1776; Lieutenant-Colonel and Aide-de-Camp to General Washington, 24th August, 1776; Colonel of one of the Sixteen Additional Continental Regiments, 11th January, 1777; retired 22d April, 1779; Commissioner of the Board of War, 7th December, 1779; resigned 10th September, 1781. (Died 12th March, 1790)

Greaton, John (Mass). Lieutenant-Colonel of Heath's Massachusetts Regiment, 19th May, 1775; Colonel, 1st July, 1775; Colonel 24th Continental Infantry, 1st January, 1776; Colonel 3d Massachusetts, 1st November, 1776; Brigadier-General Continental Army, 7th January, 1783, and served to close of war. (Died 16th December, 1783.)

Greaton, John Wheelwright (Mass). Ensign 3d Massachusetts, 16th July, 1782; retained in Jackson's Continental Regiment, November, 1783, and remained in service to 20th June, 1784.

Greaton, Richard Humphrey (Mass). Ensign 3d Massachusetts, 30th November, 1781, and served to November, 1783; Lieutenant 2d United States Infantry, 4th March, 1791; wounded in action with Miami Indians near Fort Recovery, Ohio (St. Clair's defeat), 4th November, 1791; assigned to 2d Sub Legion, 4th September, 1792; Captain, 18th February, 1793; assigned to 2d United States Infantry, 1st November. 1796; honorably discharged 1st June, 1802. (Died 18th July, 1815.)

Greaves, John.—See Graves.

Greece, Ernest (Pa). Ensign 6th Pennsylvania, 15th February, 1777; taken prisoner at Short Hills, 26th June, 1777; made his escape and retired from service, 1st July, 1778; name also spelled Grace.

Green, Berryman (Va). Paymaster 1st Continental Dragoons, 31st March, 1777, with rank of Captain from 1st January, 1778; resigned 9th April, 1779.

Green, Burwell (Va). Ensign 14th Virginia, 30th August, 1777; resigned 18th June, 1778.

Green, Charles (Va). Surgeon Hospital Department, 1777-1781.

Green, David (Md). Ensign 7th Maryland, 26th January, 1780; retired 1st January, 1781.

Green, David (Mass). Colonel Massachusetts Militia, 1775.

Green, Ebenezer (N. H.). Captain of Bedel's Regiment New Hampshire Rangers, 22d January, 1776; taken prisoner at the Cedars, 19th May, 1776; held as a hostage to 1777, and was prisoner of war on parole to 9th February, 1782.

Green, Ezra (N. H.). Surgeon 3d New Hampshire, 27th June to December, 1775; Surgeon 2d Continental Infantry, 1st January to 31st December, 1776; Surgeon in United States Navy, October, 1777, to August, 1781. (Died 25th July, 1847.)

Green, Francis (Mass). 1st Lieutenant 1st Massachusetts, 1st January, 1777; Captain, 30th August, 1780, and served to 3d November, 1783. (Died 5th September, 1831.)

Green, Gabriel (Va). Ensign 6th Virginia, 12th October, 1780; 2d Lieutenant, 25th July, 1781; retired 1st January, 1783.

Green, James (Conn). Captain Connecticut Militia, 1776. (Died 1809.)

Green, James (Mass). Private in Lexington Alarm, April, 1775; Sergeant in Doolittle's Massachusetts Regiment, May to December, 1775; Quartermaster-Sergeant 13th Massachusetts, 6th January, 1777; Ensign and Regimental Quartermaster, 20th March, 1778; Lieutenant, 29th March, 1780; transferred to 6th Massachusetts, 1st January, 1781; resigned 13th July, 1781.

Green, James (Va). Ensign 6th Virginia, 13th October, 1780, to ——.

Green, James W. (N. C.). Surgeon's Mate 10th North Carolina, 10th June, 1778; Surgeon, 7th December 1779; taken prisoner at Charleston, 12th May, 1780; exchanged 14th June, 1781; transferred to 1st North Carolina, 6th February, 1782; served to close of war.

Green, Joel (Mass). Captain of Learned's Massachusetts Regiment, April to December, 1775

Green, Joel (Mass). 1st Lieutenant 6th Massachusetts, 1st January, 1777; discharged 9th May, 1778; Captain Massachusetts Militia, 1778-1779.

Green, John (Ga). Captain 1st Georgia, 7th January, 1776, and served to ——.

Green, John, (Mass). Sergeant 2d Continental Infantry, 1st January to 31st December, 1776; Ensign 8th Massachusetts, 1st January, 1777; 2d Lieutenant, 5th January, 1777; 1st Lieutenant, 1st April, 1779; dismissed 26th March, 1782.

Green, John (Pa). Ensign of Colonel McElvain's Regiment Pennsylvania Militia; taken prisoner at Bristol, Pennsylvania, 17th April, 1777; exchanged 26th March, 1781.

Green, John (Va). Captain 1st Virginia, 6th September, 1775; Major, 13th August, 1776; wounded at Mamaroneck-21st October, 1776; Lieutenant-Colonel, 22d March, 1777; Colonel, 10th Virginia, 26th January, 1778; transferred to 6th Virginia, 14th September, 1778; retired 1st January, 1783. (Died 1793.)

Green, John (Va). 2d Lieutenant 1st Virginia, — November, 1776; 1st Lieutenant, 12th August, 1777; died 29th April, 1778.

Green, Joseph (N. C.). Commissary 8th North Carolina, 11th December, 1776, to ——.

Green, Robert (Va). Ensign 6th Virginia, 11th October, 1780; 2d Lieutenant, 10th July, 1781; retired 1st January, 1783.

Green, Samuel Ball (Va). Lieutenant Virginia Militia, 1779-1782.

Green, Timothy (Pa). Captain 1st Pennsylvania Battalion of the Flying Camp, June to December, 1776.

Green, William (Conn). 1st Lieutenant of Ward's Connecticut State Regiment, 14th May, 1776; 1st Lieutenant 5th Connecticut, 1st January, 1777; Captain, 17th March, 1778; resigned 1st April, 1779.

Green, William (Mass). Adjutant of Prescott's Massachusetts Regiment, 19th May, 1775; wounded at Bunker Hill, 17th June, 1775. (Died 1810.)

Green, William (Mass). 1st Lieutenant 8th Massachusetts, 5th January, 1777; retired 1st January, 1781.

Green, William (N .Y.). 1st Lieutenant New York Militia, ——; killed 26th July, 1777; where not stated.

Green, William (N. C.). Captain 1st North Carolina, 1st September, 1775; resigned 4th January, 1776.

Green, William (N. C.). Ensign 6th North Carolina, 6th June, 1776; 2d Lieutenant, 28th October, 1776; 1st Lieutenant, 27th August, 1777; served to ——.

Green, Willis (Va). Ensign of Grayson's Additional Continental Regiment, 23d January, 1777; 2d Lieutenant, 8th June, 1777; resigned 18th April, 1778. (Died 1813.)

Greenawalt, Philip L. (Pa). Colonel Pennsylvania Militia, 1776-1777. (Died 1802.)

Greene, Benjamin (R. I.). Surgeon's Mate 3d Rhode Island, June to December, 1775.

Greene, Christopher (R. I.). Major of Varnum's Rhode Island Regiment, 3d May, 1775; Lieutenant-Colonel, ——; taken prisoner at Quebec, 31st December, 1775; Colonel 1st Rhode Island, 27th February, 1777, to rank from 1st January, 1777. By the Act of 4th November, 1777, it was "Resolved, that Congress have a high sense of the merit of Colonel Greene, and the officers and men under his command, in their late gallant defence of the Fort at Red Bank, on the Delaware River, and that an elegant sword be provided by the Board of War and presented to Colonel Greene." Killed 14th May, 1781, by Delancey's Tories in Westchester County, New York.

Greene, Daniel (R. I.). 2d Lieutenant of Tallman's Rhode Island State Regiment, 12th December, 1776; Ensign 1st Rhode Island, 11th April, 1777; taken prisoner 2d November, 1777; where not stated; died 30th April, 1778.

Greene, Griffin (R. I.). Paymaster 1st Rhode Island, 18th July, 1777; resigned 31st May, 1778.

Greene, Job (R. I.). 2d Lieutenant of Stanton's Rhode Island State Regiment, 12th December, 1776, to May, 1777.

Greene, John Morley (R. I.). Ensign 2d Rhode Island, 1st March, 1779; wounded at Springfield, 23d June, 1780; Lieutenant, ——, 1780; retained in Olney's Rhode Island Battalion, 14th May, 1781, and served to 15th December, 1783.

Greene, Nathaniel (R. I.). Brigadier-General Rhode Island troops, 3d May, 1775; Brigadier-General Continental

Army, 22d June, 1775; Major-General, 9th August, 1776; (Quartermaster-General, 2d March, 1778, to 30th September, 1780.) By the Act of 29th October, 1781, it was "Resolved, that the thanks of the United States in Congress assembled be presented to Major-General Greene, for his wise, decisive and magnanimous conduct in the action of the 8th of September last, near the Eutaw Springs, in South Carolina, in which, with a force inferior in number to that of the enemy, he obtained a most signal victory * * * that a British stand of colors be presented to Major-General Greene as an honorable testimony of his merit, and a golden medal emblematical of the battle and victory aforesaid."

By the Act of 17th January, 1783, it was "Resolved, that the thanks of the United States in Congress assembled be presented to Major-General Greene, for his many signal and important services, and that he be assured that Congress retain a lively sense of the frequent and uniform proofs he has given of prudence, wisdom and military skill during his command in the Southern Department."

By the Act of 18th October, 1783, it was "Resolved, that two pieces of the field ordnance taken from the British Army, at the Cowpens, Augusta, or Eutaw, be presented by the Commander-in-Chief of the Armies of the United States to Major General Greene, as a public testimony of the wisdom, fortitude and skill which distinguished his command in the Southern Department, and of the eminent services, which amidst complicated difficulties and dangers, and against an enemy greatly superior in numbers he has successfully performed for his country; and that a memorandum be engraved on said pieces of ordnance expressive of the substance of this resolution."

Served to 3d November, 1783. (Died 19th June, 1786)

Greene, William (Ga). Captain Georgia Militia; killed at Ogechee Ferry, 5th November, 1781.

Greenleaf, Moses (Mass). Captain 11th Massachusetts, 6th November, 1776; resigned 15th October, 1780.

Greenleaf, William (Mass). Private in Nixon's Massachusetts Regiment, May to December, 1775; Private 4th Continental Infantry, January to December, 1776; Corporal 13th Massachusetts, 16th February, 1777; Sergeant, 1st September, 1777; Ensign, 1st September, 1777; Lieutenant, 13th February,

1778; transferred to 6th Massachusetts, 1st January, 1781; transferred to 3d Massachusetts, 1st January, 1783, and served to 3d June, 1783. (Died 10th July, 1803.)

Greenlief, William (—). Surgeon's Mate Hospital Department in 1776.

Greenman, Jeremiah (R. I.). Sergeant 2d Rhode Island, 1st January, 1777; Ensign, 1st May, 1779; transferred to 1st Rhode Island, 1st January, 1781; Lieutenant, ——, 1781; retained in Olney's Rhode Island Battalion, 14th May, 1781; Adjutant, 1st October, 1782, and served to 15th December, 1783.

Greensburry, Thomas (N. C.). Captain 3d North Carolina, 16th April, 1776; resigned 28th December, 1777.

Greenup, Christopher (Va). 1st Lieutenant of Grayson's Continental Regiment, 2d February, 1777; resigned 1st April, 1778; was subsequently Colonel Virginia Militia. (Died 24th April, 1818.)

Greenway, George (Va). Sergeant 11th Virginia, 21st January, 1777; Ensign, 30th May, 1777; resigned 20th July, 1777.

Greenway, Joseph (Pa). Ensign 1st Continental Infantry, 20th January, 1776, to ——.

Greer, Charles (Va). Surgeon's Mate 4th Virginia, 1st August, 1777; taken prisoner at Brandywine, 11th September, 1777; rejoined regiment, 15th December, 1777; transferred to 3d Virginia, 14th September, 1778, and served to January, 1780; also mentioned in orders and correspondence as a Surgeon.

Greer, Henry (Pa). 2d Lieutenant of Captain Coran's Company Pennsylvania Artillery, 1st April, 1777; 2d Lieutenant, 22d July, 1779; transferred to Flower's Artillery Artificer Regiment, 1st January, 1781; 1st Lieutenant 4th Continental Artillery, 1st July, 1781, and served to 17th June, 1783.

Greer, John (Pa). Ensign Pennsylvania Militia; taken prisoner at his home in Bristol, 17th April, 1778.

Greer, Robert (N. C.). 2d Lieutenant 8th North Carolina, 28th November, 1776; 1st Lieutenant, 24th April, 1777; retired 1st June, 1778.

Greese, Ernest (Pa). Ensign 6th Pennsylvania, 15th February, 1777; retired 21st June, 1778.

Gregg, George (Pa). 2d Lieutenant 4th Pennsylvania Batalion, 8th January, 1776, to ——.

Gregg, James (N. Y.). 2d Lieutenant 3d New York, 28th June, 1775; 1st Lieutenant of DuBois' New York Regiment, 26th June, 1776; Captain 3d New York, 21st November, 1776; wounded and scalped by Indians near Kingston, New York, 13th October, 1777; transferred to 1st New York, 1st January, 1783, and served to 3d June, 1783.

Gregg, James (S. C.). Captain South Carolina Militia at the Siege of Charleston, — May, 1780.

Gregg, John (Pa) 2d Lieutenant Pennsylvania State Regiment, 18th April, 1777; regiment designated 13th Pennsylvania; 12th November, 1777; transferred to 2d Pennsylvania, 1st July, 1778; 1st Lieutenant, 12th March, 1779; resigned 3d September, 1779.

Gregg, Robert (Pa). Sergeant in Pennsylvania State Regiment, November, 1776; Ensign, 6th January, 1777; 2d Lieutenant, 3d February ,1777; cashiered 10th August, 1777.

Gregg, Robert (Pa). 1st Lieutenant 4th Pennsylvania Battalion, 5th January to 26th November, 1776; 1st Lieutenant 5th Pennsylvania, 1st January, 1777; Captain, 7th June, 1777; retired 1st July, 1778.

Gregg, William (N. H.). Major and Lieutenant-Colonel New Hampshire Militia, 1776 to 1780. (Died 16th September, 1815.)

Gregory, Dempsey (N. C.). Captain 10th North Carolina, 19th April, 1777; resigned 22d May, 1778.

Gregory, Isaac (N. C.). Brigadier-General North Carolina Militia; wounded at Camden, 16th August, 1780.

Gregory, Jabez (Conn). Captain Connecticut Militia, 1776.

Gregory, John (Va). Captain 15th Virginia, 19th November, 1776; regiment designated 11th Virginia, 14th September, 1778; resigned — May, 1779.

Gregory, John M. (Va). 2d Lieutenant 6th Virginia, 26th February, 1776; killed at Trenton, 2d January, 1777.

Gregory, Matthew (Conn). Sergeant 8th Connecticut, 10th June, 1777; Quartermaster-Sergeant, 15th October, 1778; Sergeant-Major, 18th November, 1778; Ensign, 10th April, 1779; transferred to 5th Connecticut, 1st January, 1781; Lieutenant, 28th December, 1781; transferred to 3d Connecticut, 1st January, 1782; retired 1st January, 1783.

Gregory, William (Va). Captain 6th Virginia, 26th February, 1776; died 30th May, 1776.

Grennell, John (N. Y.). Captain 2d New York, 28th June, 1775; Captain New York Artillery Company, 22d March, 1776; resigned 27th March, 1776.

Grice, Francis (Pa). 1st Lieutenant of Mifflin's Regiment Pennsylvania Militia; taken prisoner near Germantown, 25th September, 1777.

Gridley, John (Mass). 1st Lieutenant of Gridley's and Craft's Regiments Massachusetts Artillery in 1776; Captain Lieutenant 3d Continental Artillery, 1st January, 1777, and served to 3d June, 1783; Brevet Captain, 30th September, 1783. (Died 1st December, 1830.)

Gridley, Richard (Mass). Was a half-pay officer of the British Army when he entered the service of the United States as Colonel Massachusetts Artillery Regiment, May, 1775; wounded at Bunker Hill, 17th June, 1775; Colonel and Chief of the Continental Artillery, 20th September to 17th November, 1775; Colonel and Chief Engineer, June, 1775, to 5th August, 1776; was retained in service as Colonel and Engineer to 1st January, 1781, when retired. (Died 21st June, 1796.)

Gridley, Samuel (Mass). Captain of Gridley's Regiment Massachusetts Artillery, May, 1775, to July, 1775.

Gridley, Scarborough (Mass). Major of Gridley's Regiment Massachusetts Artillery, May, 1775; dismissed 24th September, 1775, for misconduct at Bunker Hill.

Grier, David (Pa). Captain 6th Pennsylvania Battalion, 9th January, 1776; Major 2d Pennsylvania Battalion, 1st June, 1776; Lieutenant-Colonel 7th Pennsylvania, 12th January, 1777, to rank from 2d October, 1776; severely wounded at Paoli, 20th September, 1777; never rejoined regiment. (Died 3d June, 1790)

Grier, James (Pa). 1st Lieutenant of Thompson's Pennsylvania Rifle Battalion, 25th June, 1775; 1st Lieutenant 1st Continental Infantry, 1st January, 1776; Captain, 7th March, 1776; Captain 1st Pennsylvania, 1st January, 1777, to rank from 7th March, 1776; wounded at Brandywine, 11th September, 1777; Major 10th Pennsylvania, 23d October, 1777; transferred to 6th Pennsylvania, 17th January, 1781; transferred to 3d Pennsylvania, 1st January, 1783, and served to November, 1783; Brevet Lieutenant-Colonel, 30th September, 1783. (Died 9th May, 1803.)

Grier, John (Pa). 1st Lieutenant 6th Pennsylvania Battalion, 9th January,

1776; taken prisoner 24th July, 1776, on the Sorrel River, Canada; exchanged in 1778, and did not return to the army.

Griffin, Corbin (Va). Hospital Surgeon 29th February, 1776, to 31st May, 1777. Volunteer Hospital Surgeon at Yorktown, Va., October, 1781.

Griffin, Jacob (N. Y.). Captain New York Militia, 1775; Lieutenant-Colonel New York Militia, 1778-1779. Died 1779.

Griffin, John (N. H.). 1st Lieutenant 2d New Hampshire, 23d May to December, 1775.

Griffin, Samuel (Va). Aide-de-Camp to General Lee, August, 1775; Colonel Deputy Adjutant-General Flying Camp, 19th July, 1776; wounded at Harlem Heights, 12th October, 1776.

Griffing, Daniel (N. Y.). Captain 3d New York, 28th June, 1775 to January, 1776.

Griffing, Stephen (N. Y.). Sergeant 4th New York, 6th February, 1777; Ensign, 1st June, 1779, to date from 1st January, 1778; resigned 2d April, 1781. (Died 1841.)

Griffith, Benjamin (Pa). 1st Lieutenant 9th Pennsylvania, 15th November, 1776; Resigned 30th November, 1777.

Griffith, Charles (Md). 2d Lieutenant 3d Maryland, 20th February, 1777; taken prisoner at Monmouth 28th June, 1778, and was a prisoner to close of war.

Griffith, Charles Greenberry (Md). Colonel 1st Maryland Battalion of the Flying Camp, July to December, 1776.

Griffith, David (Va). Surgeon and Chaplain 3d Virginia, 28th February, 1776; resigned 18th March, 1779. (Died 3d August, 1789.)

Griffith, John (Md). Ensign 1st Maryland Battalion of the Flying Camp, July to December, 1776; 1st Lieutenant 7th Maryland, 10th December, 1776; resigned 22d March, 1777.

Griffith, Joseph (S. C.). Captain South Carolina Militia, 1775-1776

Griffith, Levi (Pa). Ensign 4th Pennsylvania Battalion, 8th January, 1776; 1st Lieutenant 5th Pennsylvania, 1st January, 1777; retired 1st January, 1783. (Died 30th January, 1825.)

Griffith, Philemon (Va). Captain of Stephenson's Maryland and Virginia Rifle Regiment, 11th July, 1776; taken prisoner at Fort Washington, 16th November, 1776; exchanged in 1778; was appointed Captain in Rawling's

Continental Regiment in January, 1777, but does not appear to have joined it. (Died 29th April, 1838.)

Griffith, Samuel (Md) Captain 3d Maryland, 10th December, 1776; wounded at Marmouth, 28th June, 1778. Resigned 3d August, 1778. (Died 1833.)

Griggs, John (Mass). Ensign and Lieutenant in Danielson's Massachusetts Regiment, May to December, 1775.

Griggs, John (N H..). 2 Lieutenant of Bodel's New Hampshire Rangers, January, 1776; taken prisoner at the Cedars, 19th May, 1776; Captain 3d New Hampshire, 8th November, 1776. Resigned 4th May, 1777.

Grimball, Thomas (S. C.). Captain Lieutenant 4th South Carolina (Artillery), 17th June, 1775; Captain 12th May, 1776; Major ——, 1780; taken prisoner at Charleston, 12th May, 1780; on parole to August, 1780; then sent as prisoner to St. Augustine; released September, 1781, and served to close of war, ——.

Grimes, Benjamin (Va). Lieutenant of Grayson's Continental Regiment ——. Resigned 20th March, 1779.

Grimes, William (Va). Captain 15th Virginia 1st January, 1777. Died 1st August, 1777.

Grimke, John Faucherand (S. C.). Major and Aide-de-Camp to General Howe, 29th November, 1777, to August, 1778; Lieutenant-Colonel South Carolina Artillery, 20th June, 1779; taken prisoner at Charleston, 12th May, 1780. (Died 9th August, 1819.)

Griner, John (Ga). Captain Independent Georgia Company, 16th October, 1775 to ——.

Griswold, Adonijah (Conn). Lieutenant of Burrall's Connecticut State Regiment, June to November, 1776.

Griswold, Andrew (Conn). Corporal in the Lexington Alarm, April, 1775; Corporal 3d Connecticut, 5th May to 10th December, 1775; Ensign 4th Connecticut, 1st January, 1777; wounded at Germantown, 4th October, 1777; 2d Lieutenant 15th November, 1777; 1st Lieutenant, 5th June, 1778; transferred to 1st Connecticut, 1st January, 1781. Resigned 31st July, 1782. (Died 1st October, 1825.)

Griswold, George (Conn). 1st Lieutenant of Ward's Connecticut State Regiment, 14th May, 1776, to May, 1777. (Died — 1823.)

Griswold, Shubael (Conn). Captain 4th Connecticut, 1st May, to 10th December, 1775; Captain Connecticut Militia in 1779. (Died 1807.)

Griswold, Stephen (N. H.). Lieutenant New Hampshire Militia, 1777.

Groesbeck, Garret (N. Y.). Captain New York Militia, 1781-1783.

Groesbeck, John W. (N. Y.). Major New York Militia' in 1775.

Groesbeck, Walter N. (N. Y.). Captain New York Militia, 1775-1776.

Grometh, Jacob (Md). Ensign German Regiment, 12th July, 1776; 2d Lieutenant, 12th May, 1777; 1st Lieutenant, 4th January, 1778; retired 1st January, 1781. (Name also spelled Gomath.)

Groom, George (——). 1st Lieutenant of Rangers, ——; in service in 1779 and 1780.

Grosh, Adam (Md). 1st Lieutenant 1st Maryland Battalion of the Flying Camp, July to December, 1776; Captain 7th Maryland, 10th December, 1776; Major, 8th June, 1779. Resigned 7th April, 1780.

Gross, John (Pa). 1st Lieutenant 2d Pennsylvania Battalion, 5th January, 1776; Captain, 25th November, 1776; Captain, 3d Pennsylvania, 1st April, 1777; cashiered, 11th July, 1777. (Died 1823.)

Grosvenor, Leicester (Mass). Captain of Cady's Massachusetts Battalion on the expedition to Canada, January to June, 1776.

Grosvenor, Lemuel (Conn). Ensign of Mott's Connecticut State Regiment, June to December, 1776.

Grosvenor, Thomas (Conn). 2d Lieutenant 3d Connecticut, 23d May, 1775; wounded at Bunker Hill, 17th June, 1775; Captain 20th Continental Infantry, 1st January, 1776; Major 3d Connecticut, 1st January, 1777; Lieutenant-Colonel, 13th March, 1778; transferred to 1st Connecticut, 1st January, 1781; Lieutenant-Colonel Commandant, 29th May, 1782; reired 1st January, 1783. (Died 1825.)

Grout, Benjamin (N. H.). 2d Lieutenant of Bedel's Regiment New Hampshire Rangers, 22d January to October, 1776.

Grout, David (Mass). Sergeant in Lexington Alarm, April, 1775; Lieutenant Massachusetts Militia in 1776; 1st Lieutenant, 15th Massachusetts, 1st January, 1777; retired 23d April, 1779; Captain Massachusetts Militia in 1780.

Grout, Jacob (——). Captain ——; was a prisoner in 1776; when and where taken not stated.

Grover, Jonathan (Mass). Captain of Doolittle's Massachusetts Regiment, May to December, 1775.

Grover, Phineas (Conn). Sergeant 2d Connecticut, 3d May to 17th December, 1775; Ensign of Swift's Connecticut State Regiment, July to November, 1776; 2d Lieutenant 7th Connecticut, 1st January, 1777; 1st Lieutenant 2d December, 1777; Captain-Lieutenant, 5th October, 1780. Retired 1st January, 1781.

Grover, Thomas (N. H.). 1st Lieutenant 3d New Hampshire Regiment, 23d May, to December, 1775; 1st Lieutenant 2d Continental Infantry, 1st January, 1776; retired May, 1776.

Groves. See Graves.

Groves, William (N. C.). 1st Lieutenant 5th North Carolina, 16th April, 1776; Captain, 17th August, 1777; retired 1st June, 1778. (Name also spelled Graves.)

Grubb, Curtis (Pa). Colonel Pennsylvania Militia, 1776.

Grubb, Peter (Pa). 3d Lieutenant of Thompson's Pennsylvania Rifle Battalion, 17th July, 1775; resigned 10th September, 1775; Captain 2d Battalion of Miles' Pennsylvania Rifle Regiment, 12th March, 1776; Captain, 10th Pennsylvania, 27th November, 1776; Captain of Patton's Continental Regiment, 13th January, 1777; resigned 6th July, 1778.

Grymes, Benjamin (Va). 1st Lieutenant of Grayson's Additional Continental Regiment, 18th January 1777; resigned 26th March, 1779. (Died 1803.)

Grymes, William (Va). Captain 15th Virginia, 21st November, 1776. "Killed 1st August, 1777;" where not stated.

Guernsey, Joseph (Conn). Captain Connecticut Militia, 1776-1777.

Guerrant, John, Jr. (Va). Sergeant 2d Virginia, 1st August, 1777; Ensign, 1st January, 1779; Regimental Paymaster, 25th May to 25th November, 1779; Lieutenant ——, 1781; served to close of war. (Died 7th December, 1813.)

Guest, Isaac (Md). Quartermaster 2d Maryland Battalion of the Flying Camp, July, 1776, to ——.

Guild, Jonathan (Mass). 1st Lieutenant of Whitcomb's Massachusetts Regiment, May to December, 1775.

Guild, Joseph (Mass). Captain in Lexington Alarm, April, 1775; Captain of Heath's Massachusetts Regiment, April to November, 1775 Captain 24th Continental Infantry, 1st January to 31st December, 1776. (Died 1794.)

Guild, Ralph (N. J.). 2d Lieutenant 3d New Jersey, 7th February, 1776; resigned 17th February, 1776.

Guion, Isaac (N. Y.). 2d Lieutenant of Nicholson's Continental Regiment, March to November, 1776; 2d Lieutenant 2d Continental Artillery, 1st January, 1777; 1st Lieutenant, 12th September, 1778; Regimental Paymaster, 1st September, 1779; Captain-Lieutenant, 21st August, 1780; retired 3d June, 1783; Captain Infantry United States Army 5th March, 1792; assigned to 3d Sub Legion, 4th September, 1792, and to 3d United States Infantry, 1st November, 1796; Brigade-Inspector, 1st November, 1799, to 25th October, 1801; Major 3d United States Infantry, 15th February, 1801. Honorably discharged, 1st June, 1802. (Died 17th September, 1823.)

Guion, Isaac (N. C.). Surgeon 1st North Carolina, 1st September, 1775; resigned — December, 1775; Commissary and Paymaster 7th North Carolina, 11th March, 1776; retired 1st July, 1778.

Gunby, John (Md). Captain of a Maryland Independent Company, 14th January, 1776; Lieutenant-Colonel 7th Maryland, 10th December, 1776; Colonel, 17th April, 1777; transferred to 2d Maryland, 1st January, 1781; transferred to 1st Maryland, 1st January, 1783; retained as Colonel of the Maryland Battalion, April, 1783, and served to 15th December, 1783; Brevet Brigadier-General, 30th September, 1783.

Gunn, James (Va). Private and Sergeant 1st Continental Dragoons, January, 1777, to February, 1779; Lieutenant, February, 1779; Captain, ———. retired 9th November, 1782. (Died 30th July, 1801.)

Gunnison, Samuel (N. H.). Captain New Hampshire Militia in 1777.

Gurley, William (N. C.). Captain 8th North Carolina 28th November, 1776, to ———.

Gurney, Francis (Pa). Lieutenant-Colonel 11th Pennsylvania, 21st August, 1776; wounded at Iron Hill, 3d September, 1777; resigned 22d October, 1777. (Died 25th May, 1815.)

Gurney, Zachariah (Mass). 1st Lieutenant of Thomas' Massachusetts Regiment, May to December, 1775; Lieutenant in Marshall's Massachusetts Regiment, June to December, 1776. (Died 1813.)

Guthrie, George (Pa). Cornet of Cavalry, Pulaski Legion, — July, 1779; Lieutenant 4th Continental Dragoons, ———, 1781; served to close of war. (Name also spelled Guthrey.)

Guthrie, James (Pa). 2d Lieutenant 8th Pennsylvania, 9th August, 1776, to ———.

Guthrie, John (Pa). Ensign 8th Pennsylvania, 21st December, 1778; 2d Lieutenant, — February, 1780; retired 17th January, 1781; Captain of Gibson's Regiment of Levies, 1791; killed 4th November, 1791, at Fort Recovery, Ohio (St. Clair's defeat.)

Gwinnett, Button (Ga). A signer of the Declaration of Independence; was Governor of Georgia; wounded in a duel with General McIntosh, 16th May, 1777, of which he died 27th May, 1777.

Guy, Alexander (N. Y.). 2d Lieutenant 2d Continental Artillery, 1st January, 1777; cashiered, 8th February, 1778.

H.

Habacker, George. See Haubacker.

Habersham, John (Ga). 1st Lieutenant 1st Georgia, 7th January, 1776; Captain, 8th May, 1776; Brigadier-Major to General Howe, 25th December, 1777; Major 1st Georgia, 1st April, 1778; taken prisoner at Savannah, 29th December, 1778, and again taken prisoner at Briar Creek, 3d March, 1779, and served to close of war. (Died 17th December, 1799.)

Habersham, Joseph (Ga). Major 1st Georgia, 7th January, 1776; Lieutenant-Colonel, 5th July, 1776; Colonel, 17th September, 1776; resigned 31st March, 1778. (Died 17th November, 1815.)

Hackenberg, Peter (Pa). Ensign Pennsylvania Militia; was a prisoner in 1780; when and where taken not shown.

Hackett, Samuel (N. J.). Ensign 3d New Jersey, 5th November, 1776; 2d Lieutenant, 1st January, 1777; resigned 31st October, 1777.

Hackley, Henry (Pa). Ensign 5th Pennsylvania, 2d June, 1778; retired 1st July, 1778.

Hackley, John (Va). Sergeant 10th Virginia, 4th November, 1776; Ensign,

28th May, 1777; 2d Lieutenant, 10th July, 1777; 1st Lieutenant, 30th August, 1778; transferred to 6th Virginia, 14th September, 1778; transferred to 1st Virginia, 12th February, 1781; retired 1st January, 1783.

Hadaway, Joel (S. C.). 1st Lieutenant 1st South Carolina,——; on roll for March, 1781.

Hadden, Thomas (N. J.). Captain Major and Lieutenant-Colonel New Jersey Militia, 1777-1778.

Haden, Josiah.—See **Hayden.**

Hadley, Joshua (N. C.). 1st Lieutenant 6th North Coralina, 1st April, 1776; transferred to 1st North Carolina, 1st June, 1778; Captain ,13th June, 1779; wounded at Eutaw Springs, 8th September, 1781; served to close of war. (Died 8th February, 1830.)

Hagan, Francis (N. J.). Surgeon Hospital Department, 10th June, 1777; Hospital Surgeon and Physician, 6th October, 1780; resigned 25th May, 1781.

Hagan, John (N. J.). Ensign 3d New Jersey, 7th Feburary, 1776; 2d Lieutenant, April, 1776; resigned 19th July, 1776.

Hagan, Robert (N. J.). 1st Lieutenant 3d New Jersey, 9th February, 1776; resigned 19th July, 1776; Captain 3d New Jersey, 29th November, 1776; resigned 1st November, 1777.

Hager, Arthur (Ga). 1st Lieutenant of a Georgia Regiment in 1779 and 1780.

Hager, Jacob (N. Y.). Captain New York Militia, 1776-1777.

Haggett, Oliver (Mass). Ensign of Woodbridge's Massachusetts Regiment, May to December, 1775.

Haig, John James (S. C.). Paymaster 3d South Carolina, 24th November, 1778, to ——.

Haight, Benjamin (N. Y.). Lieutenant and Captain New York Militia, 1775-1780.

Haight, Joseph (N. J.). Major and Lieutenant-Colonel New Jersey Militia, 1777-1779.

Hain, Henry (Md). Private German Regiment, 18th July, 1776; Corporal, 1st March, 1777; Sergeant, 12th June, 1778; Ensign, 23d July, 1778; resigned 20th June, 1779.

Haines, Samuel (Pa). 1st Lieutenant of Lewis' Pennsylvania Battalion of the Flying Camp, July to December, 1776.

Hair, John L. (N. C.). Lieutenant 1st North Carolina, 16th August, 1777, to ——.

Hairwood, Peter (Mass). Captain of Learned's Massachusetts Regiment, May, 1775, to ——.

Hait, David (Conn). Captain Connecticut Militia in 1776.

Hait, Joseph (Conn). Captain 7th Connecticut, 6th July to 10th December, 1775; Captain 19th Continental Infantry, 1st January to 31st December, 1776; Major 8th Connecticut, 1st January, 1777; Lieutenant-Colonel, 15th September, 1777; transferred to 2d Connecticut, 28th October, 1779; retired 1st January, 1781.

Hait, Samuel (Conn). Sergeant 8th Connecticut, 13th May, 1777; Quartermaster-Sergeant, 15th December, 1778; Ensign, 5th May, 1779; 2d Lieutenant, 29th May, 1782; transferred to 3d Connecticut, 1st January, 1783, and served to 3d June, 1783.

Hait, Samuel (Conn). Ensign 5th Connecticut, 1st May to 5th October, 1775; 1st Lieutenant 17th Continental Infantry, 1st January to 31st December, 1776; Captain 5th Connecticut, 1st January, 1777; retired 1st January, 1781. (Died 30th December, 1832.)

Hake, John (——). Cornet Von Heer's Independent Company of Dragoons, 1st January, 1782, and served to June, 1783.

Hale, Aaron (Conn). Ensige 8th Connecticut, 6th July to 10th December, 1775; 2d Lieutenant 17th Continental Infantry, 1st January to 31st December, 1776; 1st Lieutenant 1st Connecticut, 1st January, 1777; retired 15th November, 1778. (Died 25th May, 1829.)

Hale, Enoch (N. H.). Colonel New Hampshire Militia, 1777 to 1780.

Hale, John (N. H.). Captain New Hampshire Militia in 1775; Surgeon 1st New Hampshire, 2d April, 1777; resigned 11th January, 1780. (Died 22d October, 1791.)

Hale, Isaac (Mass). Captain of Gardner's Massachusetts Regiment, May to December, 1775.

Hale, John (N. H.). 1st Lieutenant 1st New Hampshire, 23d April, 1775; Captain, 18th June to December, 1775; Captain 5th Continental Infantry, 1st January to 31st December, 1776; Captain New Hampshire Militia, 1777-1778. (Died 1813.)

Hale, Jonathan (Conn). Captain of Wolcott's Connecticut State Regiment, December, 1775. Died 7th March, 1776.

Hale, Jonathan (Mass). Captain Massachusetts Militia, 1777

Hale, Jonathan (N. H.). Major New Hampshire Militia in 1775.

Hale, Joseph (Conn). Ensign of Ward's Connecticut State Regiment, 14th May, 1776; taken prisoner at Fort Washington, 16th November, 1776.

Hale, Mordecai (N. Y.). Surgeon's-Mate 2d Continental Artillery, 1st December, 1782; transferred to Corps of Artillery, 17th June, 1783, and served to 3d November, 1783; Post Surgeon United States Army, 13th February, 1818; honorably discharged, 1st June, 1821; Assistant-Surgeon United States Army, 27th October, 1821; died 9th December, 1832.

Hale, Nathan (Conn). 1st Lieutenant 7th Connecticut, 6th July, 1775; Captain, 1st September to 10th December, 1775; Captain 19th Continental Infantry, 1st January, 1776; taken prisoner and hanged as a spy by the British, 22d September, 1776.

Hale, Nathan (N. H.). Captain New Hampshire Minute Men, 19th April, 1775; Major 3d New Hampshre, 23d April, 1775; Major 2d Continental Infantry, 1st January, 1776; Lientenant-Colonel 2d New Hampshire, 8th November 1776; Colonel, 2d April, 1777; taken prisoner at Hubbardton, 7th July, 1777, and died while in prison, 23 September, 1780.

Hale, Samuel (N. H.). Surgeon's-Mate New Hampshire Militia, 1777-1779.

Halkerstone, John (Md). 2d Lieutenant of Beall's Independent Maryland Company, 14th January, 1776; 1st Lieutenant, july, 1776, and served to ——.

Halkerstone, Robert (Md). Sergeant 3d Maryland, 5th February, 1777; Ensign 4th Maryland, 26th January, 1780; transferred to 1st Maryland, 1st January, 1781; 2d Lieutenant, 25th April, 1781; retained in Maryland Battalion, April, 1783, and served to 15th November, 1783. (Died 17th February, 1825.)

Hall, Alexander (Pa). 2d Lieutenant of Lewis' Pennsylvania Battalion of the Flying Camp, July to December, 1776.

Hall, Aquilla (Md). Captain Maryland Militia, 1775; Colonel of same, 1776-1779. (Died 1779.)

Hall, Asaph (Conn). 1st Lieutenant 4th Connecticut, 1st May to December, 1775. (Died 1800.)

Hall, Caleb (Conn). Captain Connecticut Militia, 1776-1777.

Hall, Clement (N. C.). 1st Lieutenant 2d North Carolina, 1st September, 1775; Captain, 19th April, 1777; Brevet Major, 30th September, 1783; served to close of war.

Hall, David (Del). Captain Delaware Regiment, 15th January, 1776; Colonel, 5th April, 1777; wounded at Germantown, 4th October, 1777; did not rejoin regiment on account of wounds, and was retired 17th May, 1782; was subsequently Governor of Delaware. (Died 18th September, 1817.)

Hall, Edward (N. J.). Major New Jersey Militia in 1776.

Hall, Edward (Va). 1st Lieutenant of Grayson's Continental Regiment, — February, 1777; taken prisoner at Staten Island, 22d August, 1777; exchanged 5th November, 1780, and did not return to service.

Hall, Elias (Mass). Ensign of Learnel's Massachusetts Regiment, May to December, 1775.

Hall, Elihu (Md). Ensign 1st Maryland, 17th April, 1777; taken prisoner at Staten Island, 22d August, 1777; exchanged 25th October, 1780; promoted 1st Lieutenant to rank from 15th July, 1779; resigned 12th May, 1781; served subsequently as Lieutenant-Colonel Maryland Militia. (Died 1790.)

Hall, Elisha (Conn). Captain-Commander Militia, 1776-1777.

Hall, Highland (Conn). Sergeant of Webb's Continental Regiment, 12th February, 1777; Issuing-Commissary Connecticut Brigade, 15th November, 1778; retired 31st March, 1780.

Hall, Isaac (Mass). Captain of Company Minute Men in the Lexington Alarm, April, 1775; Captain of Gardner's Massachusetts Regiment, April to December, 1775. (Died 1778.)

Hall, Jacob Jr. (Mass). Surgeon's-Mate, 14th Massachusetts, 18th June, 1778; Surgeon 3d New Hampshire, 1st October, 1778; resigned 5th April, 1781.

Hall, James (Mass). Sergeant in Knox's Regiment Continental Artillery, February to December, 1776; 2d Lieutenant 3d Continental Artillery, 1st January, 1777; 1st Lieutenant, 12th September, 1777; Captain-Lieutenant, 12th April, 1780, and served to close of war. (Died 3d April, 1819.)

Hall, James (N. C.). Captain 9th North Carolina, ——, 1777, to ——;

was Lieutenant-Colonel North Carolina Militia, and was killed at Cowan's Ford, 1st February, 1781.

Hall, John (S. C.). Lieutenant and Regimental Quartermaster 2d South Carolina, 1st July, 1776; resigned in December, 1776, and joined the enemy; was captured and hanged for treason at Ninety-Six 17th April, 1779.

Hall, John B. (Md). 1st Lieutenant 2d Maryland Battalion of the Flying Camp, July, 1776, to ——.

Hall, Josias Carvil (Md). Colonel 2d Maryland Battalion of the Flying Camp, July to December, 1776; Colonel 4th Maryland, 10th December, 1776; retired 1st January, 1781. (Died 1814.)

Hall, Levi (R .I.). Lieutenant-Colonel Rhode Island Militia, 1775-1776.

Hall, Lyman (Ga). A signer of the Declaration of Independence; was subsequently Governor of Georgia. (Died 19th October, 1790.)

Hall Matthew (Mass). Corporal in the Lexington Alarm, April, 1775; Sergeant in Paterson's Massachusetts Regiment, May to December, 1775; ensign 15th Continental Infantry, 1st January, 1776; 2d Lieutenant, 12th September to 31st December, 1776; 1st Lieutenant of Sherburnes Continental Regiment, 14th January, 1777. Died 12th August, 1777.

Hall, Moses (Conn). 1st Lieutenant 8th Connecticut, 6th July to 18th December, 1775.

Hall, Nathaniel (Conn). Ensign 6th Connecticut, 1st May, 1775; 2d Lieutenant, 1st July to 10th December 1775; 1st Lieutenant 10th Continental Infantry, 1st January to 31st December, 1776. (Died 4th November, 1821.)

Hall, Noah (Mass). 1st Lieutenant of Walker's Massachusetts Regiment, May to December, 1775; Captain Massachusetts Militia, 1776-1780. (Died May, 1835.)

Hall, Philemon (Conn). Private 1st Connecticut, 1st May to 28th November, 1775; Ensign 7th Connecticut, 1st January, 1777; 2d Lieutenant, 10th March, 1778; 1st Lieutenant, 12th March, 1780; transferred to 2d Connecticut, 1st January, 1781; retired 1st January, 1783.

Hall, Robert (N. C.). Surgeon 3d North Carolina, 17th April, 1776; resigned 28th February, 1777.

Hall, Samuel (Conn). Captain Connecticut Light Horse in 1776.

Hall, Stephen (Conn). 1st Lieutenant 1st Connecticut, 1st May to 20th December, 1775; 1st Lieutenant 10th Continental Infantry, 31st December, 1776; Captain 7th Connecticut, 1st January, 1777; retired 1st January, 1781. (Died 25th April, 1783.)

Hall, Street (Conn). Lieutenant-Colonel 7th Connecticut, 6th July to 19th December, 1775; Lieutenant-Colonel 19th Continental Infantry, 1st January to 31st December, 1776.

Hall, Tallmadge (Conn). Private 5th Connecticut, 9th May to 30th October, 1775; Sergeant 7th Connecticut, 1st January, 1777; Ensign, 25th September, 1777; wounded at Stony Point, 16th July, 1779; Lieutenant Invalid Regiment, 16th September, 1780, and served to 23d April, 1783.

Hall, Thomas (N. J.). Captain and Major New Jersey Militia, 1776-1777.

Hall, Thomas (N. C.). Ensign 1st North Carolina, 24th December, 1776; 2d Lieutenant, 8th February, 1777; resigned 3d April, 1777.

Hall, Thomas (S. C.). 2d Lieutenant 2d South Carolina, 17th June, 1775; 1st Lieutenant, — May, 1776; wounded at Sullivan's Island, 28th June, 1776; Captain, 1st August, 1779, and served to ——.

Hall, Timothy (Mass). Surgeon's Mate 5th Massachusetts, 5th February, 1780; retired 1st January, 1781. (Died 1844.)

Hall, Titus (Conn). Private in the Lexington Alarm, April, 1775; Sergeant of Baldwin's Artillery Artificer Regiment, 10th April, 1777; 2d Lieutenant, 1st July, 1779; retired, 1st January, 1781. (Died 23d January, 1824.)

Hall, William (N. J.). Sergeant of Baldwin's Artillery Artificer Regiment, 10th December, 1777; Lieutenant, 1st July, 1779; resigned 20th October, 1780.

Hall, William (N. C.). Captain North Carolina Militia, 1779-1781; served as Colonel and Brigadier-General Tennessee Militia during the war of 1812. (Died 3d June, 1825.)

Hallam, Edward (Conn). 2d Lieutenant of Seldon's Connecticut State Regiment, June to December, 1776.

Hallam, Robert (Conn). Sergeant in the Lexington Alarm, April, 1775; 2d Lieutenant 20th Continental Infantry, 1st January to 31st December, 1776; 1st Lieutenant 4th Connecticut, 1st January, 1777; Captain, 31st July, 1777; resigned 20th May, 1779. (Died March, 1835.)

Haller, Henry (Pa). Colonel Pennsylvania Battalion of the Flying Camp in 1776.

Hallett, James (N. J.). 2d Lieutenant 4th New Jersey, 28th November, 1776; 1st Lieutenant, 17th February, 1777; resigned, 1st October, 1777; served subsequently in New Jersey Militia.

Hallett, Jonah (N. Y.). Ensign New York Militia Regiment, 18th June, 1776; 2d Lieutenant of Malcolm's Continental Regiment, 26th July, 1777; resigned 23d April, 1779; Lieutenant 4th Continental Dragoons, 2d October, 1779, and served to November, 1782.

Hallett, Jonathan (N. Y.). 2d Lieutenant 3d New York, July, 1775; 1st Lieutenant and Adjutant, March, 1776; Captain 2d New York, 21st November, 1776, and served to 3d June, 1883.

Halling, Solomon (N C.). Surgeon 4th North Carolina in 1779 to close of war.

Halsey, Elias Henry (Conn). Captain Connecticut Militia, ——; killed at Groton Heights, 6th September, 1781.

Halsey, Jeremiah (Conn). Sergeant in the Lexington Alarm, April, 1775; 2d Lieutenant 6th Connecticut, 1st May, 1775; discharged on account of sickness, 13th November, 1775; Captain Connecticut Militia Regiment, 1776 and 1777.

Halsey, Luther (N. J.). Sergeant 2d New Jersey, November, 1775; Regimental Adjutant 2d New Jersey, 28th November, 1776; Lieutenant, 9th November, 1777; retained in New Jersey Battalion, April, 1783; Brevet Captain, 30th September, 1783, and served to 3d November, 1783. (Died 27th February, 1830.)

Halstead, Benjamin (N. Y.). Lieutenant New York Militia; taken prisoner at Fort Montgomery, 6th October, 1777.

Halstead, Caleb (N. J.). Hospital Physician and Surgeon, 1779-1781. (Died 1827.)

Halsted, John (—). Appointed Commissary for the Army before Quebec, 17th February, 1776, and served to ——.

Halsted, Mathias (N. J.). Regimental Quartermaster, 1st New Jersey, 20th December, 1775; resigned 25th August, 1776; served subsequently as Brigade Major and Aide-de-Camp to General Dickinson.

Halsted, Robert (N. J.). Surgeon New Jersey Militia; taken prisoner at Fort Lee, New Jersey, 18th November, 1776. (Died 1825.)

Ham, William (R. I.). 2d Lieutenant of Elliott's Regiment Rhode Island State Artillery, 12th December, 1776, to May, 1777.

Hambleton, John (Va). 1st Lieutenant 13th Virginia, 16th November, 1776; regiment designated 9th Virginia, 14th September, 1778; resigned 23d November, 1778.

Hambleton, William (Md). Major Maryland Militia, 1778-1782.

Hambright, Frederick (N. C.). Captain North Carolina Militia, 1776; Lieutenant-Colonel North Carolina Riflemen Militia; wounded at King's Mountain, 7th October, 1780. (Died — March, 1817.)

Hambright, Henry (Pa). Captain 1st Pennsylvania Battalion of the Flying Camp, June, 1776; taken prisoner at Fort Washington 16th November, 1776; exchanged 4th November, 1780. (Died 2d March, 1835.)

Hambright, John (Pa). Sergeant-Major 10th Pennsylvania, February, 1777; Ensign, 2d June, 1778; resigned ——, 1779; served subsequently as Captain Pennsylvania Militia.

Hamill, Samuel (Pa). 2d Lieutenant of Montgomery's Pennsylvania Battalion of the Flying Camp, July to December, 1776.

Hamilton, Alexander (N. Y.). Captain Provincial Company New York Artillery, 14th March, 1776; Lieutenant-Colonel and principal Aide-de-Camp to General Washington, 1st March, 1777, to 23d December, 1783; Brevet Colonel, 30th September, 1783; Major-General and Inspector-General United States Army, 19th July, 1798; honorably discharged 15th June, 1800. (Mortally wounded in a duel with Aaron Burr, 11th July, and died 12th July, 1804.)

Hamilton, Andrew (S. C.). Captain and Major South Carolina Militia, 1775-1781. (Died 1835.)

Hamilton, David (Mass). 1st Lieutenant in the Lexington Alarm, April, 1775; 1st Lieutenant of Danielson's Massachusetts Regiment, May to December, 1775; served subsequently in Massachusetts Militia.

Hamilton, Edward (Md). Ensign 2d Maryland, 1st August, 1781; 2d Lieutenant, 8th September, 1781; retired 1st January, 1783.

Hamilton, George (Md). Ensign Maryland Battalion of the Flying Camp,

July to December, 1776; 1st Lieutenant 5th Maryland, 10th December, 1776; Captain, 25th January, 1778; taken prisoner at Camden, 16th August, 1780; transferred to 4th Maryland, 1st January, 1781; retained in Maryland Battalion, April, 1783, and served to 15th November, 1783. (Died 1798.)

Hamilton, Hanse (N. C.). Surgeon 7th North Carolina, — April, 1777, to ——.

Hamilton, James (N. Y.). Regimental Quartermaster 3d New York, 30th June, 1775, to January, 1776.

Hamilton, James (Pa). 2d Lieutenant 2d Battalion of Miles' Pennsylvania Rifle Regiment, 16th March, 1776, and served to ——. (Was in service in October, 1776.)

Hamilton, James (Pa). Captain 1st Continental Infantry, 10th March, 1776; Captain 1st Pennsylvania, 1st January, 1777, to rank from 10th March, 1776; taken prisoner at Brunswick, 24th December, 1777; Major 2d Pennsylvania, 10th December, 1778; retired 1st January, 1783.

Hamilton, James (S. C.). Paymaster South Craolina Dragoons, 5th April to September, 1781.

Hamilton, James (Va). Ensign 10th Virginia, 3d December, 1776; 2d Lieutenant, 23d March, 1777; taken prisoner at Brandywine, 11th September, 1777; 1st Lieutenant, 13th January, 1778; regiment designated 6th Virginia, 14th September, 1778; taken prisoner at Charleston, 12th May, 1780, and was on parole until retired, 1st January, 1783.

Hamilton, John (Md). Regimental Paymaster 4th Maryland, 27th May, 1778; 1st Lieutenant, 1st June, 1779; transferred to 1st Maryland, 1st January, 1781; retired 1 st January, 1783.

Hamilton, John (S. C.). 2d Lieutenant and Adjutant 1st South Carolina, ——, 1777; Brigade Major to Colonel Pinckney, 10th May, 1778; wounded at Stono Ferry, 20th June, 1779; 1st Lieutenant, 30th July, 1779; taken prisoner at Charleston, 12th May, 1780

Hamilton, John (Va). Captain 13th Virginia, 16th December, 1776; regiment designated 9th Virginia, 14th September, 1778; resigned 23d November, 1778

Hamilton, John (Va). Lieutenant Virginia Militia, 1778-1779

Hamilton, John A. (Md). Ensign 4th Maryland, 10th December, 1776; 2d

Lieutenant, 28th May, 1777; 1st Lieutenant, 1st February, 1778; transferred to 2d Maryland, 1st January, 1781; Captain, 25th October, 1781; retired 1st January, 1783.

Hamilton, Joseph (S. C.). Captain South Carolina Artillery Company in 1775.

Hamilton, Robert (Mass). Lieutenant of Woodbridge's Massachusetts Regiment, May to December, 1775.

Hamilton, Robert (Pa). Ensign 3d Pennsylvania, 3d May, 1779; retired 17th October ,1780.

Hamilton, Samuel (Md). Ensign 6th Maryland, 27th May, 1779; resigned 10th July, 1780.

Hamilton, Thomas (Pa). Ensign 12th Pennsylvania, 16th October, 1776; 2d Lieutenant, 28th March, 1777; resigned 26th January, 1778.

Hamilton, Thomas (Va). Captain 1st Virginia State Regiment, 3d March, 1777, to January, 1781. (Died 1786.)

Hamlin, Africa (Mass). Corporal 4th Massachusetts, 1st June, 1777; Sergeant, 1st September, 1777; Ensign, 1st January, 1781, and served to 1st November, 1783.

Hamlin, Daniel (Conn). Sergeant of Webb's Additional Continental Regiment, 24th May, 1777; Ensign 16th May,1778; dismissed 5th January, 1779.

Hamlin, Eleazer (Mass). Captain of Thomas' Massachusetts Regiment, May to December, 1775; Captain 23d Continental Infantry, 1st January, 1776, to ——.

Hamlin, Nathaniel (Conn). 1st Lieutenant of Gay's Connecticut State Regiment, 20th June to 25th December, 1776.

Hamlin, William (Va). 1st Lieutenant 4th Virginia, 21st March, 1776, to ——.

Hamman, James (N. Y.). Lieutenant-Colonel New York Militia; taken prisoner, when and where not stated; was Colonel New York Militia, 1779-1780.

Hammett, Malachai (R. I.). 1st Lieutenant of Richmond's Rhode Island State Regiment, 1st November, 1775; Captain, 19th August, 1776; Captain of Stanton's Rhode Island State Regiment, 12th December, 1776, to June, 1777.

Hammit, John (N. J.). 1st Lieutenant of Spencer's Continental Regiment, 7th March, 1777; omitted March, 1779.

Hammon Frederick (Mass). Private 10th Massachusetts, 17th March, 1777; Corporal 1st July, 1779; Sergeant, 1st April, 1780; Ensign, 12th December, 1780; resigned 1st August, 1782.

Hammond, — (Mass). Ensign 10th Massachusetts; resigned 1st August, 1782.

Hammond, Abijah (Mass). 2d Lieutenant 3d Continental Artillery, 1st January, 1777; 1st Lieutenant, 2d December, 1778, and served to June, 1783. (Died 30th December, 1832.)

Hammond, Andrew (Md). Ensign 3d Maryland Battalion of the Flying Camp, July, 1776, to ——.

Hammond, Benjamin (Pa). 2d Lieutenant 11th Pennsylvania, 30th September, 1776; 1st Lieutenant 21st April, 1777; killed 20th February, 1778, where and how not stated.

Hammond, David (Pa). Sergeant 1st Continental Infantry, 1st January to 31st December, 1776; 2d Lieutenant 1st Pennsylvania, 13th May, 1777; 1st Lieutenant, 8th December, 1778; wounded at Block House, 21st July, 1780; transferred to 3d Pennsylvania, 1st January, 1783; served to June, 1783. (Died 27th April, 1801)

Hammond, Edward (Mass). Captain Company of Minute Men in Lexington Alarm, April, 1775; Captain of Cotton's Massachusetts Regiment, May to December, 1775; served subsequently as Lieutenant-Colonel and Colonel-Major Militia.

Hammond, Elisha (Mass). Ensign 5th Massachusetts, 1st January, 1777; Regimental Quartermaster, 7th November, 1777, to 5th April, 1780; 2d Lieutenant, 1st April, 1779; 1st Lieutenant, 14th October, 1780; resigned 19th May, 1782.

Hammond, George (N. C). Lieutenant North Carolina Militia; wounded at Eutaw Springs, 8th September, 1781.

Hammond, John (S. C). Captain South Carolina Militia, 1775-1776.

Hammond, Joseph (N. H.). Lieutenant-Colonel New Hampshire Militia, 1777.

Hammond, Le Roy (S. C). Colonel South Carolina Militia, 1776 to 1781.

Hammond, Samuel (Va). Major Virginia Militia at Kings Mountain, October, 1780; wounded at Black Storks, 20th November, 1780, and at Eutaw Springs, 8th September, 1781. (Died 11th September, 1842.)

Hammond, Thomas (Md). Captain 3d Maryland Battalion of the Fying Camp, July, 1776, to ——.

Hamner, Francis (N. Y.). Ensign 5th New York, 21st November, 1776; Regimental Quartermaster, 14th July, 1780; retired 1st January, 1781.

Hampton, Andrew (N. C). Captain North Carolina Militia in 1776, and Colonel North Carolina Militia at Kings Mountain, October, 1780. (Died 8th October, 1805.)

Hampton, Edward (S. C). 2d Lieutenant 2d South Carolina, November, 1776; 1st Lieutenant, 23d January, 1778; killed at Fair Forrest Creek, N. C., in October, 1780.

Hampton, Henry (S. C). Captain 6th South Carolina in 1779 and was Lieutenant-Colonel South Carolina Dragoons April to September, 1781.

Hampton, John (N. J.). Captain New Jersey Militia; taken prisoner at Brunswick, 26th October, 1777; exchanged, — October, 1780.

Hampton, John (S. C). Captain South Carolina Dragoons ——, 1779, to ——.

Hampton, Wade (S. C). Lieutenant and Paymaster 1st South Carolina in 1776; Captain in 1777; Colonel South Carolina Militia, commanding a Brigade under General Sumter in 1781; Colonel Light Dragoons U. S. A., 10th October, 1808; Brigadier-General, 15th February, 1809; Major-General, 2d March, 1813; resigned 16th March, 1814. (Died 4th February, 1835.)

Hamtramck John Francis (N. Y.). Captain 5th New York, 21st November, 1776; transferred to 2d New York, 1st January, 1783; Captain United States Infantry Regiment, 12th April, 1785; Major, 20th October, 1786; Major 1st Infantry United States Army, 29th September, 1789; assigned to 2d Sub Legion, 4th September, 1792; Lieutenant-Colonel Commandant 1st Sub Legion, 18th February, 1793; assigned to 1st United States Infantry, 1st November, 1796; Colonel, 1st April, 1802; died 11th April, 1803.

Hanchet, Oliver (Conn). Lieutenant in the Lexington Alarm, April, 1775; Captain 2d Connecticut, 1st May, 1775; taken prisoner at Quebec, 31st December, 1775; exchangd 10th January, 1777.

Hancock, Belcher (Mass). Corporal in Lexington Alarm, April, 1775; Ensign 15th Continental Infantry, 1st January to 31st December, 1776; 1st Lieutenant 1st Massachusetts, 1st January, 1777;

Captain-Lieutenant, 18th March, 1779; Captain, 6th January, 1780; resigned 2d November, 1780. (Died 14th May, 1813.)

Hancock, Ebenezer (Mass). Deputy Paymaster-General, 12th June, 1776, and served to ——. (Died 1819.)

Hancock, George (Ga). Captain 2d Georgia, 1778-1782.

Hancock, John (Ga). Captain 2d Georgia ——; on roll for August, 1778.

Hancock, John (Mass). A signer of the Declaration of Independence; Major-General Massachusetts Militia, 1776; subsequently Governor of Massachusetts. (Died 8th October, 1793.)

Hand, Abraham (Conn). Private and Sergeant Baldwin's Artillery Artificer Regiment, 26th February, 1777, to 1st November, 1779; Lieutenant 1st November, 1779; retired 1st January, 1781.

Hand, Daniel (Conn). Captain Connecticut Militia in 1776. (Died 1816.)

Hand, Edward (Pa). Lieutenant-Colonel of Thompson's Pennsylvania Rifle Battalion, 25th June, 1775; Lieutenant-Colonel 1st Continental Infantry, 1st January, 1776; Colonel, 7th March to 31st December, 1776; Colonel 1st Pennsylvania, 1st January, 1777, to rank from 7th March, 1776; Brigadier-General Continental Army, 1st April, 1777; Adjutant-General Continental Army, 8th January, 1781; to 3d November, 1783; Brevet Major-General, 30th September, 1783; Maor-General United States Army, 19th July, 1798; honorably discharged, 15th June, 1800. (Died 3d September, 1802.)

Hand, Elijah (N. J.). Lieutenant and Colonel New Jersey Militia, 1777-1779.

Hand, Henry (N. J.). Lieutenant-Colonel New Jersey Militia in 1776.

Hand, John (N. J.). Major New Jersey Militia, 1776-1780.

Handcock, William (N. C.). Ensign 6th North Carolina, 28th April, 1777; 2d Lieutenant, 1st August, 1777; resigned 27th August, 1777.

Handley, George (Ga). 1st Lieutenant 1st Georgia, 7th January, 1776; Captain, 19th October, 1776; taken prisoner at Augusta, 18th September, 1780; served to close of war; Brevet Major, 30th September, 1783. (Died 17th September, 1793.)

Handy, George (Md). Ensign 5th Maryland, 17th April, 1777; Lieutenant, 10th May, 1777; resigned 26th August, 1778; Lieutenant of Lee's Battalion of Light Dragoons, 1st July, 1779; Captain, 20th November, 1780; served to close of war.

Handy, John (R. I.). Regimental Quartermaster of Richmond's and Tallman's Rhode Island State Regiments, 15th January, 1776, to January, 1777. (Died 2d March, 1828.)

Handy, Levin (Md). 2d Lieutenant 4th Maryland Battalion of the Flying Camp, June, 1776; 1st Lieutenant, August, 1776; Captain 5th Maryland, 10th December, 1776; resigned 1st May, 1780.

Hankinson, Aaron (N. J.). Colonel New Jersey Militia, 1777.

Hannah, James (Pa). Ensign 1st Pennsylvania, 1st May, 1777, to ——.

Hannah, Stephen (Pa). 3d Lieutenant 2d Battalion of Miles' Pennsylvania Rifle Regiment, 19th March, 1776; 2d Lieutenant 6th December, 1776, but declined further service.

Hannum Gideon (Mass). Regimental Quartermaster of Woodbridge's Massachusetts Regiment, May to December, 1775.

Hannum, John (Pa). Colonel Pennsylvania Militia in 1777; was a prisoner in 1780; when and where taken not stated. (Died 1799.)

Hansbrough, James (Va). Quartermaster-Sergeant 3d Virginia, 15th August, 1776; Regimental Quartermaster 3d Virginia, September, 1777; resigned 10th February, 1778.

Hansford, Cary H. (Va). Surgeon's Mate Hospital Department, 1780-1781.

Hanson, Aaron (N. H). 2d Lieutenant 2d Continental Infantry 1st January to 31st December, 1776.

Hanson, Alexander Contee (Md). Assistant Secretary to General Washington 21st June, 1776, and served to ——. (Died 1806.)

Hanson, Dirck (N. Y.). 1st Lieutenant 2d New York, 28th June, 1775; Captain of Nicholson's New York Regiment, 15th April, 1776 Captain 1st Canadian |Livingston's) Regiment, 18th December, 1776, to rank from 15th April, 1776; retired 1st January, 1781.

Hanson, Henry (N. Y.). Lieutenant of Wempell's Regiment New York Militia; killed 2d May, 1780; where not stated.

Hanson, Isaac (Md). Ensign 4th Maryland, 8th November, 1779; Lieutenant, 15th December, 1779; wounded and taken prisoner at Camden, 16th August, 1780.

Hanson, Peter Contee (Md). 2d Lieutenant 1st Maryland Battalion of the Flying Camp, July, 1776; 1st Lieutenant of Stephenson's Maryland Rifle Battalion, 17th September, 1776; wounded and taken prisoner at Fort Washington, 16th November, 1776, and died in New York, December, 1776, while a prisoner.

Hanson, Samuel (Md). Ensign 1st Maryland, 24th July, 1777; Regimental Quartermaster, 1st October, 1778; Lieutenant, 15th July, 1779; transferred to 5th Maryland, 1st January, 1781; retired, April, 1783.

Hanson, Samuel (Md). Surgeon at General Washington's Headquarters, 1st March, 1778; resigned 26th March, 1779. (Died 29th June, 1781.)

Hanson, Thomas (Md.) Captain 3d Maryland Battalion of the Flying Camp, July to December, 1776.

Hanson, Thomas (Pa). Adjutant 12th Pennsylvania, 16th October, 1776; died 13th August, 1777.

Hanson, William (Md). 2d Lieutenant 2d Maryland, 25th October, 1781; transferred to 4th Maryland, 1st January, 1783; retained in Maryland Battalion, April, 1783, and served to 15th November 1783.

Hard, Philo (N. H.). 2d Lieutenant Green Mountain Boys, 27th July to December, 1775.

Hardaway, Joel (S. C.). 1st Lieutenant 3d South Carolina, — May, 1776, to ——.

Hardcastle, Peter (Md). Sergeant 6th Maryland, 10th December, 1776; Ensign, 10th February, 1777; 2d Lieutenant, 30th November, 1777; 1st Lieutenant, 14th September, 1778; transferred to 4th Maryland, 1st January, 1781; resigned, 12th September, 1782.

Harden, Elias (Md). Captain Maryland Militia in 1776.

Harden, William (S. C.). Captain South Carolina Artillery Company, 17th June, 1775; Colonel Georgia Militia; captured British party at Four Holes, S. C., 7th April, 1781.

Hardenbergh, Abraham (N. Y.). Ensign 4th New York, May, 1776; 2d Lieutenant 1st New York 21st November, 1776, and served to June, 1783.

Hardenbergh, Cornelius (N. Y.). Captain 3d New York, 12th April, 1776; cashiered, 8th October, 1776.

Hardenbergh, Johannes (N. Y.). Colonel New York Militia, 1777-1778.

Hardenbergh, John L. (N. Y.). 2d Lieutenant of Graham's New York Militia Regiment, June to November, 1776; 2d Lieutenant 2d New York, 21st November, 1776; 1st Lieutenant, 21st June, 1777; Regimental Adjutant, January, 1780; retired 1st January, 1781; served subsequently as Captain New York Militia. (Died 25th April, 1806.)

Hardin, John (Pa). 2d Lieutenant 8th Pennsylvania, 11th August, 1776; 1st Lieutenant, 13th July, 1777; wounded at Stillwater, 19th September, 1777; with Colonel Morgan in November, 1777; resigned in 1779; subsequently Brigadier-General Kentucky Militia; murdered by Indians in Ohio in April, 1792.

Harding, Amos (Mass). Private in Lexington Alarm April, 1775; Private in Colonel Bailey's Massachusetts Regiment, May to September, 1775; Sergeant 2d Massachusetts, 28th February, 1777; Ensign, 28th March, 1778; killed at King's Bridge, 3d July, 1781.

Harding, Stephen (Pa). Captain Pennsylvania Militia; taken prisoner at Wyoming, 2d July, 1778. (Died 1789.)

Hardman, Henry (Md). 3d Lieutenant of Stephenson's Rifle Battalion, 11th July, 1776; Captain 1st Maryland Battalion of the Flying Camp, July, 1776; taken prisoner at Fort Washington, 16th November, 1776; exchanged 26th August, 1778; Captain 7th Maryland, 10th December, 1776; Major 6th Maryland, 22d May, 1779; transferred to 3d Maryland, 1st January, 1781; retired April, 1783.

Hardman John (Md). 2d Lieutenant 2d Maryland, 14th January, 1777; 1st Lieutenant, 17th April, 1777; Captain, ——, 1780; wounded and taken prisoner at Camden 16th August, 1780, and died a prisoner, 1st September, 1780.

Hardy, Christopher (S. C.). Lieutenant South Carolina Militia; killed by "Bloody Bill Cunningham" at Hayes' Station, South Carolina 9th November, 1781.

Hardy, Daniel (Mass). Adjutant of Frye's Massachusetts Regiment, 20th May to December, 1775.

Hardy, Eliphalet (Mass). Ensign in Lexington Alarm, April, 1775; 2d Lieutenant of Frye's Massachusetts Regiment, 20th May to December, 1775.

Hardy, Thomas (N. H.). 1st Lieutenant 1st New Hampshire, 23d April to December, 1775; 1st Lieutenant 2d New Hampshire, 8th May, 1777; resigned 27th August, 1778.

Hardy, Thomas Dent (Md). Lieutenant 1st Maryland, 19th July, 1776; resigned 6th July, 1778.

Hardy, William (N. C.). Paymaster Battalion North Carolina Light Dragoons, 10th September, 1777, to —.

Hardyman John (Va). 2d Lieutenant 2d Virginia State Regiment, — March, 1777; 1st Lieutenant, 24th September, 1778; served to January, 1780.

Hardyman, Joseph (S. C.). Ensign South Carolina Militia in 1776.

Hardyman, Thomas (S. C.). Captain South Carolina Militia in 1776.

Hargrave, Robert (S. C.). Captain South Carolina Militia, 1777-1778.

Hargrave, Samuel (S. C.). Lieutenant South Carolina Militia in 1776.

Hargis, Abraham (Pa). 3d Lieutenant of Miles' Pennsylvania Rifle Regiment, 2d September, 1776; 2d Lieutenant 10th Pennsylvania 2d December, 1776; 1st Lieutenant, 1st June, 1778; resigned 1st August, 1778; served subsequently as Captain Pennsylvania Militia. (Died 1811.)

Hargis, Benjamin (Pa). 3d Lieutenant 1st Battalion of Miles' Pennsylvania Rifle Regiment, 6th April, 1776, to January, 1777. (Died 1790.)

Hargis, John (Va). Ensign 13th Virginia 9th January, 1777; retired 14th September, 1778.

Haring, John (N Y.). Brigade-Major to General Clinton in 1776 and 1777.

Hargrave, William (N. C.). Ensign 10th North Carolina, 16th January, 1778; transferred to 1st North Carolina, 1st June, 1778; Lieutenant, 30th March, 1780; taken prisoner at Charleston, 12th May, 1780; exchanged 14th June, 1781; retired 1st January, 1783.

Harjett, Frederick (N. C.). Captain 8th North Carolina, 28th November, 1776, to ——.

Harkenburgh, Peter (Pa). Ensign of Baxter's Pennsylvania Battalion of the Flying Camp; taken prisoner at Fort Washington, 16th November, 1776.

Harker, Daniel (N. J.). Lieutenant-Colonel New Jersey Militia in 1777.

Harker, Joseph (N. J.). 2d Lieutenant of Martin's Regiment New Jersey Militia July to November, 1776; 1st Lieutenant 4th New Jersey, 14th January, 1777; wounded at Lackawaxon, Pennsylvania, 22d July, 1779, and did not return to service.

Harkness John (N. H.). 2d Lieutenant 3d New Hampshire 23d April to December, 1775.

Harleston, Isaac (S. C.). Captain 2d South Carolina 17th June, 1775; Major, 30th December, 1778; taken prisoner at Charleston 12th May, 1780; served to close of war.

Harleston, John (S. C.). Colonel South Carolina Militia in 1777 and 1778.

Harlow, Benjamin (S. C.). Lieutenant South Carolina Militia in 1776.

Harlow, James (Mass). Captain Massachusetts Militia in 1778.

Harman, William (Mass). 2d Lieutenant of Heath's Massachusetts Regiment, May to December, 1775.

Harmar, Josiah (Pa). Captain 1st Pennsylvania Battalion 27th October, 1775; Major 3d Pennsylvania, 1st October, 1776; Lieutenant-Colonel 6th Pennsylvania, 6th June, 1777; Lieutenant-Colonel Commandant 7th Pennsylvania, 9th August, 1780; transferred to 3d Pennsylvania, 17th January, 1781; transferred to 1st Pennsylvania, 1st January, 1783; Colonel, 30th September, 1783, and served to 3d November, 1783; Lieutenant-Colonel Commandant of United States Infantry Regiment and also Commander of the Army from 12th August, 1784, to 29th September 1789; Lieutenant-Colonel Commandant 1st United States Infantry, 29th September, 1789, to 1st January, 1792, and also commander of the United States Army from 29th September, 1789, to 4th March, 1791; Brevet Brigadier-General, 31st July, 1787; resigned 1st January, 1792. (Died 20th August, 1813.)

Harmil, David (N. Y.). Major New York Militia; was a prisoner; when and where taken not stated.

Harmon, Edward (Mass). Captain of Cotton's Massachusetts Regiment, May to December, 1775.

Harmon, John (Conn). Captain of Wolcott's Connecticut Regiment, December, 1775, to March, 1776; Captain of Mott's Connecticut State Regiment, June to December 1776; Captain 4th Connecticut, 1st January, 1777; resigned 12th January, 1780.

Harmon, William (Mass). 2d Lieutenant 24th Continental Infantry, 1st January, 1776, to ——.

Harnden, John (Mass). Lieutenant in Lexington Alarm, April, 1775; Captain of Bridge's Massachusetts Regiment May to December 1775.

Harney, Jonathan (Del). 1st Lieutenant Delaware Regiment, 15th January, 1776; wounded and taken prisoner at Long Island, 27th August, 1776; rejoined Regiment, 25th November, 1777; resigned 7th September, 1778.

Harney, Selby (N. C.). Major 8th North Carolina, 26th November, 1776; Lieutenant-Colonel, 6th November, 1777; transferred to 2d North Carolina, 1st June, 1778; taken prisoner at Charleston, 12th May, 1780; exchanged ——; transferred to 3d North Carolina, 6th February, 1782; Colonel, 30th September, 1783, and served to close of war.

Harper, Alexander (N. Y.). Captain New York Militia; was a prisoner; when and where taken not stated.

Harper, Andrew (Pa). Surgeon's Mate 9th Pennsylvania in July and August, 1777.

Harper, Andrew (N. C.). Brigade-Major to General Hogun in 1779.

Harper James (Va). 2d Lieutenant 1st Virginia State Regiment 7th December 1778; Regimental Quartermaster, 1st July, 1779; served to January, 1782.

Harper, John (N. H.). 1st Lieutenant 3d New Hampshire, 23d April to December, 1775.

Harper, John (N. Y.). Captain, Lieutenant-Colonel and Colonel New York Militia, 1776-1781.

Harper, John (Pa). Regimental Quartermaster 4th Pennsylvania Battalion, 9th February ,1776; Ensign 12th October 1776; 1st Lieutenant 5th Pennsylvania, 1st January, 1777; Brigade-Major, August, 1777; taken prisoner at Brandywine, 11th September, 1777; exchanged 4th November, 1780, and did not re-enter service.

Harper, Jonathan (N. C.) Lieutenant-Colonel North Carolina Militia, 1780-1781.

Harper, Joseph (N .Y). Ensign 2d New York, 21st November, 1776; resigned 20th September 1778.

Harper, Robert (Pa). 1st Lieutenant 11th Pennsylvania, January, 1777; retired 1st July, 1778.

Harper, Samuel (N. H.). Captain New Hampshire Militia, 1777-1778.

Harrington, Ebenezer (Mass). 1st Lieutenant 4th Massachusetts, 1st January, 1777; resigned 1st April, 1778.

Harrington, John (Mass). Captain of Baldwin's Artillery Artificer Regiment, 28th January, 1777, to ——.

Harrington, Nathaniel (Mass). Surgeon's Mate of Glover's Massachusetts Regiment, May to December, 1775; Surgeon's Mate 14th Continental Infantry, 1st January to 31st December, 1776.

Harrington, William Henry (S. C.). Brigadier-General South Carolina Militia.

Harris, Arthur (Md). Ensign 5th Maryland, 27th August 1779; Lieutenant, 26th October, 1779; transferred to 2d Maryland, 1st January, 1781, and served to April, 1783.

Harris, Benjamin (Va). 1st Lieutenant 2d Virginia, 28th December, 1776, to ——. (Died 1812.)

Harris, David (Pa). Paymaster of Thompson's Pennsylvania Rifle Battalion 25th June, 1775; 3d Lieutenant, 8th November, 1775; 1st Lieutenant 1st Continental Infantry, 5th January, 1776; Captain, 25th September, 1776; Captain 1st Pennsylvania, January, 1777; resigned 20th October, 1777. (Died 16th November, 1809)

Harris, Edward (Vt). Lieutenant Vermont Militia in 1777.

Harris Francis Henry (Ga). Captain 1st Georgia, 7th January, 1776; Major, 5th July 1776; Lieutenant-Colonel, 17th September, 1776, to ——.

Harris Jacob (N. J.). Surgeon's Mate 1st New Jersey, 28th November, 1776; Surgeon's Mate 4th New Jersey, 24th February 1777; transferred to 1st New Jersey, 1st July, 1778; Surgeon, 16th November, 1782; retained in New Jersey Battalion April, 1783, and served to November, 1783.

Harris, James (Va). 1st Lieutenant 15th Virginia, 25th November, 1776; Captain, 4th July, 1777; resigned 11th March, 1778; served subsequently as LieutenantColonel Virginia Militia.

Harris, Jonathan (—). Lieutenant ——; was a prisoner in November, 1782; when and where taken not stated.

Harris, John (Conn). 2d Lieutenant 17th Continental Infantry, 1st January to 31st December 1776; 1st Lieutenant 2d Connecticut, 1st January, 1777; killed at Whitemarsh, 7th December, 1777.

Harris, John (Mass). 2d Lieutenant 3d Continental Artillery, 1st February, 1777; resigned 4th August 1779.

Harris, John (Pa). Captain 12th Pennsylvania, 1st October, 1776; resigned 1st March, 1777.

Harris, John (Va). Ensign 1st Virginia, 11th February, 1781; 2d Lieutenant, September ,1781; transferred to Baylor's Consolidated Regiment of Dragoons 9th November, 1782, and served to close of war. (Died 1815.)

Harris, Jordan (Va). Ensign 3d Virginia, 15th May, 1782; Lieutenant, October, 1782, and served to close of war.

Harris, Joseph (Conn). Major and Lieutenant-Colonel Connecticut Militia, 1777-1783.

Harris Joseph (R. I.). Ensign 2d Rhode Island 28th June to December, 1775.

Harris Josiah (Mass). Captain of Gardner's Massachusetts Regiment May to December, 1775; Captain 25th Continental Infantry, 1st January, 1776; resigned April, 1776.

Harris, Robert (Md). Captain Maryland Militia in 1776; Captain 6th Maryland, 10th December, 1776; resigned 1st November, 1777.

Harris, Robert (Mass). 1st Lieutenant of Glover's Massachusetts Regiment, May to December, 1775; 1st Lieutenant of Spencer's Continental Regiment, 27th February, 1777; omitted December, 1777.

Harris, Robert (Pa). Surgeon's-Mate 2d Pennsylvania, 1st November, 1777; transferred to 1st Pennsylvania, 17th January, 1781; retired 1st January, 1783. (Died 4th March, 1785.)

Harris, Thomas (N. C.). Captain 4th North Carolina, 16th April, 1776; reported as Major in 1781; served to——. (Died 31st August, 1826.)

Harris, Tucker (S. C.). Surgeon South Carolina Militia, 1775-1778.

Harris, West (N. C.). Lieutenant 9th North Carolina, 28th November, 1776; Lieutenant North Carolina Dragoons, ——, 1777, to January, 1780.

Harris, William (Mass). Paymaster of Henley's Additional Continental Regiment, 1st April, 1777. Died 30th October, 1778.

Harris, William (Pa). 2d Lieutenant Pennsylvania State Regiment, 18th April, 1777; resigned 22d June, 1777.

Harrison, Battaile (Va). Lieutenant of Rawlings' Maryland and Virginia Rifle Regiment; killed at Fort Washington, 16th November, 1776.

Harrison, Benjamin (Va). Captain 13th Virginia, 16th December, 1776; regiment designated 9th Virginia, 14th September, 1778; was in service in 1780; retired 12th February, 1781, with rank of Major.

Harrison, Benjamin (Va). A signer of the Declaration of Independence; subsequently Governor of Virginia. Died 24th April, 1791.

Harrison, Benjamin Jr. (Va). Deputy Paymaster-General of Virginia troops, 15th February, 1776; elected to Congress, 10th October, 1776. (Died 24th April, 1791.)

Harrison, Charles (N. J.). Captain New Jersey Militia in 1776.

Harrison, Charles (Va). Colonel Virginia Regiment of Artillery, 30th November, 1776; Colonel 1st Continental Artillery, 1st January, 1777, to rank from 30th November, 1776, and retired 1st January, 1783. (Died 1794.)

Harrison, Cuthbert (Va). Lieutenant Virginia Dragoons, 15th June, 1776; Captain 1st Continental Dragoons, 12th February, 1777, and served to ——.

Harrison, Elisha (Md). Surgeon's-Mate 4th Maryland, 15th October, 1781; retired 1st January, 1783.

Harrison, James (Va). 2d Lieutenant 11th Virginia, 25th January, 1777; killed at Saratoga, 7th October, 1777.

Harrison, John (Va). Ensign 13th Virginia, 16th December, 1776; 2d Lieutenant, 1st January, 1777; regiment designated 9th Virginia, 14th September, 1778; 1st Lieutenant, 1st October, 1778; Captain Lieutenant, 1st January, 1781; transferred to 7th Virginia, 12th February, 1781; retired 1st January, 1783.

Harrison, John Peyton (Va). Ensign 2d Virginia, 21st September, 1775; 1st Lieutenant, 12th May, 1776; Captain, 4th May, 1777; retired 12th February, 1781.

Harrison, Lawrence (Va). 2d Lieutenant 13th Virginia, 5th April, 1778; regiment designated 9th Virginia, 14th September, 1778; 1st Lieutenant, 1st October, 1778; transferred to 7th Virginia, 12th February, 1781; retired 1st January, 1783.

Harrison, Love (Va). Ensign 8th Virginia, 25th September, 1779, to ——.

Harrison, Peyton (Va). Ensign 2d Virginia, 21st September, 1775; 2d Lieutenant, 23d January, 1776; 1st Lieutenant, 25th February, 1777; Captain, 11th March, 1777, and served to ——.

Harrison, Richard (N. C.). Major North Carolina Militia in 1780.

Harrison, Richard (Va). 1st Lieutenant 2d Virginia State Regiment, 1778 to 1780.

Harrison, Robert Hanson (Va). Lieutenant 3d Virginia, September, 1775; Lieutenant-Colonel Aide-de-Camp to General Washington, 5th November, 1775; Military Secretary to General Washington, 16th May, 1776, to 25th March, 1781. (Died 2d April, 1790.)

Harrison, Valentine (Va). Ensign 2d Virginia, — February, 1776; 2d Lieutenant, 28th December, 1776; 1st Lieutenant, 13th June, 1777; Captain, ——, 1779; retired 1st January, 1780.

Harrison, William (Md). 1st Lieutenant of Veazey's Independent Maryland Company, 14th January, 1776; in Smallwood's Maryland Regiment, June, 1776; Captain, 27th August, 1776; wounded at Long Island, 27th August, 1776. Died of wounds in 1777.

Harrison, William (N. J.). Major of Forman's Additional Continental Regiment, 1st May, 1777; resigned 19th July, 1778.

Harrison, William (N. C.). Ensign 7th North Carolina, 11th December, 1776; 2d Lieutenant, 19th December, 1776; 1st Lieutenant, 15th July, 1777; Captain, ——, 1779; served to close of war. (Died 18th July, 1831.)

Harrison, William Butler (Va). Cornet of Lee's Battalion of Light Dragoons, ——, 1779; served to close of war. (Died 28th February, 1835.)

Hart, Anthony (N. C.). 2d Lieutenant 3d North Carolina, 16th April, 1777; 1st Lieutenant, 22d November, 1777; taken prisoner at Charleston, 12th May, 1780; exchanged 14th June, 1781; Captain, 1781; served to close of war.

Hart, Benjamin (Va). Cornet and Regimental Quartermaster 3d Continental Dragoons, 26th July, 1778; Lieutenant in 1779; served to 9th November, 1782.

Hart, Derrill (S. C.). Major South Carolina Militia, 1780-1781.

Hart, Hawkins (Conn). 1st Lieutenant of Douglas' Connecticut State Regiment, June to December, 1776.

Hart, James (Mass). Adjutant of Ward's Massachusetts Regiment, May to December, 1775; 2d Lieutenant and Adjutant 21st Continental Infantry, 1st January to 31st December, 1776. (Died May, 1825)

Hart, John (Conn). 1st Lieutenant of Selden's Connecticut State Regiment, 20th June to December, 1776; Captain of Webb's Additional Continental Regiment, 1st January, 1777; resigned 9th April, 1780. (Died 28th April, 1828.)

Hart, John (Mass). Surgeon of Prescott's Massachusetts Regiment, May to August, 1775; Surgeon 7th Continental Infantry, 1st January to 31st December, 1776; Surgeon 2d Massachusetts, 1st January, 1777; retained in Jackson's Regiment Continental Army, November, 1783, and served to 20th June, 1784. (Died 27th April, 1826.) Name also spelled Heart.

Hart, John (N. J.). A signer of the Declaration of Independence; Captain of Jersey Blues in the campaign against Quebec in 1775. Died 9th May, 1779.

Hart, John (N. C.). 2d Lieutenant 6th North Carolina, 7th May, 1776; 1st Lieutenant, ——, ——; Captain, 6th August, 1779, and served to ——.

Hart, John (S. C.). Captain 2d South Carolina, 18th August 1779; resigned 19th October, 1779; 2d Lieutenant 2d South Carolina, 28th February 1780; taken prisoner at Charleston, 12th May, 1780; 1st Lieutenant, 21st November, 1781; served to close of war.

Hart, Joseph (Pa). Colonel Pennsylvania Battalion of the Flying Camp; taken prisoner at Fort Washington, 16th November, 1776.

Hart, Joseph Jr (Pa). Ensign of Hart's Pennslyvania Battalion of the Flying Camp, July to December, 1776.

Hart, Josiah (Conn). Surgeon's-Mate 6th Connecticut, 6th July to 10th December, 1775; Surgeon 10th Continental Infantry, 1st January to 31st December, 1776; Surgeon Connecticut Militia, 1777-1780. (Died August, 1812.)

Hart Nathaniel (N. C.). Captain North Carolina Rangers; killed by Indians at Blue Lick Springs, Kentucky, 19th August, 1782.

Hart, Oliver (S. C.). Surgeon's Mate 2d South Carolina, — November, 1776; resigned 14th July, 1777; Surgeon's-Mate of a South Carolina Regiment; taken prisoner at Charleston, 12th May, 1780; exchanged ——, ——; served to close of war.

Hart, Samuel (Conn). Lieutenant Cook's Regiment Connecticut Militia, ——; wounded at Stillwater, 19th September, 1777. (Died 13th January, 1825.)

Hart, Samuel (N. C.). Lieutenant 9th North Carolina, 28th November, 1776, to ——.

Hart, Samuel (S. C.). See Heart.

Hart, Thomas (N. C.). Commissary 6th North Carolina, 23d April to 28th October, 1776.

Hart, William (Mass). Captain 18th Continental Infantry, 1st January to 31st December, 1776.

Hart, William (Pa). Captain of Hart's Pennsylvania Battalion of the Flying Camp, July to December, 1776.

Hartley, Thomas (Pa). Lieutenant-Colonel 6th Pennsylvania Battalion, 10th January, 1776; Colonel of one of the Sixteen Additional Continental Regiments, 1st January, 1777; regiment designated 11th Pennsylvania, 16th December, 1778; resigned 13th February, 1779. (Died 21st December, 1800.)

Hartshorn, Jedediah (Conn). Sergeant 4th Connecticut, 26th November, 1776; Sergeant-Major, 20th November, 1777; Ensign, 25th October, 1778; resigned 19th June, 1779.

Hartshorn, John (Md). Sergeant 4th Maryland, 26th November, 1776; Ensign, 1st January, 1777; 2d Lieutenant, 1st February, 1778; 1st Lieutenant and Regimental Adjutant, 21st May, 1779; transferred to 3d Maryland, 1st January, 1781; retained in Maryland Battalion, April, 1783, and served to 15th November, 1783.

Hartshorn, Thomas (Mass). Sergeant in Bridge's Massachusetts Regiment, May to December, 1775; Ensign 16th Continental Infantry, 1st January to 31st December, 1776; 1st Lieutenant 8th Massachusetts, 1st January, 1777; Captain Lieutenant, 30th October, 1778; Captain, 26th July, 1779, and served to 3d June, 1783. (Died 6th May, 1819.)

Hartwell, Ephriam (Mass). Regimental Quartermaster of Walker's Massachusetts Regiment, June to November, 1775.

Hartwell, Isaac (Mass). 2d Lieutenant 14th Massachusetts, 1st January, 1777; dismissed 30th November, 1777. (Died 12th June, 1831.)

Hartwell, John (Mass). Sergeant in Lexington Alarm, April, 1775; 2d Lieutenant of Nixon's Massachusetts Regiment, May to December, 1775.

Harvey, Elisha (Mass). Sergeant in Knox's Regiment Continental Artillery, 3d May to 10th December, 1776; 2d Lieutenant 2d Continental Artillery, 1st

January, 1777; 1st Lieutenant, 28th June, 1778; Captain Lieutenant, 25th June, 1781, and served to June, 1783. (Died 11th February, 1821.)

Harvey, Ithamar (Conn). 2d Lieutenant of Wadsworth's Connecticut State Regiment, June to December, 1776; 1st Lieutenant 1st Connecticut, 1st January, 1777; Captain, 1st January, 1778; resigned 20th June, 1779.

Harvey, James (N. C.). Paymaster 7th North Carolina, 11th December, 1776, to ——.

Harvey, John (N. H.). Sergeant 3d New Hampshire, 22d February, 1777; Ensign 1st May, 1778; transferred to 1st New Hampshire, 1st January, 1781; Lieutenant, 12th May, 1781, and served to close of war. (Died 1841.)

Harvey, John (N. C.). Captain North Carolina Militia at King's Mountain in October, 1780.

Harvey, Josiah (Mass). Surgeon's-Mate of Fellow's Massachusetts Regiment, 28th June, 1775; Surgeon 4th Massachusetts, 1st April, 1778; resigned April, 1782. (Died 1802.)

Harvey, Moses (Mass). Captain of Brewer's Massachusetts Regiment, May to December, 1775.

Harvie, Alexander (Ga). Surgeon of a Georgia Regiment in 1779

Harvie, John (Va). Colonel Virginia Militia, 1776-1781. (Died 1807.)

Harwood, Peter (Mass). 1st Lieutenant in Lexington Alarm, April, 1775; Captain 3d Continental Infantry, 1st January, 1776; taken prisoner at White Plains, 28th October, 1776; Captain 6th Massachusetts, 6th November, 1776; Major 6th Massachusetts, 19th December, 1777; resigned 18th October, 1780.

Harwood, Thomas (Md). 1st Lieutenant of Smallwood's Maryland Regiment, 14th January, 1776; Captain 1st Maryland, 10th December, 1776; resigned 10th June, 1777. (Died 1791.)

Hasbrouck, Abraham (N. Y.). Lieutenant-Colonel and Colonel New York Militia, 1775-1776. (Died 1791.)

Hasbrouck, Elias (N. Y.). Captain 3d New York, 28th June, 1775, to January, 1776; served subsequently as Captain of Company of New York Rangers.

Hasbrouck, Jonathan (N. Y.). Colonel New York Militia in 1775.

Hasbrouck, Joseph. (N. Y.). Lieutenant and Adjutant of Malcolm's New

York Militia Regiment in 1780. (Died 1821.)

Haselton, John (Mass). See Hazelton.

Haskell, Andrew (Mass). Captain of Whitcomb's Massachusetts Regiment, May, 1775, to ——.

Haskell, Benjamin (Conn). Sergeant 6th Connecticut, 8th May to 10th December, 1775; Ensign 10th Continental Infantry, 1st January to 31st December, 1776.

Haskell, Elnathon (Mass). Sergeant of Cotton's Massachusetts Regiment, May to November, 1775; 2d Lieutenant 10th Continental Infantry, 5th July to 31st December, 1776; 1st Lieutenant and Adjutant 14th Massachusetts, 1st January, 1777; Captain, 1st April, 1778; Brigade-Major, 12th May, 1778; transferred to 4th Massachusetts, 1st January, 1781; Aide-de-Camp to General Howe, 2d September, 1782, to 3d November, 1783; retained in Jackson's Continental Regiment, November 1783, and served to 20th June, 1784.

Haskell, Henry (Mass). Captain Company of Minute Men in the Lexington Alarm, April, 1775; Lieutenant-Colonel 15th Massachusetts, 1st January, 1777; omitted, 1st July, 1779. (Died — June, 1807.)

Haskell, Jonathan (Mass). Ensign 14th Massachusetts, 13th January, 1777; Lieutenant and Adjutant, 4th February, 1779; transferred to 7th Massachusetts, 1st January, 1781; transferred to 2d Massachusetts, 12th June, 1783; retained in Jackson's Continental Regiment, 3d November, 1783, and served to 20th June, 1784; Brevet-Captain, 30th September, 1783; Captain 2d United States Infantry, 4th March, 1791; assigned to 2d Sub Legion, 4th September, 1792; resigned 5th December, 1793; Major 4th Sub Legion, 20th March, 1794; Adjutant-General and Inspector to the Army, 27th February to 1st August, 1796; honorably discharged, 1st November, 1796. (Died 13th December, 1814.)

Haskell, Nathaniel (Mass). Ensign of Phinney's Massachusetts Regiment, May to December, 1775; Lieutenant Massachusetts Militia, 1776. (Died 1794.)

Haskins, Jacob (Mass). 2d Lieutenant in Woodbridge's Massachusetts Regiment, May to December, 1775; 1st Lieutenant 25th Continental Infantry, 1st January to 31st December, 1776; Captain Massachusetts Militia in 1778. (Died 4th January, 1819.)

Haskins, Nathan (Mass). Captain of Paterson's Massachusetts Regiment, May to December, 1775.

Haslet, John (Del). Colonel Delaware Militia in 1775; Colonel Delaware Regiment, 19th January, 1776; killed at Princeton, 3d January, 1777.

Hastings, Abijah (Mass). Private in Lexington Alarm, April, 1775; Sergeant in Gerrish's Massachusetts Regiment, May to December, 1775; Ensign 26th Continental Infantry, 1st January to 31st December, 1776. (Died 25th February, 1826.)

Hastings, Benjamin (Mass). Captain in Lexington Alarm April, 1775; Captain of Whitcomb's Massachusetts Regiment, 30th June, 1775, to December, 1775.

Hastings, Edward (Pa). Captain Pennsylvania Militia; taken prisoner from his home, 26th May, 1778.

Hastings, Eliphalet (Mass) Ensign of Brewer's Massachusetts Regiment, May to December, 1775; Captain Massachusetts Militia, 1778. (Died 16th November, 1824.)

Hastings, John (Mass). Served in the Army in 1775; Captain of Lee's Additional Continental Regiment, 20th May, 1777; transferred to Jackson's Regiment, 22d April, 1779; regiment designated 16th Massachusetts, 23d July, 1780; transferred to 9th Massachusetts, 1st January, 1781; transferred to 7th Massachusetts, 1st January, 1783, and served to June, 1783; Brevet-Major, 30th September, 1783. (Died 16th February, 1839.)

Hastings, Walter (Mass). Surgeon of Bridge's Massachusetts Regiment, 28th June to December, 1775; Surgeon 8th Massachusetts, 1st January, 1777; retired 1st January, 1781. (Died 1782.)

Hasty, William (Mass). Ensign 11th Massachusetts, 6th November, 1776; 2d Lieutenant, 3d April, 1777; 1st Lieutenant, 28th March, 1779; Regimental Adjutant, 25th June, 1779; resigned 18th March, 1780. (Died 23d December, 1831.)

Hatch, Fisher (Mass). Private in Lexington Alarm, April, 1775; Sergeant in Bailey's Massachusetts Regiment, May to December, 1775; Sergeant 11th Massachusetts, 1st January, 1777; Ensign, 1st November, 1777; resigned 17th October, 1778.

Hatch, Jabez (Mass). Lieutenant-Colonel and Colonel Massachusetts Militia, 1776 to 1780. (Died 1802.)

Hatch, Joseph (N. Y.). Captain of Hoisington's Battalion of Rangers, 6th August, 1776, to ——.

Hatch, Nailer (Mass). Captain of Gardner's Massachusetts Regiment, May to December, 1775; Captain 25th Continental Infantry, 1st January to 31st December, 1776.

Hatch, Zacheus (Mass). Lieutenant Massachusetts Militia, 1776-1779.

Hatchet, Archibald (Ga). Captain of a Georgia or South Carolina Regiment in 1777.

Hatfield, Moses (N. Y.). Captain Company of Minute Men in 1775; Major of Drake's Regiment New York Militia, 1776; taken prisoner at Montressor's Island, 24th September, 1776; exchanged in 1778; Colonel New York Militia in 1780 and 1781.

Hathaway, Abraham (Mass). 2d Lieutenant of Walker's Massachusetts Regiment, June to December, 1775. (Died August, 1835.)

Hathaway, Benoni (N. J.). Captain, Major and Lieutenant-Colonel New Jersey Militia, 1776-1780.

Hathaway, John (Mass). Lieutenant-Colonel and Colonel Massachusetts Militia, 1776-1780. (Died 1800.)

Hatherston, Robert (Md). Lieutenant 4th Maryland, 25th April, 1781, and served to ——.

Hathorn, John (N. Y.). Colonel New York Militia, 1777-1779. (Died 1824.)

Hatton, Josiah (Ga). Lieutenant 3d Georgia, ——; on roll for August, 1778.

Haubecker, George (Pa). 2d Lieutenant German Battalion, 12th July, 1776; 1st Lieutenant, 10th August, 1777; resigned January ——, 1778.

Haussegger, Nicholas (Pa). Major 4th Pennsylvania Battalion, 4th January, 1776; Colonel German Regiment, 17th July, 1776; taken prisoner at Princeton, 4th January, 1777; superseded 19th March, 1777, having joined the enemy. (Died July, 1786.)

Havens, William (N. Y.). 2d Lieutenant 3d New York, 28th June, 1775, to January, 1776; 1st Lieutenant 4th New York, 21st November, 1776; resigned 7th November, 1777.

Haviland, Ebenezer (N. Y.). Surgeon 4th New York, 4th August, 1775, to January, 1776; Surgeon 4th New York, 27th April, 1776; Surgeon 2d New York, 21st November, 1776. Died 28th June, 1778.

Haviland, John (N. J.). Lieutenant New Jersey Militia; was a prisoner in 1780; when and where taken not stated.

Hawes, Benjamin. Colonel Massachusetts Militia, 1778-1780.

Hawes, Samuel (Va). Captain 2d Virginia, 19th February, 1776; Major 10th Virginia 4th October, 1777; Lieutenant-Colonel, 1st March, 1778; regiment designated 6th Virginia 14th September, 1778; transferred to 5th Virginia, 1st January, 1783, and served to 15th November, 1783

Hawkes, William (Mass). Ensign 14th Continental Infantry, 1st January to 31st December, 1776; 1st Lieutenant of Lee's Additional Continental Regiment 1st January 1777; cashiered, 17th November, 1778.

Hawkins, Elijah (R. I.). Ensign 2d Rhode Island, 10th May, 1777; resigned 14th July, 1778.

Hawkins, Henry (Md). Ensign 5th Maryland, 1st August, 1781; Lieutenant, 1st September, 1782; retained in Maryland Battalion April, 1783, and served to 15th November, 1783.

Hawkins, John (Md). 1st Lieutenant 4th Maryland Battalion of the Flying Camp, July to December, 1776; 1st Lieutenant 5th Maryland, 10th December, 1776; Captain, 20th February, 1777; resigned 1st June, 1781. (Died 1786.)

Hawkins, John (Va). Ensign and Adjutant 3d Virginia, 28th December, 1776; Lieutenant, 11th September, 1777; Captain, 13th May, 1780; taken prisoner at Charleston, 12th May, 1780; prisoner on parole to close of war. (Died 1805.)

Hawkins, Moses (Va). Captain 14th Virginia, 6th February, 1777; killed at Germantown, 4th October, 1777.

Hawkins, Nathaniel (R. I.). 1st Lieutenant 1st Rhode Island, 3d May to December, 1775; Captain 9th Continental Infantry, 1st January to 31st December, 1776; served subsequently as Major and Lieutenant-Colonel Rhode Island Militia.

Hawkins, Philemon (N. C.). Colonel North Carolina Militia, 1776-1781. (Died 1801.)

Hawkins, Reuben (Va). Ensign 10th Virginia, —— March, 1777; resigned —— December, 1777.

Hawkins, William Adrian (N. H.). Sergeant of Reed's New Hampshire Regiment, May, 1775; Ensign, June to December, 1775; 2d Lieutenant 2d Continental Infantry, 1st January, 1776;

1st Lieutenant 3d New Hampshire, 8th November, 1776; Captain, 22d May, 1779; resigned 5th July, 1780.

Hawley, Abner (N. Y.). 1st Lieutenant New York Militia in 1775.

Hawley, Gideon (Conn). Private 2d Continental Dragoons, 16th April, 1777; Corporal, 16th September, 1777; Sergeant, 7th January, 1778; Quartermaster-Sergeant, 5th September, 1778; Cornet, 14th June, 1781, and served to close of war.

Hawley, Wm (Conn). 2d Lieutenant of Bradley's Connecticut Regiment, June to December, 1776.

Hawthorne, James (S. C.). 1st Lieutenant 6th South Carolina, ——, 1777; Captain, 22d February, 1778, to ——; was Lieutenant-Colonel South Carolina Regiment at Kings Mountain in October, 1780, and was wounded at Camden 25th April, 1781. (Died 1809.)

Hay, A. Hawkes (N. Y.). Colonel New York Militia, 1778-1780.

Hay, David (Pa). 2d Lieutenant 1st Pennsylvania, 22d February 1777; resigned 1st December, 1777.

Hay, John (Pa). See **Hays.**

Hay, John (Pa). Major Pennsylvania Militia, 1777-1778.

Hay, Joseph (Va). Surgeon Hospital Department, 6th July, 1776, to ——, 1781.

Hay, Patrick (Pa). 1st Lieutenant of Cunningham's Pennsylvania Battalion of the Flying Camp, July, 1776; discharged for disability September, 1776.

Hay, Samuel (Pa). Captain 6th Pennsylvania Battalion, 9th January, 1776; Major 7th Pennsylvania, 5th October, 1776; Lieutenant-Colonel 10th Pennsylvania, 2d February, 1778; wounded at Stony Point, 16th July, 1779; retired 17th January, 1781. (Died December, 1803.)

Hay, Udny (Pa). Assistant Deputy Quartermaster-General, 30th July, 1776; brevet Lieutenant-Colonel and Assistant Deputy Quartermaster-General, 9th January, 1777; discharged 29th May, 1778; served subsequently as Lieutenant-Colonel and Deputy Quartermaster-General to close of war. (Died ——, 1806)

Hay, William (Pa). Lieutenant-Colonel of Cunningham's Pennsylvania Battalion of the Flying Camp, June to December, 1776. (Died 1812.)

Hayden, Josiah (Mass). Captain Company of Minute Men in Lexington Alarm, April, 1775; Captain of Thomas' Massachusetts Regiment, May to December, 1775; Major 23d Continental Infantry, 1st January to 31st December, 1776. (Died 2d September, 1818.)

Hayden, Thomas (Conn). Sergeant in the Lexington Alarm, April, 1775; Sergeant-Major 8th Connecticut, 11th August to 16th December, 1775; 2d Lieutenant 17th Continental Infantry, 1st January, 1776; Regimental Adjutant, 20th October to 31st December, 1776; 1st Lieutenant 3d Connecticut, 1st January, 1777; Regimental Adjutant, 8th April, 1777; resigned 15th April, 1778; served subsequently in 1781 and 1782 as Lieutenant Connecticut Militia. (Died 28th November, 1817.)

Hayes, Arthur (Ga). 2d Lieutenant 3d Georgia, 1st October, 1777; taken prisoner at Beaufort, 3d February, 1779; 1st Lieutenant, 1779; served to ——.

Hayes, Joseph (S. C.). Colonel South Carolina Militia at Kings Mountain, October, 1780, captured and hanged by the British at Hayes Station, S. C., 19th November, 1781.

Hayes, Samuel (N. J.). Major New Jersey Militia; taken prisoner in 1780; when and where not stated.

Hayes, Thomas (Md). 2d Lieutenant of Maryland Battalion of the Flying Camp, September to December, 1776.

Hayes, Thomas (Va). 1st Lieutenant 2d Virginia State Regiment, 24th September 1778, and served to January, 1780.

Haymond, Owen (Md). 2d Lieutenant 6th Maryland, 10th October, 1777; killed at Monmouth, 28th June, 1778.

Hayne, Ezekiel (Md.) Surgeon's-Mate 2d Maryland, 1st August, 1779; Surgeon 1st Maryland, 1st January, 1781; retained in Maryland Battalion, April, 1783, and served to 15th November, 1783. Name also spelled Haynie.

Hayne, Isaac (S. C.). Colonel South Carolina Militia, ——; taken prisoner at Charleston, 12th May, 1780, and paroled ——; taken prisoner at Horse Shoe, S. C., 8th July, 1781, and was executed by the British at Charleston, 4th August, 1781.

Haynes, Aaron (Mass). Captain in Lexington Alarm, April, 1775; Captain of Brewer's Massachusetts Regiment,

May to December, 1775; Captain 6th Continental Infantry, 1st January to 31st December, 1776; Captain 13th Massachusetts, 1st January, 1777; retired 8th April, 1779.

Haynes, Joseph (Vt). 2d Lieutenant of Bedel's Vermont Regiment, 1st April, 1778, to 1st April, 1779.

Haynie, Ezekiel. See Hayne.

Haynie, Holland (Md). 2d Lieutenant 1st Continental Artillery, 13th January, 1777; 1st Lieutenant, 30th November, 1777, and served to June, 1783.

Hays, Andrew (Va) Ensign 5th Virginia, 15th February, 1781, to ——.

Hays, James (N. C.). Lieutenant 7th North Carolina, 28th November, 1776, to ——.

Hays, John (N. J.). Private 4th New Jersey, 1st April, 1777; Ensign, 1st June, 1777. Died 3d November, 1777, of wounds received at Germantown, 4th October, 1777.

Hays, John (Pa). 2d Lieutenant 12th Pennsylvania, 16th October, 1776; dismissed 11th January, 1778. (Name also spelled Hay.)

Hays, John (Va). Captain 9th Virginia, 16th March, 1776; taken prisoner at Germantown, 4th October, 1777; Major 3d Virginia, 23d April, 1778; retired 12th February, 1781.

Hays, Robert (N. C.). Ensign 4th North Carolina, 16th August, 1777; 2d Lieutenant, 1st January, 1778; transferred to 1st North Carolina, 1st June, 1778; 1st Lieutenant, 16th February, 1780; taken prisoner at Charleston, 12th May 1780; exchanged 14th June, 1781; served to close of war.

Hays, Robert (Va). Ensign 4th Virginia, 4th July, 1779; taken prisoner at Charleston, 12th May, 1780.

Hays, Thomas (Va). Lieutenant Virginia Militia, 1780-1781.

Hayward Abner (Mass). Sergeant in Lexington Alarm April 1775; 2d Lieutenant of Thomas' Massachusetts Regiment May to December, 1775; 1st Lieutenant 23d Continental Infantry, 1st January to 31st December, 1776; 1st Lieutenant 2d Massachusetts, 1st January, 1777; Captain, 19th September, 1777; resigned 12th May, 1781. (Name also spelled Haywood.)

Hayward, John (Mass). 2d Lieutenant of Captain Isaac Davis' Company Massachusetts Minute Men at Concord, 19th April, 1775; 2d Lieutenant of Learned's Massachusetts Regiment, May to December, 1775; served subsequently as Captain Massachusetts Militia. (Died 13th February, 1825.)

Hayward, John (Va). 2d Lieutenant 13th Virginia, 16th April, 1777; resigned 14th November, 1777.

Hayward, Joshua (N. H.). Captain New Hampshire Militia, 1775-1778.

Hayward, Lemuel (Mass). Surgeon Hospital Department, 1775-1776. (Died 20th March 1822.)

Hayward, Thomas (Va). Ensign 13th Virginia, — December, 1776; 2d Lieutenant, 16th April, 1777; resigned 14th November, 1777.

Hayward, William (S. C.). See Heyward.

Haywood, Seth (Mass). 1st Lieutenant of Whitcomb's Massachusetts Regiment, May to December, 1775.

Haywood, Seth (N. H.). Captain New Hampshire Militia, 1775-1778.

Haywood, William (N. H.). Major New Hampshire Militia, 1775-1778.

Hazard, Samuel (Conn). 2d Lieutenant of Swift's Connecticut State Regiment, July to December, 1776.

Hazelton, John (Mass). 1st Lieutenant of Learned's Massachusetts Regiment, May to December, 1775. Name also spelled Haselton.

Hazen, Joshua (Vt). Captain Vermont in 1777.

Hazen, Moses (Canada). Was a Lieutenant in the British Army, on half pay when appointed Colonel 2d Canadian Regiment 22d January, 1776; Brevet Brigadier-General, 29th June, 1781; retired June, 1783. (Died 3d February, 1803.)

Hazlet, James (Pa). 2d Lieutenant of Lewis' Pennsylvania Battalion of the Flying Camp, July to December, 1776.

Hazleton, Simeon (Mass). Captain of Fellows' Massachusetts Regiment, May, 1775, to ——.

Hazlett, Samuel (N. J.). 2d Lieutenant 3d New Jersey, 7th February, 1776; resigned 19th July 1776.

Hazzard, Cord (Del). Ensign Delaware Regiment, 13th January, 1776; 2d Lieutenant, 16th January, 1776; 1st Lieutenant, 30th November, 1776; wounded at Princeton, 3d January, 1777; Captain, 5th April, 1777; resigned 27th January, 1778. (Died 3d March, 1831.)

Hazzard, Jonathan J. (R. I.). Adjutant 1st Rhode Island, 1st January, 1777; resigned in 1778. (Died 1812.)

Hazzard, Samuel (N. Y.). Lieutenant 2d Continental Dragoons, 21st January, 1777; resigned 25th December, 1777.

Hazzard, William (S. C.). Lieutenant 1st South Carolina, 24th November, 1779; taken prisoner at Charleston, 12th May, 1780.

Heacock, Amos, Jr. (Conn). 2d Lieutenant of Swift's Connecticut State Regiment, June to December, 1776. (Name also spelled Hecock.)

Heacock, Daniel (Conn). Ensign 5th Connecticut, 1st May to 17th October, 1775.

Head, James (N. H.). Major of Stickney's New Hampshire Regiment, 20th July, 1777; killed at Bennington, 16th August, 1777.

Head, Richard M. (S. C.). Cornet of Dragoons, Armand's Legion, 1779 and 1780. (Died 15th May, 1827.)

Headley, Francis (N. J.). Major New Jersey Militia in 1777.

Heald, John (Mass). Lieutenant in Lexington Alarm, April, 1775; 1st Lieutenant of Nixon's Massachusetts Regiment, May to December, 1775; Lieutenant Massachusetts Militia in 1776. (Died 1820.)

Heald, Thomas (N. H.). Captain Company of Minute Men in Lexington Alarm; served subsequently as Lieutenant-Colonel New Hampshire Militia. (Died 1806.)

Healey, Martin (Va). Captain of a Virginia State Regiment, 1779, to ——.

Healey, Nathaniel (Mass). Captain of Learned's Massachusetts Regiment, May to December, 1775; Captain Massachusetts Militia, 1776-1779.

Heard, James (N. J.). Cornet of Lee's Continental Dragoons, Pulaski Legion, 1st April, 1779; Lieutenant and Regimental Paymaster, 1st February, 1780; Captain, March, 1782, and served to close of war. (Died 26th March, 1831.)

Heard, Jethro (N. H.). 2d Lieutenant 2d New Hampshire, 23d May to December, 1775; 2d Lieutenant 8th Continental Infantry, 1st January, 1776; 1st Lieutenant 2d New Hampshire, 8th November, 1776; resigned 8th May, 1777.

Heard, John (N. J.). 2d Lieutenant Eastern Company New Jersey Artillery, 1st March to December, 1776; 1st Lieutenant 4th Continental Dragoons, 20th

January, 1777; Captain, 8th February, 1778; served to close of war. (Died 1826.)

Heard, Nathaniel (N. J.). Colonel New Jersey Militia, November, 1775, to February, 1777; Brigadier-General New Jersey Militia, 12th February, 1776, to close of war.

Heart, John (Conn). Sergeant 2d Connecticut, February, 1779; Ensign, 1st August, 1780; Brigade Quartermaster 4th August, 1780, and served to 3d June, 1783.

Heart, Jonathan (Conn). Served as a volunteer with 2d Connecticut, May to December, 1775; Ensign 22d Continental Infantry, 1st January, 1776; 2d Lieutenant, 10th August, 1776; Adjutant 3d Connecticut, 1st January, 1777; Captain Lieutenant, 1st July, 1779; Captain, 1st May, 1780; transferred to 1st Connecticut, 1st January, 1781; Brigade-Major and Inspector, 2d January, 1781, to June, 1783; retained in Swift's Connecticut Battalion in June, 1783, and served to 3d November, 1783; Captain United States Infantry Regiment, 9th June, 1785; Captain 1st United States Infantry, 29th September, 1789; Major 2d United States Infantry, 4th March, 1791; killed 4th November, 1791, in action with Indians at St. Clair's defeat, near Fort Recovery, Ohio.

Heart, Samuel (S. C.). Chaplain 1st South Carolina, 12th February, 1778, to ——. Name also spelled Hart.

Heart, Selah (Conn) Captain of Walcott's Connecticut State Regiment, December, 1775, to February, 1776; Lieutenant-Colonel of Gay's Connecticut State Regiment, 20th June, 1776; taken prisoner 15th September, 1776, on the retreat from New York; exchanged March, 1777; Brigadier-General Connecticut Militia, 1779, to close of war.

Heaston, Edward (Pa). Lieutenant Pennsylvania Militia; taken prisoner at his home in Philadelphia, 26th May, 1778. Name also spelled Heston.

Heath, Jonathan (N. H.). Ensign 8th Continental Infantry, 1st January to 31st December, 1776.

Heath, Nathaniel (N. Y.). Lieutenant New York Militia; killed at Oriskany, 6th August, 1777.

Heath, Peleg (R. I.). Ensign of Richmond's Rhode Island State Regiment, 1st November, 1775, to June, 1776; 1st Lieutenant 3d Connecticut, 1st January, 1777; Captain Lieutenant, 1st May, 1779; retired 1st January, 1781. (Died 1786.)

Heath, Peleg (R. I.). Major Rhode Island Militia, 1777-1779.

Heath, William (Mass). Was a Colonel of a Massachusetts Regiment at Lexington and Concord, April to June, 1775; appointed Major-General, Massachusetts Militia, 20th June, 1775; Brigadier-General, Continental Army, 22d June, 1775; Major-General, Continental Army, 9th August, 1776, and served to close of war. (Died 24th January, 1814.)

. **Heatley, Charles** (S. C.). 1st Lieutenant 3d South Carolina, 17th June, 1775; Captain, 12th August, 1775, and served to ——.

Heaton, William (Vt). Captain Vermont Militia in 1777.

Hedden, James (Mass). Ensign of Baldwin's Artillery Artificer Regiment, 10th July, 1778; omitted May, 1779.

Hedrick, Adolph William (Pa). Captain 11th Pennsylvania, 13th November, 1776; retired 1st July, 1778.

Heimberg, Frederick (Va). Surgeon's-Mate 8th Virginia, 19th April, 1777; Surgeon 1st North Carolina, 15th March, 1778; retired 1st June, 1778. Name also spelled Helmburg.

Hellen, John (Md). 1st Lieutenant 1st Maryland Battalion of the Flying Camp, July to December, 1776.

Helm, Christian (Pa). Ensign German Regiment, 12th July, 1776; 2d Lieutenant, 13th May 1777; superceded 12th September, 1777.

Helm, John (Pa). 1st Lieutenant 6th Pennsylvania Battalion, 6th January, 1776; taken prisoner at Fort Washington, 16th November, 1776; exchanged 26th August, 1778, and did not re-enter service.

Helm, Thomas (Va). 2d Lieutenant 3d Virginia, 8th March, 1776; 1st Lieutenant, 8th November, 1776; resigned 29th November, 1777. (Died 1816.)

Helm, William (R. I.). Lieutenant Rhode Island Militia in 1776-1777.

Helmer, George (N. Y.). Lieutenant New York Militia; wounded at Oriskany, 6th August, 1777. (Died 1823.)

Helms, Robert (R. I.). Ensign 2d Rhode Island, 10th March, 1777; resigned 25th November, 1777.

Helms, William (N. J.). Ensign 2d New Jersey, 7th November, 1775; 2d

Lieutenant, 25th December, 1775; 1st Lieutenant, 1st January, 1777; Captain, 1st December, 1777; transferred to 1st New Jersey, 1st January, 1783; retained in New Jersey Battalion, April, 1783; Brevet Major, 30th September, 1783, and served to 3d November, 1783. (Died ——, 1813.)

Helphinstone, Peter (Va). Major 8th Virginia, 1st March, 1776; resigned 7th August, 1776.

Hender, Caleb (Conn). Captain Connecticut Militia in 1775.

Hender, Joshua (N. H.). Captain New Hampshire Militia in 1777.

Hender, Thomas (Conn). Private in the Lexington Alarm, April, 1775; Sergeant 2d Connecticut, 17th May to 10th December, 1775; Ensign 22d Continental Infantry, 1st January, 1776; taken prisoner at Fort Washington, 16th November, 1776.

Henderson, Alexander (Pa). Captain and Deputy Commissioner of Military Stores, 10th September, 1777; resigned 3d July, 1779.

Henderson, Andrew (Pa). Ensign 4th Pennsylvania, 4th July, 1779; Lieutenant, 29th July, 1781; transferred to 2d Pennsylvania, 1st January, 1783, and served to 3d June, 1783; Ensign United States Infantry Regiment, 12th August, 1784; resigned 21st October, 1784. (Died 1831.)

Henderson, Gustavus. See John Rose.

Henderson, John (Pa). Ensign 11th Pennsylvania, 30th September, 1776; Cornet 4th Continental Dragoons, 20th January, 1777; Regimental Quarter-master, 1st July, 1778; omitted September, 1778.

Henderson, John (Pa). 2d Lieutenant 12th Pennsylvania, 1st October, 1776; transferred to 3d Pennsylvania, 1st July, 1778; Captain Lieutenant, 1st July, 1778; Captain, 12th May, 1779; resigned 11th December, 1781.

Henderson, John (S. C.). Lieutenant-Colonel South Carolina Militia; wounded at Eutaw Springs, 8th September, 1781.

Henderson, Matthew (Pa). Captain 9th Pennsylvania, 14th November, 1776; retired 1st July, 1778.

Henderson, Michael (N. C.). Captain 9th North Carolina, 28th November, 1776, to ——.

Henderson, Pleasant (N. C.). Lieutenant 6th North Carolina, 16th April, 1776, to ——; Major North Carolina Militia, 1780-1781. (Died 1842.)

Henderson, Richard (N. C.). Captain North Carolina Militia, 1780-1781.

Henderson, Richard (Pa). 2d Lieutenant of Lewis' Pennsylvania Battalion of the Flying Camp, July to December, 1776.

Henderson, Thomas (N. J.). Major New Jersey Militia in 1776; Lieutenant-Colonel of Forman's Additional Continental Regiment, 12th January, 1777; omitted — October, 1777. (Died 15th December, 1824.)

Henderson, William (Pa). Ensign Pennsylvania Musket Battalion 20th March, 1776; taken prisoner at Long Island, 27th August, 1776; exchanged 9th December 1776; 1st Lieutenant 4th Pennsylvania, 3d January, 1777; Captain, 16th May, 1778; retired 1st January, 1783. (Died 1811.7

Henderson, William (Pa). Captain 11th Pennslyvania, 30th September, 1776; Paymaster 4th Continental Dragoons, 22d February, 1777; resigned 31st March, 1780.

Henderson, William (S. C.). Major 6th South Carolina, 17th June, 1775; Lieutenant-Colonel, 16th September, 1776; transferred to 3d South Carolina, 11th February, 1780; taken prisoner at Charleston, 12th May, 1780; exchanged November, 1780; transferred to 1st South Carolina, 1st January, 1781; Colonel, 30th September, 1783; wounded at Eutaw Springs, 8th September, 1781, and served to close of war, also served as Brigadier-General South Carolina State Troops in 1781-1782. (Died 1787.)

Henderson, William (Va). 1st Lieutenant 9th Virginia, 11th March, 1776; Captain, 4th January, 1777; resigned 30th May, 1778.

Hendrick, Peter (Conn). Lieutenant in the Lexington Alarm, April, 1775; 1st Lieutenant 5th Connecticut, 1st May to 5th December, 1775.

Hendricks, James (Va). Major 6th Virginia, 13th February, 1776; Lieutenant-Colonel 6th Virginia, 13th August, 1776; Colonel 1st Virginia, 29th September, 1777, and served to 10th February, 1778. (Supposed to have resigned.)

Hendricks, William (Pa). Captain of Thompson's Pennsylvania Rifle Battalion, 25th June, 1775; killed at Quebec, 31st December, 1775.

Hendricks, William (S. C.) Captain South Carolina Militia, 1780-1782.

Hendrickson, Daniel (N. J.). Colonel 3d New Jersey Militia Regiment, 9th July, 1776; taken prisoner, 9th June, 1779, at ——.

Hendrickson, Garetson (N. J.). 1st Lieutenant New Jersey Militia, 25th September, 1777; wounded at Middletown, New Jersey, 12th June, 1780. (Died 21st December, 1801.)

Hendry, Samuel (N. J.). Ensign 2d New Jersey, 28th October, 1775; 2d Lieutenant, 30th November, 1776; Captain Lieutenant, 1st January, 1779; Captain, 5th July, 1779; retained in New Jersey Battalion, April, 1783, and served to 3d November, 1783. (Died 15th October, 1823.)

Hendry, Thomas (N. J.). Brigade Surgeon New Jersey Militia; taken prisoner at Salem, 26th March, 1778.

Henly, David (Mass). Appointed Brigade-Major to General Heath, 15th August, 1775; Deputy Adjutant-General for General Spencer, 6th September, 1776; Lieutenant-Colonel, 5th Massachusetts, 1st Noember, 1776; Colonel of one of the Sixteen Additional Continental Regiments, 1st January, 1777; retired 23d April, 1779. (Died 1st January, 1823.)

Henly, George. See Handley.

Henly, Henry (Pa). Ensign 4th Pennsylvania, 2d July, 1779; Lieutenant, 17th April, 1780; transferred to 2d Pennsylvania, 1st January, 1783 and served to 3d June, 1783.

Henly, Samuel (Mass). 2d Lieutenant 15th Massachusetts, 1st January, 1777; 1st Lieutenant of Henly's Additional Continental Regiment, 1st April, 1777; transferred to 15th Massachusetts, 23d April, 1779; Captain Lieutenant, 3d February, 1780; transferred to 4th Massachusetts, 1st January, 1781; Captain, 9th August, 1781; transferred to 9th Massachusetts, 3d May, 1782; retired 1st January, 1783.

Henly, Thomas (R. I.). 2d Lieutenant of Varnum's Rhode Island Regiment, August, 1775; Adjutant of Knox's Continental Artillery Regiment, 15th December, 1775; Major and Aide-de-Camp to General Heath, 13th August, 1776; killed at Montressor's Island, 24th September 1776.

Hennington, John (S. C.). Was a Captain in 3d South Carolina in 1779.

Hennion, Cornelius (N. J.). Ensign 3d New Jersey, 7th February, 1776; 2d Lieutenant, 19th July, 1776; 1st Lieutenant, 29th November, 1776; Captain, 1st November, 1777; severely wounded at Short Hills, 26th June, 1777; resigned 1st April, 1778. (Died 28th March, 1800.)

Henry, James (Md). Ensign 4th Maryland Battalion of the Flying Camp, July, 1776; 2d Lieutenant, 5th September, 1776; Captain 5th Maryland, 10th December, 1776; resigned 25th January, 1778.

Henry, James (N. Y.). 2d Lieutenant 2d Continental Artillery, 1st January, 1777; resigned 25th March, 1778.

Henry, John (Pa). Volunteer in Canadian Campaign; taken prisoner at Quebec 31st December, 1775; Cornet 1st Continental Dragoons, to rank from 14th June, 1776; Lieutenant 24th December, 1776; resigned 20th February, 1777, having been appointed Captain 1st Continental Artillery, to rank from 7th February, 1777; resigned 27th August, 1778.

Henry, John (R. I.). Ensign Rhode Island Militia in 1776.

Henry, Malcolm (Mass). Captain of Brewer's Massachusetts Regiment, May, 1775, to ——.

Henry, Nathaniel (N. Y.). 2d Lieutenant of Nicholson's Continental Regiment, June to November, 1776; 2d Lieutenant 1st New York, 21st November, 1776; wounded at Peekskill, 22d March, 1777; resigned 5th April, 1781. (Died 14th June, 1824.)

Henry, Patrick (Va). Colonel and Commander-in-Chief of the Virginia forces, September, 1775; resigned 28th February, 1776; Colonel 1st Virginia, 13th February, 1776, which he declined; was subsequently Governor of Virginia. (Died 6th June, 1799.)

Henry, Robert R. (N. H.). Hospital Surgeon's-Mate, 17th March, 1777; Surgeon 2d New Hampshire, 24th October, 1779; transferred to 1st New Hampshire, 1st January, 1781, and served to close of war.

Henry, Thomas (Pa). 1st Lieutenant of Montgomery's Pennsylvania Battalion of the Flying Camp, July to December, 1776.

Henry, William (Md). Captain Maryland Militia, 1776.

Henry, William (Pa). Captain of Montgomery's Pennsylvania Battalion

Flying Camp; taken prisoner at Fort Washington, 16th November, 1776.

Henshaw, Benjamin (Conn). Ensign of Ward's Connecticut State Regiment, 14th May, 1776; 2d Lieutenant 5th Connecticut, 1st January, 1777; resigned 7th January, 1778. (Died 17th May, 1828.)

Henshaw, William (Conn). Ensign 5th Connecticut, 1st January, 1777; 2d Lieutenant, 4th January, 1778; Regimental Paymaster, 1st September, 1778, to 1st January, 1783; 1st Lieutenant 20th July, 1780; transferred to 2d Connecticut, 1st January, 1781; retired 1st January, 1783. (Died 1796.)

Henshaw, William (Mass). Colonel Massachusetts Minute Men, 19th April to 16th June, 1775; Colonel Adjutant-General, 27th June to 3d July, 1775; Lieutenant-Colonel 12th Continental Infantry, 1st January to 31st December, 1776. (Died 20th February, 1820.)

Henshaw William (Va). Lieutenant of Morgan's Company Virginia Riflemen, July, 1775, to January, 1776.

Hanson, Samuel (Va). Cadet 3d Virginia, March, 1777; retired 30th September, 1778

Herbert Stewart (Pa). Ensign 12th Pennsylvania, 1st October, 1776; 2d Lieutenant, 1st May, 1777; wounded at Short Hills, 26th June, 1777; 1st Lieutenant, 1st October, 1777; transferred to 6th Pennsylvania, 1st July, 1778; wounded and taken prisoner at Green Springs, Va., 6th July, 1781; transferred to 1st Pennsylvania 1st January, 1783, and served to June, 1783; Brevet-Captain, 30th September, 1783; 1st Lieutenant and Adjutant United States Infantry Regiment, 12th August, 1784; resigned 8th September, 1785.

Herbert, Thomas (Pa). Ensign 1st Virginia, 25th February, 1776; Captain Pennsylvania Musket Battalion, 15th March, 1776; taken prisoner at Long Island, 27th August, 1776; exchanged, November, 1776; Captain 10th Pennsylvania, 4th December, 1776; resigned 12th February, 1777.

Herkimer, Nicholas (N. Y.). Brigadier-General New York Militia, ——; wounded at Oriskany, 6th August, 1777, and died of his wounds, 16th August, 1777.

Hermanse, John (N. Y.). Captain New York Militia in 1780.

Herndon, Benjamin (N. C.). Major North Carolina Militia at King's Mountain in October, 1780. (Died 31st December, 1819.)

Herndon, Edward (Va). Captain Virginia Convention Guards, 1779-1780.

Herndon, Joseph (N. C.). Captain North Carolina Militia at King's Mountain, October 1780.

Herndon, Reuben (Va). 2d Lieutenant 7th Virginia, 7th February, 1776; 1st Lieutenant, 26th April, 1776; resigned April, 1778.

Heron, James Gordon (N. J.). 1st Lieutenant 2d Canadian.(Hazen's) Regiment, July, 1776; Captain, 3d November, 1776; taken prisoner at Staten Island, 22d August, 1777; resigned 1st July, 1780. (Died 1809.)

Herrick, Joseph (Mass). Private in Lexington Alarm, April, 1775; Ensign of Mansfield's Massachusetts Regiment, 12th May to 31st December, 1775; 2d Lieutenant 27th Continental Infantry, 1st January to 31st December, 1776; served subsequently in Massachusetts Militia.

Herrick, Martin (Mass). Sergeant of Glover's Massachusetts Regiment, May to December, 1775; Surgeons-Mate — Continental Infantry, March to December, 1776; Surgeon in Navy, 1778 to 1782. (Died 25th July, 1820.)

Herrick, Nathaniel (Mass). 1st Lieutenant of Frye's Massachusetts Regiment, May to December, 1775.

Herrick, Rufus (N. Y.). Captain 4th New York, 28th June, 1775, to May, 1776; served subsequently as Captain and Lieutenant-Colonel New York Militia. (Died 1811.)

Herrick, Samuel (Vt). Colonel Vermont Rangers, 1777. (Died 1798.)

Herring, Benjamin (N. Y.). Sergeant 3d New York, 7th January, 1777; Ensign 28th May, 1778; transferred to 1st New York, 1st January, 1781, and served to 3d June, 1783.

Herrington, Ebenezer (Mass). Lieutenant 4th Massachusetts, 1st January, 1777; resigned 1st May, 1778.

Herriot, Robert (S. C.). Colonel South Carolina Militia; taken prisoner at Charleston, 12th May, 1780. (Died 1792.)

Herritage, John (N. C.). 1st Lieutenant 2d North Carolina, 1st September, 1775; Captain, 3d May, 1776; resigned 15th May, 1777.

Herron, Armwell (N. C.). Captain 10th North Carolina, 19th April, 1777; retired 1st June, 1778.

Heston, Edward (Pa). Lieutenant Pennsylvania Militia; taken prisoner at his home in Philadelphia, 26th May, 1778. Name also spelled Heaston.

Heth, Andrew (Va). Lieutenant of Captain Henry Heth's Independent Company for service at Fort Pitt and on the frontier, October, 1777, to January, 1782.

Heth, Henry (Va). Captain of a Virginia Independent Company for service at Fort Pitt and on the frontier, October, 1777, to January, 1782. (Died 1793.)

Heth, John (Va). Ensign 11th Virginia, 21st January, 1777; discharged 6th August, 1778; Ensign 2d Virginia, 8th March, 1780; taken prisoner at Charleston, 12th May, 1780; exchanged, 14th June, 1781; 2d Lieutenant, 26th May, 1781; transferred to 1st Virginia, 1st January, 1783, and served to close of war.

Heth, William (Va). Lieutenant of Morgan's Company Virginia Riflemen, July, 1775; taken prisoner at Quebec, 31st December, 1775; Major 11th Virginia, 13th November, 1776; Lieutenant-Colonel 3d Virginia, 1st April, 1777; Colonel, 30th April, 1778; taken prisoner at Charleston, 12th May, 1780; prisoner on parole to close of war. (Died 15th April, 1808.)

Hevelman, Arnold (—). 1st Lieutenant 2d Canadian (Hazen's) Regiment, 3d November, 1776; Captain, 1st August, 1777; omitted, — August, 1779.

Hewell, William (N. C.). Lieutenant 5th North Carolina, 20th April, 1777, to ——. Name also spelled Ewell.

Hewes, Joseph (N. C.). A sign of the Declaration of Independence. Died 10th November, 1779.

Hewins, Elijah (Mass). Surgeon's-Mate of Gridley's Regiment Massachusetts Artillery, June to December, 1775; Surgeon Massachusetts Militia, 1776-1779. (Died 1827.)

Hewitt, Charles (R. I.). Lieutenant Rhode Island Militia in 1776.

Hewitt, John (Mass). Sergeant in Whitcomb's Massachusetts Regiment, May to December, 1775; 2d Lieutenant of Whitcomb's Massachusetts Regiment, June, 1776; 1st Lieutenant 10th Massachusetts, 6th November, 1776; resigned 15th December, 1778.

Hewitt, Reuben (R. I.). Lieutenant of Lippitt's Rhode Island State Regiment, 19th August 1776, to May, 1777.

Hewitt, Richard (Conn). 2d Lieutenant 6th Connecticut, 1st May, 1775; 1st Lieutenant, 1st July to 10th December, 1775; 1st Lieutenant 10th Continental Infantry, 1st January to 31st December, 1776.

Hewitt, Thomas (Va). Captain 14th Virginia, 24th February, 1777; taken prisoner at Germantown, 4th October, 1777.

Hewson, John (Pa). Captain Pennsylvania Militia, 1780-1781. (Died 1821.)

Hext, William (S. C.). 2d Lieutenant 1st South Carolina, November, 1776; 1st Lieutenant, 1st January, 1777; Captain, 1st May, 1778; wounded at Stono Ferry, 20th June, 1779; served to close of war.

Heydrick, Adolph. See **Hedrick.**

Heyser, William (Pa). Captain German Battalion, 12th July, 1776; resigned 21st May, 1778.

Heyward, Daniel Jr. (S. C.). Captain South Carolina Militia, 1776.

Heyward, John (S. C.). Ensign South Carolina Militia in 1776.

Heyward Thomas (S. C.). Was a signer of the Declaration of Independence; Captain South Carolina Artillery Company in 1776; wounded at Beaufort, 9th February, 1779; taken prisoner at Charleston, 12th May, 1780; released April, 1781. (Died 6th March, 1809.)

Heyward, William (S. C.). Lieutenant 1st South Carolina, ——; resigned 22d October, 1777.

Heywood, Benjamin (Mass). Lieutenant of Nixon's Massachusetts Regiment, May to December 1775; 2d Lieutenant 4th Continental Infantry, 1st January, 1776; Regimental·Paymaster, 14th September, 1776; Lieutenant and Paymaster 6th Massachusetts, 1st January, 1777; Captain, 10th April, 1779, and served to 3d June, 1783. (Died 6th December, 1816.)

Hibbard, Augustine (N. H.). Chaplain of Bedel's Regiment New Hampshire Rangers, 21st January to August, 1776; Chaplain 2d New Hampshire, 8th November, 1776, to June, 1777;·Chaplain New Hampshire Militia, 1777-1778.

Hibbard, Thomas (N. H.). Adjutant of Bedel's Regiment New Hampshire Rangers, 15th June to December, 1775, and again of same, 22d January, 1776; taken prisoner at the Cedars, 19th May, 1776; exchanged, December, 1776; Lieutenant and Adjutant of Bedel's Vermont Regiment, December, 1777, to 1st April, 1779.

Hibbard, Thomas (N. H.). Adjutant of Bedel's Regiment New Hampshire Rangers, 22d January to October, 1776.

Hickling, William (Mass). Paymaster 7th Massachusetts, 1st January, 1777; resigned 30th September, 1778. (Died 1790.)

Hickman, Ezekiel (Pa). 1st Lieutenant 8th Pennsylvania, July, 1776, and served to ——.

Hickman, William (N. C.). Lieutenant 4th North Carolina, ——, 1777, to ——.

Hickock, Benjamin (Vt). Captain Vermont Militia in 1776.

Hickock, John (N Y.). Major New York Militia, 1775.

Hickock, Samuel (Conn). Sergeant-Major 2d Connecticut, 1st January, 1777; Ensign, 1st September, 1777; 1st Lieutenant, 1st September, 1779; resigned 3d April, 1780.

Hickox, Benjamin (Conn). Ensign of Silliman's Connecticut State Regiment, July to December, 1776.

Hickox, Benjamin (N. H.). Lieutenant of Baldwin's Regiment New Hampshire Militia, 20th September, 1776; 1st Lieutenant 3d New Hampshire, 8th November, 1776; cashiered, 20th June, 1777. Deserted to the enemy.

Hickox, James (Conn). Ensign of Chester's Connecticut State Regiment, June to December, 1776.

Hicks, Benjamin (N. Y.). Captain 1st New York, 21st November, 1776; to rank from 16th February 1776, and served to 3d June, 1783. (Died 4th April, 1833.)

Hicks, George (S. C.). Colonel South Carolina Militia, 1776-1777.

Hicks Isaac (Ga). Captain 3d Georgia, July, 1776; taken prisoner at Briar Creek, 3d March, 1779; did not rejoin regiment after release in fall of 1779. (Died 1817.)

Hicks, Jacob Giles (Pa). 2d Lieutenant 11th Pennsylvania, 9th April, 1777; 1st Lieutenant, 30th October, 1777; transferred to 10th Pennsylvania, 1st July, 1778; Captain Lieutenant, 1st March, 1780; resigned 6th March, 1781; was a prisoner, but when and where taken not stated.

Hicks, Samuel (R. I.). Ensign of Richmond's Rhode Island State Regiment 19th August, 1776; 1st Lieutenant 1st Rhode Island, 1st January, 1777; resigned 21st February, 1778.

Hicks, Thomas (N. Y.). Ensign 1st New York, 21st November, 1776; deserted 2d December, 1777.

Hicks, William (N. C.). Ensign 9th North Carolina, 28th November, 1776, to ——; was Captain North Carolina Militia in 1781.

Hide, Ebenezer (N. H.). 1st Lieutenant of Warner's Continental Regiment, 5th July, 1776, to ——.

Hide, Jedediah (Conn). Lieutenant in the Lexington Alarm, April, 1775; 1st Lieutenant 6th Connecticut, 1st May to 10th December, 1775.

Hide, Jedediah (Conn). Quartermaster-Sergeant 4th Connecticut, 1st January, 1777, to 1st January, 1780; Conductor of Military Stores, 1st January to 20th July, 1780.

Hiester, Daniel (Pa). Brigadier-General Pennsylvania Militia, 27th May, 1782, to close of war. (Died 7th March, 1804.)

Hiester, John (Pa). Colonel Pennsylvania Militia, 1779-1780. (Died 15th October, 1821.)

Hiester, Joseph (Pa). Captain of Lutz's Battalion Pennsylvania Militia; taken prisoner at Long Island, 27th August, 1776; exchanged, 9th December, 1776; Lieutenant-Colonel Pennsylvania Militia, 1777 to 1780; wounded at Germantown 4th Octoer, 1777.

Higgins, Cornelius (Conn). Sergeant 8th Connecticut, 9th July, to 10th December, 1775; Ensign 17th Continental Infantry, 1st January, 1776; taken prisoner at Long Island, 27th August, 1776; exchanged, 8th December, 1776; 2d Lieutenant 5th Connecticut, 1st January, 1777; 1st Lieutenant, 17th March, 1778; resigned 16th August, 1779.

Higgins, James (Va). 2d Lieutenant 8th Virginia, 22d March, 1776; 1st Lieutenant, 3d March, 1777; Captain, —— February, 1778; retired 30th September, 1778.

Higgins, John (N. J.). 2d Lieutenant 2d New Jersey, 9th December, 1775. Died 12th July, 1776.

Higgins, Joseph (Conn). Surgeon's-Mate 5th Connecticut, 1st June, 1779; transferred to 1st Connecticut, 1st January, 1781, and served to 3d June, 1783.

Higgins, Peter (Va). Ensign 4th Virginia, 9th March, 1777; 2d Lieutenant, 4th October, 1777; 1st Lieutenant, 23d September, 1779, and served to close of war. (Died 1809.)

Higgins, Robert (Va). 1st Lieutenant 8th Virginia, 12th March, 1776;

Captain, 1st March, 1777; taken prisoner at Germantown, 4th October, 1777; retained in 2d Virginia, 12th February, 1781, and served to close of war; Brevet-Major, 30th September, 1783.

Higgins, Sylvanus (Conn). Private 8th Connecticut, 9th July to 10th December 1775; Ensign 1st Connecticut, 1st January, 1777; resigned 30th November, 1777.

Higgins, William (Conn). Private 6th Connecticut, 21st December, 1775; Quartermaster-Sergeant, 1st January, 1777; Regimental Quartermaster, 23d July, 1777; Ensign, 15th November, 1778; transferred to 1st Connecticut, 1st January, 1781; 2d Lieutenant, 25th June, 1781; 1st Lieutenant, 28th October, 1781, and served to June, 1783.

Hildredth, Samuel (Mass). Surgeon Massachusetts Militia in 1777; served subsequently in Navy and was a prisoner in April 1782, when and where taken not stated. (Died 1823.)

Hildredth, William (Mass). Sergeant 8th Massachusetts 16th May, 1777; Ensign, 18th October 1779; Lieutenant, 14th September, 1780, and served to 3d June, 1783.

Hill, Aaron (Mass). Ensign of Lee's Additional Continental Regiment, 26th April, 1777; resigned 14th January, 1778; Surgeon's Mate 5th Massachusetts, 1st September, 1778; resigned 4th January, 1779.

Hill, Andrew (N. Y.). Captain and Major New York Militia, 1775-1779. (Died 1810.)

Hill, Baylor (Va). Cornet 1st Continental Dragoons, 4th December, 1776; Lieutenant, ——, 1777; Captain, ——, 1780; served to January, 1783.

Hill, Charles (N. H.). Ensign of Bedel's Regiment New Hampshire Rangers, 22d January, 1776; taken prisoner at the Cedars, 19th May, 1776; exchanged in December, 1776; Lieutenant of Bedel's Vermont Regiment, 15th December, 1777, to 1st April, 1779.

Hill, Daniel (Mass). Private in Scammon's Massachusetts Regiment, May to December, 1775; Sergeant 18th Continental Infantry, 1st January 1776; Ensign, 10th June, 1776; Ensign 1st Massachusetts, 1st January, 1777; resigned 14th February, 1778.

Hill, Ebenezer (N. Y.). 1st Lieutenant 2d New York, March to November, 1776.

Hill, Henry (Conn). Sergeant 6th Connecticut, 8th May to 18th December,

1775; Ensign 10th Continental Infantry, 1st January to 31st December, 1776; 1st Lieutenant 1st Connecticut, 1st January, 1777; resigned 30th June, 1779.

Hill, James (Ga). Lieutenant 2d Georgia in August, 1778, and served to ——.

Hill, James (Mass). Lieutenant 15th Massachusetts, 1st January, 1777; resigned 31st October, 1778.

Hill, James (Va). Ensign 15th Virginia, 15th June, 1777; 2d Lieutenant, 1st April, 1778; regiment designated 11th Virginia, 14th September, 1778, and served to ——; was in service October, 1779.

Hill, Jeremiah (Mass). Captain of Scammon's Massachusetts Regiment, May to December, 1775; Captain 18th Continental Infantry, 1st January to 31st December, 1776; Captain 1st Massachusetts, 1st January, 1777; resigned 4th November, 1777. (Died 11th June, 1820.)

Hill, Jeremiah (Mass). Private in Lexington Alarm, April, 1775; 2d Lieutenant of Henley's Additional Continental Regiment, 23d June, 1777; transferred to Jackson's Regiment, 22d April, 1779; 1st Lieutenant, 25th October, 1779; regiment designated 16th Massachusetts, 23d July, 1780 transferred to 9th Massachusetts, 1st January, 1781; transferred to 2d Massachusetts, 1st January, 1783, and served to 3d November, 1783. (Died 16th July, 1801.)

Hill, John (Mass). 2d Lieutenant 15th Massachusetts, 1st January, 1777; discharged 31st October, 1778.

Hill, John (N. H.). Captain New Hampshire Militia, 1778.

Hill, John (N. C.). Ensign 10th North Carolina, 4th April, 1781; Lieutenant, 5th July, 1781; transferred to 4th North Carolina, 6th February, 1782; served to close of war.

Hill, Jonathan (Mass). Sergeant in Lexington Alarm, April, 1775; 2d Lieutenant of Nixon's Massachusetts Regiment, May to December, 1775; 1st Lieutenant 4th Continental Infantry, 1st January to 31st December, 1776.

Hill, Philip (Md). 2d Lieutenant 2d Maryland, 10th April, 1777; taken prisoner at Staten Island, 22d August, 1777; 1st Lieutenant, 9th May, 1778; exchanged about February, 1781, and was with regiment at Yorktown in October, 1781; transferred to 3d Maryland, 1st January, 1783, and served to April, 1783.

Hill, Richard (Va). 2d Lieutenant 1st Continental Artillery, 13th January, 1777; 1st Lieutenant, 20th October, 1777; resigned 1st April, 1779.

Hill, Squier (Conn). Sergeant in the Lexington Alarm, April, 1775; Ensign 3d Connecticut, 1st May to 18th December, 1775; Captain Connecticut Militia in 1778. (Died 1826.)

Hill, Stephen (Del). 1st Lieutenant Delaware Battalion of the Flying Camp, July to December, 1776.

Hill, Thomas (Va). 1st Lieutenant 7th Virginia, 7th February, 1776; Captain, 13th November, 1776; transferred to 5th Virginia, 14th September, 1778; Major, 4th July, 1779; retired 12th February, 1781.

Hill, William (Md). Lieutenant 2d Maryland, ——; taken prisoner at Charleston, 12th May, 1780; released on parole 30th December, 1780.

Hill, William (S. C.). Colonel South Carolina Militia; wounded at Hanging Rock, 6th August, 1780.

Hill, William (N. C.). Lieutenant 1st North Carolina, 1st September, 1775, to ——.

Hill, William (Va). Cadet 6th Virginia, 25th March, 1776, to ——.

Hillard, John (Mass). Captain Massachusetts Artificer Regiment in 1777.

Hillary, Christopher (Ga). Regimental Quartermaster-Sergeant 2d Georgia, ——, 1777; 2d Lieutenant, 1st August, 1778; 1st Lieutenant, ——, 1780; served to ——.

Hillary, George (Pa). Ensign of Hartley's Continental Regiment, 1st February, 1777; 2d Lieutenant, 1st June, 1777, to ——; name also spelled Hillery.

Hillary, Rignal (Md). Ensign 1st Maryland, 10th December, 1776; 2d Lieutenant, 1st April, 1777; taken prisoner at Staten Island, 22d August, 1777; exchanged 25th October, 1780; 1st Lieutenant, 15th July, 1779; transferred to 3d Maryland, 1st January, 1783, and served to April, 1783.

Hiller, Jacob (N. Y.). Ensign New York Militia; killed at Oriskany, 6th August, 1777.

Hilliard, Joseph (Conn). Sergeant in the Lexington Alarm, April, 1775; Ensign 7th Connecticut, 2d July, 1775; 2d Lieutenant, 1st September to 10th December, 1775; Ensign of Mott's Connecticut State Regiment, June to December, 1776.

Hillhouse, James (N. J.). Captain New Jersey Militia in 1779. (Died 29th December, 1832.)

Hilliard, Zebulon (N. H.). 1st Lieutenant 2d New Hampshire, 23d May to December, 1775.

Hillman, Josiah (N. J.). Lieutenant-Colonel New Jersey Militia in 1776.

Hills, Andrew (N. Y.). Captain New York Militia, 1777.

Hills, Ebenezer (Conn). Captain 7th Connecticut, 6th July to 27th December, 1775; 1st Lieutenant 7th Connecticut, 1st January, 1777; Captain, 1st November 1777; transferred to Invalid Regiment, 13th September, 1780; honorably discharged 23d April, 1783.

Hillyer, Andrew (Conn). 2d Lieutenant 8th Connecticut, 6th July, 1775; Adjutant, 28th August to 10th December, 1775; Captain Connecticut Light Horse in 1776. (Died 1828.)

Hilsley, James (Va). 2d Lieutenant ᵗ Virginia, 29th February, 1776, to ——.

Hilton, Edward (N. H.). Captain New Hampshire Militia in 1778.

Hilton, Eliakim (Mass). Private iʰ ᵛington **Alarm, April, 1775;** Ensign ᵔd Massachusetts, 1st January, 1777; resigned 16th August, 1778.

Hilton, Joseph (N. H.). 2d Lieutenant 3d New Hampshire, 8th November, 1776; wounded at Stillwater, 7th October, 1777; retired 1st September, 1778. (Died 26th November, 1826.)

Hilton, William (N. C.). 2d Lieutenant 6th North Carolina, 1st April, 1777; 1st Lieutenant, 12th October, 1777; transferred to 1st North Carolina, 1st ᵗly, 1778; **killed at Stony Point, 15th** July, 1779.

Hilyard, David (R. I.). Colonel Rhode Island Militia, 1778.

Hinckley, Ichabod (Conn). Lieutenant in the Lexington Alarm, April, 1775; Lieutenant of Sage's Connecticut State Regiment, 20th June to December, 1776; Captain 2d Connecticut, 1st January, 1777; retired 1st January, 1781.

Hindman, Edward (Md). 3d Lieutenant of Hindman's Independent Maryland Company, 14th January, 1776; 2d Lieutenant, April, 1776; Captain 3d Maryland, 10th December, 1776; resigned 15th October, 1777.

Hindman, James (Md). Captain Independent Maryland Company, 14th

January, 1776; Lieutenant-Colonel 5th Maryland, 10th December, 1776; resigned 4th April, 1777.

Hindman, John (Md). Surgeon Maryland Battalion of the Flying Camp, ᵗuly to December, 1776; Surgeon 5th Maryland, 10th December, 1776; resigned 13th January, 1778.

Hinds, Bartlett (Mass). 1st Lieutenant 10th Massachusetts, 6th November, ᵗ776; Captain, 10th March, 1780; resigned 12th September, 1780.

Hinds, Jacob (N. H.). Captain 3d New Hampshire, 23d April to December, 1775; Captain 2d Continental Infantry, 1st January, 1776, to ——.

Hinds, Nehemiah (Mass). Surgeon's Mate of Woodbridge's Massachusetts Regiment, May to December, 1775.

Hine, Ambrose (Conn). 2d Lieutenant of Douglas' Connecticut State Regiment, June, 1777; Captain Connecticut Militia, 1777.

Hines, Andrew (Md). Captain 6th Maryland, 10th December, 1776; resigned 1st March, 1779; name also spelled Hynes.

Hines, William ·(Pa). Ensign of Hart's Pennsylvania Battalion of the Flying Camp, July to December, 1776.

Hinman, Benjamin (Conn). Colonel 4th Connecticut, 1st May to 20th December, 1775; subsequently Colonel Connecticut Militia. (Died 22d March, 1810.)

Hinman David (Conn). 1st Lieutenant 4th Connecticut, 1st May to 20th December, 1775. (Died 1829.)

Hinman, Elijah (Conn). Captain Connecticut Militia in 1776.

Hinman, Joel (Conn). Ensign 17th Continental Infantry, 1st January, 1776; taken prisoner at Long Island, 27th August, 1776.

Hipp, George (S. C.). Captain South Carolina Militia in 1778.

Hitchcock, Asahel (Md). 1st Lieutenant 2d Maryland Battalion of the Flying Camp, July to December, 1776.

Hitchcock, Daniel (R. I.). Colonel Rhode Island Regiment, 3d May to December 1775; Colonel 11th Continental Infantry, 1st January to 31st December, 1776; Colonel 2d Rhode Island, 1st January, 1777; died 13th January, 1777.

Hitchcock, David (Conn). Ensign of Douglas' Connecticut State Regiment, June to December, 1776.

Hitchcock, Enos (Mass). Chaplain 3d Continental Infantry, 13th March to 31st December, 1776; Chaplain 10th Massachusetts, 1st January, 1777; Brigade Chaplain of Paterson's Massachusetts Brigade, 27th August, 1778, to close of war. (Died 27th February, 1803.)

Hitchcock, Gad (Mass). Surgeon's Mate of Thomas' Massachusetts Regiment, 30th June to December, 1775; served subsequently as Surgeon Massachusetts Militia. (Died 8th August, 1803)

Hitchcock, John (Conn). 1st Lieutenant of Elmore's Continental Regiment, 15th April, 1776; cashiered 27th August, 1776.

Hitchcock, Lemuel (Conn). Ensign of Douglas' Connecticut State Regiment, June to December, 1776; 2d Lieutenant 8th Connecticut, 1st January, 1777; 1st Lieutenant, 10th March, 1778; resigned 19th May, 1779. (Died 27th February, 1803.)

Hitchcock, Luke (Mass). 1st Lieutenant 12th Massachusetts, 1st January, 1777; Captain, 5th July, 1779; transferred to 1st Massachusetts, 1st January, 1781; killed in a duel with Lieutenant Nathaniel Stone at West Point, New York, 21st February, 1782.

Hitchcock, Lyman (Conn). 2d Lieutenant of Elmore's Continental Regiment, 15th April, 1776, to April, 1777; Major of New York Levies in 1780. (Died 15th February, 1819.)

Hite, Abraham (Va). 2d Lieutenant 12th Virginia, 15th November, 1776; 1st Lieutenant, 8th January, 1777; Captain Lieutenant, May, 1778; regiment designated 8th Virginia, 14th September, 1778; Regimental Paymaster, 1st January, 1779; Captain, 4th April, 1779; taken prisoner at Charleston, 12th May, 1780; prisoner on parole to close of war. (Died 1832.)

Hite, George (Va). Ensign 8th Virginia, 10th September, 1780; transferred to 3d Continental Dragoons, August, 1782; Lieutenant, October, 1782, and served to close of war.

Hite, Isaac (Va). Ensign 8th Virginia, 1st July, 1780; 1st Lieutenant, 1st July, 1781; retired 1st January, 1783. (Died 30th November, 1836.)

Hite, Joseph (Va). Cadet 8th Virginia, 21st February, 1778; Lieutenant, — February, 1779; resigned 8th January, 1780.

Hite, Matthias (Va). 1st Lieutenant 8th Virginia, 23d January, 1776; Captain, 10th August, 1777; resigned 7th May, 1778. (Died 9th January, 1823.)

Hite, William (Va). Ensign 8th Virginia, — August, 1777; retired 1st July, 1778.

Hiwell, John (Mass). Sergeant in Knox's Regiment Continental Artillery, December, 1775, to December, 1776; 2d Lieutenant 3d Continental Artillery, 1st January, 1777; 1st Lieutenant, 22d February, 1780, and served to June, 1783.

Hixt.—See **Hext.**

Hoagland, Oakley (N. J.). Captain, Major and Lieutenant-Colonel New Jersey Militia, 1776-1780.

Hoagland, Rome (N. Y.). Adjutant of Lasher's Regiment New York Militia in 1776.

Hoar, John (Mass). Lieutenant in Lexington Alarm, April, 1775; 1st Lieutenant of Whitcomb's Massachusetts Regiment, August to December, 1775; Lieutenant Massachusetts Militia, 1776-1777.

Hoard, ——. See **Hord**, as names are spelled both ways.

Hoare, Samuel (Mass). Lieutenant in Lexington and Concord Alarm, April, 1775; Lieutenant Massachusetts Militia, 1775-1776.

Hobart, David (N. H.). Colonel New Hampshire Militia, 1776-1779.

Hobart, John (Conn). Ensign 6th Connecticut, 1st March, 1777; 2d Lieutenant, 13th March 1778; transferred to 8th Connecticut, 15th November, 1778; 1st Lieutenant 20th May, 1779; transferred to 4th Connecticut, 1st January, 1781; transferred to 3d Connecticut, 1st January, 1783, and served to June, 1783.

Hobart, Peter (Mass). 1st Lieutenant 25th Continental Infantry, 1st January to 31st December, 1776; Surgeon's Mate and Surgeon Hospital Department, 1778-1781. (Died 1793.)

Hobb, Josiah (S. C.). 1st Lieutenant of a South Carolina Regiment, 15th July, 1778; taken prisoner at Charleston, 12th May, 1780.

Hobbs, Samuel (Md). Captain of an Independent Maryland Company; killed at Guilford, 15th March, 1781.

Hobby, Caleb (N. Y.). Lieutenant 1st New York, February to November, 1776.

Hobby, David (N. Y.). Captain 3d New York, 28th March to November, 1776; served subsequently as Major New York Miilita, ——; prisoner of war, 3d September to 22d October, 1781.

Hobby, John (Mass). 1st Lieutenant of Jackson's Additional Continental Regiment, 1st February, 1777; Captain Lieutenant, 24th April, 1779; regiment designated 16th Massachusetts, 23d July, 1780; transferred to 9th Massachusetts, 1st January, 1781; Captain 24th July, 1781; transferred to 3d Massachusetts, 3d May, 1782; retained in Jackson's Continental Regiment, 3d November, 1783, and served to 20th June, 1784. (Died ——, 1802.)

Hobby, Thomas (Conn). Major 5th Connecticut, 1st May to 13th December, 1775; wounded near St. John's Canada, 6th September, 1775; Lieutenant-Colonel of Bradley's Regiment Connecticut Militia May, 1776; taken prisoner at Fort Washington, 16th November, 1776. (Died 1798.)

Hobby, Thomas, Jr (Conn). Ensign of Silliman's Connecticut State Regiment, July to December, 1776.

Hobson, Joseph (Va). 2d Lieutenant 7th Virginia, 7th March, 1776; 1st Lieutenant, 28th November, 1776; resigned 20th May, 1778. (Died 1815.)

Hobson, Nicholas (Va). 1st Lieutenant 6th Virginia, 16th February, 1776; Captain, 10th April ,1776; resigned 23d September 1777.

Hockaday, John (Va). 1st Lieutenant 6th Virginia, 10th March, 1776; Captain, 15th April, 1777; resigned 23d July, 1777.

Hockaday, Philip (Va). 2d Lieutenant 6th Virginia, 2d February, 1777; killed at Brandywine, 11th September, 1777.

Hockaday, William H. (Va). 2d Lieutenant 6th Virginia, 11th March, 1776, to ——.

Hodgdon, Caleb (N. H.). Captain New Hampshire Militia, 1776-1777.

Hodgdon, Samuel (Pa). Commissary of Military Stores, 1st February, 1777; Deputy Commissary-General of Military Stores, 11th February, 1778; Commissary-General of Military Stores, 10th July, 1781, and continued in service to 20th June, 1784; Quartermaster United States Army, 4th March, 1791; superseded 12th April, 1792. (Died 1824.)

Hodge, Asahel (Conn). Ensign 4th Connecticut, 1st May to December, 1775; 2d Lieutenant of Burrall's Continental Regiment, January, 1776; 2d Lieutenant 8th Connecticut, 1st January, 1777; 1st Lieutenant, 16th January, 1778. Adjutant, 24th May, 1778; Captain Lieutenant, 21st April ,1779; Captain 28th October, 1779; transferred to 5th Connecticut, 1st January, 1781; retired 1st January, 1783. (Died 19th February 1824.)

Hodge, Hugh (Pa). Surgeon 3d Pennsylvania Battalion, 7th February, 1776; taken prisoner at Fort Washington, 16th November, 1776. (Died 1798.)

Hodges, Isaac (Mass). Captain Massachusetts Militia, 1776-1779.

Hodges, John (N. C.). Ensign 5th North Carolina, 4th May, 1776; Lieutenant, 1st October, 1776; was in service as a Captain in 1780 and 1781; served to ——.

Hodges, Seth (Vt). Captain Vermont Militia, 1777.

Hodgkins, Francis (N. H.). Surgeon's-Mate New Hampshire Militia, 1775-1776.

Hodgkins, Joseph (Mass). Lieutenant in Lexington Alarm, April, 1775; 1st Lieutenant of Little's Massachusetts Regiment, 19th May, 1775; 1st Lieutenant 12th Continental Infantry, 1st January, 1776; Captain 15th Massachusetts, 1st January, 1777; omitted — July, 1779.

Hodgkins, Thomas (Mass). Regimental Quartermaster of Little's Massachusetts Regiment, May to December, 1775; Captain Massachusetts Militia, 1779-1780. (Died 1797.)

Hodgson, Robert (Del). Major Delaware Militia in 1775; Lieutenant-Colonel Delaware Battalion of the Flying Camp, July to December, 1776.

Hodgton, Alvery (N. C.). Lieutenant and Adjutant 3d North Carolina in 1777, and served to ——.

Hoevenburgh, Rudolph Van.—See **Van Hoevenburgh.**

Hoey, Benjamin (Mass). Lieutenant of Flower's Artillery Artificer Regiment, 1st August, 1780, and served to June, 1783.

Hoffler, William (Va). Captain 1st Virginia State Regiment, 9th January, 1777, to October, 1780.

Hoffman, Michael (Pa). Ensign 1st Pennsylvania, 28th May, 1779; Lieutenant, 1st October, 1779; died 18th July, 1780.

Hoffman, Philip.—See **Huffman.**

Hoffman, Robert (N. Y.). Major and Lieutenant-Colonel New York Militia, 1775-1782. (Died 1790.)

Hoffman, Valentine (Pa). Captain Lieutenant of Flower's Artillery Artificer Regiment, 12th February, 1777; deserted 16th April, 1777.

Hoffner, George (Pa). Ensign 2d Pennsylvania Battalion, 4th July, 1776; 2d Lieutenant 3d Pennsylvania, 11th November, 1776; 1st Lieutenant, 1st January, 1777; 1st Lieutenant and Adjutant 3d Continental Artillery, 14th April, 1777; resigned 14th February, 1780.

Hogan, ——. (S. C.). Captain 5th South Carolina; wounded at Savannah, 9th October, 1779.

Hogan Henry (N. Y.). Lieutenant New York Militia, 1775-1776.

Hogan, Philip (S. C.). Hospital Physician and Surgeon, October, 1780, to close of war.

Hoge, John (Pa). 2d Lieutenant 6th Pennsylvania Battalion, 9th January, 1776; taken prisoner at Isle aux Noix, 24th June, 1776; exchanged 20th April, 1778. (Died 4th August, 1824.)

Hogeboom, Cornelius (N. Y.). 1st Lieutenant and Captain New York Militia, 1775-1776.

Hogeboom, Stephen (N. Y.). Lieutenant-Colonel New York Militia in 1775.

Hogenbach, Henry (Pa). Captain of Kachlein's Battalion Pennsylvania Militia, ——; taken prisoner at Long Island, 27th August, 1776; exchanged 9th December, 1776.

Hogg, Ebenezer (Mass). Sergeant of Nixon's Massachusetts Regiment, April to November, 1775; Sergeant 18th Continental Infantry, 1st January, 1776; Ensign, 18th May, 1776; cashiered, 31st July, 1776.

Hogg, Samuel (Va). Ensign 1st Virginia, November, 1776; 2d Lieutenant, 11th January, 1777; Captain Lieutenant, 18th December, 1777; taken prisoner at Charleston, 12th May, 1780; exchanged 14th June, 1781; Captain, 15th May, 1782, and served to close of war.

Hogg, Thomas (N. C.). 1st Lieutenant 1st North Carolina, 1st September, 1775; Captain, 10th April, 1776; Major 5th North Carolina, 19th September, 1777; transferred to 3d North Carolina, 1st June, 1778; taken prisoner at Charleston, 12th May, 1780; exchanged

March, 1781, and served to close of war; Brevet Lieutenant-Colonel, 30th September, 1783.

Hogun, James (N. C.). Major Georgia Militia in 1776; Colonel 7th North Carolina, 26th November, 1776; transferred to 3d North Carolina, 1st June, 1778; Brigadier-General Continental Army, January 9th, 1779; taken prisoner at Charleston, 12th May, 1780, and died in captivity 4th January, 1781.

Hoisington, Joab (N.Y.). Major Commandant Battalion of Rangers, 6th August, 1776, to 1st January, 1781.

Hoit, Benjamin (Conn). Ensign 4th Connecticut, 1st January, 1777; resigned 30th December, 1777.

Hoit, Micah (N. H.). 2d Lieutenant 26th Continental Infantry, 1st January to 31st December, 1776; 2d Lieutenant New Hampshire, 8th November, 1776; 1st Lieutenant, 22d December, 1777; furloughed 30th April, 1779, and did not return to service.

Hoit, Nathan (N. H.). Ensign 3d New Hampshire, 8th November, 1776; Regimental Quartermaster, 1st August, 1778, to 15th September, 1780; 2d Lieutenant, 1st May, 1778; Lieutenant, 28th October, 1778; transferred to 1st New Hampshire, 1st January, 1781; retired March, 1782. (Died 6th January, 1820.)

Hoit, Stephen (N. H.). 2d Lieutenant 1st New Hampshire, 23d April, 1775; 1st Lieutenant 18th June to December, 1775.

Holbrook, Amos (Mass). Surgeon's Mate 24th Continental Infantry, 1st January, 1776; Surgeon, — May to 31st December, 1776. (Died July, 1842.)

Holbrook, Benjamin (N. H.). Ensign of Bedel's Regiment New Hampshire Rangers, January 1776; taken prisoner at the Cedars, 19th May, 1776.

Holbrook, David (Mass). Lieutenant Massachusetts Militia in 1776; 1st Lieutenant 4th Massachusetts, 1st January, 1777; Captain, 14th April, 1780, and served to 3d June, 1783. (Died 13th January, 1834.)

Holbrook, Ichabod (Mass). Sergeant in Lexington Alarm, April, 1775; Sergeant in Lincoln's Massachusetts Regiment, May to December, 1775, 2d Lieutenant 16th Continental Infantry, 1st January to 31st December, 1776. (Died 31st March, 1823.)

Holbrook, Nathan (Mass). Private in Lexington Alarm, April, 1775; Sergeant in Read's Massachusetts Regiment, April to November, 1775; 2d Lieutenant 6th Massachusetts, 1st January, 1777; 1st Lieutenant, 1st March, 1777; Regimental Quartermaster, 3d July, 1779; retired 1st August, 1782. (Died 8th September, 1819.)

Holbrook, Royal (Mass). Lieutenant of Read's Massachusetts Regiment, May to December, 1775.

Holbrook, Silas (Mass). Surgeon's Mate 13th Massachusetts, — October, 1778, to ——.

Holcomb, Benjamin (Conn). Ensign of Ward's Connecticut State Regiment, 14th May, 1776, to May, 1777. (Died 1807.)

Holcomb, George (N. J.). Major New Jersey Militia, 1780-1781.

Holcomb, Timothy (Conn.) 1st Lieutenant 4th Connecticut, 1st May to 10th December, 1775.

Holcombe, Henry (Va). Captain Virginia Dragoons, 1779-1780. (Died 22d May, 1824.)

Holcombe, John (Va) 1st Lieutenant 4th Virginia, 19th February, 1776; Captain, 28th November, 1776; wounded at Germantown, 4th October, 1777, and served to ——; was Colonel Virginia Militia, 1780-1781.

Holcombe, Philemon (Va). 1st Lieutenant of Captain Thomas Watkins' Company Virginia Dragoons at Guilford in March 1781. (Died 1833.)

Hold, Joseph (Va). 1st Lieutenant 10th Virginia, 12th January, 1777; resigned 1st April, 1778.

Holden, Aaron (Mass). Sergeant in Lexington Alarm, April, 1775; Sergeant in Brewer's Massachusetts Regiment, April to December, 1775; 2d Lieutenant 6th Continental Infantry, 1st January, 1776; 1st Lieutenant, 28th June, 1776; 1st Lieutenant 7th Massachusetts, 1st January, 1777; taken prisoner at Cherry Valley, 10th November, 1778, and was a prisoner when retired, 1st January, 1781. (Died 1810.)

Holden, Abel (Mass). Sergeant in Lexington Alarm, April, 1775; Adjutant of Nixon's Massachusetts Regiment, May to December, 1775; 2d Lieutenant and Adjutant 4th Continental Infantry, 1st January to 31st December, 1776; Captain 6th Massachusetts, 1st January, 1777; resigned 8th May, 1781. (Died 2d August, 1818).

Holden, Benjamin (Mass). Lieutenant-Colonel of Minute Men in the Lexington Alarm, April, 1775; Lieutenant-

Colonel of Doolittle's Massachusetts Regiment, May to December, 1775; Lieutenant-Colonel 27th Continental Infantry, 1st January to 31st December, 1776.

Holden Charles (R. I.). Paymaster 2d Rhode Island, 1st January, 1777, to ——; omitted July, 1778.

Holden, Isaac (R. I.). 1st Lieutenant 9th Continental Infantry, 1st January, 1776. (Died 29th June, 1827.)

Holden, John, Jr. (Mass). Private and Sergeant in Read's Massachusetts Regiment, May to December, 1775; Sergeant 13th Continental Infantry, January to December, 1776; Ensign 6th Massachusetts, 1st January, 1777; 2d Lieutenant, 17th April, 1778; 1st Lieutenant, 13th April, 1780; transferred to 2d Massachusetts, 12th June, 1783, and served to 3d November, 1783. (Died 13th March, 1828.)

Holden, John (Mass). Adjutant of Read's Massachusetts Regiment, May to December, 1775; 1st Lieutenant 13th Continental Infantry, 1st January to 31st December, 1776; Captain Lieutenant 6th Massachusetts, 1st January, 1777; Captain, 6th March, 1779; resigned 13th April, 1780.

Holden, John (R I.). Ensign 1st Rhode Island, 3d May to December, 1775; 1st Lieutenant 9th Continental Infantry, 1st January to 31st December, 1776; 1st Lieutenant and Adjutant 1st Rhode Island, 1st January, 1777; Captain, 10th October, 1777; retained in Olney's Rhode Island Battalion, 14th May, 1783, and served to November, 1783; Brevet Major, 30th September, 1783.

Holden, Levi (Mass). Served as a private in a Massachusetts Regiment in 1775; Sergeant and Sergeant-Major 4th Continental Infantry, 1st January to 31st December, 1776; Ensign 6th Massachusetts, 1st January, 1777; 2d Lieutenant, 22d December, 1777; 1st Lieutenant, 6th March, 1779; retired 1st January, 1783. (Died 28th April, 1828.)

Holden, Nathaniel (Mass). Lieutenant in Lexington Alarm, April, 1775; 1st Lieutenant of Bridge's Massachusetts Regiment, May to December, 1775.

Holden, Phineas (Mass). Surgeon of Walker's Massachusetts Regiment, May to December, 1775.

Holden, Thomas (R. I.). Captain 1st Rhode Island, 3d May to December, 1775, and served subsequently as Brigadier-General Rhode Island Militia.

Holden, William (Vt). Captain of Bedel's Regiment Vermont Militia, 1777-1778.

Holder, John (Va). Ensign 2d Virginia, 27th November, 1775; Lieutenant, 23d February, 1776. (In service April, 1777.)

Holding, Matthew (S. C.). Lieutenant South Carolina Militia in 1776.

Holdridge, Hezekiah (Conn). Private in the Lexington Alarm, April, 1775; 1st Lieutenant 4th Connecticut, 1st May to 10th December, 1775; Captain 22d Continental Infantry, 1st January, 1776; Major, 3d September, 1776; Major 2d Connecticut, 1st January, 1777; Lieutenant-Colonel 7th Connecticut, 25th May, 1778; retired 1st January, 1781.

Holdridge, John (Mass). Sergeant 3d Massachusetts, 20th December, 1776; Ensign, 26th November, 1777; Lieutenant, 8th May, 1782, and served to 3d June, 1783. (Died 30th November, 1834.)

Hole —— (Pa). Surgeon's Mate 5th Pennsylvania Battalion, March, 1776, to ——.

Holgate, Matthew (Pa) 2d Lieutenant of Lewis' Pennsylvania Battalion of the Flying Camp, July to December, 1776.

Holland, Francis (Md). Captain Maryland Militia, 1776.

Holland, George (Va). 2d Lieutenant 14th Virginia ,10th March 1777; 1st Lieutenant, 4th October, 1777; transferred to 10th Virginia, 14th September, 1778; resigned 12th October, 1779.

Holland, Ivcry (Mass). Private Company of Minute Men, April to December, 1775; Sergeant in Holmes New York Regiment, January to December, 1776; 2d Lieutenant 5th Massachusetts, 2d April, 1777; 1st Lieutenant, 11th November, 1778; Regimental Quartermaster 25th April, 1781, and served to 3d June, 1783. (Died 1820.)

Holland, James (N. C.). Lieutenant and Captain North Carolina Militia, 1776-1781.

Holland, Park (Mass). Private in Holman's Regiment in 1776; Ensign 5th Massachusetts, 7th November 1777; Lieutenant, 3d October, 1780, and served to 3d June, 1783. (Died 21st May 1844.)

Holland, Spier (N. C.). Ensign 5th North Carolina, 24th March, 1776; 1st Lieutenant, 25th October, 1777, and served to ——.

Holland, Thomas (Del). Adjutant 4th Pennsylvania Battalion, 8th January, 1776; resigned 15th March, 1776; 2d Lieutenant Delaware Regiment, 25th April, 1776; 1st Lieutenant and Adjutant, August, 1776; Captain, 4th December, 1776; died 13th October, 1777, of wounds received 4th October, 1777, at Germantown.

Hollenbeck, Daniel (Va). Ensign 12th Virginia, — December, 1776; resigned — August, 1777.

Hollenbeck, John (Conn). Ensign of Burrall's Continental Regiment, 23d January, 1776; 1st Lieutenant 7th Connecticut, 1st January, 1777; Captain Lieutenant, 12th January, 1780; resigned 18th March, 1780.

Hollenbeck, Matthew (Conn). Eisign of Ransom's Wyoming Valley Company 26th August, 1776; retired 27th July, 1778.

Holliday, Clement (Md). 1st Lieutenant Maryland Battalion of the Flying Camp, July to December, 1776; Paymaster 5th Maryland, 10th December, 1776; resigned 24th February, 1779.

Holliday, James (Pa). Ensign 1st Continental Infantry, 16th February, 1776; 2d Lieutenant, 10th August, 1776; 2d Lieutenant 1st Pennsylvania, 1st January, 1777; killed at Brandywine, 11th September, 1777.

Holliday, John (Pa). 1st Lieutenant of Thompson's Pennsylvania Rifle Battalion, 25th June, 1775; 1st Lieutenant 1st Continental Infantry, 1st January, 1776; Captain, 25th September, 1776; taken prisoner at Fort Washington 16th November, 1776; Captain 1st Pennsylvania, 1st January, 1777, to rank from 25th September, 1776; resigned 1st March, 1778. (Died 19th August, 1823.)

Holliday, John (Pa). 1st Lieutenant of Watt's Pennsylvania Battalion of the Flying Camp, 10th July, 1776; taken prisoner at Fort Washington 16th November, 1776.

Holliday, Joseph (Va). Ensign 6th Virginia, 16th February, 1776; 2d Lieutenant, 11th September, 1776;. 1st Lieutenant, — March, 1777; resigned 23d July, 1777; Captain Virginia Militia, 1780-1781.

Holliday, Philip (Va). Cadet 6th Virginia, 17th July, 1776, to ——.

Hollinbreck, John (Conn). Ensign of Burrall's Continental Regiment, 23d January, 1776; 1st Lieutenant 7th Connecticut, 8th January, 1777; Captain Lieutenant, 12th January, 1780; resigned 18th March, 1780.

Hollinshead, John (N. J.). 1st Lieutenant 2d New Jersey, 28th October, 1775; Captain, 30th November, 1776; Major 3d New Jersey, 4th August, 1779; transferred to 2d New Jersey, 1st January, 1781; resigned 27th November, 1781. (Died 1798.)

Hollingsworth, Charles (N. C.). Lieutenant 4th North Carolina, ——, 1777, to ——.

Hollingsworth, Henry (Md). Lieutenant-Colonel and Colonel Maryland Militia, 1776-1781. (Died 1803.)

Hollis, Moses (S. C.). Lieutenant South Carolina Militia, 1780-1782.

Hollis, Silas (Mass). Private in Lexington Alarm, April, 1775; 1st Lieutenant 16th Continental Infantry, 1st January to 31st December, 1776.

Hollister, Jesse (Mass). Corporal in Lexington Alarm, April, 1775; Sergeant in Paterson's Massachusetts Regiment, April to December 1775; Sergeant 15th Continental Infantry, 1st January, 1776; Ensign 12th September, 1776; 1st Lieutenant to 1st Massachusetts, 1st January, 1777; Captain Lieutenant, 6th January, 1780; Captain, 21st March, 1782; transferred to 4th Massachusetts, 1st January, 1783, and served to November, 1783. (Died 19th January, 1831.)

Hollister, Jonathan (Conn). Ensign 3d Connecticut, 1st January, 1777; died 22d March, 1777.

Hollister, Thomas (Conn). Ensign of Wolcott's Connecticut State Regiment, December, 1775, to March, 1776; 1st Lieutenant of Gay's Connecticut Regiment, June to December, 1776. (Died 1813.)

Holloway, —— (Va). Captain of Anderson's Regiment Virginia Militia, killed in the expedition against Cherokee Indians, April 1, 1782.

Holloway, James (Va). Ensign 12th Virginia, 28th September, 1777; 2d Lieutenant, 29th November, 1777; retired 14th September, 1778. (Died 1829.)

Holloway, Joseph (R. I.). Captain 1st Rhode Island, 3d May to December, 1775.

Hollowell, Samuel (N. C.). Lieutenant 8th North Carolina, 20th September, 1777; retired 1st June, 1778.

Holman, Edward (Mass). 2d Lieutenant of Glover's Massachusetts Regiment, 19th May, 1775, to ——.

Holman, John (Mass). Colonel Massachusetts Militia in 1777.

Holman, Jonathan (Mass). Major of Learned's Massachusetts Regiment, April to December, 1775; Colonel Massachusetts Militia, 1776. (Died 1814.)

Holman, William Jr. (Va). Ensign 9th Virginia, 13th March, 1776, to ——.

Holme, Benjamin (N. J.). Colonel New Jersey Militia, 1777-1778.

Holme, John (N. J.). Colonel New Jersey Militia in 1777.

Holmer, Christian (Va). Sergeant of Artillery, June, 1775, to May, 1776; 2d Lieutenant of Artillery, May, 1776; Major 1st Continental Artillery, 30th November, 1776; retired 1st January, 1781.

Holmes, Abijah (Pa). Lieutenant Colonel Pennsylvania Militia, 1777.

Holmes, Asa (N. Y.). Ensign of Nicholson's Continental Regiment, March, 1776, to — November, 1776.

Holmes, Asher (N. J.). Colonel New Jersey Militia; taken prisoner at Shoal Harbor, 30th December, 1779. (Died 1808.)

Holmes, Benjamin (Va).—See **Hoomes.**

Holmes, David (Conn). Surgeon 8th Connecticut, 1st January, 1777; died 20th March, 1779.

Holmes, David (Pa). Ensign of Wilson's Battalion to guard stores at Carlisle, Pa., 20th October, 1777, to January, 1783.

Holmes, David (Va). Surgeon 9th Virginia, 5th May, 1779; transferred to 7th Virginia, 12th February, 1781, and served to close of war.

Holmes, Eliphalet (Conn). Captain in Selden's Connecticut State Regiment, 20th June to December, 1776; Captain 1st Connecticut, 1st January, 1777; resigned 27th August, 1780.

Holmes, Elisha (N. J.). 2d Lieutenant 4th New Jersey, 28th November, 1776; 2d Lieutenant, 17th February, 1777; retired 1st July, 1778.

Holmes, Esiah (N. Y.). Ensign of Nicholson's Continental Regiment, March to November, 1776.

Holmes, Hardy (N. C.). 2d Lieutenant 1st North Carolina, — November, 1776; 1st Lieutenant, ——, 1777, to ——; Captain, ——; wounded at Eutaw Springs, 8th September, 1781; served to close of war.

Holmes, Hugh (R. I.) 1st Lieutenant of Sherburne's Continental Regiment, 10th March, 1777; dismissed 10th July, 1778.

Holmes, Isaac (Va). Ensign 2d Virginia State Regiment, 2d September, 1777; 1st Lieutenant, 15th September, 1778, and served to January, 1781.

Holmes, James (N. J.). Surgeon 2d New Jersey, 20th December, 1775, to November, 1776. Served subsequently as Surgeon New Jersey Militia.

Holmes, James (N. J.). Captain 4th New Jersey, 23d November, 1776; resigned 17th March, 1778.

Holmes, James (N. Y.). Colonel 4th New York, 30th June, 1775, and served to December, 1775, when he renewed his obligations to Great Britain. (Died 8th July, 1824.)

Holmes, James (Pa). 3d Lieutenant 1st Battalion of Miles' Pennsylvania Rifle Regiment, 15th April, 1776; resigned 31st December, 1776.

Holmes, James (Va). Ensign 2d Virginia, 25th January, 1776, to ——.

Holmes, John (Conn). 1st Lieutenant of Chester's Connecticut State Regiment, 20th June, 1776; died 27th August, 1776.

Holmes, John (Ga). Chaplain 1st Georgia, 16th February, 1776, to ——. (Died 1806.)

Holmes, John (N. J.). 2d Lieutenant 1st New Jersey, 9th February, 1776; 1st Lieutenant, 28th November, 1776; Captain, 1st February, 1779, and served to April, 1783.

Holmes, Jonathan (N. J.). Ensign of Forman's New Jersey Regiment, June to November, 1776; 2d Lieutenant 4th New Jersey, 28th November, 1776; 1st Lieutenant, 1st January, 1777; taken prisoner at Trenton, 2d January, 1777; transferred to 2d New Jersey, 1st July, 1778; Captain, 16th April, 1780, and served to April, 1783.

Holmes, Lemuel (Mass). 1st Lieutenant of Sargeant's Massachusetts Regiment, May to December, 1775; 1st Lieutenant 16th Continental Infantry, 1st January, 1776; Captain, 15th October, 1776; taken prisoner at Fort Washington, 16th November, 1776; exchanged 8th November, 1778. (Died 2d November, 1822.)

Holmes, Silas (Conn). Surgeon's Mate 8th Connecticut, 6th July to 10th December, 1775; Surgeon's Mate 17th Continental Infantry, 1st January,

1776; taken prisoner at Long Island, 27th August, 1776; exchanged January, 1777.

Holmes, Thomas (Conn). Captain Connecticut Militia in 1776.

Holmes, Thomas C. (Va). Lieutenant Virginia Militia, 1780-1781.

Holmes, Uriel (Conn). 2d Lieutenant of Ward's Connecticut State Regiment, 14th May, 1776, to May, 1777.

Holmes, William (N. J.). 1st Lieutenant 2d New Jersey, 28th November, 1776; Captain, 1st December, 1777; retired 1st January, 1781.

Holt, James (Conn). 2d Lieutenant 20th Continental Infantry, 1st January to 31st December, 1776; 2d Lieutenant 4th Connecticut, 1st January, 1777; died 11th May, 1777.

Holt, James (Va). Ensign 15th Virginia, 15th March, 1778; 2d Lieutenant, 1st April, 1778; regiment designated 11th Virginia, 14th September, 1778; 1st Lieutenant, 12th August, 1779; taken prisoner at Charleston, 12th May, 1780; exchanged 14th June, 1781; transferred to 4th Virginia, 12th February, 1781, and served to close of war.

Holt, John Hunter (Va). 1st Lieutenant 1st Virginia State Regiment, 29th April, 1777; Captain, 29th September, 1778, and served to January, 1781.

Holt, Joseph (Va) Ensign 4th Virginia, 23d February, 1776; 2d Lieutenant, 17th August, 1776; 1st Lieutenant, 6th January, 1777; wounded at Trenton, 2d January, 1777; resigned 1st April, 1778.

Holt, Silas (Conn). Private 3d Connecticut, 6th May to 10th December, 1775; Ensign, 4th Connecticut, 1st January, 1777; 2d Lieutenant, 13th January, 1778; 1st Lieutenant, 20th May, 1779; transferred to 1st Connecticut, 1st January, 1781, and served to 3d June, 1783.

Holt, Thomas (Mass). Surgeon's Mate of Sargeant's Massachusetts Regiment, May to December, 1775.

Holt, Thomas (Va). Sergeant 1st Virginia, — February, 1776; Ensign, — September, 1776; 2d Lieutenant, 9th August, 1777; retired 30th September, 1778.

Holt, Thomas (Va). Ensign 15th Virginia, 15th June, 1777; 2d Lieutenant, 4th October, 1777, to ——.

Holt, Timothy (Conn). 2d Lieutenant of Sage's Connecticut State Regiment, June to December, 1776.

Holton, Jonathan (N. H.). Lieutenant of Nichols' Regiment New Hampshire Militia, ——; wounded at Bennington, 16th August, 1777. (Died 19th November, 1821.)

Holton, William (—). Volunteer, ——; wounded and taken prisoner at Quebec, 31st December, 1775.

Holtzendorf, Louis Casimer de (France). Lieutenant-Colonel Continental Army, 20th November, 1776; resigned 31st January, 1778.

Homans, Edward (Mass). Lieutenant of Glover's Massachusetts Regiment, May to December, 1775.

Homans, John (Mass). Surgeon of Woodbridge's Massachusetts Regiment, May to August, 1775; Surgeon 2d Continental Infantry, 1st January to 31st December, 1776; Surgeon 2d Continental Dragoons, 18th December, 1776; resigned 4th August, 1781. (Died 18th June, 1800.)

Honeyman, William (Pa). 2d Lieutenant 2d Pennsylvania, 15th January, 1777; wounded at Iron Hill, 3d September, 1777; transferred to Invalid Regiment 1st July, 1778; resigned 20th July, 1781.

Honeywell, Israel (N. Y.). Captain New York Militia; was a prisoner; when and where taken not stated.

Honeywell, Richard. — See **Hunnewell.**

Hood, Edward (Ga). Captain 2d Georgia, ——; on roll for August, 1778.

Hood, Samuel (Mass). Captain of Ward's Massachusetts Regiment, 23d May, 1775, to ——.

Hood, Wm. (Pa). Ensign of Calderwood's Independent Company, 23d January, 1777; transferred to 11th Pennsylvania, 13th January, 1779; retired 1st January, 1781.

Hooe, Seymour (Va). 2d Lieutenant 2d Virginia, 29th September to November, 1775; 2d Lieutenant 2d Virginia, 25th January, 1776; retired 14th September, 1778.

Hooghkerk, John (N. Y.). 1st Lieutenant 4th New York, 21st March, 1776; 1st Lieutenant 1st New York, 21st November, 1776, to rank from 21st March, 1776; resigned 13th January, 1779.

Hoogland, Jeronimus (N. Y.). Lieutenant and Adjutant of Lasher's New York Militia Regiment, June, 1776; taken prisoner at Long Island, 27th August, 1776; exchanged, January, 1777; Lieutenant and Adjutant 2d Continental Dragoons, 7th October, 1777; Captain, 20th November, 1778, and served to close of war.

Hooke, Arendt (N. Y.). 2d Lieutenant 1st New York, February to November, 1776.

Hooke, James (Va). Captain 13th Virginia, 19th December, 1776; resigned 21st April, 1778. (Died 23d January, 1824.)

Hooke, John (Va). Ensign 8th Virginia, 16th March, 1777; resigned 21st April, 1778.

Hooker, Noadiah (Conn). Captain 2d Connecticut, 1st May to 18th December, 1775; Captain of Wolcott's Connecticut State Regiment, December, 1775 to November, 1776; served subsequently as Colonel Connecticut Militia. (Died 3d June, 1823.)

Hooker, Roger (Conn). Sergeant 2d Connecticut, 4th May to 18th December 1775; 2d Lieutenant 22d Continental Infantry, 1st January to 1st December, 1776; Brigade-Major Connecticut Militia in 1781.

Hooker, Zibeon (Mass). Drummer of a company of Minute Men at Bunker Hill in June, 1775; Sergeant 6th Continental Infantry, 1st October, 1776; Ensign 5th Massachusetts, 1st January, 1777; 2d Lieutenant, 27th November, 1777; 1st Lieutenant, 11th April, 1780, and served to June, 1783. (Died 24th December, 1840.)

Hoomes, Benjamin (Va). Ensign 2d Virginia, 29th September, 1775; 2d Lieutenant, 10th May, 1776; 1st Lieutenant, 28th June, 1776; Captain, 24th April, 1778; retired 14th September, 1778. Name also spelled Holmes.

Hoomes, Thomas C. (Va). 2d Lieutenant 2d Virginia State Regiment, 2d March, 1778; Regimental Quartermaster, 21st August, 1778; 1st Lieutenant, 1st June, 1779; died 13th August, 1779. Name also spelled Holmes and Homes.

Hooper, Henry (Md). Brigadier-General Maryland Militia, 6th January, 1776, to 1783.

Hooper, John (N. H.). 1st Lieutenant 3d New Hampshire, 23d May, to December, 1775.

Hooper, Robert (Pa). 2d Lieutenant 10th Pennsylvania, 29th April, 1777; 1st Lieutenant, 1st June, 1778; retired 1st July, 1778.

Hooper, Robert Lettis Jr (N. J.). Deputy Quartermaster-General, 1777 to 1782. (Died 1785.)

Hooper, William (N. C.). A signer of the Declaration of Independence. Died 11th October, 1790.

Hooper, William E. (Md). Surgeon's-Mate 5th Maryland, 15th July, 1777; resigned 28th April, 1778.

Hoops, Adam (Md). 2d Lieutenant 2d Canadian (Hazen's) Regiment, 10th December, 1776; 1st Lieutenant, 15th October, 1777; Captain, 15th October, 1779; transferred to 4th Maryland, 15th November, 1779; taken prisoner at Camden, 16th August, 1780; transferred to 2d Maryland, 1st January, 1781, but was a prisoner on parole to close of war.

Hoops, Robert (N. J.). Brigade-Major to General Dickinson in 1776; Deputy Commissary-General of Issues, 1st July, 1777; resigned 6th August, 1777.

Hopes, Robert (Pa). Ensign 6th Pennsylvania Battalion, 9th January, 1776; wounded at Three Rivers, 8th June, 1776; Regimental Quartermaster, 17th October, 1776; Captain of Hartley's Additional Continental Regiment, 13th January, 1777; killed at Brandywine, 11th September, 1777.

Hopewell, William (Md). Major 4th Maryland Battalion of the Flying Camp, July to December, 1776.

Hopkins, Benjamin (N. H.). 2d Lieutenant and Adjutant of Warner's Continental Regiment, 16th September, 1776; 1st Lieutenant, 2d May, 1778; killed 6th September, 1780, near Lake George.

Hopkins, Charles (Conn). Adjutant 17th Continental Infantry, 1st January, 1776; taken prisoner at Long Island, 27th August, 1776; exchanged, 9th December, 1776; 1st Lieutenant of Webb's Continental Regiment, 1st January, 1777; resigned 23d February, 1779.

Hopkins, Christopher (R. I.) 2d Lieutenant and Regimental Quartermaster, 11th Continental Infantry, 1st January to 31st December, 1776.

Hopkins, David (S. C.) 2d Lieutenant 3d South Carolina, 17th June, 1775; was a Captain in 1779, and served to ——.

Hopkins, David (Va). Served as a volunteer with General Arnold at Quebec in 1775; Captain 4th Continental Dragoons, 21st January, 1777; Major 1st Continental Dragoons, ——, 1780; served to close of war. (Died 4th March, 1824.)

Hopkins, Elisha (Conn). Sergeant 17th Continental Infantry 1st January, 1776; Lieutenant and Regimental Adjutant, May, 1776; taken prisoner at Long Island, 27th August, 1776; exchanged 8th December, 1776; Lieutenant and Adjutant of Webb's Continental Regiment, 1st January, 1777; taken prisoner on the Expedition to Long Island, 10th December, 1777; exchanged 17th December, 1780; Captain, 10th October, 1779; transferred to 3d Connecticut, 1st January, 1781; retained in Swift's Connecticut Regiment, June, 1783, and served to 3d November, 1783.

Hopkins, Ezekiel (Pa). Ensign of Montgomery's Pennsylvania Battalion of the Flying Camp; taken prisoner at Fort Washington, 16th November, 1776.

Hopkins, John (——). Assistant Deputy Quartermaster-General, 14th July, 1777, to ——.

Hopkins, Joseph (R. I.). Ensign of Tallman's Rhode Island State Regiment, 12th December, 1776, to May, 1777.

Hopkins, Roswell (N. Y.). Lieutenant-Colonel and Colonel New York Militia, 1775-1781. (Died 1827.)

Hopkins, Samuel (Va). Captain 6th Virginia, 26th February, 1776; Major, 29th November, 1777; wounded at Germantown, 4th October, 1777; Lieutenant-Colonel 14th Virginia, 19th June, 1778; Regiment designated 10th Virginia, 14th September, 1778; taken prisoner at Charleston, 12th May, 1780; exchanged ——; transferred to 1st Virginia, 12th February, 1781, and served to close of war. (Died October, 1819.)

Hopkins, Stephen (R. I.). A signer of the Declaration of Independence. Died 13th July, 1785.

Hopkins, Stephen (R. I.). 1st Lieutenant of Richmond's Rhode Island State Regiment, 19th August, 1776, to March, 1777.

Hopkins, Wait (N. H.). Captain Green Mountain Boys, 27th July, 1775; Captain of Warner's Continental Regiment, 5th July, 1776; killed near Stony Point, 15th July, 1779.

Hopkinson, Francis (N. J.). A signer of the Declaration of Independence. Died 9th May, 1791.

Hopper, John (N. J.). Ensign 2d New Jersey, 21st June, 1781; retained in New Jersey Battalion, April, 1783, and served to 3d November, 1783. (Died 4th November, 1819.)

Hopper, Jonathan (N. J.). Captain New Jersey Militia, ——; murdered by Tories at New Barbadoes, N. J., 21st April, 1779.

Hopper, William (Va). Captain Virginia Militia, 1780 1781.

Hoppin, Benjamin (R. I.). Lieutenant 2d Rhode Island, 15th January, 1776; Captain of Lippitt's Rhode Island Regiment, 19th August, 1776, to February, 1777; Captain Rhode Island Militia in 1779. (Died 1809.)

Hopson, Henry (Va). Captain Virginia Militia, 1775. (Died 1780.)

Hopson, Joseph (Va). See Hobson.

Hopson, Linus (Conn). Sergeant of Baldwin's Artillery Artificer Regiment, 1st August, 1777; Ensign, 13th August, 1778; Lieutenant, 12th November, 1779; resigned 31st October, 1780.

Hord, James (Va). Ensign 7th Virginia, 13th January, 1777; resigned 7th March, 1778, and served subsequently as Captain Virginia Militia.

Hord, John (Va). Lieutenant 4th Continental Dragoons, 20th January, 1777; was a Captain in Lee's Light Dragoons in 1779, and served to ——.

Hord, Thomas (Va). 2d Lieutenant 10th Virginia, 13th December, 1776; 1st Lieutenant, 1st March, 1777; Captain Lieutenant, 10th September, 1778; regiment designated 6th Virginia, 14th September, 1778; wounded and taken prisoner at Charleston, 12th May, 1780; Captain, 18th February, 1781; prisoner on parole to close of war.

Horne, Benjamin (N. J.). Ensign 4th New Jersey, 3d December, 1776; 2d Lieutenant, 1st January, 1777; 1st Lieutenant, 1st February, 1779; transferred to 3d New Jersey, 1st July, 1778; resigned 4th March, 1780.

Horry, Daniel (S. C.). Captain 2d South Carolina, 17th June, 1775; was Colonel South Carolina Dragoons in 1779, and served to ——.

Horry, Hugh (S. C.). Major and Lieutenant-Colonel South Carolina Regiment, 1779-1781.

Horry, Peter (S. C.). Captain 2d South Carolina, 17th June, 1775; Major, 16th September, 1776; wounded at Eutaw Springs, 8th September, 1781; served to close of war. Also reported as Colonel South Carolina Militia in 1779-1781.

Horse, Seymour (Va). 2d Lieutenant 2d Virginia, 25th January, 1776, to ——.

Horsey, John (Md). Lieutenant Maryland Militia, 1777-1778.

Horseford, Obadiah (Conn). Lieutenant-Colonel Connecticut Militia in 1776.

Horton, Ambrose (N. Y.). Captain 4th New York, 28th June, to November 1775.

Horton, Azariah (——). Lieutenant-Colonel Deputy Commissary-General of Musters, 6th April, 1779, to ——.

Horton, Elisha (Mass). Sergeant Major 6th Massachusetts, 1st January, 1777. Ensign 2d April, 1781; transferred to 12th Massachusetts, 12th June, 1783; retained in Jackson's Continental Regiment, November, 1783, and served to 20th June, 1784.

Horton, James (Conn). Sergeant of Baldwin's Artillery Artificer Regiment, 1st August, 1777; Lieutenant, 18th November, 1778; Captain, 1st June, 1779; retired March, 1781. (Died 30th July, 1825.)

Horton, Jonathan (N. J.). Surgeon New Jersey Militia, February to December, 1776; Hospital Surgeon Northern Department, May, 1779; died 26th February, 1780.

Horton, Joseph (N. J.). Captain New Jersey Militia, ——; wounded at Middletown, 12th July, 1780.

Horton, Jotham (Mass). 1st Lieutenant of Griddey's Regiment, Massachusetts Artillery, 30th April to November, 1775; Captain-Lieutenant of Knox Regiment, Continental Artillery, 1st January, 1776; taken prisoner at Fort Washington, 16th November, 1776; (broke his parole. It does not appear that he joined the latter regiment.) Captain 3d Continental Artillery, 1st January, 1777; resigned 12th September, 1778.

Horton, Thomas (N. Y.). Captain New York Militia, ——; taken prisoner at Fort Clinton, 6th October, 1777, and died in captivity, 30th January, 1778.

Horton, Timothy (Mass). Surgeon Massachusetts Militia, 1777-1778.

Horton, William (N. Y.). 2d Lieutenant of Nicholson's New York Regiment, —— July, 1776; cashiered 5th December, 1776.

Hosford, Amos (Conn). Lieutenant of Wolcott's Connecticut State Regiment, December, 1775, to March, 1776.

Hosman, Joseph (Del). Ensign Delaware Regiment, 5th April, 1777, 2d

Lieutenant, 6th August, 1778; 1st Lieutenant, 12th June, 1780. Retired 17th May, 1782.

Hosmer, Joseph (Mass). Lieutenant of company of Minute Men and acting Adjutant of troops at Concord, 19th April, 1775; Captain Massachusetts Militia, 1775-1776. (Died 1821.)

Hosmer, Prentice (Conn). Ensign 3d Connecticut, 1st January, 1777; 2d Lieutenant, 25th April, 1778; 1st Lieutenant 1st January, 1781; transferred to 4th Connecticut, 1st January, 1781. Resigned 15th August, 1782.

Hosmer, Timothy (Conn). Surgeon 2d Continental Artillery, 1st January, 1777; Surgeon 6th Connecticut, 10th May, 1779; retired 1st January, 1781. (Died 1815.)

Hosterman, Peter (Pa). Colonel Pennsylvania Militia, 1779.

Hotchkiss, Caleb (Conn). Captain of Spencer's Continental Regiment, —— January, 1776; killed in the attack at New Haven, 5th July, 1779.

Hotchkiss, Levi (Conn). Private in Lexington Alarm, in April, 1775; Ensign 8th Connecticut, 1st January, 1777; 2d Lieutenant, 21st March, 1778; resigned 1st May, 1779.

Houdin, Michael Gabriel (Mass). 1st Lieutenant 15th Massachusetts, 1st January, 1777; Captain, 28th June, 1779; transferred to 5th Massachusetts, 1st January, 1781; transferred to 2d Massachusetts, 12th June, 1783, and served to 3d November, 1783; Brevet Major, 6th February, 1784. (Died 4th February, 1802.)

Hough, John (Conn). Lieutenant in Lexington Alarm, April, 1775; 1st Lieutenant 1st Connecticut, 1st May to 1st December, 1775; Captain Connecticut Militia, 1776-1777.

Hough, Samuel (Conn). Private 1st Connecticut, 1st May to 20th November, 1775; Private of Baldwin's Artillery Artificer Regiment, 2d October, 1777; Sergeant, 1st November, 1778; Lieutenant, October, 1779; resigned 1st November, 1779. (Died 20th April, 1824.)

Houghberry, Henry (Pa). Ensign Pennsylvania Battalion of the Flying Camp; taken prisoner at Fort Washington, 16th November, 1776.

Houghton, Jacob (N. J.). Captain and Lieutenant-Colonel New Jersey Militia, 1776-1780.

Houghton, John (N. H.). Captain New Hampshire Militia in 1776.

Houghton, Jonathan (Mass). Lieutenant in Lexington Alarm, April, 1775, 1st Lieutenant of Whitcomb's Massachusetts Regiment, May to December, 1775; Captain Massachusetts Militia, 1776. (Died 1829.)

House, John (N. H.). Lieutenant of Bedel's New Hampshire Regiment 22d January, to 1st July, 1776; Captain of Baldwin's Regiment, New Hampshire Militia, 20th September, 1776; Captain 1st New Hampshire, 8th November, 1776; resigned 4th March, 1778. (Died 17th February, 1825.)

House, Joseph (Mass). 2d Lieutenant of Bridge's Massachusetts Regiment, May to December, 1775; 2d Lieutenant 23d Continental Infantry, 1st January, to 31st December, 1776; 2d Lieutenant 2d Massachusetts, 1st January, 1777; resigned 16th August, 1778.

House, Joseph (R. I.). 2d Lieutenant of Bailey's Massachusetts Regiment, May to December, 1775; 2d Lieutenant of Sherburne's Continental Regiment, 28th February, 1777; resigned 6th January, 1778.

House, Lawrence (Va). Captain Virginia Militia, 1779-1781.

House, Simeon (Conn). Ensign of Mott's Connecticut State Regiment, June to December, 1776; 2d Lieutenant 1st Connecticut, 1st January, 1777; resigned, 29th December, 1777.

Houston, Alexander (——). Lieutenant of Patton's Continental Regiment, 14th January, 1777 to ——.

Houston, Christopher (N. C.). Captain North Carolina Rangers, 1776 to 1782. (Died 12th May, 1837.)

Houston, James (N. C.). Captain North Carolina Rangers, 1777 to 1780; wounded at Ramsour's Mill, 20th June, 1780. (Died 2d August, 1819.)

Houston, John (N. Y.). 2d Lieutenant 1st New York, 28th June to December, 1775; Captain 3d New York, 1st November, 1776; omitted February, 1777; deserted to the enemy.

Houston, John (Pa). Hospital Surgeon, 1776-1777. (Died 1809.)

Houston, William (Pa). Ensign of Hartley's Continental Regiment, 30th September, 1776; taken prisoner at Fort Washington, 16th November, 1776; 2d Lieutenant and Adjutant, 2d June, 1778; regiment designated, 11th Pennsylvania, 16th December, 1778; 1st Lieutenant, 24th February, 1780; transferred to 6th Pennsylvania, 1st January, 1781; transferred to 2d Pennsylvania, 1st January, 1783, and served to 3d June, 1783. (Died 1834.)

Houstown, James (Ga). Surgeon 1st Georgia, 1778 to close of war.

Hovenbergh, Rudolph Van. See **Van Hoevenbergh.**

**Hovenden, —— ** (Ga). Lieutenant Pulaski Legion; wounded at Fishdam Ford, 9th November, 1780.

Hovenden, Edward (Pa). Ensign 5th Pennsylvania Battalion, 8th January, 1776; taken prisoner at Fort Washington, 16th November, 1776.

Hovenden, Thomas (Ga). Lieutenant-Colonel 4th Georgia, 1st February, 1777. Died 16th April, 1778.

Hovey, Dominicus (Mass). Lieutenant 4th Massachusetts 1st January, 1777; retired 1st April, 1779; served subsequently as Lieutenant and Captain Massachusetts Military.

Hovey, Ivory (N. H.). Surgeon 3d New Hampshire, 8th November, 1776; resigned 1st April, 1778; Surgeon 13th Massachusetts to rank from 16th Februray, 1778; resigned 31st August, 1779.

Howard, Abner (Mass). Ensign of Learned's Massachusetts Regiment, May to December, 1775.

Howard, James (Va). Ensign 7th Virginia, 13th Janaury, 1777, to ——.

Howard, John (Mass). Ensign of Learned's Massachusetts Regiment, May to December, 1775.

Howard, John Eager (Md). Captain 2d Maryland Battalion of the Flying Camp, July, 1776; Major 4th Maryland, 22d February, 1777; Lieutenant-Colonel 5th Maryland, 11th March, 1778; transferred to 2d Maryland, 22d October, 1779. By the act of 9th March, 1781, it was "Resolved, That a medal of silver be presented to Lieutenant-Colonel Howard of the Infantry, with emblems and mottoes discriptive of his conduct at the battle of Cowpens, January 17th, 1781." Wounded at Eutaw Springs, 8th September, 1781; retired April, 1783. (Died 12th October, 1827.)

Howard, Joshua (N. H.). Captain New Hampshire Militia in 1777. (Died 1839.)

Howard, Thomas (Va). 2d Lieutenant 12th Virginia, 1st April, 1777; served to ——.

Howard, Thomas H. (Md).. Surgeons-Mate 1st Maryland, 1st April, 1778; resigned 10th June, 1779.

Howard, Vashel D. (Va). Captain 4th Continental Dragoons, 24th January, 1777; died 15th March, 1778.

Howe, Abraham (Mass). Ensign 12th Continental Infantry, 1st January to 31st December, 1776.

Howe, Baxter (Mass). 2d Lieutenant 21st Continental Infantry, 1st January, 1776; 1st Lieutenant, 12th July, 1776; taken prisoner at Long Island, 27th August, 1776; 1st Lieutenant 2d Continental Artillery, 1st January, 1777; Captain-Lieutenant, 9th November, 1778. Died 20th September, 1781.

Howe, Bezaleel (N. H.). Private in Reed's New Hampshire Regiment, 23d April to 8th July, 1775; 2d Lieutenant, 1st New Hampshire, 8th November, 1776; wounded at Stillwater, 19th September, 1777; 1st Lieutenant 23d June, 1779; Captain, 10th October, 1783; served to close of war; Lieutenant 2d United States Infantry, 4th March, 1791; Captain 4th Sub Legion, 4th November, 1791; Major, 20th October, 1794; honorably discharged, 1st November, 1796. (Died 3d September, 1825.)

Howe, Caleb (Ga). 1st Lieutenant 1st Georgia, 7th January, 1776; Captain ——, 1777, and served to ——; was Colonel Georgia Militia in 1780.

Howe, Darius (Mass). Corporal in Fellow's Massachusetts Regiment, April to November, 1775; Corporal, 12th Massachusetts, 25th February, 1777; Quartermaster Sergeant, 31st August, 1777; Ensign 20th November, 1779; Lieutenant, 14th October, 1780; transferred to 1st Massachusetts, 1st January, 1781; resigned 14th May, 1781.

Howe, Estes (Mass). Surgeon of Brewer's Massachusetts Regiment, 24th April, to 1st August, 1775; Surgeon 5th Massachusetts, 1st January, 1777; resigned 1st May, 1779.

Howe, Ezekiel (Mass). Colonel Massachusetts Militia in 1780.

Howe, James (N. H.). Surgeon's-Mate and Surgeon New Hampshire Militia.

Howe, Mark (N. H.). Surgeon 3d New Hampshire 10th October, 1780; retired 1st January 1781.

Howe, Moses (Mass). Sergeant in Lexington Alarm, April, 1775; 2d Lieutenant of Brewer's Massachusetts Regiment, April to November, 1775.

Howe, Richard Surcombe (Mass). Ensign 10th Massachusetts 22d June, 1782; transferred to 4th Massachusetts 1st January, 1783, and served to close of war; 2d Lieutenant United States Infantry, 4th March, 1791; assigned to 4th Sub Legion, 4th September, 1792; Captain, 27th November, 1792. Died 22d January, 1793.

Howe, Robert (Ga). Lieutenant and Regimental Quartermaster 2d Georgia, ——, 1778 to —— October, 1782.

Howe, Robert (N. C.). Colonel 2d North Carolina, 1st September, 1775; Brigadier-General Continental Army, 1st March, 1776; Major-General, 20th October, 1777, and served to close of war. (Died 12th November, 1785.)

Howe, Solomon (Conn). Surgeon's-Mate 8th Connecticut, 1st January, 1777; died 10th June, 1778.

Howe, Squire (R. I.). Lieutenant of Elliott's Regiment, Rhode Island Artillery, 1777-1778.

Howe, Zadock (Conn). Priate in the Lexington Alarm, April, 1775; Private 4th Connecticut, 24th May to 28th December, 1775; 1st Lieutenant of Sherburne's Continental Regiment, 1st January, 1777; resigned 5th April, 1780. (Died 7th November, 1819.)

Howell, Caleb (Ga). 1st Lieutenant 1st Georgia, 7th January, 1776, to ——.

Howell, Ebenezer (N. J.). Major 4th New Jersey, 28th November, 1776; resigned 17th February, 1777; served also as Major New Jersey Militia. (Died 1791.)

Howell, Elias (N. C.). Ensign 8th North Carolina, 12th November, 1776; 2d Lieutenant, 12th July, 1777; retired 1st July, 1778.

Howell, Ezekiel (Pa). 2d Lieutenant 2d Continental Artillery 1st February, 1777; 1st Lieutenant 4th Continental Artillery 1st January, 1781, and served to 17th June, 1783.

Howell, James (N. J.). Ensign 2d New Jersey, 29th November, 1776; resigned 5th February, 1777.

Howell, John (N. J.). Ensign 1st New Jersey, 29th November, 1776; 2d Lieutenant 26th April, 1777; 1st Lieutenant, 29th October, 1777; Captain, 20th November, 1781, and served to

April, 1783. (Died 18th September, 1830.)

Howell, Joseph (Pa). Captain Pennsylvania Musket Battalion, 15th March, 1776; taken prisoner at Long Island, 27th August, 1776; exchanged, 9th December, 1776; Paymaster, 2d Pennsylvania, 27th August, 1778; resigned 1st October, 1778; Commissioner of Army Accounts and acting Paymaster General United States Army, 28th August, 1778 to 8th May, 1792. (Died 8th August, 1798.)

Howell, Lewis (Del). 1st Lieutenant Delaware Regiment, 13th January, 1776 to January, 1777.

Howell, Lewis (N. J.). Surgeon 2d New Jersey, 28th November, 1776; died 5th June, 1778.

Howell, Richard (N. J.). Captain 2d New Jersey, 29th November, 1775; Brigade-Major to General Stark's Brigade, 4th September, 1776; Major 2d New Jersey, 28th November, 1776; resigned 7th April, 1779. (Died 28th April, 1802.)

Howell, Silas (N. J.). Captain 1st New Jersey, 14th November, 1775; resigned 4th January, 1779.

Howelman, —— de (——). Lieutenant and Quartermaster of Armand's Corps, 9th December, 1776; Lieutenant 1st Cavalry Pulaski Legion, 1st March, 1779; resigned 1st September, 1779.

Howlett, Davis (N. H.). Captain New Hampshire Militia, 1777-1778.

Hoxie, Gideon (R. I.). Lieutenant-Colonel of Richmond's Rhode Island State Regiment, 1st November to December, 1776. (Died 1805.)

Hoxie, John (R. I.). Captain-Lieutenant of Varnum's Rhode Island Regiment, 3d May, 1775, to ——.

Hoxie, Peleg (R. I.). Lieutenant of Lippitt's Rhode Island State Regiment, 19th August, 1776, to March, 1777. (Died 1818.)

Hoyt, Stephen (N. H.). 2d Lieutenant 1st New Hampshire, 23d May to December, 1775; Lieutenant New Hampshire Militia, 1776-1777. (Died 1824.)

Hubbard, Charles Holby (Mass). Paymaster 16th Continental Infantry, 13th September 1776; killed at Montressor's Island, 23d September, 1776.

Hubbard, Elihu (Conn). 1st Lieutenant, 8th Connecticut, 6th July to 10th December, 1775; Captain 17th Continental Infantry, 1st January, to 31st December, 1776.

Hubbard, George (Conn). Ensign of Sage's Connecticut State Regiment, 20th June to December, 1776; 1st Lieutenant 2d Connecticut, 1st January, 1777; resigned 29th December, 1777.

Hubbard, Hezekiah (Conn). Sergeant 2d Connecticut, 5th May to 10th December, 1775; Ensign 22d Continental Infantry, 1st January to 31st December, 1776; 2d Lieutenant 3d Connecticut, 1st January, 1777; 1st Lieutenant, 1st July, 1779; retired June, 1783.

Hubbard, John (Conn). 2d Lieutenant 8th Connecticut, 21st March, 1778; 1st Lieutenant, 20th May, 1779. Retired 1st January, 1781.

Hubbard, John (Mass). Lieutenant in Lexington Alarm, April, 1775; 1st Lieutenant of Fellows' Massachusetts Regiment, May to December, 1775.

Hubbard, John (R. I.). Ensign 1st Canadian (Livingston's) Regiment, 18th December, 1776; transferred to 2d Rhode Island, 1st February, 1779; Lieutenant, 18th May, 1779, and served to May, 1781.

Hubbard, John (R. I.). Ensign 2d Rhode Island 1st February, 1779; 2d Lieutenant, 18th May, 1779; retained in Olney's Rhode Island Battalion, 14th May, 1781, and served to November, 1783.

Hubbard, Jonas (Mass). Lieutenant in Lexington Alarm, April, 1775; Captain of Ward's Massachusetts Regiment, 23d May, 1775; wounded and taken prisoner at Quebec, 31st December, 1775; died 1st January, 1776.

Hubbard, Jonathan (Conn). 2d Lieutenant 5th Connecticut, 1st January, 1777; resigned 3d January, 1778.

Hubbard, Nehemiah (Conn). 2d Lieutenant and Paymaster of Burrall's Continental Regiment, 31st July, 1776, to 31st January, 1777; Deputy Quartermaster General, November, 1778 to close of war. (Died 1837.)

Hubbard, Oliver (Conn). Ensign of Sage's Connecticut State Regiment, 20th June to 25th December, 1776.

Hubbard, Philip (Mass). Captain of Scammon's Massachusetts Regiment, May to December, 1775; Captain Massachusetts Militia, 1776. (Died 1792.)

Hubbard, Thomas (Va). Sergeant and Sergeant Major 1st Virginia, 13th

February, 1776; Regimental Quartermaster, —— October, 1777 to 1st May, 1778; retired 30th September, 1778; was Captain of Virginia Militia in 1779 and 1780.

Hubbell, Isaac (Conn). Private in Lexington Alarm, April, 1775; Private in 5th Connecticut, 17th May to 17th November, 1775; 1st Lieutenant and Adjutant 2d Continental Artillery, 1st January, 1777, to 1st July, 1779; Captain-Lieutenant, 13th September, 1778; Regimental Paymaster, 1st January, 1781, to June, 1783; transferred to Corps Artillery, 17th June, 1783, and served to 3d November, 1783. (Died 1842.)

Hubbard, Isaac (N. Y.). 2d Lieutenant 3d New York, June, 1775 to March, 1776; 1st Lieutenant of Nicholson's New York Regiment, May to November, 1776.

Hubbell, John (Mass). Ensign 12th Massachusetts, 1st January, 1777; 2d Lieutenant, 5th July, 1777; resigned 28th July, 1780.

Hubbell, Salmon (Conn). Private 7th Connecticut, 22d July to 23d December, 1775; Ensign 8th Connecticut, 1st January, 1777; 2d Lieutenant, 26th March, 1778; 1st Lieutenant, 20th April, 1779; transferred to 5th Connecticut, 1st January, 1781; Regimental Paymaster, 1st November, 1781; retired 1st January, 1783. (Died 11th March, 1830.)

Hubbell, Shadrach (Conn). 2d Lieutenant of Swift's Connecticut State Regiment, July to November, 1776.

Hubbell, William (Conn). Private 5th Connecticut, 10th May to 17th November, 1775; Ensign of Elmore's Connecticut State Regiment, 15th April, 1776; 2d Lieutenant 2d Continental Artillery, 1st January, 1777; 1st Lieutenant, 12th September, 1778; resigned 1st October, 1780. (Died, 1830.)

Hubbell, William G. (Conn). Captain 7th Connecticut 6th July to 23d December, 1775; Captain of Sullivan's Connecticut State Regiment, 20th June to December, 1776; Captain Connecticut Militia in 1777.

Hubley, Adam (Pa). Captain 1st Pennsylvania Battalion 27th October, 1775; Major 10th Pennsylvania, 6th December, 1776; transferred to Hartley's Continental Regiment, 12th January, 1777; Lieutenant-Colonel 10th Pennsylvania, 12th March, 1777, to rank from 4th October, 1776; Lieutenant-Colonel

Commandant 11th Pennsylvania, 13th February, 1779; retired 17th January, 1781. (Died May, 1793.)

Hubley, Bernard (Pa). 1st Lieutenant German Battalion, 12th August, 1776; Captain, 24th February, 1778; retired 1st January, 1781. (Died 1808.)

Hubley, Frederick (Pa). 2d Lieutenant and Regimental Quartermaster of Thompson's Pennsylvania Rifle Battalion, 25th June, 1775; 1st Lieutenant and Regimental Quartermaster 1st Continental Infantry, 1st January to 31st December, 1776. (Died 23d December, 1822.)

Hubley, George (Pa). Captain German Regiment, 8th July, 1776; Major, 9th April, 1777; died 7th February, 1779.

Huddy, Joshua (N. J.). Captain New Jersey State Artillery Company, ——; taken prisoner at Tom's River, New Jersey, 2d April, 1782, and hanged by the Tories, 12th April, 1782.

Hudson, Charles (Va). Regimental Quartermaster 14th Virginia, 22d February, 1777; resigned 28th April, 1777.

Hudson, Hooper (Md). 3d Lieutenant of Barrett's Independent Maryland Company, 14th January, 1776; 1st Lieutenant 2d Maryland, 10th December, 1776; marked "dead" on roll for December, 1777.

Hudson, John (Va). 1st Lieutenant 2d Virginia State Regiment, September, 1777; Captain, 1st October, 1778, and served to January, 1781.

Hudson, Martin (Va). 2d Lieutenant 9th Virginia, 21st July, 1776; resigned 25th April, 1778.

Hudson, Robert (Del). Lieutenant-Colonel Delaware Battalion of the Flying Camp, July to December, 1776; Lieutenant-Colonel Delaware Militia; taken prisoner at his home, 7th February, 1778.

Hudson, William (Va). Sergeant 6th Virginia, 16th February, 1776; Sergeant-Major, 2d September, 1776; Ensign, 28th April, 1777; 2d Lieutenant, 26th May, 1777; retired 30th September, 1778.

Huffman, Philip (Va). Ensign 8th Virginia, 16th March, 1777; taken prisoner at Germantown, 4th October, 1777; escaped 1st June, 1778; 2d Lieutenant, 2d November, 1777; transferred to 4th Virginia, 14th September, 1778; 1st Lieutenant, 9th March, 1779, to ——; in service March, 1781.

Hufnagel, Michael (Pa). Adjutant 1st Continental Infantry, 7th September, 1776; Captain 8th Pennsylvania, 16th March, 1777; retired 1st July, 1778. (Died 31st December, 1819.)

Huger, Benjamin (S. C.). Lieutenant 4th South Carolina (Artillery), 17th June, 1775; Major 5th South Carolina, 16th September, 1776; killed at Charleston, 11th May, 1779.

Huger, Francis (S. C.). Captain 2d South Carolina, 17th June, 1775; Lieutenant-Colonel Deputy Quartermaster-General Southern Department in 1777; resigned in 1778. (Died 18th August, 1811.)

Huger, Isaac (S. C.). Lieutenant-Colonel 1st South Carolina, 17th June, 1775; Colonel, 5th South Carolina, 16th September, 1776; Brigadier-General Continental Army, 9th January, 1779; wounded at Stono Ferry, 20th June, 1779, and at Guilford, 15th March, 1781; served to close of war. (Died 17th October, 1797.)

Huger, John (S. C.). Captain South Carolina Militia, 1776, 1777.

Hugg, Samuel (N. J.). Captain Western Company New Jersey Artillery, 1st March, 1776, to June, 1777.

Huggins, Benjamin (S. C.). Ensign 2d South Carolina, April, 1781; Lieutenant, 1782, and served to close of war.

Huggins, John (S. C.). Captain South Carolina Militia, 1778-1779.

Hughes, Greenburry (Pa). 2d Lieutenant 6th Pennsylvania, 15th February, 1777; retired 1st July, 1778.

Hughes, Henry (Va). Ensign 7th Virginia, 10th October, 1776; resigned — October, 1777; Captain Virginia Militia, 1779-1781.

Hughes, Henry (S. C). 2d Lieutenant 2d South Carolina, 17th June, 1775, to ——.

Hughes, Hugh (N. Y.). Commissary of Military Stores, 16th February, 1776; Assistant to Quartermaster-General, 11th May, 1776, to 6th December, 1781. (Died 1804.)

Hughes, Isaac (Pa). Lieutenant-Colonel of Lewis' Pennsylvania Battalion of the Flying Camp, July to December, 1776. (Died 1782.)

Hughes, James (Conn). 2d Lieutenant of Elmore's Connecticut State Regiment, 15th April to December, 1776; 2d Lieutenant 2d Continental Artillery, 1st February, 1777; dropped 8th September, 1777, with remark, transferred to a Georgia Regiment.

Hughes, James M. (N. Y.). 2d Lieutenant 1st New York, 22d July, 1775; 1st Lieutenant, 24th February, 1776; 1st Lieutenant 2d New York, 21st November, 1776; resigned 7th December, 1776. Served subsequently as Brigade Major New York Levies.

Hughes, Jasper (Va). Cornet 1st Continental Dragoons, —, 1781; transferred to Baylor's Consolidated Regiment of Dragoons, 9th November, 1782, and served to close of war.

Hughes, John (Md). 1st Lieutenant 2d Canadian (Hazen's) Regiment, 3d November, 1776; Captain, 1st September, 1778; resigned 1st November, 1781.

Hughes, John, Sr. (Pa). Ensign 6th Pennsylvania Battalion, 23d June, 1776; 2d Lieutenant 7th Pennsylvania, 20th March, 1777; resigned 13th May, 1777.

Hughes, John, Jr. (Pa). Sergeant 6th Pennsylvania Battalion, 29th January, 1776; Ensign 21st June, 1776; Ensign 7th Pennsylvania, January, 1777; 2d Lieutenant, 25th September, 1777; Regimental Quartermaster, 1st June, 1778; 1st Lieutenant, 25th April, 1779; transferred to 4th Pennsylvania, 17th January, 1781, and served to close of war. (Died 1818.)

Hughes, John (Pa). 2d Lieutenant of Hartley's Continental Regiment, 12th January, 1777; 1st Lieutenant, 1st June, 1777, to ——.

Hughes, John (Pa). 2d Lieutenant 1st Pennsylvania, 22d February, 1777; 1st Lieutenant 20th March, 1778; Captain Lieutenant, 1st October, 1779; retired 17th January, 1781.

Hughes, John (Pa). 1st Lieutenant 8th Pennsylvania, 9th August, 1776; resigned 23d November, 1778.

Hughes, John (Va). Quartermaster-Sergeant 1st Continental Dragoons, February, 1777; Regimental Quartermaster, 27th December, 1777; Captain, 31st March, 1781; transferred to Baylor's Consolidated Regiment of Dragoon's, 9th November, 1782, and served to close of war.

Hughes, John (Va). 2d Lieutenant 7th Virginia, ——; 1st Lieutenant, 25th April, 1779; taken prisoner at Charleston, 12th May, 1780.

Hughes, Joseph (S. C.). Captain South Carolina Militia at Eutaw Springs in 1781. (Died 1834.)

Hughes, Peter (Pa). 1st Lieutenant 1st Pennsylvania Battalion, 27th October, 1775; 1st Lieutenant 2d Pennsylvania, 25th October, 1776; Aide-de-Camp to General Gates 14th October, 1776; resigned 1st January, 1777.

Hughes, Pratt (Va). Ensign 1st Virginia State Regiment, 7th December, 1778; 2d Lieutenant, 16th July, 1779, and served to January, 1781.

Hughes, Samuel (Mass). 2d Lieutenant 12th Continental Infantry, 1st January to 31st December, 1776; name also spelled Huse. (Died 22d October, 1820.)

Hughes, Thomas (Md). Lieutenant-Colonel Maryland Militia in 1776.

Hughes, Thomas (R. I.). Ensign 3d Rhode Island, June to December, 1775; 2d Lieutenant 11th Continental Infantry, 1st January, 1776; wounded at Long Island, 27th August, 1776; 1st Lieutenant 2d Rhode Island, 1st January, 1777; Captain, 23d June, 1777; retained in Olney's Rhode Island Battalion, 14th May, 1781, and served to November, 1783; Brevet Major, 30th September, 1783. (Died 10th December, 1821.)

Hughes, Thomas (S. C.). Lieutenant South Carolina Artillery, 1778.

Hughes, Thomas (Va). 2d Lieutenant 2d Virginia, 21st October, 1775; Paymaster 7th Virginia, 1st December, 1776; dismissed 8th March, 1778.

Hughes, Timothy (N. Y.). 2d Lieutenant 1st New York, 28th June to December, 1775; 2d Lieutenant of Nicholson's New York Regiment, 21st April, 1776; Captain 1st Canadian (Livingston's) Regiment, 18th December, 1776; resigned 25th October, 1778.

Hugo, Thomas Brogden (Md). 2d Lieutenant 5th Maryland, 20th February, 1777; 1st Lieutenant, 26th January, 1778; transferred to 1st Maryland, 1st January, 1781; Captain, 12th June, 1781; wounded at Eutaw Springs, 8th September, 1781; resigned October, 1781.

Hulbert, John (N. Y.). Captain 3d New York, 28th June, 1775, to January, 1776; served subsequently as Lieutenant-Colonel and Colonel New York Militia.

Huling, John (Pa). Captain 2d Pennsylvania Battalion, 5th January, 1776; Captain 3d Pennsylvania, 1st January, 1777; Major, 1st August, 1777; retired 1st July, 1778.

Huling, Thomas (Pa). Ensign 3d Pennsylvania, 19th June, 1778; retired 1st January, 1781. (Died 1808.)

Hull, David (Conn). Private 2d Connecticut, 6th May to 19th December, 1775; 2d Lieutenant of Elmore's Continental Regiment, 15th April, 1776; 1st Lieutenant 6th Connecticut, 1st January, 1777; Captain Lieutenant, 19th April, 1779; resigned 2d May, 1779. (Died 8th December, 1831.)

Hull, Edwin (Va). Captain 15th Virginia, 25th November, 1776; retired 30th September, 1778; killed in service 15th September, 1780, where not stated.

Hull, Elias (R. I.). Ensign 9th Continental Infantry, 1st Januay to 31st December, 1776; Ensign 1st Rhode Island, 1st January, 1777; 2d Lieutenant, 17th February, 1777; resigned 26th April, 1778.

Hull, Isaac (N. J.). 1st Lieutenant of Spencer's Continental Regiment, 17th February, 1777; resigned 22d November, 1777.

Hull, Jehiel (Conn). Ensign 4th Connecticut, 1st May to 10th December, 1775.

Hull, Joseph (Conn). Ensign of Bradley's Connecticut State Regiment, 10th June, 1776; taken prisoner at Fort Washington, 16th November, 1776; exchanged 18th September, 1778. (Died 1825.)

Hull, Miles (Conn). 2d Lieutenant of Douglas' Connecticut State Regiment, June to December, 1776.

Hull, William (Conn). Captain Lieutenant 7th Connecticut, 6th July, 1775; Captain, 9th October, 1775; Captain 19th Continental Infantry, 1st January to 31st December, 1776; Major 8th Massachusetts, 1st January, 1777; Lieutenant-Colonel 3d Massachusetts, 12th August, 1779; retained in Jackson's Continental Regiment, 3d November, 1783, and served to 20th June, 1784; Brigadier-General United States Army, 8th April, 1812; cashiered 25th April, 1812. (Died 29th November, 1825.)

Humberg, Frederick.—See **Heimberger.**

Hume, Alexander (S. C.). Lieutenant 2d South Carolina, 1777; killed at Savannah, 9th October, 1779.

Hume, William (N. Y.). Captain New York Militia, 1781-1783.

Humphrey, Cornelius (N. Y.). Lieutenant-Colonel and Colonel New York Militia, 1775-1781.

Humphrey, Elihu (Conn). Captain 8th Connecticut, 6th July to 10th December, 1775; Major 17th Continental Infantry, 1st January, 1776; wounded and taken prisoner at Long Island, 27th August, 1776; died of wounds in September, 1777.

Humphrey, Jacob (Pa). Captain 6th Pennsylvania, 8th September, 1776; Adjutant, 29th October, 1780; transferred to 1st Pennsylvania, 1st January, 1783, and served to June, 1783. (Died 1826.)

Humphrey, James (N. Y.). Captain New York Militia; taken prisoner at Fort Montgomery, 6th October, 1777.

Humphrey, William (N. Y.). Colonel New York Militia, 1775-1777.

Humphrey, William (R. I.). Lieutenant 2d Rhode Island 17th May, 1775; taken prisoner at Quebec, 31st December, 1775; paroled 11th August, 1776; 1st Lieutenant 2d Rhode Island, 1st January, 1777; Captain, 22d October, 1777; retained in Olney's Rhode Island Battalion, 14th May, 1781, and served to November, 1783; Brevet Major, 30th September, 1783. (Died 1st July, 1832.)

Humphreys, David (Conn). Captain 6th Connecticut, 1st January, 1777; transferred to 4th Connecticut, 1st January, 1781; transferred to 2d Connecticut, 1st January, 1783; Brigade Major to General Parsons, 29th March, 1777; Major and Aide-de-Camp to General Putnam, 18th December, 1778; Aide-de-Camp to General Green, May, 1780, and Lieutenant-Colonel Aide-de-Camp to General Washington, 23d June, 1780; resigned 1st April, 1783. By the act of 3d November, 1781, it was "Resolved, that an elegant sword be presented in the name of the United States, in Congress assembled, to Colonel Humphreys, Aide-de-Camp to General Washington, to whose care the standards taken under the capitulation of York were consigned, as a testimony of their opinion of his fidelity and ability, and that the Board of War take order therein." (Died 21st February, 1818.)

Humphreys, Elijah (Conn). Paymaster 19th Continental Infantry, 22d September to 31st December, 1776; Captain 6th Connecticut, 1st January, 1777; retired 1st January, 1781.

Humphreys, John (Pa). Ensign of Lee's Battalion of Light Dragoons, 2d August, 1779; transferred to 6th Pennsylvania, 25th August, 1779; transferred to 2d Pennslyvania, 17th January, 1781; 2d Lieutenant 4th Continental Artillery, 2d April 1782, and served to 17th June, 1783.

Humphreys, Jonathan (Conn). Sergeant 8th Connecticut, 6th July to 10th December, 1775; 2d Lieutenant and Adjutant, 17th Continental Infantry, 1st January to 31st December, 1776. (Died 18th April, 1822.)

Humphreys, Nathaniel (Conn). 2d Lieutenant 2d Connecticut, 1st May to 10th December, 1775; 1st Lieutenant 22d Continental Infantry, 1st January to 31st December, 1776.

Humphreys, William (N. H.). Adjutant of Ashley's Regiment New Hampshire Militia, 1777.

Humphries, John (Va). 1st Lieutenant of Morgan's Company Virginia Riflemen, September, 1775; killed at Quebec, 31st December, 1775.

Humpton, Richard (Pa). Lieutenant-Colonel Continental Army, 16th July, 1776; Colonel 11th Pennsylvania, 25th October, 1776; transferred to 10th Pennsylvania, 1st July, 1778; transferred to 6th Pennsylvania, 17th January, 1781; transferred to 2d Pennsylvania, 1st January, 1783; Brevet Brigadier-General, 30th September, 1783, and served to 3d November, 1783. (Died 21st December, 1804.)

Hungate, William (Va). Ensign Virginia Militia in August, 1775 .(Died 1822.)

Hungerford, Benjamin (Conn). 2d Lieutenant 4th Connecticut, 1st May, 1775; died 4th September, 1775.

Hungerford, John P. (Va). Lieutenant and Captain of a Virginia State Regiment in 1779 and 1780.

Hungerford, Thomas (Va). 2d Lieutenant 3d Virginia, 15th January, 1777; 1st Lieutenant, 11th September, 1777; retired 30th September, 1778.

Hunkins, Robert (Vt). 2d Lieutenant of Bedel's Vermont Regiment in 1778.

Hunn, Thomas (N. J.). Major New Jersey Militia; cashiered 21st February, 1781.

Hunn, William (N. Y.). Lieutenant New York Militia in 1775.

Hunkins, Robert (Vt). Lieutenant of Bedel's Regiment Vermont Militia in 1777 and 1778.

Hunnewell, Israel (N. Y.). Captain New York Militia; taken prisoner at Westchester, 24th June, 1779.

Hunnewell, Richard (R. I.). Ensign 11th Continental Infantry, 1st January to 31st December, 1776; 2d Lieutenant of Stevens' Battalion of Artillery, 1st February, 1777, which was merged into the 3d Continental Artillery in September, 1778; resigned 25th November, 1778; Lieutenant-Colonel 15th United States Infantry, 3d March, 1799; honorably discharged 15th June, 1800. (Died 8th May, 1823.)

Hunt, Abraham (Mass). Adjutant of Gerrish's Massachusetts Regiment, May to December, 1775; 2d Lieutenant and Adjutant 25th Continental Infantry, 1st January to 31st December, 1776; Captain 1st Massachusetts, 1st January, 1777; resigned 31st August, 1780.

Hunt, David (N. Y.). Private 2d New York, 5th May, 1778, to 17th February, 1779; Regimental Quartermaster 5th New York, 1st July, 1780; retired 1st January, 1781. (Died 1819.)

Hunt, Ephraim (Mass). Ensign of Jackson's Additional Continental Regiment, July, 1777; 2d Lieutenant, 1st May, 1778; regiment designated 16th Massachusetts 23d July, 1780; transferred to 9th Massachusetts, 1st January, 1781; 1st Lieutenant, 9th August, 1781; transferred to 4th Massachusetts, 12th January, 1782, and served to close of war. (Died 16th October, 1805.)

Hunt, Jesse (N. C.). Captain North Carolina Militia, 1778.

Hunt, Jonathan (Vt). Lieutenant-Colonel Vermont Militia in 1776 and 1777.

Hunt, Joseph (Va). Hospital Surgeon's Mate, 28th June, 1775, to May, 1776.

Hunt, Nathaniel (N. J.). Colonel New Jersey Militia in 1776.

Hunt, Oliver (Mass). 2d Lieutenant 1st Massachusetts, 1st January 1777; 1st Lieutenant, 4th November; 1777; resined 4th May, 1780.

Hunt, Samuel (N. H.). Lieutenant-Colonel New Hampshire Militia, 1777-1778.

Hunt, Seth (Mass). Private in Lexington Alarm, April, 1775; Regimental Quartermaster of Fellows' Massachusetts Regiment, May to December, 1775.

Hunt, Stephen (N. J.). Colonel New Jersey Militia, 1776.

Hunt, Thomas (Mass). Sergeant in Captain Craft's Company of Minute Men at Lexington and Concord, April, 1775; Ensign in a Massachusetts Regiment, May to December, 1775; Ensign and Adjutant 25th Continental Infantry, 1st January, 1776; Brigade Major, 20th October, 1776; Captain Lieutenant of Jackson's Additional Continental Regiment, 1st February, 1777; Captain, 1st March, 1779; wounded at Stony Point, 16th July, 1779; regiment designated 16th Massachusetts, 23d July, 1780; transferred to 9th Massachusetts, 1st January, 1781; wounded at Yorktown, 14th October, 1781; transferred to 3d Massachusetts 1st January, 1783; retained in Jackson's Continental Regiment, November, 1783, and served to 20th June, 1784; Captain 2d United States Infantry, 4th March, 1791; assigned to 2d Sub Legion, 4th September, 1792; Major, 18th February, 1793; assigned to 1st United States Infantry, 1st November, 1796; Lieutenant-Colonel, 1st April, 1802; Colonel, 11th April, 1803; died 18th August, 1808.

Hunt, Thomas (N. Y.). 2d Lieutenant 4th New York, 21st November, 1776; 1st Lieutenant, 9th November, 1777 ;retired 1st January, 1781; served subsequently as Captain New York Levies.

Hunt, Thomas (Va). 1st Lieutenant 14th Virginia, 10th March, 1777; regiment designated 10th Virginia, 14th September 1778; Captain, 12th March, 1779; taken prisoner at Charleston, 12th May, 1780, and was a prisoner to May, 1783.

Hunter, Alexander (Pa). Paymaster 1st Pennsylvania 12th April, 1777, to ——.

Hunter, Andrew (N. J.). Chaplain 3d New Jersey, 1st June, 1777; Brigade Chaplain, 5th August, 1778, and served to close of war. (Died 1823.)

Hunter, Daniel (Pa). Colonel Pennsylvania Militia, 1776-1777.

Hunter, David (S. C.). Captain South Carolina Militia in 1775-1781.

Hunter, Elijah (N. Y.). 1st Lieutenant 4th New York, 28th June, 1775; Captain, January, 1776; Captain 2d New York ,21st November, 1776, which he declined, and retired from service 7th December, 1776.

Hunter, Ephraim (Pa). Lieutenant of Watt's Pennsylvania Battalion of the Flying Camp, June, 1776; taken prisoner at Fort Washington, 16th November, 1776; released 8th December, 1780.

Hunter, George (Pa). Surgeon's Mate Hospital Department, 1777-1778.

Hunter, James (N. C.). Major North Carolina Militia at Guilford in March, 1781.

Hunter, James (Pa). 2d Lieutenant and Paymaster 3d Pennsylvania Battalion 12th April, 1776; Captain and Paymaster 4th Pennsylvania, 31st January, 1777 ,to 1st June, 1779.

Hunter, James (S. C.). Surgeon's Mate South Carolina Militia, 1781-1783.

Hunter, John (N. Y.). 1st Lieutenant of Hardenbergh's New York Regiment, August, 1776; Captain of Malcolm's Continental Regiment, 10th April, 1777; taken prisoner at Fort Montgomery, 6th October, 1777; resigned 22d December, 1777.

Hunter, John (Va). 2d Lieutenant of Thruston's Continental Regiment, 20th April, 1777; resigned — June, 1778.

Hunter, Moses (Va). Was Paymaster 4th Virginia in 1777.

Hunter, Patrick (—). Ensign, ——; was a prisoner in 1781-1782; when and where taken not stated.

Hunter, Robert (N. Y.). Ensign of Malcolm's Continental Regiment 1st November, 1777; Lieutenant, 15th March, 1778; retired 22d April, 1779; served subsequently as Captain New York Militia. (Died 7th May, 1835.)

Hunter, Robert (R. I.). Ensign of Olney's Rhode Island Battalion, 1st July, 1781, and served to 15th November, 1783.

Hunter, William (Va). Paymaster 1st Virginia State Regiment, 1777-1778.

Huntington, Amos (Vt). Captain Vermont Militia; taken prisoner at Hubbardton, 7th July ,1777. (Died 1820.)

Huntington, Ebenezer (Conn). Served in the Lexington Alarm, April, 1775; 1st Lieutenant 2d Connecticut, 8th September to 10th December, 1775; 1st Lieutenant 22d Continental Infantry, 1st January, 1776; Captain, May, 1776; Brigade Major to General Heath, August, 1776; Major of Webb's Continental Regiment, 1st January, 1777; Lieutenant-Colonel, 10th October, 1778; transferred to 3d Connecticut, 1st January, 1781; transferred to 1st Connecticut, 1st January, 1783; retained in Swift's Connecticut Regiment, June, 1783, and served to 3d November, 1783; Brigadier-General United States Army, 19th July, 1798; honorably discharged, 15th June, 1800. (Died 17th June, 1834.)

Huntington, Hezekiah (Conn). Major Connecticut Militia in 1775. (Died 1807.)

Huntington, Jabez (Conn). Major-General Connecticut Militia, December,

1776, to May, 1779. (Died 5th October, 1786.)

Huntington, Jedediah (Conn). Colonel in the Lexington Alarm April, 1775; Colonel 8th Connecticut, 6th July to 10th December, 1775; Colonel 17th Continental Infantry, 1st January to 31st December, 1776; Colonel 1st Connecticut, 1st January, 1777; Brigadier-General Continental Army, 12th May, 1777, and served to close of war; Brevet Major-General, 30th September, 1783. (Died 25th September, 1818.)

Huntington, Joshua (Conn). 1st Lieutenant 3d Connecticut, 1st May to 16th December, 1775; Captain of Selden's Connecticut State Regiment, 26th June to 25th December, 1776.

Huntington, Samuel (Conn). A signer of the Declaration of Independence; subsequently Governor of Connecticut; died 5th January, 1796.

Huntington, Simeon (Conn). Ensign in the Lexington Alarm, April, 1775; 1st Lieutenant 17th Continental Infantry, 1st January to 31st December, 1776.

Huntley, Warren (Conn). Regimental Quartermaster 2d Connecticut, 13th May, 1775; Ensign 26th September to 10th December, 1775; was Secretary to General Wooster, 29th July to December, 1775; 2d Lieutenant 22d Continental Infantry, 1st January to 31st December, 1776.

Huntoon, Joseph (N. H.). 2d Lieutenant 8th Continental Infantry, 1st January, 1776; 1st Lieutenant 3d New Hampshire, 8th November 1776; wounded at Stillwater, 7th October, 1777, and retired from service 1st September, 1778. (Died 1812.)

Huntoon, Nathaniel (N. H.). Captain New Hampshire Militia in 1776.

Hurd, Asahel (Conn). Ensign 4th Connecticut, 1st May to 10th December, 1775; 2d Lieutenant of Burrall's Continental Regiment, 23d January, 1776; died 29th August, 1776.

Hurd, Isaac (Mass). Surgeon Massachusetts Militia, June to December, 1776.

Hurd, John J., Jr. (Mass). Ensign 9th Massachusetts, 18th June, 1781; transferred to 2d Massachusetts, 1st January, 1783, and served to 3d November, 1783. (Died 21st August, 1784.)

Hurd, Nathan (Conn). Captain of Silliman's Connecticut State Regiment, June to December, 1776.

Hurd, Samuel (Conn). 2d Lieutenant of Swift's Connecticut State Regiment, June to December, 1776.

Hurlbut, George (Conn). Private in the Lexington Alarm, April, 1775; Sergeant 7th Connecticut, 8th July to 10th December, 1775; Ensign 19th Continental Infantry, 1st January to 31st December, 1776; Cornet 2d Continental Dragoons, 12th April, 1777; Lieutenant, 25th December, 1777; Captain, 1st August, 1779; wounded near Tarrytown, New York, 15th July, 1781, and died of wounds 8th May, 1783.

Hurlbut, John (Conn). 1st Lieutenant of Chester's Connecticut State Regiment, 20th June, 1776; cashiered, 7th October, 1776.

Hurlbut, Samuel (Conn). Private in the Lexington Alarm, April, 1775; Ensign 7th Connecticut, 6th July to 6th December, 1775; 1st Lieutenant 19th Continental Infantry, 1st January, 1776, to February, 1777.

Hurlbut, Simeon (Mass). Ensign 21st Continental Infantry, 1st January, to 31st December, 1776; Lieutenant 4th Massachusetts, 1st January, 1777; resigned 30th October, 1777. (Died 16th August, 1825.)

Hurley, Martin (N. J.). Private and Sergeant 1st New Jersey, November, 1775, to November, 1776; Ensign 1st New Jersey, 29th November, 1776; killed at Germantown, 4th October, 1777.

Hurst, —— (—). Captain ——; taken prisoner at Long Island 27th August, 1776.

Hurt, John (Va). Chaplain 6th Virginia, 1st October, 1776; Brigade Chaplain, 18th August, 1778, to close of war; Chaplain United States Army, 4th March, 1791; resigned 30th April, 1794.

Huston, Alexander (Pa). Ensign Pennsylvania Musket Battalion, 20th March, 1776 ;taken prisoner at Long Island, 27th August, 1776; exchanged 9th December, 1776; Lieutenant of Patton's Continental Regiment, 11th January, 1777; killed at Brandywine, 11th September, 1777.

Huston, John (Va). Ensign 9th Virginia, 10th September, 1776; 2d Lieutenant, 1st April, 1777; resigned 8th September, 1777; name also spelled Hughston.

Hutchins, Amos (N. Y.). Captain 3d New York, 24th February, 1776; Captain 5th New York, 21st November, 1776; resigned 9th May, 1778.

Hutchins, Benjamin (Conn). Captain, Major and Lieutenant-Colonel Connecticut Militia, 1775-1781.

Hutchins, Gordon (N H.). Captain 1st New Hampshire, 23d April to December, 1775; wounded at Bunker Hill, 17th June, 1775; served subsequently as Lieutenant-Colonel New Hampshire Militia. (Died 8th December 1815.)

Hutchins, Hezekiah (N. H.). Captain 3d New Hampshire, 23d May to December, 1775.)

Hutchins, John (N. J.). Ensign of Forman's New Jersey State Regiment, August, 1776; 2d Lieutenant 2d New Jersey, 5th February, 1777; 1st Lieutenant, 1st December, 1777; taken prisoner at Cooper's Ferry, 5th April, 1778, and did not rejoin regiment.

Hutchins, Nathaniel (N. H.). 2d Lieutenant 1st New Hampshire ,23d April, 1775; taken prisoner at Quebec, 31st December, 1775; 1st Lieutenant 5th Continental Infantry, 1st January ,1776; Captain Lieutenant 25th September, 1776; Captain Lieutenant 1st New Hampshire, 8th November, 1776; Captain 2d April, 1777; retired 1st January, 1781. (Died 10th January, 1832.)

Hutchins, Thomas (—). Geographer, ——, to 3d November, 1783.

Hutchins, Thomas (Va). Captain 6th Virginia, 21st March, 1776, to ——.

Hutchins, William (N. H.). Ensign 4th Continental Infantry, 1st January to 31st December, 1776; 2d Lieutenant 1st New Hampshire, 8th November, 1776; 1st Lieutenant, 5th March, 1778; resigned 23d June, 1779. (Died 3d June, 1826.)

Hutchinson, Ebenezer N. Y.). Surgeon's Mate 5th New York, 12th June, 1778; retired 1st January, 1781.

Hutchinson, Elisha (Mass). Regimental Quartermaster-Sergeant of Mansfield's Massachusetts Regiment April to November, 1775; Ensign 27th Continental Infantry, 1st January to 31st December, 1776.

Hutchinson, Israel (Mass). Captain in Lexington Alarm, April, 1775; Lieutenant-Colonel of Mansfield's Massachusetts Regiment, 27th May to December, 1775; Colonel 27th Continental Infantry, 1st January to 31st December, 1776. (Died 16th March, 1811.)

Hutchinson, James (Pa). Surgeon's Mate Hospital Department 31st July, 1778; Surgeon, 1st February, 1779; Surgeon-General of Pennsylvania, 6th Oc-

tober, 1781, to close of war. (Died 6th September, 1793.)

Hutson, Thomas (S. C.). Captain South Carolina Militia; wounded at the siege of Savannah in October, 1779.

Hutton, Christopher (N. Y.). Regimental Adjutant of Meade's New York Militia Regiment, 23d September, 1776; Ensign 3d New York, 21st November, 1776; Regimental Adjutant, 28th May, 1778; Lieutenant, 6th February, 1779; transferred to 2d New York, 1st January, 1783, and served to 3d June, 1783.

Hutton, George (N. Y.). 2d Lieutenant 2d Continental Artillery, 1st January, 1777; resigned 4th May, 1779.

Hutton, James (Pa). Lieutenant of Baldwin's Artillery Artificer Regiment, 20th March, 1780; retired — May, 1781.

Huysradt, Adam (N. Y.). Captain New York Militia in 1775.

Hyatt, Abraham (N. Y.). 2d Lieutenant of Swartwout's New York Militia Regiment, July, 1776; 2d Lieutenant 4th New York, 21st November 1776; 1st Lieutenant, 9th November, 1777; retired 1st January, 1781. (Died 1820.)

Hyatt, John Vance (Del). Ensign Delaware Regiment, 3d December 1776; 2d Lieutenant, 5th April, 1777; taken prisoner at his home, 26th April 1778; 1st Lieutenant 7th September, 1778; exchanged 31st March, 1781, but did not rejoin regiment. (Died 1806.)

Hyde, Caleb (Mass). Colonel Massachusetts Militia in 1777.

Hyde, Elijah (Conn). Major Connecticut Light Horse; wounded at Stillwater, 7th October, 1777.

Hyde, James (Conn). Sergeant 4th Connecticut, 17th March, 1777; Ensign, 27th December, 1777; Lieutenant, 15th November, 1781; retired 13th August, 1782. (Died 1809.)

Hyde, Jedediah (Conn). Captain 22d Continental Infantry, 1st January to 31st December 1776; Captain 4th Connecticut, 1st January, 1777; resigned 31st July, 1777. (Died 1822.)

Hyde, Thomas (R. I.). Lieutenant 11th Continental Infantry 1st January, 1776; wounded at Long Island, 27th August, 1776.

Hyde, William (Md). Captain of Smallwood's Maryland Regiment, 14th January, 1776; Lieutenant-Colonel 2d Maryland Battalion of the Flying Camp, July, 1776, to ——.

Hyer, Jacob (N. J.). Lieutenant-Colonel and Colonel New Jersey Militia, 1776-1778.

Hyer, Jacob, Jr. (N. J.). Private 2d New Jersey, 1st April, 1780; Ensign, 13th May, 1781, and served to April, 1783.

Hyland, John (Md). Lieutenant Maryland Militia, 1776.

Hynes, Andrew.—See **Hines.**

Hyrne, Edmund (S. C.). Captain 2d South Carolina, 17th June ,1775; Major 12th May, 1779; Aide-de-Camp to General Greene in 1781; Deputy Adjutant-General Southern Department, 17th November, 1778, to close of war. By the act of 29th October, 1781, it was "Resolved, that Major-General Greene be desired to present the thanks of Congress to Major Hyrne ,his Aide-de-Camp in testimony of his particular activity and good conduct during the whole action at Eutaw Springs, S. C." Brevet Lieutenant-Colonel, 30th September, 1783.

Hyrne, Henry (S. C.). Captain South Carolina Militia 1775-1776.

I.

Iarber, Anathasis (Va). Regimental Quartermaster 11th Virginia, 1st November, 1777; resigned 2d April, 1778.

Ijams, John Jr. (Md). 3d Lieutenant of Watkins' Independent Maryland Company of Cannoneers, January, 1776, to ——.

Imbert, Jean Louis (France). Captain-Engineer Continental Army, 19th September, 1776; permitted to return to San Domingo, 12th April, 1777.

Imhoff, John Lewis P. (S. C.). 1st Lieutenant South Carolina Rangers, 17th June, 1775, to ——.

Imlay, Gilbert (N. J.). 1st Lieutenant of Forman's Continental Regiment, 11th January, 1777; resigned 24th July, 1778.

Imlay, William Eugene (N. J.). Captain 3d New Jersey, 7th February to December, 1776; served also as Captain New Jersey Militia.

Ingersoll, George (Mass). Private and Sergeant in Gridley's Regiment Massachusetts Artillery, June to December, 1775, and Sergeant in Knox's Regiment Continental Artillery, December, 1775, to November, 1776; 2d Lieutenant of Stevens' Battalion of Artillery, 9th November, 1776, which

became part of the 3d Continental Artillery; 1st Lieutenant, 10th June, 1779, and served to June, 1783; Lieutenant Artillery Battalion, United States Army, 4th March, 1791; Captain, 2d April, 1792; of the Artillerists and Engineers, 9th May, 1794; Regiment of Artillerists, 1st April, 1802; Major, 8th July, 1802; resigned 1st December, 1804. (Died 11th July, 1805.)

Ingersoll, Peter (Mass). Captain of Brewer's Massachusetts Regiment, May to December, 1775; Captain Massachusetts Militia, 1776-1777.

Ingersoll, Simon (Conn.) 1st Lieutenant of Silliman's Connecticut State Regiment, July to December, 1776.

Inglas, John (N. C.). 1st Lieutenant 2d North Carolina, 3d May, 1776; Captain, 24th October, 1777; taken prisoner at Charleston 12th May, 1780; exchanged June, 1781; served to close of war; Brevet Major, 30th September, 1783.

Ingram, James (N. C.). Lieutenant-Colonel 8th North Carolina, 27th November, 1776; resigned 8th July, 1777.

Inman, Joshua (Ga). Captain Georgia Rangers, 1779-1780.

Inman, Shadrach (Ga). Captain Georgia Militia, ——; killed at Musgrove's Mill, 18th August, 1780.

Innis, Brice (Pa). Surgeon's Mate 3d Pennsylvania, 15th August, 1776; died — May, 1778.

Innis, James (Pa). Ensign 9th Pennsylvania, 4th February, 1779; retired 17th January, 1781.

Innis, James (Va). Lieutenant-Colonel 15th Virginia, 13th November, 1776; retired 30th September, 1778; Judge Advocate of the Army, 9th July to 18th September, 1782.

Ioor, Joseph (S. C.). 1st Lieutenant 1st South Carolina, 17th June, 1775; Captain, May, 1776. He and his whole company were blown up and killed on the Randolph, near Charleston, in April, 1778.

Irby, Edmund (S. C.). Lieutenant South Carolina Militia; wounded at Stono Ferry, 20th June, 1779; served subsequently as Captain South Carolina Militia.

Ireland, George (Md). 2d Lieutenant 6th Maryland, 10th December, 1776; 1st Lieutenant, 1st November, 1777; resigned 4th October, 1778.

Irish, George (R. I.). Colonel Rhode Island Militia, 1776-1777.

Irish, Nathaniel (Pa). Captain of Flower's Artillery Artificer Regiment, 7th February, 1777; omitted December, 1780. (Died 11th September, 1816.)

Irvine, Andrew (Pa). 2d Lieutenant 6th Pennsylvania Battalion, 9th January, 1776; 1st Lieutenant 7th Pennsylvania, 20th March, 1777; Captain, 25th September, 1777; wounded at Paoli, 20th September, 1777; transferred to 4th Pennsylvania, 17th January, 1781; transferred to 1st Pennsylvania, 1st January, 1783, and served to 3d June, 1783. Brevet-Major, 30th September, 1783. (Died 4th May, 1789.)

Irvine, Charles (Md). Ensign 4th Maryland, 10th December, 1776; resigned or died about September, 1777.

Irvine, James (Pa). Lieutenant-Colonel 1st Pennsylvania Battalion, 25th November, 1775; Colonel 9th Pennsylvania, 25th October, 1776; transferred to 2d Pennsylvania, 12th March, 1777; resigned 1st June, 1777; Brigadier General Pennsylvania Militia, 26th August, 1777; wounded and taken prisoner at Chestnut Hill, 5th December, 1777; exchanged 1st June, 1781; Major General Pennsylvania Militia, 27th May, 1782, to close of war. (Died 28th April, 1819.)

Irvine, Matthew (N. Y.). Captain of Malcolm's Continental Regiment, 12th May, 1777; resigned 20th January, 1778.

Irvine, Matthew (Pa). Surgeon's Mate of Thompson's Pennsylvania Rifle Battalion, July to December, 1775; Surgeon of Lee's Battalion of Light Dragoons, 20th July, 1778, to close of war. (Died 31st August, 1827.)

Irvine, William (Pa). Colonel 6th Pennsylvania Battalion, 9th January, 1776; taken prisoner at Three Rivers, 8th June, 1776; paroled 3d August, 1776; exchanged 6th May, 1778; Colonel 7th Pennsylvania, January, 1777, to rank from 9th January, 1776; Brigadier General Continental Army, 12th May, 1779, and served to close of war; Superintendent of Military Stores, 13th March, 1800; died 29th July, 1804.

Irvin, Edward (Va). Cadet 6th Virginia, 25th March, 1776, to ——.

Irwin, Gerard (Pa). 1st Lieutenant 9th Pennsylvania, 18th December, 1776; omitted January, 1777.

Irwin, Henry (N. C.). Lieutenant-Colonel 5th North Carolina, 15th April, 1776; killed at Germantown 4th October, 1777.

Irwin, John (N. C.). Ensign 1st North Carolina, 28th March, 1777; 2d Lieutenant, 4th April, 1777; resigned 28th August, 1777; Colonel North Carolina Militia in 1780 and 1781.

Irwin, John (Pa). 2d Lieutenant of Hart's Pennsylvania Battalion of the Flying Camp, July to December, 1776; Ensign 1st Continental Infantry, 1st January, 1776; 2d Lieutenant, 10th August, 1776; 1st Lieutenant 2d Pennsylvania, 1st January, 1777; wounded at Paoli, 20th September, 1777; Captain, 16th May, 1780; retired 1st January, 1781. (Died 11th May, 1808.)

Irwin, John Lawson (Ga). Captain Georgia Militia, November, 1775, to December, 1778.

Irwin, Joseph (Pa). Captain 9th Pennsylvania, 15th November, 1776. retired 1st July, 1778.

Irwin, Matthew (Pa). Captain of Malcolm's Additional Continental Regiment, 12th May, 1777 ;resigned 20th January, 1778; Lieutenant 2d Cavalry Pulaski Legion, May, 1779, and served to close of war. (Died 10th March, 1800.)

Isaacs, Elisha (N. C.). Colonel North Carolina Militia, ——; wounded and taken prisoner at Camden, 16th August, 1780; exchanged July, 1781.

Israel, Isaac (Va). 2d Lieutenant 8th Virginia, 9th September, 1776; 1st Lieutenant, 3d August, 1777; Captain, 10th August, 1777; taken prisoner at Brandywine, 11th September, 1777. He was transferred to the 4th Virginia 14th September, 1778, and was dropped from rolls 23d September, 1779, with remark "never joined."

Isham, John Jr. (Conn). Captain of Chester's Connecticut State Regiment, June to December, 1776 . (Died 1828.)

Israel, John (Va). Cadet 12th Virginia, 25th December, 1776, to ——.

Ittigs, Michael (N. Y.). Captain New York Militia, 1780.

Ivers, Thomas (N. Y.). Captain-Lieutenant of Lamb's Company, New York Artillery, 30th June to December, 1775. (Died 1800.)

Ives, Bezaleel (Conn). Captain Connecticut Militia, 1776-1777.

Ives, Lazarus (Conn). 1st Lieutenant of Wadsworth's Connecticut State Regiment, June to December, 1776.

Ives, Levi (Conn). Surgeon's Mate 1st Connecticut, July to December, 1775.

Ivey, Curtis (N. C.). Ensign 5th North Carolina, 23d April, 1777; 1st Lieutenant 10th October, 1777; transferred to 3d North Carolina, 1st June, 1778; Captain, 1st February, 1779; transferred to 4th North Carolina, 6th February, 1782; served to close of war. Name also spelled Ivory.

J.

Jack, John (Va). Captain Virginia Militia in 1777.

Jack, Matthew (Pa). 1st Lieutenant 8th Pennsylvania, 9th August, 1776; Captain, 13th April, 1777; lost his left hand by bursting of gun at Bound Brook, 13th April, 1777; did not rejoin regiment and was retired 31st January, 1779.

Jack, Patrick (Pa). Captain Pennsylvania Militia in 1777.

Jack, Samuel (Ga). Colonel Georgia Militia, 1776-1781.

Jack, William (Pa). 2d Lieutenant of Morehead's Company, guard at Kittanning, Pennsylvania, 22d January, 1777, to June, 1778.

Jackson, Amasa (Mass). Fifer, Corporal, and Sergeant 8th Massachusetts, 1st January, 1777, to 3d March, 1780; Ensign 8th Massachusetts, 13th October, 1782; transferred to 3d Massachusetts, 12th June, 1783; retained in Jackson's Continental Regiment, 3d November, 1783, and served to 20th June, 1784.

Jackson, Basil (S. C.). Lieutenant 1st S. C., ——, 1776, to ——.

Jackson, Charles (Mass). Fifer 8th Massachusetts, 1st March, 1777; Fife-Major, 1st May, 1780; Ensign, 4th February, 1783; transferred to 3d Massachusetts, 12th June, 1783; retained in Jackson's Continental Regiment, 3d November, 1783, and served to 20th June, 1784.

Jackson, Daniel (Mass). Sergeant of Gridley's Regiment Massachusetts Artillery, May to December, 1775, and in Knox's Regiment Continental Artillery, December, 1775, until taken prisoner at Fort Washington, 16th November, 1776; exchanged 10th December, 1776; 2d Lieutenant 3d Continental Artillery, 1st January, 1777; 1st Lieutenant, 12th September, 1778; transferred to Corps of Artillery, 17th June, 1783, and served

to 3d November, 1783; Major 2d Artillerists and Engineers, 4th June, 1798; in Artillerists, 1st April, 1802; resigned 30th April, 1803.

Jackson, Daniel (N. Y.). Lieutenant and Adjutant New York Militia Regiment in 1776; Ensign of Malcolm's Additional Continental Regiment, 11th March, 1777; resigned 8th April, 1777.

Jackson, Daniel (S. C.). Captain 2d South Carolina, ——; resigned 22d January, 1778.

Jackson, David (Pa). Hospital Physician, 1777, to June, 1780; Hospital Physician and Surgeon, 6th October, 1780; resigned 5th December, 1780; served subsequently as Quartermaster-General State of Pennsylvania. (Died 17th September, 1801.)

Jackson, Ebenezer (Mass). Private, Corporal, and Sergeant 3d Continental Artillery, 3d March, 1777, to 3d March, 1780; 2d Lieutenant 3d Continental Artillery, 27th June, 1781; transferred to Corps of Artillery, 17th June, 1783, and served to 3d November, 1783.

Jackson, Elias (R. I.). Lieutenant Rhode Island Militia, 1776-1777.

Jackson, Ephraim (Mass). 1st Lieutenant of Thomas' Massachusetts Regiment, May to December, 1775; Lieutenant-Colonel 10th Massachusetts, 6th November, 1776; died 19th December, 1777.

Jackson, George (N. J.). Ensign of Forman's Additional Continental Regiment, — March 1777; resigned 7th January, 1778. (Died 1818.)

Jackson, George Hamilton (N. Y.). 2d Lieutenant 3d New York, 28th June to November, 1775.

Jackson, Giles (Mass). Lieutenant-Colonel Massachusetts Militia in 1777. (Died 1810.)

Jackson, Hall (N. H.). Surgeon of Long's Regiment New Hampshire Militia, 1776 and 1777.

Jackson, Henry (Mass). Colonel of one of the Sixteen Additional Continental Regiments, 12th January, 1777; regiment designated 16th Massachusetts, 23d July, 1780; transferred to 9th Massachusetts, 1st January, 1781; transferred to 4th Massachusetts, 1st January, 1783; brevet Brigadier-General, 30th September, 1783; retained as Colonel of Continental or 1st American Regiment, 3d November, 1783, and served to 20th June, 1784. (Died 4th January, 1809.)

Jackson, James (Ga). Captain of a Georgia Regiment of Provincials in 1776; Brigade-Major in 1778; wounded at Medway Church, 24th November, 1778; subsequently Colonel of the Georgia Legionary Corps; received the Keys of Savannah when the British evacuated that city, 11th July, 1782; wounded in a duel with Lieutenant-Governor Wells of Georgia in 1780. (Died 19th March, 1806.)

Jackson, Jehiel (Mass). 2d Lieutenanvt 15th Continental Infantry, 1st January, 1776; discharged September, 1776.

Jackson, Jeremiah (Mass). Ensign 4th Massachusetts, 1st January, 1777; retired 1st April, 1779.

Jackson, Jeremiah (Pa). 1st Lieutenant of Hartley's Additional Continental Regiment, 14th January, 1777; regiment designated 11th Pennsylvania 16th December, 1778; Captain-Lieutenant, 23d April, 1779; Captain, 16th March, 1780; transferred to 6th Pennsylvania, 17th January, 1781; transferred to 3d Pennsylvania, 1st January, 1783, and served to 3d June, 1783.

Jackson, John (Md). Ensign 4th Maryland Battalion of the Flying Camp, July to December, 1776.

Jackson, John (Mass). 2d Lieutenant of Jackson's Additional Continental Regiment, 15th January, 1777; 1st Lieutenant, 1st May, 1777; resigned 27th October, 1778.

Jackson, John (S. C.). Lieutenant South Carolina Militia, 1781-1782.

Jackson, Joseph (Mass). Paymaster 27th Continental Infantry, 24th September to 31st December, 1776.

Jackson, Michael (Mass). Captain Company of Minute Men at Lexington and Concord, 19th April, 1775; Major of Gardner's Massachusetts Regiment, 3d June to December, 1775; wounded at Bunker Hill, 17th June, 1775; Lieutenant-Colonel 16th Continental Infantry, 1st January to 31st December, 1776; wounded at Montressor's Island 24th September, 1776; Colonel 8th Massachusetts, 1st January, 1777; transferred to 3d Massachusetts, 12th June, 1783; brevet Brigadier-General, 30th September, 1783; served to 3d November, 1783. (Died 10th April, 1801.)

Jackson, Michael Jr. (Mass). Quartermaster's Sergeant 8th Massachusetts, 1st January, 1777; Ensign and Paymaster 8th Massachusetts, 2d October,

1777; 2d Lieutenant, 15th December, 1779; transferred to 3d Massachusetts 12th June, 1783, and served to 3d November, 1783.

Jackson, Nathan Peet (Conn). Ensign 8th Connecticut, 1st January, 1777; 2d Lieutenant, 16th January, 1778; 1st Lieutenant, 21st March, 1778; resigned 16th May, 1779.

Jackson, Patten (N. Y.). Served in New York Militia in 1776; 1st Lieutenant 5th New York, 21st November, 1776; taken prisoner at Fort Montgomery 6th October, 1777; exchanged 10th January, 1781, and did not return to service.

Jackson, Samuel (Ga). Lieutenant of a Georgia Regiment in August, 1778, to ——.

Jackson, Simon (Mass). Private in Gardner's Massachusetts Regiment, May to October, 1775; 1st Lieutenant and Paymaster 8th Massachusetts, 1st January, 1777; Captain Lieutenant, 5th October, 1780; Captain, 1st April, 1782; transferred to 6th Massachusetts 1st January, 1783; transferred to 2d Massachusetts, 12th June, 1783; retained in Jackson's Continental Regiment, November, 1783, and served to 20th June, 1784. (Died 17th October, 1818.)

Jackson, Stephen (S. C.). Captain South Carolina Militia, 1779-1781.

Jackson, Thomas (Mass). 2d Lieutenant of Knox's Regiment Continental Artillery, 10th December, 1775; 1st Lieutenant, August, 1776; Captain Lieutenant 3d Continental Artillery, 1st January, 1777; Captain, 22d February, 1780, and served to June, 1783. (Died ——, 1790.)

Jackson, Thomas Tredwell (Conn). Cornet 2d Continental Dragoons, —— January, 1779; Lieutenant, 15th November, 1779; Major and Aide-de-Camp to General Alexander, 8th July, 1781, to 15th January, 1783.

Jackson, William (N. Y.). Captain 4th New York, 21st November, 1776; resigned 26th September, 1777; served subsequently as Captain New York Militia.

Jackson, Wm. (S. C.). 2d Lieutenant 1st South Carolina, —— May, 1776; 1st Lieutenant, 18th August, 1777; Captain, 9th October, 1779; Major and Aide-de-Camp to General Lincoln in 1780; taken prisoner at Charleston, 12th May, 1780; prisoner on parole to May, 1783. (Died 17th December, 1828.)

Jackson, Wm. (Va). 2d Lieutenant 14th Virginia, 24th December, 1777; retired 1st June, 1778.

Jacobs, George (Md). Ensign 6th Maryland, 10th December, 1776; 2d Lieutenant, 4th July, 1777; 1st Lieutenant, 14th September, 1778; resigned 16th March, 1781.

Jacobs, George (Mass). Corporal in Lexington Alarm, April, 1775; Sergeant in Scammon's Massachusetts Regiment, May to December, 1775; 2d Lieutenant 1st Massachusetts, 1st January, 1777; retired 1st April, 1779. (Died 4th June, 1831.)

Jacobs, John (Mass). Major of Thomas' Massachusetts Regiment,, May to December, 1775; Lieutenant-Colonel 23d Continental Infantry, 1st January to 31st December, 1776; Colonel Massachusetts Militia in 1778.

Jacobs, John (N. C.). Ensign 6th North Carolina, 2d June, 1776; 2d Lieutenant, 1st November, 1776; resigned 1st March, 1778.

Jacobs, John Jeremiah (Md). 2d Lieutenant 6th Maryland, 10th December, 1776; 1st Lieutenant, 10th October, 1777; resigned 20th February, 1780.

Jacobs, Joshua (Mass). 2d Lieutenant in Lexington Alarm, April, 1775; 1st Lieutenant of Thomas' Massachusetts Regiment, April to December, 1775; Captain 23d Continental Infantry, 1st January to 31st December, 1776. (Died 1808.)

Jacques, Lancelot (Conn). Surgeon 7th Connecticut, 4th May, 1778; resigned 28th February, 1779.

Jacques, Moses (N. J.). Colonel New Jersey Militia, 1777-1778. (Died 1816.)

James, Alexander (S. C.). Lieutenant South Carolina Militia, 1779-1781.

James, Elijah (Mass). Cornet 2d Continental Dragoons, 16th November, 1779; Lieutenant and Paymaster, 24th November, 1779; taken prisoner at Fort St. George, 23d November, 1780; rejoined regiment in 1781, and served to close of war.

James, John (Md). Ensign 3d Maryland, 1st April, 1777; 2d Lieutenant, 10th April. 1777; 1st Lieutenant, 13th July, 1779; resigned 11th January, 1780. (Died 1794.)

James, John (N. C.). Captain 6th North Carolina, 16th April, 1776, to ——.

James, John (S. C.). Major South Carolina Militia, 1779 to 1781.

James, John Jr. (S. C.). Captain South Carolina Militia, 1780-1781.

James, Samuel (Mass). Ensign of Phinney's Massachusetts Regiment, May to December, 1775.

James, Thomas (Pa). Ensign of Montgomery's Battalion Pennsylvania Flying Camp; taken prisoner at Fort Washington, 16th November, 1776;

Jameson, John (Conn). Ensign 5th Connecticut, 1st January, 1777; resigned 22d July, 1777; Lieutenant Connecticut Militia; killed at Wyoming 8th July, 1778.

Jameson, John (Pa). Captain of Baxter's Pennsylvania Battalion of the Flying Camp, 17th September, 1776; wounded and taken prisoner at Fort Washington 16th November, 1776.

Jameson, John (Va). Captain of Virginia Regiment of Dragoons, 16th June, 1776; Major 1st Continental Dragoons, 31st March, 1777; transferred to 2d Continental Dragoons, 7th April, 1777; wounded near Valley Forge, 21st January, 1778; Lieutenant-Colonel, 1st August, 1779, and served to close of war.

Jamieson, Adam (Md). Lieutenant 5th Maryland, 1st June, 1781; retired 1st January, 1783.

Jamieson, Daniel (Pa). Lieutenant of Baxter's Pennsylvania Battalion of the Flying amp, June, 1776; taken prisoner at Fort Washington 16th November, 1776; exchanged 26th March, 1781.

Jamieson, Samuel (Mass). Regimental Quartermaster 5th Massachusetts, ——; resigned 8th July, 1779.

Janes, Elijah (Conn). Cornet 2d Continental Dragoons, 16th November, 1779; Lieutenant, 24th November, 1779; wounded and taken prisoner at Ft. St George, 23d November, 1780; rejoined regiment in 1781; Regimental Paymaster, ——, 1782, and served to close of war. (Died 22d February, 1823.)

Janney, Thomas (Pa). Lieutenant 5th Pennsylvania Battalion, 5th January, 1776; taken prisoner at Fort Washington 16th November; 1776.

Jansen, Cornelius I. (N. Y.). 1st Lieutenant 3d New York, 28th June, 1775; Captain, 26th June, 1776; Captain 3d New York, 21st November, 1776; transferred to 1st New York 1st January, 1781, and served to June, 1783.

Jansen, Dirck (N. Y.). Captain New York Militia in 1775.

Jansen, Johannes (N. Y.). Colonel New York Militia in 1780.

Jaquet, Joseph (Pa). 3d Lieutenant of Miles' Pennsylvania Rifle Regiment, 6th April, 1776; 2d Lieutenant, 28th May, 1776; killed at Long Island, 27th August, 1776.

Jaquett, Peter (Del). Ensign Delaware Regiment, 17th January, 1776; 2d Lieutenant, 27th November, 1776; 1st Lieutenant, 1st December, 1776; Captain, 5th April, 1777; taken prisoner at Camden, 16th August, 1780; Brevet Major, 30th September, 1783; served to close of war. (Died 13th September, 1834.)

Jaroloman, James (N. J.). Lieutenant New Jersey Militia; wounded near Springfield, New Jersey, 7th June, 1780.

Jarvis, John (N. C.). Captain 10th North Carolina, 19th April, 1777, to ——.

Jarvis, Nathaniel (Mass). Captain of Jackson's Additional Continental Regiment, 1st February, 1777; resigned 27th October, 1778. (Died 1801.)

Jarvis, Samuel (N. C.). Colonel North Carolina Militia in 1780.

Jay, John (N. Y.). Colonel New York Militia, 1775; was subsequently Governor of New York. (Died 17th May, 1829)

Jay, Joseph (N. J.). Ensign 2d New Jersey, 29th October, 1776; 2d Lieutenant, 26th April, 1777; cashiered 23d May, 1778.

Jayne, Timothy (Pa). Captain of Kachlein's Battalion Pennsylvania Militia, ——; taken prisoner at Long Island, 27th August, 1776; exchanged 9th December, 1776.

Jeans, Henry (—). Lieutenant, ——; was a prisoner in 1780; when and where taken not stated.

Jefferds, Samuel (Mass). Sergeant in Knox's Regiment Continental Artillery, February to December, 1776; 2d Lieutenant 3d Continental Artillery, 1st January, 1777; 1st Lieutenant, 1st October, 1778; transferred to Corps of Artillery, 17th June, 1783, and served to 20th June, 1784.

Jefferson, Thomas (Va). A signer of the Declaration of Independence; First Secretary of State under General Washington, 1789 to 1793; Third President of the United States, 4th March,

1801, to 4th March, 1809; died 4th July, 1826.

Jeffrey, Edward (Conn). Ensign of Selden's Connecticut State Regiment, June to December, 1776.

Jeffries, Bowker (Va). 2d Lieutenant 15th Virginia, 21st February, 1777; 1st Lieutenant, 21st October, 1777; resigned 15th May, 1778.

Jeffries, Francis Jacob (Pa). Lieutenant-Colonel York County, Pennsylvania Militia, in 1777.

Jeffries, Isaac (Va). Sergeant 7th Virginia, 29th December, 1776; transferred to 5th Virginia, 14th September, 1778; Ensign, 25th September, 1779. Died — December, 1779.

Jeffries, Joseph (Pa). Colonel Pennsylvania Militia in 1777.

Jenckes, Amos (R. I.). Lieutenant 2d Rhode Island, June to December, 1775; 1st Lieutenant 11th Continental Infantry, 1st January to 31st December, 1776. (Died 1825.)

Jenckes, Lowry (R. I.). Lieutenant Rhode Island Militia in 1780.

Jenckes, Oliver (R. I.). 2d Lieutenant 2d Rhode Island, 1st January, 1777; 1st Lieutenant, 25th June, 1777; retained in Olney's Rhode Island Battalion, 14th May, 1781, and died 3d February, 1782.

Jenifer, Daniel (Md). Hospital Surgeon's Mate, 27th August, 1776, to 6th October, 1780; Hospital Physician and Surgeon, 20th September, 1781, and served to October, 1782. (Died 6th November, 1790.)

Jenkins, Benjamin (S. C.). Lieutenant South Carolina Militia, 1775-1776.

Jenkins, George (Pa). 2d Lieutenant of Thompson's Pennsylvania Rifle Battalion, 27th October, 1775; 1st Lieutenant 1st Pennsylvania Battalion, 19th January, 1776; Captain 2d Pennsylvania, 1st January, 1777; wounded at Paoli, 20th September, 1777, and did not rejoin regiment.

Jenkins, Joel (Mass). Sergeant 8th Massachusetts, 1st March, 1777; Ensign, 26th November, 1779; Lieutenant, 16th April, 1782, and served to 3d June, 1783. (Died 23d June, 1827.)

Jenkins, John (Ga). 2d Lieutenant 1st Georgia, 7th January, 1776, to ——.

Jenkins, John (Conn). 2d Lieutenant of Spalding's Independent Wyoming Valley Company, 23d June, 1778; transferred to 1st Connecticut, 1st January, 1781; resigned — March, 1782. (Died 19th March, 1827.)

Jenkins, John (Mass). Ensign of Henley's Additional Continental Regiment, 1st June, 1777; resigned 21st March, 1778.

Jenkins, John (S. C.). Captain South Carolina Militia, 1775-1776.

Jenkins, Joseph (S. C.). 2d Lieutenant 1st South Carolina, 17th June, 1775, to ——.

Jenkins, Josiah (Mass). Sergeant in Phinney's Massachusetts Regiment, May to December, 1775; Ensign, 18th Continental Infantry, 1st January, 1776; 2d Lieutenant, 1st February to 31st December, 1776; Captain 12th Massachusetts, 1st January, 1777; resigned 25th June, 1779. (Died 1831.)

Jenkins, Nathaniel (N. J.). 2d Lieutenant 2d New Jersey, 5th February, 1777; 1st Lieutenant, 12th November, 1777; died 27th April, 1779.

Jenkins, Reuben (S. C.). Lieutenant South Carolina Militia, 1781-1782.

Jenkins, Samuel (Mass). Ensign 12th Massachusetts, 26th November, 1779; retired 1st January, 1781.

Jenkins, Stephen (Mass). 2d Lieutenant in Lexington Alarm, April, 1775; Adjutant of Little's Massachusetts Regiment, 19th May to December, 1775; 1st Lieutenant 12th Continental Infantry, 1st January to 31st December, 1776; Captain Connecticut Militia, 1777-1779.

Jenkins, Thomas (Conn). 1st Lieutenant of Spalding's Independent Wyoming Valley Company, 6th July, 1778; transferred to 1st Connecticut, 20th November, 1781, and served to close of war.

Jenkins, Thomas (S. C.). Captain South Carolina Militia in 1776.

Jenkins, William (Pa). Captain 1st Pennsylvania Battalion, 27th October, 1775; resigned 6th September, 1776.

Jenkins, William (Va). 2d Lieutenant 14th Virginia, 28th November, 1776; 1st Lieutenant, 22d December, 1777; regiment designated 10th Virginia, 14th September, 1778; dismissed 12th February, 1779.

Jenney, Thomas (Pa). 2d Lieutenant 5th Pennsylvania Battalion, 8th

January, 1776; 1st Lieutenant, 12th October, 1776; taken prisoner at Fort Washington, 16th November, 1776; exchanged 25th October, 1780, and did not re-enter service.

Jennings, Michael (Pa). Surgeon 11th Pennsylvania, 17th December, 1776; transferred to Hartley's Continental Regiment, 14th February, 1777; regiment designated 11th Pennsylvania, 16th December, 1778; omitted 1779.

Jennings, Simeon (R. I.). Ensign 2d Rhode Island, 1st January, 1777; 2d Lieutenant, 24th June, 1777; died 21st April, 1778.

Jennings, Wm. (R. I.). Lieutenant Rhode Island Militia, ——; died 25th May, 1778.

Jennison, Daniel (Md). Hospital Surgeon, 1779-1781.

Jennison, Samuel (Mass). 2d Lieutenant 6th Massachusetts, 1st January, 1777; Regimental Quartermaster, 30th July, 1778; resigned 11th July, 1779. (Died 1st September, 1826.)

Jennison, William (Mass). Sergeant in Lexington Alarm, April, 1775; Regimental Quartermaster of Read's Massachusetts Regiment, May to December, 1775.

Jerauld, Dutee (R. I.). Ensign 9th Continental Infantry, 1st January to 31st December, 1776; 2d Lieutenant 2d Rhode Island, 1st January, 1777; 1st Lieutenant, 11th February, 1777; Captain, 24th June, 1780; transferred to 1st Rhode Island 1st January, 1781; retained in Olney's Rhode Island Battalion, 14th May, 1781; resigned 21st June, 1782. (Lost at sea in 1786.)

Jervey, George (S. C.). Captain 5th South Carolina, ——; wounded at Beaufort, 3d February, 1779.

Jesson, William (Conn). Surgeon 2d Connecticut, 1st May, to 10th December, 1775.

Jesup, Ebenezer (Conn). Surgeon Hospital Department, 1779-1781. (Died 1812.)

Jetson, Amos (R. I.). Captain of Elliott's Regiment Rhode Island Artillery, 1777-1778.

Jewell, Daniel (N. H.). Captain New Hampshire Militia in 1780.

Jewett, David H. (Conn). Surgeon of Selden's Connecticut State Regiment, 27th September to 17th November, 1776.

Jewett, Gibbons (Conn). Surgeon of Selden's Connecticut State Regiment, 20th June to 26th August, 1776.

Jewett, James (Conn). Lieutenant of Baldwin's Artillery Artificer Regiment, 1st January, 1777; omitted March, 1779.

Jewett, Joseph (Conn). Captain 8th Connecticut, 6th July, to 10th December, 1775; Captain 17th Continental Infantry, 1st January, 1777; severely wounded and taken prisoner at Long Island, 27th August, 1776, and died in captivity, 31st August, 1776.

Jewett, Thomas (Vt). Lieutenant Vermont Militia at Bennington, August, 1777. (Died 1812.)

Jiggett, Edward Roe (Va). Ensign 4th Virginia, 10th February, 1776; 2d Lieutenant, 28th September, 1776; resigned 12th August, 1777.

Jill, Samuel (Va).—See **Gill.**

Jillson, Amos (R. I.). 1st Lieutenant of Elliott's Regiment Rhode Island State Artillery, 12th December, 1776, to June, 1777.

Johnson (—).—See also **Johnston.**

Johnson, Amos (Conn). Sergeant 7th Connecticut, 12th July to 20th December, 1775; Ensign 19th Continental Infantry, 1st January, to 31st December, 1776.

Johnson, Barent (N. Y.). Captain New York Militia; taken prisoner at Long Island, 27th August, 1776. (Died 1782.)

Johnson, Charles (N. H.). Lieutenant-Colonel New Hampshire Militia in 1775.

Johnson, Daniel (Mass). Ensign 21st Continental Infantry, 1st January to 31st December, 1776.

Johnson, David (Conn). 2d Lieutenant 4th Connecticut, 1st May, 1775; 1st Lieutenant, 1st September to 20th December, 1775; 1st Lieutenant of Wolcott's Connecticut State Regiment, December, 1775, to March, 1776.

Johnson, David (Mass). Sergeant in Lexington Alarm, April, 1775; Sergeant of Paterson's Massachusetts Regiment, 5th May to December, 1775; Ensign 15th Continental Infantry, 1st January, 1776; 2d Lieutenant, 7th October to 31st December, 1776; Lieutenant Massachusetts Militia, 1777-1781.

Johnson, David (R. I.). Ensign 1st Rhode Island, 1st January, 1777; 2d

Lieutenant, 10th February, 1777; died 22d November, 1780.

Johnson, Edmund (R. I.). Captain 1st Rhode Island, 3d May to December, 1775.

Johnson, Gideon (Va). Captain of a Virginia State Regiment, 1779-1781. (Died 6th December, 1825.)

Johnson, James (Md). Colonel Maryland Militia, 1776.

Johnson, James (Mass). Lieutenant of Phinney's Massachusetts Regiment, May to December, 1775.

Johnson, James (N. J.). Sergeant 2d New Jersey, November, 1775, to November, 1776; Ensign 2d New Jersey, 1st January, 1777; resigned 15th November, 1777. (Died 1st July, 1828.)

Johnson, James (N. C.). Regimental Quartermaster 6th North Carolina, 2d April, 1777; retired 1st June, 1778; Captain North Carolina Militia at King's Mountain, — October, 1780. (Died 23d July, 1805.)

Johnson, James (Va). Captain 6th Virginia, 16th February, 1776; Major, 1st April, 1777; resigned 15th August, 1777.

Johnson, John (Mass). Ensign 15th Continental Infantry, 1st January, 1776, to ——.

Johnson, John (N. Y.). 2d Lieutenant 1st New York, July, 1775; 1st Lieutenant, 24th February, 1776; Captain 2d New York, 21st November, 1776, which he declined and retired from service, 7th December, 1776.

Johnson, John (N. Y.). Captain 1st New York, 28th June, 1775, to January, 1776; Captain 5th New York, 21st November, 1776; retired 1st January, 1781.

Johnson, John (Pa). Lieutenant and Adjutant of Baxter's Pennsylvania Battalion of the Flying Camp, July, 1776; taken prisoner at Fort Washington, 16th November, 1776; exchanged 2d November, 1780, and did not re-enter service.

Johnson, Jonas (Mass). 2d Lieutenant of Gerrish's Massachusetts Regiment, 19th May to December, 1775.

Johnson, Jonathan (Conn). Captain of Bradley's Connecticut State Regiment, 10th June to December, 1776; Major 5th Connecticut, 1st January, 1777; Lieutenant-Colonel, 25th May, 1778; transferred to 2d Connecticut, 1st

January, 1781, and served to 3d June, 1883.

Johnson, Joseph (Mass.) Ensign 15th Continental Infantry, 1st January, 1776, to ——.

Johnson, Joshua (N. C.). Lieutenant 9th North Carolina, 28th November, 1776, to ——.

Johnson, Lambert (N. J.). Ensign New Jersey Militia, ——; taken prisoner at ——, 13th February, 1777, and died in captivity, 15th April, 1777.

Johnson, Martin (N. Y.). 2d Lieutenant Lamb's Company, New York Artillery, 30th June to December, 1775.

Johnson, Moses (Vt). Lieutenant Vermont Militia in 1777.

Johnson, Nathaniel (Conn). Captain of Douglas' Connecticut State Regiment, 20th June to 29th December, 1776.

Johnson, Obadiah (Conn). Lieutenant-Colonel in the Lexington Alarm, April, 1775; Major 3d Connecticut, 1st May to 16th December, 1775; Lieutenant-Colonel of Ward's Connecticut State Regiment, 14th May, 1776, to May, 1777; Colonel Connecticut Militia, 1777 to 1783. (Died 1801.)

Johnson, Peter (Conn). 2d Lieutenant 7th Connecticut, 6th July to 20th December, 1775; served subsequently as Captain Connecticut Militia. (Died 1813.)

Johnson, Peter (Va). Was a Private, Corporal, and Sergeant in a Virginia regiment, 1777 to 1779; was a Cornet of Lee's Battalion of Light Dragoons in 1779 and a Lieutenant in 1780; served to ——.

Johnson, Reuben (R. I.). Ensign of Olney's Rhode Island Battalion, 26th August, 1781; deserted 6th April, 1782.

Johnson, Richard (N. J.). 2d Lieutenant 1st New Jersey, 14th November, 1775, to November, 1776; Captain New Jersey Militia in 1777.

Johnson, Richard (S. C.). Captain South Carolina Militia, 1779-1780.

Johnson, Richard (Va). Major Virginia Militia in 1778.

Johnson, Robert (N. Y.). Captain 3d New York, 28th June to December, 1775; Captain of Nicholson's Continental regiment, 8th March, 1776; Captain of Spencer's Continental Regiment, 29th March, 1777, to ——.

Johnson, Roger (Md). Major Maryland Militia, 1776-1777. (Died 1831.)

Johnson, Samuel (Conn). Ensign of Burrall's Continental Regiment, 23d January, 1776; taken prisoner at the Cedars, 19th May, 1776; served subsequently as Major Connecticut Militia.

Johnson, Samuel (Mass). Lieutenant in Lexington Alarm, April, 1775; 1st Lieutenant of Frye's Massachusetts Regiment, May to December, 1775; served subsequently as Colonel Massachusetts Militia. (Died 1796.)

Johnson, Samuel (N. C.). Lieutenant 10th North Carolina, ——; wounded at King's Mountain, 7th October, 1780. (Died 15th September, 1834.)

Johnson, Seth (N. J.). Ensign 4th New Jersey, 2d November, 1776; 1st Lieutenant, 17th February, 1777; Captain-Lieutenant, 2d December, 1777; Captain, 7th April, 1779; transferred to 3d New Jersey, 1st July, 1778; resigned 30th March, 1780.

Johnson, Seybourne (Ga). 2d Lieutenant of Phoenix's Company Georgia Artillery, 6th November, 1776, to ——.

Johnson, Stephen (Conn). Chaplain 6th Connecticut, 20th May to 20th December, 1775.

Johnson, Thomas, Jr. (Md). Brigadier-General Maryland Militia, 6th January 1776, to ——. (Died 16th October, 1819.)

Johnson, Thomas (N. H.). Captain New Hampshire Militia, 1775-1776.

Johnson, Thomas (Vt). Colonel Vermont Militia; taken prisoner at Dresden in March, 1781

Johnson, Thomas (Va) Captain 3d Virginia, 21st March, 1776; resigned 18th October, 1776.

Johnson, Timothy (Mass). Lieutenant in Lexington Alarm, April, 1775; 1st Lieutenant of Frye's Massachusetts Regiment, May to November, 1775; Captain Massachusetts Militia, 1776-1777.

Johnson, William (N. Y.). Captain Lieutenant of Stevens' Battalin of Artillery, 9th November, 1776, which became part of the 3d Continental Artillery; transferred to Corps of Artillery, 17th June, 1783, and served to 20th June, 1784. (Died 20th February, 1819.)

Johnson, William (Va). Surgeon's Mate 1st Continental Dragoons, March, 1778; resigned — January, 1780.

Johnston, ———. See also **Johnson.**

Johnston, Alexander (Pa). 1st Lieutenant 4th Pennsylvania Battalion, 6th January, 1776; Captain 5th Pennsylvania, 1st January, 1777; resigned 23d January, 1778.

Johnston, Andrew (Pa). Regimental Quartermaster 1st Pennsylvania, 1st January, 1778; 2d Lieutenant, 24th March, 1778; wounded at Monmouth, 28th June, 1778; 1st Lieutenant, 12th May, 1779; retired 1st January, 1781.

Johnston, Francis (Pa). Lieutenant-Colonel 4th Pennsylvania Battalion, 4th January, 1776; Colonel 5th Pennsylvania, 27th September, 1776; retired 17th January, 1781. (Died 22d February, 1815.)

Johnston, George (N. Y.). 2d Lieutenant 2d New York, 21st November, 1776; resigned 9th April, 1778.

Johnson, George (Va). Captain 2d Virginia, 21st September, 1775; Major 5th Virginia, 13th August, 1776; Lieutenant-Colonel Aide-de-Camp to General Washington, 20th January, 1777; resigned 15th August, 1777.

Johnston, Gideon (Va). Captain of a Virginia State Regiment, 1779, to ———.

Johnston, Gilbert (N. C.). Captain North Carolina Rangers under Marion in 1780 and 1781. (Died 1794)

Johnston, Isaac (R. I.). 2d Lieutenant of Stanton's Rhode Island State Regiment, 12th December, 1776, to ———; Lieutenant-Colonel Rhode Island Militia, 1777-1779.

Johnston, James (N. Y.). Sergeant-Major 5th New York, 28th December, 1776; Ensign, 25th June, 1777; Regimental Quartermaster, 23d December, 1779; Regimental Adjutant, 14th July, 1780; transferred to 2d New York, 1st January, 1781; Lieutenant, 11th October, 1781, and served to close of war.

Johnston, James (N. C.). Captain North Carolina Militia, 1776, and at King's Mountain in 1780. (Died 23d July, 1805.)

Johnston, James (Pa). Regimental Paymaster 2d Pennsylvania, 10th January, 1777; retired 1st July, 1778.

Johnston, James (Pa). Lieutenant-Colonel Pennsylvania Militia, 1776-1777.

Johnston, James (Pa). Ensign 5th Pennsylvania, 1st January, 1777; wounded at Brandywine, 11th September, 1777; resigned — May, 1778. (Died 19th December, 1842.)

Johnston, John (Mass). Lieutenant of Gridley's Regiment Massachusetts Artillery, May to December, 1775; Captain Lieutenant of Knox's Regiment Continental Artillery, 1st January, 1777; severely wounded and taken prisoner at Long Island, 27th August, 1776; exchanged 2d May, 1777, but on account of his wounds did not return to the service. (Died 28th June, 1818.)

Johnston, John (N. C.). Captain North Carolina Militia, 1779-1781.

Johnston, John Boswell (Va). 2d Lieutenant 14th Virginia, 5th December, 1776; 1st Lieutenant, 10th March, 1777; regiment designated 10th Virginia, 14th September, 1778; taken prisoner at Charleston, 12th May, 1780; transferred to 1st Virginia, 12th February, 1781; Captain, 15th February, 1781, and served to close of war.

Johnston, Jonas (N. C.). Colonel North Carolina Militia; killed at Stono Ferry, 20th June, 1779.

Johnston, Joseph (N. C.). Ensign 9th North Carolina, 28th November, 1776; transferred to 1st North Carolina, 1st June, 1778; 1st Lieutenant, 1st February, 1779; taken prisoner at Charleston, 12th May, 1780; exchanged June, 1781; served to close of war.

Johnston, Josiah (Md). Ensign 4th Maryland Battalion of the Flying Camp, July to December, 1776; Captain 5th Maryland, 10th December, 1776; resigned 20th May, 1779.

Johnston, Launcelot (N. C.). Surgeon 9th North Carolina, 22d December, 1776; retired 1st June, 1778; Surgeon North Carolina Militia in 1779-1780 (Died 19th September, 1832.)

Johnston, Michael (Pa). Lieutenant Pennsylvania Militia; wounded and taken prisoner and died in captivity; when and where wounded and taken prisoner, not stated.

Johnston, Philip (N. J.). Lieutenant-Colonel of Hunt's Regiment New Jersey Militia, 14th June, 1776; Colonel, 1st August, 1776; killed at Long Island, 27th August, 1776.

Johnston, Robert (Pa). Surgeon 6th Pennsylvania Battalion, 9th January, 1776, to January, 1777; Hospital Physician and Surgeon, 20th March, 1780; Hospital Physician and Surgeon Southern Department, 15th May, 1781, to close of war. (Died 25th November, 1808.)

Johnston, Samuel (R. I.). Lieutenant Adjutant of Sherburne's Continental Regiment, 1st January, 1777; 1st Lieutenant of Baldwin's Artillery Artificer Regiment, 21st August, 1778; resigned 8th August, 1779.

Johnston, Thomas (Pa). 3d Lieutenant Pennsylvania Battalion of the Flying Camp; wounded at Long Island, 27th August, 1776; 1st Lieutenant Pennsylvania State Regiment, 18th April, 1777; resigned 20th June, 1777. (Died 1819.)

Johnston, Thomas (Vt). Captain Vermont Militia in 1776.

Johnston, William (N. C.). Captain North Carolina Militia at King's Mountain in October, 1780.

Johnston, William (Pa). Ensign 13th Pennsylvania, 8th May, 1777; resigned 10th February, 1778.

Johnston, William (Va). Captain 15th Virginia, 24th December, 1776; regiment designated 11th Virginia, 14th September, 1778; transferred to 7th Virginia, May, 1779; taken prisoner at Charleston, 12th May, 1780; exchanged June, 1781; transferred to 3d Virginia, 12th February, 1781; transferred to 1st Virginia, 1st January, 1783, and served to close of war; Brevet Major, 30th September, 1783.

Johnston, William E. (Va). Surgeon's Mate, 1st Continental Dragoons in 1778.

Johnston, Hugo (N. C.). Captain North Carolina Militia; wounded at Wiggins' Mill, Georgia, in April, 1781. (Died 1794.)

Johonot, Gabriel (Mass). Lieutenant-Colonel of Glover's Massachusetts Regiment, 21st May to December, 1775; Lieutenant-Colonel 14th Continental Infantry, 1st January to 31st December, 1776. (Died 9th October, 1820.)

Johonot, William (Mass). Apothecary, 1st January, 1777; Assistant and Apothecary Hospital Department, 6th October, 1780; drowned 23d July, 1782.

Joiner, John (S. C.). Captain South Carolina Artillery, 1776-1777.

Jolibois, John (Canada). 1st Lieutenant 1st Canadian (Livingston's) Regiment, 16th February, 1776; was allowed pay of Lieutenant to 3d November, 1783.

Jolliff, John (Va). 2d Lieutenant 8th Virginia, 16th February, 1776; 1st Lieutenant, 27th March, 1776; died 5th April, 1777.

Jolly, Maybury (Pa). 2d Lieutenant 11th Pennsylvania, 30th September.

1776; 1st Lieutenant, 9th April, 1777; Captain, 31st March, 1778; retired 1st July, 1778.

Jones, —— (—). Lieutenant of Marion's Brgiade; killed at Quinby's Bridge, 17th July, 1781.

Jones, Abraham P. (Ga). Lieutenant 2d Georgia; on roll for August, 1778; served to ——. (Died 28th January, 1831.)

Jones, Adam (S. C.). Captain South Carolina Militia, 1775-1776.

Jones, Adam C. (S. C.) Captain South Carolina Militia in 1775.

Jones, Albrigdon (Va). 2d Lieutenant 4th Virginia, 11th March, 1776; 1st Lieutenant, 28th September, 1776; resigned 6th January 1777; Adjutant 15th Virginia, 12th March, 1777; regiment designated 11th Virginia, 14th September, 1778; served as Adjutant to 10th May, 1779; 2d Lieutenant 9th September, 1778; transferred to 4th Virginia, 1st January, 1781, and served to close of war.

Jones, Allen (N. C.). Lieutenant-Colonel, and Colonel and Brigadier-General North Carolina Militia, 1775 to 1782. (Died 10th November, 1798)

Jones, Benjamin (N. Y.). Ensign 1st New York, 27th April to November, 1776; served subsequently as Lieutenant New York Militia.

Jones, Binns (Va). 2d Lieutenant 15th Virginia, 25th November, 1776; Regimental Quartermaster, 6th May, 1778; regiment designated 11th Virginia, 14th September, 1778; was in service in 1780.

Jones, Cadwallader (Va). Captain 3d Continental Dragoon's, 6th February, 1777, to 9th November, 1782; Aide-de-Camp to General Lafayette, 1778-1781. (Died 1796)

Jones, Catesby (Va). 1st Lieutenant 2d Virginia, 28th September, 1775, to ——.

Jones, Charles (Va). Paymaster 10th Virginia, 3d August, 1777; 2d Lieutenant, 9th September, 1778; regiment designated 6th Virginia, 14th September, 1778; taken prisoner at Charleston, 12th May, 1780; 1st Lieutenant, 18th February, 1781; retired 1st January, 1783.

Jones, Churchill (Va). Captain 3d Continental Dragoons, 1st June, 1777; transferred to Baylor's Consolidated Regiment of Dragoons, 9th November, 1782, and served to close of war; Brevet-Major, 30th September, 1783

Jones, Daniel (N. C.). Captain 3d North Carolina, 12th May, 1776; retired 1st June, 1778.

Jones, David (Mass). Surgeon of Gerrish's Massachusetts Regiment, 19th May to December, 1775; Surgeon 26th Continental Infantry, 1st January to 31st December, 1776. (Died 27th March, 1822.)

Jones, David (N. Y.) Captain New York Militia in 1775.

Jones, David (N. C). 1st Lieutenant 4th North Carolina, 27th November, 1776; omitted 1st January, 1778.

Jones, David (Pa). Chaplain 3d Pennsylvania Battalion, 27th April, 1776; Chaplain 4th Pennsylvania, 1st January, 1777; Brigade Chaplain, 25th May, 1778; transferred to 3d Pennsylvania, 1st January, 1783, and served to close of war; Chaplain United States Army, 13th May, 1794; honorable discharged, 15th June, 1800; Chaplain United States Army, 2d April, 1813; honorably discharged, 15th June, 1815. (Died 5th February, 1820.)

Jones, Edward (S. C.). Captain South Carolina Militia, 1779-1780.

Jones, Gabriel (Va). Captain of a Virginia State Regiment, 1778, to 1781.

Jones, Gibbs (Pa). Captain Lieutenant of Roman's Independent Company Pennsylvania Artillery, 6th February, 1776; Captain, 1st June, 1778; resigned 14th April, 1780.

Jones, Israel (Conn). Sergeant 4th Connecticut, 1st May to 28th November, 1775; Ensign 7th Connecticut, 1st January, 1777; 2d Lieutenant, 25th October, 1777; resigned 2d May, 1779.

Jones, Jacob (Md). Ensign 5th Maryland, 20th February, 1777; Lieutenant, 14th July, 1777; resigned 27th January, 1778.

Jones, James (Mass). Captain of Jackson's Additional Continental Regiment, 1st February, 1777; resigned 23d April, 1779.

Jones, James (Pa). Lieutenant Pennsylvania Battalion of the Flying Camp, July, 1776; taken prisoner at Fort Washington, 16th November, 1776; exchanged 29th January, 1781, and did not re-enter the service.

Jones, James (Pa). Surgeon's Mate 4th Pennsylvania, 16th February, 1778; transferred to 6th Pennsylvania, 1st May, 1779; Surgeon 4th Pennsylvania, February, 1780; retired 17th January, 1781. (Died 29th April, 1830.)

Jones, James (Pa). 2d Lieutenant Pennsylvania Militia; taken prisoner at his home, 14th February, 1778.

Jones, James Morris (Pa). Ensign 1st Pennsylvania, 3d November, 1776; 1st Lieutenant 2d Pennsylvania, 12th March, 1777; transferred to 1st Pennsylvania, 1st January, 1783, and served to 3d June, 1783.

Jones, Joel (N. Y.). Lieutenant-Colonel New York Militia at Saratoga, October, 1777. (Died 1832.)

Jones, John (Ga). Colonel Georgia Militia; wounded at Prince's Fort, Ga., 16th July, 1780, and at Beach Island, Ga., in September, 1780.

Jones, John Jr. (Ga). Major and Aide-de-Camp to General Howe, 10th May, 1778; Aide-de-Camp to General McIntosh in 1778-1779; killed at the siege of Savannah, 9th October, 1779.

Jones, John (Mass). Ensign 24th Continental Infantry, 1st January, 1776, to ——.

Jones, John (Mass). Surgeon's Mate 10th Massachusetts, 1st September, 1777; Surgeon, 24th September, 1777; resigned 14th May, 1781.

Jones, John Jr. (Mass). .Private in Lexington Alarm, April, 1775; Captain of Doolittle's Massachusetts Regiment, May to December, 1775. (Died 1797.)

Jones, John (N. H.). Captain 2d Continental Infantry, 1st January, 1776, to ——.

Jones, John (N. C.). Colonel North Carolina Partisan Rangers, ——; wounded at Pacolett River, N. C, 14th July, 1780.

Jones, John (S. C.). Was a Lieutenant in 6th South Carolina in 1777.

Jones, John (Va). Captain 6th Virginia, 9th April, 1776; retired 30th September, 1778.

Jones, John Courts (Md). 2d Lieutenant 1st Maryland Battalion of the Flying Camp, June to December, 1776; 1st Lieutenant 7th Maryland, 10th December, 1776; Captain, 20th September, 1777; transferred to 4th Maryland, 1st January, 1781; transferred to 1st Maryland 1st January, 1783, and served to April, 1783.

Jones, John C. (Mass). 1st Lieutenant in Lexington Alarm, April, 1775;

Captain of Doolittle's Massachusetts Regiment, 19th April to December, 1775; Captain 2d Continental Infantry, 1st January, 1776; died 4th July, 1776.

Jones, Jonathan (Pa). Captain 1st Pennsylvania Battalion, 27th October, 1775; Major 2d Pennsylvania, 25th October, 1776; Lieutenant-Colonel, 12th March, 1777; resigned 5th April, 1777. (Died 26th September, 1782.)

Jones, Joseph (Pa). Captain of Lewis' Pennsylvania Battalion of the Flying Camp, July to December, 1776.

Jones, Joshua (Conn). Cornet 2d Continental Dragoons, 16th November, 1779, to ——

Jones, Llewellyn (Va). Captain Virginia Regiment of Dragoons, 17th June, 1776; Captain 1st Continental Dragoons, 31st March,⁴ 1777, to ——. (In service December, 1778.)

Jones, Maurice (N. C.). Lieutenant 6th North Carolina, 15th June, 1776, to ——.

Jones, Nathaniel (Conn). Ensign of Selden's Connecticut State Regiment, June to December, 1776.

Jones, Nathaniel (Mass). Surgeon of Mitchell's Regiment Massachusetts Militia in the Bagaduce expedition, July to September, 1779; died 4th September, 1779.

Jones, Peter (Pa). 2d Lieutenant 11th Pennsylvania, 30th September, 1776; 1st Lieutenant, 11th April, 1777; retired 1st July, 1778.

Jones, Peter (Va). 1st Lieutenant 14th Virginia, 9th April, 1776; Captain, 18th November, 1776; regiment designated 10th Virginia, 14th September, 1778; resigned 15th December, 1779. (Died 10th February, 1833.)

Jones, Philip (N. C.). Lieutenant 8th North Carolina, 28th November, 1776; Captain Lieutenant of Kingsbury's Independent Company North Carolina Artillery, 19th July, 1777; taken prisoner at Charleston, 12th May, 1780.

Jones, Samuel (Md). 2d Lieutenant 3d Maryland Battalion of the Flying Camp, July to December, 1776; 1st Lieutenant 3d Maryland, 10th December, 1776; Captain, 6th August, 1777; resigned 11th February, 1780.

Jones, Samuel (N. Y.). Captain New York Militia, ——; killed at Minnisink, 22d July, 1779.

Jones, Samuel (N. C.). Ensign 8th North Carolina, 28th November, 1776; 1st Lieutenant 10th North Carolina, 4th October, 1777; transferred to 3d North Carolina, 1st June, 1778; Captain, 11th September, 1781; retired 1st January, 1783.

Jones, Samuel (N. C.). Ensign 2d North Carolina, ——. Died 7th July, 1778.

Jones, Samuel (Va). 2d Lieutenant 15th Virginia, 25th November, 1776; Regimental Paymaster, 7th January, 1777; 1st Lieutenant, 1st September, 1777; dismissed 6th June, 1778; restored 11th June, 1778, and retired 1st January, 1780.

Jones, Samuel (Va). 2d Lieutenant 15th Virginia, 22d January, 1777; 1st Lieutenant, 1st April, 1778; regiment designated 11th Virginia, 14th September, 1778; Captain, 1st January, 1780; retired 12th February, 1781.

Jones, Solomon (Mass). Ensign 6th Massachusetts, 1st January, 1777; retired 1st March, 1779.

Jones, Strother (Va). Captain of Grayson's Additional Continental Regiment, 14th May, 1777; transferred to Gist's Regiment, 22d April, 1779; retired 1st January, 1781.

Jones, Thomas (Md). Sergeant 5th Maryland, 20th December, 1776; Ensign, 20th February, 1777; resigned 13th October, 1778; served subsequently as Major Maryland Militia. (Died 1812.)

Jones, Thomas (N. H.). Ensign of Bedel's New Hampshire Regiment, January to July, 1776.

Jones, Thomas (N. C.). Ensign 7th North Carolina, 7th April, 1777; Lieutenant, 15th August, 1777; retired 1st June, 1778.

Jones, Thomas (Va). 1st Lieutenant 2d Virginia, 19th February, 1776; resigned 7th May, 1777.

Jones, Timothy (N. C.). Lieutenant 10th North Carolina, 19th April, 1777; retired 1st June, 1778.

Jones, Walter (Va). Physician General of Hospital Middle Department, 11th April, 1777; resigned 1st July, 1777. (Died 31st December, 1815.)

Jones, William (Del). 2d Lieutenant of McLane's Delaware Partisan Company, 13th January, 1777; killed at Wyoming, 23d April, 1779.

Jones, Wm. (Mass). 2d Lieutenant 14th Continental Infantry, 1st January to 31st December, 1776.

Jones, Wm. (N. C.). Brigadier-General North Carolina Militia, 1780-1781.

Jones, Wm. (Pa). Lieutenant Pennsylvania Militia in 1776 and 1777; served subsequently in Navy; Secretary of the Navy, — January, 1813, to — December, 1814. (Died 5th September, 1831)

Jones, William (R. I.). 1st Lieutenant of Babcock's Rhode Island State Regiment, 15th January, 1776; Captain of Lippitt's Rhode Island State Regiment, 19th August, 1776, to March, 1777; served subsequently as Captain of Marines, and was taken prisoner at Charleston 12th May, 1780 (Died 22d April, 1822.)

Jones, William (Va). Cornet of a Virginia Regiment Dragoons, 15th June, 1776; resigned 18th December, 1776; 2d Lieutenant of Grayson's Continental Regiment, 6th March, 1777; 1st Lieutenant, 1st December, 1777; resigned 7th February, 1778.

Jones, Windsor (Mass). Ensign 3d Massachusetts, 1st April, 1777; resigned 11th May, 1778.

Jones, Wood (Va). 1st Lieutenant 2d Virginia, 8th March, 1776; Captain, 25th December, 1776; retired 14th September, 1778.

Jordan, Cox (Del). 2d Lieutenant Delaware Regiment, 2d December, 1776; resigned 4th April, 1777.

Jordan, Griffith (Del). Ensign Delaware Regiment, 1st December, 1776; 2d Lieutenant, 5th April, 1777; resigned 6th October, 1777.

Jordan, John (Md). Ensign of Smallwood's Maryland Regiment, 14th January, 1776; 1st Lieutenant 1st Maryland, 10th December, 1776; Captain, 20th December, 1777; transferred to 2d Maryland, 1st January, 1781; retired 1st January, 1783.

Jordan, John (Pa). Captain Lieutenant of Flower's Artillery Artificer Regiment, 17th February, 1777; Captain, 7th May, 1778; retired 1st January, 1783.

Jordan, John (Va). Cadet 6th Virginia, 26th March, 1776; 2d Lieutenant, 4th January, 1777; 1st Lieutenant 3d September, 1777; transferred to 2d Virginia 14th September, 1778; taken prisoner at Charleston 12th May, 1780; exchanged April, 1781; Captain, 8th September, 1781, and served to close of war.

Jordan, Jonathan (S. C.). Lieutenant South Carolina Militia in 1775-1776.

Jordan, Nathaniel (Mass). Lieutenant-Colonel of Mitchell's Regiment on the Bagaduce expedition, July to September, 1779.

Jordan, William (Ga). 2d Lieutenant 1st Georgia, January, 1778; 1st Lieutenant, 1780, and served to close of war.

Joslyn, Joseph (R. I.). Surgeon 9th Continental Infantry, 1st January to 31st December, 1776.

Jouett, Matthew (Va). Captain 7th Virginia, 18th March, 1776; died 15th November, 1777.

Jouett, Robert (Va). Ensign 7th Virginia, 28th October, 1776; 2d Lieutenant, 28th September, 1777; transferred to 5th Virginia, 14th September, 1778; 2d Lieutenant 1st Continental Artillery, 1st January, 1779; 1st Lieutenant, 12th May, 1779; wounded at Eutaw Springs, 8th September, 1781; served to close of the war.

Jourdine, Charles (Ga). Captain Georgia Militia, ——; killed near Augusta, September, 1780.

Joynes, Levin (Va). Captain 9th Virginia, 10th February, 1776; Major 11th Virginia, 10th February, 1777; Lieutenant-Colonel 12th Virginia, 11th December, 1777; wounded and taken prisoner at Germantown, 4th October, 1777, and did not rejoin the Army.

Joynes, Reuben (Va). 2d Lieutenant 9th Virginia, 10th February, 1776; 1st Lieutenant, ——; resigned 27th March, 1777

Judd, William (Conn). Major Connecticut Militia, August to October, 1775; Captain 3d Connecticut, 1st January, 1777; retired 1st January, 1781. (Died 3d November, 1804.)

Judkins, Charles (Va). 2d Lieutenant 4th Virginia, 21st March, 1776, to ——.

Judson, Amos (Conn). Ensign 8th Connecticut, 1st January, 1777; resigned 1st January, 1778.

Judson, David (Conn). 2d Lieutenant 8th Connecticut, 1st January, 1777; 1st Lieutenant, 14th February, 1778; transferred to 4th Connecticut 1st January, 1781; Captain, 29th November, 1781; transferred to 1st Connecticut 1st

January, 1783, and served to 3d June, 1783; was Brigade Quartermaster 17th December, 1778, to 20th June, 1781. (Died 18th February, 1818.)

Judson, Ephraim (Conn). Chaplain of Ward's Connecticut State Regiment, August, 1776, to May, 1777.

Judson, James (Conn). Lieutenant Connecticut Light Horse in 1777.

Judson, Noah (Conn). 2d Lieutenant of Silliman's Connecticut State Regiment, June to December, 1776.

Julian, John (Va). Surgeon of Virginia State Troops, 5th June, 1776, to close of war. (Died 1787)

Jump, George (Va). 1st Lieutenant 2d Virginia, 27th November, 1775, to ——.

Justice, John (Pa). Ensign 11th Pennsylvania, 10th May, 1777, to ——.

K.

Kachlein, Andrew (Pa). 1st Lieutenant 2d Pennsylvania Battalion, 5th January, 1776; discharged 21st June, 1776; served subsequently as Colonel Pennsylvania Militia. (Name also spelled Kichlein.)

Kachlein, Peter (Pa). 2d Lieutenant of Baxter's Pennsylvania Battalion of the Flying Camp; wounded and taken prisoner at Fort Washington 16th November, 1776; exchanged 1778. Name also spelled Kichlein (Died 1789.)

Karr, Henry (Ga) Captain Georgia Militia, ——; wounded at Fish Dam Ford, 9th November, 1780.

Karr, James (N. C.). Lieutenant of a North Carolina Regiment in 1781. (Died 13th March, 1823.)

Karr, Jesse (N. H.). 2d Lieutenant 1st New Hampshire, 23d April, 1775, to ——

Kasson, Adam (Mass). Captain Massachusetts Militia, 1779-1780.

Kasson, Archibald (R. I.). Major, Lieutenant-Colonel, and Colonel Rhode Island Militia, 1775-1781.

Kavleman.—See **Howelman.**

Kay, John.—See **Key.**

Kay or Kays, Robert.—See **Keyes.**

Keais, Nathaniel (N. C.). Captain 2d North Carolina, 1st September, 1775; retired 1st June, 1778.

Keane, Thomas (Del). Captain of Patterson's Delaware Battalion of the Flying Camp, July to December, 1776 (Died 1802.)

Kearney, James (Pa). 1st Lieutenant of Hartley's Continental Regiment, 25th January, 1777; Captain, 9th September, 1777, to ——.

Kearsley, Samuel (Pa). Captain of Malcolm's Continental Regiment, 28th February, 1777; transferred to Spencer's Continental Regiment, 23d April, 1779; resigned 25th April, 1779. (Died 22d March, 1830.)

Keays, John (Pa). Sergeant 1st Pennsylvania Battalion, 1776; Ensign 2d Pennsylvania, 5th February, 1777, to ——.

Keeler, Aaron (Conn). Sergeant 5th Connecticut, February, 1777; Ensign, 22d April, 1781; transferred to 5th Connecticut, 1st January, 1783, and served to 3d June, 1783.

Keeler, Isaac (Conn). Ensign 2d Connecticut, 1st January, 1777; 2d Lieutenant, 27th May, 1777; 1st Lieutenant, 1st August, 1779; Regimental Quartermaster, 1st September, 1780; transferred to 3d Connecticut, 1st January, 1781, and served to 3d June, 1783. (Died 26th August, 1808.)

Keeler, Isaac (N. Y.). Lieutenant New York Militia; taken prisoner at Combond 24th June, 1779, and was a prisoner to 24th March, 1781.

Keeler, James (——). Lieutenant, ——; was a prisoner in 1780; when and where taken not stated

Keeler, Samuel (Conn). 1st Lieutenant 5th Connecticut, 1st May to 2d November, 1775; Captain of Bradley's Connecticut State Regiment, 10th June, 1776; taken prisoner at Fort Washington, 16th November, 1776; exchanged 19th March, 1781.

Keeler, Thaddeus (Conn). Sergeant 2d Connecticut, 13th July to 23d December, 1775; Sergeant in Silliman's Connecticut State Regiment, June to December, 1776; 2d Lieutenant 5th Connecticut, 1st January, 1777; 1st Lieutenant, 25th May, 1778; Regimental Quartermaster, 8th May, 1780; transferred to 2d Connecticut, 1st January, 1781; retired 1st June, 1783.

Keene, Lawrence (Pa). Captain Patton's Additional Continental Regiment, 13th January, 1777; regiment designated 11th Pennsylvania, 13th January, 1779; Aide-de-Camp to General

Mifflin, 5th June, 1778, to 25th February, 1779; transferred to 3d Pennsylvania, 17th January, 1781; transferred to 2d Pennsylvania 1st January, 1783, and served to 3d June, 1783.

Keene, Samuel Y. (Md). Surgeon's Mate 1st Maryland, ——, 1781, and served to April, 1783.

Keep, Caleb (Mass). Sergeant in Lexington Alarm, April, 1775; 1st Lieutenant of Danielson's Massachusetts Regiment, May to December, 1775; 1st Lieutenant 3d Continental Infantry, 1st January to 31st December, 1776; Captain 4th Massachusetts, 1st January, 1777; resigned 13th April, 1778; Captain Massachusetts Militia in 1779.

Keep, Jabez (Mass). Sergeant in Lexington Alarm, April, 1775; 2d Lieutenant of Whitcomb's Massachusetts Regiment, May to December, 1775.

Keep, Leonard (N. H.). Regimental Quartermaster of Ashley's New Hampshire Militia Regiment, 1777.

Keeports, George (Md. 3d Lieutenant of Smith's Baltimore Company Independent Maryland Artillery, 14th January, 1776; Captain German Battalion, 8th July, 1776; resigned 4th May, 1777.

Keiser, William (Md). Captain German Battalion, September, 1776, and served to ——

Keith, Alexander (S. C.). 2d Lieutenant 5th South Carolina, — January, 1777; 1st Lieutenant, 21st January, 1778 to ——.

Keith, Alexander (Va). Cadet 3d Virginia, 29th August, 1776; 1st Lieutenant 10th Virginia, 20th March, 1777; transferred to 6th Virginia, 14th September, 1778; resigned 13th October, 1778. (Died 1824.)

Keith, Isham (Va). 2d Lieutenant 3d Virginia, 18th March, 1776; 1st Lieutenant, 30th January, 1777; resigned 8th April, 1778.

Keith, Israel (Mass). Major and Aide-de-Camp to General Heath, 13th August, 1776, to 23d May, 1778.

Keith, James (Mass). Captain of Sargeant's Massachusetts Regiment, 1st July to December, 1775; Captain 16th Continental Infantry, 1st January to 31st December, 1776; Captain 8th Massachusetts, 1st January, 1777; Major,

12th August, 1779; retired 1st January, 1783. (Died 14th May, 1829.)

Keith, Robert (Pa). Chaplain of Hart's Pennsylvania Battalion of the Flying Camp, July to December, 1776.

Kellar, Abraham (Va). Captain of Clark's Illinois Regiment, 1779-1782.

Keller, Adam (Pa). Ensign 10th Pennsylvania, 20th April, 1777; 2d Lieutenant, 1st November, 1777; 1st Lieutenant, 3d June, 1778; retired 1st July, 1778.

Keller, Stoeffel (Pa). Ensign of Hart's Pennsylvania Battalion of the Flying Camp, July to December, 1776.

Kelley, David (N. H.). 2d Lieutenant 2d New Hampshire, 23d May to December, 1775.

Kelley, Moses (N. H.). Lieutenant-Colonel and Colonel New Hampshire Militia, 1776-1781.

Kelley, Wm. (Va). 2d Lieutenant of Shepard's Company of Virginia Riflemen, 9th July, 1776; taken prisoner at Fort Washington, 16th November, 1776; Captain of Hartley's Continental Regiment, 16th January, 1777. Died 9th September, 1777.

Kelley, Wm. Dennis (Va). Ensign 4th Virginia, 10th July, 1777; 2d Lieutenant, 22d March, 1778; 1st Lieutenant and Adjutant, 9th September, 1778; retired 30th September, 1778.

Kellock, Royall (Mass). 1st Lieutenant of Read's Massachusetts Regiment, May, 1775, to ——.

Kellogg, John (Mass). Captain Massachusetts Militia, 1777.

Kellogg, Moses (Mass). Lieutenant in Lexington Alarm, April, 1775; 1st Lieutenant of Ward's Massachusetts Regiment, May to December, 1775; Lieutenant Massachusetts Militia, 1776.

Kelly.—See also **Kelley.**

Kelly, Daniel (S. C.). Lieutenant South Carolina Militia in 1776.

Kelly, James (S. C.). Lieutenant South Carolina Militia, 1777-1778.

Kelly, Thaddeus (Va). Captain of a Virginia State Regiment, 1778 to 1781.

Kelsey, Aaron (Conn). Lieutenant of Cook's Connecticut Regiment, ——; wounded at Stillwater, 19th September, 1777.

Kelsey, Enos (N. J.). Major New Jersey Militia, 1776-1779.

Kelson, Samuel (Mass). Captain of Paterson's Massachusetts Regiment, May, 1775, to ——.

Kelty, ——. See **Kilty.**

Kemp, James (Va). Ensign of a Virginia State Regiment in 1780.

Kemp, Lawrence (Mass). Captain Massachusetts Militia, 1776-1781.

Kemp, Peter (Va). Captain of a Virginia State Regiment, 1779-1781.

Kemp, Thomas (Pa). Lieutenant of Flower's Artillery Artificer Regiment, ——, 1779, to 18th March, 1780. (Died 25th May, 1825.)

Kemp, Thomas (Va). Surgeon's Mate Virginia State troops, 1779 to 1781.

Kemper, Jacob (N. J.). Ensign 1st New Jersey, 14th November, 1775; 1st Lieutenant of Stevens' Battalion of Artillery, 9th November, 1776; Battalion formed part of 3d Continental Artillery in 1778; Captain Lieutenant, 2d December, 1778, and served to June, 1783.

Kempton, Thomas (Mass). Captain in Lexington Alarm, April, 1775; Captain of Davidson's Massachusetts Regiment, May to December, 1775; Lieutenant-Colonel Massachusetts Militia, 1776.

Kendall, Custis (Va). 1st Lieutenant 9th Virginia, 14th August, 1776; Captain, 26th May, 1778; transferred to 1st Virginia, 14th September, 1778; taken prisoner at Charleston, 12th May, 1780; transferred to 5th Virginia, 12th February, 1781; transferred to 1st Virginia, 1st January, 1783, and served to close of war.

Kendall, Thomas (Mass). Chaplain of Knox's Regiment Continental Artillery, March to December, 1776.

Kendall, Waffendal (Va). 1st Lieutenant 5th Virginia, 9th March, 1776; Captain, — April, 1777, and served to ——.

Kendrick, John (Mass). 1st Lieutenant of Whitcomb's Massachusetts Regiment, May to December, 1775.

Kenley, Benjamin (Va). Captain Virginia Militia, 1778-1779.

Kenna, Asa (R. I.). Ensign of Stanton's Rhode Island State Regiment, 12th December, 1776, to May, 1777.

Kennedy, Daniel (Pa). Sergeant 6th Pennsylvania, 1st September, 1776; Adjutant, 15th February, 1777; Ensign, 2d June, 1777; taken prisoner at Bristol, 17th April, 1778; exchanged 1st August, 1780, and did not return to service.

Kennedy, James (S. C.). 2d Lieutenant 1st South Carolina, 21st December, 1779; taken prisoner at Charleston, 12th May, 1780; exchanged June, 1781; 1st Lieutenant, 21st December, 1781, and served to close of war.

Kennedy, James (Va). Adjutant of Virginia Militia Regiment in 1779.

Kennedy, John (Mass). : Ensign 21st Continental Infantry, 1st January to 31st December, 1776; Ensign 15th Massachusetts, 1st January, 1777; Lieutenant, 19th April, 1779; transferred to 5th Massachusetts, 1st January, 1781, and served to June, 1783.

Kennedy, Joseph (Va). Ensign of a Virginia Regiment in 1777.

Kennedy, Robert (N. C.). Captain North Carolina Militia at Kings Mountain, October, 1780.

Kennedy, Samuel (Pa). Surgeon 4th Pennsylvania Battalion, 24th February to 31st December, 1776; Hospital Surgeon, 1st May, 1777; died 17th June, 1778.

Kennedy, Samuel (Pa). Ensign 6th Pennsylvania Battalion, 1st June, 1776; 2d Lieutenant, 1st October, 1776; 2d Lieutenant 7th Pennsylvania, 1st January, 1777, to rank from 1st October, 1776; 1st Lieutenant, 20th March, 1777; Captain Lieutenant, 17th April, 1779; Captain, 12th May, 1779; transferred to 2d Pennsylvania, 17th January, 1781; retired 1st January, 1783.

Kennedy, Thomas (N. C.). Captain North Carolina Militia; wounded at Ramsour's Mill, 20th June, 1780. (Died 19th June, 1836.)

Kenney, James (Pa). Captain of Hartley's Additional Continental Regiment, 13th January, 1777; resigned 13th January, 1779.

Kenney, James (S. C.). 2d Lieutenant 5th South Carolina, 23d November, 1777, to ——.

Kenney, Samuel (Pa). 2d Lieutenant Pennsylvania State Regiment, 18th April, 1777; 1st Lieutenant, 22d June, 1777; retired 1st July, 1778.

Kennon, John (N. C.). Lieutenant 6th North Carolina, 16th April, 1776, to ——.

Kennon, John (Va). 2d Lieutenant 2d Virginia, 13th August, 1776; 2d Lieutenant, 14th September, 1777, and served to ——.

Kennon, John (Va). Paymaster 6th Virginia, 1st May, 1777, to ——.

Kennon, Richard (Va). 2d Lieutenant 5th Virginia, 1st March, 1776; 1st Lieutenant, 17th December, 1776; retired 14th September, 1778; served subsequently in Virginia Militia. (Died 1802.)

Kennon, William (N. C.). Lieutenant and Commissary 1st North Carolina, 1st September, 1776; resigned April, 1777.

Kent, Daniel (Va). Ensign Virginia State troops, ——; in service in 1780.

Kent, Ebenezer (Mass). Sergeant-Major of Jackson's Additional Continental Regiment, February, 1777; regiment designated 16th Massachusetts, 23d July, 1780; transferred to 9th Massachusetts, 1st January, 1781; Ensign, 5th March, 1781; resigned 14th November, 1782.

Kent, James (Md). Captain Maryland Militia, 1776.

Kent, John Jr. (Maryland). Lieutenant Maryland Militia, 1777.

Kent, Moses (Mass). 1st Lieutenant of Little's Massachusetts Regiment, 19th May to December, 1775; 1st Lieutenant 12th Continental Infantry, 1st January to 31st December, 1776.

Keran, Edward (Va). 2d Lieutenant 13th Virginia, 16th December, 1776; dismissed 15th December, 1777.

Kerber, Paul (Pa). Regimental Quartermaster of Haller's Pennsylvania Battalion of the Flying Camp, July to December, 1776.

Kerlevan, —— (France). Lieutenant 1st Cavalry Pulaski Legion, 1st March, 1779, to ——.

Kermovan, John de (—). Lieutenant-Colonel Engineer, 16th July, 1776; discharged 9th February, 1778.

Kerney, James.—See **Kearney.**

Kerney, John (Va). Captain Virginia Militia, 1778-1782.

Kerr, John (Pa). Lieutenant Pennsylvania Militia, taken prisoner 29th April, 1776; near Crooked Billet.

Kerr, Thomas (—). Surgeon Hospital Department.

Kerr, William (N. J.). Ensign 4th New Jersey, 28th November, 1776; retired 17th February, 1777.

Kersey, William (N. J.). Private and Corporal 3d New Jersey, March, 1776, to 1st May, 1777; Ensign, 1st May, 1777; 2d Lieutenant, 1st November, 1777; 1st Lieutenant, 30th March, 1780; transferred to 1st New Jersey, 1st January, 1781; retained in New Jersey Battalion, April, 1783, and served to 3d November, 1783; Ensign United States Infantry Regiment, 12th August, 1784; Lieutenant 1st United States Infantry, 29th September, 1789; Captain, 4th June, 1791; assigned to 1st Sub Legion, 4th September, 1792; Major 4th Sub Legion, 30th June, 1794; retained in 3d United States Infantry, 1st November, 1796; died 21st March, 1800.

Kershaw, Eli (S. C.). Captain 3d South Carolina, 17th June, 1775; resigned 7th October, 1777. He was taken prisoner at Charleston, 12th May, 1780, and while being transported to Honduras as a prisoner he died about November, 1780.

Kershaw, Joseph (S. C.). Colonel South Carolina Militia, 1776-1780; taken prisoner at Charleston, 12th May, 1780.

Kershaw, William (S. C.). Brigade Major South Carolina troops, 1776 to ——.

Kertan, Peter (N. Y.). Ensign of Nicholson's New York Regiment, March to November, 1776.

Ketcham, Alexander (N. Y.). 2d Lieutenant 3d New York, 14th July, 1775, to January, 1776.

Kettle, Nicholas (N. Y.). Ensign 2d New York, June to November, 1776.

Key, Amasa (Conn). Captain Connecticut Light Horse, 1776.

Key, John (Va). Sergeant 8th Virginia, 16th February, 1776; Ensign 3d February, 1777; resigned 24th April, 1778; name also spelled Kay.

Key, John Ross (Md). 2d Lieutenant Maryland Rifle Company, 20th June, 1775; 1st Lieutenant in Stephenson's Maryland Rifle Battalion in 1776, and served to ——.

Key or **Kee, Thomas** (S. C.). Captain South Carolina Militia, 1781.

Keyes, Benjamin (Mass). Captain Massachusetts Militia, 1777.

Keyes, Danforth (Mass). Lieutenant-Colonel in Lexington Alarm, April, 1775; Lieutenant-Colonel of Learned's Massachusetts Regiment, May to December, 1775; Colonel Massachusetts Militia, 1777. (Died 1826.)

Keyes, John (Conn). 1st Lieutenant 3d Connecticut, 1st May to 10th December, 1775; Captain 20th Continental Infantry, 1st January to 31st December, 1776; served subsequently as Adjutant-General Connecticut Militia.

Keyes, Robert (Va). Sergeant 4th Virginia, 28th September, 1776; Ensign, 4th July, 1779; Lieutenant, 18th February, 1781; served to —— (name also spelled Kays).

Keyes, Stephen (Conn). 1st Lieutenant 10th Continental Infantry, 1st January to 31st December, 1776 Died 2d August, 1804.)

Keyes, Wm. (N. H.). Captain New Hampshire Militia, 1777-1778. (Died 1813.)

Keys, Richard (Pa). 3d Lieutenant 1st Pennsylvania Battalion of the Flying Camp, June, 1776; discharged September, 1776.

Keyser, John (N. Y.). Captain New York Militia, ——; prisoner of war, 15th March, 1780, to 3d September, 1781; where taken not stated.

Keyser, John Jr. (N. Y.). 2d Lieutenant 2d New York, 15th July, 1775; died November, 1775.

Kichlein.—See Kachlein.

Kidd, Charles (Del). Sergeant Delaware Regiment, January to December, 1776; Ensign Delaware Regiment, 5th April, 1777; wounded 1st June, 1778; where not stated; 2d Lieutenant, 7th September, 1778, and served to 14th May, 1782.

Kidd, John (Md). 2d Lieutenant of Smallwood's Maryland Regiment, 14th January, 1776; cashiered 8th October, 1776.

Kilby, William (N. C.). Ensign 2d North Carolina, 6th June, 1776; died 6th April, 1777.

Kilgore, Benjamin (S. C.). Captain South Carolina Militia; taken prisoner at Charleston, 12th May, 1780 (Died 1810.)

Kilgore, David (Pa). Captain 8th Pennsylvania, 9th August, 1776, to January, 1777. (Died 11th July, 1814.)

Killam, Joseph (Mass). Sergeant of Mansfield's Massachusetts Regiment, 9th May to 9th August, 1775; 2d Lieutenant 27th Continental Infantry, 5th May to 31st December, 1776; 1st Lieutenant 5th Massachusetts, 1st January, 1777; Captain Lieutenant, 1st March, 1779; Captain, 14th October, 1780; transferred to 1st Massachusetts, 12th June, 1783, and served to 3d November, 1783.

Killby, Wm. Tyler (N. C.). Ensign 2d North Carolina, 6th June, 1776; died 6th April, 1777.

Kilpatrick, William (Mass). Sergeant in Lexington Alarm, April, 1775; Ensign 24th Continental Infantry, 1st January, 1776; 2d Lieutenant, 3d August to 31st December, 1776.

Kilty, John (Md). Ensign Maryland Battalion of the Flying Camp, July to December, 1776; 2d Lieutenant 4th Maryland, 10th December, 1776; taken prisoner at Germantown, 4th October, 1777; 1st Lieutenant, 6th November, 1777; Captain 3d Continental Dragoons, 1st July, 1778; retired 9th November, 1782.

Kilty, Wm. (Maryland). Surgeon's Mate 5th Maryland, 5th March, 1778; Surgeon, 1st April, 1780; taken prisoner at Charleston, 12th May, 1780; transferred to 4th Maryland, 1st January, 1781; retired 1st January, 1783.

Kimball, Asa (N. H.). Lieutenant New Hampshire Militia in 1780.

Kimball, Asa (R. I.). Captain of Babcock's Rhode Island State Regiment, 15th January, 1776, to 1777.

Kimball, Benjamin (Mass). Captain of Mansfield's Massachusetts Regiment, May to December, 1775; Captain 27th Continental Infantry, 1st January to 31st December, 1776. (Died 1779.)

Kimball, Benjamin (N. H.). 1st Lieutenant 2d New Hampshire, 25th May to December, 1775; 1st Lieutenant 8th Continental Infantry, 1st January, 1776; Captain, 6th September, 1776; Paymaster 1st New Hampshire, 8th November, 1776; accidentally killed 23d August, 1779.

Kimball, Frederick (S. C.). Lieutenant-Colonel South Carolina Militia, 1780-1781.

Kimball, James (Mass). 1st Lieutenant of Nixon's Massachusetts Regiment, May to December, 1775; 1st Lieutenant 4th Continental Infantry, 1st January to 31st December, 1776.

Kimball, Jesse (Conn). 1st Lieutenant 7th Connecticut, 6th July to 20th December, 1775; 1st Lieutenant of Burrall's Continental Regiment, 23d January, 1776; Captain, 19th September, 1776; Captain 8th Connecticut, 1st January, 1777; resigned 15th December, 1777.

Kimball, John (Conn). 2d Lieutenant of Chester's Connecticut State Regiment, June to December, 1776.

Kimball, Peter (N. H.). Captain New Hampshire Militia, ——; wounded at Bennington, 16th August, 1777. (Died 1811.)

Kimball, Stephen (R. I.). Captain Lieutenant 2d Rhode Island, 3d May to December, 1775; Captain 11th Continental Infantry, 1st January to 31st December, 1776; Colonel Rhode Island Militia, 1779-1783.

Kimberly, Ephraim (Conn). 2d Lieutenant 8th Connecticut, 1st January, 1777; 1st Lieutenant, 8th January, 1778; transferred to 2d Connecticut 1st January, 1781; Captain, 13th April, 1782, and served to 3d June, 1783.

Kimberly, Silas (Conn). Captain Connecticut Militia; taken prisoner at West Haven, Conn., 1st September, 1781. (Died 1803.)

Kimbrough, John (S. C.). Captain South Carolina Militia in 1775.

Kimmel, Adam (Pa). 1st Lieutenant 4th Pennsylvania Battalion, 5th January to December, 1776.

Kimmell, Michael (Pa). 1st Lieutenant 4th Pennsylvania Battalion, 6th January, 1776; Regimental Paymaster, 5th Pennsylvania, 15th March, 1777; retired with rank of Captain, 1st July, 1778. (Died 1818.)

Kincaid, James (S C.). Captain South Carolina Dragoons, under Marion, 1779-1780. Died 1801.

Kincaid, Joseph (Va). Ensign of a Virginia regiment in 1781.

Kincaid, Wm. (Va). 2d Lieutenant 12th Virginia, 28th December, 1776; Resigned 31st December, 1777.

Kincannon, Andrew (Va). Captain Virginia Militia at Kings Mountain, October, 1780. (Died 1829.)

King, Alexander (Conn). Ensign of Mott's Connecticut State Regiment, June to December, 1776.

King, Caleb (Mass). Fifer in Lexington Alarm, April, 1775; Private in Thomas' Massachusetts Regiment, May to October, 1775; Sergeant 9th Massachusetts, 11th December, 1776; Ensign, 2d June, 1778; resigned 28th April, 1780.

King, Elijah (Va). Sergeant 14th Virginia, 1st January, 1777; regiment designated 10th Virginia, 14th September, 1778; Ensign, 4th July, 1779; Lieutenant, 15th February, 1781; transferred to 3d Continental Dragoons, ——, 1781; retired 9th November, 1782.

King, Eliphalet (Conn). Ensign 2d Connecticut, 1st May to 10th December, 1775; 2d Lieutenant 22d Continental Infantry, 1st January, 1776; 1st Lieutenant, 10th August, 1776; discharged 31st December, 1776.

King, Elisha (Va). Sergeant 14th Virginia, 1st January, 1777; transferred to 10th Virginia, 14th September, 1778; Ensign 10th Virginia, 4th July, 1779; transferred to 1st Virginia, 12th February, 1781; Lieutenant, 15th February, 1781, and served to 9th November, 1782.

King, Gideon (N. Y.). 1st Lieutenant 2d New York, 28th June, 1775, to January, 1776; served subsequently as Captain New York Militia.

King, Henry (Md). Sergeant Maryland Line, 25th May to 20th October, 1778; Assistant Commissary of Issues, 10th May, 1780, to 10th September, 1781.

King, Hugh (Pa). 1st Lieutenant of Baxter's Battalion Pennsylvania Flying Camp, June, 1776; taken prisoner at Fort Washington, 16th November, 1776; exchanged 8th December, 1780.

King, James (N. C.). Ensign 1st North Carolina, 1st June, 1776; 2d Lieutenant, 15th August, 1776; 1st Lieutenant, 3d April, 1777; Captain, 30th March, 1780; taken prisoner at Charleston, 12th May, 1780, and died in captivity.

King, James (R. I.). 2d Lieutenant 11th Continental Infantry, 1st January, 1776, to ——.

King, John (Mass). Sergeant in Woodbridge's Massachusetts Regiment, 9th May, 1775; 2d Lieutenant, 17th June to November, 1775; 2d Lieutenant 3d Continental Infantry, 1st January to 31st December, 1776. (Died 1829.)

King, John (Pa). Ensign 6th Pennsylvania, 17th October, 1776; killed at Germantown, 4th October, 1777.

King, Jonathan (Mass). Surgeon 4th Massachusetts, 1st January, 1777; resigned 1st April, 1778.

King, Joseph (N. J.). Regimental Adjutant, 4th New Jersey, 28th November, 1776; wounded and taken prisoner at Short Hills, 26th June, 1777; Paymaster of Baldwin's Artillery Artificer Regiment, 6th February, 1780; retired May, 1781.

King, Joseph (Pa). Paymaster Corps of Artificers, 6th February, 1780, to 1781.

King, Joshua (Mass). Fifer in Lexington Alarm, April, 1775, and in Thomas' Massachusetts Regiment, 1st May to 8th July, 1775; Sergeant 1st Massachusetts, 20th February, 1777; Cornet 2d Continental Dragoons, 16th November, 1779; Lieutenant, 20th November, 1779; wounded at Eutaw Springs, 8th September, 1781; Regimental Quartermaster in 1782, and served to close of war. (Died 1839.)

King, Josiah (Mass). Captain of Brewer's Massachusetts Regiment, May to December, 1775; served subsequently in Massachusetts Militia. (Died 1839.)

King, Lovin (Md). Ensign 5th Maryland, 20th February, 1777; resigned 8th November, 1777.

King, Miles (Va). Surgeon's Mate, 1st Virginia, 26th October, 1775; retired 14th September, 1778.

King, Peter (Mass). 2d Lieutenant of Knox's Regiment Continental Artillery, 10th December, 1775; 1st Lieutenant, August, 1776, and served to December, 1776.

King, Robert (Pa). 2d Lieutenant 12th Pennsylvania, 1st October, 1776; 1st Lieutenant, 20th May, 1777; retired 1st July, 1778; served subsequently as a Captain of Militia in Western Pennsylvania.

King, Rufus (Mass). Appointed Captain and Aide-de-Camp to General Glover, 16th August, 1778, and served to July, 1782. (Died 29th April, 1827.)

King, Samuel (Mass). Captain Massachusetts Militia, 1775-1776; Captain 10th Massachusetts, 6th November, 1776. Died 15th March, 1781; was he not killed at Guilford on that date? He served as Major and Aide-de-Camp to General De Kalb, 7th October, 1779, to 16th August, 1780, when the General was killed at Camden.

King, William (Mass). Captain of Fellow's Massachusetts Regiment, May

to December, 1775; Captain 21st Continental Infantry, 1st January to 31st December, 1776.

King, Zebulon (Mass). 1st Lieutenant 14th Massachusetts, 1st January, 1777; Captain, 4th October, 1780; transferred to 7th Massachusetts, 1st January, 1781; transferred to 4th Massachusetts, 12th June, 1783, and served to 3d November, 1783. (Killed by Indians in Ohio, 1st May, 1789.)

Kingman, Edward (Mass). Ensign 2d Massachusetts, 1st January, 1777; died 1st October, 1777, of wounds received near Saratoga, 26th September, 1777.

Kingsbury, Andrew (Conn). Superintendent of Military Stores, Hospital Department, 15th December, 1778, to 13th March, 1781.

Kingsbury, Asa (Conn). Lieutenant in Lexington Alarm, April, 1775; Captain 8th Connecticut, 6th July to 5th September, 1775; Surgeon's Mate 4th Continental Infantry, 1st January to 31st December, 1776.

Kingsbury, Eleazer (Mass). Captain Company of Minute Men, ——; wounded at Concord, 19th April, 1775.

Kingsbury, Jacob (Conn). Private and Corporal 8th Connecticut, 11th July to 16th December, 1775; Sergeant Selden's Connecticut State Regiment, June to December, 1776; Ensign of Webb's Continental Regiment, 26th April, 1780; transferred to 3d Connecticut 1st January, 1781; retained in Swift's Connecticut Regiment, June, 1783, and served to 3d November, 1783; Lieutenant United States Infantry Regiment, 15th October, 1787; Lieutenant 1st United States Infantry, 29th September, 1789; Captain, 28th September, 1791; assigned to 1st Sub Legion, 4th September, 1792; assigned to 1st United States Infantry, 1st November, 1796; Major 2d Infantry, 15th May, 1797; Lieutenant-Colonel 1st Infantry, 11th April, 1803; Colonel, 18th August, 1808. (Colonel Inspector-General, 8th April, 1813 to 31st October, 1814.) Honorably discharged upon the reorganization of the Army, 15th June, 1815. (Died 1st July, 1837.)

Kingsbury, John (N. C.). Captain Independent Company North Carolina Artillery, 19th July, 1777; taken prisoner at Charleston, 12th May, 1780.

Kingsley, Eliphalet (Conn). Sergeant of Baldwin's Regiment Artillery

Artificers, 6th October, 1777; Lieutenant, 1st December, 1778; Captain, 1st May, 1779; resigned 1st May, 1780.

Kinley, Benjamin (Va). Ensign 8th Virginia, 16th February, 1776; 2d Lieutenant, 9th March, 1777; wounded at Germantown, 4th October, 1777; retired 30th September, 1778, with rank of 1st Lieutenant; Captain Virginia State Regiment, 1778-1781.

Kinloch, Francis (S. C.). Captain South Carolina Regiment in 1776; wounded at the siege of Savannah in September, 1779; taken prisoner at Charleston, 12th May, 1780; prisoner on parole to close of war.

Kinnard, Nathaniel (Md). 2d Lieutenant 4th Maryland Battalion of the Flying Camp, July to December, 1776

Kinney, Abraham (Pa). Ensign 3d Pennsylvania, 24th May, 1779; Leiutenant 2d Continental Dragoons, 14th June, 1781; retired 17th October, 1780

Kinney, John (N. J.). Ensign 3d New Jersey, 29th July to 10th November, 1776; Ensign 3d New Jersey, 29th November, 1776; 1st Lieutenant, 6th January, 1778; resigned August, 1778. (Died 17th July, 1832.)

Kinney, Thomas (N. J.). Private 3d New Jersey, December, 1775; Ensign 3d New Jersey, 19th July to 10th November, 1776.

Kinsey, Jonathan (N. J.). Captain 4th New Jersey, 23d November, 1776. Died 16th November, 1777.

Kinsman, Aaron (N. H.). Captain 1st New Hampshire, 23d April to December, 1775; served subsequently as Captain New Hampshire Militia.

Kinsman, John (Conn). Sergeant 8th Connecticut, 12th July, 1775; Ensign, 21st October to 10th December, 1775; Ensign 17th Continental Infantry, 1st January, 1776; wounded and taken prisoner at Long Island, 27th August, 1776.

Kirby, Ephraim (R. I.). Private 2d Continental Dragoons, 24th December, 1776, to 7th August, 1779; Ensign of Olney's Rhode Island Battalion, 23d August, 1782 to 25th December, 1783 (Died 1804.)

Kirk, John (Pa). Ensign Pennsylvania Musket Battalion, 20th March to December, 1776.

Kirk, Robert (Va). Ensign of Grayson's Continental Regiment, 23d July,

1777; 2d Lieutenant, 19th April, 1778; transferred to Gist's Regiment, 22d April, 1779; retired 1st January, 1781. (Died 28th August, 1828.)

Kirkland, Daniel (Mass). 2d Lieutenant of Fellow's Massachusetts Regiment in 1775.

Kirkland, Moses (S. C.). Captain 3d South Carolina (Rangers), 17th June, 1775, and in August, 1775, he deserted with his company to the enemy.

Kirkland, Peter (N. Y.) Lieutenant-Colonel New York Militia; taken prisoner at Long Island, 27th August, 1776.

Kirkland, Samuel (N. Y.). Chaplain to Fort Schuyler, 16th October, 1779, and served to 3d November, 1783. (Died 28th February, 1808.)

Kirkpatrick, Abraham (Va). 1st Lieutenant 8th Virginia, 22d March, 1776; Regimental Adjutant(2d April, 1777; Captain, 10th August, 1777; transferred to 4th Virginia, 14th September, 1778; transferred to 1st Virginia, 12th February, 1781, and served to close of war; Brevet-Major, 30th September, 1783. (Died 17th November, 1817.)

Kirkpatrick, David (N. Y.). Ensign of Malcolm's Continental Regiment, 24th April, 1777; 2d Lieutenant, 20th January, 1778; transferred to Spencer's Regiment, 22d April, 1779; 1st Lieutenant, 24th April, 1779; retired 1st January, 1781; Captain Sappers and Miners, 25th July, 1781; wounded at Yorktown, 14th October, 1781; served to 3d June, 1783. (Died 1839.)

Kirkwood, Robert H. (Del). 1st Lieutenant Delaware Regiment, 17th January, 1776; Captain, 1st December, 1776, and served to close of war, Brevet Major, 30th September, 1783; Captain 2d United States Infantry, 4th March, 1791; killed 4th November, 1791, in action with Indians at St. Clair's defeat near Fort Recovery, Ohio.

Kirtland, Daniel (Mass). Sergeant in Lexington Alarm, April, 1775; 2d Lieutenant of Fellows' Massachusetts Regiment, May to December, 1775; Lieutenant Massachusetts Militia, 1776-1780.

Kirtland, Martin (Conn). 2d Lieutenant 6th Connecticut, 1st May to 18th December, 1775; Captain 6th Connecticut, 1st January, 1777; resigned 15th November, 1778.

Kirtland, Nathaniel (Conn). Private 6th Connecticut, 10th May to 18th December, 1775; Ensign 6th Connecticut, 12th March, 1777; Lieutenant, June,

1777; died 12th October, 1777, of wounds received at Stillwater, 7th October, 1777.

Kirtley, James (Va). 1st Lieutenant 8th Virginia, 16th January, 1776; discharged 10th June, 1777.

Kirtley, William (Va). Captain Convention Guards, 1779-1781.

Kittredge, Thomas (Mass). Surgeon of Frye's Massachusetts Regiment, 20th May to December, 1775; served subsequently as Surgeon Massachusetts Militia. (Died October, 1818.)

Klauman, Charles (Va). Captain Virginia Militia in 1777.

Kleckner, Christian.—See **Glackner.**

Klein, David (Pa). Deputy Commissary of Prisoners, 12th December, 1777, to ——.

Klein, William (Pa). Major German Battalion, 17th July, 1776; Lieutenant Colonel, 3d September, 1778; retired 21st June, 1779, and granted permission to return to Europe.

Klock, Adam (N. Y.). 1st Lieutenant New York Exempts, ——; killed at Oriskany. 6th August, 1777.

Klock, Jacob (N. Y.). Colonel New York Militia in 1776.

Klock, Jacob Conrad (N. Y.). Lieutenant New York Militia, ——; prisoner, 6th October, 1780, to 21st May, 1783; where taken not stated.

Klock, Jacob I. (N. Y.). Ensign 1st New York, 21st November, 1776; resigned 16th May, 1780, and joined the British Army.

Klotz, Jacob (Pa). Colonel Pennsylvania Battalion of the Flying Camp, July to December, 1776.

Klotz, Nicholas (Pa). Lieutenant-Colonel of Haller's Pennsylvania Battalion of the Flying Camp; taken prisoner at Long Island, 27th August, 1776. (Died 1807.)

Knapp, Job (Mass). 1st Lieutenant of Read's Massachusetts Regiment, May to December, 1775; Captain Massachusetts Militia, 1776-1781-

Knapp, John (S. C.). Sergeant 3d South Carolina ——, January, 1777; Regimental Quartermaster, 2d January, 1778; Adjutant, 6th March, 1778; Lieutenant, 18th December, 1778; transferred to 1st South Carolina, 1st January, 1781, and served to close of war.

Knapp, Joshua (Conn). Ensign 1st Connecticut, 15th November, 1781, and served to 3d June, 1783. (Died 19th July, 1829)

Knapp, Moses (Mass). Sergeant in Lexington Alarm, April, 1775; Captain of Read's Massachusetts Regiment, May to December, 1775; Captain 13th Continental Infantry, 1st January to 31st December, 1776; Captain 4th Massachusetts, 1st January, 1777; Major 11th Massachusetts, 5th November, 1778; transferred to 10th Massachusetts, 1st January, 1781; transferred to 5th Massachusetts, 1st January, 1783, and served to 12th June, 1783. (Died 7th November, 1809.)

Knapp, Samuel (N. Y.). Lieutenant New York Militia, —— ; killed at Minnisink, 22d July, 1779.

Knickerbocker, John (N. Y.). Colonel New York Militia, 1775-1778; wounded at Saratoga, 16th October, 1777. (Died 1802.)

Knight, Artemas (Mass). Private in the Lexington Alarm and in Colonel Ward's Massachusetts Regiment, April to November, 1775; 2d Lieutenant 3d Continental Artillery, 1st February, 1777; retired November, 1779. (Died 1838.)

Knight, John (Pa). Paymaster 7th Pennsylvania, 20th March 1777; retired 1st July, 1778.

Knight, John (Va). Corporal 13th Virginia, 16th December, 1777; Surgeon's Mate, 9th August, 1778; regiment designated, 9th Virginia, 14th September, 1778; transferred to 7th Virginia, 12th February, 1781; retired 1st January, 1783. (Died 1835.)

Knight, Jonathan (Conn). Surgeon's Mate 4th Connecticut, 1st February, 1778; retired 1st January, 1781. (Died 1829.)

Knight, Joseph (Mass). Lieutenant in Lexington Alarm, April, 1775; 2d Lieutenant of Gerrish's Massachusetts Regiment, 19th May to December, 1775; 2d Lieutenant 26th Continental Infantry, 1st January, to 31st December, 1776. (Died 1824.)

Knight, Joseph (Mass). 2d Lieutenant of Mitchell's Regiment, Massachusetts Militia, on the Bagaduce Expedition, July to September, 1779. (Drowned 9th September, 1799.)

Knight, Joseph (R. I.). Major Rhode Island Militia in 1779.

Knott, William (N. C.). Lieutenant 4th North Carolina ——, 1777, to ——.

Knowles, Charles (Conn). Regimental Quartermaster 2d Connecticut, 9th May to 10th December, 1775; Paymaster of Knox's Regiment Continental Artillery, 23d September, 1776; Paymaster 3d Continental Artillery, 1st January, 1777; 1st Lieutenant 12th September, 1778; Captain-Lieutenant, 13th September, 1780; transferred to Corps of Artillery, 17th June, 1783, and served to 3d November, 1783. (Died ——, 1796.)

Knowles, Charles (Mass). Captain-Lieutenant of Walker's Massachusetts Regiment, May to October, 1775.

Knowlton, Daniel (Conn). Ensign of Chester's Connecticut State Regiment; taken prisoner at Fort Washington, 16th November, 1776; served subsequently as Captain Connecticut Militia.

Knowlton, Thomas (Conn). Captain in the Lexington Alarm, April, 1775; Captain 3d Connecticut, 1st May to 10th December, 1775; Major 20th Continental Infantry, 1st January, 1776; Lieutenant-Colonel, 12th August, 1776; killed at Harlem Plains, 16th September, 1776.

Knox, .George (Pa). Ensign 9th Pennsylvania, February, 1777; 2d Lieutenant, March, 1778; 1st Lieutenant, 9th February, 1779. By the act of 26th July, 1779, it was "Resolved, unanimously, that Congress warmly approve and applaud the cool, determined spirit with which Lieutenant * * and Knox led on the forlorn hope (Stony Point), braving danger and death in the cause of their country, and that a brevet of Captain be given Lieutenant Knox." Resigned 20th April, 1780.

Knox, Henry (Mass). Served as a volunteer at Bunker Hill in June, 1775; Colonel Continental Regiment of Artillery, 17th November, 1775; Brigadier-General and Chief of Artillery Continental Army, 27th December, 1776; Major-General, 22d March, 1782, to rank from 15th November, 1781; Commander-in-Chief of the Army, 23d December, 1783, to 20th June, 1784; Secretary of War, 8th March, 1785, to 31st December, 1794. (Died 25th October, 1806.)

Knox, Hugh (S. C.). Captain South Carolina Militia; wounded at Hanging Rock, 6th Angust, 1780. (Died 1821.)

Knox, James (Va). Captain 8th Virginia, 4th April, 1776; Major 9th Virginia, 6th July, 1778. Retired 30th September, 1778.

Knox, Matthew (Pa). 1st Lieutenant 3d Pennsylvania Battalion, 6th January, 1776; Captain, 11th October, 1776; taken prisoner at Fort Washington, 16th November, 1776; exchanged 22d October, 1778, and did not re-enter service.

Knox, Robert (Pa). Colonel Pennsylvania Militia, 1776.

Knox, William (Pa). Ensign Pennsylvania Battalion of the Flying Camp, July to December, 1776; 2d Lieutenant, 10th Pennsylvania, 4th December, 1776; 1st Lieutenant, 30th April 1777; retired, 1st July, 1778.

Kobb, Abal (S. C.). Colonel South Carolina Militia in 1776.

Koen, Caleb (N. C.). Lieutenant 10th North Carolina, 19th April, 1777 to ——.

Koggen, Peter.—See **Roggen.**

Kolb, Abel (S. C.). Colonel South Carolina Militia, 1780-1782; killed and his house burned by the enemy near Dorchester, S. C., 26th April, 1782.

Kolb, Josiah (S. C.). 2d Lieutenant 2d South Carolina, 12th December, 1776; 1st Lieutenant, 15th July, 1777; taken prisoner at Charleston, 12th May, 1780; served to close of war.

Kolkauski, —— Count (Poland). Captain Pulaski Legion, 10th December, 1778, to——.

Kollock, Shepherd (N. Y.). Lieutenant of a New York Militia Regiment in 1776; 1st Lieutenant 2d Continental Artillery, 1st January, 1777; resigned 3d January, 1779. (Died 28th July, 1839.)

Kosciuszko, Thaddeus (Poland). Colonel-Engineer, 18th October, 1776; "brevet Brigadier-General, 13th October, 1783, to signify that Congress entertain a high sense of his long, faithful and meritorius services." Served to close of war. (Died 16th October, 1817.)

Kotz, Jacob (Md). 2d Lieutenant German Battalion, 12th July, 1776; 1st Lieutenant, 25th September, 1776; resigned 8th April, 1778.

Kowatz, Michael de (Poland). Colonel Commandant Pulaski Lancers of the Pulaski Legion, 18th April, 1778; killed before Charleston, 11th May, 1779.

Kring, John (N. Y.). Lieutenant New York Militia; was a prisoner 5th September, 1781 to 21st May, 1783; where taken not stated.

Kroesen, John (Pa). 1st Lieutenant of Hart's Pennsylvania Battalion of the Flying Camp, July to December, 1776.

Kronkhite, James (N. Y.). Captain of Drake's Regiment New York Militia, 1776; taken prisoner at Fort Washington, 16th November, 1776; exchanged 17th December, 1780

Kuhn, Adam (Pa). Suregon and Physician of Hospital in Pennsylvania, 8th July, 1776, to February, 1777. (Died 5th July, 1817.)

Kuyper, Hendricus (N. J.). Captain New Jersey Militia; wounded and lost a leg, 14th May, 1781, at Croton River, New York. (Died 17th August, 1783.)

Kyle, William (Pa). 2d Lieutenant 7th Pennsylvania, 13th May, 1777; resigned 25th September, 1777.

L.

Laboteaux, John (N. Y.). Captain of Malcolm's New York Regiment, March to November, 1776.

Lacey, Edward (S. C.). Captain South Carolina Militia, 1780-1781. (Drowned 20th March, 1813.)

Lacey, John (N. C.). Ensign 2d North Carolina, 20th May, 1779, to ——.

Lacey, John (Pa). Captain Pennsylvania Associaters, 21st August, 1775; Captain, 5th Pennsylvania Battalion, 5th January to 10th November, 1776; Brigadier-General, Pennsylvania Militia, 9th January, 1778, to —— February, 1781. (Died 17th February, 1814)

Lacey, Josiah (Conn). Private in the Lexington Alarm, April, 1775; Ensign, 5th Connecticut, 1st May to 13th December, 1775; 1st Lieutenant of Silliman's Connecticut State Regiment, 20th June, to 25th December, 1776; Captain 5th Connecticut, 1st January, 1777; resigned 20th July, 1780.

Lacey, Thaddeus (Conn) Captain of Swift's Connecticut State Regiment, June to December, 1776.

Lackey, Christopher (N. C.). 2d Lieutenant 5th North Carolina, 3d May, 1776; 1st Lieutenant ——, 1777; transferred to 3d North Carolina, 1st June, 1778; served to ——.

Lackey, John (Del). Ensign Delaware Battalion of the Flying Camp, July to December, 1776.

Lackland, James (Md). 2d Lieutenant Maryland Militia in 1776

la Close, —— (France). Lieutenant 1st Cavalry, Pulaski Legion, 1st March, 1779; brevet Captain, 19th July, 1780, and permitted to return to Europe. (Name also spelled La Clause.)

Ladd, Ezekiel (Vt). Captain of Bedel's Regiment, Vermont Militia, 1778-1779. (Died 1818.)

Ladd, James (Vt). Private in Bedel's New Hampshire Regiment in 1775; Lieutenant of same, January to June, 1776; Lieutenant of Bedel's Vermont Regiment, 1st April, 1778 to 1st April, 1779.

Ladd, Samuel (N. H.). 1st Lieutenant New Hampshire Militia in 1776.

Ladd, William (R. I.). Captain-Lieutenant of Church's Rhode Island Regiment, 3d May to December, 1775.

Ladley, Andrew (Pa). Surgeon 12th Pennsylvania, 18th January, 1777; retired 1st July, 1778.

Ladson, Abraham (S. C.). Lieutenant South Carolina Militia in 1776.

Ladson, James (S. C.) 1st Lieutenant 4th South Carolina, 17th June, 1775; Captain 4th November, 1775; Brigadier Major to General Howe, 1777-1778; Lieutenant-Colonel South Carolina Militia, 1779-1781. (Died 1812.)

Ladson, Thomas (S. C.). Captain and Major South Carolina Militia, 1779-1781.

Lafayette, Marie Jean Paul Joseph Roch Yves Gilbert du Motier —— Marquis de (France). Major-General Continental Army, 31st July, 1777; wounded at Brandywine, 11th September, 1777. By the act of 21st October, 1778, it was "Resolved, that the Marquis de la Fayette, Major-General in the service of the United States, have leave to go to France, and that he return at such time as shall be most convenient to him. Resolved, that the President write a letter to the marquis de la Fayette, returning him the thanks of Congress for that disinterested zeal which led him to America, and for the services he hath rendered to the United States, by the exertion of his courage and abilities on many signal occasions. Resolved, that the Minister Plenipotentiary of the United States of America at the court of Versailles be directed to cause an elegant sword, with proper devices, to be made and presented in the name of the United States, to the Marquis de la Fayette."

Sailed for France, 11th January, 1779; returned to the United States, 27th April, 1780. By the act of 25th November, 1781, it was "Resolved, that Major-General, the Marquis de la Fayette have permission to go to France, and that he return at such time as shall be most convenient to him; that he be informed, that on a review of his conduct throughout the past campaign, and particularly during the period in which he had the chief command in Virginia, the many new proofs which present themselves of his zealous attachment to the cause he has espoused, and of his judgment, vigilance, gallantry and address in its defence, have greatly added to the high opinion entertained by Congress of his merits and military talents; that he make known to the officers and troops whom he commanded during that period, that the brave and enterprising services with which they seconded his zeal and efforts, and which enabled him to defeat the attempts of an enemy far superior in numbers, have been beheld by Congress with particular satisfaction and approbation." ——; returned to France, 22d December, 1781. (Died 30th May, 1834.)

Lagare, James. See **Legare.**

Lahoye, Deconteria (——). Lieutenant in Armand's Legion in 1781.

Laird, David (Va). Captain 10th Virginia, 3d December, 1776; dismissed 13th January, 1778.

Laird, James (Va). Ensign Virginia Riflemen; mortally wounded at King's Mountain, 7th October, 1780, and died 11th October, 1780.

Lajournade, Alexander (Va). Surgeon's-Mate 1st Continental Artillery, 15th March, 1778; resigned 9th August, 1778.

Lake, Ephriam (N. Y.). Captain New York Militia, 1775-1778.

Lake, Henry (Md). Captain Maryland Militia, 1776. (Died 1804.)

Lakin, Nathaniel (Mass). 1st Lieutenant of Prescott's Massachusetts Regiment, May, 1775, to December, 1775; Captain Massachusetts Militia in 1779. (Name also spelled Leakin.)

Lamar, Cincinnatus A. L. (Ga). Captain Georgia Militia, 1777.

Lamar, Marion (Pa). Captain 1st Pennsylvania Battalion, 27th October, 1775; Major 4th Pennsylvania, 30th

September, 1776; killed at Paoli, 20th September, 1777.

Lamar, William (Md). Ensign 7th Maryland, 14th February, 1777; Lieutenant, 15th November, 1777; transferred to 1st Maryland, 1st January, 1781; Captain, 8th September, 1781; retired 1st January, 1783. (Died 8th January, 1838.)

Lamarque, Timothy (N. Y.). Surgeon's Mate, 1st Canadian (Livingston's) Regiment, 14th August, 1777; resigned 26th September, 1778.

La Marzelle —— (S. C.). Lieutenant 4th South Carolina; resigned 13th September, 1777. Name also spelled Marretta.

Lamb, Abner (N. C.). Ensign 1st North Carolina ——, 1780; Lieutenant 1st June, 1781; wounded at Eutaw Springs, 8th September, 1781; served to close of war.

Lamb, Gideon (N. C.). Major 6th North Carolina, 15th April, 1776; Lieutenant-Colonel, 6th May, 1776; Colonel, 26th January, 1777. Retired 1st June, 1778.

Lamb, John (N. Y.). Captain Independent Company New York Artillery, 30th June, 1775; wounded and taken prisoner at Quebec, 31st December, 1775 (lost an eye); Major-Commandant of Artillery Northern Department, 9th January, 1776, to rank from 1st January, 1776; Colonel 2d Continental Artillery, 1st January, 1777; wounded at Compo Hill, 28th April, 1777; served to June, 1783. (Died 31st May, 1800.)

Lamb, Richard (Pa). Lieutenant of Baldwin's Artillery Artificer Regiment, ——, 1777; Captain, 30th June, 1778; resigned 30th April, 1779.

Lamb, Thomas (Mass). Lieutenant of Jackson's Additional Continental Regiment, 1st February, 1777; resigned 24th April, 1779.

Lambert, George (Va). Ensign 1st Virginia, 15th December, 1775; Lieutenant 3d February, 1776; Captain 14th Virginia, 24th February, 1777; cashiered 18th January, 1778.

Lambert, Joseph Emanuel (Pa). Lieutenant 4th Pennsylvania, ——, 1777, to ——.

Lambert, Josiah (Mass). Sergeant 11th Massachusetts, 20th January 1777; Ensign, 1st November, 1777; deserted 16th December, 1777. (Name also spelled Lumberd.)

Lambson, Caleb (Mass). 1st Lieutenant of Little's Massachusetts Regiment, 19th May to November, 1775; 1st Lieutenant 12th Continental Infantry, 1st January to 31st December, 1776.

Lamme, Nathan (Va). 2d Lieutenant 10th Virginia, 3d October, 1776; 1st Lieutenant, 3d March, 1777; Captain 31st December, 1777; transferred to 6th Virginia, 14th September, 1778; transferred to 3d Virginia, 12th February, 1781, and served to close of war. (Died 15th January, 1834.)

Lancaster, Thomas (Mass). Chaplain of Mitchell's Regiment, Massachusetts Militia on the Expedition, July to September, 1779. (Died 12th January, 1831.)

Land, Charles (Va). Surgeon's-Mate, 3d Virginia, 21st August, 1777; resigned May, 1778.

Landenberger, John (Md). 2d Lieutenant German Battalion, 12th July, 1776; 1st Lieutenant 4th Continental Artillery, 1st January, 1777; Captain-Lieutenant, 27th April, 1777; resigned 3d February, 1779.

Landrum, Thomas (Va). Surgeon's-Mate Hospital Department, September, 1779-1781.

Lane, Aaron (N. J.). Ensign 2d New Jersey, 28th October, 1775; 2d Lieutenant, 29th November, 1776; 1st Lieutenant, 10th July, 1777; cashiered, 25th August, 1778.

Lane, Abial (Mass). Corporal in Lexington Alarm, April, 1775; Ensign Massachusetts Militia in 1776; Ensign 4th Massachusetts, 1st January, 1777; retired, 30th April, 1779.

Lane, Abraham, (N. J.). Ensign 1st New Jersey, 29th October, 1775; 2d Lieutenant, 29th November, 1776; omitted in October, 1777.

Lane, Daniel (Mass). Captain 7th Massachusetts, 1st January, 1777; taken prisoner in the Burgoyne Campaign in New York, 21st July, 1777; resigned 18th October, 1779. (Died 1811.)

Lane, Derick (N. J.). 2d Lieutenant 4th New Jersey, 28th November, 1776; 2d Lieutenant 2d New Jersey, 5th February, 1777; 1st Lieutenant, 8th November, 1777; Regimental Quartermaster, 3d April, 1779; Captain-Lieutenant, 5th July, 1779; Captain, 11th February, 1783; retained in New Jersey Battalion, April, 1783, and served to 3d November, 1783; Captain United States Infantry

Regiment, 12th August, 1784; resigned 24th November, 1785. (Died 1831.)

Lane, Ebenezer (Va). 2d Lieutenant 12th Virginia, 10th February, 1777; resigned 9th August, 1777.

Lane, Ezekiel (N. H.). Lieutenant New Hampshire Militia; killed at Bennington, 16th August, 1777.

Lane, Isaac (N. C.). Lieutenant North Carolina Militia at King's Mountain in October, 1780.

Lane, Jabez (Mass). Private in Lexington Alarm, April, 1775; 1st Lieutenant, 9th Continental Infantry, 1st January to 31st December, 1776; Captain 6th Massachusetts, 1st January, 1777; resigned 10th June, 1779. (Died 25th October, 1825.)

Lane, John (Mass). Captain 9th Continental Infantry, 1st January, 1776. Deserted September, 1776.

Lane, Joseph (Ga). Captain 3d Georgia ——, February, 1776; Major, 2d April, 1778; taken prisoner at Sunbury, 9th January, 1779, and did not rejoin regiment, and was retired about October, 1780.

Lane, Samuel (Mass). 2d Lieutenant in Lexington Alarm, April, 1775; 1st Lieutenant of Walker's Massachusetts Regiment, May, 1775, to December, 1775.

Lane, William, Jr. (Va) 2d Lieutenant 5th Virginia, 5th March, 1776, to ——.

Lang, James (Pa). Ensign Pennsylvania Musket Battalion, 19th March, 1776; 1st Lieutenant, 15th July, 1776; Captain 10th Pennsylvania, 27th November, 1776; resigned 1st April, 1779. (Name also spelled Long.)

Lang, Robert (N. Y.). Lieutenant and Quartermaster of Drake's Regiment, New York Militia; wounded on Staten Island, 15th September, 1776.

Langbourne, William (Va). Ensign 6th Virginia, 27th April, 1777. By the act of 6th October, 1783, it was "Resolved, whereas William Langburn hath served from the commencement of the war in the Army of the United States, with equal disinterestedness and reputation, that a brevet commission of Lieutenant-Colonel be given him." (Name also spelled Langburn.)

Langdon, John (Mass). Captain Massachusetts Militia, 1775-1776; Captain of Jackson's Continental Regiment, 1st February, 1777; resigned 23d October, 1778. (Died 1822.)

Langdon, John (N. H.). Colonel New Hampshire Militia, 1776-1777. (Died 19th September, 1819.)

Langdon, John (N. Y). 2d Lieutenant 3d New York, 28th June to November, 1775; served subsequently as Lieutenant-Colonel New York Militia (Died 12th March, 1819.)

Langdon, Jonathan (Va). Captain 12th Virginia, 27th November, 1776; resigned 14th September, 1778.

Langdon, Josiah (N. H.). Surgeon's-Mate 5th Continental Infantry, 1st January to 31st December, 1776

Langdon, Paul (Mass). Captain in Lexington Alarm, April, 1775; Captain of Danielson's Massachusetts Regiment, 9th May to November, 1775.

- Langdon, Samuel (Mass). Brigade Chaplain to Massachusetts Troops, June, 1775, to April, 1776. (Died 29th November, 1797.)

Langdon, Thomas (S. C.). Captain South Carolina Militia, November, 1775, to March, 1776

Langford, Alloway (N C.). Ensign 8th North Carolina, 8th February, 1777; 2d Lieutenant, 1st August, 1777; 1st Lieutenant, 12th October, 1777; retired 1st June, 1778.

Langford, Daniels (S. C.). 2d Lieutenant 2d South Carolina, January, 1777; 1st Lieutenant, 3d October, 1777; taken prisoner at Charleston, 12th May, 1780; exchanged ——; Brevet-Captain, 30th September, 1783; served to close of war.

Langham, Elias (Va) Served as Private, Corporal and Sergeant, 1st Continental Artillery, 19th February, 1777, until appointed 2d Lieutenant 1st Continental Artillery, 7th February, 1782, and served to June, 1783. (Died 3d April, 1830)

Lanman, James (Mass) Private 15th Massachusetts, 3d March, 1777; Ensign, 1st January, 1778 Died 18th October, 1778.

Lanier, David (N. C.). Lieutenant North Carolina Militia, 1780.

Lanier, James (N. C.). Ensign 8th North Carolina, 28th November, 1776; 2d Lieutenant, 26th August, 1777. Retired 1st June, 1778.

Lanier, William (N. C.). Ensign North Carolina Militia, 1780.

Lansdale, Thomas (Md). 1st Lieutenant Maryland Battalion of the Flying Camp, July to December, 1776; Captain 4th Maryland, 10th December, 1776; Major, 3d Maryland, 19th February, 1781; retained in Maryland Battalion, April, 1783, and served to 15th November, 1783; also appears to have been a prisoner in March, 1780, but when and where taken, not stated.

Lansing, Garrett G. (N. Y.). Ensign 3d New York, 6th February, 1779; transferred to 1st New York, 1st January, 1781, and served to 3d June, 1783. (Died 27th May, 1831.)

Lansing, Jacob (N. Y.) Captain New York Militia in 1780.

Lansing, Jacob, Jr. (N. Y.) Colonel New York Militia, 20th October, 1775, to 3d March, 1780

Lansing, Jacob G. (N. Y.) Lieutenant New York Militia in 1775

Lansing, John (N. Y.) 2d Lieutenant 1st New York, 21st November, 1776; resigned 8th December, 1776; served subsequently as Adjutant New York Militia Regiment, and as Military Secretary to General Schuyler. (Died 12th December, 1829.)

Lansing, John G. (N. Y.). 2d Lieutenant 2d New York, 28th June, 1775; 1st Lieutenant of Nicholson's Continental Regiment, March, 1776, to April, 1777

La Plaigneur, F. P. De (Ga). Captain in 1st Georgia in 1776. (Name not plainly written)

Lapham, King (Mass). 1st Lieutenant of Thomas' Massachusetts Regiment, April to October, 1775. Lieutenant Massachusetts Militia, 1776-1780.

Lapsley, John (Va). Ensign 7th Virginia, 20th March, 1776; 2d Lieutenant 28th November, 1776; wounded at Germantown, 4th October, 1777; 1st Lieutenant, 30th April, 1778; transferred to 5th Virginia, 14th September, 1778; resigned 7th May, 1779.

Lapsley, Samuel (Va). Captain of Gist's Additional Continental Regiment, 10th March, 1777; retired April, 1779.

Larey, James (Mass). Ensign 7th Massachusetts, 1st January, 1777; 2d Lieutenant, 19th November, 1777; cashiered, 31st December, 1777

Larks, Isaiah (Va). 1st Lieutenant 11th Virginia, 5th December, 1776, to ——.

Larnard, Simon (Mass). Ensign of Brewer's Massachusetts Regiment, May to December, 1775; Captain of Militia,

1779-1782; served for a time as Aide-de-Camp to General Glover. (Died 1817.)

Larned, .William (Mass). Major Massachusetts Militia, 1776-1778. (Died 1806.)

La Roche —— (S. C.). Lieutenant South Carolina Militia; killed at Cockspur, 4th March, 1776. .

La Roche, James (S. C.). Major South Carolina Militia, 1775.

Larrabee, Benjamin (Mass). Captain of Mitchell's Regiment, Massachusetts Militia, on the Bagaduce Expedition, July to September, 1779. (Died 17th April, 1829.)

Larrabee, Nathaniel (Mass). Major of Mitchell's Regiment on the Bagaduce Expedition, July to September, 1779.

Larrabee, Timothy (Conn). Paymaster of Mott's Connecticut State Regiment, June to December, 1776.

Lasell, John (N. H.). Captain New Hampshire Militia, 1777.

Lasher, John (N. Y.). Colonel New York Militia, 1775 to 1783. (Died 22d February, 1806.)

Lasiter, Jethro (N. C.). Ensign 7th North Carolina, 28th November, 1776; 2d Lieutenant, —— December, 1776; 1st Lieutenant, 12th October, 1777. Retired 1st June, 1778

Latham, Edward (Conn). Captain Connecticut Militia, ——; wounded and taken prisoner at Groton Heights, 6th September, 1781. (Died 1792.)

Latham, William (Conn). Ensign 6th Connecticut, 1st May to 18th December, 1775; Captain Connecticut Militia, ——; wounded at Groton Heights, 6th September, 1781.

Lathrop, Andrew (Conn). Captain Connecticut Light Horse, 1776.

Latimer, George (Del). Lieutenant-Colonel of Patterson's Delaware Battalion of the Flying Camp, July to December, 1776. (Died 12th June, 1825.)

Latimer, Henry (Del). Hospital Physician and Surgeon, 22d April, 1777, and served to close of war. (Died 19th December, 1819.)

Latimer, James (Del). Lieutenant-Colonel Delaware Militia in 1777.

Latour, John Conrad (Canada). Ensign 2d Canadian (Hazen's) Regiment, 3d November, 1776; 2d Lieutenant,

2d April, 1777; 1st Lieutenant of Ottendorf's Battalion, to rank from 3d March, 1777; dismissed August, 1779.

Lattimer, George (Conn). Ensign 6th Connecticut, 1st May to 17th December, 1775.

Lattimer, Jonathan (Conn). Major 7th Connecticut, 6th July to 19th December, 1775; Lieutenant-Colonel of Selden's Connecticut State Regiment, 20th June to 11th December, 1776; served subsequently as Colonel Connecticut Militia. (Died 1794.)

Laucks, George (N. Y.). Lieutenant New York Militia, ——; prisoner of war, 6th October, 1781, to 6th December, 1782; where taken not stated. (Name also spelled Loucks.)

Laudermilk, Jacob (Md). Ensign German Battalion, 19th November, 1776; 2d Lieutenant, 13th May, 1777; resigned 8th April, 1778.

Laudiman, —— (——). Lieutenant of Armand's Partisan Corps, 15th January, 1780, to rank from 1st June 1779, and served to ——.

Laughlin, James (Pa). Captain of Lewis' Pennsylvania Battalian of the Flying Camp, July to December, 1776.

Laumoy —— **de** (France). Served as a volunteer in Armand's Partisan Corps in 1778; Brevet Lieutenant, 13th January, 1779, and retired from the service.

Laumoy, —— **de Mons** (France). Colonel Engineers, 17th November, 1777; wounded at Stono Ferry, 20th June, 1779; taken prisoner at Charleston, 12th May, 1780; exchanged, 1781; Brevet Brigadier General, 30th September, 1783. Retired 10th October, 1783.

Laurance, John W. (Pa). 1st Lieutenant 5th Pennsylvania Battalion, 6th January, 1776; Captain 12th October, 1776; taken prisoner at Fort Washington, 16th November, 1776; exchanged, 26th August, 1778, and did not re-enter service.

Laurence, Caleb (N. Y.). Captain New York Militia; was a prisoner; when and where taken, not stated.

Laurens, John (S. C.). Volunteer Aide-de-Camp to General Washington, 6th September, 1777; wounded at Germantown, 4th October, 1777, and at Monmouth, 28th June, 1778, and taken prisoner at Charleston, 12th May, 1780; By the act of 5th November, 1778, it was "Resolved, that John Laurens,

Esq., Aide-de-Camp to General Washington, be presented with a Continental Commission of Lieutenant-Colonel, in testimony of the sense which Congress entertain of his patriotic and spirited services as a volunteer in the American Army, and of his brave conduct in several actions, particularly in that of Rhode Island on the 29th of August last, and that General Washington be directed, whenever an opportunity shall offer, to give Lieutenant-Colonel Laurens command agreeable to his rank." Declined the above proffered appointment with thanks, 6th November, 1778; Lieutenant-Colonel and Aide-de-Camp to General Washington, 29th March, 1779; mortally wounded, 27th August, 1782, in action near Combahee Ferry, South Carolina. Died same day.

Laverswyler, Jacob (Pa.). Quartermaster 1st Battalion of Miles' Pennsylvania Rifle Regiment, 24th October, 1776; Captain-Paymaster Pennsylvania State Regiment, 15th February, 1777; taken prisoner at Staten Island, 22d August, 1777; resigned 11th April, 1778.

Laverswyler, Thomas (Pa.). Sergeant 9th Pennsylvania, January, 1777; Ensign, 5th August, 1777; 2d Lieutenant 16th March, 1778. Retired 1st July, 1778.

Law, Jacob (———). Captain of Baldwin's Artillery Artificer Regiment, 16th December, 1776 to March, 1781.

Law, John (Mass). Captain 27th Continental Infantry, 1st January to 31st December, 1776.

Lawer, Conrad (N. Y.). Lieutenant New York Militia, ———; prisoner of war, 16th October, 1780, to 6th December, 1782; where taken not stated.

Lawer, John (N. Y.). Lieutenant New York Militia, ———; prisoner of war, 16th October, 1780, to 6th December, 1782; where taken not stated.

Lawler, Thomas (Va). Regimental Quartermaster 3d Virginia, — September, 1777, to May, 1778.

Lawless, William (R. I.). 1st Lieutenant of Tallman's Rhode Island State Regiment, 12th December, 1776, to May, 1777.

Lawrance, Joshua (Mass). 2d Lieutenant 10th Massachusetts, 6th November, 1776; resigned 21st October, 1778.

Lawrence, Andrew (N. Y.). 2d Lieutenant 3d New York, 28th June, 1775; 1st Lieutenant, 5th New York, 21st November, 1776. Resigned 11th March, 1777.

Lawrence, Asa (Mass). Captain of Prescott's Massachusetts Regiment, May to November, 1775. (Died 1804.)

Lawrence, Benjamin (N. J.). 2d Lieutenant 4th New Jersey, 23d November, 1776; 1st Lieutenant, 3d October, 1777; resigned 29th December, 1777.

Lawrence, Daniel (N. Y.). Lieutenant New York Militia, 1775-1776; 2d Lieutenant 4th New York, February, 1776; 2d Lieutenant 5th New York, 21st November, 1776; resigned ——— August, 1777.

Lawrence, Daniel (R. I.). Sergeant 2d Rhode Island, 10th March, 1777; Sergeant-Major, 2d April, 1777; Ensign, 12th June, 1777; dismissed 9th June, 1778.

Lawrence, Elihu (Conn). Ensign in the Lexington Alarm, April, 1775; Ensign 3d Connecticut, 1st May to 14th December, 1775.

Lawrence, Elisha (N. J.). Colonel New Jersey Militia in 1777.

Lawrence, John (N. Y.). 2d Lieutenant 4th New York, 1st August, 1775; Paymaster 1st New York, 15th August, 1776; Judge-Advocate Continental Army, 10th April, 1777; resigned 3d June, 1782. (Died November, 1810.)

Lawrence, John (Va). Brigade Major of Virginia Militia in 1777.

Lawrence, Jonathan (N. Y.). Lieutenant of Malcolm's Additional Continental Regiment, 10th January, 1777; retired 22d April, 1779; Captain Sappers and Miners, 12th June, 1781; resigned 25th November, 1782. (Died 27th April, 1802.)

Lawrence, Joseph (N. H.). Ensign 1st New Hampshire, 8th November, 1776; died 4th June, 1777.

Lawrence, Levin (Md). 1st Lieutenant of Watkin's Maryland Artillery Company, May 1776; Captain 6th Maryland, 1st April, 1777; wounded at Germantown, 4th October, 1777; resigned 1st April, 1778. (Name also spelled Laurance.)

Lawrence, Nathaniel (N. C.). Ensign 3d North Carolina, 1st June, 1777; taken prisoner at Fort Fayette, 1st June, 1779; exchanged 18th April, 1781; retained as Lieutenant 2d North Carolina, to rank from 23d January, 1781; retired 1st January 1783.

Lawrence, Oliver (N. Y.). 2d Lieutenant of Malcolm's New York Regiment, May, 1776; 2d Lieutenant 2d Continental Artillery, 1st January, 1777; 1st Lieutenant, 12th September, 1778; Aide-de-Camp to General Parsons, July, 1779, to July, 1782; resigned 19th September, 1782.

Lawrence, Richard (N. Y.). Lieutenant New York Militia in 1780.

Lawrence, Samuel (Mass). Corporal Company of Minute Men at Lexington and Concord, 19th April, 1775; Sergeant in Prescott's Massachusetts Regiment May to December, 1775; Ensign 7th Continental Infantry, 1st January to 31st December, 1776; Major Massachusetts Militia, 1777 and 1778. (Died 8th November, 1827.)

Lawrence, William (Pa). Paymaster 3d Pennsylvania Battalion 13th August to December, 1776.

Lawrie, James (N. J.). Captain 2d New Jersey, 28th October, 1775, to — November, 1776; Captain 2d New Jersey, 29th November, 1776; wounded and taken prisoner at Short Hills, 26th June, 1777, and died 13th July, 1777, while prisoner of war.

Lawson, Benjamin (Va). Sergeant 4th Virginia April, 1776; Regimental Paymaster 3d August, 1777, to June, 1779; 2d Lieutenant 3d March, 1778, 1st Lieutenant, ——, 1780; transferred to 2d Virginia, 12th February, 1781, and served to close of war.

Lawson, Claiborne Whitehead (Va). Ensign 1st Virginia, 7th October, 1775; 1st Lieutenant 2d December, 1776; Captain 18th October, 1777; mortally wounded at Hanging Rock 6th August, 1780, and died shortly after.

Lawson, Hugh (Ga). Captain Georgia Militia, ——; wounded at Augusta, Georgia, 14th September, 1780. (Died 20th February, 1802.)

Lawson, Robert (Va). Major 4th Virginia, 13th February, 1776; Lieutenant-Colonel, 13th August, 1776; Colonel, 19th August, 1777; resigned 17th December, 1777; served subsequently as Brigadier-General Virginia Militia.

Lawson, William (Va). 2d Lieutenant 2d Virginia State Regiment, March, 1777; 1st Lieutenant, 1st September, 1777; resigned 23d September, 1778.

Lawson, William (Va). 1st Lieutenant 4th Virginia, 1st January, 1777; retired 30th September, 1778.

Lawton, William (Mass). Surgeon's Mate 15th Massachusettts, 20th April, 1780; transferred to 5th Massachusetts, 1st January, 1781, and served to June, 1783. (Died 1799.)

Lay, Asa (Conn). Corporal 6th Connecticut, 8th May to 18th December, 1775; 1st Lieutenant 6th Connecticut, 1st January, 1777; taken prisoner at Loyd's Neck, 27th June, 1779; released 3d December, 1780; Captain, 28th August, 1780; transferred to 4th Connecticut, 1st January, 1781; resigned 30th October, 1782.

Lay, Lee (Conn). Captain Connecticut Militia; wounded and taken prisoner at Greenwich, 19th June, 1779. (Died 3d February, 1813.)

Layman, William (Md). Ensign 1st Maryland, 10th April, 1777; 2d Lieutenant, 10th June, 1777; resigned 4th June, 1779.

Leach, James (Mass). Captain Massachusetts Militia, 1777.

Leach, Simon (Mass). Lieutenant in Lexington Alarm, April, 1775; 1st Lieutenant of Reed's Massachusetts Regiment, May to December, 1775; 1st Lieutenant Massachusetts Militia in 1776.

Leadbetter, Drury (Ga). Colonel Georgia Militia, 1776.

Leaming, Thomas (Pa). Captain Pennsylvania Militia, 1776-1777. (Died 1797.)

Learmonth, John (Del). 2d Lieutenant Delaware Regiment, 16th January, 1776; 1st Lieutenant 28th November, 1776; Captain, 4th January, 1777; taken prisoner at Camden, 16th August, 1780, and was a prisoner to close of war; Brevet Major, 30th September, 1783.

Learned, David (Mass). Colonel Massachusetts Militia, 1777.

Learned, Ebenezer (Mass). Colonel of a Massachusetts Regiment, 19th April to December, 1775; Colonel 3d Continental Infantry, 1st January, 1776; Brigadier-General Continental Army, 2d April, 1777; resigned 24th March, 1778. (Died 1st April, 1801.)

Learned, Samuel (Mass). 1st Lieutenant of Learned's Massachusetts Regiment, May to December, 1775.

Learned, Simon (Mass). 2d Lieutenant of Brewer's Massachusetts Regiment 19th May to December, 1775; 1st Lieutenant 3d Continental Infantry, 1st January, 1776; Regimental Paymaster, 13th September, 1776; 1st Lieutenant and Adjutant 4th Massachusetts, 1st January, 1777; Captain, 20th March, 1778; Brigade Major, 9th March, 1779; Aide-de-Camp to General Glover in 1782, served to June, 1783; Colonel 9th United States Infantry, 12th March, 1812; honorably discharged 15th June, 1815. (Died 16th November, 1817.)

Leavenworth, David (Conn). Lieutenant in Lexington Alarm in April, 1775; 1st Lieutenant 1st Connecticut, December, 1775, to ——;Captain Connecticut Militia, 1777-1779. (Died 1820.)

Leavenworth, Eli (Conn). Captain 7th Connecticut, 6th July to 10th December, 1775; Captain 19th Continental Infantry, 1st January to 31st December, 1776; Captain 6th Connecticut 1st January, 1777; Major, 27th May, 1777; retired 1st January, 1781.

Leavenworth, Jesse (Conn). Lieutenant in Lexington Alarm, April, 1775; 1st Lieutenant 1st Connecticut, May to December, 1775; served subsequently in Quartermaster's Department. (Died 1824.)

Leavenworth, Nathaniel (Mass). Surgeon's Mate 8th Massachusetts 1st February, 1780; transferred to 2d Massachusetts, 1st January, 1783; retained in Jackson's Continental Regiment, November, 1783, and served to 20th June, 1784. (Died 9th January, 1799)

Leaver, William (Pa). 1st Lieutenant 11th Pennsylvania, 13th November, 1776; resigned 8th September ,1777.

Leavitt John (Mass). Ensign in Lexington Alarm, April, 1775; 2d Lieutenant of Thomas' Massachusetts Regiment, May to December, 1775; 2d Lieutenant 23d Continental Infantry, 1st January to 31st December, 1776; Lieutenant Massachusetts Militia, 1778-1780.

Leavitt, Moses (N. H.). 1st Lieutenant 2d New Hampshire, 23d May to December, 1775; 1st Lieutenant, 18th Continental Infantry, 1st January, 1776; Captain, 10th August to 31st December, 1776; Captain New Hampshire Militia, 1777-1780.

Leavitt, Nathaniel (N. H.). Ensign 3d New Hampshire, 8th November, 1776; Lieutenant, 1st June, 1778; transferred to 2d New Hampshire, 1st January, 1781; retired 1st September, 1782. (Died — February, 1825.)

Leavitt, Thomas (N. H.). Lieutenant of Poor's New Hampshire Regiment, May, 1775; Captain, 20th August to December, 1775; served subsequently as Captain New Hampshire Militia.

Leaycraft, George (N. Y.). 2d Lieutenant 2d Continental Artillery, 1st January, 1777; 1st Lieutenant, 21st August, 1780, and served to June, 1783. (Died April, 1811.)

Leaycraft, William (N. Y.). 2d Lieutenant 2d Continental Artillery, 27th June, 1781, and served to June 1783. (Died 7th June, 1827.)

Le Brun, de Bellecour (France). 2d Lieutenant 3d Continental Artillery, 1st January, 1777; Captain of Cavalry Pulaski Legion, 3d April, 1778, and served to close of war; Brevet Major, 6th February ,1784. (He signed "Bellecour.")

Le Brun, Christian Colerus.—See **Colerus.**

Ledlie, Andrew (Pa). Surgeon 12th Pennsylvania, 18th January 1777; retired 1st July, 1778. (Died 1785.)

Ledyard, Benjamin (N. Y.). Captain 1st New York, 28th June, 1775; Major 4th New York 21st November, 1776; transferred to 1st New York, 29th April, 1778; resigned 26th March, 1779. (Died 1803.)

Ledyard, Isaac (N. Y.). Surgeon's Mate, 1st New York, 20th March to November, 1776; Assistant Purveyor Hospital Department, 6th October, 1780, and served to 23d July, 1782. (Died 28th August, 1803.)

Ledyard, William (Conn). Lieutenant-Colonel Connecticut Militia, ——; killed 6th September, 1781, at Fort Griswold, Connecticut, after the surrender; Lieutenant-Colonel Ledyard commanded this post, and in the defense thereof, 6 of the garrison were killed and 18 wounded, while in the subsequent butchery, after the surrender, 79 were killed.

Ledyard, Youngs (Conn). Captain Connecticut Militia, ——; killed 6th September, 1781, at Fort Griswold, Connecticut.

Lee, Andrew (Conn). Chaplain 4th Connecticut, 1st January, 1777; resigned 15th October, 1777. (Died 25th August, 1832.)

Lee, Andrew (Pa). Ensign 2d Canadian (Hazen's) Regiment, 3d November, 1776; taken prisoner at Fort Schuyler, 22d August, 1777; Lieutenant, September, 1779, and served to ——. (Died 22d June, 1821.)

Lee, Charles (Va). Major-General Continental Army, 17th June, 1775. By the act of 20th July, 1776, it was "Resolved, that the thanks of the United States of America be given to Major-General Lee * * * and the officers and soldiers under their command, who, on the 28th June last, repulsed with so much valor, the attack which was made on that day on the State of South Carolina by the fleet and army of his Britannic majesty." Taken prisoner at Baskenridge, 13th December, 1776; exchanged 6th May, 1778; informed that his services were no longer required, 10th January, 1780 (Died 2d October, 1782.)

Lee, Daniel (Mass). Lieutenant 3d Massachusetts, 1st January, 1777; Regimental Quartermaster, 1st January to 1st October, 1777; Regimental Paymaster, 1st October, 1777, to 21st September, 1778; Brigade Major, September, 1778, to 21st December, 1778; Captain Lieutenant, 31st March, 1780; Captain, 1st February, 1781; retired 1st January, 1783.

Lee, Elisha (Conn). Sergeant in the Lexington Alarm, April, 1775; 2d Lieutenant 6th Connecticut, 1st May to 19th December, 1775; 1st Lieutenant 10th Continental Infantry, 1st January to 31st December, 1776; Captain 4th Connecticut, 1st January, 1777; resigned 22d May, 1778 (Died 15th October, 1815.)

Lee, Ezra (Conn). Sergeant 10th Continental Infantry, 1st January, 1776; Ensign, 11th October, 1776; Ensign 1st Connecticut, 1st January, 1777; 2d Lieutenant, 1st January, 1778; 1st Lieutenant, 5th June, 1778; Regimental Quartermaster, 16th November, 1778, to 1st January, 1781; transferred to 5th Connecticut, 1st January, 1781, and paymaster of same, June, 1781, to June, 1782, when retired. (Died 29th October, 1821.)

Lee, Francis Lightfoot (Va). A signer of the Declaration of Independence; died 3d April, 1797.

Lee, Henry (Va). ("Light Horse Harry.") Captain of a Company Virginia Dragoons, 18th June, 1776; company attached to and formed part of the 1st Continental Dragoons, 31st March, 1777. By the act of 7th April, 1778, it was "Resolved, whereas Captain Henry Lee, of the Light Dragoons, by the whole tenor of his conduct during the last campaign, has proved himself a brave and prudent officer rendered essential service to his country, and acquired to himself and the corps he commanded, distinguished honor, and, it being the determination of Congress

to reward merit, Resolved, that Captain H. Lee be promoted to the rank of Major-Commandant; that he be empowered to augment his present corps by enlistment of two troops of horse to act as a separate corps." By the act of 24th September, 1779, it was "Resolved, that the thanks of Gongress be given to Major Lee for the remarkable prudence, adress and bravery displayed in the attack on the enemy's fort and work at Powles' Hook, and that they approve the humanity shewn in circumstances prompting to severity, as honorable to the arms of the United States, and correspondent to the noble principles on which they were assumed, and that a gold medal emblematic of this affair be struck under the direction of the Board of Treasury, and presented to Major Lee." On 21st October, 1780, his Battalion was designated Lee's Partisan Corps; Lieutenant-Colonel of same, 6th November, 1780, and served to close of war; Major-General United States Army, 19th July, 1798; honorably discharged, 15th June, 1800. (Died 25th March, 1818.)

Lee, Isaac (Conn). Colonel Connecticut Militia, 1775-1776. (Died 1802.)

Lee, James (Pa). Captain 2d Continental Artillery, 1st January, 1777; resigned 11th December, 1779; name also spelled Lees.

Lee, John (Va. Ensign 1st Virginia, 6th September, 1775, to ——; Captain 2d Virginia State Regiment, March, 1777; Major, 1st February, 1778, to October, 1781.

Lee, John (Va). Ensign 7th Virginia, 4th July, 1779, to ——. (Name also spelled Leigh.)

Lee, Jonathan (Mass). Surgeon's Mate of Paterson's Massachusetts Regiment, May to December, 1775; Surgeon's Mate 15th Continental Infantry, 1st January to 31 December, 1776.

Lee, Joseph (Mass). Captain 14th Conutinental Infantry, 1st January to 31st December, 1776.

Lee, Noah (Conn). Lieutenant 2d Canadian (Hazen's) Regiment, 3d November, 1776; Captain, 1st June, 1778, and served to June, 1783. (Died 1840.)

Lee, Parker Hall (Md). Ensign 4th Maryland, 1st January, 1777; 2d Lieutenant, 19th November, 1777; 1st Lieutenant, 16th October, 1778, resigned 14th February, 1780.

Lee, Philip Richard Francis (Va). Captain 3d Virginia, 8th March, 1776;

mortally wounded at Brandywine, 11th September, 1777.

Lee, Richard Henry (Va). A signer of the Declaration of Independence; died 19th June, 1794.

Lee, Samuel (Conn). Surgeon 4th Connecticut. 1st January, 1777; resigned 3d April, 1778; served subsequently as Surgeon in Navy.

Lee, Seward (Mass). 2d Lieutenant of Glover's Massachusetts Regiment, 19th May to December, 1775; 2d Lieutenant 14th Continental Infantry, 1st January to 31st December, 1776.

Lee, Thomas (N. H.). Captain Independent Company New Hampshire Rangers, 1776 to 1781.

Lee, Thomas (N. Y.). 2d Lieutenant 4th New York, 28th June, 1775; 1st Lieutenant, 3d August, 1775; Captain 5th New York, 21st November, 1776; resigned 19th May, 1778; served subsequently as Captain New York Militia. (Died 1814.)

Lee, Thomas (Va). Adjutant of Grayson's Continental Regiment, 5th February, 1777; resigned 21st April, 1778.

Lee, William (N. H.). 1st Sergeant of Reed's New Hampshire Regiment, May to December, 1775; Ensign 2d Continental Infantry, 1st January, 1776; 2d Lieutenant 1st New Hampshire 8th November, 1776; resigned 9th January, 1778.

Lee, William B. (Va). Ensign of Grayson's Additional Continental Regiment, 8th June, 1777, to ——. (In service August, 1778.)

Lee, William Raymond (Mass). Captain of Glover's Massachusetts Regiment, 19th May, 1775; Major, June to December, 1775; Major 14th Continental Infantry, 1st January to 31st December, 1776; Colonel of one of the Sixteen Additional Continental Regiments, 1st January, 1777; resigned 24th January, 1778. (Died 26th October, 1824.)

Leeman, Samuel (N. H.). Ensign 3d New Hampshire, 8th November, 1776; killed at Hubbardton, 7th July, 1777.

Lees, James (Pa).—See **Lee.**

Leet, Daniel (Va). Regimental Quartermaster 13th Virginia, 1st January, 1777; Regimental Paymaster, 1st October, 1777; retired 30th September, 1778; Brigade Major of a Virginia Brigade, 21st December, 1778, to close of war. (Died 1830.)

Leffingwell, Daniel (Conn). Lieutenant in Ely's Connecticut State Regiment in 1777. (Died 1778.)

Leffiingwell, Elisha (Conn). Ensign 8th Connecticut, 6th July to 17th December, 1775.

Le Fievre, —— (France). Served as a volunteer in Armand's Corps in 1778, and was appionted Brevet Lieutenant Continental Army, 13th January, 1779, and retired from the service.

Lefoy, Thomas (N. Y.). 2d Lieutenant 4th New York, 7th July, 1775; 1st Lieutenant 1st New York, 28th March to November, 1776.

Leftwich, Augustine (Va). 1st Lieutenant Virginia Militia in 1780, and Captain, 1781-1782.

Leftwich, Thomas (Va). Captain Virginia Militia, 1780-1782.

Legare, Benjamin (S. C.). Lieutenant South Carolina Militia in 1775.

Legare, James (S. C.). 2d Lieutenant 2d South Carolina, ——; 1st Lieutenant, 9th October, 1779; taken prisoner at Charleston, 12th May, 1780; served to close of war. (Died 14th January, 1831.)

Leggett, Abraham (N. Y.) Ensign 5th New York, 21st November, 1776; taken prisoner at Fort Montgomery. 6th October, 1777, and did not rejoin regiment. (Died 1842.)

L'Hommedieu, Samuel H. (N. Y.) Captain New York Militia, 1776-1777. (Died 1804.)

Leighton, Samuel (Mass). Captain of Scammon's Massachusetts Regiment, May to December, 1775; Captain Massachusetts Militia, 1776-1780.

Leitch, Andrew (Va). Captain 3d Virginia, 5th February, 1776; Major 1st Virginia, 18th March, 1776; died 1st October, 1776, of wounds received 16th September, 1776, at Harlem Plains.

Leitheiser, Herman (Pa). Ensign 6th Pennsylvania, 15th February, 1777; resigned — October, 1777. (Died 11th February, 1829.)

Leland, Ebenezer (Mass). Private in Lexington Alarm, April, 1775; Sergeant in Jackson's Continental Regiment, 9th June, 1777; Sergeant-Major, 1st February, 1778; Ensign, 4th June. 1779; resigned 20th March, 1780.

Leland, John (Mass). Captain of Doolittle's Massachusetts Regiment, 1775-1776. (Died 1826.)

Leland, Joshua (Mass). Ensign of Brewer's Massachusetts Regiment, May to December, 1775.

Leland, Joseph (Mass). Private in Lexington Alarm, April, 1775; Corporal in Ward's Massachusetts Regiment, May to December, 1775; Ensign 9th Massachusetts, 1st January, 1777; 2d Lieutenant, 28th December, 1777; 1st Lieutenant, 12th July, 1779; transferred to 8th Massachusetts, 1st January, 1781, and served to June, 1783. (Died 1839.)

Lemmon, James (Pa). 1st Lieutenant of Hartley's Continental Regiment, 13th January, 1777; killed at Brandywine, 11th September, 1777.

Lemmon, William (Pa). 2d Lieutenant of Hartley's Continental Regiment, January, 1777; 1st Lieutenant, 23d July, 1778; regiment designated 11th Pennsylvania, 16th December, 1778; resigned 11th March, 1780.

Lemmy, Joseph (N. C.). Ensign 1st North Carolina, 4th January, 1776; 2d Lieutenant, 18th January, 1776; died — July, 1776. (Name also spelled Mc-Lemmy.)

Lemon, John (Va). Captain 13th Virginia, 18th December, 1776; resigned 16th March, 1778.

Lemont, John (Mass). Captain 14th Massachusetts, 1st January, 1777; retired 10th September, 1778. (Died 23d February, 1837.)

Lemont, William (Mass). Ensign of Nixon's Massachusetts Regiment, 21st April to October, 1775; 2d Lieutenant 4th Continental Infantry, 1st January to 31st December, 1776; 1st Lieutenant 6th Massachusetts, 1st January, 1777; transferred to Invalid Regiment, 1st March, 1779; dismissed 1st August, 1782.

Lenear, James (N .C.). Ensign 8th North Carolina, 28th November, 1776; resigned 12th October, 1777; name also spelled Lneoir.

L'Enfant, Pierre Charles (France). Captain Corps of Engineers, 3d April, 1779, to rank from 18th February, 1778; wounded at Savannah, 9th October, 1779; taken prisoner at Charleston, 12th May, 1780; exchanged — November, 1780; Brevet Major, 2d May, 1783; served to close of war. (Died 14th June, 1825.)

Lenington, Thomas (N. Y.). Ensign 3d New York, 1st July, 1775; Ensign of Nicholson's Continental Regiment, 21st April, 1776; taken prisoner while in charge of a prize on the St. Lawrence, 8th May, 1776; exchanged in December, 1776, after the discharge of his regiment. (Died 1829.)

Lennox, David (Pa). Captain 3d Pennsylvania Battalion, 5th January, 1776; wounded and taken prisoner at Fort Washington, 16th November, 1776; exchanged May, 1778, and did not reenter service.

Lenoir, William (N. C.). Captain North Carolina Rangers, ——, 1776; wounded at King's Mountain, 7th October, 1780. (Died 6th May, 1839.)

Lent, Abraham (N. Y.). Colonel New York Militia in 1775.   ..

Leonard, —— (S. C.). Captain South Carolina Militia; killed at Hayes' Station, 9th November, 1781.

Leonard, Abiel (Conn). Chaplain 3d Connecticut, 1st May to 16th December, 1775; Chaplain of Knox's Regiment Continental Artillery, 1st January to 31st December, 1776. (Died 1778.)

Leonard, David (Mass). Major of Danielson's Massachusetts Regiment, April to November, 1775; served subsequently in Massachusetts Militia.

Leonard, Jacob (Mass). Musician in Bailey's Massachusetts Regiment, May to November, 1775, and in 25th Continental Infantry, February to December, 1776; Fife-Major and Sergeant, 2d Massachusetts, 1st January, 1777, until appointed Ensign, 27th February, 1782, and served to June, 1783. (Died April, 1841.)

Leonard, Nathaniel (Mass). Major in Lexington Alarm, April, 1775; Lieutenant-Colonel of Walker's Massachusetts Regiment, May to November, 1775.

Leonard, Nathaniel (N. J.). Sergeant 2d New Jersey, 5th November, 1775; Ensign 3d New Jersey, 9th February to November, 1776; 2d Lieutenant 3d New Jersey, 29th November, 1776; 1st Lieutenant, 26th October, 1777; Captain Lieutenant, 30th March, 1780; transferred to 2d New Jersey, 1st January, 1781; Captain, 6th September, 1781, and served to April, 1783.

Leonard, Noadiah (Mass). Captain in Lexington Alarm, April, 1775; Captain of Woodbridge's Massachusetts Regiment, May to December, 1775. (Died 1790.)

Leonard, Samuel (Mass). Regimental Quartermaster of Woodbridge's Massachusetts Regiment, 4th October to December, 1775.

Leonard, William (N. Y.). Captain of Lasher's New York Militia Regiment, June to December, 1776.

Leonard, Zaphaniah (Mass). Lieutenant-Colonel Massachusetts Militia, 1776.

Le Roy, Francis (N. Y). 2d Lieutenant 4th New York, 28th June, 1775, to January, 1776.

Le Roy, Nicholas George (Pa). Ensign 2d Pennsylvania, 28th July, 1779; Lieutenant, 2d January, 1781; transferred to 1st Pennsylvania, 1st January, 1783; Brevet Captain, 6th February, 1784; retained in service to 20th June, 1784.

Lesesne, Thomas (S. C.). 1st Lieutenant 2d South Carolina, 17th June, 1775; Captain, ———; resigned in 1779.

Lester, Ebenezer (Conn). Ensign 4th Connecticut, 1st January, 1777; died 24th February, 1778.

Lester, John (Conn). Ensign Connecticut Militia; killed at Groton Heights, 6th September, 1781.

Lesure, John (Mass). Sergeant-Major 12th Massachusetts, 1st January, 1777; Ensign, 10th August, 1777; retired 8th September, 1778. (Died 12th April, 1792.)

Letts, Ezekiel (Pa). Ensign 4th Pennsylvania Battalion, 5th January, 1776; resigned 11th October, 1776.

Le Vasche, de, St. Marie (S. C.). 2d Lieutenant 1st South Carolina, October, 1776; 1st Lieutenant, 12th October, 1777; Captain, ———, 1779; taken prisoner at Charleston, 12th May, 1780; exchanged June, 1781, and served to close of war.

Leverett, William (Mass). Lieutenant of Jackson's Continental Regiment, 1st February, 1777; resigned 8th November, 1778.

Levering, Aaron (Pa). Captain of Lewis' Pennsylvania Battalion of the Flying Camp, July to December, 1776. (Died 1794.)

Levers, Robert (Pa). Paymaster 12th Pennsylvania, 13th November, 1776, to 29th April, 1777.

Levers, William (Pa). 1st Lieutenant 11th Pennsylvania, 13th November-1776; resigned 29th September, 1777.

Levington, Robert James.—See Livingston.

Levy, Asher (N. J.). Ensign 1st New Jersey, 12th September, 1778; resigned 14th July, 1779 Also called Lewis.

Lewis, Aaron (Mass). Ensign of Ward's Massachusetts Regiment, May to November, 1775.

Lewis, Abijah (R. I.). Lieutenant 1st Rhode Island, June to December, 1775.

Lewis, Abraham (Pa). 2d Lieutenant 4th Pennsylvania, 3d January, 1777; 1st Lieutenant, 15th May, 1777; taken prisoner at Germantown, 4th October, 1777; retired 1st July, 1778.

Lewis, Addison (Va). 2d Lieutenant Virginia Dragoons, 19th June, 1776; 1st Lieutenant, 25th November, 1776; Captain 1st Continental Dragoons, 15th March, 1777, and served to ———.

Lewis, Andrew (Va). Brigadier-General Continental Army, 1st March, 1776; resigned 15th April, 1777. (Died 26th September, 1781.)

Lewis, Andrew (Va). Ensign 13th Virginia, 14th September, 1776; 2d Lieutenant, 10th May, 1777; regiment designated, 9th Virginia, 14th September, 1778; 1st Lieutenant, 2d October, 1778; retired 12th February, 1781.

Lewis, Archilaus (Mass). Private in Lexington Alarm, April, 1775; Sergeant in Phinney's Massachusetts Regiment, May to December, 1775; Ensign 18th Continental Infantry, 1st January, 1776; 2d Lieutenant, 18th April to 31st December, 1776; 2d Lieutenant 1st Massachusetts, 1st January, 1777; resigned 20th February, 1779. (Died 1834.)

Lewis, Charles (Va). Colonel 14th Virginia, 12th November, 1776; resigned 28th March, 1778.

Lewis, Elijah (Conn). Regimental Quartermaster of Gay's Connecticut State Regiment, June to December, 1776.

Lewis, Elijah (R. I.). 1st Lieutenant 1st Rhode Island, 3d May to December, 1775; Captain 9th Continental Infantry, 1st January to 31st December, 1776; Captain 1st Rhode Island, 1st January, 1777; retired 14th May, 1781.

Lewis, Evans (Ga). Captain — Georgia Continental Regiment, ———; mentioned in 1778 and 1779.

Lewis, Fielding (Va). Brigadier-General Virginia Militia at the beginning of the war and was Superintendent of the Arsenal at Fredericksburg, 1776-1777. (Died 7th January, 1781.)

Lewis, Francis (N. Y.). A signer of the Declaration of Independence; died 30th December, 1802

Lewis, George (Va). Captain 3d Continental Dragoons, 12th December, 1776, to ——. (Died 1821.)

Lewis, Henry (N. Y.). Ensign of Vischer's Regiment New York Militia, ——; wounded at Oriskany, 6th August, 1777.

Lewis, Ichabod (Conn). Lieutenant-Colonel of Ward's Connecticut State Regiment in 1776.

Lewis, Isaac (Conn). Chaplain of Bradley's Connecticut State Regiment, May to December, 1776. (Died 27th August, 1840.)

Lewis, James Martin (N. C.). Lieutenant North Carolina Militia; wounded at King's Mountain, 7th October, 1780.

Lewis, Joel (N. C.). Lieutenant 10th North Carolina, 1st August, 1779; Captain 4th North Carolina, ——; wounded at King's Mountain, 7th October, 1780; was a Major in 1782, and served to ——. (Died 22d November, 1816.)

Lewis, John (Conn). Captain of Douglas' Connecticut State Regiment, 20th June to 29th December, 1776.

Lewis, John (Md). 2d Lieutenant 4th Maryland, 10th December, 1776; 1st Lieutenant 2d Virginia State Regiment, 7th March, 1778; Captain, 1st January, 1779, and served to January, 1780.

Lewis, John (Mass). 2d Lieutenant of Bridge's Massachusetts Regiment, May to December, 1775, ——; 1st Lieutenant 5th Massachusetts, 1st January, 1777; retired — April, 1779.

Lewis, John (Pa) Ensign 4th Pennsylvania, 1st January, 1777; 2d Lieutenant, 29th April, 1777; retired 30th September, 1778

Lewis, John (Va). Ensign 4th Virginia, 17th August, 1776; 2d Lieutenant, 5th January, 1777; Captain in 1780. Died 5th October, 1780.

Lewis, John (Va). Ensign 9th Virginia, 16th March, 1776; 2d Lieutenant, 7th November, 1776; 1st Lieutenant, 14th May, 1778; resigned 15th August, 1778; Captain Virginia Militia, 1780-1781. (Died 1823)

Lewis, Joseph (N. H) Surgeon New Hampshire Militia in 1777

Lewis, Joseph (Conn). Lieutenant Connecticut Militia, ——; killed at Groton Heights, 6th September, 1781.

Lewis, Joseph (Md). Ensign Maryland battalion of the Flying Camp, July, 1776; 1st Lieutenant 2d Canadian

(Hazen's) Regiment, 3d November, 1776; resigned 16th November, 1780.

Lewis, Joseph (N. C.). Lieutenant 8th North Carolina, 28th November, 1776; resigned 10th October, 1777.

Lewis, Joseph (Vt). Surgeon Vermont Militia in 1777.

Lewis, Micajah (N. C.). Captain 1st North Carolina, 25th July, 1777; transferred to 4th North Carolina, 1st June, 1778; Major, ——; wounded at King's Mountain, 7th October, 1780; died 28th February, 1781, of wounds received at Pyle's defeat, 25th February, 1781.

Lewis, Morgan (Mass). Captain Lexington Alarm, April, 1775; 1st Lieutenant of Scammon's Massachusetts Regiment, 3d May, 1775; Captain, 19th August to December, 1775.

Lewis, Morgan (N. Y.). Colonel and Deputy Quartermaster-General Northern Department, 12th September, 1776, to close of war; Brigadier-General and Quartermaster-General United States Army, 3d April, 1812, to 2d March, 1813; Major-General United States Army, 2d March, 1813; honorably discharged, 15th June, 1815. (Died 7th April, 1844.)

Lewis, Nathaniel (Mass). Lieutenant in Lexington Alarm, April, 1775; 1st Lieutenant of Cotton's Massachusetts Regiment, May to November, 1775. (Died 1839.)

Lewis, Nicholas (Va). Colonel Virginia Militia in October, 1781.

Lewis, Robert (Conn). Ensign 7th Connecticut, 6th July to 10th December, 1775; 1st Lieutenant 19th Continental Infantry, 1st January to 31st December, 1776; Captain 2d Connecticut, 1st January, 1777; killed at Peekskill, 22d March, 1777.

Lewis, Robert (Pa). Colonel Pennsylvania Battalion of the Flying Camp, August to December, 1776.

Lewis, Samuel (N. Y.). Ensign 3d New York, 21st November, 1776; Lieutenant, 7th January, 1780; transferred to 1st New York, 1st January, 1781, and served to 3d June, 1783 (Died 25th August, 1822)

Lewis, Samuel (Pa). Lieutenant Pennsylvania Militia; killed by Indians in 1778.

Lewis, Stephen (Va). Sergeant of Lee's Battalion of Light Dragoons, 1778;

August, 1778; Lieutenant and Regimental Quartermaster, 20th August, 1779, and served to close of war.

Lewis, Thomas (Va). 2d Lieutenant 15th Virginia, 21st November, 1776; 1st Lieutenant, 20th March, 1777, regiment designated 11th Virginia, 14th September, 1778; retired 12th February, 1781; Captain United States Infantry, 5th March, 1792; assigned to 1st Sub Legion, 4th September, 1792; assigned to 3d Infantry, 1st November, 1796; resigned 9th March, 1801. (Died 1809.)

Lewis, William (N. C.). Lieutenant 9th North Carolina, March, 1777, to ——.

Lewis, William (Va). 1st Lieutenant 1st Virginia, 2d October, 1775; Captain, 4th September, 1776; Brigade Inspector of Muhlenberg's Brigade, 7th April, 1778; Major 10th Virginia, 12th May, 1779; taken prisoner at Charleston, 12th May, 1780; transferred to 3d Virginia, 12th February, 1781, and was a prisoner to close of war. (Died 1811.)

Lewis, William (Va). Lieutenant of Lee's Battalion of Dragoons, 1778; killed 14th September, 1779, at Genesee, New York.

L'Hommedieu, Samuel H. (N. Y.). Captain New York Militia, 1776-1777. (Died 1804.)

Libby, James (N. H.). Captain New Hampshire Militia, 1777-1778.

Libby, Jonathan (Mass). Ensign 11th Massachusetts, 6th November, 1776; 2d Lieutenant, January, 1777; 1st Lieutenant, 27th November, 1778; resigned 18th March, 1880.

Libby, Josiah (Mass). 1st Lieutenant of Mitchell's Regiment Massachusetts Militia in the Bagaduce Expedition, July to September, 1779. (Died 1st March, 1824.)

Lide, Robert (S. C.). Captain South Carolina Militia in 1776.

Lide, Thomas (S. C.). Captain South Carolina Militia, 1776-1777.

Lidell, George (S. C.). Sergeant 2d South Carolina, 19th August, 1775; Sergeant 3d South Carolina, 24th July, 1776; 2d Lieutenant, 1st January, 1777; 1st Lieutenant, ——, 1777; Captain, 20th December, 1778, and served to close of war.

Liebert, Philip (Canada). Captain 2d Canadian (Hazen's) Regiment, 10th February, 1776; transferred to Invalid Regiment, 3d March, 1782; resigned 23d April, 1783.

Light, Ebenezer (N. H.). Ensign 26th Continental Infantry, 1st January, 1776; 2d Lieutenant 2d New Hampshire, 8th November, 1776; 1st Lieutenant, 22d December, 1777; cashiered 12th July, 1780.

Lightfoot, Philip (Va). Lieutenant 1st Continental Artillery, ——, 1778; retired 1st January, 1781. (Died 1786.)

Lighthall, William (N. H.). Sergeant of Warner's Additional Continental Regiment, 12th March, 1777; Ensign, 14th August, 1778; Lieutenant, —— March, 1780; taken prisoner at Fort Keyser, 19th October, 1780; on parole December, 1782, to close of war. (Died 5th October, 1822.)

Ligman, John (N. C.). Captain North Carolina Militia, 1780-1781.

Lilley, Reuben (Mass). Private in Lexington Alarm, April, 1775; Sergeant in Danielson's Massachusetts Regiment, 29th April to November, 1775; Sergeant 4th Continental Infantry, February to 31st December, 1776; Ensign 6th Massachusetts, 1st January, 1777; 2d Lieutenant, 17th April, 1778; 1st Lieutenant, 11th November, 1779; transferred to 2d Massachusetts, 12th June, 1783, and served to 3d November, 1783.

Lillie, David (Conn). Ensign 7th Connecticut, 6th July to 22d December, 1775; name also spelled Lilley. (Died 1827.)

Lillie, John (Mass). 2d Lieutenant of Gridley's Regiment Massachusetts Artillery, May to December, 1775; 2d Lieutenant of Knox's Regiment Continental Artillery, 10th December, 1775; 1st Lieutenant, August, 1776; Captain-Lieutenant 3d Continental Artillery, 1st January, 1777; Captain, 1st November, 1778; Aide-de-Camp to General Knox, October, 1778, to close of war; transferred to Corps of Artillery, 17th June, 1783, and served to 3d November, 1783; Captain 2d Artillerists and Engineers United States Army, 16th February, 1801; died 22d September, 1801.

Lillington, John (N. C.). Lieutenant 1st North Carolina, 1st September, 1775; resigned —— May, 1776; Colonel North Carolina Militia, 1779-1782.

Lillington, John Alexander (N. C.). Colonel 6th North Carolina, 15th April, 1776; resigned 16th May, 1776; Brigadier-General North Carolina Militia, 1776 to 1783. (Died 1786.)

Lincoln, Abijah (Mass). Ensign of Brewer's Massachusetts Regiment, May to December, 1775; 2d Lieutenant 13th

Continental Infantry, 1st January, 1776; 1st Lieutenant, 10th August to 31st December, 1776.

Lincoln, Benjamin (Mass). Major-General Continental Army, 19th February, 1777; wounded at Saratoga, 7th October, 1777. By the act of 4th November, 1777, it was "Resolved, that the thanks of Congress in their own name, and in behalf of the thirteen United States, be presented to Major-General Gates, Commander-in-Chief of the Northern Department, and to Major-Generals Lincoln and Arnold, and the rest of the officers and troops under his command, for their brave and successful efforts in support of the independence of their country, whereby an army of the enemy of 10,000 men has been totally defeated; one large detachment of it, strongly posted and entrenched, having been conquered at Bennington, another repulsed with loss and disgrace from Fort Schuyler, and the main army under General Burgoyne, after being beaten in different actions and driven from a formidable post and strong entrenchments, reduced to the necessity of surrendering themselves upon terms honorable and advantageous to these States, on the 17th day of October last, to Major-General Gates."

Surrendered at Charleston, 12th May, 1780; prisoner of war until exchanged, November, 1780; Secretary War, 30th October, 1781; resigned 29th October, 1783, but requested by Congress to perform the duties thereof to 12th November, 1783. By the act of 29th October, 1783, it was "Resolved, that the resignation of Major-General Lincoln, as Secretary of War for the United States, be accepted in consideration of the earnest desire which he expresses (the objects of the war being so highly accomplished) to retire to private life, and that he be informed that the United States in Congress assembled entertain a high sense of his perseverance, fortitude, activity, fidelity and capacity in the execution of the office of the Secretary of War, which important trust he has discharged to their entire satisfaction" (Died 9th May, 1810.)

Lincoln, Hannaiah (Pa). 1st Lieutenant 12th Pennsylvania, 1st October, 1776; Captain, 20th May, 1777; resigned 17th October, 1777.

Lincoln, John (Mass). Ensign 24th Continental Infantry, 1st January to 31st December, 1776; 2d Lieutenant 2d

Massachusetts, 1st January, 1777; resigned 20th May, 1778.

Lincoln, Loring (Mass). 2d Lieutenant of Ward's Massachusetts Regiment, May to December, 1775.

Lincoln, Rufus (Mass). Corporal in Lexington Alarm, April, 1775; 2d Lieutenant of Marshall's Masachusetts Regiment, 13th May to October, 1776; 1st Lieutenant 14th Massachusetts, 1st January, 1777; taken prisoner near Schuylkill, 28th December, 1777; Captain-Lieutenant, 8th October, 1779; Captain, 13th April, 1780; transferred to 7th Massachusetts, 1st January, 1781, and served to June, 1783. (Died 4th February, 1838.)

Lincoln, Thomas (Pa). Ensign Pennsylvania State Regiment, 8th May, 1777; regiment designated 13th Pennsylvania, 12th November, 1777; resigned 4th July, 1778.

Lind, Adam (Va). Ensign 3d Virginia, 8th February, 1776; resigned May, 1776.

Lind, Arthur (Va). Sergeant Major 4th Virginia, November, 1776; Ensign, 15th August, 1777; 2d Lieutenant, 12th September, 1777; 1st Lieutenant, 8th November, 1777; transferred to 3d Virginia, 14th September, 1778; Regimental Quartermaster, 16th November, 1778; Captain Lieutenant, — October, 1780; retired 1st January, 1783; name also spelled Lynd.

Lind, Benjamin.—See **Lynds.**

Lindenberger, John (Pa). Ensign German Regiment, 12th July, 1776; 1st Lieutenant 4th Continental Artillery, 20th April, 1777; resigned 17th March, 1778.

Lindenmuth, Michael (Pa). Major Pennsylvania Militia, 1776.

Linder, Daniel (S. C.). Captain South Carolina Militia in 1776.

Lindley, Levi (Mass). Sergeant of Read's Massachusetts Regiment, May to November, 1775; 2d Lieutenant 13th Continental Infantry, 1st January to 31st December, 1776; 2d Lieutenant 1st Massachusetts, 1st January, 1777; 1st Lieutenant, ——, 1778; cashiered 10th December, 1778.

Lindsay, John (Ga). Major Georgia Militia; wounded at Charlotte 26th September, 1780, and at Rugley's Mills, South Carolina, 4th December, 1780.

Lindsay, Samuel (Pa). Lieutenant of Montgomery's Pennsylvania Battalion of the Flying Camp; wounded and taken prisoner at Fort Washington 16th November, 1776 (lost an eye), and rendered no subsequent service (Died 16th April, 1800.)

Lindsay, Thomas (Pa). 1st Lieutenant 1st Battalion Pennsylvania Flying Camp, July to December, 1776.

Lindsay, William (Va). Cornet Virginia Dragoons, 16th June, 1776; 3d Lieutenant 1st Continental Dragoons, 15th March, 1777; wounded near Valley Forge, 21st January, 1778; Captain of Lee's Battalion of Light Dragoons, 7th April, 1778; resigned 1st Ocotber, 1778. (Died 1st September, 1797)

Lindsey, Eleazer (Mass). Captain of Gerrish's Massachusetts Regiment, May, 1775; dismissed 25th August, 1775

Lindsley, Eleazer (N. J). Lieutenant-Colonel of Spencer's Continental Regiment, 15th January, 1777; resigned 27th May, 1779.

Lindsley, Joseph (N. J.). Captain New Jersey Militia, 1778. (Died 1826.)

Lindsley, Joseph (Va). Captain Virginia Militia in 1780. (Died 1822.)

Lingan, James McCubbin (Md). 2d Lieutenant of Stephenson's Maryland and Virginia Rifle Regiment, 22d July, 1776; taken prisoner at Fort Washington, 16th November, 1776; exchanged 25th October, 1780; Captain of Rawling's Continental Regiment, to rank from 10th December, 1778; retired 1st January, 1781. (Killed 28th July, 1812)

Lingan, Thomas (Md). Ensign 2d Maryland Battalion of the Flying Camp, June, 1776; 2d Lieutenant, August, 1776; discharged with Battalion, 1st December, 1776; 1st Lieutenant of Rawlings' Continental Regiment, 26th January, 1777, to ——. (Died 28th May, 1825.)

Linkensdorf, Louis de.—See **De Linkensdorf.**

Linn, Janus (N. J.). Major New Jersey Militia, 1776-1781 (Died 29th December, 1820.)

Linn, John (Pa). Director of Hospital District of Quebec, 30th September, 1776, to — January, 1777.

Linn, William (Pa) Chaplain 5th Pennsylvania Battalion, 15th February to December, 1776. (Died 8th January, 1808.)

Linnard, Wm. (Pa). Captain Pennsylvania Artillery Company. Militia, 1779. (Died 1835)

Linning, Charles (S. C.). Lieutenant 1st South Carolina, — May, 1776; Captain, 20th July, 1778; taken prisoner at Charleston, 12th May, 1780; exchanged June, 1781, and served to close of war.

Linton, John (Va). Sergeant of Grayson's Additional Continental Regiment, 5th March, 1777; Sergeant-Major, 7th October, 1777; Ensign, 1st November, 1777; 2d Lieutenant, 29th April, 1778; resigned 14th March, 1778; Cornet 3d Continental Dragoons, April, 1779; Lieutenant, May, 1780; transferred to Baylor's Consolidated Regiment of Dragoons, 9th November, 1782, and served to close of war. (Died 1824.)

Linton, Wm. (N. C.). 2d Lieutenant 3d North Carolina, 24th July, 1776; 1st Lieutenant, 14th April, 1777, and served to ——. (Died 28th February, 1827.)

Linton, Wm. (Va). Cadet of Grayson's Continental Regiment, 28th May, 1777; Ensign, 1st November, 1777; resigned, — March, 1778.

Lippitt, Charles (R. I.). Lieutenant of Richmond's Rhode Island State Regiment, 1st November, 1775, to May, 1776. (Died August, 1845.)

Lippitt, Christopher (R. I.). Lieutenant-Colonel of Babcock's Rhode Island State Regiment, 15th January, 1776; Colonel of same regiment, May to June, 1776; Colonel 2d Rhode Island Militia Regiment, 19th August, 1776, to 18th January, 1777; served subsequently as Brigadier-General Rhode Island Militia. (Died 18th June, 1824.)

Lipscomb, Bernard (Va). Captain of a Virginia State Regiment, December, 1778, to March, 1782.

Lipscomb, Reuben (Va). 1st Lieutenant 7th Virginia, 26th February, 1776; Captain, 28th November, 1776; transferred to 5th Virginia, 14th September, 1778; died 3d October, 1778.

Lipscomb, Thomas (Va). Ensign 7th Virginia, 28th October, 1776; resigned 20th May, 1778. (Died 1799.)

Lipscomb, Yancey (Va). 1st Lieutenant Virginia State Troops, 13th May, 1778; Captain-Lieutenant, — August, 1779, and served to — March, 1782.

Liscomb, Francis (Mass). Captain of Walker's Massachusetts Regiment, May to December, 1775.

Liscombe, John (N. C.). Ensign 6th North Carolina, 28th April, 1777, to ——.

Lisle, Charles Noel Romand de (—). Major Continental Artillery, 12th November, 1776; permitted to return to San Domingo, 12th April, 1777.

Lisle, John (S. C.). Lieutenant-Colonel South Carolina Militia in 1775; joined the enemy in 1780.

Liston, Thomas (S. C.). 1st Lieutenant South Carolina Artillery, 20th May, 1779; taken prisoner at Charleston, 12th May, 1780; exchanged June, 1781, and served to close of war.

Liswell, John (Mass). 2d Lieutenant 3d Continental Artillery, 1st January, 1777; transferred to Corps of Artillery, 17th June, 1783, and served to 3d November, 1783.

Lithgow, Wm. (Mass). Captain Massachusetts Militia in 1776; Major 11th Massachusetts, 1st January, 1777; wounded at Saratoga, 7th July, 1777; resigned 29th July, 1779. (Died 17th February, 1796.)

Littell, Eliakim (N. J.). 1st Lieutenant 1st New Jersey, 26th April, 1777; resigned — May, 1778.

Little, Eleazer (N J) 1st Lieutenant of Baldwin's Artillery Artificer Regiment, 2d March, 1777; Captain Lieutenant, 12th November, 1779, and served to March, 1781.

Little, George (S. C.). Captain of a South Carolina Regiment, 20th December, 1778; taken prisoner at Charleston, 12th May, 1780.

Little, James (Ga). Captain Georgia Militia in 1779, and Colonel Georgia Militia in 1781.

Little, John (N. Y.). Captain New York Militia, ——; killed at Minnisink, 22d July, 1779.

Little, John (N. Y.). Captain New York Militia, ——; wounded at Johnstown, 24th October, 1781.

Little, Moses (Mass). Captain in Lexington Alarm, April, 1775; Colonel Massachusetts Regiment, 19th May to December, 1775; Colonel 12th Continental Infantry, 1st January to 31st December, 1776. (Died 27th May, 1798.)

Little, Moses (N. H.). 1st Lieutenant 1st New Hampshire 23d April to December, 1775; Lieutenant New Hampshire Militia in 1778. (Died 1813.)

Little, Nathaniel (Mass). Ensign 2d Massachusetts, 26th November, 1779; resigned 17th April, 1782. (Died 1835.)

Little, Theophilus (N. J.). Lieutenant New Jersey Militia; was a prisoner; when and where taken not stated.

Little, Thomas (N. J.). Captain New Jersey Militia; taken prisoner at Monmouth, 27th June, 1778, and was a prisoner to September, 1780. (Died 1810.)

Little, Wm. (Mass). Surgeon's Mate 15th Massachusetts, 1st January, 1777; resigned 1st December, 1778.

Littlefield, Daniel (Mass). 2d Lieutenant 14th Continental Infantry, 1st January, 1776, to ——.

Littlefield, Jeremiah (Mass). 2d Lieutenant of Scammon's Massachusetts Regiment, May to December, 1775; 2d Lieutenant 15th Continental Infantry, 1st January to 31st December, 1776.

Littlefield, John (Mass). Ensign 11th Massachusetts, 1st January, 1777; resigned 20th June, 1780.

Littlefield, Noah Moulton (Mass). Captain in Lexington Alarm, April, 1775; Lieutenant-Colonel Massachusetts Militia in 1776; Lieutenant-Colonel 11th Massachusetts, 6th November, 1776; retired 1st January, 1781. (Died 25th October, 1821.)

Littlefield, Wm. (R. I.). Ensign 12th Continental Infantry, 1st January to 31st December, 1776; Captain Lieutenant 2d Rhode Island, 1st January, 1777; discharged 20th June, 1780.

Litzinger, William (Pa). Sergeant German Regiment, 15th July, 1776; Ensign, 14th August, 1777; resigned 1st June, 1778.

Livermore, Daniel (N. H.). 2d Lieutenant 1st New Hampshire, 23d April to December, 1775; 1st Lieutenant 5th Continental Infantry, 1st January, 1776; Captain 3d New Hampshire, 8th November, 1776; transferred to 1st New Hampshire, 1st January, 1781; dismissed 8th August, 1781; reinstated 28th August, 1781; retired 1st March, 1782.

Livermore, Joseph (Mass). 1st Lieutenant of Ward's Massachusetts Regiment, 23d May to December, 1775; Captain Massachusetts Militia in 1779.

Livingston, Abraham (N. Y.). Captain 1st Canadian (Livingston's) Regiment, 18th December, 1776; retired 1st January, 1781; served subsequently as Captain New York Levies.

Livingston, Gilbert James (N. Y.). Ensign 3d New York, 1st September,

1776; 2d Lieutenant 2d New York, 21st November, 1776; 1st Lieutenant 1st April, 1778; resigned 5th April, 1780; served subsequently as Captain New York Militia.

Livingston, Gilbert R. (N. Y.). Ensign 1st New York, 24th February, 1776; 2d Lieutenant 3d New York, 21st November, 1776; deserted 12th October, 1776; was subsequently captured and hanged.

Livingston, Henry (N. Y.) Colonel New York Militia, 1775-1780. (Died 1828.)

Livingston, Henry Beekman (N. Y.). Captain 4th New York, 28th June, 1775; Aide-de-Camp to General Montgomery (his brother-in-law), July to December, 1775. By the act of 12th December, 1775, it was "Resolved that this Congress will make a present of a sword of the value of $100 to Captain Henry B. Livingston, as a testimonial of his services (at Chambly) to this country, and that they will embrace the first opportunity of promoting him in the Army." Colonel 4th New York, 21st November, 1776; resigned 13th January, 1799; was Major and Aide-de-Camp to General Schuyler, February to November, 1776. (Died 5th November, 1831.)

Livingston, Henry Brockholst (N. J.). Captain and Aide-de-Camp to General Schuyler in 1775; Major 3d New York, December, 1775; Lieutenant-Colonel and Aide-de-Camp, 8th March, 1776; Aide-de-Camp to General St. Clair in 1776 and 1777. Was granted leave for 12 months to accompany John Jay as Secretary and was taken prisoner by the British on his return voyage in 1782; sent to New York and released shortly after his arrival there. (Died 19th March, 1823.)

Livingston, Henry P. (N. Y.). 1st Lieutenant of Captain Caleb Gibb's Company Washington Guards, 12th June, 1777; Captain, 4th December, 1778; resigned 26th March, 1779.

Livingston, James (N. Y.). Colonel 1st Canadian Regiment, 20th November, 1775; retired 1st January, 1781. (Died 1832.)

Livingston, James (Pa). Lieutenant and Regimental Quartermaster of Flower's Artillery Artificer Regiment, 1777, to ——.

Livingston, John Justice (Va). Surgeon's Mate Hospital Department, 1st July to 31st December, 1776.

Livingston, Peter R. (N. Y.). Colonel New York Militia in 1775. (Died 1794.)

Livingston, Philip (N. Y.). A signer of the Declaration of Independence; died 12th June, 1778.

Livingston, Richard (N. Y.). Lieutenant-Colonel 1st Canadian Regiment, 18th December, 1776; taken prisoner at Fort Montgomery, 6th October, 1777; resigned 2d November, 1779. (Died ——, 1786.)

Livingston, Robert H. (N. Y.). 2d Lieutenant 2d Continental Artillery, 29th June, 1781, and served to June, 1783.

Livingston, Robert James (Va). Ensign 5th Virginia, 15th October, 1776; taken prisoner at Trenton, 26th December, 1776; 2d Lieutenant, 1st April, 1777; retired 14th September, 1778; being a prisoner. Name also spelled Levington.

Livingston, Walter (N. Y.). Commissary of Stores and Provisions, New York Department, 17th July, 1775; resigned 14th September, 1776.

Livingston, William (N. J.). Brigadier-General New Jersey Militia, 28th October, 1775, to 31st August, 1776. (Died 25th July, 1790.)

Livingston, Wm. (S. C.). Captain South Carolina Militia, 1779-1781.

Livingston, William Smith (N. Y.) Major of Lasher's Regiment New York Militia, July, 1776; Aide-de-Camp to General Greene, 12th August, 1776, to 14th January, 1777; Lieutenant-Colonel of Webb's Continental Regiment, 1st January, 1777; resigned 10th October, 1778:

Llewellyn, John (Pa). Ensign of Montgomery's Pennsylvania Battalion of the Flying Camp, July to December, 1776; Ensign 9th Pennsylvania, 7th December, 1776; resigned 11th July, 1777.

Lloyd, Bateman (N. J.). 2d Lieutenant 4th New Jersey, 23d November, 1776; 1st Lieutenant, 10th February, 1777; Captain, 12th November, 1777; taken prisoner in a skirmish at Salem, N. J., 24th March, 1778; exchanged 1st April, 1781, and resigned 6th September, 1781.

Lloyd, Benjamin (S. C.). Lieutenant of a South Carolina Artillery Company; taken prisoner at Charleston 12th May, 1780.

Lloyd, Edward (S. C.). 1st Lieutenant 4th South Carolina (Artillery),

———; wounded at Savannah, 9th October, 1779 (lost an arm), and taken prisoner at Charleston, 12th May, 1780.

Lloyd, James (Pa). 1st Lieutenant 4th Continental Artillery, 14th March, 1777; Captain Lieutenant, 9th February, 1779, and served to ———.

Lloyd, John (N. Y.). 1st Lieutenant 4th New York, 21st November, 1776; cashiered 24th March, 1778.

Lloyd, Martin (S. C.). Lieutenant South Carolina Militia, 1776.

Lloyd, Peter Z. (Pa). Captain Pennsylvania Musket Battalion, 15th March to December, 1776; Aide-de-Camp to General Ewing, 11th August to November, 1776.

Lloyd, Richard (N. J.). 1st Lieutenant 3d New Jersey, 15th April to November, 1776; 1st Lieutenant 2d Canadian (Hazen's) Regiment, 3d November, 1776; Captain, 20th September, 1777; retired June, 1783.

Lobdell, Isaac (N. Y.). Lieutenant New York Militia; was a prisoner 1st April, 1780, to 21st May, 1783; where taken not stated.

Lochman, Charles (S. C.). Hospital Surgeon's Mate, 1779 to close of war.

Lochrey, Archibald (Pa). Colonel Pennsylvania Rangers, ———; killed by Indians on the Miami, Ohio, 24th August, 1781.

Lochrey, Jeremiah (Pa). Captain 6th Pennsylvania, 15th February, 1777; deserted from arrest in October, 1777.

Locke, Benjamin (Mass). Captain of Gardner's Massachusetts Regiment, May to December, 1775; Captain Massachusetts Militia in 1776.

Locke, Francis (N. J.). Captain New Jersey Militia; killed at Elizabethtown, N. J., 15th September, 1777.

Locke, Francis (N. C.). Colonel North Carolina Militia, 1779-1781. (Died 8th January, 1823.)

Locke, George (N. C.). Lieutenant North Carolina Militia; killed at Charlotte 26th September, 1780.

Locke, Thomas (Mass). 2d Lieutenant of Gerrish's Massachusetts Regiment, May to November, 1775; 2d Lieutenant 9th Massachusetts, 1st January, 1777; resigned 20th April, 1778. (Died 18th February, 1831.)

Locke, Timothy (R. I.). Lieutenant Rhode Island Militia in 1775; 1st Lieutenant 9th Continental Infantry, 1st January to 31st December, 1776; 1st Lieutenant 1st Rhode Island, 1st January, 1777, and served to ———.

Lockerman, Thomas Wyer (Md). 1st Lieutenant 4th Maryland Battalion of the Flying Camp, July, 1776, to ———.

Lockett, John (Va). Captain Virginia Militia in 1779.

Lockhart, Philip (Pa). 2d Lieutenant of Montgomery's Pennsylvania Battalion of the Flying Camp; taken prisoner at Fort Washington 16th November, 1776.

•**Lockhart, Samuel** (N. C.). Major 3d North Carolina, 15th April, 1776; Lieutenant-Colonel 8th North Carolina, 12th October, 1777; resigned 19th October, 1777; was taken prisoner at Charleston 12th May, 1780; is then called Colonel.

Lockwood, Jacob (N. Y.). Captain New York Militia, 1779.

Lockwood, James (Conn). Secretary and Brigade-Major to General Wooster, 1st May, 1775, to May, 1776. (Died 24th August, 1795.)

Lockwood, John (Conn). Paymaster of Webb's Additional Continental Regiment, 1st January, 1777; resigned 1st May, 1778.

Lockwood, Samuel (Conn). 2d Lieutenant 5th Connecticut, 1st May, 1775; Captain Assistant Engineer, 5th November, 1775, to 5th November, 1776; taken prisoner at Quebec, 31st December, 1775; Captain 2d Continental Artillery, 1st January, 1777; resigned February, 1779.

Lockwood, Samuel (Conn). 2d Lieutenant 5th Connecticut, 1st January, 1777; resigned 13th January, 1778.

Lockwood, William (Mass). Brigade Chaplain, 12th October, 1780, to June, 1783. (Died 23d June, 1828.)

Lodge, Benjamin (Pa). Ensign 12th Pennsylvania, 16th October, 1776; 2d Lieutenant, 1st March, 1777; 1st Lieutenant, 11th October, 1777; transferred to 6th Pennsylvania, 1st July, 1778; transferred to 3d Pennsylvania, 1st January, 1783, and served to 3d June, 1783. (Died 1801.)

Loeffler, John (N. Y.). Ensign of Warner's Continental Regiment, 7th January, 1777; resigned 4th August, 1777; name also spelled Laffler. (Died 30th October, 1823.)

Logan, Francis (S. C.). Captain South Carolina Militia in 1775.

Logan, George (S. C.). Captain South Carolina Rangers; killed at Black Mingo, S. C., 14th September, 1780.

Logan, Samuel (N. Y.). Major New York Militia, 1775-1776; Major 5th New York, 21st November, 1776; taken prisoner at Fort Montgomery, 6th October, 1777; exchanged 21st December, 1780, and retired from service, 1st January, 1781; served subsequently as Major New York Levies.

Logan, Samuel (S. C.). Captain South Carolina Militia in 1776.

Logan, Thomas (N. Y.). Ensign of Nicholson's Continental Regiment, March to November, 1776.

Loisiau, Augustin (N. Y.). Captain 1st Canadian (Livingston's) Regiment, 18th December, 1776, to rank from 20th November, 1775; dismissed 5th January, 1779; name also spelled Loizeau and Loiseau.

Loller, Robert (Pa.). Major Pennsylvania Associaters, 1776-1777; wounded at Germantown 4th October, 1777. (Died 21st October, 1808.)

Lomagne, John Baptisti, Viscount (France). Captain 3d Cavalry, Pulaski Legion, 9th February, 1778; Major, 11th April, 1781; retired 24th September, 1781.

Long, Andrew (Pa.). Captain 1st Battalion of Miles' Pennsylvania Rifle Regiment, 6th April, 1776; resigned 14th October, 1776 (Died 1812.)

Long, Gabriel (Va.). Captain 11th Virginia, 23d July, 1776; regiment designated 7th Virginia, 14th September, 1778; resigned 13th May, 1779. (Died 3d February, 1827.)

Long, Hugh (Pa.). Captain of Hart's Pennsylvania Battalion of the Flying Camp, July to December, 1776. (Died 1778.)

Long, James.—See James Lang.

Long.. John (Va.). Ensign of Thruston's Continental Regiment, 25th July, 1777, to — July, 1778.

Long, Nehemiah (N. C.). Lieutenant 5th North Carolina, 4th October, 1776, to ——.

Long, Nicholas (N. C.). Colonel North Carolina Militia in 1775; Colonel Deputy Quartermaster, General Southern Department, 7th May, 1776, to ——; Colonel 43d United States Infantry, 4th August, 1813; honorably discharged 15th June, 1815. (Died 22d August, 1819.)

Long, Nicholas (Va). Sergeant of a Virginia Regiment, — November, 1776; 2d Lieutenant, — November, 1777; retired 30th September, 1778.

Long, Pierce (N. H.). Colonel New Hampshire Militia, 1776 to 1778. (Died 3d April, 1789.)

Long, Reuben (Va). Sergeant 11th Virginia, 26th September, 1776; Ensign, 16th December, 1776; 2d Lieutenant, 1st June, 1777; regiment designated 7th Virginia, 14th September, 1778; 1st Lieutenant, 10th May, 1779; transferred to 3d Virginia, 12th February, 1781, and served to close of war. (Died 1791.)

Long, Solomon (Md). 2d Lieutenant of Captain Watkin's Independent Maryland Company, 14th January, 1776; Captain Maryland Independent Company, 3d October, 1776; Captain 2d Maryland, 10th December, 1776; resigned 4th June, 1778.

Long, William (Va). 1st Lieutenant 2d Virginia State Regiment, 10th May, 1777; Captain, ——, 1780, and served to 6th February, 1781.

Longley, Robert (Mass). Captain of Whitcomb's Massachusetts Regiment, May to December, 1775; Lieutenant-Colonel of Jonathan Smith's Massachusetts Militia Regiment in 1776.

Longley, Zachariah (Mass). Regimental Quartermaster of Prescott's Massachusetts Regiment, May to December, 1775.

Longstreet, Elias (N. J.). Captain 1st New Jersey, 29th October, 1775, to 10th November, 1776; Captain 1st New Jersey, 29th November, 1776; taken prisoner at Springfield, 17th December, 1776; never rejoined regiment.

Longstreet, Gilbert (N. J.). 1st Lieutenant of Forman's New Jersey Regiment, July to December, 1776.

Loomis, Abner (N. C.). Ensign 8th North Carolina, 8th February, 1776; 2d Lieutenant, 27th August, 1777; resigned 15th November, 1777.

Loomis, Joel (Conn). Captain Connecticut Light Horse in 1776.

Loomis, Jonathan (N. C.). Surgeon 8th North Carolina, 26th November, 1776; transferred to 3d North Carolina 1st June, 1778; taken prisoner at Charleston, 12th May, 1780; exchanged 14th June, 1781; served to close of war.

Loomis, Lebbeus (Conn). Private in Lexington Alarm, April, 1775; Private 2d Connecticut, 10th May to 17th December, 1775; Sergeant-Major 4th Connecticut, 1st January, 1777; Ensign, 25th November, 1777; 2d Lieutenant, 13th January, 1778; 1st Lieutenant, 5th June, 1778; Regimental Adjutant, 1st August, 1778, to November, 1783; transferred to 1st Connecticut 1st January, 1781; retained in Swift's Connecticut Regiment, June, 1783, and served to 3d November, 1783. (Died 10th January, 1836.)

Loomis, Michael (Mass). 2d Lieutenant of Fellow's Massachusetts Regiment, April to December, 1775.

Looney, David (N. C.). Major North Carolina Militia, 1779-1782. (Died 1810.)

Loop, Henry (N. Y.). Ensign New York Militia, ——; taken prisoner at Skeenesborough, 7th March, 1780; released 24th November, 1782.

Lorah, John (Md). 2d Lieutenant 3d Maryland Battalion of the Flying Camp, June, 1776; 1st Lieutenant German Battalion, 12th July, 1776; Captain, 28th March, 1777; resigned 23d February, 1778.

Lord, James (Conn). Ensign 1st Connecticut, 1st January, 1777; 2d Lieutenant, 1st January, 1778; 1st Lieutenant 1st June, 1778; Regimental Paymastetr, 15th November, 1778; transferred to 4th Connecticut, 1st January, 1781; transferred to 2d Connecticut, 1st January, 1783, and served to 3d June, 1783.

Lord, James (Mass). 2d Lieutenant of Little's Massachusetts Regiment, 19th May to December, 1775; 1st Lieutenant 12th Continental Infantry, 1st January to 31st December, 1776. (Died 13th February, 1830.)

Lord, Jeremiah (Mass). Sergeant of Scammon's Massachusetts Regiment, May to November, 1775; Corporal and Sergeant 1st Massachusetts, 21st May, 1777, until appointed Ensign, 15th June, 1781; transferred to 2d Massachusetts, 12th June, 1783; retained in Jackson's Continental Regiment, 3d November, 1783, and served to 20th June, 1784. (Died 1795.)

Lord, Josiah (Mass). Surgeon's Mate of Little's Massachusetts Regiment, May to November, 1775.

Lord, Nathan (Mass). 2d Lieutenant of Scammon's Massachusetts Regiment, May to December, 1775; 2d Lieutenant 15th Continental Infantry, 1st January, 1776; wounded and taken prisoner at the Cedars, 19th May, 1776. (Died 1807.)

Lord, Simeon (Mass). Ensign 7th Continental Infantry, 1st January to 31st December, 1776; 1st Lieutenant 2d Massachusetts, 1st January, 1777; Captain Lieutenant, 21st June, 1779; Captain, 12th May, 1781; Assistant to Adjutant-General, 1st February, 1783, and served to close of war (Died 1815.)

Lord, William (Conn). Sergeant 6th Connecticut, 1st April, 1777; Ensign, 11th April, 1779; transferred to 3d Connecticut, 1st January, 1781; 2d Lieutenant, 6th December, 1781; retired 1st January, 1783.

Lord, William (N. C.). Paymaster 1st North Carolina,. 12th December, 1776; resigned 5th March, 1777; Lieutenant 10th North Carolina, 1st August, 1779, and served to ——.

Loring, Ephraim (N. J.). Surgeon's Mate, 3d New Jersey, 20th February, 1777; retired 1st January, 1781.

Loring, Joseph (Conn). Surgeon's Mate 2d Continental Dragoons, 20th February, 1777; resigned 16th May, 1778.

Loring, Joseph (Mass). Ensign of Gridley's Regiment Massachusetts Artillery, October, 1775; 2d Lieutenant of Knox's Regiment Continental Artillery, 10th December, 1775; Captain Lieutenant 3d Continental Artillery, 1st January, 1777; was taken prisoner at Long Island, 27th August, 1776; contracted smallpox, disabled, and was discharged as supernumerary, 12th September, 1778.

Loring, Jotham (Mass). Captain in Lexington Alarm, April, 1775; Captain of Heath's Massachusetts Regiment, May to November, 1775; Major 24th Continental Infantry, 1st January, 1776; Lieutenant-Colonel, 1st November, 1776; Lieutenant-Colonel 3d Massachusetts, 1st January, 1777; dismissed 12th August, 1779.

Loring, Samuel (Mass). Sergeant in Cotton's Massachusetts Regiment, May to November, 1775; 2d Lieutenant 23d Continental Infantry, 1st January to 31st December, 1776.

Lotbiniere, Louis (Canada). Chaplain 1st Canadian (Livingston's) Regiment, 26th January, 1776; retired 1st January, 1781.

Lothrop, Daniel (Mass). Captain in Lexington Alarm, April, 1775; Captain of Thomas' Massachusetts Regiment, May to November, 1775; Captain Massachusetts Militia, 1776-1777.

Lothrop, Thomas (Mass). Major and Lieutenant-Colonel and Colonel Massachusetts Militia, 1775-1776. (Died 1813.)

Lott, Abraham P. (N. Y.). Colonel New York Militia in 1775.

Lott, Peter (N. J.). Ensign 1st New Jersey, 29th November, 1776; 2d Lieutenant and Regimental Quartermaster, 25th February, 1778; 1st Lieutenant, 22d January, 1779; resigned 27th March, 1780.

Lott, Richard (N. J.). Lieutenant-Colonel New Jersey Militia, 1776-1777.

Lotz, Nicholas.—See **Klotz.**

Lounsbery, Edward (N. Y.). Captain Lieutenant 3d New York, July, 1776; Captain 2d New York, 21st November, 1776; resigned 14th October, 1778. (Died 1801.)

Love, Amos (N. C.). Lieutenant 6th North Carolina, 16th April, 1776, to ——.

Love, David (N. C.). Surgeon North Carolina Brigade, 18th August, 1779, to 1st August, 1781; was taken prisoner, but when and where not stated.

Love, Philip (Va). Brigade Major Virginia Militia, 1777.

Love, Robert (Va). Sergeant and Lieutenant Virginia Militia, 1780-1781. (Died 1845.)

Love, Wm. (S. C.). 1st Lieutenant 3d South Carolina, 3d November, 1776; taken prisoner at Charleston 12th May, 1780; marked on a list as "deserted." Name also spelled Lowe.

Lovejoy, Joshua (N. H.). 2d Lieutenant 8th Continental Infantry, 1st January, 1776, to ——.

Lovejoy, Obadiah (Mass). Private in Lexington Alarm, April, 1775; Sergeant 14th Massachusetts, 19th February, 1777; Ensign, 28th March, 1779; 2d Lieutenant, 18th March, 1780; 1st Lieutenant, 13th July, 1780; transferred to 10th Massachusetts 1st January, 1781; retired 1st January, 1783.

Lovell, Ebenezer.—See **Lowell.**

Lovell, James (Mass). Ensign of Lee's Continental Regiment, 25th May, 1777; Regimental Adjutant, 10th May,

1778; transferred to Jackson's Regiment, 22d April, 1779; transferred to Lee's Battalion of Light Dragoons in March, 1780, and was Adjutant of same to close of war. (Died 10th July, 1850.)

Lovell, Nehemiah (Vt). Captain of Bedel's Regiment Vermont Militia, 15th December, 1777, to 1st April, 1778.

Lovell, Robert (Va). Lieutenant of Virginia State Regiment, 1779 to 1781.

Lovell, Solomon (Mass) Colonel Massachusetts Militia, 1776-1779, and Brigadier-General Massachusetts Militia, 1779-1782. (Died 1801.)

Lovell, Wm. (Mass). Lieutenant and Adjutant of Lee's Battalion of Light Dragoons, August, 1778, to ——.

Lovett, Thomas (Ga). 1st Lieutenant of Grimes' Independent Georgia Company, October, 1775, to ——.

Loveley, Wm. Lewis (Va). Ensign 8th Virginia, 25th May, 1776; 2d Lieutenant, January, 1777; 1st Lieutenant, 26th March, 1778; transferred to 4th Virginia, 14th September, 1778; Captain, 18th February, 1781, and served to close of war.

Lovewell, Nehemiah (Vt). Lieutenant Vermont Militia, 1777; taken prisoner ——; when and where not stated.

Lovewell, Noah (N H.). Colonel New Hampshire Militia, 1778-1781.

Low, Ebenezer (Mass). 1st Lieutenant of Little's Massachusetts Regiment, 19th April to December, 1775

Low, Edward (Mass). Sergeant in Lexington Alarm, April, 1775; 2d Lieutenant of Scammon's Massachusetts Regiment, May, 1775, to August, 1775.

Low, Jacob (N. H.). Ensign 8th Continental Infantry, 1st January to 31st December, 1776; Captain of Baldwin's Artillery Artificer Regiment, 16th December, 1776; resigned 1st January, 1778.

Low, John (Mass). Captain of Mansfield's Massachusetts Regiment, May to December, 1775; Captain 27th Continental Infantry, 1st January to 31st December, 1776.

Low, John (N. Y.). Joined 2d New York as 2d Lieutenant, 29th May, 1782, and deserted 18th December, 1782.

Low, John (Pa). Ensign 1st Pennsylvania Battalion, 20th January, 1776; died 29th July, 1776.

Low, John (R. I.). Lieutenant-Colonel Rhode Island Militia, 1775-1776.

Lowden, Anthony (N. J.). 2d Lieutenant New Jersey Militia; taken prisoner at Hancock's Bridge, 21st March, 1778.

Lowdon, John (Pa). Captain of Thompson's Pennsylvania Rifle Battalion, 25th June to December, 1775; wounded at Montreal, 12th November, 1775; Captain 1st Continental Infantry, 1st January, 1776, to ——. (Died February, 1798.)

Lowe, John (N. C.). Lieutenant 10th North Carolina, 19th April, 1777; retired 1st June, 1778. (Died 1826.)

Lowe, John Hawkins (Md). Captain 3d Maryland Battalion of the Flying Camp, July to 1st December, 1776; wounded at Harlem Plains, 16th September, 1776; Captain 3d Maryland, 10th December, 1776; resigned 10th October, 1777.

Lowe, John Tolson (Md). Sergeant 2d Maryland, 10th January, 1777; transferred to 1st Maryland, 1st January, 1780; 2d Lieutenant, 20th January, 1781, and served to April, 1783.

Lowe, Philip (N. C.). Ensign 2d North Carolina, 1st September, 1775; Lieutenant 3d May, 1776; resigned 1st February, 1777; Major 4th Georgia, 18th June, 1778; Lieutenant-Colonel, ——, 1780; retired 1st October, 1780.

Lowe, William.—See **Love.**

Lowell, Ebenezer (Mass). Ensign of Jackson's Continental Regiment, 1st February, 1777; killed at Indian Field, New York, 31st August, 1778. (Name also spelled Lovell.)

Lowell, Oliver (Vt). Major Vermont Militia in 1776-1777.

Lowes, James (Pa). Sergeant 2d Pennsylvania Battalion, February, 1776; Sergeant 3d Pennsylvania, November, 1776; Ensign, 1st April, 1777; resigned 31st October, 1777. (Died 1810.)

Lowrey, Alexander (Pa). Colonel Pennsylvania Associaters, 1776-1777. (Died 31st January, 1805.)

Lowrey, Thomas (N. J.). Colonel New Jersey Militia, 1776-1777.

Lowther, Wm. (Pa). Ensign Pennsylvania Battalion of the Flying Camp; taken prisoner at Fort Washington 16th November. 1776.

Lowther, Wm. (Va). Captain Virginia Militia, 1777.

Lucas, Barton (Md). Captain of Smallwood's Maryland Regiment, 14th January, 1776; resigned 11th October, 1776.

Lucas, James (Del). Adjutant Delaware Battalion of the Flying Camp, July to December, 1776; Lieutenant and Adjutant Delaware Regiment, 27th November, 1776; resigned 15th August, 1778.

Lucas, James (Vt). Paymaster of Bedel's Regiment Vermont Militia, 15th December, 1777, to 1st April, 1779.

Lucas, James (Va). Captain 4th Virginia, 19th March, 1776; Major 1st Virginia, 23d April, 1778; transferred to 3d Virginia, 14th September, 1778; retired 16th May, 1779.

Lucas, John (Ga). Captain 3d Georgia, 1st March, 1777, to close of war; Brevet Major, 30th September, 1783; served as Aide-de-Camp to General McIntosh in 1779.

Lucas, John (Va). Captain Virginia Militia, 1779-1780.

Lucas, Nathaniel (Va). Ensign 4th Virginia, 19th March, 1776; 2d Lieutenant, 28th September, 1776; 1st Lieutenant, 7th June, 1777; Regimental Quartermaster, 28th May, 1778, to ——, 1780.

Lucas, Thomas (N. Y.). 1st Lieutenant of Malcolm's Continental Regiment, 23d January, 1777; Captain, 22d December, 1777; cashiered 11th May, 1778. (Died 3d November, 1823.)

Lucas, Thomas (Pa). 2d Lieutenant 11th Pennsylvania, 30th September, 1776; Adjutant, 17th December, 1776; 1st Lieutenant, 23d January, 1777; killed at Germantown, 4th October, 1777.

Luce, Francis.—See **Luse.**

Luckett, David (Md). Ensign of Gist's Continental Regiment, 4th July, 1779; Lieutenant, 7th April, 1780; transferred to 3d Maryland, 1st January, 1781; retained in Maryland Battalion April, 1783, and remained in command of a company at Fort Pitt, Pennsylvania, to 7th June, 1785, when ordered to be discharged.

Luckett, Thomas Hussey (Md). 1st Lieutenant of Stephenson's Rifle Regiment, 11th July, 1776; taken prisoner at Fort Washington 16th November, 1776;

exchanged 2d November, 1780, and did not rejoin the service.

Luddington, Henry (N. Y.). Captain New York Militia, 1778, and Colonel New York Militia, 1780. (Died 1817.)

Ludemann, —— (France). Lieutenant 3d Cavalry, Pulaski Legion, 1st January, 1779; resigned 25th April, 1780, and permitted to return to France.

Ludiman, John Wm. (Va). Ensign 6th Virginia, 23d May, 1780; Lieutenant, 15th June, 1781; served to close of war.

Ludlam, Jacob (N. J.). Ensign 1st New Jersey, 29th November, 1776; resigned March, 1777.

Ludlow, Cornelius (N. J.). Lieutenant-Colonel New Jersey Militia; wounded at Germantown, 4th October, 1777. (Died 1812.)

Luds, Carey (Conn). Captain Connecticut Militia, ——; killed at Groten Heights, 6th September, 1781.

Ludwig, Charles (Pa). Surgeon German Regiment, 15th November, 1776; resigned 12th November, 1777.

Ludwig, John (Pa). Captain Pennsylvania Battalion of the Flying Camp, July to December, 1776.

Lukens, Charles (Pa). Major and Commissary of Military Stores, 1776; also Major of Flower's Artillery Artificer Regiment, 8th March, 1777; retired from service at his own request, 30th August, 1780.

Lukens, Matthias (Pa). 2d Lieutenant 3d Pennsylvania, 1st April, 1777; died 21st March, 1778.

Lumberd, James.—See Lambert.

Lumos, Jonathan (N. C.). Surgeon 3d North Carolina, 26th November, 1776; retired 1st January, 1783.

Lund, John (N. H.). 1st Lieutenant of Wyman's Regiment New Hampshire Militia, May to September, 1776.

Lunsford, Wm. (Va). Cornet of Lee's Continental Battalion of Light Dragoons, ——, 1778; Lieutenant in 1781; served to ——.

Lunt, Daniel (Mass). Member of Company of Minute Men at Lexington and Concord, April, 1775; Sergeant in Phinney's Massachusetts Regiment, May to December, 1775; Sergeant Continental Regiment in 1776; 2d Lieutenant 11th Massachusetts, 6th November, 1776; 1st Lieutenant, 3d April, 1777;

Captain, 18th March, 1780; transferred to 10th Massachusetts, 1st January, 1781; transferred to 1st Massachusetts, 1st January, 1783, and served to 3d June, 1788.

Lunt, James (Mass). 2d Lieutenant 7th Massachusetts, 1st January, 1777; 1st Lieutenant, 24th August, 1777; retired 1st April, 1779.

Lunt, Ezra (Mass). Captain of Little's Massachusetts Regiment, 19th May to December, 1775; Captain 12th Continental Infantry, 1st January to 31st December, 1776; Captain of Henley's Additional Continental Regiment, 14th August, 1777; retired 23d April, 1779.

Lunt, James (Mass). 2d Lieutenant 7th Massachusetts, 1st January, 1777; 1st Lieutenant, 24th August, 1777; retired 1st April, 1779.

Lunt, Paul (Mass). Sergeant Lexington Alarm, April, 1775; 1st Lieutenant of Little's Massachusetts Regiment, 19th May to December, 1775.

Luse, Francis (N. J.). Private, Corporal and Sergeant New Jersey troops, November, 1775, to June, 1780; Ensign 2d New Jersey, 16th May, 1780; transferred to 1st New Jersey, 1st January, 1783; retained in New Jersey Battalion, April, 1783, and served to 3d November, 1783; Ensign United States Infantry Regiment, 17th March, 1786; Ensign 1st United States Infantry, 29th September, 1789; resigned 1st May, 1790. Name also spelled Luce.

Luse, Henry (N. J.). 1st Lieutenant 2d New Jersey, 25th December, 1775, to 1st November, 1776; 1st Lieutenant 2d New Jersey, 29th November, 1776; Captain, 5th February, 1777; resigned 10th February, 1779.

Luse, Nathan (N. J.). Lieutenant-Colonel New Jersey Militia in 1776.

Lush, Stephen (N. Y.). Captain of Spencer's Continental Regiment, January, 1777; Major and Aide-de-Camp to Governor Clinton, ——; taken prisoner at Fort Montgomery, 6th October, 1777.

Lush, —— (S. C.). Lieutenant South Carolina State troops, ——; killed at Eutaw Springs, 8th September, 1781.

Lusk, William (Pa). Ensign 6th Pennsylvania Battalion, 9th January, 1776; 1st Lieutenant 7th Pennsylvania, 20th March, 1777; Captain-Lieutenant, 17th April, 1779; Captain, 12th May, 1779; transferred to 2d Pennsylvania,

17th January, 1781; retired 1st January, 1783. (Died 25th August, 1799.)

Luton, James (N. C.). Ensign 2d North Carolina, 1st April, 1777; resigned 3d March, 1778.

Lutterlough, Henry E. (N. Y.). Deputy Quartermaster-General, 1777-1780.

Luttrell, John (N. C.). Lieutenant-Colonel 9th North Carolina, 27th November, 1776; retired 1st June, 1778.

Lutz, Nicholas (Pa). Lieutenant-Colonel Pennsylvania Battalion of the Flying Camp, June, 1776; wounded and taken prisoner at Long Island, 27th August, 1776; exchanged 10th September, 1779; did not re-enter service. (Died 28th November, 1807.)

Lyford, Thomas (N. H.). 2d Lieutenant 2d New Hampshire, 27th May to December, 1775; 1st Lieutenant 8th Continental Infantry, 1st January, 1776; 1st Lieutenant of Whitcomsb's New Hampshire Rangers, 4th November, 1776, to December, 1779.

Lyle, Robert (S. C.). Was a Captain in 3d South Carolina in 1779.

Lyles, Henry (Md). 2d Lieutenant 3d Maryland, 10th December, 1776; 1st Lieutenant, 20th February, 1777; taken prisoner at Staten Island, 22d August, 1777; exchanged 22d December, 1780, and did not rejoin the regiment.

Lyman, Cornelius (Mass). Ensign 2d Massachusetts, 1st January, 1781, and served to 3d November, 1783; Lieutenant 2d United States Infantry, 4th March, 1791; Captain, 30th July, 1792; assigned to 2d Sub Legion, 4th September, 1792; assigned to 2d United States Infantry, 1st November, 1796; transferred to 1st Infantry, 1st April, 1802; died 23d March, 1805.

Lyman, Daniel (Mass). Brigade Major Massachusetts Militia in 1776; Captain of Lee's Continental Regiment, 10th June, 1777; Brigade Major of General Fellow's Brigade, 17th October, 1776; Aide-de-Camp to General Heath, 9th May, 1777, to close of war; Brevet Major, 30th September, 1783. (Died 16th October, 1830.)

Lyman, Elihu (Conn). Ensign 17th Continental Infantry, 1st January, 1776; wounded and taken prisoner at Long Island, 27th August, 1776; exchanged 10th May, 1778, and did not re-enter service.

Lyman, Elijah (Mass). 2d Lieutenant of Ward's Massachusetts Regiment,

May to November, 1775; 1st Lieutenant 4th Massachusetts, 1st January, 1777; retired 1st April, 1779. Name also spelled Elihu.

Lyman, James (S. C.). Physician and Surgeon- General South Carolina Militia, ——, 1779, to 1782.

Lyman, Josiah (Mass). Captain Massachusetts Militia in 1776 and 1777.

Lyman, Moses (Conn). Colonel Connecticut Militia, 1777. (Died 1829.)

Lyman, Oliver (Mass). Lieutenant in Lexington Alarm, April, 1775; 1st Lieutenant of Fellow's Massachusetts Regiment, May to December, 1775; served subsequently in Massachusetts Militia.

Lynch, Charles (Va). Colonel Virginia Militia, 1781. (Died 29th October, 1796.)

Lynch, Cornelius (Conn). Ensign of Elmore's Connecticut State Regiment, 15th April, 1776, to April, 1777.

Lynch, James (S. C.). Surgeon Pulaski Legion and South Carolina State troops, 1779-1781. (Died 1809.)

Lynch, John (Md). 2d Lieutenant 4th Maryland Battalion of the Flying Camp, June, 1776; 1st Lieutenant, August, 1776; Captain 5th Maryland, 10th December, 1776; taken prisoner at Camden, 16th August, 1780; transferred to 4th Maryland, 1st January, 1781; Major, 8th September, 1781; retired 1st January, 1783.

Lynch, John (N. C.). Lieutenant 7th North Carolina, 28th November, 1776, to ——.

Lynch, Thomas, Jr. (S. C.). A signer of the Declaration of Independence; Captain 1st South Carolina, 17th June, 1775; elected to Congress; drowned at sea in 1779.

Lynd, Arthur.—See Lind.

Lynd, John (Pa). Chaplain 5th Pennsylvania Battalion, March to December, 1776.

Lynde, Benjamin (Mass). Ensign 6th Massachusetts, 1st January, 1778; 2d Lieutenant 9th May, 1778; resigned 14th October, 1780. (Died 14th March, 1827.)

Lyne, George (Va). Captain Virginia State Forces, 8th March, 1776; Major 13th Virginia, 12th November, 1776; Lieutenant-Colonel 9th Virginia, 28th September, 1777; resigned 14th November, 1777.

Lynn, Adam (Va). Ensign 3d Virginia, 6th February, 1776, to ——.

Lynn, David (Md). Ensign 1st Maryland Battalion of the Flying Camp, July to 1st December, 1776; 2d Lieutenant 7th Maryland, 10th December, 1776; 1st Lieutenant, 17th April, 1777; Captain-Lieutenant, 18th May, 1779; Captain, 18th May, 1779; transferred to 4th Maryland, 1st January, 1781, and served to April, 1783. (Died 11th April, 1835.)

Lynn, John (Md). Ensign 6th Maryland, 26th May, 1779; Lieutenant, 1st June, 1779; transferred to 5th Maryland, 1st January, 1781; wounded at Eutaw Springs, 8th September, 1781; retained in Maryland Battalion, April, 1783, and was in service to 20th June, 1784.

Lynn, John L. (N. Y.). Surgeon 1st New York, 28th June, 1775, to October, 1776.

Lynn, William (Conn). Sergeant 2d Connecticut, 1st January, 1777; Ensign 29th December, 1777; 2d Lieutenant 9th April, 1780; transferred to 3d Connecticut 1st January, 1781; retained in Swift's Connecticut Regiment, June, 1783 and served to 3d November, 1783.

Lynn, William (Va). Captain of a Virginia Regiment in 1777.

Lyon, Abraham (N. J.). Captain 2d New Jersey Militia in 1776; Captain 4th New Jersey, 28th November, 1776; retired 11th February, 1779.

Lyon, Archibald (N. J.). 3d Lieutenant 4th Continental Artillery, 1st April, 1777; resigned 1st March, 1778

Lyon, Asa (Conn). 2d Lieutenant of Sherburne's Continental Regiment, 19th November, 1777; Regimental Quartermaster, 18th December, 1777, to 30th April, 1780; 1st Lieutenant, 1st June, 1778; ᷱ Regimental Paymaster, 19th April, 1780; retired 1st January, 1781.

Lyon, Benjamin (Pa). 3d Lieutenant 1st Continental Infantry, 25th September, to 31st December, 1776 2d Lieutenant 1st Pennsylvania, 1st January, 1777; 1st Lieutenant, 6th July, 1777; Captain-Lieutenant, 8th December, 1778; resigned 18th May, 1779. (Died 1826.)

Lyon, Daniel (Conn) Captain 8th Connecticut, 6th July, to 17th December, 1775.

Lyon, David (N Y.). Captain 1st New York, 28th June, 1775, to October, 1776; Captain of Spencer's Continental Regiment, 12th January, 1777; resigned 10th April, 1778. (Died 1802.)

Lyon, Ephraim (Conn). Ensign in the Lexington Alarm, April 1775; 1st

Lieutenant 3d Connecticut, 1st May to 16th December, 1775. (Died 1813.)

Lyon, Gilbert (N. Y.). Captain New York Militia, ——; prisoner of war, 11th December, 1780, to 11th April, 1781; where taken not stated.

Lyon, Guthrie (S. C.). Captain South Carolina Militia, 1779-1781.

Lyon, Humberson (Va). Ensign Virginia Riflemen, ——; killed at King's Mountain, 7th October, 1780.

Lyon, Jacob (Mass). Sergeant in Lexington Alarm, April, 1775; Sergeant in Paterson's Massachusetts Regiment, May to December, 1775; 2d Lieutenant 18th Continental Infantry, 1st January, 1776. Died 15th April, 1776.

Lyon, John (Va). Surgeon's-Mate Hospital Department, 1779-1780.

Lyon, Matthew (N. H.). Lieutenant Green Mountain Boys, July, 1776; cashiered, 16th October, 1776; Paymaster of Warner's Continental Regiment, 13th July, 1777; Superceded 1st April, 1778. (Died 1st August, 1822.)

Lyon, Robert (Pa). Sergeant 12th Pennsylvania, October, 1776; Ensign 6th Pennsylvania, 15th February, 1777; 2d Lieutenant 8th July, 1777, and served to ——. (Died 19th August, 1823.)

Lyon, Samuel (Pa). Colonel Pennsylvania Militia, 1777-1778

Lyon, Stephen (Conn). Captain of Chester's Connecticut State Regiment, June to December, 1776.

Lyon, Theophilus ᷱMass). Lieutenant in Lexington Alarm. April, 1775; 1st Lieutenant of Heath's Massachusetts Regiment, 19th April to December, 1775.

Lyon, Thomas (N. H.). 2d Lieutenant of Warner's Continental Regiment, 27th October, 1776; wounded at Skernsborough 7th July, 1777, when his leg was fractured and did not rejoin regiment. (Died 3d September, 1827.)

Lyon, William (Conn): Lieutenant 3d Connecticut, 1st May to 1st December, 1775

Lyon, Zebulon (——). 2d Lieutenant of Hoisington's Battalion of Rangers, 6th August, 1776, to ——.

Lyth, John (Va). Surgeon 13th Virginia, 1st October, 1777. Died 13th January, 1778.

Lytle, Andrew (Pa). Quartermaster 1st Battalion of Miles' Pennsylvania Rifle Regiment, 1st April, 1776; Ensign and Regimental Quartermaster 13th Pennsylvania, 24th October, 1776, to 1st July, 1778; 1st Lieutenant, 20th January, 1777; transferred to 5th Pennsylvania, 1st July, 1778; transferred to 1st Pennsylvania, 1st January, 1783, and served to November, 1783.

Lytle, Archibald (N. C.). Captain 6th North Carolina, 16th April, 1776; Lieutenant-Colonel, 6th North Carolina, 26th January, 1777; wounded at Stono Ferry, 20th June, 1779; taken prisoner at Charleston, 12th May, 1780; exchanged, 9th February, 1782; Colonel, 30th September, 1783; served to close of war.

Lytle, Micajah (N. C.). Lieutenant 3d North Carolina, 3d May, 1776, to ——.

Lytle, William (N. C.). Ensign 9th North Carolina, 6th December, 1776; Lieutenant, 16th April, 1777; transferred to 1st North Carolina, 1st June, 1778; Captain, 28th January, 1779; transferred to 4th North Carolina, 6th February, 1782; served to close of war. (Died 1829.)

MAC & MC.

(Mc arranged as if spelled Mac.)

McAdams, John (Va.). 2d Lieutenant 5th Virginia, 26th February, 1776; 1st Lieutenant, 15th April, 1777; Captain, 16th March, 1778; retired May, 1779.

McAdams, Joseph (Va.). Hospital Surgeon's-Mate, 1778 to 1781

McAllister, Abdiel (Pa.). 2d Lieutenant 6th Pennsylvania Battalion, 9th January, 1776; taken prisoner at Isle Aux Noix, 21st June, 1776; exchanged 8th May, 1778, and · did not re-enter service.

McAllister, Archibald (Pa.). Captain of Hartley's Continental Regiment, 13th January, 1777; resigned 19th November, 1777. (Died 1831.)

McAllister, George (Pa.). Captain of Hartley's Additional Continental Regiment, 13th January, 1777; died in 1777.

McAllister, John (Pa.). Regimental Quartermaster of Hartley's Continental Regiment, 17th April, 1777, to ——.

McAllister, Neil (N. C.). Ensign 1st North Carolina, 1st September, 1775; 2d Lieutenant, 4th January, 1776; 1st Lieutenant, 29th June, 1776; resigned 20th June, 1777.

McAllister, Richard (Pa.). Colonel Pennsylvania Battalion of the Flying

Camp, June to December, 1776. (Died 1795.)

McAllister, William (Mass). Corporal in Doolittle's Massachusetts Regiment, May to November, 1775; Sergeant 12th Continental Infantry, February to December, 1776; Ensign 13th Massachusetts, 1st January, 1777. Died 27th October, 1777.

McArthur, Alexander (N. Y.). 2d Lieutenant 5th New York, 21st November, 1776; taken prisoner at Fort Montgomery, 6th October, 1777; exchanged, December, 1780; served subsequently as Lieutenant New York Levies.

McBride, John (Pa.). Ensign of Hartley's Continental Regiment, 2d February, 1777; killed Ensign Robert A. McClean, 8th Virginia, 27th September, 1777.

McBride, Robert (Pa.). 2d Lieutenant, 9th Pennsylvania, 15th November, 1776; 1st Lieutenant, 15th May, 1777; resigned 1st July, 1778.

McCabe, Edward (Pa.). 2d Lieutenant 12th Pennsylvania, 4th October, 1776; resigned 20th December, 1777.

McCabe, John (Md.). Lieutenant Maryland Battalion of the Flying Camp, July, 1776; drowned —— October, 1776.

McCall, George (Del.). 2d Lieutenant Delaware Regiment, 15th January to December, 1776.

McCall, Hugh (S. C.). Major South Carolina Militia, 1780-1781.

McCall, James (S. C.). Captain South Carolina Rangers; taken prisoner at Cherokee Town, 26th June, 1776, and shortly after made his escape from the Indians; was Lieutenant-Colonel South Carolina troops when wounded at Rugley's Mills, 4th December, 1780, and at Long Cane, S. C., 11th December, 1780; died May, 1781, of smallpox.

McCall, John (S. C.). Lieutenant South Carolina Militia, 1780-1781.

McCall, William (N. J.). 2d Lieutenant of Spencer's Additional Continental Regiment, 6th May, 1777; resigned 3d March, 1778.

McCalla, Daniel (Pa.). Chaplain 2d Pennsylvania Battalion, 16th January, 1776; taken prisoner at Three Rivers, 8th June, 1776; paroled in August, 1776; did not return to the army. (Died 6th April, 1809.)

McCalla, Thomas H. (Pa.). Surgeon's-Mate 4th Continental Dragoons, 1st

May, 1778; Surgeon, 1st June, 1780, and served to November, 1782.

McCalla, William (Pa). Captain Pennsylvania Militia, 1775-1781.

McCalley, Hugh (Mass). Private in Learned's Massachusetts Regiment, April to November, 1775; Sergeant 3d Continental Infantry, February to December, 1776; 2d Lieutenant 3d Massachusetts, 1st January, 1777; resigned 10th April, 1778.

McCallister, Archibald (Md). Lieutenant Maryland Battalion of the Flying Camp, —— July, 1776; Ensign 2d Maryland, 10th December, 1776; 2d Lieutenant, 1st Maryland, 17th April, 1777; 1st Lieutenant, 27th May, 1778. By the act of 24th September, 1779, it was "Resolved, that Congress justly esteem the military caution so happily combined with daring activity, by Lieutenants McCallister and Rudolph in leading on the forlorn hope (in the attack on the enemy's works at Paulus' Hook), and that the brevet of Captain be given them." Died 16th January, 1781.

McCallum, Robert.—See **McCollom.**

McCalmont, James (Md). Surgeon 2d Maryland 1st January, 1778; resigned 10th June, 1779.

McCalmont, James (Pa). Ensign of Hartley's Continental Regiment, 5th February, 1777; 2d Lieutenant, 1st June, 1777, to ——.

McCammon, John (Pa). Ensign of Hart's Pennsylvania Battalion of the Flying Camp, July to December, 1776.

McCammon, William (Del). 2d Lieutenant Delaware Battalion of the Flying Camp, July to December, 1776.

McCann, John (N. C.). Lieutenant 6th North Carolina, 16th April, 1776; killed 4th October, 1777, at Germantown, Pa.

McCarraher, Alexander (Pa). 2d Lieutenant of Montgomery's Pennsylvania Battalion of the Flying Camp; taken prisoner at Fort Washington, 16th November, 1776.

McCarter, Charles (Va). Surgeon 11th Virginia, 10th June, 1777; retired 30th September, 1778; Surgeon 4th Pennsylvania, 1st January, 1779; retired 1st January, 1781.

McCarthy, Florence (N. C.). Ensign 4th North Carolina, 1st May, 1777, to ——.

McCarthy, Timothy (R. I.). Ensign 2d Rhode Island, 1st April, 1777; cashiered, 1st November, 1777.

McCarty, Daniel (Va). 1st Lieutenant of Grayson's Continental Regiment, 5th February, 1777; resigned 1st December, 1777.

McCarty, Richard (Va). Captain of Clark's Illinois Regiment, 1778 to 1781.

McCarty, William (Mass). Regimental Quartermaster, 15th Massachusetts, 1st January, 1777; omitted July, 1779.

McCauley, James (N. H.). 1st Lieutenant 5th Continental Infantry, 1st January to 31st December, 1776.

McCauley, James (S. C.). Captain in Marion's Brigade in 1781.

McCauley, Matthew (N. C.). Lieutenant 10th North Carolina, 19th April, 1777, to ——.

McCauley, Nathaniel (N. H.). 1st Lieutenant 1st New Hampshire, 8th November, 1776. Died 30th August, 1779, of wounds received at Chemung, N. Y., August 29, 1779.

McCauley, Thomas H. (Pa). Surgeon's-Mate 4th Continental Dragoons, 1st May, 1778; Surgeon, 1st June, 1780, and served to close of war.

McCay, Daniel (Mass). Private 15th Massachusetts, 1st January, 1777; Corporal, 1st June, 1777; Sergeant 1st April, 1779; Sergeant-Major, 20th December, 1779; transferred to 5th Massachusetts, 1st January, 1781; Ensign, 10th May, 1782; transferred to 1st Massachusetts, 1st June, 1783, and served to 3d November, 1783.

McClallan, Carey (Mass). 2d Lieutenant 18th Continental Infantry, 1st January, 1776; 1st Lieutenant, 3d August, 1776, to 31st December, 1776.

McClammy, Joseph (N. C.). Ensign 2d North Carolina, 20th October, 1775, to ——.

McClanachan, Alexander (Va). Lieutenant-Colonel 7th Virginia, 29th February, 1776; Colonel, 22d March, 1777, to rank from 7th October, 1776; resigned 13th May, 1778.

McClannen, William (Mass). 1st Lieutenant 18th Continental Infantry, 1st January, 1776; deserted August, 1776.

McClary, Andrew (N. H.). Major 1st New Hampshire, 23d April, 1775; killed at Bunker Hill, 17th June, 1775.

McClary, David (N. H.). 1st Lieutenant New Hampshire Militia, ——; killed at Bennington, 16th August, 1777.

McClary, John (N .H.). Colonel New Hampshire Militia, 1779.

McClary, Michael (N. H.). 2d Lieutenant 1st New Hampshire, 23d April to December, 1775; 1st Lieutenant 5th Continental Infantry, 1st January, 1776; Captain 3d New Hampshire, 8th November, 1776; retired 1st September, 1778.

McClaughrey, James (N. Y.). Colonel New York Militia, 1779-1780.

McClaughry, John (N. Y.). Ensign 5th New York, 21st November, 1776; taken prisoner at Fort Montgomery, 6th October, 1777; exchanged, 1778; Lieutenant, 30th March, 1780; transferred to 2d New York, 1st January, 1781; died 27th October, 1781.

Maclay, Samuel (Pa.). Lieutenant-Colonel Pennsylvania Militia, 1777-1781. (Died 5th October, 1811.)

McClean, James (Pa.). Ensign 10th Pennsylvania, 2d June, 1778; Lieutenant, 21st March, 1779; transferred to Invalid Regiment, 3d February, 1781, and served to close of war, 1783. (Died 28th October, 1804.)

McClean, Moses (Pa.). Captain 6th Pennsylvania Battalion, 9th January, 1776; taken prisoner at Isle Aux Noix, 24th June, 1776; exchanged 27th March, 1777. (Died 25th August, 1810.)

McClean, Robert Anthony (Pa.). Ensign 8th Pennsylvania, 13th July, 1777; killed by Ensign McBride, 27th September, 1777.

McClellan, John (Pa.). 1st Lieutenant of Thompson's Pennsylvania Rifle Battalion, 25th June, 1775; died 3d November, 1775, on the march to Quebec.

McClellan, John (Pa.). 2d Lieutenant 1st Pennsylvania, 1st January, 1777; 1st Lieutenant, 11th September, 1777; Captain, 1st October, 1779; wounded at Green Springs, 6th July, 1781; retired 1st January, 1783.

McClellan, Joseph (Pa.). 1st Lieutenant Pennsylvania Musket Battalion, 20th March, 1776; Captain, 15th July, 1776; Captain 9th Pennsylvania, 1st January, 1777, to rank from 15th July, 1776; transferred to 2d Pennsylvania, 17th January, 1781; resigned 10th June, 1781. (Died 24th October, 1834.)

McClellan, Samuel (Conn). Major Connecticut. Militia, 1775; Lieutenant-Colonel in 1776; Colonel, 1777-1779, and Brigadier-General Connecticut Militia to close of war. (Died 1807.)

McClellan, Samuel (Pa). 1st Lieutenant of Montgomery's Pennsylvania Battalion of the Flying Camp, June, 1776; taken prisoner at Fort Washington, 16th November, 1776; exchanged 7th December, 1780.

McClellan, Samuel (Conn). Brigadier General Connecticut Militia. (Died 17th October, 1707.)

McClellan, Thomas (N. Y.). 2d Lieutenant of Nicholson's Continental Regiment, June, 1776; 1st Lieutenant 3d New York, 21st November, 1776; cashiered, ——, 1779, and joined the enemy Name also spelled McClallan.

McClellan, William (Pa). 2d Lieutenant 10th Pennsylvania, 4th December, 1776, to ——.

McClelland, Daniel (N. C.). Captain in a North Carolina Regiment in 1780 and 1781.

McClelland, John (Pa). Lieutenant-Colonel Pennsylvania Militia; killed in action against Indians in Ohio, 11th June, 1782.

McClelland, William (Pa). 2d Lieutenant 6th Pennsylvania Battalion, 9th January, 1776; resigned 23d March, 1776.

McClintock, Alexander (Pa). 2d Lieutenant 4th Pennsylvania Battalion, 8th January, 1776; 1st Lieutenant, 12th October, 1776; 1st Lieutenant, 5th Pennsylvania, 1st January, 1777; died 18th September, 1777 of wounds received at Brandywine, 11th September, 1777.

McClintock, Nathaniel (N. H.). 2d Lieutenant 8th Continental Infantry, 1st January, 1776; 2d Lieutenant and Adjutant 2d New Hampshire, 8th November, 1776; Brigade-Major, 2d April, 1777, and served to ——.

McClintock, Samuel (N. H.). Chaplain 2d New Hampshire, June to July, 1775. (Died 27th April, 1804.)

McClintock, —— (S. C.). Captain 6th South Carolina ——; died 24th June, 1778.

McClosky, Alexander (N. Y.). Colonel New York Militia, 1776.

McClune, William (N. Y.). 1st Lieutenant 2d New York, 21st June, 1775, to January, 1776.

McClure, David (Conn). 1st Lieutenant of Mott's Connecticut State Regiment, June to December, 1776.

McClure, David (Pa). Chaplain 8th Pennsylvania, 12th September, 1776, to May, 1777. (Died 25th June, 1820.)

McClure, James (N. H.). Adjutant of Long's New Hampshire Militia Regiment, 25th September, 1776; Captain-Lieutenant 2d Continental Artillery, 1st January, 1777; Captain 4th Continental Artillery, 19th April, 1781; retired 1st January, 1783.

McClure, James (N. C.). Ensign North Carolina Militia; wounded at Hanging Rock, 6th August, 1780.

McClure, James (Pa). Captain of Montgomery's Pennsylvania Battalion of the Flying Camp; taken prisoner at Fort Washington, 16th November, 1776; exchanged in 1781.

McClure, John (Ga). Captain and Major Georgia Militia, 1776-1777.

McClure, John (S. C.). Captain South Carolina Rangers. Died 18th August, 1780, of wounds received at Hanging Rock, 6th August, 1780.

McClure, Neil (S. C.). Colonel South Carolina Militia in 1780.

McClure, William (N. C.). Surgeon 6th North Carolina, 17th April, 1776; transferred to 2d North Carolina, 1st June, 1778; transferred to 1st North Carolina, ——, 1780; taken prisoner at Charleston, 12th May, 1780; exchanged 14th June, 1781; served to close of war. (Died 25th October, 1828.)

McClurg, James (Va). Surgeon of a Virginia State Regiment and Surgeon-General Virginia State Troops, 1777 to 1782. (Died 1825.)

McClurg, Walter (Va). Surgeon Hospital Department, 1778-1780.

McCobb, Samuel (Mass). Captain in Lexington Alarm, April, 1775; Captain of Nixon's Massachusetts Regiment, May to December, 1775; Captain 5th Continental Infantry, 1st January to 31st December, 1776; served subsequently as Colonel Massachusetts Militia. (Died 1791.)

McColloch, James.—See **McCullough.**

McCollom, Robert (Pa). 3d Lieutenant of Nelson's Independent Pennsylvania Rifle Company, 30th January, 1776; resigned 12th July, 1776. Name also spelled McCullam and McCallum.

McConnell, Hugh (N. Y.). Sergeant 4th New York, 24th February, 1776; Ensign, 10th August, 1776; served to November, 1776.

McConnell, Jonathan (N. H.). 2d Lieutenant of Warner's Continental Regiment, 1st October, 1776; resigned 18th November, 1778. (Died 10th May, 1829.)

McConnell, Nathan (Pa). 2d Lieutenant of Thompson's Pennsylvania Rifle Battalion, 25th June, 1775; 2d Lieutenant 1st Continental Infantry, 1st January, 1776; 1st Lieutenant, 7th March, 1776; transferred to 2d Canadian (Hazen's) Regiment, 31st November, 1776; Captain, 8th April, 1777; wounded and taken prisoner at Brandywine, 11th September, 1777; transferred to Invalid Regiment, 12th February, 1781, and served to close of war; Brevet Major, 30th September, 1783. (Died 11th March, 1816.)

McConnell, Robert (Pa). 1st Lieutenant 4th Continental Artillery, 14th March, 1777; Captain-Lieutenant, 3d June, 1779, and served to June, 1783. (Died 1829.)

McConnell, Samuel (N. H.). Captain New Hampshire Militia, 1776-1778.

McCorkle, John (Va). Ensign Virginia Militia; mortally wounded at Cowpens, 17th January, 1781, and died soon after.

McCormick, Alexander (Pa). Ensign 1st Pennsylvania, April, 1780, and served to ——.

McCormick, George (Va). Captain 13th Virginia, 16th December, 1776; retired 30th September, 1778. (Died 30th January, 1820.)

McCormick, Henry (Pa). Adjutant 1st Pennsylvania, 16th April, 1777; Brigade Major to General Hand, 27th December, 1777; resigned 16th May, 1780.

McCormick, John (Pa). Ensign 10th Pennsylvania, 2d June, 1778, to ——.

McCoskry, Samuel Allen (Pa). 1st Lieutenant of Wilson's Battalion to Guard stores at Carlisle, 20th October, 1777; Surgeon of Flower's Artillery Artificer Regiment, 16th July, 1778; retired 10th May, 1782; name also spelled McCloskrey.

McCoskry, William (Pa). Surgeon's-Mate of Flower's Artillery Artificer Regiment, 16th January, 1778; retired

3d May, 1782; name also spelled Mc-Closkrey.

McCottry, William (S. C.). Captain in Marion's Brigade, 1780-1782.

McCowan, John.—See **McGowan.**

McCoy, Daniel.—See **McCay.**

McCoy, John (Md). Lieutenant 4th Maryland, 1st January, 1781; retired 1st January, 1783. (Died 30th June, 1831.)

McCoy, Robert (Pa). Captain Pennsylvania Militia; killed at Crooked Billet, 1st May, 1778.

McCoy, Thomas (Pa). Ensign 6th Pennsylvania Battalion, 1st August, 1776; taken prisoner in Canada, 1st October, 1776; exchanged, 10th August, 1777; 2d Lieutenant 9th Pennsylvania, to rank from 15th January, 1777; dismissed, 11th November, 1778.

McCoy, William (N. Y.). 1st Lieutenant of Malcolm's Continental Regiment, 11th March, 1777; resigned 8th March, 1778.

McCracken, Hugh (Del). Captain Delaware Militia, 1780.

McCracken, Isaac (Md). 1st Lieutenant 6th Maryland, 10th December, 1776; left the service, 12th November, 1777.

McCracken, Joseph (N. Y.). Captain 2d New York, 28th June, 1775, to November, 1776; Captain 1st New York, 21st November, 1776, to rank from 16th February, 1776; wounded (lost an arm) at Monmouth, 28th June, 1778; Major 4th New York, 29th May, 1778; resigned 11th April, 1780; served subsequently as Lieutenant-Colonel New York Militia. (Died 5th May, 1825.)

McCracken, William (Pa). 2d Lieutenant Pennsylvania State Regiment, 18th April, 1777; regiment designated, 13th Pennsylvania, 12th November, 1777; retired 4th July, 1778. (Died 1803.)

McCrea, John (N. Y.). Colonel New York Militia, 1776-1781.

McCrea, Stephen (N. Y.). Surgeon 2d New York, 28th June, 1775, to January, 1776; Hospital Surgeon, —— October, 1776; retired 6th October, 1780.

McCreery, John (Md). Ensign 6th Maryland, 20th February, 1777; discharged 7th August, 1777.

McCreery, Robert (S. C.). Captain South Carolina Militia in 1775; Lieutenant-Colonel South Carolina Militia, 1778. (Name also spelled McCrary.

McCrory, Thomas (N. C.). Captain 9th North Carolina, 28th November, 1776, to ——.

McCubbin, Zachariah (Md). Captain 2d Maryland Battalion of the Flying Camp, July to December, 1776.

McCullam, John (Pa). Ensign 7th Pennsylvania, 13th March, 1777; 2d Lieutenant, 25th September, 1777; Regimental Adjutant, 22d August, 1778, to 1st June, 1779; 1st Lieutenant, 16th April, 1779; transferred to 4th Pennsylvania, 17th January, 1781; transferred to 2d Pennsylvania, 1st January, 1783, and served to 3d June, 1783. (Died ——, 1834.)

McCullam, Robert.—See **McCollom.**

McCulloch, Thomas (Va). Lieutenant Virginia Riflemen, ——; died 12th October, 1780, of wounds received 7th October, 1780, at King's Mountain.

McCullough, James (Pa). 2d Lieutenant 5th Pennsylvania, 1st January, 1777; 1st Lieutenant, 23d September, 1777; died 15th July, 1782.

McCullough, George (S. C.). Captain South Carolina Militia in 1776.

McCullough, William (Pa). 2d Lieutenant 1st Pennsylvania Battalion of the Flying Camp, July to December, 1776.

McCully, George (Pa). Ensign 2d Pennsylvania Battalion 20th March, 1776; 2d Lieutenant, 20th September, 1776; 1st Lieutenant 3d Pennsylvania, 1st January, 1777; Captain, 20th October, 1777; retired 17th January, 1781. (Died 1793.)

McCune, William (N. Y.) 1st Lieutenant, 2d New York, 28th June, 1775; Captain of Warner's Continental Regiment, 16th September, 1776; retired 18th November, 1778. (Died 1807.)

McCurdy, James (Pa). 2d Lieutenant of Hartley's Continental Regiment, 16th January, 1777; 1st Lieutenant, 19th September, 1777, and served to ——.

McCurdy, John (Pa). 2d Lieutenant of Wilson's Pennsylvania Battalion, to guard stores at Carlisle, 20th October, 1777, to October, 1778.

McCurdy, William (Pa). Private of Miles Pennsylvania Rifle Regiment, 9th April, 1776; taken prisoner at Long Island, 27th August, 1776; exchanged 19th December, 1776; Ensign of Hartley's Continental Regiment, 26th January, 1777; 2d Lieutenant, 12th November, 1777; 1st Lieutenant, 19th November, 1778; regiment designated, 11th Pennsylvania, 16th December, 1778; Captain-Lieutenant, 2d October, 1780; transferred to 1st Pennsylvania, 17th January, 1781; Captain, 18th May, 1781; served to 3d June, 1783; Captain United States Infantry, 12th August, 1784; Captain 1st United States Infantry, 29th September, 1789; resigned 4th June, 1791. (Died, 1822.)

McDaniel, Archibald (S. C.). Captain South Carolina Militia in 1776.

McDaniel, John (Pa). Captain Pennsylvania Battalion of the Flying Camp; taken prisoner at Fort Washington, 16th November, 1776.

McDolo, Joseph (Pa). 1st Lieutenant 8th Pennsylvania, —— 1776; deserted —— February, 1777.

McDonald, Adam (S. C.). Captain 1st South Carolina, 17th June, 1775; Major, 16th September, 1776; was killed in 1777, the date and place not stated.

McDonald, Alexander (Del). Regimental Quartermaster, Delaware Battalion of the Flying Camp, July to December, 1776.

McDonald, Barney (Va). Ensign 4th Virginia, 6th January, 1777; 2d Lieutenant, 29th November, 1777; deserted 7th March, 1778.

McDonald, Daniel (N. J.). Major New Jersey Militia, 1777-1778.

McDonald, Donald (Pa). 2d Lieutenant 3d Pennsylvania, 1st January, 1777; omitted, March, 1777.

McDonald, James (S. C.). Captain 1st South Carolina, 17th June, 1775; was Captain South Carolina Dragoons in 1777.

McDonald, John (Pa). 1st Lieutenant 6th Pennsylvania Battalion, 9th January, 1776; Captain of Swope's Pennsylvania Battalion of the Flying Camp, July, 1776; taken prisoner at Fort Washington, 16th November, 1776; exchanged 2d November, 1780, and did not return to the army.

McDonald, William (Ga). Lieutenant 4th Georgia, 1779 and 1780.

McDonald, William (N. J.). 2d Lieutenant 3d New Jersey, 21st March, 1776; cashiered, 1st August, 1776.

MacDonough, James (Del). 2d Lieutenant Delaware Regiment, 20th January, 1776. Died 9th April, 1776.

MacDonough, Thomas (Del). Major Delaware Regiment, 22d March, 1776; wounded at Long Island, 27th August, 1776, and did not rejoin regiment; Colonel Delaware Militia, 1781-1782.

McDougall, Alexander (N. Y.). Colonel 1st New York, 30th June to November, 1775; Brigadier-General Continental Army, 9th August, 1776; Major-General, 20th October, 1777, and served to close of war. (Died 8th June, 1786.)

McDougall, James (N. C.). Cornet 3d Continental Dragoons, 8th January, 1777, to ——.

McDougall, John A. (N. Y.). 1st Lieutenant 1st New York, 28th June, 1775, to January, 1776.

McDougall, Ronald T. (N. Y.). 2d Lieutenant 1st New York, 28th June, 1775; taken prisoner at Quebec, 31st December, 1775.

McDougall, Stephen (N. Y.). Major and Aide-de-Camp to General McDougall, 1777, to close of war.

McDowell, Alexander (Conn). Ensign 3d Connecticut, 23d March, 1777; resigned 25th June, 1779.

McDowell, Bernard (Va). Ensign 4th Virginia, 6th January, 1777; 2d Lieutenant, 29th November, 7777; deserted 24th March, 1778.

McDowell, Charles (N. C.). Colonel North Carolina Militia, 1779-1781. (Died 31st March, 1815.)

McDowell, John (Pa). Captain of Montgomery's Pennsylvania Battalion of the Flying Camp, July to December, 1776; Lieutenant-Colonel Pennsylvania Militia, 1777-1778.

McDowell, John (Pa). 1st Lieutenant 6th Pennsylvania Battalion, 9th January, 1776; 1st Lieutenant 7th Pennsylvania, 1st January, 1777, to rank from 9th January, 1776; Captain, 20th March, 1777; resigned 2d February, 1778; Surgeon, 6th Pennsylvania, 5th February, 1778; transferred to 1st Pennsylvania; 1st January, 1783, and served to 3d November, 1783; Surgeon United States Infantry Regiment, 12th August, 1784; resigned 24th July, 1788. (Died 1825.)

McDowell, John, Jr. (Va). Ensign 12th Virginia, 30th September, 1776; 2d Lieutenant, 10th May, 1777; transferred to 4th Virginia, 14th September, 1778; 1st Lieutenant and Regimental Quartermaster, 7th September, 1778, to 12th

February, 1779; resigned 1st December, 1779.

McDowell, Joseph, Sr. (N. C.). Major North Carolina Militia at King's Mountain, October, 1780, and at Cowpens in January, 1781; served subsequently as Colonel and Brigadier-General in North Carolina Militia. (Died 11th August, 1801.)

McDowell, Joseph (N. C.). Captain North Carolina Militia, 1780-1781; (was cousin of Joseph McDowell, Sr.); died 27th February, 1795.

McDowell, Samuel (Va). Colonel Virginia Militia, 1780-1781. (Died 1817.)

McDowell, William (Pa). 2d Lieutenant 1st Pennsylvania, 13th May, 1777; 1st Lieutenant, 22d March, 1778; transferred to 2d Pennsylvania, 1st January, 1783, and served to 3d November, 1783. (Died 19th June, 1835.)

McDuffee, Daniel (N. H.). Captain New Hampshire Militia, 1777-1778.

McDuffee, John (N. H.). Lieutenant-Colonel 2d New Hampshire, 20th May to December, 1775; Lieutenant-Colonel 8th Continental Infantry, 1st January to 31st December, 1776.

McDuffee, William (N. H.). Captain New Hampshire Militia, 1776.

McElderry, John (Pa). Ensign 11th Pennsylvania, 30th September, 1776; 2d Lieutenant, 9th April, 1777; resigned 30th October, 1777.

McElhaney, John (Va). Captain of Virginia Militia, 1780-1781.

McElhatton, John (Pa). Captain of Watt's Pennsylvania Battalion of the Flying Camp; taken prisoner at Fort Washington, 16th November, 1776. (Died 21st February, 1831.)

McElhatton, Samuel (Pa). Ensign of Watts' Pennsylvania Battalion of the Flying Camp, July, 1776; taken prisoner at Fort Washington, 16th November, 1776; released from prison, 8th December, 1780, and did not return to the army. Name also spelled McHatton.

McElhatton, William (Pa). 1st Lieutenant 12th Pennsylvania, 1st October, 1776; wounded at Bordentown, 8th May, 1778; transferred to 6th Pennsylvania, 1st July, 1778, with rank of Captain-Lieutenant from 1st October, 1776; transferred to Invalid Regiment, 6th July, 1779, and remained in service to close of war. (Died 26th April, 1807.) Name also spelled McHatton.

McElheney, John (Va). 2d Lieutenant 2d Virginia State Regiment, 9th October, 1777; 1st Lieutenant, 11th July, 1778; Captain 25th August, 1779, and served to January, 1780. Name also spelled McIlheney.

McElhenny, James (S. C.). Captain South Carolina Dragoons, 1781.

McEwen, John (N. J.). Sergeant of Spencer's Continental Regiment, 1st February, 1777; Sergeant-Major, 1st April, 1778; Ensign, 12th May, 1779; Regimental Quartermaster, 10th July, 1779; retired 1st January, 1781.

McFadden, James (N. C.). Captain North Carolina Militia, 1776.

McFaddon, James (Va). 2d Lieutenant 1st Continental Artillery, 1st January, 1777; 1st Lieutenant, 22d March, 1777; Captain-Lieutenant, 1st November, 1779; served to close of war.

McFall, Patrick (Pa). 1st Lieutenant Pennsylvania State Regiment, 8th April, 1777; regiment designated 13th Pennsylvania, 12th November, 1777; retired 1st July, 1778.

McFarland, George (N. J.). Ensign 4th New Jersey, 28th November, 1776; resigned December, 1776. (Died 19th March, 1792.)

McFarland, Moses (Mass). Captain of Nixon's Massachusetts Regiment, May to December, 1775; wounded at Bunker Hill, 17th June, 1775; Captain 4th Continental Infantry, 1st January to 31st December, 1776; Captain 6th Massachusetts, 1st January, 1777; transferred to Invalid Regiment, 16th March, 1779, and served to close of war; Brevet Major, 30th September, 1783.

McFarland, Samuel (N. J.). Lieutenant New Jersey Militia; taken prisoner at his home, 6th September, 1778.

Macfarlane, Andrew (Pa). 1st Lieutenant of Moorhead's Company, guarding stores at Kittanning, Pennsylvania, 22d January, 1777, and served to ——.

McFarlane, James (Pa). Lieutenant of Watt's Pennsylvania Battalion of the Flying Camp; taken prisoner at Fort Washington, 16th November, 1776; 2d Lieutenant 1st Pennsylvania, 13th May, 1777; 1st Lieutenant, 21st March, 1778, and served to November, 1783. (Died 1812.)

McFarlane, William (Pa). Captain of Watt's Pennsylvania Battalion of the Flying Camp; taken prisoner at Fort Washington, 16th November, 1776.

McFerran, Samuel (Pa). 2d Lieutenant 6th Pennsylvania Battalion, 9th January, 1776; 1st Lieutenant, 23d June, 1776; taken prisnoer at Isle Aux Noix, 24th June, 1776.

McGaffey, Andrew (N. H.). Sergeant New Hampshire Regiment, May to December, 1775; wounded at Bunker Hill, 17th June, 1775; 2d Lieutenant of Wingate's New Hampshire Militia Regiment, June to November, 1776; 1st Lieutenant 3d New Hampshire, 8th November, 1776; discharged, 1st June, 1779.

McGaffey, Neal (N. H.). **Seregant 3d** New Hampshire, 25th January, 1777; Sergeant Major, 23d December, 1778; Ensign 1st May, 1779, to rank from 14th November, 1777; transferred to 2d New Hampshire, 1st January, 1781; 2d Lieutenant, 1st June, 1781; retired 1st July, 1782.

McGavock, Hugh (Va). Lieutenant of a Virginia State Regiment in 1779 and 1780.

McGeary, William.—See **Geary.**

McGee, Robert (Pa). Lieutenant Pennsylvania Militia, ——; wounded at Millstone, 20th January, 1777.

McGee, William (Pa). 1st Lieutenant 8th Pennsylvania, January, 1777; resigned 17th April, 1777.

McGibbony, Patrick (N. C.). Ensign 4th North Carolina, 27th November, 1776; Lieutenant, 9th December, 1776; served to ——.

McGill, —— (—). Major, appointed Aide-de-Camp to General Gates, 9th August, 1780, and served to close of war.

McGlaughlan, John (N. C.). Captain 7th North Carolina, 28th November, 1776, to ——.

McGowen, —— (Ga). Lieutenant Georgia Battalion; killed at Amelia Island, 18th May, 1777.

McGowan, John (Pa). 3d Lieutenant 1st Battalion of Miles' Pennsylvania Rifle Regiment, 9th August, 1776; Regimental Adjutant, September, 1776; Captain, 24th October, 1776; Captain 4th Pennsylvania, 3d January, 1777, to rank from 24th October, 1776; Brigade-Major, September, 1777; wounded at Germantown, 4th October, 1777; transferred to Invalid Regiment, 3d February, 1781, and served to close of war; Brevet Major, 30th September, 1783. (Died November, 1805.)

McGregor, David (N. H.). 1st Lieutenant 3d New Hampshire, 8th November, 1776; Captain, 4th August, 1777; transferred to 2d New Hampshire, 1st January, 1781, and served to March, 1782.

McGregor, John (Conn). 2d Lieutenant 6th Connecticut, 1st May to 15th December, 1775; 1st Lieutenant 10th Continental Infantry, 1st January to 31st December, 1776; Captain 4th Connecticut, 1st January, 1777; retired 1st January, 1781. (Died 26th February, 1821.)

McGuire, Archibald (Pa). 2d Lieutetnant of Hartley's Continental Regiment, March, 1777; 1st Lieutenant, ——, 1778; regiment designated 11th Pennsylvania, 16th December, 1778; transferred to Invalid Regiment, ——, and served to January, 1781.

McGuire, James (Va). Captain of Grayson's Continental Regiment, 5th February, 1777; resigned 21st April, 1778.

McGuire, John (Md). Sergeant 3d Maryland, 26th March, 1777; Sergeant-Major, 26th September, 1777; Ensign and Adjutant 3d Maryland, 27th March, 1778; resigned 27th May, 1780.

McGuire, John (Va). Served as a volunteer on the Expedition to Canada, and was taken prisoner at Quebec, 31st December, 1775; Captain Grayson's Additional Continental Regiment, 5th February, 1777; wounded at Germantown, 4th October, 1777; resigned 19th April, 1778.

McGuire, Matthew (Pa). 2d Lieutenant 4th Continental Artillery, 1st February, 1777; Regimental Paymaster, 3d March, 1777; 1st Lieutenant, 18th December, 1778; Captain Lieutenant, 26th September, 1780; wounded and taken prisoner at Eutaw Springs, 8th September, 1781; on parole until retired 1st January, 1783. (Name also spelled Maguire.)

McGuire, Merry (S. C.). Sergeant 3d South Carolina, 24th July, 1776; Sergeant-Major, 20th April, 1777; 2d Lieutenant, 1778; 1st Lieutenant and Adjutant, 1st July, 1779; taken prisoner at Charleston, 12th May, 1780; exchanged June, 1781; served to close of war. Name also spelled Maguire.

McGuire, Wm. (Va). Lieutenant 1st Continental Artillery, ——; taken prisoner at Charleston, 12th May, 1780, and was a prisoner to May, 1783.

McGuire, Wm. (Va). 2d Lieutenant 1st Virginia State Regiment, March,

1777; resigned 31st October, 1777; Ensign 3d Virginia, ——, 1779; Lieutenant, ——, 1780; wounded at Eutaw Springs 8th September, 1781.

McHaney, James (Va). 1st Lieutenant 5th Virginia, 25th March, 1776, to ——.

Machenheimer, John (Md). Sergeant German Regiment, 29th July, 1776; Ensign, 17th August, 1777; resigned 31st May, 1778.

McHenry, Charles (Pa). 2d Lieutenant 4th Pennsylvania Battalion, 8th January, 1776; 1st Lieutenant 5th Pennsylvania, 1st January, 1777; Captain, 23d January, 1778; retired 1st July, 1778.

McHenry, James (Pa). Surgeon 5th Pennsylvania Battalion, 10th August, 1776; taken prisoner at Fort Washington 16th November, 1776; prisoner of war on parole until exchanged 5th March, 1778; Assistant Secretary to General Washington, 15th May, 1778; Major Continental Army, 25th May, 1781, to rank from 30th October, 1780; Major Aide-de-Camp to General Lafayette, 30th October, 1780, to 22d December, 1781; Secretary of War, 29th January, 1796, to 13th May, 1800. (Died 8th May, 1816.)

McIlhaney, James (Va). 1st Lieutenant 10th Virginia, 25th March, 1776, Captain, 5th November, 1777; resigned 18th June, 1778.

McIlhaney, John (Va). See **McElheney.**

McIlwaine, Stringer (N. C.). Lieutenant 2d North Carolina in 1777.

Machin, Thomas (Mass). Lieutenant in Gridley's Regiment Massachusetts Artillery, June to December, 1775; wounded at Bunker Hill, 17th June, 1775; 2d Lieutenant of Knox's Regiment Continental Artillery, 10th December, 1775; 1st Lieutenant, November, 1776; Captain-Lieutenant 2d Continental Artillery, 1st January, 1777; wounded at Fort Montgomery, 6th October, 1777; Captain, 21st August, 1780, and served to June, 1783; Captain 29th United States Infantry, 30th April, 1813; resigned 20th December, 1813. (Died 3d April, 1816.)

McIntire, Thomas (Pa). Ensign 3d Pennsylvania Battalion, 8th January, 1776; 2d Lieutenant, 8th March, 1776; wounded and taken prisoner at Fort Washington 16th November, 1776; exchanged 7th August, 1777; Lieutenant

of an Independent Company in Western Pennsylvania, 30th December, 1777; Captain, 8th March, 1779, and served to May, 1782.

McIntosh, Alexander (S. C.). Major 2d South Carolina, 17th June, 1775; Lieutenant-Colonel 3d South Carolina, — July, 1775, to ——. (Died ——, 1780.)

McIntosh, John (Ga). "Come and take it" Captain 1st Georgia, 7th January, 1776; Major, 14th September, 1776; Lieutenant-Colonel Commandant 3d Georgia, 1st April, 1778; wounded and taken prisoner at Briar Creek, 3d March, 1779; served to close of war. (Died 12th November, 1825.)

McIntosh, Lachlan (Ga). Colonel 1st Georgia, 7th January, 1776; Brigadier-General Continental Army, 16th September, 1776; wounded in a duel with Governor Gwinett of Georga, 16th May, 1777; taken prisoner at Charleston, 12th May, 1780; exchanged December, 1780, and served to close of war; Brevet Major General, 30th September, 1783. (Died 20th February, 1806.)

McIntosh, Lachlan Jr. (Ga). 1st Lieutenant 1st Georgia, 7th January, 1776; Brigade-Inspector, October, 1776, and served to ——.

McIntosh, William (Ga). Ensign 1st Georgia, 7th January, 1776; 2d Lieutenant, March, 1776; 1st Lieutenant, December, 1776; Captain, 17th September, 1777, and served to close of war; Brevet Major, 30th September, 1783.

McIntosh, Wm. (Mass). Colonel Massachusetts Militia, 1776-1782. (Died 1813.)

McJunkins, Joseph (S. C.). Captain South Carolina Militia in 1777.

Mack, Orlando (Conn). 2d Lieutenant 8th Connecticut, 1st January, 1777; 1st Lieutenant, 16th February, 1777; retired 15th November, 1778.

Mackay, Eneas (Pa). Colonel 8th Pennsylvania, 20th July, 1776; died 14th February, 1777.

McKay, Fitzhugh (Va). Chaplain 15th Virginia, 25th April, 1777; regiment designated 11th Virginia, 14th September, 1778; resigned 1st October, 1778.

McKean, Robert (N. Y.). Captain of Wynkoop's Regiment New York Militia, 1st March to November, 1776; Captain 1st New York, 21st November, 1776, to rank from 1st March, 1776;

resigned 29th January, 1778 served subsequently as Captain New York Levies
and was killed in action with Indians at
Fort Plain, 10th July, 1781.

McKean, Thomas (Del). A signer of
the Declaration of Independence;
Colonel Pennsylvania Militia in 1776;
was subsequently Governor of Pennsyl-
vnaia; died 24th June, 1817.

McKean, Thomas (Pa). Colonel
Philadelphia Associaters, 1775-1777.
(Died 1817.)

McKee, David (Pa). Ensign 8th
Pennsylvania, October, 1776; dismissed
— March, 1777.

McKee, Wm. (Va). Captain Virginia
Militia in 1776. (Died 1816.)

Mackell, James.—See Merkle.

McKendry, William (Mass). Private
Lexington Alarm, April, 1775; Private
in Greaton's Massachusetts Regiment,
May to August, 1775; Adjutant of
Wheelock's Massachusetts Regiment Militia in 1776; Regimental Quartermaster
7th Massachusetts, 1st January, 1777;
Ensign, 1st October, 1788; 2d Lieutenant, ——, 1782; transferred to 4th Massachusetts, 12th June, 1783, and served
to 3d November, 1783. (Died 23d August, 1798.)

McKennan, Wm. (Del). Lieutenant
Delaware Battalion of the Flying Camp,
July, 1776; 2d Lieutenant Delaware
Regiment, 29th November, 1776;
wounded at Germantown, 4th October,
1777; 1st Lieutenant, 5th April, 1778;
Captain, 15th December, 1779; served
to close of war. (Died — February,
1803.)

McKenney, Wm. (Mass). Sergeant
11th Massachusetts, 1st January, 1777;
Ensign, 1st April, 1777; 2d Lieutenant,
28th March, 1779; transferred to 10th
Massachusetts, 1st January, 1781; resigned 18th June, 1781; died 27th January 1823; name also spelled McKinney.

McKenzie, Robert (Pa). 2d Lieutenant of Thompson's Pennsylvania Rifle
Battalion, 25th June, 1775; 2d Lieutenant 1st Continental Infantry, 1st January, 1776; died 12th February, 1776.

McKenzie, Samuel (Pa). Surgeon
2d Pennsylvania Battalion, 30th March,
1776; taken prisoner at Three Rivers,
8th June, 1776; served subsequently as
Surgeon Hospital Department.

McKenzie, Wm. (S. C.). Captain
South Carolina Militia under General
Sumter in 1780. (Died 1816.)

Mackey, James (Pa). 2d Lieutenant
11th Pennsylvania, 9th April, 1777; 1st
Lieutenant, 23d December, 1777; retired
1st July, 1778.

Mackey, John (N. J.). Colonel New
Jersey Militia, 1777-1778.

Mackey, Robert (Va). Surgeon 11th
Virginia, 13th November, 1776; resigned
1st December, 1777.

Mackey, William (Md). Lieutenant
Maryland Militia, 1776-1777.

Mackey, William (Pa). 1st Lieutenant 11th Pennsylvania, 30th September,
1776; wounded and taken prisoner at
Brandywine, 11th September, 1777;
Captain, 30th October, 1777; exchanged
November, 1777; transferred to 9th
Pennsylvania, 1st July, 1778; retired
17th January, 1781. (Died 4th November, 1812.)

McKinley, Henry (Pa). Captain 12th
Pennsylvania, 16th October, 1776; resigned 18th June, 1778.

McKinley, James (Del). Colonel Delaware Militia, 1775.

McKinley, John (Va). Sergeant 13th
Virginia, 16th March, 1776; 2d Lieutenant, 1st April, 1777; resigned April,
1778. He joined Colonel Crawford's
expedition against Indians in 1781, and
was killed in June, 1782.

McKinley, John (Del). Brigadier-
General Delaware Militia, 1778 to close
of war. (Died 31st August, 1796.)

Machinett, Charles (Pa). Ensign 6th
Pennsylvania, 23d August, 1777, to ——.

McKinney, James (N. C.). Ensign
5th North Carolina, 9th May, 1776, to
——.

McKinney, John (Ga). Lieutenant
3d Georgia, ——; dismissed 12th March,
1778.

McKinney, John (Pa). Ensign 9th
Pennsylvania, 15th November, 1776;
2d Lieutenant, 29th April, 1777; 1st
Lieutenant, 18th March, 1778; transferred to 5th Pennsylvania, 17th January, 1781; transferred to 3d Pennsylvania, 1st January, 1783, and served to
3d June, 1783; Deputy Commissary of
Purchases, U. S. A., 25th April, 1812;
honorably discharged 1st June, 1821.
(Died 25th November, 1833.)

McKinney, John (S. C.). Lieutenant
of a South Carolina Regiment in 1780
and 1781.

McKinney, Moses (Mass). Ensign of
Phinney's Massachusetts Regiment,
May to November, 1775.

McKinsey, John (Va). Captain Virginia Militia, 1779-1780.

Mackinson, James (N. Y.). 1st Lieutenant 2d Continental Artillery, 1st February, 1777; killed at Fort Mifflin 15th November, 1777.

McKinstry, John (Mass). Captain of Paterson's Massachusetts Regiment, May to November, 1775; Captain 15th Continental Infantry, 1st January to 31st December, 1776; was wounded in Canada in December, 1775.

McKinstry, John (N. Y.). Major New York Militia in 1775.

McKinstry, Thomas (Mass). 1st Lieutenant of Paterson's Massachusetts Regiment, May to November, 1775; 1st Lieutenant 15th Continental Infantry, 1st January to 31st December, 1776; served subsequently in Militia.

McKissack, Wm. (Pa). Captain of Baxter's Pennsylvania Battalion of the Flying Camp, 8th August, 1776; taken prisoner at Fort Washington, 16th November, 1776; was appointed Captain 11th Pennsylvania, 1st January, 1777, to rank from 30th September, 1776, and did not join the regiment (Died 1831.)

McKissick, Daniel (N. C.). Captain North Carolina Militia; wounded at Ramsour's Mill 20th June, 1780.

McKlewaine, Samuel (N. C.). 2d Lieutenant 2d North Carolina, 16th May, 1776; resigned 24th October, 1777.

McKnight, Charles (Pa). Surgeon Pennsylvania Battalion of the Flying Camp, July to December, 1776; Surgeon-General of Hospital, Middle Department, 21st February, 1778; Chief Hospital Physician, 6th October, 1780; served to 3d January, 1782 (Died 10th November, 1791.)

McKnight, David (Pa). 2d Lieutenant 9th Pennsylvania, 10th August, 1779; 1st Lieutenant, 23d July, 1780; transferred to 5th Pennsylvania, 17th January, 1781; transferred to 1st Pennsylvania, 1st January, 1783, and served to 3d June, 1783.

McKnight, Michael (N. Y.). Captain New York Militia; taken prisoner at his home 11th June, 1779, and died in prison, date not stated.

McKowan, John (Pa). Captain 1st Battalion Pennsylvania Flying Camp, July to December, 1776; name also spelled McCowan.

McLane, Allen (Del). Lieutenant Delaware Militia, 1776; Captain of Paterson's Continental Regiment, 13th January, 1777; his company anneved to Delaware Regiment 16th December, 1778, and to Lee's Battalion Partisan Corps 13th July, 1779; retired 9th November, 1782. (Died 22d May, 1829.)

McLane, Benjamin (Del). Ensign Delaware Regiment, 4th December, 1776; 2d Lieutenant, 7th October, 1777; resigned 20th May, 1778. (Died 28th September, 1823.)

McLane, Daniel (Mass). 2d Lieutenant of Stevens' Battalion of Artillery, 9th Noyember, 1776; Battalion formed part of the 3d Continental Artillery; wounded at Monmouth, 28th June, 1778; 1st Lieutenant, 12th September, 1778; served to June, 1783; Lieutenant Battalion of Artillery, United States Army, 4th March, 1791; Captain, 4th November, 1791; resigned 2d April, 1793

McLane, John (Del). 1st Lieutenant Delaware Battalion of the Flying Camp, July to December, 1776.

McLane, John (N. C.). Captain 4th North Carolina, 16th April, 1776, to ——.

McLane, Wm. (N. C.). Surgeon's Mate 10th North Carolina, 1st January, 1783, to close of war. (Died 25th Octover, 1828.)

McLarey, James (N. Y.). Lieutenant-Colonel New York Militia; taken prisoner at Fort Montgomery, 6th October, 1777.

McLaughlan, John (N. C.). Lieutenant 1st North Carolina, 6th May, 1776; Captain in 1780, and served to ——.

McLaughlan, Thomas (S. C.). Captain — South Carolina Militia; wounded at Beaufort, 9th February, 1779; killed at Horse Neck 8th July, 1781.

McLaughlin, Thomas (N. H.). 1st Lieutenant 1st New Hampshire, 24th April, 1775; Captain, 18th June to December, 1775.

McLawrence, James (Va). Cadet 7th Virginia, — January, 1777; discharged 16th June, 1777.

McLean, Moses (Pa). Captain 6th Pennsylvania Battalion, 9th January, 1776; taken prisoner at Isle aux Noix, 24th June, 1776.

McLean, William (N. C.). Surgeon's Mate 1st North Carolina in 1779 to 1781; name also spelled McLane. (Died 25th October, 1828.)

McLellan, Alexander (Mass). Captain of Mitchell's Massachusetts Regiment on the Bagaduce Expedition, July to September, 1779. Died 4th October, 1779.

McLellan, Carey (Mass). 2d Lieutenant 18th Continental Infantry, 1st January, 1776; 1st Lieutenant, 3d August to 31st December, 1776.

McLellan, Wm. (Mass). 1st Lieutenant 18th Continental Infantry, 1st January, 1776; deserted 3d August, 1776.

McLemmy, Joseph.—See **Lemmy.**

McLowrey, Alexander (Conn). Sergeant of Warner's Additional Continental Regiment, 1st January, 1777; Ensign, 2d May, 1779; killed at Fort George, 11th October, 1780

McMechen, William (Va). Surgeon 4th Virginia, 14th October, 1776; in 3d Virginia June, 1779; served to October, 1779. (Name also spelled McMahon.)

McMichael, James (Pa). Sergeant 2d Battalion of Miles' Pennsylvania Rifle Regiment, 22d April, 1776; 2d Lieutenant Pennsylvania State Regiment, 18th April, 1777; 1st Lieutenant, 20th June, 1777; regiment designated 13th Pennsylvania, 12th November, 1777; transferred to 7th Pennsylvania, 1st July, 1778; transferred to 4th Pennsylvania, 17th January, 1781; transferred to 1st Pennsylvania, 1st January, 1783, and served to 3d June, 1783.

McMichael, William (N. J.). 1st Lieutenant 3d New Jersey, 7th February, 1776; deserted to the enemy, 14th August, 1776, and was killed by Indians in September, 1776.

McMichael, Wm. (Pa). Ensign Pennsylvania State Regiment, 20th June, 1777; regiment designated 13th Pennsylvania 12th November, 1777; dismissed 11th March, 1778.

McMires, Andrew (N. J.). Captain 1st New Jersey, 15th December, 1775, to 10th November, 1776; Captain 1st New Jersey, 29th November, 1776; killed at Germantown, 4th October, 1777. (Name also spelled McMyers.)

McMordie, Robert (Pa). Chaplain 11th Pennsylvania, 17th May, 1777; Brigade Chaplain, 15th July, 1780, and served to June, 1782. Name also spelled McMurdie.

McMullan, John (Va). 1st Lieutenant of Thruston's Continental Regiment, 12th January, 1778, to ——.

McMullan, Nathan (Pa). Private 2d Pennsylvania Battalion, 2d February, 1776; Sergeant, March, 1776; Ensign, 20th September, 1776; 2d Lieutenant 3d Pennsylvania, 1st April, 1777; died 18th October, 1777, of wounds received at Germantown 4th October, 1777.

McMurphy, Daniel (N. H.). Lieutenant in Hobart's Regiment, New Hampshire Militia; wounded at Bennington, 16th August, 1777.

McMurran, John (Conn). Ensign of Wolcott's Connecticut State Regiment, December, 1775, to March, 1776.

McMurray, William (Pa). 2d Lieutenant of Doyle's Independent Pennsylvania Rifle Company, 17th July, 1776; company attached to 11th Pennsylvania, 16th December, 1777; 1st Lieutenant, 2d June, 1778; transferred to 10th Pennsylvania, 1st July, 1778; Captain, 1st April, 1779; transferred to Sappers and Miners, 1780; resigned 1st June, 1781.

McMurtrie, John (Pa). Private and Corporal 1st Pennsylvania, February, 1777, to October, 1779; Ensign 1st Pennsylvania, 1st October, 1779; resigned 1st August, 1780; Captain Kentucky Militia, 1779; killed in action against Indians near Old Chilicothe, Ohio, 22d October, 1791.

McMyers, Andrew.—See **McMires.**

McNair, James (N. Y.). 1st Lieutenant 2d Continental Artillery, 1st January, 1777; killed at Monmouth, 28th June, 1778.

McNall, Joseph (Mass). Lieutenant of Brewer's Massachusetts Regiment, April to November, 1775; 1st Lieutenant 6th Continental Infantry, 1st January to 31st December, 1776; 1st Lieutenant 13th Massachusetts, 1st January, 1777; Captain, 1st January, 1778; retired 9th April, 1779; Captain Massachusetts Militia, 1779-1780.

McNamara, Michael (Va). 2d Lieutenant 1st Continental Artillery, 13th January, 1777; 1st Lieutenant, 1st January, 1778; Regimental Adjutant, 1st July, 1778; cashiered 25th August, 1778.

McNaughton, John (N. C.). 2d Lieutenant 8th North Carolina, 28th November, 1776; 1st Lieutenant, 5th August, 1777; retired 1st June, 1778.

McNees, John (N. C.) . 2d Lieutenant 3d North Carolina, 8th March, 1777; 1st Lieutenant, 20th November, 1777; taken prisoner at Charleston, 12th May,

1780; exchanged 14th June, 1781; transferred to 1st North Carolina 1st January, 1781; was in 3d North Carolina February, 1782, and served to close of war.

McNeil, Charles.—See **Meil.**

McNeil, Hector (N. C.). 1st Lieutenant 1st North Carolina, 1st September, 1775; deserted 3d February, 1776.

McNeil, John (Mass). 1st Lieutenant of Brewer's Massachusetts Regiment, May to December, 1775.

McNeil, Joseph (Mass). Captain of Wigglesworth's Regiment Massachusetts Militia in 1776; was wounded, but when and where not stated.

McNett, Charles (Pa). Ensign 6th Pennsylvania, 3d August, 1777; resigned 19th November, 1778.

Macomber, Ebenezer (R. I.). 1st Lieutenant of Richmond's Rhode Island Regiment, 19th August to November, 1776; 1st Lieutenant of Tallman's Rhode Island State Regiment, 12th December, 1776; 1st Lieutenant 2d Rhode Island, 12th June, 1777; transferred to 1st Rhode Island, 1st January, 1781; Captain, 17th March, 1782, and served to 17th March, 1783. (Died 5th April, 1829.)

Macomber, Gideon (Mass). Private in Lexington Alarm, April, 1775; Sergeant of Read's Massachusetts Regiment, May to November, 1775; 2d Lieutenant 13th Continental Infantry, 1st January to 31st December, 1776.

Macomber, Joseph (Mass). Sergeant of Brewer's Massachusetts Regiment, May to November, 1775; 1st Lieutenant 13th Continental Infantry, 1st January to 31st December, 1776.

Macomber, Matthew (Mass). Sergeant in Sargent's Massachusetts Regiment, May to November, 1775; Ensign 13th Continental Infantry, 1st January, 1776; cashiered 22d September, 1776.

Mason, John (N. C.). 1st Lieutenant 7th North Carolina, 28th November, 1776; Captain, 11th December, 1776; retired 1st June, 1778.

McPherson, James Frederick (Pa). Ensign 6th Pennsylvania, 15th February, 1777; 2d Lieutenant, 8th October, 1777; 1st Lieutenant, 15th January, 1779; transferred to 1st Pennsylvania, 1st January, 1783; served to 3d June, 1783.

Macpherson, John (Del). Captain and Aide-de-Camp to General Montgomery, July, 1775; killed at Quebec, 31st December, 1775.

Macpherson, Mark (Md). Sergeant 1st Maryland, 10th December, 1776; Lieutenant 2d Maryland, 1st January, 1781; retained in Maryland Battalion April, 1783, and served to November, 1783; Lieutenant 1st United States Infantry, 3d June, 1790; Captain 5th March, 1792; resigned 1st September, 1792.

McPherson, Murdock (Pa). Ensign 2d Canadian (Hazen's) Regiment, 25th February, 1776; Lieutenant, 8th April, 1777; transferred to Invalid Regiment in 1782, and served to June, 1783; Brevet Captain, 30th September, 1783.

McPherson, Robert (Pa). 2d Lieutenant 7th Pennsylvania, 20th January, 1777; 1st Lieutenant, 1st September, 1777; resigned 24th April, 1779. (Died 19th February, 1789.)

McPherson, Robert (Pa). Colonel Pennsylvania Militia, 1775-1776.

McPherson, Samuel (Md). Ensign 1st Maryland, 10th December, 1776; 2d Lieutenant, 17th April, 1777; 1st Lieutenant, 27th May, 1778; transferred to 2d Maryland, 1st January, 1781; Captain, 25th April, 1781; retained in Maryland Battalion April, 1783, and served to 15th November, 1783.

Macpherson, William (Pa). 2d Lieutenant 1st Battalion of Miles' Pennsylvania Rifle Regiment, 15th March, 1776; taken prisoner at Long Island 27th August, 1776; exchanged 20th April, 1778; Brevet Major, 16th September, 1779; Major Aide-de-Camp to General Lincoln, June, 1781, to close of war; Brigadier-General United States Army, 11th March, 1799; honorably discharged 15th June, 1800. (Died 18th November, 1813.)

McQueen, Alexander (S. C.). 1st Lieutenant 1st South Carolina, 17th June, 1775, to ——.

McQueen, John (S.. C.). Captain South Carolina Militia, 1775-1776.

McQueen, William (Va). Ensign 1st Virginia State Regiment, 4th April, 1777; resigned 31st October, 1777; Ensign 7th Pennsylvania, July, 1777; retired 1st July, 1778.

McRae, Duncan (S. C.). Lieutenant South Carolina Militia in 1776.

McRee, Griffith John (N. C.) Captain 6th North Carolina, 16th April,

1776; transferred to 1st North Carolina 1st June, 1778; taken prisoner at Charleston, 12th May, 1780; Major, 3d North Carolina, 11th September, 1781, and served to close of war; Captain Artillerists and Engineers, 2d June, 1794; resigned 24th April, 1798. (Died 3d October, 1801.)

McReynolds, Robert (N. C.). Ensign 10th North Carolina, 19th April, 1777, to ——.

McReynolds, Thomas (Va). 2d Lieutenant 5th Virginia, 12th March, 1776; 1st Lieutenant, 10th May, 1777; resigned 15th February, 1778.

McRory, James (N. C.). Ensign 9th North Carolina, 2d May, 1777, to ——.

McSheehy, Miles (N. C.). Adjutant 9th North Carolina, 12th February, 1777, to ——.

Macumber, Ebenezer (R. I.). 1st Lieutenant 2d Rhode Island, 1st January, 1777; retained in Olney's Rhode Island Battalion, 14th May, 1781; Captain, 17th March, 1782, and served to 3d November, 1783.

McVain, —— (—). Major, ——; was a prisoner in November, 1776.

McWheeling, Alexander (Pa). Ensign 7th Pennsylvania, 24th April, 1777, to ——.

McWheeling, Robert (Pa). 2d Lieutenant 7th Pennsylvania, 20th March, 1777, and served to ——.

McWhorter, Alexander (N. J.). Brigade Chaplain of Knox's Artillery Brigade, 1778 to 1779. (Died 20th July, 1807.)

McWilliam, Stephen (Del). 2d Lieutenant Delaware Regiment, 24th October, 1779; taken prisoner at Camden, 16th August, 1780; retired 21st May, 1783.

McWilliams, William (Va). Captain 3d Virginia, February, 1776; Brigade Major to General Weedon, 7th October, 1776; Major Aide-de-Camp to General Alexander, October, 1777, to 7th May, 1778.

M.

Maag, Henry (Pa). Sergeant German Regiment, 10th July, 1776; Ensign, 15th August, 1777; cashiered 26th March, 1779.

Mabon, James.—See **Maybon**; also called **Mabin**.

Mabrey, Robert (Va). 2d Lieutenant 15th Virginia, 25th November, 1776; 1st Lieutenant, 19th March, 1777; regiment designated 11th Virginia, 14th September, 1778; Captain Lieutenant, 14th May, 1779, and served to ——. (Was in service in 1780; name also spelled Mawbry.)

Madison, Ambrose (Va). Lieutenant and Paymaster 3d Virginia, 1st February, 1777; retired 14th September, 1778; Captain Virginia Convention Guards, 18th January to 23d September, 1779.

Madison, Gabriel (Va). Captain Virginia Militia, 1776-1779.

Madison, Rowland (Va). 2d Lieutenant 7th Virginia, 20th March, 1776; Captain 12th Virginia, 16th December, 1776; resigned 7th March, 1778.

Madison, William (Va). Lieutenant of Virginia Artillery Company, September, 1781, to close of war.

Magaw, Robert (Pa). Major of Thompson's Pennsylvania Rifle Battalion, 25th June, 1775; Colonel 5th Pennsylvania Battalion, 3d January, 1776; taken prisoner at Fort Washington, 16th November, 1776; exchanged 25th October, 1780; did not re-enter service. (Died 7th January, 1790.)

Magaw, William (Pa). Surgeon of Thompson's Pennsylvania Rifle Battalion, 25th June, 1775; Surgeon 1st Continental Infantry, 1st January to 31st December, 1776; Surgeon 1st Pennsylvania, 16th January, 1777; transferred to 4th Pennsylvania, 17th January, 1781; transferred to 1st Pennsylvania, 1st January, 1783, and served to 3d November, 1783. (Died 1st May, 1829.)

Magee, James (N. Y.). Captain New York Militia in 1780.

Magee, John (Pa). Ensign 7th Pennsylvania, 20th March, 1777; 2d Lieutenant, 13th October, 1777; served to ——.

Magee, Peter (N. Y.). Ensign 3d New York, 21st November, 1776; 2d Lieutenant, 23d May, 1779; transferred to 1st New York 1st January, 1781, and served to close of war.

Magee, Wm. (Pa). Sergeant 4th Pennsylvania Battalion, 30th January, 1776; Ensign 5th Pennsylvania, 1st January, 1777; died 20th September, 1777, of wounds received at Brandywine 11th September, 1777.

Magett, David (N. H.). Ensign 1st New Hampshire, 8th November, 1776; discharged 20th November, 1777.

Magill, Charles (Va). 2d Lieutenant 11th Virginia, January, 1777; Regimental Adjutant, 1st November, 1777; resigned 18th April, 1778; served subsequently as Major and Colonel of a Virginia State Regiment.

Magill, James (Pa). 2d Lieutenant 1st Pennsylvania, 13th May, 1777; resigned 1st January, 1778.

Magness, Wm. (N. C.). Captain North Carolina Militia, 1776-1777.

Magruder, Alexander Howard (Md). Captain 3d Maryland Battalion of the Flying Camp, July, 1776, to December, 1776.

Magruder, Nathaniel (Md.) Lieutenant Maryland Militia, 1778-1779.

Magruder, Samuel Wade (N. Y.). Major New York Militia, 1777-1780. (Died 1792.)

Maguire, Matthew and **Merry.**—See McGuire.

Maham, Hezekiah (S. C.). Captain South Carolina Riflemen in 1776; Major South Carolina State Dragoons in 1779; Lieutenant-Colonel in 1780; Colonel in 1781; taken prisoner at his home in August, 1782. (Died 1789.)

Mahew, Thomas (Mass). Lieutenant in Lexington Alarm, April, 1775; Captain of Cotton's Massachusetts Regiment, May to November, 1775; Captain 25th Continental Infantry, 1st January, 1776; taken prisoner at Long Island, 27th August, 1776; Captain Massachusetts Militia, 1777-1778.

Mahon, John (Pa). Ensign of Hartley's Continental Regiment, 25th February, 1777; 2d Lieutenant, 15th September, 1777; regiment designated 11th Pennsylvania, 16th December, 1778; transferred to 6th Pennsylvania, 17th January, 1781; transferred to 2d Pennsylvania, 1st January, 1783, and served to 3d June, 1783.

Majastram, —— Monsieur (—). Volunteer in Armand's Corps, ——; brevetted Lieutenant, 13th January, 1779, and retired from service.

Major, Peacock (Pa). 2d Lieutenant of Lewis' Pennsylvania Battalion of the Flying Camp, July to December, 1776; served subsequently as Lieutenant Pennsylvania Militia. (Died 1829.)

Makepeace, Ebenezer (Mass). Surgeon's Mate 4th Massachusetts, 8th June, 1778; resigned 13th May, 1779.

Makepeace, Solomon (Conn). Sergeant 8th Connecticut, 10th July to 18th December, 1775; 2d Lieutenant 17th Continental Infantry, 1st January, 1776; wounded and taken prisoner at Long Island 27th August, 1776, and died in captivity shortly afterwards.

Malbone, John (R. I.). Colonel Rhode Island Militia in 1775.

Malcolm, John (N. Y.). 1st Lieutenant of Malcolm's Additional Continental Regiment, 29th April, 1777; retired 22d April, 1779.

Malcolm, William (N. Y./. Served as Major and Colonel New York Regiment in 1776; Colonel of one of the Sixteen Additional Continental Regiments, 30th April, 1777, to 22d April, 1779, when regiment was consolidated with Spencer's and was retired 9th May, 1779; Deputy Adjutant General Northern Department, 2d June to October, 1778; served subsequently as Colonel New York Levies. (Died 1792.)

Mallett, Daniel (N. C.). Commissary 1th North Carolina, 23d April, 1776, to ——.

Mallett, Peter (N. C.). Commissary 6th North Carolina, 28th October, 1776; of the 5th North Carolina 23d April, 1777, to 1st June, 1778, when retired.

Mallory, Francis (Va). Colonel Virginia Militia; killed at Tompkin's Bridge, Va., 8th March, 1781.

Mallory, Philip (Va). 2d Lieutenant 15th Virginia, 22d November, 1776; 1st Lieutenant, 1st April, 1778; regiment designated 11th Virginia, 14th September, 1778; Captain, 14th May, 1779; taken prisoner at Charleston, 12th May, 1780; transferred to 4th Virginia, 12th February, 1781, and served to close of war.

Malmedy, Francis Marquis de (France). Brevet Major Continental Army, 19th September, 1776; served as Brigadier-General Rhode Island troops, December, 1776, to March, 1777; Colonel Continental Army, 10th May, 1777, and served to April, 1780.

Maloy, James (Pa). Ensign 5th Pennsylvania Battalion, January to November, 1776.

Manchester, Christopher (R. I.). Captain and Major Rhode Island Militia, 1st November, 1775, to 1781.

Manchester, Cyrus (R. I.). Lieutenant of Elliott's Rhode Island State Regiment, 1776 and 1777.

Manchester, Gilbert (R. I.). Lieutenant of Church's Rhode Island Regiment, 3d May to November, 1775.

Mancke, Christian (Pa). 1st Lieutenant of Captain Schott's Company of Ottendorff's Corps Pulaski Legion, 4th February, 1777; resigned 6th November, 1779; served subsequently in Armand's Corps to close of war

Maney, William (Va). 2d Lietuenant 6th Virginia, 1st March, 1776, to ——.

Mangers, Nicholas (Md). 2d Lieutenant 3d Maryland, 20th February, 1777; 1st Lieutenant, 15th April, 1779; transferred to 4th Maryland, 1st January, 1781; retired 1st January, 1783.

Manifold, Peter (Pa). Cornet 4th Continental Dragoons, 14th April, 1778; Lieutenant 1st May, 1778; Captain 14th April, 1779; resigned 30th October, 1780.

Manley, John (Ga). 1st Lieutenant 3d Georgia, 4th February, 1777, and served to — October, 1782.

Manlove, Tredwell (Del). Lieutenant Delaware Battalion of the Flying Camp, July to December, 1776.

Manlove, Matthew (Del). Captain of Patterson's Delaware Battalion of the Flying Camp, July to December, 1776.

Manlove, Wm. (Pa). Captain Pennsylvania Battalion of the Flying Camp, July to December, 1776.

Mann, Aaron (R. I.). Captain Rhode Island Militia, 1776-1777.

Mann, Andrew (Pa). 2d Lieutenant 8th Pennsylvania, 9th August, 1776; died June, 1777.

Mann, Benjamin (N H.). Captain 3d New Hampshire, 23d April to December, 1775; Captain 2d Continental Infantry, 1st January to 31st December, 1776.

Mann, David (Va). Lieutenant of a Virginia State regiment, June, 1778, to May, 1781.

Mann, James (Mass). Surgeon 4th Massachusetts, 5th July, 1779; resigned 14th April, 1782.

Mann, Obadiah (Mass). 2d Lieutenant of Ward's Massachusetts Regiment, 23d May to December, 1775; 2d Lieutenant 21st Continental Infantry, 1st

January to 31st December, 1776. (Died 4th February, 1825.)

Mann, Silas (Mass). 2d Lieutenant of Nixon's Massachusetts Regiment, 19th May to December, 1775; Lieutenant Massachusetts Militia in 1776.

Manna, Rees (Pa). Ensign of Lewis' Pennsylvania Battalion of the Flying Camp, July to December, 1776.

Manning, Ephraim (Conn). Captain in the Lexington Alarm, April, 1775; Captain 3d Connecticut, 1st May to 19th December, 1775; Captain 20th Continental Infantry, 1st January to 31st December, 1776.

Manning, Lawrence (Pa). Sergeant 2d Canadian (Hazen's) Regiment, 10th December, 1776; Sergeant-Major, 1st March, 1777; wounded and taken prisoner at Staten Island, 22d August, 1777; Ensign, 19th September, 1778; Lieutenant and Adjutant, 1st July, 1779; transferred to Lee's Battalion of Light Dragoons, March, 1780; wounded at Eutaw Springs, 8th September, 1781, and served to close of war; Major 8th United States Infantry, 12th March, 1812; Lieutenant-Colonel 15th August, 1813; Honorably discharged, 15th June, 1815.

Manning, William (Conn). 1st Lieutenant of Ward's Connecticut State Regiment, 14th May, 1776; Captain 2d Connecticut, 1st January, 1777; retired 15th November, 1778. (Died 1807.)

Mansfield, Isaac, Jr. (Mass). Chaplain of Thomas' Massachusetts Regiment, May to November, 1775; Chaplain 6th and 27th Continental Infantry, 1st January to 31st December, 1776.

Mansfield, John (Conn). Sergeant 1st Connecticut, 1st May to 28th November, 1775; Ensign of Douglas' Connecticut State Regiment, 20th June to 25th December, 1776; 2d Lieutenant 6th Connecticut, 1st January, 1777; 1st Lieutenant, 19th April, 1779; transferred to 4th Connecticut, 1st January, 1781; wounded at Yorktown, 14th October, 1781; transferred to 2d Connecticut, 1st January, 1783, and served to 3d June, 1783. (Died 1823.)

Mansfield, John (Mass). Lieutenant-Colonel in Lexington Alarm, April, 1775; Colonel Massachusetts Regiment, 3d May to 15th September, 1775.

Mansfield, Joseph (Conn). 1st Lieutenant of Douglas' Connecticut State Regiment, 20th June to 25th December, 1776; Captain 6th Connecticut, 1st January, 1777; resgined 10th May, 1780.

Mansfield, Samuel (Conn). Served as a volunteer in the Canadian Expedition in 1776; Captain 2d Continental Artillery, 1st January, 1777; resigned 7th November, 1778; was volunteer Aide-de-Camp to Governor Walton during the Siege of Savannah, in September and October, 1779. (Died 3d February, 1810.)

Manson, Eneas.—See **Munson.**

Mantz, Peter (Md). Captain 1st Maryland Battalion of the Flying Camp, July, 1776; Major, 5th September to 1st December, 1776.

Maquett, David (N. H.). Ensign 1st New Hampshire, 8th November, 1776; discharged 20th November, 1777.

Marble, Cyrus (Mass). Sergeant in Lexington Alarm, April, 1775; 2d Lieutenant of Fye's Massachusetts Regiment, May to November, 1775; served subsequently in Massachusetts Militia.

Marble, Henry (Mass). Sergeant 15th Massachusetts, 28th April, 1777; Sergeant-Major, 1st December, 1778; 2d Lieutenant, 28th June, 1779; transferred to 5th Massachusetts, 1st January, 1781, and served to 3d June, 1783. (Died 22d September, 1841.)

Marbury, Francis (Va). Adjutant 1st Virginia State Regiment, 1777-1778.

Marbury, Joseph (Md). Regimental Quartermaster of Smallwood's Maryland Regiment, 14th January, 1776; Captain 3d Maryland, 10th December, 1776; transferred to 1st Maryland, 1st January, 1783, and served to April, 1783.

Marbury, Leonard (Ga). Colonel Georgia Militia at the siege of Savannah, September and October, 1779.

Marbury, Luke (Md). Colonel Maryland Militia; taken prisoner at Germantown, 4th October, 1777; exchanged, 26th March, 1781.

Marcellin, de (——). See **De Marcellin.**

March, John (Mass). Lieutenant 1st Massachusetts, 1st January, 1777; died 18th October, 1777.

March, Samuel (Mass). Lieutenant-Colonel of Phinney's Massachusetts Regiment, 24th April to 1st August, 1775; Lieutenant-Colonel, 18th Continental Infantry, 1st January to 31st December, 1776.

Marcy, John (N. H.). Captain 3d New Hampshire, 23d April to December, 1775.

Marcy, Reuben (Conn). Lieutenant in Lexington Alarm, April, 1775; Captain of Chester's Connecticut State Regiment, June to December, 1776.

Marcy, Samuel (Conn). 2d Lieutenant of Chester's Connecticut State Regiment, June to December, 1776.

Marcy, Samuel (N. H.). Surgeon's-Mate, 2d New Hampshire ——; resigned 22d August, 1782.

Marim, John (Del). 1st Lieutenant Delaware Battalion of the Flying Camp, July to December, 1776. (Died 1815.)

Marion, Benjamin (S. C.). Captain and Major South Carolina Militia, 1775-1777.

Marion, Francis "Swamp Fox" (S. C.). Captain 2d South Carolina, 17th June, 1775; Major, 14th November, 1775; Lieutenant-Colonel Commandant, 16th September, 1776; Colonel, 30th September, 1783, to close of war; Brigadier-General South Carolina State Troops, August, 1780. By the act of 29th October, 1781, it was "Resolved, that the thanks of the United States in Congress assembled be presented to Brigadier-General Marion, of the South Carolina Militia for his wise, gallant and decided conduct in defending the liberties of his country, and particularly for his prudent and intrepid attack on a body of the British troops on the 30th of August last (Parker's Ferry), and for the distinguished part he took in the battle of the 8th of September (Eutaw Springs.)" Served to close of war. (Died 27th February, 1795.)

Markham, Barzilla (Conn). Sergeant in the Lexington Alarm, April, 1775; Ensign 8th Connecticut, 6th July, 1775; resigned 7th October, 1775.

Markham, John (Va). Captain 1st Virginia, 16th September, 1775; Major 2d Virginia, 7th May, 1776; Lieutenant-Colonel 8th Virginia, 22d March, 1777; cashiered, 26th October, 1777.

Markland, John (Pa) Ensign 9th Pennsylvania, 20th August, 1777; 2d Lieutenant, 31st May, 1778; 1st Lieutenant, 1st February, 1779; transferred to 6th Pennsylvania, 17th January, 1781; transferred to 3d Pennsylvania, 1st January, 1783; served to 3d November, 1783. (Died 25th February, 1837.)

Markle, Charles (Md). Lieutenant 2d Canadian Regiment, November, 1776; 1st Lieutenant of Ottendorff's Battalion, 22d February, 1777; Captain 3d Cavalry Pulaski Legion, 8th February, 1778, to

——; was in service in April, 1780. (Name also spelled Markell and Merkle.)

Markle James (Md). Captain Maryland Militia, 1776-1779. Name also spelled Mackall.

Markle, John (Md). 2d Lieutenant 6th Maryland, 17th April, 1777; resigned 1st August, 1777.

Maroney, Philip (Md). Captain 1st Maryland Battalion of the Flying Camp, July to December, 1775.

Marks, Elisha (N. H.). Captain New Hampshire Militia in 1777.

Marks, Isaiah (Va). 2d Lieutenant 11th Virginia, 11th November, 1776; 1st Lieutenant, 15th March, 1777; wounded at Brandywine, 11th September, 1777; Regiment designated, 7th Virginia, 14th September, 1778; Captain, 10th May, 1779; transferred to 2d Virginia, 12th February, 1781, and served to 1st January, 1783.

Marks, John (Va). 1st Lieutenant 2d Virginia, 21st October, 1775; Captain 14th Virginia, 24th February, 1777; regiment designated, 10th Virginia, 14th September, 1778; resigned 15th February, 1781.

Marsden, George (Mass). (Was a deserter from the British army). Adjutant of Scammon's Massachusetts Regiment, May to December, 1775; Adjutant 7th Continental Infantry, 1st January to 31st December, 1776; 1st Lieutenant of Sherburne's Continental Regiment, 1st October, 1777; resigned 10th August, 1778.

Marsh, Abel (Vt). Captain Vermont Militia in 1777.

Marsh, Joel (Vt). Colonel Vermont Militia in 1778.

Marsh, John (Conn). Cornet Connecticut Light Horse in 1777.

Marsh, John (N. H.). 2d Lieutenant 3d New Hampshire, 1st May to December, 1775.

Marsh, John (N. Y.). Sergeant 1st New York, 15th December, 1776; Sergeant-Major, 22d June, 1780; Ensign, 29th September, 1780; served to June, 1783.

Marsh, Joseph (Vt). Lieutenant-Colonel and Colonel Vermont Militia, 1775-1777. (Died 9th February, 1811.)

Marsh, Samuel (Mass). Private 6th Continental Infantry, 1st January, 1776; Corporal, 22d April, 1776; Sergeant, 11th

November, 1776; Ensign, 13th Massachusetts, 1st January, 1777; resigned 16th October, 1778.

Marsh, Timothy (Mass). Ensign 3d Massachusetts, 1st January, 1777; resigned 27th April, 1778.

Marshall, Abraham (Pa). Captain Pennsylvania Musket Battalion, 15th March, 1776; resigned 12th July, 1776.

Marshall, Benjamin (Pa). Ensign 5th Pennsylvania, 21st April, 1779; Lieutenant, 13th June, 1779; retired 1st July, 1782.

Marshall, Christopher (Mass). Adjutant of Marshall's Massachusetts Regiment in 1776; Captain, 10th Massachusetts, 6th November, 1776; transferred to 1st Massachusetts, 1st January, 1783, and served to 3d November, 1783; Brevet Major, 30th September, 1783.

Marshall, David (Pa). Ensign 5th Pennsylvania, 4th January, 1777; 2d Lieutenant, 1st March, 1777; 1st Lieutenant, 5th November, 1778; transferred to 2d Pennsylvania, 1st January, 1783, and served to 3d June, 1783.

Marshall, Dixon (N. C.). Ensign 1st North Carolina, 28th March, 1777; 2d Lieutenant, 26th April, 1777; 1st Lieutenant, July, 1779; taken prisoner at Charleston, 12th May, 1780; exchanged, 14th June, 1781; served to close of war. (Died 22d August, 1824.)

Marshall, Elihu (N. Y.). Adjutant 2d New York, 21st November, 1776; Brigade-Major of Poor's Brigade, 26th April to 29th August, 1778; Captain, 23d April, 1779; retired 1st January, 1781; served subsequently as Captain New York Levies.

Marshall, Humphrey (Va). Captain of Virginia Dragoons, April, 1777, to 1781. (Died 1st July, 1841.)

Marshall, James M. (Va). Lieutenant and Captain of a Virginia State Regiment, 1778 to 1781.

Marshall, John (Pa). Captain Pennsylvania Musket Battalion, 14th March, 1776; Captain Pennsylvania State Regiment, 18th April, 1777, to rank from 14th March, 1776; regiment designated, 13th Pennsylvania, 12th November, 1777; resigned, 25th September, 1778.

Marshall, John (Pa). Ensign 2d Battalion of Miles' Pennsylvania Rifle Regiment, April, 1776; 2d Lieutenant 3d Pennsylvania, 11th November, 1776; 1st Lieutenant, 10th June, 1777; Captain-Lieutenant, 12th May, 1779; Captain,

13th August, 1779; retired 1st January, 1783.

Marshall, John (Va). 1st Lieutenant 3d Virginia, 30th July, 1776; Captain-Lieutenant 15th Virginia, December, 1776, to rank from 31st July, 1776; Deputy Judge-Advocate, 20th November, 1777; Captain, 1st July, 1778; transferred to 7th Virginia, 14th September, 1778; retired 12th February, 1781. (Chief Justice of the United States, 31st January, 1801; died 6th July, 1825.

Marshall, Thomas (Mass). Colonel Massachusetts Militia, 30th April, 1776; Colonel 10th Massachusetts, 6th November, 1776; retired 1st January, 1781. (Died 18th November, 1800.)

Marshall, Thomas (Mass). Ensign 25th Continental Infantry, 1st January to 31st December, 1776.

Marshall, Thomas (S. C.). 1st Lieutenant 3d South Carolina, —— April, 1776; Captain, 7th October, 1777, and served to ——.

Marshall, Thomas (Va). Captain Virginia Militia in 1775; Major, 3d Virginia, 13th February, 1776; Lieutenant-Colonel, 13th August, 1776; Colonel 21st February, 1777; resigned 4th December, 1777; taken prisoner at Charleston, 12th May, 1780. (Died 22d June, 1802.)

Marshall, Thomas, Jr. (Va). Captain of a Virginia State Regiment, May, 1778, to April, 1780. (Died 1817.)

Marshall, William (Md). Surgeon's-Mate, 2d Maryland ——, 1777; Surgeon Hospital Department, 1st May, 1779, to ——, 1781.

Marsteller, Philip (Pa). Major Pennsylvania Militia in 1776.

Marston, John (Va). 2d Lieutenant 1st Virginia State Regiment, 1777; 1st Lieutenant, 3d July, 1779, and served to May, 1781. (Died 1835.)

Marston, Simon (N. H.). Captain New Hampshire Militia, 1775-1778.

Martin, Absalom (N. J.). Paymaster 4th New Jersey, 23d November, 1776; 1st Lieutenant 1st New Jersey, 2d March, 1777; Regimental Paymaster, 1st February, 1779, to June, 1783; Captain, 6th January, 1783, and served to April, 1783; Captain 27th United States Infantry, 20th May, 1813; honorably discharged 1st June, 1814.

Martin, Adam (Mass). 1st Lieutenant in Lexington Alarm, April, 1775; Captain of Learned's Massachusetts Regiment, April to November, 1775;

Captain, 15th Massachusetts, 1st January, 1777; resigned 28th June, 1779.

Martin, Alexander (N. C.). Lieutenant-Colonel 2d North Carolina, 1st September, 1775; Colonel, 7th May, 1776; resigned 22d November, 1777. (Died 12th November, 1807.)

Martin, Alexander (Pa). Sergeant 3d Pennsylvania Battalion, 30th January, 1776; Ensign, 19th September, 1776; 2d Lieutenant, 5th Pennsylvania, 1st January, 1777; 1st Lieutenant, 7th June, 1777; resigned, 1st February, 1779.

Martin, Daniel (N. Y.). Captain New York Militia; taken prisoner 31st January, 1779; where, not stated.

Martin, Daniel (S. C.). 2d Lieutenant 5th South Carolina, ——, 1777; 1st Lieutenant, 21st January, 1778; was a Captain and a prisoner in 1780; when and where taken, not stated.

Martin, Ebenezer (Vt). 1st Lieutenant of Bedel's Regiment, Vermont Militia, April, 1778, to April, 1779.

Martin, Ephraim (N. J.). Colonel New Jersey Militia Regiment, 14th June, 1776; wounded at Long Island, 27th August, 1776; appointed Colonel 4th New Jersey, 23d November, 1776, but never joined the regiment. (Died 1806.)

Martin, Francis (Canada). 2d Lieutenant 2d Canadian (Hazen's) Regiment, 6th December, 1776; 1st Lieutenant, 6th May, 1777; died —— October, 1778.

Martin, Hudson (Va). Ensign 9th Virginia, 11th March, 1776; 2d Lieutenant, 26th July, 1776, and served to ——.

Martin, Hugh (Va). Surgeon's-Mate 12th Virginia, 28th April, 1778; transferred to 8th Virginia, 10th August, 1778; Surgeon, 8th Pennsylvania, 7th March, 1780; retired 1st January, 1781.

Martin, Isaac (N. H.). 1st Lieutenant of Lee's Independent Company, New Hampshire Rangers, 9th December, 1776, to ——.

Martin, Jacob (N. J.). 1st Lieutenant of Forman's Regiment, New Jersey Militia, June, 1776; 1st Lieutenant, 4th New Jersey, 23d November, 1776; Captain, 16th April, 1777; resigned 23d December, 1777.

Martin, James (N. C.). 1st Lieutenant 2d North Carolina, 3d May, 1776; Captain, 5th North Carolina, 20th April, 1777; retired 1st June, 1778; Colonel North Carolina Militia, 1780-1781.

Martin, James (S. C.). Surgeon 3d South Carolina, 24th July, 1776; taken prisoner at Charleston, 12th May, 1780.

Martin, John (Ga). 1st Lieutenant 1st Georgia, 7th January, 1776; Captain, 5th July, 1776; killed at the siege of Augusta, 15th September, 1780.

Martin, John (N. J.). Ensign in Forman's New Jersey Militia Regiment, June to November, 1776; 2d Lieutenant 4th New Jersey, 23d November, 1776; 1st Lieutenant, 12th February, 1777; resigned 1st November, 1777.

Martin, John (R. I.). Brigade Surgeon Rhode Island troops, 28th June to November, 1775.

Martin, John (S. C.). 2d Lieutenant 2d South Carolina, 16th February, 1777; 1st Lieutenant, 13th March, 1778; Captain, ——, 1779; taken prisoner at Charleston, 12th May, 1780; exchanged November, 1780, and served to close of war.

Martin, Joseph (Pa). 1st Lieutenant of Baxter's Pennsylvania Battalion of the Flying Camp, June, 1776; taken prisoner at Fort Washington, 16th November, 1776; exchanged 2d November, 1780, and did not re-enter the service.

Martin, John (Va). Captain of Clark's Illinois Regiment, 1779-1782.

Martin, Marshall (Ga). Captain Georgia Militia, 1780-1781. (Died 1819.)

Martin, Moses (N. Y.). 1st Lieutenant 2d New York, 28th June, 1775; Captain, May, 1776, and served to November, 1776.

Martin, N—— (S. C.). Captain South Carolina State Troops, ——; wounded at Eutaw Springs, 8th September, 1781.

Martin, Nathaniel (Pa). Ensign 11th Pennsylvania, 30th September, 1776; 2d Lieutenant, 9th April, 1777; taken prisoner at Brandywine, 11th September, 1777, and did not rejoin regiment.

Martin, Nathaniel (R. I.). Colonel Rhode Island Militia, 1776-1779. (Died 1806.)

Martin, Peter (Pa). 2d Lieutenant 11th Pennsylvania, 30th September, 1776; killed at Brandywine, 11th Septetmber, 1777.

Martin, Philip (R. I.). Sergeant of Lippitt's Rhode Island Militia Regiment, June, 1776; Ensign, 19th August to December, 1776.

Martin, Robert (Pa). Ensign 10th Pennsylvania, 19th July, 1779; Lieutenant, 1st April, 1780; transferred to 1st Pennsylvania, 17th January, 1781; retired 1st January, 1783.

Martin, Samuel (Mass). Ensign 15th Continental Infantry, 1st January, 1776; 2d Lieutenant, 12th September to 31st December, 1776.

Martin, Samuel (N. C.). 1st Lieutenant 2d North Carolina, 8th June, 1776; Captain, — June, 1780; served to ——. (Died 26th November, 1836.)

Martin, Simeon (R. I.). 1st Lieutenant of Babcock's Rhode Island State Regiment, 15th January, 1776; Captain of Lippitt's Rhode Island Regiment, 19th August, 1776, to February, 1777.

Martin, Solomon (Mass). Corporal and Sergeant in Paterson's Massachusetts Regiment, 29th April to November, 1775; 2d Lieutenant, 15th Continental Infantry, 1st January to 31st December, 1776; 1st Lieutenant, Massachusetts Militia in 1777.

Martin, Sylvanus (Conn). Sergeant in the Lexington Alarm, April, 1775; Ensign 4th Connecticut, 1st May, 1775; 2d Lieutenant, 1st September to 6th December, 1775.

Martin, Thomas (Va). Ensign 9th Virginia, 31st August, 1776; 2d Lieutenant, 10th March, 1777; taken prisoner at Germantown, 4th October, 1777; 1st Lieutenant, 4th January, 1778; transferred to 5th Virginia, 12th February, 1781; Captain, ——, 1781, and served to close of war; 1st Lieutenant 1st United States Infantry, 3d June, 1790; Captain, 5th March, 1792; assigned to 1st Sub Legion, 4th September, 1792; assigned to 1st United States Infantry, 1st November, 1796; Honorably discharged, 1st June, 1802; Military Storekeeper, 23d July, 1804. (Died 18th January, 1819.)

Martin, William (N. Y.). 2d Lieutenant 3d New York, 28th June, 1775; 1st Lieutenant of Nicholson's Continental Regiment, — March, 1776; 1st Lieutenant of Spencer's Continental Regiment, 10th February, 1777; "killed in a fight, 31st May, 1777."

Martin, William (Pa). 1st Lieutenant 4th Continental Artillery, 1st April, 1777; taken prisoner at Hancock's Bridge, 21st March, 1778; released, 4th December, 1780; Captain-Lieutenant, 1st June, 1778; Captain, 1st January, 1782; retired 1st January, 1783.

Martin, William (S. C.). 2d Lieutenant South Carolina Rangers, 17th June, 1775, to ——; also shown as Captain Georgia Militia; killed at White House, near Augusta (Ga)., 15th September, 1780.

Martindale, Sion (R. I.). Captain of 3d Rhode Island, 3d May to December, 1775.

Marvin, Benjamin (N. Y.). 1st Lieutenant 3d New York, 28th June, 1775; 1st Lieutenant, 4th New York, 21st November, 1776; Captain, 2d September, 1777; resigned 23d April, 1778. (Died 26th June, 1822.)

Marvin, Elihu (Conn). Adjutant 4th Connecticut, 1st January, 1777; retired 1st July, 1778. (Died 13th September, 1798.)

Marvin, Ephraim (N. Y.). Lieutenant New York Militia; taken prisoner, when and where, not stated.

Marvin, Joseph (N. Y.). .Surgeon's-Mate, 1st New York, 30th August, 1775; Surgeon of Nicholson's New York Regiment March, 1776, to April, 1777.

Marvin, Ozias (Conn). Captain Connecticut Militia, 1776.

Mash, Ralph (N. J.). 1st Lieutenant of Forman's New Jersey Militia Regiment, May to December, 1776.

Mash, Simeon (N. J.). Ensign 1st New Jersey, 29th November, 1776; omitted, March, 1777.

Mason, Abel (Mass). Sergeant in Lexington Alarm, April, 1775; 1st Lieutenant of Learned's Massachusetts Regiment, April to November, 1775; Captain Massachusetts Militia, 1776-1780.

Mason, Caleb (Md). Corporal 2d Maryland, 11st January, 1777, to 11st January, 1780; Ensign, 2d Maryland, 26th January, 1780; killed at Camden, 16th August, 1780.

Mason, David (Mass). Major of Gridley's Regiment Massachusetts Artillery, May to December, 1775; Major of Knox's Regiment Continental Artillery, 10th December, 1775; Lieutenant Colonel, 25th May to 10th December, 1776; Deputy Commisssary-General of Military Stores at Springfield, Mass., February, 1777, to 26th July, 1780. (Died 1794.)

Mason, David (Mass). 2d Lieutenant 3d Continental Artillery, 1st February, 1777; 1st Lieutenant, 13th October, 1782, and served to June, 1783.

Mason, David (Va). Colonel 15th Virginia, 12th November, 1776; resigned 31st July, 1778.

Mason, David (Va). 1st Lieutenant 15th Virginia, 22d November, 1776; Captain, 1st April, 1778; regiment designated 11th Virginia, 14th September, 1778; resigned 14th May, 1779.

Mason, George, Jr. (Va). Captain Virginia Militia, 1775-1776.

Mason, James (Va). Captain 15th Virginia, 25th November, 1776; resigned —— February, 1778; served subsequently as Lieutenant-Colonel of Virginia Militia.

Mason, Jeremiah (Conn). Captain of Wadsworth's Connecticut State Regiment, June to December, 1776; Colonel Connecticut Militia in 1779. (Died 1813.)

Mason, John (N. Y.). Chaplain 3d New York, 21st November, 1776; resigned 19th July, 1777; appointed Chaplain to posts on the Hudson, 31st October, 1778, and served to close of war. (Died 1792.)

Mason, Lemuel B. (N. H.). Private 2d New Hampshire, 15th November, 1776; Sergeant, 15th December, 1779; Ensign, 30th March, 1781; 2d Lieutenant, 30th August, 1782, and served to June, 1783.

Mason, Littleburry (Va). Paymaster 15th Virginia, 12th March, 1777; retired 14th September, 1778.

Mason, Luke.—See **Mayson.**

Mason, Nathaniel (Va). Captain 4th Virginia, 14th March, 1776; resigned 14th May, 1779.

Mason, Richard (N. C.). Ensign 2d North Carolina, 4th September, 1778; Lieutenant, ——, 1779; Captain, 1781, and served to close of war.

Mason, Richard (S. C.). 1st Lieutenant 2d South Carolina, ——; Captain, 25th November, 1778; taken prisoner at Charleston, 12th May, 1780; served to close of war.

Mason, Stephen (N. H.). Captain New Hampshire Militia in 1776.

Mason, Thomas (Md). Ensign 4th Maryland Battalion of the Flying Camp, July to December, 1776; 2d Lieutenant 7th Maryland, 10th May, 1777; 1st Lieutenant, 17th April, 1779; Captain-Lieutenant, 22d May, 1779; Captain, 8th June, 1779; transferred to 2d Maryland, 1st January, 1781; retired 1st January, 1783.

Mason, William (S. C.). Captain 2d South Carolina, 17th June, 1775, to ——.

Massenburg, Nicholas (Va). 1st Lieutenant 4th Virginia, 14th March, 1776, to ——.

Massey, John (Md). 1st Lieutenant Maryland Militia; taken prisoner at Germantown, 4th October, 1777.

Massey, John (Va). Cornet and Paymaster, 1st Continental Dragoons, ——, 1781; transferred to Baylor's Consolidated Regiment of Dragoons, 9th November, 1782, and served to close of war.

Massey, William (S. C.). Lieutenant-Colonel Deputy Mustermaster-General, 20th October, 1777, to ——.

Massie, Thomas (Va). Captain 6th Virginia, 11th March, 1776; Major 11th Virginia, 20th February, 1778; transferred to 2d Virginia, 14th September, 1778; resigned 25th June, 1779. (Died 2d February, 1834.)

Masury, Joseph (R. I.). Sergeant 2d Rhode Island, 28th January, 1777; Ensign, 1st May, 1779; 2d Lieutenant, 24th June, 1780; retained in Olney's Rhode Island Battalion, 14th May, 1781, and served to 3d November, 1783.

Masterson, James (N. C.). Ensign North Carolina Militia in 1780.

Mather, Elias (Conn). Regimental Quartermaster 10th Continental Infantry, 9th September to 31st December, 1776; Regimental Quartermaster 6th Connecticut, 1st January, 1777; 2d Lieutenant, 15th November, 1778; resigned 12th September, 1780. (Name also spelled Matthew.)

Mather, John (Conn). Regimental Quartermaster of Webb's Continental Regiment, 1st January, 1777; died, —— November, 1778.

Mather, Timothy (Conn). Surgeon's-Mate 7th Connecticut, 1st August, 1778; Surgeon, 1st January, 1780; retired 1st January, 1781.

Mathews, George (Va). Lieutenant Colonel 9th Virginia, 4th March, 1776; Colonel, 10th February, 1777; wounded and taken prisoner at Germantown 4th October, 1777; exchanged 5th December, 1781; attached to 3d Virginia, 21st December, 1782, and served to close of war. Brevet Brigadier General, 30th September, 1783. He subsequently was Brigadier-General, Georgia Militia, and as Governor of Georgia. (Died 30th August, 1812.)

Mathews, William (Ga). Captain Assistant Mustermaster General for State of Georgia, 3d January, 1778, to ——.

Matlack, Timothy (Pa). Captain Pennsylvania Militia in 1777. (Died 1829.)

Matson, James (Pa). 3d Lieutenant of Thompson's Pennsylvania Rifle Battalion, 25th June, 1775; 2d Lieutenant, 13th August, 1775; 1st Lieutenant 1st Continental Infantry, 1st January to 31st December, 1776; taken prisoner at Fort Washington, 16th November, 1776.

Matthewman, William (N. Y.). 2d Lieutenant 4th New York, 28th June to November, 1775.

Matthews, Caleb (R. I.). Ensign of Lippitt's Rhode Island Regiment, 19th August, 1776, to ——.

Matthews, Henry (Md). 1st Lieutenant Maryland Militia, 1776-1777.

Matthews, Henry (Pa). Captain of Baldwin's Regiment Artillery Artificers, 20th March, 1780; died 25th January, 1781.

Matthews, James (Mass). 2d Lieutenant of Mansfield's Massachusetts Regiment, May to December, 1775; 1st Lieutenant 8th Continental Infantry, 1st January, 1776; cashiered, 5th September, 1776.

Matthews, Stephen (Conn). Captain of Swift's Connecticut State Regiment, June to December, 1776. (Died 1821.)

Matthews, Thomas (Va). Captain 4th Virginia, 25th March, 1776; resigned 15th November, 1777; served subsequently as Lieutenant-Colonel Virginia Militia. (Died 20th April, 1812.)

Mattingly, Edward (Md). Ensign 3d Maryland Battalion of the Flying Camp, June, 1746; wounded at Fort Washington, 16th November, 1776.

Mattocks, John (Va). Captain Virginia Rangers, —— ; killed at King's Mountain, 7th October, 1780.

Mattocks, Samuel (Conn). Ensign of Walcott's Connecticut Regiment, December, 1775, to March, 1776; 2d Lieutenant of Chester's Connecticut State Regiment, June to December, 1776; Captain, 8th Connecticut, 1st January, 1777; resigned 20th April, 1779. (Died 1804.)

Mattoon, Ebenezer (Mass). Lieutenant, Captain and Major Massachusetts Militia, 1777-1780. (Died 11th April, 1842.)

Maury, Abraham (Va). 2d Lieutenant 14th Virginia, 14th November, 1776; 1st Lieutenant, 8th December, 1777; Regimental Adjutant, 1st January, 1778; regiment designated 10th Virginia, 14th September, 1778; resigned —— February, 1781.

Maus, Matthew (Pa). Volunteer Surgeon in the campaign in Canada, under General Montgomery, October, 1775, to January, 1776; Surgeon's-Mate, 4th Pennsylvania Battalion, 5th January, 1776; Surgeon Hospital Department, 13th July, 1776; Surgeon Invalid Regiment, 7th October, 1780. Retired 23d April, 1783. (Died 23d September, 1787.)

Mauser, Jacob (Pa). Captain of Lutz's Battalion Pennsylvania Militia, ——; taken prisoner at Long Island, 27th August, 1776; exchanged 9th December, 1776.

Mauvide, John (R. I.). Surgeon's-Mate 1st Rhode Island, June to December, 1775.

Mawbrey, Robert.—See Mabrey.

Maxon, James (R. I.). Lieutenant-Colonel Rhode Island Militia, 1777-1778.

Maxon, Jonathan (R. I.). Lieutenant-Colonel Rhode Island Militia, 1779-1780.

Maxwell, Anthony (N. Y.). Sergeant of Malcolm's Continental Regiment, 1st May, 1777; Ensign, 1st July, 1777; 2d Lieutenant, 28th February, 1778; transferred to Spencer's Regiment, 22d April, 1779; 1st Lieutenant, 24th April, 1779; retired 1st January, 1781. (Died 1825.)

Maxwell, David (Del). 2d Lieutenant Delaware Battalion of the Flying Camp, July to December, 1776.

Maxwell, Hugh (Mass). Lieutenant of a Company of Minute Men at Lexington, 19th April, 1775; Captain of Presscott's Massachusetts Regiment, 10th May to December, 1775; wounded at Bunker Hill, 17th June, 1775; Captain 7th Continental Infantry, 1st January to 31st December, 1776; Captain 2d Massachusetts, 1st January, 1777; Major 15th Massachusetts, 7th July, 1777; transferred to 2d Massachusetts, 1st July, 1779; Lieutenant-Colonel, 8th Massachusetts, 1st August, 1782; transferred to 3d Massachusetts, 12th June, 1783, and servedto 3d November, 1783. (Died 14th October, 1799.)

Maxwell, James (Md). Captain Maryland Militia in 1776.

Maxwell, James (N. J.). 1st Lieutenant 2d New Jersey, 29th October, 1775, to 10th November, 1776; 1st Lieutenant, 2d New Jersey, 29th November, 1776; Captain, 5th February, 1777; resigned, 1st December, 1777.

Maxwell, John (N. J.). Captain of Spencer's Additional Continental Regiment, 16th January, 1777; resigned 11th April, 1778. (Died 1828.)

Mexwell, Josiah (Ga). 2d Lieutenant 3d Georgia, ——, 1777; 1st Lieutenant, 16th April, 1778; served to close of war.

Maxwell, Thomas (Ga). Captain 2d Georgia, —— January, 1776; also mentioned as Major and as Colonel in 1780-1782.

Maxwell, Thompson (N. H.). 2d Lieutenant 3d New Hampshire, 23d April to December, 1775; 2d Lieutenant 2d Continental Infantry, 1st January to 31st December, 1776. (Died 1825.)

Maxwell, William (N. J.). Colonel 2d New Jersey, 8th November, 1775; Brigadier General Continental Army, 23d October, 1776; resigned 25th July, 1780. (Died 12th November, 1798.)

May, George (Pa). Captain Pennsylvania Battalion of the Flying Camp, July to December, 1776.

May, Hezekiah (Vt). Lieutenant Vermont Militia in 1777.

May, James (N. C.). Captain 8th North Carolina, 28th November, 1776; resigned 5th August, 1777.

May, John (Mass). Captain Massachusetts Militia in 1778. (Died 16th July, 1812.)

May, Nehemiah (Mass). Captain Massachusetts Militia in 1777.

Maybank, Andrew (Ga). Captain 1st Georgia, 12th December, 1775, to ——; mentioned as Colonel Georgia Militia in 1781.

Maybank, Joseph (S. C.). Colonel South Carolina Militia; wounded at Hickory Hill, 28th June, 1779.

Mayberry, Richard (Mass). Captain 11th Massachusetts, 6th November, 1776; retired 11st September, 1778; Captain Massachusetts Militia in 1778.

Maybon, James (Va). Ensign 6th Virginia, 29th April, 1777; 2d Lieutenant, 27th May, 1777; 1st Lieutenant, 23d December, 1777; transferred to 2d

Virginia, 14th September, 1778; taken prisoner at Charleston, 12th May, 1780; exchanged June, 1781; Captain, 15th May, 1782, and served to close of war. (Name also spelled Mabon and Mabin.)

Mayers, Lawrence.—See **Myers.**

Mayhew, Thomas.—See **Mahew.**

Maynard, Adam (Mass). Sergeant in Lexington Alarm, April, 1775; 2d Lieutenant of Doolittle's Massachusetts Regiment, June to December, 1775.

Maynard, John (Mass). Acting Ensign of Nixon's Massachusetts Regiment; wounded at Bunker Hill, 17th June, 1775; Ensign 3d Massachusetts, 1st January, 1777; Lieutenant and Regimental Quartermaster, 11th November, 1777; taken prisoner at Young's House, 3d February, 1780; retired June, 1783. (Died 21st January, 1823.)

Maynard, Jonathan (Mass). Lieutenant of Nixon's Massachusetts Regiment, May to November, 1775; 1st Lieutenant 7th Massachusetts, 1st January, 1777; taken prisoner at Coverskill, 30th May, 1778; exchanged 22d December, 1780; Captain-Lieutenant 20th September, 1780; Captain, 25th January, 1781; retired 1st January, 1783. (Died 17th July, 1835.)

Maynard, Nathaniel (Mass). Ensign in Lexington Alarm, April, 1775; 1st Lieutenant of Brewer's Massachusetts Regiment, April to November, 1775; Captain Massachusetts Militia, 1776-1779. (Died 1805.)

Maynard, William (Mass). 1st Lieutenant of Nixon's Massachusetts Regiment, May to December, 1775; severely wounded at Bunker Hill, 17th June, 1775; Lieutenant Invalid Regiment, 1st June, 1779, and served to 23d April, 1783. (Died ——, 1788.)

Mayo, John (Mass). 2d Lieutenant of Woodbridge's Massachusetts Regiment, June to December, 1775; 1st Lieutenant 3d Continental Infantry, 1st January, 1776, to December, 1776.

Mayo, Thomas (Md). 1st Lieutenant 3d Maryland Battalion of the Flying Camp, July to 31st December, 1776.

Mayson, Luke (S. C.). 1st Lieutenant 3d South Carolina in 1779.

Mayson, James (S C.). Major 3d South Carolina (Rangers), 17th June, 1775; Liutenant-Colonel, —— May, 1776; served to close of war. Brevet-Colonel, 30th September, 1783. (Died 1800.)

Maysick, Daniel (S. C.). 1st Lieutenant 2d South Carolina, January, 1777; Captain, 6th May, 1778; taken prisoner at Charleston, 12th May, 1780; exchanged June, 1781, and served to close of war.

Mazick, Stephen (S. C.). Ensign 2d South Carolina, 10th March, 1780; taken prisoner at Charleston, 12th May, 1780; exchanged June, 1781, and served to close of war.

Mazuzen, Mark (Conn). Private in the Lexington Alarm, April, 1775; served in the Campaign of Canada in 1775; 1st Lieutenant of Elmore's Connecticut State Regiment, 15th April, 1776; 1st Lieutenant 2d Canadian (Hazen's) Regiment, 3d November, 1776; taken prisoner at Brandywine, 11th September, 1777, and was drowned 30th November, 1777, in attempting to escape from prison-ship.

Meacham, John (Mass). Ensign 3d Massachusetts, 1st January, 1771; 2d Lieutenant, 11th November, 1777; 1st Lieutenant, 1st January, 1779; Adjutant, 1st August, 1780; cashiered 19th December, 1782, for being absent without leave.

Mead.—See also **Meade.**

Mead, Abraham (Conn). Captain of Silliman's Connecticut State Regiment, July to December, 1776.

Mead, Giles (N. H.). 1st Lieutenant 1st New Jersey, 10th December, 1775, to 10th November, 1776; 1st Lieutenant 1st New Jersey, 29th November, 1776; Captain, 29th October, 1777, and served to April, 1783.

Mead, James (Vt). Colonel Vermont Militia, 1777-1780. (Died 1804.)

Mead, Jasper (Conn). Quartermaster-Sergeant 5th Connecticut, 1st January, 1777; 2d Lieutenant, 1st June, 1778; Regimental-Quartermaster, 15th December, 1777, to 8th May, 1780; resigned 8th May, 1780. (Died 1830.)

Mead, John (Conn). Colonel Connecticut Militia, 1777-1781, and Brigadier-General Connecticut Militia, to close of war.

Mead, John (Mass). 2d Lieutenant of Whitcomb's Massachusetts Regiment, May to December, 1775.

Mead, Matthew (Conn). Captain 5th Connecticut, 1st May, to 13th December, 1775; wounded at St. Johns, Canada, 16th September, 1775; Major of Silliman's Connecticut State Regiment, 20th June to 25th December, 1776; Lieutenant-Colonel, 5th Connecticut, 1st January, 1777; resigned 25th May, 1778; Colonel Connecticut Militia, 1779, 1781. (Died 1816.)

Mead, Silvanus (Conn). Lieutenant 6th Connecticut, 6th July to 24th December, 1775; 1st Lieutenant of Bradley's Connecticut State Regiment, May, 1776; taken prisoner at Fort Washington, 16th November, 1776.

Meade, Everard (Va). Captain 2d Virginia, 8th March, 1776; Major and Aide-de-Camp to General Lincoln, 1778, to close of war. (Died 1808.)

Meade, John (Va). Ensign 14th Virginia, 10th March, 1777; Brigade Commissary, 12th October, 1777; retired 30th September, 1778.

Meade, Richard Kidder (Va). Captain 2d Virginia, 24th October, 1775; Lieutenant-Colonel Aide-deCamp to General Washington, 12th March, 1777, to close of war. (Died 1805.)

Meade, William (N. Y.). Surgeon 1st New York, 21st November, 1776; resigned 13th October, 1779. (Died 1st February, 1829.)

Meade, William (Va). Ensign 8th Virginia, 16th February, 1776; died 20th November, 1776.

Meadle, John (Va). Captain Virginia Militia; taken prisoner, ——; when and where not stated.

Meanly, John (Ga). 1st Lieutenant 3d Georgia, 4th February, 1777; retired in 1779.

Means, James (Mass). Private in Lexington Alarm, April, 1775; Sergeant in Phinney's Massachusetts Regiment, May to October, 1775; Sergeant 18th Continental Infantry, 1st January, 1776; Ensign, 3d August, 1776; 1st Lieutenant 12th Massachusetts, 1st January, 1777; Captain, 5th July, 1779; transferred to 2d Massachusetts, 1st January, 1781, and served to 3d November, 1783. (Died 18th October, 1832.)

Mears.—See **Mease** as name is spelled both ways.

Mears, Samuel (Conn). Private in the Lexington Alarm, April, 1775; Private in the 4th Connecticut, 23d May to 20th December, 1775; Sergeant of Webb's Additional Continental Regiment, 22d April, 1777; Ensign, 16th May, 1778; 2d Lieutenant, 15th March, 1779; resigned 20th November, 1780.

Measam, George (—). Major and Commissary of Clothing, Continental Army, 16th October, 1776, to ——.

Mearse, Jacob (Pa). 2d Lieutenant of Miles' Pennsylvania Rifle Regiment, 16th March 1776; 1st Lieutenant Pennsylvania State Regiment, 21st October, 1776; regiment designated 13th Pennsylvania, 12th November, 1777; retired 1st July, 1778.

Mease, James (Pa). Commissary to Pennsylvania Troops, 25th January, 1776; Clothier General Continental Army, January, 1777, to —, 1780.

Mease, John (Pa). Captain 4th Pennsylvania, 3d July, 1777; wounded at Brandywine, 11th September, 1777; did not rejoin regiment. (Died 21st November, 1825.)

Mebane, Robert (N. C.). Lieutenant-Colonel 7th North Carolina, 26th November, 1776; transferred to 1st North Carolina, 1st June, 1778; Lieutenant-Colonel Commandant 3d North Carolina, 7th June, 1779; taken prisoner at Charleston, 12th May, 1780.

Mecklin, Dewalt (Pa). Ensign 8th Pennsylvania, 9th August, 1776; resigned 18th April, 1777.

Medaris, John (N. C.). 1st Lieutenant 3d North Carolina, 15th April, 1777; Captain, 23d December, 1777, transferred to 1st North Carolina, 6th February, 1782, and served to close of war; Brevet Major, 30th September, 1783.

Medbury, Hezekiah (R. I.). Ensign 2d Rhode Island, 24th February, 1777; died 24th March, 1777.

Medbury, Isaac, Jr. (R. I.). Captain-Lieutenant Rhode Island Militia, 1780.

Medbury, John (Mass). Private in Lexington Alarm April, 1775; Private and Corporal in Walker's Massachusetts Regiment, May to November, 1775; 2d Lieutenant 15th Massachusetts, 29th April, 1777; retired 23d April, 1779. (Died 2d November, 1825.)

Medici, Cosmo de (N. C.). Captain Independent Company North Carolina Light Horse, 3d March, 1777; company discharged 1st January, 1779.

Medow, —— (Pa). Lieutenant of Kachlein's Battalion Pennsylvania Flying Camp; taken prisoner at Long Island, 27th August, 1776.

Meeker, Joseph (N. J.). Captain 1st New Jersey, 10th December, 1775, to 20th November, 1776.

Meeker, Obediah (N. J.). Cornet, Lieutenant and Captain New Jersey Light Horse, 1777-1782.

Meeker, Samuel (N. J.). Captain and Major New Jersey Militia, 1776-1779; wounded at Minisink, 22d July, 1779.

Meeker, Uzial (N. J.). Ensign of Spencer's Additional Continental Regiment, 10th February, 1777; 2d Lieutenant, 1st November, 1777; 1st Lieutenant, 10th February, 1779; retired 1st January, 1781. (Died 3d September, 1829.)

Meeks, Edward (N. Y.). Captain of Malcolm's New York Regiment, March to November ,1776.

Meeks, John (N. Y.). Captain of Malcolm's New York Regiment, March to November, 1776.

Mehelm, John (N. J.). Colonel and Quartermaster-General New Jersey Militia, 1776-1780.

Meigs, Jehiel (Conn). Ensign in the Lexington Alarm, April, 1775; 2d Lieutenant 1st Connecticut, 1st May to 20th December, 1775; Captain of Ward's Connecticut State Regiment, 14th May, 1776; died 1776.

Meigs, John (Conn). Ensign of Webb's Additional Continental Regiment, 1st January, 1777; 2d Lieutenant, 15th February, 1778; 1st Lieutenant, 1st June, 1778; transferred to 3d Connecticut, 1st January, 1781; Regimental Adjutant, 15th February, 1778, to 3d June, 1783; Captain 13th United States Infantry, 13th February, 1799; honorably discharged, 15th June, 1800. (Died 24th November, 1826.)

Meigs, Return Jonathan (Conn). Major 2d Connecticut, 1st May, 1775; taken prisoner at Quebec, 31st December, 1775; exchanged 10th January, 1777; Lieutenant-Colonel of Sherburne's Additional Continental Regiment, 22d February, 1777. By the act of 25th July, 1777, it was "Resolved, that Congress have a just sense of the merit of Lieutenant-Colonel Meigs, and the officers and men under his command, who distinguished their prudence, activity, enterprise and valor in the late expedition to Long Island, and that an elegant sword be provided by the Commissary-General of Military Stores, and presented to Lieutenant-Colonel Meigs." Colonel 6th Connecticut, 10th September, 1777, to rank from 12th May, 1777; retired 1st January, 1781. (Died 23d January, 1823.)

Meil, Charles (Conn). Private in Lexington Alarm, April, 1775; Sergeant 6th Connecticut, 5th May to 8th December, 1775; 1st Lieutenant 7th Connecticut, 1st January, 1777; Captain-Lieutenant, 12th January, 1778; Captain, 3d September, 1780; resigned 5th October, 1780. (Name also spelled Miel.) (Died May, 1836.)

Meil, Jacob (Pa). Regimental Quartermaster German Regiment, 24th October, 1776, to July, 1778.

Mellen, James (Mass). Private in Lexington Alarm, April, 1775; Captain of Ward's Massachusetts Regiment, April to December, 1775; Captain 21st Continental Infantry, 1st January, 1776; Major, 15th August, 1776; Lieutenant-Colonel 9th Massachusetts, 1st November, 1776; transferred to 4th Massachusetts, 1st January, 1781; Lieutenant-Colonel Commandant 3d Massachusetts, 7th January, 1783; served to 3d June, 1783 (Died 1812.)

Mellish, Samuel (Mass). 2d Lieutenant and Regimental Quartermaster 3d Massachusetts, 1st January, 1777; 1st Lieutenant and Regimental Paymaster, 16th September, 1778, and served to 3d June, 1783. (Died — September, 1797.)

Meloon, Josiah (N. H.). Sergeant 8th Continental Infantry, February, 1776; Ensign 2d New Hampshire, 8th November, 1776; retired 1st July, 1778.

Meloy, John (S. C.). Lieutenant 3d South Carolina, ——; died 23d February, 1778.

Melton, John (S. C.). Captain South Carolina Militia under General Marion, 1780-1782.

Melven, George (Ga). Regimental Quartermaster 3d Georgia, ——; Captain, 1st March, 1777; taken prisoner at Charleston, 12th May, 1780; exchanged April, 1781; retired 12th July, 1782.

Melville, David (R .I.). Ensign of Lippitt's Rhode Island State Regiment, 19th August, 1776, to March, 1777.

Melville, Thomas (Mass). Major Massachusetts State Artillery, 9th May to 1st November, 1776. (Died 16th September, 1832.)

Menema, Daniel (N. Y.). Surgeon's Mate 3d New York, 27th April, 1776; Surgeon 2d New York, 1st August, 1778, and served to June, 1783. (Died 20th January, 1810.)

Meng, Christopher (Pa). Lieutenant-Colonel Assistant Deputy Quartermaster-General, 18th September, 1779, to January, 1782. (Died 1833.)

Meng, Wollory (Pa). Captain of Flower's Regiment Artillery Artificers, 1st April, 1777, to ——.

Mentges, Francis (Pa). Adjutant of Pennsylvania Musket Battalion, 22d March, 1776; 1st Lieutenant, 9th August, 1776; Major 11th Pennsylvania, 27th September, 1776; transferred to 7th Pennsylvania, 1st July, 1778; Lieutenant-Colonel 5th Pennsylvania, 9th October, 1778; retired 1st January, 1783.

Menzies, George (Va). Ensign 15th Virginia, 7th April, 1777; 2d Lieutenant, ——, 1777; retired 14th September, 1778.

Menzies, Samuel Peachy (Va). Lieutenant Virginia Militia at Yorktown, October, 1781. (Died 1833.)

Mercer, Henry (Va). Ensign 3d Virginia, 15th August, 1777, to ——.

Mercer, Hugh (Va). Colonel 3d Virginia, 13th February, 1776; Brigadier-General Continental Army, 5th June, 1776; died 12th January, 1777, of wounds received at Princeton, 3d January, 1777.

Mercer, John (N. J.). Ensign 1st New Jersey, 7th November, 1775; 1st Lieutenant, 14th November, 1775, to November, 1776; Captain 1st New Jersey, 15th February, 1777; taken prisoner at ——, 1st February, 1777; exchanged 6th November, 1780, and did not rejoin regiment; Lieutenant United States Infantry, 18th August, 1784; Captain, 24th November, 1785; Captain 1st Infantry United States Army, 29th September, 1789; resigned 26th November, 1790.

Mercer, John (N. C). Ensign 7th North Carolina, 28th November, 1776; resigned 22d November, 1777.

Mercer, John Francis (Va). 1st Lieutenant 3d Virginia, 26th February, 1776; wounded at Brandywine, 11th September, 1777; Captain, September, 1777, to rank from 27th June, 1777; Major Aide-de-Camp to General Lee, 8th June, 1778; resigned 2d July, 1779; Lieutenant-Colonel Virginia Militia, October, 1780, to November, 1781. (Died 30th August, 1821.)

Merchant, David (Pa). Captain Pennsylvania Militia in 1777.

Meredith, Samuel (Pa). Brigadier-General Pennsylvania Militia, 5th April,

1777, to 9th January, 1778. (Died 10th March, 1817.)

Meredith, Samuel (Pa). Major Pennsylvania Militia, 1776-1777. (Died 1817.)

Meredith, William (Va). Captain 1st Continental Artillery, 13th January, 1777; wounded and taken prisoner at Camden, 16th August, 1780; prisoner on parole to close of war. (Died 20th February, 1833.)

Meredith, Wm. (N. C.). Captain North Carolina Militia at King's Mountain, October, 1780.

Merriam, Jonathan (Mass). Lieutenant in Lexington Alarm, April, 1775; 2d Lieutenant of Whitcomb's Massachusetts Regiment, 27th April to September, 1775.

Merrick, Samuel (Mass). Sergeant 12th Massachusetts, 15th November, 1776; Ensign, 20th November, 1779; Regimental Quartermaster, 1st August, 1780; 2d Lieutenant, 5th September, 1780; retired 1st January, 1781.

Merrikin, Joshua (Md). 2d Lieutenant 3d Maryland Battalion of the Flying Camp, July, 1776, to ——.

Merrill, Daniel (Mass). Lieutenant in Scammon's Massachusetts Regiment, May to November, 1775; 1st Lieutenant 18th Continental Infantry, 1st January, 1776; Captain 12th Massachusetts, 1st January, 1777; retired 1st April, 1779. (Died 1804.)

Merrill, Joshua (Mass). Ensign of Phinney's Massachusetts Regiment, May to November, 1775.

Merrill, Moses (Mass). Captain of Phinney's Massachusetts Regiment, May to November, 1775.

Merrill, Nathan (Mass). Captain of Mitchell's Regiment Massachusetts Militia on the Bagaduce Expedition, July to September, 1779.

Merrill, Samuel (Mass). Lieutenant of Scammon's Massachusetts Regiment, May to November, 1775.

Merriman, Samuel (Mass). Captain Massachusetts Militia, 1779-1780.

Merritt, John (Mass). 1st Lieutenant of Glover's Massachusetts Regiment, May to December, 1775; served subsequently as Captain Massachusetts Militia. (Died 28th June, 1818)

Merritt, Samuel (Mass). 1st Lieutenant of Scammon's Massachusetts Regiment, May to December, 1775.

Merriwether, David (Va). Ensign 14th Virginia, 14th November, 1776; 2d Lieutenant, 26th November, 1777; regiment designated 10th Virginia, 14th September, 1778; 1st Lieutenant, 7th May, 1779; taken prisoner at Savannah, 9th October, 1779; exchanged ——; taken prisoner at Charleston, 12th May, 1780; transferred to 1st Virginia, 12th February, 1781, and served to close of war. (Died 16th November, 1822.)

Merriwether, James (Va). 2d Lieutenant 1st Virginia State Regiment, ——, 1777; Adjutant, 19th March, 1778; Lieutenant, 10th July, 1778, and served to December, 1780; Cornet 3d Continental Dragoons, ——, 1781; retained in Baylor's Regiment Continental Dragoons, 9th November, 1782, anad served to close of war.

Merriwether, James (Va). Lieutenant of Clark's Illinois Regiment, 1778-1781.

Merriwether, Thomas (Va). Captain 1st Virginia State Regiment, 1st February, 1777; Major, 1st June, 1778, and served to February, 1781.

Merrow, Joshua (N. H.). Ensign 2d New Hampshire, 2d April, 1777; taken prisoner at Hubbardton, 7th July, 1777; Lieutenant, 12th July, 1779; retained in Jackson's Continental Regiment in November, 1783, and served to 20th June, 1784.

Merwin, Israel (Mass). Ensign of Warner's Continental Regiment, 20th October, 1776; killed at Hubbardton, 7th July, 1777.

Meseroe, Elisha (Mass). 1st Lieutenant 18th Continental Infantry, 1st January to 31st December, 1776.

Meseroe, Solomon (Mass). Ensign 18th Continental Infantry, 1st January to 31st December, 1776. (Died 2d August, 1823.)

Meserve, Elisha (Mass). Lieutenant of Phinney's Massachusetts Regiment, May to November, 1775; 1st Lieutenant 18th Continental Infantry, 1st January to 31st December, 1776.

Meserve, Gideon (Mass). Adjutant of Mitchell's Regiment Massachusetts Militia on the Bagaduce Expedition, July to September, 1779.

Meserve, Solomon (Mass). Sergeant of Phinney's Massachusetts Regiment, May to November, 1775; Ensign 18th Continental Infantry, 1st January, 1776;

dismissed 30th September, 1776. (Died 2d August, 1823.)

Messenger, Wigglesworth (Mass). 1st Lieutenant in Lexington Alarm, April, 1775; 1st Lieutenant of Read's Massachusetts Regiment, 23d April to 8th July, 1775.

Messick, Jacob (N. C.). Ensign 8th North Carolina, 28th November, 1776; Lieutenant, 24th April, 1777; retired 1st June, 1778.

Metcalf, James (Mass). Major Massachusetts Minute Men, April, 1775; Captain 13th Continental Infantry, 1st January to 31st December, 1776; Major and Lieutenant-Colonel Massachusetts Militia, 1777, to close of war. (Died 1803.)

Metcalf, Jonathan (Mass). Lieutenant of Craft's Regiment Massachusetts State Artillery; killed near New Bedford 5th September, 1778.

Mettinger, Jacob.—See **Mytinger.**

Metz, Jacob (Pa). 1st Lieutenant 13th Pennsylvania, 18th April, 1777; superceded 20th October, 1777.

Meyer, Christopher.—See **Myer.**

Meyer, Godfrey (Pa). 2d Lieutenant of Baxter's Pennsylvania Battalion of the Flying Camp; taken prisoner at Fort Washington 16th November, 1776. Name also spelled Myer.

Meyer, Ludwig (Pa). 1st Lieutenant of a Pennsylvania Battalion of the Flying Camp, July to December, 1776.

Meyers, Christian (Md). 2d Lieutenant German Battalion, 12th July, 1776; 1st Lieutenant, 12th May, 1777; Captain, 12th March, 1778; retired 1st January, 1781.

Meyers, Lawrence.—See **Myers.**

Michaux, Joseph (Va). Captain 14th Virginia, 19th February, 1777; resigned 24th December, 1777. (Died 1807.)

Mickey, Daniel (Pa). 2d Lieutenant 8th Pennsylvania, 9th August, 1776; 1st Lieutenant, 14th October, 1777; retired 31st January, 1779. (Died 1807.)

Micou, Henry (Va). Private 1st Continental Dragoons, March, 1777; Ensign, — August, 1777; retired September, 1778.

Middagh, Derrick (N. J.). Major and Lieutenant-Colonel New Jersey Militia, 1776-1777.

Middagh, Ephraim (N. Y.). Ensign New York Militia, ——; killed at Minnisink, 22d July, 1779.

Middagh, —— (Pa). Lieutenant of Kachlein's Battalion Pennsylvania Flying Camp; taken prisoner at Long Island, 27th August, 1776.

Middlebrook, Ephraim ,Conn). Lieutenant Connecticut Militia, ——; killed at Ridgefield, 27th April, 1777.

Middlesworth Tennis (Pa). 1st Lieutenant of Hart's Pennsylvania Battalion of the Flying Camp, July to December, 1776.

Middleton, Arthur (S. C.). A signer of the Declaration of Independence; was taken prisoner at Charleston 12th May, 1780; exchanged in June, 1781; died 1st January, 1788.

Middleton, Basil (Va). Surgeon's Mate 1st Virginia State Regiment, — March, 1777; Surgeon 9th Virginia, 10th January, 1778; retired 30th September, 1778; Surgeon 5th Virginia, 20th February, 1779; taken prisoner at Charleston 12th May, 1780.

Middleton, Charles S. (Ga). Captain Georgia Militia, 1776-1777.

Middleton, Hugh (S. C.). 1st Lieutenant 3d South Carolina, 17th June, 1775; Captain, November, 1775, to ——; Lieutenant-Colonel South Carolina Militia; wounded at Eutaw Springs 8th September, 1781.

Middleton, John (S. C.). Lieutenant of Lee's Battalion of Light Dragoons, 1780-1782.

Middleton, Samuel (Mass). Ensign 9th Massachusetts, 1st January, 1777; retired March, 1779.

Middleton, Theodore (Md). 2d Lieutenant 2d Maryland, 6th April, 1779, and served to — October, 1781.

Middleton, William (Va). Cornet of Lee's Battalion of Light Dragoons in 1779.

. Miffit, Francis A. (Canada). Ensign 2d Canadian (Hazen's) Regiment, 1st September, 1777; 2d Lieutenant, 22d May, 1778; resigned 2d May, 1779.

Mifflin, Jonathan (Pa). Brigade-Major to General Mifflin, 29th June, 1776; Paymaster 5th Pennsylvania Battalion, 3d September, 1776, to January, 1777; Deputy Quartermaster-General, 30th June, 1777, to 1781. (Died 1840.)

Mifflin, Thomas (Pa). Major and Aide-de-Camp to General Washington, 4th July, 1775; Major and Quartermaster-General Continental Army, 14th August, 1775; with rank of Colonel, 22d December, 1775; with rank of Brigadier-General, 16th May, 1776, and with rank of Major-General, 19th February, 1777; resigned as Quartermaster-General, 7th November, 1777, but continued in the performance of that duty to 8th November, 1777; Member Board >f War, 7th November, 1777; resigned as Major-General, 25th February, 1779. (Died 20th January, 1800.)

Mighill, Thomas (Mass). Captain in Lexington Alarm, April, 1775; Captain of Gerrish's Massachusetts Regiment, May to November, 1775; Captain 26th Continental Infantry, 1st January to 31st December, 1776; Captain Massachusetts Militia in 1780. (Died 26th August, 1807.)

Mildeberger, Oliver (N. Y.). 1st Lieutenant of Lasher's Regiment New York Militia, ——; cashiered 28th September, 1776.

Miles, Abel (Del). 2d Lieutenant Delaware Battalion of the Flying Camp, July to December, 1776.

Miles, Charles (Mass). Captain Company of Minute Men, ——; wounded at Concord, 19th April, 1775.

Miles, Jeremiah (Mass). Lieutenant 3d Continental Artillery, 1st February, 1777; retired 12th September, 1778.

Miles, John (N. Y.). 1st Lieutenant 2d Continental Artillery, 1st January, 1777; Captain-Lieutenant, 20th September, 1779; resigned 19th December, 1782. (Died 31st March, 1830.)

Miles, Joshua (Md). 1st Lieutenant 2d Maryland Battalion of the Flying Camp, July to December, 1776; 1st Lieutenant 6th Maryland, 10th December, 1776; Captain, 12th October, 1777; resigned 18th May, 1779.

Miles, Samuel (Pa). Colonel Pennsylvania Rifle Regiment, 13th March, 1776; taken prisoner at Long Island, 27th August, 1776; exchanged 20th April, 1778; appointed Brigadier-General Pennsylvania State Troops, 28th December, 1776, and served to ——. (Died 29th December, 1805.)

Millan, James (Mass). Captain of Ward's Massachusetts Regiment, May to November, 1775.

Millan, Wm. (Del). Paymaster Delaware Battalion of the Flying Camp, July to December, 1776.

Millar, Elisha (Ga). Captain 2d Georgia, ——; on roll for August, 1778.

Millard, Thomas (Pa). Lieutenant Pennsylvania Militia; taken prisoner at his home in Bucks County, 14th February, 1778.

Miller, Abraham (Mass). 2d Lieutenant 12th Massachusetts, 6th November, 1776, to ——.

Miller, Abraham (Pa). Captain of Thompson's Pennsylvania Rifle Battalion, 25th June, 1775; resigned 9th November, 1775; Captain Pennsylvania Militia in 1776. (Died 1815.)

Miller, Benjamin (N. Y.). Surgeon New York Militia, 1780-1781.

Miller, Benjamin (Pa). Ensign 2d Pennsylvania Battalion, 5th January, 1776; 2d Lieutenant, 21st May, 1776; 1st Lieutenant 3d Pennsylvania, 1st January, 1777, and served to ——.

Miller, Charles (Conn). Sergeant 2d Connecticut, 11th May to 10th December, 1775; Ensign 22d Continental Infantry, 1st January, 1776; 2d Lieutenant 3d Connecticut, 1st January, 1777; 1st Lieutenant, 14th April, 1778; transferred to 1st Connecticut, 1st January, 1781; retained in Swift's Connecticut Regiment, June, 1783, and served to 3d November, 1783. (Died 17th February, 1821.)

Miller, David (Va). Ensign 5th Virginia, 24th September, 1776; 2d Lieutenant, 21st February, 1777; transferred to 3d Virginia, 14th September, 1778; 1st Lieutenant, 14th April, 1779; Captain, 1st May, 1779; taken prisoner at Charleston, 12th May, 1780; retired 1st January, 1782.

Miller, Elisha (Ga). Was Captain in 2d Georgia in August, 1778, and is also mentioned as having served to close of war.

Miller, Henry (Pa). Chaplain Pennsylvania State Regiment, 24th April, 1777; Chaplain to the Germans in the Army, 18th May, 1778; resigned 7th August, 1779. (Died 16th September, 1829.)

Miller, Henry (Pa). 1st Lieutenant of Thompson's Pennsylvania Rifle Battalion, 25th June, 1775; Captain, 15th October, 1775; Captain 1st Continental Infantry, 1st January, 1776; Major 1st Pennsylvania, 12th March, 1777, to rank from 28th September, 1776; Lieutenant-Colonel 2d Pennsylvania, 1st July, 1778, to rank from 1st March, 1777; resigned

8th December, 1778. (Died 5th April, 1824.)

Miller, Jacob (Mass). Captain of Doolittle's Massachusetts Regiment, May to November, 1775.

Miller, James (N. C.). Lieutenant North Carolina Militia in 1777; Captain North Carolina Militia at King's Mountain, October, 1780.

Miller, James (R. I.). 1st Lieutenant and Captain Rhode Island Militia, 1777-1780.

Miller, James (N. Y.). 1st Lieutenant 2d New York, 21st November, 1776; resigned 7th April, 1778.

Miller, James (S. C.). Captain South Carolina Militia; killed at Cowpens, 17th January, 1781.

Miller, Javan (Va). Sergeant in 4th Virginia, 1st April, 1776; Ensign, 4th July, 1779; taken prisoner at Charleston 12th May, 1780; exchanged April, 1781; Lieutenant, May, 1781, and served to close of war.

Miller, Jeremiah (Mass). Sergeant of Paterson's Massachusetts Regiment, May to December, 1775; Ensign 15th Continental Infantry, 1st January to 31st December, 1776; Captain 1st Massachusetts, 1st January, 1777; wounded at Monmouth, 28th June, 1778; served to 3d November, 1783; Brevet Major, 30th September, 1783. (Died 3d August, 1785.)

Miller, Jeremiah (N. Y.). Ensign 1st New York, 21st November, 1776; retired January, 1779.

Miller, John (Mass). Surgeon's Mate Massachusetts Militia, 1776-1777.

Miller, John (Pa). Captain 5th Pennsylvania Battalion, 5th January, 1776; died 17th November, 1776, of wounds received at Fort Washington 16th November, 1776

Miller, John (S C). Captain South Carolina Militia; taken prisoner at Carr's Fort, 10th February, 1779.

Miller, John (Va). Captain Virginia Militia in 1779.

Miller, Jonas (N. Y.). 1st Lieutenant 2d New York, 21st November, 1776; resigned 7th April, 1778.

Miller, Joseph (Mass). Sergeant-Major 13th Massachusetts, 1st January, 1777; Ensign, 30th March, 1779; 2d Lieutenant, 25th May, 1780; Regimental Adjutant, July, 1780; transferred to

6th Massachusetts, 1st January, 1781, and served to June, 1783.

Miller, Joseph (Mass). Lieutenant 14th Massachusetts, 1st January, 1777; resigned 17th December, 1777. (Also called Josiah Miller.)

Miller, Josiah (Mass). Ensign in Cary's and Willard's Regiments Massachusetts Militia in 1776; 1st Lieutenant 12th Massachusetts, 6th November, 1776; resigned 15th December, 1777.

Miller, Lemuel (Mass). Corporal of Scammon's Massachusetts Regiment, 8th May to 31st December, 1775; Sergeant 18th Continental Infantry, 1st January to 31st December, 1776; 1st Lieutenant 12th Massachusetts, 1st January, 1777; resigned 5th September, 1780. (Died 18th August, 1842.)

Miller, Leonard (Mass). 2d Lieutenant 13th Massachusetts, 1st January, 1777; 1st Lieutenant, 5th January, 1778; resigned 29th September, 1780.

Miller, Matthias Burnet (N. Y.). Surgeon New York Militia, 1777. (Died 1792.)

Miller, Nathan (R. I.). Brigadier-General Rhode Island Militia, 1775 to 1781.

Miller, Nathaniel (Mass). Sergeant 6th Massachusetts, 1st April, 1777; Ensign, 10th June, 1779; resigned 8th May, 1781.

Miller, Nicholas (Pa). Captain 12th Pennsylvania, 1st October, 1776; retired 1st July, 1778.

Miller, Philip (Md). Ensign 7th Maryland, 17th April, 1777; resigned 1st October, 1777.

Miller, Richard (Pa). Ensign 10th Pennsylvania, 4th April, 1779; retired 17th January, 1781.

Miller, Robert (Pa). Ensign 9th Pennsylvania, 8th July, 1777; resigned 25th October, 1777.

Miller, Samuel (Pa). Captain 8th Pennsylvania, 9th August, 1776; died 10th January, 1778.

Miller, Stephen (S. C.). Major South Carolina Militia, 1775.

Miller, Thomas (Mass). 2d Lieutenant of Gardner's Massachusetts Regiment, May to December, 1775.

Miller, Thomas (Va). Ensign 8th Virginia, 18th May, 1777; taken prisoner at Brandywine, 11th September, 1777, and did not rejoin regiment. (Died 17th July, 1821.)

Miller, Thomas (Va). 2d Lieutenant 4th Virginia, 4th April, 1778; 1st Lieutenant, 22d November, 1778; wounded at Eutaw Springs, 8th September, 1781; transferred to 1st Virginia, 12th February, 1782, and served to close of war.

Miller, William (Pa). Ensign 6th Pennsylvania Battalion, 9th January, 1776; 2d Lieutenant 7th Pennsylvania, December, 1776; 1st Lieutenant, 20th March, 1777; Captain Lieutenant, 2d February, 1778; Captain, 17th April, 1779; retired 17th January, 1781. (Died 1831.)

Miller, William (Va). 1st Lieutenant 1st Continental Artillery, 13th January, 1777; Captain Lieutenant, 15th August, 1778; retired 1st January, 1783.

Miller, William Turner (R. I.). Lieutenant-Colonel 3d Rhode Island, 3d May to December, 1775.

Milligan, James (N. C.). Ensign 1st North Carolina, 28th March, 1777; 2d Lieutenant, 23d April, 1777; 1st Lieutenant, 29th August, 1777; dismissed 13th July, 1778.

Milligan, James (Pa). Ensign 7th Pennsylvania, 19th March, 1777; 2d Lieutenant, 1st September, 1777; 1st Lieutenant, 16th April, 1779; transferred to 4th Pennsylvania, 17th January, 1781; transferred to 1st Pennsylvania, 1st January, 1783, and served to 3d June, 1783.

Milligan, Nathaniel (N. Y.). Lieutenant New York Militia, ——; killed at Fort Montgomery, 6th October, 1777.

Milliken, Edward (Mass). Ensign of Phinney's Massachusetts Regiment, May to November, 1775; Lieutenant 18th Continental Infantry, 1st January to 31st December, 1776. (Died 1812.)

Milliken, Lemuel (Mass). Sergeant of Phinney's Massachusetts Regiment, May to December, 1775; 2d Lieutenant of Mitchell's Regiment Massachusetts Militia on the Bagaduce Expedition, July to September, 1779.

Milling, Hugh (S. C.). Served as Lieutenant and Captain 6th South Carolina from 1777 until retired in July, 1780.

Mills, Amasa (Conn). Lieutenant in Lexington Alarm, April, 1775; 1st Lieutenant 2d Connecticut, 1st May to 10th December, 1775; Captain 22d Continental Infantry, 1st January to 31st December, 1776. (Died 1821.)

Mills, Benjamin (Conn). Sergeant in the Lexington Alarm, April, 1775; 1st

Lieutenant 4th Connecticut, 1st May to December, 1775; Captain of Bradley's Connecticut State Regiment, June to December, 1776.

Mills, Benjamin (N. C.). 1st Lieutenant 8th North Carolina, 28th November, 1776; resigned 12th July, 1777; 1st Lieutenant North Carolina Dragoons, 15th July, 1777, and served to January, 1781.

Mills, Daniel (N. Y.). Captain 4th New York, 28th June, 1775; Captain 2d New York, 21st November, 1776, to rank from 9th February, 1776; died 22d April, 1777.

Mills, Elijah (Mass). Sergeant 9th Massachusetts, 1st January, 1777; Ensign, 1st January, 1780; transferred to 8th Massachusetts, 1st January, 1781; resigned 6th June, 1781.

Mills, James (N. C.). 1st Lieutenant 8th North Carolina, 28th November, 1776; transferred to 1st North Carolina, June, 1778; appears to have been a Captain in 10th North Carolina in 1779, and is reported to have been killed in a skirmish in March, 1781.

Mills, John (Conn). Sergeant 5th Connecticut, 8th May, 1775; Regimental Quartermaster, 21st June, 1775; Regimental Adjutant, 11th July to 26th November, 1775; Captain 2d Connecticut, 1st January, 1777; resigned 13th May, 1778. (Died 14th November, 1821.)

Mills, John (Mass). Ensign in Whitcomb's Massachusetts Regiment, May to December, 1775; Ensign 6th Continental Infantry, 1st January, 1776; 2d Lieutenant 1st Massachusetts, 1st January, 1777; 1st Lieutenant, 26th March, 1777; Captain, 16th April, 1779; retained in Jackson's Regiment, November, 1783, and served to 20th June, 1784; Captain 2d United States Infantry, 4th March, 1791; assigned to 2d Sub Legion, 4th September, 1792; Major, 19th February, 1793; Adjutant and Inspector of the Army, 13th May, 1794, to 27th February, 1796; died 8th July, ·1796.

Mills, John (N. H.). Sergeant 3d New Hampshire, 23d April to December, 1775; 2d Lieutenant of Bedel's Regiment New Hampshire Rangers, 22d January, 1776; taken prisoner at the Cedars, 19th May, 1776.

Mills, John (S. C.). Captain South Carolina Dragoons, April to September, 1781.

Mills, John (Va). Private 13th Virginia, 2d February, 1778; regiment designated 9th Virginia, 14th September, 1778; Ensign, 6th August, 1779; transferred to 7th Virginia, 12th February, 1781; 2d Lieutenant, 26th May, 1781, and served to 1st January, 1783. (Died 23d November, 1833.)

Mills, Joseph (N. H.). Ensign 1st New Hampshire, 20th September, 1777; Regimental Adjutant, 1st May, 1780; Lieutenant, 5th July, 1780; retired 1st January, 1781.

Mills, Peter (Conn). Private in the Lexington Alarm, April, 1775; 2d Lieutenant 7th Connecticut, 6th July to 21st December, 1775; Captain of Baldwin's Artillery Artificer Regiment, 16th August, 1777; resigned 15th February, 1781. (Died 10th October, 1830.)

Mills, Samuel (Conn). Quartermaster-Sergeant 2d Continental Dragoons, 12th January, 1777; taken prisoner on Long Island 14th December, 1777; exchanged 8th August, 1780; Lieutenant 2d Continental Dragoons, to rank from 2d June, 1778; resigned 11th October, 1780. (Died 17th February, 1814.)

Mills, Wm. (Conn). Captain of Baldwin's Artillery Artificer Regiment, 1st January, 1777; omitted July, 1779.

Mills, William (Mass). 1st Lieutenant of Glover's Massachusetts Regiment, 19th May to December, 1775; 1st Lieutenant 11th Continental Infantry, 1st January to 31st December, 1776; 1st Lieutenant 14th Massachusetts, 1st January, 1777; Captain Lieutenant, 4th January, 1780; transferred to 7th Massachusetts, 1st January, 1781; Captain, 11th May, 1781; transferred to 4th Massachusetts, 12th June, 1783, and served to November, 1783.

Milton, John (Ga). Ensign 1st Georgia, 7th January, 1776; 1st Lieutenant, November, 1776; taken prisoner at Fort Howe, 8th February, 1777; Captain, 15th September, 1777; Aide-de-Camp to General Lincoln in 1780, and to General Marion in 1781; retired 15th July, 1782 (Died 1803.)

Minger, Edmund (—). Adjutant 2d Canadian (Hazen's) Regiment, — November, 1776; turned over to the civil authorities of Pennsylvania, 29th March, 1777, on the charge of murder.·

Minnis, Alexander (Va). Was Surgeon of the 8th Virginia; retired 14th September, 1778.

Minnis, Callohill (Va). Ensign 1st Virginia, 22d February, 1776; 1st Lieutenant, 23d December, 1776; Captain,

18th November, 1777; taken prisoner at Charleston 12th May, 1780; transferred to 7th Virginia 12th February, 1781, and served to close of war; Brevet Major, 30th September, 1783.

Minnis, Francis (Va). Ensign 1st Virginia, December, 1776; 2d Lieutenant, 2d December, 1776; 1st Lieutenant, 9th August, 1777; Aide-de-Camp to General Muhlenberg in 1779; Captain, 25th April, 1780; taken prisoner at Charleston, 12th May, 1780.

Minnis, Holman (Va). 2d Lieutenant 1st Virginia, February, 1776; 1st Lieutenant, 2d January, 1777; Captain, 12th May, 1779; taken prisoner at Charleston, 12th May, 1780; transferred to 7th Virginia 12th February, 1781, and served to close of war.

Minor, Garret (Va). Major Virginia Militia, 1778-1779.

Minor, Peter (Va). 2d Lieutenant 5th Virginia, 12th February, 1776; 1st Lieutenant, 15th September, 1776; Captain, 10th February, 1778; retired 30th September, 1778.

Minor, Thomas (Va). 1st Lieutenant 5th Virginia, January, 1777; Captain 2d Virginia State Regiment, 23d April, 1778, to February, 1780; as Aide-de-Camp to General Stevens of the Virginia Militia at Yorktown in 1781. (Died 21st July, 1834.)

Minor, Timothy (Mass). Volunteer Surgeon at Concord, 19th April, 1775. (Died 1st August, 1804.)

Minor, Samuel (N. Y.). Captain of Carpenter's Regiment New York Militia in 1776.

Minot, Ephraim (Mass). Sergeant of Nixon's Massachusetts Regiment, 23d April to November, 1775; Ensign 4th Continental Infantry, 1st January to 31st December, 1776; 1st Lieutenant 6th Massachusetts, 1st January, 1777; wounded at Princeton, 3d January, 1777; transferred to Invalid Regiment 18th February, 1778, and served to ——. (Died 30th September, 1794.)

Minthorn, John (N. Y.). Captain of Hathorn's New York Militia Regiment in 1779.

Mitchell, Abiel (Mass). Captain in Lexington Alarm, April, 1775; Major of Walker's Massachusetts Regiment, 24th May to December, 1775; served subsequently as Colonel Massachusetts Militia. (Died 1821.)

Mitchell, Alexander (N. J.). 1st Lieutenant 4th New Jersey, 23d No-

vember, 1776; Captain, 1st November, 1777; transferred to 1st New Jersey 1st July, 1778, and served to April, 1783.

Mitchell, Andrew (N. Y.). Major New York Militia, 1775-1778.

Mitchell, Ephraim (S. C.). 2d Lieutenant 1st South Carolina, 17th June, 1775; 1st Lieutenant, November, 1775; Captain 4th South Carolina, May, 1776; Major, 20th June, 1779; taken prisoner at Charleston 12th May, 1780.

Mitchell, George (N. C.). Captain 6th North Carolina, 16th April, 1776, to ——.

Mitchell, James (Del). Major Delaware Militia in 1780.

Mitchell, James (S. C.). Captain 4th South Carolina, ——; wounded at Stono Ferry 20th June, 1779; served to close of war.

Mitchell, John (Ga). 1st Lieutenant 1 Georgia, 5th April, 1778; resigned 22d October, 1782.

Mitchell, John (Md). 2d Lieutenant 1st Maryland, 10th December, 1776; 1st Lieutenant, 10th June, 1777; Regimental Adjutant, 1st May, 1779; Captain, 15th July, 1779; transferred to 4th Maryland, 1st January, 1781, and served to April, 1783.

Mitchell, Jonathan (Mass). Colonel Massachusetts Militia Regiment on the Bagaduce Expedition, July to September, 1779.

Mitchell, Joseph (Va). Captain 12th Virginia, 9th December, 1776; resigned 3d September, 1777.

Mitchell, Nathaniel (Del). Adjutant Delaware Regiment in 1775; Captain of Patterson's Delaware Battalion of the Flying Camp, July to December, 1776; Captain of Grayson's Additional Continental Regiment, 20th January, 1777; Major, 23d December, 1777; transferred to Gist's Regiment, 22d April, 1779; retired 1st January, 1781. (Died 21st February, 1814.)

Mitchell, Nathaniel (Mass). Ensign 12th Continental Infantry, 1st January, 1776, to ——.

Mitchell, Rotheus (Mass). Private in Lexington Alarm, April, 1775; Private in Bailey's Massachusetts Regiment, May to December, 1775; Sergeant and Ensign 23d Continental Infantry, January to December, 1776; Ensign 2d Massachusetts, 1st January, 1777; 2d Lieutenant, 21st June, 1779; resigned 17th May, 1781. (Died 1816.)

Mitchell, Thomas (Ga). Was a Lieutenant of a Georgia Regiment in 1779, and a Captain in 1780. (Died 1840.)

Mitchell, Thomas (Mass). Major of Thomas's Massachusetts Regiment, May, 1775; Lieutenant-Colonel, 1st July, 1775, to ——.

Mitchell, Thomas (N. Y.). Captain of Malcolm's New York Regiment, March to November, 1776.

Mitchell, Wm. (S. C.). 2d Lieutenant 4th South Carolina, 17th June, 1775; 1st Lieutenant, ——, 1776; Captain, ——, 1780; killed at Charleston, 12th May, 1780.

Mitchels, Nathaniel (N. C.). Regimental Quartermaster 3d North Carolina, ——; dismissed 31st October, 1778.

Mitler, John (R. I.). Second Lieutenant Rhode Island Militia in 1781;

Mix, Caleb (Conn). Captain Connecticut Militia; killed at New Haven, 5th July, 1779.

Mix, John (Conn). Sergeant 7th Connecticut, 10th July to 20th December, 1775; Ensign of Douglas' Connecticut State Regiment, 20th June to 25th December, 1776; Ensign 3d Connecticut, 1st January, 1777; Lieutenant and Adjutant 2d Connecticut, 1st June, 1778; retired June, 1783. (Died 19th April, 1834.)

Mix, Timothy (Conn). Private 2d Connecticut, 6th May to 1st December, 1775; Sergeant 2d Continental Artillery, 19th April, 1777; 2d Lieutenant, 12th September, 1778; 1st Lieutenant, 20th September, 1782, and served to June, 1783. (Died 11th June, 1824.)

Mixer, Joseph (Mass). Ensign of Nixon's Massachusetts Regiment, April to October, 1775.

Moaagg, Henry (Pa). Sergeant German Regiment, 10th July, 1776; Ensign, 15th August, 1777; dismissed 3d August, 1778.

Moat, John (S. C.). 1st Lieutenant 1st South Carolina, 17th June, 1775, to ——.

Moers, Benjamin (Mass). Ensign 2d Canadian (Hazen's) Regiment, ——, 1779; Lieutenant, 1780, and served to January, 1783.

Moffett, John (S. C.). Captain South Carolina Militia at King's Mountain in October, 1780, and in the South Carolina campaign of 1781. (Died 1829.)

Molhollon, William (Md). 2d Lieutenant 3d Maryland, 10th December, 1776; resigned 1st July, 1778.

Molloy, Hugh.—See Mulloy.

Molton, Michael (Mass). Captain Massachusetts Militia in 1779.

Moncrief, Richard (S. C.). 2d Lieutenant 5th South Carolina, ——, 1777; 1st Lieutenant, 21st January, 1778, to ——.

Monell, James (N. Y.). 1st Lieutenant of Malcolm's Additional Continental Regiment, 20th March, 1777; wounded at Monmouth, 28th June, 1778; resigned 23d April, 1779.

Monell, Robert (N. Y.). Lieutenant New York Militia, ——; killed at Fort Montgomery, 6th October, 1777.

Monro, George (Va). Surgeons Mate 6th Virginia, 10th February, 1779; Surgeon, — May, 1779; was a Hospital Surgeon, 1781 to 1783. (Died 11th October, 1819.)

Munro, John (Va). 2d Lieutenant 2d Vigrinia, 28th September, 1775; resigned May, 1776.

Monroe, James (Va). 2d Lieutenant 3d Virginia, 28th September, 1775; 1st Lieutenant, ——, 1776; wounded at Trenton, 26th December, 1776; Major and Aide-de-Camp to General Alexander (Lord Stirling), 20th November, 1777; resigned 20th December, 1778; Fith President of the United States, 4th March, 1817, to 4th March, 1825. (Died 4th July, 1831.)

Monroe, Robert (Mass). Ensign of Company of Minute Men, ——; killed at Lexington, 19th April, 1775.

Monson.—See Munson, ——. Name spelled both ways.

Montague, James (Va). Colonel Virginia Militia, 1779-1781.

Montague, Moses (Mass). Captain Massachusetts Militia, 1779-1780. (Died 1792.)

Montee, Francis (Canada). Lieutenant 1st Canadian (Livingston's) Regiment, 20th November, 1775, to ——.

Montford, Joseph (N. C.). 1st Lieutenant 3d North Carolina, 16th April, 1776; Captain Lieutenant, February, 1777; Captain, 9th January, 1779; taken prisoner at Charleston 12th May, 1780, exchanged, and served to close of war; Captain 1st United States Infantry, 3d

June, 1790; killed 27th April, 1792, by Indians, near Fort Jefferson, Ohio.

Montfort, Julius de.—See **De Montfort.**

Montgomery, —— (S. C.). Lieutenant 2d South Carolina, ——; resigned 5th February, 1778.

Montgomery, Hugh (Pa). Lieutenant of Marines in 1776; 1st Lieutenant 4th Continental Artillery, 14th March, 1777; died 15th May, 1777.

Montgomery, James (Pa). 2d Lieutenant 2d Pennsylvania Battalion, 5th January, 1776; 1st Lieutenant 3d Pennsylvania, 1st January, 1777; resigned 1st September, 1777.

Montgomery, James (Pa). Captain Independent Company Pennsylvania Artillery, 2d December, 1776. Died 26th August, 1777.

Montgomery, James (Va). Lieutenant of a Virginia State Regiment, 1778 to 1781.

Montgomery, James (Va). Captain of Clark's Illinois Regiment, 1778-1781.

Montgomery, John (Pa). Colonel Pennsylvania Militia in 1777.

Montgomery, John (Va). Lieutenant-Colonel of a Virginia State Regiment, 1778 to 1781.

Montgomery, John (Va). Lieutenant of Virginia Cavalry, 1781.

Montgomery, Joseph (Del). Chaplain Delaware Regiment, 13th January to December, 1776; Brigade Chaplain, 27th April, 1778, to ——, 1780.

Montgomery, Michael (Va). 1st Lieutenant of 2d Canadian (Hazen's) Regiment, 3d November, 1776; left on three months' furlough in October, 1780, and did not rejoin, and was retired 1st January, 1781.

Montgomery, Nathaniel (Mass). Corporal in Lexington Alarm, April, 1775; 2d Lieutenant of Little's Massachusetts Regiment, 19th May to December, 1775; 2d Lieutenant 12th Continental Infantry, 1st January, 1776, to ——.

Montgomery, Richard (N. Y.). Brigadier-General Continental Army, 22d June, 1775; Major-General, 9th December, 1775; killed in the assault on Quebec, 31st December, 1775.

Montgomery, Samuel (Pa). Ensign 6th Pennsylvania Battalion, 9th January, 1776; 2d Lieutenant, 1st June, 1776; Captain 7th Pennsylvania, 20th

March, 1777; transferred to 4th Pennsylvania, 17th January, 1781; wounded at Green Springs 6th July, 1781; transferred to 3d Pennsylvania, 1st January, 1783, and served to June, 1783.

Montgomery, Wm. (N. J.). Major New Jersey Militia, 1777-1778. (Died 1815.)

Montgomery, Wm. (Pa). Colonel Pennsylvania Battalion of the Flying Camp; taken prisoner at Fort Washington, 16th November, 1776. (Died 1816.)

Montgomery, William (Pa). Ensign of Wilson's Pennsylvania Battalion to guard stores at Carlisle, Pa., 20th October, 1777, to October, 1778.

Montour, John (—). Captain of a Company of Delaware Indians, 1780-1781.

Monty, Francis (Conn). Ensign 1st Canadian (Livingston's) Regiment, 25th November, 1775; 2d Lietuenant, 18th December, 1776; 1st Lieutenant, 20th November, 1777; wounded at Quaker Hill, 29th August, 1778; retired 1st January, 1781 (Died 8th February, 1809.)

Moodie, Andrew (N. Y.). 2d Lieutenant of Lamb's Company New York Artillery, 30th June, 1775; 1st Lieutenant, 6th November, 1775; taken prisoner at Quebec, 31st December, 1775; Captain 2d Continental Artillery, 1st January, 1777, and served to June, 1783. (Died 18th September, 1787.)

Moodie, Robert (Pa). Colonel Pennsylvania Militia in 1776.

Moody, Edward (Va). 2d Lieutenant 8th Virginia, 16th February, 1776; 1st Lieutenant, 6th August, 1776; dropped on roll for June, 1777, with remark "promoted to Captain Virginia Artillery," possibly a State or Militia Regiment; reportetd to have died in March, 1781.

Moody, James (Va). 1st Lieutenant 2d Virginia State Regiment, 23d April, 1778; Captain, 3d April, 1779, and served to January, 1781.

Moody, John (N. H.). Captain New Hampshire Militia in 1776.

Moody, William (Del). Major of Patterson's Delaware Battalion of the Flying Camp, July to December, 1776.

Mooers, Benjamin (N. Y.). Lieutenant New York Militia in 1776 and

1777; Ensign 2d Canadian (Hazen's) Regiment, 20th March, 1778; Lieutenant and Regimental Adjutant, March, 1780, and served to close of war. (Died 20th February, 1838.)

Moon, Archelaus (Va). 1st Lieutenant 14th Virginia, 23d December, 1776; resigned 13th November, 1777.

Moon, Hugh (Va). Lieutenant of a Virginia Regiment in 1780. (Died 24th October, 1833.)

Moon, Jacob (Va). Paymaster 14th Virginia, 28th April, 1777; resigned 28th August, 1778.

Mooney, Benjamin (N. H.). 1st Lieutenant of Wyman's Regiment New Hampshire Militia, 20th June, 1776; cashiered, 2d October, 1776.

Mooney, Hercules (N. H.). Lieutenant-Colonel and Colonel New Hampshire Militia, 1776 to 1780. (Died 1787.)

Moor, Daniel (N. H.). Colonel New Hampshire Militia in 1775. (Died 1811.)

Moor, John (N. H.). 2d Lieutenant 1st New Hampshire, 23d April to December, 1775; 1st Lieutenant 1st New Hampshire, 8th November, 1776; wounded at Stillwater, 19th September, 1777; retired 1st September, 1778. (Died 1809.)

Moor, John (N. H.). Captain 1st New Hampshire, 23d May, 1775; Major, 18th June to December, 1775; Major 5th Continental Infantry, 1st January to 31st December, 1776.

Moor, William (Mass). Sergeant-Major 3d Continental Artillery, March, 1777; 2d Lieutenant, 29th September, 1778; transferred to Corps of Artillery, 17th June, 1783; 1st Lieutenant, July, 1783, and served to 3d November, 1783; Lieutenant United States Artillery Battalion, 20th October, 1786; Lieutenant Artillery Battalion United States Army, 29th September, 1789; died 10th September, 1790.

Moore, Alexander (Va). 2d Lieutenant 14th Virginia, 7th January, 1777; 1st Lieutenant, 4th October, 1777; resigned 10th January, 1778.

Moore, Alfred (N. C.). Captain 1st North Carolina, 1st September, 1775; resigned 8th March, 1777. (Died 15th October, 1810.)

Moore, Andrew (Conn). 1st Lieutenant of Burrall's Continental Regiment, 23d January, 1776; died in July, 1776, of smallpox.

Moore, Andrew (Va). 1st Lieutenant 9th Virginia, 16th March, 1776; Captain, 25th December, 1777; resigned 14th May, 1778; served subsequently as Brigadier General Virginia Militia.

Moore, Cato (Va). 1st Lieutenant of Grayson's Additional Continental Regiment, 3d February, 1777; wounded at Brandywine, 11th September, 1777; resigned 3d February, 1778.

Moore, Cleon (Va). Captain of Grayson's Additional Continental Regiment, 29th January, 1777; wounded at Brandywine, 11th September, 1777; resigned 5th July, 1778.

Moore, Daniel (N. H.). Captain 1st New Hampshire, 23d April to December, 1775; Captain 5th Continental Infantry, 1st January to 31st December, 1776; served subsequently as Colonel New Hampshire Militia. (Died 19th July, 1820.)

Moore, David (Mass). Captain of Nixon's Massachusetts Regiment, 24th April to December, 1775.

Moore, David (N. J.). 2d Lieutenant 3d Continental Artillery, 1st January, 1777; 1st Lieutenant ——, 1778; resigned, 26th October, 1778.

Moore, Dempsey (N. C.). 1st Lieutenant 6th North Carolina, 16th April, 1776; resigned 27th August, 1777.

Moore, Elijah (N. C.). 1st Lieutenant, 10th North Carolina, 12th October, 1777; transferred to 1st North Carolina, 1st June, 1778; Captain, 11th September, 1781; transferred to 4th North Carolina, 6th February, 1782; retired 1st January, 1783.

Moore, Ezra (N. H.). Private of Bedel's New Hampshire Regiment, June 1775; 2d Lieutenant, 22d January, 1776, and served to July, 1776; 1st Lieutenant of Bedel's Vermont Regiment, 15th December, 1777, to 1st April, 1779.

Moore, Francis (Ga). Captain 2d Georgia, 5th July, 1776; also reported as Major; killed in action with Indians at Reid's Bluff, in the fall of 1782.

Moore, George (Vt). 1st Lieutenant of Bedel's Regiment Vermont Militia, 15th December, 1777, to 1st April, 1779.

Moore, Henry (N. Y.). Surgeon's-Mate, Hospital Department, 1780,1782.

Moore, Henry (S. C.). Lieutenant 4th South Carolina (Artillery), 25th October, 1778; taken prisoner at Charleston, 12th May, 1780.

Moore, Hervey (N. H.). 2d Lieutenant 2d New Hampshire, 23d May to December, 1775.

Moore, Isaac (N. C.). Captain 10th North Carolina, 19th April, 1777; transferred to 1st North Carolina, 1st June, 1778. Died 10th July, 1778.

Moore, Isham (S. C.). Lieutenant South Carolina Light Horse in 1775.

Moore, Jacob (Va). Ensign of a Virginia Regiment in 1779.

Moore, James (Del). 1st Lieutenant Delaware Regiment, 19th January, 1776; Captain, 2d December, 1776; taken prisoner at Newtown, 20th January, 1778; exchanged, 7th December, 1780; served to close of war; Brevet Major, 30th September, 1783.

Moore, James (N. Y.). Lieutenant of Lamb's Company New York Artillery, 30th June, 1775; Captain Lieutenant, 14th March, 1776; died —— January, 1777.

Moore, James (N. Y.). Ensign 1st New York, 21st November, 1776; resigned 28th February, 1778.

Moore, James (N. C.). Colonel 1st North Carolina, 1st September, 1775; Brigadier-General Continental Army, 1st March, 1776; died 9th April, 1777.

Moore, James (N. C.). Ensign 1st North Carolina, ——, 1780; Lieutenant, 1st July, 1781; wounded at Eutaw Springs, 8th September, 1781; did not rejoin regiment.

Moore, James (Pa.) Colonel Pennsylvania Militia in 1776.

Moore, James (Pa). Captain 4th Pennsylvania Battalion, 5th January, 1776; Captain 5th Pennsylvania, December, 1776, to rank from 5th January, 1776; Major 1st Pennsylvania, 20th September, 1777; transferred to 2d Pennsylvania, 1st January, 1783, and served to November, 1783; Brevet Lieutenant-Colonel, 30th September, 1783. (Died 1813.)

Moore, James (Va). Captain Virginia Militia in 1781; killed by Indians in 1786.

Moore, James Francis (Pa). 1st Lieutenant of Miles' Pennsylvania Rifle Regiment, 19th March, 1776; Captain Pennsylvania State Regiment, 25th October, 1776; regiment designated, 13th Pennsylvania, 12th November, 1777; transferred to 8th Pennsylvania, 1st July, 1778; resigned 2d August, 1779.

Moore, James W. (S. C.). Surgeon South Carolina Militia and in Hospital Department, 1778-1782.

Moore, John (N. C.). Lieutenant 7th North Carolina, 17th December, 1776, to ——.

Moore, John (Pa). Major of Lewis' Pennsylvania Battalion of the Flying Camp, July to December, 1776; Colonel Pennsylvania Militia in 1777.

Moore, John (Va). Ensign 12th Virginia, 1st March, 1777; 2d Lieutenant, 15th November, 1777; resigned 30th March, 1778.

Moore, John (Va). Regimental Quartermaster, 14th Virginia, 2d May, 1777; retired 30th September, 1778; shown also a Captain of a Virginia Regiment in 1780; possibly of Militia.

Moore, Joseph (Mass). Captain of Prescott's Massachusetts Regiment, May to December, 1775; Captain 7th Continental Infantry, 1st January to 31st December, 1776.

Moore, Joseph (Pa). 1st Lieutenant Pennsylvania Musket Battalion, May, 1776; killed at Long Island, 27th August, 1776.

Moore, Maurice (N. C.). Ensign 1st North Carolina, 1st September, 1775; 2d Lieutenant, 4th January, 1776; killed 18th January, 1776, at ——.

Moore, Merritt (Va). Ensign 2d Virginia, 3d October, 1775; 2d Lieutenant, August, 1776; 1st Lieutenant, 13th January, 1777; retired 30th September, 1778.

Moore, Nicholas Ruxton (Md). 2d Lieutenant of Fulford's Company Maryland Cannoneers, March, 1776; Lieutenant 4th Continental Dragoons, 2d February, 1777; Captain, 15th March, 1778; resigned 31st December, 1778; Captain Maryland Cavalry Militia in 1781. (Died 9th March, 1816.)

Moore, Peter (Va). Sergeant 8th Virginia, November, 1776; Lieutenant in 1777; Lieutenant and Captain of a Virginia State Regiment, 1778 to 1781.

Moore, Richard N. (Pa). Lieutenant 4th Continental Dragoons, —— February, 1777; Captain, 15th March, 1778; resigned 21st December, 1778.

Moore, Robert (N. C.). Ensign 9th North Carolina, 28th November, 1776; was a Captain in 1778 and 1779.

Moore, Roger (N. C.). Captain 4th North Carolina, 16th April, 1776; resigned —— November, 1776.

Moore, Samuel (Pa). 1st Lieutenant 2d Pennsylvania Battalion, 5th January, 1776 Captain 3d Pennsylvania, 11th November, 1776; retired 1st July, 1778. (Died 1795.)

Moore, Samuel (N. H.). Surgeon's-Mate of Wingate's Regiment New Hampshire Militia, July, 1776, to March, 1777.

Moore, Smith (Md). 2d Lieutenant 5th Maryland, 10th December, 1776; resigned 10th May, 1777.

Moore, Stephen (N. C.). Lieutenant-Colonel North Carolina Militia; taken prisoner at Charleston, 12th May, 1780.

Moore, Thomas (Va). 1st Lieutenant 13th Virginia, 16th November, 1776; Captain, 23d January, 1778; regiment designated 9th Virginia 14th September, 1778, and served to January, 1780. (Died 1829.)

Moore, Thomas Lloyd (Pa). 1st Lieutenant 2d Pennsylvania Battalion, 5th January, 1776; Captain, 21st May, 1776; Captain 3d Pennsylvania, 1st January, 1777; to rank from 21st May, 1776; Major 9th Pennsylvania, 12th May, 1779; transferred to 5th Pennsylvania, 17th January ,1781; retired 1st January, 1783; Lieutenant-Colonel 10th United States Infantry, 8th January, 1799; honorably discharged, 15th June, 1800. (Died, 1819.)

Moore, Willard (Mass). Major in Lexington Alarm, April, 1775; Major of Doolittle's Massachusetts Regiment, 23d April, 1775; killed at Bunker Hill, 17th June, 1775.

Moore, William (Del). Captain Delaware Militia, 1780-1781.

Moore, William (Mass). 2d Lieutenant 3d Continental Infantry, 1st January to 31st December, 1776; 1st Lieutenant 4th Massachusetts, 1st January, 1777; Captain, 15th June, 1779, and served to 3d June, 1783. (Died 6th August, 1819.)

Moore, William (Pa). Sergeant 3d Battalion of Miles' Pennsylvania Rifle Regiment, 26th March, 1776; 3d Lieutenant, 6th July, 1776; transferred to Pennsylvania State Regiment, October, 1776; 1st Lieutenant, 18th April, 1777; wounded at Germantown, 4th October, 1777; regiment designated 13th Pennsylvania, 12th November, 1777; transferred to 2d Pennsylvania, 1st July, ·1778; transferred to 1st Pennsylvania, 1st January, 1783, and served to 3d November, 1783; Brevet Captain, 30th

September, 1783. (Died 6th June, 1824.)

Moore, William (Pa). Sergeant-Major 3d Continental Artillery, 3d March, 1777; 2d Lieutenant, 1st August, 1778; served to June, 1783.

Moore, William (N. C.). Surgeon's-Mate, 10th North Carolina, 19th January, 1778; resigned, —— May, 1778.

Moore, William (Va). Sergeant 3d Virginia, 10th April, 1777; Ensign 15th August, 1777; 2d Lieutenant, 28th October, 1777;. retired —— May, 1779. (Died 1818.)

Moore, Zedakiah (Md). Quartermaster Sergeant, 2d Maryland, 3d June, 1777; 2d Lieutenant, 27th May, 1779; 1st Lieutenant, 10th September, 1780; died April, 1783.

Moorehouse, Andrew (N. Y.). Lieutenant-Colonel New York Militia, 1776-1778. (Died 1801.)

Moorehouse, Solomon (Conn). Captain Connecticut Militia, 1776.

Moran, Edmond (Md). Sergeant 6th Maryland, 5th December, 1776; 2d. Lieutenant Regimental Quartermaster, 17th April, 1777; 1st Lieutenant, 21st. May, 1779; dismissed, 15th July, 1780. (Died 1812.)

Morehead, James (N. C.). Lieutenant 10th North Carolina, 23d March, 1779, to ——.

Morehead, Samuel (Pa). Captain Pennsylvania Independent Company, guarding stores at Kittanning; Pa., 22d January, 1777, to 1778.

Morey, Ephriam (Vt). 1st Lieutenant of Bedel's Regiment, Vermont Militia, 15th December, 1777, to 1st April, 1778.

Morey, Isaac (Mass). Sergeant 3d Continental Artillery, 2d February, 1777; 2d Lieutenant, 1st January, 1778; omitted November, 1779. (Died 17th October, 1830.)

Morey, Israel (N. H.). Colonel New Hampshire Militia, 1779-1780. (Died 1809.)

Morey, Samuel (N. H.). Surgeon's-Mate 2d New Hampshire, in 1780; resigned 1st August, 1782.

Morfit, Henry (Pa). Lieutenant Pennsylvania Battalion of the Flying Camp, June, 1776; taken prisoner at Long Island, 27th August, 1776, and was a prisoner to close of war. (Died 1794.)

Morgan, Abel (Pa). Surgeon 11th Pennsylvania, 14th February, 1777; transferred to 8th Pennsylvania, 1st July, 1778; resigned —— February, 1779. (Died, July, 1785.)

Morgan, Abner (Mass). Major of Porter's Regiment, Massachusetts Militia, 1775-1778. (Died 7th November, 1837.)

Morgan, Benjamin (Mass). Surgeon's-Mate 1st Massachusetts, 21st March, 1782, and served to 3d November, 1783.

Morgan, Benjamin (N. C.). Ensign 3d North Carolina, 28th November, 1776, to ——.

Morgan, Daniel (Va). Captain Company of Virginia Riflemen, July, 1775; taken prisoner at Quebec, 31st December, 1775; Colonel 11th Virginia, 12th November, 1776; regiment designated 7th Virginia, 14th September, 1778; Brigadier General Continental Army, 13th October, 1780. By the act of 9th March, 1781, "The United States in Congress assembled, considering it as a tribute due to distinguished merit to give a public approbation of the conduct of Brigadier-General Morgan, and of the officers and men under his command on the 17th day of January last, when, with 80 cavalry and 237 infantry of the troops of the United States and 553 militia from the States of Virginia, North Carolina, South Carolina and Georgia, he obtained a complete and important victory over a select and well-appointed detachment of more than 1,100 British troops, commanded by Lieutenant-Colonel Tarleton, do therefore resolve, that the thanks of the United States in Congress assembled be given to Brigadier-General Morgan, and the officers and men under his command, for their fortitude and good conduct displayed in the action at the Cowpens, in the State of South Carolina, on the 17th day of January last; that a medal of gold be presented to Brigadier-General Morgan, with emblems and mottoes descriptive of his conduct on that memorable day." Served to close of war. (Died 6th July, 1802.)

Morgan, David (Md). Sergeant German Regiment, 5th November, 1776; Ensign, 13th August, 1777; Lieutenant, 8th April, 1778; retired 1st January, 1781.

Morgan, Enoch (Pa). Paymaster 6th Pennsylvania, 15th February, 1777; retired 1st July, 1778.

Morgan, Ephriam (Conn). Quartermaster-Sergeant 1st Connecticut, 19th April, 1777; Ensign and Issuing Commissary 2d Connecticut Brigade, 1st January, 1778; retired 1st January, 1783.

Morgan George (Pa). Appointed Agent for Indian Affairs, 10th April, 1776, with rank and pay of Colonel Continental Army; also appointed Deputy Commissioner-General of Purchases Western District, 20th November, 1777, and served to close of war. (Died 10th March, 1810.)

Morgan, Haynes (Va). Colonel Virginia Militia, 1776-1779.

Morgan, Jacob, Jr. (Pa). Major and Colonel Pennsylvania Militia, 1775-1779. (Died 1792.)

Morgan, James (Conn). Captain Connecticut Militia in 1776; wounded at Fort Griswold, 6th September, 1781.

Morgan, John (Pa). Had been Surgeon in British Army, ——; Director-General and Chief Physician of Hospital, 17th October, 1775; dismissed 9th January, 1777; his conduct vindicated, 12th June, 1779; see act of Congress of that date. (Died 15th October, 1789.)

Morgan, John (Pa). 1st Lieutenant 5th Pennsylvania Battalion, 6th January, 1776; Captain, 17th November, 1776; taken prisoner at Fort Washington, 16th November, 1776; exchanged 26th August, 1778.

Morgan, John (Va). Ensign 13th Virginia, —— January, 1777; died 25th October, 1777.

Morgan, Mordacai (Pa). 1st Lieutenant of Lewis' Pennsylvania Battalion of the Flying Camp, July, 1776; 1st Lieutenant, 9th Pennsylvania, 15th November, 1776; retired 1st July, 1778.

Morgan, Nathaniel (Conn). Ensign in the Lexington Alarm, April, 1775; Ensign 6th Connecticut, 1st May to 15th December, 1775; 1st Lieutenant of Ward's Connecticut State Regiment, 14th May, 1776; died —— September, 1776.

Morgan, Nicholas (N. J.). Lieutenant New Jersey Militia; mortally wounded 9th December, 1782; where, not stated.

Morgan, Simon (Va). Ensign 8th Virginia, 10th December, 1775; 1st Lieutenant 13th Virginia, 15th December, 1776; Captain, 15th March, 1778; regiment designated 9th Virginia, 14th September, 1778; transferred to 7th Virginia, 12th February, 1781; wounded at Eutaw Springs, 8th September, 1781; served to close of war.

Morgan, Spencer (Va). Ensign 7th Virginia, 4th July, 1779; was in service in April, 1781.

Morgan, William (S. C.). Lieutenant South Carolina Artillery, 1779-1780.

Moritz, Gilbert (—). Surgeon's Mate of Armand's Partisan Corps, 1777-1779.

Morrell, Henry (Mass). Captain, Lieutenant-Colonel and Colonel Massachusetts Militia, 1776-1777. (Died 1778.)

Morrell, John (Ga). Captain Georgia Militia, 1777-1779.

Morrell, Nathaniel (Vt). Lieutenant Vermont Militia in 1777.

Morrell, Thomas (N. J.). Captain 4th New Jersey, 28th November, 1776; Major, 17th February, 1777; resigned 29th October, 1777. (Died 9th August, 1838.)

Morrill, Amos (N. H.). 1st Lieutenant 1st New Hampshire, 23d May to December, 1775; Captain 5th Continental Infantry, 1st January, 1776; Captain 1st New Hampshire, 8th November, 1776; Major 2d New Hampshire, 24th March, 1780; retained in New Hampshire Battalion, 1st March, 1782, and served to close of war. (Died January, 1810.)

Morrill, Joseph (N. Y.). Sergeant 4th New York, 10th December, 1776; Sergeant-Major, 1st March, 1779; Ensign 1st June, 1779; transferred to 1st New York, 1st January, 1781, and served to June, 1783.)

Morrill, Simon (N. H.). Ensign 1st New Hampshire, 8th November, 1776; 2d Lieutenant, 19th September, 1777; resigned 20th May, 1780.

Morris, Abel (Pa). 2d Lieutenant Pennsylvania Battalion Flying Camp, June, 1776; 2d Lieutenant 2d Pennsylvania, November, 1776; retired 1st July, 1778.

Morris, Anthony, Jr. (Pa). Surgeon of troops in Canada and at Lake George, June to August, 1776; Ensign Pennsylvania Associaters; killed at Princeton, 3d January, 1777.

Morris, Anthony James (Pa). Major 1st Pennsylvania Battalion, 25th No-

vember, 1775; Major 1st Continental Infantry, 1st January, 1776, to rank from 25th November, 1775; Lieutenant-Colonel 2d Pennsylvania, 25th October, 1776; Colonel 9th Pennsylvania, 12th March, 1777, which he declined, 7th June, 1777, and retired from the service. (Died 20th May, 1831.)

Morris, Asa (Conn). 2d Lieutenant 3d Connecticut, 1st May, 1775; died 30th July, 1775.

Morris, Benjamin (Pa). Ensign 9th Pennsylvania, 4th August, 1777; killed at Brandywine, 11th September, 1777.

Morris, David (Conn). Captain Connecticut Militia, ——; taken prisoner at ——, 20th October, 1780; sent to Prison-ship, from which he escaped.

Morris, Gottlieb (Pa). Surgeon Hospital Department in 1776; Surgeon of Armand's Partisan Corps, 1780 to 1782.

Morris, Jacob (N. Y.). Major New York Militia, 1775; Major and Aide-de-Camp to General Lee, October, 1776, to October, 1778; wounded at Monmouth, 28th June, 1778; Major and Aide-de-Camp to General Greene, May, 1781, to 1782.

Morris, James (Conn). Ensign of Gay's Connecticut State Regiment, 20th June to 25th December, 1776; 1st Lieutenant 5th Connecticut, 1st January, 1777; taken prisoner at Germantown, 4th October, 1777; exchanged 3d January, 1781; Captain-Lieutenant 5th Connecticut, 20th July, 1780; Captain, 22d August, 1780; transferred to 2d Connecticut, 1st January, 1781; retired 1st January, 1783. It is also stated that he did not rejoin the army after exchange. (Died 20th April, 1820.)

Morris, James (Pa). Ensign 1st Pennsylvania Battalion, 3d November, 1776, to January, 1777.

Morris, John (Pa). Surgeon 1st Battalion of the Pulaski Legion, subsequently Armand's Corps, 1779 to 1782.

Morris, Jonathan (Md). 1st Lieutenant 7th Maryland, 10th December, 1776; Captain, 14th April, 1777; wounded and taken prisoner at Camden, 16th August, 1780; transferred to 2d Maryland, 1st January, 1781, and served to April, 1783.

Morris, Jonathan Ford (N. J.). Ensign 1st New Jersey, 14th September, 1776; 2d Lieutenant 4th Continental Artillery, 14th March, 1777; 1st Lieutenant, 14th April, 1778 resigned 28th November, 1778; served as Surgeon's-Mate in Hospital Department, 6th March, 1780 to June, 1782; also as Surgeon New Jersey Militia.

Morris, Joseph (N. J.). Captain 1st New Jersey, 8th November, 1775, to 20th November, 1776; Captain 1st New Jersey, 29th November, 1776; Major, 1st January, 1777; died 4th January, 1778, of wounds received at White Marsh, 5th December, 1777.

Morris, Lewis (N. Y.). A signer of the Declaration of Independence; Brigadier-General and Major-General New York Militia; died 22d July, 1798.

Morris, Lewis, Jr. (N. Y.). Brigade-Major New York Militia, 7th June, 1776; Major Aide-de-Camp to General Sullivan, 14th August, 1776, to 12th June, 1779; brevetted Lieutenant-Colonel Continental Army by the act of 9th September, 1778, "for bringing forward to Congress the account of the repulse of the British forces on Rhode Island on the 29th of August last, and who, on the late expedition, as well as on several other occasions, behaved with great spirit and good conduct." Aide-de-Camp to General Greene, 12th June, 1779, to close of war.

Morris, Lewis R. (N. Y.). Ensign 2d New York, 29th June, 1781; resigned 30th November, 1782.

Morris, Nathaniel G. (Va.). 1st Lieutenant 9th Virginia, 13th March, 1776; Captain, 10th February, 1777; retired 14th September, 1778. (Died 15th September, 1824.)

Morris, Robert (Pa). A signer of the Declaration of Independence; Superintendent of Finances of the United States, 1781 to close of war; died 8th May, 1806.

Morris, Samuel (Pa). Captain Philadelphia Light Horse, 1777-1780. (Died 7th July, 1812.)

Morris, William Walton (N. Y.). 2d Lieutenant 2d Continental Artillery, 20th August, 1781; Regimental Quartermaster, 1st January, 1783, and served to June, 1783. (Died 5th April, 1832.)

Morrison, Isaac (N. J.). 1st Lieutenant 1st New Jersey, 15th December, 1775, to 10th November, 1776; 1st Lieutenant, 1st New Jersey, 20th November, 1776; Captain, 1st January, 1777; wounded at Germantown, 4th October, 1777; did not rejoin regiment.

Morrison, James (Pa). Ensign 8th Pennsylvania, 21st December, 1778; retired 1st January, 1781.

Morrison, John (Ga). Ensign 1st Georgia, 7th January, 1776; 1st Lieutenant 2d Georgia, 5th February, 1777; Captain, 1779; retired 22d October, 1782.

Morrison, Joseph (Pa). 1st Lieutenant of Montgomery's Pennsylvania Battalion of the Flying Camp; taken prisoner at Fort Washington, 16th November, 1776.

Morrison, Robert (N. Y.). Surgeon's Mate 5th New York, 1st June, 1777; retired 1st July, 1778.

Morrison, Samuel (Pa). Ensign of Hartley's Continental Regiment, 15th January, 1777; 2d Lieutenant, 11th May, 1777; regiment designated, 11th Pennsylvania, 16th December, 1778; 1st Lieutenant, 13th January, 1779; transferred to 6th Pennsylvania, 17th January, 1781, and served to close of war.

Morrow, John (Va). Colonel Virginia Militia, 1778-1781.

Morrow, Robert (Md). Ensign 2d Maryland Battalion of the Flying Camp, July to December, 1776; Cornet 3d Continental Dragoons, 20th February, 1777; Regimental Adjutant, 1st June, 1777; wounded and taken prisoner at Tappan, 28th September, 1778; Lieutenant ,3d January, 1779; Captain, ——1781, and served to 9th November, 1782.

Morse, Anthony (Mass). Drummer in Lexington Alarm, April, 1775; Sergeant of Fellow's Massachusetts Regiment, April to November, 1775; Sergeant 26th Continental Infantry, April to December, 1776; Ensign, 9th Massachusetts, 1st January, 1777; resigned 14th February, 1778.

Morse, Jesse (Conn). Captain of Wadsworth's Connecticut State Regiment, June to December, 1776.

Morse, Joseph (Mass). Captain of Paterson's Massachusetts Regiment April to November, 1775; Captain 7th Continental Infantry, 1st January to 31st December, 1776; Captain 5th Massachusetts, 1st January, 1777; Major 14th Massachusetts, 11th November, 1778; died 15th December, 1779.

Morse, Joshua (Mass). Regimental Quartermaster of Cady's Battalion on the Expedition to Canada, January to June, 1776.

Morse, William (Mass). 1st Lieutenant in Lexington Alarm, April, 1775; 1st Lieutenant of Ward's Massachusetts Regiment, 27th April to December,

1775; Captain Massachusetts Militia, 1776-1781. (Died 1802.)

Morton, Dimond (Mass). Captain of Gridley's Regiment, Massachusetts Artillery, April to December, 1775; Captain of Knox's Regiment, Continental Artillery, 10th December, 1775, to December, 1776.

Morton, Hezekiah (Va). 2d Lieutenant 12th Virginia, January, 1777; 1st Lieutenant, 21st July, 1777; regiment designated 8th Virginia, 14th September, 1778; Captain, 15th July, 1781, and served to close of war. (Died 30th June, 1831.)

Morton, Hugh (Pa). Surgeon 8th Pennsylvania, 7th March, 1780; retired 1st January, 1781.

Morton, Isaac (Mass). Ensign 10th Massachusetts, 6th November, 1776; 2d Lieutenant, 1st November, 1777; discharged 4th December, 1777; Captain Massachusetts Militia in 1778. (Died December, 1827.)

Morton, James (Va). Ensign 4th Virginia, 28th September, 1776; 2d Lieutenant, 20th October, 1777; Regimental Quartermaster, 1st April, 1778; 1st Lieutenant, 9th September, 1778; taken prisoner at Charleston, 12th May, 1780, and was in prison to 1st May, 1783.

Morton, John (Pa). A signer of the Declaration of Independence; died April, 1777.

Morton, John (Pa). Surgeon's-Mate 4th Continental Artillery, 11th February, 1778, to ——.

Morton, John (Va). Captain 4th Virginia, 19th February, 1776; resigned 12th March, 1777; served subsequently as Lieutenant-Colonel of Virginia Militia.

Morton, Perez (Mass). Major and Aide-de-Camp to General Hancock in 1778.

Morton, Silas (Mass). Private Company of Minute Men in 1775; 1st Lieutenant 2d Massachusetts, 1st January, 1777; brevet Captain, 30th September, 1783, and served to 30th October, 1783. (Died 25th March, 1840.)

Morton, Simeon (N. H.). Captain New Hampshire Militia, 1776.

Mosby, John (Ga). Captain 2d Georgia ——, on roll for August, 1778.

Mosby, Littlebury (Ga). Captain 2d Georgia, 23d July, 1776; taken prisoner at Savannah, 18th October, 1779; ex-

changed December, 1779, when he returned to Virginia and was Colonel Virginia Militia, 1780-1782.

Mosby, Robert (Ga). Lieutenant 2d Georgia ——; on roll for August, 1778.

Mosby, William (Va). 1st Lieutenant 5th Virginia, 24th February, 1776; Captain, 18th December, 1776; resigned 2d June, 1778.

Moseley, Benjamin (Va). Ensign 5th Virginia in 1777; 2d Lieutenant, 10th September, 1778; 1st Lieutenant, 29th August, 1779; taken prisoner at Charleston, 12th May, 1780; exchanged June, 1781; retired 1st January, 1783; Captain 28th United States Infantry, 20th May, 1813; resigned 20th February, 1814. (Died, ——, 1819.)

Moseley, Benjamin (Va). 2d Lieutenant 1st Continental Artillery, 29th April, 1779; taken prisoner at Camden, 16th August, 1780; prisoner to 1st May, 1783.

Moseley, Ebenezer (Conn). Lieutenant Company of Minute Men in the Lexington Alarm, April, 1775; Captain 3d Connecticut, 1st May to 7th December, 1775.

Moseley, Increase (Conn). Colonel Connecticut Militia in 1778.

Moseley, John (Md). 2d Lieutenant 1st Continental Artillery, 1st January, 1779; taken prisoner at Camden, 16th August, 1780.

Moseley, John (Mass). Colonel Massachusetts Militia in 1777.

Moseley, Robert (Pa). 1st Lieutenant 8th Pennsylvania, 9th August, 1776; resigned 16th May, 1777.

Moseley, William (N. C.). Paymaster 6th North Carolina, 11th December, 1776; resigned —— May, 1777.

Moseley, William (Va). 1st Lieutenant 7th Virginia, 29th February, 1776; Captain, 13th December, 1776; wounded at Trenton, 2d January, 1777; transferred to 5th Virginia, 14th September, 1778; taken prisoner at Charleston, 12th May, 1780; exchanged November, 1780; Major 3d Virginia, 12th February, 1781, which he declined and was retired as of that date with rank of Major.

Moseman, Marcus (N. Y.). Captain New York Militia, ——; prisoner of war, 20th November, 1780, to 18th April, 1781; where taken not stated.

Moser, Jacob (Pa). Captain 6th Pennsylvania, 15th February, 1777; retired 1st July, 1778. (Name also spelled Mouser.)

Mosher, John (Mass). Sergeant in Lexington Alarm, April, 1775; 2d Lieutenant of Prescott's Massachusetts Regiment, May to December, 1775; 2d Lieutenant 7th Continental Infantry, 1st January to 31st December, 1776; 1st Lieutenant 8th Massachusetts, 1st January, 1777; retired 15th December, 1778, on account of ill health.

Moslander, Abel (N. C.). Lieutenant 4th North Carolina, 25th January, 1777, to ——.

Mosman, Timothy (Mass). Sergeant in Lexington Alarm, April, 1775; Sergeant of Whitcomb's Massachusetts Regiment, April to November, 1775, and in 1776; 1st Lieutenant 14th Massachusetts, January, 1777; omitted in January, 1780, on account of being a prisoner, but when and where taken, not stated.

Moss, Jesse (Conn). Captain Connecticut Militia, 1776-1777.

Moss, Henry (Va). 2d Lieutenant 2d Virginia, 13th January, 1777; 1st Lieutenant, 11th July, 1777; taken prisoner at Charleston, 12th May, 1780; exchanged April, 1781; Captain, 26th May, 1781; retired 1st January, 1783.

Moss, John (Va). 1st Lieutenant 1st Virginia, 22d February, 1776; Captain, 15th September, 1776; resigned 18th November, 1777.

Moss, Titus (Conn). Ensign 7th Connecticut. 6th July, 1775; 2d Lieutenant, 11th October to 19th December, 1775. (Died 1818.)

Mossam, Richard (N. C.). Ensign 10th North Carolina, 4th September, 1778, to ——.

Mott, Atwood (Mass). Corporal in Lexington Alarm, April, 1775; 1st Lieutenant of Thomas' Massachusetts Regiment, May to October, 1775; 1st Lieutenant 23d Continental Infantry, 1st January to 31st December, 1776.

Mott, Ebenezer (N. Y.). 2d Lieutenant of Graham's Regiment New York Militia, September to November, 1776; 2d Lieutenant 5th New York, 21st November, 1776; taken prisoner at Fort Montgomery, 6th October, 1777; 1st Lieutenant 22d December, 1779; retired 1st January, 1781; served subsequently as Lieutenant New York Levies.

Mott, Edward (Conn). Captain 6th Connecticut, 1st May, 1775, to 10th

February, 1776; Major of Gay's Connecticut State Regiment, 2d July to December, 1776.

Mott, Gershom (N. Y.). Captain 1st New York, 28th June, 1775; Captain of Nicholson's Continental Regiment, 8th March, 1776; Captain, 2d Continental Artillery, 1st January, 1777, and served to June, 1783. (Died 27th May, 1786.)

Mott, James (N. J.). Major New Jersey Militia, 1775-1776.

Mott, John (N. J.). 1st Lieutenant 3d New Jersey, 9th February, 1776; Captain, 20th November, 1776; retired 26th September, 1780; served subsequently as Captain New Jersey Militia. (Died 31st May, 1831.)

Mott, John (N. H.). 2d Lieutenant of Lee's Independent Company, New Hampshire Rangers, 9th December, 1776; resigned 5th March, 1778. (Died 1831.)

Mott, Samuel (Conn). Colonel Connecticut State Regiment, July to December, 1776.

Motte, Abraham (S. C.). Lieutenant Colonel 2d South Carolina, 17th June, 1775, to ——.

Motte, Charles (S. C.). Captain 2d South Carolina, 17th June, 1775; Major, ——, 1779; killed at Savannah, 9th October, 1779.

Motte, Isaac (S. C.). Lieutenant-Colonel 2d South Carolina, 17th June, 1775; Colonel, 16th September, 1776; taken prisoner at Charleston, 12th May, 1780; exchanged 14th June, 1781; Brevet Brigadier-General, 30th September, 1783; served to close of war. (Died 8th May, 1795.)

Moulder, William (Pa). 2d Lieutenant 4th Pennsylvania Battalion, 15th March, 1776; resigned 1st September, 1776. (Died 1798.)

Moulton, Jonathan (N. H.). Colonel New Hampshire Militia, 1775-1777. (Died 1787.)

Moulton, Johnson (Mass). Captain in Lexington Alarm, April, 1775; Lieutenant-Colonel of Scammon's Massachusetts Regiment, May to December, 1775; Lieutenant-Colonel 7th Continental Infantry, 1st January to 31st December, 1776. (Died 13th June, 1793.)

Moulton, Micah (R. I.). Ensign 9th Continental Infantry, 1st January, 1776; 2d Lieutenant, 10th September, 1776; 1st Lieutenant 2d Rhode Island,

1st January, 1777, to ——. (Died 18th December, 1820.)

Moulton, Stephen (Conn). Lieutenant-Colonel Connecticut Militia, ——; taken prisoner 15th September, 1776, on the retreat from New York. (Died 1819.)

Moulton, William (N. Y.). Sergeant 4th New York, in 1775; 2d Lieutenant 2d New York Regiment, 16th September, 1776; 1st Lieutenant of Warner's Additional Continental Regiment, 16th November, 1776; Captain, 1st March, 1778; retired 1st January, 1781. (Died 3d July, 1831.)

Moultrie, Alexander (S. C.). Captain South Carolina Militia in 1776.

Moultrie, Thomas (S. C.). 1st Lieutenant 2d South Carolina, 17th June, 1775; Captain, ——; killed at the siege of Charleston, 24th April, 1780.

Moultrie, William (S C.). Colonel 2d South Carolina, 17th June, 1775; by the act of 20th July, 1776, it was "Resolved, that the thanks of the United States of America be given to * * * Colonel William Moutrie * * * and the officers and soldiers under their command, who on the 28th of June last, repulsed, with so much valor, the attack which was made that day on the State of South Carolina by the fleet and army of His Britannic Majesty." Brigadier-General Continental Army, 16th September, 1776; taken prisoner at Charleston, 12th May, 1780, and was on parole to November, 1781; Major-General, 15th October, 1782, and served to close of war. (Died 27th September, 1805.)

Moultrie, William, Jr. (S. C.). 2d Lieutenant 2d South Carolina, 17th June, 1775, to ——.

Mountfort, Julius de.—See **De Montfort.**

Mountjoy, Alvin (Va). 2d Lieutenant 3d Virginia, 25th February, 1776; 1st Lieutenant, 15th January, 1777; resigned 10th December, 1777.

Mountjoy, John (Va). Captain 10th Virginia, 14th January, 1777; retired 30th September, 1778.

Mountjoy, William (Va). Regimental Quartermaster 3d Virginia, 10th April, 1776; Regimental Paymaster, 9th August, 1776; resigned 19th September, 1779.

Mountour, John (—). Captain of a Company of Delaware Indians, 1776; 1781.

Mountz, William (Pa). 2d Lieutenant 8th Pennsylvania, 9th August, 1776; resigned 20th April, 1777.

Mouser, Jacob.—See **Moser.**

Mouzon, Henry (S. C.). Lieutenant 3d South Carolina, ——, 1777; Captain, ——; wounded at Black Mingo, 14th September, 1780.

Mowatt, —— (S. C.). Captain 1st South Carolina, ——; resigned 18th August, 1777.

Mowry, Daniel (R. I.). Captain Rhode Island Militia, 1780-1781.

Moxley, Rhodom (Va). Sergeant 2d Virginia, —— September, 1777; Ensign and Regimental Quartermaster, 9th September, 1778; 2d Lieutenant ——, 1779, and served to ——.

Moylan, Stephen (Pa). Mustermaster-General Continental Army, 11th August, 1775; Aide-de-Camp to General Washington, 6th March, 1776; Colonel Quartermaster General, 5th June, 1776; resigned as Quartermaster-General, 28th September, 1776, but remained on staff of General Washington until appointed Colonel 4th Continental Dragoons, 5th January, 1777, and served to 3d November, 1783; brevet Brigadier-General, 3d November, 1783. (Died 11th April, 1811.)

Mudge, Jervis (N. Y.). 1st Lieutenant 2d New York, 28th June, 1775, to October, 1775. (Died 1810.)

Mudgett, David (N. H.). Ensign 1st New Hampshire, 8th November, 1776; resigned 20th November, 1777.

Muhlenberg, Peter (Va). Colonel 8th Virginia, 1st March, 1776; Brigadier-General Continental Army, 21st February, 1777, and served to close of war. Brevet Major-General, 30th September, 1783. (Died 1st October, 1807.)

Muir, Francis (Va). 1st Lieutenant of Gist's Additional Continental Regiment, January, 1777; Captain-Lieutenant, 23d April, 1779; Captain, —— May, 1780; retired 1st January, 1781.

Mulford, Job (N. Y.). Adjutant 4th New York, 2d August, 1775, to November, 1776.

Muller, Jeremiah Christopher (N. Y.). 2d Lieutenant 1st New York, 21st November, 1776; resigned 20th April, 1780; Captain New York State troops; wounded at Fort Keyser, 19th October, 1780. (Died 15th March, 1811.)

Mullens, Thomas (France). Brigadier-Major to General De Borre, 19th

Mulloy							407							Murdock

May to 14th September, 1777; Aide-de-Camp and Brigade-Major to General Conway, 3d October, 1777, to 28th April, 1778; brevet Lieutenant-Colonel Continental Army, 11th June, 1778, and permitted to return to France.

Mulloy, Hugh (Mass). Ensign 11th Massachusetts, 6th November, 1776; 2d Lieutenant, 1st January, 1777; resigned 20th April, 1780.

Mulloy, James (Pa). Ensign 5th Pennsylvania Battalion 8th January, 1776; deserted 2d November, 1776.

Mumford, David (Conn). Surgeon's-Mate 2d Continental Dragoons, 16th May, 1778; resigned as Surgeon's-Mate and appointed Lieutenant same regiment, 14th November, 1779; resigned 11th June, 1780.

Mumford, Giles (Conn). 2d Lieutenant of Webb's Continental Regiment, 1st January, 1777; taken prisoner on the Long Island Expedition, 10th December, 1777; exchanged, 10th April, 1778; 1st Lieutenant, 10th May, 1778; resigned 27th May, 1779.

Mumford, Isaac (R. I.). Adjutant of Varnum's Rhode Island Regiment, May, 1775; killed at the Siege of Boston, 27th August, 1775.

Mumford, Joseph (N. C.). Captain 1st North Carolina, 9th January, 1779; taken prisoner at Charleston, 12th May, 1780.

Mummey, Jacob (Pa). Ensign of Baxter's Pennsylvania Battalion of the Flying Camp, June, 1776; taken prisoner at Fort Washington, 16th November, 1776; exchanged 8th December, 1780.

Muncey, John (N. Y.). Lieutenant New York Militia, ——; killed at Moses Kill, 2d August, 1777.

Munday, William (N. Y.). Sergeant 1st New York, 1st July, 1775; Ensign, 10th August, 1776; 2d Lieutenant 2d New York, 21st November, 1776; wounded at Stillwater, 19th September, 1777; 1st Lieutenant, 10th October, 1777; Regimental Quartermaster, 5th May, 1778; dismissed 11th October, 1781. (Died 1830.)

Munford, William Green (Va). Colonel Deputy Commissary-General of Issues, 18th June, 1777, to ——.

Mungen, Jehiel (Mass). Lieutenant of Brewer's Massachusetts Regiment, May to December, 1775.

Munro, Edmund (Mass). Captain in Lexington Alarm, April, 1775; Regimental Quartermaster 13th Continental Infantry, 20th August to 31st December, 1776; Captain 15th Massachusetts, 1st January, 1777; killed at Monmouth, 28th June, 1778.

Munro, Josiah (N. H.). Ensign 16th Continental Infantry, 1st January, 1776; 2d Lieutenant 1st New Hampshire, 8th November, 1776; 1st Lieutenant, 20th September, 1777; Regimental Quartermaster, 23d August, 1778; Captain Lieutenant, 24th March, 1780; Captain, 5th July, 1780, and served to close of war. (Died 1801.)

Munson, Aeneas (Conn). Surgeon's Mate of Webb's Continental Regiment, March, 1779; transferred to 4th Connecticut, 1st January, 1781; transferred to 3d Connecticut, 1st January, 1783; retained in Swift's Connecticut Regiment, June, 1783, and served to November, 1783. (Died 16th June, 1826.)

Munson, John (N. J.). Colonel New Jersey Militia, 1776-1777.

Munson, Levi (Conn). Private in Lexington Alarm, April, 1775; served under Ethan Allen, and was taken prisoner at Montreal, 25th September, 1775; was sent to England, and exchanged in 1776; 2d Lieutenant 6th Connecticut, 1st January, 1777; resigned 8th September, 1780.

Munson, Theophilus (Conn). 1st Lieutenant 14th Continental Infantry, 1st January to 31st December, 1776; Captain 8th Connecticut, 1st January, 1777; transferred to 4th Connecticut, 1st January, 1781, and served to 3d June, 1783. (Died 30th March, 1795.)

Munson, William (Conn). 1st Lieutenant of Elmore's Continental Regiment, 15th April, 1776; 1st Lieutenant 2d Canadian (Hazen's) Regiment, 3d November, 1776; Captain, 9th January, 1778, and served to June, 1783.

Murdaugh, James (Va). Captain Virginia Militia, 1777-1780. (Died 1798.)

Murdock, Benjamin (Md). Ensign 7th Maryland, 17th April, 1777; 2d Lieutenant, 4th July, 1777; resigned 12th April, 1779.

Murdock, William (Md). Ensign 6th Maryland, 11th September, 1779; Lieutenant, 1st April, 1780; transferred to 2d Maryland, 1st January, 1781; resigned, April, 1782.

Murdock, William (—). Cornet of Cavalry Pulaski Legion in 1781.

Murfits, Henry (Pa). Lieutenant Pennsylvania Battalion of the Flying Camp, July, 1776; taken prisoner at Fort Washington, 16th November, 1776; exchanged 29th January, 1781.

Murfree, Hardy (N. C.). Captain 2d North Carolina, 1st September, 1775; Major, 1st February, 1777; Lieutenant-Colonel 1st North Carolina, 1st April, 1778, and served to July, 1782. (Died 6th April, 1809.)

Murnan, John Barnard de (France). Major Corps of Engineers, 13th January, 1779, to rank from 1st March, 1778, with pay from 1st February, 1778; Brevet Lieutenant-Colonel Continental Army, 15th September, 1783; resigned 3d February, 1784, and by the act of 3d February, 1784, it was resolved "That Congress entertain a due sense of Lieutenant-Colonel Murnan's abilities and services, and that the Secretary deliver him a copy of this act, as a testimony of their approbation of his conduct."

Murphy, Archibald (N. C.). Colonel North Carolina Militia in 1777. (Died 1817.)

Murphy, Daniel (N. H.). Lieutenant New Hampshire Militia in 1780.

Murphy, Maurice (S. C.). Captain South Carolina Militia in 1776.

Murran, William (Pa). Ensign 2d Pennsylvania, 19th May, 1779; Regimental Quartermaster, 8th August, 1779; 2d Lieutenant, 23d July, 1780; retired 1st January, 1781.

Murray, —— (—). Appointed Captain Sappers and Miners, 7th February, 1780, to rank from 2d August, 1779, and served to ——.

Murray, Alexander (Md). 2d Lieutenant of Smallwood's Maryland Regiment, 14th January, 1776; 1st Lieutenant, August, 1776; Captain 1st Maryland, 10th December, 1776; resigned 10th June, 1777, and joined the Navy. (Died 6th October, 1821.)

Murray, Francis (Pa). Captain Pennsylvania Musket Battalion, 15th March, 1776; taken prisoner at Long Island, 27th August, 1776; exchanged 9th December, 1776; Major Pennsylvania State Regiment, 2d May, 1777; regiment designated 13th Pennsylvania, 12th November, 1777; taken prisoner 21st February, 1778, while on his way home; exchanged 25th December, 1780; did not return to service. (Died 30th November, 1816.)

Murray, John (Pa). Ensign 6th Pennsylvania Battalion, 9th January,

1776; Captain of Miles' Pennsylvania Rifle Regiment, 7th March, 1776; Major Pennsylvania State Regiment, 18th March, 1777; regiment designated 13th Pennsylvania 12th November, 1777; transferred to 2d Pennsylvania, 1st July, 1778; Lieutenant-Colonel, 10th December, 1778; retired 17th January, 1781. (Died 3d February, 1798.)

Murray, John (R. I.). Chaplain to Rhode Island Regiments, 17th September to December, 1775. (Died 3d September, 1815.)

Murray, Seth (Mass). Captain of Woodbridge's Massachusetts Regiment, April to November, 1775; Colonel Massachusetts Militia in 1780. (Died 1795.)

Murray, William (N. C.). Ensign 4th North Carolina, 1st April, 1777, to ——.

Murry, Abraham (Va). 2d Lieutenant 14th Virginia, 10th March, 1777; 1st Lieutenant, 8th December, 1777, and served to ——.

Muse, Richard (Va). Ensign 15th Virginia, 25th November, 1776; 2d Lieutenant, 2d December, 1776; 1st Lieutenant, 20th March, 1777; regiment designated 11th Virginia, 14th September, 1778; resigned 14th May, 1779.

Muse, Walker (Md). Ensign of Smallwood's Maryland Regiment, 14th January, 1776; 2d Lieutenant, — May, 1776; taken prisoner at Long Island, 27th August, 1776; exchanged 8th December, 1776; 1st Lieutenant 1st Maryland, 10th December, 1776; Captain, 10th January, 1777; retained in Maryland Battalion in April, 1783; Brevet Major, 30th September, 1783, and served to 15th November, 1783.

Musser, George (Pa). Captain Pennsylvania Militia, 1776.

Mussey, Daniel (Mass). 1st Lieutenant of Mitchell's Regiment Massachusetts Militia on the Bagaduce Expedition, July to September, 1779. (Died 31st August, 1828.)

Muzzey, Robert (Mass). Ensign 13th Continental Infantry, 1st January to 31st December, 1776; 2d Lieutenant 2d Massachusetts, 1st January, 1777; resigned 30th April, 1782.

Myer, Christopher (Va). 2d Lieutenant 8th Virginia, 9th May, 1777; 1st Lieutenant, 22d November, 1777; transferred to 4th Virginia, 14th September, 1778; resigned 9th March, 1779.

Myer, Godfrey (Pa). Lieutenant of Baxter's Pennsylvania Battalion of the

Flying Camp; taken prisoner at Fort Washington, 16th November, 1776.

Myer, Henry (N. Y.). Ensign New York Militia, ——; prisoner of war, 13th April 1780, to 5th October, 1782; where taken not stated.

Myers, Jacob (N. Y.). Lieutenant New York Militia; killed at Johnson's Hall, 24th October, 1781.

Myers, Jacob (Pa). Ensign Pennsylvania Battalion of the Flynig Camp; taken prisoner at Fort Washington, 16th November, 1776.

Myers, Lawrence (Md). 2d Lieutenant 2d Canadian (Hazens) Regiment, 3d November, 1776; Lieutenant of Ottendorff's Battalion Armand's Corps, 3d March, 1777, and served to close of war. (Name also spelled Meyers and Mayers.)

Myrick, John (N. C.). Ensign 7th North Carolina, 28th November, 1776; Lieutenant, 11th December, 1776, to ——.

Myrick, Samuel (Mass). Private in Bond's Massachusetts Regiment, June to December, 1775; Sergeant in 25th Continental Infantry, January to December, 1776; Regimental Quartermaster 12th Massachusetts, 1st January, 1777; Ensign, 2t6h November, 1779; 2d Lieutenant, 5th September, 1780; transferred to 2d Massachusetts, 1st January, 1781, and served to 3d November, 1783.

Mytinger, Jacob (Pa). 1st Lieutenant of Von Heer's Independent Company of Light Dragoons, 1st August, 1778, and served to close of war; name !so spelled Mettinger. (Died 1793.)

N.

Nagel, George (Pa). Captain of Thompson's Pennsylvania Rifle Battalion, 25th June, 1775; Major 5th Pennsylvania Battalion, 5th January, 1776; Lieutenant-Colonel 9th Pennsylvania, 25th October, 1776, to rank from 21st August, 1776; Colonel 10th Pennsylvania, 7th February, 1777; retired 1st July, 1778.

Nagel, Peter (Pa). Captain Pennsylvania Militia, 1777-1778. (Died 1834.)

Nagle, Charles (Va). Adjutant 10th Virginia, 1st November, 1777, to ——. Retired 30th September, 1778.

Naglee, Samuel (N. J.). Ensign 2d New Jersey, 29th November, 1775; 2d Lieutenant, 29th November, 1776; resigned 8th April, 1780.

Nankley, Henry (Pa). 2d Lieutenant 5th Pennsylvania, 3d June, 1778, to ——.

Nasburgh, Peter I. (N. Y.). Lieutenant of Livingston's Regiment New York Militia in 1779.

Nash, Clement (N. C.). 1st Lieutenant 2d North Carolina, 3d May, 1776; resigned 1st February, 1777; Captain 3d Georgia, 10th April, 1777; was taken prisoner at Briar Creek, 3d March, 1779; exchanged ——; taken prisoner at Charleston, 12th May, 1780.

Nash, Francis (N. C.). Lieutenant-Colonel 1st North Carolina, 1st September, 1775; Colonel, 10th April, 1776; Brigadier-General Continental Army, 5th February, 1777; died 7th October, 1777, of wounds received at Germantown, 4th October, 1777.

Nash, Isaac (N. H.). Captain New Hampshire Militia; killed at Bennington, 16th August, 1777.

Nash, John (Va). Colonel Virginia Militia, 1779-1781.

Nash, Thomas (N. H.). Colonel New Hampshire Militia, 1776-1777.

Nash, William H. (Pa). 2d Lieutenant of Patton's Continental Regiment, 15th January, 1777; resigned 25th September, 1778.

Nasson, Joshua (Mass). Private in Scammon's Massachusetts Regiment, May to November, 1775; Corporal and Sergeant 18th Continental Infantry, 1st January to 31st December, 1776; Sergeant 12th Massachusetts, 1st February, 1777; Ensign, 1st November, 1777; resigned 31st August, 1780.

Nasson, Nathaniel (Mass). Sergeant in Scammon's Massachusetts Regiment, May to December, 1775, and in 7th Continental Infantry in 1776; 2d Lieutenant 1st Massachusetts, 1st January, 1777; 1st Lieutenant, 18th October, 1777; Brevet Captain, 30th September, 1783; served to 3d November, 1783. (Died.27th July, 1818.)

Nasson, Samuel (Mass). Regimental Quartermaster of Scammon's Massachusetts Regiment, May to December, 1775; Ensign and Regimental Quartermaster 7th Continental Infantry, 1st January to 31st December, 1776; Captain Massachusetts Militia in 1777.

Nay, Samuel (N. H.). Captain of Wingate's Regiment New Hampshire Militia in 1776.

Nazro, Nathaniel (Mass). Captain Lieutenant of Gridley's Regiment Massachusetts Artillery in 1775, and in

Craft's Regiment Massachusetts Artillery in 1776; Adjutant 15th Massachusetts, 12th August, 1777; resigned 17th November, 1778.

Neal, Andrew (N. C.). Lieutenant North Carolina Militia, 1776.

Neal, Ferdinand (Va). Corporal 1st Continental Dragoons, — July, 1777; Cornet of Lee's Battalion of Light Dragoons, 22d April, 1778; Lieutenant, 5th April, 1779; killed at Rocky Mount, 30th July, 1780.

Neal, James (Va). Captain 13th Virginia, 19th December, 1776; regiment designated 9th Virginia, 14th September, 1778; resigned 3d January, 1779.

Neal, Thomas (Ga). Colonel Georgia Militia; killed at Rocky Mount, 30th July, 1780.

Neal, William (N. C.). Lieutenant 9th North Carolina, 28th November, 1776, to ——; was a Captain North Carolina Militia at King's Mountain in October, 1780.

Neale, Henry (Md). 3d Lieutenant of Allen's Independent Maryland Company, 14th January to December, 1776; Captain 2d Maryland, 20th February, 1777; resigned 15th March, 1777.

Neale, Henry (N. C.). Ensign 1st North Carolina, 1st September, 1775; 2d Lieutenant, 4th January, 1776; 1st Lieutenant, 28th March, 1776; Captain, 5th February, 1777; resigned 3d April, 1777; name also spelled Neill.

Neely, Abraham (N. Y.). 1st Lieutenant of Malcolm's Continental Regiment, 25th March, 1777; wounded at Monmouth, 28th June, 1778; Captain, 10th October, 1778; transferred to Spencer's Regiment, 22d April, 1779; retired 1st January, 1781. (Died 24th February, 1822.)

Neely, Benjamin (Pa). Ensign 8th Pennsylvania, 9th August, 1776; 2d Lieutenant, 13th July, 1777; 1st Lieutenant, 4th October, 1777; retired 17th January, 1781.

Neely, William (Pa). Captain of Hart's Pennsylvania Battalion of the Flying Camp, July to December, 1776.

Neff, Rudolph (Pa). Captain of Lewis' Pennsylvania Battalion of the Flying Camp, July to December, 1776. (Died 1809.)

Neil, Daniel (N. J.) Captain Lieutenant Eastern Company New Jersey Artillery, 1st March, 1776; Captain, 9th May, 1776; killed at Princeton, 3d January, 1777.

Neil, John (S. C.). Lieutenant South Carolina Militia; killed at Hayes Station, South Carolina, 9th November, 1781.

Neill, Henry (Del). Major Delaware Battalion of the Flying Camp, July to December, 1776; Lieutenant-Colonel Delaware Militia in 1780 and 1781.

Neilson, Alexander (Md). 2d Lieutenant 1st Continental Artillery, 5th April, 1778; resigned 23d May, 1779.

Neilson, John (N. J.). Captain Company of Minute Men, July, 1775; Colonel Regiment of Minute Men, 31st August, 1775; Colonel New Jersey Militia Regiment, 1776 and 1777; Brigadier-General New Jersey Militia, 21st February, 1777; also Deputy Quartermaster-General of State to 1783. (Died 3d March, 1833.)

Nellis, George (N. Y.). Lieutenant New York Militia, ——; prisoner of war, 15th July, 1782, to 21st May, 1783; where taken not stated.

Nelson, Alexander (N. C.). Ensign 4th North Carolina, 1st July, 1777, to ——.

Nelson, Charles (N. H.). 2d Lieutenant of Bedels' Regiment New Hampshire Rangers, 17th June to December, 1775; Captain of Bedel's Regiment Vermont Militia, April, 1778, to April, 1779.

Nelson, Henry (Mass). Private in Lexington Alarm, April, 1775; Private in Read's Massachusetts Regiment, April to November, 1775; Sergeant 2d Massachusetts, 20th May, 1777; Quartermaster-Sergeant, 1st January, 1778; Ensign and Regimental Quartermaster, 1st March, 1778; Lieutenant, 15th March, 1782; transferred to 3d Massachusetts, 1st January, 1783; Regimental Paymaster, 1st April, 1783; retained in Jackson's Continental Regiment, November, 1783, and served to 20th June, 1784.

Nelson, John (Md). Sergeant of Gist's Continental Regiment, 7th March, 1777; Sergeant-Major, 1st January, 1778; 2d Lieutenant, 4th July, 1779; retired, 1st January, 1781. (Died — May, 1806.)

Nelson, John (N. J.). Captain, Colonel and Brigadier-General New Jersey Militia, 1775-1783. (Died 3d March, 1833.)

Nelson, John (N. C.). Captain 4th North Carolina, 16th April, 1776; Major 1st North Carolina, 3d February, 1778; taken prisoner at Charleston, 12th May, 1780; exchanged March, 1781; transferred to 1st North Carolina, February, 1782; retired 1st January, 1783.

Nelson, John (Pa). Captain Independent Pennsylvania Rifle Company, 30th January, 1776; Captain 9th Pennsylvania, 15th November, 1776; cashiered 15th May, 1777.

Nelson, John (Va). Captain Virginia Dragoons 19th June, 1776; assigned to 1st Continental Dragoons, January, 1777; resigned 12th February, 1777; Major Virginia State Regiment, 1779-1781.

Nelson, John (Va). Captain 7th Virginia, 28th October, 1776; retired 14th September, 1778. (Died 1827.)

Nelson, John (Va). Ensign 7th Virginia, 2d May, 1776; 2d Lieutenant, 28th December, 1776; 1st Lieutenant, 20th May, 1778; transferred to 5th Virginia, 14th September, 1778; was taken prisoner at Charleston, 12th May, 1780; exchanged November, 1780; Captain, 29th May, 1780; transferred to 6th Virginia, 12th February, 1781, and served to close of war.

Nelson, Roger (Md). 2d Lieutenant 5th Maryland, ——, 1779; 1st Lieutenant, 15th July, 1780; wounded and taken prisoner at Camden, 16th August, 1780; exchanged December, 1780; wounded at Guilford, 15th March, 1781; transferred to Baylor's Regiment Continental Dragoons, 9th November, 1782, and served to close of war. (Died 7th June, 1815.)

Nelson, Thomas (Va). 1st Lieutenant 3d Virginia, 8th March, 1776, to ——.

Nelson, Thomas, Jr. (Va). A signer of the Declaration of Independence; Captain 1st Virginia, 22d February, 1776; resigned 7th August, 1777; Commander of Virginia State forces, August, 1777, to 1782. By the act of 8th August, 1778, it was "Resolved, that the thanks of Congress be given to the Honorable General Nelson and the officers and gentlemen for their brave, generaus and patriotic efforts in the cause of their country." Was Governor of Virginia in 1781, and participated in the Siege of Yorktown. (Died 4th January, 1789.)

Nelson, William (Pa). 3d Lieutenant Pennsylvania Battalion of the Flying Camp, July to December, 1776.

Nelson, William (Va). Served as a private in a Virginia Company in 1775; Major 7th Virginia, 29th February, 1776; Lieutenant-Colonel, 7th October, 1776; resigned 25th October, 1777. (Died 8th March, 1813.)

Nelson, William (Va. 1st Lieutenant 3d Virginia, 18th March, 1776; died December, 1776.

Nesbit, Robert (Pa). Ensign 10th Pennsylvania, 15th September, 1780; transferred to 1st Pennsylvania, 17th January, 1781, and served to ——.

Nesmith, John (Mass). 2d Lieutenant of Jackson's Continental Regiment, 1st September, 1777; 1st Lieutenant, 16th July, 1777; resigned 25th October, 1779. (Died 1815.)

Nesmith, John (N. H.). Sergeant 1st New Hampshire, 23d April to December, 1775; Captain of Wingate's Regiment New Hampshire Militia, July to December, 1776.

Nestle, Peter (N. Y.). 2d Lieutenant 2d Continental Artillery, 1st January, 1777; 1st Lieutenant, 1st February, 1779; Captain Lieutenant, 20th September, 1781; retired 17th June, 1783.

Netherland, Benjamin (Ga). Lieutenant Georgia Regiment in 1779 and 1781.

Netherland, Thomas (Ga). Lieutenant Georgia Regiment in 1780.

Nettles, William (S. C.). Captain South Carolina Militia, 1779.

Neufville, Edward (S. C.). Lieutenant South Carolina Militia, 1779-1780.

Neufville, William (S. C.). Surgeon of a South Carolina Regiment in 1779 and 1780; taken prisoner at Charleston, 12th May, 1780; exchanged 14th June, 1781.

Neuville, Noirmont de la, Sr. (France). Inspector of the Army under General Gates, 14th May, 1778; Brevet Brigadier-General Continental Army, 14th August, 1778; retired 4th December, 1778, and permitted to return to France.

Neuville, Noirmont de la, Jr. (France). Aide-de-Camp to General Conway, 3d December, 1777, to 28th April, 1778; Deputy Inspector of the Army under General Gates, 14th May, 1778; Brevet Major Continental Army, 20th July, 1778; Brevet Lieutenant-Colonel, 18th October, 1779, and permitted to retire from the service.

Neville, George (Va). Cornet 1st Continental Dragoons, ——, 1780, to 29th November, 1782.

Neville, John (Md). 2d Lieutenant 4th Maryland Battalion of the Flying Camp, July 1776, to ——.

Neville, John (Va). Lieutenant-Colonel 12th Virginia, 12th November, 1776; Colonel 8th Virginia, 11th December, 1777; transferred to 4th Virginia, 14th September, 1778, and served to close of war; Brevet Brigadier-General, 30th September, 1783. (Died 29th July, 1803.)

..**Neville, Joseph** (Va). Brigadier-General Virginia Militia, ——. (Died 4th March, 1819.)

. **Neville, Presley** (Va). 1st Lieutenant 12th Virginia, 9th November, 1776; transferred to 8th Virginia, 14th September, 1778; Captain Lieutenant, 15th December, 1778; Captain, 10th May, 1779; Major and Aide-de-Camp to General Lafayette in 1778; Brevet Lieutenant-Colonel, 27th October, 1778; taken prisoner at Charleston 12th May, 1780; exchanged May, 1781. (Died 1st December, 1818.)

Nevins, David (Conn). Ensign 6th Connecticut, 1st May to 19th December, 1775; 1st Lieutenant 10th Continental Infantry, 1st January, 1776; Captain, 10th September to 31st December, 1776.

Nevins, Wm. (Mass). Sergeant of Prescott's Massachusetts Regiment, May to December, 1775; Ensign 7th Continental Infantry, 1st January to 31st December, 1776.

Nevius, Abraham (N. J.). Captain and Major New Jersey Militia, 1776-1777.

New, Anthony (Va). Colonel Virginia Militia, 1780-1781. (Died 2d March, 1833.)

Newark, Thomas (N. J.). Captain Lieutenant Western Company New Jersey Artillery, 1st March, 1776; resigned — October, 1776.

Newberry, Nicholas (Conn). Sergeant of Baldwin's Artillery Artificer Regiment, 1st February, 1777; Lieutenant, 12th November, 1779; resigned 5th March, 1781.

Newberry, Roger (Conn). Colonel Connecticut Militia, 1777-1778; Brigadier-General Connecticut Militia, 1781 to close of war.

Newbound, William (Pa). Sergeant 4th Continental Artillery, January, 1777; 3d Lieutenant, 1st April, 1777; died 14th September, 1778.

Newby, John (Pa). Ensign 3d Pennsylvania, 20th April, 1777; resigned 31st July, 1777.

Newcomb, Silas (N. J.). Colonel New Jersey Militia, 14th June, 1776; Colonel 1st New Jersey, 28th November, 1776; Brigadier-General New Jersey Militia, 15th March, 1777; resigned 4th December, 1777.

Newell, Ebenezer (Mass). Lieutenant of Phinney's Massachusetts Regiment, May to November, 1775.

Newell, Jonathan (Mass). Captain of Scammon's Massachusetts Regiment, May to December, 1775; Captain 7th Continental Infantry, 1st January to 31st December, 1776.

Newell, Samuel (Va). Lieutenant of Virginia Riflemen, ——; wounded at King's Mountain, 7th October, 1780; served subsequently as Captain Virginia Militia. (Died 21st September, 1841.)

Newell, Simeon (Conn). Sergeant 8th Connecticut, 11th July to 18th December, 1775; 2d Lieutenant 17th Continental Infantry, 1st January to 31st December, 1776. (Died 1813.)

Newhall, Eliphalet (Mass). Captain Lieutenant of Gridley's Regiment Massachusetts Artillery, May to December, 1775, and Captain of Knox's Regiment Continental Artillery, 10th December, 1775, to December, 1776.

Newhall, Ezra (Mass). Captain in Lexington Alarm, April, 1775; Captain of Mansfield's Massachusetts Regiment, May to December, 1775; Captain 27th Continental Infantry, 1st January to 31st December, 1776; Major 5th Massachusetts, 1st January, 1777, to rank from 1st November, 1776; Lieutenant-Colonel, 17th May, 1777; transferred to 4th Massachusetts, 1st January, 1783, and served to November, 1783; Brevet Colonel, 30th September, 1783. (Died 1798.)

Newhall, Thomas (Mass). 1st Lieutenant of Scammon's Massachusetts Regiment, May to November, 1775.

Newkirk, Charles (N. Y.). 1st Lieutenant 2d New York, 21st November, 1776; Regimental Adjutant, June, 1778, ʼo January, 1780.; Captain Lieutenant, 1st October, 1778; resigned 17th December, 1782. (Died November, 1822.)

Newman, Daniel (Ga). Surgeon in Hospital Department in 1778 and 1779.

Newman, Joseph (N. Y.). Lieutenant New York Militia, ——; prisoner of war, 2d March, 1780, to 21st May, 1783; where taken not stated.

Newman, Samuel (Mass). Ensign in Knox's Regiment Continental Artillery in 1776; Lieutenant in Lee's Additional Continental Regiment, 20th May, 1777; resigned December, 1778; served subsequently in United States Navy, ——; Lieutenant 2d United States Infantry, 4th March, 1791; killed 4th November, 1791, in action with Indians near Fort Recovery, Ohio.

Newman, Wm. (Pa). Captain Pennsylvania Militia; taken prisoner at Crooked Billet, 24th February, 1778.

Newman, Wingate (Pa). Commander of the Privateer Hancock in 1776; Captain Independent Company Pennsylvania Artillery, 2d December, 1776, to ——.

Newsom, Benjamin (S. C.). Was Captain 2d South Carolina in 1779; killed in action with Indians in Georgia in March, 1779.

Newton, Isaac (Mass). Captain Massachusetts Militia in 1780.

Newton, Joseph (Conn). 2d Lieutenant of Wadsworth's Connecticut State Regiment, June to December, 1776.

Newton, Seth (Mass). Captain Massachusetts Militia in 1778.

Neyle, Philip (S. C.). 2d Lieutenant 2d South Carolina, 17th June, 1775; 1st Lieutenant, ——, 1776; Aide-de-Camp to General Moultrie; killed at Charleston, 12th May, 1780.

Nice, John (Pa). Captain Pennsylvania Musket Battalion, 14th March, 1776; taken prisoner at Long Island, 27th August, 1776; exchanged 9th December, 1776, and transferred to Pennsylvania State Regiment; regiment designated 13th Pennsylvania, 12th November, 1777; transferred to 6th Pennsylvania, 1st July, 1778; transferred to 2d Pennsylvania, 17th January, 1781, and served to June, 1783. (Died 1806.)

Nicholas, George (Va). Captain 2d Virginia, 3d October, 1775; Major, 10th Virginia, 13th November. 1776; Lieutenant-Colonel 11th Virginia. 26th September, 1777; resigned 27th November, 1777.

Nicholas, Henry (Va). Cornet 1st Continental Dragoons in 1782.

Nicholas, John (Va). Ensign 2d Virginia, 24th October, 1775; 1st Lieutenant 9th Virginia, 14th February, 1776; Captain 1st Virginia State Regiment, 1st February, 1777, to January, 1780. (Died 1836.)

Nichols, Bella (Mass). Corporal in Greaton's Massachusetts Regiment, May to December, 1775; Sergeant of Stevens' Battalion Continental Artillery, 22d January, 1777, until appointed Ensign and Quartermastter of the Battalion, 11th July, 1778; transferred to 2d Continental Artillery in August, 1778; 1st Lieutenant, 1st March, 1779; resigned 7th April, 1780; name also spelled Bata Nichols. (Died 18th November, 1831.)

Nichols, Benjamin (Conn). Sergeant in the Lexington Alarm, April, 1775; Ensign 5th Connecticut, 1st May to 28th November, 1775; 1st Lieutenant in Swift's Connecticut Battalion, July to November, 1776.

Nichols, Caleb (Mass). 1st Lieutenant of Thomas' Massachusetts Regiment, May to November, 1775.

Nichols, Francis (Pa). 2d Lieutenant of Thompson's Pennsylvania Rifle Battalion, 25th June, 1775; taken prisoner at Quebec, 31st December, 1775; exchanged 10th October, 1776; Captain 9th Pennsylvania, 16th December, 1776; to rank from 1st January, 1776; Major, 7th February, 1777; resigned 12th May, 1779. (Died 13th February, 1812.)

Nichols, Isaac (Mass). Sergeant of Doolittle's Massachusetts Regiment, April to November, 1775; Ensign 4th Continental Infantry, 1st January to 31st December, 1776; 2d Lieutenant 6th Massachusetts, 1st January, 1777; Brigade Quartermaster, 3d July, 1778; retired 11th May, 1779. (Died 6th January, 1822.)

Nichols, Isaac (N. Y.). 1st Lieutenant 3d New York, 28th June, 1775; 1st Lieutenant of Nicholson's Continental Regiment, 21st April, 1776; 1st Lieutenant 1st Canadian (Livingston's) Regiment, 18th December, 1776; resigned 20th December, 1779. (Died 1835.)

Nichols, James (N. H.). 2d Lieutenant 2d New Hampshire, 2d April, 1777; 1st Lieutenant, 12th July, 1779; cashiered 12th July, 1780.

Nichols, Moses (N. H.). Colonel New Hampshire Militia, 1777-1782. (Died 23d May, 1790.)

Nichols, Nathaniel (Mass). 1st Lieutenant of Heath's Massachusetts Regiment, May to December, 1775; 1st Lieutenant 24th Continental Infantry, 1st January to 31st December, 1776.

Nichols, Noah (Mass). Captain of Stevens' Battalion of Artillery, 9th November, 1776; in 2d Continental Artillery, 1778; resigned 3d April, 1780. (Died 30th June, 1833.)

Nichols, Thomas (Mass). 1st Lieutenant of Sargent's Massachusetts Regiment, May to November, 1775.

Nichols, Wm. (Conn). Paymaster 7th Connecticut, 1st January, 1777; omitted August, 1778.

Nichols, Wm. (Pa). Ensign 6th Pennsylvania Battalion, 9th January, 1776; 2d Lieutenant, 23d June, 1776; Regimental Quartermaster, 1st August, 1776; Captain of Hartley's Continental Regiment, 12th January, 1777; resigned 11th March, 1778. (Died 1804.)

Nicholson, George Chadine (N. Y.). Major 1st Canadian (Livingston's) Regiment, 1st April, 1777; retired 1st January, 1781.

Nicholson, John, N .Y.). Captain 3d New York, 28th June to November, 1775; Colonel Continental Regiment, 8th March to November, 1776.

Nicholson, Robert (N. C.). 1st Lieutenant 10th North Carolina, 19th April, 1777; transferred to 1st North Carolina 1st June, 1778 resigned 25th June, 1779. (Died 21st May, 1819.)

Nicholson, Thomas (N. Y.). 2d Lieutenant of Nicholson's Continental Regiment, June to November, 1776; 1st Lieutenant 1st Canadian (Livingston's) Regiment, 18th December, 1776; resigned 3d May, 1779.

Nicodemus, Frederick (Md). Lieutenant Maryland Militia in 1776.

Nicola, Lewis (Pa). Colonel Invalid Regiment, 20th June, 1777, to close of war; Brevet Brigadier General, 30th September, 1783. (Died 9th August, 1807.)

Nicoll, Isaac (N. Y.). Colonel New York Militia in 1776.

Nicols, Edward (N. Y.). Lieutenant 1st New York in 1776.

Niebel, Gottlieb (Pa). Sergeant German Regiment, 15th July, 1776; Ensign, — August, 1777; died 11th October, 1777, of wounds received at Germantown, 4th October, 1777.

Niles, Jeremiah (Mass). Adjutant of Gridley's Regiment Massachusetts Artillery, June to December, 1775; Adjutant of Knox's Regiment Continental Artillery, 10th December, 1775;

Captain Lieutenant 3d Continental Artillery, 1st January, 1777; resigned 9th September, 1778. (Died 29th September, 1829.)

Niles, Nathaniel (Mass). Lieutenant in Lexington Alarm, April, 1775; 1st Lieutenant of Heath's Massachusetts Regiment, May to December, 1775; 1st Lieutenant 24th Continental Infantry, 1st January to 31st December, 1776.

Niles, Sands (Conn). Ensign of Ely's Connecticut Militia Regiment, June, 1777; taken prisoner on the expedition to Long Island, 10th December, 1777; exchanged 19th March, 1781.

Nimblett, Robert (Mass) 2d Lieutenant of Glover's Massachusetts Regiment, 19th May to December, 1775; 1st Lieutenant 14th Continental Infantry, 1st January to 31st December, 1776; Lieutenant of Baldwin's Artillery Artificer Regiment, 10th January, 1777; omitted April, 1779. (Died 9th October, 1819.)

Niseler, John Adams (Ga). 3d Lieutenant of Grimes, Independent Georgia Company, 4th November, 1775, to ——.

Niven, Daniel (N. Y.). 1st Lieutenant of Malcolm's Additional Continental Regiment, — October, 1776; Captain, 2d July, 1777; Captain Sappers and Miners, 25th April, 1779; Captain of Engineers, 4th March, 1780; to rank from 25th April, 1779, and served to close of war.

Nixon, Andrew (Del). Ensign Delaware Regiment, January, 1776, to January, 1777; Lieutenant and Adjutant 1st Continental Dragoons, 12th February, 1777; Captain, ——, 1780; retired — November, 1782.

Nixon, Charles (Del). Captain Delaware Militia in 1780.

Nixon, Henry (Va). Private 1st Continental Dragoons, January, 1777; Ensign 3d Virginia, 15th August, 1777, and served to ——.

Nixon, John (Mass). Captain Company of Minute Men at Lexington, 19th April, 1775; Colonel of a Massachusetts Regiment, 24th April to December, 1775; wounded at Bunker Hill, 17th June, 1775; Colonel 4th Continental Infantry, 1st January, 1776; Brigadier-General Continental Army, 9th August, 1776; resigned 12th September, 1780. (Died 24th March, 1815.)

Nixon, John (Pa). Colonel Pennsylvania Associaters, 1775-1777. (Died 31st December, 1808.)

Nixon, John (S C.). Lieutenant-Colonel South Carolina Militia at King's Mountain in October, 1780, and was killed soon after by Tories.

Nixon, Robert (N. J.). Captain and Major New Jersey Militia, 1776-1777.

Nixon, Thomas Jr. (Del). Ensign Delaware Regiment, 19th January to December, 1776.

Nixon, Thomas (Mass). Captain Company of Minute Men at Lexington, 19th April, 1775; Lieutenant-Colonel of Nixon's Massachusetts Regiment, 19th May, 1775; Lieutenant-Colonel 4th Continental Infantry, 1st January, 1776; Colonel, 9th August, 1776; Colonel 6th Massachusetts, 1st January, 1777, to rank from 9th August, 1776; retired 1st January, 1781. (Died 12th August, 1800.)

Nixon, Thomas (N. C.). Captain 8th North Carolina, 28th November, 1776; resigned 20th September, 1777.

Noble, Alexander (S. C.). Captain South Carolina Militia in 1775.

Noble, Caleb (Mass). Private and Corporal of Fellow's Massachusetts Regiment, April to December, 1775; Sergeant 21st Continental Infantry, January, 1776; Ensign 20th July to 31st December, 1776; 2d Lieutenant 9th Massachusetts, 1st January, 1777; retired 4th March, 1779.

Noble, David (Mass). Captain in Lexington Alarm, April, 1775; Captain in Paterson's Massachusetts Regiment, May to December, 1775; Captain 15th Continental Infantry, 1st January, 1776; died — July, 1776.

Noble, Enoch (Mass). Surgeon Massachusetts Militia in 1778, and Captain of Militia in 1780.

Noble, Jonathan (N. H.). 2d Lieutenant Green Mountain Boys, 27th July to December, 1775.

Noble, Morgan (Conn). 2d Lieutenant 4th Connecticut, 1st May to 18th December, 1775.

Noble, Nathan (Conn). Sergeant in the Lexington Alarm, April, 1775; Sergeant 2d Connecticut, 7th May to 17th December, 1775; Ensign 4th Connecticut, 1st January, 1777; 2d Lieutenant, 22d November, 1777; discharged 27th December, 1777.

Noble, Obadiah (N. H.). Chaplain New Hampshire Militia in 1777.

Noble, Oliver (Mass). Chaplain for 11th and 12th Continental Infantry, 1st January to 31st December, 1776. (Died 1792.)

Noble, Wm. (N. C.). Lieutenant 7th North Carolina, 28th November, 1776, to ——.

Noel, John (Va). Cadet 4th Virginia, 1st February, 1777; Ensign, 14th April, 1777; resigned 3d April, 1778.

Noel, N. (—). Hospital Surgeon, — September, 1777; Surgeon United States Navy, 1st September, 1778, to 1st October, 1780.

Norcross, Aaron (Pa). 1st Lieutenant 1st Pennsylvania, 19th December, 1776; Captain, 14th Septtember, 1777; Regimental Adjutant, 20th February, 1778; resigned 13th May, 1779.

Norcross, William (N. J.). Ensign 3d New Jersey, December, 1775; Regimental Quartermaster, 16th March, 1776; 2d Lieutenant, 29th November, 1776; resigned 1st November, 1777.

Norris, Aaron Burr (Pa). Ensign 11th Pennsylvania, 22d April, 1777; 2d Lieutenant, 25th October, 1777; resigned 15th February, 1778

Norris, Benjamin B. (Md). Captain and Major Maryland Militia, 1776-1778. (Died 1793.)

Norris, George (Pa). 1st Lieutenant of Flower's Artillery Artificer Regiment, 8th February, 1777; retired 1st May, 1781. (Died 9th April, 1819.)

Norris, Jacob (Md). Ensign 6th Maryland, 15th May, 1777; 2d Lieutenant, 10th October, 1777; 1st Lieutenant, 26th November, 1778; wounded and taken prisoner at Camden, 16th August, 1780; Captain, 4th November, 1782; prisoner on parole to close of war; Captain 9th United States Infantry, 8th January, 1799: honorably discharged 15th June, 1800.

Norris, James (N. H.). Captain 2d New Hampshire, 23d May to December, 1775; Captain 8th Continental Infantry, 1st January, 1776; Captain 2d New Hampshire, 8th November, 1776; wounded and taken prisoner at Hubbardton, 7th July, 1777; Major 3d New Hampshire, 20th September, 1777; resigned 5th July, 1780. (Died 1814.)

Norris, James (Pa). 1st Lieutenant 4th Continental Artillery, 1st April, 1777; resigned 16th October, 1779.

Norris, Martin (Va). Lieutenant Virginia Artillery in 1779-1780.

Norris, Thomas (Va). Ensign 5th Virginia, 22d March, 1776; 2d Lieutenant, 20th February, 1777; died 12th July, 1777.

North, Caleb (Pa). Captain 4th Pennsylvania Battalion, 5th January, 1776; Major 10th Pennsylvania, 12th March, 1777; Lieutenant-Colonel 11th Pennsylvania, 22d October, 1777; transferred to 9th Pennsylvania, 1st July, 1778; transferred to 2d Pennsylvania, 17th January, 1781; retired 1st January, 1783. (Died 7th November, 1840.)

North, Edward (—). Captain, ——; was a prisoner in 1780; when and where taken not stated.

North, George (Mass). Lieutenant-Colonel Deputy Commissary-General of Musters, 11th April, 1777; resigned 1st April, 1779.

North, George (Pa). Sergeant 5th Pennsylvania Battalion, 16th January, 1776; Ensign, 12th October, 1776; 2d Lieutenant 5th Pennsylvania, 1st January, 1777; 1st Lieutenant, 11th September, 1777; retired 1st January, 1783.

North, Noah (Pa). Regimental Quartermaster, 5th Pennsylvania, ——, 1777, to — October, 1778.

North, William (Mass). 2d Lieutenant of Knox's Regiment Continental Artillery, 9th May, 1776, to 1st January, 1777; Captain of Lee's Continental Regiment, 10th May, 1777; transferred to Spencer's Regiment, 22d April, 1779; Regiment designated 16th Massachusetts, 23d July, 1780; Aide-de-Camp to Baron Steuben, May, 1779, to November, 1783; was transferred to 9th Massachusetts, 1st January, 1781, and to 4th Massachusetts, 1st January, 1783; Brevet Major, 11th September, 1783; Maor and Inspector of the Army, 15th April, 1784, to 25th June, 1788; Brigadier-General, Adjutant-General, United States Army, 19th July, 1798; honorably discharged 15th June, 1800 (Died 4th January, 1836.)

North, William (Pa). Ensign of Lewis' Pennsylvania Battalion of the Flying Camp, July to December, 1776.

Northrup, Gamaliel (Conn). 2d Lieutenant 7th Connecticut, 6th July to 23d December, 1775; Captain of Silliman's Connecticut State Regiment, June to December, 1776.

Norton, Benjamin (Conn). Private in Lexington Alarm, April, 1775; Private 1st Connecticut, 1st May to 28th November, 1775; Sergeant 6th Connecticut, 6th March, 1777; Ensign, 29th April, 1779; transferred to 4th Connecticut, 1st January, 1781; 2d Lieutenant, 1st March, 1782; resigned — November, 1782.

Norton, Berich (Mass) Colonel Massachusetts Militia in 1776.

Norton, Charles (Conn). Ensign of Douglas' Connecticut State Regiment, June to December, 1776; Captain Connecticut Militia in 1777.

Norton, Elias (Conn). Surgeon's Mate of Wadsworth's Connecticut State Regiment, January to March, 1776.

Norton, Elisha (Mass) Ensign 1st Massachusetts, 2d April, 1781, to June, 1783.

Norton, Ichabod (Conn). Captain of Mott's Connecticut State Regiment, June to December, 1776.

Norton, John (Vt). Major Vermont Militia in 1776-1777.

Norton, Nathaniel (N. Y.). 2d Lieutenant 3d New York, 28th June, 1775; 1st Lieutenant 4th New York, 21st November, 1776; Captain, 23d April, 1778; retired 1st January, 1781. (Died 1837.)

Norton, Thomas (Pa). Sergeant 2d Pennsylvania, 4th January, 1777; Ensign, 12th March, 1777; 2d Lieutenant, 24th April, 1777; Regimental Quartermaster, 5th September, 1778, to August, 1779; 1st Lieutenant, 13th March, 1779; resigned 3d September, 1779.

Norvell, Lipscomb (Va). Private 5th Virginia, ——, 1777; Regimental Paymaster, 15th January, 1778; 2d Lieutenant, 9th September, 1778; transferred to 3d Virginia, 14th September, 1778; 1st Lieutenant, — February, 1780, and served to close of war. (Died 1843.)

Norwood, Edward (Md). Captain Maryland Battalion of the Flying Camp, July to December, 1776; Captain 4th Maryland, 10th December, 1776; dismissed 30th September, 1778.

Nottingham, William (N. Y.). Private and Sergeant 1st New York, June, 1775, to November, 1776; Ensign 2d New York, 21st November, 1776; resigned 4th May, 1779; Captain New York Militia in 1780.

Nowell, Jonathan (Mass). Captain of Scammon's Massachusetts Regiment, May to December, 1775; Captain 7th

Continental Infantry, 1st January to 31st December, 1776. (Died 5th January, 1821.)

Nowell, Richard (Va). Sergeant 3d Continental Dragoons, February, 1777; 2d Lieutenant, ——, 1781; served to ——. (Died 17th January, 1800.)

Nowell, Thomas (Mass). 1st Lieutenant of Scammon's Massachusetts Regiment, May to December, 1775; 1st Lieutenant 7th Continental Infantry, 1st January to 31st December, 1776.

Nowell, Zachariah (Mass). Private in Phinney's Massachusetts Regiment, May to December, 1775; Sergeant 21st Continental Infantry, February to December, 1776; Sergeant 11th Massachusetts, 24th December, 1776, to 24th December, 1779; Ensign 15th Massachusetts, 26th September, 1780 2d Lieutenant, 27th October, 1780; transferred to 10th Massachusetts, 1st January, 1781; retired 1st January, 1783.

Nowland, Thomas (Md). 1st Lieutenant 1st Maryland Battalion of the Flying Camp, June, 1776, to ——.

Noyes, John (Conn). Surgeon's Mate 4th Massachusetts, 22d October, 1777; Surgeon 1st Connecticut, 1st November, 1779; transferred to 4th Connecticut, 1st January, 1781; retained in Swift's Connecticut Regiment, 3d June, 1783, and served to 3d November, 1783. (Died 11th July, 1808)

Noyes, John (Mass). 2d Lieutenant of Gerrish's Massachusetts Regiment, 19th May to December, 1775; 2d Lieutenant 26th Continental Infantry, 1st January to 31st December, 1776.

Noyes, Joseph (Mass). Private in Lexington Alarm, April, 1775; Corporal in Gerrish's Massachusetts Regiment, April to November, 1775; Sergeant 26th Continental Infantry, January to December, 1776; 2d Lieutenant 9th Massachusetts, 1st January, 1777; retired 1st January, 1781. (Died 28th June, 1824.)

Noyes, Joseph (R. I.). Colonel Rhode Island Militia, 1776-1780.

Noyes, Samuel (Mass). Captain of Phinney's Massachusetts Regiment, May to November, 1775.

Noyes, Thomas (R. I.). Ensign of Babcock's Rhode Island Regiment, 15th January, 1776; Lieutenant of Lippitt's Rhode Island State Regiment, 19th August, 1776; 1st Lieutenant 1st Rhode Island, 1st January, 1777, and served to ——.

Noyes, Wadleigh (Mass). Sergeant in Lexington Alarm, April, 1775; Sergeant in Gerrish's Massachusetts Regiment, April to November, 1775; Ensign 26th Continental Infantry, 1st January to 31st December, 1776; 1st Lieutenant 9th Massachusetts, 1st January, 1777; died 27th October, 1777, of wounds received at Saratoga, 7th October, 1777

Nute, James (N. H.). Captain New Hampshire Militia, 1779-1780.

Nute, Samuel (N. H.). Ensign 8th Continental Infantry, 1st January, 1776; 2d Lieutenant 2d New Hampshire, 8th November, 1776; resigned 16th September, 1777. (Died 21st March, 1828.)

Nuthall, Nathaniel (N. C.). Ensign 9th North Carolina, 20th May, 1777; Adjutant, 26th May, 1777; transferred to 3d North Carolina, 1st June, 1778; dismissed 31st October, 1778.

Nutting, John (Mass). Captain in Lexington Alarm, April, 1775; Captain of Prescott's Massachusetts Regiment, May to December, 1775; Captain 7th Continental Infantry, 1st January to 31st December, 1776; Captain Massachusetts Militia, 1777-1779. (Died 1816.)

Nye, Benjamin (Mass). Captain massachusetts Militia in 1776.

Nye, Stephen (Mass). Lieutenant 14th Massachusetts, 1st January, 1777; resigned 29th November, 1777.

O.

Oakes, Josiah (Mass). 2d Lieutenant of Heath's Massachusetts Regiment, May to December, 1775.

Oakley, Elijah (N. Y.). 2d Lieutenant 1st New York, July, 1775; cashiered 10th June, 1776.

Oakley, John (Pa). Ensign Pennsylvania Militia; was a prisoner in 1780; when and where taken not shown.

Oakley, Miles (N. Y.). 2d Lieutenant 4th New York, 28th June, 1775, to January, 1776.

Oates, —— (S. C.) Lieutenant South Carolina Militia; killed at Cockspur 4th March, 1776.

Oates, James (Pa). Ensign 3d Pennsylvania, 11h November, 1776; and served to ——.

O'Brian, Thomas (Conn). 2d Lieutenant 8th Connecticut, 1st January, 1777; resigned 24th December, 1777.

Odell, John (Conn). Sergeant in the Lexington Alarm, April, 1775; Ensign 7th Connecticut, 6th July to 23d December, 1775; 2d Lieutenant 5th Connecticut, 1st January, 1777; resigned 15th December, 1777; served subsequently as Captain Connecticut Militia. (Died 26th October, 1835.)

Odingsell, Benjamin (Ga). 1st Lieutenant 1st Georgia, 7th January, 1776, and served to ——.

Odlum, Digby (N. Y.). 1st Lieutenant 1st New York, 28th June to 28th November, 1775; 1st Lieutenant of Nicholson's Continental Regiment, March to December, 1776.

Odom, Daniel (S. C.). Captain South Carolina Militia in 1779.

Ogden, Aaron (N. J.). Paymaster New Jersey, 8th December, 1775, to November, 1776; 1st Lieutenant 1st New Jersey, 29th November, 1776; Regimental Paymaster, 1st February, 1777, 7th March, 1778; Brigade Major to Maxwell's Brigade, 7th March, 1778, to July, 1780; Captain 1st New Jersey, 2d February, 1779; wounded at Yorktown 14th October, 1781, and served to close of war; Lieutenant-Colonel 11th United States Infantry, 8th January, 1799; honorably discharged 15th June, 1800. (Died 19th April, 1839.)

Ogden, Abraham (N. J.). Captain, Major and Lieutenant-Colonel New Jersey Militia, 1776-1779.

Ogden, Barney (N. J.). Ensign of Spencer's Additional Continental Regiment, 8th February, 1777; Lieutenant, 16th September, 1777; retired 12th May, 1779. (Died 4th October, 1823.)

Ogden, Matthias (N. J.). Served as a Brigade Major in the Expedition to Canada, and was wounded at Quebec, 31st December, 1775; Lieutenant-Colonel 1st New Jersey, 7th March, 1776; Colonel 1st January, 1777; taken prisoner at Elizabethtown, N. J., 5th October, 1780; exchanged April, 1781; granted leave 21st April, 1783, to visit Europe and did not return to the army; Brevet Brigadier-General, 30th September, 1783. (Died 21st March, 1791.)

Ogden, Moses (N. J.). Private of Spencer's Additional Continental Regiment, 20th March, 1777; Sergeant, 1st October, 1777; Ensign, 12th May, 1779; killed at Elizabethtown, 6th June, 1780.

Ogden, Nathaniel (N. J.). Sergeant of Spencer's Continental Regiment, 2d

March, 1777 Regimental Quartermaster, 1st October, 1777; retired 30th April, 1779. (Died 1809.)

Ogier, George (S. C.). 2d Lieutenant 2d South Carolina, ——, 1777; 1st Lieutenant, 14th August, 1779; taken prisoner at Charleston, 12th May, 1780.

Ogier, Lewis (S. C.). Lieutenant South Carolina Militia, 1779-1780. Died 1780.

Ogilby, James (Md). 2d Lieutenant Maryland Battalion of the Flying Camp, July to December, 1776.

Ogilby, John (Va). 2d Lieutenant 2d Virginia, 8th March, 1776; 1st Lieutenant, 28th September, 1776; resigned 21st January, 1778. (Died 1809.)

Ogilby, William (Va). 1st Lieutenant 2d Virginia, 25th September, 1776; retired 14th September, 1778.

Olgivie, John (Md). Captain Maryland Battalion of the Flying Camp, July to December, 1776.

Ogle, James (Md). Captain Maryland Militia, 1776-1777.

O'Hara, Henry (N. Y.). Captain New York Militia in 1775.

O'Hara, Henry (Pa). Captain 2d Canadian (Hazen's) Regiment, 3d November, 1776; resigned 20th September, 1777.

O'Hara, James (Pa). Brigadier-General Pennsylvania Militia, 1781-1782; Quartermaster-General United States Army, 19th April, 1792; resigned 1st May, 1796. (Died 21st December, 1819.)

Olcott, Peter (Vt). Colonel and Brigadier General Vermont Militia, 1777-1782.

Olcutt, Hezekiah (Conn). Sergeant of Baldwin's Artificer Regiment, 1st October, 1777; 2d Lieutenant, 12th November, 1779, and served to March, 1781.

Old, John (Pa). Captain Pennsylvania Battalion of the Flying Camp, July to December, 1776.

Old, William (Pa). Ensign 3d Pennsylvania Battalion, 8th January, 1776; taken prisoner at Fort Washington 16th November, 1776.

Oldenbruck, Daniel (Pa). Captain Pennsylvania Battalion of the Flying Camp, July to December, 1776.

Oldham, Conway (Va). 2d Lieutenant 12th Virginia, 9th November, 1776; 1st Lieutenant, 2d April, 1777; regiment designated 8th Virginia, 14th September, 1778; Captain, ——, 1780; killed at Eutaw Springs, 8th September, 1781.

Oldham, Edward (Md). 1st Lieutenant Maryland Battalion of the Flying Camp, July to December, 1776; 1st Lieutenant 4th Maryland, 10th December, 1776; Captain, 20th May, 1777; transferred to 5th Maryland, 1st January, 1781; transferred to 1st Maryland, 1st January, 1783; retained in Maryland Battalion, April, 1783, and served to 3d November, 1783; Brevet Major, 30th September, 1783.

Oldham, George (Va). 2d Lieutenant 9th Virginia, 13th March, 1776; 1st Lieutenant, 22d July, 1776; resigned 6th August, 1778.

Oldham, John (N. C.). Captain North Carolina Militia at Guilford in March, 1781. (Died 1831.)

Oldham, William (Pa). 1st Lieutenant of Nelson's Independent Rifle Company, 30th January, 1776; Captain, 15th December, 1776; transferred to 5th Pennsylvania, 24th March, 1777; resigned 9th January, 1779; Lieutenant-Colonel Kentucky Militia; killed at St. Clair's Defeat, near Fort Recovery, Ohio, 4th November, 1791.

Olendorf, Christian (Md). 2d Lieutenant Maryland Battalion of the Flying Camp, July, 1776; taken prisoner at Fort Washington, 16th November, 1776.

Olin, Gideon (Vt). Major Vermont Militia, 1777-1778. (Died 1823).

Oline, Benjamin (N. Y.). Lieutenant New York Militia; was a prisoner; when and where taken not stated.

Oliphant, David (S. C.). Director General of Hospitals in South Carolina, 22d March, 1780; taken prisoner at Charleston, 12th May, 1780; exchanged 9th November, 1780, and served to close of war.

Oliphant, James (N. J.). Captain New Jersey Militia, 1776-1777.

Oliphant, William (S. C.). 1st Lieutenant 2d South Carolina, 17th June, 1775; Captain, —— -, 1776; resigned 21st October, 1777.

Oliver, Alexander (Mass). Corporal of Brewer's Massachusetts Regiment, July to December, 1775; Regimental Quartermaster of Baldwin's Artillery Artificer Regiment, 25th June to December, 1777; Sergeant 5th Massachu-

setts, 29th June, 1779; Ensign, 19th October, 1781, and served to June, 1783.

Oliver, Andrew (Conn). Surgeon's Mate 19th Continental Infantry, 1st January, 1776, to ——.

Oliver, Drury (Va). 1st Lieutenant 14th Virginia, 10th March, 1777; regiment designated 10th Virginia, 14th September, 1778; resigned 7th May, 1779.

Oliver, John (N. C.). Ensign 2d North Carolina, 1st September, 1775, to ——.

Oliver, Nathaniel (Mass). Surgeon's Mate of Mansfield's Massachusetts Regiment, May to November, 1775; Surgeon's Mate 27th Continental Infantry, 1st January to 31st December, 1776.

Oliver, Richard (N. Y.). 2d Lieutenant of Malcolm's Continental Regiment, 11th March, 1777; 1st Lieutenant, 12th October, 1777; transferred to Spencer's Regiment, 22d April, 1779; retired 1st January, 1781.

Oliver, Robert (Mass). Lieutenant Company of Minute Men in April, 1775; Captain of Doolittle's Massachusetts Regiment, 12th June to December, 1775; Captain 2d Continental Infantry, 1st January to 31st December, 1776; Captain 3d Massachusetts, 1st January, 1777; Major, 1st November, 1777; transferred to 2d Massachusetts, 1st January, 1783; Brevet Lieutenant-Colonel, 30th September, 1783; served to 3d November, 1783. (Died May, 1810.)

Oliver, William (Mass). 2d Lieutenant of Gerrish's Massachusetts Regiment, 19th May to December, 1775. (Died 22d June, 1831.)

Oliver, William (N. J.). Lieutenant New Jersey Militia, ——; wounded at Rahway Meadow, 26th June, 1781.

Oliver, William (Va). Captain Lieutenant of a Virginia State Regiment, 1779 to 1780.

Olivia, Lawrence (Canada). 1st Lieutenant 2d Canadian (Hazen's) Regiment, 1st November, 1776; Captain, 8th April, 1777; Major, 1st May, 1782, and served to June, 1783.

Olmstead, Joseph (Mass). 2d Lieutenant of Steven's Battalion Continental Artillery, 9th November, 1776; resigned 15th December, 1777.

Olmsted, Aaron (Conn). Private in Lexington Alarm, April, 1775; Sergeant 4th Connecticut, 22d May, 1775; Regimental Adjutant, 10th July to December, 1775.

Olmsted, Ebenezer (Conn). Sergeant 5th Connecticut, 8th May to 13th December, 1775; Ensign of Silliman's Connecticut State Regiment, June to December, 1776; 2d Lieutenant 5th Connecticut, 1st January, 1777; resigned 15th December, 1777. (Died 1801.)

Olmsted, James (Conn). Sergeant 8th Connecticut, 2d March, 1777; Ensign, 24th December, 1777; 2d Lieutenant, 24th January, 1780; transferred to 5th Connecticut, 1st January, 1781; resigned 14th August, 1782. (Died 1811.)

Olmsted, James (Conn). Lieutenant of Baldwin's Artillery Artificer Regiment, 1st December, 1776; resigned 15th December, 1777.

Olney, Christopher (R. I.). Captain 2d Rhode Island, 3d May to December, 1775; served subsequently as Lieutenant-Colonel and Colonel Rhode Island Militia.

Olney, Coggeshall (R. I.). 1st Lieutenant 2d Rhode Island, 3d May to December, 1775; Captain 11th Continental Infantry, 1st January to 31st December, 1776; Captain 2d Rhode Island, 1st January, 1777; retained in Olney's Rhode Island Battalion, 14th May 1781; Major, 25th August, 1781, and served to 17th March, 1783.

Olney, Esnor (R. I.). Captain Rhode Island Militia, 1776-1777.

Olney, Ezekiel (—). Ensign Rhode Island Militia, 1778.

Olney, Jeremiah (R. I.). Captain 2d Rhode Island, 3d May to December, 1775; Captain 11th Continental Infantry, 1st January to 31st December, 1776; Lieutenant-Colonel 2d Rhode Island, 13th January, 1777; transferred to 1st Rhode Island, 1st January, 1781; Lieutenant-Colonel Commandant Rhode Island Battalion, 14th May, 1781; served to close of war; Colonel, 30th September, 1783. (Died 10th November, 1812) (The 1st Rhode Island Regiment after May, 1781, was also known as Olney's Rhode Island Battalion.)

Olney, Job (R. I.). Captain in Babcock's Rhode Island State Regiment, 15th January to December, 1776.

Olney, Nathan· (R. I.). Ensign 11th Continental Infantry, 1st January,

1776; 2d Lieutenant, 10th August to 31st December, 1776.

Olney, Stephen (R. I.). Ensign 2d Rhode Island, 3d May to December, 1775; 1st Lieutenant 11th Continental Infantry, 1st January to 31st December, 1776; 1st Lieutenant 2d Rhode Island, 1st January, 1777; Captain, 11th February, 1777; wounded at Springfield, 23d June, 1780; retained in Olney's Rhode Island Battalion, 14th May, 1781; wounded at Yorktown, 14th October, 1781; resigned 17th March, 1782. (Died 23d November, 1832.)

O'Neal, Charles (N. C.). Ensign 3d North Carolina, 18th April, 1777; 2d Lieutenant, 20th July, 1777; retired 1st July, 1778.

O'Neal, Francis (Pa). Surgeon 10th Pennsylvania, 1st September, 1777; dismissed 10th October, 1779.

O'Neill, Ferdinand (France). Cornet of Lee's Battalion of Light Dragoons, 22d April, 1777; Lieutenant, 5th September, 1779; Captain, — October, 1780, and served to close of war. Name also spelled O'Neal.

O'Neill, Henry (Pa). Ensign 9th Pennsylvania, ——, 1777; resigned 1st November, 1777.

Orcutt, Solomon (Conn). 2d Lieutenant 8th Connecticut, 6th July to 10th December, 1775; 1st Lieutenant 17th Continental Infantry, 1st January, 1776; wounded and taken prisoner at Long Island, 27th August, 1776. (Died 26th February, 1826.)

Orcutt, William (Conn). Lieutenant-Colonel Connecticut Militia; dismissed 10th September, 1778.

Orendorff, Christian (Md). 1st Lieutenant Maryland Battalion of the Flying Camp, July, 1776; taken prisoner at Fort Washington, 16th November, 1776; 1st Lieutenant 6th Maryland, 10th December, 1776; Captain, 1st April, 1778; transferred to 1st Maryland, 1st January, 1781, and served to April, 1783.

Orne, Azor (Mass). Major-General Massachusetts Militia in 1776. (Died 6th June, 1796.)

Orne, Joshua (Mass). Private in Lexington Alarm, April, 1775; 2d Lieutenant of Glover's Massachusetts Regiment, 19th April to December, 1775; 1st Lieutenant 14th Continental Infantry, 1st January to 31st December, 1776; Captain of Lee's Continental

Regiment, 10th January, 1777; resigned 1st October, 1778.

Orr, Alexander (Mass). Sergeant 6th Continental Infantry, January, 1776; Ensign, 12th September, 1776; 1st Lieutenant 1st Massachusetts, 1st January, 1777; resigned — July, 1780. (Died 27th January, 1832.)

Orr, James (S. C.). Surgeon 6th South Carolina, 1778-1780.

Orr, John (N. J.). 2d Lieutenant of Spencer's Additional Continental Regiment, 23d February, 1777; severely wounded at Bennington, 16th August, 1777; 1st Lieutenant, 10th October, 1778; retired 1st January, 1781. (Died 23d December, 1822.)

Orr, Robert (—). Captain, ——; was a prisoner in 1782; no further record of him.

Orr, William (Pa). Ensign 10th Pennsylvania, 4th December, 1776; 2d Lieutenant, 17th October, 1777; cashiered 16th April, 1778.

Orrell, Thomas (N. C.). Ensign 10th North Carolina, 14th March, 1778; retired 1st June, 1778.

Osborn, Alexander (N. C.). Colonel North Carolina Militia, 1775-1776. Died 1776.

Osborn, John (Conn). Drummer in 7th Connecticut, 10th July to 10th December, 1775; 2d Lieutenant of Baldwin's Artillery Artificer Regiment, 1st November, 1777; resigned 4th October, 1778. (Died 30th May, 1825.)

Osborn, John (Pa). Lieutenant Pennsylvania Militia; taken prisoner at his home, 14th February, 1778.

Osborn, Samuel (Conn). Ensign 1st Connecticut, 1st May to 10th December, 1775.

Osborn, Stephen (Conn). 1st Lieutenant of Baldwin's Artillery Artificer Regiment, 26th July, 1777; Captain, 1st May, 1778; resigned 31st May, 1779.

Osgood, David (N. H.). Chaplain 1st New Hampshire, 23d May to December, 1775.

Osgood, James (N. H.). Captain of Bedel's Regiment New Hampshire Rangers, 6th July to December, 1775; Captain of Bedel's New Hampshire Rangers, 22d January to October, 1776. (Died 1816.)

Osgood, Kendall (Mass). Surgeon's Mate 8th Massachusetts, 1st January, 1777; resigned 22d October, 1777.

Osgood, Samuel (Mass). Captain in Lexington Alarm, April, 1775; Major and Aide-de-Camp to General Ward, 20th July, 1775, to 23d April, 1776. (Died 12th August, 1813.)

Osmon, Benajah (N. J.). Regimental Quartermaster 2d New Jersey, 1st January, 1777; 2d Lieutenant, 12th September, 1778; taken prisoner at Charleston 24th April, 1780; 1st Lieutenant, 1st January, 1781, and served to April, 1783.

Osterhout, John (N. Y.). Captain New York Militia in 1775.

Ostrander, Arendt (N. Y.). Lieutenant and Captain New York Militia, 1775-1776.

Ostrander, John (N. Y.). Ensign 4th New York, June, 1776; 2d Lieutenant 1st New York, 21st November, 1776; 1st Lieutenant 1st Canadian (Livingston's) Regiment, 1st February, 1777; resigned 16th January, 1779; subsequently served as Lieutenant and Adjutant of New York Levies in 1780 and 1781.

Ostrander, Thomas (N. Y.). 2d Lieutenant in Swartwout's New York Militia Regiment, July, 1776; 2d Lieutenant 3d New York, 21st November, 1776; omitted May, 1778; served subsequently as Lieutenant in New York Levies.

Oswald, Eleazer (Conn). Private in the Lexington Alarm, April, 1775; served as a volunteer in the Expedition to Canada, and was taken prisoner at Quebec, 31st December, 1775; exchanged 10th January, 1777; Lieutenant-Colonel 2d Continental Artillery, 1st January, 1777; resigned 28th June, 1778. (Died 1st October, 1795.)

Oswald, William (S. C.). Lieutenant South Carolina Militia in 1776.

Otis, James (Mass). Adjutant 2d Continental Infantry, 1st January to 31st December, 1776; Ensign of Jackson's Additional Continental Regiment, 14th May, 1777; retired 23d April, 1779.

Otis, James (Pa). 2d Lieutenant 3d Pennsylvania, 1st April, 1777; resigned 31st May, 1777.

Ott, Abraham (S. C.). Lieutenant South Carolina Militia in 1776.

Ott, Adam (Pa). 2d Lieutenant of Nelson's Independent Pennsylvania Rifle Company, 30th January, 1776;

1st Lieutenant 5th Pennsylvania, 24th March, 1777; resigned 20th April, 1777.

Ottendorff, Nicholas Dietrich Baron de (—). Brevet Captain Continental Army, 8th November, 1776; Major of a Battalion of three companies raised in Pennsylvania, to rank from 5th December, 1776; battalion was merged into Armand's Partisan Corps, October, 1780; served to close of war.

Otterson, Samuel (S. C.). Lieutenant in 1776; Captain in 1778; Major South Carolina Militia in 1782.

Otto, Bodo (N. J.). Colonel New Jersey Militia, 1777-1778; Hospital Physician and Surgeon, 6th October, 1780; died 26th January, 1782.

Otto, Frederick (Pa.) Surgeon of Hospital Department, 6th July, 1776, to 1st August, 1780

Oury, Wendel (Pa). Captain 8th Pennsylvania, 9th August, 1776; resigned 11th October, 1777.

Ousby, Thomas (S. C.). Private, Sergeant, and Quartermaster-Sergeant 4th South Carolina, July, 1775, to June, 1779; 2d Lieutenant and Regimental Quartermaster, 15th April, 1780; taken prisoner at Charleston 12th May, 1780; prisoner to close of war; name also spelled Ousley.

Ousley William (Va). Ensign 3d Virginia, 9th February, 1776; resigned — May, 1776; name also spelled Ouby.

Outlaw, Edward (N. C.). Ensign 6th North Carolina, 16th April, 1776, to —.

Outwater, John (N. J.). Captain New Jersey Militia, 1780-1781.

Overstreet, John (Va). Cadet 4th Virginia, February to December, 1777; Captain Virginia Militia, 1780-1781.

Overton, James (Va). Ensign of Taylor's Regiment Virginia Convention Guards, January, 1779 to 1781.

Overton, John (Va). 1st Lieutenant 14th Virginia, 10th March, 1777; Captain, 4th October, 1777; regiment designated 10th Virginia, 14th September, 1778; transferred to 1st Virginia, 12th February, 1781; retired 1st January, 1783.

Overton, Thomas (Va). 2d Lieutenant 9th Virginia, 14th August, 1776; 1st Lieutenant, 9th March, 1778; resigned 22d July 1778; Lieutenant and Adjutant 4th Continental Dragoons, 1st

July, 1779; Captain, 24th April, 1781, and served to close of war.

Owen, —— (S. C.). Captain South Carolina Militia; killed at Hayes' Station, S. C., 9th November, 1781.

Owen, Caleb (Vt). Lieutenant Vermont Militia in 1777 and 1778.

Owen, Stephen (N. C.). Ensign 8th North Carolina, January, 1777; Lieutenant, 15th August, 1777; retired 1st June, 1778.

Owen, Thomas (S. C.) Captain South Carolina Militia in 1782.

Owens, Barnaby (N. Y.). 2d Lieutenant 2d New York, 25th November, 1775, to November, 1776; Adjutant 4th Pennsylvania, 2d May, 1777; 2d Lieutenant 8th Pennsylvania, 13th July, 1777, and served to —.

Owens, John (N. C.). Lieutenant 6th North Carolina, 7th May, 1776, to —.

Ozier, George.—See **Ogier.**

P.

Paca, Aquila (Md). Captain 2d Maryland Battalion of the Flying Camp, July, 1776, to December, 1776.

Paca, William (Md). A signer of the Declaration of Independence. Died 1799.

Packard, Isaac (Mass). Corporal and Sergeant of Gridley's Regiment Massachusetts Artillery, May to November, 1775; 1st Lieutenant of Knox's Regiment Continental Artillery, 10th December, 1775, to November, 1776.

Packard, John (Mass). Lieutenant in Lexington Alarm, April, 1775; Captain of Brewer's Massachusetts Regiment, May to December, 1775.

Packard, Rhodes (R. I.). 2d Lieutenant of Elliott's Regiment Rhode Island State Artillery, 19th August, 1776; 1st Lieuenant, 12th December, 1776, and served to May, 1777.

Paddock, Isaac (N. Y.). 2d Lieutenant 4th New York, 28th June, 1775; 1st Lieutenant, August, 1775, to January, 1776; Lieutenant New York Militia in 1777

Paddock, Jonathan (N. Y.). Major New York Militia, 1779-1780.

Padelford, Philip (R. I.). Surgeon Rhode Island Militia in 1778; served subsequently in the Navy.

Page, Carter (Va). 1st Lieutenant 3d Continental Dragoons, 8th January, 1777; Captain, 10th April, 1778; Aide-de-Camp to General Lafayette, June to November, 1781; served to close of war. (Died April, 1825.)

Page, David (N. H.). Lieutenant and Captain New Hampshire Militia, 1775-1777.

Page, Enoch (N. H.). Captain New Hampshire Militia, 1777-1778.

Page, Jeremiah (Mass). Captain in Lexington Alarm, April, 1775; Lieutenant-Colonel Massachusetts Militia in 1776. (Died 1806.)

Page, Jesse (N. H.). Captain New Hampshire Militia, 1777 1778.

Page, Moses (N. H.). Sergeant 3d New Hampshire, 16th March, 1777; Ensign, 1st May, 1779; transferred to 2d New Hampshire, 1st January, 1781; Lieutenant, 13th September, 1781; retained in New Hampshire Battalion, 21st March, 1782, and served to close of war. (Died 5th October, 1832.)

Page, Peter (Mass). Ensign of Scammon's Massachusetts Regiment, May to December, 1775; 2d Lieutenant 24th Continental Infantry, 1st January to 31st December, 1776; 1st Lieutenant 13th Massachusetts, 1st January, 1777; Captain, 30th March, 1779; resigned 20th May, 1780.

Page, Samuel (Mass). Lieutenant in Lexington Alarm, April, 1775; Captain Massachusetts Militia in 1776; Captain 11th Massachusetts, 1st January, 1777; resigned 18th March, 1780. (Died — September, 1814.)

Page, William (R. I.). 1st Lieutenant of Elliott's Regiment Rhode Island State Artillery, 12th December, 1776, to May, 1777; served subsequently in Navy.

Pagget, —— (Va). Captain Virginia Militia; killed at Stono Ferry, 20th June, 1779.

Paige, Timothy (Mass). Captain Massachusetts Militia in 1777. (Died 1790.)

Paine, Aaron (Mass). 1st Lieutenant of Heath's Massachusetts Regiment, May to December, 1775; 1st Lieutenant 24th Continental Infantry, 1st January to 31st December, 1776.

Paine, John (Mass). 1st Lieutenant of Walker's Massachusetts Regiment, May to December, 1775; Major Massachusetts Militia, 1776-1779.

Paine, John (N J.). Captain New Jersey Militia, —— -; killed near Spanktown, N. J., 25th September, 1781.

Paine, Phineas (Mass). 1st Lieutenant of Heath's Massachusetts Regiment, May to December, 1775; Major Massachusetts Militia, 1776-1777.

Paine, Robert Treat (Mass). A signer of the Declaration of Independence. Died 11th May, 1814.

Paine, Samuel (N. H.). Captain New Hampshire Militia, 1777.

Paine, Stephen (R. I.). Ensign of Babcock's Rhode Island State Regiment, 15th January, 1776, to November, 1776.

Painter, Elisha (Conn). Private in the Lexington Alarm, April, 1775; Captain of Wooster's Connecticut Regiment in 1775; Major of Warner's Additional Continental Regiment, 5th July, 1776; removed 18th January, 1777; order removing him repealed, 25th April, 1777; dismissed 13th October, 1778; granted a new trial, and while his case was pending, died 13th January, 1781.

Painter, Gamaliel (Conn). 1st Lieutenant of Warner's Additional Continental Regiment, 5th July, 1776; Captain of Baldwin's Artillery Artificer Regiment, 12th July, 1777; retired April, 1782. (Died 21st May, 1819.)

Palfrey, William (Mass). Major and Aide-de-Camp to General Lee, 16th July, 1775; Lieutenant-Colonel and Aide-de-Camp to General Washington, 6th March, 1776; Paymaster-General, 27th April, 1776, with rank of Lieutenant-Colonel from 9th July, 1776; appointed United States Consul to France, 4th November, 1780; vessel on which he sailed was lost at sea in December, 1780.

Pallaseure, James (R. I.). Surgeon's Mate 1st Rhode Island, 1st April, 1777; resigned 1st February, 1778.

Palmer, Abraham (N. H.) 1st Lieutenant of Bedel's Regiment New Hampshire Rangers, 15th June, 1775, to January, 1776.

Palmer, David (N. Y.). 1st Lieutenant 4th New York, 28th June, 1775; Captain, 11th August, 1775, to January, 1776.

Palmer, Edward (Conn). 1st Lieutenant 5th Connecticut, 1st January, 1777; wounded at Stony Point, 16th July, 1779; resigned 20th July, 1780.

Palmer, Elias Sanford (Conn). 1st Lieutenant of Selden's Connecticut

State Regiment, June to December, 1776. (Died 1821.)

Palmer, Fenner (N. Y.). Captain New York Militia in 1775.

Palmer, James (N. Y.). Captain New York Militia in 1775.

Palmer, John (S. C.). Captain South Carolina Militia under General Marion in 1780.

Palmer, Jonathan (Conn). 1st Lieutenant of Selden's Connecticut State Regiment, June to December, 1776.

Palmer, Joseph (Mass). Colonel Massachusetts Militia, 2d February, 1776; Brigadier-General Massachusetts Militia, 9th May, 1776, to close of war.

Palmer, Joseph (N. C.). Ensign 5th North Carolina, 6th June, 1776, to ——.

Palmer, Philip (R. I.) Ensign of Richmond's Rhode Island State Regiment, 19th August. 1776, to March, 1777.

Palmer, Thomas (N. Y.). Colonel New York Militia, 1776-1777.

Palmer, Walter (R. I.). 2d Lieutenant of Richmond's Rhode Island State Regiment, 1st November, 1775; to 1st May, 1776; 1st Lieutenant of Richmond's Rhode Island State Regiment, 19th August, 1776, to 19th November. 1776; 1st Lieutenant of Tallmann's Rhode Island Militia Regiment, 12th December, 1776, to May, 1777.

Palmer, William (—). Lieutenant Pulaski Legion, 13th February, 1778; resigned 19th March, 1779.

Pancoast, David (Pa). Captain of Flower's Artillery Artificer Regiment, 10th February, 1777; resigned — April, 1778.

Pancoast, Joseph (N. J.) . Captain New Jersey Militia in 1776.

Pannell, Abraham (Mass). Ensign 24th Continental Infantry, 1st January, 1776, to ——.

Pannell, David (Va). Captain Virginia Militia in 1777.

Pannill, Joseph (Ga). Major 2d Georgia, 5th July, 1776; Lieutenant-Colonel 4th Georgia, 16th April. 1778; retired 22d October, 1782.

Papst, —— (Pa). Major of Kachlein's Battalion Pennsylvania Flying Camp June, 1776; dismissed 10th September, 1776.

Pardee, Aaron (Mass). 2d Lieutenant 3d Continental Artillery, 17th October,

1781, and served to June, 1783. (Died 1837.)

Parham, James (S. C.). Sergeant and Quartermaster Sergeant 1st South Carolina, 1777 to March, 1778; 2 Lieutenant 1st South Carolina, 19th March, 1778; Regimental Quartermaster, April, 1778; taken prisoner at Charleston, 12th May, 1780.

Parke, John (Pa). Lieutenant-Colonel of Patton's Continental Regiment, 11th January, 1777; resigned 29th October, 1778.

Parke, John (Pa). Assistant to the Quartermaster-General, 16th August, 1775; Ensign 2d Pennsylvania Battalion, May, 1776; discharged 3d September, 1776; Ensign Pennsylvania State Regiment, 18th April, 1777; 2d Lieutenant, 1st August, 1777; regiment designated 13th Pennsylvania, 12th November, 1777; transferred to 2d Pennsylvania, 1st July, 1778; 1st Lieutenant, 15th April, 1779; died 23d July, 1780, of wounds received at Block House, N. J., 19th July, 1780.

Parke, Theophilus (Pa). 1st Lieutenant of Flower's Artillery Artificer Regiment, 7th May, 1778; Captain Lieutenant, August, 1779; cashiered. 25th March, 1780. (Name also spelled Parks.)

Parke, Thomas (Pa). Ensign 2d Pennsylvania Battalion, 5th January, 1776; discharged 20th June, 1776.

Parke, William (Mass). Corporal of Gardner's Massachusetts Regiment, May to December, 1775; 2d Lieutenant of Marshall's Regiment Massachusetts Militia in 1776; 1st Lieutenant 10th Massachusetts, 1st January, 1777; Captain Lieutenant, 15th December, 1778; Captain, 18th March, 1780; dismissed 14th January, 1782.

Parker, Aaron (Mass). Private in Lexington Alarm, April, 1775; 2d Lieutenant of Little's Massachusetts Regiment, 19th May to December, 1775.

Parker, Abel (Conn). Sergeant 2d Connecticut, 3d May to 17th December, 1775; Ensign 2d Connecticut, 1st January, 1777; resigned 3d February, 1778. (Died 1831.)

Parker, Alexander (Pa). 2d Lieutenant 6th Pennsylvania Battalion, 9th January, 1776; 1st Lieutenant, 1st June, 1776; Captain 7th Pennsylvania, 20th March, 1777; transferred to 4th Pennsylvania, 17th January, 1781; transferred to 2d Pennsylvania, 1st January, 1783, and served to 3d June, 1783. (Died 1792.)

Parker, Alexander (Va). Ensign 2d Virginia, 28th September, 1775; 2d Lieutenant, 24th January, 1776; 1st Lieutenant, 25th December, 1776; Captain, 1st June, 1777; taken prisoner at Charleston, 12th May, 1780, and served to close of war; Colonel 5th United States Infantry, 3d May, 1808; resigned 31st December, 1809.

Parker, Alexander (Va). Regimental Quartermaster, 6th Virginia, 1st June, 1776; resigned 24th August, 1777.

Parker, Asa (Mass). Captain of Prescott's Massachusetts Regiment, May to December, 1775.

Parker, Avery (Mass). 2d Lieutenant Lexington Alarm; 1st Lieutenant of Danielson's Massachusetts Regiment, May to December, 1775; Captain Massachusetts Militia, 1776-1781.

Parker, Benjamin (Mass). Ensign 9th Massachusetts, 1st January, 1777; 2d Lieutenant, 27th October, 1777; 1st Lieutenant, 10th July, 1779; retired 1st January, 1783. (Died ——, 1801.)

Parker, Clarke (R. I.). Lieutenant Rhode Island Militia, 1776-1777.

Parker, Daniel (Mass). Surgeon of Walker's Massachusetts Regiment, 3d May to December, 1775. (Also called David Parker.)

Parker, Daniel (Mass). 2d Lieutenant of Knox's Regiment Continental Artillery, 10th December, 1775; Captain Lieutenant 3d Continental Artillery, 1st January, 1777; resigned 25th October, 1778.

Parker, Danial (Mass). Private, Corporal and Sergeant 8th Massachusetts, 3d March, 1777, until appointed Ensign in August, 1778; transferred to 10th Massachusetts, 1st January, 1781; cashiered, 20th August, 1782. (Died 2d February, 1822.)

Parker, Eli (Mass). Captain Massachusetts Militia in 1777.

Parker, Elias J. (Mass). Cadet 3d Continental Artillery, 11th May, 1777; 2d Lieutenant, 12th September, 1777; 1st Lieutenant, 2d November, 1780; transferred to 1st Massachusetts, 1st January, 1781, and served to 3d November, 1783. (Died 8th December, 1798.)

Parker, Elisha (R. I.). Ensign of Richmond's Rhode Island State Regiment, 19th August, 1776, to ——.

Parker, Enos (Mass). Ensign in Lexington Alarm, April, 1775; 2d Lieutenant Paterson's Massachusetts Regiment, May to November, 1775; Captain Massachusetts Militia, 1776-1779.

Parker, Gideon (Mass). Captain of Little's Massachusetts Regiment, 19th May to December, 1775; Captain 12th Continental Infantry, 1st January, 1776, and served to ——.

Parker, Isaac (Mass). Lieutenant in Lexington Alarm, April, 1775; Lieutenant of Bridge's Massachusetts Regiment, May to December, 1775; 1st Lieutenant 8th Massachusetts, 1st January, 1777; resigned 3d October, 1778.

Parker, James (Mass). Surgeon 10th Massachusetts, 1st January, 1777; died 23d September, 1778.

Parker, James (R. I.). Captain of Tallmann's Rhode Island State Regiment, 12th December, 1776, to May, 1778.

Parker, John (Mass). Captain of Company of Minute Men at Lexington and Concord, 19th April, 1775. Died 17th September, 1775.

Parker, John (N. H.). Captain of Bedel's Regiment New Hampshire Rangers, 15th June, 1775, to 1st January, 1776.

Parker, Jonas (Mass). 2d Lieutenant of Bridge's Massachusetts Regiment, May to December, 1775; 2d Lieutenant 6th Continental Infantry, 1st January, 1776; 1st Lieutenant, 10th August, 1776; 1st Lieutenant 7th Massachusetts, 1st January, 1777; Captain Lieutenant, 1st October, 1778; Captain, 5th July, 1779; dismissed 24h January, 1781.

Parker, Jonathan (Conn). Private in Lexington Alarm, April, 1775; 1st Lieutenant 2d Connecticut, 1st May to 17th December, 1775; Captain of Sage's Connecticut Regiment, June to December, 1776; Captain 2d Connecticut, 1st January, 1777; resigned 17th June, 1778.

Parker, Joseph (N. H.). 2d Lieutenant in Lexington Alarm, April, 1775.

Parker, Joseph (Pa). 2d Lieutenant 4th Continental Artillery, 14th March, 1777; resigned 14th March, 1778. (Died 7th December, 1831.)

Parker, Joseph (Va). Captain Virginia Militia, 1775-1776.

Parker, Joshua (Mass). Sergeant in Lexington Alarm, April, 1775; Captain of Prescott's Massachusetts Regiment, May to December, 1775; Captain Massachusetts Militia, 1776-1779.

Parker, Josiah (Va). Major 5th Virginia, 13th February, 1776; Lieutenant-Colonel, 13th August, 1776; Colonel, 1st April, 1777; resigned 12th July, 1778; Colonel Virginia Militia in 1781. (Died 21st March, 1810.)

Parker, Kedar (N. C.). 2d Lieutenant 6th North Carolina, 7th May, 1776; 1st Lieutenant, 19th September, 1776; retired 1st June, 1778.

Parker, Levi (Mass). Private Lexington Alarm, April, 1775; Ensign 7th Massachusetts, 1st January, 1777; 1st Lieutenant, 20th September, 1780; transferred to 6th Massachusetts, 14th May, 1782; retired 1st January, 1783. (Died 10th September, 1825.)

Parker, Moses (Mass). Lieutenant-Colonel of Bridge's Massachusetts Regiment, 27th May, 1775; wounded and taken prisoner at Bunker Hill, 17th June, 1775, and died of his wounds, 4th July, 1775.

Parker, Nicholas Jr. (Va). 2d Lieutenant 4th Virginia, 1st April, 1776; 1st Lieutenant, 28th September, 1776. Died 7th June, 1777.

Parker, Oliver (Mass). 1st Lieutenant in Lexington Alarm, April, 1775; Captain of Prescott's Massachusetts Regiment, May, 1775; cashiered 2d August, 1775.

Parker, Paul (Pa). 1st·Lieutenant of Hartley's Continental Regiment, 16th January, 1777; Captain, 19th September, 1777; served to ——.

Parker, Phineas (Mass). Ensign of Baldwin's Artillery Artificer Regiment, 1st January, 1777; Lieutenant, 27th March, 1778; Captain, 1st January, 1779, and served to 29th March, 1781.

Parker, Richard (Va). Captain 2d Virginia, 28th September, 1775; Major 6th Virginia, 13th August, 1776; Lieutenant-Colonel 2d Virginia, 10th February, 1777; Colonel 1st Virginia, 10th February, 1778; died 8th May, 1780, of wounds received at the Siege of Charleston.

Parker, Robert (Pa). 2d Lieutenant 2d Continental Artillery, 1st January, 1777; 1st Lieutenant 4th Continental Artillery, 1st January, 1781; Captain Lieutenant, 4th October. 1782, and served to June, 1783.

Parker, Samuel Franklin (N. J.). Captain and Major New Jersey Militia, 1776-1779. Died 1779.

Parker, Stephen (Mass). Paymaster of Jackson's Additional Continental Regiment, 1st May, 1777; retired 23d April, 1779.

Parker, Thomas (Va). Ensign 2d Virginia, 4th January, 1777; Lieutenant, 13th October, 1777; wounded and taken prisoner at Savannah, 9th October, 1779; exchanged 22d December, 1780; served to close of war; Brevet-Captain, 30th September, 1783.

Parker, Thomas (Va). 1st Lieutenant 9th Virginia, 4th July, 1776; taken prisoner at Germantown, 4th October, 1777; Captain, 23d April, 1778; transferred to 5th Virginia, 12th February, 1781; transferred to 1st Virginia, 1st January, 1783, and served to close of war; Lieutenant-Colonel 8th United States Infantry, 8th January, 1799; honorably discharged 15th June, 1800; Colonel 12th United States Infantry, 12th March, 1812; Brigadier-General, 12th March, 1813; resigned 1st November, 1814. (Died 24th January, 1820.)

Parker, Warham (Mass). Captain of Danielson's Massachusetts Regiment, May to December, 1775.

Parker, William (N. H.). Surgeon's Mate 8th Continental Infantry, 1st January, 1776; Surgeon 2d New Hampshire, 8th November, 1776; resigned 30th November, 1778. (Died 15th September, 1798.)

Parker, William (Pa). Colonel Pennsylvania Militia, 1777-1778.

..**Parker, William** (Pa). Captain Pennsylvania Militia, 1776-1777.

Parkhurst, Ebenezer (Vt). Lieutenant Vermont Militia in 1777.

Parkinson, Henry (N. H.). Regimental Quartermaster 1st New Hampshire, 4th July to December, 1775; Regimental Quartermaster 5th Continental Infantry, 1st January to 31st December, 1776.

Parkinson, James (N. C.). 1st Lieutenant 2d North Carolina, — May, 1777. Died 26th March, 1778.

Parks, James (Va). 1st Lieutenant 13th Virginia, 16th December, 1776; regiment designated 9th Virginia, 14th September, 1778; killed 6th November, 1778, where or how not stated.

Parks, John (Pa). Ensign Pennsylvania State Regiment, 18th April, 1777; 2d Lieutnant, 1st August, 1777; regiment designated 13th Pennsylvania, 12th November, 1777; transferred to 2d Pennsylvania, 1st July, 1778; served to ——.

Parks, James, Theophilus and William. See Parke.

Parks, Warham (Mass). Captain of Danielson's Masschusetts Regiment, May to December, 1775; Captain 3d Continental Infantry, 1st January, 1776; Major 4th Massachusetts, 1st January, 1777; wounded at Saratoga, 7th October, 1777; resigned 1st July, 1778. (Died 1801.)

Parley, Abraham (Mass). Surgeon's-Mate of Prescott's Massachusetts Regiment, May to December, 1775; Surgeon's-Mate 7th Continental Infantry, 1st January to 31st December, 1776. (Name also spelled Perley.)

Parley, Benjamin (Mass). 2d Lieutenant of Fry's Massachusetts Regiment, May to December, 1775.

Parley, William (Mass). Captain of Fry's Massachusetts Regiment, May to December, 1775.

Parmelee, Jeremiah (Conn). Private in Lexington Alarm, April. 1775; Ensign 1st Connecticut, 1st May to 20th December, 1775; Captain of Elmore's Connecticut Regiment, 15th April, 1776; Captain 2d Canadian (Hazen's) Regiment, 3d November, 1776; wounded at Brandywine, 11th September, 1777 Died 24th March, 1778.

Parmelee, Oliver (Conn). 2d Lieutenant 4th Connecticut, 1st May to 20th December, 1775; Captain of Burrall's Continental Regiment, 19th January to December, 1776

Parr, James (Pa). 1st Lieutenant of Thompson's Pennsylvania Rifle Regiment, 25th June, 1775; 1st Lieutenant 1st Continental Infantry, 1st January, 1776; Captain, 9th March, 1776; Captain 1st Pennsylvania, 1st January, 1777; Major 7th Pennsylvania, 9th October, 1778; retired 17th January, 1781.

Parramore, Thomas (Va). 1st Lieutenant 9th Virginia, 12th February, 1776; Captain, 4th July, 1776; resigned 26th May, 1778.

Parran, Thomas (Md). Surgeon's-Mate 7th Maryland, 18th April, 1777; Surgeon 6th Maryland, 11th August, 1778; resigned 12th July, 1780.

Parran, William (Md). Quartermaster 3d Maryland Battalion of the Flying Camp, July to December, 1776.

Parris, Peter (Pa). Surgeon German Regiment, 1st September, 1778; retired 1st January, 1781.

Parrish, John (R. I.). Surgeon's-Mate 2d Rhode Island, 27th August, 1777; transferred to 1st Rhode Island, 31st March, 1778; retired 14th May, 1781.

Parrott, Jacob (Va). Ensign 8th Virginia, 4th March, 1776; 2d Lieutenant, 1st March, 1777; dismissed 9th May, 1777.

Parrott, Silas (N. J.). 2d Lieutenant of Spencer's Continental Regiment, 4th January, 1778; retired 23d April, 1779; Ensign 1st New Jersey, 1st June, 1780; to rank from 4th January, 1778, and served to April, 1783. (Died 5th October, 1819.)

Parrott, Thomas (S. C.). Captain South Carolina Militia, 1779-1781.

Parrott, William (N. J.). Ensign 2d New Jersey, 28th November, 1775; 2d Lieutenant, 29th November, 1776; 1st Lieutenant, 5th February, 1777; resigned 30th January, 1778.

Parry, Caleb (Pa). Lieutenant-Colonel Pennsylvania Musket Battalion, 3d March, 1776; killed at Long Island, 27th August, 1776.

Parsons, ——— (S C.). Lieutenant 5th South Carolina; wounded at Savannah, 9th October, 1779.

Parsons, Abraham (N. J.). Lieutenant New Jersey Militia, ———; taken prisoner at Block House, 19th July, 1780; exchanged 26th March, 1781.

Parsons, Charles (N. Y.). 2d Lieutenant 2d New York, October, 1775; 1st Lieutenant, 21st February. 1776; 1st Lieutenant 1st New York, 21st November, 1776, to rank from 21st February, 1776; Captain Lieutenant 1st September, 1778; Captain, 26th March, 1779; served to June, 1783. (Died 1814.)

Parsons, David (Conn). 1st Lieutenant of Douglas' Connecticut State Regiment, July, 1776; 2d Connecticut, 1st January, 1777; taken prisoner at King's Bridge, 1st July, 1777; exchanged 3d October, 1778; transferred to 3d Connecticut, 1st January, 1781. Died 15th November, 1781.

Parsons, Edward (N. H.). 2d Lieutenant and Adjutant 8th Continental Infantry, 1st January, 1776. Died October, 1776.

Parsons, Eli (N. Y.). 2d Lieutenant 3d New York, 1st February to November, 1776; 2d Lieutenant 3d Continental Artillery, 1st January, 1777; wounded at Germantown, 4th October, 1777; resigned 7th May, 1779; served subsequently as Commissary of Issues, June, 1779, to May, 1780. (Died 25th September, 1830.)

Parsons, Enoch (Mass). 2d Lieutenant of Little's Massachusetts Regiment, 19th May to December, 1775; 2d Lieutenant 12th Continental Infantry, 1st January, 1776, to ——.

Parsons, Hezekiah (Conn). Captain in the Lexington Alarm, April, 1775; Captain 4th Connecticut, 1st May to 18th December, 1775; Captain in Sage's Connecticut State Regiment, 20th June to 25th December, 1776. (Died 1813.)

Parsons, Jabez (Conn). Private in the Lexington Alarm, April, 1775; Sergeant in Wolcott's Connecticut Regiment, December, 1775, to March, 1776; Quartermaster-Sergeant 2d Connecticut, 1st September, 1777; Regimental Quartermaster, 1st June, 1778; 1st Lieutenant, 1st August, 1779; transferred to 3d Connecticut, 1st January, 1781; resigned 4th May, 1781. (Died 1836)

Parsons, Joseph (N. H.). Captain New Hampshire Militia, 1777-1781.

Parsons, Josiah (Mass). Sergeant in Lexington Alarm, April, 1775; Sergeant of Scammon's Massachusetts Regiment, May to December, 1775; Sergeant of Gridley's and Knox's Regiments of Artillery in 1776; 2d Lieutenant 11th Massachusetts, 1st January, 1777; retired 11th September, 1778.

Parsons, Marshfield (Conn). Lieutenant-Colonel Connetcicut Militia, 1776-1781.

Parsons, Nathan (Mass). Ensign 10th Massachusetts, 1st January, 1777; Regimental Adjutant, 1st September, 1777; retired 1st March, 1779. (Name also spelled Persons.) (Died 1824.)

Parsons, Samuel Holden (Conn). Colonel in the Lexington Alarm, April, 1775; Colonel 6th Connecticut, 1st May to 10th December, 1775; Colonel 10th Continental Infantry, 1st January, 1776; Brigadier-General Continental Army, 9th August, 1776; Major-General, 23d October, 1780. By the Act of 5th February, 1781, it was "Ordered that the letter of Major-General Parsons, with the papers enclosed, relative to his successful enterprise against the enemy's post at Morisiana, with so much of the General's letter as relates thereto be referred to the Committee of Intelligence, and that the Commander-in-Chief return the thanks of Congress to Major-General Parsons, and the officers and men under his command, and inform him that Congress have directed this publication to be made in testimony of their approbation of his judicious arrangements and of the spirit and military conduct displayed by the officers and men employed under him on the occasion." Retired 22d July, 1782. (Drowned 17th November, 1789.)

Parsons, Simeon (Conn). 1st Lieutenant of Wadworth's Connecticut State Regiment, June to December, 1776.

Parsons, Theodore (—). Surgeon in Hospital Department, 1776-1781.

Parsons, Thomas (Pa.). Lieutenant Pennsylvania Militia; wounded at Princeton, 3d January, 1777, and died shortly afterwards.

Parsons, William (Va). Cadet 6th Virginia, 25th March, 1776; Cornet 3d Continental Dragoons, 6th February, 1777; taken prisoner at Tappan, 27th September, 1778; Lieutenant, 1st January, 1779; Captain, November, 1779; retained in Baylor's Consolidated Regiment of Dragoons, 9th November, 1782, and served to close of war. (Died 1825.)

Partridge, Jesse (Mass). 2d Lieutenant in Lexington Alarm, April, 1775; 2d Lieutenant of Phinney's Massachusetts Regiment, May to December, 1775; Captain Massachusetts Militia, 1776; Captain 3d Massachusetts, 1st April, 1778; resigned 16th November, 1778.

Paschke, Frederick (Pa.) 2d Lieutenant 4th Continental Artillery, 14th March, 1777; Captain Pulaski Legion, 14th March, 1779; retired 18th May, 1780; served subsequently as Deputy Quartermaster in the Southern Department to 13th July, 1783.

Pasteur, John (N. C.). Lieutenant 6th North Carolina, 2d July, 1776, to ——.

Pasteur, Thomas (N. C.). Ensign 4th North Carolina, 15th July, 1777; 2d Lieutenant, 29th December, 1777; transferred to 1st North Carolina, 1st June, 1778; Regimental Adjutant, 26th June, 1779; 1st Lieutenant, 10th November, 1779; taken prisoner at Charleston, 12th May, 1780; exchanged December, 1780, and served to close of war; Lieutenant Infantry United States Army, 3d June, 1790; Captain 1st United States Infantry, 5th March, 1792; assigned to 1st Sub Legion, 4th September, 1792; assigned to 1st United States Infantry, 1st November, 1796; Major 2d Infantry, 11th April, 1803.Died 29th July, 1806.

Pasteur, William (N. C.). Paymaster 4th North Carolina, 12th December, 1776, to ——.

Pasteur, William (N. C.). Surgeon 2d North Carolina, 1st September, 1775, to June, 1776.

Patch, Samuel (Mass) Captain of Prescott's Massachusetts Regiment, May to December, 1775; Captain 7th Continental Infantry, 1st January to 31st December, 1776.

Patchen, Samuel (N. Y.). Lieutenant New York Militia, ——; prisoner of war, 17th May, 1781, to 8th December. 1782; where taken not stated.

Paterson, Edward (N. J.). Ensign 3d New Jersey, 21st March, 1776; 2d Lieutenant. 29th October, 1776; 1st Lieutenant 2d New Jersey, 29th November, 1776; resigned 6th January, 1778.

Paterson, John (Mass). Colonel of a Massachusetts Regiment, April to December, 1775; Colonel 15th Continental Infantry, 1st January, 1776; Brigadier-General Continental Army, 21st February. 1777, and served to close of war; Brevet Major-General, 30th September. 1783. (Died 19th July, 1808.)

Patrick, John (Mass). 2d Lieutenant of Brewer's Massachusetts Regiment, April to October, 1775; Lieutenant Massachusetts Militia in 1776. Died 6th March, 1807.

Patrick, William (Mass). Captain 7th Massachusetts, 1st January, 1777; killed 30th May, 1778, at Coverskill, N. Y.

Pattee, Asa (N. H.). 1st Lieutenant of Bedel's Regiment New Hampshire Rangers, 15th June to 16th December, 1775.

Pattee, Benjamin (Mass). Sergeant in Lexington Alarm, April, . 1775; 1st Lieutenant of Nixon's Massachusetts Regiment, May to December, 1775; Captain Massachusetts Militia, 1776-1779.

Patten, David (Conn). 1st Lieutenant of Sage's Connecticut State Regiment, June to December, 1776.

Patten, John (Del). 1st Lieutenant Delaware Regiment, 15th January, 1776; Captain, 30th November, 1776; Major, 14th December, 1779; taken prisoner at Camden, 16th August, 1780; on parole to close of war. (Died 17th June, 1801.)

Patten, John (N. C.). Major 2d North Carolina, 1st September, 1775; Lieutenant-Colonel, 10th April, 1776; Colonel, 22d November, 1777; taken prisoner at Charleston, 12th May, 1780; retired 1st January, 1783.

Patten, Jonathan (Mass). Lieutenant-Colonel Massachusetts Militia in 1781.

Patten, Thomas (Pa). Captain Lieutenant of Baldwin's Artillery Artificer Regiment, 21st December, 1779, to rank from 1st March, 1779, and served to 9th June, 1783.

Patten, William (N. C.) . Surgeon 2d North Carolina, 1st September, 1775, to ——.

Patterson, Alexander (Pa). Captain 12th Pennsylvania, 1st October, 1776; retired 1st July, 1778.

Patterson, Benjamin (Va). Cadet 1st Virginia, 27th February, 1776; Ensign, November, 1776; cashiered, 14th May, 1777.

Patterson, David (Mass). Private in Lexington Alarm, April, 1775; Corporal in Thomas' Massachusetts Regiment, May to November, 1775, and Sergeant in Marshall's Massachusetts Regiment in 1776; Lieutenant 14th Massachusetts, 1st January, 1777; dismissed 3d September, 1780; also called Peterson

Patterson, Ephriam (Vt). 2d Lieutenant of Bedel's Regiment Vermont Militia, 1778-1779.

Patterson, Ezra (Pa). 2d Lieutenant 2d Continental Artillery, 1st January, 1777; 1st Lieutenant, ——, 1779; resigned 7th April, 1781.

Patterson, Gabriel. See Peterson.

Patterson, John (Md). Ensign 2d Maryland Battalion of the Flying Camp, June, 1776, to ——-.

Patterson, John (Pa). Adjutant 1st Pennsylvania Battalion, 5th January, 1776; 2d Lieutenant, 5th September, 1776; Captain 2d Pennsylvania, 1st January, 1777; retired 1st January, 1783. (Died 1790.)

Patterson, Matthew (Conn). Ensign 4th Connecticut, 1st May to 9th December, 1775; 2d Lieutenant of Burrall's Continental Regiment, 23d January, 1776; taken prisoner at the Cedars, 19th May, 1776; 1st Lieutenant, 19th September, 1776; never rejoined regiment.

Patterson, Samuel (Del). Colonel Delaware Militia in 1775; Colonel Delaware Detachment of the Flying Camp, June, 1776, and Brigadier-General Delaware Militia, 1776 to 1781.

Patterson, Thomas (N. J.). Captain 3d New Jersey, 21st March, 1776; resigned 8th September, 1778.

Patterson, Thomas (Va). Captain 6th Virginia, 24th February, 1776; died ——, 1776.

Patterson, William (Pa). 2d Lieutenant 1st Pennsylvania Battalion of the Flying Camp, July, 1776; supposed to have been killed at Long Island, 27th August, 1776.

Patterson, William (Va). Ensign of Grayson's Additional Continental Regiment, 24th May, 1777; 2d Lieutenant, 8th June, 1777; resigned 28th May, 1778.

Patterson, William Augustus (Mass). 1st Lieutenant 15th Continental Infantry, 1st January, 1776; Captain, 12th September to 31st December, 1776; served as Engineer in 4th Continental Artillery, April, 1777, to July, 1778.

Patton, James (N. J.) . Corporal 2d Continental Dragoons, 14th February, 1777; Sergeant, 22d March, 1777; Cornet, 11th October, 1777; Lieutenant, 2d June, 1778; resigned 25th May, 1779. (Died 16th November, 1816.)

Patton, John (N. H.). Quartermaster-Sergeant 1st New Hampshire, 23d April to December, 1775; 2d Lieutenant 5th Continental Infantry, 1st January to 31st December, 1776.

Patton, John (Pa). Major 2d Battalion of Miles' Pennsylvania Rifle Regiment, 13th March, 1776; Major 9th Pennsylvania, 25th October, 1776; Colonel of one of the Sixteen Additional Continental Regiments, 11th January, 1777; resigned 3d February, 1778. (Died 1804.)

Patton, Robert (Pa). 1st Lieutenant of Klotz' Pennsylvania Battalion of the Flying Camp; taken prisoner at Fort Washington, 16th November, 1776; exchanged 3d January, 1781.

Patton, Robert (Pa). 2d Lieutenant 11th Pennsylvania, 30th September, 1776; taken prisoner in a skirmish near White Plains, 27th October, 1776; 1st Lieutenant, 13th November, 1776; transferred to 10th Pennsylvania, 1st July, 1778; Captain Lieutenant, 1st April, 1779; Captain, 1st March, 1780; transferred to 6th Pennsylvania, 17th January, 1781, and served to close of war.

Patton, William (Pa). 1st Lieutenant of Swope's Pennsylvania Battalion of the Flying Camp; taken prisoner at Fort Washington, 16th November, 1776.

Patton, William (Pa). 2d Lieutenant 1st Continental Infantry, 16th January, 1776; 2d Lieutenant of Patton's Continental Regiment, 15th January, 1777; killed at Germantown 4th October, 1777.

Paul, David (N. J.). Captain New Jersey Militia; taken prisoner at Bil-

lingsport, 2d November, 1777; was a prisoner in August, 1778.

Paul, James (N. J.). Sergeant 2d New Jersey, 30th October, 1775, to November, 1776; Sergeant 2d New Jersey, 15th December, 1776; Ensign, 1st July, 1777; wounded at Short Hills, 26th June, 1777; 2d Lieutenant, 1st December, 1777; taken prisoner at Bargin Point, 3d April, 1779; exchanged June, 1780; retired 1st January, 1781. (Died 30th October, 1831.)

Paul, Peter (Pa). Ensign Pennsylvania Battalion of the Flying Camp; taken prisoner at Fort Washington, 16th November, 1776.

Paulding, John (N. Y.). By the act of 3d November, 1780, it was "Resolved, Whereas Congress have received information that John Paulding, David Williams and Isaac Van Wart, three young volunteer Militia men of the State of New York, did on the 23d day of September last intercept Major John Andre, Adjutant-General of the British Army, on his return from the American lines, in the character of a spy, and notwithstanding the large bribes offered them for his release, nobly disdaining to sacrifice their country for the sake of gold, secured and conveyed him to the commanding officer of the district, whereby the dangerous and traitorous conspiracy of Benedict Arnold was brought to light, the insidious designs of the enemy baffled and the United States rescued from impending danger. Resolved that Congress have a high sense of the virtuous and patriotic conduct of the said John Paulding, David Williams and Isaac Van Wart, in testimony whereof ordered that each of them receive annually out of the public treasury two hundred ($200) dollars in specie, or an equivalent in the current money of these States during life, and that the board of war procure for each of them a silver medal, on one side of which shall be a shield with this inscription: 'Fidelity!' and on the other the following motto: 'Vincit amor patrias!' and forward them to the Commander-in-Chief, who is requested to present the same, with a copy of this resolution and the thanks of Congress for their fidelity and the eminent services they have rendered their country." (Died 18th February, 1818.)

Paulett, Richard (Va). Lieutenant Virginia Militia, 1779-1780.

Paulint, Antoine (Canada). Captain of an Independent Company Canadian Volunteers, 20th November, 1775; Captain 2d Canadian (Hazen's) Regiment, 3d November, 1776; retired 1st July, 1782. (Died 1816.)

Pawling, Albert (N. Y.). 2d Lieutenant 3d New York, 28th June, 1775; Brigade Major of Clinton's Brigade, November, 1775, to May, 1776; Captain of DuBois' New York Regiment, 26th June, 1776; Major of Malcolm's Continental Regiment, 27th January, 1777; resigned 23d April, 1779; Lieutenant-Colonel and Colonel New York Levies, 1779, to close of war .

Pawling, Henry (N. Y.). 1st Lieutenant 5th New York, 21st November, 1776; taken prisoner at Fort Montgomery, 6th October, 1777; exchanged — February, 1781; transferred to 2d New York, 1st January, 1781; Captain, 6th November, 1782, and served to close of war. (Died 1836.)

Pawling, Henry (N. Y.). Lieutenant of Pawling's Regiment New York Militia, 1779-1780.

Pawling, Henry (Pa). Captain of Lewis' Pennsylvania Battalion of the Flying Camp, July to December, 1776.

Pawling, Levi (N. Y.). Colonel New York Militia, 1775-1778.

Paxton, John (Pa). Captain Lancaster County, Pennsylvania, Militia, ——, 1776-1777.

Paxton, Thomas (Pa). Captain Pennsylvania Militia, 1776, and Lieutenant-Colonel in 1777. (Died 1811.)

Paxton, William (Va). Captain Virginia Militia, 1779-1781. (Died 1795.)

Payne, Edward (Conn). Private in Lexington Alarm, April, 1775; Ensign 4th Connecticut, 1st May to 28th November, 1775; 1st Lieutenant of Sage's Connecticut State Regiment, 20th June to 25th December, 1776.

Payne, Francis (N. H.). Sergeant-Major of Warner's Continental Regiment, 1st January, 1777; Ensign, 18th August, 1778; 2d Lieutenant, 2d May, 1779; was a prisoner in 1782; when and where taken not stated.

Payne, George (N. J.). Captain and Major New Jersey Militia, 1777-1780. (Died 1795.)

Payne, James William (N. Y.). 1st Lieutenant 1st New York, 28th June to November, 1776.

Payne, John (N. H.). 2d Lieutenant of Warner's Continental Regiment, 20th October, 1776; resigned 1st May, 1778.

Payne, Joseph (Va). Sergeant 9th Virginia, 13th May, 1776; Ensign, 4th January, 1777; taken prisoner at Germantown, 4th Otcober, 1777; released 3d December, 1780, and did not return to regiment; name also spelled Josiah Payne. (Died 1782.)

Payne, Joshua (N. H.). Chaplain 3d Continental Infantry, 1st January to 31st December, 1776.

Payne, Michael (N. C.). Captain 2d North Carolina, 1st September, 1775, to ——.

Payne, Tarlton (Va). Ensign 1st Virginia, — January, 1776; 2d Lieutenant, 5th October, 1776; 1st Lieutenant, 20th January, 1777; Captain, 18th November, 1777; taken prisoner at Charleston, 12th May, 1780; transferred to 7th Virginia, 12th February, 1781, and served to January, 1783.

Payne, Thomas (Ga). Lieutenant 2d Georgia, 1st December, 1777, and served to close of war; Brevet Captain, 30th September, 1783.

Payne, Thomas (Va). Ensign 13th Virginia, 30th December, 1776; Lieutenant, 18th October, 1777; taken prisoner at Germantown, 4th October, 1777; regiment designated 9th Virginia, 14th September, 1778; Captain Lieutenant, 9th December, 1779; taken prisoner at Charleston, 12th May, 1780; exchanged 22d December, 1780; Captain, 14th May, 1782, and served to close of war.

Payne, William (Va). Captain 1st Virginia State Regiment, 1777-1778.

Payson, Samuel (Mass). Captain in Lexington Alarm, April, 1775; Captain of Read's Massachusetts Regiment, May to December, 1775; Captain 13th Continental Infantry, 1st January to 31st December, 1776; Captain Massachusetts Militia, 1777-1780. (Died 19th June, 1819.)

Peabody, Ebenezer (Mass). Sergeant in Lexington Alarm, April, 1775; Sergeant of Fry's Massachusetts Regiment, 25th April to December, 1775; 2d Lieutenant of Wigglesworth's Massachusetts Regiment, May to November, 1776; 1st Lieutenant, 7th Massachusetts, 1st January, 1777; resigned 9th February, 1780. (Died 23d January, 1829.)

Peabody, Nathaniel (N. H.). Adjutant General New Hampshire Militia in 1777. (Died 27th June, 1823)

Peabody, Richard (Conn). Ensign of Chester's Connecticut State Regiment, June to December, 1776.

Peabody, Stephen (N. H.). Adjutant 3d New Hampshire, 23d April to December, 1775; Major of Wyman's Regiment New Hampshire Militia, July to December, 1776; Captain of Militia in 1777, and Lieutenant-Colonel of same, 1778 to 1779; died 1779.

Peabody, Stephen (N. H.). Major, Lieutenant-Colonel and Colonel New Hampshire Militia, 1776-1781.

Peabody, Thomas (N. H.). Surgeon New Hampshire Militia, 1777-1778.

Peachey, William (Va). Colonel 5th Virginia, 13th February, 1776; resigned 7th May, 1776.

Peacock, Richard (N. Y.). 1st Lieutenant of Malcolm's Additional Continental Regiment, 9th July, 1777; retired 22d April, 1779; served subsequently as Lieutenant in New York Levies; also called Hugh Peacock.

Peake, William (—). Quartermaster of Lee's Battalion of Light Dragoons, 7th April, 1778; resigned 28th February, 1779.

Peale, Charles Willson (Pa). Lieutenant and Captain Pennsylvania Militia, 1775-1777. (Died 23d February, 1827.)

Peale, James (Md). Ensign of Smallwood's Maryland Regiment 14th January, 1776; 1st Lieutenant 1st Maryland, 10th December, 1776; Captain, 1st March, 1778; resigned 3d June, 1779. (Died 1831.)

Pearce, George (N. C.). Ensign 9th North Carolina, 28th November, 1776, to ——.

Pearce, James (N. C.). Captain North Carolina Militia in 1780. (Died 1st April, 1833.)

Pearce, Job (R. I.). Captain of Richmond's Rhode Island State Regiment, 1st November, 1775, to February, 1776; Major of Elliott's Regiment Rhode Island State Artillery, 12th December, 1776, to May, 1777.

Pearce, John (R. I.) Ensign of Richmond's Rhode Island State Regiment, 19th August, 1776; Captain of Stanton's Rhode Island State Regiment, 12th December, 1776; Lieutenant 1st Rhode Island, 17th February, 1777; wounded at Red Bank, 22d October, 1777; wounded at Rhode Island, 29th August, 1778; resigned 15th October, 1778. (Died 7th November, 1819.) Name also Pearse.

Pearce, Nathaniel (Mass). 2d Lieutenant of Glover's Massachusetts Regiment, 19th May to December, 1775

Pearce, Philip (R. I.). Ensign 9th Continental Infantry, 1st January to 31st December, 1776.

Pearce, Thomas (R. I.). Ensign of Tallman's Rhode Island State Regiment, 12th December, 1776, to May, 1777.

Pearcy, Henry.—See **Piercy.**

Pearcy, Jonathan (N. Y.). 1st Lieutenant 1st New York, 28th June, 1775, to January, 1776; 1st Lieutenant of DuBois' New York Regiment, 26th June, 1776; Captain 4th New York, 21st November, 1776; resigned, 23d April, 1778; served subsequently as Captain New York Levies.

Pearl, James (N. C.). Ensign 8th NorthCarolina, 28th November, 1776; Lieutenant, 29th October, 1777; transferred to 1st North Carolina, 1st June, 1778; Captain, 17th July, 1780; retired 1st January, 1783.

Pearl, Stephen (Mass). Captain of Woodbridge's Massachusetts Regiment, June to November, 1775; Adjutant 1st Massachusetts, 1st January, 1777; resigned 8th March, 1778.

Pearly, Benjamin (Mass). 2d Lieutenant of Frye's Massachusetts Regiment, May to December, 1775.

Pearly, William (Mass). Captain of Frye's Massachusetts Regiment, May to December, 1775.

Pearman, Thomas (S. C.). Major South Carolina Rangers in 1779 and 1780.

Pearre, Nathaniel (Ga). 1st Lieutenant and Adjutant 3d Georgia, 29th April, 1778; was a Captain in 1781, and served to close of war.

Pearson, —— (—). Lieutenant, ——; killed by Tarlton's troops at Waxhaw, 29th May, 1780.

Pearson, John (Pa). 1st Lieutenant 11th Pennsylvania, 30th September, 1776; Captain, 7th September, 1777; transferred to 9th Pennsylvania, 1st July, 1778; transferred to 2d Pennsylvania, 17th January, 1781; transferred to 1st Pennsylvania, 1st January, 1783, and served to June, 1783; Brevet Major, 30th September, 1783.

Pearson, Moses (S. C.). Captain South Carolina Militia, 1780-1781.

Pearson, Thomas (Va). Ensign 10th Virginia, 18th November, 1776; 2d Lieutenant, 15th March, 1777; 1st Lieutenant, 3d April, 1778; transferred to 6th Virginia, 14th September, 1778; taken prisoner at Charleston, 12th May, 1780, and was a prisoner on parole to close of war. (Died 10th July, 1826.)

Pease, Abiel (Conn). 1st Lieutenant 8th Connecticut, 6th July to 16th December, 1775; subsequently served as Captain and Major Connecticut Militia.

Pease, Abner (Mass). 2d Lieutenant of Woodbridge's Massachusetts Regiment, May to December, 1775.

Peaslee, Zacheus (Canada). Private 2d Canadian (Hazen's) Regiment, 25th May, 1779; Ensign, 5th January, 1782; served to June, 1783. (Died 1810.)

Peck, Allen (R. I.). Captain Rhode Island Militia in 1777.

Peck, Cornelius (N. J.). 1st Lieutenant 3d New Jersey, 3d March, 1776; died 9th April, 1776; also called Constant Peck.

Peck, Daniel (Mass). 2d Lieutenant of Doolittle's Massachusetts Regiment, May to December, 1775.

Peck, Darius (Conn). Private in the Lexington Alarm, April, 1775; Ensign 1st Connecticut, 1st January, 1777; 2d Lieutenant, 7th February, 1778; resigned 1st May, 1779. (Died 1804.)

Peck, George (Conn). Captain Connecticut Militia, 1777.

Peck, George (R. I.). Colonel Rhode Island Militia, 1780-1781.

Peck, Hiel (N. Y.). Sergeant 2d Continental Artillery, 17th April, 1777; 2d Lieutenant, 29th June, 1781, and served to June, 1783.

Peck, James (Conn). Lieutenant in the Lexington Alarm, April, 1775; Ensign 1st Connecticut, 1st May to 1st December, 1775; 2d Lieutenant of Ward's Connecticut State Regiment, 14th May, 1776, to April, 1777; Captain Connecticut Militia, 1777-1779.

Peck, Jesse (Conn). Private 7th Connecticut, 1st August to December, 1775; Corporal in Wolcott's Connecticut State Regiment, December, 1775, to February, 1776; 2d Lieutenant of Sherburne's Additional Continental Regiment, 1st January, 1777; resigned 17th April, 1780.

Peck, John (Conn). Lieutenant of Baldwin's Artillery Artificer Regiment, 26th August, 1777; resigned 20th November, 1778.

Peck, John (N. J.). 2d Lieutenant 2d New Jersey, 29th November, 1776; 1st Lieutenant, 10th November, 1777;

Regimental Paymaster, 1st January, 1777, to April, 1783; retained in New Jersey Battalion, April, 1783; brevet Captain, 30th September, 1783; served to 3d November, 1783; served also as Captain New Jersey Militia.

Peck, Loring (R. I.). Captain of Babcock's Rhode Island State Regiment, 15th January to July, 1776; Captain of Lippitt's Rhode Island State Regiment, 19th August, 1776, to February, 1777.

Peck, Samuel (Conn). Captain 1st Connecticut, 1st May to 1st December, 1775; Captain of Douglas' Connecticut State Regiment, 20th June to 29th December, 1776. (Died 1822.)

Peck, William (R. I.). Adjutant 17th Continental Infantry, 1st January, 1776; Brigade Major to General Spencer, 28th July, 1776; Major and Aide-de-Camp to General Spencer, 14th August, 1776, to January, 1778; served also as Colonel and Deputy Adjutant-General of Forces in Rhode Island, 20th May, 1777, until he resigned, about October, 1781. (Died 19th May, 1832.)

Pecker, James (Mass). Surgeon 11th Massachusetts, 1st January, 1777. Died 22d September, 1778.

Peckham, Barber (R. I.). Ensign of Tallman's Rhode Island State Regiment, 12th December, 1776, to May, 1777; Lieutenant of Topham's Rhode Island Militia in 1778.

Peckham, Benjamin L. (R. I.). Regimental Quartermaster 2d Rhode Island, 1st January, 1777; Ensign, 11th February, 1777; Lieutenant, 15th April, 1779; transferred to 1st Rhode Island, 1st January, 1781; retained in Olney's Rhode Island Battalion, 14th May, 1781; Captain, 21st June, 1782, and served to 3d November, 1783. (Died 1821.)

Peckham, Thomas (R. I.). Captain Rhode Island Militia, 1775-1776.

Peebles, Robert (Pa). 2d Lieutenant 7th Pennsylvania, 24th April, 1777; 1st Lieutenant, 16th April, 1779; Regimental Quartermaster, 8th September, 1779; transferred to 4th Pennsylvania, 17th January, 1781; transferred to 3d Pennsylvania, 1st January, 1783, and served to 3d November, 1783.

Peebles, William (Pa). Captain 2d Battalion of Miles' Pennsylvania Rifle Regiment, 9th March, 1776; taken prisoner at Long Island, 27th August, 1776, and died while prisoner of war, in October, 1776.

Peers, Valentine (Va). Major Virginia Militia in 1776; Brigade Major to General Weedon in 1777. (Died 1830.)

Peet, David (Conn). 2d Lieutenant 5th Connecticut, 1st May to 22d July, 1775.

Peirce, Abraham (Mass). Captain Massachusetts Militia in 1778.

Peirce, Benjamin (R. I.). Captain of Babcock's Rhode Island State Regiment, 15th January to November, 1776.

Peirce, Charles (R. I.). Ensign 1st Rhode Island, 11th February, 1777; 2d Lieutenant, 10th October, 1777; resigned 7th June, 1779.

Peirce, Daniel (R. I.). Ensign Rhode Island Regiment, 1st September, 1775; 2d Lieutenant 9th Continental Infantry, 1st January to 31st December, 1776; 1st Lieutenant 1st Rhode Island, 11th February, 1777; resigned 31st May, 1779. (Died 12th February, 1823.)

Peirce, George (R. I.). Lieutenant-Colonel Rhode Island Militia in 1775.

Peirce, Hardy (Mass). Corporal and Sergeant in Paterson's Massachusetts Regiment, May to December, 1775; 2d Lieutenant of Knox's Regiment, Continental Artillery, 10th December, 1775; killed at Fort Lee, 18th November, 1776.

Peirce, Henry (Mass). 1st Lieutenant of Brewer's Massachusetts Regiment, May to December, 1775; Captain Massachusetts Militia, 1777-1781.

Peirce, Isaac (Mass). Major and Aide-de-Camp to General Gates, 7th June, 1776, to close of war. (Died 1821.)

Peirce, John (Md). Surgeon 5th Maryland, 13th January, 1778, to ——.

Peirce, John (Mass). 2d Lieutenant of Mansfield's Massachusetts Regiment, May to December, 1775; 1st Lieutenant 27th Continental Infantry, 1st January to 31st December, 1776; 1st Lieutenant 15th Massachusetts, 1st January, 1777; Captain-Lieutenant, ——, 1778; Captain, 1st March, 1779; resigned 21st December, 1780. (Also called Joshua Pierce.)

Peirce, John (Mass). 2d Lieutenant of Knox's Regiment Continental Artillery, June, 1776; 1st Lieutenant 3d Continental Artillery, 1st January, 1777; Captain-Lieutenant, 12th September, 1778; transferred to Corps of Artillery, 17th June, 1783, and served to 3d November, 1783; Lieutenant United States

Artillery Battalion, 20th October, 1786; Lieutenant Artillery Battalion United States Army, 29th September, 1789; Captain, 15th October, 1791; Artillerists and Engineers, 9th May, 1794; died 24th July, 1798.

Peirce, Joseph (Mass). Sergeant of Ward's Massachusetts Regiment, May to December, 1775; Sergeant 15th Massachusetts, 19th March, 1777; Quartermaster Sergeant, 10th March, 1778; Regimental Quartermaster, 18th June, 1779; transferred to 4th Massachusetts, 1st January, 1781; retired 1st January, 1783.

Peirce, Silas (Mass). Sergeant of Prescott's Massachusetts Regiment, May to December, 1775; Sergeant 7th Continental Infantry, February to December, 1776; 1st Lieutenant, 8th Massachusetts, 1st January, 1777; Captain, 5th December, 1779, and served to June, 1783. (Died 22d November, 1809.)

Pelcerf, Francis (Va). Surgeon's-Mate of Grayson's Continental Regiment, 1st May, 1778. Resigned 8th September, 1778.

Pelham, Charles (Va). 1st Lieutenant 1st Virginia, 25th February, 1776; Captain, 11th November, 1776; Major 2d Virginia, 25th June, 1779; taken prisoner at Charleston, 12th May, 1780; Prisoner on parole to close of war. (Died 29th August, 1829.)

Pelham, Peter (Va). Captain Virginia Militia, 1776-1777.

Pelham, William (Va). Surgeon's Mate Hospital Department in Virginia, 6th July, 1776, to 28th February, 1777.

Pell, Philip (N. Y.). Deputy Judge Advocate in 1777.

Pell, Saler (Conn). Surgeon of Bradley's Connecticut State Regiment, June to December, 1776; Surgeon 5th Connecticut, 1st January, 1777; resigned 26th July, 1777.

Pell, Samuel Treadwell (N. Y.). 1st Lieutenant 4th New York, 28th June, 1775, to January, 1776; Captain 2d New York, 21st November, 1776; served to June, 1783. (Died 29th December, 1786.)

Pelliser, Christopher (France). Lieutenant-Colonel Engineer, 29th July, 1776, to ——.

Pelton, Benjamin (N. Y.). 1st Lieutenant 1st New York, 28th June, 1775; 1st Lieutenant of Nicholson's Continental Regiment, March to November, 1776;

Captain, 2d New York, 21st November, 1776; Resigned 13th March, 1778. (Died 1830.)

Pemberton, Robert (N. J.). 1st Lieutenant of Forman's Continental Regiment, 14th June, 1777; Regimental Adjutant, 10th October, 1777; Captain, 1st January, 1780; retired 1st January, 1781.

Pemberton, Thomas (Va). Cornet 1st Continental Dragoons, 5th December, 1776; 2d Lieutenant, 18th December, 1776; 1st Lieutenant —— 1778; Captain, 12th June, 1779; retired, 9th November, 1782.

Pendergast, William (Md). 2d Lieutenant 5th Maryland, 29th October, 1779; transferred to 3d Maryland, 1st January, 1781; retained in Maryland Battalion, April, 1783, and served to 15th November, 1783.

Pendleton, Daniel (Conn). Captain of Baldwin's Artillery Artificer Regiment, 26th August, 1777, and served to May, 1781.

Pendleton, James (Va). Ensign 7th Virginia, 7th February, 1776; 2d Lieutenant, 26th April, 1776; resigned 13th January, 1777; Captain 1st Continental Artillery, 7th February, 1777; Brevet-Major, 30th September, 1783, and served to close of war.

Pendleton, Nathaniel (Va). Ensign 10th Continental Infantry, 1st January, 1776; 1st Lieutenant 11th Virginia, 23d July, 1776; Captain, 13th March, 1777; taken prisoner at Fort Washington, 16th November, 1776; exchanged, 18th October, 1880; transferred to 3d Virginia, 12th February, 1781; Aide-de-Camp to General Greene, November, 1780, to close of war; Brevet-Major, 30th September, 1783. By the act of 29th October, 1781, it was "Resolved, that Major-General Greene be desired to present the thanks of Congress to Captain Pendleton, his Aide-de-Camp, in testimony of his particular activity and good conduct during the whole action at Eutaw Springs, South Carolina." (Died 20th October, 1821.)

Pendleton, Philip (Va). Colonel Virginia Militia, 1777-1781.

Pendleton, Solomon (N. Y.). 2d Lieutenant 4th New York, November, 1775; 1st Lieutenant, June, 1776; 1st Lieutenant 5th New York, 21st November, 1776; taken prisoner at Fort Montgomery, 6th October, 1777; exchanged, 8th February, 1781, and did not return to the army.

Penét, Ignatius (France). Volunteer Aide-de-Camp to General Washington, with Brevet rank of Captain Continental Army, 14th October, 1776, to ——;. Lieutenant in Armand's Partisan Corps, 6th January, 1781, and served to close of war.

Penfield, John (Conn). Lieutenant-Colonel Connecticut Militia, 1777-1781. (Died 1797.)

Penfield, Peter (Conn). 1st Lieutenant Silliman's Connecticut State Regiment, July to December, 1776; Captain Connecticut Militia, 1777-1778. (Died 1812.)

Penn, Abram (Va). Captain Virginia Militia, 1776; Colonel, 1780 and 1781. (Died 1801.)

Penn, John (N. C.). A signer of the Declaration of Independence. Died 14th September, 1788.

Penn, William (Va). 1st Lieutenant Virginia Dragoons, 16th June, 1776; Captain 1st Continental Dragoons, 25th November, 1776; died 15th March, 1777.

Pennell, Abraham (Mass). 2d Lieutenant in Lexington Alarm, April, 1775; 2d Lieutenant of Doolittle's Massachusetts Regiment, May to December, 1775.

Penniman, Adna (N. H.). 2d Lieutenant 3d New Hampshire, 8th November, 1776; 1st Lieutenant, 1st May, 1778; Captain-Lieutenant, 5th July, 1780; retired 1st January, 1781. (Died 4th November, 1820.)

Pennington, William Sanford (N. J.). Sergeant 2d Continental Artillery, 7th March, 1777; 2d Lieutenant, 12th September, 1778, and served to June, 1783; Lieutenant United States Infantry Regiment, 18th August, 1784; resigned 24th November, 1785. (Died 17th September, 1826.)

Pennoyer, John (Mass). 2d Lieutenant of Paterson's Massachusetts Regiment, April to November, 1775; 2d Lieutenant 15th Continental Infantry, 1st January to 31st December, 1776.

Penrose, Joseph (Pa). Lieutenant-Colonel 5th Pennsylvania Battalion, 3d January, 1776; Colonel 10th Pennsylvania, 25th October, 1776; resigned 7th February, 1777.

Peppin, Andrew (N. Y.). 1st Lieutenant 1st Canadian (Livingston's) Regiment, 20th November, 1775; left regiment, June 23d, 1779, on leave for 12 months, and did not rejoin.

Perault, Michael (Va). Captain of Clark's Illinois Regiment, 1779, to 1782.

Percival, Paul (Conn). Regimental Quartermaster 1st Connecticut, 1st January, 1777; Issuing Commissary 2d Connecticut Brigade, 1st January, 1778; resigned 31st March, 1780.

Percival, Timothy (Conn). Lieutenant in the Lexington Alarm, April, 1775; 1st Lieutenant 8th Connecticut, 6th July to 10th December, 1775; Captain 17th Continental Infantry, 1st January, 1776; taken prisoner at Long Island, 27th August, 1776. (Died 1815.)

Peres, Peter (Pa). Surgeon German Regiment, 1st September, 1778; retired 1st January, 1781.

Periam, Joseph (N. J.). Regimental Quartermaster 1st New Jersey, 28th November, 1776; omitted May, 1778.

Perkins, Adam (N. C.). Lieutenant Colonel 10th North Carolina, 7th April, 1777, to ——.

Perkins, Archelaus (Va). Ensign 5th Virginia, 11th September, 1780; 2d Lieutenant, 24th November, 1781; retired 1st January, 1783.

Perkins, Benjamin (Mass). 1st Lieutenant Lexington Alarm, April, 1775; Captain of Little's Massachusetts Regiment, 19th May to December, 1775; Captain 12th Continental Infantry, 1st January to 31st December, 1776.

Perkins, David (S. C.). Ensign South Carolina Militia in 1776.

Perkins, Ebenezer (Conn). Sergeant in the Lexington Alarm, April, 1775; Sergeant 8th Connecticut, 10th July, 1775; Ensign, 18th September to 10th December, 1775; 2d Lieutenant 17th Continental Infantry, 1st January, 1776; 1st Lieutenant 1st Connecticut, 1st January, 1777; Captain, 1st January, 1778; resigned 1st July, 1780. (Died 16th April, 1831.)

Perkins, Elisha (Conn). Surgeon of Douglas' Connecticut State Regiment, January to March, 1776. (Died 1799.)

Perkins, Hardin (Va). Ensign 6th Virginia, 21st March, 1776; 2d Lieutenant, 27th October, 1776; 1st Lieutenant, 15th April 1777; resigned 26th April, 1778. (Died 1838.)

Perkins, Isaac (Md). Captain 4th Maryland Battalion of the Fling Camp, July to December, 1776.

Perkins, Jacob (N. J.). Major New Jersey Militia, 1778-1779. (Died 1792.)

Perkins, James (Mass). Sergeant in Wigglesworth's Regiment Massachusetts Militia in 1776; Ensign, 21st September, 1776; 2d Lieutenant 15th Massachusetts, 1st January, 1777; resigned 24th February, 1778. (Died 4th March, 1830.)

Perkins, John (Del). 2d Lieutenant Delaware Regiment, 21st January, to December, 1776.

Perkins, John (Mass). Private and Sergeant in Phinney's Massachusetts Regiment, May to November, 1775; Ensign, 18th Continental Infantry, 1st January, 1776; died 18th April, 1776.

Perkins, John (Mass). 2d Lieutenant and Regimental Quartermaster 25th Continental Infantry, 1st January to December, 1776.

Perkins, Jonathan (N. H.). Sergeant 1st. New Hampshire, 23d April to December, 1775; Sergeant, 1st New Hampshire, 8th November, 1776; Ensign, 29th July, 1777; 2d Lieutenant, 24th March, 1780; served to close of war. (Died 11th August, 1824.)

Perkins, Obadiah (Conn). Lieutenant Connecticut Militia, ——; wounded at Groton Heights, 6th September, 1781. (Died 1813.)

Perkins, Peter (Va). Lieutenant-Colonel Virginia Militia, 1777-1781.

Perkins, Solomon (Conn). Captain Connecticut Militia, ——; wounded at Groton Heights, 6th September, 1781.

Perkins, William (Mass). Lieutenant of Gridley's Regiment Massachusetts Artillery, May, 1775; Captain of Knox's Regiment Continental Artillery, 10th December, 1775; Captain 3d Continental Artillery, 1st January, 1777; Major, 12th September, 1778. Discharged, 1st November, 1779. (Died 27th October, 1802.)

Perkins, William Harding (Va). Colonel Virginia Militia, 1777-1781.

Perley, Abraham.—See **Parley.**

Perley, Eliphalet (Mass). Corporal in Lexington Alarm, April, 1775; Corporal and Sergeant of Mansfield's Massachusetts Regiment, April to November, 1775; Ensign, 25th Continental Infantry, 1st January to 31st December, 1776. (Died 15th April, 1822.)

Perritt, Peter (Conn). Captain 7th Connecticut, 6th July to 10th December, 1775; Captain 19th Continental Infantry, 1st January, 1776; taken prisoner at Fort Washington, 16th November, 1776; exchanged 18th September, 1778; served subsequently as Captain Connecticut State Regiment.

Perronneau, John (S. C.). 2d Lieutenant 1st South Carolina, 17th June, 1775; 1st Lieutenant, 9th November, 1777; resigned 12th December, 1777.

Perry, Abel (Mass). 1st Lieutenant of Ward's Massachusetts Regiment, 23d May to December, 1775. (Died 1808.)

Perry, Abner (Mass). Colonel Massachusetts Militia in 1780.

Perry, Benjamin (Pa). Surgeon's-Mate 2d Pennsylvania, 1st January, 1777; Surgeon, 10th July, 1777; retired 1st July, 1778.

Perry, David (Conn). 2d Lieutenant 3d Connecticut, 1st May to 6th September, 1775.

Perry, Ebenezer (N. H.). 1st Lieutenant New Hampshire Militia, ——; killed at Bennington, 16th August, 1777.

Perry, George (N. C.). Major North Carolina Militia in 1776.

Perry, James (Mass). Captain in Lexinton Alarm, April, 1775; Captain of Sargeant's Massachusetts Regiment, April to November, 1775; Captain, 16th Continental Infantry, 1st January to 31st December, 1776. (Died 1815.)

Perry, John (Mass). Captain in Lexington Alarm, April, 1775; Captain of Walker's Massachusetts Regiment, May to November, 1775; Captain Massachusetts Militia, 1776-1777.

Perry, John (Va). Cornet 3d Continental Dragoons ——, 1781; 2d Lieutenant, ——, 1782; retained in Baylor's Regiment of Dragoons, 9th November, 1782, and served to close of war.

Perry, Joseph (Mass). 2d Lieutenant of Frye's Massachusetts Regiment, May to December, 1775.

Perry, Joseph (R. I.). Lieutenant 3d Rhode Island, 28th June to December, 1775; 1st Lieutenant 6th Continental Infantry, 1st January, 1776; 1st Lieutenant of Stevens' Battalion (subsequently part of 3d Continental Artillery), 9th November, 1776; resigned 6th March, 1780.

Perry, Joseph (Conn). Chaplain of Wolcott's Connecticut Regiment, December, 1775, to February, 1776.

Perry, Nathaniel (Ga). 2d Lieutenant 3d Georgia, May, 1777; 1st Lieutenant, 29th April, 1778; was a Captain when he was killed at Quinby's Bridge, 17th July, 1781.

Perry, Sylvanus (Conn). Private in the Lexington Alarm, April, 1775; Ensign in Sage's Connecticut State Regiment, 20th June to 25th December, 1776; 1st Lieutenant 3d Connecticut, 1st January, 1777; retired 1st January, 1781. (Died 5th October, 1821.)

Perry, William (Mass). Ensign 14th Massachusetts, 1st January, 1777; died 10th October, 1777, of wounds received at Germantown, 4th October, 1777.

Persons, Jacob (Mass). Captain of Cady's Massachusetts Battalion in the Quebec campaign, January to June, 1776.

Persons, Nathan.—See Parsons.

Peters, Andrew (Mass). Captain of Read's Massachusetts Regiment, May to December, 1775; Captain 13th Continental Infantry, 1st January to 31st December, 1776; Major 2d Massachusetts, 1st January, 1777; Lieutenant-Colonel 15th Massachusetts, 1st July, 1779; resigned 26th November, 1779. (Died 5th February, 1822.)

Peters, Nathan (Mass). Captain of Danielson's Massachusetts Regiment, 19th May to December, 1775; Captain 3d Continental Infantry, 1st January to 31st December, 1776. (Died 6th February, 1824.)

Peters, Richard (Pa). Captain Pennsylvania Militia, 1775-1776. (Died 21st August, 1828.)

Peters, William (N. Y.). Ensign 2d New York, 29th June, 1781, and served to June, 1783; Lieutenant United States Infantry Regiment, 24th November, 1785; Lieutenant 1st Infantry United States Army, 29th September, 1789; Captain, 4th November, 1791; assigned to 1st Sub Legion, 4th September, 1792; Major 4th Sub Legion, 1st July, 1794; assigned to 4th Infantry, 1st November, 1796; honorably discharged, 1st June, 1802.

Peterson, Derick (N. J.). Major New Jersey Militia in 1777.

Peterson, Gabriel (Pa). Ensign 8th Pennsylvania, 9th August, 1776; 2d Lieutenant, 13th July, 1777; 1st Lieutenant, 26th July, 1777; wounded at Bound Brook, 13th April, 1777; transferred to 2d Pennsylvania, 1st January, 1783, and served to June, 1783. Name also spelled Patterson.

Peterson, John (N. J.). Captain New Jersey Militia, 1776-1777.

Petri, Jacob (N. Y.). Ensign New York Militia, ——; prisoner of war, 14th June, 1780, to 14th December, 1782; where taken not stated.

Petri, Richard (N. Y.). Lieutenant New York Militia; killed at Oriskany, 6th August, 1777.

Petrie, Alexander (S. C.). 1st Lieutenant 2d South Carolina, 1777; Captain, 21st January, 1778; wounded at Savannah, 9th October, 1779. Name also spelled Patrie.

Petrie, George (S. C.). 2d Lieutenant 1st South Carolina, 23d December, 1779; taken prisoner at Charleston, 12th May, 1780. (Died 12th July, 1831.)

Pettee, Benjamin (Mass). Lieutenant of Nixon's Massachusetts Regiment May to November, 1775.

Pettee, Thomas (Mass). 1st Lieutenant of Read's Massachusetts Regiment, May to November, 1775.

Pettibone, Abel (Conn). Captain 2d Connecticut, 1st May to 10th December, 1775; Captain 22d Continental Infantry, 1st January to 31st December, 1776. (Died 1815.)

Pettibone, Jonathan (Conn). Colonel Connecticut Militia, 1775-1776. Died 26th September, 1776.

Pettibone, Jonathan, Jr. (Conn). Ensign 2d Connecticut, 1st May to 10th December, 1775; 2d Lieutenant 22d Continental Infantry, 1st January, 1776; 1st Lieutenant, September to December, 1776. (Died 1825.)

Pettibone, Ozias (Conn). Captain of Ward's Connecticut State Regiment, 14th May, 1776, to May, 1777; served subsequently as Lieutenant-Colonel and Colonel Connecticut Militia. (Died 1812.)

Pettigrew, James (Pa). Ensign of Patton's Continental Regiment, 1st June, 1778; transferred to 11th Pennsylvania, 16th December, 1778; Lieutenant 13th February, 1779; retired 17th January, 1781.

Pettingall, Samuel (N. Y.). Captain New York Militia; killed at Oriskany, 6th August, 1777.

Pettingill, Joseph (Mass). 2d Lieutenant of Gerrish's Massachusetts Regiment, 19th May to December, 1775; Captain 26th Continental Infantry, 1st January to 31st December, 1776; Cap-

tain 9th Massachusetts, 1st January, 1777; Major, 26th July, 1779; transferred to 1st Massachusetts, 1st January, 1783, and served to November, 1783. (Died ——, 1785.)

Pettingill, Samuel (N. H.). 2d Lieutenant 3d New Hampshire, 23d April to December, 1775; 1st Lieutenant 2d Continental Infantry, 1st January to 31st December, 1776; Captain of New York Militia in 1777, and killed at Oriskany, 6th August, 1777.

Pettit, —— (——). Captain Pulaski Legion; wounded at Flat Rock. 17th July, 1780.

Pettit, Charles (N. J.). Assistant Quartermaster-General, 2d March, 1778; resigned 20th June, 1781. (Died 4th September, 1806.)

Pettus, John (Va). 2d Lieutenant 1st Virginia, 2d October, 1775; 1st Lieutenant, January, 1776; died —— May, 1777.

Petty, John (N. J.). Captain New Jersey Militia, 1777.

Petty, John (Vt). Captain Vermont Militia in 1777-1778.

Peyton, Dade (Va). Cornet 4th Continental Dragoons, 2d March, 1779; Lieutenant, 2d June, 1779, and served to ——.

Peyton, George (Va). Ensign 3d Virginia, 1776-1777; marked "dead."

Peyton, Henry (Va). Cornet Virginia Cavalry, 18th June, 1776; 2d Lieutenant 1st Continental Dragoons, 12th February, 1777; Captain Lieutenant of Lee's Battalion of Light Dragoons, 7th April, 1778; Captain, 2d July, 1778; Major, 17th February, 1780; killed at Charleston, 12th May, 1780.

Peyton, John (Va). 1st Lieutenant 3d Virginia, 5th February, 1776; Captain, 19th June, 1776; wounded at Brandywine, 11th September, 1777; retired 30th September, 1778; served as Clothier General, 1780-1781. (Died 1790.)

Peyton, Robert (Va). Ensign 3d Virginia, November, 1776; 2d Lieutenant, 1st January, 1777; killed at Brandywine, 11th September, 1777.

Peyton, Valentine (Va). 2d Lieutenant 3d Virginia, 5th February, 1777; 1st Lieutenant, 15th August, 1777; Captain, 12th September, 1777; Brevet-Major, 30th September, 1783; served to close of war. (Died 1786.)

Peyton, Valentine (Va). Was Surgeon 3d Virginia in 1777. (Died 1802.)

Phelon, Edward (Mass). Ensign of Henley's Additional Continental Regiment, 1st July, 1777; transferred to Jackson's Regiment, 22d April, 1779; wounded at ——; regiment designated 16th Massachusetts, 23d July, 1780; transferred to 9th Massachusetts, 1st January, 1781; Lieutenant, 14th October, 1781; Aide-de-Camp to General Putnam, 1781 to 1783; transferred to 4th Massachusetts, 12th June, 1783; Captain, 30th September, 1783, and served to 3d November, 1783. (Died 7th January, 1810.)

Phelon, John (Mass). Ensign 13th Massachusetts, 1st January, 1777; 2d Lieutenant, 22d October, 1777; 1st Lieutenant, 1st January, 1778; wounded at Quaker Hill, Rhode Island, 29th August, 1778; transferred to 3d Massachusetts, 1st January, 1781, and served to 3d November, 1783. (Died 14th September, 1827.)

Phelon, Patrick (Mass). 1st Lieutenant of Henley's Additional Continental Regiment, 20th June, 1777; transferred to Jackson's Regiment, 22d April, 1779; regiment designated 16th Massachusetts, 23d July, 1780; transferred to 9th Massachusetts, 1st January, 1781; transferred to 3d Massachusetts, 1st January, 1783; Brevet-Captain, 30th September, 1783; retained in Jackson's Continental Regiment, November, 1783, and served to 20th June, 1784; Captain 2d United States Infantry, 4th March, 1791; killed 4th November, 1791, in action with Indians at St. Clair's defeat, near Fort Recovery, Ohio.

Phelps, Davenport (Vt). Captain of Bedel's Regiment, Vermont Militia, 1777-1779.

Phelps, Ebenezer (Conn). 2d Lieutenant of Sage's Connecticut State Regiment, June to December, 1776.

Phelps, Elisha (Conn). Served with Ethan Allen at Ticonderoga, May, 1775; Deputy Commissary-General for Connecticut Troops, 8th June, 1775; died ——, 1776.

Phelps, Noah (Conn). Served with Ethan Allen at Ticonderoga in May, 1775; Captain in Ward's Connecticut State Regiment, 14th May, 1776, to May, 1777; served subsequently as Lieutenant-Colonel and Colonel Connecticut Militia. (Died 4th March, 1809.)

Phelps, Noah (Conn). Sergeant in the Lexington Alarm, April, 1775; Sergeant in Wolcott's Connecticut State Regiment, December, 1775, to March, 1776; Ensign 2d Connecticut, 1st January, 1777; 2d Lieutenant, December, 1777; killed 16th March, 1778, at ——; where not stated. (Name also spelled Phillips.)

Phelps, Othneil (Mass). Regimental-Quartermaster 1st Massachusetts, 13th November, 1776; resigned 6th September, 1777.

Phelps, Reuben (Conn). Ensign of Gay's Connecticut State Regiment, June to December, 1776.

Phelps, Roger (Conn). Ensign of Wadsworth's Connecticut State Regiment, June to December, 1776.

Phelps, Seth (Conn). 2d Lieutenant 20th Continental Infantry, 1st January to 31st December, 1776; 1st Lieutenant 4th Connecticut, 1st January, 1777; wounded at Princeton, 3d January, 1777; Captain, 25th May, 1778; wounded at Stony Point, 15th July, 1779; transferred to Invalid Regiment, 26th October, 1780; retired 9th October, 1782. (Died 1826.)

Phelps, Thomas (Conn). Sergeant 2d Connecticut, 4th May to 4th December, 1775; Ensign 22d Continental Infantry, 1st January to 31st December, 1776; Lieutenant of Baldwin's Artillery Artificer Regiment, 24th July, 1777; resigned 1st May, 1779. (Died 28th February, 1789.)

Phelps, Winslow (Mass). Private in Whitcomb's Massachusetts Regiment, April to November, 1775; Corporal, 6th Continental Infantry, 1st January, 1776; Sergeant, 1st August, 1776; Ensign 13th Massachusetts, 1st January, 1777; resigned 27th October, 1777.

Phiddeman, Philip (Md). Captain of Richardson's Battalion of the Flying Camp, July to December, 1776.

Phifer, Caleb (N. C.). Colonel North Carolina Militia, 1776-1777. (Died 1811.)

Phifer, Martin (N. C.). Captain Independent Company North Carolina Light Horse, March, 1777, to April, 1780 (Died 1837.)

Phile, Charles (Pa). 1st Lieutenant 5th Pennsylvania Battalion, 6th January, 1776; taken prisoner at Fort Washington, 16th November, 1776; was promoted Captain 6th Pennsylvania, to rank from 1st February, 1777; exchanged 26th August, 1778, and did not return to the army.

Phillips, Christopher (R. I.). Lieutenant Rhode Island Militia in 1776.

Phillips, George (Ga). 3d Lieutenant 1st Georgia, 12th December, 1775, to ——.

Phillips, James (Va). Ensign Virginia Riflemen Militia, ——; killed at King's Mountain, 7th October, 1780.

Phillips, John (Ga). Captain-Lieutenant 3d Georgia, ——; on roll for August, 1778.

Phillips, John (N. J.). Ensign 2d New Jersey, 1st January, 1777; resigned 14th November, 1777. (Died 25th May, 1831.)

Phillips, Jonathan (N. J.). 2d Lieutenant 2d New Jersey, 20th November, 1775; 1st Lieutenant, 29th November, 1776; Captain, 1st December, 1777, and served to April, 1783.

Phillips, Jonathan H. (N. J.). Ensign of Baldwin's Artillery Artificer Regiment, 14th October, 1777; omitted, November, 1778.

Phillips, Joseph (N. J.). Major, Lieutenant-Colonel and Colonel New Jersey Militia, June, 1776, to August, 1780.

Phillips, Joseph (N. C.). Captain 4th North Carolina, 16th April, 1776, to ——.

Phillips, Noah.—See **Phelps.**

Phillips, Peter (R. I.). Commissary 11th Continental Infantry, 26th February, 1776, to ——.

Phillips, Samuel (R. I.). Captain of Richmond's Rhode Island State Regiment, 19th August, 1776, to March, 1777; Major of Topham's Regiment Rhode Island Militia in 1778. (Died 1808.)

Phillips, Samuel (Va). Sergeant 11th Virginia, 10th August, 1776; transferred to 7th Virginia, 14th September, 1778; Ensign, 4th July, 1779; killed at Charleston, 12th May, 1780.

Phillips, Thomas (R. I.). Lieutenant of Varnum's Rhode Island Regiment, 3d May to December, 1775.

Phinney, Edmund (Mass). Colonel of Massachusetts Regiment, 19th May to December, 1775; Colonel 18th Continental Infantry, 1st January to 31st December, 1776.

Phinney, Nelson (Mass). 1st Lieutenant 3d Continental Infantry, 1st January to 31st December, 1776.

Philpot, Bryan (Md). Ensign of Smallwood's Maryland Regiment, 14th January, 1776, to ——.

Phoenix, George (Ga). Captain Georgia Artillery Company, 6th November, 1776, to ——.

Piatt, Daniel (N. J.). Captain 1st New Jersey, 16th December, 1775; Major, 4th January, 1778; died 16th April, 1780.

Piatt, Jacob (N. J.). Ensign 1st New Jersey, 16th December, 1775; 2d Lieutenant, 29th November, 1776; 1st Lieutenant, 10th January, 1777; wounded at Monmouth, 28th June, 1778; Captain-Lieutenant, 2d February, 1779; Captain, 26th October, 1779; resigned 11th March, 1780. (Died 1834.)

Piatt, William (N. J.). Private and Sergeant 1st New Jersey, December, 1775, to August, 1776. 2d Lieutenant, 20th August, 1776; 1st Lieutenant, 15th January, 1777; Captain, 11th March, 1780, and served to April, 1783.

Pickard, Bartholomew (N. Y.). Lieutenant New York Militia, ——; prisoner of war, 3d April, 1780, to 1st May, 1783; where taken not stated.

Pickard, John (N. Y.). Lieutenant New York Militia; wounded and taken prisoner at Oriskany, 6th August, 1777, and was a prisoner to 11th November, 1782. (Died 4th May, 1783.)

Pickens, Andrew (S. C.. Served as Captain, Major and Colonel South Carolina Militia and as Brigadier-General South Carolina State Troops, ——, 1775, to close of war. By the act of 9th March, 1781, it was "Resolved, that a sword be presented to Colonel Pickens, of the Militia, in testimony of his spirited conduct at the battle of Cowpens, S. C." Wounded at Eutaw Springs, 8th September, 1781. (Died 17th August, 1817.)

Pickens, John (Mass). 2d Lieutenant of Danielson's Massachusetts Regiment, May to December, 1775.

Pickens, Joseph (S. C.). Captain South Carolina Militia; killed at Ninety-Six, in June, 1781.

Pickering, James (Pa). Lieutenant Pennsylvania Militia, ——; wounded at Bristol, Pennsylvania, 17th April, 1778.

Pickering, Timothy (Mass). Colonel of a Massachusetts Militia Regiment at commencement of the war; Colonel Adjutant-General to General Washington, 18th June, 1777, to 13th January,

1778; elected member of the Board of War, 7th November, 1777; Colonel and Quartermaster General Continental Army, 5th August, 1780, to 25th July, 1785; Secretary of War, 2d January to 10th December, 1795. (Died 29th January, 1829.)

Pickett, Martin (Va). Colonel Virginia Militia, 1778-1779.

Pickett, Thomas (N. C.). Ensign 1st North Carolina, 20th October. 1775, to January, 1776.

Pickett, William (N C.). Captain 1st North Carolina, 1st September, 1775, to 4th January, 1776, when his company was broken up.

Pickett, William (Va). Major Virginia Militia, 1777-1778.

Pickron, Aaron (Ga). 2d Lieutenant of Grimes' Independent Georgia Company, 16th October, 1775, to ——.

Pidgin, Moses (Mass). Captain of Baldwin's Artillery Artificer Regiment, 12th May, 1777; omitted June, 1778.

Pier, Ethan (Vt). Lieutenant Vermont Militia in 1777.

Pierce.—See also **Peirce.**

Pierce, Amos (N. H.). Lieutenant New Hampshire Militia, ——; wounded at Bennington, 16th August, 1777.

Pierce, Benjamin (Mass). Private in Bridge's Massachusetts Regiment, April to December, 1775; Sergeant 16th Continental Infantry, January to December, 1776; Sergeant 8th Massachusetts, 1st January, 1777; Ensign, 7th October, 1777; Lieutenant, 7th July, 1782; transferred to 1st Massachusetts, 1st January, 1783, and served to November, 1783. (Died 1st April, 1839.)

Pierce, Caleb (Pa). Ensign 5th Pennsylvania, 1st January, 1777; resigned 9th April, 1777.

Pierce, Ethan (Vt). Lieutenant Vermont Militia, 1776.

Pierce, George (Pa). Captain Chester County, Pennsylvania, Militia, 1776-1777.

Pierce, John (Conn). Assistant Paymaster-General Continental Army, 10th February, 1776; Deputy Paymaster-General, 1st June, 1779; Paymaster-General, 17th January, 1781; died 1st August, 1788.

Pierce, Joshua (Mass). Ensign 2d Massachusetts, 1st January, 1777; resigned 10th April, 1779.

Pierce, Phineas (Conn). Lieutenant of Spalding's Wyoming Valley Company; resigned 10th November, 1778, on account of wounds received in 1776.

Pierce Samuel (Mass). Lieutenant-Colonel Massachusetts Militia, 1776-1780. (Died 1815.)

Pierce, Thomas (Mass). Captain of Gridley's Regiment Massachusetts Artillery, May to December, 1775; Captain of Knox's Regiment Continental Artillery, 10th December, 1775, to December, 1776.

Pierce, Timothy (Pa). Sergeant in Ransom's Wyoming Valley Company, August, 1776; Ensign, 3d December, 1777; 2d Lieutenant, 17th January, 1778; killed 3d July, 1778, at the Wyoming Valley massacre.

Pierce, William (Va). Captain of the 1st Continental Artillery, 30th November, 1776; served as Aide-de-Camp to Generals Sullivan and Greene throughout the war. By the Act of 29th October, 1781, it was "Resolved, that Major-General Greene be desired to present the thanks of Congress to Captain Pierce, his Aide-de-Camp, in testimony of his particular activity and good conduct during the whole action at Eutaw Springs, (S. C.), and that a sword be presented to Captain Pierce, who bore the General's dispatches, giving an account of the victory, and that the Board of War take order herein." Brevet-Major, 30th September, 1783.

Piercy, Christian (Pa). Captain Pennsylvania Militia; wounded at Paoli, 20th September, 1777.

Piercy, Henry (Pa). Sergeant 1st Pennsylvania Battalion of the Flying Camp, June to December, 1776; was wounded at Long Island, 27th August, 1776; 2d Lieutenant 2d Pennsylvania, 1st January, 1777; 1st Lieutenant, 12th March, 1777; wounded at Green Springs 6th July, 1781; transferred to 3d Pennsylvania, 1st January, 1783, and served to 3d June, 1783; Captain 8th United States Infantry, 10th January, 1799; honorably discharged 15th June, 1800; name also spelled Pearcy.

Piercy, Jonathan.—See **Pearcy.**

Pierson, Daniel (N. J.). 2d Lieutenant 3d New Jersey, 15th April to November, 1776; 1st Lieutenant 4th New Jersey, 1st January, 1777; resigned 9th December, 1778.

Pierson, John (N. J.). 1st Lieutenant 4th New Jersey, 17th February,

1777; transferred to Baldwin's Artillery Artificer Regiment, — June, 1777; resigned 20th April, 1778.

Pierson, Jonathan (N. J.). Captain of Spencer's Additional Continental Regiment, 6th February, 1777; wounded at Germantown, 4th October, 1777; resigned 8th October, 1778.

Pierson, Nathan (Conn). 2d Lieutenant 1st Connecticut, 1st May to 23d December, 1775; 1st Lieutenant of Douglas' Connecticut State Regiment, June to December, 1776.

Pierson, Thomas (N. J.). 1st Lieutenant 4th New Jersey, 23d November, 1776; Captain, 6th February, 1777; resigned 13th March, 1777.

Piggott, James (Pa). Captain Pennsylvania Associators, 6th April, 1776; Captain 8th Pennsylvania, 9th August, 1776; resigned 22d October, 1777; served subsequently as Captain in Clarke's Illinois Regiment on the Ohio.

Pike, Benjamin (Mass). Sergeant in Lexington Alarm, April, 1775; Sergeant of Read's Massachusetts Regiment, April to November, 1775; Ensign 13th Continental Infantry, 1st Januaryto 31st December, 1776; 1st Lieutenant 6th Massachusetts, 1st January, 1777; Captain-Lieutenant, 11th April, 1780; Captain, 16th October, 1780; retired 1st January, 1783.

Pike, Benjamin (N. C.). 1st Lieutenant 6th North Carolina, 16th April, 1776; Captain, 28th April, 1777; died 12th October, 1777.

Pike, Daniel (Mass). Ensign of Doolittle's Massachusetts Regiment, May to December, 1775.

Pike, Robert (N. H.). Ensign 8th Continental Infantry, 1st January, 1776; 2d Lieutenant, 9th November to 31st December, 1776; served subsequently as Captain New Hampshire Militia.

Pike, Samuel (Mass). Ensign 7th Massachusetts, 1st January, 1777; deserted 11th July, 1778

Pike, Thomas (Mass) 1st Lieutenant of Gerrish's Massachusetts Regiment, 19th May to December, 1775

Pike, William (Mass). Private 2d Continental Dragoons, 18th February, 1777; Sergeant, 16th March, 1778; Cornet, 14th June, 1781, and served to close of war

Pike, Zebulon (N. J.). Cornet 4th Continental Dragoons, 1st March, 1777; Regimental Adjutant, 20th November,

1777; Lieutenant, 15th March, 1778; Captain, 25th December, 1778; Regimental Paymaster, 1st June, 1780, and served to close of the war; Captain in the Levies in 1791; Captain United States Infantry, 5th March, 1792; assigned to 3d Sub Legion, 4th September, 1792; assigned to 3d Infantry, 1st November, 1796; Major, 21st March, 1800; transferred to 1st Infantry, 1st April, 1802 ;Brevet Lieutenant-Colonel, 10th July, 1812 honorably discharged 15th June, 1815. (Died 27th July, 1834.)

Piles, William (Va). 1st Lieutenant of Stephenson's Maryland and Virginia Rifle Regiment, 23d July, 1776; in Rawlins' Continental Regiment in 1777; dropped on roll for September, 1778, with remark "Prisoner broke parole."

Pilley, John (N. C.). Ensign 2d North Carolina, 11th December, 1776, to ——.

Pilsbury, Daniel (Mass). 1st Lieutenant 24th Continental Infantry, 1st January to 31st December, 1776; Captain 13th Massachusetts, 1st January, 1777; transferred to 6th Massachusetts, 1st January, 1781; retired 1st January, 1783.

Pinchon, Walter (Mass). 2d Lieutenant of Danielson's Massachusetts Regiment, May to December, 1775.

Pinckney, Charles Cotesworth (S. C.) Captain 1st South Carolina, 17th June, 1775; Lieutenant-Colonel, ——; Colonel, 16th September, 1776; taken prisoner at Charleston, 12th May, 1780; exchanged ——, and served to 3d November, 1783; Brevet Brigadier-General 3d November, 1783; Major-General United States Army, 19th July, 1798; honorably discharged 15th June, 1800. (Died 16th August, 1825.)

Pinckney, Thomas (S. C.). Captain 1st South Carolina, 17th June, 1775; Major, 1st May, 1778; Aide-de-Camp to General Lincoln in 1779; Aide-de-Camp to General Gates, 3d August, 1780; was wounded and taken prisoner at Camden, 16th August, 1780; exchanged December, 1780, and served to close of war; Major-General United States Army, 27th March, 1812; honorably discharged 15th June, 1815. (Died 2d November, 1828.)

Pindell, Richard (Md). Surgeon's Mate 4th Maryland, January, 1777; Surgeon, 14th November, 1777; transferred to 1st Maryland, 1st January, 1781; retained in Maryland Battalion, April, 1783, and served to 15th November, 1783

Pinto, Solomon (Conn). Ensign 6th Connecticut, 18th March, 1780; transferred to 7th Connecticut, 26th July, 1780; transferred to 2d Connecticut, 1st January, 1781, and served to June, 1783. (Died 28th March, 1824.)

Piper, Andrew (N. Y.). Ensign New York Militia, ——: prisoner of war 14th ne, 1780, to 14th December, 1782; where taken not stated.

Piper, George (Pa). Ensign Philadelphia County, Pennsylvania, Militia, 1776-1777.

Piper, James (Pa) Lieutenant-Colonel Commandant 1st Battalion of Miles' Pennsylvania Rifle Regiment, 13th March, 1776, wounded and taken prisoner at Long Island, 27th August, 1776, and died September, 1776, while in captivity.

Piper, John (N. J.). 1st Lieutenant of Martin's Regiment New Jersey Militia, June, 1776, 1st Leieutenant 4th New Jersey, 23d November, 1776; resigned 3d October, 1777

Piper, John (Del). Ensign Delaware Militia Regiment in 1780.

Piper, John (Pa). Colonel Pennsylvania Militia, 1776-1777.

Piper, John (Va). 2d Lieutenant 1st Virginia State Regiment, — March, 1777; 1st Lieutenant 1st June, 1778, and served to February, 1781.

Piper, Samuel (N. H.). Lieutenant of Mooney's Regiment New Hampshire Militia, 1779-1780.

Pitcher, John (Mass). Surgeon in Lexington Alarm, April, 1775; Surgeon of Cotton's Massachusetts Regiment, May to November, 1775; Surgeon 25th Continental Infantry, 1st January to 31st December, 1776; Surgeon Massachusetts Militia, 1777-1780.

Pitkin, George (Conn). Lieutenant-Colonel in Lexington Alarm, April, 1775; Lieutenant-Colonel 4th Connecticut, 1st May to 20th December, 1775; Lieutenant-Colonel Connecticut Militia in 1776.

Pitkin, Richard (Conn). 1st Lieutenant of Wolcott's Connecticut State Regiment, December, 1775, to March, 1776.

Pitman, Isaac (R. I.). Captain of Elliott's Regiment Rhode Island Artillery, 1775-1776.

Pitt, John (Pa). Captain Pennsylvania Militia, 1782.

Pitt, John (Va). Surgeon Hospital Department, 1780-1781.

Pitts, John (N. C.). Captain North Carolina Militia in 1780.

Pitts, Peter (Mass). Captain of Walker's Massachusetts Regiment, May to November, 1775.

Pixley, Asa (Mass). Sergeant 9th Massachusetts, 1st January, 1777; Ensign, 1st July, 1777; resigned 3d July, 1779. (Died 26th March, 1825.)

Pixley, David (Mass). 1st Lieutenant Paterson's Massachusetts Regiment, May to December, 1775; Lieutenant Massachusetts Militia in 1777.

Place, David (N. H.). Captain 2d Continental Infantry, 1st January to December, 1776.

Place, Morris (N. Y.). Major New York Militia in 1775.

Plater, Phillips F. (S. C.). 1st Lieutenant 4th South Carolina (Artillery) Regiment, 28th October, 1778; taken prisoner at Charleston, 12th May, 1780.

Platt, Daniel (Conn). Ensign 6th Connecticut, 1st May to 18th December, 1775; served subsequently as Lieutenant and Captain Connecticut Militia. (Died 1826.)

Platt, John (Del). Surgeon's Mate Delaware Battalion of the Flying Camp, July to December, 1776; Surgeon's Mate Delaware Regiment, 5th April, 1777, to close of war. (Died 1823.)

Platt, Jonathan (N. Y.). Captain 4th New York, 28th June. 1775, to January, 1776.

Platte, Richard (N. Y.). 2d Lieutenant 1st New York, 28th June, 1775; 1st Lieutenant, November, 1775; Captain, 21st November, 1776, to rank from 26th June, 1776; Brigade Major to General McDougall, 11th August, 1776; Major and Aide-de-Camp to General McDougall, December, 1776, to close of war; Battalion Paymaster Corps of Artillery, United States Army, 21st November, 1817; resigned 25th November, 1820. (Died 3d March, 1830)

Platt, Samuel (Pa). Surgeon's Mate 9th Pennsylvania, 25th January, 1778; retired 1st January, 1781.

Platt, Zaphania (N. Y.). Colonel New York Militia 1779-1782.

Pleasants, John (Va). Captain 5th Virginia, 24th February, 1776; resigned 18th December, 1776.

Pleasants, John, Jr. (Pa). Captain 5th Pennsylvania Battalion, 24th February, 1776; resigned August, 1776.

Pledger, Joseph (S. C.). 2d Lieutenant 3d South Carolina, 17th June, 1775, to ——.

Plessis, de Maduit du (France). Captain Continental Artillery, 15th April, 1777. In Congress, January 19, 1778, "a letter of the 13th, from General Washington, was read, wherein he recommended the Chevalier de Maduit du Plesis to be promoted to the rank of Lieutenant-Colonel, adding that the gallant conduct of this young gentleman at Brandywine, Germantown, and his distinguished services at Fort Mercer, where he united the office of Engineer and Commandant of Artillery, entitle him to the particular notice of Congress; that he made several judicious alterations in the works at Red Bank, shewed great good conduct during the action, in which the Hessians were repulsed; that after the evacuation was determined on, he became the means of saving some valuable artillery and stores, and cheerfully undertook, as volunteer, the hazardous operation of blowing up the magazine, &c., without apparatus usually provided upon such occasions." Concluding in Mr. du Plessis' favor, that "he possesses a degree of modesty not always found in men who have performed brilliant actions;" whereupon "Resolved, that a brevet of Lieutenant-Colonel be granted the Chevalier de Maudit du Plessis, as a reward for his services and an encouragement to merit, and that his commission bear date 26th November, 1777, in order that the recompense may more immediately follow the services which he has done."

By the act of 5th November, 1778, it was "Resolved, that the Chevalier Maduit du Plessis have leave to withdraw from the service of these United States, and that the President give him a written testimonial of the high sense which Congress entertain of his zeal, bravery and good conduct during his service in America." (Died ——, 1791.)

Plumb, William (Mass). Chaplain of Marshall's Massachusetts Regiment, March, 1776; Chaplain 10th Continental Infantry, 25th June to 31st December, 1776; Brigade Chaplain, 20th August, 1777; retired 1st January, 1781. (Died 2d June, 1843.)

Plunkett, David (Md). 2d Lieutenant of Smallwood's Maryland Regiment, 14th January to December, 1776; Captain 4th Continental Dragoons, 10th January, 1777; taken prisoner, 20th October, 1777; where taken not stated; resigned 13th March, 1779.

Plummer, George W. (Va). Captain Virginia Militia, 1776-1777.

Plympton, Ezekiel (Mass). 2d Lieutenant of Read's Massachusetts Regiment, May to December, 1775; 2d Lieutenant 13th Continental Infantry, 1st January to 31st December, 1776.

Pobb, Mathias (Pa). Ensign 4th Pennsylvania, 3d January, 1777; retired 1st July, 1778.

Poe, David (Md). Appointed Quartermaster at Baltimore, 19th November, 1777, and served to ——. (Died May, 1820.)

Poe, James (Pa). Captain Pennsylvania Militia, 1776-1777.

Pointer, William (Va). Ensign 14th Virginia, 2d December, 1776; 2d Lieutenant, 8th December, 1777; regiment designated 10th Virginia, 14th September, 1778, and served to ——. (In service January, 1780.)

Polhemus, John (N. J.). Captain 1st New Jersey, 29th October, 1775, to 10th November, 1776; Captain 1st New Jersey, 22d November, 1776; taken did not rejoin regiment, and was retired 1st January, 1781. (Died 1831.)

Polhemus, Tobias (N. J.). Lieutenant New Jersey Militia; taken prisoner from his home at Monmouth, 13th February, 1777, and was a prisoner in 1782.

Polehouse, Thomas (Pa). Surgeon's Mate German Regiment, 4th October, 1776, and served to ——.

Polk, Charles (N. C.). Lieutenant 4th North Carolina, 25th April, 1777, to ——.

Polk, Ezekiel (S. C.). Captain 3d South Carolina (Rangers), 17th June, 1775; deserted with his company to the enemy in August, 1775, but returned in November, 1775, and was permitted to command a company to January, 1776, under Colonel Richardson; he subsequently served as Lieutenant-Colonel South Carolina Militia. (Died 1824.)

Polk, Thomas (N. C.). Colonel North Carolina Regiment, 21st December, 1775; Colonel 4th North Carolina, 16th April, 1776; resigned 28th June, 1778; Brigadier-General North Carolina Militia, 1781, to close of war. (Died 1793.)

Polk, William (N. C.). Major 9th North Carolina, 27th November, 1776; wounded at Germantown, 4th October, 1777; retired 1st June, 1778; Colonel North Carolina Militia and State troops, 1779-1781. (Died 4th January, 1834.)

Polk, William (S. C.). Lieutenant South Carolina State troops; killed at Eutaw Springs, 8th September, 1781.

Pollard, Benjamin (Mass). 2d Lieutenant of Learned's Massachusetts Regiment, May to December, 1775; 2d Lieutenant 6th Continental Infantry, 1st January to 31st December, 1776; 1st Lieutenant 13th Massachusetts 1st January, 1777; resigned 6th February, 1778.

Pollard, Benjamin (Mass). Captain of Baldwin's Artillery Artificer Regiment, 1st January, 1777 resigned 7th August, 1778.

Pollard, Jonathan (Mass). Aide-de-Camp to General Heath, 2d October, 1776, to September, 1778.

Pollard, Richard (S. C.). Sergeant 6th South Carolina, 6th May, 1776; Sergeant-Major, 2d June, 1776; Lieutenant, February, 1777; Captain, 20th June, 1779; wounded at Stono Ferry, 20th June, 1779; transferred to 1st South Carolina, July, 1780; taken prisoner at Charleston, 12th May, 1780; served to ——.

Polley, William (Mass). Sergeant in Lexington Alarm, April, 1775; 2d Lieutenant of Learned's Massachusetts Regiment, May to December, 1775; Lieutenant Massachusetts Militia in 1776.

Pollock, Jacob. Lieutenant 4th North Carolina, 12th November, 1776, to ——.

Pomeroy, Abner (Mass). 2d Lieutenant in Lexington Alarm, April, 1775; Captain of Fellow's Massachusetts Regiment, 27th April to September, 1775; served subsequently as Lieutenant and Captain Massachusetts Militia.

Pomeroy, Benjamin (Conn). Chaplain 3d Connecticut, 1st January, 1777; resigned 1st July, 1778. (Died 22d December, 1784.)

Pomeroy, Ebenezer (Mass). Captain of Fellow's Massachusetts Regiment, May to December, 1775.

Pomeroy, John (Pa). Lieutenant-Colonel Westmoreland County, Pennsylvania, Militia in 1778; name also spelled Pumeroy.

Pomeroy, Nathaniel (Conn). 2d Lieutenant of Mott's Connecticut State Regiment, June to December, 1776; served subsequently as Captain Connecticut Militia.

Pomeroy, Oliver (Conn). 2d Lieutenant of Wolcott's Connecticut State Regiment, December, 1775, to March, 1776.

Pomeroy, Ralph (Conn). Paymaster 22d Continental Infantry, 1st January to 31st December, 1776; Paymaster 3d Connecticut, 1st January, 1777; 2d Lieutenant, 1st June, 1778; 1st Lieutenant, 8th September, 1778; retired, 1st January, 1781. (Died 19th March, 1819.)

Pomeroy, Seth. (Mass). Was a Brigadier General of the Massachusetts Militia at the commencement of the War of the Revolution and was engaged in the battle of Bunker Hill, 17th June, 1775; Major-General Massachusetts Militia, 20th June, 1775, and served as such until he died at Peekskill New York, 19th February, 1777; he was appointed first Brigadier-General of the Continental Army, 22d June, 1775, but did not serve as such or accept the appointment.

Pond, Charles (Conn). Ensign 7th Connecticut, 6th July to 21st December, 1775; 1st Lieutenant 19th Continental Infantry, 1st January to 31st December, 1776; Captain 6th Connecticut, 1st January, 1777; resigned 19th April, 1779; subsequently joined the Nvay as Captain of the "New Defence;" was taken prisoner in a naval engagement. (Died 1832.)

Pond, Enoch (Mass). Ensign of Lee's Continental Regiment, 4th January, 1777, to ——.

Pond, Oliver (Mass). Captain in Lexington Alarm, April, 1775; Captain of Read's Massachusetts Regiment, April to December, 1775; Captain 13th Continental Infantry, 1st January to 31st December, 1776.

Pontiere, Louis de (France). Captain of Horse by brevet and Aide-de-Camp to General Steuben, 18th February, 1778, to 15th April, 1784; Brevet Major, 30th September, 1783.

Pontigbeau, —— (France). Captain and Aide-de-Camp to General Lafayette, 1781 and 1782.

Poole, Abijah (Mass). Ensign of Wigglesworth's Massachusetts Militia Reiment in 1776; Lieutenant 13th Massachusetts, 1st January, 1777; retired 19th April, 1779. (Died 9th May, 1820.)

Poole, Jacob (Mass). Lieutenant in Lexington Alarm, April, 1775; 1st Lieutenant of Whitcomb's Massachusetts Regiment, May to December, 1775; Captain 6th Continental Infantry, 1st January to 31st December, 1776.

Poole, Jonathan (N. H.). Surgeon's Mate, 1st New Hampshire, 2d April, 1777; resigned 11th June, 1780 (Died 25th July, 1797.)

Poole, Mark (Mass). 1st Lieutenant of Bridge's Massachusetts Regiment. May to December, 1775.

Poole, Richard (Mass). 1st Lieutenant 10th Massachusetts, 6th November, 1776; discharged 27th November, 1777.

Poole, Thomas (Conn). Cornet 2d Continental Dragoons, 10th January, 1777; Lieutenant, 7th April, 1777; resigned 11th September, 1778. (Died 26th January, 1826.)

Poor, Abraham (Mass). 2d Lieutenant of Frye's Massachusetts Regiment, May to December, 1775.

Poor, David (Mass). 2d Lieutenant of Doolittle's Massachusetts Regiment, May to December, 1775; 2d Lieutenant 27th Continental Infantry, 1st January, 1776; taken prisoner at Fort Washington, 16th November, 1776; exchanged 17th December, 1780.

Poor, Enoch (N. H.). Colonel 2d New Hampshire, 23d May to December, 1775; Colonel 8th Continental Infantry, 1st January, 1776; Colonel 2d New Hampshire, 8th November, 1776; Brigadier-General Continental Army, 21st February, 1777; died 8th September, 1780.

Poor, Joseph (S. C.). 1st Lieutenant 1st South Carolina, 17th June, 1775, to ——.

Poor, Thomas (Mass). Major of Frye's Massachusetts Regiment, 20th May to December, 1775; Lieutenant-Colonel 5th Continental infantry, 1st January to 31st December, 1776; Colonel Massachusetts Militia, 1778. (Died 1804.)

Pope, Charles (Del). Captain Delaware Regiment, 17th January, 1776; wounded at Mamaroneck, 21st October, 1776; Lieutenant-Colonel, 5th April, 1777; resigned 13th December, 1779. (Died 16th February, 1803.)

Pope, Edward (Mass). Colonel Maschusetts Militia, 1776-1778.

Pope, Frederick (Mass). Captain of Sargeant's Massachusetts Regiment, May to December, 1775 Captain 16th Continental Infantry, 1st January to

31st December, 1776; Major and Lieutenant-Colonel Massachusetts Militia, 1777-1780. (Died 1812.)

Pope, Henry (N. C.). Ensign 1st North Carolina, 1st September, 1775; Captain 8th North Carolina, 28th November, 1776; retired 1st June, 1778.

Pope, Isaac (Mass). Private Company of Minute Men, April, 1775; 1st Lieutenant of Cotton's Massachusetts Regiment, May to December, 1775; 1st Lieutenant 23d Continental Infantry, 1st January to 31st December, 1776; Captain 4th Massachusetts, 1st January, 1777; Major 3d Massachusetts, 12th October, 1782; retired June, 1783. (Died 21st June, 1820.)

Pope, Jacob (Mass). 2d Lieutenant 21st Continental Infantry, 1st January, 1776; cashiered 17th October, 1776.

Pope, John (Va). Ensign 10th Virginia, 25th November, 1776; resigned 11th July, 1777; Colonel Virginia Militia in 1781.

Pope, Matthew (Va). Surgeon of a Virginia State Regiment in 1779.

Popham, William (Del). 2d Lieutenant Delaware Regiment, 17th January, 1776; Captain 2d Canadian (Hazen's) Regiment, 3d November, 1776; served as Aide-de-Camp to General Clinton, 1777 to 1779, and as Major and Aide-de-Camp to General Steuben to close of war; Brevet Major, 30th September, 1783. (Died 1847.)

Popkin, John (Mass). Captain of Gridley's Regiment Massachusetts Artillery, May, 1775; Captain of Knox's Regiment Continental Artillery, 10th December, 1775; Major 3d Massachusetts, 1st January, 1777; Lieutenant-Colonel 3d Continental Artillery, 15th July, 1777, and served to 17th June, 1783. (Died 8th May, 1827.)

Porter, Amos (Mass). Ensign of Paterson's Massachusetts Regiment, May to November, 1775.

Porter, Andrew (Md). 1st Lieutenant Maryland Battalion of the Flying Camp, July to December, 1776; 1st Lieutenant 5th Maryland, 10th December, 1776, but does not appear to have joined the regiment.

Porter, Andrew (Pa). Captain of Marines, 1775-1776; Captain 2d Continental Artillery, 1st January, 1777; transferred to 4th Continental Artillery 1st January, 1781; Major, 19th April, 1781; Lieutenant-Colonel, 1st January,

1782, and served to 17th June, 1783. (Died 16th November, 1813.)

Porter, Benjamin (Ga). Captain 2d Georgia, July, 1776; Major, 16th April, 1778; Lieutenant-Colonel, ——, and served to ——.

Porter, Benjamin Jr. (Va). 2d Lieutenant 2d Virginia, 8th May,1776, to ——.

Porter, Benjamin Jones (Mass). Surgeon's Mate 11th Massachusetts, 11th May, 1780; transferred to 10th Massachusetts, 1st January, 1781; transferred to 4th Massachusetts, 12th June, 1783, and served to 3d November, 1783.

Porter, Billy (Mass). Captain in Lexington Alarm, April, 1775; Captain of Mansfield's Massachusetts Regiment, April to December, 1775; Captain 27th Continental Infantry, 1st January to 31st December, 1776; Captain 11th Massachusetts, 1st January, 1777; Major 10th Massachusetts, 26th October, 1780; transferred to 7th Massachusetts, 1st January, 1781; transferred to 3d Massachusetts, 12th June, 1783, and served to 3d November, 1783. (Died 1813.)

Porter, Charles (Md). Sergeant Maryland, 10th December, 1776; Ensign 7th Maryland, 19th April, 1777; 2d Lieutenant, 7th July, 1777; 1st Lieutenant, 22d May, 1779; retired 19th February, 1780.

Porter, David (Pa). Battalion Quartermaster Cumberland County, Pennsylvania, Militia, 1776-1777.

Porter, Eleazer (Mass). Surgeon's Mate 12th Massachusetts, 1st June, 1777; died 22d February, 1778.

Porter, Elisha (Mass). Colonel Massachusetts Militia, 1776-1777. (Died 1796.)

Porter, James (N. C.). Major North Carolina Militia, ——; died 16th October, 1780, of wounds received at King's Mountain, 7th October, 1780.

Porter, James (Pa). 1st Lieutenant 1st Pennsylvania Battalion of the Flying Camp, July to December, 1776.

Porter, James (Pa). Lieutenant Lancaster County, Pennsylvania, Militia, 1776-1777.

Porter, John (Mass). Sergeant in Lexington Alarm, April, 1775; 1st Lieutenant in Sargeant's Massachusetts Regiment, May to December, 1775; 1st Lieutenant 21st Continental Infantry, 1st January, 1776; Captain, 1st July, 1776, being Paymaster of the Regiment 12th September to 31st December, 1776; Captain 13th Massachusetts 1st January, 1777; Major, 30th May, 1777; transferred to 6th Massachusetts, 1st January, 1781; discharged 12th October, 1782. (Died December, 1790.)

Porter, John (N. Y.). Lieutenant New York Militia, ——; prisoner of war 8th March to 10th August, 1778; where taken not stated.

Porter, Jonathan (Mass). Sergeant 15th Massachusetts, 8th January, 1777; Quartermaster Sergeant, 10th March, 1777; Ensign, 31st March, 1779; 2d Lieutenant, 28th June, 1779; resigned 21st December, 1780; was a prisoner, but when and where taken not stated.

Porter, Joshua (Conn). Lieutenant-Colonel of Cook's Connecticut Regiment at Saratoga in October, 1777. (Died 12th September, 1825.)

Porter, Moses (Mass). Ensign 6th Massachusetts, 1st January, 1777; 2d Lieutenant 3d Continental Artillery, 21st April, 1779; transferred to Corps of Artillery, 17th June, 1783, and served to 3d November, 1783; Lieutenant United States Artillery Battalion, 20th October, 1786; Lieutenant Artillery United States Army, 29th September, 1789; Captain, 4th November, 1791; 1st Artillerists and Engineers, 9th May, 1794; Major, 26th May, 1800; retained in Artillerists, 1st April, 1802; Colonel Light Artillery, 12th March, 1812; transferred to 1st Artillery, 1st June, 1821; Brevet Brigadier-General, 10th September, 1813, for distinguished services in the campaign of 1813; died 14th April, 1822.

Porter, Nathaniel (N. H.). Chaplain of Wingate's Regiment New Hampshire Militia, July, 1776; Chaplain 3d New Hampshire, 8th November, 1776, to July, 1777. (Died 1810.)

Porter, Oliver (Ga). Major Georgia Militia, 1779-1780.

Porter, Phineas (Conn). Captain 1st Connecticut, 1st May to 10th December, 1775; Major of Douglas' Connecticut State Regiment, 10th June, 1776; taken prisoner on the retreat from New York, 15th September, 1776; served subsequently as Major and Colonel Connecticut Militia. (Died 1804.)

Porter, Robert (Md). 2d Lieutenant 3d Maryland, 10th December, 1776; 1st Leutenant, 20th February, 1777; resigned 15th April, 1777.

Porter, Robert (N. C.). Captain North Carolina Militia, 1776-1779.

Porter, Robert (Pa). Cadet 4th Continental Artillery, 9th January, 1779; 2d Lieutenant, 2d July, 1781; served to 17th June, 1783. (Died 1842.)

Porter, Robert (S. C.). Lieutenant South Carolina State Dragoons, 5th April, 1781; resigned — July, 1781.

Porter, Stephen (Pa). 1st Lieutenant of Lewis' Pennsylvania Battalion of the Flying Camp, July to December, 1776.

Porter, Thomas (Pa). Colonel Pennsylvania Militia, 1776-177.

Porter, William (Pa). Ensign Westmoreland County, Pennsylvania, Militia in 1778.

Porter, William (Va). 2d Lieutenant 12th Virginia. (Died 20th June, 1807.)

Porter, William.—See **Porter, Billy.**

Porter, William (Va). Ensign 2d Virginia, 4th May, 1777; 2d Lieutenant, 15th June, 1777 1st Lieutenant, — December, 1777; retired 30th September, 1778.

Porter, William (Va). 2d Lieutenant 12th Virginia, 21st July, 1777; regiment designated 8th Virginia, 14th September, 1778; 1st Lieutenant, 14th April, 1779; taken prisoner at Charleston, 12th May, 1780, and was a prisoner on parole to close of war. (Died 8th July, 1828.)

Porterfield, Charles (Va). Served as a volunteer in the Canada Campaign and was taken prisoner at Quebec 31st December, 1775; Captain 11th Virginia, 3d February, 1777; Brigade-Major of Woodford's Brigade, 13th July, 1778; transferred to 7th Virginia, 14th September, 1778; resigned 2d July, 1779; Lieutenant-Colonel of a Virginia State Regiment, 14th August, 1779; mortally wounded and taken prisoner at Camden, 16th August, 1780, and died in October, 1780.

Porterfield, Dennis (N. C.). Ensign 6th North Carolina, 16th April, 1776; Lieutenant, 2d April, 1777; transferred to 1st North Carolina 1st June, 1778; Captain, 1st February, 1779; killed 8th September, 1781, at Eutaw Springs.

Porterfield, Robert (Va). 2d Lieutenant 11th Virginia, 24th December, 1776; 1st Lieutenant, 1st June, 1777; Adjutant, 19th April, 1778; transferred to 7th Virginia, 14th September, 1778;

Captain Lieutenant, 2d July, 1779; Captain, 16th August, 1779; taken prisoner at Charleston, 12th May, 1780; exchanged December, 1780; transferred to 2d Virginia, 12th February, 1781, and served to close of war. (Died 13th February, 1843.)

Posey, Belair (Md). Captain 3d Maryland Battalion of the Flying Camp, July to December, 1776.

Posey, Thomas (Va). Captain 7th Virginia, 20th March, 1776; Major 2d Virginia, 30th April, 1778; transferred to 7th Virginia, 14th September, 1778; Lieutenant-Colonel, 8th September, 1782; transferred to 1st Virginia, 1st January, 1783; retired 10th March, 1783; Brigadier-General United States Army, 14th February, 1793; resigned 28th February, 1794. (Died 19th March, 1818.)

Post, Abraham (Conn). Ensign of Swift's Connecticut State Regiment, June to November, 1776.

Post, Anthony (N. Y.). Captain of Artificers, 2d Continental Artillery, 1st January, 1777; retired 22d June, 1781. (Died 29th May, 1832.)

Post, Jacobus (N. J.). Major New Jersey Light-Horse Militia, 1775-1776.

Post, Jeremiah (N. H.). Captain New Hampshire Militia, ——; died 26th August, 1777, of wounds received at Bennington, 16th August, 1777.

Post, John (N. Y.). Commissary of Issues, New York Brigade, 1776 to 1783.

Postell, Benjamin (S. C.). Lieutenant 1st South Carolina; taken prisoner at Charleston, 12th May, 1780.

Postell, James (S. C.). Lieutenant-Colonel South Carolina Militia; taken prisoner at Charleston, 12th May, 1780; exchanged June, 1781. (Died 1824.)

Postell, John (S. C.). Captain South Carolina Militia; taken prisoner at Charleston 12th May, 1780. (Possibly James and John are same.)

Postlethwaite, Samuel (Pa). Captain of Wilson's Battalion guarding stores at Carlisle, Pennsylvania; also Assistant Deputy Quartermaster, 6th October, 1777, to December, 1782.

Potan, Mathew (N. Y.). Ensign 3d New York, 1st June, 1777; omitted May, 1778.

Potan, Matthew (Pa). Ensign 4th Pennsylvania, 3d January, 1777; 2d

Lieutenant, August, 1777; 1st Lieutenant, 11th May, 1779; resigned 26th December, 1779.

Potter, —— (Mass). Ensign 5th Massachusetts; resigned 9th January, 1783.

Potter, David (N. J.). Colonel New Jersey Militia; taken prisoner near Frankford, 25th September, 1777. (Died 1805.)

Potter, Holliman (R. I.). Sergeant Rhode Island Regiment in 1775; Ensign 11th Continental Infantry, 1st January to 31st December, 1776; Ensign 2d Rhode Island, 1st January, 1777, and served to ——.

Potter, Israel (Conn). 1st Lieutenant of Douglas' Connecticut State Regiment, 20th June to 25th December, 1776; 1st Lieutenant 6th Connecticut, 1st January, 1777; retired 15th November, 1778.

Potter, James (Pa). Colonel Pennsylvania Militia in 1776 and 1777; wounded at Princeton, 3d January, 1777; Brigadier-General Pennsylvania Militia, 5th April, 1777; Major-General Pennsylvania Militia, 23d May, 1782, and served to close of war. (Died November, 1789.)

Potter, Jared (Conn). Surgeon Hospital Department in 1775; Surgeon 1st Connecticut, 20th May to 20th December, 1775; Surgeon of Douglas' Connecticut State Regiment, 3d July to 29th December, 1776. (Died 30th July, 1810.)

Potter, Joseph (N. H.). 2d Lieutenant 2d New Hampshire, 8th November, 1776; 1st Lieutenant, 22d December, 1777; Regimental Quartermaster, 23d August, 1778; transferred to 1st New Hampshire, 1st March, 1782; Captain, 1st March, 1782; retained in Jackson's Continental Regiment, November, 1783, and served to 20th June, 1784.

Potter, Josiah (N. H.). Captain New Hampshire Militia, 1777.

Potter, Nathaniel (N. J.). Major New Jersey Militia; taken prisoner at Quibbeltown, New Jersey, 22d January, 1777.

Potter, Oliver (N. H.). Captain Green Mountain Boys, 27th July to December, 1775.

Potter, Reuben (N. J.). Major New Jersey Militia, 1776-1778.

Potter, Samuel (N. J.). Captain 3d New Jersey, 8th March to 20th November, 1776; Lieutenant-Colonel New Jersey Militia in 1777. (Died 1802.)

Potter, Stephen (Conn). 1st Lieutenant 7th Connecticut, 6th July to 20th December, 1775; 1st Lieutenant of Douglas' Connecticut State Regiment, 20th June to 25th December, 1776; 1st Lieutenant 6th Connecticut, 1st January, 1777; Captain, 19th April, 1779; transferred to 4th Connecticut, 1st January, 1781; transferred to 2d Connecticut, 1st January, 1783, and served to 3d June, 1783.

Potter, Stephen (R. I.). Colonel Rhode Island Militia in 1775.

Potter, Thomas (R. I.). Colonel Rhode Island Militia, 1779-1780. (Died 1793.)

Potter, William (R. I.). Ensign 1st Rhode Island, 3d May to December, 1775; 1st Lieutenant 9th Continental Infantry, 1st January to 31st December, 1776; 1st Lieutenant 2d Rhode Island, 1st January, 1777; Captain, 11th February, 1777; retired 1st April, 1779. (Died 14th October, 1822.)

Potter, Zabdiel (Md). Captain 4th Maryland Battalion of the Flying Camp, July, 1776, to ——.

Potts, James (Pa). Major Pennsylvania Musket Battalion, 6th April, 1776; resigned 11th July, 1776.

Potts, John (Ga). Captain Georgia Militia, ——; killed at Wofford's Iron Works, 8th August, 1780.

Potts, Jonathan (Pa). Surgeon for the troops on the Canadian Expedition, 6th June, 1776; Deputy Director-General of Hospital, Northern Department, 11th April, 1777. By the act of 6th November, 1777, it was "Resolved, that the unremitted attention shown by Dr. Potts, and the officers of the General Hospital in the Northern Department, as represented in General Gates' letter to Congress of the 20th of October, to the sick and wounded under their care, is a proof not only of their humanity, but of the zeal for the service of the United States, so deeply interested in the preservation of the health and lives of the gallant asserters of their country's cause, and that Congress therefore can not but entertain a high sense of their services which they have rendered during this campaign, by a diligent discharge of their respective functions." Transferred to the Middle Department, 22d January, 1778; retired 6th October, 1780. (Died —— October, 1781.)

Potts, Joseph (Pa). 1st Lieutenant 4th Pennsylvania Battalion, 6th January, 1776; Captain, 12th October, 1776; Captain 5th Pennsylvania, January, 1777, to rank from 12th October, 1776; wounded and taken prisoner at Brandywine 11th September, 1777; did not rejoin regiment.

Poulson, John Va). 1st Lieutenant 9th Virginia, 5th February, 1776; Captain, 17th July, 1776; taken prisoner near Germantown, 5th October, 1777; exchanged 2d November, 1780; retained as Major 8th Virginia, 12th February, 1781, to rank from 12th May, 1779; retired 1st January, 1783.

Powell, Elisha (Vt). 2d Lieutenant of Bedel's Regiment Vermont Militia, 15th December, 1777, to 1st April, 1778.

Powell, George Gabriel (S. C.). Colonel South Carolina Militia in 1775.

Powell, Isaac (N. C.). Lieutenant North Carolina Militia, 1780-1781.

Powell, John (Md). Adjutant of a Maryland Battalion of the Flying Camp, July to December, 1776.

Powell, John (Vt). Captain Vermont Militia; taken prisoner at St. Johns, Canada, — December, 1777.

Powell, John (Va). Lieutenant-Colonel Virginia Militia, 1777-1778.

Powell, Levin (Va). Major Virginia Militia, 1775-1776; Lieutenant-Colonel of Grayson's Continental Regiment, 11th January, 1777; resigned 15th November, 1778. (Died 6th August, 1810.)

Powell, Peyton (Va). Sergeant 11th Virginia, 22d November, 1776; regiment designated 7th Virginia, 14th September, 1778; Ensign, 4th July, 1779; taken prisoner at Charleston, 12th May, 1780; transferred to 3d Virginia, 12th February, 1781; 2d Lieutenant, 18th February, 1781, and served to close of war.

Powell, Robert (Va). 1st Lieutenant 3d Virginia, 12th February, 1776; Captain, 18th October, 1776; resigned 2d July, 1779; Major Virginia Militia, 1781. (Died 1829.)

Powell, Thomas (N. H.). Lieutenant of Bedel's Regiment New Hampshire Rangers, 22d January, 1776, to ——.

Powell, Thomas (Va). 1st Lieutenant of a Virginia State Regiment, 1778; died ——.

Powell, William (Va). 2d Lieutenant 11th Virginia, 24th December, 1776;

regiment designated 7th Virginia, 14th September, 1778; resigned 18th March, 1779.

Power, Robert (Pa). Cornet of Lee's Battalion of Light Dragoons, ——, 1780; Lieutenant, ——, 1781, and served to close of war. (Died 20th January, 1811.)

Power, William (Pa). Captain Lieutenant 2d Continental Artillery, 1st January, 1777; transferred to 4th Continental Artillery, 1st January, 1781; Captain, 17th October, 1781; retired 1st January, 1783. (Died 1835.)

Powers, Alexander (Pa). Regimental Quartermaster of Miles' Pennsylvania Rifle Regiment, 6th April to 13th October, 1776; Lieutenant of Baldwin's Artillery Artificer Regiment, ——, 1779; retired 31st May, 1781.

Powers, James (N. C.). 2d Lieutenant 7th North Carolina, 28th November, 1776; 1st Lieutenant, 20th April, 1777; transferred to 3d North Carolina, 1st June, 1778; served to ——. (Died 1818.)

Powers, Nahum (Mass). 2d Lieutenant of Paterson's Massachusetts Regiment, May to December, 1775.

Pownal, John (Mass). Ensign 25th Continental Infantry, 1st January to 31st December, 1776; 1st Lieutenant 3d Massachusetts, 1st January, 1777; retired 16th September, 1778.

Pownal, Thomas (N. Y.). Leiutenant New York Militia; was a prisoner, when and where taken not stated.

Poynier, Isaac (N Y.). Ensign and 2d Lieutenant in 1st New York in 1776.

Poynter, John (N. C.). Captain 7th North Carolina, 28th November, 1776, to ——.

Poytress, William (Va). 1st Lieutenant 1st Continental Artillery, 20th October, 1777; omitted — May, 1780.

Praideau, Zebedee (Mass). 1st Lieutenant of Walker's Massachusetts Regiment, May to December, 1775.

Prather, Basil (Pa). 1st Lieutenant 8th Pennsylvania, 9th August, 1776; resigned 31st March, 1779.

Pratt, David (N. Y.). Major New York Militia in 1775.

Pratt, Edward (Md). Ensign of Smallwood's Maryland Regiment, 14th January to November, 1776.

Pratt, Jacob (N. J.). Captain New Jersey Militia, 1777-1778.

Pratt, Joel (Mass). Ensign 15th Massachusetts, 1st January, 1777; Lieutenant, 1st March, 1779; transferred to 4th Massachusetts, 1st January, 1781, and served to June, 1783.

Pratt, Joel (N. Y.). Captain New York Militia, May, 1775; Captain 2d New York, 28th June, 1775, to January, 1776. (Died 1844.)

Pratt, John (Mass). Ensign 24th Continental Infantry, 1st January, 1776; dismissed 13th October, 1776.

Pratt, John (Pa). Ensign 4th Pennsylvania, 1st July, 1779; Lieutenant, 1st May, 1780; transferred to 3d Pennsylvania, 1st January, 1783; Regimental Quartermaster, 22d May, 1783, and served to June, 1783; Lieutenant United States Infantry, 15th July, 1785; Regimental Quartermaster, 3d October, 1786; Lieutenant 1st Infantry United States Army, 29th September, 1789; Captain, 4th March, 1791; assigned to 1st Sub Legion, 4th September, 1792; resigned 5th December, 1793.

Pratt, Seth (Mass). 2d Lieutenant of Walker's Massachusetts Regiment, May to December, 1775.

Pratt, Shubael (Va). Surgeon — Virginia Regiment, 12th March, 1778, to 12th June, 1779.

Pratt, William (R. I.). Sergeant 2d Rhode Island, 22d February, 1777; Ensign, 1st May, 1779; retained in Olney's Rhode Island Battalion, 14th May, 1781; Lieutenant, 25th August, 1781, and served to 25th December, 1783. (Died 1845.)

Praul, Edward (Md). Ensign of Smallwood's Maryland Regiment, 14th January, 1776; 2d Lieutenant, March, 1776; taken prisoner at Long Island, 27th August, 1776; exchanged 2d December, 1776; 1st Lieutenant 1st Maryland, 10th December, 1776; Captain, 10th June, 1777; retired 1st January, 1783.

Pray, John (Mass). Sergeant of Scammon's Massachusetts Regiment, May to December, 1775; Ensign 18th Continental Infantry, 1st January to 31st December, 1776; 1st Lieutenant 12th Massachusetts, 1st January, 1777; Captain, 5th July, 1779; transferred to 1st Massachusetts, 1st January, 1781, and served to June, 1783 (Died — Septtember, 1812.)

Preble, Jedediah (Mass). Was a Brigadier General Massachusetts Militia at the commencement of the war. In June, 1775, he was appointed General and Commander-in-Chief of the Massachusetts Militia, but declined further service on account of his age. (Died 11th March, 1784.)

Preble, Samuel (N. Y.). Ensign of Nicholson's Continental Regiment, March to November, 1776.

Prentice, Ichabod (R. I.). 2d Lieutenant of Lippitt's Rhode Island State Regiment, 19th August to December, 1776.

Prentice, Jesse (Conn). Sergeant 6th Connecticut, 5th May to 10th December, 1775; 2d Lieutenant 10th Continental Infantry, 1st January to 31st December, 1776.

Prentice, Jonas (Conn). Private in the Lexington Alarm, April, 1775; Captain of Douglas' Connecticut Regiment, 20th June to 29th December, 1776; Captain 6th Connecticut, 1st January, 1777; resigned 31st March, 1779.

Prentice, Joshua (Mass). 1st Lieutenant of Glover's Massachusetts Regiment, May to December, 1775.

Prentice, Nathaniel S. (N. H.). Captain New Hampshire Militia, 1776.

Prentice, William (Mass). Surgeon's Mate 21st Continental Infantry, 1st January to 31st December, 1776.

Prentiss, Samuel (Cann). Major 6th Connecticut, 1st May to 10th December, 1775; Major 10th Continental Infantry, 1st January, 1776; Lieutenant-Colonel, 12th August, 1776; Lieutenant-Colonel 1st Connecticut, 1st January, 1777; resigned 27th May, 1778. (Died 1807.)

Prescott, Benjamin (Mass). Private in Lexington Alarm, April, 1775; Lieutenant of Prescott's Massachusetts Regiment, May, 1775; killed at Bunker Hill, 17th June, 1775.

Prescott, Dudley (N. H.). Lieutenant of Peabody's Regiment New Hampshire Militia, 1778-1779.

Prescott, Joseph (N. H.). Major New Hampshire Militia, 1777-1778.

Prescott, Joseph (S. C.). Surgeon's Mate Hospital Department, May, 1779, to November, 1783.

Prescott, Joshua (N. H.). Captain New Hampshire Militia in 1776.

Prescott, Oliver (Mass). Brigadier-General and Major-General Massachusetts Militia, 1776 to 1781 (Died 17th November, 1804.)

Prescott, Samuel (Mass). Volunteer Surgeon at Lexington, 19th April, 1775.

Prescott, William (Mass). Colonel of a Massachusetts Regiment, 19th May to December, 1775; Colonel 7th Continental Infantry, 1st January to 31st December, 1776. (Died 13th October, 1795.)

Preston, David (Mass). 2d Lieutenant of Knox's Regiment Continental Artillery, 10th December, 1775, to November, 1776.

Preston, Isaac (N. J.). Colonel New Jersey Militia, 1776-1777; died 1777.

Preston, William (Pa). 2d Lieutenant of Flower's Artillery Artificer Regiment, 7th April, 1777; taken prisoner at Bustle Town, Pa., 14th February, 1778; exchanged 29th April, 1781, and did not rejoin regiment.

Preston, William (Va). Captain Virginia Rangers, 1777; Colonel Virginia Militia, 1777-1781; wounded at Guilford 15th March, 1781 (Died 1783.)

Preveaux, Adrian.—See **Proveaux.**

Price, Asa (Mass). Captain Lexington Alarm, April, 1775; Captain of Mansfield's Massachusetts Regiment, May to November, 1775; Captain 19th Continental Infantry, 1st January to 31st December, 1776.

Price, Benjamin (Md). 1st Lieutenant 2d Maryland, 14th January, 1777; Captain Lieutenant, 26th May, 1778; Captain, 1st July, 1779; transferred to 3d Maryland, 1st January, 1781, and served to April, 1783

Price, Charles (Ga). Lieutenant Georgia Militia, ——; killed at Savannah, 9th October, 1779.

Price, George (Va). Captain 11th Virginia, ——, 1777, to ——.

Price, John (N. Y.) 1st Lieutenant New York Militia, 20th October, 1775, to ——.

·**Price, Joseph** (Pa). 1st Lieutenant Philadelphia Battalion Pennsylvania Militia in 1776.

Price, Rufus (Conn). Ensign 2d Connecticut, 1st January, 1777; 2d Lieutenant, 7th December, 1777; 1st Lieutenant, 1st June, 1778; resigned 24th February, 1779.

Price, Thomas (Md). Captain Maryland Rifle Company, 21st June, 1775;

Major of Smallwood's Maryland Regiment, 14th January, 1776; Colonel 2d Maryland, 10th December, 1776; resigned 21st April, 1780.

Price, Thomas Jr. (Md). Ensign and Paymaster, 3d Maryland, 27th May, 1778; Lieutenant, 11th February, 1780; retired 1st April, 1783.

Price, Thomas (Va). Captain Virginia Militia at King's Mountain, October, 1780.

Price, Thomas R. (Va). Captain Virginia Militia at Yorktown in October, 1781.

Price, William (Md). 2d Lieutenant 2d Maryland, 10th December, 1776; 1st Lieutenant, 10th April, 1777; Captain, 1st July, 1779; transferred to 3d Maryland, 1st January, 1781; retired 1st January, 1783.

Price, William (Mass). Private, Corporal and Sergeant of Gridley's Regiment Massachusetts Artillery in 1775; 2d Lieutenant of Knox's Regiment Continental Artillery, 1st May, 1776; 2d Lieutenant 3d Continental Artillery, 1st January, 1777; 1st Lieutenant, 12th September, 1778; transferred to Corps of Artillery, 17th June, 1783; Deputy Commissary of Ordnance and Military Stores, 1st January, 1784, and served to 22d March, 1787. (Died — July, 1790.)

Price, William (Pa). 1st Lieutenant of Montgomery's Pennsylvania Battalion of the Flying Camp, June, 1776; Captain, 10th August to December, 1776.

Pride, Reuben (Conn). Private in Lexington Alarm, April, 1775; Sergeant 3d Connecticut, 8th May to 10th December, 1775; Ensign 3d Connecticut, 1st January, 1777; 2d Lieutenant, 11th November, 1777; Regimental Adjutant, 11th September, 1780; 1st Lieutenant, 1st January, 1781; transferred to 1st Connecticut, 1st January, 1781; retired 1st January, 1783.

Pride, William (Va). Sergeant 5th Virginia, 1st January, 1777; Ensign, 10th March, 1777; 2d Lieutenant, 10th November, 1777; Regimental Quartermaster, — January, 1778; transferred to 3d Virginia, 14th September, 1778. Died 11th June, 1779.

Priest, Job (Mass). Private in Lexington Alarm, April, 1775; Sergeant of Gardner's Massachusetts Regiment, May to December, 1775; Ensign 15th Continental Infantry, 1st January to 31st December, 1776; 2d Lieutenant 1st Massachusetts, 1st January, 1777; resigned 4th November, 1777.

Priestley, John (Pa). 1st Lieutenant 5th Pennsylvania Battalion, 6th January, 1776; Captain, 12th October, 1776; taken prisoner at Fort Washington, 16th November, 1776; exchanged 26th August, 1778, and did not return to the army.

Prince, Asa (Mass). Captain in Lexington Alarm, April, 1775; Captain of Mansfield's Massachusetts Regiment, April to November, 1775; Captain 27th Continental Infantry, 1st January to 31st December, 1776; Captain Massachusetts Militia, 1777-1778.

Prince, Frank (S. C). Captain 5th South Carolina, May, 1776, to ——.

Prince, Sylvanus (Va) Captain Virginia Militia, 1777-1779.

Prince, Thomas (S. C.). 2d Lieutenant 5th South Carolina, 11th June, 1777; killed at Stono Ferry, 20th June, 1779.

Prines, Peter (N. J.). Captain New Jersey Militia in 1781.

Prioleau, Hext (S. C.). Lieutenant South Carolina Militia in 1776.

Prioleau, Samuel (S. C.). Lieutenant South Carolina Militia; taken prisoner at Charleston, 12th May, 1780.

Prior, Abner William (Conn). Captain of Ward's Connecticut State Regiment, 14th May, 1776; Captain 5th Connecticut, 1st January, 1777; Major 1st Connecticut, 17th August, 1780; transferred to 4th Connecticut, 1st January, 1781; resigned 28th Decebber, 1781.

Prior, Abner (N. Y.). Surgeon's-Mate 4th New York, 1st January, 1780; transferred to 2d New York, 1st January, 1781, and served to 3d November, 1783; Ensign United States Infantry Regiment, 21st October, 1786; Ensign 1st Infantry United States Army, 29th September, 1789; Lieutenant, 26th November, 1790; Captain, 2d June, 1792; assigned to 3d Sub Legion, 4th September, 1792; assigned to 1st Infantry, 1st November, 1796. Died 5th December, 1800.

Prior, Jesse (Conn). Private 2d Connecticut, 8th May to 18th December, 1775; Private in Sage's Connecticut State Regiment, June to December, 1776; Ensign of Baldwin's Artillery Artificer Regiment, 18th October, 1777; 2d Lieutenant, 1st October, 1778; resigned 2d June, 1779. (Died 10th February, 1822.)

Prior, Luke (S. C.). Captain South Carolina Militia in 1776.

Pritchard, Jeremiah (N H.). 2d Lieutenant 1st New Hampshire, 8th November, 1776; wounded at Skenesborough, 7th July, 1777; Regimental Adjutant, 1st January, 1778; 1st Lieutenant, 5th March, 1778; resigned 5th July, 1780. (Died 3d December, 1813.)

Pritchard, Rees (Va). Ensign 8th Virginia, 9th December, 1776; resigned 1st March, 1777. (Died 25th September, 1830.)

Pritchard, Thomas (Mass). Sergeant in Lexington Alarm, April, 1775; Sergeant of Gardner's Massachusetts Regiment, April to November, 1775; Ensign 5th Continental Infantry, 1st January, 1776; 2d Lieutenant, 14th August, 1776; 1st Lieutenant 3d Massachusetts, 1st January, 1777; Captain Lieutenant, 20th June, 1779; Captain, 24th March, 1780, and served to June, 1783.

Proctor, Edward (Mass). 1st Lieutenant 3d Continental Artillery, 1st January, 1777; resigned 10th June, 1779.

Proctor, Ephriam (Mass). Sergeant of Prescott's Massachusetts Regiment, April to December, 1775; Sergeant 7th Continental Infantry, 1st January, 1776; Ensign, 10th August to 31st December, 1776.

Proctor, Francis (Pa). Lieutenant 1st Company Pennsylvania Artillery, 27th October, 1775; was a prisoner in 1776, when and where taken not stated; Captain 4th Continental Artillery, 3d March, 1777; dismissed 14th May, 1778.

Proctor, Francis Jr. (Pa). 2d Lieutenant of Proctor's Battalion Pennsylvania Artillery, 5th October, 1776; Captain Lieutenant 4th Continental Artillery, 3d March, 1777; Captain, 16th July, 1777; Major, 24th December, 1782, to rank from 1st January, 1782; retired 1st January, 1783.

Proctor, Jonas (Mass). Ensign of Doolittle's Massachusetts Regiment, May to November, 1775.

Proctor, Samuel (Mass). Sergeant of Little's Massachusetts Regiment. May to December, 1775; Ensign 12th Continental Infantry, 1st January to 31st December, 1776.

Proctor, Thomas (Pa). Captain 1st Company Pennsylvania Artillery, 27th October, 1775; Major Pennsylvania Artillery Battalion, 14th August, 1776; Colonel 4th Continental Artillery, 5th

February, 1777; resigned 18th April, 1781. (Died 16th March, 1806.)

Prouty, David (Mass). Lieutenant of Learned's Massachusetts Regiment, May to December, 1775.

Proveaux, Adrian (S. C.). 1st Lieutenant 2d South Carolina, — January, 1777; Captain, 27th April, 1778; taken prisoner at Charleston, 12th May, 1780. Name also spelled Preveaux.

Provost, Robert (N. Y.). Paymaster 3d New York, 15th August, 1776; Paymaster 2d New York, 21st November, 1776, to 1st January, 1781, with rank of Ensign from 1st June, 1778.

Prowell, Joseph (Pa). Captain of Patton's Continental Regiment, 11th January, 1777; Major, 1st January, 1778; transferred to 11th Pennsylvania, 13th January, 1779; retired 5th June, 1779.

Prux, William (Pa). Ensign German Battalion, 24th July, 1778, to ——.

Pruyn, Casparus (N. Y.). Lieutenant New York Militia in 1775.

Pry, Thomas (Pa). 1st Lieutenant 2d Canadian (Hazen's) Regiment, 3d November, 1776; Captain, 1st February, 1777; served to close of war.

Pryor, John (Va). Captain Lieutenant 1st Continental Artillery, 13th February, 1777; Major Aide-de-Camp to General Alexander, 9th June, 1779, to 14th January, 1783; retired 14th January, 1783.

Pugh, —— (Ga). Lieutenant Georgia Rangers; dismissed 23d August, 1776.

Pugh, John (Pa). Captain Pennsylvania State Regiment, 18th March, 1777; resigned 12th August, 1777.

Pugh, Jonathan (Pa). Sergeant 4th Pennsylvania Battalion, 16th June, 1776; Ensign 5th Pennsylvania, 1st January, 1777; 2d Lieutenant, 20th April, 1777; wounded at Brandywine, 11th September, 1777; transferred to Invalid Regiment, 6th October, 1778; Regimental Adjutant, 1st June, 1779; Captain Lieutenant, — November, 1779, and served to close of war.

Pugh, Whitmill (N. C.). Ensign 2d North Carolina, 1st September, 1775, to ——.

Pugh, Willis (Va). Ensign 15th Virginia, 19th November, 1776; killed 1st May, 1777, at ——; where not stated.

Pulaski, Casimer (Poland). Brigadier-General Continental Army and Chief of Dragoons, 15th September, 1777; designated as commander of an independent corps, known as the Pulaski Legion, 28th March, 1778; died 11th October, 1779, of wounds received 9th October, 1779, at the Siege of Savannah.

Pullen, William (R. I.). Ensign of Lippitt's Rhode Island State Regiment, 19th August, 1776; Lieutenant of Sherburne's Continental Regiment, 10th March, 1777; omitted October, 1777.

Punderson, John (N. Y.). Ensign 4th New York, 21st November, 1776; resigned 1st November, 1777.

Purcell, George (Va). Ensign 13th Virginia, 13th December, 1776; wounded at Germantown, 4th October, 1777, and did not return to regiment.

Purcell, Henry (S. C.). Lieutenant-Colonel Deputy Judge Advocate General for South Carolina and Georgia, 3d April, 1778, to ——.

Purcell, Henry (S. C.). Chaplain 2d South Carolina, 7th May, 1776; Brigade Chaplain, 7th April, 1779, to June, 1781.

Purcell, Henry D. (Pa). Ensign 2d Pennsylvania, 4th January, 1777; 2d Lieutenant, 4th October, 1777; Deputy Judge-Advocate-General to General Gates' Army, 29th January, 1778, to — February, 1779; 1st Lieutenant 3d Pennsylvania, 3d September, 1779, and served to close of war.

Purdy, Aaron (Mass). 2d Lieutenant 3d Continental Artillery, 17th October, 1781, and served to June. 1783. (Name also spelled Purdie.)

Purdy, Robert (Pa). Paymaster of Patton's Continental Regiment, January, 1777, to ——.

Purdy, Monmouth (N. J.). Lieutenant of Baldwin's Artillery Artificer Regiment, 1st August, 1777; Captain, 12th April, 1778; retired — March, 1781.

Purington, James (Mass). 1st Lieutenant of Lincoln's Regiment, Massachusetts Militia, 1776-1777.

Purviance, James (N. C.). Captain North Carolina Militia, 1779-1781.

Purvis, George (Del). Regimental Quartermaster Delaware Battalion of the Flying Camp, July to December, 1776; 2d Lieutenant Delaware Regiment, 3d December, 1776; 1st Lieutenant, 14th October, 1777; Adjutant, 16th August, 1778; Captain, ——; taken prisoner at Camden, 16th August, 1780. served to close of war; also reported as prisoner to close of war.

Purvis, James (Va). Sergeant 1st Virginia, September, 1775; Ensign, — April, 1777; resigned — February, 1778; Lieutenant Virginia Convention Guards, January, 1779; Captain. 8th October, 1779, and served to June 1781.

Purvis, John (S. C.). Captain South Carolina Rangers, 17th June. 1775, to ——; Lieutenant-Colonel South Carolina Militia, 1779-1781.

Putnam, Aaron (Mass). Surgeon's-Mate of Frye's Massachusetts Regiment, 28th June to December, 1775; Surgeon's Mate 26th Continental Infantry, 1st January to 31st December, 1776; Surgeon 1st Massachusetts, 1st January, 1777; resigned 26th October, 1777.

Putnam, Benjamin (Conn). Surgeon 4th Continental Infantry, 18th March to 31st December, 1776; Surgeon 5th Connecticut, 1st August, 1777; resigned 23d May, 1778.

Putnam, Daniel (Conn). 1st Lieutenant 20th Continental Infantry, 1st January, 1776; Major and Aide-de-Camp to General Putnam, May, 1776, to June, 1783. -

Putnam, David (Mass). Sergeant of Gridley's Regiment Massachusetts Artillery, May to December, 1775, and Sergeant of Knox's Regiment Continenatl Artillery, January to December, 1776; 2d Lieutenant 3d Continental Artillery, 1st January, 1777; resigned 26th March, 1780.

Putnam, Enoch (Mass). 2d Lieutenant in Lexington Alarm, April, 1775; Captain of Mansfield's Massachusetts Regiment, April to December, 1775; Captain 27th Continental Infantry, 1st January, 1776; taken prisoner at Fort Washington, 16th November, 1776; Lieutenant-Colonel and Colonel Massachusetts Militia, 1778-1782. (Died 1796.)

Putnam, Ezra (Mass). Major of Mansfield's Massachusetts Regiment, 27th May to December, 1775; Major 27th Continental Infantry, 1st January to 31st December, 1776. (Died 19th March, 1811.)

Putnam, Francis (Mass). Ensign of Henley's Continental Regiment, June, 1777 to 1779.

Putnam, Francis (N. Y.). Ensign of Fisher's Regiment New York Militia in 1775.

Putnam, Garrett (N. Y.). Captain of Harper's Regiment New York Militia in 1780.

Putnam, Israel (Conn). Lieutenant-Colonel in the Lexington Alarm, April, 1775; Colonel 3d Connecticut, 1st May, 1775; Major-General Continental Army, 19th June, 1775; retired 3d June, 1783. (Died 19th May, 1790.)

Putnam, Israel Jr. (Conn). Captain 3d Connecticut, 1st May, 1775; Major and Aide-da-Camp to General Putnam, 22d July, 1775, to 3d June ,1783. (Died 1812.)   ,

Putnam, Jeremiah (Mass). Sergeant in Lexington Alarm, April, 1775; Sergeant of Mansfield's Massachusetts Regiment, May to November. 1775; Ensign 27th Continental Infantry, 1st January to 31st December. 1776; Captain Massachusetts Militia, 1777-1783. (Died 6th September, 1799.)

Putnam, Philip (N. H.). Captain New Hampshire Militia, 1776.

Putnam, Rufus (Mass). Lieutenant-Colonel of Brewer's Massachusetts Regiment, 19th May to December, 1775; Lieutenant-Colonel 22d Continental Infantry, 1st January, 1776; Colonel Engineer, 5th August, 1776; Colonel 5th Massachusetts, 1st November, 1776, to rank from 5th August, 1776; Brigadier-General Continental Army, 7th January, 1783, and served to close of war. (Died 1st May, 1824.)

Putnam, Tarrant (Mass). Ensign in Lexington Alarm, April, 1775; Adjutant of Mansfield's Massachusetts Regiment, April to November, 1775; 2d Lieutenant and Adjutant 27th Continental Infantry, 1st January, 1776. Died 16th April, 1776.

Putnam, Victor (N. Y.). Lieutenant of Harper's Regiment New York Militia in 1780.

Pyatt, Peter (N. C.). Lieutenant 10th North Carolina, 30th March, 1781 to ——.

Q.

Quackenboss, Henry (N. Y.). Major and Colonel New York Militia, 1775-1781. (Died 1813.)

Quackenboss, Isaac (N. Y.). Lieutenant of Harper's Regiment New York Militia in 1780.

Quackenboss, John (N. Y.). Captain 1st New York, 28th June. 1775, to January, 1776.

Quackenboss, John P. (N. Y.). Regimental Adjutant of Schuyler's Regiment New York Militia, 1779-1781.

Quarles, Henry (Va). 1st Lieutenant 15th Virginia, 13th January, 1777; resigned 14th July, 1777, and served subsequently as Captain of a Virginia State Regiment.

Quarles, James (Va). Captain 2d Virginia State Regiment, 4th January, 1777, to January, 1780; served subsequently as Major Virginia Militia.

Quarles, John (Va). 2d Lieutenant 1st Virginia, 25th February, 1776; Captain 2d Virginia State Regiment, 4th January, 1777, to 1781.

Quarles, Robert (Va). Ensign and Regimental Quartermaster 1st Virginia, 15th May, 1782, to close of war.

Quarles, Thomas (Va). Cadet 2d Virginia State Regiment, January, 1777; 2d Lieutenant, 10th September, 1778, to January, 1781.

Quarles, Wharton (Va). Lieutenant and Regimental Quartermaster 2d Virginia State Regiment, 1779-1781.

Quarles, William P. (Va). Ensign 1st Virginia, 6th October, 1780; 2d Lieutenant, 18th February, 1781; served to close of war.

Quarterferge, Pierre (Canada). Captain 2d Canadian (Hazen's) Regiment, 3d November, 1776; resigned — January, 1778.

Quelch, Andrew (S. C.) Captain South Carolina Militia in 1775-1776.

Quenowault, Paul (Del). Ensign Delaware Regiment, 27th November, 1776; 2d Lieutenant, 5th April, 1777; 1st Lieutenant, 26th January, 1778; Captain, 1st January, 1781; died 1st December, 1782.

Quick, Abraham (N. J) Colonel New Jersey Militia, 1777.

Quig, David (N. H). Ensign of Nichols' Regiment New Hampshire Militia in 1777.

Quimby Jacob (Mass). 2d Lieutenant of Nixon's Massachusetts Regiment, May to December, 1775; 2d Lieutenant 5th Continental Infantry, 1st January to 31st December, 1776

Quinby, Aaron (N. H.). Captain of Kelley's Regiment New Hampshire Militia in 1778.

Quinby, David (N. H.). Captain New Hampshire Militia, 1777-1778.

Quinby, Josiah (N. J.). 2d Lieutenant 3d New Jersey, 7th February to 20th November, 1776. (Died 1805.)

Quinn, John (N. H.). Surgeon 3d New Hampshire, 5th July, 1780; retired 1st January, 1781.

Quinn, Michael (N. C.). 1st Lieutenant 8th North Carolina, 28th November, 1776; Captain, 1st August, 1777; retired 1st June, 1778.

Quinlan, Joseph (Va). Surgeon's-Mate 3d Virginia, 29th October, 1778; resigned 6th June, 1779.

Quinn, Samuel (Pa). 2d Lieutenant 12th Pennsylvania, 16th October, 1776; retired 1st July, 1778.

Quinton, Dixon (Md). 2d Lieutenant of Long's Independent Maryland Company, 3d October, 1776, to ——.

Quirk, Thomas (Va). Ensign 7th Virginia, 7th May, 1776; 2d Lieutenant, 13th November, 1776; 1st Lieutenant, 20th May, 1778; transferred to 5th Virginia, 14th September, 1778; resigned 4th July, 1779; served subsequently as Major of a Virginia State Regiment.

R.

Rabb, Andrew (Pa). Captain Pennsylvania Militia, 1778- 1781. (Died 1804.)

Raboldt, Jacob (Md). Quartermaster-Sergeant German Regiment, 13th November, 1777; Ensign, 24th July, 1778; Regimental Quartermaster 30th July, 1778; retired 1st January, 1781. (Name also spelled Raybold)

Radcliff, William (N. Y.). Captain and Major of Graham's Regiment New York Militia, 1777-1778.

Rader, Michael (Va). Captain Virginia Militia in 1777.

Radford, John. See Raiford.

Radiere, Lewis Mons. de la (France). Lieutenant-Colonel Engineer, 8th July, 1777; Colonel, 17th November, 1777. Died ——, 1779.

Rae, John (Ga). Ensign 1st Georgia, 7th January, 1776; Lieutenant, – —, and served to ——.

Rae, Robert (Ga). Lieutenant-Colonel 3d Georgia, 5th July, 1776; Colonel 1st Georgia, 1st April, 1778; served to close of war.

Ragan, Daniel (Va). Ensign 11th Virginia, 28th November, 1776; 2d Lieutenant, 14th June, 1777; resigned 24th January, 1778.

Ragsdale, Drury (Va). Captain 1st Continental Artillery, 7th February, 1777; retired 1st January ,1783.

Rague, John (Pa). Surgeon's-Mate 10th Pennsylvania, 19th August, 1778; transferred to 1st Pennsylvania, 17th January, 1781, and served to —–

Raiford, John (N. C.). 2d Lieutenant 2d North Carolina, ——, 1777; resigned 1st February, 1778.

Raiford, Peter (N .C.). Captain in 1st North Carolina in 1779; served to ——.

Raiford, Robert (N. C.) Captain 8th North Carolina, 28th November, 1776; transferred to 2d North Carolina, 1st June, 1778; served to close of war; Brevet Major, 30th September, 1783.

Raindtree, Reuben (N. C.). Lieutenant 10th North Carolina, 19th April, 1777; omitted 1st January, 1778.

Raines, Giles (Va). 2d Lieutenant 15th Virginia, 28th November, 1776; resigned 23d December, 1777.

Raisin, William (Md). Sergeant 5th Maryland, 12th February, 1779; 2d Lieutenant, 26th January, 1780; transferred to 1st Maryland, 1st January, 1781, and served to April, 1783.

Ralph, Ephraim (Va). Sergeant 13th Virginia, 12th January, 1777; regiment designated 9th Virginia, 14th September, 1778; 2d Lieutenant, 10th September, 1779; resigned 15th February, 1780.

Ralston, Robert (Pa) Regimental Adjutant of Hartley's Continental Regiment, 16th January, 1777, to ——.

Ramke, Frederick (—). Surgeon of Armand's Partisan Corps in 1779 and 1780.

Ramsay, Alexander (Pa). 2d Lieutenant 4th Pennsylvania, 3d January, 1777; 1st Lieutenant, 3d June, 1778; resigned 26th May, 1779; also reported as retired in September, 1778.

Ramsay, Allen (N. C.). Lieutenant 7th North Carolina, 19th December, 1776; omitted January, 1778

Ramsay, David (S. C.). Surgeon 4th South Carolina, ——; taken prisoner at Charleston, 12th May, 1780; exchanged March, 1781. (Died 8th May, 1815)

Ramsay, Jesse (S. C.). Surgeon's-Mate Hospital Department in South Carolina, 1780-1783.

Ramsay, John (Va) . Surgeon 1st Virginia, — February, 1776; died 4th November, 1776.

Ramsay, Joseph (S. C.). Surgeon's Mate in Hospital Department in 1782.

Ramsay, Matthew (N. C.). Captain 9th North Carolina, 28th November, 1776; transferred to 4th North Carolina, 1st June, 1778; resigned — November, 1781.

Ramsey, Ambrose (N. C). Colonel North Carolina Militia in 1780.

Ramsey, John (Pa). Lieutenant Lancaster County, Pennsylvania, Militia, 1776-1777.

Ramsey, Joseph (Va). Lieutenant of Clark's Illinois Regiment, 1779-1781.

Ramsey, Nathaniel (Md). Captain of Smallwood's Maryland Regiment, 14th January, 1776; Lieutenant-Colonel 3d Maryland, 10th December, 1776; wounded and taken prisoner at Monmouth, 28th June, 1778; on parole until exchanged, 14th December, 1780; retired 1st January, 1781. (Died 25th October, 1817.)

Ramsey, Robert (Pa). Lieutenant Lancaster County, Pennsylvania, Militia, 1776-1777.

Ramsey, Robert (Pa). Captain of .Hart's Pennsylvania Battalion of the Flying Camp, July to December, 1776.

Rand, Daniel (N. H.). 1st Lieutenant Lexington Alarm, April, 1775; Lieutenant and Captain New Hampshire Militia, 1776-1777; name also spelled David (Died 1811.)

Rand, Ezekiel (N. H.). 2d Lieutenant 3d New Hampshire, 23d April to December, 1775; served subsequently in New Hampshire **Militia.**

Rand, John (Mass). Colonel Massachusetts Militia in 1780.

Randall, Benjamin (N. Y.). Captain in Van Rensselaer's Regiment New York Militia in 1780, and Lieutenant-Colonel of Abbott's Regiment Vermont Militia in 1781 and 1782.

Randall, Custis (Va). Lieutenant 9th Virginia, January, 1777, to ——.

Randall, John (R. I.). Captain 1st Rhode Island, 3d May, 1775, to ——.

Randall, Joseph (N. H.). Lieutenant of Peabody's Regiment New Hampshire Militia, 1779-1780.

Randall, Matthew (Mass). 1st Lieutenant of Walker's Massachusetts Regiment, May to December, 1775; Captain Massachusetts Militia in 1776.

Randall, Matthew (R. I.). 2d Lieutenant of Stanton's Rhode Island State Regiment, 12th December, 1776, to May, 1777.

Randall, Nehemiah (R. I.). Lieutenant of Babcock's Rhode Island State Regiment, 15th January to November, 1776.

Randall, Peleg (Conn). Captain of Latimer's Regiment Connecticut Militia in 1777.

Randall, Thomas (Mass). 2d Lieutenant of Gridley's Regiment Massachusetts Artillery, 24th April, 1775; 1st Lieutenant of Knox's Regiment Continental Artillery, 10th December, 1775; Captain, 10th August, 1776; Captain 3d Continental Artillery, 1st January, 1777; wounded and taken prisoner at Germantown, 4th October, 1777; exchanged, December, 1777; resigned 1st May, 1779. (Died — January, 1811.)

Randall, William Jr. (Va). Ensign 3d Virginia, 29th April, 1776; resigned 23d August, 1776.

Randolph, Beverly (Va). Colonel Virginia Militia, 1776-1779.

Randolph, Nathaniel Fitz (N. J.). Captain New Jersey Militia, ——; wounded and taken prisoner at Long Island, 27th August, 1776; exchanged 26th May, 1780; died 23d July, 1780, of wounds received at Springfield, 23d June, 1780.

Randolph, Charles (Va). Cornet 3d Continental Dragoons, February, 1777; Lieutenant, 14th June, 1777, and served to ——. (In service, January, 1780.)

Randolph. David Meade (Va). Captain of a Virginia Regiment in 1777. (Died 23d September, 1830.)

Randolph, Edmund (Va). Aide-de-Camp to General Washington, 15th August, 1775, to 25th March, 1776; Deputy Mustermaster-General Southern Department, 25th March, 1776; resigned 26th April, 1776. (Died 12th September, 1813.)

Randolph, Edward Fitz (Pa). 2d Lieutenant 4th Pennsylvania, 3d January, 1777; wounded at Paoli, 20th September, 1777; resigned 10th May, 1779. (Died 1837.) Name also spelled Fitz-Randolph.

Randolph, Robert (Va). Cornet 3d Continental Dragoons, February, 1777; Lieutenant, 14th June, 1777; wounded and taken prisoner at Tappan, 28th September, 1778.

Randolph, Samuel (N J.). Major New Jersey Militia in 1778.

Randolph, Thomas Mann (Va). Colonel Virginia Militia, 1779.

Raniston, John (Pa). Ensign 7th Pennsylvania, 24th July, 1779; resigned 30th March, 1780.

Rankin, Robert (Pa). 1st Lieutenant of Taylor's Regiment Pennsylvania Militia; taken prisoner from his home, 14th September, 1777.

Rankins, Robert (Va). Sergeant 11th Virginia, 26th July, 1776; regiment designated 7th Virginia, 14th September, 1778; Ensign, 4th July, 1779; Lieutenant. 1st January, 1780; taken prisoner at Charleston, 12th May, 1780.

Randless, John ,N. Y.). Ensign of Malcolm's Continental Regiment, — 1777; resigned 8th March, 1778.

Ranney, John (Va). Surgeon Virginia Militia, 1780-1781.

Ranney, Stephen (Va). Surgeon 12th Virginia, 21st April, 1778; retired 14th September, 1778.

Ransdell, Thomas (Va). 3d Lieutenant 11th Virginia, 31st July, 1776; 2d Lieutenant, 6th February, 1777; 1st Lieutenant, 1st July, 1777; regiment designated 7th Virginia, 14th September, 1778; transferred to 3d Virginia, 12th February, 1781; Captain, — October, 1781; retired 1st January, 1783.

Ransom, Elijah (Conn). Sergeant in the Lexington Alarm, April, 1775; 2d Lieutenant 3d Connecticut, 1st January, 1777; 1st Lieutenant, 1st May, 1780; transferred to 1st Connecticut, 1st January, 1781; retired March, 1782. (Died 1828.)

Ransom, James (Conn). 1st Lieutenant 2d Connecticut, 1st May to 17th December, 1775.

Ransom, John (Conn). 1st Lieutenant of Swift's Connecticut State Regiment, July to December, 1776.

Ransom, Peleg (N. Y.). Captain New York Militia, 1778.

Ransom, Samuel (Pa). Captain Wyoming Valley Company, 26th August, 1776; killed at the Wyoming Massacre, 3d July, 1778.

Ransom, Thomas (Pa). 1st Lieutenant of Warner's Continental Regiment, 16th September, 1776, to ——.

Rapalje, Jacques (N. Y.). Captain of Lasher's Regiment New York Militia, July, 1776, to January, 1777 and in 1778.

Rape, Christopher (N. J.). Captain New Jersey Militia in 1777.

Raphael, —— (S. C.). Lieutenant 4th South Carolina in 1776-1777.

Rathburn, Amos (Mass). Captain Massachusetts Militia in 1777.

Ravenal, Henry (S. C.). Lieutenant South Carolina Militia under General Marion, 1781-1782.

Rawlings, Isaac (Md.) 2d Lieutenant of Dorsey's Independent Company Maryland Artillery, 3d September, 1779; company formed part of 1st Continental Artillery and served to close of war.

Rawlings, Moses (Md.). 1st Lieutenant of Cresaps Maryland Rifle Company, 21st June, 1775; Captain, 21st October, 1775; Lieutenant-Colonel of Stephenson's Maryland and Virginia Rifle Regiment, 27th June. 1776; wounded and taken prisoner at Fort Washington, 16th November, 1776; Colonel of one of the sixteen additional Continental Regiments, 12th January, 1777: resigned 2d June, 1779. (Died — May, 1809.)

Rawlings, Nicholas (N. H.). Captain New Hampshire Militia, 1777-1778.

Rawson, Asa (Mass). Captain Lieutenant Knox's Regiment Continental Artillery, 10th December, 1775, to December, 1776.

Rawson, Jeduthan (Mass). Musician in Read's Massachusetts Regiment in 1775, and in 1st Continental Infantry in 1776; Fife Major 6th Massachusetts, 11th February, 1777; Ensign, 27th March, 1779; transferred to 1st Massachusetts, 1st January, 1781; resigned 18th February, 1781. (Name also spelled Jonathan.)

Rawson, Wilson (R. I.). Ensign of Babcock's Rhode Island State Regiment, 15th January, 1776; Lieutenant of Lippitt's Rhode Island State Regiment, 19th August, 1776; 1st Lieutenant 1st Rhode Island, 1st January, 1777, and served to ——.

Ray, Andrew (Va). Surgeon Hospital Department, 1779-1781.

Ray, Benjamin (Mass). Private in Lexington Alarm, April, 1775; Private in Read's Massachusetts Regiment, April to November, 1775; Sergeant in 3d Continental Infantry in 1776; Sergeant, 4th Massachusetts, 1st January, 1777; Ensign, 20th February, 1778; 2d Lieutenant and Adjutant, 4th August, 1780; resigned 14th April, 1782.

Ray, James (Va). Captain Virginia Militia in 1779-1780.

Ray, Matthew.—See **Rhea.**

Ray, William (N. H.). Lieutenant New Hampshire Militia in 1780.

Raymond, John (Conn). 2d Lieutenant 6th Connecticut, 1st May to 17th December, 1775.

Raymond, Joseph (Mass). Corporal 11th Massachusetts, 11th March, 1777; Sergeant, 1st December, 1777; Lieutenant, 26th October, 1780; resigned 6th May, 1782.

Raymond, William (Conn). 2d Lieutenant of Selden's Connecticut State Regiment, June to December, 1776.

Reab, George (Mass). Sergeant 14th Massachusetts, 5th April, 1777; Ensign, 8th October, 1779; Lieutenant, 16th April, 1780; transferred to 7th Massachusetts, 1st January, 1781; transferred to 4th Massachusetts, 12th June, 1783, and served to 3d November, 1783.

(Died 20th June, 1838.)

Read.—See also **Reed** and **Reid.**

Read, Archibald (Pa). Paymaster 8th Pennsylvania, 13th December, 1777; Ensign, 2d June, 1778; served to ——.

Read, Benjamin (Mass). 2d Lieutenant and Adjutant 13th Continental Infantry, 1st January to 31st December, 1776; 1st Lieutenant 7th Massachusetts, 1st January, 1777; killed at Stillwater 19th September, 1777.

Read, Charles (N. J.). Colonel New Jersey Militia, 1776-1777.

Read, Clements (Va). Lieutenant of a Virginia regiment in 1779; died in service, date not known.

Read, Edmund (Va). 1st Lieutenant 4th Virginia, 23d February, 1776; resigned 6th July, 1777; Captain of a Virginia State Regiment, 2d June, 1779, to January, 1782.

Read, George (Del). A signer of the Declaration of Independence. Died 21st September, 1798.

Read, Isaac (Va). Lieutenant-Colonel 4th Virginia, 13th February, 1776; Colonel 9th Virginia, 13th August, 1776; transferred to 4th Virginia, 17th December, 1777; died 4th September, 1778.

Read, James (N. C.). Ensign 1st North Carolina, 4th January, 1776; 2d Lieutenant, 6th July, 1776; 1st Lieutenant, 7th July, 1776; Captain, 8th July, 1777, to ——; Colonel North Carolina Militia; taken prisoner at Charleston, 12th May, 1780. (Died 1803.)

Read, James (Pa). Major Pennsylvania Militia in 1777. (Died 1822.)

Read, James (Va). Colonel 1st Virginia, 13th February, 1776; died 29th September, 1777.

Read, Jesse (N. C.). 2d Lieutenant 6th North Carolina, 20th October, 1776; 1st Lieutenant, 25th October, 1777; transferred to 2d North Carolina, 1st June, 1778; transferred to 3d North Carolina, 1st January, 1781; taken prisoner at Eutaw Springs, 8th September, 1781; Captain, 15th October, 1781; served to close of war.

Read, John (Md). Ensign 2d Maryland, 20th February, 1777; 2d Lieutenant, 27th May, 1778; resigned 11th April, 1779.

Read, John (Va). 2d Lieutenant 4th Virginia, —— May, 1776; died 25th June, 1777, of wounds received at Princeton, 3d January, 1777.

Read, Joseph (Mass). Lieutenant-Colonel Lexington Alarm, April, 1775; Colonel Massachusetts Regiment, 18th April to December, 1775; Colonel 13th Continental Infantry, 1st January to 31st December, 1776.

Read, Joseph (R. I.). Ensign of Lippitt's Rhode Island State Regiment, 19th August, 1776, to March, 1777.

Read, Joshua (R. I.). Captain 9th Continental Infantry, 1st January to 31st December, 1776. **See Joshua Reed.** Are they not the same?

Read Thaddeus (Mass). Private in Lexington Alarm, April, 1775; Sergeant of Read's Massachusetts Regiment, May to December, 1775; 2d Lieutenant, 13th Continental Infantry, 1st January to 31st December, 1776; Captain Massachusetts Militia, 1777-1781.

Read, Thomas C. (N. J.). Surgeon's-Mate 3d New Jersey, 9th February to 22d November, 1776.

Read, William (Mass). Captain of Thomas' Massachusetts Regiment, May to December, 1775; Captain 23d Continental Infantry, 1st January to 31st December, 1776.

Read, William (N. H.). Captain New Hampshire Militia, 1776.

Read, William (S. C.). Hospital Physician and Surgeon Southern Department, 22d March, 1780, to close of war. (Died 20th April, 1845.)

Read, Zalmon (Conn). Captain 5th Connecticut, 1st May to 28th November, 1775; Captain of Silliman's Connec-

ticut State Regiment, 20th June to 25th December, 1776.

Read, Zalmon (Conn). Ensign 4th Connecticut, 19th June, 1779; retired 1st November, 1781.

Reading, John (N. J.). Ensign 3d New Jersey, 2d April, 1776; 2d Lieutenant, 29th November, 1776; 1st Lieutenant, 1st January, 1777; resigned, 10th February, 1779. (Died 1820.)

Reading, Samuel (N. J.). 1st Lieutenant 3d New Jersey, 28th October, 1775; taken prisoner at Three Rivers, 8th June, 1776; exchanged December, 1776; Captain 2d New Jersey, 1st January, 1777; Major, 27th December, 1781; retained in New Jersey Battalion, April, 1783, and served to 3d November, 1783.

Reading, Thomas (N. J.). Captain 3d New Jersey, 2d April to 22d November, 1776. (Died 1814.)

Reading, Zebedee.—See **Redding.**

Reckless, Anthony (N. J.). Lieutenant Sappers and Miners in 1780, and served to close of war. (Died 1817.)

Reddick, John (N. C.). Lieutenant North Carolina Militia, 1780-1781.

Redding, William (Mass). Ensign 8th Massachusetts, 1st January, 1777; deserted in June, 1778.

Redding, Zebedee (Mass). Lieutenant of Walker's Massachusetts Regiment, May to December, 1775; 1st Lieutenant, 14th Continental Infantry, 1st January, to 31st December, 1776; Captain, 14th Massachusetts, 1st January, 1777; resigned, 4th October, 1780.

Redman, John (Pa). Paymaster of Miles' Rifle Regiment, October, 1776; Captain of Patton's Continental Regiment, 13th January, 1777; resigned 8th November, 1778.

Redmond, Andrew (S. C.). Corporal and Sergeant, 1st South Carolina, 1776-1779; Military Storekeeper, 1780-1783.

Redmond, John (S. C.). Captain 6th South Carolina Militia, 1780, to close of war.

Redpith, John (N. C.). Lieutenant 4th North Carolina, 20th August, 1777; died 13th October, 1777, of wounds received at Germantown, 4th October, 1777.

Reed, Bowles (N. J.). Lieutenant-Colonel and Colonel New Jersey Militia, 1776-1778.

Reed, Abraham (N. H.). 1st Lieutenant 1st New Hampshire, 23d April to 28th July, 1775. (Name also spelled Reid.)

Reed, Daniel (Conn). Ensign of Ward's Connecticut State Regiment, 14th May, 1776, to May, 1777.

Reed, Eli (Conn). Captain Connecticut Militia, 1776.

Reed, Enoch (Conn). 2d Lieutenant 10th Continental Infantry, 1st January to 31st December, 1776; Captain-Lieutenant 1st Connecticut, 1st January, 1777; Captain, 1st August 1779; transferred to 4th Connecticut, 1st January, 1781; transferred to 1st Connecticut, 1st January, 1783, and served to 3d June, 1783.

Reed, Frederick (Mass). 2d Lieutenant of Mansfield's Massachusetts Regiment, May to December, 1775.

Reed, George (N. C.). Captain North Carolina Militia; killed at Hanging Rock, 6th August, 1780.

Reed, George (S. C.). Captain South Carolina Militia in November, 1775.

Reed, Jacob (N. Y.). 2d Lieutenant of Knox's Regiment Continental Artillery, January, 1776; Captain Lieutenant 2d Continental Artillery, 1st January, 1777; Captain, 23d March, 1780, and served to 17th June, 1783. (Died 31st May, 1838.)

Reed, James (N. H.). Captain in Lexington Alarm, April, 1775; Colonel 3d New Hampshire, 23d April to December, 1775; Colonel 2d Continental Infantry, 1st January, 1776; Brigadier-General Continental Army, 9th August, 1776; became blind and retired from service, September, 1776. (Died 13th February, 1807.)

Reed, James (N. Y.). Major New York Militia, 1777-1781; was also Commissary of Purchases, ——.

Reed, Jeremiah (Mass). Sergeant of Glover's Massachusetts Regiment, May to December, 1775; Ensign 14th Continental Infantry, 1st January to 31st December, 1776; Lieutenant of Lee's Continental Regiment, 1st January, 1777; resigned 26th September, 1778.

Reed, John (Mass) Captain 7th Massachusetts, 1st January, 1777; resigned 20th October, 1780. (Died — September, 1797.)

Reed, John (N. J.). Sergeant 3d New Jersey, 24th November, 1775, to November, 1776; Ensign 3d New Jersey, 1st February, 1777; 2d Lieutenant, 3d October, 1777; 1st Lieutenant, 1st February, 1779; transferred to 1st New Jersey, 1st January, 1781, and served to April, 1783. (Died 1803.)

Reed, John (N. J.). Sergeant of Spencer's Additional Continental Regiment, 1st February, 1777; Ensign, 12th May, 1779; retired 1st January, 1781; Lieutenant in the Levies of 1791; wounded in action with Indians at St. Clair's defeat near Fort Recovery, Ohio, 4th November, 1791; Lieutenant United States Infantry, 16th March, 1792; assigned to 3d Sub Legion, 4th September, 1792; Captain, 12th November, 1793; honorably discharged, 1st November, 1796.

Reed, John (N. Y.). 3d Lieutenant of Grennell's Company New York Artillery, 16th March to November, 1776; 2d Lieutenant 2d Continental Artillery, 29th June, 1781, to rank from 17th December, 1780; transferred to Corps of Artillery, 17th June, 1783, and served to 20th June, 1784.

Reed, John (Pa). Captain 1st Pennsylvania Battalion of the Flying Camp, June, 1776, to ——.

Reed, John (Pa). Ensign 8th Pennsylvania, — August, 1776, to ——.

Reed, John (Pa). Lieutenant Westmoreland County, Pennsylvania, Militia, 1776-1777.

Reed, Jonathan (N. H.). Colonel New Hampshire Militia, 1776-1778. (Died 1790.)

Reed, Joshua (Mass). Lieutenant of Frye's Massachusetts Regiment, May to December, 1775; Captain Massachusetts Militia in 1777. See Joshua Read; were they not the same?

Reed, Joseph (Pa). Lieutenant-Colonel and Military Secretary to General Washington, 4th July, 1775, to 16th May, 1776; Colonel Adjutant-General Continental Army, 5th June, 1776; resigned 22d January, 1777; Brigadier-General Continental Army, 12th May, 1777, which he declined 9th June, 1777. (Died 5th March, 1785.)

Reed, Joseph (Pa). Ensign 9th Pennsylvania, 20th July, 1780; transferred to 5th Pennsylvania, 17th January, 1781, and served to June, 1783.

Reed, Philip (Md). Captain Maryland Militia, 1776-1777. (Died 2d November, 1829.)

Reed, Samuel (N. C.). Captain North Carolina Militia, 1780-1781. (Died 1810.)

Reed, Seth (Mass). Major in Lexington Alarm, April, 1775; Lieutenant-Colonel of Paterson's Massachusetts Regiment, 27th May to December, 1775; Lieutenant-Colonel 15th Continental Infantry, 1st January, 1776; became insane in August, 1776, and retired from the service. (Died 1797.)

Reed, Silvanus (N. H.). Ensign 2d Continental Infantry, 1st January to 31st December, 1776; served subsequently as Adjutant and as Captain New Hampshire Militia.

Reed, Thomas (Conn). Assistant Paymaster-General, 31st March, 1778, to ——.

Reed, Thomas (N. Y.). Surgeon 1st Canadian (Livingston's) Regiment, 18th December, 1776; retired 1st January, 1781. (Died 18th September, 1826.)

Reed, Thomas (Pa). Ensign 1st Pennsylvania Battalion of the Flying Camp, June, 1776; taken prisoner at Fort Washington, 16th November, 1776; exchanged, 4th November, 1780, and did not return to the service.

Reed, Timothy (Mass). Ensign of Woodbridge's Massachusetts Regiment, May to November, 1775.

Reeder, Hezekiah (Md). 2d Lieutenant 3d Maryland, 10th December, 1776; resigned 9th February, 1778.

Reese, Abel (Pa). 2d Lieutenant 9th Pennsylvania, 15th November, 1776; resigned 14th August, 1777.

Reese, David (Conn). Sergeant in Burrall's Continental Regiment, May, 1776; Ensign, 19th September, 1776, to January, 1777.

Reese, George (N. C.). Lieutenant 9th North Carolina, 28th November, 1776, to ——.

Reese, John (Pa). Captain 2d Pennsylvania Battalion, 5th January, 1776; Captain 3d Pennsylvania, January, 1777, to rank from 5th January, 1776; resigned 31st December, 1777.

Reeves, Enos (Pa). Ensign 11th Pennsylvania, 1st May, 1777; Adjutant, 11th September, 1777; 2d Lieutenant, 25th October, 1777; 1st Lieutenant, 31st March, 1778; transferred to 10th Pennsylvania, 1st July, 1778; transferred to 2d Pennsylvania, 1st January, 1781; transferred to 1st Pennsylvania, 1st January, 1783, and served to 3d November, 1783.

Reeves, Isaac (N. J.). Captain New Jersey Militia, 14th June, 1776; killed at Elizabethtown, 6th June, 1780.

Reeves, John (N. J.). Sergeant 3d New Jersey, December, 1775, to November, 1776; Ensign 2d New Jersey, 29th November, 1776; resigned 1st February, 1777.

Reeves, Nathaniel (Mass). Sergeant in Lexington Alarm, April, 1775; 2d Lieutenant of Brewer's Massachusetts Regiment, May to December, 1775.

Regnier.—See **De Roussi**.

Reid, Charles (Va). Ensign 3d Virginia, May, 1777; superceded August, 1777.

Reid, George (N. H.). Captain Company of Minute Men in April, 1775; Captain 1st New Hampshire, 23d May to December, 1775; Captain 5th Continental Infantry, 1st January, 1776; Major .1st New Hampshire, 8th November, 1776; Lieutenant-Colonel, 2d April, 1777; transferred to 2d New Hampshire, 5th March, 1778 ;retained in New Hampshire Battalion, 1st March, 1782, and served to 3d November, 1783; Colonel, 30th September, 1783. (Died — September, 1815.)

Reid, George (Pa). 2d Lieutenant of Patton's Continental Regiment, 15th January, 1777; last appears on roll for October ,1778.

Reid, James (Va). 2d Lieutenant 3d Virginia, ——, 1777; "superceded."

Reid, James Randolph (Pa). 1st Lieutenant 4th Pennsylvania Battalion, 6th January, 1776; Captain 2d Canadian (Hazen's) Regiment, 3d November, 1776; Major, 1st September, 1777; retired June, 1783.

Reid, Nathan (Va). Captain 14th Virginia, 28th January, 1777; wounded at Brandywine, 11th September, 1777; regiment designated 10th Virginia, 14th September, 1778; transferred to 1st Virginia, 12th February, 1781; retired 1st January, 1783. (Died 6th November, 1830.) Name also spelled Reed.

Reid, Philip (Md). Ensign 5th Maryland, 20th February, 1777; Lieutenant, 13th October, 1778; transferred to 3d Maryland, 1st January, 1781; taken prisoner at Camden, 16th August, 1780; Captain, 9th February, 1782; retired 12th April, 1783.

Reid, Samuel (Pa). Ensign 11th Pennsylvania, 5th August, 1779; Lieutenant, 2d October, 1780; transferred to 3d Pennsylvania, 17th January, 1781; transferred to 1st Pennsylvania, 1st January, 1783, and served to 3d June, 1783.

Reidel, Henry (Pa). Cornet Dragoons, Pulaski Legion, 1st April, 1778; Lieutenant in 1782; served to ——.

Reigart, Adam (Pa). Lieutenant-Colonel Pennsylvania Militia in 1776.

Reiley, John (Conn). 2d Lieutenant of Burrall's Continental Regiment, 19th January, 1776; 1st Lieutenant, 19th September, 1776, to January, 1777; 2d Lieutenant of Webb's Continental Regiment, 1st January, 1777; 1st Lieutenant, 1st February, 1777; Captain, 10th July, 1779; taken prisoner on the Long Island Expedition, 10th December, 1777; exchanged 3d December, 1780; transferred to 3d Connecticut, 1st January, 1781; retired 1st January, 1783.

Reiley, John (Pa). 1st Lieutenant 12th Pennsylvania, 1st October, 1776; Captain, 20th May, 1777; transferred to 3d Pennsylvania, 1st July, 1778; wounded at Bonhampton, N. J., —— April, 1777; transferred to Invalid Regiment, 12th August, 1780, and served to 24th June, 1783.

Reiley, William (Md). 2d Lieutenant Maryland Battalion of the Flying Camp, July to December, 1776; 1st Lieutenant 4th Maryland, 10th December, 1776; Captain, 13th October, 1777; transferred to 1st Maryland, 1st January, 1781, and served to April, 1783.

Reinick, Christian (Pa). Surgeon's Mate of Thompson's Pennsylvania Rifle Battalion, 25th June, 1775; Surgeon's Mate 1st Continental Infantry, 1st January to 31st December, 1776; Surgeon 1st Pennsylvania, 1st January, 1777; died 21st September, 1777, of wounds received 20th September, 1777, at Paoli, Pa.

Remick, Timothy (Mass) Sergeant of Scammon's Massachusetts Regiment, May to November, 1775; Sergeant 18th Continental Infantry, 1st January to ——, 1776; 2d Lieutenant, 13th November, 1776; 1st Lieutenant 12th Massachusetts, 1st January, 1777; Captain, 4th October, 1780; transferred to 1st Massachusetts, 1st January, 1781, and served to 3d November, 1783. (Died 1784.)

Remington, John (R. I.). Ensign 9th Continental Infantry, 1st January to 31st December, 1776; 2d Lieutenant 1st Rhode Island, 1st January, 1777, and served to ——.

Remsen, Henry (N. Y.). Colonel New York City Militia in 1775. (Died 1792.)

Rencastle, John.—See **Ruecastle.**

Rendelo, —— (—). Captain, ——; wounded at Savannah, 9th October 1778.

Renner, Francis Jacob (Pa). Lieutenant-Colonel Pennsylvania Militia in 1777.

Rennison, John (Pa). Sergeant 7th Pennsylvania, December, 1776; Ensign, 24th July, 1779; resigned — April, 1780. (Died 18th May, 1829.)

Requa, Gabriel (N. Y.). Captain of Hamman's Regiment New York Militia; was a prisoner; when and where taken not stated.

Requa, Isaac (N. Y.). Lieutenant and Adjutant New York Militia Regiment, ——; prisoner of war, 31st January, 1779, to 10th March, 1780; when and where taken not stated.

Requa, Joseph (N. Y.). Lieutenant New York Militia in 1780.

Respess, John (N. C.). Ensign 8th North Carolina, 28th November, 1776; resigned 24th April, 1777.

Reuch, John (Md). Ensign 1st Maryland Battalion of the Flying Camp, June, 1776, to ——.

Reucher, John Grant (Pa). Sergeant 5th Pennsylvania, January, 1777; 2d Lieutenant, 7th June, 1777; cashiered 15th November, 1777.

Revelly, Francis (Md). 2d Lieutenant 3d Maryland, 20th February, 1777; 1st Lieutenant, 15th April, 1777; Captain, 18th June, 1781; retained in Maryland Battalion, April, 1783, and served to 15th November, 1783.

Rew, John (Pa). Regimental Quartermaster 6th Pennsylvania, 7th December, 1777; taken prisoner at Newtown, 29th August, 1779; exchanged 25th October, 1780; served subsequently in the Navy.

Rexford, Elisha (Conn). Chaplain of Elmore's Continental Regiment, 15th April, 1776, to April, 1777.

Reynolds, Daniel (N. H.). Lieutenant-Colonel and Colonel New Hampshire Militia, 1780-1781.

Reynolds, Elisha (N. C.). Lieutenant North Carolina Militia at King's Mountain in October, 1780. (Died 13th December, 1836.

Reynolds, George (N. J.). Ensign 2d New Jersey, 25th December, 1775; 2d Lieutenant, 23d November, 1776; 1st Lieutenant, 1st January, 1777; resigned 3d January, 1778.

Reynolds, James (Conn). 1st Lieutenant of Swift's Connecticut State Regiment, June to November, 1775.

Reynolds, John (Md). Captain 1st Maryland Battalion of the Flying Camp, July to December, 1776; Captain 7th Maryland, 10th December, 1776; resigned 28th December, 1777.

Reynolds, John (Md). 2d Lieutenant 4th Maryland Battalion of the Flying Camp, July to November, 1776.

Reynolds, John (R. I.). Lieutenant of Varnum's Rhode Island Regiment, 3d May to December, 1775.

Reynolds, John (S. C.). Lieutenant South Carolina Militia in 1775.

Reynolds, Nathaniel (N. Y.). Lieutenant New York Militia; taken prisoner at Combond 24th June, 1779; exchanged 24th October, 1781.

Reynolds, Richard (S. C.). Captain South Carolina Militia, 1775-1776.

Reynolds, Thomas (N. J.). Lieutenant-Colonel New Jersey Militia; taken prisoner from his home 23d December, 1776. (Died 1803.)

Rhea, Aaron (N. J.). Ensign 1st New Jersey, 12th September, 1778; resigned 24th October, 1780; Lieutenant 2d Continental Dragoons, 17th August, 1781, and served to close of war.

Rhea, David (N. J.). Major 2d New Jersey, 28th November, 1775; Lieutenant-Colonel, 28th November, 1776; transferred to 4th New Jersey, 1st January, 1777; retired 1st July, 1778. (Died 14th June, 1821.)

Rhea, John (Pa). Regimental Quartermaster 6th Pennsylvania, 17th March, 1777; dismissed 3d January, 1778.

Rhea, John (Va). Ensign 7th Virginia, 9th January, 1777; dismissed 20th November, 1777. (Died 27th May, 1832.)

Rhea, Jonathan (N. J.). Ensign 2d New Jersey, 1st January, 1777; 2d Lieutenant, 1st April, 1778; retained in New Jersey Battalion in April, 1783, and served to 3d November, 1783.

Rhea, Matthew (Va). Regimental Quartermaster 7th Virginia, 15th June, 1777; 2d Lieutenant, 9th September, 1778; transferred to 5th Virginia, 14th September, 1778; 1st Lieutenant, 4th July, 1779; transferred to 7th Virginia, 12th February, 1781, and served to close of war.

Rhodes, Charles (R. I.). Ensign 9th Continental Infantry, 1st January, 1776, to ——.

Rhodes, John (Del). 1st Lieutenant Delaware Battalion of the Flying Camp, July to December, 1776; 1st Lieutenant Delaware Regiment, 4th December, 1776; wounded 12th May, 1777, where not stated; Captain Lieutenant, 1st March, 1779; Captain, 27th April, 1780; taken prisoner at Camden 16th August, 1780, and died 26th October, 1780.

Rhodes, Joseph (N. C.). Lieutenant 8th North Carolina, 28th November, 1776; Captain, 5th August, 1777; retired 1st June, 1778.

Rhodes, Joseph (R. I.). Surgeon's Mate to Brigade of Rhode Island State troops in 1776.

Rhodes, Joseph Thomas (N. C.). Captain 10th North Carolina, 1st August, 1777; transferred to 4th North Carolina, 1st June, 1778; wounded at Stono Ferry, 20th June, 1779; served to close of war; Brevet Major, 30th September, 1783.

Rhodes, William (Del). Lieutenant-Colonel Delaware Militia, 1775.

Rice, Asa (Mass). Lieutenant in Lexington Alarm, April, 1775; 2d Lieutenant of Ward's Massachusetts Regiment, April to December, 1775; Captain Massachusetts Militia, 1776-1779. (Died 1823.)

Rice, Benjamin (Pa). Ensign 1st Pennsylvania Battalion, 20th January, 1776; 2d Lieutenant, 6th August, 1776; served to January, 1777.

Rice, Edward (Va). 2d Lieutenant 8th Virginia, 10th December, 1775; resigned — February, 1776.

Rice, Frederick William (Pa). 1st Lieutenant German Regiment, 12th July, 1776; Captain, 4th January, 1777; retired 1st January, 1781. (Died January, 1805.)

Rice, George (Va). Captain 11th Virginia, 18th January, 1777; retired 30th September, 1778.

Rice, Hezekiah (N. C.). 1st Lieutenant 1st North Carolina, 1st September, 1775; Captain, 28th November, 1776; omitted January, 1778.

Rice, Holman (Va). Captain Virginia Militia, 1779-1781.

Rice, Jeptha (N. C.). Quartermaster-Sergeant 9th North Carolina, 28th

November, 1776; Ensign, 15th March, 1777; retired 1st June, 1778.

Rice, Joseph (Mass). Captain of Phinney's Massachusetts Regiment, May to December, 1775; Captain 18th Continental Infantry, 1st January, 1776; died 18th May, 1776.

Rice, John (N. C.). Adjutant 1st North Carolina, 10th December, 1776; Ensign, 28th March, 1777; 2d Lieutenant, 3d April, 1777; 1st Lieutenant 1st Continental Dragoons, 1st June, 1778, and served to 9th November, 1782. (Died 30th June, 1830.

Rice, John (Pa). Lieutenant-Colonel Pennsylvania Militia in 1776.

Rice, Joseph (Pa). Captain 4th Continental Artillery, 3d March, 1777; resigned 26th September, 1780.

Rice, Joseph (R. I.). Lieutenant Rhode Island Militia in 1779.

Rice, Nathan (Mass). Adjutant of Heath's Massachusetts Regiment, May to December, 1775; 2d Lieutenant and Adjutant 24th Continental Infantry, 1st January to 31st December, 1776; Major and Aide-de-Camp to General Lincoln, 7th May, 1777, to 1st January, 1781; retained as Major 4th Massachusetts, 1st January, 1781, and served to June, 1783; Lieutenant-Colonel 14th United States Infantry, 3d March, 1799; honorably discharged 15th June, 1800. (Died 17th April, 1834.)

Rice, Nathaniel (Va). Lieutenant of a Virginia State Regiment, 1778 to 1781.

Rice, Nehemiah (Conn). 1st Lieutenant of Elmore's Continental Regiment, 15th April, 1776; Adjutant 8th Connecticut, 1st January, 1777; Captain, 15th November, 1777; transferred to 5th Connecticut, 1st January, 1781; retired 1st January, 1783.

Rice, Oliver (Mass). Private in Lexington Alarm, April, 1775; Sergeant 4th Continental Infantry, 1st January to 31st December, 1776; Sergeant Major 9th Massachusetts, 1st March, 1777; Ensign, 2d June, 1778; Lieutenant, 5th September, 1780; transferred to 4th Massachusetts, 1st January, 1783, and served to 3d November, 1783.

Rice, Robert (Pa). Ensign 10th Pennsylvania, 2d June, 1778; dismissed ——, 1779.

Rice, Rufus (Conn). Ensign 2d Connecticut, 1st January, 1777; 2d Lieutenant 7th December, 1777; resigned 24th February, 1779.

Rice, Sylvanus (Mass). Captain in Lexington Alarm, April, 1775; Captain Massachusetts Militia, 1779-1780. (Died 1819.)

Rice, Thomas (R. I.). Captain Rhode Island Militia, 1776-1777.

Richborough, —— (S. C.). Captain 6th South Carolina, resigned 22d February, 1778.

Richards, Abel (Mass). Captain Massachusetts Militia in 1778.

Richards, Benjamin (Conn). Captain of Wadsworth's Connecticut State Regiment, June to December, 1776.

Richards, Bradley (N. H.). Sergeant 3d New Hampshire, 27th January, 1777; Ensign, 1st May, 1778; transferred to 2d New Hampshire, 1st January, 1781; resigned 15th June, 1781.

Richards, George (R. I.). Regimental Quartermaster of Elliott's Regiment Rhode Island State Artillery, 12th December, 1776, to May, 1777.

Richards, Jeremiah (N. H.). Lieutenant 1st New Hampshire, January, 1777; wounded at Hubbardton, 7th October, 1777; discharged 5th July, 1780.

Richards, Peter H. (Mass). Sergeant of Brewer's Massachusetts Regiment, May to December, 1775; Sergeant 6th Continental Infantry, 1st January to 31st December, 1776; 2d Lieutenant 3d Massachusetts, 1st January, 1777; resigned 10th February, 1778; Captain Massachusetts Militia; killed at Groton Heights 6th September, 1781.

Richards, Samuel (Conn). Sergeant 2d Connecticut, 4th May to 18th December, 1775; Ensign 22d Continental Infantry, 1st January to 31st December, 1776; 1st Lieutenant 3d Connecticut, 1st January, 1777; Regimental Paymaster, 8th September, 1778; retired 1st January, 1781. (Died 1841.)

Richards, Samuel (N. H.). Captain 1st New Hampshire, 23d May to December, 1775; Captain 5th Continental Infantry, 1st January to 31st December, 1776.

Richards, Thomas (N. H.). Ensign 5th Continental Infantry, 1st January, 1776, to ——.

Richards, William (Conn). Regimental Quartermaster, 6th Connecticut, 20th May to 10th December, 1775; 1st Lieutenant 10th Continental Infantry, 1st January to — December, 1776; Captain, 11th October, 1776; Captain 1st Connecticut, 1st January,

1777; transferred to 5th Connecticut, 1st January, 1781; transferred to 2d Connecticut, 1st January, 1783, and served to June, 1783. (Died 3d March, 1825.)

Richards, William (Conn). Surgeon's Mate of Gage's Connecticut State Regiment, June to December, 1776.

Richardson, Aaron (Mass). Sergeant in Lexington Alarm, April, 1775; 2d Lieutenant of Gardner's Massachusetts Regiment, May to December, 1775.

Richardson, Abijah (Mass). Surgeon's Mate, 3d Massachusetts, 1st January, 1777; taken prisoner at Fort Fayette, 1st June, 1779; exchanged September, 1779; Surgeon 5th Massachusetts, 17th July, 1780; retired 1st January, 1781. (Died 10th May, 1822.)

Richardson, Addison (Mass). Captain of Mansfield's Massachusetts Regiment, May to December, 1775; Captain 27th Continental Infantry, 1st January, 1776; taken prisoner at Long Island 27th August, 1776; exchanged 1st March, 1778; Captain Massachusetts Militia, 1779-1780.

Richardson, Bradbury (N. H.). Major New Hampshire Militia in 1776.

Richardson, Caleb (Mass). Captain of Walker's Massachusetts Regiment, May to December, 1775; Captain Massachusetts Militia, 1776-1780.

Richardson, Edward (Mass). Ensign of Nixon's Massachusetts Regiment, May to November, 1775; Captain Massachusetts Militia, 1778-1779. (Died 1834.)

Richardson, Edward (S. C.). Captain South Carolina Rangers, 17th June, 1775, to ——.

Richardson, Ephraim (Mass). Lieutenant in Lexington Alarm, April, 1775; Captain of Whitcomb's Massachusetts Regiment, May to December, 1775.

Richardson, Holt (Va). Captain 7th Virginia, 27th February, 1776; Major 15th Virginia, 13th November, 1776; Lieutenant-Colonel 7th Virginia, 9th October, 1777; transferred to 5th Virginia, 14th September, 1778; resigned 10th May, 1779.

Richardson, Isaac (Va). 1st Lieutenant 12th Virginia, 16th December, 1776; cashiered 9th May, 1777.

Richardson, John (Md). Ensign 1st Maryland Battalion of the Flying Camp, July, 1776, to ——.

Richardson, John (N. C.). Ensign 10th North Carolina, February, 1777; omitted 1st January, 1778.

Richardson, John (Pa). 1st Lieutenant 5th Pennsylvania Battalion, 6th January, 1776; Captain, 21st March, 1776; taken prisoner at Fort Washington, 16th November, 1776; exchanged 26th August, 1778, and did not return to the army.

Richardson, Jonas (Mass). Captain of Frye's Massachusetts Regiment, May to December, 1775.

Richardson, Joseph (N. C.). Ensign 6th North Carolina, January, 1777; 2d Lieutenant, 27th August, 1777; retired 1st June, 1778.

Richardson, Josiah (N. H.). Lieutenant of Nichols' Regiment, New Hampshire Militia in 1777.

Richardson, Luther (N. H.). Captain of Bedel's Regiment, New Hampshire Militia, 1775, and of Bedel's Regiment, Vermont Militia, 1778-1779.

Richardson, Richard (Pa). 2d Lieutenant 8th Pennsylvania, 9th August, 1776; 1st Lieutenant, 13th July, 1777; resigned — November 1777.

Richardson, Richard (S. C.). Colonel and Brigadier-General South Carolina Militia, 1775; taken prisoner at Charleston, 12th May, 1780; died September, 1780, in captivity.

Richardson, Richard, Jr. (S. C.). Captain South Carolina Militia in 1775.

Richardson, Stephen (Mass). Captain Massachusetts Militia, 1777.

Richardson, Walker (Va). 2d Lieutenant 1st Continental Artillery, 4th March, 1778; Regimental Quartermaster, 25th February, 1779; 1st Lieutenant, 18th August, 1779; served to ——.

Richardson, William (Md). Colonel 4th Maryland Battalion of the Flying Camp, July to December, 1776; Colonel 5th Maryland, 10th December, 1776; resigned 22d October, 1779.

Richardson, William (N. H.). Lieutenant of Peabody's Regiment New Hampshire Militia, 1778-1779.

Richardson, William (S. C.). Captain South Carolina Militia; taken prisoner at Charleston, 12th March, 1780. (Died 1786.)

Richie, William (Pa). Ensign of Baxter's Pennsylvania Battalion of the Flying Camp; taken prisoner at Fort Washington, 16th November, 1776.

Richmond, Benjamin (Mass). Ensign 14th Massachusetts, 1st January, 1777; retired, 1st April, 1779. (Died 1st July, 1825.)

Richmond, Christopher (Md). Lieutenant and Paymaster 1st Maryland, 27th February, 1778; transferred to 2d Maryland, 1st January, 1781; Captain, 20th November, 1781, and served to April, 1783.

Richmond, David (Pa). 2d Lieutenant 1st Pennsylvania, 14th September, 1777; was in service in 1780.

Richmond, David (R. I.). Lieutenant of Hitchcock's Rhode Island Regiment, 3d May to December, 1775.

Richmond, Ebenezer (R. I.). Surgeon 2d Rhode Island, June to December, 1775; Surgeon's-Mate 11th Continental Infantry, 15th January to 31st December, 1776.

Richmond, William (R. I.). Colonel Rhode Island Militia, 1775 and 1776.

Richmond, William (Va). Director and Chief Physician Hospital Department in Virginia, 11th June, 1776, to ——.

Richter, Nicholas (N. Y.). Captain of Klock's Regiment, New York Militia, was wounded, but where and when, not stated.

Rickard, William (Mass). Sergeant of Jackson's Additional Continental Regiment, 14th May, 1777; Ensign, 24th April, 1779; regiment designated 16th Massachusetts, 23d July, 1780; transferred to 9th Massachusetts, 1st January, 1781; Lieutenant, 14th April, 1782; transferred to 4th Massachusetts, 1st June, 1782; retained in Jackson's Continental Regiment in November, 1783, and served to 20th June, 1784; Lieutenant 2d United States Infantry, 4th May, 1792; assigned to 3d Sub Legion, 4th September, 1792; Captain, 30th January, 1794; resigned 15th November, 1800. (Died 9th January, 1813.)

Ricker, Abraham.—See Riker.

Ricketts, Nicolas (Md). 2d Lieutenant of Dorsey's Company, Maryland Artillery, 1st December, 1777; company attached to and formed part 1st Continental Artillery, 30th May, 1778; 1st Lieutenant, 25th August, 1778, and served to close of war.

Rickman, William (Va). Director of Hospital in Virginia, 18th May; 1776; retired 21st October, 1780.

Riddick, Jason (Va). 1st Lieutenant 4th Virginia, 2d April, 1776; Captain,

10th June, 1777; retired 30th September, 1778. (Died 1785.)

Riddick, Willis (Va). 2d Lieutenant 15th Virginia, 22d November, 1776; 1st Lieutenant, 11th September, 1777; taken prisoner at Germantown, 4th October, 1777; exchanged in 1780; assigned to 4th Virginia; Captain, 12th February, 1781, but resigned 14th February, 1781.

Riddle, Henry (Pa). Regimental Quartermaster 3d Continental Artillery, 1st April, 1778, to June, 1783.

Riddle, Isaac (——). Captain; was a prisoner in 1780, when and where taken, not stated.

Ridgely, Bazil (Md). Ensign 1st Maryland, 10th December, 1776; resigned, 7th December, 1778.

Ridgely, Frederick (Ga). Surgeon's-Mate 2d Georgia, July, 1776, to ——.

Ridgely, Frederick (N. Y.). Surgeons Mate Hospital Department, 1775-1776.

Ridgely, Henry (Md). 1st Lieutenant 3d Maryland Battalion of the Flying Camp, July to December, 1776; Captain 3d Maryland, 10th December, 1776; resigned 14th August, 1777.

Ridgely, William (Md). Ensign of Smallwood's Maryland Regiment, 14th January, 1776; 2d Lieutenant, 1st Maryland, 10th December, 1776, but never joined the regiment, having been taken prisoner at Long Island, 27th August, 1776.

Ridley, Benjamin (Va). 2d Lieutenant 8th Virginia, 9th May, 1777, to ——.

Ridley, Thomas (Va). Captain 4th Virginia, 11th March, 1776; Major 10th Virginia, 1st March, 1778; transferred to 6th Virginia, 14th September, 1778, retired 12th February, 1781. (Died 1845.)

Ridley, William (N. C.. Surgeon 3d North Carolina 21st April, 1777; resigned 21st November, 1777.

Riegor, Jacob (Pa). Surgeon 2d Battalion of Miles' Pennsylvania Rifle Regiment, 22d March to December, 1776.

Riggs, Abimelech (R. I.). Captain of Tallman's Rhode Island State Regiment, 1776 and 1777.

Riggs, John (Mass). Corporal in Lexington Alarm, April, 1775; 2d Lieutenant of Nixon's Massachusetts Regiment, May to December, 1775; 1st Lieutenant 4th Continental Infantry, 1st January, 1776; cashiered, 5th June, 1776.

Righter, John (Pa). Lieutenant Philadelphia County, Pennsylvania, Militia, 1776-1777.

Riker, Abraham (N. Y.). 1st Lieutenant 4th New York, 28th June, 1775; Captain 3d New York, 28th March, 1776; Captain 2d New York, 21st November, 1776; died 7th May, 1778. (Name also spelled Ricker.)

Riker, John Berrien (N. J.). Surgeon 4th New Jersey, 23d November, 1776; retired 11th February, 1779|

Rinehardt, Godfrey (N. J.). Captain and Major New Jersey Militia, 1777-1779.

Ringgold, James (Md). 2d Lieutenant of Smallwood's Maryland Regiment, 14th January 1776; resigned 3d July, 1776.

Rinker, Jacob (Va). 1st Lieutenant 8th Virginia, 4th March, 1776; resigned 10th May, 1777.

Rinnard, Nathaniel (Md). 2d Lieutenant of Richardson's Battalion Maryland Flying Camp, July to December, 1776.

Ripley, Hezekiah (Mass). 1st Lieutenant 2d Massachusetts, 1st January, 1777; Regimental Quartermaster, 1st June, 1779, and served to June, 1783. (Died 18th October, 1841.)

Ripley, John (Conn). Captain 8th Connecticut, 6th July to 18th December, 1775; Major of Chester's Connecticut State Regiment, 20th June to 25th December, 1776; Major 13th United States Infantry, 13th February, 1799; honorably discharged 15th June, 1800.

Rippey, William (Pa). Captain 6th Pennsylvania Battalion, 9th January, 1776; Captain, 7th Pennsylvania, 1st January, 1777; resigned 20th March, 1777. (Died 22d September, 1819.)

Risberg, Gustavus (Md). Assistant Deputy Quartermaster-General of the Flying Camp, 17th August to 1st December, 1776.

Risley, Jeremiah (N. J.). Lieutenant New Jersey Militia in 1777.

Rittenhouse, Benjamin (Pa). Captain Pennsylvania Militia, 1775-1777; also superintendent of a gun factory in Pennsylvania, 1776 to close of war. (Died 1825.)

Ritter, Charles (Pa). Surgeon's-Mate German Regiment, 20th December, 1777; resigned August, 1778.

Ritter, William (Pa). 2d Lieutenant German Regiment, 12th July, 1776;

1st Lieutenant 4th Continental Artillery, 1st April, 1777; resigned 11th March, 1779.

Ritzema, Rudolphus (N. Y.). Lieutenant-Colonel 1st New York, 30th June, 1775; Colonel, 28th November, 1775; Colonel 3d New York, 28th March, to November, 1776; subsequently joined the British army.

Rivel, Adam (——). Lieutenant; was a prisoner in 1782, when and where taken not stated:

Roane, Christopher (Va). Captain of a Virginia State Regiment, 1777, to 1782.

Robarts, Thomas.—See Roberts.

Robb, John (Pa). 2d Lieutenant 1st Battalion of Miles' Pennsylvania Rifle Regiment, 17th March to December, 1776; Captain Pennsylvania State Regiment, 18th April, 1777; regiment designated 13th Pennsylvania, 12th November, 1777; retired 1st July, 1778.

Robbins, Ammi Ruhamah (Conn). Chaplain of Burrall's Connecticut State Regiment, 20th March, 1776, to January, 1777. (Died 30th October, 1813.)

Robbins, John (Va). Cadet 9th Virginia, 11th December, 1776; Ensign 5th February, 1777; 2d Lieutenant, 14th May, 1778; 1st Lieutenant, 25th August, 1778; transferred to 1st Virginia, 14th September, 1778; taken prisoner at Germantown, 4th October, 1777; retained in 5th Virginia, 12th February, 1781; Lieutenant, 4th Continental Dragoons, 1st October, 1781, and served to close of war. (Died 1840.)

Robbins, Josiah (Conn). 1st Lieutenant of Sage's Connecticut State Regiment, June to December, 1776.

Roberdeau, Daniel (Pa). Brigadier-General Pennsylvania Militia, 4th July, 1776, to March, 1777. (Died 5th January, 1795.)

Roberts, Algernon (Pa). Lieutenant Philadelphia Battalion Pennsylvania Militia in 1776.

Roberts, Benjamin (Va). Captain of Clark's Illinois Regiment, 1778 to 1781.

Roberts, Cyrus (Va). 1st Lieutenant 14th Virginia, 28th November, 1776; Captain, 15th January, 1778; retired 30th September, 1778.

Roberts, Daniel (Ga). Lieutenant Georgia Rangers; taken prisoner at Savannah, 4th March, 1776; Major, 3d Georgia, 5th July, 1776; Lieutenant-

Colonel, 2d Georgia, 21st March, 1778; died 18th November, 1779.

Roberts, James (Mass). 2d Lieutenant of Scammon's Massachusetts Regiment, May to December, 1775; Major and Lieutenant-Colonel Massachusetts Militia, 1776-1780.

Roberts, Jesse (Pa). 2d Lieutenant of Lewis' Pennsylvania Battalion of the Flying Camp, July, 1776; 2d Lieutenant 10th Pennsylvania, 4th December, 1776, but does not appear to have joined this regiment.

Roberts, John (Mass). 1st Lieutenant of Spencer's Continental Regiment, 18th February, 1777; resigned 15th September, 1777.

Roberts, John (N. Y.). 2d Lieutenant of Malcolm's Continental Regiment, 6th February, 1777; 1st Lieutenant, 17th November, 1777; Captain-Lieutenant, 16th June, 1778; resigned 1st April, 1779; name also spelled Robert.

Roberts, John (Va). Surgeon 6th Virginia, 1st February, 1777; transferred to 4th Virginia, 14th September, 1778; transferred to 10th Virginia, 1st August, 1779; served on staff of General Lafayette in 1781; served to close of war. (Died 21st April, 1821.)

Roberts, John (Va). Lieutenant of Clark's Illinois Regiment, 1779-1782.

Roberts, John (N. C. and Va). Lieutenant 5th North Carolina, 28th March, 1777; retired 1st June, 1778; Captain Virginia Convention Guards, 11th January, 1779; Major, 5th March, 1779; retired 1st May, 1781. (Died 30th November, 1843.)

Roberts, Joseph (N. H.). Captain New Hampshire Militia, 1776.

Roberts, Moses (Mass). 1st Lieutenant 15th Massachusetts, 1st January, 1777; Captain, 1st March, 1779; killed at Young's House, 3d February, 1780.

Roberts, Owen (S. C.). Major, 1st South Carolina, 17th June, 1775; Lieutenant-Colonel, 4th South Carolina (Artillery), 14th November, 1775; Colonel, 16th September, 1776; killed at Stono Ferry, 20th June, 1779.

Roberts, Richard Brooke (S. C.). Captain 4th South Carolina (Artillery), 1779; Aide-de-Camp to General Lincoln in 1782, to close of war; Captain 2d United States Infantry, 4th March, 1791; assigned to 2d Sub Legion, 4th September, 1792; Major 3d Sub Legion, 28th February, 1793; assigned to 4th

Infantry, 1st November, 1796; died 19th January, 1797.

Roberts, Samuel (Pa). Lieutenant Pennsylvania Militia, 1776-1777.

Roberts, Thomas (Va). Surgeon 10th Virginia, 1st October, 1778; transferred to 3d Virginia, 1st August, 1779, and served to close of war.

Roberts, William (Pa). Captain of Hart's Pennsylvania Battalion of the Flying Camp, July to December, 1776.

Roberts, William (Va). Lieutenant of Clark's Illinois Regiment, 1779-1781.

Robertson, Abiather (Mass). Lieutenant 1st Massachusetts, 1st January, 1777; resigned 11th February, 1778.

Robertson, Charles (N. C.). Major North Carolina Rangers, ——; wounded at Wofford's Iron Works, 8th August, 1780.

Robertson, James (Va). Adjutant 13th Virginia, 15th October, 1777; retired 30th September, 1778; Lieutenant of Clark's Illinois Regiment, 1779-1782.

Robertson, John (Va). Adjutant 10th Virginia, 4th December, 1777; 2d Lieutenant, 9th September, 1778; regiment designated 6th Virginia, 14th September, 1778; taken prisiner at Charleston, 12th May, 1780; 1st Lieutenant, 18th February, 1781; retired 1st January, 1783. (Died 1810.)

Robertson, John (Conn). Captain 20th Continental Infantry, 1st January, to 31st December, 1776.

Robertson, Peter (Conn). 2d Lieutenant 2d Connecticut, 1st January, 1777; 1st Lieutenant, 7th November, 1777; transferred to 3d Connecticut, 1st January, 1781; Captain, 28th December, 1781, and served to June 1783.

Robertson, Robert (N. J.). Ensign 1st New Jersey, 16th December, 1775; 2d Lieutenant, 18th September, 1776; 1st Lieutenant, February, 1777; wounded at Germantown, 4th October, 1777, and resigned shortly afterward.

Robertson, Robert (Pa). Surgeon's-Mate of a Battalion, Pennsylvania Flying Camp, July to December, 1776.

Robertson, Samuel (Conn). 1st Lieutenant of Mott's Connecticut State Regiment, June to December, 1776.

Robertson, Tully (Va). 1st Lieutenant 4th Virginia, 25th March, 1776; Cashiered, 6th June, 1777. He served subsequently as Captain of a Virginia State Regiment. Major, 5th United

States Infantry, 16th January, 1809; re-signed 9th May, 1809. Name also spelled Robinson.

Robertson, William (Va). Ensign 2d Virginia, 21st October, 1775; resigned May, 1776; Adjutant, 9th Virginia, 22d May, 1777; transferred to 1st Virginia, 14th September, 1778; Lieutenant, 24th September, 1778; taken prisoner at Germantown, 4th October, 1777; re-leased, 3d December, 1780; retained in 5th Virginia, 12th February, 1781, and retired 1st January, 1783. (Died 12th November, 1831.)

Robeson, James (S. C.). 1st Lieuten-ant 3d South Carolina; wounded in action with Indians, 4th May, 1777, and again wounded in action at Amelia Island, 18th May, 1777; was a Captain in 1780. Name also spelled Robison.

Robicheux, James (N. Y.). Captain 1st Canadian in (Livingston's) Regi-ment, 20th November, 1775; retired 1st January, 1781.

Robie, William.—See **Roby.**

Robinson —— (Mass). Ensign 1st Massachusetts; resigned 7th Novem-ber, 1782.

Robinson, Abiather (Mass). Lieuten-ant 1st Massachusetts, 1st January, 1777; resigned 11th February, 1778.

Robinson, Abner (Conn). Sergeant in the Lexington Alarm, April, 1775; Ensign 3d Connecticut, 1st May to 16th December, 1775; 2d Lieutenant of Mott's Connecticut State Regiment, June to December, 1776; subsequently served as Captain Connecticut Militia.

Robinson, Andrew (Pa). 2d Lieuten-ant 11th Pennsylvania, 30th September, 1776; taken prisoner at Fort Washing-ton, 16th November, 1776; exchanged, 4th January, 1781, and did not rejoin the army.

Robinson, Caleb (N. H.). 1st Lieu-tenant 26th Continental Infantry, 1st January, 1776; Captain, 10th August, 1776; Captain 2d New Hampshire, 8th November, 1776; taken prisoner at Hubbardton, 7th July, 1777; Brigade Inspector, 13th July, 1781; Major, 2d New Hampshire, 6th October, 1781; re-tired 1st March, 1782.

Robinson, Cole (Va). Ensign of a Virginia State Regiment in 1781.

Robinson, Elias (Conn). Private in the Lexington Alarm, April, 1775; Ser-geant 4th Connecticut, 12th March, 1777; Ensign, 27th December, 1777;

Lieutenant, 26th October, 1780; resigned 15th August, 1782.

Robinson, Elijah (Conn). Corporal in the Lexington Alarm, April, 1775; Captain-Lieutenant 2d Connecticut, 1st May, 1775; Captain, 1st July to 19th De-cember, 1775; Captain of Douglas' Con-necticut State Regiment, June to De-cember, 1776; served subsequently as Captain Connecticut Militia.

Robinson, Elisha (R. I.). Major Rhode Island Militia in 1775.

Robinson, Enoch (Mass). 2d Lieu-tenant in Lexington Alarm, April, 1775; 1st Lieutenant of Walker's Massachu-setts Regiment, April to November, 1775; Captain Massachusetts Militia, 1776-1780.

Robinson, George (S. C.). Captain South Carolina Militia, 1776-1777.

Robinson, Ichabod (Vt). Captain Vermont Militia, 1781-1782.

Robinson, Increase (Mass). 2d Lieu-tenant of Thomas' Massachusetts Regi-ment, May to December, 1775; Captain Massachusetts Militia, 1776.

Robinson, James (Va). Adjutant 5th Virginia, 2d February, 1777; resigned 3d October, 1777.

Robinson, James E. (Va). Lieuten-ant of Clark's Illinois Regiment, 1778-1781.

Robinson, Jared (Conn). 2d Lieuten-ant 1st Connecticut, 1st May to 1st December, 1775; 1st Lieutenant 6th Connecticut, 1st April, 1777; retired 15th November, 1778.

Robinson, John (Mass). 1st Lieuten-ant of Frye's Massachusetts Regiment, April to December, 1775; Captain Massachusetts Militia, 1776-1781.

Robinson, John (Mass). Lieutenant-Colonel Massachusetts Militia at Con-cord, 19th April, 1775; Lieutenant-Colonel of Prescott's Massachusetts Regiment, May to December, 1775; Colonel Massachusetts Militia, 1776-1782. (Died 1805.)

Robinson, Jonathan (N. H.). Captain New Hampshire Militia, 1776.

Robinson, Lemuel (Mass). Colonel Massachusetts Militia, 1775-1776.

Robinson, Moses (Vt). Colonel Ver-mont Militia, 1777-1781. (Died 1813.)

Robinson, Noah (N. H.). Ensign 8th Continental Infantry, 6th September, 1776; 2d Lieutenant 2d New Hampshire, 8th November, 1776; wounded at Stillwater, 19th September, 1777; 1st Lieutenant, 22d December, 1777; Captain-Lieutenant, 30th November, 1779; retired 1st January, 1781. (Died 10th February, 1827.)

Robinson, Robert (Pa). Lieutenant-Colonel Pennsylvania Militia in 1776.

Robinson, Samuel (Conn). Private 2d Canadian (Hazen's) Regiment, 1st January, 1777; Corporal, 15th April, 1777; Regimental Quartermaster, 1st September, 1777; resigned 1st April, 1782.

Robinson, Samuel, Jr. (Conn). 1st Lieutenant 3d Connecticut, 1st May to 15th December, 1775.

Robinson, Samuel (Mass). 2d Lieutenant 1st Massachusetts, 1st January, 1777; resigned 10th February, 1778.

Robinson, Septimus (N. C.). Ensign 1st North Carolina, 28th March, 1776; 2d Lieutenant, 7th July, 1776; died 10th December, 1776.

Robinson, Thomas (Pa). Captain 4th Pennsylvania Battalion, 5th January, 1776; Major, 2d October, 1776; Major, 5th Pennsylvania, 1st January, 1777, to rank from 2d October, 1776; Lieutenant-Colonel, 11th June, 1777; wounded at Brandywine, 11th September, 1777; transferred to 2d Pennsylvania, 1st January, 1783; Colonel, 30th September, 1783, and served to November, 1783. (Died 1819.)

Robinson, Timothy (Mass). Lieutenant-Colonel and Colonel Massachusetts Militia, 1778-1782. (Died 1805.)

Robinson, Tully.—See Robertson.

Roby, Joseph (Mass). Captain of Little's Massachusetts Regiment, April to December, 1775.

Roby, William (N. H.). 2d Lieutenant 3d New Hampshire, 23d April to December, 1775; 1st Lieutenant of Bedel's Regiment, New Hampshire Rangers, January, 1776; wounded and taken prisoner at the Cedars, 19th May, 1776; died 15th June, 1776, of smallpox.

Roche, Edward (Del). 2d Lieutenant Delaware Regiment, 5th April, 1777; Regimental Paymaster, 15th August, 1777; taken prisoner at Camden, 16th August, 1780; prisoner on parole to close of war. (Died 6th April, 1821.)

Roche, Matthew (Ga). Lieutenant and Adjutant 2d Georgia, in 1778; served to ——.

Roche, Patrick (S. C.). Ensign South Carolina Militia in 1775.

Rochefontaine, Bechet de (France). Captain, Engineers, ——; brevet Major, 16th November, 1781, and served to close of war.

Rochel, John (N. C.). Captain 3d North Carolina, 28th November, 1776; omitted January, 1778.

Rochel, Lodowick (N. C.). 1st Lieutenant 3d North Carolina, 28th November, 1776; resigned —— November, 1777.

Rochester, Nathaniel (N. C.). Paymaster North Carolina Militia in 1775 and 1776; Colonel North Carolina Militia and Commissary-General of Militiary Stores in North Carolina, 10th May, 1776, to 1782.

Rockefeller, Philip (N. Y.). Adjutant 10th Regiment, New York Militia in 1775.

Rockefeller William (N. Y.). Lieutenant New York Militia in 1775.

Rockefeller, Tiel (N. Y.). Captain New York Militia in 1775.

Rockwell, John (Conn). Ensign 4th Connecticut, 1st May to 1st December, 1775; 1st Lieutenant of Gay's Connecticut State Regiment, June to December, 1776.

Rockwell, Thaddeus (Conn). 2d Lieutenant 5th Connecticut, 1st May to 17th September, 1775.

Rodgers, Christopher (S. C.). Was a Lieutenant in 2d South Carolina in 1779.

Rodgers, Elisha (Md). 2d Lieutenant Maryland Battalion of the Flying Camp, July to December, 1776.

Rodgers, James (N. J.). Sergeant 4th New Jersey, 1st March, 1777; Ensign 3d New Jersey, 1st February, 1779; killed at Springfield, 24th August, 1780.

Rodgers, James (Pa). Captain Pennsylvania Rifle Battalion in 1777.

Rodgers, John R. B. (Pa). Surgeon 1st Pennsylvania, 1st October, 1779; transferred to 3d Pennsylvania, 1st January, 1783, and served to 3d June, 1783. (Died 29th January, 1833.)

Rodgers, John (Pa). Major Pennsylvania Rifle Battalion, 1776-1777.

Rodgers, John (S. C.). Captain South Carolina Militia in November, 1775.

Rodgers, Peter (Va). Captain Virginia Militia, 1777-1779.

Rodgers, Zabdial (N. Y.). Major Lieutenant-Colonel and Colonel New York Militia, 1775-1782. (Died 1808.)

Rodman, Thomas (N. Y.). 1st Lieutenant of Malcolm's Regiment, 17th March, 1777; resigned 15th July, 1777.

Rodney, Caesar (Del). A signer of the Declaration of Independence; Colonel and Brigadier-General Delaware Militia, 1776-1777; died 29th June, 1784.

Rodney, Thomas (Del). Colonel Delaware Militia in 1777. (Died 1811.)

Roe, Daniel (N. Y.). Captain New York Militia, 1776-1777.

Roe, Hugh (Pa). Ensign of Patton's Additional Continental Regiment, 15th January, 1777; resigned 14th January, 1778.

Roe, James (Pa). Commissary-General of Purchases, 6th August, 1777, to ——.

Roe, Jesse (Pa). Captain of Flower's Artillery Artificer Regiment 3d February, 1777; resigned 23d January, 1778.

Roebuck, James (S. C.). Lieutenant-Colonel South Carolina Militia at King's Mountain in October, 1780; wounded and taken prisoner at Mud Lick, (S. C.), 2d March, 1781; exchanged, August, 1781. (Died 1788.)

Roger, Enos (Vt). Brigadier-General Vermont Militia.

Rogers, Andrew (Va). 2d Lieutenant 14th Virginia, 23d December, 1776; resigned 2d March, 1778.

Rogers, Edward (Conn). Captain of Gay's Connecticut State Regiment, June to December, 1776.

Rogers, Hezekiah (Conn). 1st Lieutenant 5th Connecticut, 1st January, 1777; Regimental Adjutant, 12th June, 1777, to July, 1781; transferred to 2d Connecticut, 1st January, 1781; Captain, 5th December, 1782; transferred to 3d Connecticut, 1st January, 1783; Aide-de-Camp to General Huntington, 7th July, 1781, to June, 1783; retained in Swift's Connecticut Regiment in June, 1783, and served to 3d November, 1783; Military Storekeeper, United States Army, 27th October, 1801; died 3d November, 1811.

Rogers, Jedediah (Conn). Cornet 2d Continental Dragoons, 15th February,

1778; Lieutenant 2d June, 1778, and served to close of war. Captain Light Dragoons United States Army, 4th May, 1792; resigned 25th October, 1792.

Rogers, Jacob (Mass). 2d Lieutenant of Thomas' Massachusetts Regiment, May to December, 1775.

Rogers, John (Conn). 1st Lieutenant of Webb's Additional Continental Regiment, 1st January, 1777; resigned 13th February, 1778.

Rogers, John (R. I.). Sergeant 2d Rhode Island, 6th March, 1777; Ensign, 1st May, 1779; Adjutant, 1st May, 1780, to 8th September, 1782; wounded at Connecticut Farms, 23d June, 1780; 2d Lieutenant, 4th February, 1781; retained in Olney's Rhode Island Battalion, 14th May, 1781, and served to November, 1783; Military Storekeeper, United States Army, 9th March, 1819; Honorably discharged, 1st June, 1821.

Rogers, John (Va). 2d Lieutenant 4th Virginia, 25th March, 1776; was Captain of Clark's Illinois Regiment June, 1778, to February, 1782.

Rogers, John, Jr. (N. C.). Paymaster 5th North Carolina, 11st December, 1776, to ——.

Rogers, Joseph (Va). Lieutenant of a Virginia Regiment; taken prisoner at Newberne, N. C., 26th September, 1778.

Rogers, Joseph (Conn). Ensign 2d Connecticut, 4th January, 1781, to 3d June, 1783. (Died 3d September, 1818.)

Rogers, Josanah (N. Y.). Captain of Drake's Regiment, New York Militia, in 1776.

Rogers, Nicholas (France). Major and Aide-de-Camp, 12th May, 1777; served as Aide-de-Camp to Generals Coudray and De Kalb to 10th December, 1778, when he was brevetted Lieutenant-Colonel Continental Army and retired from the service.

Rogers, Patrick (N. C.). Regimental Quartermaster 1st North Carolina, 3d November, 1776; Ensign 28th March, 1777; 2d Lieutenant 3d April, 1777; died 19th April, 1778.

Rogers, Philip (Pa). 2d Lieutenant 8th Pennsylvania, 9th August, 1776, to ——.

Rogers, Robert (R. I.). 2d Lieutenant of Tallman's Rhode Island State Regiment, 12th December, 1776; 2d Lieutenant 1st Rhode Island, 1st January, 1777; 1st Lieutenant, 19th February, 1777; resigned 24th March, 1779. (Died 5th August, 1835.)

Rogers, Samuel (Mass). 2d Lieutenant of Henley's Additional Continental Regiment, 1st January, 1777; 1st Lieutenant, 26th June, 1777; transferred to Jackson's Continental Regiment, 22d April, 1779; regiment designated 16th Massachusetts, 23d July ,1780; transferred to 9th Massachusetts, 1st January, 1781; died 20th October ,1781.

Rogers, Thomas (Mass). Sergeant in Lexington Alarm, April, 1775; 2d Lieutenant of Gerrish's Massachusetts Regiment, May to December, 1775.

Rogers, William (Mass). Captain in Lexington Alarm, April, 1775; Captain of Gerrish's Massachusetts Regiment, May to December, 1775; Captain Massachusetts Militia, 1776-1781.

Rogers, William (Pa). Chaplain of Miles' Pennsylvania Rifle Regiment, 6th April to December, 1776; Chaplain of Patton's Continental Regiment, 1st February, 1777; Brigade Chaplain, 1st June, 1778; retired 16th January, 1781. (Died 7th April, 1824.)

Rogers, William (S. C.). Lieutenant South Carolina Dragoons, 5th April, 1781; dismissed, — June, 1781.

Rogers, William (Va). 2d Lieutenant 4th Virginia, 19th March, 1776; 1st Lieutenant, 28th September, 1776; Captain, 1st April, 1778; taken prisoner 22d September, 1778; where not stated; exchanged in 1780; transferred to 5th Virginia, 12th February, 1781; retired 1st January, 1783.

Roggen, Peter (N. Y.). 2d Lieutenant 3d New York, 2d August, 1775, to January, 1776. (Died 1804.)

Rogowski, —— (Poland). Captain and Aide-de-Camp to General Pulaski; wounded at Savannah, 9th October, 1779.

Rohlwagen, Frederic.—See **Rowlwagen.**

Rohrer, John (Pa). 2d Lieutenant 1st Battalion Pennsylvania Flying Camp, July to December, 1776.

Rolando —— (S. C.). Lieutenant 5th South Carolina; resigned 28th May, 1777.

Rolston, Isaac (N. C.). Ensign 2d North Carolina, 8th June, 1776; 1st Lieutenant, January, 1777; retired 1st June, 1778.

Rolston, Robert (N. C.). Ensign 1st North Carolina, 1st September, 1775;

2d Lieutenant, 4th January, 1776; 1st Lieutenant, 28th March, 1776; Captain, 8th March, 1777; resigned 29th August, 1777.

Romans, Bernard (Pa). Captain Independent Pennsylvania Artillery Company, 8th February, 1776; resigned 1st June, 1778.

Ronells, Grindoll (Vt). Lieutenant of Williams' Regiment Vermont Militia in 1777; name also spelled Runals.

Roney, John (Va). Regimental Adjutant 5th Virginia, 25th January, 1778; 2d Lieutenant, 9th September, 1778; transferred to 3d Virginia, 14th September, 1778; 1st Lieutenant, 19th June, 1779; taken prisoner at Charleston, 12th May, 1780.

Roosevelt, Cornelius C. (N. Y.). Ensign, 1st New York in 1776.

Root, Aaron (Mass). Lieutenant-Colonel and Colonel Massachusetts Militia in 1776 ,and 1777. (Died 1809.)

Root, Elihu (Mass). Ensign 21st Continental Infantry, 1st January to 31st December, 1776; 1st Lieutenant 5th Massachusetts, 1st January, 1777; retired 5th March, 1779.

Root, Elisha (Conn). Lieutenant of Wolcott's Continental State Regiment, December, 1775; died March, 1776.

Root, Jasse (Conn). Captain Connecticut Militia in 1776; Lieutenant-Colonel Deputy Adjutant General to General Putnam, July 9th, to November, 1777. (Died 29th March, 1822.)

Root, Josiah (Conn). Conductor 2d Continental Artillery, 18th March, to July, 1777; subsequently served as Apothecary Northern Department to close of war. (Died 1841.)

Root, Nathan (Conn). 1st Lieutenant 2d Connecticut, 1st January, 1777; resigned 1st May, 1778.

Root, Oliver (Mass). Captain Massachusetts Militia in 1776.

Rosa, Isaac A. (N. Y.). Ensign 4th New York, 21st November, 1776; 2d Lieutenant, 9th November, 1777; resigned 22d January, 1778; served subsequently as Captain New York Militia.

Rosa, Jacobus (N. Y.). Captain New York Militia, ——; killed at Fort Montgomery, 6th October, 1777.

Rose, Alexander (Va). 1st Lieutenant 6th Virginia, 4th March, 1776; Captain, 17th September, 1776; retired 14th September, 1778, with rank of Major.

Ross, George (Pa). Ensign 2d Pennsylvania Battalion, 20th March, 1776; resigned 21st July, 1776, to enter the Navy, and served as Captain of Marines.

Ross, James (Pa). Lieutenant Lancaster County, Pennsylvania, Militia, 1776-1777.

Rose, John (Pa). His proper name was Baron Gustavus H. de Rosenthal. Surgeon 7th Pennsylvania, 12th June, 1777; found not competent and transferred to General Hospital as Surgeon's-Mate, under the name of Gustavus Henderson; appointed Surgeon's-Mate 7th Pennsylvania, 1st March, 1780; afterwards appointed Surgeon on the Revenge; taken prisoner in fall of 1780; when not stated; served as Aide-de-Camp to General Irvine in 1781 and 1782; Lieutenant 4th Pennsylvania, 1st April, 1781; transferred to 3d Pennsylvania, 1st January, 1783, and served to June, 1783. (Died 1829.)

Rose, John (Conn). Sergeant of Warner's Continental Regiment, 1st January, 1777; Ensign, 13th November, 1778; retired 20th February, 1780. (Died 2d December, 1818.)

Rose, John (Conn). Surgeon's-Mate of Webb's Continental Regiment, 1st August, 1778; transferred to 3d Connecticut, 1st January, 1781; Surgeon, 3d March, 1782, and served to June, 1783.

Rose, Rainsford (Conn). Adjutant of Selden's Connecticut State Regiment, 10th July to 25th December, 1776.

Rose, Robert (Va). Surgeon 6th Virginia, 9th April, 1776; Surgeon 1st Continental Dragoons, 10th December, 1776; retained in Baylor's Regiment of Consolidated Dragoons, 9th November, 1782 and served to November, 1783.

Roseburg, John (Pa). Chaplain Pennsylvania Militia in 1776-1777; killed at Trenton, 2d January, 1777.

Rosekrans, Jacob (N. J.). Captain 3d New Jersey, 29th November, 1776; resigned — March, 1777.

Rosekrans, James (N. Y.). Name also spelled Rosenkrans. Captain 4th New York, 3d August, 1775; Captain 5th New York, 21st November, 1776, to rank from 3d August, 1775; Major 3d New York, 1st March, 1780; retired 1st January, 1781.

Rosenthal, Gustavus H. de Baron.— See **John Rose.**

Ross —— (S. C.). Major South Carolina Militia; wounded in action with Indians in Georgia in March, 1779, and died 2 days afterwards.

Ross, David (Md). Major of Grayson's Additional Continental Regiment, 11th January, 1777; resigned 20th December, 1777.

Ross, Edward (R. I.). Ensign Rhode Island Militia, 1781.

Ross, Francis (N. C.). Lieutenant 9th North Carolina, 28th November, 1776, to ——.

Ross, George (N. J.). Ensign 1st New Jersey, 10th December, 1775; 2d Lieutenant 2d New Jersey, 29th November, 1776; resigned 18th December, 1777.

Ross, George (Pa). A signer of the Declaration of Independence; Colonel Pennsylvania Militia, 1775-1776; died 16th July, 1779.

Ross, George, Jr. (Pa). Adjutant 2d Battalion, 11th January, 1776; 1st Lieutenant, 11th Pennsylvania, 30th September, 1776; Captain, 11th April, 1777; resigned 1st April, 1778.

Ross, Horatio (Pa). 1st Lieutenant of Hartley's Continental Regiment, 24th January, 1777; Captain, 11th September, 1777, and served to ——.

Ross, James (Pa). Captain of Thompson's Pennsylvania Rifle Battalion, 25th June, 1775; Captain 1st Continental Infantry, 1st January, 1776; Major, 25th September, 1776; Major 1st Pennsylvania, January, 1777, to rank from 25th September, 1776; Lieutenant-Colonel, 12th March, 1777; transferred to 8th Pennsylvania, 11th June, 1777; resigned 22d September, 1777.

Ross, John (Md). Surgeon's-Mate 4th Maryland, 7th March, 1778; Surgeon Hospital Department, 1st July, 1778, to ——, 1780.

Ross, John (N. J.). Captain 3d New Jersey, 13th March, 1776; Major 2d New Jersey, 7th April, 1779; Brigade Inspector, October, 1779, to November, 1780; retired 1st January, 1781; Lieutenant-Colonel New Jersey Militia in 1782. (Died 7th September, 1796.)

Ross, John (Pa). Ensign 7th Pennsylvania, 2d February, 1778, to ——.

Ross, Perin (Conn). 1st Lieutenant of Ransom's Wyoming Valley Company, 26th August, 1776; resigned 25th October, 1777. (Killed at Wyoming, 3d July, 1778.)

Rosseter, David (Mass). Captain in Lexington Alarm, April, 1775; served subsequently as Major, Lieutenant-Colonel and Colonel Massachusetts Militia. (Died 1810.)

Rosseter, Elnathon (Conn). 1st Lieutenant 6th Connecticut, 1st May, 1775; Captain, 1st July to 17th December, 1775.

Rosseter, Timothy W. (Mass). Surgeon's-Mate of Fellow's Massachusetts Regiment, May to December, 1775; Surgeon's-Mate, 19th Continental Infantry, 1st January to 31st December, 1776.

Rosseter, William (Conn). 1st Lieutenant 7th Connecticut, 6th July to 20th December, 1775.

Rosseter, Thomas (Pa). 1st Lieutenant of Lewis' Pennsylvania Battalion of the Flying Camp, July to December, 1776.

Rotan, Peter.—See **Rutan.**

Roth, Francis Charles (Pa). 1st Lieutenant Pulaski Legion, March, 1778, to ——.

Roth, Philip (Pa). Lieutenant Pulaski Legion, 1779-1780.

Roth, William (Pa). 2d Lieutenant Pulaski Legion in 1778 and 1779.

Rothmaler, Erasmus (S. C.). Was an Ensign in 3d South Carolina, in 1781.

Rothmaler, Job (S.C.). Colonel South Carolina Militia in 1775.

Roueire, Marquis de la.—See **Charles T. Armand.**

Roulledge, William (N. C.). 1st Lieutenant 4th North Carolina, 25th January, 1777; resigned 20th August, 1777.

Roundy, Luke (Mass). Ensign 27th Continental Infantry, 1st January to 31st December, 1776; 2d Lieutenant 11th Massachusetts, 1st January, 1777; died 22d October, 1777.

Rounsevell, Levi (Mass). Captain of Brewer's Massachusetts Regiment, May to December, 1775.

Rountree, Reuben (N. C.). Lieutenant 10th North Carolina, 19th April, 1777, to ——.

Rouse, Oliver (Mass). Private in Lexington Alarm April, 1775; Sergeant in Read's Massachusetts Regiment, April to December, 1775; Ensign, 13th Continental Infantry, 1st January, to 31st December, 1776; 1st Lieutenant 5th Massachusetts, 1st January, 1777; transferred to 12th Massachusetts, 12th June,

1783; Brevet-Captain, 30th September, 1783, and served to 3d November, 1783. (Died — March, 1787.)

Rouse, Thomas (Md). Ensign 2d Maryland, 20th February, 1777; 2d Lieutenant, 17th April, 1777; taken prisoner at Staten Island, 22d August, 1777; exchanged, 25th October, 1780, when he was retained in the 5th Maryland, with rank of 1st Lieutenant from 15th September, 1779; retained in Maryland Battalion, April, 1783, and served to November, 1783.

Routt, Richard (Va). Ensign 12th Virginia, 9th December, 1776; 2d Lieutenant, 2d April, 1777; retired 14th September, 1778.

Roux, Albert (S. C.). 1st Lieutenant 2d South Carolina, 15th December, 1777; Captain, October, 1779; wounded at Savannah, 9th October, 1779; retired 1st January, 1781.

Rowan, John (N. C.). Lieutenant North Carolina Militia, 1780. (Died 27th July, 1825.)

Rowan, Robert (N. C.). Captain 1st North Carolina, 1st September, 1775; resigned 29th June, 1776.

Rowe, Caleb (Mass). Ensign of Phinney's Massachusetts Regiment, May to December, 1775; 1st Lieutenant, 18th Continental Infantry, 1st January, 1776; discharged 1st February, 1776.

Rowe, Christopher (S. C.). Colonel South Carolina Militia, 1775.

Rowe, Henry (S. C.). Captain South Carolina Militia in 1776.

Rowe, John (Mass). Private of Bridge's Massachusetts Regiment, May to December, 1775; Sergeant-Major, 8th Massachusetts, 16th April, 1777; Ensign, 15th June, 1781; transferred to 3d Massachusetts, 12th June, 1783; retained in Jackson's Continental Regiment, — November, 1783, and served to 20th June, 1784; Major, 15th United States Infantry, 8th January, 1799; Honorably discharged, 15th June, 1800.

Rowe, John (Mass). Captain of Bridge's Massachusetts Regiment, May to December, 1775.

Rowe, John (N. Y.). Captain of Graham's Regiment New York Militia in 1778.

Rowe, Winthrop (N. H.). Captain Company of Minute Men at Concord, 19th April, 1775; Captain 2d New Hampshire, 23d May to December, 1775.

Rowell, Grindall (Vt). Lieutenant Vermont Militia in 1777.

Rowell, William (N. H.). Ensign in Poor's New Hampshire Regiment, 20th September to December, 1775; 2d Lieutenant 8th Continental Infantry, 1st January, 1776; 1st Lieutenant 2d New Hampshire, 8th November, 1776; Captain, 2d April, 1777, and served to close of war; Brevet Major, 30th September, 1783.

Rowley, Aaron (Mass). 1st Lieutenant of Woodbridge's Massachusetts Regiment, May to December, 1775; served subsequently as Major Vermont Militia and was wounded at Johnstown, 24th October, 1781. (Died 1799.)

Rowley, Abijah (Conn). Captain 8th Connecticut, 6th July to 17th December, 1775; Captain of Swift's Connecticut State Regiment, July, 1776; died September, 1776.

Rowley, Nathaniel (N. Y.). 1st Lieutenant 2d New York, 28th June, 1775, to January, 1776; served subsequently as Captain New York Militia.

Rowlwagen, Frederick (Pa). 1st Lieutenant German Regiment, 19th July, 1776; cashiered 15th April, 1777. (Name also spelled Rohlwagen.)

Rowse, Thomas.—See **Rouse.**

Roxburg, Alexander (Md). 2d Lieutenant of Smallwood's Maryland Regiment, 14th January, 1776; Captain 1st Maryland, 10th December, 1776; Major, 7th Maryland, 7th April ,1780; transferred to 4th Maryland, 1st January, 1781; retired 1st January, 1783.

Roy, Beverly (Va). Sergeant 3d Virginia, 11th February, 1777; Ensign, 15th August, 1777; Lieutenant, 28th November, 1777; tken prisoner at Charleston, 12th May, 1780; Captain, September, 1781, and served to close of war.

Roy, Thomas (Va). 2d Lieutenant of Grayson's Additional Continental Regiment, 15th February, 1777; resigned 1st December, 1777.

Ruault, Victor (—). Lieutenant of Armand's Partisan Corps, 1st June, 1777, to ——.

Ruback, Jacob (Vt). Surgeon Vermont Militia, 1777-1782.

Rucker, Alcott (Va). Lieutenant Virginia Militia, 1780-1781.

Rucker Angus (Va). 1st Lieutenant 1st Virginia State Regiment, 24th June, 1777; Captain, 3d July, 1779, and served to January, 1781.

Rucker, Elliott (Va). 2d Lieutenant 1st Virginia State Regiment, 24th June, 1777; 1st Lieutenant, ——, 1778, and served to January, 1781. (Died 19th March, 1832.)

Rucker, Ephraim (Va). Lieutenant-Colonel Virginia Militia, 1777-1781.

Rudd, Jonathan (Conn). Captain of Chapman's Regiment Connecticut Militia in 1778.

Rudd, Joseph (Vt). Lieutenant Vermont Militia, 1777-1781.

Rudder, Epaphroditus (Va). 2d Lieutenant 1st Virginia State Regiment, June, 1777; 1st Lieutenant, 1st April, 1778, to October, 1779; Lieutenant 1st Continental Dragoons, 1780; retired 9th November, 1782.

Rudolph, Jacob (Pa). Captain Pennsylvania Militia; taken prisoner at Brandywine, 11th September, 1777; exchanged — June, 1778. (Died 1795.)

Rudolph, John (Md). Lieutenant of Lee's Battalion of Light Dragoons, 20th April, 1778; Captain, 1st October, 1778; Major, ——, 1781; died 8th December, 1782.

Rudolph, John (Pa). 2d Lieutenant 5th Pennsylvania Battalion, 8th January, 1776; taken prisoner at Fort Washington, 16th November, 1776; exchanged 25th October, 1780.

Rudolph, Michael (Md). Sergeant-Major of Lee's Battalion of Light Dragoons, 7th April, 1778; Regimental Quartermaster, 1st April, 1779; Lieutenant, 1st July, 1779. By the act of 24th September, 1779, it was "Resolved, that Congress greatly esteem the military caution so happily combined with daring activity by Lieutenants McCallister and Rudolph in leading on the forlorn hope (in the attack on the enemy's works at Powlus Hook), and that the brevet of captain be given them." Captain 1st November, 1779, and served to close of war; Captain 1st United States Infantry, 3d June, 1790; Major Light Dragoons, 5th March, 1792; Adjutant and Inspector of the army, 22d February, 1793; resigned 17th July, 1793. (Drowned ——, 1795.)

Rue, Lewis (N. J.. Sergaent 2d New Jersey, 31st October, 1775, to November, 1776; Ensign 2d New Jersey, 16th December, 1776; resigned April, 1777.

Ruecastle, John (N. J.). Private, Corporal and Sergeant 3d New Jersey, December, 1775, until appointed Ensign, 1st May, 1777; 2d Lieutenant, 1st November, 1777; 1st Lieutenant, 7th April, 1779; transferred to 1st New Jersey, 1st January, 1781, and served to April, 1783. Name also spelled Rencastle.

Ruffin, Thomas (Va). Captain 6th Virginia, 1st March, 1776; killed at Brandywine, 11th September, 1777.

Ruggles, Ashbel (Conn). Ensign 5th Connecticut, 1st May to 16th October, 1775.

Ruggles, Lazarus (Conn). Ensign of Silliman's Connecticut State Regiment, June to December, 1776; wounded at White Plains, 28 October, 1776. (Died 1801.)

Ruggles, Timothy (Mass). 1st Lieutenant of Cotton's Massachusetts Regiment, May to December, 1775; Captain Massachusetts Militia in 1779. (Died 1831.)

Rumford, Jonathan (Del). Captain Delaware Battalion of the Flying Camp, July to December, 1776.

Rumney, Edward (Mass). 1st Lieutenant of Gridley's Regiment Massachusetts Artillery, 13th May, 1775; Captain Lieutenant of Knox's Regiment Continental Artillery, 10th December, 1775, to December, 1776.

Rumney, William (Va). Colonel Virginia Militia, 1777-1778.

Rumney, William (Va). Surgeon — Virginia Regiment, 12th March, 1778; resigned 12th March, 1780.

Rumsey, Charles (Md). Colonel Maryland Militia in 1776. (Died 1780.)

Rumsey, David (N. Y.). Captain New York Militia, ——; prisoner of war, 11th June, 1781, to 21st May, 1783.

Runals, Daniel (N. H.). Captain New Hampshire Militia, 1776

Runals, Grindoll (Vt). Lieutenant of Williams' Regiment Vermont Militia in 1778.

Runals, James (N. H.). Sergeant and Ensign Mooney's Regiment New Hampshire Militia, 1779-1780.

Runals, Samuel (N. H.). Captain of Mooney's Regiment New Hampshire Militia, 1779-1780.

Rush, Benjamin (Pa). A signer of the Declaration of Independence; Surgeon in May, 1775-1776; Surgeon-General of Hospitals, Middle Department, 11th April, 1777; Physician General Hospitals Middle Department, 1st July, 1777; resigned 30th April, 1778. (Died 19th April, 1813.)

Rusche, John Henry (S. C.). Surgeon's Mate 2d South Carolina, 11th June, 1778, to ——.

Rushworm, William (N. C.). Lieutenant 3d North Carolina, 16th April, 1777; omitted 1st January, 1778; Cornet North Carolina Dragoons, 1778-1780.

Russ, Amaziah (Conn). 2d Lieutenant of Chester's Connecticut State Regiment, June to December, 1776.

Russell, Absalom (—). Surgeon's Mate Hospital Department, 1775-1776.

Russell, Albert (Va). Ensign 12th Virginia, 9th December, 1776; 2d Lieutenant, 20th May, 1777; regiment designated 8th Virginia, 14th September, 1778; Regimental Adjutant, 1st May, 1779; 1st Lieutenant, 15th December, 1779; transferred to 1st Virginia, 1st January, 1781; retired 1st January, 1783. (Died 1818.)

Russell, Alexander (Pa). 2d Lieutenant 7th Pennsylvania, 20th January, 1777; 1st Lieutenant, 25th September, 1777; resigned 27th April, 1779. (Died ——, 1836.)

Russell, Andrew (Va). Captain 5th Virginia, 25th March, 1776; Major, 19th June, 1777; retired 30th September, 1778. (Died 1789.)

Russell, Charles (Va). 2d Lieutenant 1st Virginia State Regiment, 12th February, 1778; 1st Lieutenant, 16th January, 1779, and served to January, 1782.

Russell, Cornelius (Conn). Corporal in Lexington Alarm, April, 1775; Private 2d Connecticut, 7th May to 19th December, 1775; Sergeant 17th Continental Infantry, January to December, 1776; Ensign 5th Connecticut, 1st Januarl, 1777; 2d Lieutenant, 15th December, 1777; 1st Lieutenant, 1st April, 1779; transferred to 2d Connecticut, 1st January, 1781, and served to June, 1783. (Died 1823.)

Russell, Edward (Conn). Captain of Douglas' Connecticut State Regiment, 20th June to 29th December, 1776.

Russell, George (N. C.). Lieutenant North Carolina Militia at King's Mountain, October, 1780.

Russell, Giles (Conn). Lieutenant-Colonel Sage's Connecticut State Regiment, 2d July, 1776; Lieutenant-Colonel 4th Connecticut, 1st January, 1777; Colonel 8th Connecticut, 5th March, 1778; died 28th October, 1779.

Russell, Isaac (Mass). Sergeant 6th Continental Infantry, 1st January; transferred 31st December, 1776; Lieutenant 13th Massachusetts, 1st January, 1777 resigned 15th March, 1778. (Died 1821.)

Russell, James (Mass). Ensign of Presscott's Massachusetts Regiment, May to November, 1775; Captain Massachusetts Militia, 1776. (Died 1821.)

Russell, James (N. Y.). Sergeant 1st New York, 10th December, 1776; Ensign, 20th February, 1777; omitted July, 1777.

Russell, John (Mass). Captain 14th Massachusetts, 1st January, 1777; resigned 2d April, 1778.

Russell, John (N. Y.). Ensign 2d Canadian (Hazen's) Regiment, 2d December, 1776 2d Lieutenant 1st January, 1777; resigned ——, December, 1777.

Russell, John (Va). 2d Lieutenant 1st Virginia State Regiment, 7th December, 1778, and served to January, 1780. (Died 1822.)

Russell Josiah (N. H.). Captain New Hampshire Militia, 1777.

Russell, Philip M. (Va). Surgeon's Mate Hospital Department, 1777-1778. (Died 11th August, 1830.)

Russell, Richard (—). Surgeon's Mate Hospital Department, 1775-1776.

Russell, Thaddeus (Mass). Captain of Brewer's Massachusetts Regiment, May to December, 1775.

Russell, Thomas (R. I.). Ensign of Sherburne's Additional Continental Regiment, 1st October, 1777; Aide-de-Camp to General Stark, 27th November, 1779; retired 1st January, 1781.

Russell, Thomas (Va). 2d Lieutenant 5th Virginia, 3d October, 1775; resigned May, 1776. (Died 28th September, 1819.)

Russell, Thomas C. (S. C.). 2d Lieutenant 1st South Carolina, 22d April, 1778; 1st Lieutenant, 9th October, 1779; taken prisoner at Charleston, 12th May, 1780.

Russell, William (Mass). 1st Lieutenant of Glover's Massachusetts Regiment, 19th May, 1775, to ——.

Russell, William (Pa). Sergeant of Thompson's Pennsylvania Rifle Regiment, 25th June to December, 1775, and in 1st Continental Infantry in 1776; Ensign 3d Pennsylvania, 21st April,

1777; wounded at Brandywine (lost a leg), 11th September, 1777 ;transferred to Invalid Regiment, 17th September, 1779, but on account of his wounds did not join his regiment. (Died 4th March, 1802.)

Russell, William (Va). Colonel 13th Virginia, 19th December, 1776; transferred to 5th Virginia, 14th September, 1778; taken prisoner at Charleston, 12th May, 1780; exchanged November, 1780, and served to 3d November, 1783; Brevet Brigadier-General, 3d November, 1783. (Died 1793.)

Russell, William, Jr. (Va). Lieutenant Virginia Militia at King's Mountain in October, 1780.

Rust, John (Va). Ensign 10th Virginia, December, 1776; 2d Lieutenant, 11th July, 1777; dismissed, 18th February, 1778.

Rutan, Peter (N. Y.). 2d Lieutenant 1st Canadian (Livingston's) Regiment, 20th November, 1775; 1st Lieutenant, 18th December, 1776; resigned 12th August, 1779. Name also spelled Rotan.

Rutherford, Griffith (N. C.). Brigadier-General North Carolina Militia; wounded and taken prisoner at Camden, 16th August, 1780; exchanged 14th June, 1781. (Died — December, 1799.)

Rutherford, John (N. C.) Major North Carolina Militia; killed at Eutaw Springs, 8th September, 1781.

Rutherford, John (Pa). Captain Pennsylvania Militia, 1777. (Died 1804.)

Rutherford, Robert (N. C.). Colonel North Carolina Militia, 1776-1780. (Died 1814.)

Rutherford, Samuel (Pa). Ensign Pennsylvania Battalion Flying Camp, July, 1776; taken prisoner at Fort Washington, 16th November, 1776; exchanged 4th November, 1780.

Rutgers, Anthony (N. Y.). Captain New York City Artillery Company, 1775-1776. (Died 1784.)

Rutgers, Henry, Jr. (N. Y.). Lieutenant New York Militia in 1775 and 1776; Lieutenant-Colonel Deputy Commissary-General of Musters, 6th April, 1779, to ——. (Died 17th February, 1830.)

Rutgers, Hermanus (N. Y.). Captain New York Militia; killed at Long Island, 27th August, 1776.

Ruth, Francis (Pa). Adjutant Pennsylvania State Regiment, 18th April, 1777; regiment designated 13th Pennsylvania, 12th November, 1777; accidentally wounded by a soldier in March, 1778; retired 1st July, 1778.

Rutledge, Edward (S. C.). A signer of the Declaration of Independence; was a Lieutenant South Carolina Artillery in 1775, and a Captain in 1776; was elected to Congress in 1776; taken prisoner at the siege of Charleston, 12th May, 1780, and was a prisoner to April, 1781; died 23d January, 1800.

Rutledge ,Joshua (Md) 2d Lieutenant 4th Maryland, 1st May, 1780; taken prisoner at Camden, 16th August, 1780; exchanged December, 1780; retained in Maryland Battalion, April, 1783, and served to 15th November, 1783.

Rutledge, Thomas (S. C.). Lieutenant South Carolina Militia in 1776.

Ryan, James (S. C.). Captain South Carolina Militia, 1779-1780.

Ryan, Michael (Pa). 2d Lieutenant 4th Pennsylvania Battalion, 5th January, 1776; Regimental Adjutant, 15th March, 1776; Brigade Major to St. Clair's Brigade, 17th September, 1776; Brigade Major to General Wayne, 21st May, 1777, to 13th June, 1779; was appointed Major 10th Pennsylvania, 23d October, 1777, which was deemed irregular, and superseded 9th May, 1778; Captain 5th Pennsylvania, to rank from 23d January, 1777; resigned 13th June, 1779; Inspector-General of Pennsylvania in 1780.

Ryan, William (Mass). 2d Lieutenant of Nixon's Massachusetts Regiment, May, 1775; cashiered 24th August, 1775.

Ryckman, Wilhelmus (N. Y.). Ensign 1st New York, 21st November, 1776; Lieutenant, 5th April, 1781, and served to June, 1783.

Ryerson, Thomas (N. J.). Ensign 2d New Jersey, 28th October, 1775; 2d Lieutenant, 18th July, 1776; taken prisoner at Fort Washington, 18th November, 1776.

Ryland, Nicholas N. (Va). Lieutenant Virginia Militia in 1779.

S.

Sabin, Zebediah (Mass). 1st Lieutenant of Paterson's Massachusetts Regiment, May, 1775; died in June, 1776, of smallpox.

Sackett, Daniel (N. Y.). Lieutenant of Malcolm's New York Regiment in 1780.

Sackett, David (Mass). 2d Lietuenant of Brewer's Massachusetts Regiment, May to December, 1775; 2d Lieutenant 3d Continental Infantry, 1st January to 31st December, 1776. (Died 6th June, 1838.)

Sackett, Israel (Mass). Corporal in Lexington Alarm, April, 1775; Sergeant of Danielson's Massachusetts Regiment, April to December, 1775; 2d Continental Infantry, 1st January to 31st December, 1776.

Sackett, James (N. J.). 1st Lieutenant of Spencer's Continental Regiment, 1st April, 1777; Surgeon's Mate Hospital Department, 15th September, 1777, to ——.

Sackett, James (Va). Surgeons Mate 14th Virginia, 18th July, 1777; resigned 24th April, 1778.

Sackett, Peter (N. Y.). Adjutant 4th New York, 21st November, 1776; resigned 10th September, 1778.

Sackett, Richard (N. Y.). Captain of Graham's Regiment New York Militia in 1778; prisoner of war, 26th December, 1781, to — February, 1782; when taken not stated.

Sackett, Samuel (N. Y.). 1st Lieutenant 4th New York, 28th June, 1775; aptain, 15th November, 1775, to April, 1776; Captain 4th New York, 21st November, 1776, to rank from 15th November, 1775; died 15th April, 1780.

Sadler, Mathias (—). Captain of Baldwin's Artillery Artificer Regiment, 1st February, 1777, to ——.

Sadler, Samuel (Md). Captain Lieutenant Marylnad Artillery Company, 3d September, 1779; resigned 1st June, 1780.

Safford, Jacob (N. H.). Sergeant of Warner's Additional Continental Regiment, 18th February, 1777; 2d Lieutenant, 18th August, 1778; resigned 18th November, 1779.

Safford, Jesse (Vt). Captain Vermont Militia in 1778.

Safford, Joseph (N. H.). 2d Lieutenant of Warner's Continental Regiment, 16th September, 1776; retired 18th November, 1778. (Died 1808.)

Safford, Joseph (Vt). Brigadier-General Vermont Militia.

Safford, Samuel (N. H.). Major Green Mountain Boys, 27th July to December, 1775; Lieutenant-Colonel of Warner's Continental Regiment, 5th July, 1776; retired 1st January, 1781; Brigadier-General Vermont Militia, 1781-1782. (Died 1813.)

Sage, Comfort (Conn). Lieutenant-Colonel of Wadsworth's Connecticut State Regiment, January to March, 1776; Colonel Connecticut State Regiment, June to December, 1776; served subsequently as Colonel Connecticut Militia. (Died 14th March, 1799.)

Sale, John (Mass). 2d Lieutenant of Henley's Additional Continental Regiment, — January, 1777; 1st Lieutenant, 20th September, 1777; retired 23d April, 1779.

Sale, John (Va). Hospital Surgeon and Physician, 1778-1781.

Salisbury, Abraham (Vt). 1st Lieutenant and Captain Vermont Militia in 1776-1779.

Salisbury, Barent Staats (N. Y.). 2d Lieutenant 1st New York, November, 1775; 1st Lieutenant, 1st March, 1776; 1st Lieutenant 1st New York, 21st November, 1776, to rank from 1st March, 1776; Captain-Lieutenant, 14th July, 1779; retired 1st January, 1781.

Salmon, John (Mass). Captain of Glover's Massachusetts Regiment, May to December, 1775.

Salmon, Nathan (N. J.). Ensign 2d New Jersey, 1st January, 1777; resigned 14th November, 1777. (Died 23d July, 1827.)

Salter, Joseph (N. J.). Lieutenant-Colonel New Jersey Militia in 1775.

Salter, James (N. C.). Commissary 2d North Carolina, 19th December, 1776, to —.

Salter, Richard (Pa). Major Pennsylvania Militia, 1781-1782. (Died 1793.)

Salter, Robert (N. C.). Commissary 2d North Carolina, 23d April, 1776; resigned 1st December, 1776.

Salter, Titus (N. H.). Captain New Hampshire Artillery Company, 1775-1778.

Saltonstall, Gurdon (Conn). Colonel Connecticut Militia, 1775 and 1776; Brigadier-General Connecticut Militia, 10th September, 1776, to May, 1777. (Died 19th September, 1785.)

Same, William, Jr. (Va). 2d Lieutenant 5th Virginia, 25th March, 1776, to —.

Sammons, Jacob (N. Y.). 2d Lieutenant 1st Canadian (Livingston's) Regiment, February, 1777; resigned March, 1778.

Sample, John (Pa). Surgeon's Mate of a Pennsylvania Battalion of the Flying Camp, July to December, 1776.

Sample, Robert (Pa). Captain 10th Pennsylvania, 4th December, 1776; taken prisoner 7th March, 1778, at Germantown; exchanged 4th November, 1780; retired 1st January, 1781, not having rejoined regiment.

Sampson, Abisha (Vt). Lieutenant Vermont Militia, 1777-1778.

Sampson, Andrew (Mass). 1st Lieutenant of Cotton's Massachusetts Regiment, May to December, 1775; Captain Massachusetts Militia, 1776-1777.

Sampson, Crocker (Mass). Regimental Quartermaster 14th Massachusetts, 1st January, 1777; Ensign, 1st April, 1778; 1st Lieutenant, 13th April, 1780. transferred to 7th Massachusetts, 1st January, 1781, and served to June, 1783. (Died 7th July, 1823.)

Sampson, Ezekiel (Mass). Lieutenant of Baldwin's Artillery Artificer Regiment, 16th August, 1777, to —.

Sampson, Joseph (Mass). 2d Lieutenant of Cotton's Massachusetts Regiment, May to December, 1775.

Sampson, Thomas (Mass). 2d Lieutenant of Cotton's Massachusetts Regiment, May to December, 1775.

Sanborn, Aaron (N. H.). 1st Lieutenant 2d New Hampshire, 27th May to December, 1775.

Sanborn, Abraham (N. H.). 2d Lieutenant 2d New Hampshire, 23d May to December, 1775; 1st Lieutenant of Tash's Regiment New Hampshire Militia, 20th September to 1st December, 1776.

Sanborn, Ebenezer (N. H.). Captain New Hampshire Militia, 1775.

Sanborn, Nathan (N. H.). Captain of Evans' Regiment New Hampshire Militia, August, 1776, to October, 1777; wounded at Bemis' Heights, 19th September, 1777. (Died 13th August, 1814.)

Sanders, Fred (S. C.). Surgeon's Mate Pulaski Legion, 1779-1780.

Sanders, James (S. C.). Lieutenant 3d South Carolina (Rangers) in 1775.

Sanders, Richard (N. C.). Captain North Carolina Militia, 1782.

Sanders, Roger P. (S. C.). Captain 1st South Carolina, 17th June, 1775, to —.

Sanders, William (S. C.). Captain South Carolina Militia in 1776.

Sanderson, Reuben (Conn). Private in the Lexington Alarm, April, 1775; Private 2d Connecticut, 8th May to 17th December, 1775; Private in Selden's Connecticut State Regiment, June to December, 1776; Sergeant 1st Connecticut, 1st January, 1777; Ensign 29th December, 1777; Lieutenant, 22d August, 1780; transferred to 5th Connecticut, 1st January,. 1781; retained in Swift's Connecticut Regiment in June, 1783, and served to 3d November, 1783. (Died 31st December, 1822.)

Sandridge, Augustine (Va). Sergeant 6th Virginia, 28th January, 1777; Regimental Quartermaster 6th Virginia, 16th August, 1777; retired 30th September, 1778.

Sands, Edward (N. Y.). Surgeon's Mate 4th New York, 17th August to December, 1775.

Sandford, John (N. Y.). 1st Lieutenant and Adjutant of Malcolm's New York Regiment, September, 1776; Captain of Malcolm's Additional Continental Regiment, 11th March, 1777; transferred to Spencer's Regiment, 22d April, 1779; retired 1st January, 1781; served subsequently as Captain New York Levies. (Died 1808.)

Sanford, Ezekiel (Conn). 1st Lieutenant 5th Connecticut, 1st May to 28th November, 1775; 1st Lieutenant of Silliman's Connecticut State Regiment, 20th June to 25th December, 1776; Captain 5th Connecticut, 1st January, 1777; resigned 17th March, 1778. (Died 1808.)

Sanford, Peter (N. J.). 1st Lieutenant New Jersey Militia in 1776.

Sanford, Samuel (Conn). Sergeant 7th Connecticut, 10th July to 10th December, 1775; 2d Lieutenant 19th Continental Infantry, 1st January to 31st December, 1776; 1st Lieutenant 8th Connecticut, 1st January, 1777; Captain, 15th December, 1777; transferred to 5th Connecticut, 1st January, 1781; retired 1st January, 1783. (Died 1804.)

Sanford, Samuel (N. Y.). Ensign 2d Canadian (Hazen's) Regiment, 2d December, 1776; 2d Lieutenant, 1st March, 1780; resigned 28th April, 1780 (Died 1804.)

Sanford, William (Va). 2d Lieutenant 2d Virginia, 21st September, 1775; 1st Lieutenant, February, 1776; Captain, 25th December, 1776; resigned 6th April, 1778.

Sanford, Thomas (Va). 2d Lieutenant 1st Virginia State Regiment, 1777-1778.

Sands, John (R. I.). Captain Rhode Island Militia in 1775.

Sands, Ray (—). Major and Lieutenant-Colonel Rhode Island Militia, 1777-1778.

Sanger, Jedediah (Mass). Private in Lexington Alarm, April, 1775; .2d Lieutenant of Paterson's Massachusetts Regiment, April to December, 1775; 2d Lieutenant 7th Continental Infantry, 1st January to 31st December, 1776; Captain Massachusetts Militia, 1777-1781.

Sansum, Philip (Va). Sergeant 1st Virginia, February, 1776; Ensign, — September, 1776; 2d Lieutenant, 28th November, 1776; 1st Lieutenant, 15th September, 1777; Captain Lieutenant, 4th October, 1777; Captain, 4th May, 1782, and served to close of war.

Santford, John.—See Sanford.

Saple, John Alexander (Pa). Surgeon's Mate 8th Pennsylvania, 14th June, 1778; transferred to Hospital Department in March, 1779, and served to close of war.

Sappington, Richard (Md). Surgeon's Mate 3d Maryland, 20th February, 1777; resigned 11th January, 1779. (Died 1828.)

Sares, Jacob.—See Sayres.

Sargent, Erastus (Mass). Captain Massachusetts Militia in 1777.

Sargent, Paul Dudley (Mass). Colonel of a Massachusetts Regiment, May to December, 1775; wounded at Bunker Hill, 17th June, 1775; Colonel 16th Continental Infantry, 1st January to 31st December, 1776; Colonel Massachusetts Militia, 1777-1781 (Died 28th September, 1828.)

Sargent, Samuel (N. H.). 1st Lieutenant of Bedel's Regiment New Hampshire Rangers, 13th January to December, 1776.

Sargent, Winthrop (Mass). Lieutenant of Gridley's Regiment Massachusetts Artillery, 7th July, 1775; Captain-Lieutenant of Knox's Regiment Continental Artillery, 10th December, 1775; Captain 3d Continental Artillery, 1st January, 1777; Brevet Major, 28th August, 1783; served as Aide-de-Camp to General Howe, June, 1780, to close of war; served as Adjutant-General of the army in the field under General St.

Clair, September, 1791, until wounded in action with Indians on the Maumee, Ohio, 4th November, 1791. (Died 3d June, 1820.)

Sartell, Nathaniel (Mass). Sergeant in Lexington Alarm, April, 1775; 2d Lieutenant of Paterson's Massachusetts Regiment, April to December, 1775; 2d Lieutenant 7th Continental Infantry, 1st January to 31st December, 1776; Lieutenant of Militia, 1777-1779. (Died 24th January, 1822.)

Sartwell, Simon (N. H.). 1st Lieutenant 4th Continental Infantry, 1st January, 1776; 1st Lieutenant 1st New Hampshire, 8th November, 1776; Captain-Lieutenant, 20th September, 1777; Captain, 24th March, 1780; resigned 12th May, 1781. (Died 1791.)

Sarzedas, David (Ga). Lieutenant Georgia Militia in 1779.

Satterlee, William (Conn). Captain of Elmore's Continental Regiment, 15th April, 1776; Captain 2d Canadian (Hazen's) Regiment, 3d November, 1776; wounded at Monmouth 28th June, 1778, and did not rejoin regiment. (Died 6th December, 1798.)

Saunders, Jesse (Mass). Captain of Sargent's Massachusetts Regiment, May, 1775; cashiered 9th August, 1775.

Saunders, Jesse (N. C.). Captain 6th North Carolina, 16th April, 1776; resigned — May, 1776.

Saunders, Joseph (Va). 2d Lieutenant 1st Virginia State Regiment, 1777-1779.

Saunders, Nathaniel (S. C.). Captain South Carolina Militia in 1776.

Saunders, Roger Parker (S. C.). Captain 1st South Carolina, 17th June, 1775, to ——; was in service in 1778.

Saunders, Robert Hyde (Va). Ensign 1st Virginia State Regiment, 30th March, 1777; resigned — February, 1778.

Saunders, William (N. C.). Ensign 6th North Carolina, 2d April, 1777; transferred to 1st North Carolina 1st June, 1778; Lieutenant, 6th February, 1779; Captain, 8th February, 1779; transferred to 4th North Carolina, 6th February, 1782; retired 1st January, 1783.

Savage, Abijah (Conn). Lieutenant 2d Connecticut, 1st May, 1775; taken prisoner at Quebec, 31st December, 1775; exchanged — October, 1776; Captain of Sherburne's Continental Regiment, 1st January, 1777; retired 1st January, 1781. (Died 1825.)

Savage, Henry (Mass). 2d Lieutenant 3d Massachusetts, 1st January, 1777; 1st Lieutenant, 1st January, 1779; Regimental Adjutant, 11th November, 1777, to 1st January, 1780; Aide-de-Camp to General Nixon, 1st January, 1780, to close of war.

Savage, John (Mass). 2d Lieutenant 10th Massachusetts, 6th November, 1776; resigned 22d January, 1778.

Savage, John (Pa). Ensign 5th Pennsylvania Battalion, 8th January, 1776; 1st Lieutenant 6th Pennsylvania, 15th February, 1777; Captain, 1st January, 1778; retired 7th September, 1778. (Died 26th April, 1825.)

Savage, John (S. C.). Colonel South Carolina Militia in 1775.

Savage, Joseph (Mass). Sergeant of Gridley's Regiment, Massachusetts Artillery, April to December, 1775; 2d Lieutenant of Knox's Regiment Continental Artillery, 10th December, 1775; Captain-Lieutenant 2d Continental Artillery, 1st January, 1777; Captain, 20th September, 1779, and served to 17th June, 1783; Captain United States Artillery Battalion, 20th October, 1786; Captain of Artillery Battalion United States Army, 29th September, 1789; resigned 15th October, 1791. (Died 20th January, 1814.)

Savage, Joseph (Va). Surgeon 2d Virginia, ——, 1779; taken prisoner at Charleston, 12th May, 1780.

Savage, Nathaniel (Va). Lieutenant Virginia Militia, 1780-1781.

Savage, Samuel H. (Vt). Lieutenant Vermont Militia in 1777.

Savage, William (S. C.). Major South Carolina Militia in 1775.

Sawyer, —— (S. C.). Lieutenant South Carolina, ——; wounded at Beaufort, 9th February, 1779.

Sawyer, Benjamin (Vt). 1st Lieutenant of Bedel's Regiment Vermont Militia, 15th December, 1777, to 1st April, 1779.

Sawyer, Ephraim (Mass). Major of Whitcomb's Massachusetts Regiment, 19th April to December, 1775; Lieutenant-Colonel Massachusetts Militia, 1776-1780.

Sawyer, Ephraim (Mass). 1st Lieutenant 11th Continental Infantry, 1st January to 31st December, 1776; 1st

Lieutenant 15th Massachusetts, 1st January, 1777; resigned 28th October, 1777; Captain of Henley's Continental Regiment, 26th December, 1777; retired 23d April, 1779. (Died 14th February, 1826.)

Sawyer, James (Mass). Captain in Lexington Alarm, April, 1775; Captain of Frye's Massachusetts Regiment, May to December, 1775.

Sawyer, James (Mass). Private of Whitcomb's Massachusetts Regiment, May to December, 1775; Sergeant 6th Continental Infantry, 1st January to 31st December, 1776; Sergeant 7th Massachusetts, 1st January, 1777; Ensign, 22d February, 1777; transferred to 4th Massachusetts, 12th June, 1783; retained in Jackson's Continental Regiment, 3d November, 1783, and served to 20th June, 1784. (Died 27th March, 1827.)

Sawyer, Jesse (N. H.). 2d Lieutenant Green Mountain Boys, 27th July to December, 1775.

Sawyer, John (Mass). Private in Lexington Alarm, April, 1775; Sergeant of Gerrish's Massachusetts Regiment, May to December, 1775; 2d Lieutenant 4th Continental Inantry, 1st January to 31st December, 1776; Lieutenant and Regimental Quartermaster, 8th Massachusetts, 1st January, 1777; resigned 27th September, 1778.

Sawyer, Jonathan (Mass). 2d Lieutenant of Phinney's Massachusetts Regiment, May to December, 1775; 1st Lieutenant 18th Continental Infantry, 1st January, 1776; Captain, 18th April, 1776; 1st Lieutenant 14th Massachusetts, 1st January, 1777; died 19th July, 1777. (Name also spelled Sayer.) setts, 1st January, 1777; died 19th July,

Sawyer, Levi (N. C.). 2d Lieutenant 2d North Carolina 15th May, 1776; resigned 16th March, 1778.

Sawyer, Samuel (Mass). 1st Lieutenant in Lexington Alarm, April, 1775; Captain of Scammon's Massachusetts Regiment, May to December, 1775; Captain 15th Continental Infantry, 1st January to 31st December, 1776; Captain of Mitchells Regiment Massachusetts Militia; mortally wounded on the Bagaduce Expedition, 29th July, and died 1st August, 1779.

Sawyer, Thomas (Vt). Captain Vermont Militia in 1777.

Sawyer, William (N. H.). Surgeon's-Mate 2d New Hampshire, 23d May to

December, 1775; Surgeon's-Mate, 8th Continental Infantry, 1st January to 31st December, 1776.

Sawyer, William (N. H.). Surgeon's Mate 2d New Hampshire, 23d May to December, .1775.

Sawyer, William (N. C.). Ensign 2d North Carolina, 15th May, 1776, to ——.

Sawyers, John (Va). Captain Virginia Militia at Kings Mountain in October, 1780. (Died 23d November, 1822.)

Saxton, Gee (N. H.). Ensign of Warner's Continental Regiment, 25th March, 1777; 2d Lieutenant, ——, 1778; retired 1st January, 1781.

Sayer, Jonathan. See Sawyer.

Sayer, Joshua (R. I.). 1st Lieutenant of Elliot's Regiment Rhode Island State Artillery, 19th August, 1776; Captain, 12th December, 1776, and served to ——.

Sayles, David (R. I.). Ensign of Babcock's Rhode Island State Regiment, 15th January, 1776; 2d Lieutenant 2d Rhode Island, 1st January, 1777; 1st Lieutenant 12th June, 1777; retained in Olney's Rhode Island Battalion, 14th May, 1781; Captain, 1st May, 1782 retired 17th March, 1783.

Sayres, Jacob (Md). Captain Maryland Militia in 1777.

Sayres, John (Va). Captain 1st Virginia, 18th September, 1775; Major 4th Virginia, 13th August, 1776; Lieutenant-Colonel 9th Virginia, 30th January, 1777; killed at Germantown, 4th October, 1777. (Name also spelled Seayres.)

Sayres, Robert (Va). 1st Lieutenant 7th Virginia, 7th May, 1776; Captain 4th April, 1777; transferred to 5th Virginia, 14th September, 1778; supernumerary, — May, 1779.

Sayres, Thomas (Va). Ensign 5th Virginia, 12th February, 1781; 2d Lieutenant, 5th May, 1782; retired 1st January, 1783

Sayres, William (Pa). 1st Lieutenant 12th Pennsylvania, 16th October, 1776; resigned 11th October, 1777

Scammell, Alexandria (N. H.). Major New Hampshire Militia, April, 1775; Brigade-Major to New Hampshire Brigade, 21st September, 1775; Aide-de-Camp to General Sullivan 14th August, 1776; Brigade Major to General Lee's Division, 29th October, 1776; Colonel 3d New Hampshire, 8th November, 1776; Adjutant-General Continental Army, on staff of General Washington, 5th January, 1778, to 1st January, 1781, when he resigned to assume command of the 1st New Hampshire; mortally wounded and taken prisoner at Yorktown, 30th September, 1781, and died while a prisoner, 6th October, 1781.

Scammell, Samuel Leslie (Mass). Ensign 13th Massachusetts 30th August, 1780; transferred to 6th Massachusetts, 1st January, 1781; transferred to 2d Massachusetts, 12th June, 1783, and served to 3d November, 1783. Died ——.

Scammon, James (Mass). Colonel of a Massachusetts Regiment, May to December, 1775. (Died 14th January, 1821.)

Scarborough, John (Va). Sergeant 9th Virginia, 8th May, 1776; Ensign, 10th February, 1777; taken prisoner at Germantown, 4th October, 1777; transferred to 1st Virginia 14th September, 1778; Lieutenant 26th December, 1778; transferred to 5th Virginia, 12th February, 1781; transferred to 1st Virginia, 1st January, 1783, and served to close of war.

Schenck, Curtenius (N. J.). 1st Lieutenant 1st New Jersey 16th December, 1775, to 20th November, 1776; 1st Lieutenant 1st New Jersey 29th November, 1776; omitted October, 1777.

Schenck, Henry (N. Y.). Major New York Militia, 1775-1776.

Schenck, Peter (N. Y.). Captain and Major New York Militia 1775-1780

Schenck, William (N. J.). Ensign of Forman's Additional Continental Regiment 1st March, 1777; resigned 1st August, 1778. (Died 1st July, 1827.)

Schermerhorn, Jacob (N. Y.). Lieutenant-Colonel New York Militia in 1775.

Schermerhorn, Jacob C. (N. Y.). Captain New York Militia in 1777. (Died 1822.)

Schermerhorn John (N. Y.). Captain New York Militia 1775-1781.

Schlatter, Grandue (Pa.). 1st Lieutenant of Lewis' Pennsylvania Battalion of the Flying Camp, July to December, 1776.

Schneider, Conrad (Pa). Captain of Watt's Pennsylvania Battalion of the Flying Camp; taken prisoner at Fort Washington 16th November, 1776.

Schneider, Jacob (Pa). 1st Lieutenant Pennsylvania State Regiment, 18th April, 1777; Regiment designated 13th Pennsylvania, 12th November, 1777; retired 1st July, 1778.

Schofield, William (Pa). 2d Lieutenant 5th Pennsylvania, 1st January, 1777; 1st Lieutenant, 23d January, 1778; retired 1st July, 1778. (Died 3d February, 1822.)

Schoonhoven, Jacobus (N. Y.). Colonel New York Militia, 1777-1778.

Schoonmaker, Abraham (N. Y.). Lieutenant of Hasbrouck's Regiment New York Militia in 1777.

Schoonmaker, Edward (N. Y.). Lieutenant and Captain in Snyder's Regiment New York Militia, 1777-1783.

Schoonmaker Frederick (N. Y.). aptain of Pawling's Regiment New York Militia, 1777-1778.

Schoonmaker, Josham (N. Y.). Captain of Pawling's Regiment New York Militia, 1777-1778.

Schott, John Paul (Pa). Captain Independent Pennsylvania Company, 6th September, 1776; attached to Ottendorff's Corps, 7th December, 1776; taken prisoner at Short Hills, 26th June, 1777; exchanged ——; in orders of 1780 is called major; served to close of war. (Died 18th June, 1829.)

Schrack, David (Pa). 1st Lieutenant Lewis' Pennsylvania Battalion of the Flying Camp, July, 1776; 1st Lieutenant 10th Pennsylvania, 4th December, 1776; Captailn 17th October, 1777; retired 1st July, 1778.

Schrader, Israel (Pa). Cornet of Dragoons Pulaski Legion in 1780 to ——.

Schrader, Philip (Pa). 2d Lieutenant German Battalion, 12th July, 1776; 1st Lieutenant, 13th May, 1777; Captain Lieutenant, 8th February, 1778; retired 1st January, 1781; Captain Pennsylvania Rangers, 1781-1782. (Died 1822.)

Schreiber, Jacob (Pa). Lieutenant Continental Artillery, 26th November, 1779; Captain Corps of Engineers, 2d March, 1780; taken prisoner at Charleston, 12th May, 1780; exchanged 1781; retired 1st May, 1783. Name also spelled Shriver.

Schroeder, George L. (N. Y.). Adjutant 3d New York, 30th June, 1775; resigned 11th September, 1775.

Schrop, John (Pa). 2d Lieutenant of Ottendorff's Corps, 19th March, 1777; omitted on roll for July, 1777.

Schureman, James (N. Y.). Lieutenant New York Militia; taken prisoner at New Brunswick in July 1777. (Died 22d January, 1824.)

Schutt, John (N. Y.). Captain New York Militia, 1775-1776.

Schuyler, Dirck (N. Y.). Ensign 2d New York 5th June, 1782, and served to close of war; Lieutenant United States Artillery Battalion 7th August, 1786; Lieutenant Artillery United States Army, 29th September, 1789; resigned 20th June, 1792

Schuyler, Harmanus (N. Y.). Assistant Commissary General Northern Department in 1776.

Schuyler, Nicholas (N. Y.). Surgeon 2d Canadian (Hazen's) Regiment 1st April, 1777, to June, 1783. (Died 24th November, 1824.)

Schuyler, Peter P. (N. Y.). Major New York Militia in 1775.

Schuyler, Philip (N. Y.). Major-General Continental Army, 19th June, 1775; resigned 19th April, 1779. (Died 18th November, 1804.)

Schuyler, Richard (N. Y.). Ensign 2d New York 5th June, 1782, and served to June, 1783.

Schuyler, Stephen J. (N. Y.). Colonel New York Militia, 1775-1781.

Schwartz, Christian (Pa). Lieutenant Pennsylvania Militia; was a prisoner in 1780, but when and where taken not stated.

Schwartz, Christopher Godfried (Pa). Ensign German Regiment, 19th July, 1776; 2d Lieutenant, 14th May,, 1777; 1st Lieutenant, 12th February, 1778; retired 1st January, 1781.

Scibbio, Thomas (N. Y.). Private 4th New York, 1st January, 1777; Sergeant, 15th July, 1777; Surgeon's-Mate, 23d October, 1778; omitted November, 1779. Name also spelled Sibbio.

Scobey, James (N. J.). Ensign 3d New Jersey, 1st May, 1777; 2d Lieutenant, 1st November 1777; resigned 15th December, 1777.

Scofield, Reuben (Conn). Sergeant 7th Connecticut, 10th July to 10th December, 1775; 2d Lieutenant 19th Continental Infantry, 1st January to 31st December, 1776; subsequently served as Captain Connecticut Militia.

Scott, Alexander (Ga). Chaplain 1st Georgia, January, 1776, to ——.

Scott, Benjamin (Md). 1st Lientenant 6th Maryland, 10th December, 1776; resigned 22d September, 1778

Scott, Calvin (Mass). Surgeon's-Mate 8th Massachusetts 1st January, 1778; resigned 29th August, 1779.

Scott, Charles (Va). Cornet 1st Continental Dragoons, ——, 1781; retained in Baylor's Regiment of Dragoons, 9th November, 1782, and served to close of war.

Scott, Charles (Va). Lieutenant-Colonel 2d Virginia, 13th February, 1776; Colonel, 5th Virginia, 7th May, 1776; Brigadier-General Continental Army, 1st April, 1777; taken priosner at Charleston, 12th May, 1780, and was a prisoner on parole to close of war; Brevet Major General, 30th September, 1793. (Died 22d October, 1813.)

Scott, Daniel (——). Surgeon's-Mate Hospital Department, 1775-1776.

Scott, David (Va). Captain 13th Virginia, 1777, to ——; retired 30th September, 1778.

Scott, Ezekiel (Conn). Captain 2d Connecticut 1st May to 10th December, 1775; Captain 22d Continental Infantry, 1st January to 31st December, 1776.

Scott, George (Va). 2d Lieutenant of Stephenson's Virginia Rifle Company, July to December, 1775; Captain Virginia Militia, 1777-1778.

Scott, James (Mass). Ensign 7th Massachusetts, 14th December, 1781; transferred to 4th Massachusetts, 12th June, 1783, and served to 3d November, 1783.

Scott, James (Va). Capt Virginia Militia, 1775-1776. (Died 1799).

Scott, Jeremiah (R. I.). Captain Rhode Island Militia in 1778.

Scott, John (Pa). Lieutenant Lancaster County, Pennsylvania, Militia, 1776-1777.

Scott, John (Va). Ensign 2d Virginia State Regiment in 1780; Ensign 1st Virginia, 10th February, 1781, and served to close of war.

Scott, John Budd (N. J.). Captain 2d New Jersey, 28th October, 1775; cashiered, 2d November, 1776, and joined the enemy.

Scott, John Day (Md). Captain of Smallwoods Maryland Regiment, 14th

January, 1776; killed at White Plains, 28th October, 1776.

Scott, John Eppes (Va). Ensign 15th Virginia, 1st January, 1777; 2d Lieutenant, 21st July, 1777; regiment designated 11th Virginia, 14th September, 1778; 1st Lieutenant, 14th May, 1779; retired 12th February, 1781.

Scott, John Morin (N. Y.). Brigadier-General New York Militia 9th June, 1776; wounded at White Plains, 28th October, 1776; served to March, 1777. (Died 14th September, 1784.)

Scott, Joseph Sr. (Va). 2d Lieutenant 1st Virginia, 16th September, 1775; 1st Lieutenant, January, 1776; Regimental Adjutant, May, 1776, to August, 1777; Captain, 9th August, 1777; Brigade-Major to General Muhlenburg, 28th August, 1777; wounded at Germantown, 4th October, 1777; transferred to 5th Virginia, 12th February, 1781, and served to close of war; Brevet Major, 30th September, 1783.

Scott, Joseph Jr. (Va). 2d Lieutenant 1st Virginia, 21st January, 1776; 1st Lieutenant, 11th September, 1777; Captain, 12th May, 1780, and served to close of war.

Scott, Joseph James (S. C.). Lieutenant South Carolina Rangers; wounded at Black Mingo, 14th September, 1780.

Scott, Matthew (Pa). 1st Lieutenant of Miles Pennsylvania Rifle Regiment, 15th March, 1776; taken prisoner at Long Island, 27th August, 1776; exchanged 8th December, 1776; Captain Pennsylvania State Regiment, 18th April 1777, to rank from 24th October, 1776; regiment designated 13th Pennsylvania, 12th November, 1777; retired 1st July, 1778 (Died 1796.)

Scott, Moses (N. J.). Hospital Physician and Surgeon, 21st February, 1777; resigned 13th December, 1780.

Scott, Walter (Va). Lieutenant of a Virginia State Regiment, 1779 to 1781.

Scott, William (Ga). Captain 3d Georgia, ——, 1777; was in service in 1782.

Scott, William (Mass). 2d Lieutenant of Sargents Massachusetts Regiment, May, 1775; taken prisoner at Bunker Hill, 17th June, 1775; 1st Lieutenant 16th Continental Infantry, 1st January to 31st December, 1776; Captain of Henley's Continental Regiment, 1st January, 1777; transferred to Jackson's Regimetn, 22d April, 1779; retired

1st January, 1781; served subsequently in Navy. (Died 1796.)

Scott, William (N. H.). Captain New Hampshire Company, April, 1775; Company attached to Sargents Massachusetts Regiment, 7th July, 1775; Captain 16th Continental Infantry, 1st January, 1776; Captain 1st New Hampshire, 8th November, 1776; wounded and taken prisoner at Stillwater 19th September, 1777; Major, 20th September, 1777; retired 1st January, 1781. (Died 1796.)

Scott, William (Pa). Captain of Clotz's Pennsylvania Battalion of the Flying Camp; taken prisoner at Fort Washington, 16th November, 1776.

Scott, William (S. C.). Captain 2d South Carolina, 17th June, 1775; Major, 1st May, 1777; Lieutenant-Colonel, ——; surrendered Fort Moultrie and taken prisoner then, 7th May 1780; exchanged June, 1781, and served to close of war.

Scott, William (Va). Captain of Thurston's Continental Regiment, 3d April, 1777; dismissed 4th April, 1778, and his company attached to Hartley's Regiment.

Scott, William (Va). Sergeant 4th Virginia, 2 9th November, 1777; Ensign 4th July 1779; retired 1st January, 1780.

Scovil, Samuel (Conn). Ensign of Douglas' Connecticut State Regiment, June to December, 1776.

Scovil, Stephen (Conn). 2d Lieutenant of Gay's Connecticut State Regiment, June to December, 1776.

Screven, Benjamin (S. C.). Captain South Carolina Dragoons, 1779.

Screven, James (Ga). Captain 3d Georgia (Rangers), 9th January, 1776; Colonel 3d Georgia, 5th July, 1776; resigned 20th March, 1778; Brigadier-General Georgia Militia; killed at Medway Church, 24th November, 1778.

Screven, John (Ga). Lieutenant Georgia Rangers, 9th January 1776, to ——. (Died 1801.)

Scribner, Nathaniel (Conn). Captain Connecticut Militia, ——; wounded at Monmouth, 28th June, 1778.

Scroggen, Robert (Md). Ensign 2d Maryland, 17th April, 1777; resigned 14th May, 1777.

Scruggs, Gross (Va). Captain 5th Virginia, 26th February, 1776 to ——.

Scudder, Henry (N. Y.). Lieutenant New York Militia; taken prisoner at Long Island, 27th August, 1776.

Scudder, Nathaniel (N. J.). Colonel New Jersey Militia, ——; killed in a skirmish at Shrewsbury, 16th October, 1781.

Scudder, William (N. J.). Major and LieutenantColonel New Jersey Militia, 1776-1778.

Scudder, William (N. Y.). Ensign 4th New York, June, 1776; 2d Lieutenant 1st New York, 21st November, 1776; taken prisoner by Indians at Minnisink, 22d July, 1779. (Died 1799).

Scull, Edward (Pa). Adjutant of Haller's Battalion Pennsylvania Flying Camp July, 1776; Captain 4th Pennsylvania, 3d January, 1777; resigned 11th May, 1779.

Scull, John (N. J.). Lieutenant New Jersey Militia in 1777.

Scull, John Gambier (N. C.). Ensign 1st North Carolina, 1st June, 1776; 2d Lieutenant, 21st November, 1776; 1st Lieutenant, 26th April, 1777; was a Captain in 1780, and served to close of war.

Scull, Nicholas (Pa). Ensign 1st Pennsylvania Battalion 20th January, 1776, to ——.

Scull, Nicholas (Pa). Surgeon's-Mate Hospital Department, 1779-1780.

Scull, Peter (Pa). 2d Lieutenant of Thompson's Pennsylvania Rifle Regiment, 17th July, 1775; Captain 3d Pennsylvania Battalion, 5th January, 1776; Brigade-Major, 23d March, 1776; Major of Patton's Continental Regiment, 11th January, 1777; resigned 1st January, 1778; secretary to the Board of War, 17th January, 1779. Died at sea 4th November, 1779.

Scull, Samuel (N. J.). Captain New Jersey Militia in 1777.

Scull, William (Pa). Captain 11th Pennsylvania, 30th September, 1776; retired 1st July, 1778, and joined the Geographers' Department.

Scurlock, James (N. C.). Lieutenant 10th North Carolina 1st September, 1780; Captain, 11th September, 1781; transferred to 4th North Carolina, 6th February, 1782; retired 1st January, 1783.

Seabrook, Thomas (N. J.). Major and Lieutenant-Colonel New Jersey Militia in 1776.

Seabury, Benjamin (R. I). Captain of Church's Rhode Island Regiment, 3d May to December 1775.

Seagrave, Edward (Mass). 1st Lieutenant in Lexington Alarm, April, 1775; Captain of Read's Massachusetts Regiment, May to December, 1775; Captain 13th Continental Infantry, 1st January to 31st December, 1776; Captain Massachusetts Militia, 1777-1781. (Died 1806).

Seargeant, Isaac (Conn). Captain Connecticut Light-Horse in 1776

Searle, David (R. I.). Lieutenant of Lippitt's Rhode Island State Regiment, 19th August, 1776, to May, 1777.

Searle, William (Mass). Private in Lexington Alarm, April, 1775; Sergeant of Little's Massachusetts Regiment, April to November, 1775; Ensign 12th Continental Infantry, 1st January, 1776, to ——.

Sears, Barnabas (Mass). 1st Lieutenant of Learned's Massachusetts Regiment, May to December, 1775; served subsequently in Militia.

Sears, George (R. I.). Lieutenant-Colonel Rhode Island Militia in 1776.

Sears, John (Md). Sergeant 2d Maryland, 10th January, 1777; Ensign, 26th January, 1780; transferred to 5th Maryland, 1st January, 1781; 2d Lieutenant, 1st January, 1781; transferred to 1st Maryland, 1st January, 1783; retained in Maryland Battalion, April, 1783, and served to 15th November, 1783.

Sears, Nathan (Mass). Private in Lexington Alarm, April, 1775; 2d Lieutenant of Cotton's Massachusetts Regiment, May to December, 1775; 2d Lieutenant 23d Continental Infantry, 1st January to 31st December, 1776.

Sears, Peter (Mass). Private of Steven's Battalion Continental Artillery, 3d March, 1778; transferred to 3d Continental Artillery, September, 1778; Lieutenant, 1st March, 1779; Captain Lieutenant, 1781; served to January, 1783.

Sears, Thomas (N. Y.). Lieutenant New York Militia, 1778- 1779.

Seaton, Augustine (Va). Regimental Quartermaster of Grayson's Additional Continental Regiment, 24th May, 1777; resigned 20th December, 1777.

Seaton, John (N. Y.). Lieutenant in Graham's Regiment New York Militia, 1776-1778.

Seaward, Shackford (N. H.). 2d Lieutenant of Long's New Hampshire Militia Regiment, — May, 1776; resigned 10th February, 1777.

Seawell, Benjamin (N. C.). Colonel North Carolina Militia, 1780-1781.

Seeber, Adolph (N. Y.). Ensign New York Militia; killed at Oriskany, 6th August, 1777.

Seeber, Jacob W. (N. Y.). Captain New York Militia; killed at Oriskany, 7th August, 1777.

Seeber, Severinus (N. Y.). 1st Lieutenant New York Militia, ——; killed at Oriskany, 6th August, 1777.

Seeber, William (N. Y.). Lieutenant Colonel New York Militia, ——; killed at Oriskany, 6th August, 1777.

Seckel, George Jr. (Pa). 2d Lieutenant 9th Pennsylvania, 15th January, 1777, to ——.

Sedam, Cornelius Ryer (N. J.). Ensign 1st New Jersey, 30th May, 1782, and served to April, 1783; Ensign United States Infantry Regiment, 17th March, 1786; Ensign 1st Infantry United States Army, 29th September, 1789; Lieutenant, 22d October, 1790; Captain, 23d April, 1792; assigned to 1st Sub Legion, 4th September, 1792; honorably discharged 1st November, 1796. (Died 10th May, 1823.)

Sedgwick, Abraham (Conn). Captain of Chester's Connecticut State Regiment, June to December, 1776.

Sedgwick, John (Conn). Captain 4th Connecticut, 1st May to 10th December, 1775; Major of Burrall's Continental Regiment, 19th January, 1776; Major 7th Connecticut, 1st January, 1777; resigned 10th February, 1778; served also as Lieutenant-Colonel Connecticut Militia. (Died 1820).

Sedgwick, Theodore (Mass). Aide-de-Camp and Brigade Major to General Thomas in the expedition to Canada, January to June, 1776. (Died 24th January, 1813.)

Segand, James (Md). Captain Pulaski Legion, 1778-1783; was a prisoner, but when and where taken not stated; Brevet Major, 30th September, 1783. Name also spelled Segond.

Segard, James. See Second.

Seegern, Frederick (Pa). Quartermaster German Battalion, 12th July, 1776; resigned 10th October, 1776; Ensign 3d Cavalry Pulaski Legion, 1st May, 1778; 1st Lieutenant, 1st June, 1779, and served to ——. (Name also spelled Seegarn and Segern.)

Seeley, Enos (N. J.). Lieutenant Colonel and Colonel New Jersey Militia, 1776-1777.

Seeley, Isaac (Pa). 2d Lieutenant 4th Pennsylvania Battalion, 5th January, 1776; 1st Lieutenant 5th Pennsylvania, January, 1777; Captain, 20th September, 1777; Brigade Major 2d Pennsylvania Brigade, 22d March, 1778; taken prisoner at Paramus 16th April, 1780; transferred to 1st Pennsylvania 1st January, 1783, and served to close of war; Brevet Major, 30th September, 1783.

Seeley, John (Pa). Sergeant 12th Pennsylvania, 13th December, 1776; Ensign, 3d February, 1777; resigned 20th August, 1777.

Seeley, Josiah (N. J.). 1st Lieutenant 3d New Jersey, 7th February, 1776; resigned 24th February, 1776.

Seeley, Samuel (N. J.). Ensign 1st New Jersey, 1st March, 1777; 2d Lieutenant, 4th October, 1777; 1st Lieutenant, 11th March, 1780; retained in New Jersey Battalion, April, 1783, and served to 3d November, 1783.

Seeley, Sylvanus (N. J.). Captain, Major, Lieutenant-Colonel and Colonel New Jersey Militia, 1776-1780.

Seelye, Abner (N. H.). Captain of Warner's Continental Regiment, 5th July, 1776; resigned 1st June, 1778; Captain Vermont Militia in 1781.

Seibert, Henry (Pa). Lieutenant 3d Cavalry, Pulaski Legion, 6th June, 1778, and served to ——. (In service January, 1780.)

Seibert, Philip (Pa). Captain Invalid Regiment, to rank from 10th February, 1776, and served to June, 1783.

Seidelin, —— (—). Lieutenant and Adjutant Pulaski Legion, 1779-1780.

Seigart, Zachariah (—). Lieutenant, ——; was a prisoner in 1778; when and where taken not stated.

Seily, Charles (Pa). 2d Lieutenant 3d Pennsylvania, 1st January to 1st April, 1777.

Seitz, Charles (Pa). 2d Lieutenant 4th Pennsylvania Battalion, 5th January, 1776; taken prisoner at Long Island 27th August, 1776; exchanged December, 1776; 1st Lieutenant 3d Pennsylvania, 1st January, 1777; Adjutant of Ottendorff's Corps, 14th April, 1777; resigned 22d September, 1777. (Died 1784.)

Seits, Peter (N. Y.). Ensign New York Militia, ——; prisoner of war 2d

June, 1778, to 9th November, 1780; where taken not stated.

Selden, Charles (Conn). 2d Lieutenant of Lee's Continental Regiment, 1st July, 1777; transferred to Jackson's Regiment, 22d April, 1779; 1st Lieutenant, 4th March, 1779; regiment designated 16th Massachusetts, 23d July, 1780; transferred to 9th Massachusetts, 1st January, 1781; transferred to 4th Massachusetts 12th June, 1783; retained in Jackson's Continental Regiment in November, 1783, and served as Regimental Adjutant, 16th June, 1783, to 20th June, 1784. (Died 1st January, 1820.)

Selden, Ezra (Conn. Sergeant 6th Connecticut, 6th May to 10th December, 1775; 2d Lieutenant 10th Continental Infantry, 1st January to 31st December, 1776; Adjutant 1st Connecticut, 1st January, 1777; Captain, 11th January, 1778; wounded at Stony Point, 16th July, 1779; transferred to 4th Connecticut 1st January, 1781; transferred to 3d Connecticut 1st January, 1783, and served to 3d June, 1783. (Died 9th December, 1784.)

Selden, James (Va). 2d Lieutenant 1st Virginia, 15th September, 1777, to ——.

Selden, John (Va). Captain Virginia Militia, 1776-1777.

Selden, Joseph (Va). 2d Lieutenant 1st Virginia State Regiment, 20th March, 1777; 1st Lieutenant, 5th February, 1778; resigned 10th July, 1778.

Selden, Samuel (Conn). Colonel Connecticut State Regiment, 20th June, 1776; wounded and taken prisoner in the retreat from New York, 15th September, 1776, and died in prison 11th October, 1776.

Selden, Samuel (Va.) 2d Lieutenant 1st Virginia, 11th June, 1777; 1st Lieutenant, 25th June, 1778; Captain Lieutenant, 23d June, 1779; taken prisoner at Charleston 12th May, 1780; exchanged November, 1780; wounded at Ninety Six, 18th June, 1781, and served to close of war.

Selden, Wilson (Va). Surgeon Virginia Militia, 1779-1780.

Selin, Anthony (Pa). Captain of Ottendorff's Corps, 10th December, 1776; also appears as Captain 2d Canadian Regiment, 10th December, 1776, and referred to as late Major of same in Journal of Congress of 24th

February, 1784; appears to have served to close of war. (Died ——, 1792.)

Selleck, Jacob (Conn). Ensign 5th Connecticut, 1st May to 9th October, 1775.

Selleck, Simeon (Conn). Regimental Quartermaster 5th Connecticut, 20th May to 20th June, 1775.

Sellers, John (Pa). Lieutenant Westmoreland County, Pennsylvania, Militia in 1778.

Sellman, Jonathan (Md). 2d Lieutenant 3d Maryland Battalion of the Flying Camp, July, 1776; 1st Lieutenant, August, 1776; Captain 4th Maryland, 10th December, 1776; transferred to 1st Maryland, 1st January, 1781; Major, 9th May, 1782; retired 1st January, 1783. (Died 1810.)

Semmes.—See **Simms**, as name is spelled both ways.

Senter, Asa (N. H.). Ensign 5th Continental Infantry, 14th August, 1776; 2d Lieutenant 1st New Hampshire, 8th November, 1776; taken prisoner at Dutch Island, 3d August, 1777; 1st Lieutenant, 5th March, 1778; Captain, 12th May, 1781, and served to close of war. (Died 1835.)

Senter, Isaac (R. I.). Surgeon 3d Rhode Island, November, 1775, to March, 1776; Hospital Surgeon, 20th July, 1776, to April, 1779; Surgeon-General Rhode Island Militia, 1779-1781. (Died 20th December, 1799.)

Senter, Joseph (N. H.). Lieutenant-Colonel of Wyman's Regiment New Hampshire Militia, 1776 to 1778. (Died 1798.)

Sere, .Daniel (Md). Chaplain of Smallwood's Maryland Regiment, June to December, 1776.

Sever, James (Mass). Ensign 7th Massachusetts, 1st February, 1781; transferred to 4th Massachusetts, 12th June, 1783; retained in Jackson's Continental Regiment, November, 1783, and served to 20th June, 1784; Post Captain United States Navy, 11th May, 1798; honorably discharged, 18th June, 1801. (Died 16th December, 1845.)

Sever, Thomas (Mass). Ensign of Ward's Massachusetts Regiment, May to December, 1775.

Sevier, John (N. C.). Colonel North Carolina Militia, 1777, to close of war; Brigadier-General United States Army,

19th July, 1798; honorably discharged 15th June, 1800. (Died 24th September, 1815.)

Sevier, Robert (N. C.). Captain North Carolina Militia; mortally wounded at King's Mountain, 7th October, 1780.

Sevier, Valentine (N. C.). Captain North Carolina Militia at King's Mountain in October, 1780. (Died 23d February, 1800.)

Sewall, Charles (Md). 2d Lieutenant 4th Maryland, 10th December, 1776; resigned or died 19th November, 1777.

Sewall, Clement (Md). Sergeant 1st Maryland, 4th March, 1777; Ensign, 12th September, 1777 ,to rank from 4th March, 1777; severely wounded at Germantown, 4th October, 1777, and rendered no further service. (Died 7th January, 1829.)

Sewall, Henry, Jr. (Mass). Corporal in Prescott's Massachusetts Regiment, May, 1775; Ensign, September to December, 1775; Ensign 18th Continental Infantry, 1st January to 31st December, 1776; 1st Lieutenant 12th Massachusetts, 1st January, 1777; Captain, 1st April, 1779; transferred to 2d Massachusetts, 3d May, 1782; Major Aidede-Camp to General Heath, 19th May, 1779, to June, 1783. (Died 11th September, 1845.)

Sewall, Stephen (Mass). Captain of Lee's Continental Regiment, 1st March, 1777; resigned 1st July, 1778; Captain Aide-de-Camp to General Glover, 16th August, 1778, to July, 1782.

Seward, John (N. J.). Captain, Lieutenant-Colonel, and Colonel New Jersey Militia, 1776 to 1783. (Died 1797.)

Seward, Richard (Pa). 1st Lieutenant 5th Pennsylvania Battalion, 1st February, 1776; taken prisoner at Fort Washington, 16th November, 1776; exchanged December, 1776; did not return to service.

Seward, Thomas (Mass). 1st Lieutenant of Gridley's Regiment Massachusetts Artillery, May, 1775; Captain-Lieutenant of Knox's Regiment Continental Artillery, 10th December, 1775; Captain 3d Continental Artillery, 1st January, 1777, and served to June, 1783; Brevet Major, 30th September, 1783. (Died 27th November, 1800.)

Seward, William C. (Va). Captain Virginia Militia in 1776.

Sexton, George (N. H.). 2d Lieutenant of Warner's Continental Regiment, 12th July, 1776; 1st Lieutenant, 28th September, 1778; resigned 26th September, 1780. (Died 1815.)

Seybert, Nicholas (Md). Ensign 1st Maryland Battalion of the Flying Camp, July to December, 1776; 2d Lieutenant 7th Maryland, 20th February, 1777; dropped 4th July, 1777.

Seymour, Horace (Conn). Sergeant 2d Continental Dragoons, 10th January, 1777; Regimental Quartermaster, 25th March, 1777; Cornet, 10th July, 1778; Lieutenant, 2d June, 1779, and served to close of war.

Seymour, Israel (Conn). Captain of Chester's Connecticut State Regiment, June to December, 1776.

Seymour, Moses (Conn). Captain Connecticut Light Horse, 1776-1777. (Died 1826.)

Seymour, Thomas Young (Conn). Lieutenant 2d Continental Dragoons, 10th January, 1777; Captain, 20th October, 1777; resigned 23d November, 1778. (Died 1811.)

Seymour, Uriah (Conn). Captain Connecticut Light Horse, 1776-1777.

Seymour, William (Conn). 2d Lieutenant 5th Connecticut, 1st May to 13th December, 1775. (Died 1821.)

Shackelford, —— (S. C.). Captain 5th South Carolina, ——; resigned 7th December, 1777.

Shackelford, William (Va). 2d Lieutenant 14th Virginia, 2d December, 1776; died 23d November, 1777.

Shade, Henry (Pa). Captain of Miles' Pennsylvania Rifle Regiment, 9th March, 1776; Captain 10th Pennsylvania, 5th December, 1776; cashiered 17th October, 1777.

Shadock, Thomas (N. Y.). Captain New York Militia; taken prisoner from his home, 11th June, 1779.

Shaffner, George (Pa). 2d Lieutenant German Regiment, 12th July, 1776; Lieutenant of Schott's Company, Ottendorff's Battalion, Pulaski Legion, 4th February, 1777; Captain 3d Cavalry Pulaski Legion, 8th February, 1778; Major, ——, and served to ——.

Shaffner, Peter (Pa). 1st Lieutenant Pennsylvania Musket Battalion, 20th March to December, 1776.

Shaick, Goose Van.—See **Van Shaick.**

Shallus, Jacob (Pa). Regimental Quartermaster 1st Pennsylvania Battalion, 19th January, 1776; Ensign, 6th August, 1776; resigned 1st January, 1777. (Died 18th April, 1796.)

Shandonet, Francis.—See **Chandonet.**

Shankland, Robert (Del). Ensign Delaware Battalion of the Flying Camp, July to December, 1776.

Shanks, Thomas (Pa). Ensign 10th Pennsylvania, 4th December, 1776; cashiered 12th October, 1777.

Shannon, Robert (Pa). Captain Pennsylvania Militia in 1777.

Shannon, Samuel (Pa). Lieutenant 2d Pennsylvania Battalion of the Flying Camp; taken prisoner at Fort Washington, 16th November, 1776; Captain Pennsylvania Militia; taken prisoner by Indians in Ohio in August, 1781, and killed by them in October, 1781.

Shannon, William (Va). Ensign 1st Virginia, February, 1776; 2d Lieutenant, November, 1776; 1st Lieutenant, 4th December, 1776; resigned July, 1777.

Shapley, Adam (Conn). Captain Connecticut Militia, ——; killed at Groton Heights, 6th September, 1781.

Sharp, Anthony (N. J.). Captain 3d New Jersey, 9th February to November, 1776; served also as Major New Jersey Militia.

Sharp, Anthony (N. C.). 1st Lieutenant 9th North Carolina, 28th November, 1776; Captain, 24th August, 1777; transferred to 1st North Carolina, 1st June, 1778; transferred to 4th North Carolina, 6th February, 1782, and served to close of war; Brevet Major, 30th September, 1783.

Sharp, Elijah (Conn). 1st Lieutenant 8th Connecticut, 6th July to 14th December, 1775; Captain of Mott's Connecticut State Regiment, June to December, 1776.

Sharp, James (S. C.). Lieutenant South Carolina Rangers in 1775.

Sharp, James Boyd (Ga). Surgeon's Mate 2d Georgia, February, 1777; Surgeon, 6th December, 1782, and served to close of war.

Sharp, John (N. C.). Ensign of Captain Pemberton's Company North Carolina Rangers; in service October, 1780.

Sharp, John (Pa). 2d Lieutenant 2d Canadian (Hazen's) Regiment, 3d No-

vember, 1776; 2d Lieutenant of Ottendorff's Corps, 3d March, 1777; Lieutenant of Cavalry, Pulaski Legion, 10th February, 1778; Captain of Armand's Partisan Corps, 1780, and served to ——.

Sharpe, Anthony (N. C.). Captain 1st North Carolina, ——; in service in 1779.

Sharpe, Joseph (N. C.). Captain North Carolina Militia, 1780-1781.

Sharpe, George (N. Y.). Lieutenant in Graham's Regiment New York Militia in 1776.

Shartel, Jacob (Pa). Captain of Hartley's Additional Continental Regiment, ——, 1777; wounded by Indians at Muncey Creek, Pennsylvania, in 1778.

Shaw, Amos (Mass). Sergeant in Lexington Alarm, April, 1775; 1st Lieutenant of Thomas' Massachusetts Regiment, May to December, 1775; 1st Lieutenant 23d Continental Infantry, 1st January to 31st December, 1776.

Shaw, Archibald (N. J.). Captain 2d New Jersey, 31st October, 1775; resigned 5th February, 1777.

Shaw, Benjamin (Mass). Sergeant of Mansfield's Massachusetts Regiment, May to December, 1775; Ensign 2d Continental Infantry, 1st January to 31st December, 1776; Sergeant-Major 11th Massachusetts, 13th February, 1777; Ensign, 2d October, 1777; Lieutenant, 18th March, 1780; transferred to 10th Massachusetts, 1st January, 1781; resigned 2d May, 1781.

Shaw, Daniel (Mass). Ensign of Woodbridge's Massachusetts Regiment, May to December, 1775.

Shaw, Daniel (N. C.). Ensign 6th North Carolina, 2d April, 1777; 2d Lieutenant, 11th October, 1777; transferred to 1st North Carolina, 1st June, 1778; 1st Lieutenant, 1st October, 1779; Regimental Quartermastter, 1st June, 1778; taken prisoner at Charleston, 12th May, 1780; exchanged 14th June, 1781, and served to close of war.

Shaw, Elijah (Mass). Ensign of Heath's Massachusetts Regiment, May to December, 1775; 1st Lieutenant 24th Continental Infantry, 1st January to 31st December, 1776. (Died 1823.)

Shaw, Francis (N. Y.). Ensign of Nicholson's Continental Regiment, June, 1776; 2d Lieutenant 2d Continental Artillery, 1st February,

1777; 1st Lieutenant, 12th September, 1778; resigned 14th February, 1779.

Shaw, James (Mass). Lieutenant 14th Massachusetts, 1st January, 1777; resigned 22d December, 1777. (Died — April, 1822.)

Shaw, James (Pa). 2d Lieutenant of Hart's Pennsylvania Battalion of the Flying Camp, July to December, 1776.

Shaw, John (Mass). 1st Lieutenant of Walker's Massachusetts Regiment, 23d April to December, 1775; served subsequently as Captain Massachusetts Militia. (Died 1835.)

Shaw, John (N. Y.). Lieutenant in New York Levies, 1780 and 1781; 2d Lieutenant 2d Continental Artillery 2d November, 1781; transferred to Corps of Artillery, 17th June, 1783, and served to 3d November, 1783. (Died 14th July, 1826.)

Shaw, John (Pa.) Captain of Montgomery's Pennsylvania Battalion of the Flying Camp, July, 1776; resigned 10th August, 1776.

Shaw, Jonathan (Pa). Ensign 6th Pennsylvania, 15th February, 1777; detectetd in horse stealing in July, 1777, and made his escape.

Shaw, Mason (Mass). Lieutenant in Lexington Alarm, April, 1775; Adjutant of Walker's Massachusetts Regiment, April to December, 1775; served subsequently as Lieutenant and Captain Massachusetts Militia.

Shaw, Samuel (Mass). 2d Lieutenant of Heath's Massachusetts Regiment, May, 1775; 2d Lieutenant of Knox's Regiment Continental Artillery, 10th December, 1775; Regimental Adjutant, May, 1776; 1st Lieutenant 3d Continental Artillery, 1st January, 1777; Captain, 12th April, 1780; transferred to Corps of Artillery, 17th June, 1783; Aide-de-Camp to General Knox, June, 1782, to November, 1783. (Died 30th May, 1794.)

Shaw, Sylvanus (R. I.). Lieutenant 3d Rhode Island, 3d May, 1775; taken prisoner at Quebec, 31st December, 1775; exchanged about August, 1776; Captain 2d Rhode Island, 4th May, 1777; killed at Red Bank, 22d October, 1777.

Shaw, Thomas (Conn). Surgeon's Mate of Ward's Connecticut State Regiment, August, 1776, to. May, 1777.

Shays, Daniel (Mass). 2d Lieutenant of Woodbridge's Massachusetts Regiment, May to December, 1775; Captain 5th Massachusetts, 1st January, 1777; resigned 14th October, 1780. (Died 29th

September, 1825.) (Name also spelled Shea and Shaes.)

Shaylor, Joseph (Conn). Ensign of Douglas' Connecticut State Regiment, 20th June to 25th December, 1776; 2d Lieutenant 6th Connecticut, 1st January, 1777; 1st Lieutenant, 15th November, 1778; transferred to 4th Connecticut, 1st January, 1781; transferred to 1st Connecticut, 1st January, 1783, and served to 3d June, 1783; Captain 2d United States Infantry, 4th March, 1791; assigned to 2d Sub Legion, 4th September, 1792; Major 3d Sub Legion, 1st October, 1793; assigned to 2d Infantry, 1st November, 1796; resigned 16th May, 1797. (Died 4th March, 1816.)

Shead, Joseph (Mass). Ensign of Prescott's Massachusetts Regiment, May to December, 1775; Ensign 7th Continental Infantry, 1st January, 1776; 2d Lieutenant, 10th August to 31st December, 1776.

Shee, John (Pa). Colonel 3d Pennsylvania Battalion, 3d January, 1776; resigned 27th September, 1776.

Sheffield, Thomas (R. I.). Captain Rhode Island Militia in 1777.

Sheftall, Mordecai (Ga). Commissary General for troops in Georgia, July, 1777; taken prisoner at Savannah, 29th December, 1778. (Died 26th January, 1809.)

Shelby, Evan (Va). Brigadier-General Virginia Militia, 1778-1783. (Died 1794.)

Shelby, Evan, Jr. (Va). Major Virginia Militia at King's Mountain in October, 1780. (Killed by Indians 18th January, 1793.)

Shelby, Isaac (Va). Colonel Virginia Militia at King's Mountain, October, 1780, and in the South Carolina Campaign in 1781. The thanks of Congress were presented to him, as late Governor of Kentucky, and to the officers and men under his and General Harrison's command, for gallantry and good conduct in defeating the combined British and Indian forces under Major-General Proctor, on the Thames, in Upper Canada, October 5, 1813. (Died 18th July, 1826.)

Shelby, Isaac, Jr. (Va). Lieutenant Virginia Militia at Kings Mountain in October, 1780.

Shelby, Moses (N. C.). Captain North Carolina Militia; wounded at Kings Mountain, 7th October, 1780, and again wounded at Augusta, Ga., in April, 1781.

Sheldon, Benjamin (R. I.). Lieutenant Rhode Island Militia in 1780.

Sheldon, Caleb (R. I.). Captain Pawtuxent Rangers, Rhode Island Militia, in 1776.

Sheldon, Daniel (Conn). Surgeon's Mate 4th Connecticut, June to December, 1775.

Sheldon, Daniel (R. I.). Ensign of Tallman's Rhode Island State Regiment, 12th December, 1776, to May, 1777.

Sheldon, Elisha (Conn). Major Commandant Battalion Connecticut Light Horse, June, 1776; Colonel 2d Continental Dragoons, 12th December, 1776, and served to close of war; Brevet Brigadier-General, 30th September, 1780.

Sheldon, Samuel (Mass). Sergeant in Lexington Alarm, April, 1775; 2d Lieutenant of Ward's Massachusetts Regiment, May to December, 1775; 2d Lieutenant 21st Continental Infantry, 1st January, 1776; 1st Lieutenant, 11th September, 1776; 1st Lieutenant 5th Massachusetts, 1st January, 1777; resigned 20th March, 1778. (Died 23d March, 1829.)

Sheldon, Samuel (N. Y.). Lieutenant and Captain New York Militia, 1775 1778.

Shelmerdine, Stephen (Md). 2d Lieutenant 4th Maryland, 10th December, 1776; 1st Lieutenant, 1st February, 1778; resigned 15th December, 1779.

Shelton, Clough (Va). 1st Lieutenant 10th Virginia, 11th December, 1776; Captain, 1st March, 1777; régiment designated 6th Virginia, 14th September, 1778; taken prisoner at Charleston, 12th May, 1780.

Sheldon, Benjamin (R. I.). Lieutenant Rhode Island Militia in 1780.

Shepard, Abraham (Conn). 2d Lieutenant of Sage's Connecticut State Regiment, June to December, 1776.

Shepard, Abraham (N. C.). Colonel 10th North Carolina, 17th April, 1777; retired 1st June, 1778.

Shepard, David (Mass). Volunteer Surgeon at Lexington and Concord, 19th April, 1775; Surgeon of Danielson's Massachusetts Regiment, May to December, 1775; Surgeon of Militia at Bennington in August, 1777. (Died 12th December, 1818.)

Shepard, Jared (Conn). Captain of Wadsworth's Connecticut State Regiment, June to December, 1776

Shepard, John (N. Y.). Private of Baldwin's Artillery Artificer Regiment,

25th August, 1777; Sergeant, 8th January, 1779; Captain, 24th November, 1779; retired — March, 1781.

Shepard, John, Jr. (Mass). 2d Lieutenant of Danielson's Massachusetts Regiment, May to December, 1775; Captain Massachusetts Militia in 1776.

Shepard, Samuel (N. J.). Adjutant 3d New Jersey, 8th February, 1776; 1st Lieutenant, 12th November, 1777; transferred to 1st New Jersey, 1st July, 1778; resigned 10th May, 1782.

Shepard, Thomas (Conn). 2d Lieutenant 1st Connecticut, 1st May to 1st December, 1775; 1st Lieutenant of Wadsworth's Connecticut State Regiment, June to December, 1776.

Shepard, William (Mass). Lieutenant-Colonel of Danielson's Massachusetts Regiment, May to December, 1775; Lieutenant-Colonel 3d Continental Infantry, 1st January, 1776; wounded at Long Island 27th August, 1776; Colonel, 2d October, 1776, to rank from 4th May, 1776; Colonel 4th Massachusetts, 1st January, 1777, to rank from 4th May, 1776; retired 1st January, 1783. (Died 11th November, 1817. Name also spelled Shepherd.)

Shepard, William, Jr. (Mass). Ensign 4th Massachusetts, 1st January, 1781, and served to November, 1783. (Name also spelled Shepherd.)

Shephard, Jonathan (N. Y.). Lieutenant of Allison's Regiment New York Militia; killed in action on the Delaware River, 22d July, 1779.

Shepherd, —— (S. C.). Captain Charleston Regiment, ——; killed at Savannah, 9th October, 1779.

Shepherd, Abraham (N. Y.). Lieutenant New York Militia; killed at Minnisink 22d July, 1779.

Shepherd, Abraham (Va). Lieutenant of Stephenson's Virginia Rifle Company, July, 1775; Captain of Stephenson's Maryland and Virginia Rifle Regiment, 9th July, 1776; taken prisoner at Fort Washington, 16th November, 1776; exchanged 26th August, 1778; was appointed Captain 11th Virginia, to rank from July, 1776, but was retired 14th September, 1778, being absent, sick. Name also spelled Shepard.

Shepherd, Charlton (N. J.). Captain New Jersey Militia, ——; wounded at Hancock's Bridge, 21st March, 1778.

Shepherd, Jonidab (N. J.). Lieutenant and Captain New Jersey Militia, 1776-1777.

Shepherd, Moses (Conn). Sergeant in Lexington Alarm, April, 1775; Ensign 4th Connecticut, 10th May to December, 1775; Lieutenant of Burrall's Continental Regiment in 1776. (Died 1818.)

Shepherd, William (N. C.). 1st Lieutenant 10th North Carolina, ——, 1777; Captain, 20th January, 1778; retired 1st June, 1778.

Sherburne, Benjamin (R. I.). Ensign of Sherburne's Additional Continental Regiment, 14th January, 1777; 2d Lieutenant, 1st September, 1777; transferred to 1st Rhode Island, 1st January, 1781; retained in Olney's Rhode Island Battalion, 14th May, 1781, and served to 25th December, 1783. (Died 16th June, 1828.)

Sherburne, Edward (N. H.). Major and Aide-de-Camp to General Sullivan, 9th October, 1776; killed at Germantown, 4th October, 1777.

Sherburne, Henry (R. I.). Major 3d Rhode Island, 8th May to December, 1775; Major 15th Continental Infantry, 1st January to 31st December, 1776; taken prisoner near the Cedars, 20th May, 1776; Major 1st Rhode Island, 1st January, 1777; Colonel of one of the Sixteenth Additional Continental Regiments, 12th January, 1777; retired 1st January, 1781.

Sherburne, John Samuel (N. H.). Brigade-Major to General Whipple's Brigade of New Hampshire Militia, ——; wounded (lost leg) at Quaker Hill, 29th August, 1778. (Died 2d August, 1830.)

Sherif, Cornelius (Pa). 1st Lieutenant, 10th Pennsylvania, 4th December, 1776, to ——.

Sherman, Asaph (Mass). 1st Lieutenant of Ward's Massachusetts Regiment, May to December, 1775.

Sherman, Ebenezer (R. I.). 2d Lieutenant of Spalding's Company Rhode Island Artillery, 15th January, 1776, to ——.

Sherman, Henry (R. I.). Ensign of Sherburn's Continental Regiment, 1st September, 1777; Lieutenant, ——, 1779; taken prisoner at Paramus, 16th April, 1780; retained in Olney's Rhode Island Battalion, 14th May, 1781, and served to 25th December, 1783. (Died 8th April, 1829.)

Sherman, Isaac (Conn). Captain 26th Continental Infantry, 1st January, 1776; Major, 10th August, 1776; Lieu-

tenant-Colonel 2d Connecticut, 1st January, 1777; Lieutenant-Colonel Commandant 8th Connecticut, 28th October, 1779; transferred to 5th Connecticut, 1st January, 1781; retired 1st January, 1783. (Died 16th February, 1819.)

Sherman, John (Conn). Paymaster 6th Connecticut, 1st January, 1777—transferred to 4th Connecticut, 1st January, 1781; transferred to 2d Connecticut, 1st January, 1783, and served to June, 1783; had rank of 2d Lieutenant from 7th October, 1777, and as 1st Lieutenant from 10th May, 1780. (Died 1801.)

Sherman, Josiah (Conn). Chaplain 7th Connecticut, 1st January, 1777; resigned 6th December, 1777. (Died 1789.)

Sherman, Roger (R. I.). A signer of the Declaration of Independence; died 23d July, 1793.

Sehrman, William (Conn). Paymaster of Warner's Continental Regiment, 6th July, 1776; retired 1st January, 1781. (Died 26th June, 1789.)

Sherwood, Adiel (N. Y.). 2d Lieutenant 1st New York, October, 1775; taken prisoner in Canada in 1775; 1st Lieutenant, 1st March, 1776; 1st Lieutenant 1st New oYrk, 21st November, 1776, to rank from 1st March, 1776; resigned 16th May, 1780; served subsequently as Captain New oYrk Levies. (Died 12th December, 1824.)

Sherwood, Isaac (N. Y.). 1st Lieutenant 2d New York, 21st November, 1776; died 10th October, 1777, of wounds received at Stillwater, 19th September, 1777.

Sherwood, Seth (N. Y.). Captain New York Militia, ——; prisoner of war, 10th October, 1780, to 11th November, 1782; where taken not stated.

Sherwood, Stephen (N. Y.). Ensign New York Militia, ——; prisoner of war, 4th to 19th March, 1782; where taken not stated.

Shethar, John (Conn). Lieutenant 2d Continental Dragoons, 31st December, 1776; Captain, 11th October, 1777; resigned 8th March, 1780.

Shick, Frederick (Ga). 1st Lieutenant 3d Georgia, 26th April, 1778, and served to October, 1782.

Shick, John (Ga). Lieutenant Georgia Militia; wounded and taken prisoner at Savannah, 18th October, 1779; lost an arm. (Died 1797.)

Shields, John (Va). 1st Lieutenant 1st Virginia State Regiment, 5th March, 1777; Captain, 8th April, 1778; died 16th January, 1779, of wounds received at Monmouth, 28th June, 1778.

Shields, Reuben (Va). 2d Lieutenant 8th Virginia, 10th May, 1777, to ——.

Shiles, Peter (Pa). 2d Lieutenant 10th Pennsylvania, 20th April, 1777; died 5th November, 1777, of wounds received 11th September, 1777, at Brandywine.

Shillington, Thomas.—See **Skillington.**

Shimer, Isaac (Pa). 3d Lieutenant of Baxter's Pennsylvania Battalion of the Flying Camp, 9th July, 1776; wounded and taken prisoner at Fort Washington, 16th November, 1776, and died shortly afterwards.

Shinn, Buddle (N. J.). 2d Lieutenant 3d New Jersey, 29th November, 1776; omitted in 1778.

Shipman, Benoni (Conn). Private in Lexington Alarm, April, 1775; Private 1st Connecticut, 25th May to 20th December, 1775; Sergeant-Major 19th Continental Infantry, 1st January, 1776; Ensign, 10th August, 1776; 2d Lieutenant 2d Connecticut, 1st January, 1777; 1st Lieutenant, 27th May, 1777; Captain Lieutenant, 1st June, 1778; retired 1st January, 1781. (Died 22d May, 1820.)

Shipman, Edward (Conn). Captain 7th Connecticut, 6th July to 18th December, 1775; Captain 19th Continental Infantry, 1st January to 31st December, 1776; served subsequently as Major Connecticut Militia and State Troops.

Shipman, James (N. C.). Captain North Carolina Militia, 1779-1780.

Shipman, Matthias (N. J.). Major anad Lieutenant-Colonel New Jersey Militia, 1776-1778.

Shippen, William, Jr. (Pa). Chief Physician of the Flying Camp, 15th July to 1st December, 1776; Director-General of all Hospitals, 11th April, 1777; resigned 3d January, 1781. (Died 4th November, 1801.)

Shircliff, William (Md). Ensign 3d Maryland Battalion of the Flying Camp, July to December, 1776; 1st Lieutenant 4th Maryland, 10th December, 1776; resigned 1st February, 1778.

Shirtliff, Joseph.—See **Shurtliff.**

Shoemaker, —— (Pa). Lieutenant of Kachlein's Battalion Pennsylvania Militia, ——; taken prisoner at Long Island 27th August, 1776.

Shoemaker, Elijah (Conn). Lieutenant Connecticut Militia, ——; killed at the Wyoming Massacre, 3d July, 1778.

Shoemaker, Jacob (Md). Ensign 4th Maryland, 26th January, 1780; 2d Lieutenant, 14th February, 1780; wounded and taken prisoner at Camden, 16th August, 1780, and died while a prisoner.

Short, William (Va). Major Virginia Militia, 1780-1781.

Shortridge, Richard (N. H.). Captain 2d New Hampshire, 23d May to December, 1775; Captain 8th Continental Infantry, 1st January, 1776; killed at Gwynn's Island, 8th July, 1776.

Shreve, Israel (N. J.). Lieutenant-Colonel 2d New Jersey, 31st October, 1775; Colonel, 28th November, 1776; retired 1st January, 1781. (Died 1799.)

Shreve, John (N. J.). Ensign 2d New Jersey, 15th December, 1776; 2d Lieutenant, 11th July, 1777; 1st Lieutenant, 3d February, 1779; resigned 20th March, 1781. (Died 8th September, 1854.)

Shreve, Samuel (N. J.). Captain and Lieutenant-Colonel New Jersey Militia, 1776-1778.

Shreve, William (N. J.). Major, Lieutenant-Colonel and Colonel New Jersey Militia, 1776-1781.

Shriver, Jacob.—See **Schreiber.**

Shriver, Samuel (Pa). Ensign 3d Pennsylvania Battalion, 8th January, 1776. Deserted 1st November, 1776.

Shrupp, Henry (Pa). Sergeant German Regiment, 20th July, 1776; Ensign, 20th August, 1777; resigned 20th June, 1779.

Shryock, Henry (Md). Lieutenant-Colonel 1st Maryland Battalion of the Flying Camp, July to December, 1776; Lieutenant-Colonel 6th Maryland, 10th December, 1776; resigned 17th April, 1777.

Shubrick, Jacob (S. C.). 2d Lieutenant 1st South Carolina, 17th June, 1775; 1st Lieutenant, 10th May, 1776; Captain, 21st October, 1777; served to ——

Shubrick, Richard (S. C.). 1st Lieutenant 2d South Carolina, 17th June, 1775; Captain 2d South Carolina Artillery, 15th November, 1776; died 8th November, 1777.

Shubrick, Thomas (S. C.). 1st Lieutenant 2d South Carolina, January, 1777; Brigade Major to General Howe, 24th May, 1777, to September, 1778; Captain, 15th January, 1778; Aide-de-Camp to General Greene in 1781. By the act of the 29th October, 1781; it was "Resolved, that Major-General Greene be desired to present the thanks of Congress to Captain Shubrick, his Aide-de-Camp, in testimony of his particular activity and good conduct during the whole action at Eutaw Springs, S. C." Served to close of war.

Shubrick, Thomas, Jr. (S. C.). Ensign South Carolina Militia in 1775.

Shugart, Martin (Md). Ensign German Regiment, 12th July, 1776; 2d Lieutenant, 15th November, 1777; 1st Lieutenant, 25th May, 1778; retired 1st January, 1781.

Shugart, Zacharias (Pa). Lieutenant of Swope's Pennsylvania Battalion of the Flying Camp, 22d August, 1776; wounded and taken prisoner at Fort Washington, 16th November, 1776; exchanged 31st December, 1780.

Shumway, John (Conn). Private in Lexington Alarm, April, 1775; Ensign 7th Connecticut, 6th July to 16th December, 1775; 1st Lieutenant 19th Continental Infantry, 1st January to 31st December, 1776; Captain 1st Connecticut, 1st January, 1777; retired 1st January, 1781.

Shurtliff, Joseph (Mass). Ensign 10th Massachusetts, 6th November, 1776, to 1st September, 1777, when he accepted position in Quartermaster's Department; taken prisoner at Tappan 28th September, 1778. (Name also spelled Shirtliff.)

Shute, Daniel (Mass). Aide-de-Camp to General Lincoln, 27th October, 1777, to January, 1778; Surgeon's Mate Hospital Department, 16th July, 1778, to 16th June, 1779; Surgeon 4th Massachusetts, 11th April, 1782, to June, 1783. (Died 18th April, 1829.)

Shute, John (Pa). 3d Lieutenant 4th Continental Artillery, 1st April, 1777; 2d Lieutenant, ——; 1st Lieutenant, ——; resigned 10th March, 1780. (Died 1848.)

Shute, Samuel Moore (N. J.). Private 2d New Jersey, 31st October, 1775; Ensign, 26th August to November, 1776; Ensign 2d New Jersey, 15th De-

cember, 1776; 2d Lieutenant, 11th September, 1777; 1st Lieutenant, 8th April, 1780; retained in New Jersey battalion April, 1783, and served to 3d November, 1783. (Died 30th August, 1816.)

Shute, Thomas (N. C.). Ensign 10th North Carolina, 19th April, 1777; retired 1st June, 1778. (Died 15th January, 1819.)

Shute, William (N. J.). Captain and Paymaster 2d New Jersey, 28th November, 1775; resigned 2d April, 1778; Ensign and Paymaster 2d New Jersey, 17th June, 1780; retained in New Jersey Battalion, April, 1783, and served to 3d November, 1783; Major 11th United States Infantry, 8th January, 1799; honorably discharged 15th June, 1800.

Shute, William (N. J.). Lieutenant-Colonel New Jersey Militia, 1777-1778.

Sias, Benjamin (N. H.). Captain New Hampshire Militia, 1777-1779.

Sibbio, Thomas.—See Scibbio.

Sibley, Henry (Mass). Private in Brewer's Massachusetts Regiment, April to December, 1775; Sergeant 6th Continental Infantry, 1st January to 31st December, 1776; Ensign 7th Massachusetts, 1st January, 1777; resigned 15th March, 1777.

Sibley, John (Mass). Surgeon's Mate Massachusetts Militia in 1776.

Sickles, Ethan (N. Y.). 2d Lieutenant of Lasher's Regiment New York Militia, ——; cashiered 27th October, 1776.

Sickles, Thomas (N. J.). Ensign 1st New Jersey, 29th December, 1775; 2d Lieutenant, 29th November, 1776; omitted March, 1777.

Sickerly, Barod (Pa). Ensign 2d Pennsylvania, 1st January, 1777; resigned November, 1777.

Sigfried, John (Pa). Major Pennsylvania Militia in 1776.

Sigismund, Ernst (Pa). 1st Lieutenant of Ottendorff's Corps, 29th April, 1777, to ——.

Sigman, John (N. C.). Captain North Carolina Militia at King's Mountain in October, 1780.

Signcross, George (Mass). 2d Lieutenant of Glover's Massachusetts Regiment, 19th May to December, 1775.

Sigourneir, Louis de (——). Captain 3d Cavalry, Pulaski Legion, 2d February, 1778; resigned — October, 1780.

Sill, David Fithian (Conn). Lieutenant in Lexington Alarm, April, 1775; Captain 6th Connecticut, 1st May to 10th December, 1775; Captain 10th Continental Infantry, 1st January to 31st December, 1776; Major 1st Connecticut, 1st January, 1777; Lieutenant-Colonel, 13th March, 1778; retired 1st January, 1781.

Sill, Richard (Conn). Regimental Quartermaster 10th Continental Infantry, 1st January, 1776; Regimental Paymaster, 7th September to 31st December, 1776; Regimental Paymaster 8th Connecticut, 1st January, 1777; 1st Lieutenant, 15th December, 1777; transferred to 1st Connecticut, 1st January, 1781; Captain, 22d April, 1781; Major-Aide-de-Camp to General Alexander, 26th September, 1781, to 15th January, 1783, when he rejoined his regiment and served to 3d June, 1783.

Sill, Thomas (Conn). Private 4th Connecticut, 1st May to 26th November, 1775; 1st Lieutenant of Warner's Additional Continental Regiment, 5th July, 1776; taken prisoner at Hubbardton, 7th July, 1777; Captain, 4th November, 1778; killed 11th October, 1780, near Fort George, Conn.

Silliman, Gold Selleck (Conn). Colonel Connecticut State Regiment, 20th June to 25th December, 1776; Brigadier-General Connecticut Militia, 1777; taken prisoner from his home, 1st May, 1779, and was on parole until exchanged in October, 1780. (Died 21st July, 1790.)

Silsby, Joseph (Pa). Lieutenant of Patton's Continental Regiment, 15th February, 1777; dropped — August, 1777.

Silver, James (Mass). 2d Lieutenant of Bridge's Massachusetts Regiment, April to December, 1775; served subsequently in Massachusetts Militia.

Sim, Patrick (Md). Captain of Smallwood's Maryland Regiment, 20th January to December, 1776; Major, 1st Maryland, 10th December, 1776; Lieutenant-Colonel, 18th February, 1777; resigned 10th June, 1777. (Died 7th January, 1819.)

Simmons, Ephraim (R. I.). Captain of Hillyard's Regiment, Rhode Island Militia, in 1778. (Died 21st February, 1836.)

Simmons, George (R. I.). Captain Rhode Island Militia in 1775.

Simmons, Isaiah (Mass). 2d Lieutenant of Knox's Regiment, Continental Artillery, 10th December, 1775, to 24th November, 1776.

Simmons, Jeremiah (Pa). 1st Lieutenant of Proctor's Company Pennsylvania Artillery, 24th February, 1776; Captain-Lieutenant, 28th May, 1776, and served to 1st October, 1776, when he joined the navy. (Died 1793.)

Simmons, Jonathan (R. I.). Lieutenant of Church's Rhode Island Regiment, 3d May to December, 1775; Lieutenant Rhode Island Militia, in 1779. (Died 1808.)

Simmons, Peleg, Jr. (R. I.). Ensign of Richmond's Rhode Island State Regiment, 19th August, 1776, to May, 1777; Captain Rhode Island Militia in 1781.

Simms, Charles (Va). Major 12th Virginia, 12th November, 1776; Lieutenant-Colonel 6th Virginia, 29th September, 1777; transferred to 2d Virginia, 14th September, 1778; resigned 7th December, 1779. (Died 1819.)

Simms, Edward (Md). Ensign 1st Maryland, 11th September, 1779; resigned 7th February, 1780.

Simms, James (Md). Ensign 1st Maryland, 10th December, 1776; 2d Lieutenant, 17th April, 1777; 1st Lieutenant, 27th May, 1778; taken prisoner at Phillip's Heights, 16th September, 1778, and was a prisoner to January, 1780; did not rejoin regiment. Name also spelled Semmes.

Simms, John (Pa). Ensign 8th Pennsylvania, August, 1776, to ——.

Simms, William (Pa). 2d Lieutenant 4th Pennsylvania, 3d January, 1777; resigned — November, 1777.

Simonds, Benjamin (Mass). Colonel Massachusetts Militia, at Bennington, in August, 1777. (Died 1807.)

Simonds, Daniel (Mass). Private in Bigelow's Massachusetts Regiment, May to December, 1775; Sergeant 15th Massachusetts, 10th March, 1777; Ensign, 1st March, 1779; Lieutenant 13th April, 1780; transferred to 5th Massachusetts, 1st January, 1781. Resigned 8th May, 1782.

Simonds, Jonas (Mass). 2d Lieutenant of Gridley's Regiment of Massachusetts Artillery, May, 1775; 1st Lieutenant of Knox's Regiment Continental Artillery, 10th December, 1775; Captain-Lieutenant, 2d Continental Artillery, 1st January, 1777; Captain, 12th November, 1778; transferred to 4th Continental Artillery, 1st January, 1781; retired 1st January, 1783.

Simonds, Richard (S. C.). Lieutenant South Carolina Dragoons; killed at Eutaw Springs, 8th September, 1781; also reported as of North Carolina Dragoons.

Simonet, John.—See **Valcour.**

Simons, James (S. C.). Cornet South Carolina Dragoons; wounded at Eutaw Springs, 8th September, 1781.

Simons, John (Conn). Captain of Wolcott's Connecticut State Regiment, December, 1775, to March, 1776.

Simons, John (S. C.). Lieutenant 1st South Carolina 10th May, 1776; was a captain in 1780; killed at Quinby's Bridge, 17th July, 1781.

Simons, Peter (N. C.). Captain 5th North Carolina, 16th April, 1776, to ——.

Simpson, Andrew (——). Ensign of Spencer's Continental Regiment, ——, 1779; retired 1st January, 1781.

Simpson, John (Conn). Surgeon 5th Connecticut, 14th August, 1778; transferred to 2d Connecticut, 1st January, 1781, and served to June, 1783.

Simpson, John (Pa). Captain Pennsylvania Battalion of the Flying Camp, taken prisoner at Fort Washington, 16th November, 1776.

Simpson, Michael (Pa). 2d Lieutenant of Thompson's Pennsylvania Rifle Battalion, 25th June, 1775; 1st Lieutenant 1st Continental Infantry, 1st January, 1776; Captain 1st Pennsylvania, 1st December, 1776; retired 17th January, 1781. (Died 1st June, 1813.)

Simpson, Robert (S. C.). Lieutenant 4th South Carolina in 1777.

Simpson, Thomas (N. H.). 2d Lieutenant 3d New Hampshire, 8th November, 1776; 1st Lieutenant, 4th October, 1777; wounded at Bemus' Heights, 19th September, 1777, and at Stillwater, 7th October, 1777; Captain-Lieutenant, 22d May, 1779; resigned 20th July, 1779.

Simrall, Alexander (Pa). 2d Lieutenant 8th Pennsylvania, 9th August, 1776; cashiered, ——, 1777.

Sinclair, James (N. H.). Captain New Hampshire Militia, 1775-1776. (Died 1811.)

Sinclair, Richard (N. H.). Captain New Hampshire Militia, 1776-1780. (Died 1813.)

Singletary, Joseph (N. C.). Lieutenant North Carolina Militia, 1777.

Singletary, William (N. C.). Lieutenant 8th North Carolina, 28th November, 1776; resigned 26th October, 1777.

Singleton, Anthony (Va). Captain 1st Continental Artillery, 7th February, 1777; retired 1st January, 1783. (Died 1795.)

Singleton, John (S. C.). Lieutenant South Carolina Light Horse in 1775.

Singleton, Matthew (S. C.). Captain South Carolina Light Horse in 1775. (Died 1784.)

Singleton, Richard (N. C.). Captain North Carolina Militia in 1776.

Singleton, Richard (S. C.). 1st Lieutenant 2d South Carolina, 17th June, 1775, to ——; was subsequently Colonel South Carolina Militia.

Singleton, Robert (N. C.). Ensign 10th North Carolina, 1777; omitted May, 1778.

Singuefield, Francis (S. C.). Captain 3d South Carolina, November, 1775, to ——.

Sinkler, Robert (N. H.). Captain New Hampshire Militia in 1776.

Sinn, Frederick (S. C.). Surgeon South Carolina Artillery Regiment, 1st January, 1780; taken prisoner at Charleston, 12th May, 1780; exchanged, October, 1780, and served to close of war.

Sinnett, Samuel (Md). Ensign 5th Maryland, 20th February, 1777; resigned 1st June, 1777.

Sitgreaves, John (N. C.). Lieutenant North Carolina Militia in 1776. (Died 4th March, 1802.)

Sizer, William (Conn). Lieutenant of Baldwin's Regiment Artillery Artificer Regiment, 26th July, 1777; Captain 1st May, 1778, and served to — March, 1782.

Skerrett, Clement (Md). 2d Lieutenant 1st Continental Artillery, 5th February, 1778; 1st Lieutenant, 1st October, 1778; Regimental Quartermaster, 6th June, 1779, and served to June, 1783.

Skidmore, John (Va). Captain Virginia Militia, 1777.

Skillings, John (Mass). Captain 11th Massachusetts, 6th November, 1776; died 2d April, 1777.

Skillington, Elijah (Del). Ensign Delaware Regiment, 5th April, 1777; 2d

Lieutenant, 8th September, 1778; taken prisoner at Camden, 16th August, 1780; prisoner on parole to close of war.

Skillington, Thomas (Del). Captain of Patterson's Delaware Battalion of the Flying Camp, July to December, 1776.

Skinner, Abraham (Pa). Ensign 1st Continental Infantry, August to December, 1776; 2d Lieutenant, 1st Pennsylvania, 1st January, 1777; 1st Lieutenant, 13th May, 1777; taken prisoner at Germantown, 4th October, 1777; exchanged June, 1778; Commissary-General of Prisoners, 15th September, 1780, to close of war. (Died 31st July, 1826.)

Skinner, Alexander (Va). Surgeon 1st Virginia, 26th October, 1775; Surgeon of Lee's Battalion of Light Dragoons, 1780 to close of war.

Skinner, Elisha (Mass). Surgeon's-Mate 10th Massachusetts, 6th November, 1776; Surgeon, 1st April, 1777; resigned 12th September, 1780. (Died November, 1827.)

Skinner, Frederick (Md). 1st Lieutenant 3d Maryland Battalion of the Flying Camp, July to December, 1776.

Skinner, James John (Md). Ensign 1st Maryland, 10th December, 1776; 2d Lieutenant 7th Maryland, 7th July, 1777; 1st Lieutenant, 18th September, 1778; transferred to 1st Maryland, 1st January, 1781; retired 1st January, 1783. (Died 1794.)

Skinner, John (Conn). Lieutenant in Lexington Alarm, April, 1775; 2d Lieutenant 4th Connecticut, 1st May to 19th December, 1775; Lieutenant of Wadsworth's Connecticut State Regiment, June to December, 1776; Major Connecticut Militia in 1779.

Skinner, Joseph (Conn). 2d Lieutenant of Chester's Connecticut State Regiment, June to December, 1776.

Skinner, Josiah (N. Y.). Lieutenant New York State Troops, 1781 and 1782.

Skinner, Thomas (Conn). Surgeon 8th Connecticut, 20th March, 1779; transferred to 5th Connecticut, 1st January, 1781, and served to June, 1783.

Skinner, Thomas (Md). 2d Lieutenant 5th Maryland, 20th February, 1777; resigned, 10th December, 1777; Lieutenant and Paymaster of Lee's Battalion of Light Dragoons, 1779 to close of war.

Skirving, Charles (S. C.). 2d Lieutenant 1st South Carolina, 20th December, 1777; was 1st Lieutenant and Regimental Adjutant in 1779; taken prisoner at Charleston, 12th May, 1780.

Skolfield, William (Pa).—See **Schofield.**

Slade, Stephen (N. C.). Quartermaster Sergeant 2d North Carolina, 12th May, 1776; Regimental Quartermaster, 1st January, 1778; Ensign, 5th September, 1778; Lieutenant 11th January, 1780; taken prisoner at Charleston, 12th May, 1780; exchanged, 14th June, 1781; 1st Lieutenant, 13th January, 1781, and served to close of war.

Slade, William (N. C.). Ensign 4th North Carolina, 2d January, 1777; 2d Lieutenant, 26th April, 1777; transferred to 1st North Carolina, 1st June, 1778; Regimental Adjutant, 1st June, 1778; resigned 18th February, 1780. (Died 1791.)

Slake, Christian (Pa).—See **Stake.**

Slangertuffle, —— (——). Captain; was a prisoner; when and where taken not stated.

Slaughter, Augustin (Va). Surgeon 7th Virginia, 1st April, 1776; transferred to 5th Virginia, 1st April, 1778; resigned 20th February, 1779.

Slaughter, George (Va). Captain 8th Virginia, 26th January, 1776; Major 12th Virginia, 4th October, 1777; resigned 23d December, 1777.

Slaughter, James (Va). Lieutenant Virginia Militia, 1778-1781. (Died 1833.)

Slaughter, John (N. C.). Captain 5th North Carolina in 1779.

Slaughter, John (Va). Ensign 12th Virginia, 9th December, 1776; 2d Lieutenant, 1st September, 1777; retired 30th September, 1778.

Slaughter, Joseph (Va). Lieutenant Virginia Militia in 1781.

Slaughter, Lawrence (Va). Lieutenant of Clark's Illinois Regiment, 1779-1781.

Slaughter, Philip (Va). 2d Lieutenant 11th Virginia, 23d July, 1776; 1st Lieutenant, 14th March, 1777; Regimental Paymaster, 14th March, 1777; regiment designated, 7th Virginia, 14th September, 1778; Captain-Lieutenant, 1st November, 1778; Captain, 13th May, 1779; retired 12th February, 1781.

Slaughter, Robert (Va). Ensign 3d Virginia, 12th February, 1776; 2d Lieutenant, 20th June, 1776; resigned 18th December, 1777.

Slaughter, Thomas (Va). Regimental Quartermaster 1st Virginia State Regiment, in 1777-1778.

Slaughter, William (Va). 2d Lieutenant 1st Virginia State Regiment, 7th December, 1778, to 1781.

Slayton, Reuben (Mass). Sergeant Lexington Alarm, April, 1775; Ensign of Learned's Massachusetts Regiment, April to December, 1775; 2d Lieutenant, 3d Continental Infantry, 1st January to 31st December, 1776; Captain 4th Massachusetts, 1st January, 1777; resigned 20th March, 1779.

Slead, Jonathan (Conn). Private in the Lexington Alarm, April, 1775; Ensign 7th Connecticut, 1st January, 1777; died 10th March, 1778.

Sledge, Arthur (N. C.). Ensign 7th North Carolina, 19th December, 1776, to ——.

Sleght, Henry I. (N. Y.). Lieutenant New York Militia in 1781. (Died 1787.)

Sloan, Alexander (Conn). 2d Lieutenant of Elmore's Continental Regiment, 15th April, 1776; 1st Lieutenant 2d Canadian (Hazen's) Regiment, 16th December, 1776; resigned 2d June, 1777.

Sloan, Archibald (N. C.). Lieutenant North Carolina Militia, 1780-1781.

Sloan, David (Pa). 3d Lieutenant of Miles' Pennsylvania Rifle Regiment, 19th March, 1776; 2d Lieutenant, 9th August, 1776; killed at Long Island, 27th August, 1776.

Sloan, John (N. H.). Captain New Hampshire Militia in 1775.

Sloan, Samuel (Mass). Captain in Lexington Alarm, April, 1775; Captain of Paterson's Massachusetts Regiment, May to December, 1775; Captain, 15th Continental Infantry, 1st January to 31st December, 1776; Captain Massachusetts Militia in 1781.

Sloan, Sturgin (Mass). Private in Lexington Alarm, April, 1775; Private in Fellow's Massachusetts Regiment, April to December, 1775; Sergeant 23d Continental Infantry, February to December, 1776; Ensign, 2d Massachusetts, 1st January, 1777; Lieutenant, 21st August, 1781; transferred to 3d Massachusetts, 12th June, 1783, and served to 3d November, 1783.

Slocum, Edward (R. I.). Lieutenant 3d Rhode Island Regiment, 2d June, 1775; taken prisoner at Quebec, 31st December, 1775; exchanged ——, 1776; 1st Lieutenant 1st Rhode Island, 1st January, 1777; Captain, 26th May, 1778; resigned 9th November, 1779.

Slocum, Ezekiel (N. C.). Lieutenant North Carolina Militia in 1776.

Slocum, Peleg (R. I.). Lieutenant of Babcock's Rhode Island State Regiment, 15th January, 1776; Captain of Stanton's Rhode Island State Regiment, 12th December, 1776, to May, 1777.

Sloper, Ambrose (Conn). 1st Lieutenant of Gay's Connecticut State Regiment, June to December, 1776. (Died 1822.)

Sloper, Daniel (Conn). Captain Connecticut Light Horse, 1777-1779. (Died 1789.)

Sloper, Samuel (Conn). Captain of Sheldon's Regiment, Connecticut Light Horse in 1776.

Sloper, Samuel (Mass). Captain Massachusetts Militia, 1779-1780.

Slough, Mathias (Pa). Colonel Pennsylvania Battalion of the Flying Camp, July to December, 1776.

Sluman, John (Mass). 1st Lieutenant of Knox's Regiment Continental Artillery, 10th December, 1775; Captain-Lieutenant 3d Continental Artillery, 1st January, 1777; wounded at Germantown, 4th October, 1777; Captain, 12th September, 1778, and served to 17th June, 1783.

Small, Henry (Pa). Regimental Quartermaster 10th Pennsylvania, 20th April, 1777; resigned — November, 1777.

Small, Jacob (N. Y.). Captain New York Militia, ——; killed at Oriskany, 6th August, 1777.

Smalley, David (N. J.). Captain New-Jersey Militia, 1776-1781.

Smalley, James (Vt). Lieutenant of Olcott's Regiment, Vermont Militia, in 1781.

Smallwood, Hebard (Va). Captain of Grayson's Continental Regiment, 4th February, 1777; resigned — October, 1778.

Smallwood, William (Md). Colonel Maryland Regiment, 14th January, 1776; wounded at White Plains, 28th

October, 1776; Brigadier-General Continental Army, 23d October, 1776; Major-General, 15th September, 1780. By the act of 14th October, 1780, it was "Resolved, that the thanks of Congress be given Brigadiers Smallwood and Gist, and to the officers and soldiers in the Maryland and Delaware Lines, the different Corps of Artillery, Colonel Porterfield's and Major Armstrong's Corps of Light Infantry, and Colonel Armand's Cavalry, for their bravery and good conduct displayed in the action of the 16th of August last, near Camden, in the State of South Carolina." Served to close of war. (Died 14th February, 1792.)

Smart, Thomas (Mass). 2d Lieutenant and Adjutant of Wigglesworth's Massachusetts Militia Regiment, May, 1776; 1st Lieutenant 13th Massachusetts, 1st January, 1777; Captain, 15th June, 1779; transferred to 3d Massachusetts, 1st January, 1781; resigned, 1st February, 1781.

Smith, —— (N. C.). Captain North Carolina Partisan Rangers, ——; killed at Ramsour's Mill, 20th June, 1780.

Smith, Aaron (N. H.). Surgeon of Bedel's Regiment, New Hampshire Rangers, 22d January, to — September, 1776.

Smith, Aaron (N. H.). Ensign of Bedel's Regiment, New Hampshire Rangers, 14th January, 1776; wounded and taken prisoner at The Cedars 19th May, 1776; exchanged December, 1776. (Died 6th June, 1819.)

Smith, Aaron (S. C.). Captain South Carolina Militia in 1775; 1st Lieutenant 2d South Carolina, 18th March, 1778; was in 3d South Carolina in 1779; taken prisoner at Charleston, 12th May, 1780. (Died 1817.)

Smith, Abijah (N. H.). Captain New Hampshire Militia in 1776. (Died 1786.)

Smith, Abraham (Pa). Captain 6th Pennsylvania Battalion, 9th January, 1776, to March, 1777.

Smith, Abraham (Pa). 3d Lieutenant of Miles' Pennsylvania Rifle Regiment, 16th April, 1776; resigned 6th July, 1776.

Smith, Adam (Md). 2d Lieutenant German Regiment, 12th July, 1776; resigned 4th May, 1777.

Smith, Alexander (Md). Private German Regiment, 20th May, 1778; Surgeon's-Mate, 1st August, 1778; retired 1st January, 1783.

Smith, Alexander Lawson (Md). Captain of Stephenson's Maryland and Virginia Rifle Regiment, 13th July, 1776; Captain of Rawlings' Continental Regiment, January, 1777, to rank from July, 13, 1776; Major, 11th September, 1777; resigned 6th September, 1780, with rank of Lieutenant-Colonel.

Smith, Arthur (Va). Captain 4th Virginia, 1st April, 1776; wounded at Germantown, 4th October, 1777, and did not rejoin regiment.

Smith, Ballard (Va). Ensign 1st Virginia, — October, 1776; 2d Lieutenant, 9th August, 1777; 1st Lieutenant, 18th November, 1777; Captain-Lieutenant, 12th May, 1779, and served to close of war; Captain, 1st United States Infantry, 3d June, 1790; Major of Infantry, 2d June, 1792; assigned to 4th Sub Legion, 4th September, 1792; died 20th March, 1794.

Smith, Burrell (Ga). Captain 3d Georgia, 5th July, 1776; resigned 4th April, 1778; Major Georgia Militia; killed at Wofford's Ironworks, 8th August, 1779.

Smith, Benjamin (S. C.). Captain South Carolina Militia in 1775.

Smith, Caleb (Mass). Lieutenant of Woodbridge's Massachusetts Regiment, May to December, 1775; Lieutenant Massachusetts Militia in 1776. (Died 1813.)

Smith, Calvin (Mass). Major of Read's Massachusetts Regiment, May to December, 1775; Major 13th Continental Infantry, 1st January, 1776; Lieutenant-Colonel 6th Massachusetts, 1st November, 1776; Lieutenant-Colonel Commandant 13th Massachusetts, 10th March, 1779; transferred to 6th Massachusetts, 1st January, 1881, and served to 12th June, 1783.

Smith, Charles (Conn). Captain Connecticut Militia in 1777.

Smith, Charles (Md). 2d Lieutenant 1st Maryland, 10th December, 1776; 1st Lieutenant, 20th February, 1778; Captain-Lieutenant, 1st August, 1779; resigned 18th February, 1780. (Died 1822.)

Smith, Charles (Mass). Lieutenant of Sargent's Massachusetts Regiment, May, 1775; deserted, July, 1775.

Smith, Christopher (R. I.). Captain 1st Rhode Island, 28th June to December, 1775; Major 9th Continental Infantry, 1st January to 31st December,

1776; Lieutenant-Colonel of Tallman's Rhode Island State Regiment, January to May, 1777.

Smith, Cotton Mather (Conn). Chaplain 4th Connecticut, June to November, 1775. (Died 27th November, 1806.)

Smith, Daniel (Va). Assistant Deputy Purveyor Southern Department, 20th September, 1781, to close of war. (Died 16th June, 1818.)

Smith, David (Conn). 2d Lieutenant 7th Connecticut, 1st January, 1777; resigned 10th March, 1778.

Smith, David (Conn). Captain of Elmore's Connecticut State Regiment, 15th April, 1776; Captain 8th Connecticut, 1st January, 1777; Major, 13th March, 1778; Brigade-Major and Brigade Inspector, 13th May, 1779, to 13th July, 1781; transferred to 5th Connecticut, 1st January, 1781; transferred to 2d Connecticut, 1st January, 1783, and served to 3d June, 1783.

Smith, Ebenezer (Mass). Private in Lexington Alarm, April, 1775; Private and Sergeant in Fellows' Massachusetts Regiment, May to December, 1775; Ensign, 6th Continental Infantry, 1st January, 1776; 2d Lieutenant, 1st October, 1776; 1st Lieutenant, 13th Massachusetts, 1st January, 1777; Captain, 30th March, 1779; transferred to 6th Massachusetts, 1st January, 1781; transferred to 2d Massachusetts, 1st January, 1783, and served to 3d November, 1783. (Died 1816.)

Smith, Ebenezer (Mass). Private and Sergeant in a Massachusetts Regiment, September, 1775, to January, 1777; 1st Lieutenant, 9th Massachusetts, 1st January, 1777; Captain-Lieutenant, 12th May, 1780; Captain, 6th October, 1780; transferred to 8th Massachusetts, 1st January, 1781; transferred to 2d Massachusetts, 12th June, 1783, and served to 3d November, 1783; Lieutenant-Colonel, 34th United States Infantry, 23d February, 1813; dropped 31st May, 1814. (Died 4th September, 1824.)

Smith, Ebenezer (N H.). Lieutenant-Colonel of Badger's Regiment, New Hampshire's Militia in 1776.

Smith, Ebenezer Augustus (Del). Surgeon's-Mate Hospital Department, August, 1781, to close of war.

Smith, Edward (Md). 2d Lieutenant of Stephenson's Maryland and Virginia Rifle Regiment, 17th July, 1776; taken prisoner at Fort Washington, 16th November, 1776.

Smith, Edward (Va). Lieutenant 7th Virginia; was a prisoner in 1780, when and where taken, not stated; retired 12th February, 1781, on account of being absent as a prisoner.

Smith, Edward Miles (Md). Private Maryland Battalion of the Flying Camp, 18th July to December, 1776; Private and Quartermaster Sergeant, 3d Maryland, 16th March, 1777, to 16th March, 1780; 2d Lieutenant, 1st Maryland, 19th February, 1781, and served to April, 1783.

Smith, Eleazer (N. H.). Lieutenant-Colonel New Hampshire Militia, 1776-1777.

Smith, Elias (Conn). Chaplain 19th Continental Infantry, 1st January, to 31st December, 1776.

Smith, Elihu (Conn). Ensign of Bradley's Connecticut State Regiment, 20th June, 1776; taken prisoner at Fort Washington, 16th November, 1776. (Died 1830.)

Smith, Elijah (Conn). Major Connecticut Militia; taken prisoner at Newark, Conn,. 15th February, 1776.

Smith, Ephraim (Mass). Sergeant in Lexington Alarm, April, 1775; 2d Lieutenant of Whitcomb's Massachusetts Regiment, May to December, 1775.

Smith, Ezra (Conn). Ensign 4th Connecticut, 1st January, 1777; 2d Lieutenant, 31st July, 1777; retired 1st January, 1781.

Smith, Francis (N. H.). Major New Hampshire Militia in 1777.

Smith, Francis (Va). Private 10th Virginia, 1st February, 1777; Corporal 9th June, 1777; Sergeant, February, 1778; Quartermaster Sergeant, March, 1778; transferred to 6th Virginia, 14th September, 1778; Ensign, 5th March, 1780; 2d Lieutenant, 26th May, 1781, and served to close of war.

Smith, Francis Joseph (France). Brevet Ensign Continental Army, 29th July, 1778, to be made use of in case of his being made prisoner while serving as a volunteer in the American Army.

Smith, Frederick (Va). Ensign 15th Virginia, 3d April, 1777; resigned — June, 1777.

Smith, George (Conn). Sergeant-Major of Webb's Additional Continental Regiment, 13th March, 1777; Ensign 16th May, 1778; resigned 6th July, 1779. (Died 13th October, 1822.)

Smith, George (Del). Captain Delaware Militia in 1780.

Smith, George (Mass). Adjutant of Phinney's Massachusetts Regiment, May to December, 1775; Lieutenant and Adjutant, 18th Continental Infantry, 1st January to 31st December, 1776; Captain, 1st Massachusetts, 1st January, 1777; resigned 3d May, 1779.

Smith, George (N. Y.). 2d Lieutenant 4th New York, 21st November, 1776; Judge Advocate Northern Department, 5th October, 1777; served to ——.

Smith, George (Pa). Captain of Lewis' Pennsylvania Battalion of the Flying Camp, July to December, 1776; Captain Delaware Militia, 1780-1781.

Smith, Granville (Va). Captain of Grayson's Continental Regiment, 4th February, 1777; resigned 15th July, 1778.

Smith, Gregory (Va). Captain 7th Virginia, 7th February, 1776; resigned 28th November, 1776; Colonel 2d Virginia State Regiment, June, 1777, to 2d May, 1779.

Smith, Hezekiah (Mass). Chaplain of Nixon's Massachusetts Regiment, May to December, 1775; Chaplain 4th Continental Infantry, 1st January, to 31st December, 1776; Chaplain, 6th Massachusetts, 1st January, 1777; Brigade Chaplain, 18th August, 1778; resigned 13th October, 1780. (Died 22d January, 1805.)

Smith, Isaac (Mass). Major in Lexington Alarm, April, 1775; Lieutenant-Colonel of Little's Massachusetts Regiment, 19th May to December, 1775; Colonel Massachusetts Militia, 1776.

Smith, Isaac (Mass). 1st Lieutenant of Walker's Massachusetts Regiment, May to December, 1775.

Smith, Isaac (N. J.). Colonel New Jersey Militia, 1776.

Smith, Isaac (N. Y.). Surgeon's-Mate 2d New York, 21st November, 1776; Surgeon's-Mate, 3d New Hampshire, 1st August, 1778; Surgeon, 5th April, 1780; resigned 5th August, 1780.

Smith, Isaac (N. Y.). 2d Lieutenant 2d Continental Artillery, 20th August, 1781, and served to 17th June, 1783.

Smith, Israel (Mass). Ensign and Lieutenant of Sargent's Massachusetts Regiment, May to December, 1775; served subsequently as Captain in Quartermaster Department.

Smith, Israel (R. I.). Ensign Rhode Island Militia in 1778.

Smith, Israel (N. Y.). Captain 4th New York, 21st November, 1776; Regimental Paymaster, 1st March, 1779; transferred to 2d New York, 1st January, 1781, and served to June, 1783.

Smith, Jabez (Conn). Surgeon's-Mate of Selden's Connecticut State Regiment, July, 1776; Surgeon's Mate, 5th Connecticut, 1st January, 1777; resigned 15th December, 1778.

Smith, Jabez (N. C.). Ensign 5th North Carolina, January, 1777; 2d Lieutenant, 1st September, 1777; retired 1st June, 1778.

Smith, Jacob (Md). Sergeant German Regiment, 15th July, 1776; Sergeant-Major, 1st October, 1776; Regimental Adjutant, 15th December, 1777; resigned 15th July, 1778.

Smith, James (Md). Captain Lieutenant of Brown's Independent Company, Maryland Artillery, 22d November, 1777; company formed part of the 1st Continental Artillery in May, 1778; transferred to Brown's Company's 24th December, 1781; killed at Combahee Ferry, (S. C.), 27th August, 1782.

Smith, James (Md). 2d Lieutenant 3d Maryland Battalion of the Flying Camp, July to December, 1776; 1st Lieutenant 4th Maryland, 10th December, 1776; Captain, 15th October, 1777; resigned 20th June, 1779.

Smith, James (Mass). Sergeant in Lexington Alarm, April, 1775; 2d Lieutenant of Cotton's Massachusetts Regiment, April to December, 1775; Lieutenant Massachusetts Militia, 1776-1780.

Smith, James (Pa). A signer of the Declaration of Independence; Colonel Pennsylvania Militia, 1775-1776; died 4th July, 1806.

Smith, James (Pa). Colonel Pennsylvania Militia, 1777-1778. (Died 1812.)

Smith, James (Pa). 2d Lieutenant 4th Continental Artillery, 14th March, 1777; taken prisoner at Hancock's Bridge, 21st March, 1778; exchanged 4th December, 1780. He was promoted to rank from 28th November, 1778; Captain-Lieutenant, 3d June, 1779, and served to 17th June, 1783. (Died 14th January, 1835.)

Smith, James (R. I.). Lieutenant 3d Rhode Island, 3d May to December, 1775; served subsequently as Captain Rhode Island Militia.

Smith, James (Va). Sergeant 7th Virginia, March, 1776; Ensign, 9th January, 1777; 2d Lieutenant, 20th May, 1778; transferred to 5th Virginia, 14th September, 1778; taken prisoner at Germantown, 4th October, 1777; omitted in May, 1779, being absent a prisoner.

Smith, Jared (Mass). 2d Lieutenant of Whitcomb's Massachusetts Regiment, May to December, 1775; 2d Lieutenant 12th Continental Infantry, 1st January, 1776, to ——.

Smith, Jeremiah (N. J.). 2d Lieutenant 2d New Jersey, 28th November, 1775, 1st Lieutenant, 29th November, 1776, and served to ——; served subsequently as Lieutenant-Colonel New Jersey Militia in 1777.

Smith, Job (Conn). Paymaster 5th Connecticut, 1st January, 1777, to 1st September, 1778, when he resigned.

Smith, Joel (Mass). Captain of Glover's Massachusetts Regiment, May to December, 1775.

Smith, Joel (Conn). Private 3d Connecticut, 20th April, 1777; Corporal, 14th February, 1778; Sergeant, 1st March, 1778; Ensign, 20th April, 1780; transferred to 4th Connecticut, 1st January, 1781; transferred to 2d Connecticut, 1st January, 1783, and served to 3d June, 1783.

Smith, John (Conn). 2d Lieutenant of Webb's Continental Regiment, 1st January, 1777; 1st Lieutenant, 8th April 1777; transferred to Sherburne's Continental Regiment, 22d April, 1779; resigned 21st March, 1780. (Died 16th February, 1807.)

Smith, John (Conn). 1st Lieutenant of Sherburne's Continental Regiment, 1st January, 1777; resigned 22d March, 1780. (Died 1811.)

Smith, John (Conn). Lieutenant Connecticut Militia; wounded at Compo Hill, 28th April, 1777. (Died 16th February, 1807.)

Smith, John (Md). 2d Lieutenant 2d Maryland Battalion of the Flying Camp, July to December, 1776; 1st Lieutenant 3d Maryland, 10th December, 1776; Captain, 1st January, 1777; wounded at Savannah, 9th October,

1779; wounded and taken prisoner at Camden, 16th August, 1780; transferred to 5th Maryland, 1st January, 1781; prisoner on parole to close of war; Brevet-Major, 30th September, 1783.

Smith, John (Md). Ensign Maryland Battalion of the Flying Camp, July to December, 1776; 1st Lieutenant 6th Maryland, 10th December, 1776; Captain, 9th November, 1777; transferred to 3d Maryland, 1st January, 1781; wounded at Guilford, 15th March, 1781; wounded and taken prisoner at Hobkirk's Hill, 25th April, 1781; exchanged, ——, 1781, and served to April, 1783.

Smith, John (N. Y.). Ensign of Lee's Additional Continental Regiment, 10th January, 1777; retired 23d April, 1779.

Smith, John (Mass). Ensign 6th Continental Infantry, 1st January, 1776; 2d Lieutenant, 5th October, 1776; 2d Lieutenant 3d Massachusetts, 1st January, 1777; 1st Lieutenant, 1st May, 1779, and served to June, 1783.

Smith, John (Mass). Sergeant in Lexington Alarm, April, 1775; 1st Lieutenant of Ward's Massachusetts Regiment, 23d May to December, 1775.

Smith, John (N. Y.). Ensign of Malcolmn's Additional Continental Regiment, February, 1777; resigned 1st March, 1778.

Smith, John (N. Y.). 2d Lieutenant 2d Continental Artillery, 29th June, 1781, and served to June, 1783; Captain United States Infantry Regiment, 21st October, 1786; Captain 1st Infantry United States Army, 29th September, 1789; Major 2d Infantry, 28th December, 1791; assigned to 4th Sub Legion, 4th September, 1792; resigned 1st October, 1793, Lieutenant-Colonel 5th United States Infantry, 24th April, 1799; honorably discharged, 15th June, 1800; Lieutenant-Colonel 3d United States Infantry, 9th January, 1809; died 6th June, 1811.

Smith, John (N. C.). Ensign 9th North Carolina, 28th November, 1776, to ——.

Smith, John (Pa). 1st Lieutenant of Montgomery's Pennsylvania Battalion of the Flying Camp; taken prisoner at Fort Washington, 16th November, 1776.

Smith, John (Va). Colonel Virginia Militia in 1776. (Died 1836.)

Smith, John (Va). Ensign 4th Virginia, 14th March, 1776; 2d Lieutenant,

1st September, 1776; 1st Lieutenant, 12th March, 1777; resigned 26th May, 1778.

Smith, John (Va). Adjutant 8th Virginia, 1st January, 1778; retired 30th September, 1778.

Smith, John Carraway (S. C.). 2d Lieutenant 2d South Carolina, 1st September, 1775; 1st Lieutenant, May, 1776; Captain, 16th September, 1776; wounded at Savannah, 9th October, 1777; was in 3d South Carolina, in 1779; taken prisoner at Charleston, 12th May, 1780; exchanged November, 1780, and served to close of war. Bervet-Major, 30th September, 1783.

Smith, John Kilby (Mass). Ensign of Brewer's Massachusetts Regiment, May to December, 1775; 2d Lieutenant 6th Continental Infantry, 1st January to 31st December, 1776; 1st Lieutenant and Adjutant 13th Massachusetts, 1st January, 1777; Captain, 12th February, 1778; transferred to 6th Massachusetts, 1st January, 1781; transferred to 2d Massachusetts, 12th June, 1783, and served to 3d November, 1783. (Died 7th August, 1842.)

Smith, John N. (Mass). 2d Lieutenant of Henley's Additional Continental Regiment, 16th July, 1777; retired 23d April, 1779.

Smith, John Sim (Va). 2d Lieutenant of Armand's Partisan Corps, 1780-1781.

Smith, Jonathan (Mass). Colonel Massachusetts Militia in 1776.

Smith, Jonathan (R. I.). Lieutenant 3d Rhode Island, 3d May to December, 1775; Lieutenant Rhode Island Militia in 1778. (Died 1841.)

Smith, Jonathan (Va). Ensign 8th Virginia, 17th March, 1777; taken prisoner at Germantown, 4th October, 1777; exchanged, 15th December, 1780; 2d Lieutenant, 4th April, 1778; 1st Lieutenant, 24th September, 1779; transferred to 5th Virginia, 12th February, 1781; retired 1st January, 1783. (Died 1847.)

Smith, Jonathan Bayard (Pa). Lieutenant-Colonel Pennsylvania Associaters in 1777. (Died 16th June, 1812.)

Smith, Joseph (Conn). 2d Lieutenant of Selden's Connecticut State Regiment, June to December, 1776.

Smith, Joseph (Conn). Captain 5th Connecticut, 1st May to 11th November, 1775. (Died 1810.)

Smith, Joseph (Md). Captain of Gist's Additional Continental Regiment, 31st May, 1777; retired 1st January, 1781.

Smith, Joseph (Mass). Sergeant of Paterson's Massachusetts Regiment, May to December, 1775; Ensign 5th Massachusetts, 1st January, 1777; Regimental Quartermaster, 10th September to 9th November, 1777; 2d Lieutenant, 7th November, 1777; 1st Lieutenant, 1st March, 1778, and served to June, 1783; Captain 45th United States Infantry, 21st April, 1814; resigned 1st September, 1814.

Smith, Joseph (Mass). 1st Lieutenant 4th Continental Infantry, 1st January, 1776, to ——.

Smith, Joseph Sim (Md). Cornet 1st Battalion of Cavalry, Armand's Partisan Corps, 1780 to 1782. (Died —— 1822.)

Smith, Josiah (Mass). 1st Lieutenant of Woodbridge's Massachusetts Regiment, May to December, 1775; Captain 10th Massachusetts, 1st January, 1777; retired 1st January, 1781.

Smith, Josiah (Mass). Private in Cotton's Massachusetts Regiment, May to December, 1775; Sergeant and Sergeant-Major, 10th Massachusetts, 9th January, 1777, until appointed Ensign, 2d April, 1779; Lieutenant, 27th March, 1780; transferred to 6th Massachusetts, 1st January, 1783, and served to June, 1783. (Died 20th June, 1848.)

Smith, Josiah (N. Y.). Colonel New York Militia in 1776.

Smith, Josiah (N. Y.). Lieutenant New York Militia; wounded at Stamford, (Conn.), 27th May, 1782.

Smith, Larkin (Va). Private Company of Minute Men, November, 1775; Cadet 6th Virginia, 10th February, 1776; Cornet 4th Continental Dragoons, 1st August, 1777; Lieutenant, 4th September, 1778; Captain, 1st April, 1780, and served to close of war.

Smith, Manassah (Mass). Chaplain of Whitcomb's Massachusetts Regiment, May to December, 1775. (Died 1823.)

Smith, Martin (Mass). Ensign 3d Continental Infantry, 1st January to 31st December, 1776; Lieutenant 4th Massachusetts, 1st January, 1777; resigned 3d January, 1778.

Smith, Matthew (Pa). Captain of Thompson's Pennsylvania Rifle Battalion, 25th June, 1775; Captain 1st Continental Infantry, 1st January, 1776; resigned November, 1776; Major 9th Pennsylvania, 11th January, 1777, to rank from 27th September, 1776; his resignation as Lieutenant-Colonel, 7th February, 1777; resigned 23d February, 1778. (Died 1794.)

Smith, Matthew (Va). Captain 1st Continental Artillery, to rank from 30th November, 1776, and served to ——.

Smith, Matthew (Va). 2d Lieutenant 1st Virginia, 22d January, 1776; 1st Lieutenant, 15th August, 1777; retired 14th September, 1778.

Smith, Minor (N. C.). Captain North Carolina Militia; wounded at King's Mountain, 7th October, 1780; is also reported as being from Virginia.

Smith, Nathan (Md). Private and Sergeant 1st Maryland, 10th May, 1777, to September, 1779; 2d Lieutenant 4th Maryland, 15th September, 1779; 1st Lieutenant, 14th February, 1780; resigned 4th July, 1781.

Smith, Nathan (Mass). 1st Lieutenant of Gardner's Massachusetts Regiment, May to December, 1775; 1st Lieutenant 25th Continental Infantry, 1st January, 1776; Captain, August to 31st December, 1776. (Died 17th February, 1825.)

Smith, Nathan (N. H.). 2d Lieutenant Green Mountain Boys, 27th July to December, 1775.

Smith, Nathan (Va). Surgeon's-Mate 6th Virginia, 1781-1783.

Smith, Nathaniel (Md). Captain Independent Company Baltimore Artillery, 14th January, 1776, to ——.

Smith, Nathaniel (Pa). Ensign 4th Pennsylvania, 5th July, 1779; 2d Lieutenant, 10th August, 1779; 1st Lieutenant, 23d July, 1780; transferred to 5th Pennsylvania, 17th January, 1781; transferred to 3d Pennsylvania, 1st January, 1783, and served to June, 1783.

Smith, Nath'l. (Vt). Captain Vermont Militia in 1777.

Smith, Obediah (Va). Ensign 5th Virginia, February, 1777; 2d Lieutenant, 10th December, 1777; transferred to 3d Virginia, 14th September 1778; resigned 25th April, 1779.

Smith, Oliver (Conn). Major, Lieutenant-Colonel and Colonel Connecticut Militia, 1775-1782.

Smith, Peter (Pa). Sergeant 2d Pennsylvania Battalion, 15th January, 1776; Ensign 3d Pennsylvania, 11th November, 1776; Regimental Quartermaster, 2d June, 1778; 2d Lieutenant, 18th June, 1778; 1st Lieutenant, 13th August, 1779; transferred to 5th Pennsylvania, 17th January, 1781; retired 1st January, 1783.

Smith, Press. (S. C.). 2d Lieutenant 2d South Carolina, 17th June, 1775, to ——.

Smith, Richard (Md). Captain Maryland Battalion of the Flying Camp, July to December, 1776.

Smith, Robert (N. Y.). Captain New York Militia in 1775; Captain of Malcolm's New York Militia Regiment, June, 1776; wounded at White Plains, 28th October, 1776; Captain of Malcolm's Continental Regiment, — January, 1777; wounded at Monmouth, 28th June, 1778; did not return to regiment. (Died 1838.)

Smith, Robert (N. C.). 1st Lieutenant 2d North Carolina, 1st September, 1775; Captain 4th North Carolina, 16th April, 1776; transferred to 3d Continental Dragoons, 9th January, 1777; resigned, 4th November, 1778.

Smith, Robert (Pa). Captain Chester County, Pennsylvania, Militia in 1775; in charge of the defences and obstructions in the Delaware river in 1776; Colonel Chester County Militia in 1777. (Died, December, 1803.)

Smith, Robert (S. C.). Chaplain in Hospital Department in South Carolina, 1780 to 1783.

Smith, Roger (S. C.). Captain South Carolina Militia in 1775.

Smith, Royal (R. I.). Ensign of Richmond's Rhode Island State Regiment, 1st November, 1775; Captain 19th August, 1776; Captain of Stanton's Rhode Island State Regiment, 12th December, 1776, to May, 1777.

Smith, Samuel (Del). Captain Delaware Regiment, 20th January, 1777, to ——.

Smith, Samuel (Md). Captain of Smallwood's Maryland Regiment, 14th January, 1776; Major 4th Maryland, 10th December, 1776; Lieutenant-Colonel, 22d February, 1777; wounded at Fort Mifflin, 23d October, 1777. By the Act of 4th November, 1777, it was "Resolved, that Congress have a high sense of the merit of Lieutenant-

Colonel Smith, and the officers and men under his command, in their late gallant defense of Fort Mifflin, on the river Delaware, and that an elegant sword be provided by the Board of War and presented to Lieutenant-Colonel Smith." Resigned 22d May, 1779; Major-General Maryland Militia 1812. (Died 22d April, 1839.)

Smith, Samuel (Md). 2d Lieutenant 2d Maryland, 20th February, 1777; died June, 1777.

Smith, Samuel (N. Y.). 1st Lieutenant 3d New York, 14th July, 1775, to January, 1776.

Smith, Samuel (N. C.). Ensign 2d North Carolina, 3d May, 1776, to ——.

Smith, Samuel (Pa). 2d Lieutenant 8th Pennsylvania, 9th August, 1776; 1st Lieutenant, 13th July, 1777; killed at Germantown, 4th October, 1777.

Smith, Samuel (Pa). 2d Lieutenant 6th Pennsylvania, 15th February, 1777; killed 27th May, 1777; where, not stated.

Smith, Samuel (Pa). 1st Lieutenant 4th Pennsylvania Battalion, 5th January, 1776; Captain 5th Pennsylvania, 1st March, 1777; retired 17th January, 1781; Brigadier-General Pennsylvania Volunteers War of 1812. (Died 17th September, 1835.)

Smith, Samuel (Pa). 2d Lieutenant 1st Pennsylvania, 13th March, 1777; resigned 26th March, 1778.

Smith, Samuel (Va). Captain 15th Virginia, 22d November, 1776; regiment designated 11th Virginia, 14th September, 1778; served to ——.

Smith, Samuel (Va). Captain Lieutenant 1st Continental Artillery, 22d November, 1777, to ——. (In service August, 1778.)

Smith, Samuel (Va). Surgeon Virginia Regiment, ——; in service in 1777.

Smith, Seth (Mass). 2d Lieutenant of Danielson's Massachusetts Regiment, May to December, 1775; 2d Lieutenant 3d Continental Infantry, 1st January to 31st December, 1776. (Died 6th July, 1830.)

Smith, Simeon (Conn). Captain of Bradley's Connecticut State Regiment, June to December, 1776.

Smith, Simeon (Mass). 1st Lieutenant in Lexington Alarm, April, 1775; 1st Lieutenant of Paterson's Massachusetts Regiment May to December, 1775;

Captain of Cady's Massachusetts Battalion in the Expedition to Canada, January to June, 1776; Captain of Warner's Continental Regiment, 5th July, 1776; taken prisoner at Fort Stanwix, 22d August, 1777; exchanged ——; retired 1st January, 1781.

Smith, Simeon (R. I.). Ensign 1st Rhode Island, 7th May, 1777; resigned 15th January, 1778.

Smith, Sylvanus (Mass). Lieutenant Company of Minute Men at Lexington, 19th April, 1775; 1st Lieutenant of Whitcomb's Massachusetts Regiment, May to December, 1775; 1st Lieutenant 12th Continental Infantry, 1st January to 31st December, 1776; Captain 15th Massachusetts, 1st January, 1777; transferred to 5th Massachusetts, 1st January, 1781; transferred to 1st Massachusetts, 12th June, 1783, and served to 3d November, 1783; Brevet Major, 30th September, 1783. (Died 12th May, 1830.)

Smith, Thomas (N. J.). Ensign 2d New Jersey, 29th November, 1776; resigned 5th February, 1777.

Smith, Thomas (Pa). Major Pennsylvania Militia in 1776 and 1777.

Smith, Thomas (Va). Captain Virginia Militia, 1778.

Smith, Timothy (Mass). Surgeon's Mate of Whitney's Regiment Massachusetts Militia, 10th April to 1st August, 1776; Surgeon's Mate 2d Massachusetts, 1st January, 1777; resigned 12th September, 1780.

Smith, Walter (Md). Surgeon Maryland Militia, 1776 and 1777.

Smith, William (Conn). Ensign 19th Continental Infantry, 1st January to 31st December, 1776; 1st Lieutenant 6th Connecticut, 1st January, 1777; Captain Lieutenant, 25th August, 1780; retired 1st January, 1781.

Smith, William (Mass). Captain Company of Minute Men at Concord, 19th April, 1775; Captain of Nixon's Massachusetts Regiment, May to December, 1775.

Smith, William (Mass). Lieutenant of Woodbridge's Massachusetts Regiment, May to December, 1775; 1st Lieutenant 8th Continental Infantry, 1st January to 31st December, 1776.

Smith, William (Pa). Surgeon 1st Battalion **Pennsylvania Flying** Camp, July to December, 1776.

Smith, William (Va). Ensign 5th Virginia, 25th March, 1776, to ——.

Smith, William (Va). 2d Lieutenant 15th Virginia, 20th December, 1776; 1st Lieutenant, 20th March, 1777; regiment designated 11th Virginia, 14th September, 1778, and served to ——. Was in service January, 1780. (Died 1823.)

Smith, William (Va). Captain 11th Virginia, 22d November, 1776; resigned 5th July, 1777.

Smith, William (Va). 2d Lieutenant 10th Virginia, December, 1776; resigned 10th July, 1777.

Smith, William (Va). 2d Lieutenant 15th Virginia, 21st November, 1776; 1st Lieutenant, 4th July, 1777; killed at Germantown, 4th October, 1777.

Smith, William Hooker (Pa). Surgeon's Mate Hospital Department at Wilkes Barre, Pa, 3d July, 1778, to close of war. (Died 1835.)

Smith, William P. (—). Surgeon's Mate in Hospital Department in 1780.

Smith, William Stephens (N. Y.). Major and Aide-de-Camp to General Sullivan, 15th August, 1776; Lieutenant-Colonel of Lee's Additional Continental Regiment, 1st January, 1777; transferred to Spencer's Regiment, 22d April, 1779; continued as Adjutant and Inspector on staff of General Lafayette, 1st January to July, 1781; Lieutenant-Colonel Aide-de-Camp to General Washington, 6th July, 1781, to 23d December, 1783. (Died 10th June, 1816.)

Smith, William Stirling (Va). Sergeant 10th Virginia, 1st February, 1777; Sergeant-Major, 8th November, 1777; Regimental Quartermaster, 1st March, 1778; 2d Lieutenant, 9th September, 1778; transferred to 6th Virginia, 14th September, 1778; 1st Lieutenant, ——, 1780; taken prisoner at Charleston, 12th May, 1780. (Died 1829.)

Smock, Barnes (N. J.). Captain New Jersey Militia; taken prisoner at Connecticut Farms, 23d June, 1780.

Smock, Hendrick (N. J.). Captain New Jersey Militia Artillery Company, 1775-1777.

Smock, John (N. J.). Lieutenant-Colonel New Jersey Militia ; taken prisoner at Bordentown, 8th May, 1778. (Died 1808.)

Smoot, William (Md). Sergeant 2d Maryland, April, 1777; 2d Lieutenant, 16th March, 1781; retired 1st January, 1783.

Smyser, Michael (Pa). Captain of Swope's Pennsylvania Battalion of the Flying Camp; taken prisoner at Fort Washington, 16th November, 1776. (Died 1810.)

Smyth, Thomas (Md). 1st Lieutenant of Smallwood's Maryland Regiment, 14th January, 1776; Captain 4th Maryland Battalion of the Flying Camp, July to December, 1776 Major 5th Maryland, 10th December, 1776; resigned 12th March, 1778. (Died 1819.)

Snead, Charles (Va). Ensign 9th Virginia, 10th February, 1776; 1st Lieutenant, 10th February, 1777 ;transferred to 8th Virginia, September, 1778; Captain, 12th May, 1779; transferred to 5th Virginia, 12th February, 1781, and served to close of war.

Snead, Smith (Va). 1st Lieutenant 9th Virginia, 10th February, 1776; Captain, 31st August, 1776; taken prisoner at Germantown, 4th October, 1777; exchanged 2d November, 1780; retained in 2d Virginia, 12th February, 1781, with rank of Major from 9th December, 1779, and served to close of war.

Snead, Thomas (Va). Captain 9th Virginia, 14th February, 1776; Major 11th Virginia, 1st April, 1777; resigned 8th March, 1778.

Snicker, S. William (Va). Captain of Thruston's Continental Regiment, — March, 1777; resigned 31st January, 1778.

Snipes, William Clay (S. C.). Captain South Carolina Rangers under General Marion, 1776-1781.

Snook, Philip (N. J.). Captain New Jersey Militia, ——; wounded at Monmouth, 28th June, 1778.

Snow, Benjamin (Mass). Private in Lexington Alarm, April, 1775; Sergeant of Learned's Massachusetts Regiment, May to December, 1775; Ensign 16th Continental Infantry, 1st January to 31st December, 1776.

Snow, Eleazer (Mass). Lieutenant of Sargent's Massachusetts Regiment, May to December, 1775.

Snow, Ephraim (N. Y.). Ensign 4th New York, 21st March, 1776; 2d Lieutenant 1st New York, 21st November, 1776; 1st Lieutenant 26th March, 1779, and served to June, 1783.

Snow, Jabez (Mass). Sergeant 21st Continental Infantry, 1st January, 1776; Ensign, 12th July, 1776; 1st Lieutenant 3d Massachusetts, 1st January, 1777; resigned 10th April, 1780.

Snow, Lemuel (Mass). 1st Lieutenant 4th Massachusetts, 1st January, 1777; resigned 23d October, 1781.

Snow, Silas (Del). Lieutenant Delaware Militia; taken prisoner from his home, 4th May, 1778.

Snow, William (S. C.). Captain South Carolina Militia in 1776.

Snowden, Jonathan (N. J.). Ensign 1st New Jersey, 26th April, 1777; 2d Lieutenant, 14th April, 1778; 1st Lieutenant, 26th October, 1779; transferred to Lee's Battalion of Light Dragoons in 1780; wounded at Guilford, 15th March, 1781; Aide-de-Camp to General Hand May, 1781, to close of war; Captain in the Levies in 1791; Military Storekeeper United States Army, 5th May, 1808; died 25th December, 1824.

Snowden, Nathaniel (N. C.). Lieutenant 10th North Carolina, 5th June, 1778, to ——.

Snowden, William (N. C.). Lieutenant 7th North Carolina, 28th November, 1776, to ——.

Snyder, Jeremiah (—). Captain; was a prisoner; when and where taken not stated; made his escape in September, 1782.

Snyder, Johannes (N. Y.). Major, Lieutenant-Colonel and Colonel New York Militia, 1775-1782. (Died 1794.)

Snyder, Philip (Pa). Ensign 6th Pennsylvania, 21st August, 1777; retired 21st June, 1778. (Died 20th October, 1793.)

Somers, James (N. J.). Lieutenant New Jersey Militia in 1777.

Somers, Richard (N. J.). Colonel New Jersey Militia, 1776-1777.

Sommervell, James (Md). Ensign Maryland Battalion of the Flying Camp, July to December, 1776; 2d Lieutenant 6th Maryland, 10th December, 1776; 1st Lieutenant, 20th February, 1777; Captain Lieutenant, 1st April, 1778; Captain, 1st June, 1779; wounded and lost an arm at Camden, 16th August, 1780; transferred to 5th Maryland, 1st January, 1781; retired 1st January, 1783. (Died 1815.)

Soper, Amasa (Mass). Lieutenant in Lexington Alarm, April, 1775; 1st Lieutenant of Danielson's Massachusetts Regiment, May to 15th November, 1775; Captain 10th Massachusetts, 6th November, 1776; resigned 30th October, 1780. (Died 1st November, 1818.)

Soper, Joseph (N. H.). Lieutenant 1st New Hampshire, 23d April to December, 1775; 2d Lieutenant 5th Continental Infantry, 1st January, 1776; 1st Lieutenant, 10th August to 31st December, 1776.

Soper, Oliver (Mass). 1st Lieutenant in Lexington Alarm, April, 1775; Captain of Walker's Massachusetts Regiment, May to December, 1775; Captain 13th Continental Infantry, 1st January to 31st December, 1776. (Died 8th August, 1821.)

Soper, Solomon (Vt). Lieutenant Vermont Militia in 1777.

Soulé, Charles W. (Mass). Ensign 6th Massachusetts, 2d April, 1781; resigned 4th December, 1782.

Soulé, John (Mass). Ensign 5th Massachusetts, 1st January, 1777; 2d Lieutenant, 26th December, 1777; 1st Lieutenant, 3d October, 1780; resigned 30th March, 1781.

Soulé, Moses (Mass). Lieutenant in Lexington Alarm, April, 1775; Captain of Fellows' Massachusetts Regiment, May to December, 1775; Captain 6th Continental Infantry, 1st January, 1776; resigned 30th September, 1776.

Southall, Stephen (Va). Ensign 15th Virginia, 12th March, 1778, 2d Lieutenant 2d North Carolina, 1st April, 1778; resigned 4th October, 1778; 1st Lieutenant 1st Continental Artillery, 1st February, 1781; retired 1st January, 1783.

Southerland, John (Va). 2d Lieutenant 4th Virginia, February 1776; died 22d February, 1777.

Southerland, Ransom (N. C.). Commissary 4th North Carolina, 23d April, 1776, to ——.

Southmayd, Danied (Conn). Surgeon's Mate 2d Connecticut May to December, 1775.

Southworth, Jedediah (Mass). 2d Lieutenant of Read's Massachusetts Regiment, May to December, 1775.

Southworth, Thomas (Va). Lieutenant of a Virginia Regiment in 1779.

Southworth, William (R. I.). Ensign 3d Rhode Island, 28th June to December, 1775.

Sowers Seth (Mass). Captain Massachusetts Militia in 1776.

Spain, Augustin (N. C.). Captain North Carolina Militia, 1780-1781.

Spalding, Ebenezer (Mass). Corporal in Lexington Alarm, April, 1775; 1st Lieutenant of Prescott's Massachusetts Regiment, May to December, 1775; 1st Lieutenant 7th Continental Infantry, 1st January to 31st December, 1776. (Died 1808.)

Spalding, Edward (Mass). 1st Lieutenant of Prescott's Massachusetts Regiment, May to December, 1775; 1st Lieutenant 23d Continental Infantry, 1st January to 31st December 1776; Captain Massachusetts Militia, 1777-1781.

Spalding Edward (R. I.). Captain of Elliott's Rhode Island State Artillery Regiment, 15th January to November, 1776.

Spalding, John (Conn). Surgeon 3d Connecticut, 1st May to 4th October, 1775; Surgeon 20th Continental Infantry 1st January to 31st December, 1776.

Spalding, Joseph (Mass). Sergeant Lexington Alarm, April 1775; 1st Lieutenant of Prescott's Massachusetts Regiment, 30th April, 1775; killed at Bunker Hill 17th June, 1775.

Spalding, Josiah (Conn). Lieutenant Connecticut Militia, ——; wounded at Quaker Hill, 29th August, 1778. (Died 1799.)

Spalding, Levi (N. H.). Captain 3d New Hampshire 23d May to December, 1775; Captain 2d Continental Infantry, 1st January to 31st December, 1776. (Died 1st March, 1825)

Spalding, Oliver (Vt). Lieutenant of Bedel's Regiment Vermont Militia, 15th December 1777, to 1st April 1778.

Spalding, Simon (Conn). 2d Lieutenant of Ransom's Wyoming Valley Company, 26th August, 1776; 1st Lieutenant, 1st January 1777; Captain, 24th June ,1778; transferred to 1st Connecticut, 1st January, 1781; retired 1st January, 1783 (Died 24th January, 1814.)

Spalding, Thomas (Mass). Sergeant of Prescott's Massachusetts Regiment, 28th April, 1775; 2d Lieutenant 17th June to December, 1775.

Spangler, Joseph (Pa). Major York County, Pennsylvania, Militia in 1775.

Sparhawk Nathaniel (Mass). Colonel Massachusetts Militia, 1776-1779.

Sparks, Daniel (S. C.). Captain South Carolina Militia, 1779-1781.

Sparks, Henry, Jr. (N. J.). Major New Jersey Militia in 1777.

Sparks John, Jr. (N. J.). Ensign 2d New Jersey 11th November, 1775; 2d Lieutenant, 10th May, 1776; 1st Lieutenant, 1st January, 1777; Captain, 1st January, 1778; resigned 8th September, 1778. (Died 30th April 1826.)

Sparks, William (Pa). Captain Westmoreland County, Pennsylvania, Militia in 1778.

Sparrow, Edward (Mass). 2d Lieutenant of Cotton's Massachusetts Regiment, May to November, 1775; 2d Lieutenant, 23d Continental Infantry, 1st January to 31st December 1776.

Speakman, Gilbert Warner (Mass). Captain 14th Continental Infantry, 1st January to 31st December, 1776; Commissary of Military Stores, 1777-1780.

Spear, Edward (Pa). Ensign Pennsylvania State Regiment, 8th May, 1777; regiment designated 13th Pennsylvania, 12th November, 1777; 2d Lieutenant, 7th February, 1778; transferred to 6th Pennsylvania, 1st July ,1778; 1st Lieutenant 16th May, 1781; transferred to 1st Pennsylvania, 1st January, 1783, and served to 3d November, 1783; Lieutenant United States Artillery Battalion, 10th September, 1787; Lieutenant Artillery United States Army, 20th September, 1779; killed 4th November, 1791, in action with Indians near Fort Recovery, Ohio ("St. Clear's defeat.")

Spear, John (Pa). 1st Lieutenant of Miles' Pennsylvania Rifle Regiment, 6th April, 1776; wounded and taken prisoner at Long Island, 27th August, 1776; Captain Pennsylvania State Regiment, 6th February, 1777; regiment designated 13th Pennsylvania, 12th November, 1777; died 8th February 1778.

Speck, Henry (Pa). Sergeant German Regiment, 30th July, 1776; Ensign, 24th July, 1778; resigned 20th June, 1779.

Speed, —— (N. C.). Captain North Carolina Militia; wounded at Stono Ferry 20th June, 1779.

Speed James (Va). Lieutenant of Cocke's Virginia Militia Regiment, ——; wounded at Guilford 15th March, 1781. (Died 1811.)

Speller Benjamin C. (Va). 2d Lieutenant 7th Virginia, 26th February, 1776, to ——.

Spencer, —— (S. C.). Captain 5th South Carolina, ——; resigned 10th December, 1777, and appointed same date as Deputy Quartermaster-General of South Carolina.

Spencer, Ebenezer (R. I.). Captain and Major Rhode Island Militia, 1775-1778.

Spencer, David (Conn). Private in Lexington Alarm, April, 1775; Sergeant 16th Connecticut, 16th May to 17th December, 1775 2d Lieutenant 1st Connecticut, 1st January, 1777; 1st Lieutenant, 6th February, 1778; wounded at Horse Neck, 14th October, 1778, and retired 15th November 1778　,

Spencer, Elihu (—). Hospital Chaplain 1777-1781.

Spencer, Gideon (Va). Lieutenant of a Virginia State Regiment ,1778 to 1781.*

Spencer, Ichabod (Conn). Sergeant in the Lexington Alarm April, 1775; Ensign 1st Connecticut, 1st January, 1777; 2d Lieutenant, 29th May, 1778; 1st Lieutenant, 20th June, 1779; transferred to 5th Connecticut, 1st January, 1781; resigned 27th February, 1781. (Died 25th September, 1821.)

Spencer, Isaac (Conn). 1st Lieutenant of Selden's Connecticut State Regiment, June to December, 1776. (Died 1818.)

Spencer, Israel (N. Y.). 2d Lieutenant 2d New York, 28th June, 1775; Captain of Burrall's Continental Regiment, 19th January, 1776, to January, 1777; served subsequently as Major New York Levies. Died 1813.

Spencer, Ithomar (N. Y.). Captain New York Militia in 1775.

Spencer, John (Conn). Sergeant of Baldwin's Artillery Artificer Regiment, 22d April, 1777; 2d Lieutenant, 12th November, 1779; retired March, 1781.

Spencer, John (Va). Lieutenant of a Virginia State Regiment 1778 to 1781.

Spencer, Joseph (Conn). Colonel in the Lexington Alarm, April, 1775; Colonel 2d Connecticut, 1st May 1775; Brigadier-General Continental Army, 22d June, 1775; Major-General, 9th August, 1776; resigned 13th January, 1778; Major-General Connecticut Militia, 1779 to close of war. (Died 13th January, 1789)

Spencer, Joseph (Va). Captain 7th Virginia, 8th May 1776; resigned 14th November, 1777. (Died 27th August, 1829.)

Spencer, Michael (R. I.). Ensign of Babcock's Rhode Island State Regiment, 15th January, 1776, to ——.

Spencer, Oliver (N. J.). Major and Lieutenant-Colonel New Jersey Militia in 1776; Colonel of one of the sixteen additional Continental Regiments 15th January, 1777; retired 1st January, 1781. (Died, 1811.)

Spencer, Robert (N. J.). Paymaster of Spencer's Continental Regiment, 6th February, 1777; retired 12th May, 1779.

Spencer, Seth (Conn). Sergeant of Burrall's Continental Regiment, February, 1776; Ensign, 19th September, 1776, and served to January, 1777.

Spencer, Thomas (Va). 2d Lieutenant 4th Virginia, 23d February 1776; 1st Lieutenant, 28th September, 1776; resigned 30th July, 1778.

Spencer, William (Va). Ensign 8th Virginia, 25th September, 1779; Lieutenant, — September, 1780; Captain in 1781; was in service to ——. (Died 1813.)

Sperry, Elijah (Conn). 2d Lieutenant of Baldwin's Artillery Artificer Regiment, 4th October, 1777; 1st Lieutenant, 14th April, 1779; resigned 31st July, 1779.

Spicer, Abel (Conn). Captain 6th Connecticut, 1st May to 18th December, 1775; Captain of Selden's Connecticut Regiment, 20th June to 25th December 1776; served subsequently as Captain Connecticut Militia.

Spicer, James.—See Spycer.

Spicer John (N. C.). Captain 2d North Carolina, 11th December, 1776, to ——.

Spies, Jacob (Pa). Lieutenant Northumberland County, Pennsylvania, Militia in 1779.

Spiller, Benjamin C. (Va). 2d Lieutenant 7th Virginia, 26th February, 1776; resigned 10th October, 1776; Captain 2d Virginia State Regiment, 9th May, 1777; resigned 12th August, 1778.

Spiller, William (Va). Captain of a Virginia State Regiment, 1778 to 1781.

Spitfathom, John (Va). Served as Private and Sergeant in the Virginia Line from December, 1775, until appointed Ensign in 4th Virginia, 17th December, 1780; retired 12th February, 1781.

Spitzer, Aaron (N. H.). Surgeon's Mate 2d New Hampshire, 10th July, 1782; retired 31st March, 1783.

Spofford, Isaac (Mass). Surgeon of Nixon's Massachusetts Regiment, 28th

June to December, 1775; Surgeon 14th Continental Infantry, 1st January to 31st December ,1776; Surgeon 3d Continental Artillery 1st January, 1777; resigned 2d June, 1778.

Spohn, John (Pa). Captain 5th Pennsylvania Battalion 5th January, 1776; resigned 4th November, 1776.

Spooner, Daniel (Vt). Ensign Vermont Militia in 1777.

Spoor, John (N. Y.). Ensign 3d New York, 21st November, 1776 ;taken prisoner 3d July, 1777; where not stated; rejoined and dismissed 31st March, 1780.

Spotswood, Alexander (Va). Major 2d Virginia 13th February, 1776; Lieutenant-Colonel, 7th May, 1776; Colonel, 21st February, 1777; resigned 9th October, 1777. (Died 20th December, 1818.)

Spotswood, John (Va). Captain 10th Virginia, 29th November, 1776; wounded at Brandywine, 11th September, 1777; wounded and taken prisoner at Germantown, 4th October, 1777; regiment designated 6th Virginia, 14th September, 1778; exchanged November, 1780; did not return to the army and was retired 12th February, 1781. (Died 1800.)

Spraggins, —— (S. C.). Lieutenant South Carolina State Troops; wounded at Eutaw Springs, 8th September, 1781.

Sprague, Elijah (N. Y.). Captain New York Militia, ——; taken prisoner at Schohaire, 17th October, 1780; released 8th December, 1782.

Sprague, James (Conn). Sergeant in the Lexington Alarm, April, 1775; Ensign 3d Connecticut, 1st May to 10th December, 1775; 1st Lieutenant 20th Continental Infantry, 1st January to 31st December, 1776; 1st Lieutenant 3d Connecticut, 1st January, 1777; retired 15th November, 1778.

Sprague, John (Mass). Surgeon's Mate of Bridge's Massachusetts Regiment, May to December, 1775; Surgeon's Mate 18th Continental Infantry, 1st January to 31st December, 1776. (Died 21st October, 1803)

Sprague, Reuben (R. I.). Ensign 2d Rhode Island, 28th June to December, 1775.

Sprague, Samuel (Mass). Captain in Lexington Alarm, April, 1775; Captain of Gerrish's Massachusetts Regiment, 19th May to December, 1775; served subsequently in Navy. (Died 1783.)

Spratt, Thomas (N. C.). Lieutenant 9th North Carolina, 28th November, 1776, to ——.

Sprigg, Thomas (Md). Ensign Maryland Battalion of the Flying Camp, September to December, 1776; served subsequently as Lieutenant Maryland Militia.

Spring, Samuel (Mass). Chaplain of Fellows' Massachusetts Regiment, May to December, 1775. (Died 4th March, 1819.)

Spring, Simeon (Mass). Ensign 4th Massachusetts, 1st January, 1777; 2d Lieutenant, 3d January, 1778; 1st Lieutenant, 20th March, 1779, and served to November, 1783.

Springer, Jacob (Va). Ensign 9th Virginia, 31st October, 1778; Lieutenant, 8th August, 1779; transferred to 7th Virginia, 12th February, 1781, and served to close of war. (Died 16th June, 1823.)

Springer, Joseph (R. I.). Ensign of Richmond's Rhode Island State Regiment, 19th August, 1776; 1st Lieutenant of Stanton's Rhode Island State Regiment, 12th December, 1776, and Captain in 1778.

Springer, Richmond (R. I.). 1st Lieutenant of Topham's Regiment Rhode Island Militia in 1778.

Springer, Samuel (N. J.) 1st Lieutenant New Jersey Militia in 1777.

Springer, Sylvester (S. C.). Surgeon's Mate, 2d South Carolina, 27th June, 1778; taken prisoner at Charleston, 12th May, 1780; exchanged October, 1780, and served to close of war.

Springer, Uriah (Va). 1st Lieutenant 13th Virginia, 19th December, 1776; Captain, 25th August, 1778; regiment designated 9th Virginia, 14th September, 1778; transferred to 7th Virginia, 12th February, 1781, and served to close of war; Captain Infantry United States Army, 7th March, 1792; assigned to 3d Sub Legion, 4th September, 1792; honorably discharged 1st November, 1796.

Sproat, William (Pa). Ensign of Pennsylvania Associators in 1776; 1st Lieutenant 4th Pennsylvania, 3d January, 1777; Regimental Adjutant, 30th June to 17th December, 1777; Captain Lieutenant, 17th April, 1779; Captain, 11th May, 1779; transferred to 3d Pennsylvania, 17th January, 1781, and served to 3d November, 1783. (Died 1793.)

Sproul, James (N. J.). Ensign 4th New Jersey, 1st January, 1777; killed at Short Hills, 26th June, 1777.

Sproul, Moses (N. J.). Private, Corporal and Sergeant 3d New Jersey, November, 1775, to 1781; Ensign 2d New Jersey, 21st June, 1781; retained in New Jersey Battalion in April, 1783, and served to November, 1783.

Sprout, Ebenezer (Mass). Captain of Cotton's Massachusetts Regiment, 23d April, 1775; Major, 27th June to December, 1775; Major 3d Continental Infantry, 1st January to 31st December, 1776; Lieutenant-Colonel 4th Massachusetts, 1st January, 1777; Lieutenant-Colonel Commandant 12th Massachusetts, 29th September, 1778; transferred to 2d Massachusetts, 1st January, 1781; Colonel, 30th September, 1783; served to 3d November, 1783. (Died February, 1805.)

Sprout, James (Pa). Hospital Chaplain Middle Department, 10th February, 1778 to 1781.

Sprowle, —— (Ga). Captain Georgia Militia; taken prisoner at Briar Creek, 3d March, 1779.

Sprowles, John (Pa). 1st Lieutenant of Flower's Regiment of Artillery Artificers, 8th February, 1777; resigned 3d December, 1780.

Spurr, John (Mass). Lieutenant of 2d Rhode Island, 3d May, 1775; Captain 11th Continental Infantry, 1st January to 31st December, 1776; Captain 6th Massachusetts, 1st January, 1777; Major, 16th October, 1780; retired 1st January, 1781. (Died 1st November, 1822.)

Spurr, Richard (Va). Captain Virginia Militia, 1779-1780.

Spurrier, Edward (Md). Ensign Maryland Battalion of the Flying Camp, July to December, 1776; 1st Lieutenant 4th Maryland, 10th December, 1776; Captain Lieutenant, 27th May, 1778; Captain, 20th May, 1779; transferred to 3d Maryland, 1st January, 1781; retained in Maryland Battalion, April, 1783, and served to 15th November, 1783.

Spycer, James (N. C.). Paymaster 5th North Carolina in 1777 and 1778; name also spelled Spicer.

Spyker, Benjamin (Md). Captain Maryland Battalion of the Flying Camp, July to December, 1776; Captain 7th Maryland, 10th December, 1776; resigned 12th May, 1779.

Staats, Barent (N. Y.). Captain New York Militia in 1775; Major in 1776, and Lieutenant-Colonel in 1778.

Staats, Garret (N. Y.). 2d Lieutenant 3d New York, 10th August, 1776; 1st Lieutenant, 23d November, 1776; resigned 1st March, 1780.

Staats, Henry (N. Y.). Lieutenant New York Militia in 1775.

Staats, Philip (N. Y.). Lieutenant New York Militia; wounded at Fort Ann, 7th July, 1777.

Staats, Rynear (N. J.). Captain New Jersey Militia; wounded at Germantown, 4th October, 1777.

Stacey, John (Mass). 1st Lieutenant of Glover's Massachusetts Regiment, 19th May to December, 1775; Lieutenant Massachusetts Militia in 1780.

Stacey, Joseph (Mass). Regimental Quartermaster of Glover's Massachusetts Regiment, April to December, 1775; Regimental Quartermaster 14th Continental Infantry, 1st January to 31st December, 1776; Regimental Quartermaster of Lee's Continental Regiment, 1st January, 1777; retired 23d April, 1779.

Stacey, William (Mass). Major of Woodbridge's Massachusetts Regiment, April to December, 1775; Lieutenant-Colonel 7th Massachusetts, 1st January, 1777; transferred to 4th Massachusetts, 29th September, 1778; taken prisoner at Cherry Valley, 11th November, 1778; prisoner of war four years; did not return to the army. (Died ——, 1804.)

Staddel, Christian (Pa). 2d Lieutenant 1st Pennsylvania Battalion, 27th October, 1775; 1st Lieutenant, 4th May, 1776; Captain 2d Pennsylvania, 1st January, 1777; retired 1st July, 1778; also called John Staddle.

Stafford, —— (—). Colonel; wounded at Parker's Ferry, 30th August, 1781.

Stafford, Daniel (R. I.). Ensign of Stanton's Rhode Island Regiment, 12th December, 1776, to May, 1777.

Stafford, Joab (N. Y.). Captain New York Militia; wounded at Bennington, 16th August, 1777. (Died 21st November, 1801.)

Stafford, John R. (Mass). Ensign and Adjutant 3d Massachusetts, 30th November, 1781, and served to November, 1783.

Stagg, John (N. Y.). 2d Lieutenant of Malcolm's Additional Continental

Regiment, 4th March, 1777; Brigade Major of Conway's Brigade, 12th January, 1778; 1st Lieutenant of Spencer's Continental Regiment, 24th April, 1779; retired 1st January, 1781. (Died 28th December, 1803.)

Stake, Christian (Pa). Captain of a Pennsylvania Battalion of the Flying Camp; taken prisoner at Fort Washington, 16th November, 1776; name also spelled Slake.

Stake, Jacob (Pa). 3d Lieutenant of Miles' Pennsylvania Rifle Regiment, 15th March, 1776; 1st Lieutenant 10th Pennsylvania, 4th December, 1776; Captain, 12th November, 1777; transferred to 1st Pennsylvania, 17th January, 1781; wounded at Green Springs, 6th July, 1781; transferred to 3d Pennsylvania, 1st January, 1783, and served to June, 1783.

Stake, John (Pa). Ensign of Hartley's Continental Regiment, 20th May, 1777, to ——; Cornet of Von Heer's Company of Dragoons, 1st January, 1782, and served to close of war.

Stanard, Larkin(Va). Cadet 6th Virginia, 1st September, 1776, to January, 1777.

Standin, Thomas (N. C.). Ensign 2d North Carolina, 20th October, 1775; Lieutenant, 3d May, 1776; Captain, January, 1777; resigned 15th May, 1777.

Stanley, Caleb, Jr. (Conn). Ensign 3d Connecticut, 1st May to 15th December, 1775.

Stanley, Gad (Conn). Captain of Gay's Connecticut State Regiment, June to December, 1776; served subsequently as Major and Lieutenant-Colonel, Connecticut Militia.

Stanley, Jeremiah (Conn). 2d Lieutenant of Ward's Connecticut State Regiment, 14th May, 1776, to May, 1777.

Stanley, John (Va). Cadet 1st Continental Artillery, 18th November, 1779; retired 1st January, 1783.

Stanley, Joseph (Pa). Ensign 4th Pennsylvania Battalion, 8th January, 1776; 2d Lieutenant 5th Pennsylvania, 5th January, 1777; 1st Lieutenant, 20th April, 1777; died 10th April, 1778.

Stanley, Oliver (Conn). Captain Connecticut Militia, 1776-1777.

Stanley, Richard (Pa). 1st Lieutenant 1st Pennsylvania Battalion, 27th October, 1775, to ——.

Stanley, Solomon (Mass). 2d Lieutenant of Walker's Massachusetts Regi-

ment, May to December, 1775. (Died 1819.)

Stanley, Valentine (Pa). Surgeon's Mate Pennsylvania Musket Battalion, 31st July, 1776, to January, 1777; served subsequently in Navy. (Died 1787.)

Stanley, William (Pa). 2d Lieutenant 5th Pennsylvania Battalion, 8th January, 1776; 1st Lieutenant, 16th November, 1776; taken prisoner at Fort Washington, 16th November, 1776; exchanged, 25th August, 1780, and did not return to army. (Name also spelled Standley.)

Stanton, Amos (Conn). 1st Lieutenant of Sherburne's Additional Continental Regiment, 1st January, 1777; Captain, 9th November, 1777; resigned 28th April, 1780; Captain Connecticut Militia Regiment in 1781; killed at Groton Heights, 6th September, 1781.

Stanton, Andrew (R. I.). Lieutenant of Topham's Regiment Rhode Island Militia in 1776.

Stanton, Augustus (R. I.). Lieutenant of Richmond's Rhode Island State Regiment, 1st November, 1775; Captain of Stanton's Rhode Island State Regiment, 15th January, 1776, to ——.

Stanton, Ebenezer (Conn). Ensign of Sherburne's Continental Regiment, 1st January, 1777; Regimental Quartermaster, 1st June to 9th November, 1777; 2d Lieutenant, 9th November, 1777; Regimental Paymaster, 13th April, 1779; resigned 18th April, 1780.

Stanton, Enoch (R. I.). Lieutenant 1st Rhode Island, 19th February, 1777; resigned 28th May, 1779; Lieutenant Rhode Island Militia; killed at Fort Griswold, 6th September, 1781.

Stanton, Isaac Wheeler (Conn). 2d Lieutenant of Selden's Connecticut State Regiment, June to December, 1776.

Stanton, Joseph (R. I). Colonel Rhode Island State Regiment, 12th December, 1776; resigned 10th November, 1777; was subsequently Brigadier-General Rhode Island Militia.

Stanton, Joshua (N. H.). 2d Lieutenant Green Mountain Boys, 27th July, 1775; Captain of Warner's Continental Regiment, 5th July, 1776, and served to January, 1777. (Died 1819.)

Stanton, William (Conn). Captain of Burrall's Connecticut State Regiment, January, 1776, to January, 1777; Paymaster 2d Continental Dragoons,

1st March, 1777, to close of war; had rank of Lieutenant from 1st April, 1778, and Captain from 8th March, 1780.

Stanwood, William (Mass). 1st Lieutenant 11th Massachusetts, 6th November, 1776; retired 11th September, 1778.

Starbird, John (Mass). Private in Lexington Alarm, April, 1775; Private in Phinney's Massachusetts Regiment, May to December, 1775; Corporal 15th Continental Infantry, 1st January to 31st December, 1776; Sergeant and Sergeant-Major 1st Massachusetts, 1st January, 1777, until appointed Ensign, 1st January ,1780; retired 1st January, 1783. (Died 4th November, 1824.)

Stark, Archibald (N. H.). Ensign 3d New Hampshire, 20th September, 1777; Lieutenant, 5th July, 1780; transferred to 1st New Hampshire, 1st January, 1781, and served to March, 1782.

Stark, Caleb (N. H.). Ensign in Stark's New Hampshire Regiment, May to December, 1775; Ensign 5th Continental Infantry, 1st January, 1776; 2d Lieutenant, 14th August, 1776; Regimental Adjutant 1st New Hampshire, 8th November, 1776; retired 1st September, 1778; Aide-de-Camp and Brigade Major to General Stark, October, 1778, to close of war. (Died 26th August, 1838.)

Stark, John (N. H.). Colonel 1st New Hampshire, 23d April to December, 1775; Colonel 5th Continental Infantry, 1st January to 31st December, 1776; Colonel 1st New Hampshire, 8th November, 1776; resigned 23d March, 1777; Brigadier-General New Hampshire Militio, 1777. By the act of 4th October, 1777, it was "Resolved, that the thanks of Congress be presented to General Stark, of the New Hampshire Militia, and to the officers and troops under his command, for their brave and successful attack upon and signal victory over the enemy in their lines at Bennington, and that Brigadier-General Stark be appointed a Brigadier-General in the Army of the United States." Brigadier-General Continental Army, 4th October, 1777, and served to close of war; Brevet Major-General, 30th September, 1783. (Died 8th May, 1822.)

Stark, John (N. H.). Captain New Hampshire Militia, ——; wounded at Bennington, 16th August, 1777.

Stark, Patrick (S. C.). Surgeon's-Mate 1st South Carolina; taken prisoner at Charleston, 12th May, 1780.

Stark, Richard (Va). Ensign 7th Virginia, 28th October, 1776; 2d Lieutenant, 1st February, 1777; transferred to 5th Virginia, 14th September, 1778; 1st Lieutenant, 7th May, 1779; taken prisoner at Charleston, 12th May, 1780; transferred to 8th Virginia, 12th February, 1781; retired 1st January, 1783.

Stark, Robert (S. C.). Colonel South Carolina Militia in 1775.

Stark, William (Va). 2d Lieutenant 6th Virginia, 9th April, 1776; 1st Lieutenant, 10th December, 1776; retired 30th September, 1778; was a Lieutenant in 1st Continental Dragoons in 1780.

Starke, John (N. J.). Major and Lieutenant-Colonel New Jersey Militia, 1777-1782.

Starr, David (Conn). 1st Lieutenant 6th Connecticut, 1st January, 1777; Captain Lieutenant, 19th April, 1779; Captain, 10th May ,1780; transferred to 4th Connecticut, 1st January ,1781; retired 1st January, 1783.

Starr, Jehosaphat (Conn). Quartermaster-Sergeant of Webb's Additional Continental Regiment, 25th March, 1777; Regimental Quartermaster, 19th November, 1777; taken prisoner on the Long Island Expedition, 10th December, 1777; exchanged — August, 1778; Ensign 2d Connecticut, 6th January, 1779; resigned 29th March, 1780.

Starr, Josiah (Conn). Captain 4th Connecticut, 1st May to December, 1775; Lieutenant-Colonel of Swift's Connecticut State Regiment, July to November, 1776; Lieutenant-Colonel 7th Connecticut, 1st January, 1777; Colonel 1st Connecticut, 27th May, 1777; retired 1st January, 1781. (Died 1813.)

Starr, Thomas (Conn). Ensign 7th Connecticut, 1st January, 1777; wounded in Danbury Raid, 27th April, 1777; 2d Lieutenant, 25th January, 1778; 1st Lieutenant, 12th March, 1780; retired 1st January, 1783. (Died 21st April, 1806.)

Starr, Thomas (Conn). Captain Connecticut Militia, 1776 and 1777; wounded at Danbury, 27th April, 1777. (Died 1806.)

Starr, William (Conn). Ensign 7th Connecticut, 1st January, 1777; 2d Lieutenant, 3d November, 1777; resigned 25th May, 1780; Captain Connecticut Militia in 1781; wounded at Groton Heights 6th September, 1781. (Died 6th June, 1823.)

Statsors, John (N. J.). Captain New Jersey Militia; was a prisoner 5th March to 20th September, 1782; where taken not stated.

Staynor, Roger (Pa). 2d Lieutenant 1st Pennsylvania Battalion, 27th October, 1775; 1st Lieutenant, 19th January, 1776; Captain 2d Pennsylvania, 1st January, 1777; taken prisoner at his home in Philadelphia, 26th September, 1777; exchanged 4th November, 1780, and did not return to the army. (Died ——, 1839.)

St. Clair, Arthur (Pa). Colonel Pennsylvania Militia in 1775; Colonel 2d Pennsylvania Battalion, 3d January, 1776; Brigadier-General Continental Army, 9th August, 1776; Major-General, 19th February, 1777, and served to close of war; Major-General and Commander United States Army, 4th March, 1791; resigned 5th March, 1792. (Died 31st August, 1818.)

St. Clair, Daniel (Pa). Ensign 2d Pennsylvania Battalion, 20th September, 1776; 2d Lieutenant 3d Pennsylvania, 1st April, 1777; 1st Lieutenant, 1st September, 1777; retired 17th January, 1781. (Died 18th February, 1833.)

Stearns, Abijah (Mass). Colonel Massachusetts Militia, 1776-1778.

Stearns, Elijah (Mass). Lieutenant in Lexington Alarm, April, 1775; Lieutenant of Doolittle's Massachusetts Regiment, May to December, 1775.

Stearns, Ephraim (Mass). Captain Massachusetts Militia in 1778.

Stearns, Jonathan (Mass). Lieutenant of Fellow's Massachusetts Regiment, May to November, 1775.

Stearns, Josiah (Mass). Lieutenant of Doolittle's Massachusetts Regiment, May to December, 1775.

Stearns, Peter (N. H.). Lieutenant of Mooney's Regiment New Hampshire Militia ,1779-1780.

Stearns, Thomas (N. H.). Surgeon New Hampshire Militia in 1777.

Stebbins, Cyrus (Mass). Private in Lexington Alarm, April, 1775; Private in Ward's Massachusetts Regiment, April to December, 1775; Corporal and Sergeant 24th Continental Infantry, 1st January to 31st December, 1776; Ensign 3d Massachusetts, 1st January, 1777; died 8th March, 1777.

Stebbins, Francis (Mass). Ensign 3d Massachusetts, 1st January, 1777; resigned 8th October, 1778.

Stebbins, Joseph (Mass). Captain of Brewer's Massachusetts Regiment, May to December, 1775.

Stedham, Joseph (Del). Captain Delaware Regiment, 13th January, 1776, to January, 1777.

Stediford, Garret (Pa). Ensign and Regimental Quartermaster 3d Pennsylvania Battalion, 9th February, 1776; taken prisoner at Fort Washington, 16th November, 1776; exchanged 10th December, 1776; 1st Lieutenant 4th Pennsylvania, January, 1777; Captain, 12th October, 1777; resigned 23d May, 1781.

Stedman, Benjamin (N. C.). Captain 5th North Carolina, 16th April, 1776, —; omitted 1st January, 1778.

Stedman, James (Ga). Lieutenant and Adjutant 4th Georgia in 1779 and 1781.

Stedman, James (Conn). Captain in the Lexington Alarm, April, 1775; Captain of Ward's Connecticut State Regiment, 14th May, 1776, to 15th May, 1777. (Died 7th September, 1798.)

Stedman, James (N. Y.). Lieutenant 2d Canadian (Hazen's) Regiment, 3d November, 1776; omitted 1st January, 1778.

Steed, Jesse (N. C.). Ensign 10th North Carolina, 1st June, 1781; Regimental Quarttermastter, 13th July, 1781; Lieutenant, 8th September, 1781; transferred to 1st North Carolina, 6th February, 1782; retired 1st January, 1783.

Steed, John (Va). 2d Lieutenant 8th Virginia, 19th February, 1776; 1st Lieutenant, 3d January, 1777; Captain, 30th March, 1778; transferred to 4th Virginia, 14th September, 1778; taken prisoner at Charleston, 12th May, 1780; exchanged October, 1780, and served to close of war.

Steel, Aaron (Mass). Sergeant in Lexington Alarm, April, 1775; 2d Lieutenant of Danielson's Massachusetts Regiment, April to December, 1775; 2d Lieutenant 25th Continental Infantry, 1st January to 31st December, 1776; 1st Lieutenant 7th Massachusetts, 1st January, 1777; died 24th November, 1777, of wounds received at Fort Mifflin 14th November, 1777.

Steel, Alexander (N. J.). 2d Lieutenant of Spencer's Continental Regiment, 23d February, 1777; Regimental Quartermaster, 1st July, 1777; omitted October, 1777.

Steel, David (Va). Captain 13th Virginia, 16th December, 1776; retired 30th September, 1778. (Died 4th February, 1819.)

Steel, Hugh (Pa). Ensign 5th Pennsylvania, 9th April, 1777; resigned 10th August, 1777.

Steel, James (Pa). Ensign 5th Pennsylvania, 1st January, 1777; resigned 3d August, 1777.

Steele, Archibald (Pa). 1st Lieutenant of Thompson's Pennsylvania Rifle Regiment, 25th June, 1775; wounded and taken prisoner at Quebec, 31st December, 1775; exchanged August, 1776; retained rank as 1st Lieutenant 1st Continental Infantry, 1st January to 31st December, 1776; Deputy Quartermaster-General, May, 1777, to October, 1781; Military Storekeeper United States Army, 28th April, 1816; honorably discharged 1st June, 1821. (Died 29th October, 1822.)

Steele, Bradford (Conn). Lieutenant in Lexington Alarm, April, 1775; 1st Lieutenant 1st Connecticut, 1st May to 20th December, 1775; served subsequently as Captain Connecticut Militia. (Died 1804.)

Steele, James (Mass). 2d Lieutenant of Knox's Regiment Continental Artillery, 10th December, 1775, to December, 1776. (Died 1st December, 1836.)

Steele, John (N. Y.). Captain of Malcolm's Continental Regiment, January, 1777; resigned 8th March, 1778

Steele, John (Pa). 1st Lieutenant 10th Pennsylvania, 4th December, 1776; wounded at Brandywine, 11th September, 1777; Captain Lieutenant, 27th May, 1778; Captain, 21st March, 1779; transferred to 1st Pennsylvania, 17th January, 1781; retired 1st January, 1783. (Died 27th February, 1827.)

Steele, John (Pa). Captain Independent Pennsylvania Company, 13th January, 1777; Company transferred to 11th Pennsylvania, 16th December, 1778; retired 17th January, 1781.

Steele, John (Va). Ensign 9th Virginia, 4th April, 1777; 2d Lieutenant, 26th May, 1778; transferred to 1st Virginia, 14th September, 1778; 1st Lieutenant, 18th February, 1781; taken prisoner at Charleston, 12th May, 1780

Steele, Robert (Pa). Ensign 4th Pennsylvania, 3d January, 1777, to ——.

Steele, William (Conn). Ensign of Burrall's Continental Regiment, 23d January, 1776; cashiered 29th July, 1776.

Steele, William (Pa). Captain 1st Pennsylvania Battalion of the Flying Camp, June to December, 1776; Captain Pennsylvania Militia in 1777 and 1778.

Steelman, Zephaniah (N. J.). Captain New Jersey Militia in 1777.

Steenbergh, Elias (N. Y.). Captain New York Militia in 1775.

Steenrod, Cornelius (N. Y.). Captain 1st New York, 27th April to November, 1776.

Stein, James (S. C.). Lieutenant-Colonel South Carolina Militia at King's Mountain in October, 1780, and in the South Carolina campaign in 1781.

Stelle, Benjamin (R. I.). Adjutant of Richmond's and Tallman's Rhode Island State Regiments, 1st November, 1775, to 1777; Deputy Paymaster, 1st June, 1779, to 1st April, 1781.

St. Elms, Gerard de (France). By the act of 13th February, 1779, it was "Resolved, that Monsieur Gerard de St. Elms, having manifestetd great zeal and encountered many difficulties to distinguish himself in the service of these States, having also made a campaign here and behaved with bravery and being now about to return to France, resolved that he be appointed to the rank of major by brevet, as a testimony of the approbation of Congress of his zeal and services."

Stephen, Adam (Va). Colonel 4th Virginia, 13th February, 1776; Brigadier-General Continental Army, 4th September, 1776; Major-General, 19th February, 1777; dismissed 20th November, 1777. (Died — November, 1791.)

Stephens, Ezra (Conn). 2d Lieutenant 5th Connecticut, 1st May to 29th October, 1775.

Stephens, James (Del). Ensign Delaware Regiment, 15th January, 1776; killed at Princeton, 3d January, 1777.

Stephens, John (Va). Captain Virginia Militia, 1780-1781.

Stephens, Simeon (N. H.). 1st Lieutenant New Hampshire Minute Men in 1775.

Stephenson, David (Va). Captain 8th Virginia, 25th March, 1776; Major 5th Virginia, 4th May, 1778; transferred to 11th Virginia, 14th September, 1778; taken prisoner at Charleston, 12th May,

1780; transferred to 6th Virginia, 12th February, 1781; retired 1st January, 1783.

Stephenson, George (Pa). Ensign 1st Pennsylvania, 17th January, 1777; 2d Lieutenant, 13th May, 1777; resigned 4th September, 1777; Surgeon's Mate 1st Pennsylvania, 28th May, 1779; resigned 1st August, 1780; Major 10th United States Infantry, 8th January, 1799; honorably discharged 15th June, 1800 (Died 15th May, 1829.)

Stephenson, Hugh (Va). Captain of a Company of Virginia Riflemen, July, 1775; Colonel Maryland and Virginia Regiment of Riflemen, 27th June, 1776; died ——. (Was dead in September, 1776.)

Stephenson, James (Va). Paymaster 13th Virginia, 16th December, 1776; resigned January, 1777.

Sterrett, John (Md). Captain Maryland Militia Company; taken prisoner at·Eutaw Springs, 8th September, 1781.

Sterrett, William (Md). 1st Lieutenant of Smallwood's Maryland Regiment, 14th January, 1776; taken prisoner at Long Island 27th August, 1776; exchanged 8th November, 1776; Captain 1st Maryland, 10th December, 1776; Major, 10th April, 1777; resigned 15th December, 1777.

Sterrett, William (Pa). Captain Pennsylvania Militia; killed at Crooked Billet 1st May, 1778.

Sterry, Cyprian (R. I.). Ensign 2d Rhode Island, 3d May to December, 1775; 2d Lieutenant and Regimental Quartermaster 11th Continental Infantry, 1st January to 31st, December, 1776; Brigade-Major to Rhode Island Brigade, 12th to 31st December, 1776. (Died 1st September, 1824.)

Stetson, Josiah (Mass). Captain 14th Massachusetts, 1st January, 1777; resigned 13th April, 1780.

Stetson, Prince (Mass). Sergeant in Lexington Alarm, April, 1775; 1st Lieutenant of Thomas' Massachusetts Regiment, May to December, 1775; 1st Lieutenant 23d Continental Infantry, 1st January to 31st December, 1776; Captain Massachusetts Militia in 1777.

Steuben, Frederick William Augustus, Baron de (Prussia). By the Act of 14th January, 1778, it was "Resolved, that whereas Baron Steuben, a Lieutenant-General in foreign service, has in a most disinterested and heroic manner offered his services to these States,

in the quality of a volunteer—resolved that the President present the thanks of Congress in behalf of these United States to Baron Steuben, for the zeal he has shewn for the cause of America, and the disinterested tender he has been pleased to make of his military talents, and inform him that Congress cheerfully accepts of his services as a volunteer in the army of these States, and wish him to repair to General Washington's headquarters as soon as convenient." Volunteer Inspector-General, 28th March, 1778; Major-General and Inspector-General Continental Army, 5th May, 1778. By the Act of 5th September, 1779, it was "Resolved, that Baron Steuben, Inspector-General, be informed by the President that Congress entertain a high sense of his merit, displayed in a variety of instances, but especially in the system of military order and discipline, formed and presented by him to Congress." By the Act of 15th April, 1784, it was "Resolved, that the resignation of Baron Steuben, late Inspector-General and Major-General, be accepted; that the thanks of the United States, in Congress assembled, be given Baron Steuben for the zeal and abilities he has discovered in the discharge of the several duties of his office; that a gold-hilted sword be presented to him as a mark of the high sense Congress entertain of his character and services, and that the Superintendent of Finance take order for procuring the same." (Died 28th November, 1794.)

Stevens, Aaron (Conn). Captain in the Lexington Alarm, April, 1775; 1st Lieutenant 7th Connecticut, 6th July to 18th December, 1775; Captain of Mott's Connecticut State Regiment, June to December, 1776; Captain 7th Connecticut, 1st January, 1777; retired 1st January, 1781. (Died 29th August, 1820.)

Stevens, Asa (Conn). Lieutenant Connecticut Militia; killed at the Wyoming Massacre, 3d July, 1778.

Stevens, Ebenezr (Conn). Corporal of Warner's Continental Regiment, 25th April, 1779; Ensign, 7th August, 1779; Regimental Quartermaster, 7th September, 1780; killed at Fort George, 11th October, 1780.

Stevens, Ebenezer (Mass). Private in Phinney's Massachusetts Regiment, May to December, 1775; Sergeant 18th Continental Infantry, 1st January, 1776; Ensign, 13th November, 1776; Ensign, 12th Massachusetts, 1st January, 1777; 2d Lieutenant, 1st November,

1777; 1st Lieutenant 2d Continental Artillery, 30th April, 1778, and served to 17th June, 1783.

Stevens, Ebenezer (R. I.). 1st Lieutenant Company of Rhode Island Artillery, May, 1775; Captain of Knox's Regiment Continental Artillery, 10th December, 1775; Major Independent Battalion of Artillery, 9th November, 1776; brevet Major Continental Army, 27th May, 1777; his battalion annexed to 3d Continental Artillery in the fall of 1778; brevet Lieutenant-Colonel Continental Army, 30th April, 1778, "in consideration of his services and the strict attention with which he discharged his duty as commanding officer of Artillery in the Northern Department during two campaigns"; Lieutenant-Colonel 2d Continental Artillery, 24th November, 1778, to rank from 30th April, 1778; served to June, 1783. (Died 2d September, 1823.)

Stevens, Edward (Va). Colonel Virginia Militia in 1775; Colonel 10th Virginia, 12th November, 1776; resigned 31st January, 1778; Brigadier-General and Major-General Virginia Militia, 1779 to 1782; wounded at Guilford 15th March, 1781. (Died 17th August, 1820.)

Stevens, Elias (Vt). Lieutenant of Bedell's Regiment Vermont Militia, 1st April, 1778, to 1st April, 1779.

Stevens, John (Conn). Captain of Burrall's Continental Regiment, 19th January, 1776; taken prisoner at the Cedars, 19th May, 1776; exchanged 11th February, 1782.

Stevens, John (N. J.). Major New Jersey Militia, 1777-1778.

Stevens, Richard (Va). Captain 10th Virginia, 25th November, 1776; regiment designated 6th Virginia, 14th September, 1778; retired 18th February, 1781.

Stevens, Safford (Conn). 2d Lieutenant of Elmore's Continental Regiment, 15th April, 1776, to April, 1777. (Died 3d June, 1822.)

Stevens, Samuel (Mass). Ensign 15th Continental Infantry, 1st January to 31st December, 1776. (Died 1782.)

Stevens, Samuel (R. I.). Lieutenant of Richmond's Rhode Island State Regiment, 19th August, 1776, to May, 1777.

Stevens, Simeon (Vt). Lieutenant Vermont Militia in 1777; Captain of Bedel's Regiment Vermont Militia, 1778-1782. (Died 1788.)

Stevens, William (Mass). Sergeant of Gridley's Regiment Massachusetts Artillery, 29th May, 1776; 2d Lieutenant, 28th June, 1775; 1st Lieutenant of Knox's Regiment Continental Artillery, 1st January, 1776; Captain Lieutenant 2d Continental Artillery, 1st January, 1777; Captain, 12th September, 1778; transferred to Corps of Artillery, 17th June, 1783, and served to 3d November, 1783.

Stevens, William (Va). Ensign 5th Virginia, 1st March, 1777; 2d Lieutenant, 21st December, 1777; transferred to 3d Virginia, 14th September, 1778; 1st Lieutenant, 19th June, 1779; taken prisoner at Charleston, 12th May, 1780, and was a prisoner on parole to close of war. (Died 28th December, 1825.)

Stevens, William Smith (S. C.). Surgeon's Mate Hospital Department in South Carolina, 1779 to 1782.

Stevenson, Frederick (N. Y.). 1st Lieutenant of Graham's Regiment New York Militia, in 1778.

Stevenson, George (Pa). Surgeon's Mate Hospital Department, 1778-1781.

Stevenson, George (Pa). 3d Lieutenant 1st Continental Infantry, 1st January to 31st December, 1776; 1st Lieutenant of Wilson's Battalion, guarding stores at Carlisle, Pa., 20th October, 1777, to 2d June, 1778.

Stevenson, John (Md). Captain 2d Maryland Battalion of the Flying Camp, July to December, 1776.

Stevenson, John (N. Y.). Surgeon's Mate 3d New York, 25th August, 1775, to November, 1776; Surgeon of Stevens' Battalion Continental Artillery, 1st April, 1777; retired — September, 1778.

Stevenson, John (Pa). 2d Lieutenant 8th Pennsylvania, 13th July, 1777; cashiered 30th November, 1777.

Stevenson, John (Va). Captain 8th Virginia, 10th December, 1775, to February, 1776; served as Major of Clark's Illinois Regiment, 1778 to 1783. (Died 1826.)

Stevenson, Silas (N. C.). 1st Lieutenant 10th North Carolina, 28th November, 1776; Captain, 19th April, 1777; retired 1st June, 1778.

Stevenson, Stephen (Pa). 2d Lieutenant 9th Pennsylvania, 15th November, 1776; 1st Lieutenant, 16th March, 1778; Captain Lieutenant, 10th October, 1779; transferred to 4th Pennsylvania, 17th January, 1781; Captain 4th Pennsylvania, 11th July, 1781; transferred to

2d Pennsylvania, 1st January, 1783, and served to June, 1783

Stevenson, Thomas (Conn). 1st Lieutenant of Bradley's Connecticut Regiment, June to December, 1776.

Stevenson, William (Va). 2d Lieutenant 1st Continental Artillery, 30th September, 1777; 1st Lieutenant, 15th June, 1778, and served to ——.

Steward, Charles Augustus (S. C.). Lieutenant-Colonel South Carolina Militia in 1775.

Stewart, Alexander Del). 2d Lieutenant Delaware Regiment, 18th January, 1776; wounded and taken prisoner at Long Island, 27th August, 1776.

Stewart, Alexander (Mass). Chaplain of Knox's Regiment Continental Artillery, March to December, 1776.

Stewart, Alexander (N. Y.). Regimental Quartermaster of Malcolm's Continental Regiment in 1780.

Stewart, Alexander (Pa). Surgeon's-Mate Hospital Department, October, 1775 to April, 1776; Surgeon of Knox's Regiment, Continental Artillery, 1st May to 31st December, 1776; Surgeon 10th Pennsylvania, 10th October, 1779; transferred to 3d Pennsylvania, 17th January, 1781; retired 1st January, 1783. (Died 1793.)

Stewart, Charles (Conn). Ensign 2d Connecticut, 1st January, 1777; retired 15th November, 1778.

Stewart, Charles (N. J). Colonel New Jersey Militia, 1775-1776; Commissary of Issues, 18th June, 1777, to 24th July, 1782. (Died 24th July, 1800.)

Stewart, Charles (N. C.). 1st Lieutenant 5th North Carolina, 23d July, 1777; transferred to 2d North Carolina, 1st June, 1778; Captain-Lieutenant, 1st January, 1779; taken prisoner at Charleston, 12th May, 1780; exchanged, 14th June, 1781; Captain, 18th May, 1781; killed at Eutaw Springs, 8th September, 1781.

Stewart, Charles (Va). Ensign 15th Virginia, 21st November, 1776; 2d Lieutenant, 28th June, 1777; regiment designated, 11th Virginia, 14th September, 1778; retired, January, 1780.

Stewart, George (N. C.). Lieutenant 9th North Carolina, 28th November, 1776, to ——.

Stewart, Jacob (Mass). Ensign 5th Massachusetts, 1st January, 1777; resigned 21st November, 1777.

Stewart, James (N. Y.). Captain of Malcolm's Continental Regiment, August, 1776; Captain 5th New York; 21st November, 1776; retired 1st January, 1781.

Stewart, John (Md). 1st Lieutenant of Thomas' Independent Maryland Company, 14th January, 1776; Captain 2d Maryland, 10th December, 1776; Major, 17th April, 1777; taken prisoner on Staten Island, 22d August, 1777. By the Act of 26th July, 1779, it was "Resolved, unanimously, that Lieutenant-Colonel Fleury and Major Stewart, who, by their situation in leading two assaults (on stony Point), had a more immediate opportunity of distinguishing themselves, have by their personal achievements, exhibited a bright example to their brother soldiers, and merit in a particular manner the approbation and acknowledgment of the United States; that a silver medal of this action be struck and presented to * * Major Satewart;" Lieutenant-Colonel 1st Maryland, 10th February, 1781. Died — December, 1782.

Stewart, John (N. J.). Ensign 4th New Jersey, 1st February, 1777; resigned 30th December, 1777.

Stewart, Joseph (N C.). Lieutenant 9th North Carolina, 28th November, 1776, to——

Stewart, Lazarus (Pa). Captain Pennsylvania or Connecticut Militia; killed at the Wyoming Massacre, 3d July, 1778.

Stewart, Lewis (Va). Surgeon's-Mate 11th Virginia, 10th May, 1778; discharged 3d October, 1778.

Stewart, Nicholas (N C). Lieutenant 2d North Carolina, 30th April, 1777, to ——.

Stewart, Philip (Va). Lieutenant 3d Continental Dragoons, ——, 1780; wounded at Eutaw Springs, 8th September, 1781; transferred to Baylor's Regiment of Dragoons, 9th November, 1782, and served to close of war; Lieutenant 2d Artillerists and Engineers, 5th June, 1798; resigned 15th November, 1800. Died 14th August, 1830.)

Stewart, Walter (Pa). Captain 3d Pennsylvania Battalion, 5th January, 1776; Major Aide-de-Camp to General Gates, 7th June, 1776. By the Act of 19th November, 1776, it was "Resolved, that Major Stewart, who brought the late intelligence from General Gates, and who is recommended as a deserving officer, have the rank of Lieutenant-Colonel by brevet, and be presented with a sword of the value of one hundred (100) dollars;" Colonel Pennsylvania State Regiment, 17th June, 1777; regiment designated 13th Pennsylvania, 12th November, 1777; transferred to 2d Pennsylvania, 1st July, 1778; retired 1st January, 1783. (Died 14th June, 1796.)

Stewart, Walter, Jr. (Pa). Ensign 2d Pennsylvania, 27th May, 1779; retired 1st January, 1783.

Stewart, William (N. Y.). Captain in Graham's Regiment New York Militia, in 1778.

Sticker, William (N. J.). 2d Lieutenant of Spencer's Continental Regiment, 4th April, 1777; taken prisoner at Monmouth, 28th June, 1778; resigned 18th November, 1778.

Stickney, Eleazer (Mass). 2d Lieutenant of Bridge's Massachusetts Regiment, May to December, 1775. (Died 1824)

Stickney, Jonathan (Mass). Captain in Lexington Alarm, April, 1775; Captain Bridges' Massachusetts Regiment, May to December, 1775.

Stickney, Thomas (Mass). Lieutenant in Lexington Alarm, April, 1775; 1st Lieutenant of Frye's Massachusetts Regiment, May to December, 1775; was Lieutenant Massachusetts Militia, 1776-1777, and was wounded at Bennington, 16th August, 1777. (Died 1808.)

Stickney, Thomas (N. H.). Colonel New Hampshire Militia, 1776 to 1780; commanded Regiment at Bennington. (Died 26th January, 1809.)

Stickney, William (Mass). 2d Lieutenant of Little's Massachusetts Regiment, May to December, 1775. (Died 25th August, 1833.)

Stiles, Jeremiah (Mass). Captain of Sargent's Massacusetts Regiment, May to December, 1775.

Stille, Aaron (Mass). 1st Lieutenant of Danielson's Massachusetts Regiment, May to December, 1775.

Stille, Edward (Pa). 2d Lieutenant 6th Pennsylvania Battalion, 9th January, 1776; taken prisoner at Isle Aux Noix, 24th June, 1776. (Supposed to have been killed).

Stillman, George (R. I.). Captain Rhode Island Militia, 1775-1776.

Stillwell, Daniel (R. I.). Lieutenant and Captain Rhode Island Artillery Militia, 1775-1781. (Died 1805.)

Stillwell, Elias (Conn). Private in the Lexington Alarm, April, 1775; Ensign 1st Connecticut, 1st May to 10th December, 1775; 2d Lieutenant 22d Continental Infantry, 1st January to 31st December, 1776; Captain-Lieutenant 3d Connecticut, 1st January, 1777; Captain, 1st July, 1779; transferred to 1st Connecticut, 1st January, 1781, and served to June, 1783.

Stillwell, Enoch (N. J.). Major and Lieutenant-Colonel New Jersey Militia, 1776-1779.

Stillwell, Nicholas (N. J.). Captain, Major, Lieutenant-Colonel and Colonel New Jersey Militia, 1776-1780.

Stinson, James (N. C.). Captain North Carolina Militia at King's Mountain in October, 1780.

Stinson, William (Md). 2d Lieutenant 5th Maryland, 20th February, 1777; resigned 1st November, 1777.

Stirk, John (Ga). Lieutenant-Colonel 2d Georgia, 5th July, 1776; Colonel 3d Georgia, 21st March, 1778; taken prisoner at Augusta, 18th September, 1780.

Stirk, Samuel (Ga). Judge Advocate Southern Department, 1779-1780.

Stith, John (Va). 1st Lieutenant 4th Virginia, 19th March, 1776; Captain, 12th March, 1777; taken prisoner at Charleston, 12th May, 1780; transferred to 2d Virginia, 12th February, 1781, Brevet Major, 30 September, 1783, and served to close of war.

Stith, John (Va). Lieutenant 3d Continental Dragoons; taken prisoner at Taffen, 28th September, 1778.

St. John, Aaron (Conn). Private 5th Connecticut, 12th May to 13th December, 1775; Sergeant 2d Connecticut, 1st March, 1777; Ensign 9th April, 1780; transferred to 3d Connecticut, 1st January, 1781; resigned 31st March, 1782.

St. John, David (Conn). 1st Lieutenant 8th Connecticut, 1st January, 1777; resigned 13th February, 1778.

St. John, John (Conn). 2d Lieutenant of Silliman's Connecticut State Regiment, 20th June to 25th December, 1776; 1st Lieutenant 5th Connecticut, 1st January, 1777; Captain, 25th May, 1778; transferred to 2d Connecticut, 1st January, 1781; resigned 2d May, 1781.

St. John, Stephen (Conn). Major and Lieutenant-Colonel Connecticut

Militia, 1775 to April, 1781; taken prisoner at his home, April, 1781.

St. Marie, Levaliet de (S. C.). Captain-Lieutenant 1st South Carolina, ——; Captain, 9th October, 1779, and served to ——.

St. Martin, —— (France). Lieutenant-Colonel Engineer Continental Army, 23d July, 1776, to ——.

Stockbridge, Samuel (Mass). Captain of Thomas' Massachusetts Regiment, May to December, 1775.

Stocker, Ebenezer (Mass). Corporal in Lexington Alarm, April, 1775; Corporal in Mansfield's Massachusetts Regiment, May to December, 1775; Sergeant, 27th Continental Infantry, 1st January to 31st December, 1776; 2d Lieutenant 3d Massachusetts, 1st January, 1777, and served to June, 1783. (Died 1806.)

Stockett, Thomas Noble (Md). Surgeon Maryland Militia, 13th February, 1776; Surgeon 4th Maryland Battalion of the Flying Camp, 26th September to 1st December, 1776; served subsequently as hospital physician in 1777. (Died 16th May, 1802.)

Stockholm, Andrew (N. Y.). Lieutenant-Colonel of Lasher's Regiment, New York Militia, in 1776.

Stockley, Charles (Va). Ensign 9th Virginia, 22d July, 1776; taken prisoner at Germantown, 4th October, 1777; Lieutenant, 25th February, 1778; transferred to 1st Virginia, 14th September, 1778; transferred to 5th Virginia, 12th February, 1781, and served to close of war.

Stockton, Benjamin B. (N. Y.). Surgeon in Hospital Department, 1777 to 1781. (Died 9th June, 1829.)

Stockton, Ebenezer (N. H.). Surgeon 2d New Hampshire, 10th July, 1782, retained in New Hampshire Battalion, 21st March, 1783, and served to 3d November, 1783.

Stockton, John (Md). 2d Lieutenant 4th Maryland Battalion of the Flying Camp, June to December, 1776; taken prisoner at Long Island, 27th August, 1776, but made his escape; 1st Lieutenant 7th Maryland, 10th December, 1776, but no record of his joining the regiment.

Stockton, Richard (N. J.). A signer of the Declaration of Independence; Colonel and Inspector of the Northern Army; taken prisoner at the home of his friend, Mr. Covenhoven, 30th November, 1776. Died 28th February, 1781.

Stockwell, Levi (N. Y.). 2d Lieutenant 4th New York, April, 1776; 1st Lieutenant 3d New York, 21st November, 1776; omitted May, 1778; served subsequently as Captain New York Militia.

Stoddard, Darius (——). Surgeon Hospital Department, 1777-1778.

Stoddard, Jonathan (Conn). Ensign Mott's Connecticut State Regiment, June to December, 1776.

Stoddard, Josiah (Conn). Served with Ethan Allen at Ticonderoga in May, 1775; 1st Lieutenant of Bradley's Connecticut State Regiment, June to December, 1776; Captain 2d Continental Dragoons, 31st December, 1776; died 28th August, 1778.

Stoddard, Luther (Conn). 2d Lieutenant 4th Connecticut, 1st May to 10th December, 1775; Captain of Burrall's Continental Regiment, 19th January, 1776, to January, 1777.

Stoddard, Nathan (Conn). Captain 8th Connecticut, 1st January, 1777; killed at Fort Miffin, 15th November, 1777.

Stoddard, Nathan (Conn). 1st Lieutenant of Burrall's Continental Regiment, 23d January to December, 1776.

Stoddard, Orringh (Mass). 2d Lieutenant in Lexington Alarm, April, 1775; 2d Lieutenant of Paterson's Massachusetts Regiment, May to December, 1775; Captain, 1st Massachusetts, 1st January, 1777. Resigned, 2d November, 1780.

Stoddard, Ralph (Conn). Captain Connecticut Militia in 1776.

Stoddard, Benjamin (Md). Captain of Hartley's Continental Regiment, 13th January, 1777; wounded at Brandywine, 11th September, 1777; resigned, 8th April, 1779; Secretary Board of War, 1779 to 1781; First Secretary of the Navy, 1798 to 1801. (Died 18th December, 1813.)

Stoddard, William Trueman (Md). Ensign 5th Maryland, 10th December, 1776; 2d Lieutenant, ——; 1st Lieutenant, 21st May, 1779; transferred to 4th Maryland, 1st January, 1781; retired 1st January, 1783.

Stokeley, Nehemiah (Pa). 1st Lieutenant 8th Pennsylvania, 9th August,

1776; Captain, 16th October, 1777; retired 31st January, 1779. (Died 1811.)

Stokeling, Thomas (Pa). Captain ——; was a prisoner in 1782.

Stokes, Hezekiah (Va). Regimental Quartermaster 8th Virginia, 1st March, 1777; Regimental Paymaster, 4th June, 1777; retired 14th September, 1778.

Stokes, John (Va). Ensign 6th Virginia, 16th February, 1776; 2d Lieutenant, 10th August, 1776; 1st Lieutenant, 28th December, 1776; Captain, 20th February, 1778; transferred to 2d Virginia, 14th September, 1778; killed at Waxhaw, 29th May, 1780.

Stokes, Peter (Md). 2d Lieutenant 5th Maryland, 13th June, 1777; resigned 24th August, 1778.

Stone, Benjamin (N. H.). Regimental Quartermaster 20th Continental Infantry, 7th September, to 31st December, 1776; Captain 3d New Hampshire, 8th November, 1776; resigned 20th May, 1779. (Died 13th February, 1820.)

Stone, Enos (Mass). Sergeant in Lexington Alarm, April, 1775; Sergeant of Paterson's Massachusetts Regiment, May to December, 1775, Captain, 12th Massachusetts, 1st January, 1777; taken prisoner at Hubbardton, 7th July, 1777; exchanged in August, 1779, and did not rejoin regiment.

Stone, Ephriam (N. H.). Lieutenant of Bedel's New Hampshire Regiment, January to June, 1776 Captain in Mooney's Regiment New Hampshire Militia, 1779-1780.

Stone, Isaac (N. H.). 1st Lieutenant 3d New Hampshire, 1st May to December, 1775; 1st Lieutenant 2d Continental Infantry, 1st January to 31st December, 1776.

Stone, Jeremiah (R. I.). Sergeant and Lieutenant Topham's Regiment Rhode Island Militia, 1776-1778

Stone, John (Pa). 1st Lieutenant of Miles' Pennsylvania Rifle Regiment, 15th March, 1776; Captain, 10th Pennsylvania, 4th December, 1776; resigned 12th November, 1777. (Died 24th March, 1825.) Name also spelled Stoner.

Stone, John (Pa). Ensign 12th Pennsylvania, 16th October, 1776; resigned 8th January, 1777. (Died —— March, 1792.)

Stone, John (Vt). Captain Vermont Militia in 1777.

Stone, John Hawkins (Md). Major of Smallwood's Maryland Regiment, 14th January, 1776; Lieutenant-Colonel 1st Maryland, 10th December, 1776; Colonel, 18th February, 1777; wounded at Germantown, 4th October, 1777; resigned 1st August, 1779. (Died 5th October, 1804.)

Stone, Jonathan (Mass). Sergeant of Learned's Massachusetts Regiment, May to December, 1775; Ensign 3d Continental Infantry, 1st January to 31st December, 1776; Paymaster 5th Massachusetts, 1st January, 1777, to 1st January, 1783, with rank of 1st Lieutenant, from 1st January, 1777; Captain-Lieutenant, 14th October, 1780, and Captain from 25th April, 1781; retired 1st January, 1783. (Died 25th March, 1801.)

Stone, Nathaniel (Mass). Ensign 1st Massachusetts, 1st January, 1777; 2d Lieutenant, 28th March, 1777; 1st Lieutenant, 6th January, 1780; retained in Jackson's Continental Regiment, November, 1783, and served to 20th June, 1784. (Killed Captain Luke Hitchcock in a duel at West Point, N. Y., 21st February, 1782.)

Stone, Josiah (Vt). Major of Bedel's Regiment, Vermont Militia, 1778-1779.

Stone, Thomas (Md). A signer of the Declaration of Independence. Died 5th October, 1787.

Stoner, John.—See Stone.

Stoner, Ebenezer (Mass). Private and Corporal in Scammon's Massachusetts Regiment, May to December, 1775; Corporal and Sergeant 18th Continental Infantry, 1st January to 31st December, 1776; Ensign 12th Massachusetts, 1st January, 1777; Regimental Paymaster, 13th October, 1778; Lieutenant, 5th July, 1779; transferred to 2d Massachusetts, 1st January, 1781, and served to 3d November, 1783. (Died 23d January, 1846.)

Storm, Thomas (N. Y). Captain New York Militia, 1775-1776.

Storrs, Experience (Conn). Lieutenant-Colonel in the Lexington Alarm, April, 1775; Lieutenant-Colonel 3d Connecticut, 1st May, 1775; Colonel 1st July to 17th December, 1775; served subsequently as Colonel Connecticut Militia. (Died 22d July, 1801.)

Storrs, John (Conn). Chaplain of Gay's Connecticut State Regiment, 20th June to 25th December, 1776; Chaplain Connecticut Militia in 1781. (Died 1799.)

Storrs, Justus (Conn). Surgeon's-Mate, 2d Connecticut, 1st February, 1780; transferred to 1st Connecticut. 1st January, 1781; retained in Swift's Connecticut Regiment, 3d June, 1783, and served to 3d November, 1783.

Story, Asa (Conn). Corporal in Lexington Alarm, April, 1775; Sergeant 6th Connecticut, 6th May to 16th December, 1775; Ensign of Selden's Connecticut State Regiment, 20th June to 25th December, 1776; 2d Lieutenant 1st Connecticut, 1st January, 1777; resigned 1st November, 1778. (Died 1828.)

Story, Elisha (Mass). Surgeon of Little's Massachusetts Regiment, May to December, 1775; Surgeon 12th Continental Infantry, 1st January to 31st December, 1776. (Died 27th August, 1805.)

Story, John (Mass). Served as a volunteer in 1775; Lieutenant and Paymaster 11th Massachusetts, 1st January, 1777; Brigade Quartermaster, June, 1777; Major Aide-de-Camp to General Alexander, January, 1778; died December, 1782.

Story, Samuel (Pa). 2d Lieutenant 4th Continental Artillery, 1st January, 1777; 1st Lieutenant 11th May, 1779; Regimental Adjutant, 13th February, 1780; Captain-Lieutenant, 7th October, 1781; died 4th October, 1782.

Story, Solomon (Conn). Private in the Lexington Alarm, April, 1775; Ensign 6th Connecticu, 1st May to 10th December, 1775; served subsequently as Lieutenant Connecticut Militia. (Died 1820.)

Story, William (Mass). Sergeant in Little's Massachusetts Regiment, May to December, 1775; Ensign 12th Continental Infantry, 1st January to 31st December, 1776; 1st Lieutenant and Adjutant 8th Massachusetts, 1st January, 1777; Captain-Lieutenant, 23d January, 1779; Captain, 12th August, 1779, and served to January, 1783. (Died ——, 1800.)

Stotesbury, John (Pa). 2d Lieutenant 11th Pennsylvania, 30th September, 1776; 1st Lieutenant, 9th April, 1777; wounded at Brandywine, 11th September, 1777; taken prisoner, 14th February, 1778; where not stated; exchanged 31st December, 1780; retained as Captain 6th Pennsylvania, 17th January, 1781, and served to June, 1783.

Stoughton, Samuel (Conn). Ensign 8th Connecticut, 1st July, 1775; resigned 25th October, 1775.

Stout, Abraham (N. J.). Sergeant 3d New Jersey, 7th February, 1776; Ensign 29th October, 1776; 2d Lieutenant 2d New Jersey, 29th November, 1776; 1st Lieutenant 1st January, 1778; taken prisoner, 5th April, 1778, at Cooper's Ferry; exchanged 3d December, 1780, and did not return to the army. (Died 1821.)

Stout, Harmon (Pa). Ensign 3d Pennsylvania Battalion, 8th January, 1776; 2d Lieutenant, 13th June, 1776; 1st Lieutenant 10th Pennsylvania, 4th December, 1776; Captain, 12th February, 1777; resigned 1st March, 1780. (Died 1803.)

Stout, Joseph (N. J.). Captain 2d New Jersey, 28th October, 1775, to 20th November, 1776; Captain 2d New Jersey, 29th November, 1776; killed at Brandywine, 11th September, 1777.

Stout, Samuel (N. J.). Captain New Jersey Militia; wounded 17th October, 1777; where not stated.

Stout, Wessel Ten Broeck (N J.). Ensign 3d New Jersey, 1st June, 1777; 2d Lieutenant, 1st November, 1777; wounded in the Long Island raid, 10th December, 1777; transferred to 1st New Jersey, 1st January, 1781; 1st Lieutenant, 12th May, 1782; retained in New Jersey Battalion, April, 1783, and served to 3d November, 1783. (Died 11th November, 1818.)

Stoughtenburg, Isaac (N. Y.). Lieutenant-Colonel of Malcolm's Continental Regiment in 1776.

Stoughtenburgh, Luke (N. Y.). Captain of Freer's Regiment New York Militia, 1777-1778.

Stoughtenburgh, Peter (N. Y.). Captain of Graham's Regiment New York Militia in 1776

Stoughtenburgh, Tobias (N. Y.). Colonel New York Militia in 1776.

Stow, Jabez (Conn). Lieutenant Connecticut Militia, ——; wounded and taken prisoner at Groton Heights, 6th September, 1781. (Died 1785.)

Stow, Josiah (Vt). Major of Bedel's Regiment, Vermont Militia, 1st April, 1778, to 1st April, 1779.

Stow, Lazarus (Pa) Ensign 11th Pennsylvania, 9th April, 1777; 2d Lieutenant, 8th September, 1777; 1st Lieutenant, 20th February, 1778; retired 1st July, 1778.

Stow, Timothy (Mass). Lieutenant of Gridley's Regiment, Massachusetts Artillery, May to December, 1775; Captain of Knox's Regiment, Continental Artillery, 10th December, 1775, to December, 1776.

Stowell, David (Vt). Captain Vermont Militia, 1777.

Stowers, John (Mass). Sergeant 15th Massachusetts, 18th September, 1777; Ensign, 26th November, 1778; Lieutenant, 20th June, 1779; transferred to 5th Massachusetts, 1st January, 1781, and served to April, 1781. (Died 11th October, 1821.)

Stoy, John (Pa). 1st Lieutenant 2d Pennsylvania, 1st January, 1777; Captain-Lieutenant, 16th May, 1779; retired 17th January, 1781.

Strachan, William (N. Y.). Regimental Quartermaster 2d Continental Artillery, 28th October, 1778, to 1st August, 1779; 2d Lieutenant, 23d September, 1779; 1st Lieutenant, 14th April, 1781, and served to 17th June, 1783.

Straight, Christian (Va). Chaplain 8th Virginia, 1st August, 1776, to July, 1777. (Name also spelled Streight.)

Strang, Gilbert (N. Y.). Lieutenant New York Militia, 1775-1776; 2d Lieutenant 4th New York, 21st November, 1776; resigned 23d April, 1778.

Strape, Henry.—See **Stroop.**

Stratton, Aaron (Mass). Ensign of Sargent's Massachusetts Regiment, May to December, 1775; 2d Lieutenant, 16th Continental Infantry, 1st January, 1776. By the Act of Congress he was allowed the pay of a Lieutenant from September 1st, 1776, to 21st January, 1781, while a prisoner; taken prisoner at Tappan, 7th December, 1776.

Strawbridge, Joseph (Pa). 1st Lieutenant of Montgomery's Pennsylvania Battalion of the Flying Camp; taken prisoner at Fort Washington, 16th November, 1776.

Strawbridge, Thomas (Pa). Captain Chester County, Pennsylvania, Militia, 1775-1776.

Strawbridge, Joseph (Pa). Lieutenant Chester County, Pennsylvania, Militia in 1775-1776.

Street, Benjamin (Pa). Ensign of Hartley's Continental Regiment, 15th January, 1777; 2d Lieutenant, 11th May,

1777; 1st Lieutenant, 30th November, 1778; regiment designated, 11th Pennsylvania, 16th December, 1778; resigned 25th May, 1780.

Stribling, Sigismund (Va). 2d Lieutenant 12th Virginia, 9th December, 1776; 1st Lieutenant, 10th May, 1777; regiment designated, 8th Virginia, 14th September, 1778; Captain, 26th May, 1781; retired 1st January, 1783.

Stricker, George (Md). Captain of Smallwood's Maryland Regiment, 14th January, 1776; Lieutenant-Colonel German Regiment, 17th July, 1776; resigned 29th April, 1777.

Stricker, John (Pa). Ensign 2d Pennsylvania, January, 1777; 2d Lieutenant, 1st October, 1777; 1st Lieutenant, 1st May, 1779; transferred to 3d Pennsylvania, 1st January, 1783, and served to June, 1783.

Stricker, John (Pa). Sergeant 4th Continental Artillery, January, 1777; 3d Lieutenant, 1st April, 1777; 2d Lieutenant, 13th May, 1779; 1st Lieutenant, 3d June, 1779; Captain-Lieutenant, 11th February, 1780, and served to 17th June, 1783.

Stringer, Samuel (Md). Director of Hospital and Chief Physician Northern Department, 14th September, 1775; dismissed 9th January, 1777.

Strobagh, John Martin (Pa). Lieutenant of Proctor's Battalion, Pennsylvania Artillery, 13th May, 1776; Captain, 5th October, 1776; Captain 4th Continental Artillery, 6th February, 1777; Lieutenant-Colonel, 3d March, 1777; died 2d December, 1778.

Strong, Adonijah (Conn). 1st Lieutenant of Bigelow's Company, Connecticut Artillery, in 1776.

Strong, David (Conn). Sergeant in Burrall's Continental Regiment, January, 1776; taken prisoner at the Cedars, 19th May, 1776; 1st Lieutenant 5th Connecticut, 1st January, 1777; Captain-Lieutenant, 20th July, 1780; transferred to 2d Connecticut, 1st January, 1781; Captain, 2d May, 1781; retired 1st January, 1783; Captain United States Infantry Regiment, 15th July, 1785; Captain 1st Infantry United States Army, 29th September, 1789; Major 2d Infantry, 4th November, 1791; assigned to 2d Sub Legion, 4th September, 1792; Lieutenant-Colonel, 19th February, 1793; assigned to 2d Infantry, 1st November, 1796; died 19th August, 1801.

Strong, Israel (Conn). Private in the Lexington Alarm, April, 1775; Private 4th Connecticut, 19th May to 20th December, 1775; Sergeant 2d Connecticut, 1st March, 1777; Ensign 7th December, 1777; 2d Lieutenant. 2d April, 1780; retired 1st January, 1781.

Strong, John (Conn). Ensign 8th Connecticut, 1st January, 1777; 2d Lieutenant, 10th March, 1778; resigned 24th January, 1780. (Died 1843.)

Strong, Joseph (Conn). Chaplain 20th Continental Infantry, March to December, 1776. (Died 1st January, 1803.)

Strong, Nathan (Conn). Chaplain 22d Continental Infantry, April to December, 1776. (Died 25th December, 1816.)

Strong, Nathan (N. Y.). Lieutenant New York Militia, February to November, 1776; Captain 4th New York, 21st November, 1776; retired April, 1779.

Strong, Solomon (Conn). Captain 5th Connecticut, 1st January, 1777; resigned 25th August, 1778.

Stroop, Henry (Pa). 1st Lieutenant of Flower's Artillery Artificer Regiment, 1st May, 1778; resigned 27th December, 1780; name also spelled Strape.

Strother, William D. (Ga). Captain 2d Georgia, 1776; killed at Medway Church, 24th November, 1778.

Stroud, Jacob (Pa). Colonel Pennsylvania Militia in 1775. (Died 1806.)

Strubling, Philip (Pa). 2d Lieutenant of Von Herr's Company of Light Dragoons, 1st September, 1779, and served to close of war; brevet Captain, 15th April, 1784.

Stryker, John (N. J.). Captain New Jersey Militia, 1777-1778. (Died 1786.)

Stuart, Alexander (Va). Major Virginia Militia; wounded and taken prisoner at Guilford, 15th March, 1781.

Stuart, Christopher (Pa). Captain 4th Pennsylvania Battalion, 5th January, 1776; Major, 20th September, 1776; taken prisoner at Fort Washington, 16th November, 1776; exchanged January, 1777; Major 5th Pennsylvania, June, 1777, to rank from 28th February, 1777; Lieutenant-Colonel 3d Pennsylvania, 17th April, 1780; retired 17th January, 1781. (Died 1799.)

Stuart, Joseph (Mass). Private and Sergeant in Phinney's Massachusetts Regiment, May to December, 1775; Sergeant, 18th Continental Infantry, 1st

January, 1776; Ensign, 18th April, 1776; deserted 6th November, 1776.

Stuart, Wentworth (Mass). Captain of Phinney's Massachusetts Regiment, May to December, 1775; Captain, 18th Continental Infantry, 1st January, 1776. Died 7th April, 1776.

Stewart, William (N. Y.). Captain New York Militia, 1775-1776; Lieutenant 2d Canadian (Hazen's) Regiment, 8th November, 1776; Regimental Adjutant, 8th October, 1777, and served to June, 1783. (Died 5th February, 1831.)

Stubblefield, Beverly (Va). Cadet 6th Virginia, 10th February, 1776; 2d Lieutenant, 28th December, 1776; 1st Lieutenant, 7th August, 1777; transferred to 2d Virginia, 14th September, 1778; taken prisoner at Charleston, 12th May, 1781; exchanged June, 1781; Captain, ——, 1781, and served to close of war.

Stubblefield, George (Va). Captain 5th Virginia, 12th February, 1776; Major 14th Virginia, 1st April, 1777; resigned 22d February, 1778; Colonel Virginia Militia, 1780-1781.

Stubblefield, Peter (Va). 1st Lieutenant 1st Virginia State Regiment, March, 1777; resigned 12th June, 1778.

Stubbs, Samuel (Mass). Sergeant of Phinney's Massachusetts Regiment, May to December, 1775; Ensign, 18th Continental Infantry, 1st January to 31st December, 1776. (Died 3d March, 1823.)

Studson, Joshua (N. J.). Lieutenant New Jersey Militia, ——; killed —— December, 1780, while boarding an enemy's vessel.

Stull, Daniel (Md). 1st Lieutenant 1st Maryland Battalion of the Flying Camp, June to December, 1776; Captain 7th Maryland, 10th December, 1776; resigned 14th September, 1778.

Sturtevant, Isaac (Mass). Sergeant of Heath's Massachusetts Regiment, May to December, 1775; 2d Lieutenant 9th Massachusetts, 1st January, 1777; transferred to 7th Massachusetts, 1st January, 1783; transferred to 4th Massachusetts, 12th June, 1783, and served to 3d November, 1783.

Sturtevant, Jesse (Mass). Lieutenant in Lexington Alarm, April, 1775; Lieutenant of Cotton's Massachusetts Regiment, May to December, 1775; 1st Lieutenant 21st Continental Infantry, 1st January to 31st December, 1776;

Captain Massachusetts Militia, 1777-1780. (Died September, 1818.)

Sturtevant, John (Mass). 1st Lieutenant 21st Continental Infantry, 1st January to 31st December, 1776.

Stymart, Jasper (N. Y.). 2d Lieutenant 2d Continental Artillery, 23d September, 1777; resigned 24th June, 1778.

Sugart, Martin.—See **Shugart.**

Suggs, George (N. C.). Lieutenant 5th North Carolina, November, 1776, to ——.

Sullivan, Ebenezer (Mass). Captain of Scammon's Massachusetts Regiment, May to December, 1775; Captain 15th Continental Infantry, 1st January, 1776; taken prisoner at the Cedars, 20th May, 1776; exchanged ——, 1778. (Died 1799.)

Sullivan, James (Va). Captain 13th Virginia, 16th December, 1776; retired 30th September, 1778.

Sullivan, John (N. H.). Brigadier-General Continental Army, 22d June, 1775; Major-General, 9th August, 1776; taken prisoner at Long Island, 27th August, 1776; exchanged December, 1776. By the Act of 9th September, 1778, it was "Resolved, that the thanks of Congress be given to Major-General Sullivan, and to the officers and troops of his command, for their fortitude and bravery displayed in the action of August 29th (Quaker Hill), in which they repulsed the British forces and maintained the field." By the act of 14th October, 1779, it was "Resolved, that the thanks of Congress be given to Major-General Sullivan and the brave officers and soldiers under his command, for effectually executing an important expedition against such of the Indian nations as, encouraged by the councils of his Britannic majesty, had perfidiously waged an unprovoked and cruel war against these United States, laid waste many of their defenseless towns, and with savage barbarity slaughtered the inhabitants thereof." Resigned 30th November, 1779. (Died 23d January, 1795.)

Sullivan, John (Pa). Cornet 4th Continental Dragoons, ——; Lieutenant, 1st October, 1777; "left the service in June, 1783, without leave before the conclusion of the war;" see Journal of Congress of 27th June, 1786.

Sullivan, Samuel (——). Captain and Quartermaster Pulaski Legion, 1779-1780.

Summers, Jacob (Pa). Lieutenant Pennsylvania Militia; taken prisoner from his home, 1st May, 1778. Name also spelled Sommers.

Summers, John (N. C.). Ensign 1st North Carolina, 28th March, 1776; 2d Lieutenant, 7th July, 1776; 1st Lieutenant, 5th February, 1777; Captain 10th July, 1778; taken prisoner at Williamson's Plantation, 12th July, 1780; retired 1st January 1783.

Summers, Peter (Pa). Ensign 4th Pennsylvania, 3d January, 1777; 2d Lieutenant, 18th October, 1777; 1st Lieutenant, 2d June, 1778; Regimental Quartermaster, 2d June, 1778 to 18th May, 1780; resigned, 1st April, 1781.

Summers, Simon (Va). Adjutant 6th Virginia, 1st March, 1776; transferred to 2d Virginia, 14th September, 1778; retired 12th February, 1781.

Sumner, Ebenezer (Conn). 1st Lieutenant 2d Connecticut, 1st May, 1775; Captain, 1st July to 18th December, 1775; Captain 22d Continental Infantry, 1st January to 31st December, 1776; served subsequently as Captain Connecticut Militia.

Sumner, Jethro (N. C.). Colonel 3d North Carolina, 15th April, 1776; Brigadier-General Continental Army, 9th January, 1779, and served to close of war. (Died 18th March, 1785.)

Sumner, Job (Mass). Ensign in Gardner's Massachusetts Regiment, May to December, 1776; 1st Lieutenant 25th Continental Infantry, 1st January, 1776, Captain 3d Massachusetts, 1st January, 1777; by the act of 7th April, 1779, he was given rank of Captain from 1st July, 1776; Major, 3d March, 1783 ,to rank from 1st October, 1782; retained as Captain in Jackson's Continental Regiment, November, 1783, and served to 20th June, 1784. (Died 16th September, 1789.)

Sumner, John (Conn). Ensign 8th Connecticut, 6th July to 10th December, 1775; Major of Mott's Connecticut State Regiment, June to December, 1776; Major 4th Connecticut, 1st January, 1777; Lieutenant-Colonel 28th April, 1777; retired 1st January, 1781. (Died 1804.)

Sumner, William (Mass). 2d Lieutenant of Heath's Massachusetts Regiment, May to December, 1775. (Died 19th November, 1846.)

Sumter, Thomas (S. C.). Colonel — South Carolina Regiment, ——; Brigadier-General South Carolina State Troops, July, 1780; wounded at Fish Dam Ford, Broad River, 9th November, 1780, and at Black Stocks, 20th November, 1780. By the act of 13th January, 1781, it was resolved that "Congress taking into consideration the eminent services rendered to the United States by Brigadier-General Sumter, of South Carolina, at the head of a number of volunteer militia from that and the neighboring States, particularly in the victory obtained over the enemy at the Hanging Rock, on the 6th day of August; in the defeat of Major Wemys and the corps of British Infantry and dragoons under his command, at Broad River, on the 9th day of November, in which the said Major Wemys was made prisoner, and in the repulse of Lieutenant-Colonel Tarleton, and the British cavalry and infantry under his command at Black Stocks, on Tyger River, on the 20th of November last, in each of which action the gallantry and military conduct of General Sumter, and the courage and perseverance of his troops were highly conspicuous; resolved therefore that the thanks of Congress be presented to Brigadier-General Sumter, and the militia aforesaid, for such reiterated proofs of their patriotism, bravery and military conduct, which entitle them to the highest esteem and confidence of their country, and that the Commanding Officer of the Southern Department do forthwith cause the same to be issued in general orders, and transmitted to General Sumter." Served to close of war. (Died 1st June, 1832.)

Sunderland, Peleg (Vt). Lieutenant Vermont Militia in 1776.

Sunn, Frederick (S. C.). Surgeon's-Mate Pulaski Legion in 1778, and Surgeon South Carolina Artillery, 1779, to 1782.

Sutcliffe, John (Ga). Captain, Assistant Deputy Quartermaster-General Southern Department, 3d February, 1778, to ——.

Sutherland, David (N. Y.). Colonel New York Militia, 1775-1778. (Died 1794.)

Sutherland, Smith (N. Y.). Captain of Graham's Regiment New York Militia in 1777.

Sutherland, Thomas (Pa). Lieutenant-Colonel Pennsylvania Militia in 1776.

Sutfin, Roeliff (N. J.). Captain New Jersey Militia; wounded at Paulus Hook, 19th August, 1779.

Sutliff, Benjamin (Conn). Private 1st Connecticut, 1st May to 28th November, 1775; Private in Douglas' Connecticut State Regiment, June to December, 1776; Sergeant 6th Connecticut, 21st May, 1777; Ensign, 2d May, 1779; transferred to 4th Connecticut, 1st January, 1781; 2d Lieutenant, 3d April, 1782; retired 1st January, 1783.

Sutter, James (Pa). Ensign Pennsylvania Musket Battalion, 28th March, 1776; 2d Lieutenant Pennsylvania State Regiment, 18th April, 1777; regiment designated 13th Pennsylvania, 12th November, 1777; retired 1st July, 1778.

Sutton, Edward (Conn). Surgeon of Burrall's Continental Regiment in 1776.

Sutton, James (N. C.). 2d Lieutenant 2d North Carolina, 16th December, 1776; resigned 10th March, 1778.

Sutton, John (S. C.). Ensign South Carolina Militia in 1776.

Sutton, John (Va). Paymaster 1st Virginia, 7th November, 1776, to May, 1779; Paymaster Virginia Militia, 1780-1781. (Died 1800.)

Sutton, Robert (S. C.). Captain South Carolina Militia in 1776.

Sutton, Thomas (N. Y.). 2d Lieutenant of Knox's Regiment Continental Artillery, May, 1776; 1st Lieutenant 2d Continental Artillery, 1st January, 1777; resigned August, 1777.

Suydam, Oke (N. Y.). Lieutenant of Snyder's Regiment New York Militia, 1779-1781.

Suydam, Cornelius R.—See **Sedam**.

Swain, Ebenezer (Pa). Ensign 9th Pennsylvania, 31st December, 1776; resigned 10th July, 1777 name also spelled Swayne.

Swan, Caleb (Mass). Corporal and Sergeant 9th Massachusetts, 1st February, 1777, until appointed Ensign, 26th November, 1779; transferred to 8th Massachusetts, 1st January, 1781; transferred to 3d Massachusetts, 12th June, 1783; retained in Jackson's Continental Regiment, November, 1783, and served to 20th June, 1784; Paymaster United States Army, 8th May, 1792; resigned 30th June, 1808. (Died 20th November, 1809.)

Swan, John (Md). Captain 3d Continental Dragoons, 26th April, 1777;

taken prisoner at Tappan, 28th September, 1778; Major 1st Continental Dragoons, 21st October, 1780 retained in Baylor's Regiment of Dragoons, 9th November, 1782, and served to close of war.

Swan, Joshua (Mass). 1st Lieutenant of Gardner's Massachusetts Regiment, May to December, 1775; 1st Lieutenant 25th Continental Infantry, 1st January, 1776, to ——.

Swan, Joseph (Va). Brigade Major of Muhlenburg's Brigade, April, 1777; resigned 25th August, 1777.

Swan, Matthew (Pa). Lieutenant and Quartermaster 1st Pennsylvania Battalion of the Flying Camp, June to December, 1776.

Swan, Nimrod (N.C .). Regimental Quartermaster 5th North Carolina, 18th June, 1777; omitted 1st January, 1778.

Swan, Thomas (R. I.). 2d Lieutenant of Tallman's Rhode Island State Regiment, 12th December, 1776, to May, 1777.

Swart, Evert W. (N. Y.). Captain New York Militia, 1775-1776.

Swartwout, Abraham (N. Y.). Captain in Clinton's New York Militia Regiment, 27th April, 1776; Captain 3d New York, 21st November, 1776; omitted May, 1778.

Swartwout, Bernardus (N. Y.). Ensign 2d New York, 1st June, 1778, and served to June, 1783.

Swartwout, Cornelius (N. Y.). 2d Lieutenant of Knox's Regiment Continental Artillery, 27th May, 1776; Captain Lieutenant 2d Continental Artillery, 1st January, 1777; Captain Lieutenant, 16th July, 1777; taken prisoner at Fort Montgomery, 6th October, 1777; exchanged 17th December ,1780; served to 17th June, 1783.

Swartwout, Henry (N. Y.). Ensign 5th New York, 21st November, 1776, to rank from 28th March, 1776; taken prisoner at Fort Montgomery, 6th October, 1777; exchanged 17th December, 1780; 2d Lieutenant, 28th February, 1780; transferred to 1st New York, 1st January, 1781, and served to close of war.

Swartwout, Jacobus (N Y.). Colonel New York Militia, 1776 to 1780; Brigadier-General New York Militia, 3d March, 1780, to close of war.

Swasey, Joseph (Mass). Captain 14th Continental Infantry, 1st January to

31st December, 1776; Major of Lee's Continental Regiment, 1st January, 1777; resigned 9th July, 1778.

Swayne, Ebenezer (Pa).—See **Swain**.

Swearingen, Joseph (Va). 1st Lieutenant 12th Virginia, 1st March, 1777; regiment designated 8th Virginia, 14th September, 1778; Captain Lieutenant, 14th April, 1779; taken prisoner at Charleston, 12th May, 1780; Captain, 18th February, 1781, and was a prisoner to close of war.

Swearingin, Van (Pa). Captain of an Independent Pennsylvania Company, 3d February, 1776; Captain 8th Pennsylvania, 9th August, 1776 wounded and taken prisoner at Stillwater, 19th September, 1777 resigned 10th August, 1779; Captain Kentucky Militia in 1791; was killed 4th November, 1791, at St. Clair's defeat near Fort Recovery, Ohio.

Sweeny, Isaac (Pa). 2d Lieutenant of Hartley's Continental Regiment, January 23d, 1777; 1st Lieutenant, 9th September, 1777; Captain, 23d July, 1778; regiment designated 11th Pennsylvania, 16th December, 1778; died 2d October, 1780.

Sweeny, James (Pa). 2d Lieutenant of Flower's Artillery Artificer Regiment, 22d February, 1777, to ——.

Sweers, Cornelius (——). Deputy Commissary-General of Military Stores, ——; dismissed for fraud and forgery, 24th August, 1778.

Sweet, Abraham (Mass). Lieutenant 13th Massachusetts, 1st January, 1777; resigned 28th February, 1778; name also spelled Swett.

Sweet, Caleb (N. Y.). Surgeon's Mate 1st New York, 21st November, 1776; Surgeon, 13th October, 1779, and served to close of war.

Sweet, Moses (Mass). 2d Lieutenant of Scammon's Massachusetts Regiment, — May to December, 1775.

Sweet, Samuel (N. H.). Ensign 1st New Hampshire, 8th November, 1776; resigned 28th September, 1777.

Sweet, Samuel (R. I.). Captain of Elliott's Regiment Rhode Island State Artillery, 12th December, 1776, to May, 1777.

Sweet, Stephen (Mass). Surgeon of Phinney's Massachusetts Regiment, May to December, 1775.

Sweet, Thomas (Mass). Lieutenant of Little's Massachusetts Regiment, May to December, 1775.

Sweet, Thomas (R. I.). Lieutenant 1st Rhode Island, 28th June to November, 1775.

Sweetland, Eleazer (Mass). Chaplain of Sargent's Massachusetts Regiment, May to December, 1775; Chaplain 16th Continental Infantry, 1st January to 31st December, 1776. (Name also spelled Eleazer Swetland.)

Swett, Abraham.—See Sweet.

Swift, Heman (Conn). Colonel Connecticut State Regiment, July to December, 1776; Colonel 7th Connecticut, 1st January, 1777; transferred to 2d Connecticut, 1st January, 1781; retained as Colonel of the Consolidated Connecticut Regiment in June, 1783; Brevet Brigadier-General, 30th September, 1783, and served to December, 1783.

Swift, Heman (Conn). Ensign of Durkee's Wyoming Valley Company, 26th August, 1776; resigned 1st July, 1778.

Swift, Isaac (Conn). Surgeon's Mate 19th Continental Infantry, 1st January to 31st December, 1776; Surgeon's Mate 7th Connecticut, 1st January, 1777; Surgeon, 6th August, 1777; resigned 1st May, 1778. (Died 1802.)

Swift, Jeriah (Conn). 1st Lieutenant 4th Connecticut, 1st May to 10th December, 1775; Captain of Burrall's Continental Regiment, 19th January, 1776; died 28th July, 1776.

Swift, Matthew (Va). 2d Lieutenant 1st Virginia, 18th September, 1775, to ——.

Swift, Nathaniel (Conn). Ensign of Burrall's Continental Regiment, 13th January, 1776, to January, 1777.

Swift, Samuel (Pa). 1st Lieutenant of Lewis' Pennsylvania Battalion of the Flying Camp, July to December, 1776.

Swinton, Alexander (S. C.). Major of South Carolina Militia of Marion's Brigade; wounded at Quinby's Bridge, 17th July, 1781.

Switz, Abraham (N. Y.). Major New York Militia in 1775.

Switz, Walter (N. Y.). 2d Lieutenant of Warner's Continental Regiment, 1st April, 1777, to ——; was in service in September, 1779.

Swogan, Robert (Md). Ensign 2d Maryland, 20th February, 1777; resigned 20th June, 1777.

Swobe, George (Pa). Lieutenant Northumberland County, Pennsylvania, Militia in 1779.

Swope, Jacob (Pa). Surgeon of Hartley's Continental Regiment, 15th January, 1777, to ——.

Swope, Michael (Pa). Colonel — Pennsylvania Battalion of the Flying Camp, June, 1776; taken prisoner at Fort Washington, 16th November, 1776; exchanged 26th January ,1781.

Sykes, William (N. C.). Ensign North Carolina Militia in 1781.

Syme, John (Va). Captain 10th Virginia, 3d December, 1776; resigned 3d January, 1778; Colonel Virginia Militia, 1780-1781.

Symmes, John Cleves (Va). Colonel Virginia Militia, 1775-1776. (Died 1814.)

Symmes, Jonathan (Va). Captain 10th Virginia, January, 1777; resigned 31st December, 1777.

Symonds, Daniel.—See Simonds.

Symonds, Francis (Mass). Lieutenant in Lexington Alarm, April, 1775; Captain of Glover's Massachusetts Regiment, May to December, 1775; Captain 11th Continental Infantry, 1st January to 31st December, 1776.

Sytez, George (N. Y.). Adjutant 3d New York, 21st November, 1776, to 28th May, 1778; Captain Lieutenant, 28th May, 1778 Captain, 7th January, 1780; transferred to 1st New York, 1st January, 1781, and served to June, 1783.

T.

Tabb, Augustin (Va). 2d Lieutenant 2d Virginia State Regiment, 3d October, 1777; 1st Lieutenant, 24th April, 1778; Captain, 10th September, 1778, and served to January, 1780.

Tabbs, Barton (Md). Surgeon 7th Marland, 20th March, 1777; resigned 3d October, 1779.

Taber, Lemuel (Mass). Ensign of Brewer's Massachusetts Regiment, May to December, 1775; served subsequently as Major Massachusetts Militia.

Taft, Peter (Mass). Sergeant in Lexington Alarm, April, 1775; 2d Lieutenant of Read's Massachusetts Regiment, May to December, 1775; 1st Lieutenant 13th Continental Infantry, 1st January to 31st December, 1776.

Taft, Robert (Mass). 2d Lieutenant of Read's Massachusetts Regiment, May to December, 1775.

Taggart, James (N. H.). 2d Lieutenant 3d New Hampshire, 8th May to December, 1775; 2d Lieutenant 2d Continental Infantry, 1st January, 1776; 1st Lieutenant 1st New Hampshire, 8th November, 1776; resigned 23d August, 1778. (Died 25th January, 1828.)

Taggart, John (N. H.). Lieutenant New Hampshire Militia; killed at Hubbardton, 7th July, 1777.

Taggart, William (N. H.). Ensign 2d New Hampshire, 8th November, 1776; 2d Lieutenant, 29th December, 1777; wounded at Ticonderoga, 6th July ,1777; lost his sight sy smallpox in 1778; resigned 4th February, 1780.

Taggart, William (S. C.). 2d Lieutenant 3d South Carolina, 12th February, 1778, to ——.

Tahis, Moses (Md). 2d Lieutenant 3d Maryland Battalion ot the Flying Camp, July, 1776, to ——.

Talbot, Benjamin (Mass). Ensign 24th Continental Infantry, 1st January, 1776; 2d Lieutenant, 3d August, 1776; dismissed 13th October, 1776.

Talbot, Jeremiah (Pa). Captain 6th Pennsylvania Battalion, 9th January, 1776; Captain 7th Pennsylvania, 15th February, 1777, to rank from 9th January, 1776; Major, 25th September, 1777; retired 1st January, 1781. (Died 19th January, 1791.)

Talbot, Richard (Md). Ensign 3d Maryland Battalion of the Flying Camp, June to December, 1776; 2d Lieutenant 4th Maryland, 10th December, 1776; 1st Lieutenant, 15th April, 1777; resigned 6th November, 1777.

Talbot, Silas (R. I.). Captain 2d Rhode Island, 28th June to December, 1775; Captain 11th Continental Infantry, 1st January to 31st December, 1776; was severely burnt on fire-ship, 14th September, 1776; Captain 1st Rhode, 1st January, 1777; ·Major, 1st September, 1777; wounded at Fort Mifflin, 23d October, 1777. By the act of 14th November, 1778, it was "Resolved, that Congress have a high sense of the bravery and good conduct of Major Silas Talbot, of the State of Rhode Island, and the officers and men under his command, in boarding and taking the armed schooner 'Pigot' of eight twelve-pounders and forty-five men, in the east passage between Rhode Is-

land and the Main, and that he, as a reward of his merit and for the encouragement of a spirit of enterprise, be presented with the commission of Lieutenant-Colonel in the Army of the United States." Lieutenant-Colonel Continental Army, 14th November, 1778; was wounded in action at sea in the spring of 1779; Captain United States Navy, 17th September, 1779; captured at sea in 1780; exchanged in 1781; served to close of war; Captain United States Navy, 11th May, 1798; resigned 21st September, 1801. (Died 30th June, 1813.)

Talcott, Elizur (Conn). Colonel Connecticut Militia, 1775-1776.

Talcott, Matthew (Conn). Colonel Connecticut Militia in 1776.

Taliaferro, Benjamin (Va). 2d Lieutenant 6th Virginia, 4th March, 1776; 1st Lieutenant, 7th August, 1776; Captain, 23d September, 1777; transferred to 2d Virginia, 14th September, 1778; taken prisoner at Charleston, 12th May, 1780; prisoner on parole to close of war; Brevet Major, 30th September, 1783. (Died 3d September, 1821.)

Taliaferro, Francis (Va). Captain 2d Virginia, March, 1776 to —, 1777.

Taliaferro, Nicholas (Va). Sergeant 10th Virginia, 25th November, 1776; Ensign, 15th August, 1777; 2d Lieutenant, 15th November, 1777; regiment designated 6th Virginia, 14th September, 1778; taken prisoner at Charleston, 12th May, 1780; transferred to 3d Virginia, 12th February, 1781; 1st Lieutenant, 18th February, 1781; retired 1st January, 1783. (Died 1812.)

Taliaferro, Philip (Va). Captain 2d Virginia, 23d September, 1777; retired 30th September, 1778.

Taliaferro, William (Va). Captain 2d Virginia, 29th September, 1775; Major 8th Virginia, 7th August, 1776; Lieutenant-Colonel 4th Virginia, 21st February, 1777; taken prisoner at Brandywine, 11th September, 1777; died 1st February, 1778

Tallmadge, Benjamin (Conn). Adjutant of Chester's Connecticut State Regiment, 20th June, 1776; Brigade Major to General Wadsworth, 11th October, 1776; Captain 2d Continental Dragoons, 14th December, 1776; Major, 7th April, 1777. By the act of 6th December, 1780, it was "Resolved, while Congress are sensible of the patriotism, courage and perseverance of the officers and privates of their regular forces, as well as of the militia throughout these United States, and of the military conduct of the principal Commanders in both, it gives them pleasure to be so frequently called upon to confer marks of distinction and applause for enterprises which do honor to the profession of arms, and claim a high rank of military achievements; in this light they view the enterprise against Fort St. George, on Long Island, planned and conducted with wisdom and great gallantry, by Major Tallmadge, of the Light Dragoons, and executed with intrepidity and complete success by the officers and soldiers of the detachment. Ordered, therefore, that Major Tallmadge's report to the Commander-in-Chief be published, with the preceding minute, as a tribute to distinguished merit, and in testimony of the sense Congress entertain of this brilliant service." Served at General Washington's Headquarters, March, 1781, to November, 1783; Brevet Lieutenant-Colonel, 30th September, 1783. (Died 17th March, 1835.)

Tallmadge, James (N. Y.). Captain New York Militia, ——; wounded at Saratoga, 7th October, 1777.

Tallmadge, Samuel (N. Y.). Sergeant 4th New York, 21st November, 1776; Ensign, 9th November, 1777; Regimental Adjutant, 9th July, 1778, to 1st January, 1781; transferred to 2d New York 1st January, 1781; 2d Lieutenant, 27th October, 1781; 1st Lieutenant, 10th April, 1782, and served to June, 1783.

Tallman, Benjamin (R. I.). Major of Richmond's Rhode Island State Regiment, 1st November, 1775, to 25th January, 1776; Colonel Rhode Island Militia and State Regiment, 12th December, 1776, to 16th March, 1780.

Tallman, Teunis (N. Y.). Lieutenant of Graham's Regiment New York Militia in 1778.

Tallman, Thomas (R. I.). Ensign of Warner's Additianol Continental Regiment, 14th August, 1778; 2d Lieutenant, May, 1780; retired 1st January, 1781. (Died 19th April, 1809.)

Tallow, James (N. Y.). Captain New York Militia; taken prisoner at Westchester, 24th December, 1779.

Tannehill, Adamson (Md). 2d Lieutenant of Stephenson's Maryland and Virginia Rifle Regiment, 11th July, 1776; 1st Lieutenant of Rawlings' Continental Regiment, — January, 1777;

Captain, 20th July, 1779, to rank from 1st April, 1778; retired 1st January, 1781; Brigadier-General Pennsylvania Volunteers in 1812. (Died 7th July, 1817.)

Tannehill, Josiah (Va). Ensign and Paymaster 9th Virginia, 6th August, 1779; transferred to 7th Virginia, 12th February, 1781; Lieutenant, October, 1781 retired 1st January, 1783. (Died 1811.)

Tannehill, Nieman (Md). 2d Lieutenant of Stephenson's Maryland and Pennsylvania Rifle Regiment, 11th July, 1776; killed at Fort Washington, 16th November, 1776.

Tanner, Ebenezer (Conn). Sergeant 7th Connecticut, 30th April, 1777; Ensign, 25th May, 1779; transferred to 2d Connecticut, 1st January, 1781; 2d Lieutenant, 28th March, 1782; retired 1st January, 1783.

Tanner, Joseph (Md). 1st Lieutenant Maryland Battalion of the Flying Camp, July to December, 1776.

Tanner, Thomas (Conn). 2d Lieutenant of Bradley's Connecticut State Regiment, 10th June, 1776; taken prisoner at Fort Washington, 16th November, 1776. (Died 1817.)

Tanner, Tryal (Conn). Ensign of Elmore's Continental Regiment, 15th April, 1776; 2d Lieutenant, 25th July, 1776; 2d Lieutenant 7th Connecticut, 1st January, 1777; 1st Lieutenant, 1st September, 1777; Regimental Adjutant, 16th December, 1777; resigned 11th April, 1780.

Tapp, William (N. Y.). Regimental Quartermaster 1st New York, 5th July to November, 1775; 2d Lieutenant of Nicholson's Continental Regiment, 26th March, 1776; 1st Lieutenant 3d New York, 21st November, 1776; resigned 20th March, 1780.

Tappan, Christopher (N Y.). Major New York Militia in 1775.

Tappan, Peter (N. Y.). Lieutenant New York Militia in 1775; Surgeon's Mate in Hospital Department, 1776 to 1780 ;2d Lieutenant 2d Continental Artillery, 20th August, 1781, and served to June, 1783.

Tarbox, Solomon (Conn). Corporal 2d Connecticut, 13th May to 17th December, 1775; Lieutenant of Wadsworth's Connecticut State Regiment, July to December, 1776; 2d Lieutenant 3d Connecticut, 1st January, 1777; died 20th December, 1777.

Tarling, —— (S. C.). Lieutenant-Colonel South Carolina Militia, 1777-1778.

Tarlton, William (Vt). Captain Bedel's Regiment Vermont Militia, 1st April, 1778, to 1st April, 1779.

Tarrant, Manlove (N. C.). Ensign 2d North Carolina, 3d May, 1776; Lieutenant, 8th June, 1776; Captain, 24th October, 1777; retired 1st June, 1778.

Tartanson, Francis (N. C.). Captain 8th North Carolina, 16th January, 1777; resigned 10th September, 1778.

Tash, Thomas (N. H.). Colonel New Hampshire Militia, 1776 to 1780.

Tate, Adam (Pa). Ensign 11th Pennsylvania, 21st April, 1777; 2d Lieutenant, 11th September, 1777; resigned 25th October, 1777.

Tate, James (N. C.). Chaplain 1st North Carolina, 13th October, 1775; Brigade Chaplain North Carolina Troops, 1st June, 1778, and served to close of war.

Tate, James (Pa). Surgeon Delaware Battalion of the Fling Camp, July to December, 1776; Surgeon's Mate 2d Maryland, 1st January, 1777; Surgeon 3d Pennsylvania, 1st August, 1777, to 31st July, 1780. (Died 1814.)

Tate, James (S. C.). Lieutenant South Carolina Militia; killed at Guilford, 15th March, 1781.

Tate, John (Pa). Ensign 11th Pennsylvania, 1st January, 1777; resigned — October, 1777; Surgeon's Mate 2d Maryland, 10th May, 1778; resigned April, 1779.

Tate, Joseph (N. C.). 1st Lieutenant 2d North Carolina, 1st September, 1775; Captain, 16th May, 1776; died 2d June, 1777.

Tate, Robert (S. C.). Captain South Carolina Dragoons, 5th April to September, 1781.

Tate, Samuel (S. C.). Captain South Carolina Militia; wounded at Guilford, 15th March, 1781. (Died 1798.)

Tate, William (S. C.). Captain Lieutenant 4th South Carolina (Artillery) Regiment, 8th October, 1779; taken prisoner at Charleston, 12th May, 1780; exchanged October, 1780, and served to close of war.

Tatum, Absolom (N. C.). 1st Lieutenant 1st North Carolina, 1st September, 1775; Captain, 29th June, 1776; resigned 19th September, 1776.

Tatum, Henry (Va). Ensign 5th Virginia, 25th March, 1776; 2d Lieutenant, 13th December, 1776; wounded at Brandywine, 11th September, 1777; retired 14th September, 1778. (Died 1836.)

Tatum, Howell (N. C.). Ensign 1st North Carolina, 1st September, 1775; 2d Lieutenant, 4th January, 1776; 1st Lieutenant, 28th March, 1776; Captain, 3d April, 1777; taken prisoner at Charleston, 12th May, 1780; exchanged 14th June, 1781; resigned 20th May, 1782.

Tatum, James (N. C.). Ensign 9th North Carolina, 12th August, 1777; 2d Lieutenant, 1st January, 1778; transferred to 3d North Carolina, 1st June, 1778; 1st Lieutenant, 14th December, 1779; taken prisoner at Charleston, 12th May, 1780, and was a prisoner on parole to close of war. (Died 10th September, 1821.)

Tatum, Zachariah (Va). Ensign 5th Virginia, 13th December, 1780; retired 1st January, 1783.

Taulman, Peter (N. Y.). Ensign of Malcolm's Continental Regiment, 11th March, 1777; Regimental Adjutant, 1st July, 1777; 2d Lieutenant, 12th October, 1777; 1st Lieutenant, 1st April, 1779; transferred to Spencer's Continental Regiment, 17th April, 1779; retired 1st January, 1781; Captain Lieutenant Sappers and Miners, 2d July, 1781, and served to close of war. (Died 16th December, 1835.)

Taylor, Andrew (N. Y.). Adjutant 1st New York, 18th March, 1776; 2d Lieutenant, 18th June to November, 1776.

Taylor, Augustine (Conn). 2d Lieutenant 7th Connecticut, 1st January, 1777; Regimental Quartermaster, 26th July, 1778; 1st Lieutenant, 20th January, 1779; transferred to 2d Connecticut, 1st January, 1781; resigned 25th June, 1781. (Died 10th February, 1816.)

Taylor, Charles (Pa). 3d Lieutenant of Miles' Pennsylvania Rifle Regiment, 19th March, 1776; killed at Long Island, 27th August, 1776.

Taylor, Charles (Va). Surgeon's Mate 2d Virginia, 19th July, 1776; Surgeon Virginia Convention Guards, 26th October, 1779, to 15th May, 1780.

Taylor, Chase (N. H.). Captain of Stickney's Regiment New Hampshire Militia, ——; severely wounded at Bennington, 16th August, 1777. (Died 1805.)

Taylor, Christopher (Pa). Surgeon's Mate Invalid Regiment, 1st May, 1782, and served to close of war.

Taylor, Christopher (N. C.). Captain North Carolina Militia at King's Mountain, October, 1780.

Taylor, Daniel (Mass). 1st Lieutenant of Nixon's Massachusetts Regiment, May to December, 1775.

Taylor, Dudley (Mass). Ensign 4th Continental Infantry, 1st January, 1776; 2d Lieutenant, 10th August to 31st December, 1776.

Taylor, Elijah (Conn). Sergeant 5th Connecticut, 1st May, 1777; Ensign, 12th May, 1779; resigned 21st July, 1781.

Taylor, Ezekiel (N. Y.). Major New York Militia, 1775-1778.

Taylor, Francis (S. C.). 2d Lieutenant 3d South Carolina, 12th September, 1775; 1st Lieutenant, 6th May, 1776; Captain, —, February, 1777; resigned 7th October, 1777.

Taylor, Francis (Va). Captain 2d Virginia, 8th May, 1776; Major 15th Virginia, 20th March, 1778; retired 14th September, 1778; Colonel Virginia Convention Guards, January, 1779, to June, 1781.

Taylor, George (N. J.). Colonel New Jersey Militia in 1776.

Taylor, George (Pa). A signer of the Declaration of Independence; died 23d February, 1781.

Taylor, Gillam (N. H.). Ensign 2d Continental Infantry, 1st January, 1776, to ——.

Taylor, Henry (Va). Lieutenant-Colonel Virginia Militia, 1776-1780.

Taylor, Ignatius (Md). Captain Maryland Militia, 1776-1777. (Died 1807).

Taylor, Isaac (Va). Captain of Clark's Illinois State Regiment, 1778 to 1781.

Taylor, James (Ga). Was a Captain 1st Georgia in 1776, and served to ——.

Taylor, James (Pa). Captain 3d Pennsylvania Battalion, 5th January, 1776; Judge Advocate Northern Department, 26th December, 1776; Major 5th Pennsylvania, 23d September, 1777; resigned 3d April, 1778. (Died 1844.)

Taylor, James (Va). Colonel Virginia Militia in 1775. (Died 1814.)

Taylor, John (N. J.). Colonel New Jersey Militia in 1777. (Died 1801.)

Taylor, John (N. C.). Ensign 1st North Carolina, 1st September, 1775, to ——.

Taylor, John (N. C.). Lieutenant and Paymaster 8th North Carolina, 24th July, 1777; omitted 1st January, 1778.

Taylor, John (Va). Captain 1st Virginia, 29th April, 1776; Judge Advocate of Continental Troops in Virginia with rank of Major in 2d Canadian Regiment, 24th January 1777, to rank from 13th November, 1776; resigned 10th February, 1779.

Taylor, John (Va). Lieutenant Virginia Militia, 1780-1781.

Taylor, Jonathan (Va). Lieutenant Virginia Convention Guards, 18th June, 1779, to 15th June, 1781. (Died 1804.)

Taylor, Joseph (Vt). Captain of Bedel's Regiment Vermont Militia, 15th December, 1777, to 1st April, 1779.

Taylor, Levi (Conn). 1st Lieutenant 5th Connecticut, 1st May to 25th October, 1775.

Taylor, Nathan (N. H.). Lieutenant of Whitcomb's Battalion New Hampshire Rangers, 1st February, 1777; resigned 6th December, 1779. (Died 1840.)

Taylor, Nathan (R. I.). Lieutenant Rhode Island Militia in 1777.

Taylor, Othniel (Mass). 2d Lieutenant 10th Massachusetts, 1st January, 1777; 1st Lieutenant, 2d March, 1778; Regimental Adjutant, 1st January, 1779; Captain, 30th October, 1780; retired 1st January, 1783. (Died 15th August, 1819.)

Taylor, Philip (N. C.). Captain 6th North Carolina, 16th April, 1776; retired 1st June, 1778.

Taylor, Reuben (Va). 1st Lieutenant 2d Canadian (Hazen's) Regiment, 3d November, 1776; Captain, 2d February, 1778; omitted — October, 1781.

Taylor, Richard (Va). 1st Lieutenant 1st Virginia, 6th September, 1775; Captain, 5th March, 1776; Major, 13th Virginia, 4th February, 1778; transferred to 9th Virginia, 14th September, 1778; Lieutenant-Colonel 2d Virginia, 7th December, 1779; retired 12th February, 1781. (Died 1826.)

Taylor, Richard (Va). Ensign 6th Virginia, 7th September, 1776; 2d Lieutenant, 5th February, 1777; 1st Lieutenant, 4th June, 1777; retired 30th September, 1778; served subsequently in Navy.

Taylor, Robert (N. J.). Captain, Major and Colonel New Jersey Militia, 1776-1777.

Taylor, Robert (Pa). Major Pennsylvania Militia, 1777.

Taylor, Samuel (Mass). 2d Lieutenant of Brewer's Massachusetts Regiment, May to December, 1775.

Taylor, Samuel (S. C.). 2d Lieutenant 3d South Carolina, 17th June, 1775; 1st Lieutenant, May, 1776; Captain, ——, 1780; wounded and lost a leg at Cowpens, 17th January, 1781. (Died 1798.)

Taylor, Severn (Va). Lieutenant 1st Virginia, 7th March, 1777; wounded at Germantown, 4th October, 1777, and did not rejoin regiment.

Taylor, Tertius (Mass). Sergeant 10th Massachusetts, 1st February, 1777; 2d Lieutenant, 18th March, 1777; transferred to 1st Massachusetts, 1st January, 1783, and served to 3d November, 1783.

Taylor, Thomas (Ga). Adjutant 4th Georgia in 1777; Colonel Georgia Militia, 1780 to 1782.

Taylor, Thomas (Pa). Colonel Pennsylvania Militia, 1777-1778. (Died 1782.)

Taylor, Thomas (S. C.). Colonel South Carolina Militia, 1779-1783.

Taylor, Thornton (Va). Ensign 4th Virginia, 15th August, 1777; Lieutenant, ——; retired 30th September, 1778.

Taylor, Timothy (Conn). Sergeant 5th Connecticut, 9th May to 11th December ,1775; Ensign of Bradley's Connecticut State Regiment, 10th June, 1776; taken prisoner at Fort Washington, 16th November, 1776; 1st Lieutenant 2d Connecticut, 1st September, 1777; transferred to 3d Connecticut, 1st January, 1781; Captain, 15th December, 1781; transferred to 2d Connecticut, 1st January, 1781; retained in Swift's Connecticut Regiment in June, 1783, and served to 3d November, 1783; Lieutenant-Colonel 13th United States Infantry, 13th February, 1799; honorably discharged, 15th June, 1800.

Taylor, William (Mass). Sergeant in Prescott's Massachusetts Regiment, May to December, 1775; Ensign, 7th Continental Infantry, 1st January to 31st December, 1776; 1st Lieutenant

2d Massachusetts, 1st January, 1777, and served to June, 1783.

Taylor, William (N. C.). Lieutenant-Colonel 6th North Carolina, 7th May, 1776, to ——.

Taylor, William (Va). 1st Lieutenant 2d Virginia, 29th January, 1776; Captain 28th December, 1776; Major 9th Virginia, 7th December, 1779; retired 12th February, 1781. (Died 14th April, 1830.)

Teackle, Arthur (Va). 2d Lieutenant 9th Virginia, 14th February, 1776; 1st Lieutenant, 26th July, 1776; resigned 26th May, 1778.

Teackle, Severn (Va). Ensign 9th Virginia, 12th February, 1776; 2d Lieutenant, 11th July, 1776; taken prisoner at Germantown, 4th October, 1777; exchanged in 1780; retained as Captain 5th Virginia, 12th February, 1781, to rank from 25th June, 1779; retired 1st January, 1783. (Died 1794.)

Tearse, Peter B. (N. Y.). Lieutenant and Adjutant 2d New York, 16th February, 1776; 1st Lieutenant and Adjutant 1st New York, 21st November, 1776, to rank from 16th February, 1776; resigned 23d April, 1781; Brigade Major to General Gansevoort's New York Militia in 1781.

Teas, Alexander (Md). 2d Lieutenant 2d Canadian (Hazen's) Regiment, 3d November, 1776; died 15th September, 1777, of wounds received at Germantown, 11th September, 1777.

Teas, William (Md). Cornet 3d Continental Dragoons, 1779 to 9th November, 1782; wounded at Camden, 16th August, 1780. (Died 1824.)

Tebbetts, Ebenezer (N. H.). Major New Hampshire Militia, 1777-1778.

Tebbs, John (Va). Ensign 3d Virginia, 5th February, 1776; 2d Lieutenant, 19th June, 1777; 1st Lieutenant, ——, 1778; retired 30th September, 1778.

Tebbs, Thomas (Va). 1st Lieutenant 2d Virginia, 23d January, 1776, to ——.

Tebbs, Willoughby (Va). Ensign of Grayson's Continental Regiment, 1st March, 1777; 2d Lieutenant, 8th June, 1777; Regimental Quartermaster, 1st July, 1778; resigned 28th September, 1778.

Tefft, Oliver (R. I.). Ensign 1st Rhode Island, 28th June to November, 1775.

Teller, James (N. Y.). Captain in Graham's Regiment New York Militia; prisoner of war, 24th June, 1779, to January, 1781; where taken not stated.

Temple, Benjamin (Va). Captain Virginia Dragoons, 15th June, 1776; Lieutenant-Colonel 1st Continental Dragoons, 31st March, 1777; transferred to 4th Dragoons, 10th December, 1779, and served to close of war; Colonel, 30th September, 1783. (Died 1802.)

Temple, John (Mass). Ensign of Baldwin's Artillery Artificers Regiment, 28th March, 1778; Lieutenant, 12th May, 1779; retired 26th March, 1781.

Templeton, Andrew (Ga). Captain — Georgia Militia; killed at Charleston, 12th May, 1780.

Ten Broeck, Abraham (N. Y.). Colonel New York Militia, 1775 to 1778, and Brigadier-General New York Militia, 25th June, 1778; resigned 26th March, 1781. (Died 19th January, 1810.)

Ten Brock, Adam (N. Y.). Ensign 1st New York, 29th June, 1781, and served to June, 1783. (Died 30th May, 1826.)

Ten Broeck, Dirck (N. Y.). Lieutenant-Colonel New York Militia, 20th October, 1775, to ——.

Ten Broeck, John (N. J.). Captain, Major and Lieutenant-Colonel New Jersey Militia, 1775-1779. (Died 1820.)

Ten Broeck, John Cornelius (N. Y.). 2d Lieutenant 4th New York, October, 1775; 1st Lieutenant, 1st March, 1776; 1st Lieutenant 1st New York, 21st November, 1776, to rank from 1st March, 1776; Captain, 5th April, 1781, and served to June, 1783. (Died 10th August, 1835.)

Ten Broeck, Leonard (N. Y.). Captain New York Militia in 1776.

Ten Broeck, Peter B. (N. Y.). Lieutenant in New York Levies in 1780.

Ten Broeck, Petrus (N. Y.). Colonel and Brigadier-General New York Militia, 1775-1781.

Ten Broeck, Samuel (N. Y.). Captain and Major New York Militia, 1775-1780.

Ten Eyck, Abraham (N Y.). Lieutenant New York Militia in 1775; Lieutenant and Paymaster 1st New York, 21st November, 1776; Regimental Quartermaster, 13th January, 1777; retired 1st January, 1781; Captain Assistant Deputy Quartermaster-General United States Army, 20th May, 1813; honor-

ably discharged, 15th June, 1815. (Died 14th November, 1824.)

Ten Eyck, Abraham (N. J.). Colonel New Jersey Militia, 1776-1779.

Ten Eyck, Barent J. (N. Y.). Captain 2d New York, 28th June, 1775, to March, 1776; Captain 2d New York, 21st November, 1776, to rank from 28th June, 1775; resigned 22d January, 1778.

Ten Eyck, Coenradt (N. Y.) Captain and Major New York Militia, 1775-1776.

Ten Eyck, Henry (Conn). Adjutant 2d Connecticut, 1st January, 1777; Captain, 13th May, 1778; transferred to 4th Connecticut, 1st January, 1781; transferred to 3d Connecticut, 1st January, 1783, and served to June, 1783.

Ten Eyck, John (N. J.). Lieutenant New Jersey Militia, ——; killed at Millstone, N. J., 17th June, 1777.

Ten Eyck, John D. P. (N. Y.). Lieutenant and Paymaster 1st Canadian (Livingston's) Regiment, 12th February, 1777 Captain Lieutenant, 24th September, 1779 retired 1st January, 1781.

Tennant, George (R. I.). Lieutenant 3d Rhode Island, 3d May, 1775, to ——.

Tennent, William (Conn). Chaplain of Swift's Connecticut State Regiment, July to December, 1776.

Tenney, Samuel (R. I.). Surgeon's Mate of Gridley's Regiment Massachusetts Artillery, June to December, 1775; Surgeon 11th Continental Infantry, 1st January to 31st December, 1776; Surgeon 2d Rhode Island, 1st January, 1777; retained in Olney's Rhode Island Battalion, April, 1783, and served to 25th December, 1783. (Died 6th February, 1816.)

Tennill, Francis (Ga).—See **Trunnell.**

Terhune, Jacob (N. J.). Captain New Jersey Militia in 1776.

Terhune, Nicholas (N. J.). Captain New Jersey Militia in 1776.

Ternant, Jean Baptiste (France). Deputy Quartermaster-General, 26th March, 1778; Lieutenant-Colonel and Inspector Continental Army, 25th September, 1778, with pay from 26th March, 1778, and served with the Pulaski Legion; taken prisoner at Charleston, 12th May, 1780; Brevet Colonel, 13th October, 1783; subsequently was by act of 22d April, 1784, appointed Colonel of Armand's Partisan Corps or Legion to date from March, 26, 1783; the date of Armand's promotion to Brigadier-

General: served to close of war. (Died April, 1816.)

Terrell, Henry (Va). Captain 5th Virginia, 12th March, 1776; resigned 11th August, 1777.

Terrell, Israel (Conn). 2d Lieutenant 1st Connecticut, 1st May to December, 1775. (Died 1811.)

Terrell, Josiah (Conn). Captain Connecticut Militia, 1776-1777.

Terrill, William (Va). Ensign 5th Virginia, 26th February, 1776; 2d Lieutenant 14th December, 1776; resigned 5th September, 1778.

Terry, Jeremiah (S. C.). Major South Carolina Militia, 1775.

Terry, Nathaniel (Va). 1st Lieutenant 14th Virginia, 2d December, 1776; regiment designated 10th Virginia, 14th September, 1778; Captain Lieutenant, 12th March, 1779; Regimental Quartermaster, 31st March, 1779; Captain, 15th December, 1779; taken prisoner at Charleston, 12th May, 1780, and was a prisoner on parole to close of war. (Died 1834.)

Terry, William (Va). Lieutenant Colonel Virginia Militia, 1777-1778.

Tetard, Benjamin (Ga). Surgeon of a Georgia Regiment, 1779-1780.

Tetard, John Peter (N. Y.). Chaplain of New York Troops, 6th July, 1775, to January, 1776; Chaplain, 4th New York, 21st November, 1776, to 27th May, 1777.

Teter, Andrew (Ga). Captain 3d Georgia, ——; cashiered 24th January, 1778.

Tew, Benedict (R. I.). Ensign 2d Rhode Island, 1st January, 1777; 2d Lieutenant, 11th February, 1777; 1st Lieutenant, 22d October, 1777; resigned 19th May, 1779.

Tew, James (R. I.). Captain of Babcock's Rhode Island State Regiment, 15th January, 1776; Major of Lippitt's Rhode Island State Regiment, 19th August, 1776, to March, 1777.

Tew, Thomas (R. I.). Captain of Church's Rhode Island Regiment, 3d May to December, 1775.

Tew, William (R. I.). Captain 3d Rhode Island, 3d May to December, 1775; Captain 11th Continental Infantry, 1st January to 31st December, 1776; Captain 2d Rhode Island, 1st January, 1777; retired 14th May, 1781. (Died 31st October, 1808.)

Texier, John Felix (—). Surgeon Pulaski Legion, 1779-1780.

Thackston, James (N. C.). Lieutenant-Colonel 4th North Carolina, 15th April, 1776; retired 1st January, 1781.

Thatcher, James (Va). Surgeon 1st Virginia State Regiment, 10th October, 1778; resigned 30th June, 1779.

Thatcher, James (Mass). Surgeon's Mate of Whitcomb's Massachusetts Regiment, July to December, 1775; Surgeon's Mate 6th Continental Infantry, 1st January to 31st December, 1776; Hospital Surgeon's Mate, 1st April, 1777; Surgeon of Jackson's Additional Continental Regiment, 10th November, 1778; regiment designated 16th Massachusetts, 23d July, 1780; transferred to 9th Massachusetts, 1st January, 1781; retired 1st January, 1783. (Died 24th May, 1844.)

Thatcher, John (Conn). Captain of Swift's Connecticut State Regiment; taken prisoner at Valcour Island, 13th October, 1776, while in command of the "Washington." (Died 17th July, 1805.)

Thatcher, Nathaniel (Mass). Ensign of Jackson's Continental Regiment, 1st February, 1777; taken prisoner at Paramus, 16th April, 1780; regiment designated 16th Massachusetts, 23d July, 1780; transferred to 9th Massachusetts, 1st January, 1781; Lieutenant, 7th October, 1781; transferred to 5th Massachusetts, 1st May, 1782, and served to 3d November, 1783. (Died February, 1809.)

Thayer, Abel (Mass). Lieutenant in Lexington Alarm, April, 1775; Captain of Fellows' Massachusetts Regiment, May to December, 1775.

Thayer, Bartholomew (Mass). Corporal 10th Massachusetts, 20th February, 1777; Sergeant, 1st November, 1777; Ensign, 6th April, 1779; Lieutenant, 12th September, 1780; retired 1st July, 1782. (Died 11th April, 1826.)

Thayer, Ebenezer (Mass). Captain Massachusetts Militia in 1780.

Thayer, Isaac (Mass). Ensign and Lieutenant of Sargent's Massachusetts Regiment, May to December, 1775; Captain Massachusetts Militia in 1776. (Died 1827.)

Thayer, Jabez (Mass). Chaplain 14th Massachusetts, 1st January, 1777; resigned — September, 1777.

Thayer, Jedediah (Mass). 2d Lieutenant of Gardiner's Massachusetts Regiment, May to December, 1775;

2d Lieutenant 25th Continental Infantry, 1st January, 1776; 1st Lieutenant, 13th April to 31st December, 1776; Captain of Baldwin's Artillery Artificer Regiment, 1st January, 1777, to ——.

Thayer, Nathan (Mass). Private of Greaton's Massachusetts Regiment, April to December, 1775; Sergeant 12th Continental Infantry, February to November, 1776; Sergeant 13th Massachusetts, 28th November, 1776; Ensign, 1st December, 1777; resigned 31st March, 1778. (Died 24th September, 1827.)

Thayer, Simeon (R. I.). Captain Lieutenant 2d Rhode Island, 3d May, 1775; taken prisoner at Quebec, 31st December, 1775; exchanged 1st July, 1777; Major 2d Rhode Island, to rank from 1st January, 1777; wounded (lost an eye) at Monmouth, 28th June, 1778; retired 14th May, 1781. (Died 14th October, 1800.)

. **Thayer, Zacheus** (Mass). Ensign of Sargent's Massachusetts Regiment, June to December, 1775; 2d Lieutenant 16th Continental Infantry, 1st January to 31st December, 1776; Lieutenant Massachusetts Militia, 1777-1780.

Thelable, Robert (Va). Ensign 15th Virginia, 13th February, 1777; 2d Lieutenant, 11th March, 1777; retired 30th September, 1778.

Theus, James (S. C.). Captain South Carolina Militia, 1779-1782.

Theus, Jeremiah (S. C.). Surgeon 2d South Carolina, 2d August, 1777; taken prisoner at Charleston 12th May, 1780; served to close of war.

Theus, Perrin (S. C.). Surgeon Hospital Department, 1777-1780.

Theus, Simeon (S. C.). 2d Lieutenant 1st South Carolina, 17th June, 1775; 1st Lieutenant, May, 1776; Captain, 18th August, 1777; taken prisoner at Charleston, 12th May, 1780; exchanged ——; served to close of war; Brevet Major, 30th September 1783.

Thibout, Henry.—See **Tiebout.**

Thomas, Abisha (Mass). Captain Deputy-Quartermaster-General, 1st May to 10th November, 1777.

Thomas, Alexander (R. I.). Lieutenant of Babcock's Rhode Island State Regiment, 15th January, 1776, and of Lippitt's Rhode Island State Regiment, 19th August, 1776, to March, 1777; Captain of Topham's Rhode Island Regiment in 1778. (Died 1812.)

Thomas, David (Mass). Sergeant in Lexington Alarm, April, 1775; Ensign of Sargent's Massachusetts Regiment, May to December, 1775; 2d Lieutenant 16th Continental Infantry, 1st January, 1776; 1st Lieutenant, 28th June to 31st December, 1776.

Thomas, Edmund Disney (N. J.). Private and Cadet 3d New Jersey, January to July, 1776; Ensign, 19th July, 1776, to 20th November, 1776; Ensign 3d New Jersey, 29th November, 1776; 1st Lieutenant, 11th November, 1777; transferred to 2d New Jersey, 1st January, 1781; retained in New Jersey Battalion, April, 1783; Brevet Captain, 30th September, 1783, and served to 3d November, 1783.

Thomas, Edward (N. J.). Colonel New Jersey Militia, 1776-1778. (Died 1795.)

Thomas, Edward (N. Y.). Lieutenant New York Militia, ——; prisoner of war, 1st March to November, 1781.

Thomas, Edward (S. C.). Lietuenant South Carolina Militia in 1775.

Thomas, Foxwell (Mass). Corporal in Lexington Alarm, April, 1775; 2d Lieutenant of Cotton's Massachusetts Regiment, May to December, 1775; 2d Lieutenant 3d Continental Infantry, 1st January to 31st December, 1776. (Died 10th September, 1829.)

Thomas, Henry (Pa). Private 12th Pennsylvania, 15th October, 1776; Sergeant-Major, — November, 1776; Ensign, 1st February, 1777; resigned 17th October, 1777.

Thomas, Jacob (N. Y.). 1st Lieutenant 4th New York, 28th June, 1775; resigned 11th August, 1775.

Thomas, John, Jr. (Md). 2d Lieutenant 4th Maryland Battalion of the Flying Camp, July to December, 1776.

Thomas, John (Mass). Surgeon's Mate of Cotton's Massachusetts Regiment, April to December, 1775; Surgeon's Mate 23d Continental Infantry, 1st January to 31st December, 1776; Surgeon 9th Massachusetts, 1st January, 1777; transferred to 8th Massachusetts, 1st January, 1781; transferred to 3d Massachusetts, 12th January, 1783, and served to close of war. (Died 30th October, 1819.)

Thomas, John (Mass). Colonel of a Massachusetts Regiment, April, 1775; Major General Massachusetts Militia, 20th June, 1775; Lieutenant-General Massachusetts Militia, January, 1776;

Brigadier General Continental Army, 22d June, 1775; Major-General Continental Army, 6th March, 1776. Died 2d June, 1776.

Thomas, John (N. Y.). Colonel New York Militia; was a prisoner, when and where taken not stated.

Thomas, John (N. C.). Ensign 9th North Carolina, 28th November, 1776, to ——.

Thomas, John (S. C.). Colonel South Carolina Militia, 1775-1776.

Thomas, John, Jr. (S. C.). Colonel South Carolina Militia, 1780-1782.

Thomas, John (R. I.). Ensign 11th Continental Infantry, 1st January, 1776; drowned 27th August, 1776.

Thomas, John (Va). Captain Virginia Militia, 1780-1781.

Thomas, John Allen (Md). Captain of an Independent Maryland Company, 14th January, 1776, to ——.

Thomas, Joseph (Mass). 2d Lieutenant of Knox's Regiment Continental Artillery, 10th December, 1775; Captain Lieutenant 2d Continental Artillery, 1st January, 1777; Captain, 26th October, 1779, and served to 17th June, 1783. (Died ——, 1804.)

Thomas, Joseph (N. H.). Ensign 1st New Hampshire, 18th October, 1775; taken prisoner at Quebec, 31st December, 1775.

Thomas, Joseph M. (N. H.). Lieutenant and Adjutant of Tash's Regiment New Hampshire Militia, August to November, 1776; 2d Lieutenant 3d New Hampshire, 8th November, 1776; 1st Lieutenant, 14th July, 1777; killed at Bemus Heights, 19th September, 1777.

Thomas, Joshua (Mass) Adjutant of Cotton's Massachusetts Regiment, May to December, 1775; 2d Lieutenant and Adjutant, 23d Continental Infantry, 1st January to December, 1776; was Aide-de-Camp to General Thomas in 1776.

Thomas, Lewis (Va). 2d Lieutenant 13th Virginia, 19th December, 1776; 1st Lieutenant, 15th July, 1777; regiment designated 9th Virginia, 14th September, 1778; Captain Lieutenant, ——, 1779; transferred to 7th Virginia, 12th February, 1781; retired 1st January, 1783.

Thomas, Mark (Va). Captaian of Clark's Illinois Regiment, 1777 to 1781.

Thomas, Philip (Mass). 2d Lieutenant of Marshall's Massachusetts Regi-

ment, June to November, 1776; Captain 10th Massachusetts, 6th November, 1776; retired 1st March, 1779.

Thomas, Philip (N. H.). Captain Lieutenant 3d New Hampshire, 23d April to December, 1775.

Thomas, . Richard (Pa). Colonel Pennsylvania Militia, 1776-1777.

Thomas, Samuel (Mass). Ensign of Phinney's Massachusetts Regiment, May to November, 1775.

Thomas, Samuel Wright (Md). 2d Lieutenant 4th Maryland Battalion of the Flying Camp, July to December, 1776.

Thomas Stephen Jones (N. H.). 2d Lieutenant 8th Continental Infantry, 1st January, 1776, to 31st December, 1776; Captain of Peabody's Regiment Rhode Island Militia, 1779-1780.

Thomas, Thomas (N. Y.). Colonel New York Militia, ——; taken prisoner at Cherry Valley, 10th November, 1778; released 15th May, 1779.

Thomas, Thomas (Va). Ensign 11th Virginia, 5th December, 1776; resigned June 7th, 1778.

Thomas, Tristam (S. C.). Colonel South Carolina Militia, 1780.

Thomas, William (Mass). Surgeon of Cotton's Massachusetts Regiment, May to December, 1775. Surgeon Massachusetts Militia in 1777.

Thomas, William (Pa). 1st Lieutenant 11th Pennsylvania, 30th September, 1776; resigned 9th April, 1777.

Thomaston, Ephraim (Conn). 2d Lieutenant of Douglas' Connecticut State Regiment, June to December, 1776.

Thompson, Alexander (N. Y.). 2d Lieutenant 2d Continental Artillery, 31st May, 1779; transferred to Corps of Artillery, 17th June, 1783, and served to 20th June, 1784; Captain 1st Artillerists and Engineers, 2d June, 1794; honorably discharged 1st June, 1802; Military Storekeeper United States Army, 27th July, 1806; died 28th September, 1809.

Thompson, Amos (Md). Chaplain of Stephenson's Maryland and Virginia Riflemen, 23d July, 1776, to ——.

Thompson, Anderson (Va). 2d Lieutenant 3d Virginia, 21st March, 1776; resigned 2d August, 1776.

Thompson, Andrew (N. J.). Sergeant 1st New Jersey, December, 1776; Ensign of Spencer's Continental Regiment, 3d April, 1777; taken prisoner at Brandywine, 11th September, 1777; exchanged 17th December, 1780; retired with rank of Lieutenant 1st January, 1781.

Thompson, Archibald (Pa). Colonel Pennsylvania Militia, 1776.

Thompson, Archibald (Pa). Captain of Lewis' Pennsylvania Battalion of the Flying Camp, July to December, 1776.

Thompson, Benjamin (Conn). Adjutant 2d Continental Dragoons, 1st March. 1777; left regiment 3d October, 1777.

Thompson, Benjamin (Mass). Lieutenant 12th Massachusetts, 1st January, 1777; retired on account of ill-health, 16th January, 1779.

Thompson, Charles (R. I.). Chaplain 1st Rhode Island, 17th March, 1777; Brigade Chaplain, 31st May, 1778; taken prisoner about June, 1778; date and place not stated.

Thompson, Cornelius (Va). 1st Lieutenant 12th Virginia, 9th December, 1776; resigned April, 1777.

Thompson, David (Va). 1st Lieutenant 1st Virginia, — February 1777, to ——.

Thompson, Elias (R. I.). Lieutenant 1st Rhode Island, 19th February, 1777; dishonorably discharged 11th February, 1780.

Thompson, George (Va). Lieutenant of a Virginia State Regiment, 1779; Major Virginia Militia in 1780 and 1781. (Died 22d March, 1834)

Thompson, Isaac (Pa). 2d Lieutenant 6th Pennsylvania, 15th February, 1777; retired 1st June, 1778. (Died 25th April, 1823.)

Thompson, Isaiah (Conn). Private 2d Connecticut, 4th May to 18th December, 1775; Sergeant of Elmore's Continental Regiment, 8th April, 1776; Ensign, 5th October 1776; 2d Lieutenant 2d Continental Artillery, 1st January, 1777; 1st Lieutenant, 12th September, 1778; Captain Lieutenant, 14th April, 1781, and served to June, 1783. (Died 1791.)

Thompson, Jabez (Conn). Major in the Lexington Alarm, April, 1775; Major 1st Connecticut, 1st May to 20th December, 1775; Lieutenant-Colonel 2d Connecticut Militia, 1776; killed in the retreat from New York, 15th September, 1776.

Thompson, James (Conn). 2d Lieutenant 4th Connecticut, 1st May to 10th December, 1775; Regimental Quartermaster 2d Canadian (Hazen's) Regiment, 10th January, 1777; 1st Lieutenant of Baldwin's Artillery Artificer Regiment, 29th January, 1778; resigned 1st May, 1780. (Died 27th February, 1804.)

Thompson, James (Va). 1st Lieutenant 12th Virginia, 9th December, 1776; Resigned 20th October, 1777.

Thompson, Jesse (N. Y.). 1st Lieutenant 4th New York, 28th June, 1775, to January, 1776.

Thompson, John (Mass). Captain Massachusetts Militia in 1777.

Thompson, John (Mass). Ensign 6th Massachusetts, 11th November, 1779; retired 1st January, 1781.

Thompson, John (Pa). Ensign Pennsylvania Militia; taken prisoner at Princeton, 3d January, 1777.

Thompson, John (Pa). 1st Lieutenant of Miles' Pennsylvania Rifle Regiment, 15th March, 1776; Captain 2d Canadian (Hazen's) Regiment, 3d November, 1776; resigned 30th October, 1777; served subsequently as Colonel Pennsylvania Militia. (Died 17th April, 1834.)

Thompson, John (Pa). 1st Lieutenant 6th Pennsylvania, 15th February, 1777; died 22d March, 1778.

Thompson, John (S. C.). Captain South Carolina Militia at King's Mountain, October, 1780, and at Cowpens January, 1781.

Thompson, John (Va). 1st Lieutenant 7th Virginia, 18th March, 1776; resigned 28th October, 1776. (Died 1833.)

Thompson, John Baptist (Md). 1st Lieutenant 1st Maryland Battalion of the Flying Camp, July to December, 1776.

Thompson, John D. (Md). Colonel Maryland Militia, 1777-1778.

Thompson, Jonathan (Mass). Sergeant 6th Massachusetts, 17th March, 1777; Ensign, 11th November, 1779; died 22d January, 1781.

Thompson, Joseph (Conn). Colonel Connecticut Militia in 1777.

Thompson, Joseph (Mass). Captain in Lexington Alarm, April, 1775; Captain of Danielson's Massachusetts Regiment, 19th May to December, 1775; Captain 4th Continental Infantry, 1st January, 1776; Major 6th Massachusetts, 1st November, 1776; Lieutenant Colonel 10th Massachusetts, 19th December, 1777; taken prisoner at Young's House 3d February, 1780; exchanged 8th December, 1780; retired 1st January, 1781. (Died 1795.)

Thompson, Joseph (Pa). Surgeon's Mate 4th Continental Dragoons, 1st June, 1780, and served to close of war.

Thompson, Joshua (Mass). Adjutant of Cotton's Massachusetts Regiment, May to December, 1775; 2d Lieutenant and Adjutant 23d Continental Infantry, 1st January to 31st December, 1776; was also Aide-de-Camp to General Thomas in 1776.

Thompson, Joshua (N. H.). Ensign 1st New Hampshire, 8th November, 1776; 2d Lieutenant, 5th March, 1778; 1st Lieutenant, 30th August, 1779, and served to close of war.

Thompson, Lawrence (N. C.). 1st Lieutenant 1st North Carolina, 1st September, 1775; Captain, 15th August, 1776; retired 1st June, 1778.

Thompson, Leonard (Va). 2d Lieutenant 7th Virginia, 18th March, 1776; resigned 2d May, 1776.

Thompson, Mark (N. J.). Colonel New Jersey Militia in 1776.

Thompson, Richard (Md). Regimental Quartermaster 1st Maryland Battalion of the Flying Camp, July to December, 1776.

Thompson, Richard (Pa). 1st Lieutenant 6th Pennsylvania, 15th February, 1777; died 21st March, 1777.

Thompson, Robert (Pa). Colonel Pennsylvania Militia in 1776.

Thompson, Robert (Va). Was Lieutenant and Adjutant 4th Virginia in 1777.

Thompson, Rodger (Va). Captain Virginia Militia, 1777-1778.

Thompson, Samuel (Mass). 1st Lieutenant of Doolittle's Massachusetts Regiment, May to December, 1775; 1st Lieutenant 26th Continental Infantry, 1st January to 31st December, 1776. (Died 1820.)

Thompson, Samuel (N. H.). Sergeant 1st New Hampshire, 3d May, 1777; Ensign, 10th January, 1778; cashiered 1st August, 1781.

Thompson, Samuel (N. C.). Lieutenant 6th North Carolina, 16th April, 1776, to ——.

Thompson, Samuel (Va). Captain Virginia Militia, 1777-1779.

Thompson, Thaddeus (Mass). Surgeon's Mate 6th Massachusetts, 15th January, 1778; Surgeon, 1st May, 1779; retired 1st January, 1781.

Thompson, Thomas (N. Y.). Sergeant in Hamilton's Company New York Artillery, March, 1776; 2d Lieutenant, 15th August, 1776; Captain Lieutenant 2d Continental Artillery, 1st January, 1777; killed at Springfield 23d June, 1780.

Thompson, Thomas (N. Y.). Colonel New York Militia; taken prisoner at Westchester 16th September, 1777.

Thompson, Thomas (Pa). Private 1st Canadian (Hazen's) Regiment, 1st November, 1779; Ensign and Regimental-Quartermaster, 1st May, 1782, to June, 1783.

Thompson, Thomas (R. I.). Captain of Stanton's Rhode Island State Regiment, 12th December, 1776, to May, 1777.

Thompson, William (Conn). Lieutenant Connecticut Militia; killed on the Danbury Raid, 27th April, 1777.

Thompson, William (Mass). 1st Lieutenant of Cotton's Massachusetts Regiment, May to December, 1775; 1st Lieutenant of Jackson's Continental Regiment, 1st February, 1777; resigned 16th March, 1778; Lieutenant of Marines, 1778-1780. Died 1816.)

Thompson, William (Mass). Surgeon Massachusetts Militia in 1776.

Thompson, William (N. C.). Captain North Carolina Militia in 1778-1779.

Thompson, William (Pa). 2d Lieutenant 8th Pennsylvania, 9th August, 1776; Regimental Adjutant 9th Pennsylvania, 15th November, 1776; 2d Lieutenant, 2d June, 1778; 1st Lieutenant, 16th June, 1778; retired 17th January, 1781.

Thompson, William (Pa). Colonel Pennsylvania Rifle Regiment, 25th June, 1775; Colonel 1st Continental Infantry, 1st January, 1776; Brigadier-General Continental Army, 1st March, 1776; taken prisoner at Three Rivers, 8th June, 1776; exchanged 25th October, 1780; died 3d September, 1781.

Thompson, William (S. C.). Lieutenant-Colonel 3d South Carolina (Rangers), 17th June, 1775; Colonel, 16th May, 1776. By the Act of 20th July, 1776, it was "Resolved, that the thanks of the United States of America be given * * * Colonel William Thompson, and the officers and soldiers under their command, who, on the 28th of June last, repulsed, with so much valor, the attack which was made that day on the State of South Carolina by the fleet and army of his Britannic Majesty;" taken prisoner at Charleston, 12th May, 1780; prisoner on parole to close of war. (Brevet Brigadier-General, 30th September, 1783.) (Died 22d November, 1796.)

Thompson, William (Va). Captain of a Virginia State Regiment, June, 1777, to April, 1781.

Thompson, William Russell (S. C.). Colonel South Carolina Rangers in 1779.

Thoms, Samuel (Mass). 2d Lieutenant of Phinney's Massachusetts Regiment, April to December, 1775; 1st Lieutenant 11th Massachusetts, 6th November, 1776; Captain, 3d April, 1777; retired 22d November, 1778. (Died 13th February, 1823.)

Thorn, Samuel (N. Y.). 2d Lieutenant 1st New York, 21st November, 1776; resigned 27th December, 1777.

Thornburgh, Joseph (Pa). Wagonmaster-General, with rank of Lieutenant-Colonel Continental Army, 18th June, 1777, and served to 1781.

Thornbury, Francis (Pa). Ensign of Hartley's Continental Regiment, 2d February, 1778; regiment designated 11th Pennsylvania, 16th December, 1778; 2d Lieutenant, 25th May, 1780; transferred to 3d Pennsylvania, 17th January, 1781; retired 1st January, 1783.

Thornbury, Jeremiah (Pa). 2d Lieutenant 11th Pennsylvania, 2d October, 1778, to ——.

Thorne, Joseph (N. J.). Captain New Jersey Militia in 1776.

Thornton, Frank (Va). Cornet of Lee's Battalion of Light Dragoons, 21st April, 1778; resigned 1st January, 1779.

Thornton, John (Va). Captain 3d Virginia, 12th February, 1776; Major of Grayson's Continental Regiment, 20th March, 1777; Lieutenant-Colonel, 15th November, 1778; retired 20th April, 1779; Colonel Commanding Regiment of Virginia Militia at Yorktown in 1781. (Died 1822.)

Thornton, Matthew (N. H.). A signer of the Declaration of Independence; Colonel New Hampshire Militia, 1775 to 1783; died 24th June, 1803.

Thornton, Matthew, Jr. (N. H.). 1st Lieutenant of Bedel's Regiment New Hampshire Rangers, 6th July to December, 1775.

Thornton, Presley Peter (Va). Cornet 3d Continental Dragoons, 21st February, 1777; Lieutenant, ——; Lieutenant-Colonel Aide-de-Camp to General Washington, 6th September, 1777, to ——; Captain, ——, and served to June, 1783; Captain 8th United States Infantry, 10th January, 1799; honorably discharged 15th June, 1800. (Died 1811.)

Thornton, Samuel (R. I.). Lieutenant of Hitchcock's Rhode Island Regiment, 3d May to December, 1775.

Thorp, Eliphalet (Mass). Sergeant in Lexington Alarm, April, 1775; Ensign 24th Continental Infantry, 1st January to 31st December, 1776; 1st Lieutenant 7th Massachusetts, 1st January, 1777; Captain, 20th September, 1780, and served to June, 1783. (Died 1812.)

Thorp, Timothy (Va). Ensign 4th Virginia, 11th March, 1776, to ——.

Threadgill, Thomas (Ga). Captain 3d Georgia, ——; on roll for August, 1778.

Throckmorton, Albion (Va). Cornet 1st Continental Dragoons, ——, 1779; retired 9th November, 1782.

Throop, Benjamin (Conn). 1st Lieutenant 6th Connecticut, 1st May to 10th December, 1775; Captain of Burrall's Continental Regiment, 19th January, 1776; Captain 1st Connecticut, 1st January, 1777; Major 4th Connecticut, 1st May, 1778; transferred to 5th Connecticut, 1st January, 1781; retired 1st January, 1783. (Died 16th May, 1822.)

Throop, Billings (R. I.). Captain of Richmond's Rhode Island Regiment, 1st November, 1775, to May, 1776.

Throop, Daniel (Conn). 1st Lieutenant in Lexington Alarm, April, 1775; Captain Connecticut Militia, 1776-1777.

Throop, Dyer (Conn). Major of Wadsworth's Connecticut State Regiment, January to March, 1776; served subsequently as Colonel Connecticut Militia.

Throop, John Rutherford (Conn). 2d Lieutenant 2d Continental Artillery, 1st

January, 1777; 1st Lieutenant, 26th October, 1779, and served to 17th June, 1783.

Thruston, Charles Wynn (Va). Colonel of one of the sixteen Additional Continental Regiments, 15th January, 1777; wounded and lost an arm at Amboy, 8th March, 1777; resigned 1st January, 1779. His regiment was never fully completed and was consolidated with Gist's Regiment, April 12th, 1779. (Died 21st March, 1812.)

Thruston, Charles (Va). 1st Lieutenant of Thruston's Continental Regiment, 1777-1779.

Thruston, Robert (Va). Lieutenant of a Virginia State Regiment, 1778 to 1781.

Thumb, John (Pa). Corporal German Regiment, 8th August, 1776; Sergeant, 1st October, 1776; Ensign, 30th May, 1777; transferred to 11th Pennsylvania, 1st January, 1778; retired 1st July, 1778.

Thurber, Joseph (N. H.). 2d Lieutenant of Bedel's Regiment New Hampshire Rangers, 22d January to July, 1775; Adjutant of Gilman's New Hampshire Militia Regiment, December, 1776, to March, 1777.

Thurman, Thomas (Va). Captain Virginia Militia, 1779-1781.

Thurston, Benjamin (N. Y.). Lieutenant-Colonel New York Militia, ——; killed at Minnisink, 22d July, 1779.

Thurston, George (R. I.). Captain Rhode Island Militia in 1775.

Thurston, George, Jr. (R. I.). Captain of Noyes' Regiment, Rhode Island Militia in 1776.

Thurston, John A. (Va). Was a cornet in Clark's Illinois Regiment in 1780-1781.

Thweat, Thomas (Va). Captain 14th Virginia, 2d December, 1776; taken prisoner at Germantown, 4th October, 1777; paroled, 27th March, 1778; did not rejoin regiment.

Thwing, Nathaniel (N. H.). 2d Lieutenant 2d New Hampshire, 23d May, 1775; 1st Lieutenant 20th August to December, 1775.

Tibbs, Thomas (Va). 1st Lieutenant 2d Virginia, 21st September, 1775, to ——.

Tibbs, Willoughby (Va). Ensign of Grayson's Additional Continental Regiment, 5th March, 1777; 2d Lieutenant,

8th June, 1777; Regimental Quartermaster, 1st July, 1778; resigned 28th September, 1778. (Name also spelled Tebbs.)

Ticknold, Elisha (N. H.). Captain New Hampshire Militia, 1777.

Tiebout, Henry (N. Y.). 2d Lieutenant 1st New York, 24th February, 1776; Captain 3d New York, 21st November, 1776; transferred to 1st New York, 1st January, 1783, and served to 3d June, 1783; Brevet Major, 30th September, 1783.

Tierce, Peter B.—See **Tearse**.

Tiffany, Isaiah (Conn). Corporal 1st Connecticut, 14th April, 1777; Sergeant 1st June, 1777; Ensign, 1st January, 1778; transferred to 5th Connecticut, 1st January, 1781; 2d Lieutenant, 22d April, 1781; transferred to 2d Connecticut, 1st January, 1783; retained in Swift's Connecticut Regiment 3d June, 1783, and served to 3d November, 1783.

Tiffany, John (Conn). Sergeant of Burrall's Continental Regiment, January, 1776; Ensign 19th September, 1776; Ensign 1st Connecticut, 1st January, 1777; 2d Lieutenant, 31st December, 1777; 1st Lieutenant, 6th February, 1778; Captain-Lieutenant, 21st August, 1780; transferred to 4th Connecticut, 1st January, 1781; resigned 23d October, 1781.

Tilden, Daniel (Conn). Captain in the Lexington Alarm, April, 1775; 1st Lieutenant 3d Connecticut, 1st May to 19th December, 1775; 1st Lieutenant and Adjutant 20th Continental Infantry, 1st January, 1776; Captain, 7th September to 31st December, 1776. (Died September, 1832.)

Tilden, John Bell (Pa). Ensign 2d Pennsylvania, 28th May, 1779; 2d Lieutenant, 25th July, 1780; retired 17th January, 1781. (Died 1838.)

Tilden, Joshua (Conn). Ensign 8th Connecticut, 1st January, 1777; resigned 12th December, 1777. (Died 17th November, 1819.)

Tilghman, Tench (Pa). Captain of a Pennsylvania Battalion of the Flying Camp, July, 1776; on duty as a volunteer at General Washington's Headquarters, as Military Secretary from 8th August, 1776; Lieutenant-Colonel Aide-de-Camp and Military Secretary to General Washington, 1st April, 1777. By the act of 29th October, 1781, it was "Resolved, that the Board of War be directed to present to Lieutenant-

Colonel Tilghman, in the name of the United States, in Congress assembled, a horse properly caparisoned, and an elegant sword, in testimony of their high opinion of his merit and ability." Served to 23d December, 1783. (Died 18th April, 1786.)

Tillard, Edward (Md). Captain Maryland Battalion of the Flying Camp, July to December, 1776; Major 6th Maryland, 10th December, 1776; taken prisoner at Staten Island, 22d August, 1777; exchanged 25th October, 1780; Lieutenant-Colonel 4th Maryland, 22d May, 1779; retired 1st January, 1781. (Died 1830.)

Tillery, John (N. C.). Lieutenant 3d North Carolina ——, 1777; omitted 1st January, 1778.

Tilley, Edward (Conn). Ensign 1st Connecticut, 1st May, 1775; taken prisoner by the British Navy, 17th September, 1775; released 14th April, 1776; 1st Lieutenant of Swift's Connecticut State Regiment, June to December, 1776.

Tilley, Robert (Va). Paymaster of Grayson's Continental Regiment, 15th April, 1777; resigned 31st August, 1778.

Tillinghast, Daniel (R. I.). Ensign 1st Rhode Island, 11th February, 1777; resigned 5th October, 1778; Captain Rhode Island Militia, 1778-1781.

Tillinghast, Thomas (R. I.). Major, Lieutenant-Colonel, and Colonel Rhode Island Militia, 1778-1781. (Died 26th August, 1821.)

Tillman, John (N. Y.). Adjutant 2d New York, 30th June, 1775, to January, 1776.

Tillotson, Daniel (N. H.). Captain New Hampshire Militia in 1775.

Tillotson, Thomas (Md). 1st Lieutenant Maryland Militia in 1776; Hospital Physician and Surgeon, 6th October, 1780, to close of war. (Died 5th May, 1832.)

Tillotson, William (N. Y.). Surgeon 2d Canadian (Hazen's) Regiment, 10th April, 1777; resigned 22d December, 1777.

Tilton, James (Del). Surgeon Delaware Regiment, 16th January, 1776 to January, 1777; Hospital Physician, 23d April, 1777; Hospital Physician and Surgeon, 6th October, 1780, and served to close of war; Physician and Surgeon-General United States Army, 11th June, 1813; honorably discharged, 15th June, 1815. (Died 14th May, 1822.)

Tilton, John (N. H.). 2d Lieutenant 2d New Hampshire, 23d May to December, 1775.

Tilton, Philip (N. H.). Captain 2d New Hampshire, 23d May to December, 1775; Captain 8th Continental Infantry, 1st January to 31st December, 1776.

Tilton, Timothy (N. H.). Ensign New Hampshire Militia, 1776-1777.

Tilton, William (Pa). 2d Lieutenant 3d Pennsylvania Battalion, 8th January, 1776; 1st Lieutenant, 23d March, 1776; taken prisoner at Fort Washington, 16th November, 1776.

Tilton, William (Pa). 1st Lieutenant 9th Pennsylvania, 13th July, 1776; Captain-Lieutenant, 31st October, 1777; resigned 27th January, 1779.

Timberlake, Benjamin (Va). Captain Virginia Convention Guards, 13th January to 12th October, 1779.

Timmerman, Henry (N. Y.). Lieutenant New York Militia; wounded at Oriskany, 6th August, 1777. (Died 1807.)

Tinning —— (N. C.). Colonel North Carolina Militia, 1779-1780.

Tinsley, Samuel (Va). Captain of a Virginia State Regiment, 1778 to 1782; 1st Lieutenant of Infantry, United States Army, 16th March, 1792, assigned to 3d Sub Legion, 4th September, 1792; Captain, 9th February, 1794; transferred to 1st United States Infantry, 1st November, 1796; honorably discharged, 1st June, 1802. (Died 2d October, 1833.)

Tipton, Abraham (Va). 2d Lieutenant 12th Virginia, 27th November, 1776; 1st Lieutenant, 20th May, 1777; resigned 16th March, 1778; served subsequently as Captain Virginia State Regiment, and was killed by Indians near Falls of the Ohio in 1781.

Tipton, Jonathan (Va). Major Virginia Militia at King's Mountain, October, 1780. (Died 18th January, 1733.)

Tisdale, James (Mass). 2d Lieutenant of Heath's Massachusetts Regiment, 19th May, 1775; wounded and taken prisoner at Quebec, 31st December, 1775; 2d Lieutenant, 24th Continental Infantry, 1st January, 1776; 1st Lieutenant 3d Massachusetts, 1st January, 1777; Captain, 1st January, 1779, and served to 3d November, 1783.

Titcomb, Benjamin (N| H.). Captain 2d New Hampshire, 23d May to December, 1775; Captain 8th Continental Infantry, 1st January, 1776; Captain 1st New Hampshire, 8th November, 1776; Major, 2d April, 1777; wounded at Hubbardton, 7th July, 1777, and again at Chemung, 29th August, 1779; Lieutenant-Colonel, 24th March, 1780; retired 1st January, 1781. (Died 1799.)

Titus, Jonathan (N. Y.). 2d Lieutenant 1st New York November, 1775; 1st Lieutenant, July, 1776; Captain 4th New York, 21st November, 1776; retired 1st January, 1781. (Died 1808.)

Titus, Samuel (N. H.). Captain New Hampshire Militia in 1775.

Todd, Jonathan (Conn). Surgeon's-Mate 6th Connecticut, 1st January, 1777; resigned 5th March, 1777; Surgeon's Mate 7th Connecticut, 5th August, 1777; resigned 26th March, 1778.

Todd, Robert (Va). Captain of Clark's Illinois Regiment, 1778 to 1782.

Tolbert, Isham (Va). 1st Lieutenant 5th Virginia, 26th February, 1776, to ——.

Tolbert, Jacob (Pa). 2d Lieutenant 10th Pennsylvania, 7th November, 1777; retired 1st July, 1778.

Tolbert, Samuel (Pa). 2d Lieutenant 1st Pennsylvania Battalion, 15th January, 1776; Captain 2d Pennsylvania, 2d October, 1776, and served to ——.

Tollman, Thomas (R. I.). Ensign of Warner's Continental Regiment, 14th August, 1778; 2d Lieutenant, May, 1780; retired 1st January, 1781. (Died 19th April, 1809.)

Tolson, William (Md).—See **Towson.**

Tomlinson, David (Conn). Private 1st Connecticut, 15th May to 10th December, 1775; Ensign 6th Connecticut, 1st January, 1777; retired 15th November, 1778.

Tomlinson, Jabez Huntington (Conn). Ensign of Webb's Continental Regiment, 3d April, 1780; transferred to 3d Connecticut, 1st January, 1781; resigned, 24th March, 1781. (Died 14th January, 1849.)

Tompkins, Charles (Va). Captain 7th Virginia, 7th March, 1776; resigned 28th December, 1776.

Tompkins, Christopher (Va). Ensign 5th Virginia, 5th March, 1776. Died 30th October, 1776.

Tompkins, Daniel (Va). Ensign 10th Virginia, 8th December, 1776; 2d Lieutenant, 15th March, 1777; died 15th November, 1777.

Tompkins, Henry (Va). Ensign 14th Virginia, 5th December, 1776; died 3d May, 1777.

Tompkins, Robert (Va). Ensign 5th Virginia, 7th March, 1776; 2d Lieutenant, 19th September, 1776. Died 14th January, 1777.

Tomm, Nathaniel (N. Y.). Captain New York Militia in 1776; Captain of Malcolm's Continental Regiment, 17th March, 1777; transferred to Spencer's Regiment, 22d April, 1779; resigned 23d April, 1779.

Toms, John (N. J.). 1st Lieutenant New Jersey Militia, ——; taken prisoner at Long Island, 27th August, 1776.

Tonkin, Samuel (N. J.). Lieutenant Colonel New Jersey Militia, 1776-1777.

Toogood, William (Mass). Adjutant of Danielson's Massachusetts Regiment May to December, 1775; 1st Lieutenant 4th Continental Infantry, 1st January to 31st December, 1776; Captain 6th Massachusetts, 1st January, 1777; resigned 10th April, 1779.

Toole, Henry Irwin (N. C.). Captain 2d North Carolina, 1st September, 1775; resigned April, 1776.

Toole, James (Md). Lieutenant and Quartermaster Maryland Battalion of the Flying Camp; taken prisoner at Fort Washington, 16th November, 1776. (Died 18th July, 1833.)

Toombs, Robert (Va). Major Virginia Militia, 1779-1782. (Died 1815.)

Toomer, Joshua (S. C.). Captain South Carolina Militia, 1779-1780.

Toomy, John (Md). Ensign 2d Maryland, 10th December, 1776; 2d Lieutenant, 17th April, 1777; transferred to Gist's Continental Regiment, 12th May, 1777, and served to January, 1780.

Topham, Daniel (Pa). 1st Lieutenant of Miles' Pennsylvania Rifle Regiment, 28th March, 1776; taken prisoner at Long Island, 27th August, 1776; exchanged 20th April, 1778.

Topham, John (R. I.). Captain-Lieutenant 3d Rhode Island, 3d May, 1775; wounded and taken prisoner at Quebec, 31st December, 1775; Colonel 1st Rhode Island State Regiment, 9th February, 1778, to 6th May, 1780. (Died 26th September, 1793.)

Torrence, Joseph (Pa). 2d Lieutenant 7th Pennsylvania, 20th January, 1777; 1st Lieutenant, 2d February, 1778; resigned 15th April, 1779.

Torrence, Robert (Pa). 1st Lieutenant of Warner's Continental Regiment, 16th September, 1776, to ——.

Torrey, Joseph (Canada). Captain 2d Canadian (Hazen's) Regiment 3d November, 1776; Major, 9th January, 1777; Lieutenant-Colonel, 1st May, 1782; retired June, 1783. (Died 30th September, 1783.)

Torrey, William (Mass). Member Company of Minute Men at Lexington, 19th April, 1775; Sergeant in Bailey's Massachusetts Regiment, May to December, 1775; 1st Lieutenant 2d Massachusetts, 1st January, 1777; Regimental Adjutant, — March, 1779, and served to June, 1783. (Died 22d October, 1828.)

Torrey, William (Mass). Ensign 2d Canadian (Hazen's) Regiment, 1st November, 1777; 2d Lieutenant, 1st January, 1778. Retired 1st June, 1783. (Died 1831.)

Totman, Joshua (Mass). Private in Lexington Alarm, April, 1775; Sergeant of Cotton's Massachusetts Regiment, April to December, 1775; Quartermaster Sergeant, 2d Massachusetts, 1st January, 1777; Regimental Quartermaster, 1st January, 1778; retired 1st April, 1779.

Toschey, William (N. C.). Ensign 2d North Carolina, 3d May, 1776, to ——.

Tourneau le, —— (France). Served as a volunteer in Armand's Corps; brevetted 1st Lieutenant Continental Army 13th January, 1779, and permitted to return to France.

Tourtellotte, Abraham (R. I.). Ensign 2d Rhode Island, 3d May to November, 1775; Lieutenant of Lippitt's Rhode Island State Regiment, 19th August, 1776, to March, 1777. (Died 6th December, 1820.)

Tousard, Louis de (France). Joined the Continental Army as a volunteer in the summer of 1777. By the act of 27th October, 1778, it was "Resolved, that the gallantry of Monsieur Tousard in the late action on Rhode Island (when he was wounded and lost an arm) is deserving of the highest applause and that Congress in consideration of his zeal and misfortune, do promote the said Monsieur Tousard to the rank of Lieutenant-Colonel in the service of the United States, by brevet, and that he do receive a pension of thirty dollars per month, out of the Treasury of the United States during his life."

Major 1st Artillerists and Engineers United States Army, 26th February, 1795; Lieutenant-Colonel 2d Artillerists and Engineers, 26th May, 1800; honorably discharged, 1st June, 1802. (Died 18th September, 1821.)

Tower, Levi (R. I.). 1st Lieutenant of Hitchcock's Rhode Island Regiment, 3d May, 1775; Captain, 28th June to December, 1775.

Towle, Brackett (N. H.). Lieutenant of Peabody's Regiment New Hampshire Militia, 1778-1779.

Towles, Henry (Va). 2d Lieutenant 5th Virginia, 10th February, 1776, to ——.

Towles, Oliver (Va). Captain 6th Virginia, 16th February, 1776; Major, 15th August, 1777; taken prisoner at Germantown, 4th October, 1777; exchanged latter part of 1780, and was retained in 5th Virginia, 12th February, 1781, as Lieutenant-Colonel, to rank from 10th February, 1778; retired 1st January, 1783.

Town, Archelaus (Mass). Captain of Bridge's Massachusetts Regiment, May to December, 1775. (Died 1st December, 1779.)

Town, Ebenezer (Mass). Ensign 4th Massachusetts, 1st January, 1777; died 11th February, 1778.

Town, Ezra (N. H.). Lieutenant New Hampshire Minute Men, April, 1775; Captain 3d New Hampshire, 23d April to December, 1775; Captain 2d Continental Infantry, 1st January, to 31st December, 1776. (Died 1795.)

Town, Jacob (Mass). Sergeant 4th Massachusetts, 2d April, 1777; Ensign 18th August, 1779; transferred to 9th Massachusetts, 1st January, 1781; Lieutenant, 27th May, 1782; transferred to 2d Massachusetts, 1st January, 1783, and served to 3d November, 1783.

Town, Salem (Mass). Lieutenant of Regimental Quartermaster of Learned's Massachusetts Regiment, May to December, 1775; served subsequently in Massachusetts Militia.

Towne, Francis (N. H.). 2d Lieutenant in Lexington Alarm, April, 1775; Captain New Hampshire Militia in 1777.

Towner, Timothy (Conn). Ensign of Bradley's Connecticut State Regiment, July to December, 1776.

Townes, John (Va). Ensign 11th Virginia, 25th November, 1776; 2d Lieutenant, 7th February, 1777; Regiment designated, 7th Virginia, 14th September, 1778; 1st Lieutenant, 1st July, 1779; taken prisoner at Charleston, 12th May, 1780; transferred to 6th Virginia, 12th February, 1781; retired 1st January, 1783.

Townsend, Abiel (Mass). Ensign in Lexington Alarm, April, 1775; 1st Lieutenant of Cotton's Massachusetts Regiment, May, 1775; accidentally killed 17th September, 1775.

Townsend, David (Mass). Surgeon of Brewer's Massachusetts Regiment, 12th July, 1775; Surgeon 6th Continental Infantry, 1st January to 31st December,˙ 1776; Hospital Surgeon, March, 1777; Hospital Physician and Surgeon, 6th October, 1780, and served to close of war. (Died 13th April, 1829.)

Townsend, Elijah (N. Y.). Captain of Graham's Regiment New York Militia in 1780.

Townsend, Paul (S. C.). Paymaster 4th South Carolina in 1779 and 1780.

Townsend, Samuel (N. Y.). Paymaster 5th New York, 25th June, 1777; omitted, May, 1779.

Townsend, Solomon (R. I.). Regimental Quartermaster of Stanton's Rhode Island State Regiment, 12th December, 1776, to May, 1777.

Townsend, Stephen (Mass). Ensign 6th Massachusetts, ——; prisoner, ——; released 22d December, 1780; when and where taken not stated.

Towson, William (Md). 2d Lieutenant 4th Maryland, 9th May, 1782; retired April, 1783. (Name also spelled Tolson.)

Trabue, John (Va). Ensign 5th Virginia, 15th May, 1782, and served to close of war.

Tracy, —— (Pa). Surgeon's Mate of Hartley's Continental Regiment, 5th February, 1777, to ——.

Tracy, Andrew Hodges (N. Y.). Sergeant and Sergeant-Major of Stevens' Battalion Continental Artilley, 19th November, 1776, to June, 1777; 2d Lieutenant, 1st June, 1777; resigned 13th September, 1778, and joined the enemy.

Tracy, Hezekiah (Conn). 2d Lieutenant 1st Connecticut, 1st January, 1777; retired 15th November, 1778.

Tracy, Joshua (Conn). Ensign 17th Continental Infantry, 1st January to 31st December, 1776.

Tracy, Phineas Lyman (Conn). 2d Lieutenant and Adjutant 6th Connecticut, 6th July, 1775; died 26th August, 1775.

Tracy, William (Conn). Sergeant-Major 1st Connecticut, 1st March, 1777; Ensign, 30th July, 1777; resigned 9th September, 1780.

Traffam, Philip (R. I.). Captain of Topham's Regiment Rhode Island Militia in 1778.

Trafton, Joshua (Mass). Sergeant Lexington Alarm, April, 1775; Ensign of Scammon's Massachusetts Regiment, May to December, 1775; 2d Lieutenant 15th Continental Infantry, 1st January, to 31st December, 1776; Captain of Sherburne's Continental Regiment, 1st June, 1777; resigned 20th April, 1780.

Trafton, Philip (R. I.). 1st Lieutenant of Richmond's Rhode Island Regiment, 19th August, 1776, and of Stanton's Rhode Island State Regiment, 12th December, 1776, to May, 1777.

Trant, Dominick (Mass). Ensign 9th Massachusetts, 23d June, 1781; died 7th November, 1782.

Trapier, Paul, Jr. (S. C.). Captain Georgetown Company, South Carolina Artillery; 17th June, 1775, to ——.

Trask, Jonathan (Mass). 2d Lieutenant of Little's Massachusetts Regiment, April to December, 1775; 2d Lieutenant 27th Continental Infantry, 1st January, to 31st December, 1776.

Trask, Moses (Mass). 2d Lieutenant of Little's Massachusetts Regiment, 19th May to December, 1775.

Trask, Nathaniel (Mass). Private in Lexington Alarm, April, 1775; Private and Corporal in Gerrish's Massachusetts Regiment, April to December, 1775; Sergeant, 26th Continental Infantry, 1st January to 31st December, 1776; 2d Lieutenant 9th Massachusetts, 1st January, 1777; resigned 12th July, 1779.

Travis, Champion (Va). Colonel Virginia Militia in 1775.

Travis, Edward (Va). 1st Lieutenant 2d Virginia, 24th October, 1775; joined the Navy in 1776.

Travis, Jacob (N. Y.). Lieutenant New York State Troops; wounded and lost an arm at Crompo Hill, Connecticut, 28th April, 1777. (Died 10th March, 1809.)

Treadway, John (Conn). Lieutenant of Wadsworth's Connecticut State Regiment, June to December, 1776.

Treadwell, William (Mass). 2d Lieutenant of Gridley's Regiment, Massachusetts Artillery, 25th April, 1775; Captain-Lieutenant of Knox's Regiment, Continental Artillery, 10th December, 1775; Captain 3d Continental Artillery, 1st January, 1777, and served to 17th June, 1783; Brevet Major, 30th September, 1783. (Died April, 1795.)

Treat, Joseph (N. Y.). Chaplain of Malcolm's New York Regiment in 1776. (Died 1797.)

Treat, Malachi (N. Y.). Physician-General Hospital Northern Department, 11th April to August, 1777; Chief Hospital Physician, 6th October, 1780, and served to close of war.

Treat, Samuel (N. Y.). 1st Lieutenant of Knox's Regiment Continental Artillery, 10th December, 1775; Captain-Lieutenant 2d Continental Artillery, 1st January, 1777; killed at Fort Mifflin, 15th November, 1777.

Tremper, Jacob (N. Y.). Lieutenant of Graham's Regiment New York Militia, 1776-1777.

Trent, Lawrence (Va). Cornet 4th Continental Dragoons, ——, 1778; Lieutenant and Regimental Quartermaster, 1st October, 1779; Captain, ——; served to close of war.

Trescott, Lemuel (Mass). Captain of Brewer's Massachusetts Regiment, 19th May to December, 1775; Captain 6th Continental Infantry, 1st January to 31st December, 1776; Captain of Henley's Additional Continental Regiment, January, 1777; Major, 20th May, 1778; transferred to Jackson's Regiment, 22d April, 1779; regiment designated, 16th Massachusetts, 23d July, 1780; transferred to 9th Massachusetts, 1st January, 1781; transferred to 7th Massachusetts, 1st January, 1783; transferred to 4th Massachusetts, 12th June, 1783, and served to November, 1783; Major 2d United States Infantry, 4th March, 1791; resigned 28th December, 1791. (Died 10th August, 1826.)

Tressam, James (Del). Regimental Quartermaster Delaware Regiment, 21st June, 1777; resigned 15th September, 1777.

Treuson, de —— (France). Served as a volunteer in Armand's Corps, ——; brevetted Captain, 13th January, 1779, and permitted to return to France.

Trevett, Samuel Russell (Mass). Captain of Gridley's Regiment Massachusetts Artillery, May to December, 1775. (Died 19th January, 1832.)

Trezvant, John T. (Va). Surgeon 2d Virginia, 1779; taken prisoner at Charleston, 12th May, 1780; released shortly after, and served to close of war.

Trigg, Daniel (Va). 2d Lieutenant 1st Virginia, 15th December, 1775; 1st Lieutenant, 3d February, 1776; dropped on return for October, 1776, as absent without leave.

Trigg, John (Va). Captain of a Virginia Artillery Company, 1779-1781.

Trimble, James (Va). Surgeon's-Mate Hospital Department, 30th September to 20th November, 1775.

Trimble, James (Va). Captain Virginia Militia in 1778. (Died 1804.)

Tripler, George (Pa). 1st Lieutenant 10th Pennsylvania, 4th December, 1776; resigned 1st November, 1777.

Triplett, Charles (N. C.). Ensign 1st North Carolina, 19th September, 1776; died — December, 1776.

Triplett, Francis (Va). Captain Virginia Militia, 1778-1781.

Triplett, George (Va). 1st Lieutenant 1st Virginia, State Regiment, 12th September, 1777, to January, 1781; Captain Virginia Militia in 1781.

Triplett, Hedgeman (Va). Lieutenant Virginia Militia, 1779-1780.

Triplett, Roger (Va). Lieutenant 2d Virginia State Regiment, 1777-1778; cashiered, 22d August, 1779.

Triplett, Thomas (Va). Captain of Grayson's Additional Continental Regiment, 13th January, 1777; resigned 29th April, 1778. (Died 28th February, 1833.)

Triplett, William (Va). Ensign of Grayson's Continental Regiment, 1st November, 1777; Lieutenant, 10th May, 1778; Regimental Paymaster, 10th January, 1779; transferred to Gist's Regiment, 22d April, 1779; retired 1st January, 1781.

Tripp, William (N. Y.). 2d Lieutenant 1st New York, 24th April to November, 1776.

Tripp, Stephen (R. I.). Ensign of Church's Rhode Island Regiment, 3d May, 1775, to ——.

Tripp, William (R. I.). Captain Rhode Island Militia in 1776.

Trotter, John (Mass). Ensign of Read's Massachusetts Regiment, May to December, 1775; Ensign 13th Continental Infantry, 1st January to 31st December, 1776; 1st Lieutenant 5th Massachusetts, 1st January, 1777; Regimental Adjutant, 1st January, 1779; Captain, 18th October, 1780; Aide-de-Camp to General Putnam, 20th January, 1783, to close of war.

Troup, Robert (N. Y.). 1st Lieutenant of Lasher's Regiment New York Militia, May, 1776; taken prisoner at Long Island, 27th August, 1776; exchanged 9th December, 1776; Major Aide-de-Camp to General Gates, February, 1777; Lieutenant-Colonel Aide-de-Camp to General Gates, 4th October, 1777; Secretary to the Board of Treasury, 29th May, 1779; resigned 8th February, 1780. (Died 14th January, 1832.)

Trousdale, James (N. C.). Captain North Carolina Militia, 1780-1781. (Died 1818.)

Trout, Henry (Md). Ensign 2d Maryland, 14th January, 1777; resigned, 10th July, 1777.

Troutwine, George Jacob (Va). Surgeon's-Mate 11th Virginia, 13th November, 1776; resigned 22d November, 1777.

Trow, Bartholomew (Mass). Lieutenant of Gardner's Massachusetts Regiment, May to December, 1775; 1st Lieutenant 25th Continental Infantry, 1st January, 1776; Captain, — April to December, 1776.

Trowbridge, Caleb (Conn). Captain 1st Connecticut, 1st May to 10th December, 1775; Captain 17th Continental Infantry, 1st January, 1776; wounded and taken prisoner at Long Island, 27th August, 1776, and died of wounds, 29th August, 1776.

Trowbridge, Elihu (Conn). 2d Lieutenant 2d Connecticut, 1st January, 1777; resigned 4th December, 1777. (Died 23d March, 1826.)

Trowbridge, John (Conn). 2d Lieutenant, 6th Connecticut, 1st January, 1777; 1st Lieutenant, 29th April, 1779;

transferred to 4th Connecticut, 1st January, 1781; transferred to 3d Connecticut, 1st January, 1783, and served to June, 1783.

Trowbridge, John (Conn). 1st Lieutenant 7th Connecticut, 6th July, to 21st December, 1775; 1st Lieutenant of Swift's Connecticut State Regiment, July to November, 1776.

Trawbridge, John (Mass). Major, Lieutenant-Colonel and Colonel Massachusetts Militia in 1778-1780. (Died 1807.)

Trowbridge, Luther (Mass). 2d Lieutenant 7th Massachusetts, 1st January, 1777; 1st Lieutenant, 5th July, 1779; Regimental Adjutant, 1780 to 1783; served to June, 1783. (Died 19th February, 1802.)

Truby, Christopher (Pa). Captain Westmoreland County, Pennsylvania, Militia in 1778.

True, Bradbury (Mass). Lieutenant of Phinney's Massachusetts Regiment, May to December, 1775.

Truelock, Henry (Md). Ensign 5th Maryland, 20th February, 1777; resigned 7th December, 1777.

Trueman, Alexander (Md). Ensign 3d Maryland Battalion of the Flying Camp, June to December, 1776; Captain 6th Maryland, 10th December, 1776; transferred to 2d Maryland, 1st January, 1781; retired 1st January, 1783; Captain 1st Infantry United States Army, 3d June, 1790; Major of Infantry, 11th April, 1792; wounded in action with Indians on the Miami, Ohio, 4th November, 1791; found dead about 20th April, 1792, having been killed, scalped and stripped by Indians in Ohio. See American State papers, Indian affairs, volume 1, page 243.

Trueman, John (Md). Ensign of Ewing's Battalion Maryland Flying Camp, July to December, 1776; Ensign 3d Maryland, 26th January, 1780; transferred to 1st Maryland, 1st January, 1781; 2d Lieutenant, 16th March, 1781; wounded and taken prisoner at Camden, 16th August, 1780, and was a prisoner to close of war. (Died 4th February, 1809.)

Truesdel, Ebenezer (Conn). Ensign 1st Connecticut, 1st to 28th May, 1775.

Truitt, Joseph (Del). 1st Lieutenant Delaware Regiment, 16th January, 1776, to 21st January, 1777.

Trumbull, Benjamin (Conn). Chaplain 1st Connecticut, May to December,

1775; Chaplain of Douglas' Connecticut State Regiment, 24th June to 29th December, 1776. (Died 2d February, 1820.)

Trumbull, Jonathan (Conn). Paymaster-General Northern Department, 28th July, 1775; resigned 29th July, 1778; Lieutenant-Colonel and Military Secretary to General Washington, 8th June, 1781, to 23d December, 1783. (Died 7th August, 1809.)

Trumbull, Jonathan, Jr. (Conn). Adjutant 2d Connecticut, 28th May, 1775; Lieutenant-Colonel and Aide-de-Camp to General Washington, 27th July, 1775; Brigade Major to General Spencer, 15th August, 1775; Deputy Adjutant-General Northern Department, 28th June, 1776; resigned 19th April, 1777. (Died 10th November, 1843.)

Trumbull, Joseph (Conn). Commissary-General of Connecticut Troops, April, 1775; Commissary-General of Stores Continental Army, 19th July, 1775; Commissary-General of Purchases, 18th June, 1777; resigned 2d August, 1777; Commissioner for the Board of War, 27th November, 1777; resigned 18th April, 1778. (Died 23d July, 1778.)

Trunbower, Philip (Pa). 1st Lieutenant of Hart's Pennsylvania Battalion of the Flying Camp, July to December, 1776.

Trunnell, Francis (Ga). 1st Lieutenant 2d Georgia, 20th June, 1777; was a Captain in 1782, and served to close of war. (Name also spelled Tannell.)

Trux, William (Md). Private German Regiment, 21st July, 1776; Sergeant, 1st March, 1777; Ensign 25th July, 1778; resigned 1st July, 1779.

Tubbs, Joel (Mass). 2d Lieutenant of Walker's Massachusetts Regiment, April to December, 1775.

Tubbs, Samuel (Mass). Captain of Walker's Massachusetts Regiment, May to December, 1775; Major 14th Massachusetts, 1st January, 1777; furloughed 15th October, 1778, and did not return to the army.

Tucker, Benjamin (Mass). Private 12th Massachusetts, 1st January, 1777; Corporal, 1st August, 1777; Ensign 26th November, 1779; retired 1st January, 1781.

Tucker, Gideon (Mass). Ensign of Swift's Connecticut State Regiment, June to December, 1776.

Tucker, John (Mass). Sergeant of Mansfield's Massachusetts Regiment,

May to December, 1775; Ensign, 27th Continental Infantry, 1st January, to 31st December, 1776; 1st Lieutenant 5th Massachusetts, 1st January, 1777; resigned, 10th July, 1779. (Died 16th January, 1831.)

Tucker, Joseph (Mass). Ensign 7th Massachusetts, 1st January, 1777; Lieutenant, 9th February, 1780; Paymaster of Regiment, 1st October, 1778, to June, 1783. (Died 1812.)

Tucker, St. George (Va). Secretary and Aide-de-Camp to General Nelson, of Virginia, in 1779; Major and Lieutenant-Colonel Virginia Militia, 1780-1781; wounded at Guilford, 15th March, 1781. (Died 10th November, 1828.)

Tucker, Thomas Tudor (S. C.). Hospital Physician and Surgeon, 20th September, 1781, to close of war. (Died 2d May, 1828.)

Tucker, William (Va). Ensign 14th Virginia, 3d February, 1777; 2d Lieutenant, 24th December, 1777; regiment designated 10th Virginia, 14th September, 1778; resigned 6th March, 1779. (Died 23d May, 1819.)

Tuckerman, Abraham (Mass). 2d Lieutenant of Brewer's Massachusetts Regiment, April to December, 1775; 2d Lieutenant and Adjutant of 6th Continental Infantry, 1st January, 1776; 1st Lieutenant 5th October to 31st December, 1776; Captain 1st Massachusetts, 1st January, 1777; retired 1st April, 1779; Brigade Quartermastter, 1st April, 1779, to January, 1781.

Tudor, George (Pa). 1st Lieutenant 3d Pennsylvania Battalion, 6th January, 1776; Captain, 13th June, 1776; taken prisoner at Fort Washington, 16th November, 1776; exchanged 10th May, 1778; Captain 4th Pennsylvania, to rank from 13th June, 1776; Major 5th Pennsylvania, 17th April, 1780; retired 17th January, 1781.

Tudor, William (Mass). Judge Advocate Continental Army, 29th July, 1775, with rank of Lieutenant-Colonel, 10th August, 1776; resigned 9th April, 1778; was also Lieutenant-Colonel of Henley's Additional Continental Regiment, January, 1777; resigned 9th April, 1778. (Died 8th July, 1819.)

Tufts, Francis (Mass). Sergeant of Wheelock's Regiment, Massachusetts Militia in 1776; Sergeant-Major 8th Massachusetts, 21st February, 1777; Ensign, 9th October, 1777; Lieutenant, 12th August, 1779; Regimental Adjutant, 27th April, 1780; transferred to

3d Massachusetts, 12th June, 1783, and served to 3d November, 1783.

Tufts, Grimes (Mass). Sergeant in Lexington Alarm, April, 1775; 2d Lieutenant of Mansfield's Massachusetts Regiment, May to December, 1775; Lieutenant Massachusetts Militia in 1776.

Tufts, Moses (Mass). 1st Lieutenant 8th Massachusetts, 1st January, 1777; resigned 27th February, 1778.

Tukerburry, Henry (N. H.). Lieutenant New Hampshire Militia, 1776-1777.

Tunison, Cornelius (N. J.). Captain New Jersey Militia 1777-1778.

Tunison, Garret (N. J.). Surgeon's-Mate Hospital Department, May, 1776; Surgeon 2d Continental Artillery, 1st February, 1779, and served to June, 1783.

Tupper, Anselm (Mass). Lieutenant and Adjutant 11th Massachusetts, 1st September, 1780; transferred to 10th Massachusetts, 1st January, 1781; transferred to 6th Massachusetts, 1st January, 1783; transferred to 2d Massachusetts, 3d June, 1783, and served to 3d November, 1783.

Tupper, Benjamin (Mass). Major of Fellow's Massachusetts Regiment, April, 1775; Lieutenant-Colonel, 4th November, 1775; Lieutenant-Colonel 21st Continental Infantry, 1st January, 1776; Lieutenant-Colonel 2d Massachusetts, 1st November, 1776; Colonel 11th Massachusetts, 7th July, 1777; transferred to 10th Massachusetts, 1st January, 1781; transferred to 6th Massachusetts, 1st January, 1783, and served to 12th June, 1783; Brevet Brigadier General, 30th September, 1783. (Died 1st July, 1792.)

Tupper, Simeon (Mass). 2d Lieutenant 2d Massachusetts, 1st January, 1777; resigned 28th March, 1778.

Turbee, William (N. C.). Lieutenant 3d North Carolina, 6th July, 1777. (In service, January, 1780.)

Turberville, George Lee (Va). Captain 15th Virginia, 2d December, 1776; Major Aide-de-Camp to General Lee, 26th May, 1778; retired 30th September, 1778.

Turbett, Thomas (Pa.). Captain Pennsylvania Militia in 1777; subsequently Lieutenant-Colonel Pennsylvania Militia.

Turk, Andrew (Va). 2d Lieutenant 8th Virginia, 12th March, 1777; resigned — May, 1777.

Turnbull, Charles (Pa). 2d Lieutenant of Proctor's Battalion Pennsylvania Artillery, 5th October, 1776; Captain-Lieutenant 4th Continental Artillery, 3d March, 1777; taken prisoner at Bound Brook, 13th April, 1777; exchanged 3d April, 1780; Captain, 16th July, 1777; served to June, 1783; Brevet Major, 30th September, 1783. (Died 19th December, 1795.)

Turnbull, Stephen (Va). Captain Virginia Militia, 1779-1780.

Turner, Amos (Mass). Captain in Lexington Alarm, April, 1775; Captain of Thomas' Massachusetts Regiment, May to December, 1775; Captain Massachusetts Militia, 1776-1780.

Turner, Berryman (N. C.). Ensign 1st North Carolina, 1st September, 1775, to ——.

Turner, Edward (Mass). Sergeant in Lexington Alarm, April, 1775, and in Doolittle's Massachusetts Regiment, April to December, 1775; 1st Lieutenant 5th Massachusetts, 1st January, 1777; died 26th December, 1777.

Turner, George (N. H.). Captain New Hampshire Artillery Company, 1775-1776.

Turner, George (S. C.). 2d Lieutenant 1st South Carolina, 17th June, 1775; 1st Lieutenant, 16th May, 1776; Captain, 28th April, 1777; taken prisoner at Charleston, 12th May, 1780; exchanged ——; served to close of war. Brevet-Major, 30th September, 1783.

Turner, Hezekiah (Va). Paymaster 3d Virginia, September, 1777, to May, 1778.

Turner, Ichabod (N. Y.). Captain New York Militia, 1775 and 1777.

Turner, Isaac (Conn). Sergeant 8th Connecticut, 8th July to 18th December, 1775; 1st Lieutenant of Mott's Connecticut State Regiment, June to December, 1776; 1st Lieutenant 2d Connecticut, 1t Janpary, 1777; resigned 15th May, 1778. (Died 1829.)

Turner, Jacob (N. C.). Captain 3d North Carolina, 16th April, 1776; killed at Germantown, 4th October, 1777.

Turner, James (Pa). 2d Lieutenant 1st Pennsylvania Battalion of the Flying Camp, June to December, 1776.

Turner, John, Jr. (Mass). Lieutenant in Lexington Alarm, April, 1775; 1st

Lieutenant of Thomas' Massachusetts Regiment, May to December, 1775; Captain Massachusetts Militia, 1776-1780. (Died 1820.)

Turner, John (Va). Ensign 11th Virginia, 7th December, 1776, to ——.

Turner, Jonathan (Mass). Ensign in Lexington Alarm, April, 1775; Lieutenant Massachusetts Militia in 1776; 2d Lieutenant 10th Massachusetts, 6th November, 1776; 1st Lieutenant, 1st November, 1777; Captain, 4th October, 1780; transferred to 5th Massachusetts, 1st January, 1783, and served to June, 1783. (Died — November, 1821.)

Turner, Marlbry (Mass). Private in Lexington Alarm, April, 1775; Corporal in Thomas' Massachusetts Regiment, April to December, 1775; Sergeant 23d Continental Infantry, 1st January to 31st December, 1776; Ensign 2d Massachusetts, 1st January, 1777; Lieutenant, 10th August, 1781, and served to close of war.

Turner, Moses (R. I.). Ensign 3d Rhode Island, May to December, 1775.

Turner, Peleg (Mass). Sergeant 10th Massachusetts, 1st March, 1777; Ensign, 1st November, 1777; 2d Lieutenant, 1st April, 1779; resigned 14th August, 1781.

Turner, Peter (R. I.). Surgeon 1st Rhode Island, 15th March, 1777; retired 14th May, 1781. (Died 14th February, 1822.)

Turner, Philip (Conn). Volunteer Surgeon at Bunker Hill, June, 1775; Surgeon 8th Connecticut, 6th July to 16th December, 1775; Physician and Surgeon to Connecticut Troops, October, 1776; Surgeon-General Hospital Eastern Department, 11th April, 1777; Hospital Physician and Surgeon, 6th October, 1780; retired 13th June, 1781. (Died 20th April, 1815.)

Turner, Robert (N. C.). Lieutenant 10th North Carolina, — February, 1778; retired 1st June, 1778.

Turner, Thomas (Mass). 1st Lieutenant of Jackson's Additional Continental Regiment, 1st February, 1777; Captain, 24th April, 1779; regiment designated 16th Massachusetts, 23d July, 1780; transferred to 9th Massachusetts, 1st January, 1781; transferred to 7th Massachusetts, 1st January, 1783, and serv :d to June, 1783.

Turner, Thomas (Mass). Captain 14th Massachusetts, 1st January, 1777; resigned 9th October, 1779.

Turner, William (Mass). Captain and Aide-de-Camp to General Gates in 1776,

and Colonel Massachusetts Militia in the Rhode Island Campaign in 1781. (Died 1807.)

Turner, William (Ga). Lieutenant 2d Georgia, ——; on roll for August, 1778.

Turpin, Thomas (Va). Ensign 15th Virginia, 28th August, 1777; resigned 11th March, 1778; also called Horatio Turpin.

Tusten, Benjamin (N. Y.). Lieutenant-Colonel New York Militia; killed at Minnisink, 18th August, 1779.

Tuthill, Azariah (N. Y.). Sergeant-Major 4th New York, 1st January, 1777; Ensign, 9th November, 1777; Lieutenant, 11th April, 1780; retired 1st January, 1781; served subsequently as Lieutenant New York Levies.

Tuthill, Barnabas (N. Y.). Major 4th New York, 30th June, 1775, to January, 1776; Major, 1st New York, 27th April, 1776; resigned 4th September, 1776. (Died 1781.)

Tuthill, John (N. Y.). Adjutant 4th New York, 28th June, 1775, to January, 1776.

Tuthill, Samuel (N. J.). Lieutenant-Colonel New Jersey Light Horse, 1775-1776.

Tutt, Benjamin (S. C.). Captain South Carolina Militia in 1775.

Tutt, Charles (Va). 2d Lieutenant 6th Virginia, 16th February, 1776; 1st Lieutenant, 19th June, 1776; was Aide-de-Camp to General Stephen until killed at Brandywine, 11th September, 1777.

Tuttle, David (Conn). Sergeant in Lexington Alarm, April, 1775; Ensign 2d Connecticut, 1st May to 26th June, 1775.

Tuttle, David (N. J.). 2d Lieutenant 3d New Jersey, 7th February, 1776; 1st Lieutenant 5th March to November, 1776.

Tuttle, George (N. H.). Captain New Hampshire Militia, 1777-1778.

Tuttle, Nathaniel (Conn). Captain 7th Connecticut, 6th July to 20th December, 1775; Captain 19th Continental Infantry, 1st January to 31st December, 1776.

Tuttle, Samuel (Mass). 2d Lieutenant 3d Massachusetts, 1st January, 1777; retired 1st October, 1778.

Tuttle, Timothy (Conn). Sergeant of Elmore's Connecticut State Regiment, 28th March, 1776, to April, 1777; Sergeant 8th Connecticut, 24th May, 1777;

Ensign, 16th January, 1778; resigned 11th May, 1779.

Tuttle, William (N. J.). Private, Corporal and Sergeant 1st and 3d New Jersey, 1776 to 1781; Ensign 1st New Jersey, 15th June, 1781, and served to April, 1783. (Died January; 1836.)

Twaddle, James (Pa). Lieutenant Chester County, Pennsylvania, Militia, 1776-1777.

Twiggs, John (Ga). Brigadier-General Georgia Militia; wounded at Camden, 16th August, 1780. (Died 29th March, 1816.)

Twining, Nathaniel (Md). Ensign 4th Maryland, 10th December, 1776; 2d Lieutenant, 15th October, 1777; resigned 1st June, 1779.

Twombley, William (N. H.). Sergeant 2d New Hampshire, 15th November, 1776; Ensign, 9th October, 1777; resigned 8th July, 1780.

Tyler, Abraham (Conn). Captain in the Lexington Alarm, April, 1775, Captain 17th Continental Infantry, 1st January to 31st December, 1776; served subsequently as Major and Lieutenant-Colonel Connecticut Militia. (Died 1804.)

Tyler, Abraham (Mass). Captain of Phinney's Massachusetts Regiment, May to December, 1775; Captain Massachusetts Militia in 1778.

Tyler, Charles (Va). Ensign 11th Virginia, 25th November, 1776; resigned 23d December, 1777.

Tyler, Dudley (Mass). Sergeant of Nixon's Massachusetts Regiment, May to December, 1775; 2d Lieutenant 4th Continental Infantry, 1st January to 31st December ,1776; 1st Lieutenant 6th Massachusetts, 1st January, 1777; wounded at Princeton, 3d January, 1777; left regiment on 3 months' leave, March, 19th, 1779, and did not rejoin, and was dropped.

Tyler, Jacob (Mass). Captain Massachusetts Militia at Bunker Hill in June, 1775. (Died — December, 1795.)

Tyler, Jacob (Mass). 1st Lieutenant of Baldwin's Artillery Artificer Regiment, 1st February, 1778, to ——.

Tyler, John (Conn). Lieutenant-Colonel 6th Connecticut, 1st May to 10th December ,1775; Lieutenant-Colonel 10th Continental Infantry, 1st January, 1776; Colonel, 12th August to 31st December, 1776; Brigadier-General Connecticut Militia, 1777 and 1778. (Died 1804.)

Tyler, John (Va). 1st Lieutenant 3d Virginia, 9th February, 1776; resigned 7th August, 1776.

Tyler, John, Jr. (Va). Ensign 3d Virginia, 19th March, 1776; died, January, 1777.

Tyler, John Steel (Mass). 1st Lieutenant 14th Continental Infantry, 1st January, 1776; Captain, August to 31st December, 1776; Major of Jackson's Continental Regiment, 1st February, 1777; resigned 1st March, 1779; Lieutenant-Colonel Massachusetts Militia in 1780.

Tyler, Samuel (Conn). Ensign Lexington Alarm, April, 1775; 1st Lieutenant of Mott's Connecticut State Regiment, July to December, 1776; served subsequently as Major Connecticut Militia. (Died 1820.)

Tyler, William (R. I.). Adjutant of Babcock's Rhode Island State Regiment, 15th January, 1776, to ——.

Tyrell, Thomas (Conn). Ensign Lexington Alarm, April, 1775; 1st Lieutenant 8th Connecticut, 6th July, 1775; resigned 18th October, 1775.

Tyrie, James (Va). 2d Lieutenant 1st Continental Artillery, 23d April, 1778; resigned 8th October, 1778.

U.

Udall, Samuel (Vt). Lieutenant Vermont Militia in 1777-1778.

Udree, Daniel (Pa). Colonel Pennsylvania Militia, 1775-1781.

Uechritz, Louis Augustus de Baron (—). Lieutenant of Ottendorff's Battalion, 29th April, 1777; taken prisoner at the head of the Elk, 2d September, 1777; exchanged ——, 1780; Captain in Armand's Partisan Corps, ——, 1781, and served to close of war . Name also spelled Uttricht.

Ulmer, Philip (Mass). Lieutenant 1st Massachusetts, 1st January, 1777; resigned 14th February, 1778.

Ulricht, Nathan (Md). 2d Lieutenant 3d Maryland, 7th January, 1781; supposed to have been killed at Camden, 25th April, 1781.

Underhill, Abraham (Vt). Captain of Allen's Regiment Vermont Militia in 1781.

Underhill, Isaac (Vt). Lieutenant of Allen's Regiment Vermont Militia in 1781.

Underwood, Benjamin (R. I.). Captain Rhode Island Militia in 1775.

Upham, Benjamin Allen (Mass). Surgeon's Mate 3d Continental Artillery, 14th March, 1778; resigned 20th May, 1782.

Upp, Valentine (Pa). Captain of Hart's Pennsylvania Battalion of the Flying Camp, July to December, 1776.

Upshaw, James (Va). 2d Lieutenant 2d Virginia, 19th February, 1776; 1st Lieutenant, 13th August, 1776, and served to ——; appears also to have been a Captain of a Virginia State Regiment.

Upshaw, Thomas (Va). Captain of a Virginia State Regiment, 1778, to 1781.

Upson, Samuel (Conn). Captain Connecticut Militia in 1779. (Died 1816.)

Upton, John (Mass). Ensign in Lexington Alarm, April, 1775; 1st Lieutenant of Mansfield's Massachusetts Regiment, May to December, 1775; 1st Lieutenant 19th Continental Infantry, 1st January to 31st December, 1776.

Usher, Robert (Conn). Surgeon of Wadsworth's Connecticut State Regiment, January to March, 1776; Hospital Surgeon, 1777-1781. (Died 1820.)

Usher, William (N. C.). Surgeon 3d North Carolina, 4th December, 1776, to March, 1777.

Utley, Samuel (N. Y.). Lieutenant of Malcolm's New York Militia Regiment in 1780.

V.

Vacher, John Francis (N. Y.). Surgeon 4th New York, 1st January, 1777; retired 1st January, 1781. (Died 4th December, 1807.)

Vail, Benjamin (N. Y.). Captain New York Militia, ——; killed at Minnisink, 22d July, 1779.

Vail, Edward (N. C.). 1st Lieutenant 2d North Carolina, 1st September, 1775; Captain, 21st August, 1776; cashiered 21st December, 1777; name also spelled Veal.

Vail, Israel (N. Y.). Captain of Swartwout's Regiment New York Militia in 1777.

Vail, Josiah (N. Y.). Captain of McClaughrey's Regiment New York Militia, 1777-1778.

Vail, Micah (N. H.). Captain Green Mountain Boys, 27th July to November, 1775. (Died 1777.)

Vail, Thomas (Vt). Lieutenant of Marsh's Regiment Vermont Militia at the battle of Bennington in 1778.

Valcour, John Simonet de (France). Cornet 2d Continental Dragoons, 20th April, 1777; Lieutenant, 1st January, 1778; Brevet Captain, 1st December, 1778, and permitted to retire from the service.

Valentine, Edward (Va). Captain of a Virginia State Regiment, 1778, to 1781.

Valentine, Henry (Pa). Ensign Pennsylvania Musket Battalion, 20th March, 1776; resigned 10th October, 1776.

Valentine, Jacob (Va). 1st Lieutenant 1st Virginia State Regiment, —— February, 1777; Captain, 1st February, 1778; resigned 3d July, 1779.

Valentine, Josiah (Va). 2d Lieutenant and Regimental Quartermaster, 1st Virginia, 1st March, 1778; resigned 1st September, 1778.

Valentine, William (S. C). Deputy Commissary-General Southern Department, 13th March, 1778, to ——.

Vallance, David (N. Y.). Lieutenant of Warner's Additional Continental Regiment, 27th October, 1776; resigned 15th September, 1779.

Vallenais, —— (France). Captain and Aide-de-Camp to Colonel La Balme, Inspector of Cavalry, 8th July, 1777, and served to 11th October, 1777.

Van Aelen, Barent (N. Y.). Lieutenant New York Militia in 1775.

Van Anglen, John (N. J.). 1st Lieutenant 1st New Jersey, 25th November, 1775, to 20th November, 1776; 1st Lieutenant 1st New Jersey, 29th November, 1776; Captain, 4th October, 1777; retired 1st January, 1781. (Died 14th October, 1812.)

Van Alstyne, Abraham I. (N. Y.). Colonel New York Militia in 1777-1780.

Van Alstyne, Philip (N. Y.). Lieutenant-Colonel New York Militia in 1775.

Van Bergen, Anthony (N. Y.). Colonel New York Militia, 1775-1780.

Van Brunne, John De Lavacher (Md). 2d Lieutenant 2d Maryland, 10th March, 1777; taken prisoner on Staten Island, 22d August, 1777; sailed for Europe on leave, 4th August, 1782, and was lost at sea.

Van Brunt, Hendrick (N. J.). Lieutenant, Captain and Major New Jersey Militia, 1776-1780; was a prisoner in

September, 1780; when and where taken not stated.

Van Brunt, Richard (N. Y.). Colonel New York Militia in 1776.

Van Bunchoten.—See **Bunchoten.**

Van Buren, Herman (N. Y.). Major New York Militia, 1776-1779.

Van Buren, Leonard (N. Y.). Lieutenant New York Militia; was a prisoner; when and where taken not stated.

Van Buren, Tobias (N. Y.). Captain New York Militia, 1778-1782. (Died 1821.)

Vance, David (Pa). Ensign Westmoreland County, Pa., Militia in 1778.

Vance, David (N. C.). Ensign 2d North Carolina, 20th April, 1776; 1st Lieutenant, 8th June, 1776; retired 1st June, 1778; Captain North Carolina Militia at King's Mountain in October, 1780, and in the South Carolina campaign in 1781. (Died 1813.)

Vance, John Carlow (N. C). 1st Lieutenant of Captain Kingsbury's Company North Carolina State Artillery, 19th July, 1777; taken prisoner at Charleston, 12th May, 1780; exchanged 14th June, 1781.

Vance, Robert (Va). 1st Lieutenant 13th Virginia, December, 1776; Captain, 19th August, 1778; regiment designated 9th Virginia, 14th September, 1778; resigned 31st December, 1780.

Vance, William (Va). Captain 12th Virginia, 3d January, 1777; regiment designated 8th Virginia, 14th September, 1778; retired 12th February, 1781.

Van Cleve, Benjamin (N. J.). 1st Lieutenant, Captain and Major New Jersey Militia, 1776-1777.

Van Cleve, William (N. J.). Lieutenant and Captain New Jersey Militia, 1777-1778.

Van Cleve, William (N. J). Sergeant New Jersey Troops, November, 1775, to November, 1776; Ensign 3d New Jersey, 29th November, 1776 omitted June, 1777.

Can Cortlandt, Nicholas (N. Y.). Major and Aide-de-Camp to General Sullivan, 9th November, 1777, to ——.

Van Cortlandt, Philip (N. Y.). Lieutenant-Colonel 4th New York, 30th June, 1775; Colonel 2d New York, 21st November, 1776, and served to close of war; Brevet Brigadier-General, 30th September, 1783. (Died 5th November, 1831.)

Van Cortlandt, Pierre (N. Y.). Colonel New York Militia, 1777.

Vancourt, John (Pa). Ensign 10th Pennsylvania, 15th September, 1780; transferred to 6th Pennsylvania, 17th January, 1781; Regimental Quartermaster, 22d May, 1781; 2d Lieutenant 4th Conntiental Artillery, 2d April, 1782, and served to 17th June, 1783.

Vanderburgh, Bartholomew (N. Y.). Ensign 5th New York, 1st May, 1778; transferred to 2d New York, 1st January, 1781, and served to June, 1783.

Vanberburgh, Garret (N. Y.). Colonel New York Militia, 1777-1778.

Vanderburgh, Henry (N. Y.). 2d Lieutenant 3d New York ,15th November, 1775; 1st Lieutenant 5th New York, 21st November, 1776; Captain Lieutenant, 1st September, 1778; Captain, 31st March, 1780; transferred to 2d New York, 1st January, 1781. and served to close of war.

Vanderburgh, Henry J. (N. Y.). Ensign 5th New York, 21st November, 1776; resigned 5th June, 1779.

Vanderburgh, James (N. Y.). Colonel New York Militia in 1775 and 1778.

Vanderburgh, Johannes (N. Y.). Captain New York Militia, 1777-1779.

Vanderheyden, Nanning (N. Y.). 2d Lieutenant 2d New York, May, 1776; 1st Lieutenant 3d New York, 21st November, 1776; omitted — May, 1778.

Vanderhoof, Hendrick (N. Y.). Captain New York Militia in 1775.

Vanderhorst, John (S. C.) 1st Lieutenant 2d South Carolina, 17th June, 1775, to ——; was a Captain in 1777, and a Major in 1781, but of what organization not known.

Vanderlynn, Peter (Mass). Surgeon 12th Massachusetts, 1st January, 1777. "Ran away 20th December, 1777." Was Surgeon of Rawling's Regiment New York Militia in 1781.

Vanderslice, Jacob (Pa). 2d Lieutenant 9th Pennsylvania, 15th November, 1776; 1st Lieutenant, 16th March, 1778; resigned — June, 1778.

Vanderventer, Jacob (N. J.). Captain New Jersey Militia in 1776.

Vandeventer, Per (N. J.). Ensign 1st New Jersey, 29th November, 1776; dropped February, ₁777.

Vanduval, Mark (Va). 2d Lieutenant 1st Virginia, 25th October, 1777; 1st Lieutenant, 4th February, 1778;

taken prisoner at Charleston, 12th May, 1780; retired 1st January, 1783.

Van Duzer, Christopher (N. Y.). Captain New York Militia, 1777-1778. (Died 1812.)

Van Dyke, Abraham C. (N. Y.). Captain of Lasher's Regiment New York Militia, ——; taken prisoner at Fort Washington, 16th November, 1776; exchanged May, 1778.

Van Dyke, Cornelius (N. Y.). Captain 2d New York, 28th June, 1775; Lieutenant-Colonel 1st New York, 21st November, 1776, and served to close of war; Colonel, 30th September, 1783.

Van Dyke, Henry (N. J.). Colonel New Jersey Militia, 1777-1780.

Van Dyke, John (N. Y.). 1st Lieutenant 2d Continental Artillery, 1st January, 1777; Captain Lieutenant, 1779; was in service in June, 1779.

Van Emburgh, John (N. J.). Major New Jersey Militia; taken prisoner at Tonis River, 14th May, 1780, but shortly after escaped.

Van Etten, Anthony (N. Y.). Captain New York Militia; killed in action with Indians near Cherry Valley in November, 1778.

Van Eetten, Johannes (Pa). Captain Pennsylvania Militia in 1781.

Van Gaasbeck, Thomas (N. Y.). Sergeant 3d New York, June to December, 1775; Ensign of Malcolm's Additional Continental Regiment, 8th April, 1777; resigned 16th December, 1777.

Van Hoevenbergh, Rudolph (N. Y.). Ensign 4th New York, 21st November, 1776; 2d Lieutenant, 13th March, 1777; 1st Lieutenant, 9th November, 1777; retired 1st January, 1781. (Died 1808.)

Van Hook, Arant (N. Y.). 2d Lieutenant 1st New York, 24th February to November, 1776.

Van Hook, Lawrence (N .J.). Lieutenant and Captain New Jersey Militia, 1776-1777.

Van Horne, David (N. Y.). Captain of Lee's Continental Regiment, 5th June, 1777; retired 23d April, 1779. (Died 12th May, 1807.)

Van Horne, Isaac (Pa). Ensign 5th Pennsylvania Battalion, 8th January, 1776; 2d Lieutenant, 12th October, 1776; taken prisoner at Fort Washington, 16th November, 1776; 1st Lieutenant 6th Pennsylvania, 15th February, 1777; Captain Lieutenant, 1st July, 1779;

transferred to 2d Pennsylvania, 17th January, 1781; Captain, 10th June, 1781; retired 1st January, 1783. (Died 2d February, 1834.)

Van Horne, Robert (—). Lieutenant; was a prisoner in 1780; when and where taken not stated.

Van Horne, William (Pa). Pennsylvania Brigade Chaplain, 30th June, 1779; resigned 1st June, 1780. (Died 31st October, 1807.)

Van Houten, Resolvert (N. Y.). Lieutenant in Graham's Regiment New York Militia in 1778.

Van Ingen, Dirck (N. Y.). Hospital Physician and Surgeon, 1779-1782.

Van Keuren Hendrick (N. Y.). Captain New York Militia, 1779-1780.

Van Kleeck, Barent (N. Y.). Captain New York Militia, 1775-1776.

Van Lear, John (Pa). 2d Lieutenant 9th Pennsylvania, 15th November, 1776; 1st Lieutenant, 3d March, 1777; Captain Lieutenant, 27th January, 1779; Captain, 10th October, 1779; wounded at Green Springs, 6th July, 1781; retired 1st January, 1783.

Vanmetre, Garrett (Va). Colonel Virginia Militia, 1775-1776. (Died 1788.)

Vanmetre, Jacob (Va). Sergeant 12th Virginia, 14th January, 1777; regiment designated 8th Virginia, 14th September, 1778; Ensign, 8th September, 1779; retired 1st January, 1781.

Van Ness, David (N. Y.). Captain New York Militia in 1775; Captain 2d New York, 16th February to November, 1776; Captain 1st New York, 21st November, 1776, to rank from 16th February, 1776; omitted May, 1778; served subsequently as Captain and Major New York Militia. (Died 1818.)

Van Ness, John (N. Y.). Colonel New York Militia in 1775; died in 1776.

Van Ness, John Jacob (N. Y.). 2d Lieutenant 2d New York, June to November, 1776; served subsequently as Lieutenant and Captain New York Militia.

Van Ness, Peter (N. Y.). Colonel New York Militia Regiment, 1775-1780.

Van Neste, Abraham (N. J.). Captain New Jersey Militia in 1777. (Died 1833.)

Van Orden, Ignatius (N. Y.). Major New York Militia, 1775-1779.

Vanoy, Andrew (N. C.). Captain 10th North Carolina, 19th April, 1777; retired 1st June, 1778.

Van Pelt, John (Pa). 2d Lieutenant Pennsylvania State Regiment, 18th April, 1777; regiment designated 13th Pennsylvania, 12th November, 1777; retired 1st July, 1778.

Van Rensselaer, Henry Kilian. Colonel New York Militia in 1775, and wounded at Fort Ann, 8th July, 1777. (Died 1781.)

Van Rensselaer, James (N. Y.). Aide-de-Camp to General Montgomery, August to 31st December, 1775; Captain 2d New York, April ,1776; Aide-de-Camp to General Schuyler, June to August, 1776; resigned August, 1776. (Died 1827.)

Van Rensselaer, Jeremiah (N. Y.). Ensign 3d New York, 21st November, 1776; Regimental Paymaster, 28th May, 1778, to June, 1783; transferred to 1st New York, 1st January, 1781; Lieutenant, 5th April, 1781, and served to close of war. (Died 17th February, 1810.)

Van Rensselaer, John (N. Y.). Major and Lieutenant-Colonel New York Militia, 1775-1776.

Van Renssellaer, Nicholas (N. Y.). 2d Lieutenant 2d New York, 28th June, 1775; 1st Lieutenant, 16th February, 1776; 1st Lieutenant 1st New York, 21st November, 1776, to rank from 16th February, 1776; Captain, 1st September, 1778; retired 1st January, 1781. (Died 29th March, 1848.)

Van Rensselaer Peter (N. Y.). Captain 1st Canadian (Livingston's) Regiment, 28th June, 1776; resigned 20th December, 1779; served subsequently as Captain New York Levies.

Van Rensselaer, Robert (N .Y.). Colonel New York Militia, 1775 to 1780; Brigadier-General New York Militia, 16th June, 1780, to close of war. (Died 11th September, 1802.)

Van Riper, Richard (N. J.). Captain New Jersey Militia in 1776.

Vansandt, Nathaniel (Pa). Captain 5th Pennsylvania Battalion, 5th January, 1776; taken prisoner at Fort Washington, 16th November, 1776; exchanged 20th November, 1778; did not return to army.

Van Santvoort, Cornelius (N. Y.). Captain New York Militia in 1778.

Van Schaick, Cornelius (N. Y.). Major New York Militia in 1775.

Van Schaick, Goose (N. Y.). Colonel 2d New York, 28th June, 1775; Colonel 1st New York, 8th March, 1776; wounded at Ticonderoga, 6th July, 1777. By the act of 10th May, 1779, it was "Resolved, that the thanks of Congress be presented to Colonel Van Schaick, and the officers and soldiers under his command, for their activity and good conduct in the late expedition against the Onondagas." Brevet Brigadier-General, 10th October, 1783; served to November, 1783. (Died 4th July, 1787.)

Van Schaick, Jacob (N. Y.). Major New York Militia, 1775-1779.

Van Schoonhoven, Jacobus (N. Y.). Colonel New York Militia, 1775-1779.

Van Slyke, Cornelius (N. Y.). 1st Lieutenant 2d New York, 28th June, 1775, to January, 1776.

Van Slyke, Herman (N. Y.). Major New York Militia, ——; killed at Oriskany, 6th August, 1777.

Van Slyke, John (N. Y.). Killed 22d July, 1781; where or how not stated.

Van Steenburgh, Benjamin (N. Y.). Lieutenant of Graham's Regiment New York Militia in 1776.

Van Steenburgh, John (N. Y.). Captain of Graham's Regiment New York Militia, 1781-1782. (Died 1810.)

Van Swearingen, Charles (Md). Major Maryland Militia, 1779-1781. (Died 1818.)

Van Tassell, Cornelius (N. Y.). Lieutenant New York Militia; taken prisoner at Tarrytown, 17th November, 1777.

Van Tassell, Jacob (N. Y.). Lieutenant New York Militia, ——; prisoner of war, 17th November, 1777, to October, 1778, and again July, 1779, to 27th November, 1781; where taken not stated. Died 24th August, 1840.)

Van Valkenburgh, Bartholomew, Jacob (N. Y.). 2d Lieutenant 1st New York, 21st November, 1776; 1st Lieutenant, 29th September, 1780; retired 1st January, 1781. (Died 4th August, 1831.)

Van Veghten, Anthony (N. Y.). 1st Lieutenant 2d New York, 28th June, 1775, to ——.

Van Vechten, Cornelius (N. Y.). Lieutenant-Colonel and Colonel New York Militia, 1775-1781.

Van Veghten, Derick (N. Y.). Captain New York Militia; died 8th August, 1777, of wounds received at Oriskany ,6th August, 1777.

Van Veghten, Samuel (N. Y.). 2d Lieutenant 4th New York, July, 1775; 1st Lieutenant, 3d August, 1775; Captain, March, 1776; Captain 1st New York, 21st November, 1776; resigned — December, 1776. (Died 1813.)

Van Veghten, Tobias (N. Y.). 2d Lieutenant 2d New York, May, 1776; 1st Lieutenant 1st New York, 21st November, 1776; killed 26th July, 1778, at ——; where not stated.

Van Veghten, Tunis T. (N. Y.). Lieutenant New York Militia in 1775.

Van Veghten, Volkert (N. Y.). Captain and Lieutenant-Colonel New York Militia, 1775-1776.

Van Vleiland, Cornelius (S. C.). 2d Lieutenant 2d South Carolina, 1777; killed at Savannah, 9th October, 1779.

Van Vliet, John (N. J.). Captain and Major New Jersey Militia, 1776-1777.

Van Voorst, Cornelius (N. J.) Lieutenant-Colonel New Jersey Militia, 1775-1776.

Van Voorst, Jellis D. (—). Lieutenant of Lee's Battalion of Light Dragoons in 1779 and 1780.

Van Vranken, John (N. Y.). Lieutenant and Captain New York Militia, 1775-1778.

Van Vranken, Nicholas (N. Y.). Lieutenant New York Militia, 1775-1778.

Van Wagenen, Garret H. (N. Y.). 2d Lieutenant 1st New York, 28th June, 1775; 1st Lieutenant, 26th June, 1776; taken prisoner at Long Island, 27th August, 1776; exchanged June, 1778; served subsequently as Deputy Commissary of Prisoners. (Died 20th November, 1835.)

Van Wegenen, Tunis (N. Y.). Ensign 2d New York, 21st November, 1776; 2d Lieutenant, 10th October, 1777; 1st Lieutenant, 5th April, 1780; retired 1st January, 1781; served subsequently as Captain New York Levies|

Van Wart, Abraham (N. Y.). Lieutenant and Regimental Quartermaster of Graham's Regiment New York Militia in 1778.

Van Wart, Isaac (N. Y.). By the act of 3d November, 1780, it was "Resolved, whereas, Congress have received information that John Paulding, David Williams and Isaac Van Wart, three young volunteer Militia men of the State of New York, did, on the 23d day of September last, intercept Major John Andre, Adjutant General of the British

Army, on his return from the American lines, in the character of a spy, and, notwithstanding the large bribes offered them for his release, nobly disdaining to sacrifice their country for the sake of gold, secured and conveyed him to the commanding officer of the district, whereby the dangerous and traitorous conspiracy of Benedict Arnold was brought to light, the insidious design of the enemy baffled, and the United States secured from impending danger, Resolved, that Congress have a high sense of the virtuous and patriotic conduct of the aforesaid John Paulding, David Williams and Isaac Van Wart. In consideration whereof, ordered that each of them receive annually out of the public treasury $200 dollars in specie or an equivalent in the current money of these States during life, and that the Board of War procure for each of them a silver medal, on one side of which shall be a shield with this inscription, 'Fidelity,' and on the other the following motto, 'Vincent amor Patrias,' and forward them to the Commander-in-Chief, who is requested to present the same, with a copy of this resolution, and the thanks of Congress for their fidelity, and the eminent services they have rendered their country." (Died 23d May, 1828.)

Van Winckle, John (Pa). Ensign Pennsylvania State Regiment, 18th April, 1777; taken prisoner in 1777; date and place not stated.

Van Woert, Henry (N. Y.). Regimental Quartermaster 2d New York, 30th June, 1775, to March, 1776; 2d Lieutenant and Regimental Quartermaster 1st New York, 21st November, 1776; 1st Lieutenant ,16th May, 1780, and served to close of war. (Died 30th July, 1831.)

Van Woert, Isaac (N. Y.). Lieutenant New York Militia in 1775; 2d Lieutenant 4th New York, 3d August, 1775; 1st Lieutenant 2d New York ,21st November 1776; Captain, 15th October, 1778; resigned 23d April, 1779.

Van Woert, Lewis (N. Y.). Colonel New York Militia, 1775-1780:

Van Woert, Peter (N. Y.). Captain New York Militia in 1775.

Van Wyck, Abraham (N. Y.). Captain 1st New York, 28th June, 1775; killed by lightning, 21st August, 1776.

Van Wyck, Cornelius (N. Y.). Captain New York Militia; killed at White Plains, 31st October, 1776.

Van Wyck, Richard (N. Y.). Major New York Militia in 1775. (Died 6th October, 1780.)

Van Zandt, Jacobus (N. Y.). Captain of Lasher's Regiment New York Militia in 1776.

Varcaze, James (N. C.). Lieutenant 10th North Carolina, 17th March, 1778; retired 1st June, 1778.

Varick, Richard (N. Y.). Captain 1st New York, 28th June, 1775, to 24th September, 1776; Aide-de-Camp and Secretary to General Schuyler, June, 1776; Deputy Mustermaster General Northern Army, 25th September, 1776; Lieutenant-Colonel and Deputy Commissary-General of Musters, 10th April, 1777, and served to June, 1780; served subsequently as Aide-de-Camp to General Arnold from August, 1780, until the treason of that officer was known; joined General Washington's Staff and served as his private and confidential Secretary, 25th May, 1781, to 14th December, 1799; date of General Washington's death. (Died 30th July, 1831.)

Varner, Robert (N. C.). Ensign 1st North Carolina, 28th March, 1776; 2d Lieutenant, 7th July, 1776 1st Lieutenant, 8th March, 1777; cashiered 1st October ,1779.

Varnum, Benjamin (Mass). Surgeon's Mate of Frye's Massachusetts Regiment, May to December, 1775.

Varnum, Ebenezer (Mass). 2d Lieutenant of Bridge's Massachusetts Regiment, April to December, 1775.

Varnum, James (Mass). Private in Lexington Alarm, April, 1775; Sergeant of Bridge's Massachusetts Regiment, April to November 1775; 1st Lieutenant 9th Continental Infantry, 1st January, 1776; Captain, 10th August, 1776; Captain 8th Massachusetts, 1st January, 1777, to rank from 10th August, 1776; resigned 6th October, 1780. (Died 2d December, 1832.)

Varnum, James Mitchell (R. I.). Colonel Rhode Island Regiment, 3d May to December, 1775; Colonel 9th Continental Infantry, 1st January to 31st December, 1776; Colonel 1st Rhode Island, 1st January, 1777; Brigadier-General Continental Army, 27th February, 1777; resigned 5th March, 1779; was also Major-General Rhode Island Militia. (Died 10th January, 1789)

Vaughan, Benjamin (N. C.). Captain North Carolina Militia in 1776.

Vaughan, Claiborne (Va). Surgeon's Mate 6th Virginia, 1st November, 1776;

transferred to 1st Virginia, 14th September, 1778; transferred to 1st Continental Dragoons, 3d April, 1779; retained in Baylor's Regiment of Dragoons, 9th November, 1782, and served to close of war.

Vaughan, George H. (Md). Lieutenant of a Maryland Regiment; wounded at Guilford, 15th March, 1781. (Died 2d December, 1820.)

Vaughan, George (Pa). Regimental Quartermaster 12th Pennsylvania, October, 1777; retired 1st July, 1778.

Vaughan, James (N. C.). 1st Lieutenant 7th North Carolina, 28th November, 1776; Captain, 6th July, 1777; resigned 27th August, 1777.

Vaughan, John (Conn). Ensign 8th Connecticut, 6th July to 17th December, 1775; served subsequently as Captain Connecticut Militia.

Vaughan, John (Del). Ensign Delaware Regiment, 28th October, 1780; retired 1st January, 1783.

Vaughan, John (Pa). Ensign of Montgomery's Pennsylvania Battalion of the Flying Camp; taken prisoner at Fort Washington, 16th November, 1776.

Vaughan, John (Va). Lieutenant of a Virginia State Regiment, ——; on list for 1779.

Vaughan, Joseph (Del). Captain Delaware Regiment, 21st January, 1776; Major, 5th April, 1777; Lieutenant-Colonel, 14th December, 1779; Colonel, 30th September, 1783; taken prisoner at Camden, 16th August, 1780; prisoner on parole to close of war. (Died 1802.)

Vaughan, William (Del). Ensign Delaware Regiment, 21st January, 1776; 1st Lieutenant, 2d December, 1776; died 22d March, 1777, of wounds received at Brunswick, 1st December, 1776.

Vaughter, William (Va). Sergeant 1st Virginia State Regiment, February, 1777; Ensign, 7th December, 1778; 2d Lieutenant, 1st June, 1779; retired 1st January, 1780. Name also spelled Vawter.

Vause, William (Va). Captain 12th Virginia, 8th January, 1777; regiment designated 8th Virginia, 14th September, 1778; retired 12th February, 1781. (Name also spelled Voss).

Veazie, John (Mass). 2d Lieutenant 25th Continental Infantry, 1st January to 31st December, 1776. (Died 1820.)

Veazy, Edward (Md). Captain of Smallwood's Maryland Regiment, 14th

January, 1776; killed at Long Island, 27th August, 1776.

Veazy, William (Md). 1st Lieutenant 4th Maryland Battalion of the Flying Camp, July to December, 1776.

Veeder, Garret S. (N. Y.). Captain 4th New York, April to November, 1776; Captain 1st New York, 21st November, 1776, which he declined; served subsequently as Captain New York Militia. (Died 18th February, 1836.)

Veeder, Volkert (N. Y.). Major New York Militia in 1775.

Venable, Samuel (Va). Lieutenant of Virginia Dragoons at Guilford in March, 1781.

Verbryck, William (N. J.). Major New Jersey Militia in 1777.

Verdier, Baptiste (France). Lieutenant 1st Cavalry Pulaski Legion, 1st March, 1777; Brevet Captain, 6th February, 1784; served to close of war.

Vergereau, Peter (N. Y.). Ensign 1st New York, 3d Otcober, 1775; 2d Lieutenant, 24th February ,1776; killed by lightning, 21st August, 1776.

Vermonet, Jean Arthur de (France). Brevet Captain Continental Army, 29th July, 1776; Brevet Major, 18th September, 1776.

Vernejoux, Jean Louis de (France). Brevet Captain Continental Army, 19th September, 1776; Captain 2d Continental Dragoons to rank from 18th December, 1776; ran away 15th October, 1777, and was dismissed by General Gates, 20th October, 1777.

Verner, James (N. C.). Captain Lieutenant 1st North Carolina, 8th May, 1777, and served to ——. (In service January, 1780.)

Vernie, Peter J. F. (—). Major 1st Cavalry Pulaski Legion, 23d February, 1779; mortally wounded at Monk's Corner, 14th April, 1780.

Vernon, Frederick (Pa). Captain 4th Pennsylvania Battalion, 5th January, 1776; Captain 5th Pennsylvania, January, 1777, to rank from 5th January, 1776; Major 8th Pennsylvania, 7th June, 1777; transferred to 4th Pennsylvania, 17th January, 1781; transferred to 1st Pennsylvania, 1st January, 1783, and served to close of war; Brevet Lieutenant-Colonel, 30th September, 1783.

Vernon, Job (Pa). Ensign 4th Pennsylvania Battalion, 5th January, 1776; 2d Lieutenant, 1st October, 1776; 1st Lieutenant 5th Pennsylvania, 1st January, 1777; Captain Lieutenant, 23d January, 1778; Captain, 13th June, 1779; retired 1st January, 1783. (Died ——, 1810.)

Vernon, Richard (N. C.). Lieutenant and Captain North Carolina Militia, 1779-1781.

Verrier, James (N. C.). Adjutant 5th North Carolina, 1st October, 1776; Ensign, 20th August, 1777; 2d Lieutenant, 1st June, 1778; transferred to 3d North Carolina, 1st June, 1778; resigned 10th September, 1779.

Verstille, William (—). Ensign of Webb's Continental Regiment 1st January, 1777; 2d Lieutenant, 16th May, 1778; resigned 3d February, 1779.

Vial, John (R. I.). Sergeant 2d Rhode Island, 12th January, 1777; Ensign 24th June, 1777; omitted 9th October, 1778.

Vickers, Oliver (—). Ensign Rhode Island Militia in 1780.

Vickers, Samuel (S. C.). Hospital Physician and Surgeon Southern Department, 14th April, 1777, to close of war.

Victor, Felix (Canada). Ensign 2d Canadian (Hazen's) Regiment, 1st November, 1776; resigned — June, 1777.

Vieland, —— (S. C.). Lieutenant 2d South Carolina, ——; wounded at Savannah 9th Octover, 1779.

Vienna, ——. See **de Vienna**.

Villefranche, —— (France). Captain-Engineer on staff of General du Coudray, 11th August to 15th September, 1777; Major Engineer, 1st January, 1778; Brevet Lieutenant-Colonel, 2d May, 1783.

Villepontoux, Benjamin (S. C.). Paymaster 4th South Carolina, ——; taken prisoner at Charleston, 12th May, 1780.

Vinal, William (Mass). Surgeon's Mate of Gardner's Massachusetts Regiment, May to December, 1775; Surgeon's Mate 25th Continental Infantry, 1st January to 31st December, 1776; Hospital Surgeon's Mate, 8th April, 1777, to 1st January, 1781.

Vincent, George (Va). Ensign Virginia Militia in 1777; Captain in 1782.

Vincent, Jeremiah (N. Y.). Captain New York Militia in 1775.

Vinton, John (Mass). Captain in Lexington Alarm, April, 1775; Captain Massachusetts Militia in 1775; Captain 16th Continental Infantry, 1st January to 31st December, 1776. (Died 1803.)

Visscher, Frederick (N. Y.). Colonel New York Militia in 1777.

Visscher, John (N. Y.). Captain 2d New York, 1st July, 1775; Major, October, 1775; Major 4th New York, 8th March, 1776; Lieutenant-Colonel of Nicholson's Continental Regiment, 26th June, 1776; wounded at Johnstown, 22d May, 1780.

Visscher, Matthew (N. Y.). Lieutenant New York Militia in 1775.

Visscher, Nanning N. (N. Y.). Captain New York Militia, 1775-1779.

Visson, Henry (N. C.). Ensign 2d North Carolina, 1st September, 1775, to ——.

Voglesun, Armand (Va) Captain Virginia Militia, 1779-1780.

Vonck, Peter (N. Y.). Regimental Quartermaster 4th New York, 15th January, 1777; dismissed 24th March, 1778.

Von Heer, Bartholomew (Pa). Adjutant of Ottendorff's Battalion, 19th March, 1777; Captain 4th Continental Artillery, 14th April, 1777, to rank from 3d March, 1777; Captain Provost Company of Light Dragoons, 1st June, 1778; Brevet Major, 30th September, 1783, and served to close of war.

Von Plater, Frederick (S. C.). 1st Lieutenant 3d South Carolina, 28th October, 1778, to ——.

Voorhees, John (N. J.). Captain New Jersey Militia, 1776.

Voorhees, John, Jr. (N. J.). Captain New Jersey Militia in 1776.

Voorhees, Peter Van (N. J.). 2d Lieutenant 1st New Jersey, 29th Otcober, 1775; 1st Lieutenant, 18th September to 20th November, 1776; 1st Lieutenant 1st New Jersey, 29th November, 1776; Captain, 1st November, 1776; taken prisoner and murdered by Tories near New Brunswick, N. J., 26th October, 1779.

Voorhies, David (N. J.). Lieutenant New Jersey Militia in 1781

Vosburgh, Isaac P. (N. Y.). Captain New York Militia, 1777-1778.

Vosburgh, Peter Isaac (N. Y.). 2d Lieutenant 2d New York, — September, 1775; 1st Lieutenant, 16th February, 1776; 1st Lieutenant 1st Canadian (Livingston's) Regiment, December, 1776, to rank from 16th February, 1776; Regimental Quartermaster, 1st September, 1778; retired 1st January, 1781. (Died 29th January, 1830.)

Vose, Bill (Mass). Lieutenant of Heath's Massachusetts Regiment, May to December, 1775; Lieutenant and Regimental Quartermaster 24th Continental Infantry, 1st January to 31st December, 1776; Paymaster 1st Massachusetts, 1st January, 1777; resigned 1st April, 1779.

Vose, Elijah (Mass). Captain of Heath's Massachusetts Regiment, May to December, 1775; Captain 24th Continental Infantry, 13th January to 31st December, 1776; Major 1st Massachusetts, 1st January, 1777; Lieutenant-Colonel, 21st January, 1777; Colonel, 30th September, 1783, and served to November, 1783. (Died 21st March, 1822.)

Vose, Joseph (Mass). Major of Heath's Massachusetts Regiment, 19th May, 1775; Lieutenant-Colonel, 1st July, 1775; Lieutenant-Colonel 24th Continental Infantry, 1st January to 31st December, 1776; Colonel 1st Massachusetts, 1st January, 1777; Brevet Brigadier-General, 30th September, 1783, and served to 3d November, 1783. (Died 22d May, 1816.)

Vose, Thomas (Mass). 2d Lieutenant of Gridley's Regiment Massachusetts Artillery, 8th May to December, 1775; 2d Lieutenant of Knox's Regiment Continental Artillery, 10th December, 1775; Captain Lieutenant of Stevens' Battalion of Artillery, 9th November, 1776; Captain 3d Continental Artillery, 2d December, 1778; transferred to Corps of Artillery, 17th June, 1783, and served to November, 1783. (Died 28th December, 1810.)

Voss, William.—See **Vause.**

Vowles, Charles (Va). Lieutenant of a Virginia State Regiment, 1776 to 1780.

Vowles, Henry (Va) Adjutant 7th Virginia, 5th December, 1776; 2d Lieutenant, 20th May, 1778; Brigade Major of Woodford's Brigade, 21st January, 1778; transferred to 5th Virginia, 14th September, 1778; 2d Lieutenant 1st Continental Artillery, 1st January, 1779; resigned 10th May, 1779; served subsequently as Captain Lieutenant of a Virginia State Regiment.

Vowles Walter (Va) Lieutenant and Captain of a Virginia State Regiment, 1778, and died ——.

Vowles, William (Va). Lieutenant of a Virginia State Regiment in 1779.

Vrecourt, de —— Count (—). Colonel and Engineer, 12th April, 1777, to ——.

Vredenburgh, John (N. Y.). 2d Lieutenant of Lasher's New York Militia

Regiment, July to December, 1776; 2d Lieutenant 2d Continental Artillery, 1st January, 1777; resigned 23d July, 1777.

Vroom, Peter Dumont (N. J.). Lieutenant-Colonel and Colonel New Jersey Militia, 1776-1777.

Vrooman, Ephraim (N. Y.). Lieutenant New York Militia, ——; prisoner of war, 9th August, 1780, to 31st August, 1781.

Vrooman, Peter (N. Y.). Colonel New York Militia, 1778-1781.

Vrooman, Walter (N. Y.). Captain New York Levies, ——; taken prisoner at Kanasaroga, 23d Ocotber, 1780, and was a prisoner to 29th July, 1783.

W.

Waddell, Samuel (Pa). 2d Lieutenant 6th Pennsylvania, January, 1777; resigned — August, 1777.

Waddle, James (Pa). 2d Lieutenant 6th Pennsylvania, 15th February, 1777; resigned September, 1777.

Waddle, Robert (Pa). Ensign Westmoreland County, Pa., Militia in 1778.

Wade, Abner (Mass). 1st Lieutenant 8th Massachusetts, 1st January, 1777; Captain, 12th May, 1780, anad served to June, 1783. (Died — October, 1827.)

Wade, Amos (Mass). Captain in Lexington Alarm, April, 1775; Captain of Cotton's Massachusetts Regiment, May to December, 1775.

Wade, Edward (Va). 1st Lieutenant 7th Virginia, 7th March, 1776; died 26th April, 1776.

Wade, Elisha (Conn). Sergeant in the Lexington Alarm, April, 1775; Ensign 6th Connecticut, 1st May, 1775; 2d Lieutenant, 1st July to 1st December, 1775; 1st Lieutenant of Selden's Connecticut State Regiment, 20th June to 25th December, 1776.

Wade, Francis (Del). Colonel and Deputy Quartermaster-General, 1779-1782.

Wade, George (S. C.). Lieutenant South Carolina Militia; wounded at Savannah, 9th October, 1779. (Died 1824.)

Wade, Hezekiah (Ga). Captain 1st Georgia 12th December, 1775, to ——.

Wade, Joseph J. (N. C.) Captain 9th North Carolina, 28th November, 1776; omitted 1st January, 1778.

Wade, Nathaniel (Mass). Captain in Lexington Alarm, April, 1775; Captain of Little's Massachusetts Regiment, May to December, 1775; Captain 12th Continental Infantry, 1st January to 31st December, 1776; Lieutenant Colonel and Colonel Massachusetts Militia, 1777-1780. (Died 1826.)

Wade, Nehemiah (N. J.). Major New Jersey Militia in 1776.

Wade, Noadiah (N. J.). Captain 4th New Jersey, 22d December, 1776; resigned 31st October, 1777. (Died 1830.)

Wadington, John (Va). Lieutenant Virginia Militia in 1781.

Wadsworth, Amos (Conn). Ensign 2d Connecticut, 1st May, 1775 died 29th October, 1775.

Wadsworth, Bissell (R. I.). Surgeon of Sherburne's Continental Regiment, 1st September, 1777; resigned 17th April, 1780.

Wadsworth, Elijah (Conn). Cornet Connecticut Light Horse in 1776; Regimental Quartermaster 2d Continental Dragoons, 1st January, 1777; Cornet, 17th April, 1777; Lieutenant, 1st January, 1778; Captain, 8th March, 1780; retired 1st January, 1783. (Died 1817.)

Wadsworth, Fenn (Conn). Brigade Major to General Wadsworth, Connecticut Militia, 28th September, 1776, to April, 1779.

Wadsworth, James (Conn).· Colonel Connecticut Militia, 1775 and 1776; Brigadier-General Connecticut Militia, 20th June, 1776, and Major-General, May, 1777, to May, 1779. (Died 22d September, 1817.)

Wadsworth, Jeremiah (Conn). Deputy Commissary-General of Purchases, 18th June, 1777; resigned 6th August, 1777; Commissary-General of Purchases, 9th April, 1778; resigned 1st January, 1780. (Died 30th April, 1804.)

Wadsworth, Jonathan (Conn). Captain of Cook's Regiment Connecticut Militia, 28th August, 1777; mortally wounded at Stillwater, 19th September, 1777.

Wadsworth, Joseph (Mass). Sergeant of Cotton's Massachusetts Regiment, May to December, 1775; Ensign 23d Continental Infantry, 1st January to 31st December, 1776; Captain 14th Massachusetts, 1st January, 1777; resigned 8th October, 1779. (Died 4th July, 1824.)

Wadsworth, Joseph Bissell (Conn). Surgeon of Sherburne's Additional Continental Regiment 1st September, 1777; resigned 17th April, 1780. (Died 12th March, 1784.)

Wadsworth, Peleg (Mass). Captain in Lexington Alarm, April, 1775; Captain of Cotton's Massachusetts Regiment, May to December, 1775; Captain 23d Continental Infantry, 1st January to 31st December, 1776; Aide-de-Camp to General Ward, 13th February to 23d April, 1776; Brigadier-General Massachusetts Militia, 1777 to 1782. (Died 18th November, 1829.)

Wadsworth, Roger (Conn). 1st Lieutenant 5th Connecticut, 1st January, 1777; resigned 7th April, 1780. (Died 1810.)

Wadsworth, Samuel (Conn). Ensign of Webb's Additional Continental Regiment, 1st January, 1777; 2d Lieutenant, 16th May, 1778; resigned 6th July, 1779.

Wadsworth, Theodore (Conn). Surgeon's Mate 6th Connecticut, 18th March, 1777; Surgeon, 16th February, 1778; resigned 30th August, 1780. (Died 1808.)

Wadsworth, William (Conn). Cornet Connecticut Light Horse in 1776.

Wagenen.—See **Van Wagenen.**

Waggoner, Andrew (Va). Captain 12th Virginia, 20th June, 1776; transferred to 8th Virginia, 14th September, 1778; Major, 15th December, 1778; taken prisoner at Charleston 12th May, 1780; exchanged November, 1780; retired 1st January, 1783. (Died 27th May, 1813.)

Waggoner, John Peter (N. Y.). Colonel New York Militia at Oriskany in 1777.

Waggoner, Philip Henry (Pa). Ensign 2d Pennsylvania, 1st January, 1777; 2d Lieutenant, 12th March, 1777; 1st Lieutenant, 11th March, 1779; resigned 3d May, 1779.

Wagnor, John Peter (Ga). 2d Lieutenant 1st Georgia, 1st July, 1778; 1st Lieutenant in 1781, and served to close of war. (Died 22d August, 1828.)

Wainwright, Francis (—). Surgeon's Mate Hospital Department, 1782-1783.

Wait, Abraham (S. C.). Ensign South Carolina Militia in 1775.

Wait, Benjamin (N. Y.). Captain of Hoisington's Battalion of Rangers, 6th August, 1776, to ——, 1777. (Died 1822.)

Wait, Benjamin (Vt). Lieutenant of Marsh's Regiment Vermont Militia in 1777 and 1778.

Wait, Daniel (Conn). Sergeant 6th Connecticut, 8th May to 10th December, 1775; Ensign 10th Continental Infantry, 1st January to 31st December, 1776; 1st Lieutenant 4th Connecticut, 1st January, 1777; resigned 1st March, 1779.

Wait, Jason (N. H.). Captain of Bedel's Regiment New Hampshire Rangers, 22d January to July, 1776; Captain 1st New Hampshire, 8th November, 1776; taken prisoner at Stillwater, 19th September, 1777; Major 3d New Hampshire, 5th July, 1780; transferred to 1st New Hampshire, 1st January, 1781; retained in New Hampshire Battalion, 1st March, 1782; resigned 8th December, 1782.

Wait, Joseph (N. H.). Lieutenant-Colonel of Bedel's Regiment New Hampshire Rangers, 22d July, 1775. Died 28th November, 1776, of wounds received at Valcour Island 28th September, 1776.

Wait, Richard (Vt). Lieutenant Vermont Militia in 1777.

Walbridge, Amos (Conn). Captain in the Lexington Alarm, April, 1775; Captain 13th Continental Infantry, 1st January to 31st December, 1776; Captain 7th Connecticut, 1st January, 1777; Major 2d Connecticut, 28th April, 1777; retired 1st January, 1781.

Walbridge, Ebenezer (N. H.). Lieutenant-Colonel New Hampshire Militia, 1778-1779. (Died 1819.)

Walbridge, Holmes (Mass). Captain of Brewer's Massachusetts Regiment, May to December, 1775.

Walbron, Major (Pa). Ensign 1st Pennsylvania Battalion, 20th January, 1776; 1st Lieutenant 2d Pennsylvania, 1st January, 1777; killed at Paoli, 20th September, 1777.

Walch, Joseph (Mass). 1st Lieutenant of Paterson's Massachusetts Regiment, May to December, 1775.

Walcott, Benjamin (Mass). Captain 10th Massachusetts, 6th November, 1776; taken prisoner at Fort Ann, 8th July, 1777; rejoined regiment 9th May, 1778; retired 1st April, 1779. Name also spelled Walcutt.

Walcott, Benjamin S. (R. I.). 2d Lieutenant of Tallman's Rhode Island State Regiment, 12th December, 1776, to May, 1777.

Walcott, Christopher (Mass). Ensign 10th Massachusetts, 1st January, 1777; killed at Fort Ann 8th July, 1777.

Walcott, Erastus (Conn). See **Wolcott.**

Walden, Ambrose (N. Y.). Sergeant 2d Canadian (Hazen's) Regiment, 6th February, 1777; Ensign, 6th May, 1777; Lieutenant, 2d February, 1778; resigned 30th July, 1778

Waldo, Albigence (Conn). Clerk in the Lexington Alarm, April, 1775; Surgeon's Mate 8th Connecticut, 6th July to 10th September, 1775; Surgeon 1st Connecticut, 1st January, 1777; resigned 1st October, 1779. (Died 29th January, 1794.)

Waldo, Edward (N. H.). Lieutenant New Hampshire Militia, ——; wounded at Bennington, 16th August, 1777. (Died 22d January, 1829.)

Waldo, John (Conn). Surgeon 17th Continental Infantry, 1st January to 31st December, 1776. (Died 1786.)

Waldron, John (N. H.). Colonel New Hampshire Militia, 1775-1778.

Waldron, John (N. Y.). 2d Lieutenant 2d Continental Artillery, 1st January, 1777; 1st Lieutenant, 12th September, 1778; Captain Lieutenant, 14th April, 1781; resigned 8th April, 1782.

Wales, Ebenezer (Conn). Ensign 4th Connecticut, 1st January, 1777; 2d Lieutenant, 31st July, 1777; 1st Lieutenant, 4th March, 1779; transferred to 1st Connecticut, 1st January, 1781; retained in Swift's Connecticut Regiment, June, 1783, anad served to 3d November, 1783.

Wales, Edward Lloyd (Md). Ensign 6th Maryland, 20th February, 1777; re signed 1st January, 1778. (Name also spelled Wailes.)

Wales, Jacob (Mass). Sergeant Lexington Alarm, April, 1775; 2d Lieutenant Massachusetts Militia in 1776; 1st Lieutenant 10th Massachusetts, 6th November, 1776; Captain, 1st November, 1777; resigned 4th October, 1780

Wales, Jonathan (Mass). Lieutenant of Fellows' Massachusetts Regiment, May to November, 1775; Captain Massachusetts Militia, 1776-1777. He was appointed 1st Lieutenant 14th Continental Infantry, 1st January, 1776, which he declined.

Wales, Joseph (Mass). Ensign 10th Massachusetts, 18th July, 1780; Lieutenant 4th October, 1780; transferred to 6th Massachusetts, 1st January, 1783, and served to 3d June, 1783.

Wales, Nathaniel (Conn). Ensign 3d Connecticut, 1st May to 7th December, 1775; 2d Lieutenant of Ward's Connecticut State Regiment, 14th May, 1776, to May, 1777; served subsequently as Captain Connecticut Militia. (Died 1811.)

Wales, Nathaniel (N. H.). Quartermaster of Bedel's Regiment New Hampshire Rangers, 15th June to December, 1775; Ensign and Regimental Quartermaster Bedel's Regiment New Hampshire Rangers, 22d January to July, 1776.

Wales, Samuel (Mass). Sergeant of Gardner's Massachusetts Regiment, May to December, 1775; Ensign 24th Continental Infantry, 1st January to 31st December, 1776.

Walker, Aaron (Mass). Lieutenant in Lexington Alarm, April, 1775; 1st Lieutenant of Walker's Massachusetts Regiment, May to December, 1775.

Walker, Abel (N. H.). Captain, Major, and Lieutenant-Colonel New Hampshire Militia, 1776 to 1781. (Died 1815.)

Walker, Ambrose (N. Y.). 2d Lieutenant 2d Canadian (Hazen's) Regiment, February, 1777; 1st Lieutenant, 2d February, 1778; resigned 30th July, 1778.

Walker, Andrew (Pa). 2d Lieutenant of Hartley's Continental Regiment, 13th January, 1777; 1st Lieutenant, 1st June, 1777; Captain, 23d January, 1778; regiment designated 11th Pennsylvania, 16th December, 1778; transferred to 2d Pennsylvania, 17th January, 1781, and served to close of war.

Walker, Benjamin (Mass). Sergeant of Read's Massachusetts Regiment, May to December, 1775; Ensign 13th Continental Infantry, 1st January to 31st December, 1776; 1st Lieutenant 2d Massachusetts, 1st January, 1777; resigned 23d February, 1778.

Walker, Benjamin (Mass). Lieutenant in Lexington Alarm, April, 1775; Captain of Bridge's Massachusetts Regiment, 27th May, 1775; wounded and taken prisoner at Bunker Hill, 17th June, 1775, and died of wound — August, 1775.

Walker, Benjamin (N. Y.). 2d Lieutenant 1st New York, — August, 1775; 1st Lieutenant, 24th February, 1776; Captain 4th New York, 21st November, 1776; Major, Aide-de-Camp to General

Steuben, 3d September, 1778; Lieutenant-Colonel Aide-de-Camp to General Washington 25th January, 1782, to close of war. (Died 13th January, 1818.)

Walker, David (Va). 2d Lieutenant 14th Virginia, 18th November, 1776; 1st Lieutenant, 2d March, 1778; transferred to 10th Virginia, 14th September, 1778; wounded at Savannah 9th October, 1779; taken prisoner at Charleston 12th May, 1780; transferred to 1st Virginia 12th February, 1781, and served to close of war.

Walker, Edward (Mass). Lieutenant and Paymaster 4th Massachusetts, 1st January, 1777; retired 1st January, 1783. (Died ——, 1802.)

Walker, Felix (N. C.). Lieutenant-Colonel North Carolina Militia at King's Mountain, October, 1780. (Died 1829)

Walker, George (N. J.). 2d Lieutenant 2d New Jersey, 12th September, 1778; retained in New Jersey Battalion, April, 1783, and served to November, 1783.

Walker, George (Va). Ensign 13th Virginia, 20th July, 1777; deserted 8th September, 1777.

Walker, Jacob (Va). Captain 1st Continental Artillery, 7th February, 1777; died 5th February, 1778.

Walker, James (Md). Ensign of Gist's Continental Regiment, 20th March, 1777; cashiered 30th May, 1778.

Walker, James (Mass). Ensign 26th Continental Infantry, 1st January to 31st December, 1776.

Walker, James (Pa). Lieutenant Lancaster County, Pa., Militia, 1776-1777.

Walker, John (N. C.). Captain 1st North Carolina, 1st September, 1775; Major, 26th April, 1777; Lieutenant-Colonel and Aide-de-Camp to General Washington, 17th February, 1777; resigned 22d December, 1777. (Died 2d December, 1809.)

Walker, John (Va). Ensign 9th Virginia, 4th July, 1776; resigned May, 1777.

Walker, Jonathan (Mass). 1st Lieutenant of Cady's Battalion on the expedition to Canada, January to June, 1776; served subsequently as Colonel Massachusetts Militia.

Walker, Joseph (Conn). Ensign 26th Continental Infantry, 1st January to 31st December, 1776; 1st Lieutenant

of Webb's Continental Regiment, 1st January, 1777; Captain, 22d August, 1777; transferred to 3d Connecticut, 1st January, 1781, and served to June, 1783; was Major and Aide-de-Camp to General Parsons, 15th December, 1780, to 22d July, 1782. (Died 12th August, 1810.)

Walker, Joseph N. C.). Captain 7th North Carolina, 28th November, 1776; omitted 1st January, 1778.

Walker, Levin (Va). Ensign 2d Virginia State Regiment, 3d December, 1777; 2d Lieutenant, 27th April, 1778; 1st Lieutenant, 30th April, 1779; retired January, 1780.

Walker, Micah (Mass). Lieutenant of Phinney's Massachusetts Regiment, May to November, 1775.

Walker, Richard (Mass). Lieutenant of Jackson's Additional Continental Regiment, 12th January, 1777; killed at Quaker Hill, 29th August, 1778.

Walker, Robert (Conn). 2d Lieutenant 5th Connecticut, 1st May to November, 1775; Captain of Elmore's Continental Regiment, 15th April, 1776; Captain 2d Continental Artillery, 1st January, 1777; resigned 23d March, 1780. (Died 7th November, 1810.)

Walker, Robert (Mass). Corporal in Lexington Alarm, April, 1775; Sergeant of Phinney's Massachusetts Regiment, May to December, 1775; Sergeant 18th Continental Infantry, 1st January, 1776; Ensign, 15th April to 31st December, 1776; 1st Lieutenant 12th Massachusetts, 1st January, 1777; taken prisoner in Bucks County, Pa., 7th April, 1778; exchanged 4th April, 1781; Captain 12th Massachusetts, 15th July, 1779; transferred to 9th Massachusetts 1st January, 1781; transferred to 2d Massachusetts, 1st January, 1783, and served to June, 1783. (Died — January, 1834.)

Walker, Samuel (Va). 2d Lieutenant of Gist's Continental Regiment, 12th March, 1777; resigned 25th August, 1778; served subsequently as Captain Virginia Militia. (Died 6th July, 1830.)

Walker, Silas (Mass). 1st Lieutenant of Nixon's Massachusetts Regiment, May to December, 1775; Captain 5th Continental Infantry, 1st January to 31st December, 1776; 1st Lieutenant 15th Massachusetts, 1st January, 1777; retired 9th April, 1779; Captain Massachusetts Militia in 1780.

Walker, Solomon (N. C.). Ensign 6th North Carolina, 16th April, 1776;

2d Lieutenant, 20th April, 1777; resigned 27th August, 1777.

Walker, Sylvanus (Mass). Captain of Danielson's Massachusetts Regiment, May to December, 1775.

Walker, Thomas (Va). Captain 9th Virginia, 11th March, 1776; resigned 7th November, 1776.

Walker, Thomas Reynolds (Va). Colonel Virginia, Militia, 1776-1779.

Walker, Timothy (Mass). Colonel in Lexington Alarm, April, 1775; Colonel of a Massachusetts Regiment, April to December, 1775.

Walker, William (Mass). Adjutant of Paterson's Massachusetts Regiment, May to December, 1775; 1st Lieutenant 15th Continental Infantry, 1st January to 31st December, 1776.

Walker, William (N. H.). Captain 3d New Hampshire, 23d April to December, 1775; served subsequently as aptain New Hampshire Militia.

Walker, William (N. C.). Lieutenant 2d North Carolina, ——; taken prisoner at Charleston, 12th May, 1780; exchanged 14th June, 1781.

Walker, Zacehus (Mass). Lieutenant of Prescott's Massachusetts Regiment, May to December, 1775; 1st Lieutenant 7th Continental Infantry, 1st January to 31st December, 1776.

Wall, James (N. C.). 1st Lieutenant of Captain Kingsbury's Company North Carolina Artillery, 19th July, 1777; resigned 20th July, 1779.

Wall, William (R. I.). Lieutenant-Colonel of Elliott's Regiment Rhode Island State Artillery, 12th December, 1776, to June, 1777.

Wallace, Adam (Va). 1st Lieutenant 7th Virginia, 20th March, 1776; Captain, 29th June, 1778; transferred to 5th Virginia, 14th September, 1778, and served to January, 1780.

Wallace, Andrew (Va). Captain 12th Virginia, 13th March, 1777; transferred to 8th Virginia, 14th September, 1778; killed at Guilford, 15th March, 1781.

Wallace, Benjamin (Pa). Captain of Montgomery's Pennsylvania Battalion of the Flying Camp; taken prisoner at Fort Washington, 16th November, 1776.

Wallace, Charles (Md). Paymaster of Smallwood's Maryland Regiment, 14th January to December, 1776.

Wallace, Gustavus Brown (Va). Captain 3d Virginia, 20th February, 1776; Major 15th Virginia, 4th October, 1777; Lieutenant-Colonel, 20th March, 1778; regiment designated 11th Virginia, 14th September, 1778; taken prisoner at Charleston 12th May, 1780; transferred to 2d Virginia 12th February, 1781, and served to close of war.

Wallace, Henry (Va). 2d Lieutenant 1st Continental Artillery, 1st March, 1778; retired 1st January, 1783.

Wallace, James (N. C.). Lieutenant 10th North Carolina, 30th November, 1778; omitted 1st July, 1779.

Wallace, James (R. I.). Captain of Richmond's Rhode Island State Regiment, 1st November, 1775, to ——. (Died 4th May, 1820.)

Wallace, James (Va). Ensign 12th Virginia, 16th December, 1776; died 24th August, 1777.

Wallace, James (Va). Lieutenant 3d Continental Dragoons in 1780.

Wallace, James (Va). Surgeon 2d Virginia, June, 1777; Surgeon 3d Continental Dragoons, 1778; retained in Baylor's Regiment of Dragoons, 9th November, 1782, and served to close of war.

Wallace, John (Pa). Ensign 4th Pennsylvania Battalion, 8th January, 1776; 2d Lieutenant 5th Pennsylvania, 1st January, 1777; resigned 28th January, 1777.

Wallace, Michael (Md). Surgeon's Mate of Smallwood's Maryland Regiment, 14th January to December, 1776; Surgeon 1st Maryland, 10th December, 1776; resigned ——, 1777.

Wallace, Samuel (Pa). Captain of Montgomery's Pennsylvania Battalion of the Flying Camp, July to December, 1776.

Wallace, Thomas (Pa). Ensign 4th Pennsylvania Battalion, 5th January, 1776; resigned 1st October, 1776.

Wallace, Thomas (Va). Ensign 8th Virginia, 2d June, 1779; Lieutenant, 23d November, 1779; taken prisoner at Charleston 12th May, 1780.

Wallace, William (N. H.). 1st Lieutenant of Wyman's New Hampshire Militia Regiment, June, 1776; 1st Lieutenant 2d New Hampshire, 8th November, 1776; left regiment on furlough in October, 1777, and did not rejoin.

Wallace, William (Md). 2d Lieutenant 1st Continental Artillery, 1st May,

1779; wounded and taken prisoner at Camden 16th August, 1780.

Wallace, William (N. Y.). 1st Lieutenant 1st Canadian (Livingston's) Regiment, 6th May, 1777; resigned 17th August, 1779. (Died 25th January, 1837.)

Wallace, William B. (Va). 2d Lieutenant of Grayson's Continental Regiment, 6th March, 1777; 1st Lieutenant, 3d February, 1778; transferred to Gist's Continental Regiment, 22d April, 1779; resigned 1st June, 1779; was appointed 2d Lieutenant 1st Continental Artillery, to rank from 1st May, 1779; taken prisoner at Camden 16th August, 1780, and was a prisoner on parole to close of war.

Wallen, Jonathan (R. I.). Ensign of Richmond's Rhode Island State Regiment, 1st November, 1775; Captain, 19th August, 1776; Captain 1st Rhode Island, 1st January, 1777; retired 1st June, 1779. (Died 21st June, 1819.)

Waller, Allen (Va). Ensign 3d Virginia, 25th February, 1776; died 1st August, 1776.

Waller, Edward (Va). Major of a Virginia State Regiment in 1780.

Waller, George (Va) Major Virginia Militia in 1781. (Died 1790.)

Walling, Thomas (N. J.). Captain New Jersey Militia in 1777.

Wallingford, David (Mass). 2d Lieutenant of Bridge's Massachusetts Regiment, April, to December, 1775.

Wallingford, Samuel (N. H.). Captain New Hampshire Militia; killed 24th April, 1778; where not stated.

Wallis, George (Va). 1st Lieutenant 4th Virginia, 10th February, 1776; Captain, 27th September, 1776; resigned 2d July, 1779. Appears to have been also a Major in a Virginia State Regiment in 1781.

Wallis, James (N. C.). Ensign 3d North Carolina, 30th November, 1778, to ——.

Wallis, John (Mass). 1st Lieutenant of Fellow's Massachusetts Regiment; May to December, 1775; 2d Lieutenant 14th Continental Infantry, 1st January, 1776, to ——.

Walls, John Milburn (Md). Ensign 5th Maryland, 20th February, 1777; resigned 13th October, 1778.

Walls, Thomas —— (Va). Lieutenant of a Virginia State Regiment in 1780 and 1781.

Walsh, Enoch (Pa). Ensign Invalid Regiment, 17th July, 1777; transferred to Pulaski Legion, 14th October, 1778; resigned — December, 1779.

Walsh, John (N. C.). Captain 8th North Carolina, 28th November, 1776; omitted 1st January, 1778.

Walter, John Allen (S. C.). 1st Lieutenant 1st South Carolina, 17th June, 1775, to ——.

Walters, John (Va). Cornet 1st Continental Dragoons, 1781; retained in Baylor's Regiment of Dragoons, 9th November, 1782, and served to close of war.

Walton, Benjamin (Pa). Lieutenant Pennsylvania Militia; taken prisoner from his home in Bucks County 14th February, 1778.

Walton, Elisha (N. J.). Captain and Major New Jersey Militia, 1777-1780;

Walton, George (Ga). A signer of the Declaration of Independence; 2d Lieutenant 1st Georgia, 7th January, 1776; 1st Lieutenant, 5th July, 1776; elected to Congress in February, 1776; was Colonel Georgia Militia in 1778; wounded and taken prisoner at Savannah, 29th December, 1778; exchanged September, 1779; was Governor of Georgia ——; died 2d February, 1804.

Walton, William (N. C.). 2d Lieutenant 7th North Carolina, 20th April, 1777; transferred to 1st North Carolina 1st June, 1778; 1st Lieutenant, 15th August, 1778; taken prisoner at Charleston 12th May, 1780, and made his escape; Captain, 1st August, 1781; retired 1st January, 1783. (Died 1816.)

Walworth, Benjamin (N. Y.). Adjutant of Nicholl's New York Regiment in 1779. (Died 1812.)

Wandin, John (Ga). Lieutenant 2d Georgia, ——; on roll for August, 1778.

Waples, Samuel (Va). Ensign 2d Virginia, May, 1776; 2d Lieutenant, 30th July, 1776; taken prisoner at Brandywine 11th September, 1777; escaped 10th December, 1777; resigned 22d May, 1778. (Died 11th August, 1834.)

Ward, Andrew (Conn). Lieutenant-Colonel 1st Connecticut, 1st May to 20th December, 1775; Colonel Connecticut State Regiment, 14th May, 1776, to May, 1777; Brigadier-General Connecticut Militia, June, 1777, to close of war. (Died 1799.)

Ward, Artemus (Mass). Colonel of a Massachusetts Regiment, 23d May, 1775; Major-General Continental Army,

20th June, 1775; resigned 23d April, 1776, but at the request of General Washington continued on duty to 20th September, 1776. He was appointed General and Commander-in-Chief of the Massachusetts State Forces 19th May, 1775. (Died 28th October, 1800.)

Ward, Bernard (Pa). 2d Lieutenant Pennsylvania Musket Battalion, 20th March, 1776; 1st Lieutenant, 15th July, 1776; taken prisoner at Fort Washington 16th November, 1776; exchanged 20th January, 1779; Captain Continental Army, 7th April, 1780, and served to close of war.

Ward, Charles (Mass). Ensign 25th Continental Infantry, 1st January, 1776, to ——.

Ward, Edward (N. C.). Captain 8th North Carolina, 28th November, 1776; resigned 1st August, 1777.

Ward, John (Pa). Ensign 8th Pennsylvania, 4th November, 1776; 2d Lieutenant 1st January, 1777; 1st Lieutenant, 2d April, 1779; transferred to 2d Pennsylvania 17th January, 1781; transferred to 1st Pennsylvania 1st January, 1783, and served to close of war.

Ward, John Peter (S. C.). Lieutenant 1st South Carolina, 27th October, 1779; taken prisoner at Charleston 12th May, 1780; exchanged October, 1780, and served to close of war.

Ward, Jonas (N. J.). Captain of Spencers Additional Continental Regiment, 15th February, 1777; resigned 10th April, 1778.

Ward, Jonathan (Mass). Lieutenant-Colonel of Ward's Massachusetts Regiment, 23d May, 1775; Colonel, 17th June to December, 1775; Colonel 21st Continental Infantry, 1st January to 31st December, 1776. (Died 7th July, 1791.)

Ward, Joseph (Mass). Major and Aide-de-Camp to General Ward, 20th July, 1775, to 23d April, 1776, and Secretary to same to 20th September, 1776; Colonel and Commissary-General of Musters, Continental Army, 10th April, 1777; Commissary-General of Prisoners, 15th April, 1780, to close of war. (Died 14th February, 1812.)

Ward, Matthias (N. J.). Lieutenant-Colonel New Jersey Militia, 1776-1777; taken prisoner in New York 15th March, 1777.

Ward, Nahum (Mass). Sergeant of Brewer's Massachusetts Regiment, July to December, 1775; 1st Lieutenant 21st

Continental Infantry, 1st January, 1776; Captain, 11th September, 1776; Captain 9th Massachusetts, 1st January, 1777; died 6th March, 1778.

Ward Patrick (Conn). Lieutenant Connecticut Militia, ——; killed at Groton Heights 6th September, 1781.

Ward, Robert (Ga). Lieutenant 2d Georgia, ——; killed at Amelia Island, Fla.; 20th May, 1777.

Ward, Samuel, Jr. (R. I.). Captain 1st Rhode Island, 3d May, 1775; taken prisoner at Quebec 31st December, 1775; exchanged ——, 1776; Major 1st Rhode Island, 12th January, 1777; Lieutenant-Colonel, 26th May, 1778; retired 1st January, 1781. (Died 16th August, 1832.)

Ward, William (N. C.). Captain 5th North Carolina, 16th April, 1776, to ——.

Ward, William (S. C.). Lieutenant 1st South Carolina, 21st December, 1779; taken prisoner at Charleston 12th May, 1780.

Wardell, —— (S. C.). Lieutenant South Carolina Militia; wounded at Savannah, 9th October, 1779.

Wardlaw, Hugh (S. C.). Captain South Carolina Militia in 1776.

Wardwell, Joseph (Mass). Private, Corporal, and Sergeant 1st Massachusetts, 13th March, 1777, until appointed Ensign, 18th January, 1782, and served to 3d November, 1783. (Died 1849.)

Ware, Francis (Md.) Lieutenant-Colonel of Smallwood's Maryland Regiment, 14th January, 1776; Colonel 1st Maryland, 10th December, 1776; resigned 18th February, 1777.

Ware, Francis (Md). Ensign 5th Maryland, 1st August, 1780; 2d Lieutenant, August, 1781; retained in Maryland Battalion April, 1783, and served to 15th November, 1783.

Ware, Robert (Va). Captain Virginia Militia, 1779-1780. (Died 1817.)

Warfield, John (Md). 2d Lieutenant 5th Maryland, 10th December; 1776; resigned 7th November, 1777.

Warfield, Walter (Md). Surgeon's Mate 2d Maryland, 27th November, 1777; Surgeon, 10th June, 1779; transferred to 1st Maryland 1st January, 1781; retained in Maryland Battalion April, 1783, and served to 15th November, 1783.

Warham, Charles (S. C.). Lieutenant South Carolina Artillery, ——; killed at Charleston 12th May, 1780.

Waring, Basil (Md). 2d Lieutenant 4th Maryland, 25th October, 1781; transferred to 2d Maryland, 1st January, 1783; retained in Maryland Battalion April, 1783, and served to 15th November, 1783.

Waring, Henry (N. Y.). 1st Lieutenant 2d Continental Artillery, 1st January, 1777; Captain Lieutenant, 26th Septetmber, 1779; resigned 14th April, 1781.

Waring, Henry (Va). Ensign 7th Virginia, 5th March, 1776; 2d Lieutenant, 10th October, 1776; 1st Lieutenant, 10th October, 1777; transferred to 5th Virginia, 14th September, 1778; resigned 29th August, 1779.

Waring, Morton (S. C.). Lieutenant South Carolina Militia in 1775.

Waring, Thomas (Va). Ensign 5th Virginia, September, 1776; 2d Lieutenant, 10th May, 1777; resigned 10th November, 1777; Captain Virginia Militia; taken prisoner at Charleston 12th May, 1780.

Warley, Felix (S. C.). Lieutenant 3d South Carolina, 17th June, 1775; Captain, 24th May, 1776; taken prisoner at Charleston 12th May, 1780; exchanged June, 1781, and served to close of war; Brevet Major, 30th September, 1783.

Warley, George (S. C.). Captain 2d South Carolina, 10th June, 1777; taken prisoner at Charleston 12th May, 1780; exchanged October, 1780, and served to close of war; Brevet Major, 30th September, 1780.

Warley, Joseph (S. C.). 1st Lieutenant 3d South Carolina, 1777; Captain 10th June, 1777; taken prisoner at Charleston 12th May 1780; exchanged October, 1780, and served to close of war; Brevet Major, 30th September, 1783.

Warley, Paul (S. C.). Lieutenant 2d South Carolina, 16th November, 1776; resigned 15th June, 1777.

Warman, Thomas (Va). 1st Lieutenant of Rawlings' Continental Regiment, February, 1777; Captain Lieutenant, 23d September, 1777; taken prisoner at Germantown 4th October, 1777; exchanged 8th December, 1780; Captain, 1st November, 1778; retained in 3d Virginia in January, 1781, and served to close of war.

Warmsley, William (Conn). Corporal 3d Connecticut, 2d February, 1777; Sergeant, 11th August, 1778; Ensign 29th June, 1779; transferred to

3d Connecticut 1st January, 1781, and served to June, 1783.

Warneck, Frederick (Va). Lieutenant-Colonel of a Virginia State Regiment in 1780.

Warner, Elizur (Conn). Captain 7th Connecticut, 1st January, 1777; resigned 1st September, 1777; Captain 37th United States Infantry, 30th April, 1813; honorably discharged 15th June, 1815.

Warner, Isaac (Pa). Colonel Pennsylvania Militia in 1777.

Warner, James (Conn). 1st Lieutenant of Douglas' Connecticut State Regiment, June to December, 1776.

Warner, John (R. I.). Captain-Lieutenant of Elliott's Regiment Rhode Island State Artillery, 12th December, 1776, to May, 1777.

Warner, John (Vt). Captain Vermont Rangers in 1777.

Warner, Jonathan (Mass). Colonel in the Lexington Alarm, April, 1775; Colonel and Brigadier-General Massachusetts Militia, 17761780. (Died 1803.)

Warner, Joseph (Mass). Lieutenant in Lexington Alarm, April, 1775; Lieutenant of Fellow's Massachusetts Regiment, April to November, 1775; Captain Massachusetts Militia, 1776-1778.

Warner, Nathaniel (Mass). Captain of Little's Massachusetts Regiment, 19th May to December, 1775; Captain 12th Continental Infantry, 1st January to December, 1776; Captain Massachusetts Militia, 1777-1779.

Warner, Noadiah (Mass). Lieutenant Massachusetts Militia in 1777. (Died 16th October, 1824.)

Warner, Robert (Conn). Ensign 2d Connecticut, 1st May to 10th December, 1775; 1st Lieutenant 22d Continental Infantry, 1st January to 31st December 1776; Captain 3d Connecticut, 1st January, 1777; transferred to 1st Connecticut, 1st January, 1781; Major, 29th May, 1782; retired 1st January, 1783. (Died 10th June, 1824.)

Warner, Seth (N. H.). Lieutenant-Colonel Commandant of a Battalion of Minute Men in April, 1775; took possession of Crown Point, 12th May, 1775; Lieutenant-Colonel Green Mountain Boys, 27th July, 1775; Colonel of one of the Sixteen Additional Continental Regiments, 5th July, 1776; retired 1st January, 1781. (Died 26th December, 1784.)

Warner, Thomas (N. Y.). 2d Lieutenant of Lasher's Regiment New York Militia. June, 1776; 2d Lieutenant 3d New York, 21st November, 1776; retired — April, 1778.

Warner, Thomas (Va). 1st Lieutenant 7th Virginia, ——; retired 30th September, 1778, being absent a prisoner ——; when and where taken not stated.

Warner, William (Mass). Sergeant in Lexington Alarm, April, 1775; Sergeant of Whitcomb's Massachusetts Regiment, April to December, 1775; Adjutant of Whitney's Regiment Massachusetts Militia in 1776; Captain 10th Massachusetts. 6th November, 1776; resigned 18th March, 1780. (Died 21st July, 1822.)

Warren, Aaron (Mass). Surgeon's Mate 6th Massachusetts, 10th September, 1777; resigned 1st January, 1778; Surgeon in Navy, 1778-1780.

Warren, Adriel (Mass). Private in Lexington Alarm, April, 1775; Private of Phinney's Massachusetts Regiment, 10th May to December, 1775; Corporal and Sergeant 18th Continental Infantry. 1st January to 31st December, 1776; Ensign 12th Massachusetts, 13th November, 1776; taken prisoner at Brandywine. 11th September, 1777; 2d Lieutenant, 9th January ,1778; 1st Lieu-Lieutenant, 1st April, 1779; transferred to 1st Massachusetts, 1st January, 1781, and served to 3d November, 1783.

Warren, Benjamin (Mass). Sergeant Lexington Alarm, April, 1775; 2d Lieutenant of Cotton's Massachusetts Regiment, May to December, 1775; 1st Lieutenant 25th Continental Infantry, 1st January to 31st December, 1776; Captain 7th Massachusetts, 1st January, 1777; resigned 11th May, 1781. (Died 10th June, 1825.)

Warren, Elijah (Mass). Paymaster 12th Massachusetts, 1st January, 1777; died 13th October, 1778.

Warren, Gideon (N. H.). 1st Lieutenant Green Mountain Boys, 27th April, 1775; wounded at Ticonderoga, 10th May, 1775; served subsequently as Colonel 12th New Hampshire Militia. (Died 4th April, 1803.)

Warren, Henry (Conn). 2d Lieutenant of Silliman's Connecticut State Regiment, July to December, 1776.

Warren, Isaac (Mass). 1st Lieutenant of D. Brewer's Massachusetts Regiment, May to December, 1775; 1st Lieutenant 13th Continental Infantry, 1st January to 31st December, 1776;

Captain 2d Massachusetts, 1st January, 1777; died at Valley Forge 12th June, 1778.

Warren, James (Mass). Paymaster-General Continental Army, 27th July, 1775; resigned 19th April, 1776. (Died 27th November, 1808.)

Warren, John (Mass). Sergeant 15th Massachusetts, 15th May, 1777; Ensign, 26th November, 1779; transferred to 5th Massachusetts, 1st January, 1781; Lieutenant, 19th May, 1782, and served to June, 1783. (Died 24th December, 1823.)

Warren, John (Mass). Surgeon to Massachusetts Troops, May, 1775; wounded at Bunker Hill, 17th June, 1775; served as Surgeon Massachusetts Militia, 1776 to 1780; Hospital Physician and Surgeon, 6th October, 1780, to close of war. (Died 4th April, 1815.)

Warren, Joseph (Mass). 1st Lieutenant of Fellows' Massachusetts Regiment, May to December, 1775.

Warren, Joseph (Mass). Served at Concord, 19th April, 1775; Major-General Massachusetts State Troops, 14th June, 1775; killed at Bunker Hill, 17th June, 1775.

Warren, Josiah (Ga). Captain Georgia Militia; wounded at Savannah, 9th October, 1779.

Warren, Josiah (Mass). 1st Lieutenant of Gardner's Massachusetts Regiment, May to December, 1775; Captain Massachusetts Militia, 1776-1777.

Warren, Moses (Conn). Captain Connecticut Militia in 1777. (Died 1805.)

Warren, Pelatiah (N. H.). Surgeon's Mate 2d New Hampshire, 8th November, 1776; Surgeon 12th Massachusetts, 1st September, 1777; resigned 1st May, 1779.

Warren, Perez (Mass). 2d Lieutenant of Thomas' Massachusetts Regiment, May to December, 1775.

Warren, Peter (Mass). Captain of Mitchell's Regiment Massachusetts Militia on the Bagaduce Expedition, July to September, 1779. (Died 1825.)

Warren, Samuel (Mass). Captain of Read's Massachusetts Regiment, May to December, 1775; Captain 13th Continental Infantry, 1st January to 31st December, 1776. (Died 1825.)

Warren, Thomas (Md). 1st Lieutenant of Stephenson's Maryland and Virginia Rifle Regiment, 21st June, 1775; to ——.

Warren, William (Mass). 1st Lieutenant of Nixon's Massachusett Regiment, May to December, 1775; severely wounded at Bunker Hill, 17th June, 1775, and rendered no subsequent service. (Died 29th July, 1831.)

Warsham, Richard.—See Worsham.

Washburn, Azel (Conn). Surgeon of Warner's Additional Continental Regiment, 1st October, 1776; retired 1st January, 1781.

Washburn, Bethuel (Mass). 2d Lieutenant 13th Continental Infantry, 1st January to 31st December, 1776; Regimental Quartermaster 5th Massachusetts, 1st January, 1777; Deputy Commissary of Issues, 24th August, 1777, andserved to close of war.

Washburn, Ebenezer (Mass). Regimental Quartermaster of Brewer's Massachusetts Regiment, May to December, 1775.

Washburn, Joseph (Mass). Sergeant 15th Massachusetts, 1st January, 1777; Ensign, 1st May, 1777; 2d Lieutenant, 2d March, 1779; resigned 11th April, 1780.

Washburn, Seth (Mass). Captain of Ward's Massachusetts Regiment, 23d May to December, 1775.

Washington, George (Va). General and Commander-in-Chief of all the forces raised or to be raised, 15th June, 1775 By the resolve of 25th March, 1776, "That the thanks of this Congress, in their name and in the name of the Thirteen United States Colonies whom they represent, be presented to His Excellency, General Washington, and the soldiers under his command, for their wise and spirited conduct in the sieze and acquisition of Boston, and that a medal of gold be struck in commemoration of this great event and presented to His Excellency, and that a committee of three be appointed to prepare a letter of thanks and a proper device for the medal."

By the act of 7th October, 1777, it was "Resolved, unanimously, that the thanks of Congress be given General Washington for his wise and well-concerted attack upon the enemy's army at Germantown on the 4th inst., and to the officers and soldiers of the army, for their brave exertions on that occasion, Congress being well satisfied that the best designs and boldest efforts may sometimes fail by unforseen incidents, trusting that on future occasions the valor and virtue of the army will, by the blessing of Heaven, be crowned with complete and deserved success."

By the act of 7th July, 1778, it was "Resolved, unanimously, that the thanks of Congress be given General Washington for the activity with which he marched from the camp at Valley Forge in pursuit of the enemy; for his distinguished exertions in forming the line of battle, and for his great, good conduct in leading on the attack and gaining the important victory of Monmouth over the British grand army, under the command of Sir H. Clinton, in their march from Philadelphia to New York."

By the act of 26th July, 1779, it was "Resolved, that the thanks of Congress be given to His Excellency, General Washington, for the vigilance, wisdom and magnanimity with which he hath conducted the military operations of these States, and which are among many other signal instances manifested in his orders for the late glorious enterprise and successful attack on the enemy's fortress on the banks of Hudson River."

By the act of 24th September, 1779, it was "Resolved, that the thanks of Congress be given His Excellency, General Washington, for ordering, with so much wisdom, the attack on the enemy's fort and works at Powles' Hook."

By the act of 14th October, 1779, it was "Resolved, that the thanks of Congress be given His Excellency, General Washington, for directing an expedition against such of the Indian nations as, encouraged by the councils conducted by the officers of his Britannic majesty, had perfidiously waged an unprovoked and cruel war against these United States, laid waste many of their defenceless towns, and with savage barbarity slaughtered the inhabitants thereof."

By the act of 27th October, 1779, it was "Resolved, that the thanks of Congress be given to His Excellency, General Washington, for directing the important expedition against the Mingo and Munsey Indians and that part of the Senecas on the Allegheny River, by which the depredations of those savages assisted by their merciless instigators, subjects of the King of Great Britain, upon the defenceless inhabitants of the western frontiers have been restrained and prevented."

By the act of 29th October, 1781, it was "Resolved, that the thanks of the United States, in Congress assembled, be presented to His Excellency, General Washington, for the eminent services which he has rendered the United

States, and particularly for the well-concerted plan against the British garrisons in York and Gloucester; for the vigor, attention and military skill with which that plan was executed, and for the wisdom and prudence manifested in the capitulation. * * * and that General Washington be directed to communicate to the officers and soldiers under his command the thanks of the United States in Congress assembled, for their conduct and valor on this occasion. * * * That two stands of colors taken from the British army under the capitulation of York be presented to His Excellency, General Washington, in the name of the United States in Congress assembled."

At request, General Washington attended Congress, 26th August, 1783, and, being introduced by two members, the President addressed him as follows: "Sir, Congress feel particular pleasure in seeing your Excellency, and in congratulating you on the success of a war, in which you have acted so conspicuous a part. It has been the singular happiness of the United States that during a war so long, so dangerous and so important, Providence has been graciously pleased to preserve the life of a General, who has merited and possessed the uninterrupted confidence and affection of his fellow-citizens. In other nations, many have performed services, for which they have deserved and received the thanks of the public. But to you, sir, peculiar praise is due. Your services have been essential in acquiring and establishing the freedom and independence of your country. They deserve the grateful acknowledgments of a free and independent nation. Those acknowledgments Congress have the satisfaction of expressing to your Excellency. Hostilities have now ceased, but your country still needs your services. She wishes to avail herself of your talents in forming the arrangements which will be necessary for her in time of peace. For this reason your attendance at Congress has been requested. A committee is appointed to confer with your Excellency, and to receive your assistance in preparing and digesting plans relative to those important objects.

To which His Excellency made the following reply:

"Mr. President: I am too sensible of the honorable reception I have now experienced, not to be penetrated with the deepest feelings of gratitude. Notwithstanding Congress appear to estimate the value of my life beyond any services I have been able to render the United States, yet I must be permitted to consider the wisdom and unanimity of our national councils, the firmness of our citizens and the patience and bravery of our troops, which have produced so happy a termination of the war, as the most conspicuous effect of the Divine interposition, and the surest presage of our future happiness. Highly gratified by the favorable sentiments which Congress are pleased to express of my past conduct, and amply rewarded by the confidence and affection of my fellow-citizens, I cannot hesitate to contribute my best endeavors towards the establishment of the national security in whatever manner the sovereign power may think proper to direct, until the ratification of the definite treaty of peace, or the final evacuation of our country by the British forces; after either of which events, I shall ask permission to retire to the peaceful shade of private life. Perhaps, sir, no occasion may offer more suitable than the present to express my humble thanks to God, and acknowledgments to my country, for the great and uniform support I have received in every vicissitude of fortune, and for the many distinguished honors which Congress have been pleased to confer upon me in the course of the war."

In Congress, December, 23, 1783.

According to order, His Excellency, the Commander-in-Chief, was admitted to a public audience, and being seated, the President, after a pause, informed him that the United States, in Congress assembled, were prepared to receive his communications; whereupon he arose and addressed them as follows:

"Mr. President: The great events on which my resignation depended having at length taken place, I have now the honor of offering my sincere congratulations to Congress, and of presenting myself before them to surrender into their hands the trust committed to me, and to claim the indulgence of retiring from the service of my country.

"Happy in the confirmation of our independence and sovereignty and pleased with the opportunity afforded the United States of becoming a respectable nation, I resign with satisfaction the appointment I accepted with diffidence in my abilities to accomplish so arduous a task; which, however, was superseded by a confidence in the rectitude of our cause, the support of the supreme power of the Union and the patronage of Heaven.

"The successful termination of the war has verified the most sanguine expectations; and my gratitude for the interposition of Providence and the assistance I have received from my countrymen, increases with every review of the momentous contest.

"While I repeat my obligations to the army in general, I should do injustice to my feelings not to acknowledge in this place the peculiar services and distinguished merits of the gentlemen who have been attached to my person during the war. It was impossible the choice of confidential officers to compose my family should have been more fortunate. Permit me, sir, to recommend in particular those who have continued in the service to the present moment as worthy of the favorable notice and patronage of Congress.

"I consider it an indispensible duty to close this last act of my official life by commending the interests of our dearest country to the protection of Almighty God, and those who have the superintendence of them to His holy keeping.

"Having now finished the work assigned me I retire from the great theatre of action, and bidding an affectionate farewell to this august body, under whose orders I have so long acted, I here offer my commission and take my leave of all the employments of public life."

He then advanced and delivered to the President his commission, with a copy of his address, and, having resumed his place, the President returned him the following answer:

"Sir: The United States in Congress assembled, receive with emotions, too affecting for utterance, the solemn resignation of the authorities under which you have led their troops with success through a perilous and a doubtful war. Called upon by your country to defend its invaded rights, you accepted the sacred charge before it had formed alliances and whilst it was without funds or a government to support you. You have conducted the great military contest with wisdom and fortitude, invariably regarding the rights of the civil power through all disasters and changes. You have, by the love and confidence of your fellow-citizens, enabled them to display their martial genius, and transmit their fame to posterity. You have persevered till these United States, aided by a mag-

nanimous king and nation, have been enabled, under a just Providence, to close the war in freedom, safety and independence; on which happy event we sincerely join you in congratulations.

Having defended the standard of liberty in this new world; having taught a lesson useful to those who inflict and to those who feel oppression, you retire from the great theatre of action, with the blessings of your fellow-citizens, but the glory of your virtues will not terminate with your military command, it will continue to animate remotest ages.

"We feel with you our obligations to the army in general, and will particularly charge ourselves with the interests of those confidential officers who have attended your person to this affecting moment.

"We join you in commending the interests of our dearest country to the protection of Almighty God, beseeching Him to dispose the hearts and minds of its citizens, to improve the opportunity afforded them, of becoming a happy and respectable nation. And for you, we address to Him our earnest prayers, that a life so beloved may be fostered with all His care, and that your days may be happy as they have been illustrious, and that He will finally give you that reward which this world cannot give."

First PRESIDENT OF THE UNITED STATES, 30th April, 1789, to 4th March, 1797; Lieutenant-General and Commander of the United States Army, 3d July, 1798, until he died at Mount Vernon, Va., 14th December, 1799.

Washington, George Augustine (Va). 2d Lieutenant of Grayson's Additional Continental Regiment, 1st September, 1777; resigned 16th November, 1777; Cornet of Lee's Battalion of Light Dragoons, 20th April, 1778; resigned 31st December, 1778; Ensign 2d Virginia, ——, 1780; Lieutenant, 26th May, 1781; Aide-de-Camp to Lafayette in 1781, and served to close of war. (Died February, 1793.)

Washington, John (Va). Captain 4th Virginia, 2d April, 1776; died 14th March, 1777.

Washington, John Augustine (Va). Colonel Virginia Militia in 1775.

Washington, Robert (N. C.). Adjutant 3d North Carolina, 15th April, 1776, to ——.

Washington, Samuel (Va). Colonel Virginia Militia, 1775-1776. (Died 1781.)

Washington, Thomas (Va). 2d Lieutenant of Grayson's Continental Regiment, 13th February, 1777; 1st Lieutenant, 1st December, 1777; resigned 1st May, 1778; Lieutenant of Lee's Battalion Light Dragoons, May, 1778, and served to close of war. (Died 1794.)

Washington, William (N. C.). Ensign 9th North Carolina, 15th August, 1777; retired 1st January, 1778.

Washington, William (Va). Captain 3d Virginia, 25th February, 1776; wounded at Long Island 27th August, 1776, and at Trenton, 26th December, 1776; Major 4th Continental Dragoons, 27th January, 1777; Lieutenant-Colonel 3d Dragoons, 20th November, 1778; wounded at Cowpens, 17th January, 1781. By the act of 9th March, 1781, it was "Resolved, that a medal of silver be presented to Lieutenant-Colonel Washington of the Cavalry, with emblems and mottoes descriptive of his conduct at the battle of Cowpens, January 17th, 1781." Wounded and taken prisoner at Eutaw Springs, 8th September, 1781, and was a prisoner on parole to close of war; Brigadier-General United States Army, 19th July, 1798; honorably discharged, 15th June, 1800. (Also called William Augustine Washington.) (Died 6th March, 1810.)

Waterbury, David (Conn). Colonel 5th Connecticut, 1st May to 13th December, 1775; Brigadier-General Connecticut State Troops, 3d June, 1776; taken prisoner at Valcour's Island, 11th October, 1776; exchanged — October, 1780, and served subsequently as Brigadier-General Connecticut State Troops. (Died 29th June, 1801.)

Waterbury, Gideon (Conn). Ensign of Silliman's Connecticut State Regiment, June to Deecmber, 1776.

Waterbury, John (Conn). Private in the Lexington Alarm, April, 1775; Ensign 5th Connecticut, 1st May to December, 1775; 1st Lieutenant of Elmore's Continental Regiment, 15th April, 1776, to April, 1777.

Waterhouse, Abraham (Conn). 1st Lieutenant 6th Connecticut, 1st May to 18th December, 1775; Captain in Connecticut Light Horse, June, 1776; Captain 10th Continental Infantry, 1st January to 31st December, 1776.

Waterhouse, Josiah (Mass). Surgeon's-Mate 4th Massachusetts, 29th October, 1777. Resigned 28th February, 1778.

Waterman, Andrew (Conn). Captain in Lexington Alarm, April, 1775; Captain of Wadsworth's Connecticut State Regiment, June to December, 1776.

Waterman, Andrew (R. I.). Captain 2d Rhode Island, 3d May to December, 1775; Captain of Babcock's Rhode Island State Regiment, 15th January, 1776, to May, 1777.

Waterman, Asa (N. Y.). Lieutenant-Colonel New York Militia, 1775-1779. (Died 1817.)

Waterman, Jedediah (Mass). Ensign 8th Massachusetts 1st January, 1781; transferred to 3d Massachusetts, 12th June, 1783, and served to November, 1783. (Died 25th September, 1828.)

Waterman, Jedediah (Conn). Lieutenant in the Lexington Alarm, April, 1775; 1st Lieutenant 3d Connecticut, 1st May to 10th December, 1775; Captain 20th Continental Infantry, 1st January to 31st December, 1776.

Waterman, John (Conn). Quartermaster-Sergeant 3d Connecticut, 3d May to 10th December, 1775; 2d Lieutenant 20th Continental Infantry, 1st January to 31st December, 1776; 1st Lieutenant 4th Connecticut, 1st January, 1777; dismissed 24th July, 1777.

Waterman, John (Conn). Ensign of Elmore's Continental Regiment, 15th April, 1776, to April, 1777. (Died 16th December, 1825.)

Waterman, John (R. I.). Colonel Rhode Island Militia, 1776-1777. (Died 1812.)

Waterman, John (R. I.). Regimental Quartermaster 2d Rhode Island 11th February, 1777; died 20th April, 1778.

Waterman, Luther L. (Conn. Surgeon 25th Continental Infantry, 14th March to 31st December, 1776; Surgeon of Webb's Continental Regiment, 1st January, 1777; resigned 30th March, 1778.

Waterman, Thomas (R. I.). Colonel Rhode Island Militia, 1776-1777.

Waterman, Thomas (R. I.). Ensign 2d Rhode Island, 1st January, 1777; 2d Lieutenant, 11th February, 1777; Regimental Adjutant, 10th August, 1777; resigned 30th August, 1779. (Died 1807.)

Waters, Felix (S. C.). Captain 1st South Carolina, 24th May, 1776; taken prisoner at Charleston, 12th May, 1780.

Waters, James (N. C). Ensign 1st North Carolina, 24th December, 1776;

2d Lieutenant, 29th March, 1777; resigned 23d April, 1777.

Waters, Richard (Md). 2d Lieutenant 1st Maryland, 1st April, 1777; 1st Lieutenant, 27th May, 1778; Captain, 7th April, 1779; transferred to 3d Maryland, 1st January, 1781; retired 1st January, 1783; Brevet 1st Lieutenant, 5th November, 1777.

Waters, Richard (Md). 1st Lieutenant 1st Continental Artillery, 13th January, 1777 Regimental Adjutant, 25th September, 1778; Captain-Lieutenant, 18th August, 1779; taken prisoner at Camden, 16th August, 1780; prisoner on parole to close of war.

Waters, Richard (Md.) Surgeon's-Mate 2d Maryland, 7th May, 1778; resigned, 1st November, 1778.

Waters, Samuel (N. C.). Ensign 1st North Carolina, 24th December, 1776; 2d Lieutenant, 29th March, 1777; resigned 23d April, 1777.

Waters, Stillworthy (Conn). Major of Swift's Connecticut State Regiment, July to December, 1776.

Waters, William (N. C.). Ensign 1st North Carolina, 19th September, 1776; 2d Lieutenant, 5th February, 1777; 1st Lieutenant, 19th September, 1777; on roll for June, 1778, is reported as transferred to Cavalry Regiment, 1st June, 1778.

Waters, William (Va). Captain 1st Continental Artillery, 7th February, 1777; resigned, ——, 1778.

Waties, John (Va). Cornet 1st Continental Dragoons, 12th January, 1777; resigned 20th December, 1777.

Waties, Thomas (S. C.). Captain in Marion's Brigade, 1779-1782.

Watkins, Gassaway (Md). Sergeant of Smallwood's Maryland Regiment. 14th January, 1776; Ensign 3d Maryland, 10th December, 1776; 2d Lieutenant, 7th Maryland, 14th April, 1777; 1st Lieutenant, 14th September, 1778; transferred to 5th Maryland, 1st January, 1781; Captain 13th May, 1782 and served to April, 1783. (Died 14th July, 1840.)

Watkins, John (Md). Ensign 6th Maryland. 15th May, 1777; resigned 15th August, 1777.

Watkins, John (Md). Captain of an Independent Maryland Company, 14th January, 1776; resigned 3d October, 1776.

Watkins, John, Jr. (Va.) Captain 4th Virginia, 21st March, 1776, to ——.

Watkins, Joseph (N. Y.). Major and Commissary of Ordnance Stores, 5th February, 1777, to ——.

Watkins, John William (N. Y.). 2d Lieutenant 1st New York, 24th February to November, 1776; Captain of Malcolm's Continental Regiment, 11th March, 1777; resigned 12th October, 1777.

Watkins, Nathan (Mass). Captain in Lexington Alarm, April, 1775; Captain of Paterson's Massachusetts Regiment, May to December, 1775; Captain, 18th Continental Infantry, 1st January to 31st December, 1776; Captain, 12th Massachusetts 1st January, 1777; taken prisoner in a skirmish, 7th July, 1777; retired 8th September, 1778, on account of being absent a prisoner. (Died 1815.)

Watkins, Robert (Va). Ensign 5th Virginia, 5th February, 1776; Lieutenant, November, 1776; resigned 12th March, 1778.

Watkins, Thomas (Md). Captain Maryland Company of Artillery, 26th October, 1776, to 1777.

Watkins, Thomas (Va). Captain Virginia Dragoons at Guilford in March, 1781.

Watkins, William (Mass). Ensign of Paterson's Massachusetts Regiment, May to December, 1775.

Watkins, Zachariah (Mass). Sergeant in Lexington Alarm, April, 1775; Sergeant-Major of Thomas' Massachusetts Regiment, May to December, 1775; 2d Lieutenant 23d Continental Infantry, 1st January to 31st December, 1776; Lieutenant Massachusetts Militia, 1777-1779. (Died 24th June, 1826.)

Watrous, John Richard (Conn). Surgeon's-Mate 2d Connecticut, 1st May to 10th December, 1775; Surgeon's-Mate 22d Continental Infantry, 1st January, to 31st December, 1776; Surgeon 3d Connecticut, 1st January, 1777; transferred to 1st Connecticut, 1st January, 1781; retired 1st January, 1783.

Watrous, Josiah (Mass). Surgeon's-Mate 12th Massachusetts, 28th August, 1777; Surgeon's-Mate of Stevens' Battalion, subsequently part of the 3d Continental Artillery, 4th September, 1777; resigned 8th January, 1779. Died 14th June, 1825.)

Watson, Abraham (Mass). Captain 3d Massachusetts, 1st January, 1777;

taken prisoner at Young's House, 3d February, 1780; exchanged 22d December, 1780; resigned 12th April, 1782.

Watson, Abraham, Jr. (Mass). Surgeon of Gardner's Massachusetts Regiment, 28th June to December, 1775.

Watson, James (Conn). 2d Lieutenant of Bradley's Connecticut State Regiment, May, 1776; Captain of Webb's Continental Regiment, 1st January, 1777; resigned 1st May, 1778.

Watson, James (Pa). Colonel Pennsylvania Militia in 1777.

Watson, James (Pa). Captain Pennsylvania Battalion of the Flying Camp, July to December, 1776.

Watson, James (Va). Captain Virginia Militia, 1779-1781.

Watson. John, Jr. (Conn). Captain 4th Connecticut, 1st May to December, 1775; wounded at St. John's, 2d November, 1775. (Died 1815)

Watson, John (Del). Quartermaster Delaware Battalion of the Flying Camp, July to December, 1776.

Watson, Michael (S. C.). Captain South Carolina Militia, 1780-1782; killed near Sharon, Ga., 24th May, 1782.

Watson, Marston (Mass). 2d Lieutenant 14th Continental Infantry, 1st January to December, 1776, when he joined the Navy.

Watson, Moses (R. I.). Ensign of Richmond's Rhode Island State Regiment, 19th August, 1776, to ——.

Watson, Samuel (Pa). 1st Lieutenant 1st Pennsylvania Battalion, 27th October, 1775; Captain 2d Pennsylvania Battalion, 5th January, 1776; died 21st May, 1776.

Watson, Samuel (S. C.). 1st Lieutenant 3d South Carolina, 17th June, 1775; killed at Cowpens, 17th January, 1781.

Watson, Thomas (Del). Captain Delaware Battalion of the Flying Camp, July to December, 1776.

Watson, Thomas (N. C.). 1st Lieutenant 7th North Carolina, 28th November, 1776; resigned 12th April, 1777.

Watson, Titus (Conn). Sergeant in the Lexington Alarm, April, 1775; 2d Lieutenant 4th Connecticut, 1st May to December, 1775; Captain of Burrall's Continental Regiment, 19th January, 1776; Captain 7th Connecticut, 1st January, 1777; resigned 12th January, 1780. (Died 14th December, 1820.)

Watson, William (Mass). Ensign Lexington Alarm, April, 1775; 2d Lieutenant of Fellow's Massachusetts Regiment, May to December, 1775; 2d Lieutenant 21st Continental Infantry, 1st January to 31st December, 1776; 1st Lieutenant 9th Massachusetts, 1st January, 1777; Captain 25th July, 1779; taken prisoner at Young's House, 3d February, 1780; exchanged December, 1780; transferred to 3d Massachusetts, 1st January, 1783, and served to June, 1783. (Died 17th October, 1822.)

Watson, William (Va). Lieutenant 1st Virginia State Regiment in 1780.

Watson, Willis (S. C.). Lieutenant South Carolina Militia, 1780-1782.

Wattles, Mason (Mass). Sergeant of Nixon's Massachusetts Regiment, May to December, 1775; Ensign 4th Continental Infantry, 1st January to 31st December, 1776; 1st Lieutenant, 6th Massachusetts, 1st January, 1777; taken prisoner at Stony Point, 1st June, 1779; exchanged October, 1780; Captain, 13th April, 1780, and served to June, 1783. (Died 23d July, 1819.)

Watts, David (Mass). Sergeant in Lexington Alarm, April, 1775; Sergeant of Phinney's Massachusetts Regiment, May to December, 1775; Ensign, 18th Continental Infantry, 1st January, 1776; 1st Lieutenant, 18th April, 1776; 1st Lieutenant, 12th Massachusetts, 1st January, 1777; resigned 1st July, 1779.

Watts, Frederick (Pa). Lieutenant-Colonel of a Pennsylvania Battalion of the Flying Camp, July to December, 1776; taken prisoner at Fort Washington, 16th November, 1776 Brigadier-General Pennsylvania Militia, 28th May, 1782, to close of war. (Died 3d October, 1795.)

Watts, George (Va). Major Virginia Militia, 1777-1778.

Watts, John (Mass). Sergeant of Phinney's Massachusetts Regiment, May to December, 1775; Ensign 27th Continental Infantry, 1st January to 31st December, 1776.

Watts, John (Va). Cornet Virginia Dragoons, 17th June, 1776; Lieutenant 1st Continental Dragoons, 18th December, 1776; Captain, 7th April, 1778; wounded at Eutaw Springs, 8th September, 1781; retained in Baylor's Regiment of Dragoons, 9th November, 1782, and served to close of war; Lieutenant-Colonel Light Dragoons United States Army, 8th January, 1799; honorably discharged, 15th June, 1800. (Died 8th June, 1830.)

Watts, Thomas (Va). Captain Virginia Militia in 1780.

Watts, William (Md). Cornet 1st Continental Dragoons, 18th December, 1776; Lieutenant, 31st March, 1777; Captain, ——, 1779; wounded at Eutaw Springs, 8th September, 1781; retired 9th November, 1782. (Died 1816.)

Watts, William (Md). Surgeon's-Mate 2d Maryland, 15th August, 1781, and served to April, 1783.

Waugh, James (Pa). Captain 6th Pennsylvania, 15th February, 1777; retired 21st June, 1778. (Died 1816.)

Way, Moses (Ga). 2d Lieutenant 1st Georgia, 22d December, 1775; was a Captain in 1779.

Wayman, Abel.—See **Weyman.**

Wayne, Anthony (Pa). Colonel 4th Pennsylvania Battalion, 3d January, 1776; Brigadier-General Continental Army, 21st February, 1777; wounded at Stony Point, 16th July, 1779. By the act of 26th July, 1779, it was "Resolved, unanimously, that the thanks of Congress be presented to Brigadier-General Wayne for his brave, prudent and soldierly conduct in the spirited and well-conducted attack on Stony Point; that a gold medal emblematical of this action be struck and presented to Brigadier-General Wayne." Served to close of war; Brevet-Major-General, 30th September, 1783; Major General and Commander United States Army, 5th March, 1792; died 15th December, 1796.

Weare, Nathan (N. H.). Sergeant 3d New Hampshire, 8th April, 1777; Ensign, 4th October, 1777; Lieutenant, 5th July, 1780; transferred to 1st New Hampshire, 1st January, 1781, and sered to March, 1782.

Weare, Richard (N. H.). 1st Lieutenant 8th Continental Infantry, 1st January, 1776; Captain 3d New Hampshire, 8th November, 1776; died 2d August, 1777, of wounds received at Fort Ann, 8th July, 1777.

Weatherbee, Benjamin (N. J.). Captain of Spencer's Additional Continental Regiment 23d February, 1777; retired 1st January, 1781.

Weatherly, Isaac (S. C.). Lieutenant 1st South Carolina, May, 1776; Captain, ——; taken prisoner at Charleston, 12th May, 1780.

Weathers, James (Va). Lieutenant Virginia Militia, 1780-1781.

Weaver, Edward (N. Y.). Ensign 5th New York, 21st November, 1776;

discharged, 16th December, 1777. (Died 29th June, 1828.)

Weaver, Henry (Pa). Captain Pennsylvania Militia, 1777-1778.

Weaver, Jacob (N. Y.). 2d Lieutenant of Graham's Regiment New York Militia in 1778.

Weaver Jacob (Pa). Ensign 3d Pennsylvania Battalion, 22d April, 1776; taken prisoner at Fort Washington, 16th November, 1776; exchanged, 12th December, 1780; was retained as Captain of an independent company, to rank from 13th January, 1777; company annexed to 10th Pennsylvania, 7th November, 1777; retired 17th January, 1781. (Died 1812.)

Weaver, John (Pa). Surgeon's-Mate Invalid Regiment, 9th October, 1780, to 31st October, 1781.

Weaver, Michael (Pa). Captain Northumberland County, Pa., Militia in 1779.

Weaver, Thomas (S. C.). Captain 4th South Carolina (Artillery, ——. Died 10th October, 1779.

Webb, Charles (Conn). Colonel Connecticut Militia Regiment, May and June, 1775; Colonel 7th Connecticut, 6th July to 10th December, 1775; Colonel 19th Continental Infantry, 1st January to 31st December, 1776; Colonel 2d Connecticut, 1st January, 1777; resigned 13th March, 1778.

Webb, Charles, Jr. (Conn). Adjutant 5th Connecticut, 20th May, 1775; Adjutant 7th Connecticut, 11th July to 10th December, 1775; 2d Lieutenant and Adjutant 19th Continental Infantry, 1st January to 31st December, 1776; Paymaster 2d Connecticut, 1st January, 1777; reported to have been killed in the fall of 1778 on a gunboat on the sound near Stamford.

Webb, Ebenezer (Mass). Captain of Fellow's Massachusetts Regiment, May to November, 1775.

Webb, Elisha (N. C.). Ensign 7th North Carolina, 28th November, 1776, to ——.

Webb, George (Mass). 1st Lieutenant 3d Continental Infantry, 1st January to 31st December, 1776; Captain 4th Massachusetts, 1st January, 1777; retired 1st January, 1783. (Died 24th August 1825.)

Webb, Isaac (Va). Ensign 7th Virginia, September, 1776; 2d Lieutenant, 13th January, 1777; transferred to 5th

Virginia, 14th September, 1778; 1st Lieutenant, 30th October, 1778; Captain, ——, 1781, and served to close of war. (Died 1833.)

Webb, James (Mass). Sergeant 1st Massachusetts, 1st January, 1777; Ensign, 4th November, 1777; retired 1st January, 1781. (Died 1st September, 1825.)

Webb, James (R. I.). Lieutenant 3d Rhode Island, May, 1775; taken prisoner at Quebec, 31st December, 1775; exchanged, 1776; Captain of Sherburne's Continental Regiment, 1st March, 1777; resigned 17th April, 1780.

Webb, John (Conn). Lieutenant 2d Continental Dragoons, 10th January, 1777; Captain 1st January, 1778; Aide-de-Camp to Generals Howe and Greene, in 1781 and 1782; resigned 18th April, 1783.

Webb, John (N. C.). Commissary 3d North Carolina, 23d April, 1776, to ——.

Webb, John (Va). Captain 7th Virginia, 5th March, 1776; Major, 26th January, 1778; transferred to 5th Virginia, 14th September, 1778; Lieutenant-Colonel, 4th July, 1779; retired 12th February, 1781.

Webb, Joseph, Jr. (Conn). 1st Lieutenant of Silliman's Connecticut State Regiment, July to December, 1776.

Webb, Nathaniel (Conn). 1st Lieutenant 20th Continental Infantry, 1st January, 1776; Regimental Adjutant, 7th September to 31st December 1776; Captain 4th Connecticut, 1st January, 1777; retired 1st January, 1781. (Died 25th January, 1814.)

Webb, Samuel (Conn). Clerk in Lexington Alarm, April, 1775; Clerk, 5th Connecticut, 6th May to December, 1775; 1st Lieutenant of Elmore's Continental Regiment, 15th April, 1776; 1st Lieutenant 2d Continental Artillery, 1st January, 1777; resigned 29th May, 1778; Ensign 3d Connecticut, 26th July, 1780; Brigade Major of Waterbury's Brigade, January, 1781; resigned — April, 1781.

Webb, Samuel Blatchey (Conn). 1st Lieutenant 2d Connecticut, 1st May, 1775; wounded at Bunker Hill, 17th June, 1775; Major and Aide-de-Camp to General Putnam, 22d July, 1775; Lieutenant-Colonel and Aide-de-Camp to General Washington, 21st June, 1776; wounded at White Plains, 28th October, 1776, and at Trenton, 2d January, 1777; Colonel of one of the Sixteen Additional Continental Regiments, 11th January,

1777; taken prisoner on the expedition to Long Island, 10th December, 1777, and was a prisoner of war on parole until exchanged, December, 1780; transferred to 3d Connecticut, 1st January, 1781; brevet Brigadier-General, 30th September, 1783, and served to 3d June, 1783. (Died 3d December, 1817.)

Webb, Thomas (Mass). Ensign 23d Continental Infantry, 1st January to 31st December, 1776.

Webber, Christopher (N. H.). Captain New Hampshire Militia, 1776-1777. (Died 1803.)

Webber, Daniel (Mass). Private in Scammon's Massachusetts Regiment, May to December, 1775; Sergeant, 23d Continental Infantry, 1st January to 31st December, 1776; Sergeant 2d Massachusetts, 1st January, 1777; Ensign, 1st January, 1781; Lieutenant, 30th April, 1782, and served to June, 1783. (Died 1st February, 1827.)

Webber, Ebenezer (Mass). Captain in Lexington Alarm, April, 1775; Captain of Fellow's Massachusetts Regiment, May to December, 1775; Major, Massachusetts Militia, 1776-1780.

Webster, Alexander (N. Y.). Colonel New York Militia, 1780-1782.

Webster, Amos (N. H.). Ensign of Bedel's Regiment New Hampshire Rangers, 22d January, 1776; 2d Lieutenant 3d New Hampshire, 8th November, 1776; 1st Lieutenant, 20th June, 1777; killed at Stillwater, 7th October, 1777.

Webster, David (Vt). Lieutenant-Colonel of Bedel's Regiment, Vermont Militia, 1777-1779.

Webster, Ebenezer (N. H.). Captain New Hampshire Militia, 1777-1778.

Webster, Jacob (N. H.). 1st Lieutenant 2d New Hampshire, 23d May to December, 1775.

Webster, John (N. H.). 2d Lieutenant Bedel's Regiment New Hampshire Rangers, 22d July, 1775; taken prisoner at the Cedars 19th May, 1776; served subsequently as Colonel New Hampshire Militia. (Died 1827.)

Webster, John (N. J.). Lieutenant-Colonel and Colonel New Jersey Militia, 1778-1780.

Webster, John B. (Pa). Sergeant in Proctor's Pennsylvania Artillery Battalion, 1776; Quartermaster-Sergeant 4th Continental Artillery, January, 1777; Regimental Quartermaster, 1st November 1777; 1st Lieutenant, 11th

May, 1779; Captain-Lieutenant, 12th October, 1781, and served to June, 1783. (Died 19th March, 1834.)

Webster, Noah (Conn). Captain Connecticut Militia, 1777-1778. (Died 1813.)

Webster, Robert (Mass). Captain of Fellow's Massachusetts Regiment, May to December, 1775.

Wederstrandt, Conrod Theodore (Md). Assistant Deputy Commissary of Purchases for Maryland, 1779, 1781.

Wedgewood, James (N. H.). Ensign of Poor's New Hampshire Regiment, 20th September to December, 1775; 1st Lieutenant 3d New Hampshire, 8th November, 1776; retired 1st September, 1778. (Died 18th May, 1826.)

Weed, Seth (Conn). Private 5th Connecticut, 8th May to 15th October, 1775; 1st Lieutenant 2d Connecticut, 1st January, 1777; resigned 30th September, 1777. (Died 1822.)

Weed, Thaddeus (Conn). 2d Lieutenant of Silliman's Connecticut State Regiment, 20th June to 25th December, 1776; 1st Lieutenant 5th Connecticut, 1st January, 1777; Captain-Lieutenant, 1st June, 1778; Captain, 1st April, 1779; transferred to 2d Connecticut, 1st January, 1781; resigned 17th December, 1781.

Weeden, Ephraim (R. I.). Ensign 1st Rhode Island, June to December, 1775.

Weeden, Thomas (Mass). Private in Lexington Alarm, April, 1775; Sergeant of Cotton's Massachusetts Regiment, 2d May to December, 1775; Ensign 23d Continental Infantry, 1st January to 31st December, 1776. (Died 11th June, 1824.)

Weedon, George (Va). Lieutenant-Colonel 3d Virginia, 13th February, 1776; Colonel, 13th August, 1776; Acting Adjutant-General to General Washington, 20th February, 1777; Brigadier-General Continental Army, 27th February, 1777; resigned 11th June, 1783. (Died November, 1793.)

Weekly, John (S. C.). Lieutenant 4th South Carolina (Artillery), 26th November, 1776; Captain, 20th June, 1779; taken prisoner at Charleston, 12th May, 1780.

Weeks, Nathan (R. I.). Ensign 2d Rhode Island, 1st January, 1777; 2d Lieutenant, 17th February 1777; killed at Monmouth, 28th June, 1778.

Weeks, Thomas (Mass). Lieutenant in Lexington Alarm, April, 1775; Adjutant of Brewer's Massachusetts Regiment, May to December, 1775; Adjutant 10th Massachusetts, 6th November, 1776; omitted in 1777, having been appointed Assistant Commissary of Issues.

Weeks, William, Jr. (N. H.). Paymaster 3d New Hampshire, 8th November, 1776; resigned 1st June, 1778. (Died 1843.)

Weems, James S. (Mass). Surgeon's-Mate of Jackson's Additional Continental Regiment, 10th May, 1778; omitted September, 1778.

Wehritz, —— Baron de (——). Lieutenant of Armand's Legion, 3d March, 1777, to ——.

Weibert, Antoine Felix (——). Lieutenant-Colonel Engineer Continental Army, 14th August, 1776, "with pay from 28th June, 1776, the day he entered on duty;" served to ——.

Weidmann, John (Pa). Ensign German Regiment, 2d July, 1776; 1st Lieutenant, 14th May, 1777; taken prisoner at Brandywine, 11th September, 1777; exchanged 30th December, 1780, and retired 1st January, 1781. (Died 9th June, 1830.)

Weidmann, Mathias (Pa). 1st Lieutenant Pennsylvania Musket Battalion, 20th March, 1776; taken prisoner at Fort Washington, 16th November, 1776; exchanged, 26th August, 1778; did not return to the army.

Weisenfels, Charles Frederick (N. Y.). Ensign in Nicholson's Continental Regiment, July, 1776; 2d Lieutenant 2d New York, 21st November, 1776; 1st Lieutenant, 1st September, 1778; Regimental Quartermaster, 4th October, 1779, and served to June, 1783.

Weisenfels, Frederick (N. Y.). Captain 1st New York, 28th June, 1775; Lieutenant-Colonel 3d New York, 8th March, 1776, Lieutenant-Colonel 2d New York, 21st November, 1776; Lieutenant-Colonel Commandant 4th New-York, 13th January, 1779; retired 1st January, 1781; served subsequently as Lieutenant-Colonel New York Levies. (Died 14th May, 1806.)

Weisenthal, Frederick (Md). Surgeon of Smallwood's Maryland Regiment, February to December, 1776.

Weiser, Benjamin (Pa). Captain German Regiment, 8th July, 1776; cashiered, 31st October, 1776, for misconduct at Montressor's Island.

Weiser, Benjamin (Pa). Colonel Pennsylvania Militia in 1776.

Weiser, Frederick (Pa). 2d Lieutenant German Regiment, 8th July, 1777; resigned 1st May, 1777.

Weiser, Peter (Pa). 2d Lieutenant 1st Continental Infantry, 5th January, 1776; 1st Lieutenant, 25th September, 1776; 1st Lieutenant 1st Pennsylvania, 1st January, 1777; wounded and taken prisoner at Germantown, 4th October, 1777.

Weitzel, Caspar (Pa). Captain of Miles' Pennsylvania Rifle Regiment, 9th March, 1776, to January, 1777.

Weitzel, Jacob (Pa). Ensign of Patton's Additional Continental Regiment, 16th January, 1777; 2d Lieutenant, 2d April, 1777; transferred to Hartley's Regiment, February, 1778; regiment designated 11th Pennsylvania, 16th December, 1778; 1st Lieutenant, 11th March, 1780; transferred to 3d Pennsylvania, 17th January, 1781; transferred to 1st Pennsylvania, 1st January, 1783, and served to June, 1783.

Welch, John (N. Y.). 2d Lieutenant of Wynkoop's New York Regiment, June, 1776; 1st Lieutenant 3d New York, 21st November, 1776; cashiered, 9th January, 1779, and joined the enemy.

Welch, John (R. I.). Lieutenant Sappers and Miners, 2d August, 1779; resigned 1st July, 1781; Ensign and Regimental Quartermaster of Olney's Rhode Island Battalion, 1st January, 1782; 1st Lieutenant, 1st May, 1782, and served to close of war. (Name also spelled Welch.)

Welch, Joseph (N. H.). Major and Colonel New Hampshire Militia 1777-1780.

Welch, Nathaniel (Va). Captain of a Virginia State Regiment, 1778 to 1781.

Welch, Thomas (Mass). Volunteer Surgeon at Lexington and Concord, 19th April, 1775; Surgeon 27th Continental Infantry, January to December, 1776. (Died 9th February, 1831.)

Weld, Eleazer (Conn). 1st Lieutenant of Ward's Connecticut State Regiment, 14th May, 1776, to May, 1777.

Welles, Benjamin (Mass). Ensign 1st Massachusetts, 1st January, 1777; Lieutenant, 4th May, 1780, and served to November, 1783. (Died 3d June, 1828.)

Welles.—See also **Wells.**

Welles, Hezekiah (Conn). Captain of Walcott's Connecticut Regiment, December, 1775 to February, 1775.

Welles, Jonathan (Conn). Captain in Lexington Alarm, April, 1775; Captain of Walcott's Connecticut Regiment, December, 1775, to February, 1776; Major and Lieutenant-Colonel Connecticut Militia, 1776-1779.

Welles, Roger (Conn). 2d Lieutenant of Webb's Additional Continental Regiment, 1st January, 1777; 1st Lieutenant, 16th May, 1778; Captain, 8th April, 1780; transferred to 3d Connecticut, 1st January, 1781; retained in Swift's Connecticut Regiment, June, 1783, and served to November, 1783. (Died 27th May 1795.)

Welles, Samuel (Conn). Captain of Gay's Connecticut State Regiment, 20th June, 1776; taken prisoner, 15th September, 1776, on the retreat from New York; exchanged June, 1778.

Wells, Stephen (R. I.). Ensign 1st Rhode Island, 3d May, to December, 1775.

Wells, Bayze (Conn). Private 4th Connecticut, May to December, 1775; Ensign of Burrall's Continental Regiment, 23d January, 1776; 2d Lieutenant, 19th September, 1776; 1st Lieutenant 8th Connecticut, 1st January, 1777; resigned 21st March, 1778.

Wells, Chester (Conn). Captain of Chester's Connecticut State Regiment, June to December, 1776.

Wells, David (Mass). Lieutenant-Colonel Massachusetts Militia, 1776-1777. (Died 1814.)

Wells, Henry (Mass). 2d Lieutenant of Knox's Regiment Continental Artillery, 10th December, 1775; 1st Lieutenant, — March to November, 1776.

Wells, James (Conn). 1st Lieutenant of Durkee's Wyoming Valley Company, 26th August, 1776; killed 3d July, 1778, at the Wyoming massacre.

Wells, James (Conn). Sergeant 2d Continental Dragoons 7th May, 1777; Cornet, 1st January, 1778; Lieutenant, 2d June, 1779, and served to ——; reported as "dead;" date not stated.

Wells, James (Del). 1st Lieutenant Delaware Regiment, 18th January, 1776, to January, 1777; Captain 4th United States Infantry, 16th March, 1792; died 9th June, 1792.

Wells, James (Mass). Private and Sergeant in 4th Continental Infantry in 1776; Lieutenant 11th Massachusetts, 16th October, 1780; transferred to 10th Massachusetts, 1st January, 1781; transferred to 4th Massachusetts, 1st January, 1783, and served to June, 1783. (Died 23d February, 1806.)

Wells, James (Pa). 1st Lieutenant 4th Continental Artillery, 20th April, 1777; resigned 1st March 1778.

Wells, John.—See **Willis.**

Wells, Joshua (N. H.). Captain New Hampshire Militia in 1777.

Wells, Levi (Conn). Captain 2d Connecticut, 1st May to 10th December, 1775; Major 22d Continental Infantry, 1st January, 1776; taken prisoner at Long Island, 27th August, 1776; exchanged 9th December, 1777; served subsequently as Colonel Connecticut Militia and was taken prisoner at Horseneck, 9th December, 1780.

Wells, Stephen (Conn). Lieutenant-Colonel Connecticut Militia, ——; wounded in the Danbury Raid, 27th April, 1777.

Wells, Stephen (R. I.). Ensign of Varnum's Rhode Island Regiment, 3d May, 1775, to ——.

Wells, Thomas (Mass). 2d Lieutenant of Gridley's Regiment Massachusetts Artillery, May to December, 1775; 2d Lieutenant of Knox's Regiment Continental Artillery, 1st January, 1776; Captain Lieutenant 3d Continental Artillery, 1st January, 1777; Captain, 13th March, 1778; resigned 22d February, 1780. (Died 30th October, 1799.)

Wells, Thomas (R. I.). Captain of Richmond's Rhode Island State Regiment, 1st November, 1775, and served to 1777.

Wells, Thomas (Va). 1st Lieutenant, 15th January, 1777; Captain, 21st July, 1777; regiment designated 11th Virginia, 14th September, 1778; retired — January, 1780

Welp, Anthony (N. Y.). 1st Lieutenant 4th New York, 28th June, 1775, to March, 1776; 1st Lieutenant 1st Canadian (Livingston's) Regiment, 18th December, 1776; Captain, 26th November, 1778; retired 1st January, 1781.

Welch, Edward (S. C.). 1st Lieutenant 5th South Carolina, ——, 1777; Captain, 20th January, 1778, to ——.

Welsh, Jacob (Mass). Ensign 6th Continental Infantry, 1st January, 1776;

2d Lieutenant of Stevens' Battalion of Artillery (subsequently part of the 3d Continental Artillery), 9th November, 1776; 1st Lieutenant, 12th September, 1778; resigned 10th November, 1778; name also spelled Welch.

Welsh, John (R. I.). Ensign and Quartermaster, 12th March, 1782, to rank from 1st July, 1781; retired 15th June, 1783.

Welsh, Joseph (Mass). Lieutenant of Paterson's Massachusetts Regiment, May to December 1775; 1st Lieutenant 15th Continental Infantry, 1st January to 31st December, 1776. (Died 15th February, 1825.)

Welsh, Nathaniel (Va). 2d Lieutenant 2d Virginia State Regiment, ——, 1778; 1st Lieutenant, 13th January, 1779; Captain, 1st September, 1779; retired January, 1781.

Welsh, Patrick (S. C.). Major South Carolina Dragoons, 5th April to September, 1781.

Welsh, Peter (Mass). Sergeant of Mansfield's Massachusetts Regiment, May to December, 1775; Sergeant 27th Continental Infantry, 1st January to 31st December, 1776; 2d Lieutenant 5th Massachusetts, 1st January, 1777; resigned 30th April, 1780. Name also spelled Welch. (Died 22d August, 1831.)

Welsh, Richard (Mass). Sergeant of Bridge's Massachusetts Regiment, May to December, 1775; Ensign 16th Continental Infantry, 1st January to 31st December, 1776; 1st Lieutenant 9th Massachusetts, 1st January, 1777; dismissed 28th August, 1780.

Weltner, Ludowick (Md). Major German Regiment, 17th July, 1776; Lieutenant-Colonel, 29th April, 1777; retired 1st January, 1781.

Wempel, Abraham (N. Y.). Colonel New York Militia, 1777-1779.

Wempel, Myndert A. (N. Y.). Captain New York Militia, 1777-1778.

Wempel, Myndert M. (N. Y.). Major New York Militia in 1778.

Wendell, Cornelius (N. Y.). Lieutenant New York Militia in 1775.

Wendell, Harmanus (N .Y.). Captain New York Militia in 1775; Lieutenant-Colonel New York Militia, 1780-1781.

Wendell, Henry (N. Y.). Major New York Militia, 20th October, 1775, to ——.

Wendell, Jacob Henry (N. Y.). Ensign 1st New York, 21st November,

1776; Lieutenant, January, 1779; Regimental Adjutant, 29th September, 1780, and served to June, 1783. (Died 23d March, 1826.)

Wendell, John H. (N. Y.). Captain in Wynkoop's New York Regiment, 1st March, 1776; Captain 1st New York, 21st November, 1776; resigned 5th April, 1781. (Died 10th July, 1832.)

Wentworth, James (Pa). Lieutenant, ——; was a prisoner; when and where taken not stated.

Wentworth, Jonathan (N. H.). Captain 2d New Hampshire, 23d May to December, 1775; Captain 8th Continental Infantry, 1st January, 1776; cashiered 26th July, 1776; Major New Hampshire Militia in 1780. (Died 1790.)

Werts, Thomas (Va). Captain 11th Virginia, 21st July, 1776; died 20th December, 1776.

Wesson, James Mass). Major of Gerrish's Massachusetts Regiment, 19th May to December, 1775; Lieutenant-Colonel 26th Continental Infantry, 1st January, 1776; Colonel 9th Massachusetts, 1st November, 1776; wounded at Monmouth, 28th June, 1778; retired 1st January, 1781. (Died 15th October, 1809.)

Wesson, Nathan (N. H.). Lieutenant of Flowers' Artillery Artificer Regiment, 1779-1781.

West, Benjamin (Mass). 2d Lieutenant of Whitcomb's Massachusetts Regiment, May, 1775; killed at Bunker Hill, 17th June, 1775.

West, Benjamin (R. I.). 1st Lieutenant of Richmond's Rhode Island State Regiment, 19th August, 1776; Captain of Stanton's Rhode Island State Regiment, 12th December, 1776, to ——.

West, Cato (S. C.). 1st Lieutenant 5th South Carolina, — March, 1777; resigned — October, 1779.

West, Charles (Va). Captain 3d Virginia, 9th February, 1776; Major, 30th January, 1777; resigned 6th July, 1778.

West, Ebenezer (Conn). Sergeant 3d Connecticut, 9th May to 18th December, 1775; 2d Lieutenant of Sage's Connecticut State Regiment, 20th June to 25th December, 1776; Adjutant of Ely's Connecticut State Regiment, June, 1777; taken prisoner on Long Island Expedition, 10th December, 1777; exchanged 8th December, 1780.

West, Ebenezer (R. I.). Ensign 11th Continental Infantry, 1st January to 31st December, 1776; 1st Lieutenant

2d Rhode Island, 11th February, 1777; cashiered 12th July, 1778.

West, George (Pa). 1st Lieutenant of Miles' Pennsylvania Rifle Regiment, 9th March, 1776; taken prisoner at Long Island, 27th August, 1776, and died in captivity.

West, Jeremiah (Conn). Surgeon's Mate of Webb's Continental Regiment, 1st January, 1777; Surgeon, 5th June, 1778; transferred to 3d Connecticut, 1st January, 1781; resigned 3d March, 1782. (Died 18th October, 1806.)

West, Jacob (N. J.). Lieutenant-Colonel and Colonel New Jersey Militia, 1776-1780.

West, Nathaniel (Conn). 2d Lieutenant of Sage's Connecticut State Regiment, June to December, 1776.

West, Samuel (Mass). 2d Lieutenant of Whitcomb's Massachusetts Regiment, May to December, 1775.

West, Thomas (Va). Captain 10th Virginia, 10th November, 1776; resigned 9th September, 1778.

West, William (Pa). Captain 3d Pennsylvania Battalion, 5th January, 1776; Major, 25th October, 1776; taken prisoner at Fort Washington, 16th November, 1776.

West, William (R. I.). Colonel and Brigadier-General Rhode Island Militia, 1775-1780.

Westcoat, Arthur (N. J.). 1st Lieutenant New Jersey Militia in 1777. (Name also spelled Wescoat.)

Westcoat, Joel (Pa). Ensign 3d Pennsylvania Battalion, 8th January, 1776; 2d Lieutenant, 12th April, 1776; taken prisoner at Fort Washington, 16th November, 1776.

Westcott, Gideon (R. I.). Captain of Elliott's Regiment Rhode Island Artillery in 1777.

Westcott, Jabez (R. I.). Captain of Elliott's Regiment Rhode Island State Artillery, 12th December, 1776, to ——.

Westcott, John (N. J.). 1st Lieutenant Western Company New Jersey Artillery, 1st March, 1776; Captain Lieutenant, October, 1776; Captain, 1777, to ——.

Westcott, Nathan (R. I.). Ensign of Stanton's Rhode Island State Regiment, 12th December, 1776, to ——.

Westcott, Richard (N. J.). Major New Jersey Militia; wounded at Trenton, 2d January, 1777. (Died 1825.)

Westcott, Uriah (R. I.). 2d Lieutenant of Elliott's Regiment Rhode Island State Artillery, 12th December, 1776, to ——.

Westcott, Wright (Va). Captain Virginia Militia, 1780-1781.

Westcott, Zorobabel (R. I.). 1st Lieutenant of Richmond's Rhode Island State Regiment, 1st November, 1775, to ——.

Westfall, Abel (Va). Captain 8th Virginia, 12th March, 1776; resigned 22d November, 1777.

Westfall, Cornelius (Va). Ensign 8th Virginia, 16th March, 1777; resigned 21st April, 1778.

Westfall, Simon (N. Y.). Captain New York Militia in 1780.

Weston, Benjamin (Conn). Private in the Lexington Alarm, April, 1775; Sergeant of Webb's Continental Regiment, 10th March, 1777; Ensign, 16th May, 1778; resigned 13th July, 1779.

Weston, James (Mass). Sergeant 6th Massachusetts, 25th February, 1777; Sergeant-Major February, 1779; Ensign, 10th April, 1779; roll for February, 1780, says "never joined."

Wetherill, Obadiah (Mass). Ensign 7th Continental Infantry, 1st January to 31st December, 1776; Ensign 8th Massachusetts, 1st January, 1777; 2d Lieutenant, 5th January, 1777; resigned 14th September, 1780. Name also spelled Wetherell.

Wetherill, John (N. J.). Colonel New Jersey Militia in 1776.

Wetmore, Jacob (Conn). 1st Lieutenant of Sage's Connecticut State Regiment, June to December, 1776.

Wetzell, Michael (N. J.). 2d Lieutenant 2d Continental Artillery, 29th June, 1781; transferred to Corps of Artillery, 17th June, 1783, and served to November, 1783.

Weyman Abel (N. Y.). Ensign 1st New Jersey, 4th August to November, 1776; Ensign 4th New Jersey, 28th November, 1776; 2d Lieutenant, 17th February, 1777; 1st Lieutenant, 1st November, 1777; transferred to 2d New Jersey, 1st July, 1778; Captain, 16th April, 1780; transferred to 1st New Jersey, 1st January, 1781, and served to April, 1783. (Name also spelled Wayman.)

Weyman, Edward (S. C.). Captain South Carolina Artillery, 1779-1781.

Wharton, Carpenter (—). Commissary Continental Army, 6th July, 1776; charges were preferred against him, and was directed 26th June, 1777, to settle his accounts.

Wheatley, Andrew (Conn). Regimental Quartermaster 4th Connecticut, 15th January, 1777; resigned — April, 1778.

Wheatley, John (Conn). 2d Lieutenant of Selden's Connecticut State Regiment, 20th June, 1776; wounded and taken prisoner on the retreat from New York, 15th September, 1776.

Wheaton, Joseph (N. H.). Lieutenant of Peabody's Regiment New Hampshire Militia, 1778-1779.

Wheaton, Joseph (R. I.). Ensign 2d Rhode Island, 1st March, 1779; 2d Lieutenant, 31st August, 1779; retained in Olney's Rhode Island Battalion 14th May 1781, and served to 25th December, 1783; Captain Assistant Deputy Quartermaster-General United States Army, 28th April, 1813; Major Deputy Quartermaster-General, 15th September, 1814; appointment negatived by Senate, 3d January, 1815. (Died 23d November, 1828.)

Wheaton, Samuel (Conn). Quartermaster-Sergeant 2d Connecticut, 13th December, 1776; Regimental Quartermaster, 10th December, 1777; resigned 8th March, 1778.

Whedbee, Richard (N. C.). 2d Lieutenant 7th North Carolina, 1st May, 1777; 1st Lieutenant, 15th August, 1777; dismissed 15th January, 1778.

Wheeler, Adam (Mass). Lieutenant in Lexington Alarm, April, 1775; Captain of Doolittle's Massachusetts Regiment, May to December, 1775; Captain 4th Continental Infantry, 1st January to 31st December, 1776; Captain 6th Massachusetts, 1st January, 1777; retired 15th October, 1778. (Died 1802.)

Wheeler, Abijah (N. H.). Lieutenant of Drake's Regiment, New Hampshire Militia, 1777-1778.

Wheeler, Ephraim (Mass). Ensign 4th Continental Infantry, 1st January to 31st December, 1776; 2d Lieutenant 6th Massachusetts, 1st January, 1777; cashiered 22d December, 1777.

Wheeler, Francis (Mass). Lieutenant Company of Minute Men at Concord, 19th April, 1775.

Wheeler, John (Mass). 1st Lieutenant of Doolittle's Massachusetts Regiment, May to December, 1775; Lieutenant Massachusetts Militia, 1776-1777.

Wheeler, Joseph (N. J.). Lieutenant and Captain New Jersey Militia, 1776-1777.

Wheeler, Lemuel (Conn). Surgeon 4th Connecticut, May to November, 1775.

Wheeler, Nathan (Mass). Private in Lexington Alarm, April, 1775; Corporal of Doolittle's Massachusetts Regiment, April to December, 1775; Sergeant 4th Continental Infantry, 1st January to 31st December 1776; Quartermaster-Sergeant 6th Massachusetts, 1st February, 1777; Ensign, 6th March, 1779; resigned 5th October, 1780. (Died 15th July, 1823.)

Wheeler, Nathan (Mass). Ensign of Nixon's Massachusetts Regiment, May to December, 1775; 1st Lieutenant 4th Continental Infantry, 1st January to 31st December, 1776; 1st Lieutenant 6th Massachusetts 1st January, 1777; retired 1st March, 1779.

Wheeler, Seth (N. H.). 2d Lieutenant of Bedel's Regiment New Hampshire Rangers, 6th July, 1775, to January, 1776.

Wheeler, Silas (R. I.). Lieutenant of Barton's Regiment Rhode Island Militia in 1779.

Wheeler, Warham (Mass). Sergeant of Nixon's Massachusetts Regiment, April to November, 1775; Ensign 4th Continental Infantry, 1st January, 1776; 2d Lieutenant, 10th Massachusetts, 6th November, 1776; resigned 11th November, 1777.

Wheeler, William (Md). Ensign 2d Maryland, 14th January, 1777; resigned 20th November, 1777.

Wheeler, William (N. Y.). Surgeon of Steven's Battalion of Artillery, 4th September, 1777; resigned 18th January, 1779.

Wheelock, Ephraim (Mass. Lieutenant-Colonel in Lexington Alarm, April, 1775, and Colonel Massachusetts Militia, 1776-1777.

Wheelock, John (Vt). Captain and Lieutenant-Colonel Bedel's Regiment Vermont Militia, 1777-1778.

Wheelock, Moses (Mass). Captain of Ward's Massachusetts Regiment, 23d May to December, 1775; Captain, Major and Lieutenant-Colonel Massachusetts Militia, 17761780. (Died 1801.)

Wheelwright, Daniel (Mass). Captain Massachusetts Militia, 1775-1776; Captain 11th Massachusetts, 6th November, 1776; died 28th May 1778.

Whelp, Anthony.—See **Welp.**

Whelpley, James (Conn). Regimental Quartermaster 5th Connecticut, 1st January, 1777; resigned 15th December, 1777.

Wherry, David (Pa). Ensign 8th Pennsylvania, August, 1776, to ——.

Wherry, Joseph (Pa). 2d Lieutenant of Montgomery's Pennsylvania Battalion of the Flying Camp; taken prisoner at Fort Washington, 16th November, 1776.

Wherry, Robert (Pa). Surgeon's Mate of Malcolm's Additional Continental Regiment, 20th June, 1778; transferred to 11th Pennsylvania, 16th December, 1778; transferred to 3d Pennsylvania, 17th January, 1781; transferred to 1st Pennsylvania, 1st January, 1783, and served to close of war.

Whetmore, Hezekiah (N. Y.). Quartermaster 2d Continental Dragoons, 12th January, 1777; Adjutant of Stevens' Battalion of Artillery, 1st February, 1777; resigned 5th September, 1778. (Name also spelled Wetmore.)

Whipple, Amos (R. I.). Captain Rhode Island Militia in 1777.

Whipple, Bella (R. I.). Adjutant 2d Rhode Island, June to December, 1775.

Whipple, George (Mass). 2d Lieutenant of Read's Massachusetts Regiment, May to December, 1775; 2d Lieutenant 13th Continental Infantry, 1st January to 31st December, 1776; 2d Lieutenant 2d Continental Artillery, 1st January, 1777, to · ——.

Whipple, Job (Mass). Sergeant in Lexington Alarm, April, 1775; Lieutenant of Mansfield's Massachusetts Regiment, May to December, 1775; 1st Lieutenant 27th Continental Infantry, 1st January to 31st December, 1776; Captain 5th Massachusetts, 1st January, 1777; wounded at Bennington, 16th August, 1777; resigned 20th April, 1781. ·

Whipple, Moses (N. H.). Captain New Hampshire Militia in 1777.

Whipple, Samuel (R. I.). Ensign of Tallman's Rhode Island Regiment 12th December, 1776; 2d Lieutenant 2d Rhode Island, 11th February, 1777; resigned 18th January, 1778.

Whipple, William (N. H.). A signer of the Declaration of Independence;

Brigadier-General New Hampshire Militia in 1777-1778; died 28th November, 1785.

Whipple, William (R. I.). Ensign of Stanton's Rhode Island State Regiment, 12th December, 1776, to ——.

Whitaker, Edward (N. Y.). Lieutenant of Snyder's Regiment New York Militia in 1781-1782.

Whitaker, Hudson (N. C.). Ensign 7th North Carolina, 22d December, 1776, to ——; wounded at Hickory Hill, 28th June, 1779.

Whitaker, Stephen (N. J.). Lieutenant New Jersey Militia, 1776-1777.

Whitaker, William (Va). Lieutenant 1st Continental Artillery, 10th April, 1782, to ——.

Whitcomb, Asa (Mass). Colonel of a Massachusetts Regiment, 3d June to December 1775; Colonel 6th Continental Infantry 1st January to 31st December, 1776. (Died 1804.)

Whitcomb, Benjamin (N. H.). 2d Lieutenant of Bedel's Regiment New Hampshire Rangers, 22d January, 1776; 1st Lieutenant, 10th May, 1776; Captain, 14th October, 1776; Major Battalion New Hampshire Rangers, 10th November, 1777; retired 1st January, 1781. (Died 22d July, 1828.)

Whitcomb Elisha (N. H.). 1st Lieutenant of Bedel's Regiment New Hampshire Rangers, 22d January to December, 1776, and Captain of Vermont Militia, 15th December, 1777, to 1st April, 1778.

Whitcomb, John (Mass). Was a Brigadier-General Massachusetts Militia at the commencement of the war, also a Colonel, Massachusetts Regiment, April to December, 1775, and was also Major-General Massachusetts Militia in 1775; appointed Brigadier-General Continental Army, 5th June, 1776, which he declined. (Died 1812.)

Whitcomb Jonathan (N. H.). Captain 3d New Hampshire, 23d April to December, 1775. (Died 1792.)

Whitcomb, Joseph (N. H.). Captain New Hampshire Militia, 1777.

Whitcomb, Scottoway (Mass). Ensign and Regimental Quartermaster 3d Continental Infantry, 1st January, 1776, to December, 1776; Lieutenant Massachusetts Militia, 1777-1779.

White, Aaron (Mass). Hospital Surgeon, 1776-1779. (Died 1813.) Name also spelled Wight.

White, Andrew (N. Y.). Ensign 2d New York, 21st November, 1776; 2d Lieutenant, 1st June, 1777; resigned 5th April, 1780; served subsequently as Captain New York Levies.

White, Anthony Walton (N. J.). Lieutenant-Colonel 3d New Jersey, 18th January, 1776; Lieutenant-Colonel 4th Continental Dragoons, 15th February, 1777; Lieutenant-Colonel Commandant 1st Continental Dragoons 10th December, 1779; Colonel, 16th February, 1780; taken prisoner at Lanneaus' Ferry, 6th May, 1780; exchanged October, 1780; retired 9th November, 1782; Brigadier-General United States Army, 19th July, 1798; honorably discharged, 15th June, 1800. (Died 10th February, 1803.)

White, Haffield (Mass). Lieutenant Company of Minute Men at Lexington, 19th April, 1775; 2d Lieutenant of Mansfield's Massachusetts Regiment, May to December, 1775; 1st Lieutenant 27th Continental Infantry, 1st January to 31st December, 1776, being Regimental Adjutant from 24th April, 1776; Captain 5th Massachusetts, 1st January, 1777; retired 1st January, 1783. (Died ——, 1817.)

White, Aquilla (Pa). Ensign 8th Pennsylvania, August, 1776; left the sevice 23d February, 1777.

White, Ebenezer (N. Y.). Surgeon New York Militia; taken prisoner at Fort Montgomery, 6th October, 1777. (Died 1827.)

White, Edward (Mass). Ensign 9th Massachusetts, 1st January, 1777; 2d Lieutenant, 6th March, 1778; transferred to 8th Massachusetts, 1st January, 1781; transferred to 3d Massachusetts, 12th June, 1783, and served to 3d November, 1783. (Died 9th January, 1812.)

White, Edward (Pa). Ensign of Patton's Continental Regiment, 16th January, 1777; 2d Lieutenant, 11th September, 1777; resigned 28th May, 1778.

White, Elisha (Conn). 2d Lieutenant of Walcott's Connecticut Regiment, December, 1775 to February, 1776.

White, Elisha (Va). 2d Lieutenant 1st Virginia, 11th June, 1777; dropped as absent without leave in May, 1778.

White, Epenetus (N. Y.). Lieutenant New York Militia, ——; prisoner of war, 11th June, 1781, to 9th November, 1782; where taken not stated.

White, Francis (Pa). Ensign 10th Pennsylvania, 2d June, 1778; Lieutenant, 2d August, 1779; transferred to 1st Pennsylvania, 17th January, 1781; taken prisoner at Green Springs, 6th July, 1781; retired 1st January, 1783.

White, George (Mass). Captain Massachusetts Militia in 1776; Captain 11th Massachusetts, 6th November, 1776; resigned 25th June, 1779. (Died 26th May, 1826.)

White, George (N. J.). Lieutenant 1st Continental Dragoons, 1780; transferred to Baylor's Regiment of Dragoons, 9th November, 1782 and served to close of war.

White George (N. Y.). Captain 2d New York, 28th June to December, 1775.

White, Henry (Mass). Sergeant of Gerrish's Massachusetts Regiment, May to December, 1775; Sergeant 26th Continental Infantry, 1st January, 1776; Ensign, — July to 31st December, 1776; Ensign 9th Massachusetts, 1st January, 1777; 2d Lieutenant, 28th July, 1779; transferred to 8th Massachusetts, 1st January, 1781; retired 1st January, 1783. (Died 16th December, 1823.)

White, Henry (S. C.). Lieutenant 5th South Carolina, ——, 1777; resigned 22d January, 1778; Colonel South Carolina Militia, 1779-1782.

White, Hugh (Pa). Lieutenant-Colonel Pennsylvania Militia, 1776-1777.

White, Isaac (N. C.). Lieutenant North Carolina Militia at Kings Mountain, October, 1780. (Died 1821.)

White, James (Ga). Captain 3d Georgia, — July, 1776, to ——.

White, James (N. C.). Captain North Carolina Militia, 1779-1781. (Died 1821.)

White, John (Conn). Sergeant 6th Connecticut, 2d May, 1777; Ensign, 1st April, 1779; 2d Lieutenant, 8th September, 1780; transferred to 4th Connecticut, 1st January, 1781; transferred to 2d Connecticut, 1st January, 1783, and served to June, 1783.

White, John (Md). 2d Lieutenant Maryland Artillery Company, 13th September, 1779; resigned 15th February, 1780.

White, John (Mass). Quartermaster of Nixon's Massachusetts Regiment, April to December, 1775; 2d Lieutenant and Quartermaster 4th Continental Infantry, 1st January to 31st December, 1776; Quartermaster 6th Massachusetts, ter, 30th July, 1777, to January, 1781.

White, John (N. H.). 1st Lieutenant of Bedel's Regiment New Hampshire Rangers, 22d January to July, 1776.

White, John (N. H.). Surgeon New Hampshire Militia in 1777. (Died 1838.)

White, John (N. C.). Captain 2d North Carolina, 1st September, 1775; Major, 7th May, 1776; Colonel 4th Georgia, 1st February, 1777; wounded and taken prisoner at Savannah, 9th October, 1779; made his escape and died of wounds shortly afterwards.

White, John (Pa). Volunteer Aide-de-Camp to General Sullivan, 27th September, 1777; died 10th October, 1777, of wounds received at Germantown, 4th October, 1777.

White, John (Va). Ensign 7th Virginia, 28th December, 1776; 2d Lieutenant, 30th April, 1778; transferred to 5th Virginia, 14th September, 1778; 1st Lieutenant, 4th July, 1779; taken prisoner at Charleston, 12th May, 1780; transferred to 8th Virginia, 12th February, 1781, and served to ——.

White, John (Va). Ensign and Paymaster 7th Virginia, 6th March, 1778; transferred to 5th Virginia, 14th September, 1778; 1st Lieutenant, 4th September, 1779; retired 1st January, 1780.

White, John (Va). Cornet 1st Continental Dragoons, 25th June, 1777; Lieutenant of Lee's Battalion of Light Dragoons in 1779.

White, Joseph (N. C.). Captain North Carolina Militia at King's Mountain in October, 1780.

White, Matthew (N. C.). Lieutenant 6th North Carolina, 2d November, 1776; killed at Germantown, 4th October, 1777.

White, Moses (Mass). Captain 2d Canadian (Hazen's) Regiment, 3d November, 1776; Aide-de-Camp to General Hazen, 1st September, 1781, to close of war; Brevet Major, 30th September, 1783. (Died 28th May, 1833.)

White, Nahum (Mass). Corporal in Lexington Alarm, April, 1775; Sergeant of Brewer's Massachusetts Regiment, May to December, 1775; Ensign 6th Continental Infantry, 1st January to 31st December, 1776; Ensign 12th Massachusetts, 6th November, 1776; 2d Lieutenant, 1st January, 1777; resigned 28th October, 1777. (Name also spelled Wight.)

White, Nathaniel (Vt). Lieutenant Vermont Militia in 1777.

White, Nehemiah (Mass). 1st Lieutenant of Read's Massachusetts Regiment May to December, 1775.

White, Nicholas (Pa). Ensign 10th Pennsylvania, 2d June, 1778; Lieutenant, 2d August, 1779; resigned 1st April, 1780.

White, Peter (Mass). 2d Lieutenant of Paterson's Massachusetts Regiment, May to December, 1775; 1st Lieutenant 15th Continental Infantry, 1st January to 31st December, 1776.

White, Richard P. (Va). 1st Lieutenant Virginia Convention Guards, 13th January, 1779; Captain, ——, 1780, and served to 10th June, 1781.

White, Robert (Md). Deputy Commissary-General of Issues, 14th August, 1777; resigned 15th September, 1777.

White, Robert (Pa). 1st Lieutenant 6th Pennsylvania Battalion, 9th January, 1776; resigned 9th February, 1776.

White, Robert (Pa). Ensign 9th Pennsylvania, 15th November, 1776; 2d Lieutenant, 4th August, 1777; resigned 1st February, 1778.

White, Robert (Va). Entered service as a private in September, 1775; 2d Lieutenant 12th Virginia, 1st March, 1777; wounded at Short Hills, 26th June, 1777; 1st Lieutenant, 1st September, 1777, but did not rejoin regiment. (Died 2d November, 1831.)

White, Sims (S. C.). Captain 4th South Carolina (Artillery), 14th November, 1775; resigned 12th September, 1777; was taken prisoner at Charleston, 12th May, 1780.

White, Salmon (Mass). Sergeant 6th Massachusetts, 18th April, 1777; Ensign, 26th November, 1779; 2d Lieutenant, 30th April, 1781; retired 1st November, 1782.

White, Stephen (N. Y.). Captain New York Levies, ——; taken prisoner at Johnstown, 24th October, 1781; exchanged October, 1782.

White, Tarpley (Va). Ensign 7th Virginia, 7th March, 1776; 2d Lieutenant, 28th October, 1776; 1st Lieutenant, 29th January, 1778; transferred to 5th Virginia, 14th September, 1778; Captain Lieutenant, 29th August, 1779; Captain, ——, 1780; retired 12th February, 1781.

White, Thomas (Mass). Sergeant in Lexington Alarm, April, 1775; Sergeant in Woodbridge's Massachusetts Regiment, May to November, 1775; 2d Lieutenant 27th Continental Infantry, 1st January, 1776; 1st Lieutenant, 10th Massachusetts, 6th November, 1776; dismissed 27th March, 1780. (Died 1814.)

White, Thomas (Mass). Captain in Lexington Alarm, April, 1775; Captain Massachusetts Militia, 1775-1777.

White, Thomas (N. C.). 1st Lieutenant 6th North Carolina, 16th April, 1776; Captain, 20th January, 1777; retired 1st June, 1778.

White, Thomas (Pa). 1st Lieutenant of Montgomery's Pennsylvania Battalion of the Flying Camp, July, 1776; taken prisoner at Fort Washington, 16th November, 1776; exchanged in 1778, and did not rejoin the army.

White, Thomas (Pa). Captain York County, Pa., Militia in 1777.

White, Thomas (Va). Corporal and Sergeant 1st Virginia State Regiment, March, 1777; 2d Lieutenant, 7th December, 1778; 1st Lieutenant, 13th August, 1779, and served to January, 1781. (Died 1839.)

White, Timothy (Conn). Ensign of Douglas' Connecticut State Regiment, June to December, 1776.

White, Timothy (Mass). Surgeon Massachusetts Militia in 1777.

White, Walter (Md). 1st Lieutenant Maryland Battalion of the Flying Camp, July to December, 1776.

White, William (Mass). Sergeant in Lexington Alarm, April, 1775; Sergeant of Danielson's Massachusetts Regiment, April to December, 1775; Lieutenant of Massachusetts Militia in 1776; Adjutant 7th Massachusetts, 1st January, 1777; Lieutenant, 1st October, 1778; killed at Yorktown, 13th October, 1781.

White, William (N. C.). Ensign 7th North Carolina, 17th April, 1777; omitted — November, 1777.

White, William (Va). Ensign 1st Virginia State Regiment, 7th December, 1778; 2d Lieutenant, 1st April, 1779, and served to February, 1781. (Died 1814.)

White, William (Va). 2d Lieutenant 7th Virginia, 8th May, 1776; 1st Lieutenant, 28th September, 1777; transferred to 5th Virginia, 14th September, 1778; Captain Lieutenant, 12th May, 1779; Captain, 4th July, 1779; taken prisoner at Charleston, 12th May, 1780, and was a prisoner on parole to close of war. (Died 30th July, 1828.)

White, William (Va). 1st Lieutenant 3d Virginia, 21st March, 1776; died 16th September, 1777, of wounds received at Brandywine, 11th September, 1777.

White, Wright (N. Y.). 1st Lieutenant of Graham's Regiment New York Militia in 1778.

Whitefield, Luke (S. C). Captain South Carolina Militia in 1776.

Whitehall, Alexander (N. C.). Captain North Carolina Militia in 1780.

Whitehead, James (Pa). Ensign 2d Pennsylvania, 21st January, 1777; 2d Lieutenant, 12th March, 1777; retired 17th January, 1781.

Whitehead, John (Mass). Private in Lexington Alarm, April, 1775; Lieutenant of Baldwin's Artillery Artificer Regiment, 1st January, 1777; resigned 27th March, 1778. (Died 1783.)

Whiteley, Michard (Pa). Captain Pennsylvania Militia; taken prisoner at Chestnut Hills, Pa., 6th December, 1777, and died shortly after.

Whiteley, William (Md). Lieutenant-Colonel 4th Maryland Battalion of the Flying Camp, 16th August to 1st December, 1776.

Whiteman.—See **Weidmann.**

Whiting, Aaron (Mass). Ensign of Brewer's Massachusetts Regiment, May to December, 1775.

Whiting, Beverly (Va). Ensign 7th Virginia, 13th December, 1776; resigned 4th July, 1778.

Whiting, Bradford (N. Y.). Colonel New York Militia in 1775.

Whiting, Charles (Conn). Adjutant 2d Connecticut, 28th July to 10th December, 1775; 1st Lieutenant and Adjutant 22d Continental Infantry, 1st January, 1776; Aide-de-Camp to General Spencer, 14th August, 1776; Captain of Webb's Additional Continental Regiment, 14th February, 1777; Died 10th July, 1779; also reported as killed same date.

Whiting, Daniel (Mass). Lieutenant in Lexington Alarm, April, 1775; Captain of Brewer's Massachusetts Regiment, 19th May to December, 1775; Captain 6th Continental Infantry, 1776; Major 7th Massachusetts, 1st January, 1777; Lieutenant-Colonel 6th Massachusetts, 29th September, 1778; retired 1st January, 1781. (Died October, 1807.

Whiting, Elisha (Mass). Lieutenant of Heath's Massachusetts Regiment, May to December, 1775.

Whiting, Francis (Va). 1st Lieutenant of Thruston's Additional Continental Regiment, 28th May, 1777; Lieutenant 1st Continental Dragoons, April, 1779; transferred to Baylor's Regiment of Dragoons, 9th November, 1782, and served to close of war.

Whiting, Frederick Jones (Conn). Cornet 2d Continental Dragoons, ——, 1779; taken prisoner at Horse Neck, 15th December, 1780; Lieutenant, 14th June, 1781; Adjutant in 1782, and served to January, 1783.

Whiting, Gamaliel (Mass). 2d Lieutenant of Fellow's Massachusetts Regiment, May to December, 1775.

Whiting, Henry (Va). Ensign 4th Virginia, 25th March, 1776; 2d Lieutenant, 28th September, 1776; 1st Lieutenant 29th November, 1777; retired 14th September, 1778. (Died 1797.)

Whiting, Israel (Mass). Surgeon's Mate 21st Continental Infantry, 1st July to 31st December, 1776.

Whiting, James (—). 2d Lieutenant; was a prisoner in August, 1778; when and where taken not stated.

Whiting, John (Mass). Private in Lexington Alarm, April, 1775; Private and Corporal in Bridge's Massachusetts Regiment, April to December, 1775; Sergeant and Quartermaster-Sergeant 6th Continental Infantry, 1st January to 31st December, 1776; Quartermaster-Sergeant 12th Massachusetts, 1st January, 1777; Ensign and Regimental Quartermaster, 10th August, 1777; Lieutenant, 5th July, 1779; transferred to 2d Massachusetts 1st January, 1781, and served to 3d November, 1783; Lieutenant-Colonel 4th United States Infantry, 8th July, 1808; Acting Adjutant and Inspector of the Army, 17th July, 1809, to 17th August, 1809; Colonel 5th United States Infantry, 31st December, 1809. Died 3d September, 1810.

Whiting, John (Pa). 1st Lieutenant Chester County, Pa., Militia, 1775-1776; name also spelled Whitting.

Whiting, John (Conn). Lieutenant 2d Continental Artillery; resigned 14th March, 1781.

Whiting, Jonathan (Conn). 2d Lieutenant 5th Connecticut, 1st May to 31st December, 1775; 1st Lieutenant 8th Connecticut, 1st January, 1777; resigned 10th March, 1778.

Whiting, Judson (Conn). Ensign 5th Connecticut, 1st May to 30th September, 1775; Ensign of Bradley's Connecticut State Regiment, 20th June, 1776; taken prisoner at Fort Washington 16th November, 1776, and died 16th January, 1777.

Whiting, Matthew (Va). 2d Lieutenant 3d Virginia, 19th March, 1776; resigned — March, 1777.

Whiting, Moses (Mass). Captain of Heath's Massachusetts Regiment, May to December, 1775; Captain 24th Continental Infantry, 1st January to 31st December, 1776; Captain Massachusetts Militia, 1777-1779.

Whiting, Nathaniel Haynes (Conn). Ensign of Webb's Additional Continental Regiment, 9th April, 1780; transferred to 3d Connecticut, 1st January, 1781; Lieutenant, 10th February, 1781; retired 1st January, 1783. (Died 16th September, 1801.)

Whiting, Samuel (Conn). 2d Lieutenant 2d Continental Artillery 1st January, 1777; taken prisoner on the expedition to Long Island, 10th December, 1777; exchanged December, 1780; resigned 14th March, 1781.

Whiting, Samuel (Conn). Surgeon's Mate 5th Connecticut, May to December, 1775. (Died 1832.)

Whiting, Samuel (Conn). Lieutenant-Colonel 5th Connecticut, 1st May to 18th November, 1775; served subsequently as Colonel Connecticut Militia and State Troops. (Died 1803.)

Whiting, Timothy (Mass). Private in Lexington Alarm, April, 1775; Sergeant-Major of Bridge's Massachusetts Regiment, April to December, 1775; 2d Lieutenant 16th Continental Infantry, 1st January to 31st December, 1776; served subsequently as Assistant to Deputy Quartermaster General, 1777 to June,, 1780. (Died 10th July, 1799.)

Whiting, William Bradford (N. Y.). Colonel New York Militia in 1775-1781. (Died 1796.)

Whitlock, Ephraim Lockhart (N. J.). Ensign 4th New Jersey, 2d November, 1776; 2d Lieutenant, 1st January, 1777; 1st Lieutenant, 23d November, 1777; transferred to 1st New Jersey, 1st July, 1778; retained in New Jersey Battalion April, 1783; Brevet Captain, 30th September, 1783, and served to November, 1783; Major 15th United States Infantry, 1st May, 1812; Lieutenant-Colonel 14th Infantry, 14th November, 1813; honorably discharged 15th June, 1815.

Whitlock, James (N. J.). Major New Jersey Militia; taken prisoner at Light-House, 13th February, 1777; exchanged 22d December, 1780.

Whitlock, John (N. J.). Lieutenant New Jersey Militia, ——; killed at Middletown 13th February, 1777.

Whitlock, Reuben (Va). Sergeant-Major 2d Virginia State Regiment, — March, 1777; Ensign, December, 1777; 2d Lieutenant, 29th April, 1778; resigned 29th October, 1779.

Whitlow, Matthew (Pa). 1st Lieutenant of Roman's Independent Company Pennsylvania Artillery, 14th February, 1776; resigned 15th May, 1776.

Whitman, Samuel (Conn). Lieutenant of Webb's Continental Regiment, 1st January, 1777; resigned 7th March, 1778.

Whitman, William (Pa). 1st Lieutenant 9th Pennsylvania, 15th November, 1776; wounded at Germantown 4th October, 1777; retired 1st July, 1778.

Whitmarsh, Joseph (R. I.). 2d Lieutenant 9th Continental Infantry, 1st January to 31st December, 1776; 1st Lieutenant 1st Rhode Island, 1st January, 1777; resigned 8th March, 1778.

Whitmarsh Micah (R. I.). Ensign of Varnum's Rhode Island Regiment, 29th May, 1775; Ensign, 1st September, 1775; 2d Lieutenant 9th Continental Infantry, 1st January, 1776; 1st Lieutenant of Stanton's Rhode Island State Regiment, 12th December, 1776; 1st Lieutenant 1st Rhode Island, 14th February, 1777; resigned 25th April, 1778. (Died 30th December, 1819.)

Whitmel, Blunt.—See Blunt.

Whitmore, Thomas (Pa). Lieutenant 1st Pennsylvania Battalion of the Flying Camp, July to December, 1776.

Whitney, Abner (Mass). Private in Lexington Alarm, April, 1775; Corporal in Gerrish's Massachusetts Regiment, May to December, 1775; Sergeant 26th Continental Infantry, 1st January to 31st December, 1776; Ensign 9th Massachusetts, 1st January, 1777; resigned 15th December, 1777.

Whitney, Benjamin (Vt). Lieutenant Vermont Militia in 1777 and 1778.

Whitney, Francis (Md). 1st Lieutenant of Grayson's Continental Regiment, 28th May, 1777; retired 22d April, 1779.

Whitney, Henry (R. I.). Paymaster of Sherburne's Continental Regiment,

13th November, 1777; resigned 13th April, 1779.

Whitney, Jonathan (Conn). 1st Lieutenant 8th Connecticut, 1st January, 1777; resigned 10th March, 1778.

Whitney, Josiah (Mass). Lieutenant-Colonel of Whitcomb's Massachusetts Regiment, May to December, 1775; Colonel Massachusetts Militia in 1776 and 1777. (Died 1806.)

Whitney, Joshua (Conn). Private 3d Connecticut, 19th May to 13th November, 1775; Sergeant in Elmore's Continental Regiment, April, 1776, to April, 1777; Sergeant 8th Connecticut, 19th April, 1777; Ensign, 30th December, 1777; 2d Lieutenant, 31st December, 1777; 1st Lieutenant, 21st August, 1780; transferred to 5th Connecticut, 1st January, 1781; transferred to 3d Connecticut, 1st January, 1783; retained in Swift's Connecticut Regiment, June, 1783, and served to November, 1783.

Whitney, Josiah (Conn). Sergeant of Burrall's Continental Regiment, January, 1776; Ensign, 19th September, 1776, ·to January, 1777.

Whitney, Levi (Mass). Private in Lexington Alarm, April, 1775; 1st Lieutenant of Prescott's Massachusetts Regiment, May to December, 1775; Lieutenant Massachusetts Militia, 1777.

Whitside, James (Pa). Captain Lancaster County, Pa., Militia, 1776-1777.

Whittemore, Joseph (Mass). Lieutenant of Little's Massachusetts Regiment, May to December, 1775; wounded at Bunker Hill, 17th June, 1775. (Died 25th June, 1821.)

Whittemore, Pelatiah (N. H.). Ensign 2d Continental Infantry, 1st January, 1776; 2d Lieutenant 2d New Hampshire, 8th November, 1776; 1st Lieutenant, 22d December, 1777, and served to March, 1782.

Whittemore, Samuel (Mass). Captain Company of Minute Men, ——; wounded at Concord, 19th April, 1775.

Whitten, Elias (Mass). 1st Lieutenant of Heath's Massachusetts Regiment, May to December, 1775.

Whittier, Ebenezer, Jr. (Conn). Captain of Selden's Connecticut State Regiment, June to December, 1776.

Whittier, Josiah (Mass). 1st Lieutenant of Danielson's Massachusetts Regiment, May to December, 1775.

Whittier, Richard (Mass). Ensign 8th Massachusetts, 1st January, 1777; resigned 12th August, 1778. (Name also spelled Witter.)

Whittlesey, Charles (Conn). Sergeant 1st Connecticut, 15th May to 10th December, 1775; Ensign 19th Continental Infantry, 1st January, 1776; 2d Lieutenant, July, 1776; discharged 31st December, 1776; Regimental Quartermaster 4th Massachusetts, 1st January, 1777; omitted July, 1778.

Whittlesey, Nathan (Conn). 2d Lieutenant 19th Continental Infantry, 1st January, 1776, to ——.

Whitwell, Samuel (Mass). Surgeon 3d Massachusetts, 1st January, 1777, and served to close of war. (Died 21st November, 1791.)

Whorter, John (Mass). 2d Lieutenant 10th Massachusetts, 6th November, 1776; discharged 24th March, 1778.

Wickes, Zophar (N. Y.). 1st Lieutenant of Graham's Regiment New York Militia in 1777.

Wickham, John (S. C.). Lieutenant 2d South Carolina, 10th May, 1776; killed at Savannah, 9th October, 1779.

Wickley, John (S. C.). Captain South Carolina Artillery; taken prisoner at Charleston 12th May, 1780.

Wickom, John (S. C.). Adjutant 2d South Carolina, ——, 1779; taken prisoner at Charleston 12th May, 1780.

Wigg, William H. (S. C.). Captain South Carolina Militia in 1779. (Died 1798.)

Wiggin, Andrew (N. H.). Lieutenant New Hampshire Militia, 1776-1777.

Wiggin, Mark (N. H.). Major New Hampshire Militia, 1777-1778. (Died 23d February, 1821.)

Wiggin, Simon (N. H.). Lieutenant of Kelley's Regiment New Hampshire Militia in 1777.

Wiggins, Thomas (Pa). Surgeon of a Pennsylvania Battalion of the Flying Camp, July to December, 1776; Surgeon 11th Pennsylvania, 1st July, 1779; resigned 23d January, 1780. (Died 1798.)

Wigglesworth, Samuel (N. H.). Surgeon of Wingate's Regiment, New Hampshire Militia, 1776 and 1777.

Wigglesworth, Edward (Mass). Captain Company of Massachusetts Matrosses 29th June, 1776; Colonel Massachusetts Militia in 1776; Colonel 13th Massachusetts, 1st January, 1777; resigned 10th March, 1779. (Died 8th December, 1826.)

Wigglesworth, John (Mass). Regimental Quartermaster 13th Massachusetts, 1st January, 1777; discharged 1st September, 1777.

Wigglesworth, Samuel (N. H.). Surgeon of Wingate's Regiment New Hampshire Militia, 1776 and 1777.

Wigglesworth, William (Mass). Private in Lexington Alarm, April, 1775; Corporal in Gerrish's Massachusetts Regiment, April to November, 1775; Corporal-Sergeant 26th Continental Infantry, 1st January to 31st December, 1776; Ensign 13th Massachusetts, 1st January, 1777; 2d Lieutenant, 1st January, 1778; transferred to 6th Massachusetts, 1st January, 1781; retired 1st August, 1782.

Wight, Aaron and **Nahum.**—See **White.**

Wigneron, —— (R. I.) Surgeon Rhode Island Militia, 1776-1777.

Wigton, John (Pa). Ensign and Paymaster 3d Pennsylvania, 2d June, 1778, Lieutenant, 18th June, 1779; retired 17th January, 1781. (Name also spelled Wigdon.

Wikoff, Auke (N. J.). Lieutenant-Colonel and Colonel New Jersey Militia; taken prisoner in 1778; when and where not stated.

Wikoff, William (N. J.). Captain of Forman's Continental Regiment, 1st March, 1777; resigned 20th May, 1779.

Wilbur, Aaron (R. I.). Captain 3d Rhode Island, May to December, 1775. (Died 1802.)

Wilbur, Samuel (R. I.). Captain Rhode Island Militia in 1777.

Wilcocks, John (R. I.). Captain Rhode Island Militia, 1777.

Wilcocks, Samuel (Mass). 2d Lieutenant of Paterson's Massachusetts Regiment, May, 1775, to ——.

Wilcox.—See also **Willcox.**

Wilcox, Jarius (Conn). 1st Lieutenant of Baldwin's Artillery Artificer Regiment, 1st January, 1777; Captain, 28th July, 1777, and served to March, 1781. (Died 1807.)

Wilcox, Edward (Md). Quartermaster of Dorsey's Independent Maryland Artillery Company, May, 1777; dishonorably discharged 19th August, 1777.

Wilcox, Gershom (Conn). Sergeant 2d Connecticut, 1st May, 1775; taken prisoner at Quebec 31st December, 1775; Sergeant Major of Sherburne's Continental Regiment, 10th March, 1777; Ensign, 9th November, 1777; resigned 21st March, 1779.

Wilcox, James (Pa). Ensign 11th Pennsylvania, 30th September, 1776, to ——.

Wilcox, Robert (Del). Surgeon Delaware Militia in 1780.

Wild, Richard (Del). 2d Lieutenant Delaware Battalion of the Flying Camp, July to December, 1776.

Wild, Silas (Mass). Captain Lexington Alarm, April, 1775; Captain of Heath's Massachusetts Regiment, April to December, 1775; Captain 18th Continental Infantry to 31st December, 1776 (Died 30th September, 1807.)

Wilder, Abel (Mass). Captain in Lexington Alarm, April, 1775; Captain of Doolittle's Massachusetts Regiment, May to December, 1775.

Wilder, David (Mass). Captain in Lexington Alarm, April, 1775; Captain of Whitcomb's Massachusetts Regiment, May to December, 1775; Major Massachusetts Militia, 1779-1781. (Died 1814.)

Wilds, Ebenezer (Mass). Corporal in Brewer's Massachusetts Regiment, May to December, 1775; Sergeant 6th Continental Infantry, 1st January to 31st December, 1776; Sergeant 1st Massachusetts, 1st January, 1777; Ensign, 24th October, 1779; 2d Lieutenant, 11th May, 1781, and served to 3d November, 1783. (Died 4th December, 1794.)

Wilds, Jesse (S. C.). Lieutenant in Marion's Brigade, 1780-1781.

Wilds, Joseph (Del). Sergeant Delaware Battalion of the Flying Camp, July to December, 1776; Ensign Delaware Regiment, 2d December, 1776; 2d Lieutenant, 5th April, 1777; resigned 15th August, 1778.

Wilds, Richard (Del). 2d Lieutenant Delaware Regiment, 1st December, 1776; 1st Lieutenant, 5th April, 1777; wounded at Germantown 4th October, 1777; resigned 15th August, 1778.

Wiley, Aldrich (Mass). Corporal and Sergeant of Sargent's Massachusetts Regiment, May to December, 1775; Ensign 16th Continental Infantry, 1st January to 31st December, 1776; 1st Lieutenant 8th Massachusetts, 1st January, 1777; killed at Stillwater, 7th October, 1777.

Wiley, Aquilla (Pa). Captain York County, Pa., Militia in 1777.

Wiley, John (Mass). Captain of Gridley's Regiment Massachusetts Artillery, May, 1775; superseded 25th June, 1775; Captain 16th Continental Infantry, 1st January to 31st December, 1776; Captain 8th Massachusetts, 1st January, 1777; Major 14th Massachusetts, 15th December, 1779; retired 1st January, 1781. (Died 1805.)

Wiley, John (N. Y.). Captain 1st New York, 24th February to — November, 1776.

Wiley, John (Pa). 1st Lieutenant Pennsylvania State Regiment, 18th April, 1777; regiment designated 13th Pennsylvania, 12th November, 1777; resigned 25th January, 1778.

Wiley, Robert (Mass). Ensign 8th Massachusetts, 1st January, 1777; wounded at Bemus' Heights, 19th September, 1777; resigned 14th August, 1778.

Wiley, Robert (Pa). Captain of Flower's Artillery Artificer Regiment, 1779, and served to close of war.

Wilkie, William (S. C.)'. Lieutenant South Carolina Militia, ——; wounded at Savannah 19th October, 1779.

Wilkins, Benjamin (S. C.). Lieutenant Charleston Artillery, ——; killed at Beaufort 9th February, 1779.

Wilkins, Daniel (N. H.). 1st Lieutenant 3d New Hampshire, 23d April to December, 1775; Captain of Bedel's Regiment New Hampshire Rangers, 22d January, 1776; taken prisoner at the Cedars 19th May, 1776, and died in captivity 8th July, 1776, of smallpox.

Wilkins, John (Pa). Captain of Spencer's Additional Continental Regiment, 27th February, 1777; resigned 8th April, 1778. (Died 11th December, 1809.)

Wilkins, John, Jr. (Pa). Surgeon's Mate 4th Pennsylvania, 8th April, 1780; transferred to 1st Pennsylvania, 1st January, 1783, and served to 3d November, 1783; Quartermaster-General United States Army, 1st June, 1796; honorably discharged 1st June, 1802. (Died 29th April, 1816.)

Wilkins, Nathaniel (Va). 2d Lieutenant 9th Virginia, 12th February, 1776; 1st Lieutenant, 4th February, 1777; taken prisoner at Germantown, 4th October, 1777; escaped 11th December, 1777, and resigned in March, 1778.

Wilkins, Robert (Pa). 1st Lieutenant 5th Pennsylvania Battalion, 6th January, 1776; Captain 10th October, 1776; taken prisoner at Fort Washington 16th November, 1776; exchanged January, 1777; Captain 6th Pennsylvania, 1st January, 1777, to rank from 10th October, 1776; transferred to 2d Pennsylvania, 1st January, 1781, and served to June, 1783

Wilkins, Robert B. (N. H.). Sergeant 3d New Hampshire, 22d March, 1777; Ensign, 1st May, 1779; transferred to 2d New Hampshire 1st January, 1781; 2d Lieutenant, 19th April, 1781, and resigned — March, 1782. (Died 13th August, 1832.)

Wilkins, Stephen (Mass). 1st Lieutenant of Mansfield's Massachusetts Regiment, May to December, 1775; 1st Lieutenant 19th Continental Infantry, 1st January, 1776, to ——.

Wilkinson, Amos (Pa). 2d Lieutenant 1st Pennsylvania Battalion, 5th January, 1776; 1st Lieutenant, 4th May, 1776; Captain 4th Continental Artillery, 14th March, 1777; resigned 7th June, 1779; served subsequently in Navy. (Died 1833.)

Wilkinson, James (Md). Served as a volunteer in Thompson's Pennsylvania Rifle Battalion, 9th September, 1775, to March, 1776; Captain 2d Continental Infantry, March, 1776, to rank from 9th September, 1775; served on staff of General Greene, November, 1775, to April, 1776; Aide-de-Camp to General Arnold, 2d June to 17th July, 1776; Brigade-Major, 20th July, 1776, and as such on staff of General Gates from 13th December, 1776; Lieutenant-Colonel of Hartley's Continental Regiment, 12th January, 1777; Deputy Adjutant-General Northern Department, 24th May, 1777, to 6th March, 1778; Brevet Brigadier-General Continental Army, 6th November, 1777; resigned 6th March, 1778; Secretary to Board of War, 6th January, 1778; resigned 31st March, 1778; Clothier-General Continental Army, 24th July, 1779; resigned 27th March, 1781; Brigadier-General Pennsylvania Militia, 1782; Lieutenant-Colonel Commandant 2d United States Infantry, 22d October, 1791; Brigadier-General, 5th March, 1792; Major-General, 2d March, 1813; honorably discharged 15th June, 1815. (Died 28th December, 1825.)

Wilkinson, Nathan (N. J.). Sergeant 3d New Jersey in 1775; Sergeant-Major 3d New Jersey, 11th February, 1777; Ensign 1st May, 1777; 2d Lieutenant,

11th November, 1777; Regimental Quartermaster, — September, 1778; 1st Lieutenant, 4th March, 1780; resigned 8th November, 1782.

Wilkinson, Reuben (N. C.). Lieutenant 4th North Carolina, 20th December, 1776; retired 1st June, 1778.

Wilkinson, Reuben (N. C.). Ensign 3d North Carolina, 1st May, 1779; Lieutenant, ——, 1780; resigned 21st July, 1782.

Wilkinson, Young (Md). Sergeant of Dorseys Company Maryland Artillery, 24th November, 1777; 2d Lieutenant, 25th February, 1778; Company transferred to 1st Continental Artillery, 30th May, 1778; 1st Lieutenant, 1st April, 1779, and served to June, 1783. (Died 15th Septetmber, 1827.)

Will, George (Pa). 1st Lieutenant and Adjutant 6th Pennsylvania, 15th February, 1777; resigned 17th October, 1777.

Willard, Aaron (Mass). Colonel Massachusetts Militia in 1776.

Willard, Elias (N. Y.). Hospital Surgeon's Mate and Hospital Surgeon in New York, 1775 to 1779.

Willard, Jonathan (N. H.). Ensign 1st New Hampshire, 8th November, 1776; wounded at Stillwater 19th September, 1777; 2d Lieutenant, 10th January, 1778; 1st Lieutenant, 23d August, 1779; resigned 13th April, 1782.

Willard, Levi (Mass). Surgeon of Read's Massachusetts Regiment, 28th June to December, 1775.

Willard, Reuben (Mass). Private in Lexington Alarm, April, 1775; Private and Sergeant of Doolittle's Massachusetts Regiment, 28th April, 1775; Ensign, 27th November, 1775, to 1st January, 1776; served subsequently as Lieutenant and Captain Massachusetts Militia.

Willcox, Joseph (Conn). Corporal 6th Connecticut, 9th May to 19th December, 1775; Ensign 2d Connecticut, 1st January, 1777; 2d Lieutenant, 1st September, 1777; 1st Lieutenant, 12th January, 1780; transferred to 2d Connecticut 1st January, 1781; retired 1st January, 1783.

Willcox, Samuel (Mass). 2d Lieutenant of Cady's Battalion on the expedition to Canada, January to June, 1776.

Willcox, William (N. Y.). Captain of Lasher's New York Militia Regiment, July, 1776; Major Aide-de-Camp to

General Alexander, 13th April, 1777; resigned 20th October, 1777. (Died 20th December, 1826.)

Willes, Hezekiah (Conn). Ensign of Walcott's Connecticut Regiment, December, 1775, to February, 1776.

Willes, Solomon (Conn). Captain in the Lexington Alarm, April, 1775; Captain 2d Connecticut, 1st May to 17th December, 1775.

Willett, Augustin (Pa). Captain 1st Pennsylvania Battalion, 27th October, 1775; Captain 2d Pennsylvania, 25th October, 1776; resigned 1st January, 1777; served subsequently as Major and Lieutenant-Colonel Pennsylvania Militia, May, 1780, to close of war.

Willett, Marinus (N. Y.). Captain 1st New York, 28th June, 1775, to 9th May, 1776; Lieutenant-Colonel 3d New York, 21st November, 1776. By the act of 4th October, 1777, it was "Resolved, that Congress have a just sense of the distinguished merit of Lieutenant-Colonel Willett, for a repeated instance of his bravery and conduct in the late successful sally on the enemy investing Fort Schuyler, and that the Commissary-General of Military Stores be directed to procure an elegant sword and present the same to Lieutenant-Colonel Willett in the name of these United States." Lieutenant-Colonel Commandant 5th New York, 1st July, 1780; Colonel, November, 1780, to rank from 22d December, 1779; retired 1st January, 1781; subsequently served as Colonel New York Levies and Militia. (Died 22d August, 1830.)

Willey, John (Conn). Captain in Lexington Alarm, April, 1775; Captain Lieutenant 2d Connecticut, 1st May to 17th December, 1775; Captain of Wadsworth's Connecticut State Regiment, June to December, 1776.

Williams, —— (Ga). Lieutenant Georgia Militia; wounded and taken prisoner at Amelia Island 18th May, 1777.

Williams, Abraham (Mass). Ensign of Brewer's Massachusetts Regiment, May to December, 1775; 2d Lieutenant 6th Continental Infantry, 1st January to 31st December, 1776; 1st Lieutenant 12th Massachusetts, 1st January, 1777; Captain Lieutenant, 29th September, 1778; Captain, 6th March, 1779; transferred to 2d Massachusetts, 1st January, 1781, and served to 3d November, 1783. (Died 1790.)

Williams, Bedford (N. Y.). Surgeon's Mate 2d New York, 28th June, 1775, to

January, 1776; Surgeon Hospital Department, 1779-1781.

Williams, Benjamin (N. C.). 1st Lieutenant 2d North Carolina, 1st September, 1775; Captain, 19th July, 1776, and served to ——; was in service January, 1780.

Williams, Charles (Conn). 2d Lieutenant of Selden's Connecticut State Regiment, 20th June, 1776; taken prisoner on the retreat from New York, 15th September, 1776, and died in captivity.

Williams, Cornelius (N. J.). Captain New Jersey Militia in 1776.

Williams, Daniel (N. Y.). Lieutenant and Captain of Graham's and Pawling's Regiments New York Militia, 1777-1781.

Williams, Daniel (N. Y.). Captain New York Militia, ——; taken prisoner at Young's House, New York, 25th December, 1778; released 8th March, 1780.

Williams, Daniel (N. C.). 1st Lieutenant 6th North Carolina, 16th April, 1776; Captain, 1st April, 1777; retired 1st June, 1778; Captain North Carolina Militia, 1780-1781. (Died 1823.)

Williams, Daniel (S. C.). Captain South Carolina Militia; killed at Hayes' Station, S. C., 9th November, 1781.

Williams, David (N. Y.). By the act of 3d November, 1780, it was "Resolved, whereas Congress have received information that John Paulding, David Williams and Isaac Van Wart, three young volunteer militiamen of the State of New York, did, on the 23d of September last, intercept Major John Andre, Adjutant-General of the British Army, in the character of a spy, and notwithstanding the large bribes offered them for his release, nobly disdaining to sacrifice their country for the sake of gold, secured and conveyed him to the commanding officer of the District, whereby the dangerous and traitorous conspiracy of Benedict Arnold was brought to light, the insidious design of the enemy baffled, and the United States secured from impending danger. Resolved, that Congress have a high sense of the virtuous and patriotic conduct of the aforesaid John Paulding, David Williams, and Isaac Van Wart. In consideration whereof, ordered that each of them receive annually out of the public treasury ($200) two hundred dollars in specie, or an equivalent in the current money of these States during life, and that the Board of War procure for each of them a silver medal, on one side of which shall be a shield with this inscription, 'Fidelity,' and on the other the following motto: Vincit amor patriæ'; and forward them to the Commander-in-Chief, who is requested to present the same with a copy of this resolution, and the thanks of Congress for their fidelity and the eminent services they have rendered their country." (Died 2d August, 1831.)

Williams, David (Va). 2d Lieutenant 12th Virginia, 20th February, 1777; 1st Lieutenant, 7th March, 1778; regiment designated 8th Virginia, 14th Setember, 1778; transferred to 3d Virginia 12th February 1781; retired 1st January, 1783 (Died 8th November, 1831.)

Williams, David (Va). Ensign 11th Virginia, 1st March, 1777; 2d Lieutenant, 1st July, 1777; regiment designated 7th Virginia 14th September, 1778; 1st Lieutenant, 2d July, 1779; transferred to 3d Virginia 12th February, 1781, and served to close of war.

Williams, Ebenezer (Conn). Colonel Connecticut Militia, 1775-1776.

Williams, Ebenezer (Mass). Corporal in Lexington Alarm, April, 1775; Corporal in Paterson's Massachusetts Regiment, April to December, 1775; Sergeant 15th Continental Infantry, 1st January, 1776; Ensign, 12th September, 1776; 2d Lieutenant 1st Massachusetts, 1st January, 1777; 1st Lieutenant, 25th October, 1777; Brevet Captain, 30th September, 1783; served to 3d November, 1783.

Williams, Edward (Va). Sergeant 12th Virginia, 8th January, 1777; regiment designated 8th Virginia 14th Setember, 1778; Ensign, 4th July, 1779; resigned 30th December, 1779.

Williams, Edward Payson (Mass). Captain of Heath's Massachusetts Regiment, May to December, 1775; Captain 24th Continental Infantry, 1st January to 31st December, 1776; Major 3d Massachusetts, 1st January, 1777; died 25th May 1777.

Williams, Elisha Otho (Md.) 1st Lieutenant 1st Maryland Battalion of the Flying Camp, July to December, 1776; Captain 7th Maryland, 10th December, 1776; resigned 28th November, 1777.

Williams, Ennion (Pa). Major 1st Battalion of Miles' Pennsylvania Rifle

Regiment, 13th March, 1776; resigned 4th February, 1777.

Williams, George (Mass). Colonel Massachusetts Militia in 1777.

Williams, Hart (Mass.) Captain in Lexington Alarm, April, 1775; Captain of Phinney's Massachusetts Regiment, April to December, 1775; Captain 18th Continental Infantry, 1st January to 31st December, 1776; Captain Massachusetts Militia in 1778.

Williams, Henry (Conn). 2d Lieutenant of Sherburne's Continental Regiment, 22d February, 1777; 1st Lieutenant, 9th November, 1777; Regimental Adjutant, February, 1780; resigned 2d May, 1780; subsequently served as Lieutenant Connecticut Militia and was killed at Groton Heights 6th Septetmber, 1781.

Williams, Henry (Va). 1st Lieutenant 6th Virginia, 21st March, 1776; dismissed 16th July, 1776.

Williams, Henry Abraham (N. Y.). 1st Lieutenant 2d Continental Artillery, 12th September, 1780; 1st Lieutenant, 23d March, 1781, and served to June, 1783.

Williams, Isaac (Pa). 2d Lieutenant 10th Pennsylvania, 4th December, 1776, to ——.

Williams, Jacob (R. I.). Ensign of Babcock's Rhode Island Regiment, 15th January, 1776; Lieutenant of Lippitt's Rhode Island Regiment, 19th August 1776, to ——.

Williams, James (N. C.). 1st Lieutenant 4th North Carolina, 2d June, 1776; Captain 3d April, 1777; died 2d May, 1778.

Williams, James (R. I.). Captain 2d Rhode Island, 28th June to December, 1775; Major and Lieutenant Colonel Rhode Island Militia, 1776-1779.

Williams, James (S. C.). Captain South Carolina Militia in 1775; Colonel South Carolina Militia; killed at King's Mountain 7th October, 1780.

Williams, James (Va). 2d Lieutenant 10th Virginia, 17th December, 1776; 1st Lieutenant, 18th March, 1777; Captain-Lieutenant, 2d January, 1778; regiment designated 6th Virginia, 14th September, 1778; Captain, 19th September, 1778, and served to close of war. (Died about 1823.)

Williams, Jared (Va). Lieutenant Virginia Militia in 1781.

Williams, Jarrett (Va). 1st Lieutenant of Clark's Illinois Regiment, 1778-1781. (Died 1810.)

Williams, John (Conn). Lieutenant and Captain Connecticut Militia, 1776-1780; wounded at White Plains 28th October, 1776. (Died 1811.)

Williams, John (Mass). Sergeant in Lexington Alarm, April, 1775; 2d Lieutenant of Prescott's Massachusetts Regiment, May to December, 1775; 1st Lieutenant 7th Continental Infantry 1st January to 31st December, 1776; 1st Lieutenant 12th Massachusetts, 1st January, 1777; Captain 7th July, 1777; transferred to 1st Massachusetts, 1st January, 1781; Brevet Major, 30th September, 1783, and served to 3d November, 1783. (Died 1st July, 1822.)

Williams, John (N. Y.). Captain and Colonel New York Militia, 1775-1781.

Williams, John (N. C.). 1st Lieutenant 2d North Carolina, 1st September, 1775; retired 1st June, 1778.

Williams, John (Va). Captain of Clark's Illinois Regiment, August, 1777, to February, 1781.

Williams, John P. (N. C.). Captain 5th North Carolina, 16th April, 1776; Colonel 9th North Carolina, 26th November, 1776; retired 1st June, 1778.

Williams, Joseph (Mass). Sergeant of Brewer's Massachusetts Regiment, June to December, 1775; Ensign 6th Continental Infantry, 1st January to 31st December, 1776; 2d Lieutenant 13th Massachusetts, 1st January, 1777; resigned 5th January, 1778; served subsequently as Quartermaster of Massachusetts State Troops.

Williams, Joseph (Mass). 1st Lieutenant 24th Continental Infantry, 1st January to 31st December, 1776; Captain 3d Massachusetts, 1st January, 1777; Brevet Major, 30th September, 1783, retained in Jackson's Continental Regiment, November, 1783, and served to 20th June, 1784. (Died 21st April, 1819.)

Williams, Joseph (N. C.). Lieutenant-Colonel North Carolina Militia, 1777-1780. (Died 1827.)

Williams, Joshua (Pa). Adjutant Battalion Pennsylvania Associators, 25th May, 1775; Captain 1st Pennsylvania Battalion of the Flying Camp, June to December, 1776; Captain Independent Pennsylvania Company, March, 1777; company attached to 4th Pennsylvania, 21st October, 1777; retired 1st July, 1778. (Died 12th December, 1825.)

Williams, Lemuel (Mass). 2d Lieutenant 8th Massachusetts, 1st January, 1777; resigned 31st May, 1778.

Williams, Lilburn (Md). Ensign of Woolford's Independent Maryland Company, 2d March, 1776; 1st Lieutenant 2d Maryland, 10th December, 1776; Captain, 16th April, 1777; transferred to 3d Maryland, 1st January, 1781; wounded at Camden 10th May, 1781; retired 1st January, 1783.

Williams, Macey (Mass). Captain in Lexington Alarm, April, 1775; Captain of Walker's Massachusetts Regiment, May to December, 1775.

Williams, Nathan (Md). Ensign Maryland Battalion of the Flying Camp, July to December, 1776; 2d Lieutenant 6th Maryland, 10th December, 1776; 1st Lieutenant, 10th October, 1777; wounded at Monmouth, 28th June, 1778; Captain Lieutenant, 1st June, 1779; killed at Camden, 16th August, 1780.

Williams, Nathaniel B. (N. C.). 2d Lieutenant 8th North Carolina, 28th November, 1776; retired 1st June, 1778; 1st Lieutenant 10th North Carolina, 23d January, 1781; transferred to 4th North Carolina 6th February, 1782, and served to close of war.

Williams, Obadiah (N. H.). Surgeon 1st New Hampshire, 23d May to December, 1775; Surgeon Hospital Department, 1776-1780. (Died 1799.)

Williams, Othneil (Conn). Ensign of Walcott's Connecticut Regiment, December, 1775, to February, 1776.

Williams, Osborne (Md). Ensign 3d Maryland, 1st March, 1777; 2d Lieutenant, 4th October, 1777; 1st Lieutenant, 12th April, 1779; resigned 5th January, 1780. (Died 19th December, 1819.)

Williams, Otho Holland (Md). 1st Lieutenant of Cresap's Company Maryland Riflemen, 21st June, 1775; Major of Stephenson's Maryland and Virginia Rifle Regiment, 27th June, 1776; wounded and taken prisoner at Fort Washington, 16th November, 1776; exchanged 16th January, 1778; Colonel 6th Maryland, 10th December, 1776; transferred to 1st Maryland 1st January, 1781; Brigadier-General Continental Army, 9th May, 1782; retired 16th January, 1783. (Died 16th July, 1794.)

Williams, Peleg (N. H.). 1st Lieutenant 1st New Hampshire, 8th November, 1776; resigned 10th May, 1778.

Williams, Phineas (Vt). Captain Vermont Militia in 1777.

Williams, Ralph (N. C.). Lieutenant 9th North Carolina, 28th November, 1776; omitted 1st January, 1778.

Williams, Richard (Pa). Captain Westmoreland County, Pa., Militia in 1778.

Williams, Robert (Mass). 1st Lieutenant 14th Continental Infantry, 1st January to 31st December, 1776. (Died 10th September, 1818.)

Williams, Robert (Mass). Regimental Paymaster 14th Continental Infantry, 14th September to 31st December, 1776; Ensign of Lee's Additional Continental Regiment, 24th April, 1777; Regimental Paymaster, 3d June, 1777; transferred to Jackson's Regiment, 22d April, 1779; transferred to 9th Massachusetts, 1st January, 1781; 1st Lieutenant, 12th April, 1782; transferred to 4th Massachusetts, 1st January 1783; retained in Jackson's Continental Regiment, November, 1783, and served to 20th June, 1784. (Died 16th November, 1834.)

Williams, Robert (N. C.). Surgeon 3d North Carolina, June, 1778, to 1781. (Died 12th October, 1840.)

Williams, Robert B. (Mass). Sergeant of Baldwin's Artillery Artificer Regiment, 12th April, 1778; Lieutenant, 12th November, 1779; resigned 25th March, 1781.

Williams, Samuel (Mass). Colonel Massachusetts Militia in 1777.

Williams, Samuel (N. C.). Captain North Carolina Militia at King's Mountain in October, 1780.

Williams, Samuel (Pa). 2d Lieutenant Pennsylvania State Regiment, 18th April, 1777; regiment designated 13th Pennsylvania, 12th November, 1777; retired 1st July, 1778.

Williams, Samuel William (Conn). 2d Lieutenant 6th Connecticut, 1st May to 18th December, 1775; 1st Lieutenant of Webb's Additional Continental Regiment, 1st January, 1777; Captain, 23d March, 1778; transferred to 3d Connecticut, 1st January, 1781; retired 1st January, 1783. (Died 14th September, 1812.)

Williams, Theophilus (N. C.). Ensign 6th North Carolina, 2d April, 1777; omitted 1st January, 1778.

Williams, Thomas (Mass). Captain of Paterson's Massachusetts Regiment, May to December, 1775.

Williams, Thomas (Mass). 2d Lieutenant of Walker's Massachusetts Regiment, May to December, 1775; 1st Lieutenant 13th Continental Infantry, 1st January, 1776; cashiered 2d June, 1776. (Died 13th May, 1828.)

Williams, Thomas, Jr. (N. Y.). Regimental Quartermaster of Wynkoop's New York Regiment, July, 1776; Regimental Quartermaster 3d New York, 21st November, 1776; omitted May, 1778. (Died 13th May, 1828.)

Williams, William (Conn). A signer of the Declaration of Independence; Colonel Connecticut Militia in 1775; died 2d August, 1911.

Williams, William (N. H.). Colonel New Hampshire Militia in 1777.

Williams, William (N. C.). Ensign 2d North Carolina, 11th December, 1776, to ——.

Williams, William (N. C.). 1st Lieutenant and Adjutant 4th North Carolina, 1st September, 1775; wounded at Germantown 4th October, 1777; Captain Invalid Regiment, 1st April, 1778, anad served to 23d April, 1783.

Williams, William (Pa). Captain 1st Pennsylvania Battalion, 27th October, 1775; transferred to 2d Pennsylvania, 25th October, 1776; Major 12th March, 1777, to rank from 29th September, 1776; taken prisoner at Germantown, 4th October, 1777; escaped 20th April, 1778; Lieutenant-Colonel 3d Pennsylvania, 28th June, 1778; resigned 17th April, 1780. (Died 31st May, 1799.)

Williams, William (Vt). Colonel Vermont Militia in 1777 and 1778.

Williams, William (Va). 1st Lieutenant 13th Virginia, 8th January, 1777; dismissed, 6th February, 1778.

Williams, William B. (N. C.). Major 1st North Carolina, 13th June, 1776, to ——.

William, Zadock (R. I.). 2d Lieutenant of Tallman's Rhode Island State Regiment, 12th December, 1776, to ——.

Williamson, Andrew (Ga). Brigadier-General Georgia Militia, ——; turned traitor to American cause in July, 1780.

Williamson, James (Md). 1st Lieutenant 4th Maryland Battalion of the Flying Camp, July, 1776, to ——.

Williamson, James (Pa). 2d Lieutenant 7th Pennsylvania, 19th March, 1777; resigned 16th April, 1779.

Williamson, James (Pa). 2d Lieutenant 12th Pennsylvania, 4th October, 1776; 1st Lieutenant, 20th May, 1777; resigned 15th March, 1778.

Williamson, John (Pa). 1st Lieutenant 4th Pennsylvania Battalion, 6th January to July, 1776. (Died 1794.)

Williamson, John (S. C.). Captain 1st South Carolina, 12th May, 1779; taken prisoner at Charleston, 12th May, 1780.

Williamson, Micajah (Ga). Lieutenant Georgia Militia, 1779-1781.

Williamson, Matthias (N. J.). Colonel and Brigadier-General New Jersey Militia, October, 1775, to February, 1777; served subsequently as Quartermaster-General of New Jersey; was taken prisoner at Connecticut Farms in June, 1780.

Williamson, Ralph (Pa). Ensign 11th Pennsylvania, 30th September, 1776, to ——.

Williamson, Thomas (S. C.). Captain South Carolina Militia in 1776.

Williamson, Samuel (Conn). Chaplain 4th Continental Dragoons, 1st May, 1778; omitted May, 1779.

Willing, James (——). Captain ——; was a prisoner in August, 1778; when and where taken not stated.

Willington, Elisha (Mass). Sergeant 3d Massachusetts, 1st March, 1777; Quartermaster-Sergeant, 8th November, 1778; Ensign, 11th November, 1779; 2d Lieutenant, 26th July, 1782; transferred to 7th Massachusetts, 1st January, 1783, and served to June, 1783.

Willington, Josiah (Mass). Corporal in Lexington Alarm, April, 1775; Sergeant of Brewer's Massachusetts Regiment, April to December, 1775; Ensign 6th Continental Infantry, 1st January to 31st December, 1776; 1st Lieutenant, 13th Massachusetts, 1st January, 1777; retired 17th April, 1779.

Willington, Thomas (Mass). 1st Lieutenant of Brewer's Massachusetts Regiment, 19th May to December, 1775; 1st Lieutenant 6th Continental Infantry, 1st January, 1776; Captain, 5th October to 31st December, 1776; Captain 13th Massachusetts, 1st January, 1777; retired 10th April, 1779.

Willis, Francis (Va). Captain of Grayson's Continental Regiment, 14th January, 1777; resigned 10th May, 1778. (Died 25th January, 1829.)

Willis, Henry (Pa). Cornet 4th Continental Dragoons, June, 1777; 2d Lieutenant, 22d December, 1778; 1st Lieutenant, 25th June, 1781; Captain, ——; served to close of war.

Willis, Henry (Va). 2d Lieutenant 1st Continental Artillery, 1st March. 1778; resigned 18th November, 1778.

Willis, James (Va). Captain of Grayson's Continental Regiment, 14th January, 1777; resigned 11th May, 1778.

Willis, John (Va). 1st Lieutenant 2d Virginia, 29th September, 1775; Captain, 15th June, 1776; taken prisoner at Brandywine, 11th September, 1777; exchanged, 8th November, 1780; was promoted to Major, 5th Virginia, 12th May, 1779, but did not join regiment.

Willis, Lewis (Va). Lieutenant-Colonel 10th Virginia, 13th November, 1776; resigned 1st March, 1778.

Willis, Thomas (Va). Captain 15th Virginia, 21st July, 1777; regiment designated 11th Virginia, 14th September, 1778, and served to ——; was in service March, 1780.

Williston, Consider (Conn). Ensign in the Lexington Alarm, April, 1775; 2d Lieutenant 2d Connecticut, 1st May to 17th December, 1775.

Willoughby, John (N. H.). Captain New Hampshire Militia in 1777.

Wills, Agrippa (Mass). Captain of Whitcomb's Massachusetts Regiment, May to December, 1775.

Wills, Solomon (Conn). Lieutenant-Colonel of Chester's Connecticut State Regiment, 20th June to 25th December. 1776.

Willson, or Wilson.—See both as name is spelled both ways.

Willson, James (Pa). Lieutenant Pennsylvania Rifle Battalion in 1777.

Willson, Nathaniel (Mass). Private in Lexington Alarm, April, 1775; and in Massachusetts Militia, 1775 and 1776; 2d Lieutenant 3d Massachusetts, 1st February, 1777; 1st Lieutenant, 1st April, 1778; resigned 16th November, 1778.

Wilmot, Edward, Jr. (N. J.). Captain New Jersey Militia in 1778.

Wilmot, Robert (Md). 3d Lieutenant Baltimore Artillery Company, 5th November, 1776; 1st Lieutenant of Dorsey's Company Maryland Artillery, 24th November, 1777; 1st Continental Artillery, 30th May, 1778; retired 1st October, 1780. (Died 1809.)

Wilmot, Samuel (Conn). 1st Lieutenant 1st Connecticut, 1st May, 1775; Captain, ——, 1775; discharged 20th December, 1775.

Wilmot, William (Md). 1st Lieutenant 3d Maryland, 10th December, 1776; Captain, 15th October, 1777; transferred to 2d Maryland, 1st January, 1781; killed on John's Island, South Carolina, 4th November, 1782, by a British foraging party. The blood of Captain Wilmot was the last spilled in the war of the Revolution.

Wilson.—See also **Willson.**

Wilson —— (——). Lieutenant ——; killed at Fort Plain, 7th September, 1781. (See John Williams.)

Wilson, Abner (Conn). 2d Lieutenant of Gay's Connecticut State regiment, July to December, 1776.

Wilson, Abraham (Mass). Surgeon of Gardner's Massachusetts Regiment, May to December, 1775.

Wilson, Alexander (N. Y.). 1st Lieutenant 2d Canadian (Hazen's) Regiment, 3d November, 1776; died 26th April, 1780.

Wilson, Amos (Conn). 1st Lieutenant of Gay's Connecticut State Regiment, July to December, 1776.

Wilson, Andrew (Pa). 1st Lieutenant Chester County, Pa., Militia in 1776.

Wilson, Dorrington (Pa). 2d Lieutenant 1st Battalion, Pennsylvania Flying Camp, July to December, 1776; Lieutenant Pennsylvania Militia in 1777.

Wilson, George (Pa). Lieutenant-Colonel 8th Pennsylvania, 20th July, 1776; died — February, 1777.

Wilson, George (Va). Lieutenant-Colonel of a Virginia State Regiment, 1780 and 1781.

Wilson, Goodwin (Pa). Surgeon's-Mate in Hospital Department, 1776 to 1780; Hospital Physician and Surgeon, 20th September, 1781, and served to close of war.

Wilson, James (N. C.). Captain 10th North Carolina, 19th April, 1777; resigned 25th May, 1778.

Wilson, James (N. Y.). Captain in Graham's Regiment New York Militia, 1778-1779.

Wilson, James (Pa). A signer of the Declaration of Independence; Brigadier-General Pennsylvania Militia, 24th May, 1782, to close of war; died 28th August, 1798.

Wilson, James (Pa). 2d Lieutenant of Thompson's Pennsylvania Rifle Battalion, 25th June, 1775; 1st Lieutenant 1st Continental Infantry, 1st January, 1776; Captain 1st Pennsylvania, 16th January, 1777; retired 1st January, 1781.

Wilson, James (S. C.). 1st Lieutenant 4th South Carolina (Artillery), November, 1776; Captain-Lieutenant, 31st May, 1778; Captain, ——, 1779; taken prisoner at Charleston, 12th May, 1780; exchanged, ——; served to close of war.

Wilson, James Armstrong (Pa). Captain 6th Pennsylvania Battalion, 9th January, 1776; taken prisoner, 24th July, 1776, on the Sorrell River, Canada; exchanged ——, 1777; Major of Battalion to guard stores at Carlisle, Pennsylvania, 6th October, 1777; discharged 2d June, 1778. (Died 17th March, 1783.)

Wilson, John (Del). Ensign Delaware Regiment, 18th January, 1776 1st Lieutenant, 1st December, 1776; Captain, 1st March, 1777; retired 1st January, 1783.

Wilson, John (Ga). Was a Lieutenant in 2d Georgia, in August, 1778, and was a Captain in 1780.

Wilson, John (N. Y.). Captain in Graham's Regiment New York Militia, 1778-1779.

Wilson, John (Va). Ensign 4th Virginia, 28th December, 1776; 2d Lieutenant, 12th March, 1777; 1st Lieutenant, 1st April, 1778; killed at Eutaw Springs, 8th September, 1781.

Wilson, Jonathan (Mass). Captain of a Company of Minute Men, ——; killed at Concord, 19th April, 1775.

Wilson, Joseph (Pa). Major York County, Pa., Militia in 1777.

Wilson, Lewis (N. J.). Surgeon's-Mate Hospital Department, 7th January, 1777; Surgeon, 30th June, 1779, and served to October, 1780.

Wilson, Nathaniel (Md). 2d Lieutenant Maryland Battalion of the Flying Camp, July to December, 1776. (Died 1796.)

Wilson, Nathaniel (N. H.). Captain New Hampshire Militia, 1776-1778.

Wilson, Richard (Pa). Captain of Hartley's Continental Regiment, 15th February, 1777, to ——.

Wilson, Robert (N. H.). Major New Hampshire Militia, 1777-1778. (Died 1790.)

Wilson, Robert (N. Y.). Ensign 1st New York, 9th June, 1781, and served to close of war. (Died 1811.)

Wilson, Robert (N. C.). Surgeon 6th North Carolina, 8th June, 1776, to ——.

Wilson, Robert (Pa). 2d Lieutenant 6th Pennsylvania Battalion, 9th January, 1776; Captain 7th Pennsylvania, 20th March, 1777; wounded at Paoli, 20th September, 1777, and resigned 1st March, 1778; Assistant to Deputy Quartermaster General at Pittsburg, 1779-1783.

Wilson, Simeon W. (Del). Captain Delaware Militia in 1780.

Wilson, Simon (Pa). Ensign of Patton's Continental Regiment, 16th January, 1777; 2d Lieutenant, 11th September, 1777, and served to March, 1778.

Wilson, Thomas (Va). Lieutenant of a Virginia State Regiment, 1779 to 1781.

Wilson, Whitfield (N. C.). Regimental Quartermaster, 3d North Carolina, 24th April, 1777; resigned 1st October, 1777.

Wilson, William (Pa). 3d Lieutenant of Thompson's Pennsylvania Rifle Battalion, 25th June, 1775; 2d Lieutenant 1st Continental Infantry, 4th January, 1776; 1st Lieutenant, 25th September, 1776; Captain 1st Pennsylvania, 2d March, 1777; brevet Major, 30th September, 1783; served to 3d November, 1783. (Died, ——, 1813.)

Wilson, William (Pa). Lieutenant Philadelphia County, Pa., Militia, 1776-1777.

Wilson, William (S. C.). Captain South Carolina Rangers, July, 1775, to ——.

Wilson, Willis (Va). Ensign 1st Virginia, 30th September, 1776; 2d Lieutenant, 26th January, 1777; 1st Lieutenant, 29th November, 1779; taken prisoner at Charleston, 12th May, 1780.

Wiltbank, Abraham (—). Lieutenant of a Company of Delaware Indians 1780-1781.

Wiltbank, George (Del). Lieutenant Delaware Battalion of the Flying Camp, July to December, 1776.

Winborne, John (N. C.). Lieutenant 7th North Carolina, 28th November, 1776. Died — November, 1777.

Winchel, Nathaniel (Conn). Ensign of Chester's Connecticut State Regiment, 20th June to 25th December,

1776; served subsequently as Captain in the Connecticut Light Horse Militia.

Winchester, George (Md). Ensign 4th Maryland, 1st June, 1779; 2d Lieutenant, 15th September, 1779; retired 1st January, 1783.

Winchester, George (Md). 2d Lieutenant of Gist's Continental Regiment, 8th April, 1777; 1st Lieutenant, 1st May, 1779; taken prisoner at Charleston, 12th May, 1780.

Winchester, James (Md). Sergeant Maryland Battalion of the Flying Camp, July to December, 1776; 2d Lieutenant, 2d Maryland, 20th February, 1777; taken prisoner at Staten Island, 22d August, 1777; exchanged, ——; 1st Lieutenant, 27th May, 1778; taken prisoner at Charleston, 12th May, 1780; released 22d December, 1780; transferred to 3d Maryland, 1st January, 1781; Captain 9th February, 1782; retained in Maryland Battalion, April, 1783; served to 15th November, 1783; Brigadier-General United States Army, 27th March, 1812; resigned 31st March, 1815. (Died 27th July, 1826.)

Winchester, William (Mass). Sergeant in Lexington Alarm, April, 1775; 2d Lieutenant of Ward's Massachusetts Regiment, April to December, 1775; 2d Lieutenant, 6th Continental Infantry, 1st January, 1776; 1st Lieutenant, 5th October, 1776; 1st Lieutenant 13th Massachusetts, 1st January, 1777; retired 23d April, 1779.

Winder, Levin (Md). 1st Lieutenant of Smallwood's Maryland Regiment, 14th January. 1776; Captain 1st Maryland, 10th December, 1776; Major, 17th April, 1777; wounded and taken prisoner at Camden, 16th August, 1780; exchanged June, 1781; transferred to 4th Maryland, 1st January, 1781; Lieutenant-Colonel, 5th Maryland, 27th April, 1781; transferred to 1st Maryland, 1st January, 1783, and served to 12th April, 1783; Brigadier-General, Maryland Militia, 1812. (Died 7th July, 1819.)

Winds, William (N. J.). Lieutenant-Colonel 1st New Jersey, 7th November, 1775; Colonel, 7th March to November, 1776; subsequently served as Brigadier-General New Jersey Militia. (Died 12th October, 1789.)

Wing, Jonathan (Mass). Sergeant 5th Massachusetts, 1st January, 1777; Ensign, 19th October, 1781; transferred to 1st Massachusetts, 12th June, 1783, and served to 3d November, 1783.

Wing, Samuel (Conn). Ensign of Gay's Connecticut State Regiment, July to December, 1776.

Wingfield, John (Pa). Lieutenant Westmoreland County, Pa., Militia in 1778.

Wingate, John (Mass). Surgeon 13th Massachusetts, 1st January, 1777; transferred to 12th Massachusetts, 1st May, 1778; resigned 1st October, 1780. (Died 25th July, 1819.)

Wingate, Joshua (N. H.). Colonel New Hampshire Militia Regiment, 1775 to 1777.

Winkel, Francis (Pa). Ensign York County, Pennsylvania, Militia, in 1777.

Winlock, Joseph (Va). Corporal 9th Virginia, 25th January, 1777; Ensign 9th Virginia, 6th August, 1779; transferred to 7th Virginia, 12th February, 1781; 2d Lieutenant, 26th May, 1781, and served to close of war; Brigadier-General Virginia Militia, 1812 (Died 1831.)

Winn, Richard (S. C.). 1st Lieutenant 3d South Carolina (Rangers), 17th June, 1775; subsequently served as Colonel South Carolina Militia and was wounded at Hanging Rock, 6th August, 1780. (Died 1812.)

Winn, Samuel (Mass). Ensign of Sherburne's Continental Regiment, 12th January, 1777; 2d Lieutenant, 1st October, 1777; discharged 12th May, 1779.

Winn, William (Va). 1st Lieutenant 14th Virginia, 11th November, 1776; resigned 11th December, 1777.

Winship, Amos (Mass). Surgeon's-Mate Hospital Department, 1776-1777.

Winship, Ebenezer (Mass). Captain of Nixon's Massachusetts Regiment, 19th May, to December, 1775; Captain 4th Continental Infantry, 1st January to 31st December, 1776; Captain, 5th Massachusetts, 1st January, 1777; Deputy Commissary of Issues, 11th August, 1777 to June, 1783. (Died 1799.)

Winship, John (Mass). Sergeant of Gerrish's Massachusetts Regiment, May to December, 1775; Sergeant 26th Continental Infantry, 1st January to 31st December, 1776; Ensign 9th Massachusetts, 1st January, 1777; resigned 3d April, 1778. (Died 9th October, 1822.)

Winslow, Benjamin (Va). Ensign 5th Virginia, 12th February, 1776, to ——.

Winslow, John (Mass). Lieutenant and Paymaster of a Massachusetts Regiment in 1775; Captain 3d Continental Artillery, 8th January, 1777; Regimental Paymaster, 1st June, 1778; resigned 5th November, 1778. (Died 29th November, 1819.)

Winslow, Nathaniel (Mass). Lieutenant in Lexington Alarm, April, 1775; Captain of Thomas' Massachusetts Regiment, May to December, 1775; Captain 10th Massachusetts, 6th November, 1776; Major, 1st November, 1777; retired 1st January, 1781. (Died 27th June, 1821.)

Winsor, Stephen (R. I.). Captain Rhode Island Militia, 1777. (Died 1825.)

Winston, Anthony (Va). Captain Virginia Militia, 1779-1780. (Died 1828.)

Winston, John (Va). Captain 14th Virginia, 5th December, 1776; regiment designated 10th Virginia, 14th September, 1778; retired 12th February, 1781. (Died 1788.)

Winston, Joseph (N. C.). Major North Carolina Militia at King's Mountain, October, 1780. (Died 28th April, 1815.)

Winston, William (Va). Sergeant of Lee's Battalion of Light Dragoons, 7th April, 1778; Cornet, 1st August, 1779; Lieutenant and Adjutant, 1781, and served to close of war; Lieutenant Light Dragoons United States Army, 14th March, 1792; Captain 8th May, 1792; Major, 17th July, 1793; honorably discharged, 1st November, 1796. (Died 1804.)

Winter, Francis (Mass). Chaplain 7th Massachusetts, 1st January, 1777; resigned 16th July, 1777.

Winter, Josiah (Mass). 2d Lieutenant of Danielson's Massachusetts Regiment, May to December, 1775.

Wirt, George (Pa). 2d Lieutenant of Miles' Pennsylvania Rifle Regiment, 6th April, 1776; 1st Lieutenant, 28th May, 1776; taken prisoner at Long Island, 27th August, 1776. Died in captivity, 14th November, 1778.

Wirtenberg, Ludwig (Pa). Surgeon German Regiment, 10th May, 1778; resigned 17th August, 1778.

Wirtz, William (Pa). Captain 10th Pennsylvania, 4th December, 1776; resigned — March, 1778.

Wise, —— (Pa). 3d Lieutenant 1st Pennsylvania ——; killed at Brandywine, 11th September, 1777.

Wise, Samuel (S. C.). Captain 3d South Carolina, 17th June, 1775; Major, 18th May, 1776; killed at Savannah, 9th October, 1779.

Wishart, Thomas (Va). 1st Lieutenant 15th Virginia, 17th March, 1777; resigned 20th April, 1778; seems to have served subsequently in some capacity, as he was taken prisoner at Osborne's, 27th April, 1781, and was a prisoner until the surrender of Yorktown, and was considered by Court of Claims as having retired 15th October, 1781, and was so paid.

Wisner, Gabriel (N. Y.). Ensign New York Militia; killed at Minnisink, 22d July, 1779.

Wisner, Henry (N. Y.). Lieutenant-Colonel New York Militia, 1776-1777. (Died 1790.)

Wisner, John (N. Y.). Captain of Nicoll's New York Militia Regiment, ——; cashiered, 30th Septembered, 1776. (Died 1778.)

Witbeck, Andries (N. Y.). Colonel New York Militia in 1775.

Witherell, James (Mass). Sergeant of Wigglesworth's Massachusetts Regiment, May to December, 1776; wounded at White Plains, 28th October, 1776; Sergeant, 11th Massachusetts, 1st January, 1777; Ensign, 26th September, 1780; transferred to 10th Massachusetts, 1st January, 1781; resigned 1st August, 1782. (Died 1838.)

Withers, —— (S. C.). Lieutenant 5th South Carolina; was in service in January, 1777.

Withers, Enoch Keane (Va). Sergeant of Grayson's Continental Regiment, 28th May, 1777; Ensign, 1st November, 1777; resigned 13th March, 1778; Adjutant 4th Virginia, 1st February, 1781, and served to close of war. (Died 1818.)

Withers, James (Va). Ensign 1st Virginia State Regiment, May, 1777; resigned 15th January, 1778. (Died 1808.)

Withers, John (Va). Lieutenant Virginia Militia, 1780-1781. (Died 1834.)

Withers, William R. (S. C.). Ensign 1st South Carolina, November, 1775; was a Lieutenant in 1780, and served to ——.

Witherspoon, David (N. ·C.). Lieutenant North Carolina Militia at King's Mountain in October, 1780. (Died · 1828.)

Witherspoon, Gavin (S. C.). Captain in Marion's Brigade in 1781.

Witherspoon, James (N. J.). Brigade-Major to General Maxwell, ——; killed at Germantown, 4th October, 1777.

Witherspoon, James (S. C.). Captain South Carolina Militia under General Marion, 1780-1782. (Died 1791.)

Witherspoon, John (N. J.). A signer of the Declaration of Independence. Died 15th November, 1794.

Witherspoon, John (N. J.). Surgeon Hospital Department, 1778-1780.

Witherspoon, Thomas (Del). Captain Delaware Battalion of the Flying Camp, July to December, 1776.

Withington, Peter (Pa). Captain 12th Pennsylvania, 1st October, 1776; died 11th May, 1777.

Withrow, James (N. C.). Captain North Carolina Militia at King's Mountain in October, 1780.

Witman, William (Pa). 1st Lieutenant 9th Pennsylvania, 15th November, 1776; wounded and taken prisoner at Germantown, 4th October, 1777; paroled and became supernumerary, 1st July, 1778. (Died 12th October, 1808.)

Witson, David (Pa.). Captain Chester County, Pa., Militia, 1776-1777.

Witter, Josiah (Conn). Lieutenant Connecticut Militia; wounded and taken prisoner on Long Island in March, 1783.

Woelper, John David (Pa). 1st Lieutenant 3d Pennsylvania Battalion, 6th January, 1776; Captain German Regiment, 17th July, 1776; transferred to Invalid Regiment, 11th June, 1778, and served to 23d April, 1783.

Wohlfest —— Barron (——). Lieutenant in Pulaski Legion, 1778-1779.

Wolcott, Christopher (Conn). Surgeon's-Mate of Wolcott's Connecticut Regiment, December, 1775 to February, 1776.

Wolcott, Erastus (Conn). Colonel Connecticut Militia, 1775-1776; Brigadier General Connecticut Militia, December, 1776, to January, 1781. (Died 14th September, 1793.)

Wolcott, Erastus (Conn). Private in Lexington Alarm, April, 1775; 1st Lieutenant 2d Connecticut, 1st January, 1777; Captain, 27th May, 1777; taken prisoner at Mamaroneck, 1st July, 1777; exchanged, ——; transferred to 1st Connecticut, 1st January, 1781, and served to 3d June, 1783.

Wolcott, Giles (N. H.). Captain of Warner's Continental Regiment, 3d January, 1777; retired 1st January, 1781. (Died 4th June, 1819.)

Wolcott, Oliver (Conn). A signer of the Declaration of Independence; served as Colonel, Brigadier-General and Major-General Connecticut Militia, 1775, to close of war, subsequently Governor of Connecticut. Died 1st December, 1797.

Wolcott, Simeon .(Conn). Surgeon 6th Connecticut, 20th May to 21st December, 1775; Captain of Gay's Connecticut State Regiment, June to December, 1776.

Womack, William (N. C.). Regimental Quartermaster 1st North Carolina, January, 1778; retired 1st June, 1778.

Wood.—See also Woods.

Wood, Abraham (Pa). Ensign 5th Pennsylvania, 1st January, 1777; 2d Lieutenant, 24th March, 1777; wounded and taken prisoner at Brandywine, 11th September, 1777; transferred to Invalid Regiment, 6th October, 1778; discharged 2d January, 1782.

Wood, Clement (N. J.). Ensign 4th New Jersey, 1st February, 1777; cashiered 20th November, 1777. (Died 8th July, 1828.)

Wood, Daniel (Mass). Major of Scammon's Massachusetts Regiment, May to December, 1775; Major 26th Continental Infantry, 1st January to 10th August, 1776. (Died 1819.)

Wood, Daniel (N. Y.). Surgeon of Malcolmn's Additional Continental Regiment, 11th March, 1777; retired 23d April, 1779.

Wood, Ebenezer (Vt). Colonel Vermont Militia in 1780 and 1781.

Wood, Edward (Ga). Was Captain in 2d Georgia in 1778.

Wood, Edward (Va). Ensign 4th Virginia, 19th February, 1776, to ——.

Wood, Ezra (Mass). Colonel Massachusetts Militia in 1778. (Died 1815.)

Wood, Gerrard (Md). Surgeon's-Mate 2d Maryland, 1st August, 1781; retired 1st January, 1783.

Wood, Isaac (Mass). 1st Lieutenant in Lexington Alarm, April, 1775; Captain of Cotton's Massachusetts Regiment, May to December, 1775; Captain 3d Continental Infantry, 1st January to 31st December, 1776.

Wood, Isaiah (N. Y.). Lieutenant of Lamb's Company New York Artillery, 30th June, 1775; Captain Lieutenant, 6th November, 1775, to January, 1776.

Wood, Jeremiah (N. Y.). Captain of Malcolmn's New York Regiment in 1776.

Wood, James (Va). Colonel 12th Virginia, 12th November, 1776; regiment designated 8th Virginia, 14th September, 1778, and served to 1st January, 1783. (Died 16th July, 1813.)

Wood, John (Conn). Surgeon 5th Connecticut, May to December, 1775.

Wood, John (Mass). Ensign 26th Continental Infantry, 1st January, 1776, to ——.

Wood, John (Mass). Captain of Gerrish's Massachusetts Regiment, May to December, 1775; Captain, 26th Continental Infantry, 1st January to 31st December, 1776; Captain of Baldwin's Artillery Artificer Regiment, 4th September, 1777; resigned 18th September, 1778.

Wood, John (N. Y) Colonel New York Militia, ——; taken prisoner at Minnisink 22d July, 1779, and was a prisoner to July, 1783.

Wood, John (N. Y.). Ensign New York Militia, ——; killed at Minnisink, 22d July, 1779.

Wood, Joseph (Mass). Ensign in Lexington Alarm, April, 1775; 2d Lieutenant of Cotton's Massachusetts Regiment, May to December, 1775; 1st Lieutenant 4th Continental Infantry, 1st January, to 31st December, 1776.

Wood, Joseph (Pa). Captain 2d Pennsylvania Battalion, — November, 1775; Major, 4th January, 1776; Lieutenant-Colonel, 29th July, 1776; Colonel, 7th September, 1776; wounded at Lake Champlain, 11th October, 1776; Colonel 3d Pennsylvania, January, 1777, to rank from 30th September, 1776; resigned 31st July, 1777. (Died 12th December, 1788.)

Wood, Lemuel (Mass). Ensign in Lexington Alarm, April, 1775; 2d Lieutenant of Cotton's Massachusetts Regiment, May to December, 1775.

Wood, Matthew (N. C.). 1st Lieutenant 3d North Carolina, 24th July, 1776; Captain, 22d November, 1777; retired 1st June, 1778. (Died 28th October, 1832.)

Wood, Preserve (Conn). Surgeon's-Mate 19th Continental Infantry, 29th July to 31st December, 1776.

Wood, Robert (N. Y.). 2d Lieutenant 3d New York, June, 1776; 1st Lieutenant 2d New York, 21st November, 1776; died 21st June, 1777.

Wood, Robert (N. Y.). Ensign 2d New York, 21st November, 1776; resigned 27th March, 1778; served subsequently as Captain New York Levies. (Died 5th March, 1833.)

Wood, Samuel (Conn). Chaplain 5th Connecticut, May to December, 1775.

Wood, Samuel (Mass). Captain of Ward's Massachusetts Regiment, May to December, 1775.

Wood, Samuel (N. C.). Captain North Carolina Militia at King's Mountain in October, 1780.

Wood, Solomon (N. C.). Lieutenant 8th North Carolina, 28th November, 1776, to ——.

Wood, Spencer (Mass). Private in Lexington Alarm, April, 1775; Sergeant of Read's Massachusetts Regiment, April to December, 1775; Sergeant and Quartermaster Sergeant 4th Massachusetts, 18th May, 1777; Ensign, 18th August, 1779; resigned 16th December, 1782.

Wood, Sylvanus (Mass). Private in Lexington Alarm, April, 1775; Sergeant of Gerrish's Massachusetts Regiment, April to December, 1775; Ensign, 26th Continental Infantry, 1st January to 31st December, 1776.

Wood, William (N. Y.). Surgeon's-Mate 4th New York, 13th August, 1777; resigned 29th August, 1778.

Woodard, Nathaniel.—See Woodward.

Woodberry, John (——). Lieutenant South Carolina Militia, 1781.

Woodbridge, Benjamin Ruggles (Mass). Colonel Massachusetts Regiment, 15th May to December, 1775; Colonel of a Massachusetts Militia Regiment in 1776-1781.

Woodbridge, Christopher (Mass). Lieutenant Massachusets Militia in 1776; 1st Lieutenant 13th Massachusetts, 1st January, 1777; Captain-Lieutenant, ——, 1778; Captain, 10th April, 1779; transferred to 3d Massachusetts, 1st January, 1781, and served to November, 1783. (Died — March, 1825.)

Woodbridge, Ebenezer (Vt). Lieutenant Vermont Militia in 1776.

Woodbridge, Enoch (Mass). Adjutant of Cady's Massachusetts Battalion on the expedition to Canada, January to June, 1776; Regimental Quartermaster of Warner's Continental Regiment, 1st October, 1776, and served to ——; was appointed Commissary at Bennington, 13th November, 1776.

Woodbridge, Howell (Conn). 1st Lieutenant of Wolcott's Connecticut Regiment, December, 1775, to February, 1776; served subsequently as Colonel Connecticut Militia in 1779,1780. (Died 1796.)

Woodbridge, John (Mass). Major 10th Massachusetts, 9th November, 1776; resigned 31st October, 1777. (Died 27th December, 1782.)

Woodbridge, Joshua (Mass). Ensign of Woodbridge's Massachusetts Regiment, May to December, 1775.

Woodbridge, Theodore (Conn). 1st Lieutenant 4th Connecticut, 1st May, 1775; Captain of Wooster's Connecticut Regiment, 10th November, 1775, to March, 1776; Captain of Elmore's Continental Regiment, 15th April, 1776; Captain 7th Connecticut, 1st January, 1777; Major, 10th February, 1778; Brigade-Major and Inspector, 20th June, 1779, to 13th July, 1781; transferred to 2d Connecticut, 1st January, 1781, and retired 1st January, 1783.

Woodbridge, Theophilus (Conn). Private 2d Connecticut, 4th May to 10th December, 1775; 2d Lieutenant, 3d Connecticut, 1st January, 1777; resigned 13th April, 1780.

Woodbury, Elisha (N. H.). Captain 1st New Hampshire, 23d April to December, 1775; Captain 5th Continental Infantry, 1st January to 31st December, 1776. (Died 1816.)

Woodbury, Luke (N. H.). Ensign 2d New Hampshire, 8th November, 1776; 2d Lieutenant, 20th September, 1777; 1st Lieutenant, 30th November, 1779; resigned 17th April, 1781.

Woodford, William (Md). Ensign 1st Maryland, 17th April, 1777; Lieutenant, 1779; wounded at Eutaw Springs, 8th September, 1781; served to ——.

Woodford, William (Va). Colonel 2d Virginia, 13th February, 1776; Brigadier-General Continental Army, 21st February, 1777; wounded at Brandywine, 11th September, 1777; taken prisoner at Charleston, 12th May, 1780; died 13th November, 1780, in captivity.

Woodgate, John (Del). Captain of Patterson's Delaware Battalion of the Flying Camp, July to December, 1776.

Woodhouse, John (N. C.). Ensign 2d North Carolina, 1st September, 1775, to ——.

Woodhull, Nathaniel (N. Y.). Brigadier-General New York Militia, ——; taken prisoner and wounded after capture at Brookland, 28th August, 1776, and died of wounds, 20th September, 1776.

Woodmansee, John (R. I). Ensign 1st Rhode Island, 28th June, to November, 1775.

Woodman, Jonathan (Mass). Sergeant of Little's Massachusetts Regiment, May to December, 1775; Ensign 12th Continental Infantry, 1st January to 31st December, 1776. (Died 18th November, 1831.)

Woodmansee, Joseph (Conn). Ensign Connecticut Militia, ——; wounded at Groton Heights, 6th September, 1781. (Died 1813.)

Woodrow, Andrew (Va). Major and Lieutenant-Colonel Virginia Militia, 1779-1781.

Woodruff, Aaron (Pa). Surgeon's-Mate 12th Pennsylvania, 14th October, 1776; retired 1st July, 1778.

Woodruff, Benjamin (Conn). Regimental Quartermaster 2d Continental Dragoons, 5th April, 1777; discharged 1st January, 1778.

Woodruff, Enoch (Conn). Captain Connecticut Light Horse in 1776. (Died 1786.)

Woodruff, Ephraim (N. Y.). Sergeant 4th New York, December, 1776; Ensign, 9th November, 1777; transferred to 2d New York, 1st January, 1781; 2d Lieutenant, 30th October, 1781, and served to June, 1783. (Died 9th July, 1820.)

Woodruff, Ezekiel (N. J.). Captain and Major New Jersey Militia, 1776-1780.

Woodruff, Henloch (N. Y.). Surgeon's-Mate 1st New York, 21st July, 1775, to March, 1776; Surgeon 3d New York, 21st November, 1776; retired 1st January, 1781.

Woodruff, John (Conn). Captain Connecticut Militia, 1776-1777.

Woodruff, Joseph (Ga). Captain 1st Georgia, 12th December, 1775, to ——. Is also reported as a Major in 1776, regiment to which he belonged not shown.

Woodruff, Lewis (N. J.). 2d Lieutenant 4th New Jersey, 28th November, 1776; retired 17th February, 1777.

Woodruff, Samuel (——). Surgeon's-Mate Hospital Department, 1777-1780.

Woods, Archibald (Va). Captain Virginia Militia, 1780-1781.

Woods, Ebenezer (Mass). Lieutenant in Lexington Alarm, April, 1775; 1st Lieutenant of Whitcomb's Massachusetts Regiment, May to December, 1775; 1st Lieutenant 7th Continental Infantry, 1st January to 31st December, 1776 (Name also spelled Wood.)

Woods, Henry (Mass). Major of Prescott's Massachusetts Regiment, May to December, 1775; Major 7th Continental Infantry, 1st January to 31st December, 1776. (Died 1804.) (Name also spelled Wood.)

Woods, Samuel (Va). Ensign 8th Virginia in 1781; transferred to 3d Virginia, 1st January, 1783, and served to close of war. (Died 3d February, 1826.)

Woodside, John W. (Pa). 2d Lieutenant 3d Pennsylvania Battalion, 8th January, 1776; taken prisoner at Fort Washington, 16th November, 1776; exchanged, 8th May, 1778, and did not return to the army. (Died 18th July, 1835.)

Woodson, Frederick (Va). 2d Lieutenant 1st Virginia State Regiment, 1777; 1st Lieutenant, 1st June, 1778; Captain, ——, 1780, and served to December, 1781.

Woodson, Hughes (Va). 1st Lieutenant 10th Virginia, 3d December, 1776; Captain, 6th August, 1777; regiment designated 6th Virginia, 14th September, 1778; resigned 1st March, 1780.

Woodson, Obadiah (Va). 2d Lieutenant 4th Virginia, 19th February, 1776, to ——.

Woodson, Robert (Va). 2d Lieutenant 9th Virginia, 13th March, 1776; 1st Lieutenant, 31st August, 1776; taken prisoner at Germantown, 4th October, 1777; exchanged October, 1780; Captain, 27th May, 1778; regiment designated, 5th Virginia, 14th September, 1778, and after exchange, served to 1st January, 1783.

Woodson, Samuel (Va). Captain 9th Virginia, 13th March, 1776; resigned 29th December, 1777.

Woodson, Tarleton (Va). Ensign 1st Virginia, 16th September, 1775; Captain 10th Virginia, 3d December, 1776; Major 2d Canadian (Hazen's) Regiment, 1st May, 1777; taken prisoner on Staten Island, 22d August, 1777; exchanged, ——; resigned 1st March, 1782.

Woodward, Daniel (N. H.). Captain New Hampshire Militia in 1777.

Woodward, Elias (Conn). Lieutenant and Regimental Quartermaster of Douglas' Connecticut Regiment, December, 1775, to March, 1776.

Woodward, Ephraim (N. Y.). Captain New York Militia in 1775.

Woodward, John (Mass). Adjutant of Doolittle's Massachusetts Regiment April to December, 1775; 2d Lieutenant and Adjutant, 26th Continental Infantry, 1st January to 31st December, 1776; Lieutenant and Paymaster 9th, Massachusetts, 1st January, 1777; died 17th October, 1778.

Woodward, John (S. C.). Lieutenant South Carolina Rangers, 17th June, 1775, to ——.

Woodward, Nathaniel (N. Y.). Captain 4th New York, 28th June, 1775, to May, 1776. (Name also spelled Woodard.)

Woodward, Peter (N. Y.). 2d Lieutenant 2d Continental Artillery, 1st January, 1777; 1st Lieutenant, 23d March, 1781, and served to June, 1783

Woodward, Richard (Mass). 2d Lieutenant of Gridley's Regiment Massachusetts Artillery, May, 1775; cashiered 13th October, 1775.

Woodward, Samuel (Mass). Surgeon's-Mate 4th Massachusetts, 7th April, 1780; transferred to 3d Continental Artillery, 24th May, 1782, and served to June, 1783. (Died 29th March, 1785.)

Woodward, Thomas (S. C.). Captain South Carolina Rangers, 17th June 1775; killed by Tories in 1779; when and where not stated.

Woodworth, —— (——). Lieutenant ——; killed at Fort Plain, 7th September, 1781.

Woodworth, Elisha (Vt). Ensign Vermont Militia in 1777.

Woodworth, John (Vt). Regimental Quartermaster of Bedel's Regiment Vermont Militia, 1st April to 5th December, 1778.

Woodworth, Jonathan (Conn.). Sergeant 3d Connecticut, 5th May to 10th December, 1775; 2d Lieutenant 20th Continental Infantry, 1st January to 31st December, 1776.

Wool, Isaac (N. Y.). Captain of DuBois' New York Regiment, 26th June to November, 1776.

Wool, Isaiah (N. Y.). Lieutenant of Lamb's Company New York Artillery, 2d August, 1775; taken prisoner at Quebec, 31st December, 1775; Captain-Lieutenant 25th November, 1775; company attached to Knox's Regiment Continental Artillery, fall of 1776; Captain 2d Continental Artillery, 1st January, 1777; resigned 21st August, 1780. (Died 1794.)

Woolford, Thomas (Md). 1st Lieutenant of Barrett's Independent Maryland Company, 14th January, 1776; Captain, May, 1776; Captaain 1st Maryland, 10th December, 1776; Major, 20th February, 1777; Lieutenant-Colonel 2d Maryland, 17th April, 1777; Lieutenant-Colonel Commandant 5th Maryland, 22d October, 1779; wounded and taken prisoner at Camden, 16th August, 1780; exchanged 20th December, 1780; transferred to 4th Maryland, 1st January, 1781; retired 1st January, 1783.

Woolford, William (Md). Ensign 2d Maryland, 20th February, 1777; 2d Lieutenant, 11th April, 1777; 1st Lieutenant, 11th September, 1779; died 16th October, 1781, of wounds received at Eutaw Springs 8th September, 1781.

Woolsey, Melancthon Lloyd (N. Y.). Ensign 4th New York, 21st November, 1776; Lieutenant of Lee's Continental Regiment, 30th January, 1777; retired 23d April, 1779; Major New York Levies in 1780. (Died 21st June, 1819.)

Woolsey, William (Md). 1st Lieutenant of Smith's Baltimore Artillery Company, 14th January, 1776, to ——.

Wooster, David (Conn). Major-General Connecticut Troops, April, 1775; Colonel 1st Connecticut, 1st May, 1775; Brigadier-General Continental Army, 22d June, 1775; died 2d May, 1777, of wounds received at Ridgefield 27th April, 1777.

Wooster, Thomas (Conn). Captain of Webb's Additional Continental Regiment, 23d February, 1777; retired 6th April, 1779. (Lost at sea in 1793.)

Wooten, Shadrach (N. C.). Ensign 5th North Carolina, 28th November, 1776, to ——.

Work, Joseph (Pa). Captain 1st Pennsylvania Battalion of the Flying Camp, July to December, 1776.

Work, William (Pa). Captain 12th Pennsylvania, 16th October, 1776; cashiered 31st March, 1777.

Worman, Thomas (Va). 1st Lieutenant 11th Virginia, 21st July, 1776; 1st Lieutenant, 20th December, 1776; taken prisoner at Fort Washington 16th November, 1776.

Wormer, Isaac (N. H.). Ensign 5th Continental Infantry, 1st January, 1776, to ——.

Wormsted, Robert (Mass). Ensign 14th Continental Infantry, 1st January, 1776, to ——.

Worrell, Dennis (Pa). Captain Pennsylvania Militia; wounded at Germantown, 4th October, 1777.

Worrell, Lewis (Del). 1st Lieutenant Delaware Regiment, 18th January, 1776, to ——.

Worsham, John (Va). Ensign 2d Virginia, 8th March, 1776; 2d Lieutenant, 13th January, 1777; 1st Lieutenant, 13th June, 1777; Captain Lieutenant, 8th March, 1779; died ——, 1779.

Worsham, Richard (Va). Ensign 14th Virginia, 20th November, 1776; 2d Lieutenant, 13th November, 1777; regiment designated 10th Virginia, 14th September, 1778; 1st Lieutenant, 12th March, 1779; taken prisoner at Charleston, 12th May, 1780; transferred to 1st Virginia 12th February, 1781, and served to close of war. (Died 17th February, 1826.)

Worsham, William (Va). Quartermaster Sergeant 1st Continental Dragoons, January, 1777; Cornet, 4th February, 1778; Lieutenant, ——, 1780, and served to 9th November, 1782.

Worth, Joseph (N. C.). Ensign 2d North Carolina, 20th October, 1775; 1st Lieutenant, 3d May, 1776; died 6th April, 1777.

Worthen, Ezekiel (N. H.). Captain in Peabody's Regiment, New Hampshire Militia in 1776, and in Mooney's Regiment, New Hampshire Militia, 1779-1780.

Worthington, Edward (Va). Captain Virginia Militia, 1780-1781.

Worthington, Elias (Conn). Colonel Connecticut Militia in 1780. (Died 1822.)

Worthington, William (Conn). Lieutenant-Colonel of Mott's Connecticut State Regiment, June to December,

1776; served subsequently with Connecticut Militia.

Worthy, John (Mass). Captain of Phinney's Massachusetts Regiment, May to December, 1775.

Woulds, James (Md). Adjutant 5th Maryland, 16th March, 1777; Ensign, 22d May, 1778; resigned 23d September, 1779.

Wright, Aaron (Mass). Surgeon Hospital Department, 1776-1777.

Wright, Abraham (Conn). Ensign 8th Connecticut, 6th July to 18th December, 1775; 1st Lieutenant 17th Continental Infantry, 1st January to 31st December, 1776.

Wright, Alexander (Pa). Ensign of Lewis' Pennsylvania Battalion of the Flying Camp, July to December, 1776.

Wright, Anthony (Pa). 1st Lieutenant of Flower's Artillery Artificer Regiment, 1st March, 1777, to March, 1781.

Wright, Benjamin (Md). Ensign 6th Maryland, 14th June, 1777, 2d Lieutenant, 12th October, 1777; resigned 1st December, 1778.

Wright, Charles (Conn). Ensign of Burrall's Continental Regiment, March to November, 1776.

Wright, Daniel (N. C.). Captain North Carolina Militia, 1779-1780.

Wright, David (N. C.). Ensign 10th North Carolina, 19th April, 1777; 2d Lieutenant, 15th February, 1778; transferred to 1st North Carolina, 1st June, 1778; resigned 5th February, 1780.

Wright, Dudley (Conn). Sergeant 2d Connecticut, 6th May to 10th December, 1775; 2d Lieutenant 22d Continental Infantry, 1st January to 31st December, 1776; 1st Lieutenant 3d Connecticut, 1st January, 1777; resigned 13th April, 1778.

Worthern, Ezekiel (N. H.). Captain in Peabody's Regiment New Hampshire Militia in 1776 and in Mooney's Regiment New Hampshire Militia, 1779-1780.

Wright, Edward (Md). Ensign 7th Maryland, 1st April, 1777; 2d Lieutenant, 14th September, 1778; resigned 8th October, 1779.

Wright, Elihu (Mass). Surgeon of Fellow's Massachusetts Regiment, April to December, 1775; Surgeon 21st Continental Infantry, 1st January to 31st December, 1776.

Wright, Enoch (Pa). Sergeant-Major 5th Pennsylvania Battalion, January, 1776; Adjutant 10th Pennsylvania, 31st

January, 1777; deserted 1st November, 1777.

Wright, George (Pa). Major Pennsylvania Militia; taken prisoner from his home 14th February, 1778.

Wright, Isaac (S. C). Lieutenant South Carolina Militia in 1775.

Wright, Jacob (N. Y.). Captain of Lasher's New York Militia Regiment, May, 1776; Captain 2d New York, 21st ovember, 1776, and served to close of war.

Wright, James (Va). 2d Lieutenant 11th Virginia, 31st July, 1776; 1st Lieutenant, 25th March, 1777; regiment designated 7th Virginia, 14th September, 1778; Captain, 2d July, 1779; taken prisoner at Charleston, 12th May, 1780, and was a prisoner on parole to close of war.

Wright, Job (Conn). 2d Lieutenant of Selden's Connecticut State Regiment, June to December, 1776.

Wright, John (Ga). 1st Lieutenant 2d Georgia, November, 1776; Captain, ——, 1778; served to close of war. (Died 1809.)

Wright, John (Mass). Sergeant in Lexington Alarm, April, 1775; 2d Lieutenant of Brewer's Massachusetts Regiment, May to December, 1775; 1st Lieutenant 4th Massachusetts, 1st January, 1777; Captain, 20th March, 1779; resigned 14th April, 1780. (Died 1805.)

Wright, Joseph Allyn (Conn). 1st Lieutenant 7th Connecticut, 6th July to 10th December, 1775; 1st Lieutenant 19th Continental Infantry, 1st January to 31st December, 1776; Captain 5th Connecticut, 1st January, 1777; Major 4th Connecticut, 28th December, 1781; transferred to 2d Connecticut, 1st January, 1781; transferred to 3d Connecticut, 1st January, 1783, and served to June, 1783. (Died 2d May, 1819.)

Wright, Josiah (Mass). 2d Lieutenant in Lexington Alarm, April, 1775; 2d Lieutenant of Paterson's Massachusetts Regiment, May to December, 1775 (Died 1817.)

Wright, Jotham (——). Lieutenant of Baldwin's Artillery Artificer Regiment, 12th November, 1779, and served to March, 1781.

Wright, Nahum (Mass). Lieutenant Massachusetts Militia, ——; wounded at Bunker Hill, 17th June, 1775.

Wright, Nathan (Md). Sergeant 2d Maryland, 10th January, 1780; 2d Lieutenant 3d Maryland, 1st January, 1781; retained in Maryland Battalion, April,

1783, and served to 15th November, 1783.

Wright, Noble (N. H.). 2d Lieutenant New Hampshire Rangers, 1778-1781.

Wright, Patrick (Va). Captain of a Virginia State Regiment, 1778; resigned ——, 1780.

Wright, Robert (Md). Captain Maryland Militia in 1777.

Wright, Robert (N. Y.). Captain 1st Canadian (Livingston's) Regiment, 18th December, 1776; left regiment 28th June, 1779; on leave for 12 months, and did not rejoin.

Wright, Shadrach (Ga). 1st Lieutenant 2d Georgia, 7th January, 1776; Captain, ——, 1778, and served to October, 1782.

Wright, Samuel (Conn). 1st Lieutenant 2d Connecticut, 1st May to 10th December, 1775; Captain 22d Continental Infantry, 1st January to 31st December, 1776.

Wright, Samuel Turbutt (Md). 2d Lieutenant of Veazey's Independent Maryland Company, 14th January, 1776; taken prisoner at Long Island 27th August, 1776; exchanged 20th April, 1778; Captain 2d Maryland, 10th December, 1776; resigned 1st July, 1779.

Wright, Willard (Conn). 2d Lieutenant of Webb's Continental Regiment, 1st January, 1777; 1st Lieutenant, 16th May, 1778; resigned 10th April, 1779.

Wright, William (N. Y.). Lieutenant New York Militia; prisoner of war 16th February to 28th October, 1781; where taken not stated.

Wyatt, Cary (Va). Lieutenant of a Virginia State Regiment, — March, 1778; Captain Lieutenant, 6th December, 1778, to February, 1782.

Wyatt, Hubbard (Va). Captain Virginia Militia, 1779-1780.

Wyatt, John (Del). Ensign Delaware Regiment, 3d December, 1776; 2d Lieutenant, 29th March, 1777, and served to ——.

Wyatt, Thomas (Pa). Ensign 8th Pennsylvania, 21st December, 1778; Lieutenant, ——, 1780; retired 17th January, 1781.

Wyley, Aldrich.—See **Wiley.**

Wylie, Thomas (Pa). Captain Lieutenant of Flower's Artillery Artificer Regiment, 17th February, 1777; Captain, 1st February, 1778, and served to close of war.

Wylley, Thomas (Ga). Was an Ensign 2d Georgia in May, 1778; Captain and Deputy Quartermaster General of Georgia troops, 1779-1781.

Wyllys, Hezekiah (Conn). Captain of Chester's Connecticut State Regiment, 20th June to 25th December, 1776; served subsequently as Lieutenant-Colonel Connecticut Militia. (Died 29th March, 1827.)

Wyllys, John Plasgrave (Conn). Adjutant of Wolcott's Connecticut State Regiment, January, 1776; Brigade-Major to General Wadsworth, 7th August, 1776; taken prisoner 15th September, 1776, on the retreat from New York; exchanged 20th December, 1776; Captain of Webb's Additional Continental Regiment, 1st January, 1777; Major, 10th October, 1778; transferred to 3d Connecticut, 1st January, 1781; transferred to 1st Connecticut, 1st January, 1783; retained in Swift's Connecticut Regiment, June, 1783, and served to 25th December, 1783; Major United States Infantry Regiment, 9th June, 1785; Major 1st Infantry United States Army, 29th September, 1789; killed 22d October, 1790, in action with Indians on the Miami, Ohio.

Wyllys, Samuel (Conn). Lieutenant-Colonel 2d Connecticut, 1st May, 1775; Colonel, 1st July to 10th December, 1775; Colonel 22d Continental Infantry, 1st January to 31st December, 1776; Colonel 3d Connecticut, 1st January, 1777; retired 1st January, 1781. (Died 9th June, 1823.)

Wyman, Abijah (Mass). Sergeant in Lexington Alarm, April, 1775; Captain of Prescott's Massachusetts Regiment, April to December, 1775. (Died 1804.)

Wyman, Isaac (N. H.). Lieutenant-Colonel 1st New Hampshire, 23d April to December, 1775; served subsequently as Colonel New Hampshire Militia. (Died 1792.)

Wyman, John (Mass). 1st Lieutenant of Whitcomb's Massachusetts Regiment, May to December, 1775; 1st Lieutenant 11th Continental Infantry, 1st January, 1776, to ——.

Wyman, William (Mass). Captain of Paterson's Massachusetts Regiment, April to December, 1775; Captain 15th Continental Infantry, 1st January to 31st December, 1776.

Wyndham, Amos (S. C.). Major South Carolina Militia in 1776.

Wynkoop, Cornelius D. (N. Y.). Major 3d New York, 30th June, 1775; Lieutenant-Colonel, 2d August, 1775; Colonel 4th New York, 8th March to November, 1776; served subsequently as Colonel New York Militia.

Wynkoop, Jacobus (N. Y.). Captain 4th New York, 28th June, 1775, to January, 1776; subsequently Captain in the Navy. (Died 1795.)

Wynkoop, Petrus (N. Y.). Quartermaster 10th New York Militia Regiment in 1775.

Wynn, Samuel.—See **Winn**.

Wynn, Thomas (Pa). Lieutenant of Montgomery's Pennsylvania Battalion of the Flying Camp, June, 1776; taken prisoner at Fort Washington 16th November, 1776; exchanged 2d January, 1781. (Died 1816.)

Wynn, Walter (Pa). Lieutenant of Montgomery's Pennsylvania Battalion of the Flying Camp, June, 1776; taken prisoner at Fort Washington, 16th November, 1776; escaped in July, 1777, but did not rejoin the army.

Wythe, George (Va). A signer of the Declaration of Independence; died 8th June, 1806.

Y.

Yancey, Charles (N. C.). Lieutenant 9th North Carolina, 28th November, 1776, to ——.

Yancey, John (Va). Ensign and Regimental Quartermaster 10th Virginia, 8th January, 1777, to March, 1778; Captain Virginia Militia, 1779-1780.

Yancey, Leighton (Va). Lieutenant 1st Continental Dragoons in 1778; taken prisoner at Charleston 12th May, 1780, and was a prisoner on parole to close of war.

Yancey, Robert (Va). Cornet 1st Continental Dragoons, 20th March, 1777; Regimental Quartermastetr, 12th February, 1777; Lieutenant, ——, 1778; Captain, 13th June, 1779; taken prisoner at Charleston 12th May, 1780, and was a prisoner on parole to close of war.

Yarborough, Charles (Va). 2d Lieutenant 1st Virginia State Regiment, March, 1777; 1st Lieutenant, 1st February, 1778; Lieutenant 3d Continental Dragoons, 16th October, 1780; transferred to Baylor's Regiment of Dragoons 9th November, 1782, and served to close of war.

Yarborough, Edward (N. C.). Ensign 3d North Carolina, 8th May, 1776; Lieutenant, 16th April, 1777; Captain Lieutenant, 9th January, 1777; Captain, 10th May, 1779; retired 1st January, 1783.

Yard, Thomas (N. J.). 1st Lieutenant 2d New Jersey, 28th October, 1775; Captain, 29th November, 1776; resigned — November, 1777.

Yarnall, Peter (Pa). Surgeon's Mate 3d Pennsylvania Battalion, 7th February, 1776; transferred to Navy in August, 1776; Surgeon's Mate 4th Continental Dragoons, 22d May, 1777; resigned 15th September, 1777. (Died ——, 1798.)

Yates, Abraham L. (N. Y.). 2d Lieutenant New York Militia, October, 1775, to ——.

Yates, Bartholomew (Va). Ensign 1st Virginia, 15th June, 1776; 2d Lieutenant, November, 1776; died 9th January, 1777, of wounds received at Princeton, 3d January, 1777.

Yates, Christopher P. (N. Y.). Captain 2d New York, 15th July, 1775; Major 1st New York, 21st November, 1776; resigned 1st January, 1778; Lieutenant-Colonel New York Militia, 1778-1779; Lieutenant-Colonel and Deputy Quartermaster General under General Schuyler, 1779-1781. (Died 1785.)

Yates, George (Va). Surgeon's Mate of a Virginia Regiment, 1779 to 1st January, 1783.

Yates, John (Conn). 1st Lieutenant 7th Connecticut, 6th July to 10th December, 1775; 1st Lieutenant 19th Continental Infantry, 1st January to 31st December, 1776.

Yates, John (Del). Paymaster Delaware Regiment, 9th August to December, 1776.

Yates, John (Va). Lieutenant of a Virginia State Regiment in 1780 and 1781.

Yates, Moses (N. H.). Captain New Hampshire Militia in 1778.

Yates, Paul (Conn). 2d Lieutenant 4th Connecticut, 1st May to 10th December, 1775; served subsequently as Captain Connecticut Militia.

Yates, Peter (N. Y.). Lieutenant-Colonel 2d New York, 28th June, 1775, to March, 1776; Lieutenant-Colonel of Nicholson's Continental Regiment, 8th March to 26th June, 1776; Colonel New York Militia, 1779-1780. (Died 1807.)

Yates, Thomas (Md). Captain 2d Maryland Battalion of the Flying Camp, July to December, 1776; Captain 4th Maryland, 10th December, 1776; resigned 20th May, 1777. (Died 1815.)

Yates, Thomas (Pa). Sergeant of Baldwin's Artillery Artificer Regiment, 1st May, 1778; 1st Lieutenant, 20th March, 1780, to May, 1781; was an Aide-de-Camp to General Putnam in 1777.

Yates, William (S. C.). Lieutenant-Colonel Deputy Mustermaster General Southern Department, 1777-1780. (Died 2d December, 1789.)

Yeaton, Moses (N. H.). Captain New Hampshire Militia in 1778.

Yeaton, William (N. H.). 2d Lieutenant of Turner's Company New Hampshire Artillery, 1775-1776.

Yeomans, John (Mass). Corporal in Danielson's Massachusetts Regiment, May to December, 1775; Sergeant, 4th Massachusetts, 1st February, 1777; Ensign, 10th February, 1778; 2d Lieutenant, 15th April, 1779; 1st Lieutenant, 14th April, 1780, and served to June, 1783. (Died 12th July, 1827.)

Yeomans, Moses (N. Y.). Sergeant-Major 3d New York, 2d July to November, 1775; 2d Lieutenant 3d New York, 21st November, 1776; omitted May, 1778; served subsequently as Captain New York Militia.

York, Bartholomew (Mass). Lieutenant of Phinney's Massachusetts Regiment, May to December, 1775; 1st Lieutenant 18th Continental Infantry, 1st January, 1776; Captain, 18th May to 31st December, 1776.

Young, Aaron (N. H.). Lieutenant of Brook's Regiment New Hampshire Militia, 1777-1778.

Young, Edward (Ga). Captain of a Georgia Artillery Company in 1778, and Colonel Georgia Militia in 1779.

Young, Edward (Pa). 2d Lieutenant 5th Pennsylvania Battalion, 8th January, 1776; 1st Lieutenant 6th Pennsylvania, 15th February, 1777; resigned — April, 1777.

Young, George (Ga). Captain Lieutenant of Phoenix's Company Georgia Artillery, 6th November, 1776, to ——.

Young, Guy (N. Y.). 2d Lieutenant 2d New York, 28th June, 1775; 1st Lieutenant, 16th February, 1776; 1st Lieutenant, 1st New York, 21st November, 1776, to rank from 16th February, 1776; Captain Lieutenant, 26th March,

1777; Captain, 14th July, 1779; retired 1st January, 1781; served subsequently as Captain New York Levies.

Young, Henry (Va). 1st Lieutenant 7th Virginia, 5th March, 1776; Captain, 28th December, 1776; transferred to 5th Virginia 14th September, 1778; retired 1st January, 1783.

Young, James (Md). Captain 2d Maryland Battalion of the Flying Camp, July 1776, to December, 1776.

Young, James (Pa). Captain of Baldwin's Artillery Artificer Regiment, 1st August, 1777, to 1780. (Died 28th August, 1832.)

Young, James (Pa). 1st Lieutenant 7th Pennsylvania, 20th March, 1777; resigned 1st September, 1777.

Young, Jesse (N. H.). Lieutenant of Bedel's Regiment New Hampshire Militia, 1777-1778.

Young, John (N. H.). Surgeon of Peabody's Regiment New Hampshire Militia in 1778.

Young, John (Vt). Regimental Quartermaster of Bedel's Regiment Vermont Militia, 1778-1779.

Young, John (Pa). Sergeant 2d Pennsylvania Battalion, 20th February to 31st December, 1776; Sergeant 3d Pennsylvania, 1st January, 1777; Ensign, 20th April, 1777; resigned 31st July, 1777.

Young, John (Pa). Captain 1st Battalion Philadelphia County, Pa., Militia in 1776.

Young, John (R. I.). Surgeon's Mate Hospital Department, 1779-1781.

Young, Joseph (R. I.). Surgeon 9th Continental Infantry, 1st January to 31st December, 1776; Hospital Surgeon and Physician, 20th September, 1781, to close of war.

Young, Joshua (Vt). Lieutenant of Bedel's Regiment Vermont Militia, 1778-1779.

Young, Marcus (Pa). Private, Corporal and Sergeant German Regiment, 20th June, 1776, to June, 1777; 2d Lieutenant, 8th June, 1777; 1st Lieutenant, 12th March, 1778; retired 1st January, 1781.

Young, Nathaniel (N. Y.). 2d Lieutenant 1st New York, 13th January, 1777, to ——.

Young, Robert (Va). 2d Lieutenant 11th Virginia, 25th November, 1776; 1st

Lieutenant, 1st June, 1777; retired 14th September, 1778.

Young, Samuel (N. H.). 1st Lieutenant of Bedel's New Hampshire Regiment, 22d January to September, 1776; Captain of Bedel's Regiment New Hampshire Militia, 15th December, 1777, to 1st April, 1779.

Young, Thomas (Va). Captain Virginia Militia, 1779-1781.

Young, William (Ga). 1st Lieutenant of Beckham's Company Georgia Militia, 15th August, 1781, to 15th February, 1782. (Died 1826.)

Young, William (Mass). Quartermaster of Danielson's Massachusetts Regiment, May to December, 1775.

Young, William (Pa). Lieutenant of McAllister's Pennsylvania Battalion of the Flying Camp, July, 1776; taken prisoner at Fort Washington 16th November, 1776; exchanged 8th December, 1780

Younglove, David (N Y.). Surgeon's Mate New York Militia, 1776-1778.

Younglove, John (N. Y.). Major New York Militia, 1778-1779.

Younglove, Moses (N. Y.). Surgeon New York Militia, 1776-1778.

Yule, James (N. Y.). 1st Lieutenant of Harper's Regiment New York Militia, May to November, 1780.

Yule, James (Pa). Was a Cornet 4th Continental Dragoons in September, 1778.

Z.

Zanck, Jacob (Pa). Lieutenant of Thompson's Pennsylvania Rifle Battalion, 25th June, 1775; 1st Lieutenant 1st Continental Infantry, 1st January, 1776; resigned 25th August, 1776.

Zane, Silas (Va). 1st Lieutenant 13th Virginia, 28th December, 1776; Captain, 9th February, 1777; dismissed 25th January, 1778.

Zedwitz, Herman (N. Y.). Major 1st New York, 15th July, 1775; injured by the fall of a wall at Quebec, 31st December, 1775; Lieutenant-Colonel, 8th March, 1776; sent to prison, 22d November, 1776, under sentence to be confined during the war; released and permitted to leave the United States 14th July, 1779.

Zeizble, David (Pa). 3d Lieutenant 1st Continental Infantry, 1st January, 1776; wounded near Long Island, 26th August, 1776.

Zelly, John (—). A Lieutenant; was a prisoner in 1782; when and where taken not stated.

Ziegler, David (Pa). 3d Lieutenant and Adjutant of Thompson's Pennsylvania Rifle Battalion, 25th June, 1775; 2d Lieutenant 1st Continental Infantry, 1st January, 1776; 1st Lieutenant, 25th September, 1776; wounded at Long Island 27th August, 1776; 1st Lieutenant 1st Pennsylvania 16th January, 1777; Captain, 8th December, 1778; retired 1st January, 1783; Captain United States Infantry Regiment, 12th August, 1784; Captain 1st Infantry, United States Army, 29th September, 1789; Major, 22d October, 1790; resigned 5th March, 1792. (Died 24th September, 1811.)

Ziegler, Jacob (Pa). Ensign 1st Pennsylvania Battalion, 27th October, 1775; 2d Lieutenant, 15th January, 1776; 1st Lieutenant 2d Pennsylvania, 1st January, 1777; resigned — February, 1777.

Ziele, Peter W. (N. Y.). Lieutenant-Colonel New York Militia, 1775-1778.

Zielinski, John de (Poland). Captain of Lancers, Pulaski Legion, 18th April, 1778; died 25th September, 1779.

Zollikoffer, John Conrad (N. C.). Captain North Carolina Militia, 1778-1780. (Died 1796.)

Zollinger, Peter (Pa). Captain York County, Pa., Militia in 1777.

By the United States in Congress Assembled.

A PROCLAMATION!

Whereas, in the progress of an arduous and difficult war, the armies of the United States of America have eminently displayed every military and patriotic virtue, and are not less to be applauded for their fortitude and magnanimity in the most trying scenes of distress than for a series of heroic and illustrious achievements, which exalt them to a high rank among the most zealous and successful defenders of the rights and liberties of mankind: And, whereas, by the blessing of Divine Providence on our cause and our arms, the glorious period is arrived when our national independence and sovereignty are established, and we enjoy the prospect of a permanent and honorable peace; we, therefore, the United States, in Congress assembled, thus impressed with a lively sense of the distinguished merit and good conduct of the said armies, do give them the thanks of their country for their long, eminent and faithful services. And it is our will and pleasure that such part of the Federal armies as stands engaged to serve during the war, and as by our acts of the 26th day of May, the 11th day of June, the 9th day of August, and the 26th day of September last were furloughed, shall, from and after the 3d day of November next, be absolutely discharged, by virtue of this our proclamation from the said service, and we do declare that the further services in the field of the officers who are deranged and on furlough in consequence of our aforesaid acts can now be dispensed with, and they have our full permission to retire from service, without being longer liable from their present engagements to be called into command. And of such discharge and permission to retire from service respectively all our officers, civil and military, and all others whom it may concern, are required to take notice and to govern themselves accordingly.

Given under the seal of the United States, in Congress assembled, witness His Excellency, ELIAS BOUDINOT, our President in Congress, this 18th day of October, in the year of our Lord 1783, and of the sovereignty and independence of the United States of America the eighth.

The following official document, furnished by the War Department in 1827, is deemed of sufficient importance to reprint in connection with this work. (Exact copy from Vol. 3, American State Papers, Military Affairs, pages 529-559.)

19th Congress.]　　　　　　　　No. 342.　　　　　　　　[2d Session.

Statement of the Names and Rank of the Officers

OF THE

REVOLUTIONARY WAR, &C.

Communicated to the House of Representatives, January 10, 1827.

DEPARTMENT OF WAR, JANUARY 10, 1827.

SIR: In Compliance with the resolution of the House of Representatives of the 8th instant, directing the Secretary of War "to report to this House the name and rank of each officer of the Continental Army who served to the end of the Revolutionary War, and who were, by the resolution of Congress, entitled to half pay during life; and also, as nearly as practicable, the names of the surviving officers and their places of residence,"

I transmit herewith a list of the names and rank of the officers of the Revolutionary War, as complete as the records of the Department will furnish, with the exception of Foreign officers. There is no evidence in the department to show which of them "were by the resolution of Congress entitled to half pay," nor is it known which of them are still living, with their places of residence, except those who are on the pension list.

Very respectfully, &c.,

JAMES BARBOUR, Secretary of War.

The Speaker of the House of Representatives.

SCHEDULE

OF THE

NAMES AND RANK

OF MOST OF THE

OFFICERS OF THE WAR OF INDEPENDENCE,

Chiefly returned as belonging to the line or corps of the thirteen original United States, soon after said Army was disbanded in 1783, arranged alphabetically according to States.

NEW HAMPSHIRE.

Adams, Samuel, Lieutenant, 1st.
Adams, John, Lieutenant, 1st.
Adams, Winbourn, Lietuenant-Colonel, Hale's.
Aldrich, George, Captain, Whitcomb's Rangers.
Allen, Ethan, Colonel, ——.
Allen, David, Surgeon's Mate, 1st.
Butterfield, Jonas, ——, Whitcomb's Rangers.
Boyton, Joseph, Lieutenant, 1st.
Blodget, Caleb, Lieutenant, 1st.
Blake, Thomas, Lieutenant, 1st.
Blanchard, Thomas, Lieutenant, 1st.
Bell, M. William, Captain, 2d.
Bacon, Oliver, Lieutenant, 2d.
Brownson, Gideon, Major, Warner's.
Beach, Samuel, Lieutenant, Warner's.
Barrett, Oliver, Lieutenant, Warner's.
Barnett, Robert, Lieutenant, Invalid.
Beal, Zachary, Captain, Scammell's.
Cilley, Joseph, Colonel, ——.
Clapp, Daniel, Captain Lieutenant, ——.
Cass, Jonathan, Captain, 1st.
Carr, James, Major, ——.

Cherry, Samuel, Captain, 1st.
Cilley, Jonathan, Lieutenant, ——.
Church, Reuben, Ensign, Warner's.
Colbourn, Andrew, Lieutenant-Colonel, Scammell's.
Dearborn, Henry, Lieutenant-Colonel Commandant, ——.
Drufton, Moses, Captain, 1st.
Dustin, Moody, Captain, ——.
Dennitt, John, Captain, ——.
Dunning, Michael, Captain, Warner's.
Ellis, Benjamin, Captain, 1st.
Evans, Israel, Chaplain, ——.
Eno, Martin, Ensign, Warner's.
Frost, P. George, Captain, ——.
Farwell, Isaac, Captain, 1st.
Frye, Isaac, Captain, 1st.
Fogg, Jeremiah, Captain, 1st.
Facy, Joseph, Ensign, Scammell's.
Gilman, Nicholas, Captain, ——.
Gookin, Daniel, — Lieutenant, 2d.
Green, Ebenezer, Captain, ——.
Hutchins, Nathaniel, Captain, ——.
Henry, R. Robert, Surgeon, 1st.
Howe, Bezabeel, Lieutenant, 1st.
Harvey, John, Lieutenant, 1st.
Levitt, Nehemiah, Lieutenant, ——.
Livermore, Daniel, Captain, 1st.

Lyon, Thomas, Lieutenant, Warner's.
Penniman, Adna, Captain-Lieutenant, ——.
Potter, Joseph, Captain, 1st.
Perkins, Jonathan, Lieutenant, 2d.
Page, Moses, Lieutenant, 2d.
Payne, Francis, Lieutenant, 2d.
Robinson, Noah, Captain-Lieutenant, ——.
Rowell, William, Captain, ——.
Reid, George, Lieutenant-Colonel Commandant, 1st.
Robinson, Caleb, Major, 2d.
Reed, James, Brigadier-General.
Stark, Archibald, Lieutenant, 1st.
Scott, William, Major, 2d.
Senter, Asa, Captain, ——.
Stockton, Ebenezer, Surgeon, 2d.
Scammell, Alexander, Colonel, ——.
Smith, Simeon, Captain, Warner's.
Safford, Samuel, Lieutenant-Colonel. Warner's.
Stevens, Ebenezer, Lieutenant, Warner's.
Stark, John, Brigadier-General.
Titcomb, Benjamin, Lieutenant-Colonel.
Thompson, Joshua, Lieutenant, 2d.
Talman, Thomas, Lieutenant, Warner's.
Taylor, Nathan, Lieutenant, Whitcomb's Rangers.
Thomas, Joseph, Lieutenant, Scammell's.
Weare, Nathan, Lieutenant, 1st.
Wilkins, B. Robert, Lieutenant, 2d.
Washburn, Azel, Surgeon, 2d.
Warner, Seth, Colonel, Warner's.
Walcott, Giles, Captain, Warner's.
Whitcomb, Benjamin, Major, Rangers.
Wear, Richard, Captain, Scammell's.

MASSACHUSETTS

Allen, Noah, Major, 1st.
Allen, C. Nathaniel, Captain, 7th.
Alden, Judah, Captain, 2d.
Ames, Jotham, Lieutenant, 2d.
Abbot, Josiah, Ensign, 2d.
Ashley, Moses, Major, 6th.
Adams, Henry, Surgeon, 6th.
Armstrong, Samuel, Leutenant and Paymaster, 8th.
Abbot, Stephen, Captian, 8th.

Adams, Samuel, Hosptal Surgeon.
Andrews William, Lieutenant, Crane's Artillery.
Austin, John, Lieutenant, Crane's Artillery.
Alden, Ichabod, Colonel, Alden's.
Allen, Jacob, Captain, Bailey's.
Bailey, John, Colonel, Old 2d.
Bradford, Gamaliel, Colonel, ——.
Bassett, Barachiah, Lieutenant-Colonel, ——.
Ballard, H. William, Major, ——.
Burley, William, Captain, ——.
Buxton, James, Captain, ——.
Bates, Joseph, Captain, ——.
Bannister, Seth, Captain, ——.
Bussey, Isaiah, Lieutenant, Crane's Artillery.
Bailey, Thomas, Lieutenant, Crane's Artillery.
Bradley, Levi, Lieutenant, ——.
Buffington, Samuel, Lieutenant, ——.
Bills, Jabez, Lieutenant, ——.
Benjamin, Samuel, Lieutenant, ——.
Browne, Ezekiel, Surgeon, ——.
Bartlett, Daniel, Surgeon, ——.
Baldwin, Jeduthan, Colonel, ——.
Bigelow, Timothy, Colonel, Old 15th.
Brooks, John, Lieutenant-Colonel, Commandant, 7th.
Bramhall, Joshua, Lieutenant, 7th.
Bradford, Gamaliel, Lieutenant, 7th.
Bailey, Luther, Captain, 2d.
Bailey, Adams, Captain, 2d.
Bradford, Robert, Captain, 2d.
Bullard, Asa, Lieutenant, 2d.
Blanchard, John, Captain, 4th.
Belcom, Joseph, Lieutenant, 6th.
Brown, Ebenezer, Lieutenant, 1st.
Bowman, Samuel, Lieutenant, 1st.
Bowles, H. Ralph, Lieutenant, 1st.
Burnham, John, Major, 5th.
Benson, Joshua, Captain, 5th.
Bowman, Phineas, Captain, 5th.
Brigham, Origen, Surgeon's-Mate, 2d.
Bancroft, James, Lieutenant, 8th.
Barnet, John, Chaplain, 2d Brigade.
Baylis Hodijah, Major, ——.
Barlow, Joel, Chaplain, ——.
Burbeck, Henry, Captain, Crane's Artillery.
Bliss, Joseph, Lieutenant, ——.

Blake, Edward, Lieutenant, ——.
Ballentine, Ebenezer, Surgeon's-Mate,
Tupper's.
Burr, Ephraim, Captain, Bailey's.
Baker, Joseph, Lieutenant, Bailey's.
Barney, Jabez, Ensign, Lee's.
Cogswell, Thomas, Major, ——.
Carr, Samuel, Major, ——.
Clark, Silas, Captain, ——.
Cook, David, Captain, Artillery,
Crane's, 3d.
Cole, Thomas, Lieutenant, Infan-
try, ——.
Crane, John, Lieutenant, Infan-
try, ——.
Crane, John, Surgeon, ——.
Coburn, Asa, Captain, 7th.
Cogswell, Samuel, Lieutenant, 7th.
Cooper, Ezekiel, Captain, 2d.
Clapp, Caleb, Captain, 2d.
Condy, Thomas, Lieutenant, 4th.
Chapen, Samuel, Lieutenant, 4th.
Chambers, Matthew, Captain, 6th.
Clays, Peter, Captain, 6th.
Crook, Joseph, Lieutenant, 6th.
Cushing, Thomas, Lieutenant, 1st.
Carlton, Moses, Lieutenant, 5th.
Cushing, Nathan, Captain, 1st.
Castaing, Peter, Lieutenant, 3d.
Cobb, David, Lieutenant-Colonel,
commanding 5th
Clap, Joseph, Lieutenant and Quar-
termaster, 8th.
Cogswell, Amos, Captain, 8th.
Carey, Jonathan, Lieutenant, 8th.
Clarkson, Matthew, Major, 8th.
Crane, John, Colonel, 3d Artillery.
Callender, John, Captain-Lieutenant,
Crane's.
Crowley, Florence, Lieutenant,
Crane's.
Cooper, Samuel, Lieutenant, Crane's.
Colton, Charles, Captain, Greaton's.
Cleveland, Ephraim, Captain, M.
Jackson's.
Cartwright, Thomas, Captain, H.
Jackson's.
Carlton, Samuel, Lieutenant-Colonel,
Brewer's.
Conant, John, Paymaster, Tupper's.
Chapin, Leonard, Lieutenant, Grea-
ton's.

Chaloner, Edward, Ensign, Putnam's.
Dean, Walter, Captain, ——.
Day, Elijah, Lieutenant, ——.
Day, Luke, Captain, 7th.
Danforth, Joshua, Lieutenant, 2d.
David, John, Lieutenant, 4th.
Daniels, Japheth, Captain, 6th.
Dodge, Levi, Lieutenant, 1st.
Drew, Seth, Major, 3d.
Davis, James, Lieutenant, 3d.
Dana, Benjamin, Lieutenant, 3d.
Davis, Ebenezer, Lieutenant, 3d.
Darby, Samuel, Major, 8th.
Dix, Nathan, Captain, 8th.
Donnel, Nathaniel, Captain, Crane's
Artillery.
Duffield, John, Surgeon, Crane's Ar-
tillery.
Emmerson, Nehemiah, Captain, ——.
English, Andrew, Captain, – –.
Eldridge, Samuel, Lieutenant, ——.
Emery, Ephraim, Lieutenant, 6th.
Everett, Pelatiah, Lieutenant, 5th.
Egleston, Azariah, Lieutenant and
Paymaster, 1st.
Eysandeau, William, Lieutenant. 5th.
Edwards, Thomas, Lieutenant, ——.
Eustis, William, Surgeon, General
Hospital.
Eaton, Benjamin, Lieutenant, Crane's
Artillery.
Eddy, Joshua, Captain, Bradford's.
Ellis, Paul, Captain, Bigelow's.
Fernald, Tobias, Lieutenant-Colonel,
——.
Frye, Nathaniel, Lieutenant, ——.
Francis, Thomas, Captain, ——.
Fox, Joseph, Captain, ——.
Finlay, Samuel, Surgeon, 7th.
Freeman, D. Thomas, Lieutenant, 7th.
French, Elijah, Ensign, 7th.
Fuller, John, Captain, 4th.
Frost, Samuel, Captain, 6th.
Frye, Frederick, Ensign, 1st.
Floyd, Ebenezer, Ensign, 1st.
Foster, Elisha, Ensign, 1st.
Fisk, Joseph, Surgeon, 1st.
Finley, B. E. James, Surgeon, 5th.
Felt, Jonathan, Captain, 5th.
Fowles, John, Captain, 3d.
Foster, Thomas, Lieutenant, 8th.
Frink, Samuel, Ensign, 8th.

Frothingham, Benjamin, Captain, Crane's Artillery.
Freeman, Constant, Captain-Lieutenant, Crane's Artillery.
Fenno, Ephriam, Captain-Lieutenant, Crane's Artillery.
Ford, Chilion, Lieutenant, Crane's Artillery.
Frisby, Jonah, Lieutenant, Vose's.
Francis, Ebenezer, Colonel, 10th.
Glover, John, Brigadier-General.
Givens, Robert, Lieutenant 7th.
Garret, Andrew, Lieutenant, 6th.
Graves, Asa, Ensign, 6th.
Green, Francis, Captain, 1st.
Goodale, Nathan, Captain, 5th.
Gilbert, Benjamin, Lieutenant, 5th.
Gibbs, Caleb, Major, 2d.
Goodwin, B. L. Francis, Surgeon's-Mate, 3d.
Greenleaf, William, Lieutenant, 3d.
Greaton, H. Richard, Ensign, 3d.
Greaton, W. John, Ensign, 3d.
Green, John, Lieutenant, 8th.
Gridley, John, Captain-Lieutenant, Crane's Artillery.
George, John, Captain-Lieutenant, Crane's Artillery.
Gardner, James, Captain-Lieutenant, Crane's Artillery.
Greaton, John, Brigadier-General.
Graham, G. Isaac, Surgeon's-Mate, Sproat's.
Gage, Isaac, Lieutenant, Greaton's.
Goodrich, Ezekiel, Lieutenant, M. Jackson's.
Gray, Hugh, Lieutenant, Marshall's.
Holden, Aaron, Captain, ——.
Henly, Samuel, Captain, ——.
Holbrook, Nathan, Lieutenant, ——.
Hastings, Walter, Surgeon ——
Haskell, Jonathan, Lieutenant, 7th
Hastings, John, Captain, 7th.
Hill, Jeremiah, Lieutenant, 2d.
Hurd, John, Ensign, 2d.
Hart, John, Surgeon, 2d
Holbrook, David, Captain, 4th.
Hollister, Jesse, Captain, 4th.
Hunt, Ephraim, Lieutenant, 4th.
Hamlin, Africa, Ensign, 4th.
Hull, William, Lieutenant-Colonel, 6th.

Heywood, Benjamin, Captain, 6th.
Holden, Levi, Lieutenant, 6th.
Holden, John, Lieutenant, 6th.
Horton, Elisha, Ensign, 6th.
Howe, S. Richard, Ensign, 6th.
Hooker, Zibeon, Lieutenant, 5th.
Holland, Ivory, Lieutenant, 5th.
Holdridge, John, Lieutenant, 3d.
Hunt, Thomas, Captain, 3d.
Hobby, John, Captain, 3d.
Haskell, Elnathan, Captain, 4th.
Houdin, G. Michael, Captain, 5th.
Holland, Park, Lieutenant, 5th.
Hartshorn, Thomas, Captain, 8th.
Heldreth, William, Lieutenant, 8th.
Hiwell, John, Lieutenant, Crane's Artillery.
Heath, William, Major-General.
Hall, James, Captain-Lieutenant, Crane's Artillery.
Hammond, Abijah, Lieutenant, Crane's Artillery.
Hoey, Benjamin, Lieutenant, ——.
Henley, David, Colonel, ——.
Haines, Aaron, Captain, Wigglesworth's.
Hovey, Dominicus, Lieutenant, Shepherd's.
Jackson, Henry, Colonel, 4th.
Jackson, Simon, Captain, 6th.
Jackson, Michael, Colonel, 8th.
Jackson, Michael, Jr., Lieutenant, 8th.
Jackson, Amasa, Ensign, 8th.
Jackson, Charles, Ensign, 8th.
Jenkins, Joel, Lieutenant, 8th.
Jackson, Ebenezer, Lieutenant, Crane's Artillery.
Jackson, Thomas, Captain, Crane's Artillery.
Johnson, William, Captain-Lieutenant, Crane's Artillery.
Jackson, Daniel, Lieutenant, Crane's Artillery.
Jefferds, Samuel, Lieutenant, Crane's Artillery.
Ingersoll, George, Lieutenant, Crane's Artillery.
Jacobs, George, Lieutenant, Vose's.
Jackson, Jeremiah, Ensign, Shepherd's.
Jones, Solomon, Ensign, Nixon's.
King, Zebulon, Captain, 7th.

Kendry, William, Lieutenant, 7th.
Knapp, Moses, Major, 5th.
Killam, Joseph, Captain, 5th.
Knox, Henry, Major-General.
Kingman, Edward, Ensign, Bailey's.
Littlefield, M. Noah, Lieutenant-Colonel, ——.
Lord, Simeon, Captain, ——.
Lee, Daniel, Captain, ——.
Lunt, James, Lieutenant, ——.
Lovejoy, Obadiah, Lieutenant, ——.
Lincoln, Rufus, Captain, 7th.
Leonard, Jacob, Ensign, 2d.
Lyman, Cornelius, Ensign, 2d.
Learned, Simon, Captain, 4th.
Lilley, Reuben, Lieutenant, 6th.
Lord, Jeremy, Ensign, 6th.
Lunt, Daniel, Captain, 1st.
Leland, Joseph, Lieutenant, 8th.
Lincoln, Benjamin, Major-General.
Lockwood, W., Chaplain, 1st Brigade.
Ligwell, John, Lieutenant, Crane's Artillery.
Lillie, John, Captain and Aide-de-Camp, Crane's Artillery.
Laughton, William, Surgeon's-Mate, 1st.
Marshall, Thomas, Colonel, 10th.
Maynard, Jonathan, Captain, 10th.
Mills, William, Captain, 7th.
Means, James, Captain, 2d.
Merrick, Samuel, Lieutenant, 2d.
Morton, Silas, Lieutenant, 2d.
Moore, William, Captain, 4th.
Miller, Joseph, Lieutenant, 6th.
Miller, Jeremiah, Captain, 1st.
Marshall, Christopher, Captain, 1st.
Mills, John, Captain, 1st.
Marble, Henry, Lieutenant, 5th.
McClay, Daniel, Ensign, 5th.
Mellen, James, Lieutenant-Colonel commandant, 3d.
Maynard, John, Lieutenant and Quartermaster, 3d.
Mellish, Samuel, Lieutenant, 3d.
Maxwell, Hugh, Lieutenant-Colonel, 8th.
McLane, Daniel, Lieutenant, Crane's Artillery.
Mason, David, Lieutenant, Crane's Artillery.

Moore, William, Lieutenant, Crane's Artillery.
Morgan, Benjamin, Lieutenant, Crane's Artillery.
Moores, Benjamin, Lieutenant and Adjutant, Hazen's.
McFarland, Moses, Captain, Invalid.
Maynard, William, Lieutenant, Invalid.
Mayberry, Richard, Captain, Tupper's.
McNeil, Joseph, Captain, Wigglesworth's.
Munroe, Edmund, Captain, Bigelow's.
Nixon, Thomas, Colonel, 6th.
Newell, Ezra, Lieutenant-Colonel, 4th.
Nason, Nathaniel, Lieutenant and Quartermaster, 1st.
Nelson, Henry, Lieutenant and Paymaster, 3d.
North, William, Captain and Aide-de-Camp, 4th.
Nichols, Isaac, Lieutenant, Nixon's.
Noble, Caleb, Lieutenant, Wesson's.
Oliver, Robert, Major, 2d.
Oliver, Alexander, Ensign, 5th.
Paterson, John, Brigadier-General.
Peters, Andrew, Lieutenant-Colonel, ——.
Pike, Benjamin, Captain, ——.
Park, Levi, Lieutenant, ——.
Parker, Benjamin, Lieutenant, Wesson's.
Pilsbury, Daniel, Captain, ——.
Porter, Billy, Major, 7th.
Pratt, Joel, Lieutenant, 4th.
Pettingill, Joseph, Major, 1st.
Pray, John, Captain, 1st.
Parker, Elias, Lieutenant, 1st.
Pierce, Benjamin, Lieutenant, 1st.
Pope, Isaac, Major, 3d.
Phelon, John, Lieutenant, 3d.
Phelon, Patrick, Lieutenant, 3d.
Pritchard, Thomas, Captain, 3d.
Phelon, Edward, Lieutenant, 4th.
Pierce, Silas, Captain, 8th.
Putnam, Rufus, Brigadier-General.
Popkin, John, Lieutenant-Colonel, Crane's Artillery.
Perkins, William, Major, Crane's Artillery.
Pearce, John, Captain-Lieutenant, Crane's Artillery.

Price, William, Lieutenant, Crane's Artillery.
Porter, Moses, Lieutenant, Crane's Artillery.
Pardee, Aaron, Lieutenant, Crane's Artillery.
Pool, Abijah, Lieutenant, Wigglesworth's.
Patrick, William, Captain, Alden's.
Richardson, Abijah, Surgeon, ——.
Reab, George, Lieutenant and Quartermaster, 7th.
Ripley, Hezekiah, Lieutenant, 2d.
Rice, Nathan, Major, 4th.
Rice, Oliver, Lieutenant, 4th.
Richard, William, Lieutenant, 4th.
Rawson, Jeduthan, Ensign, 6th.
Remick, Timothy, Captain, 1st.
Rouse, Oliver, Captain, 8th.
Rowe, John, Ensign, 8th.
Root, Elihu, Ensign, Putnam's.
Richmond, Benjamin, Ensign, 12th.
Reed, Benjamin, Lieutenant, Alden's.
Smith, Calvin, Lieutenant-Colonel Commandant, ——.
Stacey, William, Lieutenant-Colonel, ——.
Spurr, John, Major, ——.
Smith, Josiah, Captain, ——.
Scott, William, Captain, ——.
Stone, Jonathan, Captain, ——.
Stratton, Aaron, Captain, ——.
Shepherd, William, Colonel, ——.
Sturtevant, Isaac, Lieutenant, 7th.
Sampson, Crocker, Lieutenant, 7th.
Scaven, James, Ensign, 7th.
Sawyer, James, Ensign, 7th.
Scott, James, Ensign, 7th.
Sprout, Ebenezer, Lieutenant-Colonel Commandant, 2d.
Sewall, Henry, Captain, 2d.
Selden, Charles, Lieutenant, 4th.
Sprung, Simeon, Lieutenant, 4th.
Shute, Daniel, Surgeon, 4th.
Shepherd, William, Ensign, 4th.
Smith, K. John, Captain, 6th.
Smith, Ebenezer, Captain, 6th.
Smith, Josiah, Lieutenant, 6th.
Scammel, L. Samuel, Ensign, 6th.
Stone, Nathaniel, Lieutenant, 1st.
Smith, Sylvanus, Captain, 5th.
Smith, Joseph, Lieutenant, 2d.

Storer, Ebenezer, Lieutenant, ——.
Savage, Henry, Lieutenant and Adjutant, 3d.
Stafford, R. John, Ensign, 3d.
Sumner, Job, Major, 3d.
Smith, John, Lieutenant, 3d.
Stocker, Ebenezer, Lieutenant, 3d.
Smith, Ebenezer, Captain, 8th.
Storey, William, Captain, 8th.
Stone, Sturgeon, Lieutenant, 8th.
Swan, Caleb, Ensign, 8th.
Shaw, Samuel, Captain and Aide-de-Camp, Crane's Artillery.
Sergeant, Winthrop, Captain and Aide-de-Camp, Crane's Artillery.
Seward, Thomas, Captain, Crane's Artillery.
Sluman, John, Captain, Crane's Artillery.
Stevens, William, Captain, Crane's Artillery.
Satterlee, William, Captain, Hazen's.
Stone, Enos, Captain, Brewer's.
Sawyer, Ephraim, Captain, Henley's.
Stanwood, William, Lieutenant, Tupper's.
Stevens, Ebenezer, Lieutenant, Brewer's.
Sale, John, Lieutenant, Henley's.
Smith, He. John, Lieutenant, Henley's.
Thompson, Joseph, Lieutenant-Colonel, ——.
Taylor, Othniel, Captain, ——.
Thayer, Bartholomew, Lieutenant, ——.
Thompson, Thadeus, Surgeon, ——.
Thacher, James, Surgeon, ——.
Trescott, Lemuel, Major, 7th.
Turner, Thomas, Captain, 7th.
Thorp, Eliphalet, Captain, 7th.
Trowbridge, Luther, Lieutenant, 7th.
Torry, William, Lieutenant, 2d.
Taylor, William, Lieutenant, 2d.
Town, Jacob, Lieutenant, 2d.
Tupper, Benjamin, Colonel, 6th.
Thacher, Nathaniel, Lieutenant, 6th.
Tupper, Anselm, Lieutenant, 6th.
Taylor, Tirteus, Lieutenant, 1st.
Turner, Jonathan, Captain, 5th.
Turner, Malbra, Lieutenant, 5th.
Trotter, John, Captain, 5th.

Tisdale, James, Captain, 3d.
Tucker, Joseph, Lieutenant, 7th.
Tufts, Francis, Lieutenant and Adjutant, 8th.
Thomas, John, Surgeon, 8th.
Townsend, David, Hospital Surgeon.
Treadwell, William, Captain, Crane's Artillery.
Thomas, Joseph, Captain, Crane's Artillery.
Tucker, Abraham, Captain, Vose's.
Tuttle, Samuel, Lieutenant, Greaton's.
Thomas, Samuel, Captain, Tupper's.
Thomas, Phillip, Captain, Marshall's.
Thompson, Benjamin, Lieutenant, Brewer's.
Tubbs, Samuel, Major, Bradford's.
Vose, Joseph, Colonel, 1st.
Vose, Elijah, Lieutenant-Colonel, 1st.
Vose, Thomas, Captain, Crane's Artillery.
Van Horne, David, Captain, Lee's.
Wesson, James, Colonel, ——.
Whiting, Daniel, Lieutenant-Colonel, ——.
Wiley, John, Major, ——.
Winslow, Nathaniel, Major, ——.
Webb, George, Captain, ——.
White, Haffield, Captain, ——.
White, Solomon, Lieutenant, ——.
Wigglesworth, William, Lieutenant, ——.
White, Henry, Lieutenant, ——.
Walker, Edward, Lieutenant, ——.
Willington, Elisha, Lieutenant, ——.
Walker, Robert, Captain, 2d.
Whiting, John, Lieutenant, 2d.
Webber, Daniel, Lieutenant, 2d.
Wells, James, Lieutenant, 4th.
Wattles, Mason, Captain, 6th.
Wales, Joseph, Lieutenant, 6th.
Williams, John, Captain, 1st.
Williams, Ebenezer, Lieutenant, 1st.
Warren, Adriel, Lieutenant, 1st.
Wells, Benjamin, Lieutenant, 1st.
Wilds, Ebenezer, Lieutenant, 1st.
Wardell, Joseph, Ensign, 1st.
Warren, John, Lieutenant, 5th.
Wing, Jonathan, Ensign, 5th.
Whitwell, Samuel, Surgeon, 3d.
Williams, Joseph, Captain, 3d.

Woodbridge, Christopher, Captain, 3d.
Watson, William, Captain, 3d.
Williams, Robert, Lieutenant, 3d.
Wade, Abner, Captain, 8th.
White, Edward, Lieutenant, 8th.
Waterman, Jedediah, Ensign, 8th.
Williams, Abraham, Captain, 2d.
Warren, John, Hospital Surgeon.
White, Moses, Captain, Hazen's.
Wheeler, Adam, Captain, Nixon's.
Watkins, Nathan, Lieutenant, Brewer's.
Wheeler, Nathan, Lieutenant, Nixon's.
Walker, Robert, Lieutenant, Brewer's.
Woolsey, L. Melancthon, Lieutenant, Lee's.
Willington, Thomas, Captain, Wigglesworth's.
Winchester, William, Lieutenant, Wigglesworth's.
Willington, Josiah, Lieutenant, Wigglesworth's.
Welsh, Joseph, Lieutenant, Paterson's.
Walker, Silas, Lieutenant. 15th.
Walcott, Benjamin, Captain, Marshall's.
Wiley, Aldrich, Lieutenant, M. Jackson's.
Walker, Richard, Lieutenant, H. Jackson's.
Walcott, Christopher, Ensign, Marshall's.
Yeomans, John, Lieutenant, 4th.

CONNECTICUT.

Allen, Timothy, Captain, S. B. Webb's.
Avery, Simeon, Lieutenant, Starr's.
Anderson, Thomas, Lieutenant, Starr's.
Allen, Robert, Lieutenant, Starr's.
Adams, David, Surgeon, Durkee's.
Avery, Thomas, Lieutenant, Starr's.
Bradley, P. Phillip, Colonel, ——.
Bernard, John, Captain, Wyllys'.
Bates, David, Captain, Warner's.
Baldwin, Caleb, Captain, Swift's.
Billings, Stephen, Captain, Swift's.
Belding, Simeon, Lieutenant, Wyllys'.
Ball, John, Lieutenant, Meigs'.

Barnam, Eli, Lieutenant, Meigs'.
Beaumont, William, Lieutenant, Chandler's.
Beach, David, Lieutenant, Bradley's.
Butler, Zebulon, Colonel, 1st.
Buell, H. John, Captain, Durkee's.
Benton, Selah, Captain, Chandler's.
Bulkeley, Edward, Captain, Webb's.
Baldwin, Abraham, Chaplain, Webb's.
Beers, Nathan, Lieutenant and Paymaster, Webb's.
Betts, Stephen, Captain, C. Webb's.
Bradley, Daniel, Lieutenant, Bradley's.
Benjamin, Aaron, Lieutenant, Chandler's.
Bushnell, David, Captain, Sappers and Miners.
Bull, Aaron, Lieutenant, Sheldon's.
Bennett, James, Lieutenant, Swift's.
Brunson, Isaac, Surgeon's Mate, Sheldon's.
Berham, Silas, Lieutenant, C. Webb's.
Barber, David, Ensign, Meigs'.
Benedict, Noble, Captain, Bradley's.
Chapman, Albert, Major, Swift's.
Clift, Wells, Major, Wyllys'.
Chipman, John, Captain, Warner's.
Converse, Thomas, Captain, Wyllys'.
Chamberlain, Ephraim, Captain, Wyllys'.
Coleman, Noah, Surgeon, C. Webb's.
Chapman, Joseph, Lieutenant, Warner's.
Clift, Lemuel, Captain, Durkee's.
Cotton, George, Ensign, Wyllys'.
Crosby, Ebenezer, Surgeon, Guards.
Cole, Abner, Ensign, Starr's.
Clarke, Joseph, Ensign, Meigs'.
Comstock, Samuel, Captain, Chandler's.
Chapman, Elijah, Captain, Bradley's.
Colfax, William, Lieutenant, Starr's.
Curtis, Giles, Lieutenant, Meigs'.
Cleveland, John, Ensign, Durkee's.
Cunningham, Henry, Lieutenant, 2d Artillery.
Clarke, James, Lieutenant, Cook's.
Cook, Jesse, Captain, Bradley's.
Durkee, John, Captain, Durkee's.
Denslow, Martin, Lieutenant, Bradley's.

Dimmuck, Benjamin, Lieutenant, C. Webb's.
Deming, Pownal, Lieutenant, Durkee's.
Dorrance, David, Captain, Starr's.
Douglas, Richard, Captain, Starr's.
Dole, James, Lieutenant, Sheldon's.
Deforrest, Samuel, Lieutenant, Bradley's.
Dagget, Henry, Lieutenant, Swift's.
Durkee's, Benjamin, Captain, Wyllys'.
Eells, Edward, Captain, Wyllys'.
Ellis, John, Chaplain, 1st Brigade.
Edwards, Nathaniel, Lieutenant, Bradley's.
Fitch, Andrew, Captain, Durkee's.
Farmer, Thomas, Lieutenant, Meigs'.
Fanning, Charles, Lieutenant and Paymaster, Durkee's.
Frothingham, Ebenezer, Lieutenant and Quartermaster, Webb's.
Fox, Jacob, Lieutenant, Starr's.
Fosdick, U. Thomas, Ensign, C. Webb's.
Grosvenor, Thomas, Lieutenant-Colonel Commandant, Wyllys'.
Grover, Phineas, Lieutenant, Swift's.
Gove, Obadiah, Lieutenant, Wyllys'.
Griswold, Andrew, Lieutenant, Durkee's.
Gregory, Matthew, Lieutenant, Chandler's.
Grant, Benoni, Lieutenant, Warner's.
Goodell, Silas, Lieutenant, Wyllys'.
Goodrich, Ozias, Ensign, Wyllys'.
Gray, Ebenezer, Lieutenant-Colonel, Meigs'.
Gorham, Nehemiah, Lieutenant, Bradley's.
Glenny, William, Lieutenant, Durkee's.
Gibbs, Samuel, Lieutenant, Invalid.
Higgins, Joseph, Surgeon's-Mate, 2d.
Hait, Joseph, Lieutenant-Colonel, Chandler's.
Holdridge, Hezekiah, Lieutenant, Colonel, C. Webb's.
Hall, Stephen, Captain, Swift's.
Hinckley, Ichabod, Captain, C. Webb's.
Humphrey, Elijah, Captain, Meigs'.
Hait, Samuel, Captain, Chandler's.

Hodge, Asahel, Captain, Chandler's.
Hosmer, Timothy, Surgeon, ——.
Heath, Peleg, Lieutenant, ——.
Hyde, James, Lieutenant, ——.
Hosman, Prentice, Lieutenant, ——.
Hubble, Solomon, Lieutenant, ——.
Hall, Philomen, Lieutenant, ——.
Henshaw, William, Lieutenant, ——.
Huntington, Ebenezer, Lieutenant-Colonel, 1st.
Higgins, William, Lieutenant and Quartermaster, 1st.
Hart, Jonathan, Captain, 1st.
Hubbard, Hezekiah, Lieutenant, 1st.
Holt, Silas, Lieutenant, 1st.
Humphreys, David, Lieutenant-Colonel Aide-de-Camp, 1st.
Hopkins, Elisha, Captain, 3d.
Hobart, John, Lieutenant, 3d.
Hait, Samuel, Lieutenant, 3d.
Harman, Jaques, Ensign, 3d.
Hogeland, Jeronimus, Captain, Sheldon's.
Hawley, Gideon, Lieutenant, Sheldon's.
Hart, John, Ensign, 2d.
Huntington, Jedediah, Brigadier-General.
Hubbell, Isaac, Captain-Lieutenant, 2d Artillery.
Hill, Ebenezer, Captain, Invalid.
Hobby, Thomas, Lieutenant-Colonel, Bradley's.
Hull, Joseph, Lieutenant, Artillery.
Harris, John, Lieutenant, C. Webb's.
Hale, Aaron, Lieutenant, Starr's.
Judd, William, Captain, Wyllys'.
Judson, David, Captain, Chandler's.
Jackson, Frederick Thomas, Lieutenant, Sheldon's.
Janes, Elijah, Lieutenant, Sheldon's.
Johnson, Jonathan, Lieutenant-Colonel, Bradley's.
Johnson, Samuel, Major, ——.
Keeler, Thaddeus, Lieutenant, Bradley's.
Knapp, Joshua, Ensign, C. Webb's.
Keeler, Isaac, Lieutenant, C. Webb's.
Kingsbury, Jacob, Ensign, C. Webb's.
Keeler, Aaron, Ensign, Chandler's.
King, Joshua, Lieutenant, Sheldon's.
Kimberly,, Ephraim, Captain, Chandler's.

Kenney, Abraham, Lieutenant, Sheldon's.
Keeler's, Samuel, Captain, Bradley's.
Leavenworth, Eli, Major, Meigs'.
Lay, Asa, Captain, Meigs'.
Lyon, Asa, Lieutenant, Meigs'.
Lord, William, Lieutenant, Meigs'
Loomis, Lebeus, Lieutenant and Adjutant, Durkee's.
Lynn, William, Lieutenant, C. Webb's.
Lyman, Daniel, Major and Aide-de-Camp, C. Webb's.
Lord, James, Lieutenant, Starr's.
Lee, Noah, Captain, Hazen's.
Meigs, J. Return, Colonel, ——.
McGregor, John, Captain, Durkee's.
Moulton, William, Captain, Warner's.
Morris, James, Captain, Bradley's.
Mather, Timothy, Surgeon, Swift's.
Miller, Charles, Lieutenant, Wyllys'.
Meigs, John, Lieutenant and Adjutant, Webb's.
Mix, John, Lieutenant, Wyllys'.
Munson, Theophilus, Captain, Chandler's.
Manifield, John, Lieutenant, Meigs'.
Manson, Eneas, Surgeon's-Mate, Webb's.
Munson, William, Captain, Webb's.
Mix, Timothy, Lieutenant, 2d Artillery.
Norton, Benjamin, Lieutenant, Meigs,.
Noyes, John, Surgeon, Starr's.
Olmstead, James, Lieutenant, Chandler's.
Parsons, H. Samuel, Major-General.
Prior, Abner, Major, Bradley's.
Parsons, David, Captain, C. Webb's.
Pomeroy, Ralph, Lieutenant, Wyllys'.
Perry, Sylvanus, Lieutenant, Wyllys'.
Phelps, Seth, Captain, Durkee's.
Pride, Reuben, Lieutenant, Wyllys'.
Putnam, Israel, Major-General.
Pendleton, Daniel, Captain, Artificers.
Pike, William, Lieutenant, Sheldon's.
Potter, Stephen, Captain, Meigs'.
Pinto, Solomon, Ensign, Meigs'.
Potter, Israel, Lieutenant, Meigs'.
Painter, Elisha, Major, Warner's.
Parrott, Peter, Captain, Artillery.
Rogers, Joseph, Ensign, Swift's.
Robinson, Peter, Captain, Chandler's.

Russell, Cornelius, Lieutenant, Bradley's.
Rice, Nehemiah, Captain, Chandler's.
Riley, John, Captain, Webb's.
Richard, Samuel, Lieutenant, Wyllys'.
Ransom, Elijah, Lieutenant, Durkee's.
Robinson, Elias, Lieutenant, Durkee's.
Reed, Enoch, Captain, Starr's.
Rose, John, Surgeon, Webb's.
Rogers, Jedediah, Captain, Sheldon's
Rhea, Aaron, Lieutenant, Sheldon's.
Richards, William, Captain, Starr's.
Robinson, Jared, Lieutenant, Meigs'.
Starrs, Justus, Surgeon's-Mate, 1st.
Stevens, John, Captain, Hostage.
Starr, Josiah, Colonel, ——.
Sherman, Isaac, Lieutenant-Colonel Commandant, C. Webb's.
Sumner, John, Lieutenant-Colonel, Durkee's.
Stevens, Aaron, Captain, Swift's.
Shumway, John, Captain, Starrs'.
Savage, Abijah, Captain, ——.
Sanford, Samuel, Captain, Chandler's.
Spaulding, Simon, Captain, Chandler's.
Starr, David, Captain, Meigs'.
Sill, Richard, Captain, Chandler's.
Strong, David, Captain, Bradley's.
Skinner, Thomas, Surgeon, Russell's.
Shipman, Benoni, Lieutenant, C. Webb's.
Smith, William, Lieutenant, Meigs'.
Stevens, Ebenezer, Ensign, Warner's.
Starr, Thomas, Lieutenant, Swift's.
Sutliff, Benjamin, Lieutenant, Meigs'.
Smith, Ezra, Lieutenant, Durkee's.
Sill, F. David, Lieutenant-Colonel, Starr's.
Stillwell, Elias, Captain, Wyllys'.
Shaylor, Joseph, Lieutenant, Meigs'.
Sanderson, Reuben, Lieutenant, Starr's.
Seldon, Ezra, Captain, Starr's.
Stanton, William, Captain, Sheldon's.
Sheldon, Elisha, Colonel, 2d. Dragoons.
Seymour, Horace, Lieutenant, 2d Dragoons.
Swift, Heman, Colonel, 2d.
Smith, David, Major, Chandler's.

Sherman, John, Lieutenant, Meigs'.
Smith, Joel, Ensign, Meigs'.
Spencer, David, Lieutenant, Starr's.
Trumbull, Jonathan, Lieutenant-Colonel Aide-de-Camp, Starr's.
Throop, Benjamin, Major, ——.
Tanner, Ebenezer, Lieutenant, Swift's.
Ten Eyck, Henry, Captain, Starr's.
Trowbridge, John, Lieutenant, Meigs'.
Talmage, Benjamin, Major, Sheldon's.
Taylor, Timothy, Captain, 2d.
Tiffany, Isaiah, Lieutenant, Starr's.
Throop, R. John, Lieutenant, 2d. Artillery.
Thompson, Isaiah, Captain-Lieutenant, 2d Artillery.
Tracey, Hezekiah, Lieutenant, Starr's.
Wyllys' Samuel, Colonel, ——.
Walbridge, Amos, Major, C. Webb's.
Woodbridge, Theodore, Major, Swift's.
Warner, Robert, Major, Wyllys'.
Webb, Nathaniel, Captain, Durkee's.
Weed, Thaddeus, Captain, Bradley's.
Woolcutt, Erastus, Captain, C. Webb's.
Williams, W. Samuel, Captain, Webb's.
Watrous, R. John, Surgeon, Wyllys'.
Wilcox, Joseph, Lieutenant, Swift's.
Whiting, H. Nathan, Lieutenant, Swift's.
Wyllys, P. John, Major, Webb's.
Wales, Ebenezer, Lieutenant, Durkee's.
Walmsby, William, Ensign, Wyllys'.
Walker, Joseph, Captain and Brevet-Major, Webb's.
Webb, B. Samuel, Colonel, ——.
Wright, A. Joseph, Major, ——.
Wells, Roger, Captain, Webbs.
Whiting, Joshua, Lieutenant, Chandler's.
Webb, John, Captain, Sheldon's.
Wadsworth, Elijah, Captain, Sheldon's.
Whiting, J. Frederick, Lieutenant, Sheldon's.
White, John, Lieutenant, Meigs'.
Wooster, Thomas, Captain, Webbs's.

RHODE ISLAND.

Allen, William, Captain, 1st.
Angel, Israel, Colonel, 2d.
Arnold, Thomas, Captain, Invalids.
Burlingame, Chandler, Lieutenant, 1st.
Brown, Zephaniah, Captain, 1st.
Barton, William, Colonel, 1st.
Bradford, William, Major, Sherburne's.
Bogart, N. Nicholas, Surgeon's-Mate, 1st.
Dexter, S. John, Major, 1st.
Dexter, S. Daniel, Captain, 1st.
Ennis, William, Lieutenant, 1st.
Flagg, Ebenezer, Major, Green's.
Green, Christopher, Colonel, Green's.
Hughs, Thomas, Captain, 1st.
Holden, John, Captain, 1st.
Humphrey, William, Captain, 1st.
Hubbard, John, Lieutenant, 1st.
Hunter, Robert, Ensign, 1st.
Kerby, Ephraim, Ensign, 1st.
Lewis, Elijah, Captain, Green's.
Macomber, Ebenezer, Captain, Angel's.
Masury, Joseph, Lieutenant, 1st.
Olney, Coggleshall, Major, Angel's.
Olney, Jeremiah, Lieutenant-Colonel commandant, Angel's.
Plumb, William, Chaplain, ——.
Peckham, L. Benjamin, Captain, Angel's.
Pratt, William, Lieutenant, 1st.
Peck, William, Major, ——.
Potter, William, Captain, Angel's.
Rogers, John, Lieutenant, 1st.
Russell, Thomas, Ensign, Sherburne's.
Sayles, David, Captain, Angel's.
Sherburne, Benjamin, Lieutenant, 1st.
Sherman, Henry, Lieutenant, 1st.
Sherburne, Henry, Colonel, ——.
Talbot, Silas, Lieutenant-Colonel, Geen's.
Tenney, Samuel, Surgeon, 1st.
Thayer, Simeon, Major, ——.
Tew, William, Captain, ——.
Turner, Peter, Surgeon, ——.
Ward, Samuel, Lieutenant-Colonel. Green's.
Wheaton, Joseph, Lieutenant, 1st.
Welsh, John, Lieutenant, 1st.
Wallen, Jonathan, Captain, Green's.

NEW YORK.

Aorson, Aaron, Captain, 1st.
Adams, Jonas, Lieutenant, 2d Artillery.
Anspach, Peter, Lieutenant, 2d Artillery.
Armstrong, Edward, Lieutenant, Malcolm's.
Beekman, Jerrick, Lieutenant, Old 2d.
Bruen, Jacobus, Lieutenant-Colonel, 3d.
Bowen, Prentice, Lieutenant, 4th.
Barrett, James, Lieutenant, 4th.
Barr, John, Ensign, ——.
Bevier, D. Phillips, Captain, 5th.
Brindley, Francis, Lieutenant, Livingston's.
Belnap, William, Lieutenant, Livingston's.
Bull, William, Captain, Spencer's.
Bagley, Josiah, Lieutenant, 1st.
Bleeker, Leonard, Captain, 1st.
Bauman, Sebastian, Major, 2d Artillery.
Bliss, T. Thomas, Captain, 2d Artillery.
Brewster, James, Captain-Lieutenant, 2d Artillery.
Brewster, Caleb, Captain-Lieutenant, 2d Artillery.
Bradford, James, Lieutenant, ——.
Burnet, Robert, Lieutenant, ——.
Conine, Philip, Captain-Lieutenant, 3d.
Cook, Samuel, Surgeon, 5th.
Codwise, Christopher, Lieutenant, 2d.
Clinton, James, Brigadier-General.
Cochran, John, Physician General of Army.
Cortlandt, Philip, Colonel, 2d.
Cochran, Robert, Lieutenant-Colonel, 2d.
Colebreath, William, Lieutenant and Quartermaster, 2d.
Connolly, Michael, Lieutenant and Paymaster, ——.
Carpenter, Nehemiah, Ensign, ——.

Clinton, Alexander, Lieutenant, 2d Artillery.

Campbell, George, Physician and Surgeon, General Hospital.

Craigie, Andrew, Apothecary, General Hospital.

Cady, Palmer, Lieutenant, Hazen's.

Cutting, J. B., Apothecary-General, General Hospital.

Dennison, J. George, Lieutenant, 3d.

Davis, John, Major, 4th.

Dunscomb, Edward, Captain, 4th.

Dodge, Henry, Captain-Lieutenant, 5th.

Doughty, John, Captain, 2d Artillery.

Dodge, Samuel, Lieutenant, 2d.

Denniston, Daniel, Lieutenant, 2d.

Dodge, Samuel, Ensign, 2d.

Demter, Henry, Lieutenant, 2d Adtillery.

Draper, George, Surgeon, General Hospital.

Drake, Joshua, Lieutenant, Malcolm's.

Dowe, Alexander, Lieutenant, Malcolm's.

Elsworth, Peter, Captain-Lieutenant, 4th.

English, Samuel, Lieutenant, 5th.

Eliott, John, Surgeon's-Mate, 1st.

Fleming, George, Captain, 2d Artillery.

Freelich, Joseph, Lieutenant, 2d.

Finch, Andrew, Captain, 1st.

French, Abner, Captain, 1st.

Fairlie, James, Lieutenant and Aide-de-Camp, 2d.

Fondy, John, Ensign, 1st.

Furman, John, Lieutenant, 1st.

Fondy, Down, Ensign, 1st.

Fish, Nicholas, Major, 2d.

Fowler, Theodosius, Captain, 2d.

Guion, Isaac, Captain-Lieutenant, 2d Artillery.

Gray, Silas, Captain, 4th.

Gildersleve, Finch, Lieutenant, Spencer's.

Goodwin, Henry, Captain, 5th.

Gansevoort, Peter, Colonel, 3d.

Graham, Charles, Captain, 2d.

Graham, John, Major, 1st.

Gregg, James, Captain, 1st.

Gilbert, Benjamin, Lieutenant, 1st.

Hardenburg, L. John, Lieutenant, 2d.

Hunt, Thomas, Lieutenant, 4th.

Hyat, Abraham, Lieutenant, 4th.

Hanmer, Francis, Lieutenant, 5th.

Hanson, Dirck, Captain, Livingston's.

Hicks, Benjamin, Captain, 1st.

Hardenberg, Abraham, Lieutenant, 1st.

Henin, Benjamin, Ensign, 1st.

Huton, Christopher, Ensign and Adjutant, 2d.

Hamtramck, F. John, Captain, 2d.

Harvey, Elisha, Captain-Lieutenant, 2d Artillery.

Hay, Udney, Lieutenant-Colonel, ——.

Hallet, Jonathan, Captain, 2d.

Hunter, Robert, Lieutenant, Malcolm's.

Johnson, John, Captain, 5th.

Janson, T. Cornelius, Captain, 1st.

Johnston, James, Lieutenant, 2d.

Kirkpatrick, David, Lieutenant, Sappers and Miners.

Ledyard, Isaac, Assistant Purveyor, General Hospital.

Logan, Samuel, Major, 5th.

Leggett, Abraham, Lieutenant, 5th.

Livingston, Abraham, Captain, Livingston's.

Lansing, Garrett, Ensign, 1st.

Lewis, Samuel, Lieutenant, 1st.

Lamb, John, Colonel, 2d Artillery.

Laycroft, George, Lieutenant, 2d Artillery.

Livingston, H. Robert, Lieutenant, 2d Artillery.

Laycraft, William, Lieutenant 2d Artillery.

Livingston, B. Henry, Lieutenant-Colonel, ——.

Lawrence, Jonathan, Lieutenant, Malcolm's.

Marshall, Elihu, Captain, 2d.

Mott, Ebenezer, Lieutenant, 2d.

Monty, Francis, Lieutenant, Livingston's.

Maxwell, Anthony, Lieutenant, Spencer's.

Morrell, Joseph, Ensign, 1st.

Marsh, John, Ensign, 1st.

Magee, Peter, Lieutenant, 1st.

Minnama, Daniel, Surgeon, 2d.

Moodie, Andrew, Captain, 2d Artillery.

Mott, Gershom, Captain, 2d Artillery.

Machin, Thomas, Captain, 2d Artillery.

Miles, John, Captain-Lieutenant, 2d Artillery.

Morris, William, Captain-Lieutenant, 2d Artillery.

McKnight, Charles, Physician and Surgeon, General Hospital.

McDougall, Alexander, Major-General.

McDougall, Stephen, Major and Aide-de-Camp.

Morris, Lewis, Major and Aide-de-Camp.

Malcolm, William, Colonel, Malcolm's.

McArthur, Alexander, Lieutenant, ——.

Neslet, Peter, Captain-Lieutenant, 2d Artillery.

Newkirk, Charles, Captain-Lieutenant, 2d.

Norton, Nathan, Captain, 4th.

Nicholson, C. George, Major, Livingston's.

Neely, Abraham, Captain, Spencer's.

Niven, Daniel, Captain, Engineers.

Platt, Richard, Major, ——.

Provost, Robert, Ensign, 3d.

Parsons, Charles, Captain, 1st.

Pell, T. Samuel, Captain, 2d.

Pawling, Henry, Captain, 2d.

Peters, William, Ensign, 2d.

Pennington, William, Lieutenant, 2d Artillery.

Peck, Hiel, Lieutenant, 2d Artillery.

Pendleton, Solomon, Lieutenant, ——.

Robecheau, James, Captain, Livingston's.

Reed, Thomas, Surgeon, Livingston's.

Ryckman, Wilhelmus, Lieutenant, 1st.

Reed, Jacob, Captain, 2d Artillery.

Reed, John, Lieutenant, 2d Artillery.

Stevens, Ebenezer, Lieutenant-Colonel, 2d Artillery.

Swartwout, Cornelius, Captain-Lieutenant, 2d Artillery.

Strachan, William, Lieutenant, 2d Artillery.

Scudder, William, Lieutenant, 1st.

Salisbury, S. Berent, Captain-Lieutenant, 5th.

Stewart, James, Captain, 5th.

Sandford, John, Captain, Spencer's.

Stagg, John, Lieutenant, Spencer's.

Sweet, Caleb, Surgeon, 1st.

Swartwout, Henry, Lieutenant, 1st.

Snow, Ephraim, Lieutenant, 1st.

Sytez, George, Captain, 1st.

Smith, Israel, Captain, 2d.

Swartwout, Barna, Ensign, ——.

Schuyler, Dirck, Ensign, 2d.

Schuyler, Nicholas, Surgeon, Hazen's.

Smith, Isaac, Lieutenant, 2d Artillery.

Shaw, John, Lieutenant, 2d Artillery.

Smith, John, Lieutenant, 2d Artillery.

Smith, William S., Lieutenant-Colonel and Aide-de-Camp.

Strong, Nathan, Captain, 4th.

Thompson, Alexander, Lieutenant, 2d Artillery.

Tappen, Peter, Lieutenant, 2d Artillery.

Titus, Jonathan, Captain, 4th.

Tuthill, Azariah, Lieutenant, 4th.

Thompson, Andrew, Lieutenant, Spencer's.

Ten Eyck, Abraham, Lieutenant, Spencers.

Taulman, Peter, Captain Sappers and Miners.

Tiebout, Henry, Captain, 1st.

Tenbroock, C. John, Captain, 1st.

Tenbroock, Adam, Ensign, 1st.

Talmage, Samuel, Lieutenant, 2d.

Treat, Malachi, Hospital Surgeon.

Van Rensselaer, N., Captain, 1st.

Van Wolkenberg, Bartholomew, Lieutenant, ——.

Van Bunschoten, Peter, Lieutenant, 4th.

Vachee, T. John, Surgeon, 4th.

Vosberg, J. Peter, Captain, Livingston's.

Van Dycke, John, Captain-Lieutenant, ——, Artillery.

Van Wagenen, Tunis, Lieutenant, 2d.

Van Schaick, Goose, Colonel, 1st.

Van Dycke, Cornelius, Lieutenant-Colonel, 1st.

Van Woert, Henry, Lieutenant and Quartermaster, 1st.

Van Rensselaer, Jeremiah, Lieutenant and Paymaster, 1st.

Van Deburg, Henry, Captain, 2d.

Van Hovenbarach, Rudolph, Lieutenant, 2d.
Van Deburg, Bartholomew, Ensign, 2d.
Van Vechten, Tobias, Lieutenant, 1st.
Woodruff, Kenlock, Surgeon, 3d.
Weisenfelts, Frederick, Lieutenant-Colonel Commandant, 4th.
Willet, Marinus, Lieutenant-Colonel Commandant, 5th.
Welp, Anthony, Captain, Livingston's.
Walker, Benjamin, Lieutenant-Colonel and Aide-de-Camp, 2d.
Wenden, H. Jacob, Lieutenant and Adjutant, 1st.
Wilson, Robert, Ensign, 1st.
Wright, Jacob, Captain, 2d.
Weisenfeldts, F. Charles, Lieutenant, 2d.
Woodruff, Ephraim, Lieutenant, 2d.
Young, Guy, Captain, 1st.
Young, Joseph, Physician and Surgeon, General Hospital.

NEW JERSEY.

Appleton, Abraham, Lieutenant, Battalion.
Anderson, J. Joseph, Captain, 1st.
Anderson, William, Ensign, 1st.
Anderson, James, Lieutenant, Hazen's.
Baldwin, Jesse, Lieutenant, Old 1st.
Baldwin, Daniel, Captain, ——.
Bennett, James, Captain, ——.
Barnett, William, Surgeon, ——.
Bowman, Nathaniel, Major, ——.
Barton, William, Captain, ——.
Burrows, John, Major, Old 2d.
Ballard, Jeremiah, Captain, ——.
Barbour, William, Major, ——.
Buck, Joseph, Lieutenant, Battalion.
Burrowes, Eden, Lieutenant, 1st.
Bonham, Absalom, Lieutenant, ——.
Bishop, John, Ensign, ——.
Brooks, Alamarine, Ensign, 1st.
Blair, John, Lieutenant, ——.
Burnet, William, Physician and Surgeon, General Hospital.
Bloomfield, Joseph, Major, 3d.
Boslick, C. William, Lieutenant, 3d.
Costigan, Lewis, Lieutenant, ——.
Darby, Ephraim, Lieutenant, ——.
Dayton, Jonathan, Captain, 1st.

De Hart, Cyrus, Captain, Battalion.
Dayton, Elias, Brigadier-General.
Day, Aaron, Lieutenant, 3d.
Elmer, Ebenezer, Surgeon, 3d.
Elmer, G. Moses, Mate, 1st.
Edgar, David, Captain, Sheldon's.
Faulker, Peter, Ensign, Battalion.
Forman, Jonathan, Lieutenant-Colonel, 1st.
Ford, Mahlon, Lieutenant, 3d.
Howell, John, Captain, ——.
Hunter, Andrew, Chaplain, ——.
Hendry, Samuel, Captain, Battalion.
Holmes, Jonathan, Captain, Battalion.
Hopper, John, Ensign, Battalion.
Halsey, Luther, Lieutenant, Battalion.
Helmes, William, Captain, 1st.
Holmes, John, Captain, 1st.
Hyre, Jacob, Ensign, ——.
Harris, Jacob, Ensign, 1st.
Heard, James, Captain, Lee's Legion.
Hutchen, John, Lieutenant, 2d.
Kemper, Jacob, Captain-Lieutenant, Crane's Artillery.
Kersey, William, Lieutenant, 1st.
Kenney, Abraham, Lieutenant, Sheldon's.
King, Joseph, Adjutant, 3d.
Lane, Derrick, Captain, ——.
Leonard, Nathaniel, Captain, 1st.
Luce, Francis, Ensign, 1st.
Lloyd, Richard, Captain, Hazen's.
Lindsley, Eleazer, Lieutenant-Colonel, Spencer's.
Lyon, Abraham, Captain, 4th.
Morrison, Isaac, Captain, Old 1st.
Meeker, Uzal, Lieutenant, ——.
McEwen, John, Ensign, ——.
Mead, Giles, Captain, ——.
Mason, John, Chaplain, ——.
Mitchell, Alexander, Captain, 1st.
Martin, Absalom, Captain, Battalion.
Mercer, John, Captain, ——.
Mott, John, Captain, 3d.
Orr, John, Lieutenant, ——.
Osmun, Benjamin, Lieutenant, ——.
Ogden, Mathias, Colonel, 1st.
Ogden, Aaron, Captain, 1st.
Ogden, Barny, Lieutenant, Spencer's.
Ogden, Nathaniel, Quartermaster, Spencer's.
Pemberton, Robert, Captain, Spencer's.

Philips, Jonathan, Captain, Spencer's.
Paul, James, Lieutenant, Spencer's.
Parrott, Silas, Lieutenant, Spencer's.
Piatt, William, Captain, 1st.
Peck, John, Lieutenant, Battalion.
Polhemus, John, Captain, Old 1st.
Read, John, Ensign, ——.
Ross, John, Major, ——.
Reading, Samuel, Major, Battalion.
Reed, John, Lieutenant, 1st.
Rencastle, John, Lieutenant, 1st.
Rhea, Jonathan, Lieutenant, ——.
Reckless, Anthony, Lieutenant Sappers and Miners.
Stout, Abraham, Lieutenant, ——.
Spencer, Oliver, Colonel, Spencer's.
Shreeve, Israel, Colonel, ——.
Shute, William, Ensign, Battalion.
Shute, M. Samuel, Lieutenant, ——.
Seely, Samuel, Lieutenant, 1st.
Sproule, Moses, Ensign, 1st.
Sedam, R. Cornelius, Ensign, 1st.
Stout, T. Wessell, Lieutenant, 1st.
Sears, Peter, Captain-Lieutenant, Artificers.
Snowden, John, Lieutenant, Lee's Legion.
Spencer, Robert, Paymaster, Spencer's
Thomas, D. Edward, Lieutenant, Battalion.
Tuttle, William, Ensign, 1st.
Tunison, Garrett, Surgeon, 2d Artillery.
Wetherby, Benjamin, Captain, 1st.
Weyman, Abel, Captain, ——.
Walker, George, Lieutenant, 1st.
Whitlock, Ephraim, Lieutenant, 1st.
Van Argle, John, Captain, 1st.

PENNSYLVANIA.

Alexander, William, Major, 9th.
Allison, Richard, Surgeon's-Mate, 2d.
Armstrong, John, Lieutenant, 3d.
Allison, Robert, Lieutenant, 3d.
Adams, William, Surgeon, 4th Artillery.
Ashton, Joseph, Captain-Lieutenant, 4th Artillery.
Armstrong, James, Captain, Lee's Legion.
Armstrong, John, Major and Aide-de-Camp.
Armor, James, Lieutenant, Old 4th.

Ashton, John, Lieutenant, 9th.
Bicker, Henry, Colonel, Old 2d.
Binney, Barnabas, Hospital Surgeon.
Butler, Thomas, Captain, Old 3d.
Boyd, John, Captain-Lieutenant, 9th.
Barclay, John, Captain-Lieutenant, 5th.
Benflead, Alexander, Lieutenant, 10th.
Brown, Joseph, Surgeon, 7th.
Butler, William, Lieutenant-Colonel Commandant, 4th.
Burke, Edward, Captain, 1st.
Bush, John, Captain, 5th.
Brady, Samuel, Captain, Old 8th.
Bicker, Henry, Captain, 4th.
Bartholomew, Benjamin, Captain, 5th.
Broadhead, Daniel, Colonel, 1st.
Brown, B. Thomas, Captain, 1st.
Bankson, John, Captain, 1st.
Bonde, Thomas, Captain, 1st.
Butler, Percival, Lieutenant, 1st.
Bevins, Wilder, Lieutenant, 1st.
Blewer, George, Lieutenant, Old 4th.
Bower, Jacob, Captain, 2d.
Bryson, Samuel, Lieutenant, 2d.
Butler, Richard, Colonel, 3d.
Bayard, Stephen, Lieutenant-Colonel, 3d.
Bush, George, Captain, 3d.
Beatty, Erkurius, Lieutenant, 3d.
Ball, W. Blackall, Lieutenant, 3d.
Butler, Edward, Lieutenant, 3d.
Beatty, Reading, Surgeon, 4th Artillery.
Bryce, John, Captain, 4th Artillery.
Banner, Jacob, Captain, German Regiment.
Boyer, Peter, Captain, German Regiment
Bond, Thomas, Purveyor, General Hospital.
Barr, Thomas, Captain -Lieutenant, Crane's Artillery.
Broadhead, Luke, Captain, 6th.
Baxter, William, Ensign, 6th.
Bickham, John, Lieutenant, 9th.
Brown, William, Lieutenant, 9th.
Boyd, Thomas, Lieutenant, 1st.
Banner, Rudolph, Lieutenant-Colonel, 3d ——.
Boyd, William, 2d Lieutenant, Old 12th.
Bush, Lewis, Major, Hartley's.
Broadhead, Daniel, Jr., Lieutenant, 3d.

Chambers, James, Colonel, Old 1st.
Church, Thomas, Major, 4th.
Craig, Samuel, Captain, 1st.
Cobea, John, Captain, 2d.
Carberry, Henry, Captain, 11th.
Craig, Thomas, Colonel, 3d.
Campbell, Thomas, Captain, 4th.
Claypoole, G. Abraham, Captain, 6th.
Coltman, Robert, Captain, 4th Artillery.
Christie, James, Captain, 2d.
Carnahan, James, Captain, 2d.
Collier, Joseph, Lieutenant, 2d.
Christie, John, Captain, 3d.
Clarke, John, Captain, 3d.
Crawford, Edward, Lieutenant, 3d.
Craig, John, Captain, 4th Dragoons.
Craig, Isaac, Major, 4th Artillery.
Crossley, Jesse, Captain-Lieutenant, 4th Artillery.
Cleckner, Christian, Ensign, German Regiment.
Cramer, Jacob, Lieutenant, German Regiment.
Crawford, William, Captain, 5th.
Chambers, Stephen, Captain, 12th.
Connelly, Robert, Captain, 4th.
Cruise, Walter, Captain, 6th.
Campbell, Archibald, Lieutenant, 6th.
Coleman, Nicholas, Lieutenant, 9th.
Cox, William, Captain, 9th.
Caruthers, John, Lieutenant, 12th.
Carmichael, Alexander, Ensign, 11th.
Caldwell, Robert, Captain, 9th.
Cox, Joseph, Lieutenant, 6th.
Caldwell, Andrew, Mate, General Hospital.
Duncan, James, Captain, Hazen's.
Dionne, Germain, Lieutenant, Hazen's.
Dunn, Budd Isaac, Captain and Aide-de-Camp, 3d.
Davis, John, Captain, 5th.
Davidson, James, Surgeon, 5th.
Douglas, Thomas, Captain, 4th Atillery.
Doyle, John, Captain, 1st.
Dunn, M. Abner, Lieutenant, 1st.
Denny, Ebenezer, Lieutenant, 1st.
Dungan, Thomas, Lieutenant, 2d.
Dixon, Sankey, Lieutenant, 2d.
De Marcellin, Anthony, Lieutenant, 2d.
Davis, Lewyllin, Lieutenant, 3d.
Doty, Samuel, Captain-Lieutenant, 4th Artillery.

Doven, Andrew, Lieutenant, 3d.
Davidson, William, Captain, 3d.
Duguid, John, Lieutenant, 3d.
Depuff, Abraham, Captain, Atlee's.
Detrick, Peter, Ensign, 2d.
De Hart, Jacob, Ensign and Aide-de-Camp, 2d.
Dill, James, Lieutenant, Hartley's.
Davis, Joseph, Captain, Patton's.
Darragh, Charles, Lieutenant, 2d.
Davis, Samuel, Lieutenant, 9th.
Darragh, Daniel, Lieutenant, 9th.
Dennis, Daniel, Lieutenant, 10th.
Dean, Samuel, Captain, 11th.
Dow, Alexander, Captain, Artificers.
Edwards, Evan, Major, 4th.
Everly, Michael, Lieutenant, 1st.
Emes, Wortley, Captain, 4th Artillery.
Erwin, James, Lieutenant, 3d.
Erwin, Joseph, Captain, 9th.
Finney, Walter, Captain, 1st.
Fishbourne, Benjamin, Captain and Aide-de-Camp, 1st.
Fullerton, Richard, Lieutenant, 1st.
Finley, John, Captain, 2d.
Finley, L. Joseph, Captain, 3d.
Ferguson, William, Captain, 4th Artillery.
Freeman, Jeremiah, Captain, 4th Artillery.
Fick, David, Captain-Lieutenant, 4th Artillery.
Franks, S. David, Major and Aide-de-Camp, 4th Artillery.
Farmer, Lewis, Lieutenant - Colonel, 12th.
Foster, John, Ensign, 6th.
Fiss, Jacob, Lieutenant, 11th.
Finley, H. John, Lieutenant, 5th.
Forrest, Andrew, Lieutenant, 3d.
Graydon, Alexander, Captain, 3d.
Gibson, James, Captain, Artificers.
Gam, H. James, Lieutenant, 4th Artillery.
Gosner, Peter, Captain, 2d.
Gray, William, Captain, 4th.
Griffith, Levi, Lieutenant, 5th.
Gilchrist, James, Lieutenant, 5th.
Glentworth, James, Lieutenant, 2d.
Grier, James, Major, 3d.
Guthry, George, Lieutenant, 4th Dragoons.

Green, Henry, Lieutenant, 4th Artillery.
Gray, Robert, Captain, 13th.
Gyer, George, Lieutenant, 13th.
Gregg, John, Lieutenant, 13th.
Gorman, Joseph, Ensign, 13th.
Gray, Samuel, Lieutenant, 4th.
Gregg, Robert, Captain, 5th.
Hoge, John, Lieutenant, 6th.
Hand, Edward, Brigadier-General.
Hubley, Adam, Lieutenant-Colonel Commandant, 11th.
Hay, Samuel, Lieutenant-Colonel, 7th.
Hughes, John, Captain-Lieutenant, 1st.
Hick, G. Jacob, Captain-Lieutenant, 10th.
Hughes, John, Lieutenant, 7th.
Hamilton, James, Major, 2d.
Henderson, William, Captain, 4th.
Harper, John, Lieutenant, 5th.
Harmon, Josiah, Lieutenant-Colonel, 1st.
Humphrey, Jacob, Captain, 1st.
Hammond, David, Lieutenant, 1st.
Henley, Henry, Lieutenant, 1st.
Harris, Robert, Surgeon's-Mate, 1st.
Humpton, Richard, Colonel, 2d.
Huston, William, Lieutenant, 2d.
Henderson, Andrew, Lieutenant, 2d.
Herbert, Stewart, Lieutenant, 2d.
Hopkins, David, Captain, 4th Dragoons.
Heard, John, Captain, 4th Dragoons.
Hallet, Jonah, Lieutenant, 4th Dragoons.
Howell, Ezekiel, Lieutenant, 4th Artillery.
Humphreys, John, Lieutenant, 4th Artillery.
Hubley, Bernard, Captain, German Regiment.
Helm, John, Captain, 5th.
Hopes, Robert, Captain, Hartley's.
Huston, Alexander, Lieutenant, Patton's.
Hulings, John, Major, 3d.
Hughes, Greenberry, Lieutenant, 6th.
Henderson, Matthew, Captain, 9th.
Harris, John, Captain, 11th.
Hooper, Robert, Lieutenant, 10th.
Johnson, Francis, Colonel, 5th.
Irwine, William, Chaplain, 2d.

Jones, James, Surgeon, 3d.
Jackson, Jeremiah, Chaplain, 3d.
Johnson, Andrew, Lieutenant, 1st.
Irvine, Andrew, Chaplain, 1st.
Jones, Morris James, Lieutenant, ——.
Irvine, William, Brigadier-General.
Irvine, Matthew, Surgeon, Lee's Legion.
Jones, David, Chaplain, — —Line.
Johnson, Robert, Physician and Surgeon, General Hospital.
Janney, Thomas, Lieutenant, Old 5th.
Jenkins, George, Captain, 2d.
Johnson, William, Ensign, 13th.
Jolly, Mayberry, Captain, 11th.
Jones, Peter, Lieutenant, 11th.
Jordan, John, Captain, Artificers.
Kennedy, Samuel, Captain, 2d.
Keene, Lawrence, Captain and Aide-de-Camp, 2d.
Kenny, Samuel, Lieutenant, 13th.
Knox, William, Lieutenant, 10th.
Keller, Adam, Lieutenant, 10th.
Knox, Matthew, Lieutenant, 3d.
Lee, Andrew, Lieutenant, Hazen's.
Lambert, Emanuel Joseph, Lieutenant, 4th.
Lusk, William, Captain, 2d.
Lodge, Benjamin, Lieutenant, 1st.
Le Roy, George, Lieutenant, 2d.
Lyttle, Andrew, Lieutenant, 3d.
Lloyd, James, Captain-Lieutenant, 4th Artillery.
Ladley, Andrew, Surgeon, 12th.
Lewis, John, Lieutenant, 4th.
Lewis, Abraham, Lieutenant, 4th.
Lowerswyler, Thomas, Ensign, 9th.
Lamar, Marian, Major, 4th.
Lucas, Thomas, Lieutenant, 11th.
Lomon, James, Lieutenant, Hartley's.
Macpherson, William, Major, ——.
MacGowan, John, Captain, Invalid.
McConnell, Matthew, Captain, Invalid.
McEllhatton, William, Captain-Lieutenant, Invalid.
McLean, James, Lieutenant, Invalid.
Maus, Matthew, Surgeon, Invalid.
Magaw, Robert, Colonel, 6th.
Murray, John, Lieutenant-Colonel, 2d.
Miller, William, Captain, 7th.
Mackay, William, Captain, 11th.
Martin, Hugh, Surgeon, 8th.

McClure, James, Captain, 4th Artillery.

Martin, Williams, Captain, 4th Artillery.

McGuire, Matthew, Captain-Lieutenant, 4th Artillery.

Marshall, David, Lieutenant, 4th Artillery.

Moore, William, Lieutenant, ——.

Moore, James, Major, 1st.

McFarlane, James, Lieutenant, 1st.

McPherson, F. James, Lieutenant, 1st.

Mulligan, James, Lieutenant, 1st.

Mcullam, John, Lieutenant, 1st.

McDowell, John, Surgeon, 1st.

Montgomery, Samuel, Captain, 3d.

McCully, George, Captain, 3d.

McMichael, James, Lieutenant, 3d.

McKinney, John, Lieutenant, 3d.

McKnight, David, Lieutenat, 3d.

Moylan, Stephen, Colonel, 4th Dragoons.

McCalla, Thomas Surgeon, 4th Dragoons.

McConnell, Robert, Captain-Lieutenant, 4th Artillery.

Morrison, James, Ensign, 8th.

McCoskey, Alexander, Surgeon, Artificers.

Manning, Lawrence, Lieutenant, Lee's Legion.

Miller, John, Captain, 5th.

McIntire, Thomas, Captain, 5th.

Marshall, Benjamin, Lieutenant, ——.

Morrison, Samuel, Lieutenant, 11th.

Mentges, Francis, Lieutenant-Colonel, 5th.

Moore, L. Thomas, Major, 3d.

McClellan, John, Captain, 1st.

Marshall, John, Captain, 3d.

McDowell, William, Lieutenant, 2d.

Mahon, John, Lieutenant, 2d.

Muvren, William, Lieutenant, 2d.

Martin, Robert, Lieutenant, 2d.

Magaw, William, Surgeon, ——.

Murray, Francis, Major, 13th.

Morris, Abel, Lieutenant, 2d.

Moore, Samuel, Captain, 3d.

Miller, Nicholas, Captain, 12th.

Mouser, Jacob, Captain, 6th.

McCowen, John, Captain, 6th.

Morgan, Enoch, Paymaster, 6th.

Morgan, Mordecai, Lieutenant, 9th.

McBride, Robert, Lieutenant, 9th.

Mackay, James, Lieutenant, 11th.

McHenry, Charles, Captain, 5th.

McClintock, Alexander, Lieutenant, 5th.

McGee, William, Ensign, 5th.

Morris, Benjamin, Ensign, 5th.

Martin, Peter, Lieutenant, 11th.

McKissack, William, Captain, 1st.

Morgan, John, Captain, 5th.

Mettinger, Jacob, Lieutenant, Vonheers.

Nichola, Lewis, Colonel, Invalid.

Nice, John, Captain, 2d.

North, Caleb, Lieutenant-Colonel, 2d.

North, George, Lieutenant, 5th.

Nagle, George, Colonel, 10th.

Neely, Benjamin, Lieutenant, 8th.

Prye, Thomas, Captain, Hazen's.

Peaseley, Zacheus, Lieutenant, Hazen's.

Pugh, Jonathan, Lieutenant, Invalid.

Paulient, Antoine, Captain, Hazen's.

Parr, James, Major, 7th.

Patterson, John, Captain, 2d.

Pierson, Johnson, Captain, 2d.

Patton, Robert, Captain, 2d.

Proctor, Francis, Major, 4th Artillery.

Power, William, Captain, 4th Artillery.

Parker, Alexander, Captain, 2d.

Piercey, Henry, Lieutenant, 2d.

Pursell, D. Henry, Lieutenant, 2d.

Pettigrew, James, Lieutenant, 2d.

Pratt, John, Lieutenant, 3d.

Peebles, Robert, Lieutenant, 3d.

Paterson, Gabriel, Lieutenant, 3d.

Pike, Zebulon, Captain, 4th Dragoons.

Porter, Andrew, Lieutenant-Colonel Commandant, 4th Artillery.

Parker, Robert, Captain, 4th Artillery.

Patton, Robert, Captain, 10th.

Peres, Peter, Surgeon, German Regiment.

Patterson, Alexander, Captain, 12th.

Potts, Joseph, Captain, 12th.

Priestly, John, Captain, 5th.

Phile, Charles, Captain, 5th.

Quinn, Samuel, Lieutenant, 12th.

Rose, John, Lieutenant and Aide-de-Camp, 2d.

Reed, R. James, Major, Hazen's.

Riely, John, Captain, Invalid.

Rogers, B. R. John, Surgeon, ——.
Reeves, Enos, Lieutenant, 1st.
Reed, Samuel, Lieutenant, 1st.
Robinson, Thomas, Lieutenant-Colonel, 2d.
Robbins, John, Lieutenant, 4th Artillery.
Reed, Archibald, Lieutenant, 8th.
Rice, William, Captain, German Regiment.
Robinson ,Andrew, Lieutenant, 11th.
Robb, John, Captain, 13th.
Ramsay, Alexander, Lieutenant, 4th.
Rudolph, John, Lieutenant, 5th.
Richardson, John, Captain, 5th.
Stewart, William, Lieutenant, Hazen's.
Sproat, William, Captain and Aide-de-Camp, ——.
Stewart, Christopher, Lieutenant-Colonel, 5th.
Simpson, Michael, Captain, 1st.
Sample, Robert, Captain, 10th.
Stoy, John, Captain-Lieutenant, 2d.
Stewart, Walter, Colonel, 2d.
Steel, John, Captain, 1st.
Stephenson, Stephen, Captain, 2d.
Smith, Samuel, Captain, 5th.
Stotesbury, John, Captain, 6th.
Smith, Peter, Lieutenant, 5th.
Stewart, Alexander, Surgeon, 3d.
Seely, Isaac, Captain, 2d.
Stucker, John, Lieutenant, 2d.
Spear, Edward, Lieutenant, 2d.
Stake, Jacob, Captain, 3d.
Smith, Nathaniel, Lieutenant, 3d.
St. Clair, Daniel, Lieutenant, 3d.
Sullivan, John, Lieutenant, 4th Dragoons.
Simonds, Jonas, Captain, 4th Artillery.
Smith, James, Captain-Lieutenant, 4th Artillery.
Stricker, John, Captain-Lieutenant, 4th Artillery.
Shrauder, Philip, Captain-Lieutenant, German Regiment.
St. Clair, Arthur, Major-General.
Smith, Hooker W., Surgeon's-Mate, General Hospital.
Saple, A. John, Surgeon's-Mate, General Hospital.
Stevenson, George, Surgeon's-Mate, General Hospital.

Scott, Matthew, Captain, 13th.
Staddle, Christian, Captain, 2d.
Skolfield, William, Lieutenant, 5th.
Savage, John, Captain, 6th.
Snyder, Philip, Ensign, 6th.
Shraik, David, Captain, 10th.
Stow, Lazarus, Lieutenant, 11th.
Smith, Samuel, Lieutenant, 8th.
Stayner, Roger, Captain, 2d.
Standley, William, Lieutenant, 5th.
Tilghman, Tench, Lieutenant-Colonel and Aide-de-Camp.
Talbot, Jeremiah, Major, 6th.
Tudor, George, Major, 4th.
Talbert, Samuel, Captain, 2d.
Tilden, B. John, Lieutenant, 2d.
Thornbury, Francis, Lieutenant, 3d.
Thompson, Joseph, Surgeon-s-Mate, 4th Dragoons.
Turnbull, Charles, Captain, 4th Artillery.
Thompson, William, Lieutenant, 9th.
Taylor, Christopher, Surgeon's-Mate, Invalid.
Tolbert, Jacob, Lieutenant, 10th.
Van Horne, Isaac, Captain, 6th.
Vernon, Job, Captain, 5th.
Van Lear, William, Captain, 5th.
Vernon, Frederick, Major, 2d.
Vancourt, John, Lieutenant, 4th Artillery.
Van Pelt, John, Lieutenant, 13th.
Vonheer, Bartholomew, Captain Vonheer's.
Walbran, Major, Lieutenant, 2d.
Woodside, W. John, Lieutenant, 3d.
Wilson, Goodwin, Surgeon, General Hospital.
Woelper, D. John, Captain, Invalid.
Wayne, Anthony, Brigadier-General.
Wilson, James, Captain, 1st.
Wigton, John, Lieutenant, 3d.
Weaver, Jacob, Captain, 10th.
Wilson, Wm. Captain, 1st.
Weitzel, Jacob, Lieutenant, 1st.
White, Francis, Lieutenant, 1st.
Wilkin, Robert, Captain, 2d.
Ward, John, Lieutenant, 2d.
Walker, Andrew, Captain, 3d.
Wilkins, John, Surgeon's-Mate, 3d.

Webster, B. John, Captain-Lieutenant, 4th Artillery.

Weidman, John, 1st Lieutenant, German Regiment.

Weidman, John, 2d Lieutenant, German Regiment.

Woodruff, Aaron, Surgeon's-Mate, 12th.

Williams, Joshua, Captain, 4th.

Waugh, James, Captain, 6th.

Young, Marcus, Lieutenant, German Regiment.

Ziegler, David, Captain, 1st.

DELAWARE.

Anderson, Thomas, Lieutenant.

Bennett, Pree Caleb, Lieutenant.

Campbell, James, Lieutenant.

Cox, Powell Daniel, Captain.

Driskill, Joseph, Lieutenant, Crane's Artillery.

Duff, Henry, Captain.

Gilder, Reuben, Surgeon.

Hosman, Joseph, Lieutenant.

Hall, David, Colonel.

Hyatt, Vance John, Lieutenant.

Haslett, John, Colonel.

Holland, Thomas, Captain.

Jacquett, Peter, Captain.

Kirkwood, Robert, Captain.

Kidd, Charles, Lieutenant.

Leavenworth, John, Captain.

Latimer, Henry, Surgeon.

McLean, Allen, Captain, Lee's.

McKennan, William, Captain.

Moore, James, Captain.

McWilliams, Stephen, Lieutenant.

Mitchel, Nathaniel, Major, Gist's.

Popham, William, Captain, Hazen's.

Patten, John, Major.

Platt, John, Lieutenant.

Purvis, George, Captain.

Roche, Edward, Lieutenant.

Shillington, Elijah, Lieutenant.

Tilton, James, Hospital Surgeon.

Vaughan, Joseph, Lieutenant-Colonel.

Vaughan, John, Lieutenant.

Wilson, John, Captain.

MARYLAND.

Adams, William, Lieutenant, Maryland Infantry.

Adams, Peter, Lieutenant-Colonel Commandant, Infantry.

Anderson, Richard, Captain, Infantry.

Brice, Jacob, Captain, Infantry.

Baker, Henry, Lieutenant, Infantry.

Benham, Malakiah, Lieutenant, Infantry.

Brevitt, John, Lieutenant, Infantry.

Belt, Sprigg John, Captain, Infantry.

Burgess, Joshua, Lieutenant, Infantry.

Burgess, Bazil, Lieutenant, Infantry.

Britton, Joseph, Lieutenant, Infantry.

Boyer, Michael, Captain, Infantry.

Batzell, Charles, Captain, Infantry.

Bruce, William, Captain, Infantry.

Baldwin, Henry, Lieutenant, Infantry.

Brookes, Benjamin, Major, Infantry.

Beatty, Thomas, Lieutenant, Infantry.

Brown, William, Major, Artillery.

Baynes, James, Lieutenant, Artillery.

Beall, Lloyd, Captain, Infantry.

Beall, B. Samuel, Lieutenant, Infantry.

Bealenent, William, Major, Infantry.

Boyd, Thomas, Lieutenant, Infantry.

Bruff, James, Captain, Infantry.

Benson, Perry, Captain, Infantry.

Carlisle, John, Captain, Hazen's.

Crawford, Jacob, Lieutenant, Infantry.

Clements, Henry, Lieutenant, Infantry.

Cross, Joseph, Lieutenant, Infantry.

Compton, Edmund, Lieutenant, Infantry.

Chapman, H. Henry, Lieutenant, Infantry.

Cavy, D. John, Lieutenant, Infantry.

Chever, John, Lieutenant, Artillery.

Dorsey, Richard, Captain, Artillery.

Davidson, John, Major, Artillery.

Dyer, Walter, Lieutenant, Infantry.

Dyson, A. Thomas, Lieutenant, Infantry.

Denwood, Levin, Surgeon, Infantry.

Davis, Rezin, Captain, Infantry.

Dyer, Edward, Captain, Infantry.

Denny, Robert, Lieutenant, ——.

Edmiston, Samuel, Surgeon, Hospital.

Edmiston, Samuel, Lieutenant, Infantry.

Ewing, James, Captain, Infantry.

Eccleston, John, Major, Infantry.

Evans, Elijah, Captain, Infantry.

Finley, Ebenezer, Lieutenant, Artillery.
Fickle, Benjamin, Lieutenant, Infantry.
Foard, Hezekiah, Lieutenant, Infantry.
Forrest, Uriah, Lieutenant-Colonel, Infantry.
Giles, Aquila, Major and Aide-de-Camp, Infantry.
Gassaway, Henry, Lieutenant, Infantry.
Goldsborough, William, Lieutenant, Infantry.
Gassaway, John, Captain, Infantry.
Gunby, John, Colonel, Infantry.
Gaither, Henry, Captain, Infantry.
Gale, John, Captain, Infantry.
Gray, Woolford James, Captain, Infantry.
Gist, John, Captain, Infantry.
Grameth, Jacob, Lieutenant, Infantry.
Gassaway, Nicholas, Lieutenant, Infantry.
Gist, Mordecai, Brigadier-General.
Gibson, Jonathan, Captain, Infantry.
Hamilton, George, Captain, Infantry.
Hanson, Samuel, Lieutenant, Infantry.
Hamilton, A. John, Captain, Infantry.
Hill, Philip, Lieutenant, ——.
Harris, Arthur, Lieutenant, Infantry.
Howard, E. John, Colonel, Infantry.
Halkerston, Robert, Lieutenant, Infantry.
Hamilton, Edward, Lieutenant, Infantry.
Hanson, William, Lieutenant, Infantry.
Hartshorn, John, Lieutenant, Infantry.
Hanie, Ezeziel, Surgeon, ——.
Hoops, Adam, Captain, ——.
Hugoei, Thomas, Captain, Infantry.
Hawkins, Henry, Lieutenant, Infantry.
Hall, Carvel Josias, Colonel, Infantry.
Hamilton, John, Lieutenant, Infantry.
Hardman, Henry, Major, Infantry.
Handy, George, Captain, Lee's Legion.
Hanson, Isaac, Lieutenant, Infantry.
Hardman, John, Captain, Infantry.
Jones, C. John, Captain, Infantry.
Jamieson, Adam, Lieutenant, Infantry.
Jennison, Daniel, Hospital Surgeon.
Kilty, William, Surgeon.

Keene, Y. Samuel, Mate.
Lansdale, Thomas, Major, Infantry.
Luckett, H. Thomas, Major, Infantry.
Laman, William, Captain, Infantry.
Luckett, David, Lieutenant, Infantry.
Lingam, M. James, Captain, Infantry.
Lynn, David, Captain, Infantry.
Lynch, John, Major, Infantry.
Lowe, T. John, Lieutenant, Infantry.
Lynn, John, Lieutenant, Infantry.
McPherson, Samuel, Captain, Infantry.
Myers, Christian, Captain, Infantry.
McPherson, Mark, Lieutenant, Infantry.
Myers, Lawrence, Lieutenant, Infantry.
Mason, Thomas, Captain, Infantry.
Morris, Jonathan, Captain, Infantry.
Mitchell, John, Captain, Infantry.
McPhadon, James, Lieutenant, Artillery.
Morgan, David, Lieutenant, Infantry.
Muse, Walker, Captain, Infantry.
McCoy, John, Lieutenant, Infantry.
Marberry, Joseph, Captain, Infantry.
McHenry, James, Major, ——.
Norris, Jacob, Lieutenant, Infantry.
Oldham, Edward, Captain, Infantry.
Pendergast, William, Lieutenant, Infantry.
Price, Thomas, Jr., Lieutenant, Infantry.
Price, Benjamin, Captain, Infantry.
Pindell, Richard, Surgeon, ——.
Prall, Edward, Captain, Infantry.
Revely, Francis, Captain, Infantry.
Roxburg, Alexander, Major, Infantry.
Rutledge, Joshua, Lieutenant, Infantry.
Razin, William, Lieutenant, Infantry.
Reiley, William, Captain, Infantry.
Raybold, Jacob, Lieutenant, Infantry.
Ramsay, Nathiel, Colonel, Infantry.
Reed, Philip, Captain, Infantry.
Ricketts, Nicholas, Lieutenant, Infantry.
Rawlings, Isaac, Lieutenant, Infantry.
Rowse, Thomas, Lieutenant, Infantry.
Richmond, Christopher, Captain, Infantry.
Rudolph, Michael, Captain, Lee's Legion.

Smith, M. Edward, Lieutenant, Infantry.
Smith, Joseph, Captain, Infantry.
Smith, Alexander, Mate, Infantry.
Spurrier, Edward, Captain, Infantry.
Sears, John, Lieutenant, Infantry.
Sillman, Jonathan, Jr., Major, Infantry.
Smith, John, Captain, Infantry.
Somerville, James, Captain, Infantry.
Smoot, William, Lieutenant, Infantry.
Smith, John, Captain, Infantry.
Smith, James, Captain, Artillery.
Sherrett, Clement, Lieutenant, Artillery.
Stoddard, T. William, Lieutenant, Infantry.
Shugart, Martin, Lieutenant, Infantry.
Smallwood, William, Major-General.
Trueman, Alexander, Captain, Infantry.
Tannehill, Adamson, Captain, Infantry.
Tillard, Edward, Lieutenant-Colonel, Infantry.
Towson, William, Lieutenant, Infantry.
Tillotson, Thomas, Physician and Surgeon, General Hospital.
Trueman, John, Lieutenant, Infantry.
Williams, H. Otho, Brigadier-General.
Watkins, Gassaway, Captain, Infantry.
Ware, Francis, Lieutenant, Infantry.
Wright, Nathan, Lieutenant, Infantry.
Winchester, James, Captain, Infantry.
Weltner, Ludwick, Colonel, German Regiment.
Waring, Bazil, Lieutenant, Infantry.
Williams, Lyburn, Captain, Infantry.
Waters, Richard, Captain, Infantry.
Woolford, Thomas, Colonel, Infantry.
Warfield, Walter, Surgeon, Infantry.
Winchester, George, Lieutenant, ——.
Wilkinson, Young, Lieutenant, Infantry.
Wilmot, Robert, Lieutenant, ——.
Winder, Levin, Lieutenant-Colonel, Infantry.

VIRGINIA.

Ashby, Benjamin, Lieutenant, 3d.
Allen, David, Lieutenant, 7th.
Anderson, John, Captain, 3d.
Archer, F. Peter, Lieutenant, 2d.
Archer, Richard, Ensign, 3d.
Anderson, C. Richard, Lieutenant-Colonel, 3d.

Ball, Daniel, Lieutenant, 8th.
Ball, Thomas, Captain, Infantry.
Barrett, William, Captain, 3d Dragoons.
Baskerville, Lieutenant, 6th.
Biggs, Benjamin, Captain, 7th.
Bruin, Peter, Major, ——.
Brackenridge, Robert, Lieutenant and Adjutant, Posey's.
Bedinger, Daniel, Ensign, Posey's.
Barbee, Thomas, Captain, 6th.
Bowne, Thomas, Captain, 6th.
Burwell, Nathan, Captain, Artillery.
Bradford, K. Samuel, Captain-Lieutenant, Artillery.
Bell, Henry, Lieutenant, 3d Dragoons.
Bowyer, Henry, Lieutenant, 1st Dragoons.
Belfield, John, Major, 1st Dragoons.
Butler, Lawrence, Captain, 4th.
Booker, Samuel, Captain, 4th.
Ball, Burgess, Lieutenant-Colonel Commandant, 4th.
Beale, Robert, Captain, 4th.
Blackwell, John, Captain, 4th.
Blackwell, Joseph, Captain, 6th.
Baylis, Henry, Ensign, Infantry.
Bradford, Charles, Lieutenant, Infantry.
Bentley, William, Captain, Infantry.
Beck, John, Lieutenant, 7th.
Brook, Francis T., Lieutenant, Artillery.
Brooke, John T., Lieutenant, Artillery.
Booker, Lewis, Captain-Lieutenant, Artillery.
Bedinger, Henry, Captain, 3d.
Buford, Abraham, Colonel, 3d.
Bohanner, Ambrose, Captain-Lieutenant, Artillery.
Baldwin, Cornelius, Surgeon, ——.
Bowyer, Thomas, Captain, 8th.
Buckner, Thomas, Captain, 8th.
Bowen, John, Lieutenant, 8th.
Brown, R. Jacob, Lieutenant, 5th.
Bowyer, Michael, Captain, ——.
Baylor, George, Colonel 3d Dragoons.
Brackenridge, Alexander, Captain, ——.
Craike, James, Physician-General, General Hospital.
Croghan, William, Major, 4th.
Carnes, Patrick, Captain, Lee's Legion.
Cruite, John, Lieutenant, 4th.
Campbell, Archibald, Lieutenant, 4th

Coleman, Jacob, Lieutenant, 7th.
Conway, Joseph, Lieutenant, Posey's.
Cannon, Luke, Lieutenant, Posey's.
Craddock, Robert, Lieutenant, Posey's.
Curry, James, Captain, 4th.
Coleman, Whitehead, Captain, Artillery.
Chrystie, Thomas, Surgeon, 1st.
Crittenden, John, Captain-Lieutenant, 1st.
Clay, Matthew, Lieutenant, 5th.
Cowherd, Francis, Captain, 2d.
Clayton, Philip, Lieutenant, 7th.
Carter, Champe John, Captain, Artillery.
Crawford, John, Lieutenant, 2d.
Coverly, Thomas, Lieutenant, 5th.
Carrington, Clement, Ensign, Lee's Legion.
Carrington, Mayo, Captain, 6th.
Clark, Edmund, Lieutenant, 6th.
Clark, Jonathan, Lieutenant-Colonel, 8th.
Cocke, Colon, Captain, 2d.
Carrington, Edward, Lieutenant-Colonel, Artillery.
Cabell, J. Samuel, Lieutenant-Colonel, 7th.
Clement, Mace, Surgeon, ——.
Call, Richard, Major, 3d Dragoons.
Crockett, Joseph, Major, ——.
Delaplaine, James, Lieutenant, 2d.
Dade, Francis, Lieutenant, 3d.
Dawson, Henry, Lieutenant, 7th.
Davis, Joseph, Surgeon, Infantry.
Darby, Nathaniel, Lieutenant, Posey's.
Dandridge, John, Captain, Artillery.
Drew, John, Lieutenant, Artillery.
Dix, Thomas, Captain-Lieutenant, Artillery.
Darke, William, Lieutenant-Colonel Commandant, ——.
Davies, William, Colonel, 1st.
Eskridge, William, Lieutenant, 2d.
Eggleston, Joseph, Major, Lee's Legion.
Epps, William, Captain-Lieutenant, Lee's Legion.
Eastin, Philip, Lieutenant, 4th.
Edmund, Thomas, Captain, 3d.
Evans, William, Lieutenant, 6th.
Eddins, Samuel, Captain, Atillery.
Eustace, Ensign, 3d.
Edwards, Le Roy, Captain, 3d.

Erskine, Charles, Lieutenant, 1st Dragoons.
Fitzgerald, John, Captain, 4th.
Field, Reuben, Captain, 4th.
Finley, Samuel, Major, Posey's.
Foster, H. John, Ensign, Posey's.
Fitzhugh, William, Cornet, 3d Dragoons.
Febiger, Christian, Colonel, 2d.
Fox, Thomas, Captain, 6th.
Fenn, Thomas, Captain-Lieutenant, Artillery.
Fitzhugh, Peregrine, Captain, 3d Dragoons.
Gill Erasmus, Captain, 4th Dragoons.
Gates, Horatio, Major-General.
Gibson, John, Ensign, 7th.
Gibson, John, Colonel, 7th.
Gamble, Robert, Captain, 8th.
Glasscock, Thomas, Lieutenant, 1st Dragoons.
Gaines, Fleming William, Captain-Lieutenant, Artillery.
Gist, Nathaniel, Colonel, Artillery.
Gray, William, Lieutenant, 1st Dragoons.
Green, John, Colonel, 6th.
Green, Robert, Lieutenant, 6th.
Green, Gabriel, Lieutenant, 6th.
Gaskin, Thomas, Lieutenant-Colonel, 3d.
Gray, Francis, Lieutenant, 6th.
Gilchrist, George, Major, 6th.
Gillison, John, Captain, 6th.
Gordon, Ambrose, Lieutenant, 3d Dragoons.
Garnett, Benjamin, Lieutenant, 3d Dragoons.
Gunn, James, Captain, 1st Dragoons.
Garland, Peter, Captain, 6th.
Harrison, Lawrence, Lieutenant, 7th.
Hughes, Jasper, Cornet, 1st Dragoons.
Hughes, Henry, Ensign, ——.
Harrison, John, Lieutenant, 7th.
Holmes, David, Surgeon, 2d.
Higgins, Peter, Lieutenant, ——.
Holt, Thomas, Captain, 1st.
Hite, George, Lieutenant, 3d Oragoons.
Hackley, John, Lieutenant, 6th.
Heth Henry, Captain, ——.
Hopkins, Samuel, Lieutenant-Colonel, 1st.
Hite, Isaac, Lieutenant, 8th.

Holmer, Christian, Major, Artillery.
Hill, Thomas, Major, Artillery.
Hughes, John, Captain, 1st Dragoons.
Holt, James, Lieutenant, 4th.
Harrison, B. William, Ensign, Lee's Legion.
Heth, William, Colonel, ——.
Hays, John, Major, ——.
Hamilton, James, Lieutenant, 6th.
Hite, Abraham, Captain, 8th.
Hogg, Samuel, Captain, 1st.
Hord, Thomas, Captain, 6th.
Harris, Jordan, Ensign, Infantry.
Hopkins, David, Major, 1st Dragoons.
Harris, John, Lieutenant, 1st Dragoons.
Heth, John, Lieutenant, 2d.
Hawes, Samuel, Lieutenant-Colonel, 6th.
Harrison, Charles, Colonel, Artillery.
Johnston, B. John, Captain, 1st.
Jones, Churchill, Captain, 3d Dragoons.
Jones, Albridgton, Lieutenant, 4th.
Jones, Charles, Lieutenant, 6th.
Johnston, Peter, Lieutenant, Lee's Legion.
Joynes, Levin, Lieutenant-Colonel Commandant, ——.
Jodan, John, Captain, 2d.
Johnston, William, Captain, 2d.
Jameson, John, Lieutenant-Colonel, ——.
King, Elisha, Lieutenant, 3d Dragoons.
Kendall, Custes, Captain, 5th.
Kirkpatrick, Abraham, Captain, 4th.
Kiltey, John, Captain, 3d Dragoons.
Kirk, Robert, Lieutenant, 1st.
Kays, Robert, Lieutenant, 4th.
Lapsley, Samuel, Captain, Infantry.
Lewis, William, Major, 3d.
Lovell, James, Cornet, Dragoons.
Langham, Elias, Lieutenant, Artillery.
Lovly, L. William, Captain, 4th.
Ludeman, W. John, Lieutenant, 6th.
Linton, John, Lieutenant, 3d Dragoons.
Long, Reuben, Lieutenant, 3d.
Lind, Arthur, Captain-Lieutenant, Infantry.
Lawson, Benjamin, Lieutenant, 2d.
Lee, Henry, Lieutenant-Colonel Commandant, Lee's Legion.
Muhlenberg, Peter, Brigadier-General.
Marks, Isaiah, Captain, 2d.
Morgan, Simon, Captain, 7th.
Muir, Francis, Captain, Infantry.

Mallory, Philip, Captain, 4th.
Miller, Thomas, Lieutenant, 2d.
Meriwether, James, Lieutenant, 1st Artillery.
Meriwether, David, Lieutenant, 1st.
Mills, John, Lieutenant, 7th.
Mosely, Benjamin, Lieutenant, 5th.
Mosely, William, Major, 5th.
Morrow, Robert, Captain, 3d Dragoons.
Morton, Hezekiah, Captain, 8th.
Munroe, George, Surgeon, ——.
Matthews, George, Colonel, 3d.
Moss, Henry, Captain, 7th.
Mabon, James, Captain, 7th.
Miller, Javan, Lieutenant, 7th.
Morgan, Daniel, Brigadier-General.
Meredith, William, Captain, Artillery.
Mosely, Benjamin, Lieutenant, Artillery.
Miller, William, Captain-Lieutenant, ——.
Miller, David, Lieutenant, 2d.
Middleton, Bazil, Surgeon, ——.
McGuire, William, Lieutenant, Artillery.
Minnis, Holman, Captain, 7th.
Minnis, Callowhill, Captain, 7th.
Martin, Thomas, Lieutenant, 5th.
Massey, John, Cornet, 1st Dragoons.
Minnis, Francis, Captain, Infantry.
Morris, G. Nathaniel, Captain, ——.
Mercer, Hugh, Brigadier-General.
Nevill, John, Colonel, 4th.
Nevill, Presley, Captain, 8th.
Nixon, Andrew, Captain, 1st Dragoons.
Norvell, Lipscomb, Lieutenant, Posey's.
Nelson, John, Captain, 6th.
Nelson, Roger, Lieutenant, 3d Dragoons.
Overton, Thomas, Captain, 4th.
Pearson, Thomas, Lieutenant, 6th.
Pearce, William, Captain and Aide-de-Camp, Artillery.
Pendleton, Nathaniel, Captain, 3d.
Payne, Josias, Ensign, Infantry.
Payne, Tarleton, Captain, 7th.
Porterfield, Robert, Captain, 2d.
Payne, Thomas, Captain, 5th.
Parker, Alexander, Captain, Posey's.
Posey, Thomas, Lieutenant-Colonel, Posey's.
Parker, Thomas, Captain, Posey's.
Pemberton, Thomas, Captain, 1st Dragoons.
Powell, Peyton, Lieutenant, 3d.

Perkins, Archelaus, Lieutenant, 5th.
Poulson, John, Major, 8th.
Pelham, Charles, Major, 7th.
Power, Robert, Cornet, Lee's Legion.
Parsons, William, Captain, 3d Dragoons.
Perry, John, Cornet, 3d Dragoons.
Porter, William, Lieutenant, 8th.
Quarles, Robert, Ensign, Posey's.
Quarles, P. William, Lieutenant, 1st.
Quarles, John, Lieutenant, ——.
Rose, Robert, Surgeon, 1st Dragoons.
Roy, Beverly, Captain, Posey's.
Roney, John, Lieutenant, 3d.
Ransdall, Thomas, Captain, 3d.
Russell, Albert, Lieutenant, 8th.
Ragsdale, Drury, Captain, Artillery.
Russell, William, Colonel, 5th.
Rudder, Epaphroditus, Lieutenant, 1st Dragoons.
Rhea, Matthew, Lieutenant, 7th.
Rankins, Robert, Lieutenant, 7th.
Reid, Nathan, Captain, 1st.
Ridley, Thomas, Major, 1st.
Robertson, William, Lieutenant, 5th.
Robertson, John, Lieutenant, 6th.
Rose, Alexander, Captain, ——.
Stockley, Charles, Lieutenant, 5th.
Sansom, Philip, Captain, 1st.
Springer, Uriah, Captain, 7th.
Springer, Jacob, Lieutenant, 7th.
Savage, Joseph, Mate, ——.
Selden, Samuel, Lieutenant, 1st.
Scott, Charles, Cornet, 1st Dragoons.
Smith, S. Williams, Cornet, 6th.
Smith, Francis, Cornet, 6th.
Settle, Strother, Ensign, Infantry.
Smith, Nathan, Mate, Posey's.
Scott, Joseph, Captain, Posey's.
Shelton, Clough, Captain, Posey's.
Smith, Ballard, Lieutenant, Posey's.
Scott, John, Ensign, Posey's.
Stuart, Philip, Lieutenant, 3d Dragoons.
Stevenson, David, Major, 6th.
Sawyers, Robert, Captain, ——.
Stevens, William, Lieutenant, 3d.
Steel, John, Lieutenant, 1st.
Stith, John, Captain, 2d.
Singleton, Anthony, Captain, Artillery.
Southall, Stephen, Lieutenant, Artillery.
Swearingen, Joseph, Captain, 8th.
Snead, Smith, Major, 2d.
Scarborough, John, Lieutenant, 5th.

Stribling, Sigismund, Captain, 8th.
Seayres, Thomas, Ensign, 5th.
Skinner, Alexander, Surgeon, Lee's Legion.
Smith, Jonathan, Lieutenant, 5th.
Scott, Charles, Brigadier-General.
Smith, James, Lieutenant, ——.
Stubblefield, Beverly, Captain, 2d.
Swan, John, Major, 1st Dragoons.
Stokes, John, Captain, 2d.
Tannehill, Josiah, Lieutenant, 7th.
Trabue, John, Ensign, Infantry.
Taylor, Richard, Lieutenant-Colonel, ——.
Terry, Nathaniel, Captain, 1st.
Throckmorton, Albion, Cornet, 1st Dragoons.
Talliaferro, Nicholas, Lieutenant, 6th.
Tatum, Zachariah, Ensign, ——.
Taliaferro, Benjamin, Captain, 2d.
Trezvant, John, Surgeon, 2d.
Towles, Oliver, Lieutenant Colonel, ——.
Thomas, Lewis, Captain, 7th.
Temple, Benjamin, Lieutenant-Colonel, 4th Dragoons.
Trant, Lawrence, Captain, 4th Dragoons.
Vaughan, Claibourne, Mate, 1st Dragoons.
Vandewall, Marks, Lieutenant, 1st Dragoons.
Wallace, James, Surgeon, 3d Dragoons.
White, Walton Anthony, Colonel, 1st Dragoons.
Weedon, George, Brigadier-General.
Wallace, B. Gustavus, Lieutenant-Colonel, 2d.
Winston, William, Lieutenant, Lee's Legion.
Winlock, Joseph, Lieutenant, 7th.
Willson, Willis, Lieutenant, 4th.
Whiting, Francis, Lieutenant, 1st Dragoons.
Woodson, Robert, Captain, 5th.
Williams, James, Captain, 6th.
Wallace, B. Williams, Lieutenant, Artillery.
Washington, William, Lieutenant-Colonel, 3d Dragoons.
White, William, Captain, 8th.
Willis, John, Major, 5th.

Williams, David, Lieutenant, 3d.
Whitaker, William, Lieutenant, Artillery.
Wright, James, Captain, 3d.
Walker, David, Lieutenant, 1st.
Waggener, Andrew, Major, 1st.
Warman, Thomas, Captain, 3d.
Walters, Richard, Captain-Lieutenant, Artillery.
Washington, A. George, Lieutenant, 2d.
Watts, John, Captain, 1st Dragoons.
Warsham, Richard, Lieutenant, 1st.
Wood, James, Colonel, 8th.
White, John, Lieutenant, 8th.
Wallace, James, Lieutenant, 3d Dragoons.
Yancey, Robert, Captain, 1st Dragoons.
Yancey, Leighton, Lieutenant, 1st Dragoons.
Young, Henry, Captain, 5th.
Yarborough, Charles, Lieutenant, 3d Dragoons.
Yates, George, Mate, ——.

NORTH CAROLINA.

Armstrong, John, Lieutenant-Colonel, 1st.
Armstrong, William, Captain, 1st.
Ashe, Samuel, Lieutenant, ——.
Armstrong, James, Colonel, 1st.
Armstrong, Thomas, Captain and Aide-de-Camp, 1st.
Ballard, Kedar, Captain, 1st.
Bradley, Gee, Captain, 1st.
Brevard, Alexander, Captain, 1st.
Bailey, Benjamin, Captain, 1st.
Budd, Samuel, Captain, 1st.
Blount, Reading, Captain, 1st.
Blyth, Joseph, Surgeon, 1st.
Bacot, Peter, Captain, 1st.
Bush, William, Lieutenant, 1st.
Brevard, Joseph, Lieutenant, 1st.
Bell, Robert, Lieutenant, 1st.
Clarke, Thomas, Colonel, ——.
Craddock, John, Captain, ——.
Callender, Thomas, Captain, ——.
Crancher, Anthony, Lieutenant, ——.
Clandennen, John, Lieutenant, ——.
Coleman, Benjamin, Captain, ——.
Carter, Benjamin, Captain, ——.
Campen, James, Lieutenant, ——.

Clark, Thomas, Lieutenant, ——.
Campbell, John, Lieutenant, ——.
Child, Francis, Captain, ——.
Donohoe, Thomas, Major, ——.
Doherty, George, Major, ——.
Davis, John, Captain, ——.
Dixon, Tilghman, Captain, ——.
Dudley, Thomas, Lieutenant, ——.
Dixon, Charles, Lieutenant, ——.
Dixon, Wayne, Lieutenant, ——.
Davidson, William, Lieutenant-Colonel, ——.
Evans, Thomas, Captain, 1st.
Fenner, Robert, Captain, ——.
Fawn, William, Captain, ——.
Fenner, Richard, Lieutenant, ——.
Finney, Thomas, Lieutenant, ——.
Ford, John, Lieutenant, ——.
Fergus, James, Surgeon, ——.
Graves, Francis, Lieutenant, 1st.
Gerrard, Charles, Lieutenant, 1st.
Green, W. James, Surgeon, ——.
Harney, Selby, Colonel, 1st.
Hogg, Thomas, Major, ——.
Hargrave, William, Lieutenant, ——.
Hall, Clement, Captain, ——.
Hadley, Joshua, Captain, ——.
Hays, Robert, Lieutenant, ——.
Holmes, Hardy, Lieutenant, ——.
Hill, John, Lieutenant, ——.
Howe, Robert, Major-General.
Halling, Solomon, Surgeon, ——.
Ingles, John, Captain, ——.
Jones, Samuel, Captain, ——.
Ivry, Curtis, Lieutenant, ——.
Jones, Philip, Captain-Lieutenant, Artillery.
Kingsbury, John, Captain, Artillery.
Lawrence, Nathaniel, Lieutenant, ——.
Lyttle, Archibald, Lieutenant-Colonel Commandant, 1st.
Lyttle, William, Captain, 1st.
Lamb, Abner, Lieutenant, 1st.
Lewis, Micajah, Captain, 1st.
Lamb, Gideon, Colonel, 1st.
Murfree, Hardy, Lieutenant-Colonel, 1st.
Mumfort, Joseph, Captain, 1st.
Mc Nees, John, Captain, 1st.
Mills, James, Captain, 1st.
Moore, Elijah, Captain, 1st.
Marshall, Dixon, Lieutenant, 1st.
Mc Ree, J. Griffith, Major, 1st.

Moor, James, Lieutenant, 1st.
McClure, William, Surgeon, 1st.
McLain, William, Mate, 1st.
Nelson, John, Major, 1st.
Nash, Francis, Brigadier-General.
Patten, John, Colonel, ——.
Pearl, James, Captain, ——.
Pasteurs, Thomas, Lieutenant, ——.
Reed, Jesse, Captain, ——.
Raiford, Robert, Captain, ——.
Rhodes, Thomas Joseph, Captain, ——.
Read, James, Captain, ——.
Stewart, Charles, Captain, ——.
Summers, John, Captain, ——.
Shaw, Daniel, Lieutenant, ——.
Slade, Stephen, Lieutenant, ——.
Saunders, William, Lieutenant, ——.
Scurlock, James, Lieutenant, ——.
Sharpe, Anthony, Captain, 1st.
Steed, Jesse, Lieutenant, ——.
Sumner, Jethro, Brigadier-General.
Tatem, James, Lieutenant, ——.
Thackston, James, Lieutenant-Colonel Commandant, ——.
Vance, John, Lieutenant, Artillery.
Walton, William, Captain, ——.
Williams, Nathaniel, Lieutenant ——.

SOUTH CAROLINA.

Axon, J. Samuel, Mate, Hospital.
Brownson, Nathan, Deputy Purveyor.
Bradwell, Nathaniel, Lieutenant, Infantry.
Brown, Charles, Lieutenant, Infantry.
Beekman, Samuel, Lieutenant, Infantry.
Beekman, Bernard, Colonel, Artillery.
Baker, B. Richard, Captain, Infantry.
Buchanan, John, Captain, Infantry.
Baker, Jesse, Captain, ——.
Budd, S. John, Captain-Lieutenant, Artillery.
De St. Marie, La Vacher, Captain, Infantry.
Doyley, Daniel, Lieutenant, Infantry.
Davis, Harman, Captain, Artillery.
Dunbar, Thomas, Lieutenant, Infantry.
Evans, George, Lieutenant Infantry.
Elliott, Bernard, Captain, Artillery.
Flagg, Collins Henry, Deputy Apothecary, 1st.

Ford, Tobias, Ensign, Infantry.
Frierson, John, Lieutenant, Infantry.
Field, James, Captain-Lieutenant, Artillery.
Favrer, Field, Captain, Infantry.
Faysoux, Peter, Physician and Surgeon, General Hospital.
Goodwin, John, Lieutenant, Infantry.
Goodwin, Uriah, Captain, Infantry.
Grimke, F. John, Lieutenant-Colonel, Artillery.
Gadsden, Thomas, Captain, Infantry.
Gray, Peter, Captain, Infantry.
Grayson, John, Lieutenant, Artillery.
Huger, Isaac, Brigadier-General.
Hyrne, Edmond, Major, Infantry.
Hamilton, John, Lieutenant and Adjutant, Infantry.
Huggins, Benjamin, Ensign, Infantry.
Henderson, William, Lieutenant-Colonel, Infantry.
Hazzard, William, Lieutenant, Infantry.
Harleston, Isaac, Major, Infantry.
Hixt, William, Captain, Infantry.
Hart, John, Lieutenant, Infantry.
Hart, Oliver, Mate, Infantry.
Jackson, William, Captain, Infantry.
Kennedy, James, Lieutenant, Infantry.
Kolb, Josiah, Lieutenant, Infantry.
Knapp, John, Lieutenant, Infantry.
Liston, Thomas, Lieutenant, Artillery.
Langford, Daniel, Lieutenant, Infantry.
Legare, James, Lieutenant, Infantry.
Lloyd, Benjamin, Lieutenant, Artillery.
Lining, Charles, Captain, Infantry.
Liddle, George, Captain, Infantry.
Lochman, Charles, Mate, ——.
Lloyd, Edward, Lieutenant, Artillery.
Moultrie, William, Major-General.
Marion, Francis, Lieutenant-Colonel Commandant, Infantry.
Martin, John, Captain, Infantry.
McGuire, Merry, Lieutenant, Infantry.
Mayzick, Stephen, Lieutenant, Infantry.
Mayzick, Daniel, Captain, Infantry.
Mitchel, James, Captain, Artillery.
Mitchel, Ephraim, Major, Artillery.
Mason, Richard, Captain, Infantry.
Moore, Henry, Lieutenant, Artillery.
Martin, James, Surgeon, Infantry.
Neufville, William, Surgeon, Infantry.

Oliphant, David, Director, General Hospital

Ogive, George, Lieutenant, Infantry.

Ousley, Thomas, Lieutenant, Artillery.

Purcell, Henry, Chaplain, ——.

Pinckney, C. Charles, Colonel, Infantry.

Pinckney, Thomas, Major, Infantry.

Preveaux, Adrian, Captain, Infantry.

Pollard, Richard, Captain, Infantry.

Rothmaler, Erasmus, Ensign, Infantry.

Roux, Albert, Captain, Infantry.

Russell, C. Thomas, Lieutenant, ——.

Roberts, Brook Richard, Captain, Artillery.

Read, William, Physician and Surgeon, Hospital.

Shubrick, Thomas, Captain and Aide-de-Camp, Infantry.

Smith, C. John, Captain, Infantry.

Scott, William, Lieutenant-Colonel, Infantry.

Smith, Aaron, Lieutenant, Infantry.

Sunn, Frederick, Surgeon, Infantry.

Springer, Sylvester, Mate, ——.

Theus, Simeon, Captain, Infantry.

Turner, George, Captain, Infantry.

Tate, William, Captain-Lieutenant, Artillery.

Tucker, Tudor Thomas, Physician and Surgeon, Hospital.

Vickers, Samuel, Physician and Surgeon, Hospital.

Withers, R. William, Ensign, 1st.

Warley, Felix, Captain, 1st.

Warley, Joseph, Captain, 1st.

Ward, P. John, Lieutenant, 1st.

Williamson, John, Captain, 1st.

Warley, George, Captain, 1st.

Wichley, John, Captain, Artillery.

Ward, William, Lieutenant, Infantry.

GEORGIA.

Allison, Henry, Lieutenant, Infantry.

Brossard, Celeron, Captain, Infantry.

Booker, Gideon, Captain, Infantry.

Bard, John, Captain, Infantry.

Cuthbert, Alexander, Captain, Infantry.

Cowan, Edward, Lieutenant, Infantry.

Collins, Cornelius, Lieutenant, Infantry.

Cook, Rains, Captain, Infantry.

Delaplaine, Peter Emanuel, Captain, Infantry.

Ducoins, John, Captain, Infantry.

Day, Joseph, Captain, Infantry.

Davenport, Thomas, Lieutenant, Infantry.

Elbert, Samuel, Colonel, Infantry.

Frazer, John, Lieutenant, Infantry.

Fitzpatrick, Patrick, Lieutenant, Infantry.

Houston, James, Surgeon, Infantry.

Hillary, Christopher, Lieutenant, Infantry.

Hayer, Arthur, Lieutenant, Infantry.

Handley, George, Captain, Infantry.

Hicks, Isaac, Captain, Infantry.

Habersham, John, Major, Infantry.

Jordan, William, Lieutenant, Infantry.

Lucas, John, Captain, Infantry.

Lane, Joseph, Major, Infantry.

Lowe, Philip, Major, Infantry.

McIntosh, Lachlan, Brigadier-General, Infantry.

McIntosh, John, Lieutenant-Colonel Commandant, Infantry.

Meanly, John, Lieutenant, Infantry.

McIntosh, Lachlan, Lieutenant, Infantry.

Morris, John, Lieutenant, Infantry.

McIntosh, William, Captain, Infantry.

Mitchell, John, Lieutenant, Infantry.

Maxwell, Josiah, Lieutenant, Infantry.

Mosby, Robert, Lieutenant, Infantry.

Melvin, George, Captain, Infantry.

Mosby, Littleberry, Captain, ——.

Milton, John, Captain, Infantry.

Moore, Francis, Major, Infantry.

Parre, Nathaniel, Lieutenant, Infantry.

Payne, Thomas, Lieutenant, Infantry.

Scott, William, Captain, Infantry.

Shick, Frederick, Lieutenant, Infantry.

Sharp, James Boyd, Mate, Infantry.

Steadman, James, Lieutenant, Infantry.

Tetard, Benjamin, Surgeon, ——.

Tannell, Francis, Lieutenant, Infantry.

Templeton, Andrew, Captain, Infantry.

Wagnon, John Peter, Lieutenant, Infantry.

LIST OF FRENCH OFFICERS

THAT SERVED WITH THE

AMERICAN ARMY,

I am indebted to the Pennsylvania Historical Society for this list, who kindly permitted me to make certain extracts from the original, which is in French, not arranged as here, as it was deemed best to follow the alphabetical style of the book, and also omitted other irrevelant matter, following, however, as near the original in the personal history of each officer as possible. The original manuscript was obtained for Mr. William B. Reed (who presented the same to the Pennsylvania Historical Society) by the Honorable Richard Rush, while Minister at Paris, and was accompanied by the following note:

JUNE, 25th, 1849.

SIR: To comply with the wish you expressed in the note, which was delivered to me by Mr. Perkins, I hastened to search, according to the very expressions of the note, for the names of the French officers who served in the Revolutionary War of the United States of America. It was in vain, unfortunately, that I searched for the muster-rolls at the *Ministere de la Marine,* or at the *Dépôt,* and in the *Archives de la Guerre,* looking through a great number of volumes and boxes. Appreciating, however, the high feeling that inspired the request, I was not willing to be conquered by difficulties, and thought that with time and perseverance it would be possible to supply the absence of the muster-rolls. The papers, which I have the honor to address you, will explain to you how I proceeded to attain that end. Taking the names of some officers well-known as having contributed to the liberty of the United States, I conceived that I could find in their *Etats de Services* the different actions in which our troops had distinguished themselves, and thus know the time when the notes for the rewards to be conferred on those who had deserved well of the two countries had been prepared in the Ministers' offices. This partly succeeded and brought me after-wards to look for the muster-rolls of the corps to which belonged the officers who had signalized themselves; but though I have added many names to my lists from that source, I cannot say that they are complete, for I could not conclude from the muster-rolls themselves that all the officers belonging to the corps had been present in America. The regiments not having sent very often more than a detachment, and the detachments sometimes having served only on shipboard, I could not designate an officer as having served in the American War, unless the fact had been indicated in some note concerning that time, and so I was obliged to confine myself to inscribing the names of the officers whom I could positively ascertain to have been engaged in the war.

I hope, sir, these lists, however incomplete, will not be without interest for the history of the two countries, nor do I regret the three weeks I have given to collecting them, though I may have been fatigued at moments by the dryness of the task. I beg you, sir, to observe, that if I have not found the whole as you desired, I have succeeded at least in that which was most important, having recovered from oblivion the names of all those whom their good behavior, their talents, and courage had rendered most conspicuous. On the other side, as a mere name is not signficant enough and does not sufficiently particularize a family and a man, you will be pleased, no doubt, to find that to each officer's name I have added the date and the place of his birth, and some other details contained in the rolls. This I know was not in the directions given me, but being occupied with historical works myself I thought it would be agreeable to the historian to whom these notes are destined, nor will I neglect to apprise him that in the course of my researches I have found some documents concerning the Independence War, which I have not seen quoted elsewhere. I have the honor to be, sir, yours, most respectfully,

PIERRE MARGRY,

11 Rue du Mont Thabor.

Mons. Rush, Minister Plenipotentiáre des Etats Unis à Paris.

LIST OF FRENCH OFFICERS

THAT SERVED WITH

THE AMERICAN ARMY.

Aboville.

Aboville, D'. See D'Aboville.

Adrien, de Buzelet, Sir Charles. Brigade-Chief in the Alexonne Regiment Royal Artillery Corps; pension granted.

Anne, Claude. See Claude.

Anselme, Bernard Joseph D'. Lieutenant-Colonel (Soissonnois); served from 1745; Captain in 1760; Major in 1774; Lieutenant-Colonel in 1777; distinguished officer; followed his regiment to America notwithstanding feeble health; Lieutenant-Colonel of the Soissonnois Regiment; thirty-eight years' service; Captain in 1760; Major in 1774; Lieutenant-Colonel in 1777; excellent officer; his gallant conduct at York obtained for him a pension of $600 in the Order of St. Louis; the oldest of the Lieutenant-Colonels in America who was not made a Brigadier; Lieutenant-Colonel, 17th July, 1777; born at Apt in Provence, 26th August, 1737; pensioned by the Order of St. Louis for gallant conduct at York.

Anselme, de la Gardette, Chevalier d'. Captain Commandant (Soissonnois); twenty-five years' service; two campaigns in America; very fine officer.

Antoine, Thomas. See Thomas, Antoine.

Arcy, Jacques Philippe d'. Captain, 5th May, 1772; born in Paris in 1742; died at Savannah.

Baudin

Autichamp, d'. Brigadier; Lieutenant-General commanding the Regiment of Agénois; served from 1759; officer in 1761; Captain in 1763; Colonel, 11th April, 1770; Brigadier, 5th December, 1781, for gallantry at York; took part in four campaigns in America, and by zeal and intelligence distinguished himself at York and St. Christopher; appointed Lieutenant-General to take rank ——.

Aymard. See D'Aymard.

Barre. See De la Barre.

Barry, D'Imbart de. Captain, en second, of the Company of Grenadiers, Regiment of Agénois; entered the service 4th May, 1759; Assistant Aide-Major, 11th August, 1771; Captain, en second, 11th June, 1776; wounded in the attack on Savannah; gunshot wound, left arm.

Barry, Du. See Du Barry.

Barthelemy, Jean. See Montaligre.

Basques, de. See Chazelle.

Bathisy, Jacques Eleonor Viscount de. Colonel, second class; born at Calais, 4th December, 1748; Lieutenant-Colonel of this regiment, 7th August, 1778; grievously wounded in 1779 at Savannah.

Baudin, de Beauregard. See Romefort.

Baudot. Captain Commandant (Soissonnois); served from 1747; Captain in 1777; engaged in the war with Germany; was buried beneath a mine at Minorca; served with zeal and intelligence.

Baudre, Olivier Victor De. Captain, 22d April, 1762; born at Bayeux, 21st May, 1736; excellent officer; honorable, zealous and intelligent; gallant conduct at York; Captain Commandant (Soissonnois); served from 1756; Captain in 1762; oldest officer of the regiment; excellent officer.

Bayac, de. See De Lasse.

Bazin, Gillaume De. Captain, 4th July, 1777; born at Marmande, in Guyenne, 24th May, 1740; decorated for gallantry at York. See De Bazin—believed to be the same.

Beaumont, Alexis Jean Francois Gorat de. Captain, July 30, 1758; born at Limoges, 25th July, 1735; pensioned for brave conduct at York.

Beaumont, Antoine Joseph Eulalie de, Count Daudechamp. Colonel, 3d October, 1779; born at Angers, 10th December, 1744; an officer of the greatest distinction, full of active talents and resolution; made Brigadier-General 5th December, 1781, for gallant conduct at York.

Beaumont, De. Captain Commandant (Sanitonge); served from 1754; Captain in 1770; officer of distinction; participated in all the war with Germany; served in India, and displayed zeal and valor at York.

Beauregard, Baudin de. See Romefort.

Bédeé, Ange Armand de Bédeé, de Boisbras. Captain, 28th August, 1777; born at Rennes, 1st March, 1742; decorated for brave conduct at York; Captain Commandant (Saintonge); twenty-four years' service; five campaigns in Cayenne; two in America.

Béhagle, Jean Baptist Emmanuel de. Captain Commandant, Grenadiers (Agénois); after twenty-six years of service, participating in the campaigns in Germany and six years' sojourn in America, his health was undermined to the extent of preventing his continuance in service; born at Paris, 3d February, 1735.

Bérage, De la Boyère Jean Pierre. Captain, 7th June, 1776; born at Aix, in Provence, 26th February, 1736; decorated for gallantry at York.

Bérard, de Mauraige, Christophe Philippe. Second Lieutenant, 4th November, 1779; born 15th March, 1759; wounded at Savannah, leg broken, 8th November, 1780, for which decorated; remained on the field of battle, and for four months was a prisoner of war in the enemy's hospitals.

Bernard, ——; born at St. Ouen, 1739; died in America, ——, 1780.

Berthelot, Augustin Clement de Villeneuve, Chevalier de. Captain, 7th August, 1779; born at Rossigne, in Anjou, 19th August, 1750; died in 1781 from wounds, received at the siege of York in said year.

Berthier, Louis Alexandre. Captain, 26th April, 1780; born at Versailles, 20th November, 1753; Topographical Engineer; participated in four campaigns as Assistant-Aide to the Quartermaster-General in America; was the coming Grand Marshal of the Empire.

Bervet. Paymaster; (Agénois); private in 1768; officer in 1779; took part in the siege of York.

Bethisy, Viscount de. Colonel, second class, Gatinois Regiment; wounded twice before Savannah, 9th October last, through left hand and in the epigastric region; entered the service in 1764; Captain of Dragoons, 1768; Colonel, second class, 1778; by his request Count D'Estaing placed him Third Commandant of the de Dillon column.

Beville. See De Beville.

Bien, De, de Cherigny. See De Bien.

Blandat, Mathieu. Born at Malan, in Franche Comté, 17th January, 1725; Private in 1742; Lieutenant, 1777; First Lieutenant, 21st April, 1779; gunshot wound through both thighs at the siege of Tournay in 1747; another gunshot wound, right thigh, at Laufeldt in 1747, and a sabre cut on the head at Warbourg in 1760, requiring trepanning; killed, 24th September, 1779, at the siege of Savannah.

Boisbras. See Bedei de Boisbras.

Bonnaforce, de Bellinay. Champagne Regiment; present at the capture of Grenada, but does not appear in the land operations.

Bonne, Jean Chevalier de. Captain, 1st August, 1780; born at Viver les Montagnes; pensioned in 1782 for gallant conduct at St. Christopher.

Bordenave, Jean Ignace Chevalier de. Captain, en second (Gatinois); twenty years' service; one campaign in Germany, six in America; Captain, 28th August, 1777; born at Montmassay, 13th December, 1742; decorated for the capture of York.

Borneot. Second Lieutenant of Grenadiers (Gatinois); private in 1765; officer in 1779; in the attack of the redoubt.

Bosnier, de Saint Cosme. Captain; entered the service in 1766; Gray Musketeer in 1766; appointed Second Lieutenant in the Regiment of Normandy up to 1772; Lieutenant (following the Columns) in 1775; Captain (following the Regiment of Armagnac) in 1777; wounded in the breast in the attack on Savannah.

Bouland. Captain of Grenadiers, Regiment of Armagnac; 37 years of service; wounded in the attack on the entrenchments at Savannah.

Boulières, Des. See Des Boulières.

Boyère, De la. See Bérage.

Bressoles, Gilbert de. Lieutenant-Colonel, 29th December, 1777; born at the Planche in Bourbonnais, 3d December, 1739; received several sabre cuts at the battle of Minden in 1759; horse killed under him in a sortie at Cassel in 1762; pension received for gallant conduct at York; Lieutenant-Colonel (Bourbonnois); served from 1757; Captain in 1769; Major in 1776; Lieutenant-Colonel in 1777; wounded several times at Minden; served with great distinction and one of the best Lieutenant-Colonels.

Brie, De. Captain commanding (Saintonge); served from 1749; Captain in 1760; served in the Grenadiers.

Brières, Des. See Des Brières.

Broglie, Prince de. Colonel of Horse, second class, of Saintonge; served from 1771; Colonel, 3d June, 1779; his exemplary conduct always merited praise.

Brosse, de la. See Londeix.

Broune, Thomas. Major, 30th January, 1778; born at Castelloppe, 12th October, 1732; killed at the siege of Savannah, 9th October, 1779.

Buzdet, de. See Adrien de Buzelet.

Cabannes, Adam Maxamilien de. Born at Nassau Sieghen, 4th January, 1741; Second Lieutenant from 18th May, 1758; Captain commandant, 30th June, 1782; decorated with the Cross of the Mérite Militaire after the action at York.

Cabannes, Charles de. Captain commandant (Royal Deux Ponts); twenty-three years and eight months' service; five campaigns in Germany, two in America.

Cabannes, Charles Guillaume de. Captain; born at Luttange, 21st April, 1742; Lieutenant, second class, 9th April, 1758; Captain commanding, 4th April, 1780; decorated with the Cross of the Mérite Militaire for gallant conduct at York.

Cadet See Le Cadet.

Cadignan, Chevalier de. See Dupleix.

Cahière. Captain commanding (Gatinois); twenty-six years' service; six campaigns in Germany, four in the colonies; commanded the Second Battalion, which formed part of the attacking column under the command of Baron de Viomeuil. (See Rouverie.)

Cahières, Charles de. See Rouverie

Caldagues, Pierre Raymond De. Captain, 12th May, 1781; born at Aurillac, 3d August, 1747; pensioned for gallant conduct at York; Captain, en second, (Soissonnois); served from 1763; Captain in 1781; served with honor.

Cambray, De. Cadet Corps of Engineers in 1770; was not made an officer, there being no vacancy; Lieutenant-Colonel in the service of the United States from 1778, date when joined its army; merited this gracious, but premature distinction for the gallant manner he served in South America; name to be presented for a majority in the provincial troops.

Cantel, Donetville, Sir. Major Royal Engineer Corps; pension granted.

Carrèze. Captain, en second, of Grenadiers (Gatinois); served from 1767; Captain in 1779.

Castille, de. See Josselin.

Catey, Francois César de. Lieutenant; participated in three actions during the war in America, and was once shipwrecked, which greatly affected his health.

Caupanes, de. See Lassaderie.

Caulanges, Jacques Scot de. Captain, 7th July, 1779; born at Epin, in Touraine, 25th July, 1742; decorated for brave conduct at York.

Cazat, de. Captain commanding (Bourbonnois); twenty-two years' service; two war campaigns.

Chabannes, Count de. Captain, on half-pay, in the Royal Redmont Regiment; officer in 1776; Captain in 1778; took part in two campaigns in America

as Assistant Quartermaster-General of the army of Count de Rochambeau, which shows that he always gave proof of the best of purpose and the greatest zeal, and that he merits much for brave conduct, as well as birth, which commend him to due consideration upon attaining the required age; will have reached twenty-three years of age 3d August, 1783, at which time his name will be presented for appointment as Colonel of Horse, second class.

Chalandar. 1st Lieutenant (Gatinois); served from 1771; was in the attack of the redoubt.

Chalendar, Jean Baptiste Marguerite, Chevalier de. Captain, 16th October, 1781; born at Bornay, Diocese of Puy, 16th April, 1751; was at York, where he distinguished himself; taken prisoner 12th April; confined on the ship Caton.

Chamerière, Gillaume. Captain 19th March, 1780; born in the parish of "L'Hermitage," in Normandy, 11th June, 1734; pension of £300 for gallantry at York.

Chandron, Chevalier de la Valette, Charles Francois. Lieutenant-Colonel, 24th February, 1774; born at Montfort, Amaury, 5th June, 1731; nominated Brigadier-General 5th December, 1781, for distinguished conduct at the capture of York.

Chappier, de Tourville, Toussaint Magloire. Lieutenant, 10th March, 1780; born at Vivier, Vivarais, 6th June, 1761; Cadet Nobleman, 6th June, 1776; Second Lieutenant, 28th August, 1777; Lieutenant, en second, 10th March, 1780; First Lieutenant, 24th April, 1784; received a gunshot wound through the chest at Savannah; taken prisoner in the action of 12th April, 1782, and confined on the ship Ardent.

Chapuy, de Tourville, Charles Bertin Gaston. Major (Gatinois); 18th April, 1776; born at Metz, 4th January, 1740; during nearly one year in

America performed the duties of a Major-General.

Chapuy, de Tourville. 2d Lieutenant; entered the service as 2d Lieutenant in the regiment of Gadenois, 6th June, 1776; gunshot wound through left breast in the action of 24th September, before Savannah.

Charles, Count de. Colonel of Horse, second class, of the Regiment of Saintonge; born 3d May, 1756; served from ——; Captain, 4th April, 1774; Colonel of Horse, second class, 23d May, 1779; upon all occasions he displayed zeal, action, modesty, subordination and courage; "it is an act of justice that Count de Rochambeau renders him when he forgets that he is the son of a minister."

Charlot. Captain commanding (Touraine); twenty-four years' service; two campaigns in Germany, two in America.

Chassepied. 2d Lieutenant of Grenadiers (Agenois); private in 1752; officer in 1779; took part in the campaigns of Germany, Savannah, and York.

Chastelleux, Chevalier de. Lieutenant-General; served from 1747; Colonel of the Regiment of March in 1759; Brigadier in 1769; Lieutenant-General, 1st March, 1780; useful services rendered to Count de Rochambeau in most of the conferences held with General Washington.

Chazelle, de Basques, Antoine. Lieutenant, 2d June, 1777; born at Salen, in Auvergne, 23d November, 1752; wounded at the Siege of York; his wound gave him trouble.

Chennevières. Captain, en second, of Grenadiers (Bourbonnois); private in 1754; officer in 1767; Captain in 1780; old and good officer, without fortune.

Chevigny, De. See De Chevigny.

Choisy, De. See De Choisy.

Chouin. 1761; Midshipman Engineer.

Christian Des Deux Ponts, Count. See Des Deux Ponts.

Claude, Anne. Born at Bonneval; took part in the expedition against Savannah, Tobago, St. Lucie and St. Christopher; served with great bravery; had his leg shattered on the ship Jason in the engagement of the 12th April, 1782.

Claude, ——. Born at Alais, 29th September, 1751.

Clozen, Jean Christophe Louis Frédéric Ignace, Baron de. Born 14th August, 1752; Second Lieutenant, 10th September, 1769; Captain en second from 4th April, 1780; Aide-de-Camp of Mr. the Count de Rochambeau; behaved well at York; was related to Baron de Clozen, a general officer in the service of France; Aide-de-Camp to Count de Rochambeau; Captain, en second, in the Regiment Royal Deux Ponts; served from 10th September, 1769; Captain, 4th April, 1780; nephew of old general officer of the same name; developed all the talents of his uncle.

Clovis. Second Lieutenant of Grenadiers (Soissonnois); thirty-four years' service; private, Sergeant, and Quartermaster officer from 1769; faithful service in war; wounded.

Collot. Aide Quartermaster-General; served from 1765; Captain from 1778; attached to the Regiment of Bercheney.

Colously, de. See D'Houdedot.

Corbière, Chevalier de la. Captain commanding (Saintonge); twenty-two years' service; five campaigns in Cayenne, two in America.

Coriolès, Jean Baptiste Etienne, Chevalier de. Lieutenant, 29th December, 1777; born at Aix, in Provence, 18th May, 1754; 1st Lieutenant (Bourbonnois); served from 1773; Lieutenant in 1777; was in the attack of the redoubt.

Corlière, De la. Captain, en second (Agénois); gallantry at York; twenty-one years' service; one campaign in 1761, one in 1762, four in the Colonies.

Couffin, De. See De Couffin.

Coulanges, de. See Scott de Coulanges.

Coussol D'Esparsac. Captain commanding (Gatinois); twenty-five years' service; four campaigns in Germany, six in America.

Cromot Dubourg, Baron de. Aide-de-Camp to Count de Rochambeau, and Captain, at half-pay in the Dragoon Regiment of Mr. ——; served from 1768; 2d Lieutenant, 18th March, 1770; Captain, 24th February, 1774; Captain, at half-pay, in 1776.

Crozet. See Du Crozet.

Custine, Count de. Brigadier commanding the Saintonge Regiment; gained the trench, and served with an indefatigable zeal, activity, and courage; Lieutenant-General; served from 1747; thirty-six years' service; Colonel of Horse in 1763; Brigadier in 1780; Lieutenant-General, 5th December, 1781; Count de Rochambeau said "it is impossible to have the discipline and instruction of a regiment more perfect with such unshaken firmness, joined to the most exacting probity.'

D'Aboville. Colonel commanding the Artillery; Colonel of Horse, en second.

D'Alausse. See Galtier D'Alausse.

Dalomine, Chevalier. Captain, 9th December, 1780.

Dalpheraus, Felix. 2d Lieutenant, ——; born 6th April, 1744; participated in the American campaigns from 1780 to 1783.; was at York.

D'Anselme de la Gardette. See Anselme de la Gardette.

D'Anselme. See Anselme.

Daudechamp, Count. See Beaumont.

Daurien, Madron. See De Brie.

D'Autichamp, Marquis. See Autichamp, d'.

D'Aymard, de Ville, Louis Francois. Captain; born at Verdun, 5th November, 1749; seriously wounded in the actions of 9th or 12th April, 1782, under Mr. the Count de Grasse.

De Barry. See Barry.

De Baudre. See Baudre.

De Bazin. Captain commanding (Soissonnois); twenty-four years and eight months' service; three campaigns in Germany, two in Corsica, 1768 and 1769; two in America; wounded at Clostercamp and in Corsica. (See Bazin.)

De Beaumont. See Beaumont.

De Béhagle. See Béhagle.

De Beville. Lieutenant - General; thirty-seven years' service; served from 1746; Lieutenant-Colonel in 1761; Brigadier in 1778; Lieutenant-General, 5th December, 1781; took part in the first war with Germany in the staff corps of the army, and was, in the American war, Quartermaster-General of the Army; made, with the whole army, two marches of more than seven miles each, crossing fifteen large streams without delay or accident, accomplished with meagre means at his disposal; for gallant conduct at the siege of York he received a pension of —1,200; made application for a Commandership in the Order of St. Louis, with hope of appointment therein.

De Béville. Aide Quartermaster-General; served from 1773; Captain on half-pay in the Dragoon Regiment of de Noailles; officer in 1775; Captain in 1780; came to America with his brother and was first appointted by Count de Rochambeau as Aide-de-Camp, then sent to the staff of the army.

De Bien, de Chevigny, Frédéric Francois Louis. Captain, 7th May, 1777; born at Avalon, 13th April, 1737; though retired, participated in the campaign at York.

De Bonne. See Bonne.

Des Boulières, de Grillières Francois. Sailor (?), Chevalier; born 28th October, 1752; gallant conduct at St. Christopher; was in the Expedition of the Hudson Bay, 13th June, 1783.

De Brie, Jean Georges Prosper Daurien de Madron. Served from 1749; Captain, 6th January, 1760; born at Brie, near Saverdun Compté de Foix; served in the Grenadiers; pension for brave conduct at York.

De Cabannes, Adam Maximilien. See Cabannes.

De Cabannes, Charles Guillaume. See Cabannes.

De Cabannes, Maximilien. Captain en second (Royal Deux Ponts); twenty-two years' service; five campaigns in Germany, two in America.

De Caldagues. See Caldagues.

De Catey. See Catey.

De Cazab. See Cazab.

De Charles. See Charles.

De Chevigny. Lieutenant of Chasseurs, Armagnac regiment; commanded this company in the absence of De Tarragon; was in the sortie of the 24th September, and in the attack on the entrenchments at Savannah, where he lost half of his command.

De Choisy. Lieutenant - General; served from 1741; forty-two years' service; Major in 1763; Lieutenant-Colonel in 1767; Brigadier in 1772; Colonel of Horse in the 4th Regiment of Chasseurs in 1779, which he left in 1780 in order to proceed to America, 5th December, 1781; obtained all the grades by brilliant actions; covered himself with glory in the defense and capture of Cracow; served in America with the zeal of a man who had a record to make; rendered signal services at Gloucester, the blockade of which was confided to him, and acquitted himself with honor in the brisk charges he made against the British Cavalry at the head of the de Lauzun Legion; was

promised a possible governorship; Brigadier; commanded the placing of troops in the county of Gloucester; was engaged in a particular action against the corps of Tarleton.

De Colanby. See Houdetot de Colanby.

De Couffin. Captain, en second, (Soissonnois); served from 1763; served in Corsica and was wounded; Captain in 1781; gallant conduct at York.

De Damas. Aide-de-Camp to Count de Rochambeau; Lieutenant, en second, in the King's Infantry Regiment; served from 9th February, 1777; Colonel from 29th April, 1781, to take rank from 1st September, following, when he will reach the age of twenty-three years. Too much cannot be said of him; possessed of brilliant courage and all the military virtues.

de Dillon. See Dillon.

D'Eccouffin Du Vales. See Du Vales.

D'Eparsac. See Eparsac.

D'Esparsac. See Coussoul D'Esparsac.

De Ferette. See Ferette.

D'Eyrous. See Eyrous.

De Fladen. Captain commanding (Royal Deux Ponts); twenty-four years and nine months' service; six campaigns in Germany, two in America.

De Fleury. See Fleury.

De Gambs. See Gambs.

De Gillègue. See Gillègue.

De Gouvion. See Gouvion.

De Haak. See Haak.

De Hoen. See Hoen.

Didier. Surgeon (Agénois); capable in his profession and none more zealous.

De James. See James.

De Kerveguen. See Gautier de Kerveguen.

De la Barre. Lieutenant of Dragoons; entered the service as Cadet in the Troops of the Columns in 1759; passed aspirant of Artillery in 1764; volunteer in the Carabiniers in 1764; 2d Lieutenant in 1770; Lieutenant in Prince Conde's Regiment 1776; wounded at the Siege of Savannah. (See Du Barry.)

De la Boyère. See Bérage.

De Lacarderie. See Lacarderie.

De la Corlière. See Corlière.

De la Roche Négley. See Négley.

De Lasse, de Bayac, Charles Joseph. Captain, 16th April, 1771; born at Fimeray, in Périgord, 11th March, 1742; decorated for gallantry at York.˙

De Lauberdiére. Aide-de-Camp to Count de Rochambeau and 2d Lieutenant in the regiment of Saintonge; cadet, gentleman, Military Academy, 6th June, 1776; 2d Lieutenant, 30th January, 1778; first cousin of Count de Rochambeau, who commissioned him Captain to date from 15th April, 1780, in the regiment of Saintonge.

Delaunay. Captain commanding (Touraine); served from 1757; Captain in 1769; took part in all the campaigns of Hanover. (See Launay.)

De Launet. See Launet.

De La Valette. Lieutenant-Colonel of the regiment of Saintonge; the oldest Colonel of this year; served with all possible zeal and action, of the best spirit, full of courage, and talented.

De Leonardy. See Leonardy.

De Longueville, Chevalier. See James.

De Losse, de Bayac. Captain commanding (Bourbonnois); twenty-two years' service three campaigns in Germany, two in America merits the praises of His Majesty; was in the action of the 16th March, on the ship Jason.

De Loucault. See Loucault.

De Lustrac. See Lustrac.

De Lutzen. See Lutzen.

De Madron. See De Brie.

De Marguerit. See Dolomnie.

De Maury. See Maury.

De Marin. See Marin.

De Menon. See Menon.

De Menonville. See Thiebault.

De Menonville. See Ménonville.

De Miolis. 2d Lieutenant (Soissonnois); served from 1778; shell wound in the face.

De Miolis. See Miolis.

De Montalègre. See Montalègre.

De Montlezun. See Montlezun.

De Mouzellan. See Mouzellan.

De Moysia. See Moysia.

De Pecanne. See La Bord De Pecanne.

De Pondeux. See Liamart.

De Ribaupierre. See Ribaupierre.

De Roussillo, Raymond de See Roussville.

Desanis. See Poquet.

Des Bordes. Captain commandant (Touraine); served from 1755; Captain in 1769.

Des Brières, Zacharie Jacques. Captain; born in Paris 26th March, 1736; his gallant conduct at York won him the Cross; Captain commandant (Saintonge); twenty-two years' service; four campaigns in the Isle of France; two in America.

Des Deux Ponts. See Deux Ponts.

De Scheldon. Colonel of Horse; attached to the Corps of Hussars.

Des Ecures. See Ecures.

Des-feyron. Major (Soissonnois); served from 1747; Captain in 1760; Major in 1780; an officer of valor and intelligence; renounced a large fortune and went to America.

Des Noes, Augustin Rouxelin. Captain, en second, 8th April, 1779; Captain Commandant, 5th March, 1781; born at Caen 9th April, 1741; decorated for brave conduct at York; resigned 3d August, 1782.

Des-peyron. See Peyron.

Des Roches, Philippe Henry. Captain, 8th September, 1778; born at Perigneux, 8th November, 1742; decorated for brave conduct at York.

Des Roches. Captain, second class (Saintonge); twenty-one years and six months' service; five campaigns in Cayenne, two in America.

De Rostaing. See Rostaing.

De St. Sauveur. See St. Sauveur.

De Sniety. Captain commanding (Soissonnois); twenty-two years' service; three campaigns in Germany, two in Corsica, two in America; officer of intelligence and capacity.

De Straack. See Straack.

De Tarlé. Aide Major-General (Aide Adjutant General); served from 1759; Captain in the Regiment de Bouillon; Lieutenant-Colonel, 24th March, 1780; served with distinction; talented; siege of York.

De Trenovay. See Trenovay.

De Tarragon. Captain commanding the company of Chasseurs; twenty-three years of service performing the functions of Major of the division of the Count de Dillon.

Deux, Ponts, Christian Marquis des. Lieutenant-Colonel of Horse, commanding the Royal Deux Ponts Regiment; officer, 20th April, 1768; Colonel in 1772, but did not assume command of the regiment till 20th September, 1775, on account of age; took part in the four campaigns in America with zeal, courage and all the necessary qualities inherent in a good corps commander; received the Cross of St. Louis and the assurance of a promotion to the rank of brigadier when the colonels of 1772 were advanced.

D'houdetot. See Houdetot.

D'Ichtensheim. See Ichtensheim.

Didier, Pierre, Captain; commissioned from 1st September, 1749; born at Dijon, 20th September, 1729; though retired, participated in the York campaign.

Dillon, Arthur, Count de. Colonel, March, 1772; born in London, 1st May, 1749.

Dillon, Barthelemy. Lieutenant-Colonel, 24th June, 1780; born in Ireland, 17th October, 1729. (Married Miss Mahé de la Bourdonnaye, widow of the Marquis de Montlezun.)

D'Imbart de Barry. See Barry.

D'Olliéres, Jean Baptiste Philippe Felix. Count of Saint Maine; born at Olliéres, diocese of Aix, 25th December, 1751; 2d Lieutenant in the —— ——? Colonel-General of Horse Regiment of the Cavalry, 16th July, 1769; Colonel of the Soissonnois, 29th June, 1775; nephew of Marshal Duellery; gallant conduct at York.

Domergue, de St. Florent Francois Isaac. Captain, 16th June, 1775; born at Couse, in Languedoc, in 1742; decorated with the insignia of St. Louis for gallant conduct at York.

Doyré, Sir. Captain Royal Engineer Corps; pension granted; his father was Lieutenant-General and director of the fortifications of the defenses of the Meuse.

Drude, de la Caterie Julien. Captain, 19th March, 1780; born at Vire, in Normandy, 1st August, 1742; decorated for gallantry at York.

Drouilhet, de Figalas. Captain, en second (Agénois); served from 1770; Captain in 1781; received a painful wound at York, from which it was feared permanent injury would result.

Drouilhet, de Sigala Ignace. Captain, 1st December, 1781; born at Mamande, 26th November, 1752; wounded in the siege of York in 1781.

Du Barry, Denis d'Hubart. Captain, 11th June, 1776; born at Puy Laurens, in Languedoc, 11th February, 1742; wounded at Savannah; brave conduct at St. Christopher.

Du Bouchet. Aide Major-General; served from 1770; Captain from 1779; served with valor and intelligence; siege of York.

Dubourg, Cromot. See Cromot Dubourg.

Du Chesne. Captain commanding (Saintonge); twenty-five years' service; three campaigns in Germany, four in the Isle of France.

Du Crozet, de Sarrazin Jean Francois. Captain, 29th May, 1778; born at Vienna, 7th January, 1733; killed in the action of 15th May, 1780, while serving in Count de Guichey's squadron.

Dudiot. Captain commanding Grenadiers (Gautinois); twenty-two years' service; three campaigns in Germany, six in America; was in the attack of the redoubt at the head of his company.

Du Drot, Marc Antoine. Captain, 23d April, 1773; born at Charleville, 16th January, 1743; decorated with the insignia of St. Louis after the capture of York.

Dune, Count de. Took part in all the engagements of the campaign. (Name also spelled O'Dune.)

Du Plessis. See Thomas.

Dupleix, Jean Baptiste Girard. Chevalier de Cadignan. Lieutenant-Colonel, 19th August, 1775; gallant conduct at St. Christopher; if engaged at said place it is quite likely he served the United States.

Dupont, D'Aubevoye de Laubardière, Louis Francois Bertrand. Second Lieutenant, 30th January, 1778; born 27th October, 1759; Aide-de-Camp to the Count de Rochambeau; obtained a discharge as Captain of Cavalry without payment therefor, for distinguished conduct at York, Pa.

Du Portail, Le Bégue. Commanded the American Engineer Corps; was promised, 25th February, 1782, the rank of Brigadier in three years by continuing in active service in America; served from 1761 in the Corps of Engineers in which he was appointed Captain in 1773; Lieutenant-Colonel attached to the Infantry Corps, 25th April, 1780; Chevalier of St. Louis, 5th December, 1781; obtained at this period a bounty of $(?)2,400; Colonel in the Army of the United States from 1777; then Brigadier-General, and after the siege of York Congress raised him to the rank of Major-General; took part in five campaigns in America; commanded the United States and French Engineers; had charge of the defense of the country; of the construction of the forts at all the important points; was present in the most important actions and sieges, and in him General Washington placed implicit confidence; upon the conclusion of peace was promoted Brigadier.

Durand de la Motte. Champagne Regiment; present at the capture of Grenada and in the naval action, but does not appear in the land operations.

Durssus, Jacques Philippe Auguste. Lieutenant, ——; born at Mondeville, district of Caen, 26th April, 1758; wounded at the siege of York.

Dursu. Lieutenant, second class (Soissonnois); served from 1774; seriously wounded at York. (Supposed to be the same as preceding name.)

Du Vales, Jean Grégoire D'Ecouffin. Captain, 15th April, 1780; born at Montmac in Languedoc, 27th January, 1746; gratuity granted for gallant conduct at York; gunshot wound through left thigh at Borzo, Corsica, 8th October, 1768.

Ecouffin D¹: Vales, d'. See Du Vales.

Ecures Des. Second Lieutenant of the Company of Chasseurs, Armagnac Regiment; received a gunshot wound through the hand in a sortie 24th September, which did not prevent him from being present in the attack on the entrenchments at Savannah.

Edouard, ——. Born 3d June, 1700.

Emery de Bois Loge, Sir Henry. Captain of Cannoneers in the Royal Artillery Corps; pension granted.

Enfant, L'. See L'Enfant.

Eparsac, Joseph Henry de Coussol d'. Captain, 28th August, 1777; born at St. Gon in Gascony, 20th March, 1736; decorated for the capture of York.

Eussebe. See Kermarec.

Eyroux, Ponteves d'. See Ponteves.

Fahègues. First Lieutenant of Chasseurs (Gatinois); served from 1755; in the attack of the redoubt.

Fahègue, Chevalier de la. See Montalègre.

Falqueirettes, de Saint Félix (Chevalier de Rebourquil), Louis Etienne Aronde. Captain Touraine regiment, 12th December, 1779; born at Milhan, in Rouergue, 16th February, 1749; promise of a majority for exhibition of zeal and talents displayed at York.

Fauste, de Mayence (sic), Charles Gaspard. Born at Blangy, in Normandy, 22d February, 1735; 2d Lieutenant, 12th March, 1780; Lieutenant, 8th April, 1784.

Ferrette, Jean Baptiste. Captain, 27th January, 1758; born at Cernay, in Alsace, 13th January, 1736; promise of a lieutenancy in the Colonel's Company for brave conduct at York; Captain (Saintonge); commanding with the rank of major; served from 1753; Captain in 1758, with rank of Major, 3d March, 1774; distinguished officer; first Captain of the regiment; *probably senior.*

Fersen, Axel, Count de. Colonel of Horse; born 4th September, 1754; gallantry at York; Lieutenant, second class, of the Royal Deux Ponts Regiment; served from 1769 in Sweden; Colonel, 20th June, 1780; First Aide-de-Camp of Count de Rochambeau and son of a Minister of State in Sweden; a man of great merit.

Feyron Des. See Des-feyron.

Figalas, de. See Drouilhet de Figalas.

Fladen, De. See De Fladen.

Flechir, Charles Francois Joseph Count de. Colonel of Horse en second, 13th April, 1780; gallant conduct at York; distinguished conduct at St. Christopher, where, with a small body of 300 Grenadiers and Chasseurs he repulsed and routed 1,400 troops the British had landed; served from 1760; Captain, 7th June, 1776; Colonel of Horse, en second, 13th April, 1780.

Fleury, Francois Louis Teissedre de. Major, 19th May; born at St. Hippolite, 20th August, 1749; decorated for distinguished conduct at York; Major (Saintonge); thirteen years and six months' service; two campaigns in Corsica, 1768 and 1769; six in the Colonies from 1776; officer of the greatest distinction; commanded a camp of Light Troops in the American service from 1777 to 1779; granted a decoration by Congress for gallantry at Stony Point; was at York and there, too, sustained his reputation.

Fontanges, Viscount de. Born 21st March, 1740, at Montlucon, Department of the Allier; Lieutenant in the Infantry Regiment of Poitou, 1st January, 1756; Captain, same regiment, 1st June, 1758; took part in all the war with Germany, from 1757 to 1763; wounded at the battle of Rosbak, 5th November, 1757; served with the rank of Captain from March, 1775; detailed in the Department of the Navy and Colonies and appointed Major of the Regiment of the Cape at San Domingo, where he arrived in the month of September, 1775; Chevalier of the Royal and Military Order of St. Louis, 1777; Lieutenant-Colonel, 1778; Colonel, 1780; Major-General of the troops of debarkation of the Naval Army of Count d'Estaing, July, 1779; seriously wounded in the siege at Savannah, Ga., 7th October, 1779; commanded in St. Domingo at the time of the Revolution, etc., etc.; died 13th June, 1822. Commanded, under the orders of M. d'Estaing, a legion composed of mulattos and free negroes of St. Domingo—this legion saved the army at Savannah by bravely covering its retreat. Among the blacks who rendered signal services at this time were: André, Regaud; —— Beauvais; —— Villatte; —— Beauregard; —— Lambert; who latterly became Generals under the Convention, including Henri Christophe, the future King of Haiti.

Forbach (Marquis des Deux Ponts) Christian, Count de. Colonel; born at the Deux Ponts, 20th September, 1752; rank of 2d Lieutenant, without pay, from 20th April, 1768; Colonel of the regiment in 1775; gallant conduct at York.

Forbach, Count des Deux Ponts, Gillaume de. Lieutenant-Colonel, en second; born at the Deux Ponts, 18th June, 1754; rank of 2d Lieutenant in the regiment, 12th November, 1768; Lieutenant-Colonel, en second, of the regiment, 2d October, 1777; wounded at the siege of York in 1781.

Forèt. Sergeant of Chasseurs (Gatinois); soldier in 1769; Sergeant in 1781; selected for the attack of the redoubt and marched thereto at the head of the Axe-Bearers.

Foucauld. Captain, second class, of Chasseurs (Gatinois); served from 1760; Captain in 1777; in the attack of the redoubt; wounded at Savannah.

Fouquet, d'Aurillac, Jean Gabriel Réné Francois Marquis de. Colonel of Horse, second in command; born at Metz, 13th March, 1751; decorated for gallantry at St. Christopher, action at Savannah; expeditions made against the enemy in the Islands of Taboga, St. Christopher, St. Lucie and the Domingo.

Francois, Marie. Born at Montpellier 1st February, 1750.

Furstenwoerther, Charles, Baron de. Captain; born at Musenheimle, 23d August, 1741; Ensign, 8th January, 1758; Captain commanding in 1776; distinguished himself at York, for which he received the Cross of the Mérite Militaire; Regiment of Royal Deux Ponts; Captain commanding; twenty-three years and ten months' service; five campaigns in Germany, two in America.

Gallatin. Lieutenant, second-class, of Grenadiers (Royal Deux Ponts); served from 1776; Lieutenant from 1780; was in the attack of the redoubt.

Galtier, D'Alansse, Joseph Philemond. Captain, 8th April, 1779; born in Languedoc, 24th December, 1742; engaged in the three actions under Count de Guichey.

Gambs, Jean Daniel de. Major (Bourbonnois); served from 1757; Captain in 1772; Major in 1777; took part in the war with Germany and Corsica; in the action in the Chesapeake; the oldest officer of this year; officer of the greatest distinction; born at Strasburg in 1741; received pension for gallant conduct at York.

Gardette, Joseph Bernard Modeste Anselme de La. . Captain, 11th May, 1769; born at Apt, in Provence, 24th July, 1740; decorated for gallantry at York.

Garavagne, Sir. Captain; Royal Engineer Corps; pension granted.

Gaston, Charles Bernard. See Chapuy.

Gautier, de Kerveguen. Captain of Infantry; Assistant to the Quartermaster-General for lodging the landing troops; entered the service in 1755 as Naval Engineer went to St. Domingo as Aide-de-Camp to Count d'Estaing; performed the duties of engineer from 1764 to 1766; Topographical Engineer of Camps in 1767; sent to Corsica up to 1769; Captain of Infantry with appointments from 1769; employed on the coasts and frontiers up to 1777; participated in all of d'Estaing's campaign and was engaged in the land actions which took place during the twenty-one months' campaign of this squadron; was one of the first in the assault of the bluff of the Grenada hospital, and at the siege of Savannah gave proof of great usefulness and valor.

Germain. See Rostaing.

Gilbert, Jacques Marie. Born in Paris, 3d August, 1760.

Gilbert, Melchoir Joseph. Captain commanding (Soissonnois); twenty-five years and three months' service two campaigns in America; served with distinction at the capture of York; Captain, 11th May, 1769; born at Dié, in Dauphiné, 4th October, 1737; decorated for gallantry at York.

Gillegue, Jean Francois de. 2d Lieutenant; born 6th October, 1761; Cadet, nobleman, 28th August, 1777; 2d Lieutenant of the Colonel's Company, 26th September, 1778; gallantry at York, where he was wounded.

Gilliaume, de Deux Ponts, Count. Colonel of Horse, second class, of the Royal Deux Ponts Regiment; born 18th June, 1754; served from 1770; Captain, 25th April, 1772; Colonel from 2d October, 1777; engaged in the attack of the redoubt with such brilliant valor that the Count de Rochambeau requested his appointment to the command of a regiment in preference to his son.

Ginville, de. See Levert.

Gouvion, De. Captain, second class, in the Corps of Royal Engineers; Col-

onel in the service of the Americans; served from 1769 in the Engineers; Captain in 1779; in America with the rank of Major since 1777, and was Lieutenant-Colonel and Colonel respectively; rendered valuable services; name presented for a Lieutenancy in the Colonel's Company, Provincial Troops.

Gouzié. 2d Lieutenant of Grenadiers (Agénois); private in 1757; officer in 1770; took part in the campaigns of Germany and York; in the latter showed gallantry.

Gorat de Beaumont. See Beaumont.

Grillière, Marin. Captain, en second, Regiment of Armagnac; commanded a picket; ten years' service; two dangerous gunshot wounds in the attack on the entrenchments at Savannah; was at the time under the orders of Count de Dillon, who had pickets from this regiment in his division.

Guichard. 2d Lieutenant Grenadiers (Soissonnois); private in 1746; officer in 1776; campaign in Germany as an inferior officer; wounded at Laufeldt and in the action of 16th March, 1781.

Haack, Frédéric Charles Baron de. Captain, en second, of Grenadiers (Royal Deux Ponts); twenty-one years' service; three campaigns in Germany, two in America; displayed great valor in the attack; born at Lappe, 14th March, 1744; Captain of Grenadiers, 8th April, 1779; Cross of the Mérite Militaire conferred 5th December, 1781, for gallant conduct at York.

Haden, Charles Louis de. Captain; born at Manheim, 17th July, 1738; Cadet in the service of the Palatinat in 1757; Captain of the Colonel's Company, 18th October, 1777; brave conduct at York, for which he received the Cross of the Mérite Militaire.

Hainault, Charles Theodore. Captain; born at Manheim, 1st October, 1738; Cadet in the service of the Palatine Prince, 20th August, 1756; Captain commanding, 22d July, 1779; Cross of the

Mérite Militaire after the action at York.

Haynault. Captain commanding (Royal Deux Ponts); twenty-four years' service; six campaigns in Germany, two in America. (Is not this the same as the one preceding?)

Henry, Emery. See Henry de Bois Loge.

Hoen, de Dillenbourg. Philippe Frédéric, Chevalier, de. Born 16th June, 1759; 2d Lieutenant of Grenadiers, 18th October, 1777; Lieutenant, second class, 22d July, 1779; gratuities for brave conduct at York.

Houdetot, Marc Joseph de Colanby. Lieutenant, second class (Agénois); served from 1775; Lieutenant, 21st April, 1779; born at St. Martin, 18th June, 1852; bayonet wound in the thigh at the siege of York.

Hubart, d'. See Du Barry.

Humbert. 2d Lieutenant of Chasseurs (Royal Deux Ponts); served from 28th August, 1777.

Humbert, Claude Jacques Francois. Born 14th August, 1757; Lieutenant, ties for brave conduct at York.

Ichtensheim, Francois Charles d'. Born 28th October, 1756; Lieutenant, second class, 30th June, 1782; gratuisecond class, 28th April, 1778; gratuities for brave conduct at York; Lieutenant, en second, of Chasseurs (Royal Deux Ponts); served from 1775; Lieutenant from 1778; was in the attack of the redoubt.

Jacques, Gilbert Marie. See Gilbert.

James, Chevalier de Longueville, Jean Joachim de. 2d Lieutenant, 7th July, 1779; born 24th August, 1762; wounded at the siege of York.

Jayet, de Baudot, Jean Baptiste Antoine. Captain, 29th December, 1777; born at Charlemont, 15th February, 1739; gunshot wound, left shoulder, at Minorca; buried in a mine; gunshot wound, right shoulder, at Borgo, in Corsica, 1768; extraordinary gratuity for gallantry at York.

Josselin, de Laumont de Castille. 2d Lieutenant (Agénois); served from 1778; received two dangerous bayonet wounds in the breast in the only sortie made by the enemy at York; gallant conduct.

Kalb, Henry Jules Alexandre, baron de. Born in Saxony, 25th November, 1753; 1st Lieutenant, 28th April, 1778; of the Grenadiers, 4th April, 1780; distinguished himself at York; 1st Lieutenant · of Grenadiers; served from 1770; Lieutenant from 1776 (Royal Deux Ponts); brave officer, engaged in the attack of the redoubt.

Kermarec, de Troron, Louis Jean Eussebe. Captain, 1st February, 1782; born at Quimperle, 8th December, 1747; gratuities given for gallant conduct at York; wounded in the action of 12th April, under M. de Grasse.

Klock, Bernard Antoine. Captain; born in the palatinat, 16th June 1736; Sergeant, 18th October, 1756; Captain commanding, 28th August, 1777; of Chasseurs, the 18th of October, following; gallantry at York, for which he received the Cross of the Mérite Militaire.

Klocker. Captain commanding Grenadiers; twenty-five years' service; two campaigns in America; engaged in the attack of the redoubt; an officer of great merit. (Is not this the same as the preceding?)

La Bade, de Pecosme, Jean Francois. Captain, 17th August, 1775; born at the Bartido in Armagnac, 7th February, 1743; decorated after the capture of York.

La Barre. See De la Barre.

La Bord, De Pecanne. Captain commanding (Gatinois); twenty-one years' service; two campaigns in Germany, six in America; good services.

La Boyére. Captain commanding (Soissonnois); twenty-five years' service; two campaigns in America; very fine officer.

Lacarderie, De. Captain, en second (Soissonnois); twenty-two years' service; three campaigns in Germany, two in Corsica, two in America; gave evidence of valor.

La Corbière, Antoine Madelaine de. Captain, 19th May, 1774; born at Avranches, 11th August, 1743; decorated for brave conduct at York.

La Corbière, Réné Anne Gilbert Francois de. Captain, 1st September, 1777; born at St. Martin de 'Julien, Diocese of Avranches, 11th February, 1742; decorated for gallantry at York.

Lafayette, Marie, Joseph, Paul, Yves, Roch Gilbert du Motier du Motier; son of Michael, Louis, Christophe, Roch Gilbert du Motier, Marquis de Lafayette, Baron de Vissac, nobleman of St. Romain and other places, and of Lady Marie Louise Julie de la Rivière; baptized 7th September, 1757, in the parish of Chavaniac, Diocese of St. Flour; born 26th September, 1757 (6th September); 9th April, 1771, musketeer in the Second Company; 7th April, 1773, rank of 2d Lieutenant in the de Noailles Dragoon Regiment; 19th May, 1774, Captain; ——, 1776, on half pay; ——, 1777, came to North America, where he commanded a Corps d'Armée; 3d March, 1779, Colonel of Horse commanding the regiment of the Dragoons of the King; 1st June, 1779, Assistant Quartermaster-General of the Army in Brittany and Normandy; 27th January, 1782, leaves the King's Regiment; 5th December, 1781, promise of the appointment to the rank of Lieutenant-General, to date from 19th October, 1781; 12th March, 1783, brevet of Lieutenant-General forwarded to date from 19th October, 1781, in order to receive its benefits, etc.; 1st April, 1788, commanding a Brigade of Infantry in the division of Languedoc and Roussillon; 15th July, 1788, the King judged proper to withdraw his service papers as Colonel of Horse, on duty; July, 1789, Com-

manding-General of the Guard of Paris; 30th June, 1791, Lieutenant-General, Commander-in-Chief, 16th August, 1792, left his post with Launnay, Laton, Maubourg, Lallemant, De Roure, Paris; came to North America in 1777, where he was appointed Major-General in the American Army; took part in the campaign as of said rank; wounded 11th September of the same year, at the battle of Brandywine; appointed Commander of a body of troops to operate against Canada; took part in the campaign of 1778, commanding a portion of the American Army; led a detachment of troops to co-operate with the French in Rhode Island; took part in the campaign of 1779 in France; was assigned to the staff of the army in Normandy; set out again in the month of March, 1780, for America and was given the command of a corps of Elite troops in advance of General Washington's army; in the beginning of 1781 was placed in command of Virginia with an effective force of 10,000 men, of which number 3,200 were Frenchmen; was engaged at Williamsburg, and during the night of the 14th of October carried by assault a redoubt at York, which surrendered on the 19th; and carried to France the news of the capture of this place in the month of November, 1781; he did not return to America, but was under the orders of the Count d'Estaing and was designated to perform the duties of Major-General of the combined armies of France and Spain against Jamaica about the time preliminaries were being made.

La Gardette. See Gardette.

Lalbeuge, Jean Francois de. Captain; born at La Tour en Quercy, 23d December, 1730; First Captain of the Regiment (Gatinois); served from 1754; Captain in 1757.

Langon, Jean Jacques de. Captain commanding (Gatinois); twenty-three years' service; six campaigns in Germany, six in the Colonies; in the attack of the redoubt; Captain, 18th June, 1776; born at Aire, in Guyenne, 14th February, 1737; decorated for gallant conduct at York.

La Perouse, ——. Commanded an expedition in the Hudson Bay.

La Pierre. Lieutenant, en second, of Grenadiers (Gatinois); private in 1746; officer in 1770; was in the attack of the redoubt.

Lassaderie de Caupanes, Pierre. Captain, commissioned 4th July, 1777; born in 1730; pension of $400 on the occasion of the siege of York.

Lauberdière, De. See De Lauberdière.

Laumont de Castille, de. See Josselin.

Launay, Jean Baptiste Réné Clément De. Captain, 27th July, 1769; born at Ruppeveil, in Normandy, in November, 1730; decorated for actions under Count de Guichey; pensioned for gallantry at York; gratuity for gallant conduct at St. Christopher.

Launay, Sir de. Captain in the Corps of Royal Engineers; Colonel in the service of the Americans; served from 1768 in the Engineers; Captain in 1777; came to America in 1777 with the rank of Major and was made Lieutenant-Colonel and Colonel respectively; name presented for a Lieutenancy in the Colonel's Company of the provincial troops.

Launet, Francois Claude de. Captain commandant Grenadiers (Bourbonnois); twenty-four years' service; three campaigns in Germany, two in America. Captain, 25th August, 1773; born at the Garde, in Berry, 11th November, 1738; decorated for gallantry at York.

Lauretz, Chevalier de. Aide Quartermaster-General; Captain, half pay, in the regiment of Royal Cavalry; twenty-six years of age; 2d Lieutenant, 29th July, 1776; rank of Captain, 6th November, 1779; received a serious

wound in the attack and fears entertained of his being crippled for life; full of courage and talented; nephew of Marshal Duke de Broglie; siege of York; request for appointment as Colonel of Horse, second class, and the Cross of St. Louis, in resigning that of Malta.

Lauzun, Duke de. Brigadier; commanded a corps of volunteers bearing his name; served from 1761; Colonel, 11th October, 1767; Brigadier, 1st March, 1780; gave proof of the greatest zeal and the most brilliant valor; siege of York.

Laval, Anne Alexandre Marie Sulpice Joseph, Marquis de. Colonel; born in Paris, 22d January, 1747; — Musketeer in the second campaign, 1762; Captain in the cavalry regiment of de Berry, 28th April, 1765; Colonel of Touraine, 3d January, 1770; of Bourbonnais, 1775; promoted to the rank of Brigadier-General, 5th December, for gallant conduct at York; Quartermaster of the army in Corsica in 1769; Lieutenant-General, 13th June, 1780, to take rank from the first promotion. Colonel of Horse; commanded the Bourbonnois Regiment; engaged in the action in the Chesapeake; two naval actions; in the last remained alone with his Major on the quarter-deck, the others having been killed or wounded; his service in America deserves the greatest praise; served in the war of Corsica. Brigadier; Colonel of Horse commanding the Bourbonnais Regiment; served from 1762; Captain in 1765; Colonel, 3d January, 1770; Brigadier from 5th December, 1781, as a reward for his gallant conduct at the siege of York; took part in two campaigns in Corsica, four in America; engaged in three actions, ——; appointed Lieutenant-General, to take rank, ——; was aboard of the ship Conqueror (Conquérant), where, during the action of the 16th March he suffered more than all others of the squadron.

La Valette. See De La Valette.

La Villebonne, de. See Le Saige de La Villebonne.

Leaumont, de Castille, Marie Robert. 2d Lieutenant, 8th April, 1780; born on the Isle at Vacae, Isle of Saint Dominique; wounded at the siege of York in 1781.

Le Bret, Jean Francois. Captain commanding Chasseurs (Soissonnois); twenty-two years' service; three campaigns in Germany, two in Corsica, two in America; distinguished officer; Captain, 4th July, 1777; born at Belusson in Normandy, 25th November, 1742; decorated for gallantry at York.

Le Cadet, Thomas. Born 6th November, 1742.

Le Cornet. Sergeant-Major of Grenadiers (Gatinois); private in 1769; Sergeant in 1781; selected for the attack of the redoubt and marched thereto at the head of the Axe-Bearers.

Le Fetre de la Faluer. Captain commanding (Saintonge); twenty-two years' service; five campaigns in Cayenne, two in America.

Lehoux, Michel. Lieutenant, 11th November, 1779; born 5th October, 1736; came to America in 1775; took part in all the campaigns.

L'Enfant. Captain in the service of the United States since 1778; was Lieutenant in the Colonial Troops, from which he passed into the American service in 1777; was at the siege of Savannah, where he was wounded and remained on the battle field; from that time he served in General Washington's army; much has been said that, like Villefranche, he spent his fortune in the United States; obtained a pension of $300, and his name to be presented for a company in the Provincial Troops.

Leonardy, Charles Joseph de. 2d Lieutenant; born 22d September, 1758; Cadet, nobleman, 20th September, 1777; 2d Lieutenant, 7th August, 1770; in

the Chasseurs, 10th March, 1780; gallantry at York.

Le Saige, de La Villebrune. Captain, en second, of Chasseurs (Agénois); served from 1762; Captain from 1779; officer of merit; gallant conduct at Pensacola and York; Servant Paul; Captain, 22d August, 1779; born at Sulliac, Diocese of St. Malo, 25th September, 1747; gallantry at the capture of York; was killed in the siege of the Castle of St. Christopher in 1782.

Lespes, Jean Joseph de. Captain, 17th August, 1774; born at Mengron, near Tardres, in Gascony, 8th October, 1731; decorated 8th October, 1781; died 7th March, 1782, from wounds received in the siege of St. Christopher.

Lestrade, Claude, Baron de. Lieutenant-Colonel to date, 19th August, 1777; born at Puy en Velay, 5th April, 1730; conspicuous at York, Va., by the most brilliant acts. Lieutenant-Colonel of the Regiment of Gatinois; served from 1746; Captain, 5th February, 1757; Lieutenant-Colonel, 17th August, 1777; marched at the head of the Grenadiers in the midst of abattis and palisades as sprightly as a man of twenty years; siege of York.

Levert, de Genville, Barthilemy Laurent. Lieutenant, 16th November, 1781; born at Raincourt, in Conté, 10th August, 1755; gallantry at York; taken prisoner in the action of 12th April, 1782; confined on the ship Hector; Lieutenant, en second, of Chasseurs (Gatinois); served from 1776; in the attack of the redoubt; Lieutenant; born 30th November, 1759; cadet, nobleman, 6th June, 1776; 2d Lieutenant, en second, 14th November, 1781; served very well at Savannah.

Liamart, Henry Francois, Viscount de Pondeux. Colonel, 13th April, 1780; born in Paris, 1st August, 1748; his father was Governor of Saint Jean Pied de Port; gallant conduct at York.

Londeix, de la Brosse, Junier. Lieutenant, 1779; born 25th April, 1761;

wounded in the face in the actions of the 9th or 12th of April, under M. de Grasse.

Loucault, Jean Simon David de. Captain, 28th August, 1777; born in the Isle de Rhé, 26th February, 1741; decorated 4th April, 1781; wounded at Savannah, and was in the engagements under M. Lamotte Piquet.

Lustrac, Jean Joseph de. Captain, 5th June, 1760; born at Liasse, in the Diocese of Aire, in Gascony, 25th November, 1733; seriously wounded at the siege of Munster in 1759; distinguished himself at the siege of York; Captain commanding (Agénois); served from 1756; Captain in 1760; engaged in the campaigns in Germany; seriously wounded at the siege of Munster; officer of merit.

Lutzen, Guillaume Frédéric Bernard de. Born 18th May, 1758; 1st Lieutenant, 4th April, 1780; wounded at the siege of York in 1781; 1st Lieutenant of Chasseurs (Royal Deux Ponts); served from 1775; Lieutenant from 1778; was in the attack of the redoubt.

Lynch, Isidore. Captain, 24th May, 1778; born 8th June, 1755; distinguished himself in India, Grenada, Savannah, and York; Aide Adjutant of Infantry; served from 1770; Captain from 1778; attached to the Dillon Regiment; served in India, Grenada, at Savannah, in America.

Macdonnall. Captain, en second Dillon Regiment; twenty-four years' service; took part in the last war with Germany; was at the capture of Grenada, naval action, and in the expedition against Savannah when d'Estaing selected him to the command of a picket of sixty volunteers in the action of the 9th October, ——.

Madron de Brie. See De Brie.

Maguois. Lieutenant, second-class (Soissonnois); forty-one years' service; private, grenadier; officer from 1763;

good officer of fortune, riddled with wounds.

Marguerit. See Dolomine.

Marguerite, Chevalier de Chalendar. See Chalendar.

Marie, Francois. See Francois.

Marin de Grillière. See de Grillière.

Marin, Jean Baptiste De. Captain, 22d April, 1762; born at Tarascon; dangerously wounded at the siege of York; died from wounds; Captain, commanding Grenadiers (Soissonnois); twenty-six years' service; two campaigns in America; received two serious wounds at the capture of York; permanently injured.

Mascaron, Philippe Louis Beau de. Captain; born at Vauvert, in Languedoc, 22d January, 1744; Captain, en second (Gatinois); served from 1767; Captain in 1779; in the attack of the redoubt; his uncle was governor of the Isle of Aix.

Maublerce. See St. Simon Maublerce.

Mauraige, de. See Bérard.

Maury, Louis Francois Philippe de. Captain, 3d June, 1779; born 3d October, 1749; pensioned for gallantry at York; Captain, second class, of Chasseurs (Bourbonnois); student of the Military Academy; served from 1767; Captain in 1779; was in the attack of the redoubt.

Menon, Louis Armand Francois De. Captain, 30th June, 1778; born at Monsegur 19th November, 1744; promise of a regiment for gallant conduct at York; nominated to the majority of the Auvergne Regiment, in 1782; Captain, en second, of Grenadiers (Soissonnois); served from 1761; Captain in 1778; a distinguished and gallant officer.

Menon, Pierre Armand, Chevalier de. Captain, 14th November, 1782; born at Monsegur, in Guyenne, 5th April, 1755.

Ménonville, Louis Antoine Thiebault De. Major, 29th September, 1775; pensioned; siege of York. (See Thibault.)

Meth, Alexandre, Chevalier de la. Captain on half-pay in the Regiment of Royal Cavalry; officer in 1778; Captain in 1779; appointed Assistant Quartermaster-General, supernumerary, in November, 1782; was a distinguished officer; granted a pension of $500.

Miolis Sixtus Alexandre Francois de. Lieutenant, 20th September, 1782; born at Aix, in Provence 18th September, 1759; dangerously wounded at siege of York.

Mirabaud, André Boniface, Louis de Regniety, Chevalier de. Colonel of Horse, 24th April, 1772; born in Paris, 30th November, 1754; was engaged in three actions under M. de Guichey in 1780; gallant conduct at St. Christopher, where he was wounded; he was father of the Tribune.

Molière, André Louis Florent de. Captain; born 17th December, 1749; Captain, en second (Gatinois); student at the military school; served from 1767; was in the attack of the redoubt.

Montalègre, Chevalier [de la Fahégue de] Jean Barthélemy. Captain, 1st July, 1782; born at Vigau, in Languedoc, 7th January, 1755; gallant conduct at York.

Montalembert, Trion de. Captain; sent to the Conty Dragoons, 6th June, 1780; Chevalier de Tressan.

Montlezun, De. Lieutenant-Colonel (Touraine); served from 1744; Captain in 1775; Lieutenant-Colonel in 1779; distinguished officer. (See Monzellan.)

Montlong. 2d Lieutenant (Agénois); served from 1777; 2d Lieutenant in 1779; was in the sieges of Pensacola and York; behaved very well.

Monzellan, Jean Francois Du Moulin de la Bartelle De. Lieutenant-Colonel, 8th April, 1779; born at Aire, in Guyenne, 14th June, 1729; received a bad

contusion in the actions of 9th and 12th April, 1782, under Count de Grasse.

Moysia, Joseph Marie Anne De. Captain, 30th January, 1778; Captain, en second (Soissonnois); student military academy; twenty-one years' service; two campaigns in Germany; two in Corsica; two in America; born at Bourges, in Bresse, 19th February, 1744; decorated for gallantry at York. (Name also spelled Moyria.)

Muhlenfels, Charles Adam. Born 23d October, 1748; 2d Lieutenant, 13th August, 1765; 2d Captain from 8th April, 1779; gratuities for brave conduct at York; Captain, en second, of Chasseurs (Royal Deux Ponts); served from 1765; Captain from 1779; was in the attack of the redoubt.

Mullens. Lieutenant in the Regiment of de Berwick, to rank as Captain; served as private from 1757; flagbearer in 1769; 2d Lieutenant in 1770; Lieutenant in 1778; rank of Captain in 1779; took part in two campaigns in Germany; two in the Isle of France, and seven in America; filled the functions of Captain des Guides with great success.

Négley, De la Roche. Lieutenant; entered the service, 6th June, 1776; engaged in the attack on the entrenchments at Savannah, where he was wounded; served in the Regiment of Gadenois.

Noes, Des. See Des Noes.

Noailles, Louis Marie Viscount de. 2d Colonel, 8th March, 1780; Colonel of Horse, Lieutenant Commandant of the King's Dragoon Regiment, 27th January, 1782, for distinguished conduct at York. Colonel of Horse, en second, of the Regiment of Soissonnois; Captain from 2d March, 1773; Colonel from 28th February, 1778, upon condition not to assume command and rank before reaching the age of twenty-three years; gave proof of his zeal from the beginning of the war, especially at York. He was charged, with Colonel Laurens, to arrange for the surrender, and acquitted himself well.

Noailles, Viscount de. Colonel of Infantry, commanding the third division; two assaults; two landings; one siege; chief in charge of several trenches; commanded a division of a thousand men.

O'Dune. See Dune.

O'Farell. Lieutenant, en second; served four years in the Regiment de Lally in India; was discharged and entered in the service in the Dillon Regiment as Cadet in 1757; was made officer in 1776; was in the assault on the bluff of the Grenada hospital, naval action, and in the assault at Savannah, where he received a gunshot wound in the leg.

Ollières. See D'Ollières.

Olonne, Chevalier d'. 2d Lieutenant in the de Schomberg Regiment from 1773; came to America as Aide-de-Camp to his uncle, Baron de Viomeuil; was detailed to the staff of the army; his gallant conduct at the siege of York gave promise of a captaincy on half-pay, which was granted.

O'Moran, Jacques. Major, 20th October, 1779; born at Elphin, in Ireland, 1st May, 1739.

O'Neil. Captain Commandant; twenty-nine years of service; he belongs to the fifth generation of those who had the honor to serve the King in the regiment (Dillon) since the passage of Irishmen into France. This officer took part in the last war with Germany; was present at the capture of Grenada naval action; in the expedition against Savannah, where he received a gunshot wound in the breast, causing violent contusion.

Paillot, Antoine. Private, 1st February, 1756; 2d Lieutenant, 21st April, 1779, of the Grenadier Company; gallantry at York; 2d Lieutenant of Grenadiers (Gatinois); private in 1756;

Officer in 1779; in the attack of the redoubt.

Parmentier, Jacques Joseph. Lieutenant 16th June, 1776; born at Heigen, 15th August, 1728; gratuity given for gallant conduct at York.

Parmentier. Lieutenant (Touraine); private in 1746; officer in 1764; very good officer of fortune; served well.

Perouse. See La Perouse.

Petitot. Champagne Regiment; present at the capture of Grenada and in the naval action, but does not appear in the land operations.

Peyron, Pierre. Major, 24th March, 1780; born at Barthelemy, in the Peche; officer of valor and intleligence (note of 1779); pensioned 5th December, 1779, for gallant conduct at York.

Pignol, de Rocreusse, Gaspard Jean Joseph Olivier. Lieutenant, 17th January, 1780. On his way to America, he saved, by his courage and firmness, one hundred and sixty-eight men of the two hundred he commanded from the shipwrecked "Three Henriettas."

Plancher, Sir. Lieutenant, Royal Engineer Corps; pension granted.

Ponteves, d'Eyroux, Marie Jean Balthazar. Lieutenant, en second (Soissonnois); served from 1777; gratuity granted for gallantry at York.

Poquet, de Pulery Desains Sauveur, Mathieu Louis Claude; Captain, 15th November, 1782; born at Martinique, 10th December, 1750; wounded at Savannah, where he distinguished himself, and at the taking of York.

Poudeux, Viscount de. Colonel of Horse; commanded the Regiment of Touraine; served from 1760; Captain, 28th April, 1768; Colonel of Horse, 14th March, 1774.

Pulery, de. See Poquet.

Querenet, Mr. Colonel without Brigade in the Royal Engineer Corps; pension granted.

Rebourquil, Chevalier de. See Falqueirrette de Saint Félix.

Rhule, De. Captain commanding (Royal Deux Ponts); twenty-three years and nine months' service; five campaigns in Germany, two in America.

Ribaupierre, Charles Royer de. Born 8th January, 1762; 2d Lieutenant from 28th April, 1778; gratuities for brave conduct at York 2d Lieutenant of Chasseurs (Royal Deux Ponts); served from 1778; was in the attack of the redoubt.

Rochambeau, Donatien Marie Joseph de Vernier, Viscount de. Colonel of Horse, second class, of the Regiment of Bourbonnois; born 9th April, 1755; served from 1769; Captain, 28th July, 1773; Colonel of Horse, second class, 22d January, 1779; commanded a Battalion of Grenadiers and Chasseurs at the time of the advance and placed them so near the enemy as to force Cornwallis to abandon the redoubts and the camp at Pigeon's Hill, which gained a very great advantage over the enemy; Colonel; born in Paris, 9th April, 1775; appointed Colonel of his Regiment, 1st July, 1783; Colonel of Horse, commanding the regiment of Saintonge; 2d Lieutenant, 5th August, 1769; Captain in 1773; Colonel, second-class, of the Bourbonnois in 1779; Colonel of Horse, commanding the Regiment of Saintonge in 1782; took part in four campaigns in America; made a trip to Europe regarding the Conference of Hartford; told the Chevalier of Malo de la Molt that the Queen desired his removal, yet he continued the same functions without pay; for a long time Commander-in-Chief, in the absence of the Marquis de Laval, of the Bourbonnois regiment, and according to the usage practiced in America fed all the officers during the marches; these expenses affected his fortune and the small fortune of Madame de Rochambeau; received the Cross of St. Louis, 5th August, 1783, and a pension of $4,000; Colonel, second-class, 22d January, 1779; born at Paris 9th April, 1755; 2d Lieutenant in the Royal Artillery Corps, 1769; Cross of St. Louis, to be decorated therewith 5th August, 1783.

Rochambeau, Jean Baptiste Donatien de Vineur Count de. Born at Vendome, Diocese of Blois, 1st July, 1725; Cornet in the Cavalry Regiment of St. Simon, 24th May, 1742; Captain, 23d July, 1743; Colonel of the Regiment of March, Infantry, 3d March, 1747; Governor of Vendome in Suriuame, 1st June, 1755; Brigadier, 23d July, 1756; detailed to the Army in Germany, 1st March, 1757; Colonel of the Auvergne Regiment, 7th March, 1759; wounded at Clostercamp, 16th October, 1760; Lieutenant-General, 20th February, 1761; Inspector-General of Infantry, 7th March, 1761; Commander of the Order of St. Louis, 1st April, 1766; Grand Cross of St. Louis, 9th December, 1771; Governor of Villefranche, 1776; detailed in Normandy and Brittany, 1st June, 1778; Governor of the City of Vendome,, 1st June, 1779, to 20th December, 1779, at the death of his father; Lieutenant-General, 1st March, 1780; Commander of the King's Army in North America, —— March, 1780; Chevalier of the King's Orders, 8th June, 1783; Commander-in-Chief in Picardy, ——, 1784; Engaged in the campaign in Minorca in 1756, and throughout the German war in 1757, and distinguished himself in both; in the war campaigns from 1742 to 1748; wounded at the battle of Lanfeldt in 1747; displayed gallantry at the head of the Auvergne Brigade in 1759; wounded at Clostercamp, 16th October, 1760; gallant conduct in 1762; commanded a corps of troops; came to America in 1780, and merits the greatest praise.

Rochefontaine. Major in the service of the United States when he came in 1778; was only Captain before the siege of York, but his gallant conduct thereat won him the majority; name to be presented for a company in the Provisional Troops.

Rochenegly, Gabriel Francois de la. Lieutenant, second-class, of Chasseurs, 7th August, 1779; born at Chamblas, 4th October, 1757; wounded at Savannah; taken prisoner in the action of 12th April, 1782; confined on the ship Caton.

Roches, Des. See Des Roches.

Rocreusse, de. See Pignol.

Romefort, Charles Pierre Baudin de Beauregard de. Major 5th June, ——; born at Cognac, 15th June, 1740.

Rostaing, Marquis de; name also Juste, Antoine Henry Marie, Germain, Brigadier; Colonel of Horse commanding the regiment Royal Auvergne or Gatinois; officer in 1760; Captain in 1765; Colonel from 1st April, 1770; Brigadier, 5th December, 1781, as a mark of distinction for gallantry at York; took part in four campaigns in America, and won a brilliant military reputation; appointed to the rank of Lieutenant-General from ——.

Roussille, Raymond de. Lieutenant, 26th September, 1778; born 16th February, 1756; conducted himself well at York; 1st Lieutenant (Gatinois); served from 1775; was orderly officer to Baron de Viomeuil; commanded the trench.

Rouverie, Charles de [Cahières Ches de.] Captain, 6th May, 1761; born at Nismes, 5th January, 1741; decorated for gallant conduct at York, Va.

Rouxelin. See Des Noes.

Royal Deux Ponts, Count. See Des Deux Ponts.

Ruhle, Charles Guillaume de. Born in Saxony, 3d December, 1740; Ensign in the service of Holland; Captain commanding, 22d August, 1779; Cross of the Mérite Militaire after the action at York.

Saint Cosme de Bosnier. See Bosnier.

Saint Maine, Count de. Colonel of Horse; commanded the Soissonnois. See St. Maine.

Sarreck, Custine Adam Phillippe, Count de. Colonel, 8th March, 1780; born at Metz, 4th February, 1740; brave conduct at York; nominated Lieutenant-General, 5th December, 1781.

Sauvage, de Serilange Jean Gaspar. Captain, 3d June, 1780; born at Quarante, diocese of Narbonne, 28th September, 1743; participated in the entire campaign in America; seriously wounded in the left leg at St. Lucie.

Sauver. See Poquet.

Scheldon, De. See De Scheldon.

Scheverin, Guillaume Henry Florus Count de Born at Wiedrauchel, 31st July, 1754; 2d Lieutenant from the 28th of August, 1777; Lieutenant, en second, 28th October, 1781; gratuities for brave conduct at York; 2d Lieutenant of Grenadiers (Royal Deux Ponts); served from 1777; was in the attack of the redoubt.

Scott de Coulanges. Captain, second class (Saintonge); twenty years' service; five campaigns in Cayenne; two in America.

Sebastien, Charles Francois. Captain; born at Falaisse, 21st March, 1746.

Ségur, Count de. Colonel of Horse, en second, of the regiment of Soissonnois actually Colonel of Horse commanding a regiment of Dragoons; served from 1769; Colonel from 1st October, 1776 gave proof at all times of zeal, courage, discipline, and good conduct.

Sequier de Tersson See Tersson.

Serilange, de. See Sauvage.

Shée, Jacques. Captain; born in Ireland, 15th February, 1735.

Sigala, de. See Drouilhet.

Silègue. 2d Lieutenant of Chasseurs (Gatinois); served from 1777; in the attack of the redoubt, where he received a gunshot wound through the thigh; 2d Lieutenant in the Royal Auvergne Regiment; served from 1777; was in the attack of the redoubt at York, and, though mounted on the parapet, he hastened to aid the Viscount deux Ponts, to reach it; he received a gunshot wound through the thigh; pension of £300 granted.

Sirinil, Jean de. Captain commanding Chasseurs (Gatinois); twenty-three years' service; three campaigns in Germany, four in America; was seriously wounded, also at Savannah; officer of great valor; Captain; born at Leinceril, in Périgord, 25th December, 1742; wounded at Savannah, and was in the three engagements under M. De Guichey; wounded at York and died from the effects of his wound in hospital at Williamsburg, 20th December, 1781, or 7th March, 1782

Sinety, Francois Bernard De. Captain, 4th July, 1777, born at Apt, in Provence, 23d July, 1743; decorated for gallantry at York.

Srack, Joseph de. Captain; born at Neukirsh, 4th March, 1734; Ensign in the Regiment of Alsace in 1758; Captain commanding, 3d June, 1779; twice wounded at Clostercamp; received the Cross of the Mérite Militaire after the action at York.

Steding, Baron de. Swede; two assaults; two landings; one siege; commanded trenches; also a column in the assault on Savannah, where he received a wound; a naval action.

St. Felix, Falquerettes de. See Falquerettes.

St. Florent.. Captain commanding (Gatinois); twenty-one years' service; three campaigns in Germany; six in the Colonies; in the attack of the redoubt.

St. Maine, Count de. Colonel of Horse, Regiment of Soissonnois; officer in 1766; Colonel, 29th June, 1775; commanded his regiment with all possible zeal and intelligence during the four campaigns in America; received assurance of an appointment to Brigadier with the Colonels of 1772.

St. Sauveur, De. 1st Lieutenant (Agénois); served from 1773; Lieutenant in 1779; wounded in the breast at the siege of Savannah; displayed great gallantry in an attack upon one of the redoubts at York, and was wounded in the thigh.

St. Simon Maublerce, Claude Anne, Marquis de. Colonel, 29th June, 1775; Lieutenant-General, 1st March, 1780; served from 1754; Colonel, 25th March, 1758; Brigadier, 3d January, 1770; Lieutenant-General from 1st March, 1780; one of the bravest men that ever lived; wounded at York.

Straack, De. Captain commanding Chasseurs (Royal Deux Ponts); twenty-three years' service; five campaigns in Germany; two in America; engaged in the attack of the redoubt.

Sundahl, Christien Louis Philippe. Captain; born at Deux Ponts, 10th May, 1734; Ensign in the service of the Prince of Waldeck in 1754; Captain commanding the Colonels' Company, 3d June, 1779; brave conduct at York, which won for him the Cross of the Mérite Militaire; Captain commandant (Royal Deux Ponts); twenty-four years and nine months' service; six campaigns in Germany; two in America.

Taaffe, Georges. Lieutenant, 10th July, 1779; born in Ireland in 1757; killed at Savannah 8th October, 1779.

Tarlé De. See De Tarlé.

Tascher. Captain; ———.

Teissedre de Fleury. See Fleury.

Tenade, Jean Marie. 1st Lieutenant of Grenadiers (Gatinois); served as private from 1752; officer in 1769; was in the attack of the redoubt; Lieutenant; born at Perosse, in Guyenne, 16th May, 1731; private in the Auvergne Regiment, 10th March, 1752; 2d Lieutenant (in second), 28th August, 1777; 1st Lieutenant, 14th November, 1781; displayed gallantry at York; name also spelled Terrade

Tersson. Sequier de. Captain of Grenadiers Regiment of Agénois; entered the service 11th March, 1756; Captain with Troop, 5th June, 1760; Captain of Grenadiers, 1st September, 1777; in the siege at Savannah, where he reached the trenches as a superior officer.

Thibault, de Menonville. Aide Major-General; served from 1756; Captain in the Engineer Corps; Lieutenant-Colonel, 24th March, 1772; served faithfully in Corsica, Poland Armenia, and siege of York. (See Menonville.)

Thomas, Antoine Chevalier de Maudinet du Plessis. Captain ,en second; First Assistant Aide of the artillery train in the army under the command of Count de Rochambeau; pension granted.

Tourville de. See Chapuy.

Trauront, Chevalier de. 1st Lieutenant (Agénois); served from 1771; Lieutenant in 1777; served well in the Grenadiers.

Trenovay, Captain De. Lieutenant in the Regiment of Foix, January, 1757; Captain in November, 1762; appointed Major by Count D'Estaing at Savannah towards the end of October, 1779.

Troron, de. See Kermarec.

Vachon, Pierre Charles Francois de. Captain, 13th November, 1761; born at Retornnac in Velay, 12th April, 1742; decorated for the capture of York; Captain commanding (Gatinois); twenty-three years' service; five campaigns in America; very fine officer.

Valette, De la. Brigadier, Lieutenant-Colonel of the Saintonge Regiment; served from 1746; Lieutenant-Colonel, 2d March, 1773; Brigadier, 5th December, 1781, for gallant conduct at the capture of York; was left at York with the siege artillery commanding a detachment of 600 men, who afterwards were sent to Baltimore; lived with the inhabitants of both these great cities in an honorable way, and the $200 pay per month he received as a brigadier

in the service of America was barely sufficient to meet his demands.

Varni, de la Chaussée, Charles Alexandre 2d Lieutenant, 22d July, 1779; born at Rouen, 3d July, 1759; wounded at the siege of York.

Vauban, Count de. Colonel of Horse, attached to the Regiment of Orleans, Infantry; formerly 2d Lieutenant of the Gendarmerie; born 9th March, 1754; served from 1770; Captain, 26th May, 1775; Standard-Bearer of Gendarmerie and rank of Lieuetnant- Colonel, 9th March, 1777; Colonel of Horse, 8th April, 1779; obtained permission to join the army in America; was in the attack under Baron de Viomeuil, and displayed gallantry at the siege of York; Colonel of Horse attached to the de Chartres Dragoon Regiment; officer in 1770; Captain in 1775; 2d Lieutenant of the Gendarmerie, with rank of Lieutenant-Colonel in 1777; Lieutenant with the rank of Colonel of Horse in 1779; assigned to the de Chartres Regiment in 1780; took part in three campaigns in America as Aide-de-Camp to Count de Rochambeau; displayed on all occasions the most brilliant valor, particularly in the attack on the redoubts at York, serving side by side with Baron de Viomeuil; name to be presented for appointment as Colonel of Horse, second class.

Villebrune de. See Le Saige.

Villefranche. Formerly Lieutenant in His Majesty's Dragoons; Topographical Engineer in 1770; 2d Lieutenant in 1772; Lieutenant in 1773; was appointed to his lieutenancy in 1782; Major in the service of the United States, 1777, when he came to America; an intelligent and exact person; scattered all his fortune in America; obtained a pension of £500 and name presented for a company of Provincial Troops.

Viomeuil, Chevalier de. Lieutenant-General; served from 1747; Colonel, 20th July, 1761; Brigadier, 3d January, 1770; Lieutenant-General, 1st March,

1780; possessed full knowledge of details, firmness and the most brilliant courage; siege of York; Lieutenant-General; served from 1740; forty-three years' service; Colonel in 1759; Brigadier in 1762; Lieutenant-General, 1770; distinguished himself in a special manner at the siege of York; appointed to the rank of Lieutenant-General after the war; Commandeur of the Order of St. Louis; gallant conduct in the first action of the Chesapeake; carried by assault, sword in hand, at the head of four hundred Grenadiers, the redoubt at York; Lieutenant-General; Colonel in 1761; Brigadier from 4th January, 1770; Lieutenant-General, 1st March, 1780; served well in the war of 1756 in Corsica and in America; commanded the Lorraine Legion with general approval.

Wisca, Jean Christophe Baron de. Captain; born in Holstein 22d May, 1730; Quartermaster in the service of the Emperor in 1756; Captain, 28th August, 1777; of Grenadiers, 4th April, 1780; wounded at York; received the Cross of the Mérite Militaire for bravery.

Wisch, Baron de. Regimental Royal Deux Ponts; Captain commanding; twenty-three years and nine months' service; five campaigns in Germany; two in America; wounded at Berghen; contused at the siege of York and incapacitated for further service.

NOTE.—Many names in the original list appear in two or three different places, names are spelled variously, and it was difficult in many instances to determine the correct spelling of the names.

CONTINENTAL ARMY BREVETS.

The following resolution was passed by the Continental Congress September 30, 1783:

On the report of a Committee, consisting of Mr. McHenry, Mr. Peters, and Mr. Bland, to whom was referred a letter of 15th May, from the Secretary of War: *Resolved,* That the Secretary of War issue to all officers in the Army, under the rank of major-general, *who hold the same rank now that they held in the year 1777, a brevet commission one grade higher than their present rank,* having respect to their seniority; and that commissions for *full colonels* be *granted to the lieut-tenant-colonels of 1777,* the resolution of *27th May, 1778, notwithstanding.*

On the report of a Committee, consisting of Mr. McHenry, Mr. Peters, and Mr. Duane, to whom were referred a letter from Captain Second, and sundry other papers:

Resolved, That Captains Second and De Pontiere, late of Pulaski's legion, be promoted to the rank of majors by brevet in the army of the United States; their relative rank to be settled according to the dates of their present commissions.

Resolved, That Lieutenant Beaulieu be promoted to the rank of captain by brevet in the Army of the United States.

On a report from the Secretary of War:

Resolved, That the brevet commission of major in the army of the United States issue to Captain Haskell, Aide-de-Camp to Major-General R. Howe.

On the report of a Committee, consisting of Mr. McHenry, Mr. Hawkins, and Mr. Madison, to whom was referred a memorial of Lieutenant Edward Phelon:

Whereas Lieutenant Edward Phelon, of the 4th Massachusetts Regiment, hath, by his memorial set forth, that while he was fighting for the liberties of the United States, he received several wounds, under which he has for four years past borne the most excruciating pains; and that during that time he has been without any other support from the public than what has been given to other officers in full health, and that he is still a cripple; and whereas the facts above set forth are certified to be true in all their parts by eleven of the general officers of the army, who have moreover recommended him as having served with reputation to himself and advantage to the United States, and as deserving the favor and confidence of Congress: therefore,

Resolved, That the Secretary of War issue to Lieutenant E. Phelon a commission of captain in the Army of the United States.

The Continental Army was finally disbanded, to take effect November 3, 1783, by a proclamation of the Continental Congress of October 18, 1783. (See page 66, this volume.)

It would appear that the larger part, if not all, of the Continental Army, was, at the time of disbandment, on furlough.

ALPHABETICAL LIST

OF

BATTLES, ACTIONS, &c.

Amboy, New Jersey, 8th March, 1777.
Amelia Island, Florida, 18th May, 1777.
Anderson, Fort, Georgia, 23d July, 1780.
Anne, Fort, New York, 8th July, 1777.
Assumpsick Bridge, N. J., 2d January, 1777.
Augusta, Georgia, 29th January, 1777, 14th to 18th September, 1780, and 16th
    April to 5th June, 1781.
Balfour, Fort, South Carolina, 12th April, 1781.
Barren Hill, Pennsylvania, 20th May, 1778.
Beaufort, South Carolina, 10th August, 1776, and 3d February, 1779.
Beattie's Mill, S. C., 21st March, 1781.
Bedford, New York, 2d July, 1779.
Breeds Hill (Bunker Hill), Massachusetts, 17th June, 1775.
Bemus Heights, New York, 19th September, 1777.
Bennington, Vermont, 16th August, 1777.
Bergen, New Jersey, 19th July, 1780.
Biggin's Bridge, South Carolina, 14th April, 1780.
Black Mingo, S. C., 14th April, 1780.
Black River, South Carolina, 25th October, 1780.
Black Stoks, South Carolina, 20th November, 1780.
Block House, New Jersey, 21st July, 1780.
Blue Licks, Kentucky, 19th August, 1782.
Bordentown, New Jersey, 8th May, 1778.
Boston, Massachusetts (siege of), 17th June, 1775, to 17th March, 1776.
Bound Brook, New Jersey, 13th April, 1777.
Brandon's Camp, S. C., 12th July, 1780.
Brandywine, Pa., 11th September, 1777.
Brattonville, South Carolina, 12th July, 1780.
Brewton Hill, Georgia, 29th December, 1778.
Brier Creek, Georgia, 3d March, 1779.
Bristol, Pennsylvania, 17th April, 1778.
Bristol, Rhode Island, 7th October, 1775.
Broad River, South Carolina, 12th November, 1780.
Brookland, Long Island, 28th August, 1776.
Brooklyn, New York, 27th August, 1776.
Bruce's Cross-Roads, North Carolina, 12th February, 1781.
Brunswick, New Jersey, 1st December, 1776, and 26th October, 1779.
Buford Massacre, S. C., 29th May, 1780.
Bulltown Swamp, Savannah, Georgia, 19th November, 1778.
Bull's Ferry, New Jersey, 21st July, 1780.

Bunker Hill (Breeds Hill), Massachusetts, 17th June, 1775.
Bushwick, Long Island, 27th August, 1776.
Butts Hill, Rhode Island, 29th August, 1778.
Camden, South Carolina, 16th August, 1780, 25th April and 10th May, 1781.
Cane Brake, South Carolina, 22d December, 1775.
Cane Creek, North Carolina, 12th September, 1780, and 13th September, 1781.
Cars, Fort, Georgia, 10th February, 1779.
Catawba Ford, South Carolina, 18th August, 1780.
Caughnawaga, New York, 22d May, 1780.
Cedars, The, Canada, 19th May, 1776.
Cedar Springs, South Carolina, 13th July and 8th August, 1780.
Chadd's Ford, Pa., 11th September, 1777.
Chambly, Canada, 19th October, 1775, and 16th June, 1776.
Charles City Court-House, Virginia, 8th January, 1781.
Charleston, South Carolina, siege of, 11th to 13th May, 1779, and 29th March to
    12th May, 1780; sortie from 24th April, 1780; occupied by the British, 12th
    May, 1780, to 14th December, 1782.
Charleston Neck, South Carolina, 11th May, 1779.
Charlestown, Massachusetts, 8th January, 1776.
Charlotte, North Carolina, 26th September, 1780.
Chatterton's Hill, New York, 28th October, 1776.
Chemung, New York, 29th August, 1779.
Cherokee Ford South Carolina, 14th February, 1779.
Cherokee Indian Town, S. C., 13th July, 1780.
Cherry Valley, New York, 10th November, 1778.
Chesapeake Bay, 8th to 10th July, 1776.
Chestnut Creek, New Jersey, 6th October, 1778.
Chestnut Hill, Pennsylvania, 6th December, 1777.
Clapp's Mill, North Carolina, 2d March, 1781.
Clinton, Fort, New York, 6th October, 1777.
Clouds Creek, S. C., 7th November, 1781.
Cobleskill, New York, 1st June, 1778.
Cock-hill Fort, New York, 16th November, 1776.
Combahee Ferry, South Carolina, 27th August, 1782.
Concord, Massachusetts, 17th April, 1775.
Connecticut Farms, New Jersey, 7th to 23d June, 1780.
Coosawhatchie, S. C., 11th to 13th May, 1779.
Coram, Long Island, 21st November, 1780.
Cornwallis, Fort, Georgia, 14th September, 1780, and 5th June, 1781.
Cowan's Ford, North Carolina, 1st February, 1781.
Cowpens, South Carolina, 17th January, 1781.
Crompo Hill, Connecticut, 28th April, 1777.
Crooked Billet, Pennsylvania, 1st May, 1778.
Croton River, New York, 14th May, 1781.
Crown Point, New York, 12th May, 1775; 14th October, 1776, and 16th June, 1777.
Cumberland, Fort, Nova Scotia, 20th November, 1776.
Currytown, New York, 9th July, 1781.
Danbury Raid, Connecticut, 25th to 27th April, 1777.
Diamond Island, New York, 23d September, 1777.
Dorchester, South Carolina, 1st and 29th December, 1781, and 24th April, 1782.
Dorchester Neck, Massachusetts, 14th February, 1776.
Dreadnought, Fort, Georgia, 21st May, 1781.

Dutch Island, Rhode Island, 2d August, 1777.
Earle's Ford, North Carolina, 15th July, 1780.
East Chester, New York, 18th January, 1780.
Ebenezer, Georgia, 23d June, 1782.
Edge Hill, Pennsylvania, 7th December, 1777.
Egg Harbor, New Jersey, 15th October, 1778.
Elizabethtown, New Jersey, 25th January, and 6th June, 1780.
Elmira, New York, 29th August, 1779.
Esopus, New York, 13th October, 1777.
Essenecca Town, South Carolina, 1st August, 1776.
Eutaw Springs, South Carolina, 8th September, 1781.
Fairfield, Connecticut, 8th July, 1779.
Falmouth, Maine, 18th October, 1775.
Fayette, Fort, New York, 1st June, 1779.
Fish Dam Ford, South Carolina, 9th November, 1780.
Fishing Creek, South Carolina, 18th August, 1780.
Flatbush, New York, 22d to 23d August, 1780.
Flat Rock, South Carolina, 20th July, 1780.
Fogland Ferry, Rhode Island, 10th January, 1777.
Fort Plain, New York, 2d August, 1780, and 7th September, 1781.
Four Corners, New York, 3d February, 1780.
Four Holes, South Carolina, 7th and 15th April, 1781.
Freehold Court-House, New Jersey, 28th June, 1778.
Freeman's Farm, New York, 19th September, 1777.
Galphin, Fort, Georgia, 21st May, 1781.
Geneseo, New York, 14th September, 1779.
George, Fort, New York, 16th November, 1776, and 11th October, 1780.
George, Fort, Long Island, 21st November, 1780.
Georgetown, South Carolina, 24th January, 1781.
German Flats, New York, 29th October, 1780.
Germantown, Pennsylvania, 4th October, 1777.
Gloucester, Mass, 13th August, 1775
Granby, Fort, South Carolina, 15th May, 1781.
Grape Island, Massachusetts, 21st May, 1775
Great Bridge, Virginia, 9th December, 1775.
Great Savannah, South Carolina, 20th August, 1780.
Green Spring, South Carolina, 1st August, 1780.
Green Springs, Virginia, 6th July, 1781.
Greenwich, Connecticut, 19th June, 1779.
Grierson, Fort, Georgia, 14th September, 1780, and 24th May, 1781.
Griswold, Fort, Connecticut, 6th September, 1781.
Groton Hill, Connecticut, 6th September, 1781.
Guilford, North Carolina, 15th March, 1781.
Gulphs Mill, Pennsylvania, 11th December, 1777.
Gum Swamp, South Carolina, 16th August, 1780.
Gwyn's Island, Chesapeake Bay, 8th to 10th July, 1776.
Hampton, Virginia, 26th October, 1775.
Hancock's Bridge, New Jersey, 21st March, 1778.
Hanging Rock, South Carolina, 1st to 6th August, 1780.
Harlem Cove, New York, 16th November, 1776.
Harlem Heights, New York, 16th October, 1776.
Harlem Plains, New York, 16th September, 1776.

Haw River, North Carolina, 25th February, 1781.
Hayes' Station, South Carolina, 9th November, 1781.
Henry, Fort, Virginia, 1st September, 1777, and 26th to 28th February, 1778.
Hickory Hill, Georgia, 28th June, 1779.
Highlands, New York, 24th March, 1777.
Hillsborough, North Carolina, 25th April, 1781.
Hobkirk Hill, South Carolina, 25th April, 1781.
Hogg Island, Massachusetts, 28th May, 1775.
Horseneck, Connecticut, 26th February, 1779, and 9th December, 1780.
Hubbardton, Vermont, 7th July, 1777.
Hunts Bluff, South Carolina, 1st August, 1780.
Hutchinson's Island, Georgia, 7th March, 1776.
Independence of United States acknowledged by Great Britain, 30th November, 1782.
Indian Field and Bridge, New York, 31st August, 1778.
Iron Hill, Delaware ,3d September, 1777.
Isle aux Noix, Canada, 24th June, 1776.
Jamaica, Long Island, 28th August, 1776.
James Island, South Carolina, —— July, 1782.
Jamestown Ford, Virginia, 6th July, 1781.
Jefferd's Neck, New York, 7th November, 1779.
Jersey City, New Jersey, 18th July, 1779.
Jerseyfield, New York, 30th October, 1781.
John's Island, South Carolina, 4th November, 1782.
Johnson, Fort, South Carolina, 14th September, 1775.
Johnson Hall, New York, 24th October, 1781.
Johnstown, New York, 22d May, 1780, and 24th October, 1781.
Kanassoraga, New York, 23d October, 1780.
Kemp's Landing, Virginia, 14th November, 1775.
Kettle Creek, Georgia, 14th February, 1779.
Keyser, Fort, New York, 19th October, 1780.
King's Bridge, New York, 17th January, 1777, and 3d July, 1781.
King's Mountain, North Carolina, 7th October, 1780.
Kingston, New York, 13th October, 1777.
Kingstree, South Carolina, 27th August, 1780.
Klock's Field, New York, 21st October, 1780.
Lake Champlain, 11th to 13th October, 1776.
Lake George, New York, 18th September, 1777.
Lanneau's Ferry, South Carolina, 6th May, 1780.
Lee, Fort, New Jersey, 18th November, 1776.
Le Nud's Ferry, South Carolina, 18th May, 1780.
Lexington, Massachusetts, 19th April, 1775.
Lindley's Mill, North Carolina, 13th September, 1781.
Lloyd's Neck, New York, 5th September, 1779.
Long Cane, South Carolina, 11th December, 1780.
Long Island, New York, 27th August, 1776, and 10th December, 1777.
Mamaroneck, New York, 21st October, 1776.
Manhattanville, New York, 16th November, 1776.
Martha's Vineyard, Massachusetts, 5th May, 1775.
McDonnell's Camp, South Carolina, 15th and 16th July, 1780.
McIntosh, Fort, Georgia, 2d to 4th February, 1777.
Medway Church, Georgia, 24th November, 1778.

Mercer, Fort, New Jersey, 22d October, 1777.

Middleburg, New York, 15th October, 1780.

Middletown, New Jersey, 27th April, 1779, and 12th June, 1780.

Mifflin, Fort, Pennsylvania, 23d October and 10th to 15th November, 1777.

Millstone, New Jersey, 22d January and 17th June, 1777.

Mincock Island, New Jersey, 15th October, 1778.

Minisink, New York, 22d July, 1779.

Mohawk Valley, New York, 2d August, 1780.

Monk's Corner, South Carolina, 14th April, 1780, and 16th October, 1781.

Monmouth, New Jersey, 28th June, 1778.

Montgomery, Fort, New York, 6th October, 1777.

Montreal, Canada, 25th September, and 12th November, 1775.

Montressor's Island, New York, 24th September, 1776.

Moore's Creek Bridge, North Carolina, 27th February, 1776.

Morris, Fort, Georgia, 9th January, 1779.

Morrisania, New York, 5th August, 1779, 22d January, 1781, and 4th March, 1782.

Moses Kill, New York, 2d August, 1777.

Motte, Fort, South Carolina, 12th May, 1781.

Moultrie, Fort, South Carolina, 28th June, 1776, and 7th May, 1780.

Mount Washington, New York, 8th November, 1776.

Musgrove's Mills, South Carolina, 19th August, 1780.

Nelson, Fort, Virginia, 9th May, 1779.

Nelson's Ferry, South Carolina, 20th August, 1780, and 14th May, 1781

Newark, New Jersey, 25th January, 1780.

New Bridge, New Jersey, 15th April, 1780.

New Haven, Connecticut, 5th July, 1779.

New London, Connecticut, 6th September, 1781.

New Rochelle, New York, 18th October, 1776.

Newtown, New York, 29th August, 1779.

New York City, New York, attack on, 29th August, 1775; occupied by British
    Troops, 15th September, 1776, to 25th November, 1783.

Ninety-Six, South Carolina, 19th and 21st November, 1775, and 22d May to 19th
    June, 1781.

Noddles Island, Massachusetts, 27th May, 1775.

Nooks Hill, Massachusetts, 8th March, 1776.

Norfolk, Virginia, 1st January, 1776, and 9th May, 1779.

Norwalk, Connecticut, 12th July, 1779.

Oconore, South Carolina, 1st August, 1776.

Ogeechee Road, Georgia, 21st May, 1782.

Old Iron Works, South Carolina, 8th August, 1780

Onondagas, New York, 20th April, 1779.

Orangeburg, South Carolina, 11th May, 1781.

Oriskany, New York, 6th August, 1777.

Osborne's, Virginia, 27th April, 1781.

Pacolett River, North Carolina, 14th July, 1780.

Paoli, Pennsylvania, 20th September, 1777.

Paramus, New Jersey, 22d March, and 16th April, 1780.

Paulus Hook, New Jersey, 19th August, 1779.

Peace, treaty of, concluded, 3d September, 1783.

Peekskill, New York, 22d March, 1777.

Pelham Manor, New York, 18th October, 1776.

Petersburg, Virginia, 25th April, 1781.

Philadelphia, Pennsylvania, occupied by the British 26th September, 1777, to 18th June, 1778.
Phillips Heights, New York, 16th September, 1778.
Phipp's Farm, Massachusetts, 9th November, 1775.
Piscataway, New Jersey, 8th May, 1777.
Plain, Fort, New York, 2d August, 1780.
Plains of Abraham, Canada, 6th May, 1776.
Pon Pon, South Carolina, 23d March, 1780.
Port Royal Island, South Carolina, 3d February, 1779.
Poundridge, New York, 2d July, 1779.
Princeton, New Jersey, 3d January, 1777.
Punk Hill, New Jersey, 8th March, 1777.
Pyles' Defeat, North Carolina, 25th February, 1781.
Quaker Hill, Rhode Island, 29th August, 1778.
Quebec, Canada, siege of, 8th to 31st December, 1775.
Quinby's Bridge, South Carolina, 17th July, 1781.
Quinton's Bridge, New Jersey, 18th March, 1778.
Rahway Meadow, New Jersey, 26th June, 1781.
Ramsour's Mill, North Carolina, 20th June, 1780.
Rayborn Creek, South Carolina, 15th July, 1776.
Red Bank, New Jersey, 22d October, 1777.
Rentowle, South Carolina, 27th March, 1780:
Rhode Island, 29th August, 1778.
Richmond, Virginia, 5th January, 1781.
Ridgefield, Connecticut, 27th April, 1777.
Rocky Mount, South Carolina, 30th July, 1780.
Roxbury, Massachusetts, 8th July, 1775.
Rugley's Mills, South Carolina, 4th December, 1780.
Sagg Harbor, New York, 23d May, 1777.
Salkahatchie, South Carolina, 8th March, 1780.
Sandusky, Ohio, 4th June, 1782.
Saratoga, New York, 7th to 17th October, 1777.
Savannah, Georgia, occupied by British troops, 29th December, 1778, to 11th July, 1782; siege of 23d September to 18th October, 1779.
Schohaire, New York, 17th October, 1780.
Schuyler, Fort, New York, 4th to 22d August, 1777.
Shallow Ford, North Carolina, 6th February, 1781.
Sharon, Georgia (near), 24th May, 1782.
Short Hills, New Jersey, 26th June, 1777.
Silver Bluff, South Carolina, 21st May, 1781.
Skenesborough, New York, 7th July, 1777.
Smith's Point, New York, 23d November, 1780.
Somerset Court-House, New Jersey, 20th January, 1777.
Spencer's Hill, Georgia, 19th November, 1778.
Spencer's Tavern, Virginia, 26th June, 1781.
Springfield, New Jersey, 17th December, 1776, and 23d June, 1780.
Sorrel River, Canada, 24th July, 1776.
Stallions, South Carolina, 12th July, 1780.
Stanwix, Fort, New York, 4th to 22d August, 1777.
Staten Island, New York, 21st and 22d August, 1777.
St. George, Fort, Long Island, 23d November, 1780.
Stillwater, New York, 19th September, and 7th October, 1777.

St. John, Fort, Canada, 14th May, 1775.
St. John's Canada, 18th September, and 3d November, 1775.
Stone Arabia, New York, 19th October, 1780.
Stonington, Connecticut, 30th September, 1775.
Stono Ferry, South Carolina, 20th June, 1779.
Stony Point, New York, 1st June and 16th July, 1779.
Sullivan, Fort, South Carolina, 28th and 29th June, 1776.
Sullivan's Island, South Carolina, 28th and 29th June, 1776, and 8th May, 1780.
Sunbury, Georgia, 6th to 9th January, 1779.
Tappan, New York, 28th September, 1778.
Tarcote, South Carolina, 4th September, 1780.
Tarcote Swamp, South Carolina, 25th October ,1780.
Tarrytown, New York, 30th August, 1779, and 15th July, 1781.
Thickety, Fort, South Carolina, 30th July, 1780.
Tomassy, South Carolina, 11th August, 1776.
Threadwell's Neck, New York, 10th October, 1781.
Three Rivers, Canada, 8th June, 1776.
Throg's Neck, New York, 12th October, 1776.
Ticonderoga, New York, 10th May, 1775, and 6th July, 1777.
Tiger River, South Carolina, 20th November, 1780.
Tiverton, Rhode Island, 31st May, 1778.
Tom's River, New Jersey, 19th July, 1780.
Torrence's Tavern, North Carolina, 1st February, 1781.
Trenton, New Jersey, 26th December, 1776, and 2d January, 1777.
Tryon, Fort, New York, 16th November, 1776.
Valcour Island, New York, 11th October, 1776.
Valley Grove, Long Island, 26th August, 1776.
Vandreuil, Canada, 26th May, 1776.
Verplanck's Point, New York, 1st June, 1779.
Vincennes, Indiana, 5th July, 1778, 17th December, 1778, and 23d February, 1779.
Wahab's Plantation, South Carolina, 21st September, 1780.
Wambaw Creek, South Carolina, 14th February, 1782.
Ward's House, New York, 16th March, 1777.
Warwarsing, New York, 22d August, 1781.
Washington, Fort, New York, 16th November, 1776.
Wateree, Ford of the, South Carolina, 15th August, 1780.
Watson, Fort, South Carolina, 15th to 23d April, 1781.
Waxhaws, South Carolina, 29th May, 1780.
Weehawken, New Jersey, 19th August, 1779.
West Canada Creek, New York, 30th October, 1781.
West Chester, New York, 16th September, 1778.
West Chester County, New York, 16th March, 1777.
West Farms, New York, 25th January, 1777.
West Greenwich, Connecticut, 26th March, 1779.
West Haven, Connecticut, 1st September, 1781.
Wetzell's or Whitsall's Mills, North Carolina, 6th March, 1781.
Wheeling, Virginia, 1st September, 1777, and 26th to 28th September, 1778.
White House, Georgia, 15th September, 1780.
Whitemarsh, Pennsylvania, 5th to 8th December, 1777.
White Plains, New York, 28th October, 1776.
Wiboo Swamp, South Carolina, 6th March, 1781.
Wiggins Hill, Georgia, —— April, 1781.

Williamson's Plantation, South Carolina, 12th July, 1780, and 31st December, 1780. ·
Wilmington, North Carolina, 1st February, 1781.
Wofford's Iron Works, South Carolina, 8th August, 1780.
Woodbridge, New Jersey, 19th April, 1777.
Wright's Bluff, South Carolina, 27th February, 1781.
Wyoming, Pennsylvania, 1st to 4th July, 1778.
Yamacrow Bluff (Savannah), Georgia, 4th March, 1776.
Yorktown, Virginia, 28th September to 19th October, 1781.
Young's House, New York, 25th December, 1778, and 3d February, 1780.

CHRONOLOGICAL LIST OF BATTLES, ACTIONS, &c.

1775.

19th April, 1775, Lexington, Massachusetts.
19th April, 1775, Concord, Massachusetts.
5th May, 1775, Martha's Vineyard, Massachusetts.
10th May, 1775, Ticonderoga, New York.
12th May, 1775, Crown Point, New York.
14th May, 1775, Fort St. John, Canada.
21st May, 1775, Grape Island, Massachusetts.
27th May, 1775, Noodle's Island, Massachusetts.
27th May, 1775, Hogg Island, Massachusetts.
17th June, 1775, Bunker Hill (Breed's Hill), Massachusetts.
17th June, 1775, to 17th March, 1776, Siege of Boston, Massachusetts.
8th July, 1775, Roxbury, Massachusetts.
13th August, 1775, Gloucester, Massachusetts
29th August, 1775, New York City, Attack on.
18th September, 1775, St. Johns, Canada.
25th September, 1775, Montreal, Canada.
30th September, 1775, Stonington, Connecticut.
7th October, 1775, Bristol, Rhode Island.
18th October, 1775, Falmouth, Maine.
19th October, 1775, Chambly, Canada.
26th October, 1775, Hampton, Virginia.
3d November, 1775, St. Johns, Canada.
9th November, 1775, Phipps' Farm, Massachusetts.
12th November, 1775, Montreal, Canada.
14th November, 1775, Kemp's Landing, Virginia.
19th and 21st November, 1775, Ninety-Six, South Carolina.
8th to 31st December, 1775, Siege of Quebec, Canada.
9th December, 1775, Great Bridge, Virginia.
22d December, 1775, Cane Brake, South Carolina.
31st December, 1775, Quebec, Canada.

1776.

1st January, 1776, Norfolk, Virginia.
8th January, 1776, Charlestown, Massachusetts.
14th February, 1776, Dorchester Neck, Massachusetts.
27th February, 1776, Moore's Creek Bridge, North Carolina.
7th March, 1776, Hutchinson's Island, Georgia.
8th March, 1776, Nook's Hill, Massachusetts.
7th March, 1776, Boston, Massachusetts, evacuated by the British.
4th March, 1776, Yamcrow Bluff, South Carolina.
6th May, 1776, Plains of Abraham, Canada.
19th May, 1776, The Cedars, Canada.

26th May, 1776, Vandreuil, Canada.
8th June, 1776, Three Rivers, Canada.
16th June, 1776, Chambly, Canada.
24th June, 1776, Isle aux Noix, Canada.
28th to 29th June, 1776, Fort Sullivan (Sullivan's Island), South Carolina.
8th to 10th July 1776, Gwyn's Island, Chesapeake Bay.
15th July, 1776, Rayborn Creek, South Carolina.
24th July, 1776, Sorrel River, Canada.
1st August, 1776, Oconore, South Carolina.
1st August 1776, Essenecca Town, South Carolina.
11th August, 1776, Tomassy, South Carolina.
22d to 23d August, 1776, Flatbush, Long Island.
26th August, 1776, Valley Grove, Long Island.
27th August, 1776, Long Island (Bushwick or Brooklyn), New York.
28th August, 1776, Jamaica (Brookland), Long Island.
15th September 1776, New York City occupied by the British.
16th September, 1776, Harlem Plains, New York.
24th September, 1776, Montressor's Island, New York.
11th October, 1776, Valcour Island, New York.
12th October 1776, Harlem Heights (Throg's Neck), New York.
13th October, 1776, Lake Champlain.
14th October, 1776, Crown Point, New York.
18th October, 1776, Pelham Manor (New Rochell), New York.
21st October, 1776, Mamaroneck, New York.
28th October, 1776, White Plains, New York.
8th November, 1776, Mount Washington, New York.
16th November, 1776, Fort Washington, New York.
16th November, 1776, Fort Tryon, New York.
16th November, 1776, Fort George, New York.
16th November, 1776, Harlem Cove (Manhattanville), New York.
16th November, 1776, Cock-Hill Fort New York.
18th November 1776, Fort Lee, New Jersey.
20th November, 1776, Fort Cumberland, Nova Scotia.
1st December, 1776, Brunskick, New Jersey.
7th December, 1776, Tappan, New York.
17th December, 1776, Springfield, New Jersey.
26th December, 1776, Trenton, New Jersey.

1777.

2d January, 1777, Assumpsick Bridge, Trenton, New Jersey.
3d January, 1777, Princeton, New Jersey.
10th January, 1777, Fogland Ferry, Rhode Island.
17th January, 1777, King's Bridge, New York.
20th January, 1777, Somerset C. H. (Millstone), New Jersey.
25th January, 1777, West Farms, New York.
29th January, 1777, Augusta, Georgia.
2d to 4th February, 1777, Fort McIntosh, Georgia.
8th March, 1777, Amboy (Punk Hill), New Jersey.
16th March, Ward's House (West Chester County), New York.
22d March, 1777, Peekskill, New York.
24th March, 1777, Highlands, New York.

13th April, 1777, Boundbrook, New Jersey.
19th April, 1777, Woodbridge, New Jersey.
25th to 27th April, 1777, Danbury Raid, Connecticut.
27th April, 1777, Ridgefield, Connecticut.
28th April, 1777, Crompo Hill, Connecticut.
8th May, 1777, Piscataway, New Jersey.
18th May, 1777, Amelia Island, Florida.
23d May, 1777, Sag Harbor, New York.
16th June, 1777, Crown Point, New York.
17th June, 1777, Millstone, New Jersey.
26th June, 1777, Short Hills, New Jersey.
6th July, 1777, Crown Point, New York, evacuated by United States Troops.
7th July, 1777, Hubbardton, Vermont.
7th July, 1777, Skenesborough, New York.
8th July, 1777, Fort Anne, New York.
2d August, 1777, Moses Kill, New York.
2d August, 1777, Dutch Island, Rhode Island.
4th to 22d August, 1777, Fort Schuyler (Fort Stanwix), New York.
6th August, 1777, Oriskany, New York.
16th August, 1777, Bennington, Vermont.
21st to 22d August, 1777, Staten Island, New York.
1st September, 1777, Fort Henry (Wheeling), Virginia.
3d September, 1777, Iron Hill, Delaware.
11th September, 1777, Chad's Ford, Delaware.
11th September, 1777, Brandywine, Delaware.
18th September, 1777, Lake George, New York.
19th September, 1777, Bemus Heights, New York.
19th September, 1777, Stillwater (Freeman's Farm), New York.
20th September, 1777, Paoli, Pennsylvania.
23d September, 1777, Diamond Island, New York.
26th September, 1777, Philadelphia, Pennsylvania, occupied by the British.
4th October, 1777, Germantown, Pennsylvania.
6th October, 1777, Forts Clinton and Montgomery, New York.
7th October, 1777, Stilwater, New York.
7th to 17th October, 1777, Saratoga, New York.
13th October, 1777, Esopus, New York.
13th October, 1777, Kingston, New York
17th October, 1777, Saratoga, New York   Surrender of General Burgoyne.
22d October, 1777, Fort Mercer (Red Bank), New Jersey.
23d October, 1777, Fort Mifflin, Pennsylvania.
10th to 15th November, 1777, Fort Mifflin, Pennsylvania.
5th to 8th December, 1777, Whitemarsh, Pennsylvania.
6th December, 1777, Chestnut Hill, Pennsylvania.
7th December, 1777, Edge Hill, Pennsylvania.
10th December, 1777, Long Island, New York.
11th December, 1777, Gulph's Mills, Pennsylvania.

1778.

18th March, 1778, Quintan's Bridge, New Jersey.
21st March, 1778, Hancock's Bridge, New Jersey.
17th April, 1778, Bristol, Pennsylvania.

1st May, 1778, Crooked Billet, Pennsylvania.
8th May, 1778, Bordentown, New Jersey.
20th May, 1778, Barren Hill, Pennsylvania.
31st May, 1778, Tiverton, Rhode Island.
1st June, 1778, Cobleskill, New York.
18th June, 1778, Philadelphia, Pennsylvania, evacuated by the British.
28th June, 1778, Monmouth (Freehold C. H.), New Jersey.
1st to 4th July, 1778, Wyoming, Pennsylvania.
5th July, 1778, Vincennes, Indiana.
29th August, 1778, Quaker Hill (Butts Hill or Rhode Island), Rhode Island.
31st August, 1778, Indian Field and Bridge, New York.
16th September, 1778, West Chester, New York.
26th to 28th September, 1778, Fort Henry (Wheeling), Virginia.
28th September, 1778, Tappan, New York.
6th October, 1778, Chestnut Creek, New Jersey.
15th October, 1778, Mincock Island (Egg Harbor), New Jersey.
10th November, 1778, Cherry Valley, New York.
19th November, 1778, Spencer's Hill (Bulltown Swamp), Georgia.
24th November, 1778, Medway Church, Georgia.
17th December, 1778, Vincennes, Indiana.
25th December, 1778, Young's House, New York.
29th December, 1778, Savannah (Brewton Hill), Georgia

1779.

9th January, 1779, Fort Morris (Sunbury), Georgia.
29th January, 1779, Augusta, Georgia, occupied by the British.
3d February, 1779, Port Royal Island, South Carolina.
3d February, 1779, Beaufort, South Carolina.
10th February, 1779, Car's Fort, Georgia.
14th February, 1779, Kettle Creek, Georgia.
14th February, 1779, Cherokee Ford, South Carolina.
23d February, 1779, Vincennes, Indiana.
26th February, 1779, Horseneck Connecticut.
3d March, 1779, Brier Creek, Georgia.
26th March, 1779, West Greenwich, Connecticut.
20th April, 1779, Onondegas, New York.
27th April, 1779, Middletown, New Jersey.
9th May, 1779, Fort Nelson, (Norfolk), Virginia.
11th May, 1779, Charleston Neck, South Carolina.
11th to 13th May, 1779, Coosawhatchie, South Carolina.
1st June, 1779, Stony Point, Verplanck's Point (Fayette), New York.
19th June, 1779, Greenwich, Connecticut.
20th June, 1779, Stono Ferry, South Carolina.
28th June, 1779, Hckory Hill, Georgia.
2d July, 1779, Poundridge, New York.
2d July, 1779, Bedford, New York.
5th July, 1779, New Haven, Connecticut.
8th July, 1779, Fairfield; Connecticut.
12th July, 1779, Norwalk, Connecticut.
16th July, 1779, Stony Point, New York.
18th July, 1779, Jersey City, New Jersey.

22d July, 1779, Minisink, New York.
5th August, 1779, Morrisania, New York.
19th August, 1779, Paulus Hook (Weehawken), New Jersey.
29th August, 1779, Newton, Chemung (Elmira), New York.
30th August, 1779, Tarrytown, New York.
5th September, 1779, Lloyd's Neck, New York.
14th September, 1779, Geneseo, New York.
23d September to 19th October, 1779, Siege of Savannah, Georgia.
19th October, 1779, Savannah, Georgia.
26th October, 1779, Brunswick, New Jersey.
7th November, 1779, Jefferd's Neck, New York.

1780.

18th January, 1780, Eastchester, New York.
25th January, 1780, Elizabethtown, New Jersey.
25th January, 1780, Newark, New Jersey.
3d February, 1780, Young's House (Four Corners), New York.
8th March, 1780, Salkahatchie, South Carolina.
23d March, 1780, Pon Pon, South Carolina.
27th March, 1780, Rentowl, South Carolina.
29th March to 12th May, 1780, Siege of Charleston.
14th April, 1780, Monk's Corner (Biggins' Bridge), South Carolina.
15th April, 1780, New Bridge, New Jersey.
16th April, 1780, Paramus, New Jersey.
24th April, 1780, Sortie from Charleston, South Carolina.
6th May, 1780, Lanneau's Ferry, South Carolina.
7th May, 1780, Fort Moultrie, South Carolina.
8th May, 1780, Sullivan's Island, South Carolina.
12th May, 1780, Surrender of Charleston, South Carolina.
18th May, 1780, Le Nud's Ferry, South Carolina.
22d May, 1780, Caughnawaga, New York.
22d May, 1780, Johnstown, New York.
29th May, 1780, Waxhaws, South Carolina.
29th May, 1780, Buford's Massacre, South Carolina.
6th June, 1780, Elizabethtown, New Jersey.
7th to 23d June, 1780, Connecticut Farms, New Jersey.
20th June, 1780, Ramsour's Mills, North Carolina.
23d June, 1780, Springfield, New Jersey.
12th July, 1780, Williamson's Plantation (Brattenville), South Carolina.
12th July, 1780, Stallians, South Carolina.
12th July, 1780, Brandon's Camp, South Carolina.
13th July, 1780, Cedar Springs North Carolina.
13th July, 1780, Cherokee Indian Town, South Carolina.
14th July 1780, Pacolett River, North Carolina.
15th July, 1780, Earle's Ford, North Carolina.
15th and 16th July, 1780, McDonnell's Camp, South Carolina.
19th July, 1780, Block House, Tom's River (Bergen), New Jersey.
21st July, 1780, Bull's Ferry, New Jersey.
30th July, 1780, Rocky Mount, South Carolina.
30th July, 1780, Fort Anderson (Thickety Fort), South Carolina.
1st August, 1780, Hunt's Bluff, South Carolina.

1st August, 1780, Green Springs, South Carolina.
2d August, 1780, Mohawk Valley (Fort Plain), New York.
6th August, 1780, Hanging Rock, South Carolina.
8th August, 1780, Wofford's Iron Works (Cedar Springs), South Carolina.
8th August, 1780, Old Iron Works, South Carolina.
15th August, 1780, Fort of the Wateree, South Carolina.
16th August, 1780, Camden, South Carolina.
16th August, 1780, Gum Swamp, South Carolina.
18th August, 1780, Musgrove's Mills, South Carolina.
18th August, 1780, Fishing Creek, South Carolina.
18th August, 1780, Catawba Ford, South Carolina.
20th August, 1780, Great Savannah (Nelson's Ferry), South Carolina.
27th August, 1780, Kingstree, South Carolina.
4th September, 1780, Tarcote, South Carolina.
12th September, 1780, Cane Creek, North Carolina.
14th to 18th September, 1780, Forts Grierson and Cornwallis (Augusta), Georgia.
14th September, 1780, Black Mingo, South Carolina.
15th September, 1780, White House, Georgia.
21st September, 1780, Wahab's Plantation, North Carolina.
26th September, 1780, Charlotte, North Carolina.
7th October, 1780, King's Mountain, North Carolina.
11th October, 1780, Fort George, New York.
15th October, 1780, Middleburg, New York.
17th October, 1780, Schoharie, New York.
19th October, 1780, Fort Keyser (Palatine or Stone Arabia), New York.
21st October, 1780, Klock's Field, New York.
23d October, 1780, Kanassoraga, New York.
25th October, 1780, Black River (Tarcote Swamp), South Carolina.
29th October, 1780, German Flats, New York.
9th November, 1780, Fish Dam Ford (Broad River), South Carolina.
12th November, 1780, Broad River, South Carolina.
20th November, 1780, Black-Storks (Tiger River), South Carolina.
21st November, 1780, Coram (Fort George), Long Island.
23d November, 1780, Fort St. George (Smith's Point), Long Island.
4th December, 1780, Rugley's Mills, South Carolina.
9th December, 1780, Horseneck, Connecticut.
31st December, 1780, Williamson's Plantation, South Carolina.

1781.

5th January, 1781, Richmond, Virginia.
8th January ,1781, Charles City Courhourse, Virginia.
17th January, 1781, Cowpens, South Carolina.
22d January, 1781, Morrisania, New York.
24th January, 1781, Georgetown, South Carolina.
1st February ,1781, Wilmington, North Carolina.
1st February, 1781, Cowan's Ford, North Carolina.
1st February, 1781, Torrence's Tavern, North Carolina.
6th February, 1781, Shallow Ford, North Carolina.
12th February, 1781, Bruce's Cross-Roads, North Carolina.
25th February, 1781, Haw River (Pyle's Defeat), North Carolina.
27th February, 1781, Wright's Bluff, South Carolina.

2d March, 1781, Clapp's Mill, North Carolina.
6th March, 1781, Wetzell's or Whitsall's Mills, North Carolina
6th March, 1781, Wiboo Swamp, South Carolina.
15th March, 1781, Guilford, North Carolina.
21st March, 1781, Beattie's Mill, South Carolina.
—— April, 1781, Wiggins' Hill, Georgia.
7th April, 1781, Four Holes, South Carolina.
12th April, 1781, Fort Balfour, South Carolina.
15th to 23d April, 1781, Fort Watson, South Carolina.
15th April ,1781, Four Holes, South Carolina.
16th April to 5th June, 1781, Augusta, Georgia, Siege of.
25th April, 1781, Hobkirk's Hill, South Carolina.
25th April 1781, Hillsborough, North Carolina.
25th April, 1781, Petersburg, Virginia.
25th April 1781, Camden, South Carolina.
27th April, 1781, Osborne's, Virginia.
10th May 1781, Camden, South Carolina.
11th May, 1781, Orangeburg, South Carolina.
12th May, 1781, Fort Motte, South Carolina.
14th May, 1781, Croton River, New York.
14th May, 1781, Nelson's Ferry, South Carolina.
15th May, 1781, Fort Granby, South Carolina.
21st May, 1781, Silver Bluff, South Carolina.
21st May, 1781, Fort Galphin (Fort Dreadnought), Georgia.
22d May to 19th June, 1781, Ninety-Six, South Carolina.
24th May, 1781, Augusta (Fort Cornwallis), Georgia.
5th June, 1781, Augusta (Forts Cornwallis and Grierson), Georgia.
5th June, 1781, Georgetown, South Carolina.
26th June, 1781, Rahway Meadow, New Jersey.
26th June, 1781, Spencer's Tavern, Virginia.
3d July, 1781, King's Bridge, New York.
6th July, 1781, Jamestown Ford, Virginia.
6th July 1781, Green Springs, Virginia.
9th July, 1781, Currytown, New York.
15th July, 1781, Tarrytown, New York.
17th July ,1781, Quinby's Bridge, South Carolina.
22d August, 1781, Warwarsing, New York.
30th August, 1781, Parker's Ferry, South Carolina.
1st September, 1781, West Haven, Connecticut.
6th September, 1781, New London, Connecticut.
6th September, 1781, Fort Griswold (Groton Hill), Connecticut.
8th September, 1781, Eutaw Springs, South Carolina.
13th September, 1781, Hillsborough, North Carolina.
13th September, 1781, Lindley's Mill (Can Creek), North Carolina.
29th September to 19th October, 1781, Yorktown, Virginia, Siege of.
10th October, 1781, Threadwell's Neck, New York.
16th October, 1781, Monk's Corner, New York.
19th October, 1781, Yorktown, Virginia, Surrender of Cornwallis.
24th October 1781, Johnson Hall (Johnstown), New York.
30th October, 1781, Jerseyfield (West Canada Creek), New York.

9th November, 1781, Hayes' Station, South Carolina.
1st December, 1781, Dorchester, South Carolina.
29th December, 1781, Dorchester, South Carolina.

1782.

14th February, 1782, Wambaw Creek, South Carolina.
4th March, 1782, Morrisania, New York.
24th April, 1782, Dorchester, South Carolina.
21st May 1782, Ogechee Road, near Savannah, Georgia.
24th May, 1782, near Sharon, Georgia.
4th June, 1782, Sandusky, Ohio.
23d June, 1782, Ebenezer, Georgia.
11th July, 1782, Savannah, Georgia, evacuated by the British.
—— July, 1782, James Island, South Carolina.
19th August, 1782, Blue Licks, Kentucky.
27th August 1782, Combahee Ferry ,South Carolina.
4th November 1782, John's Island, South Carolina.
30th November, 1782, Independence of United States acknowledged by Great
  Britain.
14th December, 1782, Charleston, South Carolina, evacuated by the British.

1783

3d September, 1783, Treaty of Peace concluded.
26th November, 1783, British troops withdrawn from New York.

CALENDAR

FOR THE YEARS OF THE REVOLUTION.

1775.

January.

S	M	T	W	T	F	S
1	2	3	4	5	6	7
8	9	10	11	12	13	14
15	16	17	18	19	20	21
22	23	24	25	26	27	28
29	30	31	:	:	:	:

February.

S	M	T	W	T	F	S
.	.	.	1	2	3	4
5	6	7	8	9	10	11
12	13	14	15	16	17	18
19	20	21	22	23	24	25
26	27	28	:	:	:	:

March.

S	M	T	W	T	F	S
.	.	.	1	2	3	4
5	6	7	8	9	10	11
12	13	14	15	16	17	18
19	20	21	22	23	24	25
26	27	28	29	30	31	:

April.

S	M	T	W	T	F	S
.	.	.	.	.	.	1
2	3	4	5	6	7	8
9	10	11	12	13	14	15
16	17	18	19	20	21	22
23	24	25	26	27	28	29
30	:	:	:	:	:	:

May.

S	M	T	W	T	F	S
.	1	2	3	4	5	6
7	8	9	10	11	12	13
14	15	16	17	18	19	20
21	22	23	24	25	26	27
28	29	30	31	:	:	:

June.

S	M	T	W	T	F	S
.	.	.	.	1	2	3
4	5	6	7	8	9	10
11	12	13	14	15	16	17
18	19	20	21	22	23	24
25	26	27	28	29	30	:

July.

S	M	T	W	T	F	S
.	.	.	.	.	.	1
2	3	4	5	6	7	8
9	10	11	12	13	14	15
16	17	18	19	20	21	22
23	24	25	26	27	28	29
30	31	:	:	:	:	:

August.

S	M	T	W	T	F	S
.	.	1	2	3	4	5
6	7	8	9	10	11	12
13	14	15	16	17	18	19
20	21	22	23	24	25	26
27	28	29	30	31	:	:

September.

S	M	T	W	T	F	S
.	.	.	.	.	1	2
3	4	5	6	7	8	9
10	11	12	13	14	15	16
17	18	19	20	21	22	23
24	25	26	27	28	29	30

October.

S	M	T	W	T	F	S
1	2	3	4	5	6	7
8	9	10	11	12	13	14
15	16	17	18	19	20	21
22	23	24	25	26	27	28
29	30	31	:	:	:	:

November.

S	M	T	W	T	F	S
.	.	.	1	2	3	4
5	6	7	8	9	10	11
12	13	14	15	16	17	18
19	20	21	22	23	24	25
26	27	28	29	30	:	:

December.

S	M	T	W	T	F	S
.	.	.	.	.	1	2
3	4	5	6	7	8	9
10	11	12	13	14	15	16
17	18	19	20	21	22	23
24	25	26	27	28	29	30
31	:	:	:	:	:	:

1776.

January.
S	M	T	W	T	F	S
	1	2	3	4	5	6
7	8	9	10	11	12	13
14	15	16	17	18	19	20
21	22	23	24	25	26	27
28	29	30	31			

February.
S	M	T	W	T	F	S
				1	2	3
4	5	6	7	8	9	10
11	12	13	14	15	16	17
18	19	20	21	22	23	24
25	26	27	28	29		

March.
S	M	T	W	T	F	S
					1	2
3	4	5	6	7	8	9
10	11	12	13	14	15	16
17	18	19	20	21	22	23
24	25	26	27	28	29	30
31						

April.
S	M	T	W	T	F	S
	1	2	3	4	5	6
7	8	9	10	11	12	13
14	15	16	17	18	19	20
21	22	23	24	25	26	27
28	29	30				

May.
S	M	T	W	T	F	S
		1	2	3	4	
5	6	7	8	9	10	11
12	13	14	15	16	17	18
19	20	21	22	23	24	25
26	27	28	29	30	31	

June.
S	M	T	W	T	F	S
						1
2	3	4	5	6	7	8
9	10	11	12	13	14	15
16	17	18	19	20	21	22
23	24	25	26	27	28	29
30						

July.
S	M	T	W	T	F	S
	1	2	3	4	5	6
7	8	9	10	11	12	13
14	15	16	17	18	19	20
21	22	23	24	25	26	27
28	29	30	31			

August.
S	M	T	W	T	F	S
				1	2	3
4	5	6	7	8	9	10
11	12	13	14	15	16	17
18	19	20	21	22	23	24
25	26	27	28	29	30	31

September.
S	M	T	W	T	F	S
1	2	3	4	5	6	7
8	9	10	11	12	13	14
15	16	17	18	19	20	21
22	23	24	25	26	27	28
29	30					

October.
S	M	T	W	T	F	S
		1	2	3	4	5
6	7	8	9	10	11	12
13	14	15	16	17	18	19
20	21	22	23	24	25	26
27	28	29	30	31		

November.
S	M	T	W	T	F	S
					1	2
3	4	5	6	7	8	9
10	11	12	13	14	15	16
17	18	19	20	21	22	23
24	25	26	27	28	29	30

December.
S	M	T	W	T	F	S
1	2	3	4	5	6	7
8	9	10	11	12	13	14
15	16	17	18	19	20	21
22	23	24	25	26	27	28
29	30	31				

1777.

January.
S	M	T	W	T	F	S
			1	2	3	4
5	6	7	8	9	10	11
12	13	14	15	16	17	18
19	20	21	22	23	24	25
26	27	28	29	30	31	

February.
S	M	T	W	T	F	S
						1
2	3	4	5	6	7	8
9	10	11	12	13	14	15
16	17	18	19	20	21	22
23	24	25	26	27	28	

March.
S	M	T	W	T	F	S
						1
2	3	4	5	6	7	8
9	10	11	12	13	14	15
16	17	18	19	20	21	22
23	24	25	26	27	28	29
30	31					

April.
S	M	T	W	T	F	S
		1	2	3	4	5
6	7	8	9	10	11	12
13	14	15	16	17	18	19
20	21	22	23	24	25	26
27	28	29	30			

May.
S	M	T	W	T	F	S
				1	2	3
4	5	6	7	8	9	10
11	12	13	14	15	16	17
18	19	20	21	22	23	24
25	26	27	28	29	30	31

June.
S	M	T	W	T	F	S
1	2	3	4	5	6	7
8	9	10	11	12	13	14
15	16	17	18	19	20	21
22	23	24	25	26	27	28
29	30					

July.
S	M	T	W	T	F	S
		1	2	3	4	5
6	7	8	9	10	11	12
13	14	15	16	17	18	19
20	21	22	23	24	25	26
27	28	29	30	31		

August.
S	M	T	W	T	F	S
					1	2
3	4	5	6	7	8	9
10	11	12	13	14	15	16
17	18	19	20	21	22	23
24	25	26	27	28	29	30
31						

September.
S	M	T	W	T	F	S
	1	2	3	4	5	6
7	8	9	10	11	12	13
14	15	16	17	18	19	20
21	22	23	24	25	26	27
28	29	30				

October.
S	M	T	W	T	F	S
			1	2	3	4
5	6	7	8	9	10	11
12	13	14	15	16	17	18
19	20	21	22	23	24	25
26	27	28	29	30	31	

November.
S	M	T	W	T	F	S
						1
2	3	4	5	6	7	8
9	10	11	12	13	14	15
16	17	18	19	20	21	22
23	24	25	26	27	28	29
30						

December.
S	M	T	W	T	F	S
	1	2	3	4	5	6
7	8	9	10	11	12	13
14	15	16	17	18	19	20
21	22	23	24	25	26	27
28	29	30	31			

January.

S	M	T	W	T	F	S
				1	2	3
4	5	6	7	8	9	10
11	12	13	14	15	16	17
18	19	20	21	22	23	24
25	26	27	28	29	30	31

February.

S	M	T	W	T	F	S
1	2	3	4	5	6	7
8	9	10	11	12	13	14
15	16	17	18	19	20	21
22	23	24	25	26	27	28

March.

S	M	T	W	T	F	S
1	2	3	4	5	6	7
8	9	10	11	12	13	14
15	16	17	18	19	20	21
22	23	24	25	26	27	28
29	30	31				

April.

S	M	T	W	T	F	S
		1	2	3	4	
5	6	7	8	9	10	11
12	13	14	15	16	17	18
19	20	21	22	23	24	25
26	27	28	29	30		

May.

S	M	T	W	T	F	S
					1	2
3	4	5	6	7	8	9
10	11	12	13	14	15	16
17	18	19	20	21	22	23
24	25	26	27	28	29	30
31						

June.

S	M	T	W	T	F	S
	1	2	3	4	5	6
7	8	9	10	11	12	13
14	15	16	17	18	19	20
21	22	23	24	25	26	27
28	29	30				

July.

S	M	T	W	T	F	S
		1	2	3	4	
5	6	7	8	9	10	11
12	13	14	15	16	17	18
19	20	21	22	23	24	25
26	27	28	29	30	31	

August.

S	M	T	W	T	F	S
						1
2	3	4	5	6	7	8
9	10	11	12	13	14	15
16	17	18	19	20	21	22
23	24	25	26	27	28	29
30	31					

September.

S	M	T	W	T	F	S
		1	2	3	4	5
6	7	8	9	10	11	12
13	14	15	16	17	18	19
20	21	22	23	24	25	26
27	28	29	30			

October.

S	M	T	W	T	F	S
			1	2	3	
4	5	6	7	8	9	10
11	12	13	14	15	16	17
18	19	20	21	22	23	24
25	26	27	28	29	30	31

Novenrber.

S	M	T	W	T	F	S
1	2	3	4	5	6	7
8	9	10	11	12	13	14
15	16	17	18	19	20	21
22	23	24	25	26	27	28
29	30					

December.

S	M	T	W	T	F	S
		1	2	3	4	5
6	7	8	9	10	11	12
13	14	15	16	17	18	19
20	21	22	23	24	25	26
27	28	29	30	31		

January.

S	M	T	W	T	F	S
					1	2
3	4	5	6	7	8	9
10	11	12	13	14	15	16
17	18	19	20	21	22	23
24	25	26	27	28	29	30
31						

February.

S	M	T	W	T	F	S
	1	2	3	4	5	6
7	8	9	10	11	12	13
14	15	16	17	18	19	20
21	22	23	24	25	26	27
28						

March.

S	M	T	W	T	F	S
	1	2	3	4	5	6
7	8	9	10	11	12	13
14	15	16	17	18	19	20
21	22	23	24	25	26	27
28	29	30	31			

April.

S	M	T	W	T	F	S
			1	2	3	
4	5	6	7	8	9	10
11	12	13	14	15	16	17
18	19	20	21	22	23	24
25	26	27	28	29	30	

May.

S	M	T	W	T	F	S
						1
2	3	4	5	6	7	8
9	10	11	12	13	14	15
16	17	18	19	20	21	22
23	24	25	26	27	28	29
30	31					

June.

S	M	T	W	T	F	S
		1	2	3	4	5
6	7	8	9	10	11	12
13	14	15	16	17	18	19
20	21	22	23	24	25	26
27	28	29	30			

July.

S	M	T	W	T	F	S
				1	2	3
4	5	6	7	8	9	10
11	12	13	14	15	16	17
18	19	20	21	22	23	24
25	26	27	28	29	30	31

August.

S	M	T	W	T	F	S
1	2	3	4	5	6	7
8	9	10	11	12	13	14
15	16	17	18	19	20	21
22	23	24	25	26	27	28
29	30	31				

September.

S	M	T	W	T	F	S
			1	2	3	4
5	6	7	8	9	10	11
12	13	14	15	16	17	18
19	20	21	22	23	24	25
26	27	28	29	30		

October.

S	M	T	W	T	F	S
					1	2
3	4	5	6	7	8	9
10	11	12	13	14	15	16
17	18	19	20	21	22	23
24	25	26	27	28	29	30
31						

November.

S	M	T	W	T	F	S
	1	2	3	4	5	6
7	8	9	10	11	12	13
14	15	16	17	18	19	20
21	22	23	24	25	26	27
28	29	30				

December.

S	M	T	W	T	F	S
			1	2	3	4
5	6	7	8	9	10	11
12	13	14	15	16	17	18
19	20	21	22	23	24	25
26	27	28	29	30	31	

1780.

January.
S	M	T	W	T	F	S
.	.	.	.	.	.	1
2	3	4	5	6	7	8
9	10	11	12	13	14	15
16	17	18	19	20	21	22
23	24	25	26	27	28	29
30	31					

February.
S	M	T	W	T	F	S
.	.	1	2	3	4	5
6	7	8	9	10	11	12
13	14	15	16	17	18	19
20	21	22	23	24	25	26
27	28	29				

March.
S	M	T	W	T	F	S
.	.	.	1	2	3	4
5	6	7	8	9	10	11
12	13	14	15	16	17	18
19	20	21	22	23	24	25
26	27	28	29	30	31	

April.
S	M	T	W	T	F	S
.	.	.	.	.	.	1
2	3	4	5	6	7	8
9	10	11	12	13	14	15
16	17	18	19	20	21	22
23	24	25	26	27	28	29
30						

May.
S	M	T	W	T	F	S
.	1	2	3	4	5	6
7	8	9	10	11	12	13
14	15	16	17	18	19	20
21	22	23	24	25	26	27
28	29	30	31			

June.
S	M	T	W	T	F	S
.	.	.	.	1	2	3
4	5	6	7	8	9	10
11	12	13	14	15	16	17
18	19	20	21	22	23	24
25	26	27	28	29	30	

July.
S	M	T	W	T	F	S
.	.	.	.	.	.	1
2	3	4	5	6	7	8
9	10	11	12	13	14	15
16	17	18	19	20	21	22
23	24	25	26	27	28	29
30	31					

August.
S	M	T	W	T	F	S
.	.	1	2	3	4	5
6	7	8	9	10	11	12
13	14	15	16	17	18	19
20	21	22	23	24	25	26
27	28	29	30	31		

September.
S	M	T	W	T	F	S
.	.	.	.	.	1	2
3	4	5	6	7	8	9
10	11	12	13	14	15	16
17	18	19	20	21	22	23
24	25	26	27	28	29	30

October.
S	M	T	W	T	F	S
1	2	3	4	5	6	7
8	9	10	11	12	13	14
15	16	17	18	19	20	21
22	23	24	25	26	27	28
29	30	31				

November.
S	M	T	W	T	F	S
.	.	.	1	2	3	4
5	6	7	8	9	10	11
12	13	14	15	16	17	18
19	20	21	22	23	24	25
26	27	28	29	30		

December.
S	M	T	W	T	F	S
.	.	.	.	.	1	2
3	4	5	6	7	8	9
10	11	12	13	14	15	16
17	18	19	20	21	22	23
24	25	26	27	28	29	30
31						

1781.

January.
S	M	T	W	T	F	S
.	1	2	3	4	5	6
7	8	9	10	11	12	13
14	15	16	17	18	19	20
21	22	23	24	25	26	27
28	29	30	31			

February.
S	M	T	W	T	F	S
.	.	.	.	1	2	3
4	5	6	7	8	9	10
11	12	13	14	15	16	17
18	19	20	21	22	23	24
25	26	27	28			

March.
S	M	T	W	T	F	S
.	.	.	.	1	2	3
4	5	6	7	8	9	10
11	12	13	14	15	16	17
18	19	20	21	22	23	24
25	26	27	28	29	30	31

April.
S	M	T	W	T	F	S
1	2	3	4	5	6	7
8	9	10	11	12	13	14
15	16	17	18	19	20	21
22	23	24	25	26	27	28
29	30					

May.
S	M	T	W	T	F	S
.	.	1	2	3	4	5
6	7	8	9	10	11	12
13	14	15	16	17	18	19
20	21	22	23	24	25	26
27	28	29	30	31		

June.
S	M	T	W	T	F	S
.	.	.	.	.	1	2
3	4	5	6	7	8	9
10	11	12	13	14	15	16
17	18	19	20	21	22	23
24	25	26	27	28	29	30

July.
S	M	T	W	T	F	S
1	2	3	4	5	6	7
8	9	10	11	12	13	14
15	16	17	18	19	20	21
22	23	24	25	26	27	28
29	30	31				

August.
S	M	T	W	T	F	S
.	.	.	1	2	3	4
5	6	7	8	9	10	11
12	13	14	15	16	17	18
19	20	21	22	23	24	25
26	27	28	29	30	31	

September.
S	M	T	W	T	F	S
.	.	.	.	.	.	1
2	3	4	5	6	7	8
9	10	11	12	13	14	15
16	17	18	19	20	21	22
23	24	25	26	27	28	29
30						

October.
S	M	T	W	T	F	S
.	1	2	3	4	5	6
7	8	9	10	11	12	13
14	15	16	17	18	19	20
21	22	23	24	25	26	27
28	29	30	31			

November.
S	M	T	W	T	F	S
.	.	.	.	1	2	3
4	5	6	7	8	9	10
11	12	13	14	15	16	17
18	19	20	21	22	23	24
25	26	27	28	29	30	

December.
S	M	T	W	T	F	S
.	.	.	.	.	.	1
2	3	4	5	6	7	8
9	10	11	12	13	14	15
16	17	18	19	20	21	22
23	24	25	26	27	28	29
30	31					

1782.

January.
S	M	T	W	T	F	S
		1	2	3	4	5
6	7	8	9	10	11	12
13	14	15	16	17	18	19
20	21	22	23	24	25	26
27	28	29	30	31		

February.
S	M	T	W	T	F	S
					1	2
3	4	5	6	7	8	9
10	11	12	13	14	15	16
17	18	19	20	21	22	23
24	25	26	27	28		

March.
S	M	T	W	T	F	S
					1	2
3	4	5	6	7	8	9
10	11	12	13	14	15	16
17	18	19	20	21	22	23
24	25	26	27	28	29	30
31						

April.
S	M	T	W	T	F	S
	1	2	3	4	5	6
7	8	9	10	11	12	13
14	15	16	17	18	19	20
21	22	23	24	25	26	27
28	29	30				

May.
S	M	T	W	T	F	S
			1	2	3	4
5	6	7	8	9	10	11
12	13	14	15	16	17	18
19	20	21	22	23	24	25
26	27	28	29	30	31	

June.
S	M	T	W	T	F	S
						1
2	3	4	5	6	7	8
9	10	11	12	13	14	15
16	17	18	19	20	21	22
23	24	25	26	27	28	29
30						

July.
S	M	T	W	T	F	S
	1	2	3	4	5	6
7	8	9	10	11	12	13
14	15	16	17	18	19	20
21	22	23	24	25	26	27
28	29	30	31			

August.
S	M	T	W	T	F	S
				1	2	3
4	5	6	7	8	9	10
11	12	13	14	15	16	17
18	19	20	21	22	23	24
25	26	27	28	29	30	31

September.
S	M	T	W	T	F	S
1	2	3	4	5	6	7
8	9	10	11	12	13	14
15	16	17	18	19	20	21
22	23	24	25	26	27	28
29	30					

October.
S	M	T	W	T	F	S
		1	2	3	4	5
6	7	8	9	10	11	12
13	14	15	16	17	18	19
20	21	22	23	24	25	26
27	28	29	30	31		

November.
S	M	T	W	T	F	S
					1	2
3	4	5	6	7	8	9
10	11	12	13	14	15	16
17	18	19	20	21	22	23
24	25	26	27	28	29	30

December.
S	M	T	W	T	F	S
1	2	3	4	5	6	7
8	9	10	11	12	13	14
15	16	17	18	19	20	21
22	23	24	25	26	27	28
29	30	31				

1783.

January.
S	M	T	W	T	F	S
			1	2	3	4
5	6	7	8	9	10	11
12	13	14	15	16	17	18
19	20	21	22	23	24	25
26	27	28	29	30	31	

February.
S	M	T	W	T	F	S
						1
2	3	4	5	6	7	8
9	10	11	12	13	14	15
16	17	18	19	20	21	22
23	24	25	26	27	28	

March.
S	M	T	W	T	F	S
						1
2	3	4	5	6	7	8
9	10	11	12	13	14	15
16	17	18	19	20	21	22
23	24	25	26	27	28	29
30	31					

April.
S	M	T	W	T	F	S
		1	2	3	4	5
6	7	8	9	10	11	12
13	14	15	16	17	18	19
20	21	22	23	24	25	26
27	28	29	30			

May.
S	M	T	W	T	F	S
				1	2	3
4	5	6	7	8	9	10
11	12	13	14	15	16	17
18	19	20	21	22	23	24
25	26	27	28	29	30	31

June.
S	M	T	W	T	F	S
1	2	3	4	5	6	7
8	9	10	11	12	13	14
15	16	17	18	19	20	21
22	23	24	25	26	27	28
29	30					

July.
S	M	T	W	T	F	S
		1	2	3	4	5
6	7	8	9	10	11	12
13	14	15	16	17	18	19
20	21	22	23	24	25	26
27	28	29	30	31		

August.
S	M	T	W	T	F	S
					1	2
3	4	5	6	7	8	9
10	11	12	13	14	15	16
17	18	19	20	21	22	23
24	25	26	27	28	29	30
31						

September.
S	M	T	W	T	F	S
	1	2	3	4	5	6
7	8	9	10	11	12	13
14	15	16	17	18	19	20
21	22	23	24	25	26	27
28	29	30				

October.
S	M	T	W	T	F	S
			1	2	3	4
5	6	7	8	9	10	11
12	13	14	15	16	17	18
19	20	21	22	23	24	25
26	27	28	29	30	31	

November.
S	M	T	W	T	F	S
						1
2	3	4	5	6	7	8
9	10	11	12	13	14	15
16	17	18	19	20	21	22
23	24	25	26	27	28	29
30						

December.
S	M	T	W	T	F	S
	1	2	3	4	5	6
7	8	9	10	11	12	13
14	15	16	17	18	19	20
21	22	23	24	25	26	27
28	29	30	31			

NUMBER OF TROOPS FURNISHED

DURING THE

WAR OF THE REVOLUTION

By the SEVERAL STATES

The exact number of men in the Continental Establishment, furnished by each State in the War of the Revolution, is not known, but an approximate estimate made by Colonel Pierce, Paymaster-General of the Continental Army, and the Treasury Accountants, in 1787, is as shown in the first column of this table. In addition, however, all the States furnished regiments or independent battalions or companies of State Troops, Militia, Rangers, Riflemen, &c., for brief services, who were called out to assist the Continental Army in emergencies, or who were raised to protect and defend their own States, many of whom were in service at two or more different periods. The exact number thus furnished can not be given, but upon examination of various estimates, I believe the figures shown in the second column of the table to be, in round figures, approximately correct:

	CONTINENTAL ARMY	STATE TROOPS, MILITIA, &c.	TOTAL
New Hampshire................	12,497	4,000	16,497
Massachusetts	67,907	20,000	87,907
Rhode Island..................	5,908	4,000	9,908
Connecticut	31,939	9,000	40,939
New York......................	17,781	10,000	27,781
New Jersey.....................	10,726	7,000	17,726
Pennsylvania	25,678	10,000	35,678
Delaware	2,386	1,000	3,386
Maryland	13,912	9,000	22,912
Virginia	26,678	30,000	56,678
North Carolina.................	7,263	13,000	20,263
South Carolina.................	6,417	20,000	26,417
Georgia	2,679	8,000	10,679
Total.....................	231,771	145,000	376,771

The total here given is excessive as to the number that served in the army, for many served two, three and even four terms. Many of the men who entered the service in 1775, re-entered in 1776, again in 1777, and again in 1780, and were therefore counted two, three, or four times, and from the best information attainable it is fair to assume that the number of individuals actually engaged in the military service during the war did not exceed 250,000. ·

Addenda

to

Heitman's Historical Register

of

Officers of the Continental Army

during the

War of the Revolution

APRIL 1775 TO DECEMBER 1783

---

by
ROBERT H. KELBY
New York Historical Society

Copied June, 1932
By Alma Rogers Van Hoevenberg
or THE SOCIETY OF THE CINCIN

Adams, Jonas. See Addoms, Jonas (N. Y.)

Alden, Austin (Mass.) 2d Lieutenant, 18th May, 1776.

Allen, Lathrop (N.Y.) Elmore's Continental Regiment.

Allin. See Allyn.

Allyn, Samuel. See Allyn, Simeon.

Andrews, William (Conn.) Elmore's Continental Regiment.

Aorson, Aaron (1741-   ). 1st Lieutenant, 1st New York Continental Regiment, Colonel Alexander McDougall, 28th June, 1775-15th April, 1776, at Quebec; appointed 1st Lieutenant of regiment to be raised by Colonel Lewis DuBois, 26th June, 1776; resigned 8th July, 1776; Captain 3d Regiment, New York Line, Colonel Peter Gansevoort, 21st November, 1776; transferred to 1st Regiment, New York Line, Colonel Goose Van Schaick, 1st January, 1783; Brevet Major, 30th September, 1783; served to close of war.

Armstrong, John. Deputy-Adjutant-General, 1779. (1914 ed. has 1780.)

Armstrong, Thomas (N. C.) Lieutenant, transferred to 2d North Carolina, 1st June, 1778.

Armstrong, Thomas (N. C.) Adjutant, 5th North Carolina, 28th March, 1782. (Query: Same man as Lieut.?)

Atkin, James. See Aitkin, James.

Babcock, Joshua (R. I.) Major-General. (Died 1st April, 1783.)

Bane, John (N: Y.) 3d Lieutenant, New York Provincial Artillery, Captain Alexander Hamilton, 3d February, 1776.

Banks, Moses (Mass.) Cashiered 26th July, 1776.

Bankson, John (Pa.) 1881, 1883—should be 1781, 1783.

Barrett, James (Mass.) Captain, —, 19th April, 1775. (Died 11 April, 1779.)

Beekman, Tjerck. (Died 23d December, 1791, aged 37 years), buried in Dutch Churchyard, Kingston, N.Y. See Poucher and Terwilliger, Old Gravestones of Ulster Co., N. Y.

Benedict, Elisha (N. Y.) Served as Captain in Nicholson's Continental Regiment, 8th March, 1776 to March, 1777.

Blackburn, Thomas (Va.) Lieutenant-Colonel, 2d Regiment, Virginia State Troops, 20th December, 1776, to 11th June, 1777. (From Ms. Roster—in possession of Asa Bird Gardiner.)

Blackley, John (N.Y.) Nicholson's Continental Regiment.

Bliss, Theodore } same man.
——, Thomas Theodore }

Bowman, Joseph (N.C.) Also called Joshua Bowman.

Bradish, John (Mass.) Captain. See Bradish, David.

Brandon, William. Resigned 17th March, 1776.

Brewer, Samuel (N.C.) Colonel, 12th North Carolina, January, 1777; cashiered 29th September, 1778. (Died 1781.) (See Brewer, Samuel (Mass.) in 1914 ed.)

Brewster, Lott (N.C.) Major, 7th North Carolina, 27th November, 1776.

Brindley, Francis (N.Y.) Nicholson's Continental Regiment.

Brogdan, John (N.Y.) Nicholson's Continental Regiment, 21st March, 1776, to March, 1777.

Brown, Eli (Conn.) Elmore's Continental Regiment.

Brown, John (Conn.) Lieutenant-Colonel, Elmore's Continental Regiment.

Brown, Peter W. (Mass.) Roster in N.Y. Hist. Soc. has Peter.

Bryan, Benjamin (N.C.) Ensign, 7th North Carolina.

Bullard, Seth (Mass.) Captain, —, Walpole, Mass.; Major 4th Regiment, Suffolk Co., Mass., Militia, 1777 to 1780. (Died 1st August, 1811.)

Bush, John (N.C.) Ensign, 5th North Carolina, 1776; Lieutenant, 8th North Carolina, ——, February, 1777; Adjutant 7th August, 1781.

Bush, William (N.C. Adjutant, 12th May, 1781.

Cady, Palmer (Conn.) Sergeant, Elmore's Continental Regiment.

Campbell, James (N.C.) Ensign, 2d North Carolina, 11th December, 1776. (Also as Campen.)

Campen, James. See Campbell, James.

Canfield, Jabez. See Campfield, Jabez.

Chapman, Albert (Conn.) Elmore's Continental Regiment.

Chapman, James (Conn.) Elmore's Continental Regiment.

Cheeseboro, John (N.C.) Ensign, 25th April, 1779.

Child, Abraham. See Childs, Abraham.

Church, Uriah (Conn.) Elmore's Continental Regiment.

Clajon, William. Secretary to Gen. Gates and Interpreter to Northern Department. (Died 30th July, 1784, Philadelphia) (From Freeman's Journal, Phila.) "native of France . . . principal par of life in America . . . resident of Phila . . from commencement of hostilities with Great Britain, he acted as secretary . . .

Clark, Othneil (Conn.) (Died 22d July, 1782, Fishkill, N.Y

Clark, Thomas (N.C) Major, Brevet Brigadier-General, 30th September, 1783.

Clinch, Joseph (N.C.) See Clinch, James.

Cochrane. See Cochran.

Cochrane, Robert (N.Y.) Captain. (Also as Robert Cochran.)

Cogswell, Samuel (Conn.) Brigade Major to Colonel Jackson's Brigade. (West Point Garrison Orders, 11th September, 1778.)

Coleman. See Colman.

Coleman, Theophilus. See Coleman, Theophebus (1914 ed.).

Colman, Charles (N.C.) Quartermaster, 3d North Carolina, 14th October, 1777. (See Coleman, Charles, in 1914 ed.)

Cooper, Ezekiel (Mass.) Ensign of 27th Continental Infantry.

Costigan, Lewis Johnston (N.J.) (Died 9th November, 1822.)

Cowan, Daniel (N. C.) See Cowan, David.

Crosby, Ebenezer, (Conn.) (Died 15th July, 1788.)

Cutler. See Cutler.

Cutter. See Cutler.

Darby. See Derby.

Darke, William (Va.) Wounded, —, 4th November, 1791.

Dawes, Abraham (N.C.) Adjutant, 7th North Carolina, 22d December, 1776. (See Davis, Abraham.)

Dawes. See Davis in 1914 ed.

Dawson, Henry (N.C.) Lieutenant-Colonel, 8th North Carolina, 19th October, 1777.

Dayley. See Daley.

Dean, John (Md.) Captain, Colonel Josias Hall's 4th Regiment ——. (See Annapolis (Md.) Gazette, 3d April, 1777, p. 3, col. 2.)

De Costia. See Du Coines (Coin).

Deheyser. See DeKeyser.

DeKeyser. See Deheyser.

Demont. See Dement.

Dennis, William (N.C.) Captain, 20th September, 1777.

Derby. See Darby.

Dickinson, Joel (Conn.) Elmore's Continental Regiment.

Doherty, George (N.C.) Major, 17th July, 1782.

Dondel. Spelled Donnald in Roster in N.Y. Hist. Soc.

DuBois, Lewis (N.Y.) Nicholson's Continental Regiment.

Du Coines—Du Coin, John. Son of Duke DeCostia, a sugar planter in Hispaniola, near Cape Francois; in consequence of a duel with Lewis Fopa, in which the latter fell, DeCostia fled to St. Domingo, where he resided several months; afterward came to Philadelphia, changed his name to John DuCoin and enlisted in McIntosh's Regiment ——; his real name was John Francis Borigan DeCostia. (See letter of Gen. McIntosh, 15th October, 1783, Steuben Papers in N.Y. Hist. Soc.)

Dyer, Asa. 1st Lieutenant——, 19th May to December, 1775.

Eagle, Joseph (N.C.) Ensign, 1st North Carolina.

Eason. See Easton.

Eckert, Valentine (Pa.) (Died — December, 1821.)

Elderkin, Vine (Conn.) (Died 15th August, 1800.)

Elmore, Samuel (Conn.) Colonel, Continental Regiment, raised in Canada.

Elmore, Samuel, Jr. 2d Lieutenant, Elmore's Continental Regiment.

Engle, Andrew. (Died 2d June, 1810.)

Evans, Benjamin (N.Y.) Nicholson's Continental Regiment.

Evans, Israel, (N.Y.) Chaplain of Nicholson's Continental Regiment.

Everit. See Everett.

Everett, Abner (Pa.) Lieutenant, ——, July, 1776.

Ewing, Alexander. Captain, 1780.

Febiger. See Fehiger, 1914 ed.

Febiger, Christian (Denmark).

Feeley, Timothy, (Died 8th May, 1782.) See certificate of Timothy Feely in Misc. Ms. F. (N.Y. Hist. Soc.)

Fehiger. Should be Febiger.

Fergus, James (N.C.) See Fergus, Janus (1914 ed.) Surgeon's Mate, 10th North Carolina, ——, 1782.

Ferrell, William (N.C.) Ensign, 2d North Carolina, 8th September, 1777.

Finley, Samuel (Pa. and Va.) Same man.

Fiske, John (Conn.) Elmore's Continental Regiment.

Foard. See Ford.

Ford. See Foard.

Ford, John (N.C.) Lieutenant, 1780. (Also spelled Foard.)

Foster, Jacob. See Forster, Jacob.

Gallaudet, Edgar (N.J.) See Gaudilet.

Gatling, Levi. Cashiered, 28th August, 1778.

Geyer. See Geiger. (Also spelled Gyer.)

Gillespie, Robert (N.C.) 2d Lieutenant, ——, August, 1777.

Godwin, Henry (N.Y.) (Died 10th March, 1782.) Also spelled Goodwin.

Goodin, Christopher (N.C.) Captain, 5th North Carolina, January, 1779.

Goodwin. See Godwin.

Gorham, Shubael. Elmore's Continental Regiment.

Gosselin, Clement. Wounded at Yorktown, 16th October, 1781.

Graham, John (N.Y.) (Died 7th May, 1832, at Schuyler, N. Y., near Utica.)

Graves, Francis (N.C.) Regimental Quartermaster, 6th November, 1778.

Guion, Isaac (N.C.) Surgeon, Commissary, 9th North Carolina, 11th December, 1776.

Guion, Isaac (N.C.) probably misprint for N. Y. (in 1914 ed.) Nicholson's Continental Regiment.

Gyer. See Geiger.

Hagan, Francis. Hospital Surgeon, January, 1777.

Hair, John L. (N.C.) 2d Lieutenant, ——, 1777.

Hall, James (N.C.) Captain, ——, May, 1777.

Hancock. See Handcock.

Hanson, Dirck (N.Y.) Nicholson's Continental Regiment.

Hargett, Frederick. See Harjett, Frederick.

Harkenburgh, Peter (Pa.) Ensign, ——, July, 1776.

Harrison, William (N.C.) Ensign, 2d North Carolina, 11th December, 1776.

Helmburg. See Heimberg.

Herrick, Rufus (N.Y.) (Died 28th January, 1811.)

Hoffman, Philip. See Huffman. Is called Captain; killed at Guilford, 15th March, 1781.

Holmes, Asa (N.Y.) Nicholson's Continental Regiment, June, 1776; served as Sergeant in a New York Regiment from June, 1775.

Horton, William (N.Y.) Nicholson's Continental Regiment.

Houston, Christopher (N.C.) (Died 17th May, 1837.)

Hovey, Ivory. (Died Boxford, Mass., aged 82.) (See N.Y. Gazette, 7th September, 1832.)

Hubbell, William (Conn.) Elmore's Continental Regiment.

Huffman. See Hoffman.

Hughes, James (Conn.) Elmore's Continental Regiment.

Hughes, Timothy (N.Y.) 1st Lieutenant, Nicholson's Continental Regiment, 21st April, 1776.

Hull, Titus, see Hall, Titus.

Ingles, John. See Inglas, John.

Irvine, Mathew (Pa.) See Irvine, William (in 1914 ed.).

Ivey, Curtis (N.C.) 2d Lieutenant, 10th October, 1777.

Jacobs, John (N.C.) Ensign, 2d North Carolina, 6th June, 1776; 1st Lieutenant, ——, 1st November, 1776.

Jewett, Joseph. 1st January, 1777— should be 1776.

Johnson, Martin (N.Y.) 1st Lieutenant, New York Provincial Artillery, Captain Alexander Hamilton, 3d February, 1776.

Jones, John (Mass.) Captain ——, 19th April, 1775. (Died 4th July, 1776.)

Jones, Philip (N.C.) 1st Lieutenant, 8th North Carolina, 28th November, 1776.

Jones, Thomas (N.C.) Ensign, ——, 17th April, 1777.

Keeler, Isaac (Conn.) Lieutenant, Continental Line. (Died 25th July, 1825, aged 71 years, New York City.)

Keeler, Isaac. (N.Y.) Lieutenant Isaac Keeler, who died 26th August, 1808, was an Invalid Pensioner formerly Lieutenant in Lieutenant-Colonel Thaddeus Crane's Regiment (4th Regiment), Westchester Co. Militia. Prisoner of war, from 1779 to 1781.

Kemp, Peter. Captain, ——, Regiment of Artillery to 23d April, 1780.

Keyes, Stephen. (Died 4th August, 1804.)

Kilby. See Killby.

Lansing, John G. (N.Y.) 1st Lieutenant, Nicholson's Continental Regiment, 8th March, 1776.

Lewis, Archilaus (Mass.) Ensign, 1st February, 1776. Is Archibald in Roster in N. Y. Hist. Soc.

Lincoln, Rufus. Great-grandson, James Minor Lincoln (deceased), New York City, had Captain Rufus Lincoln's Papers. (See Papers of Captain Rufus Lincoln, compiled by J. M. Lincoln, 1904.)

Lithgow, William. Wounded at Saratoga, October, 1777.

Little. See Lytle.

Livingston, Henry, Jr. (N.Y.) Major, 3d New York Continental Regiment, 2d August to December, 1775. (Died 1828.) (See Livingston, Henry, in 1914 ed.)

Lord, William (N.C.) 1st Lieutenant. 10th North Carolina, 1st August, 1779.

Lowe, Philip (N.C.) 1st Lieutenant, ——, 3d May, 1776.

Lyman, David. See Lyman, Daniel.

Lynch, Cornelius (Conn.) Elmore's Continental Regiment.

McArthur, Alexander (N.Y.) (Died 8th October, 1782, Fishkill, N.Y.)

McClammy. See Lemmy, McLemmy.

McClellan, Carey. See McClallan.

McClellan, William. See McClannen.

McCrary, Thomas (N.C.) See McCrory, Thomas.

McFarland, Moses (Mass.) (Died 7th April, 1802). (See Little. History of Clan Macfarland, p. 108, for Roster of MacFarland's Company and sketch of his life.)

Maclaine. See McLane.

McLemmy, Joseph. See Lemmy, McClammy.

McNees, John (N.C.) Captain, ——, 2d November, 1782.

McRee, Griffith John (N.C.) Major, 4th September, 1781.

Macon, John (N.C.) Lieutenant, 7th North Carolina, 28th November, 1776; Captain, 11th December, 1776.

Madearis (or Medaris). See Medaris.

Malcolm, William (N.Y.) (Died 1st September, 1791, in his 47th year.)

March, Samuel (Mass.) (Died 30th October, 1804.)

Markland, John (Pa.) 3d, not 2d Lieutenant, 19th October, 1777.

Martin, James (N.C.) Captain, 2d North Carolina, 20th April, 1777.

Martin, William (N.J.) See Martin, William (N.Y.)

Martin, William (N.Y.) 1st Lieutenant, ——, 8th March, 1776.

Mazuzen, Mark (Conn.) Elmore's Continental Regiment.

Mekbane. See Mebane.

Mersowey, Solomon, is Meserve. Discharged 30th September, 1776.

Metcalf, Jonathan (Mass.) (Died 28th September, 1778, of wounds received near New Bedford, 5th September, 1778.)

Milliken, Edward. Quartermaster 27th July, 1776.

Mills, James (N.C.) Captain, 10th North Carolina — January, 1779.

Mills, John (N.H.) Sergeant, Captain Joshiah Crosby's Company, Colonel James Read's New Hampshire Regiment. 23d April to December, 1775; 1st Lieutenant, Colonel M. Nichol's Regiment New Hampshire Militia, 18th July to 27th September, 1777; Captain, 5th Regiment New Hampshire Militia, 24th September, 1781.

Monro, John (Va.) Under Munro, John, but arranged with Monro.

Moore, James (N.Y.) Captain-Lieutenant, New York Provincial Artillery, Captain Alexander Hamilton.

Moore, William (N.C.) Retired 1st June, 1778.

Morris, Lewis, Jr. (N.Y.) (Died 22d November, 1824, aged 71.)

Moyen, Jacob (Pa.) Ensign, Swope's Pennsylvania Battalion of the Flying Camp, July, 1776; taken prisoner at Fort Washington, 16th November, 1776.

Munro. See Monro.

Myer, Godfrey (Pa.) Lieutenant, ——, July, 1776.

Nelson, John (N.C.) Captain, ——, 10th April, 1776.

Odlum, Digby (N.Y.) 1st Lieutenant, ——, 8th March, 1776, to March, 1777.

Otto, Bodo (Pa.) (Died 30th June, 1787.)

Parke, Theophilus. Cashiered. (See order printed in Pennsylvania Packet, 18th April, 1780.)

Parmelee, Jeremiah. Elmore's Continental Regiment.

Patton, John (N.C.) See Patten, John.

Patton, Robert (Pa.) 2d Lieutenant, ——, August, 1776.

Peacock, Richard (N.Y.) (Died in 82d year, Fredericksburg, Va.) See N. Y. Gazette, 11th August, 1832.

Pendleton, Nathaniel. 1880 should be 1780.

Perkins, James (Mass.) Ensign, 18th Regiment, Massachusetts Continental Infantry, 1st August, 1776.

Perkins, John (Mass.) (Died 17th April, 1776.)

Peyton, Valentine. Killed at Charleston, 12th May, 1780.

Piatt. See Pyatt.

Platt, Richard (N.Y.) (Died 4th March, 1830, aged 74 years.)

Pope, Charles. Captain, 19th January, 1776.

Pyatt. See Piatt.

Reed. See Read, Reid.

Reed, James (N.C.) Captain, North Carolina Militia. (Died 18th August, 1780, of wounds received at Hanging Rock, 6th August, 1780.)

Reed, William (S. C.) see Read, William.

Reid. See Read, Reed.

Reid, George (N.H.) (Died 17th September, 1815.)

Rhodes, Joseph J. (N.C.) See Rhodes, Joseph Thomas.

Rice, John (Mass.) See Rice, Joseph.

Romans, Bernard. See Saffel. See Phillips, P. L. Notes on life and works of Bernard Romans, 1924. (Fla. State Hist. Soc. Publications.)

Ross, James (Pa.) Major, 3rd Pennsylvania.

Rowe, Caleb (Mass.) 2d Lieutenant, 18th Regiment, —, 1st January, 1776.

Rull, Thomas (N.C.) Surgeon's Mate, 10th North Carolina, ——, 1782.

Scott, Moses. Senior Hospital Physician and Surgeon, to date from 1st June, 1777.

Scurlock, James (N.C.) Lieutenant, 10th North Carolina, 1st September, 1781.

Sewall, Henry (Mass.) 1st Lieutenant, 13th November, 1776.

Sill, Richard (Conn.) (Died 4th June, 1790.)

Simons, James (S.C.?) Captain, 3d Regiment Continental Dragoons, Lieutenant-Colonel William A. Washington; Lieutenant, 1781; Adjutant, 2d June to 26th December, 1781; Captain, same Brigade; Major, 27th December, 1781, to 30th June, 1782; Brevet-Colonel. (See Johnson, Joseph (M. D.) Traditions of the Revolution in the South, 1851, p. 300.) (N. Y. Hist. Soc. owns Geo Bancroft copy, with additions.)

Singletary, Richa.. (N.C.) Ensign, 6th North Carolina, 16th April, 1776.

Smith, David (Conn.) Captain, Elmore's Continental Regiment.

Smith, Ebenezer (Mass.) (Died 8th September, 1816.)

Snead, Charles (Va.) Taken prisoner at Brandywine, 11th September, 1777.

Spicer, John (N.C.) Paymaster, 2d North Carolina, 11th December, 1776.

Stedman, James (Conn.) (Died 7th April, 1788.)

Stewart, Wentworth (Mass.) (Died 17th April, 1776.) Spelled Stuart in Roster in N. Y. Hist. Soc.

Story, Samuel. (Died ——, in South Carolina.) See Freeman's Journal (Philadelphia), 4th December, 1782.

Stuart, Joseph (Mass.) Deserted, 31st October, 1776.

Stuart, Wentworth. See Stewart, Wentworth.

Stubbs, Samuel. 2d Lieutenant, 1st August, 1776.

Suydam. See Sedam. (Suydam probably correct form, well-known name in New York and New Jersey. A. R. V. H.)

Swartwout, Bernardus, (N.Y.) (Died 8th October, 1824, in his 63d year.)

Swearingen. See Van Swearingen.

Swearingen, Joseph (Md.) Captain. See Saffell, page 433, "Officers entitled to half-pay." See Family Historical register—Swearingen, p. 8.

Swearingen, Joseph (Va.) (Died August, 1821.)

Swearingen, Van. See Family Historical register—Swearingen, p. 7-8.

Thatcher, John (Conn.) Captain, ——, June, 1776.

Thomas, John (Mass.) Surgeon's Mate of Cotton's Massachusetts Regiment, April to December, 1775; Surgeon's Mate 23d Continental Infantry, 1st January to 31st December, 1776; Surgeon 9th Massachusetts, 1st January, 1777; transferred to 8th Massachusetts, 1st January, 1781; transferred to 3d Massachusetts 12th January, 1783, and served to close of war. (Died 30th October, 1818.)

Thomas, Thomas (N.Y.) Colonel Militia. (Died 19th June, 1824, in 79th year.)

Thompson, William (Mass.) Lieutenant. (Died 14th March, 1816.)

Thorn (or Thorne), Samuel. Resigned (?26th) December, 1777. (See N.Y. Balloting book, p. 107.)

Titcomb, Benjamin. Wounded at Chemung, 29th August, 1778.

Town, Archelaus (Mass.) Captain, 1st Regiment New Hampshire Line, Colonel John Stark, June to December, 1775; at Bunker Hill; private Continental Army, 24th July to October, 1777; at Saratoga; private, 5th Regiment, New Hampshire Militia, Colonel Moses Nichols, raised to fill up 3d New Hampshire Battalion, 21st June, 1779. (Died — November, 1779, Fishkill, N.Y.)

Trumbull, Jonathan, Jr. (Conn.) Deputy Adjutant-General, by General Gates, 28th June, 1776; by Congress, 12th, September, 1776.

Tryon, Simeon (N.Y.) Lieutenant, 2d New York, 19th February, 1776. Died in service (West Point), 1778.

Tucker, St. George (Va.) Secretary, ——, May, 1779.

Tuttle, Timothy (Conn.) Elmore's Continental Regiment.

Tyler, Abraham (Mass.) Captain, 18th Regiment, Massachusetts Continental Infantry, 1st January to 31st December, 1776. (See Tyler, Abraham (Conn.))

Van Cortlandt, Nicholas Bayard (N.Y.) Aide-de-camp to Major General Sullivan. (Died at Persippany, N.J., May 1, 1782.)

Vanderburgh, Henry (N.Y.) Also Vanderburgh.

Van Duyck, John (N.?C.) 1st Lieutenant, Captain Clark's Company, North Carolina Artillery, 1st February, 1777; was in service as late as June, 1779. 1914 ed. has this under Van Dyke, John (N.Y.)

Van Dyck. See Van Duyck.

Van Heer. See Von Heer.

Van Swearingen. See Swearingen.

Vascher. See Vacher.

Von Heer. Also spelled Van Heer.

Wallace, Benjamin (Pa.) Captain, July, 1776.

Walsh. See Welch, Welsh.

Ward, Artemus. (Died 27th October, 1800.)

Watts, David (Mass.) Ensign, ——, 17th April, 1776; 2d Lieutenant, 3d August, 1776.

Welch. See Walsh, Welsh.

Welles, Benjamin (Mass.) (Died 19th April, 1813.) See under Wells.

Wells. See Welles.

Welsh. See Walsh, Welch.

White, John (N.C.) Captain, ——, died of wounds, in Virginia.

White, John (N.C.) Adjutant, 2d North Carolina, 1st September, 1775.

White, Tarpley (Va.) Captain, 6th Virginia, ——, 1780.

White, William (Mass.) Killed 14th October, 1781.

Williams, James (N.C.) 7th June, 1776.

Williams, John (N.C.) Lieutenant, retired 1st June, 1783.

Williams, Nathaniel (N.C.) Lieutenant, 10th North Carolina, January, 1782.

Williams, William (N.C.) Adjutant, 9th North Carolina, 15th April, 1776; Lieutenant, 9th December, 1776.

Wright, Job (N.Y.) Captain, 1st Regiment, New York Line. (See Calendar of Hist. Ms.: Revolution 2:45.)